Microsoft®
Windows® Vista
IN DEPTH

Robert Cowart

Brian Knittel

que®

Pearson Education Limited
Edinburgh Gate
Harlow
Essex CM20 2JE
England

and Associated Companies throughout the world

Visit us on the World Wide Web at:
www.pearsoned.co.uk

Original edition, entitled SPECIAL EDITION USING MICROSOFT WINDOWS VISTA, 2nd edition, 9780789737816 by COWART, ROBERT; KNITTEL, BRIAN, published by Pearson Education, Inc, publishing as Que Publishing, Copyright © 2008 Robert Cowart and Brian Knittel.

All rights reserved. No part of this publication may be reproduced or transmitted in any form or by any means, electronic, mechanical, including photocopying, recording or by any information storage retrieval system without permission from Pearson Education, Inc.

European edition published by PEARSON EDUCATION LTD, Copyright © 2008

This edition is manufactured in the USA and available for sale only in the United Kingdom and Europe.

The right of Robert Cowart and Brian Knittel to be identified as authors of this work has been asserted by them in accordance with the Copyright, Designs and Patents Act 1988.

All trademarks used herein are the property of their respective owners. The use of any trademark in this text does not vest in the author or publisher any trademark ownership rights in such trademarks, nor does the use of such trademarks imply any affiliation with or endorsement of this book by such owners.

ISBN: 978-0-273-72162-8

British Library Cataloguing-in-Publication Data

A catalogue record for this book is available from the British Library

10 9 8 7 6 5 4 3 2 1

12 11 10 09 08

Printed and bound in the United States of America

The publisher's policy is to use paper manufactured from sustainable forests.

Associate Publisher
Greg Wiegand

Executive Editor
Rick Kughen

Development Editor
Rick Kughen

Technical Editor
Mark Reddin

Managing Editor
Patrick Kanouse

Project Editor
Seth Kerney

Indexer
Ken Johnson

Publishing Coordinator
Cindy Teeters

Multimedia Developer
Dan Scherf

Book Designer
Anne Jones

Contents at a Glance

I Introducing Windows Vista
1 Introducing Windows Vista 3
2 Installing and Upgrading Windows Vista 41
3 The First Hour 77

II Using Windows Vista
4 Using the Windows Vista Interface 121
5 Managing Files and Searching 163
6 Printing 203
7 Sidebar and Other Supplied Accessories . . .233

III Multimedia and Imaging
8 Windows Media Player 259
9 Windows Imaging Tools 287
10 Scanning and Faxing .307
11 Producing Videos with Windows Movie Maker 323
12 Sound Recorder, DVD Maker, and Other Multimedia Tools 349
13 Windows Media Center 361

IV Windows Vista and the Internet
14 Getting Connected 393
15 Using Internet Explorer 7 423
16 Email and Newsgroups with Windows Mail 471
17 Troubleshooting Your Internet Connection . . .527
18 Hosting Web Pages with Internet Information Services .553

V Networking
19 Overview of Windows Networking 589
20 Creating a Windows Network 611
21 Mix and Match with Old Windows and Macs 663
22 Connecting Your Network to the Internet . .701
23 Using a Windows Network 739
24 Troubleshooting Your Network 785

VI Maintaining Windows Vista
25 Windows Management and Maintenance . .803
26 Tweaking the GUI 897
27 Managing Hard Disks 929
28 Troubleshooting and Repairing Problems . .961
29 Keeping Windows and Other Software Up to Date 985
30 Installing and Replacing Hardware 1009
31 Editing the Registry .1037
32 Command-Line and Automation Tools . . .1069

VII Security
33 Protecting Windows from Viruses and Spyware 1131
34 Protecting Your Data from Loss and Theft . .1149
35 Protecting Your Network from Hackers and Snoops 1205
36 Protecting Yourself from Fraud and Spam . .1243

VIII Windows on the Move
37 Wireless Networking 1261
38 Hitting the Road 1279
39 Meetings, Conferencing, and Collaboration . .1311
40 Remote Desktop 1329
41 Tablet PC Features 1355

IX Appendixes
A Windows Programs and Services 1379
B What's New in Service Pack 1 (SP-1) 1421

Index 1431

Contents

Introduction xxxix
    Welcome xxxix
    Why This Book? xl
    How Our Book Is Organized xlii
    Conventions Used in This Book xliv

I Introducing Windows Vista

1 Introducing Windows Vista 3
    An Overview of Windows Vista 4
    A Little Windows History 6
    So What's New in Windows Vista? 8
        Interface Improvements 12
        System Security Enhancements 18
        Performance Improvements 20
        System Management and Stability Improvements 22
        Data Security Enhancements 23
        New or Improved Accessories 24
        Networking 27
        Productivity 29
        Internet Explorer 7 30
        Entertainment 31
    Differences Among Versions of Vista 32
    How Does Windows Vista Compare to UNIX and Linux? 35
        UNIX 36
        Linux 37
    Windows Vista on the Corporate Network 39

2 Installing and Upgrading Windows Vista 41
    General Considerations for Windows Vista 42
    Windows Vista Hardware Requirements 42
        Option 1: Using What You've Got: Ensuring Compatibility via the
            Windows Vista Upgrade Advisor 43
        Option 2: Choosing a Windows Vista Premium Ready PC 48
        Option 3: Upgrading Your Computer 48
    Performing a New Installation of Windows Vista 49
        Typical Clean Setup Procedure 49
    Upgrading Older Versions of Windows to Vista 62

Upgrading One Version of Vista to Another 65
Multibooting Windows Vista 66
Activating Windows Vista 70
The Virtual Machine Approach 73
Tips from the Windows Pros: Editing Your Windows Vista Boot Menu Entries 74

3 The First Hour 77

The First Things to Do After Starting Windows Vista 78
A Quick Tour of Vista's Important Features 78
    The Welcome Screen 78
    The Welcome Center 80
    The New Start Menu 81
    The New Windows Explorer 82
    The Redesigned Control Panel 83
    User Account Control 84
Windows Vista User Accounts 88
    Create New Accounts 89
    Change Account Settings 90
    Before You Forget Your Password 91
    Adjust Your Own User Account 92
    Just One User? 93
Set Up Internet Access 94
Download Critical Updates 95
Personalize Windows 95
    Personalize Screen Settings 95
    Set Up the Quick Launch Bar 96
    Adjust the Explorers 97
Transfer Information from Your Old Computer 99
    Windows Easy Transfer 100
    Windows Easy Transfer Companion 102
Log Off or Shut Down 104
More Than You Wanted to Know 105
    Where's My Stuff, or the User Profile Structure 105
    Compatibility and Virtualization 110
    Creating User Groups 112
    After You Forget Your Password 112
    Using a Password Recovery Disk 115
    Accessing the Real Administrator Account 115
Tips from the Windows Pros: Configuring the Default User Profile 116

II Using Windows Vista

4 Using the Windows Vista Interface ... 121
- Who Should Read This Chapter? ... 122
- Logging In to Windows Vista ... 123
  - Logging On from the Welcome Screen ... 123
- Using Windows Vista—The User Experience ... 124
  - Parts of the Windows Vista Screen ... 125
  - Dialog Box Changes ... 130
  - Putting Items on the Desktop ... 131
  - Saving Files on the Desktop from a Program ... 132
  - Properties and the Right-Click ... 132
  - Using Windows Explorer ... 135
- The Taskbar, the Start Menu, and Other Tools ... 138
  - Uninstall or Change Programs ... 140
  - Add New Programs ... 143
  - Installing Programs from the Network ... 145
- Running Your Applications ... 145
  - How to Launch Your Apps ... 145
  - Using Documents, Pictures, and Music ... 149
  - Using Speech Recognition ... 150
- Using the Help System ... 153
- Exiting Windows Gracefully ... 154
- Dealing with a Crashed Application or Operating System ... 156
- Troubleshooting ... 157
- Tips from the Windows Pros: Working Efficiently ... 159

5 Managing Files and Searching ... 163
- What's New in Windows Explorer ... 164
  - The Legacy of WebView ... 167
- Buttons, Breadcrumbs, Toolbars, and More ... 170
  - Breadcrumbs in the Computer Window ... 172
  - Breadcrumbs in Windows Explorer ... 175
  - User Profiles ... 176
- Navigating the File System ... 177
  - Right-Clicking ... 180
  - Selecting Several Items ... 181
  - Viewing Meta-Information ... 182
  - Turning Panes On and Off ... 184
- Customizing File and Folder Views ... 185
  - Customize This Folder ... 187
  - Setting Folder Options ... 187

Searching	189
Changing Search and Indexing Settings	190
Searching As You Type	192
The Search Pane	195
Grouping and Stacking	197
Zipping and Packing Files	198
File and Folder Security	200
Troubleshooting	201
Tips from the Windows Pros: Using the Search Tool from the Start Menu	202

6 Printing 203

Windows Printing Primer	204
The Printers Folder	205
Installing and Configuring a Printer	206
Adding a New Printer	208
Installing a Local Printer	208
If the Printer Isn't Found or Is on a Serial (COM) Port	210
What to Do If Your Printer Isn't Listed	212
Changing a Printer's Properties	214
Comments About Various Settings	216
Removing a Printer from the Printers Folder	219
Printing from Windows Applications	220
Preprinting Checklist	220
Printing by Dragging Files into the Print Manager	221
Printing Offline	222
Printing from DOS Applications	222
Working with the Printer Queue	223
Deleting a File from the Queue	224
Canceling All Pending Print Jobs on a Given Printer	224
Pausing, Resuming, and Restarting the Printing Process	224
Viewing and Altering Print Document Properties	225
Advanced Printer Management	225
XPS Print Output	226
Print to Disk Option	227
Faxing	228
Troubleshooting	228
Tips from the Windows Pros: Does the Green Ink Have You Seeing Red?	230

7 Sidebar and Other Supplied Accessories 233

Using Gadgets and the Sidebar 234
    Running Sidebar 235
    Adding new Gadgets 238
    Downloading New Gadgets 239
    Hiding the Sidebar 241
    Adjusting a Gadget's Settings 242
    Moving Gadgets Around 243
    Adding a Gadget More Than Once 244
    Changing Opacity of Gadgets 245
    Bringing Gadgets to the Front 245
    Removing Gadgets 245

Calendar 247
    Creating a Calendar 248
    Entering Appointments 248
    Subscribing to and Publishing Calendars 249
    Setting Up Tasks 251
    Setting Options 251

The Other Accessories 252

Troubleshooting 254

Tips from the Windows Pros: Receiving Email on a Pocket PC or Blackberry 255

III Multimedia and Imaging

8 Windows Media Player 259

Learning the Basics 260
    Media Types Compatible with Media Player 260
    Getting Around Windows Media Player 11 261
    Playing Audio and Video in Windows Media Player 11 265

Getting Music and Video on Your Computer 266
    Ripping Songs from CDs onto Your Computer 266
    Shopping for Music and Video from Online Stores 269
    Adding Items from Your Computer to Your Library 271

Taking Your Music and Video on the Go 272
    Burning Customized CDs 272
    Syncing Files to Your Portable Media Player 274
    Sharing Media Throughout Your Home 277

Organizing Your Music Collection 279
    Creating Your Own Custom Playlists 279
    Creating and Editing Auto Playlists 279
    Organizing your Media Collection 281

Updating Media Information and Album Art 282
    Adding or Editing Media Information 283
    Adding or Changing Album Art 284

Tips from the Windows Pros: Playing Audio from Your Portable Device
Through Your Car Stereo 285

9 Windows Imaging Tools 287

Image Manipulation in Windows Vista 288

What's Built in to Windows Vista for Photographs? 288

Windows Photo Gallery 288
    Importing Files into Windows Photo Gallery 290
    Organizing Photos and Movies in Windows Photo Gallery 290

Working with Scanners and Cameras 290
    Using Windows Photo Gallery with a Scanner 291
    Using Windows Photo Gallery with a Digital Camera 292
    Manipulating Pictures in Windows Photo Gallery 295
    Printing Your Masterpiece 297
    Sharing Your Photos with Others Electronically 299

Burning Your Pictures to CD 300
    Writing Photos to CD Using Windows Explorer 300
    Making CDs and DVDs from Windows Photo Gallery 301
    Which Output Option to Use 303

Troubleshooting 303

Tips from the Windows Pros: Archiving Your Company's History 305

10 Scanning and Faxing 307

Introducing Windows Fax and Scan 308
    Preparations for Using Windows Fax and Scan 309

Configuring the Fax Service 309
    Configuring Fax-Receiving Options 310
    Setting Up Sender Information 310
    Creating a Customized Cover Page 310
    Configuring Fax Settings 312

Sending Faxes from Windows Fax and Scan 313
    Adding Scanned Pages 314
    Previewing the Fax 314
    Setting Up Dialing Rules 315
    Sending the Fax 315
    Monitoring Outgoing Faxes 315

Receiving Faxes 316
    Printing Received Faxes Automatically 316

Scanning Documents with Windows Fax and Scan 316
    Scanning Images 317
    Editing Scan Profile Defaults 318
    Creating a New Scan Profile 319
    Emailing Scans 319
    Faxing Scans 319
    Manipulating Scanned Images 319

Troubleshooting 320

Tips from the Windows Pros: Scanning and Faxing Slides and Transparencies 322

11 Producing Videos with Windows Movie Maker 323

Multimedia, Imaging, and Windows 324

Video Capture and Editing with Microsoft Movie Maker 6 324
    Steps of Movie Production with Movie Maker 325
    Video Formats You Can Import 325
    Connecting Your Camcorder 326

Capturing Your Video Clips 327
    Importing Digital Still Camera Movies, Snaps, and Sound Files 332
    Organizing Your Clips 332
    Turning Your Video Clips into a Simple Movie 333
    Editing Your Movie 334
    Adding Transitions Between Clips 336
    Adding Video Effects (Filters) to Your Clips 337
    Adding Narration to Your Movie 338
    Adding Titles to Your Movie 339
    Saving Your Project and Saving Your Movie 340
    AutoMovie 343
    Movie Maker Advanced Settings 344
    Beyond Windows Movie Maker 345
    Help Sites and Resources for Digital Video 345

Troubleshooting 346

Tips from the Windows Pros: Adding Impact to Your Movies 346
    Effects and Transitions Are Overrated 346
    Color and Exposure Correction 347
    Who's Zoomin' Who(m)? 348

12 Sound Recorder, DVD Maker, and Other Multimedia Tools 349

Become a Recording Star 350

Windows Sound Recorder 350

Volume Control 351

Viewing Images 354
    Using Windows Explorer to View Your Photos 354
    Using a Slideshow 355
    Using Your Own Photos as a Screen Saver 356

Recording to DVD 357

Troubleshooting 360

13 Windows Media Center 361

Windows Media Center—What's the Hubbub? 362

The WMC Hardware 364
    The New WMC PC Form Factors 365
    Is Windows Media Center Based on Home or Business Versions? 366

    Can I Upgrade My NonMedia Center PC to a Windows Media Center PC? 367
    Basic WMC PC Hookup 368
    Media Center Extender 370
The WMC Functions 370
    TV + Movies 372
    Pictures + Video 376
    Music 378
Some Tricks of the Trade 378
    Playing DVDs and Other Video Files 378
    Viewing TV Shows on Your HDTV or Projector 380
    Broadcasting TV Shows to Your TV or Projector 381
    Burning DVDs from Recorded TV 383
    Setting Parental Control Ratings 385
Troubleshooting 387
Tips from the Windows Pros 388
    Converting Your Videos to DivX to Save Disk Space 388
    Burn DivX to DVD 390

IV Windows Vista and the Internet

14 Getting Connected **393**

Going Worldwide 394
Connection Technologies 394
    Analog Modem 394
    ISDN 395
    DSL 395
    Cable Modem 396
    Satellite Service 397
    Wireless 397
    Choosing a Technology 397
Choosing an Internet Service Provider 398
    Travel Considerations 399
Choosing Equipment 400
Ordering the Service 401
Installing the Hardware 401
    Installing a Modem in Windows Vista 401
    Changing the Modem Type 404
    Installing Internal ISDN Adapters 404
    Installing a Network Adapter 405
    Installing a Satellite or Wireless Connection 406

Configuring Your Internet Connection 406
    Configuring an ISP Account 407
Adjusting Dial-Up Connection Properties 409
Configuring a High-Speed Connection 411
    Configuring a PPPoE Broadband Connection 412
Making and Ending a Dial-Up Connection 416
    Checking the Connection Status 418
    Hanging Up a Dial-Up Connection 418
Changing the Default Connection 418
Managing Multiple Internet Connections 419
Troubleshooting 420
Tips from the Windows Pros: Staying Connected While Traveling Abroad 421

15 Using Internet Explorer 7 423

Origins and Development of the World Wide Web 424
What's New in Internet Explorer 7? 425
Internet Explorer 7 Quick Tour 426
    Entering URLs 428
    Browsing in Tabbed Pages 430
    Adding Sites to Your Favorites 432
    Working Offline 433
    Saving a Single Web Page for Later Viewing 434
Using Multimedia Browsing and Downloading 435
    Images 435
    Audio and Video 436
    Downloading Programs 442
    Protecting Against Bad Downloaded Programs 443
    Protecting Against "Drive-By" Downloads of IE Add-Ons 445
Customizing the Browser and Setting Internet Options 448
    Setting Default Mail, News, and HTML Editor Programs 451
    Setting Security and Privacy Preferences 453
    Blocking Pop-Ups and Pop-Unders 457
    Controlling Objectionable Content 459
    Other Internet Settings 461
Effectively Searching the Web 462
Safer Alternatives to IE 464
Getting a Microsoft Live ID 465
    Hey, Who's Afraid of Microsoft Live ID? 465
Troubleshooting 467
Tips from the Windows Pros: Finding and Using PDF Documents
    on the World Wide Web 468

16 Email and Newsgroups with Windows Mail 471

Choosing an Email Client 472
- What If You Like Outlook 97, 98, 2000, 2003, or 2007? 474
- Other Email Clients 475

Windows Mail Quick Tour 476
- Setting Up an Email Account 478
- Reading and Processing Incoming Messages 481
- Deleting Messages 483

Creating and Sending New Mail 483
- Sending and Receiving Attachments 485
- Guarding Yourself Against Email Viruses 486
- Setting Up a Signature 487
- Requesting Receipts 488
- Formatting Options for Mail 489
- Sending and Receiving Secure Messages 490

Using the Windows Contacts Address Book 492
- Adding, Editing, and Removing Entries 492
- Creating Distribution Lists 493
- Finding People Who Aren't in Your Address Book 495

Handling Unique Mail Situations 495
- Modifying an Existing Email Account 495

Additional Security Features in Windows Mail 496
- Limiting Spam 496
- Protecting Against HTML Scripts 498
- Handling Multiple Email Accounts for the Same User 498
- Organizing Your Mail 500
- Compacting Your Mail Folder 501
- Filtering Your Mail 501
- Checking Your Messages While Traveling 503
- Backing Up Windows Mail Data 505
- Dealing with Spam 508

Newsgroups and the Internet 509
- What About Mailing Lists? 510
- Locating News Servers 511

Setting Up a Newsgroup Account in Windows Mail 512
- Downloading the Newsgroup List 512

Finding and Reading Newsgroups 513
- Subscribing to Newsgroups 514
- Reading and Posting Messages to a Newsgroup 515
- Managing Messages 517
- Reading News Offline 518

Troubleshooting Email 519

Troubleshooting Newsgroups 521

Tips from the Windows Pros: Creating Formatted Email 523
Tips from the Windows Pros: Newsgroups—For More Than Just News 524

17 Troubleshooting Your Internet Connection 527

It's Great When It Works, but… 528
Before You Run into Trouble 528
Troubleshooting Step by Step 531
Identifying Software-Configuration Problems 535
    Troubleshooting a Dial-Up Connection 535
    Troubleshooting a Cable or DSL Modem Connection 536
    Troubleshooting a LAN Connection 537
Identifying Network Hardware Problems 539
    Identifying Modem Hardware Problems 540
    Identifying Modem Connectivity Problems 542
Troubleshooting Internet Problems with Windows TCP/IP Utilities 543
    ipconfig 544
    ping 545
    tracert 546
    pathping 547
    route 548
Third-Party Utilities 549
    Speed Check 549
    whois Database 550
    Reverse tracert 550
    WS_Ping Pro Pack 551
Tips from the Windows Pros: Pinging with Larger Packets 551

18 Hosting Web Pages with Internet Information Services 553

Overview of Internet Information Services 7.0 554
    What Does a Web Server Do? 555
    A Directory by Any Other Name… 556
    Default Documents 556
    MIMEs Make It Happen 557
    To Run or Not to Run 557
IIS Services and Requirements 558
    Do You Really Want to Do This? 559
    Before You Get Started 560
    Name Service 561
Installing IIS 562
    Opening the Firewall 566
    Setting File Permissions 567
Setting Up a Simple Website 567
Managing Your Site with the Computer Management Console 569
    Important IIS Settings and Components 570

Managing the FTP Server	575
Using the FTP Service to Publish Website Content	576
Using the FTP Service to Exchange Files	577
Managing FTP Connections	579
Log Files	580
Making the Site Available on the Internet	580
Security Issues for Internet Services	582
Keeping Up-to-Date	582
File Security	583
Troubleshooting	584
Tips from the Windows Pros: Scripting for Interactive Sites	585

V Networking

19 Overview of Windows Networking 589

Networking for Everybody	590
Why You Really Need a Network	590
Why It Won't Cost Much	591
Windows Vista's Network Personalities	591
Network Hardware Options	593
Wired Ethernet Networks	593
Unshielded Twisted-Pair (UTP) Cable	594
Wireless Networks	595
Powerline and Phoneline	597
Network Terminology	598
Windows Vista Network Services	600
What's Changed in Vista	600
File and Printer Sharing	602
Link Layer Discovery Protocol (LLDP)	603
Roaming User Profiles	603
Distributed Applications	603
.NET	604
Virtual Private Networking	605
Remote Access Service (RAS)	605
Internet Connection Sharing	606
Windows Firewall	606
Universal Plug and Play	606
Active Directory	607
IntelliMirror	609
Intranet/Internet Services and Tools	609
Security	610
Tips from the Windows Pros: Becoming a Networking Professional	610

20 Creating a Windows Network 611

Creating or Joining a Network 612
Planning Your Network 612
    Are You Being Served? 613
    When to Hire a Professional 615
    Planning for Adequate Capacity 616
    Printers 616
    Backup System 616
    Power Surprise 617
Choosing a Network and Cabling System 617
    10/100BASE-T Ethernet 618
    1000Mbps Ethernet (Gigabit Ethernet) 620
    Phone Line and Power Line Networking 620
    802.11g Wireless Networking 622
    Mixed Networking 624
    Printing and Faxing 624
    Providing Internet Connectivity 625
    Providing Remote Access 625
Installing Network Adapters 625
    Checking Existing Adapters 626
    Installing Multiple Network Adapters 627
Installing Network Wiring 628
    Cabling for Ethernet Networks 628
    General Cabling Tips 629
    Wiring with Patch Cables 630
    Installing In-Wall Wiring 631
    Connecting Just Two Computers 632
    Connecting Multiple Hubs 634
    Installing a Wireless Network 635
    Setting Up a New Wireless Network 638
    Joining an Existing Wireless Network 641
Configuring a Peer-to-Peer Network 642
    Adding Network Clients, Services, and Protocols 642
    Configuring the TCP/IP Protocol 644
    Choosing Your Network Location 649
    Setting Your Computer Identification 651
    Configuring Windows Firewall 652
    Advanced Features 653
Joining a Windows Domain Network 653
Network Security 655
Checking Out the Neighborhood 655
Installing and Configuring Backup Software 656
    File and Folder Backup 657
    System Backup 657

Bridging Two Network Types with Windows Vista 658
Troubleshooting 659
Tips from the Windows Pros: Grassroots Networking 661

21 Mix and Match with Old Windows and Macs 663

Networking with Other Operating Systems 664

Internetworking with Windows XP and Windows 2000 665
    Setting TCP/IP As the Default Network Protocol 666
    Installing the LLDP Responder for Windows XP 667
    Password Protection and Simple File Sharing 667

Internetworking with Windows 95, 98, and Me 670

Internetworking with UNIX and Linux 672
    The SMB/CIFS Protocol 673
    Samba 673
    Samba Client Tools 673
    Samba Server Tools 674
    Telnet 676
    Services for NFS 678
    The Berkeley "r" Commands 680
    Subsystem for UNIX-Based Applications 680

Internetworking with Macintosh 683
    Planning for Compatibility 683
    Working with Mac OS X 685

Advanced Networking Services 690
    Setting Network Bindings 690
    Installing Optional Network Components 691

Troubleshooting 696

Tips from the Windows Pros: The Hosts File 699

22 Connecting Your Network to the Internet 701

It's a Great Time to Connect Your LAN to the Internet 702

The Nuts and Bolts of the Connection 702
    The Need for Speed 702
    Ways to Make the Connection 703
    Managing IP Addresses 705
    NAT and Internet Connection Sharing 706
    Running Your Own Web Servers 709
    A Warning for Business Users 710
    Frame Relay 711
    Special Notes for Wireless Networking 711
    Special Notes for Cable Service 712
    Special Notes for ISDN Service 713

Configuring Your LAN 713
    Scheme A—Microsoft Internet Connection Sharing with a Dial-Up Connection 714
    Scheme B—Microsoft Internet Connection Sharing with a Broadband Connection ...718
    Scheme C—Sharing Router with a Broadband or Dial-Up Connection 719
    Using Universal Plug and Play 722
    Scheme D—Cable Internet with Multiple Computers 724
    Scheme E—Cable Internet with Multiple Computers and a Separate LAN 725
    Scheme F—Routed Service Using a Router 726

Making Services Available 728
    Enabling Access with Internet Connection Sharing 728
    Enabling Access with a Sharing Router 733

Troubleshooting 736

Tips from the Windows Pros: Speeding Up Vista? 737

23 Using a Windows Network 739

Windows Vista Was Made to Network 740
    Workgroup Versus Domain Networking 742

File Sharing in Windows Vista 742
    What's in a Name? 743
    The UNC Naming Convention 743

The Network and Sharing Center in Windows Vista 744
    The Major Components of the Network and Sharing Center 745
    Finding Network Shares 745

Using Shared Folders 747

Exploring and Searching the Network 748
    A Look at Shared Resources 748
    Searching the Network 749
    Advanced Active Directory Searching 752
    Using a Shared Disk Drive 753
    Using Internet-Based File Storage Services 754
    Mapping Drive Letters 754

Using Printers on the Network 757
    Installing Network Printers 759
    Using a Network Printer 761
    Using Printers over the Internet with IPP 762
    Using Other IPP Printers 763
    Using UNIX and LPR Printers 764
    Using AppleTalk Printers 765
    Using Other Network-Connected Printers 766

Using Network Resources Effectively 766
    Use Network Explorer 766
    Make Folder Shortcuts 767
    Use Offline Network Folders 767
    Put Tools and Documentation Online 767
    Organize Your Network to Fit Your Users 767

Sharing Resources 767

Sharing Folders and Drives 768
    Sharing Folders on a Workgroup or Domain Network 768

Sharing Printers 771
    Installing Extra Printer Drivers 772
    Setting Printer Permissions 773
    Tracking Printer Users 774
    Changing the Location of the Spool Directory 775
    Printer Pooling 776
    Separator Pages 776

Managing Network Use of Your Computer 778

Managing Network Resources Using the Command Line 778
    Mapping Drives with net use 779

Troubleshooting 781

Tips from the Windows Pros: Using Command-Line Utilities 782

24 Troubleshooting Your Network 785

When Good Networks Go Bad 786

Getting Started 786

Diagnostic Tools 788
    The Network Window 788
    Network and Sharing Center 789
    Network Diagnostics 790
    Windows Firewall 791
    Event Viewer 792
    Device Manager 793

Testing Network Cables 794

Checking Network Configuration 795
    ipconfig 795
    Computer 796
    Network Connections 797

Testing Network Connectivity 797
    ping 797

Diagnosing File and Printer Sharing Problems 799

Tips from the Windows Pros: Monitoring Your LAN 799

VI Maintaining Windows Vista

25 Windows Management and Maintenance 803

Overview 803

The Windows Vista Control Panel 804
    Breaking Down the Category View 805
    What Should You Use? 816

AutoPlay 820

Date and Time 821

Default Programs 823
    Set Your Default Programs 824
    Set Associations 824
    Set Program Access and Computer Defaults 825

Device Manager 825

Understanding and Resolving Hardware Conflicts 827
    IRQs 828
    DMA Channels 832
    I/O Port Assignments 833
    Memory Addresses 834
    Checking a Device's Resources 835
    Using Device Manager to Deal with Resource Conflicts 835

Ease of Access Center 837
    Accessibility Keyboard Settings 838
    Accessibility Sound Settings 839
    Accessibility Display Settings 840
    Accessibility Mouse Settings 841

Fonts 841
    Fonts 101 842
    Font Types 842
    Font and Font Information Sources 843
    Font Substitutions 844
    Font Installation and Management 845

Game Controllers 846

Keyboard 846

Mouse 847

Performance Information and Tools 850
    The Windows Experience Index 850
    Interpreting the Windows Experience Index 851
    Manage Startup Programs with Windows Defender 853
    Adjust Visual Effects 854
    Adjust Indexing Options 855
    Other Performance Options 856
    Advanced Tools 856

Reliability and Performance Monitor ... 857
    Resource Overview ... 857
    Performance Monitor ... 858
    Reliability Monitor ... 858
    Data Collector Sets and Reports ... 859

System Diagnostics Report ... 860

Power Options ... 860

Programs and Features ... 861
    Uninstall or Change a Program ... 861
    View Installed Updates ... 863
    Windows Marketplace ... 863
    Digital Locker ... 864
    Enable/Disable Windows Features ... 866

Regional and Language Options ... 867

System ... 868
    Remote Settings ... 869
    System Protection ... 869
    Advanced System Settings ... 870
    Data Execution Prevention (DEP) ... 871
    Environment Variables ... 871

Windows SideShow ... 872

Administrative Tools ... 872

Computer Management ... 874
    Event Viewer ... 876
    Shared Folders ... 879
    Local Security Policy ... 879
    Print Management ... 879

Services ... 880

Task Scheduler ... 881

System Configuration ... 881

Task Manager ... 883
    Applications Tab ... 884
    Processes Tab ... 885
    Services Tab ... 887
    Performance Tab ... 887
    Networking Tab ... 888
    Users Tab ... 889

System Information ... 889

Adjust Visual Effects and Performance Options ... 890

Using the iSCSI Initiator ... 891

System Tools Folder in Start Menu ... 892
    Character Map ... 892

Troubleshooting 895

Tips from the Windows Pros: Creating and Using Shortcuts to
    Your Favorite Control Panel Applets 895

26 Tweaking the GUI **897**

GUI: To Tweak or Not to Tweak 898

Start Menu Pizzazz! 898
    Tweaking the Taskbar 900

Display Properties 902
    Windows Color and Appearance 903
    Desktop Background 906
    Screen Savers 909
    The Sounds Link 911
    The Recording and Playback Tabs 914
    Changing Your Theme 914
    Display Settings 915

Tweak UI 919

Miscellaneous GUI Tips 920
    Fonts Preview Trick 920
    Which Windows Are You Using? 920
    Limiting Flip 3D 921
    More Visual Effects 922
    Administrator Tools Not Showing Up 922
    Changing the Location of the Documents and other Special Folders 923
    Cascading Elements off the Start Menu 924
    Switch Ctrl, Alt, and Caps Lock Keys 924
    Auto Scrolling with a Three-Button Mouse 924

Configuring the Recycle Bin 925

Troubleshooting 925

27 Managing Hard Disks **929**

Hard Disk Management 930

Windows Vista File and Storage Systems 930
    Basic Disks 930
    Dynamic Storage 931

Organizational Strategies 933

Windows Vista's Disk-Management Tools 934

Disk Management 935
    Assigning Drive Letters and Joining Volumes 936
    Dynamic Disk Management 939
    Extending a Disk 940
    Shrinking a Disk 940
    Creating a Spanned Volume 940
    Creating a Striped Volume 941

Removable Storage 942
Disk Defragmenter 943
    The MFT 944
    Configuring Defrag 946
Detecting and Repairing Disk Errors 946
Convert 947
Compression: How It Works, How to Use It 948
Disk Cleanup Utility 949
    Using Internet Explorer's Cache Cleanup 952
Zipping or Compressing Files 953
Third-Party Management Tools 953
Hard Disk Troubleshooting 954
    Take the Mental Approach First 955
    Problems and Solutions 956
Tips from the Windows Pros: Quieting a Noisy System 958

28 Troubleshooting and Repairing Problems 961

Troubleshooting 101 962
Easy Repair Options at Boot Time 962
    Using System Recovery 962
Startup Repair 963
System Restore 964
    Configuring System Restore 964
    Creating Restore Points 965
    Restoring Your System to an Earlier Time 966
Windows Complete PC Restore 967
Windows Memory Diagnostic Tool 968
Command Prompt 970
Repairing a System That Won't Start with Regedit 970
Boot Options 972
As a Last Resort 975
Preventing Problems 976
Fixing Application Problems with the Program Compatibility Wizard 977
    Adjusting Settings with the Compatibility Tab 978
Using Problem Reports and Solutions 979
Finding and Using Windows Vista Troubleshooting Resources 981
Black Magic of Troubleshooting 982
Tricks of the Windows Masters: Recovering Data from the
    System Recovery Options Menu 983

29 Keeping Windows and Other Software Up to Date 985

Windows Vista and Keeping Up to Date 986
Windows Update 986
    Windows Automatic Updates 987
    Windows Update Applet and Functions 988
    Other Windows Update Settings 989
    Viewing and Changing Installed Updates 991
Updating Drivers 992
    Manually Update Drivers 992
Service Packs 994
    Basic Service Pack Information 994
    Installation of Service Packs 995
Ultimate Extras 996
    Power Toys 997
Installing and Removing Software 998
    Installation Via CD or DVD 998
    Installation Via Downloaded Program 999
    Uninstalling or Changing a Program Applet 999
    Uninstalling Software 1000
    Compatibility Issues in 64-Bit Version 1002
    Other Program Compatibility Issues 1002
    Side-by-Side Installs 1003
    Virtual Registries and Folders 1004
Troubleshooting 1005
Tips from the Windows Pros: Windows Update Driver Settings 1007

30 Installing and Replacing Hardware 1009

Upgrading Your Hardware 1010
    BIOS Settings 1010
    Upgrading Your Hard Disk 1011
    Adding RAM 1012
Adding Hardware 1013
    Providing Drivers for Hardware Not in the List 1017
Removing Hardware 1018
Installing and Using Multiple Monitors 1019
Installing a UPS 1023
    Choosing a UPS 1025
    Installing and Configuring a UPS 1026
    Testing Your UPS Configuration 1028

How Many Upgrades Are Allowed before EULA and SPP Barf? 1028
    Upgrading Hardware in the Same Box and Complying with EULA 1030

Troubleshooting 1032

Tips from the Windows Pros: Upgrading and Optimizing Your Computer 1034
    Keep Your Eye on the Hardware Compatibility List 1034
    Sleuthing Out Conflicts 1035
    Optimizing Your Computer for Windows Vista 1035

31 Editing the Registry **1037**

What Is the Registry? 1038

How the Registry Is Organized 1039

Registry Contents 1041
    HKEY_LOCAL_MACHINE 1041
    HKEY_CURRENT_CONFIG 1042
    HKEY_CLASSES_ROOT 1042
    HKEY_USERS 1042
    HKEY_CURRENT_USER 1043

New Registry Features in Windows Vista 1043
    Registry Virtualization 1044
    Registry Reflection 1045

Backing Up and Restoring the Registry 1046
    Backing Up the Registry 1046
    Restoring the Registry 1048

Using Regedit 1050
    Viewing the Registry 1050
    Searching in the Registry 1051
    Editing Keys and Values 1053
    Advanced Registry Editing 1056
    Editing the Registry of a Remote Computer 1056
    Editing Registry Entries for Another User 1057
    Editing Registry Entries for Another Windows Installation 1059
    Editing Registry Security 1059

Other Registry Tools 1061
    X-Setup Pro 1061
    Registry Toolkit 1061
    Registrar Registry Manager 1061
    TweakVI 1062
    Registry-Hacker Websites 1062
    Google 1062

Registry Privileges and Policies 1063

Troubleshooting 1063

Tips from the Windows Pros: Deploying Registry Settings with REG Files 1066

32 Command-Line and Automation Tools 1069

Command-Line Tools 1070
The Windows Vista Command Prompt Environment 1070
  Command-Line Syntax 1071
  Quoting Filenames with Spaces 1072
  The Current Drive and Current Directory 1073
  Editing Command Lines 1074
  Filename Completion 1075
  Redirection and Pipes 1075
  Cut and Paste in the Command Prompt Window 1078
  Command-Line Tips 1078
  Getting Information About Command-Line Programs 1080
Command-Line Management Tools 1081
  The net use Command 1081
  The sc Command 1083
  The Shutdown Command 1085
Setting Environment Variables 1085
  Setting the PATH Environment Variable 1090
  Specifying the Location of Temporary Files 1091
Setting Command Prompt Window Properties 1092
  Keeping a Command Prompt Window Open After Execution 1094
The MS-DOS Environment 1094
  Customizing AUTOEXEC.NT and CONFIG.NT 1096
  Issues with DOSKEY and ANSI.SYS 1099
  Editing Advanced Settings for a DOS Application 1100
  Custom Startup Files 1102
  Unavailable MS-DOS Commands 1102
Batch Files 1104
  Batch File Basics 1104
  Batch File Programming 1107
  Batch File Tips 1112
Windows Script Host 1113
  How WSH works 1113
  Creating Scripts 1114
  Some Sample Scripts 1117
Task Scheduler 1123
Troubleshooting 1127
Tips from the Windows Pros: Getting More Information 1128

VII Security

33 Protecting Windows from Viruses and Spyware 1131

Malicious Software: Ignorance Is Not Bliss 1132
    Viruses Past and Present 1132
    Worms: "Look, Ma! No Hands!" 1133
    Spyware 1133
    Rootkits and Beyond 1134

Antimalware Strategy: Defense in Depth 1134
    Windows Security Center 1135
    Choosing and Installing an Antivirus Client 1136
    Windows Defender for Spyware Protection 1138
    Personal Firewalls: A Layer of Protection from Worms 1142
    Automatic Updates: Remove the Side Doors 1142
    Data Execution Prevention (DEP) 1142
    User Account Control (UAC) 1144
    Service Hardening 1146
    Internet Explorer 7 Malware Protection 1147

Tips from the Windows Pros: Avoiding Malware 1147

34 Protecting Your Data from Loss and Theft 1149

The Backup and Restore Center 1150
    Differences in the Backup and Restore Center 1150
    File and Folder Backups Versus Complete PC Backups 1152

Creating a File and Folder Backup 1153
    Working with Removable Media During Backups 1155
    How Backups Created with Back Up Files Are Stored 1156

Restoring Data from a File and Folder Backup 1157
    Restoring the Current User's Data 1157
    Performing an Advanced Restore 1158

Creating a Complete PC (Image) Backup 1160
    WBADMIN Command-Line System Backup and Restore 1162
    Using VHDMount with Complete PC Backup Images 1164

Restoring a Complete PC Backup Image 1172

Encrypted File System (EFS) 1173
    Using CIPHER 1175
    Rules for Using Encrypted Files 1177
    Suggested Folders to Encrypt 1178
    Protecting and Recovering Encrypted Files 1178

Disk Organization for Data Safety 1181

BitLocker Disk Encryption 1182
    BitLocker System Requirements 1183
    Using the BitLocker Drive Preparation Tool 1183
    Manual Preparation of the Hard Disk for Use with BitLocker 1184
    Enabling the TPM 1185

- Encrypting the Drive with BitLocker 1186
- BitLocker Drive Encryption Recovery 1187
- How BitLocker Protects Your Information 1188
- Differences Between BitLocker and EFS Encryption 1189

Recovering Previous Versions of a File 1190

NTFS File Permissions 1192
- Inheritance of Permissions 1194
- Advanced Security Settings 1195
- Viewing Effective Permissions 1196
- Access Auditing 1196
- Taking Ownership of Files 1197
- Assigning Permissions to Groups 1198
- Securing Your Printers 1199

Security Policy Configuration Options 1199

Third-Party Disc-Backup Tools 1200

Troubleshooting 1201

Tips from the Windows Pros: Restoring NTBACKUP Files 1203

35 Protecting Your Network from Hackers and Snoops 1205

It's a Cold, Cruel World 1206
- Who Would Be Interested in My Computer? 1206
- Types of Attack 1207
- Your Lines of Defense 1209

Network Security Basics 1210

Advantages of a NAT (Shared) Connection and Separate Router 1212
- Set Up Firewalls and NAT (Connection-Sharing) Devices 1212
- Windows Firewall 1213
- Packet Filtering 1213
- Using NAT or Internet Connection Sharing 1215
- Add-On Products for Windows 1216
- Secure Your Router 1216

Passwords Versus Passwordless File Sharing 1217
- Set Up Restrictive Access Controls 1218

Testing, Logging, and Monitoring 1219
- Test Your Defenses 1219
- Monitor Suspicious Activity 1221

Disaster Planning: Preparation for Recovery After an Attack 1222
- Make a Baseline Backup Before You Go Online 1222
- Make Frequent Backups When You're Online 1222
- Write and Test Server Restore Procedures 1222
- Write and Maintain Documentation 1223
- Prepare an Incident Plan 1223

Specific Configuration Steps for Windows Vista 1224
    If You Have a Standalone Windows Vista Computer 1224
    If You Have a LAN 1225
    Enabling Windows Firewall 1225
    Keep Up-to-Date 1226
    Tightening Local Security Policy 1227

Configuring Windows Firewall 1230
    Enabling and Disabling the Firewall 1231
    Enabling Exceptions 1231
    Advanced Firewall Settings 1234

Windows Firewall with Advanced Security 1235
    Configuring Windows Firewall with Advanced Security on a Local Computer 1236
    Firewall Rules 1238

More About Security 1240

Troubleshooting 1240

Tips from the Windows Pros: Having Professionals Audit Your Network 1242

36 Protecting Yourself from Fraud and Spam 1243

Phishing (Fishing) for Information 1244
    Live Phish: A Real-World Example 1244
    More Help from Internet Explorer 1249
    Two-Way Authentication 1250
    Two-Factor Authentication 1250
    Identity-Management Software 1251
    Avoiding Phishing 1252

Spam Not Fit for Consumption 1252
    Antispam Tactics 1253

Tips from the Windows Pros: Take Action Against Email Abuse 1257

VIII Windows On the Move

37 Wireless Networking 1261

Wireless Networking in Windows Vista 1262
    Types of Wireless Networks 1262

Wireless Security Issues 1262
    Plain Old Snooping 1263
    Man in the Middle 1264
    Wireless Security Keys 1264
    Longer Is Better 1264
    Take Care When You Share 1266

Joining a Wireless Network 1267
    In the Corporate Environment 1267
    At Home or the Small Office 1267

In Someone Else's Office 1269
　　　At a Public Hot Spot 1270
　Ad Hoc Networks and Meetings 1271
　Managing Wireless Network Connections 1271
　　　Switching Between Wireless Networks 1271
　　　Advanced Wireless Network Settings 1272
　Troubleshooting 1273
　Tips from the Windows Pros: The Wireless Command Line 1277

38 Hitting the Road 1279
　Windows Unplugged: Mobile and Remote Computing 1280
　Managing Mobile Computers 1280
　　　Windows Mobility Center 1281
　　　Getting the Most Out of Your Battery 1283
　VPN and Dial-Up Networking 1286
　　　Setting Up VPN and Dial-Up Networking 1288
　　　Setting a VPN or Dial-Up Connection's Properties 1289
　　　Managing Dial-Up Connections from Multiple Locations 1292
　　　Establishing a VPN or Dial-Up Connection 1293
　　　Using Remote Network Resources 1295
　　　Email and Network Connections 1295
　　　Monitoring and Ending a VPN or Dial-Up Connection 1296
　　　Routing Issues 1296
　Incoming VPN and Dial-Up Access 1297
　　　Setting Up VPN and Dial-Up Access 1298
　　　Enabling Incoming VPN Connections with NAT 1300
　Offline Folders 1301
　　　Identifying Files and Folders for Offline Use 1302
　　　Using Files While Offline 1303
　　　Sync Center 1305
　　　Managing and Encrypting Offline Files 1306
　　　Making Your Shared Folders Available for Offline Use by Others ...1307
　Multiple LAN Connections 1308
　Troubleshooting 1308
　Tips from the Windows Pros: Manually Adding Routing Information 1309

39 Meetings, Conferencing, and Collaboration 1311
　Vista: Plays Well with Others 1312
　Making Presentations with a Mobile Computer 1312
　　　Adjusting Presentation Settings 1312
　　　External Display 1314
　　　Network Projectors 1315

Windows Meeting Space 1315
    Setting Up Windows Meeting Space 1316
    Joining an Existing Meeting 1319
    Working in Windows Meeting Space 1319
    Sharing Documents as Handouts 1321
    Leaving a Meeting 1321

Remote Assistance 1322
    Enabling Remote Assistance 1322
    Requesting Remote Assistance 1323
    Responding to an Assistance Request 1326

Tips from the Windows Pros: It's Not All About the Bullets 1328

40 Remote Desktop **1329**

Using Your Computer Remotely 1330

Setting Up Access to Your Own Computer 1332
    Enabling Remote Desktop Access to Your Computer 1333
    Establishing 24×7 Access 1334
    Static IP Address or Dynamic DNS 1335
    Port Forwarding 1338

Connecting to Other Computers with Remote Desktop 1342
    Connection Options 1343
    Using the Remote Connection 1346
    Keyboard Shortcuts 1347
    Setting Up the Web-Based Client 1349

Troubleshooting 1350

Tips from the Windows Pros: Making More Than One Computer Available 1351

41 Tablet PC Features **1355**

Importance of Handwriting 1356

History of Tablets 1356

Who Needs a Tablet? 1358

What Does Tablet Vista Have That Regular PCs Don't? 1359

What's New in Tablet Vista? 1360

Choosing a Tablet PC 1360

Using Your Tablet PC—Differences and Similarities of Functions 1361

Input Methods Using the Input Panel 1361
    Writing Methods Using the Input Panel 1362
    Stylus Pen 1362
    Input Panel Options 1363

Gestures and Pen Flicks 1363
    Scratch-Out Gestures 1363
    Pen Flicks 1364

Handwriting Recognition 1364
    Specific Handwriting Recognition Errors 1365
    Teach the Recognizer Your Style 1365
AutoComplete 1366
Sticky Notes and the Snipping Tool 1366
    Sticky Notes 1367
    Snipping Tool 1367
Windows Journal 1369
Tablet PC Settings and Pen and Input Devices 1370
    Tablet PC Settings Menu 1370
    Pen and Input Devices Menu 1372
Troubleshooting 1374
Tips from the Windows Pros: A Whole New Level of Pen Flicks 1375

IX Appendixes

A Windows Programs and Services 1379

Windows Programs 1380
    Executable Programs 1380
    MS-DOS Applications 1399
    Control Panel Applets 1400
    Microsoft Management Console Plug-Ins 1401
    Screensavers 1402
Windows Services 1403

B What's New in Service Pack 1 (SP-1) 1421

Service Packs, Updates and Hotfixes, Oh My! 1422
Windows Vista Service Pack 1 1423
Obtaining and Installing Service Pack 1 1424
    Windows Update Method 1425
    The Update Process Itself 1426
Free Support from Mirosoft 1427
    Standalone Method 1427
Uninstalling Service Pack 1 1428
Making Service Pack 1 Permanent 1428

Index 1431

About the Authors

Robert Cowart has written more than 40 books on computer programming and applications, with more than a dozen on Windows. His titles include *Windows NT Unleashed*, *Mastering Windows 98*, *Windows NT Server Administrator's Bible*, and *Windows NT Server 4.0: No Experience Required*. Several of his books have been bestsellers in their category and have been translated into more than 20 languages. He has written on a wide range of computer-related topics for such magazines as *PC Week*, *PC World*, *PC Magazine*, *PC Tech Journal*, *Mac World*, and *Microsoft Systems Journal*. In addition to working as a freelance consultant specializing in small businesses, he has taught programming classes at the University of California Extension in San Francisco. He has appeared as a special guest on the PBS TV series *Computer Chronicles*, CNN's *Headline News*, ZD-TV's *The Screen Savers*, and ABC's *World News Tonight with Peter Jennings*. Robert lives in Berkeley, California. In his spare time he is involved in the music world, producing chamber-music concerts and playing various genres of music. He meditates regularly in hopes of rewiring his inner computer.

Brian Knittel has been a software developer for more than 30 years. After doing graduate work in nuclear medicine and magnetic resonance imaging technologies, he began a career as an independent consultant. An eclectic mix of clients has led to long-term projects in medical documentation, workflow management, real-time industrial system control, and most importantly, 20 years of real-world experience with MS-DOS, Windows, and computer networking in the business world. Previously, he coauthored *Special Edition Using Microsoft Windows 2000 Professional*, *Special Edition Using Microsoft Windows XP*, and contributed to several of Bob Cowart's other Windows books. Brian also coauthored *Upgrading and Repairing Microsoft Windows*, with Scott Mueller, and is the sole author of *Windows XP Under the Hood*. Brian lives in Oakland, California, and spends his free time restoring antique computers and trying to perfect his wood-fired pizza recipes.

About the Contributors

Everette Beatley is a fourth-year computer engineering major at Christopher Newport University in Newport News, Virginia. He currently works for Southern Electronics, Inc. in Kilmarnock, Virginia, as a System Administrator. When not in school, Everette lives in Lancaster, Virginia, where he enjoys road cycling and waterskiing on the Rappahannock River.

Eric Butow has authored or coauthored seven books since 2000, including *Master Visually Windows 2000 Server*, *Teach Yourself Visually Windows 2000 Server*, *FrontPage 2002 Weekend Crash Course*, *C#: Your Visual Blueprint*, *Creating Web Pages Bible*, and *Dreamweaver MX 2004 Savvy*. His most recent book is *The PDF Book for Microsoft Office*, an e-book produced by ExcelUser.com. He is also the CEO of Butow Communications Group (BCG), a technical writing and web design firm based in Roseville, California. Butow also writes for Addison-Wesley.

Greg Dickinson lives in Birmingham, Alabama, and has 10 years experience with computer networking. He works for one of the top 30 banks in the country, packaging and distributing software packages and updates to the bank's 6,000 desktops. When not wrestling with the intricacies of enterprise networks, Greg likes to spend his time recording training videos and singing in a barbershop chorus.

Diana Huggins is currently the Information Services Technical Communication Specialist for Great-West Life. She also works as an independent contractor providing both technical writing and consulting services. Diana has authored/coauthored several certification study guides, including *Windows 2000 Directory Services Design (Exam Cram 70-219)* as well as *MCSE Planning and Maintaining a Microsoft Windows Server 2003 Network Infrastructure (Exam 70-293)*. To complement this, she also spends a portion of her time providing technical-editing services and developing certification practice exams.

Alex G. Morales first managed networked computer systems in the 1980s and has since managed some of the world's largest Internet sites. Along with several industry certifications, he holds a bachelor's degree in anthropology from the University of Texas, and currently leads a stalwart team of engineers in the global deployment of Windows Vista at Dell, Inc. Alex lives in Austin, Texas, with his muse, Gwen, her son Evan, and Molly the Border Collie.

Will Schmied, MCSE, is a Senior Systems Administrator for a world-renowned children's research hospital. As a freelance writer, Will has worked with many publishers, including Microsoft and Pearson. Will has also worked directly with Microsoft in the MCSE exam-development process and is the founder of the popular Internet certification portal, www.mcseworld.com. Will currently resides in northern Mississippi with his wife, Chris; their children, Christopher, Austin, Andrea, and Hannah; their dogs, Charlie and Jack; and their cats, Smokey, Evin, and Socks.

Mark Edward Soper has worked with computers and related technologies since 1983 and specializes in technology education through training, writing, and public speaking. He has taught computer troubleshooting and other subjects to thousands of students, and is the author or coauthor of 17 books, most recently *Upgrading and Repairing Networks*, 5th edition, published by Que Publishing, and has also written more than 150 magazine articles. He has CompTIA A+ and Microsoft MCP certifications and provides online self-help content for Skywire Software, technology screening questions for ReviewNet. He also teaches applied technology classes for IvyTech Community College of Indiana. Mark lives in Evansville, Indiana, and blogs at www.markesoper.com.

Steve Suehring is a technology architect and author with a diverse background of computing experience. In recent years, Steve has worked on several books and magazine articles and has been an editor for a popular technology magazine. Steve has spoken at conferences and meetings internationally and currently works with clients to help them optimize and better utilize technologies, both old and new.

Brent Thal is a Virginian who is a senior at Christopher Newport University in computer engineering and plans to attend graduate school in computer science and applied physics. Brent comes from a long line of engineers. His grandfather was a mechanical engineer, and his father is a registered professional engineer (P.E.) in civil engineering and an adjunct professor of engineering at the University of Virginia. After graduate school, Brent plans to work in the computer engineering field for a highly reputable company and continue to write as a contributing author.

Dedication

In memory of my mother, Geraldine, for teaching me that the devil is in the details. —Bob

To my mother and father, for their encouragement. —Brian

Acknowledgments

This book, as much as the product it covers, is the product of a team effort. We couldn't have produced this without the great team at Que, the assistance of contributing writers, the patience and support of our friends, and so…

We feel privileged to be part of the consistently professional *Special Edition Using* family. Producing these highly technical, state-of-the art books requires a dedicated and knowledgeable staff, and once again the staff at Que did an amazing job. Executive editor Rick Kughen has provided unflagging, cheerful support and guidance through our four *SE Using* volumes. Also serving as development editor, Rick did double duty keeping us on schedule, as well as helping us to shape this tome. Rick pored over every word on every page of this new Vista edition, just as he has on numerous past editions, and offered invaluable direction and tuning. This is a much better book than it could have been without him.

We'd like to acknowledge the efforts of our technical editor, Mark Reddin. We also would like to thank the editorial, indexing, layout, art, proofing, and other production staff at Que—Patrick Kanouse, Seth Kerney, and Ken Johnson. You did a marvelous job.

We'd like to thank Everette Beatley, Eric Butow, Greg Dickinson, Diana Huggins, Arthur Knowles, Alex Morales, Mark Soper, Steve Suehring, Brent Thal, and Will Schmied for their expertise and hard work: Your contribution made this a better book and let it get to press on time (more or less!). You were a great writing team to work with. In addition to his writing skills, Everette Beatley deserves extra kudos for his always-available-by-IM invaluable backstage sleuthing of Vista issues and factoids. Special thanks to first-time authors but big-time computer pros Alex Morales and Brent Thal, and encouragement to keep writing! No book could make it to market without the real-world personal relationships developed between booksellers on the one hand, and the sales and marketing personnel back at the publishers. We've had the opportunity to meet sales and marketing folks in the computer publishing world and know what a difficult job selling and keeping up with the thousands of computer titles can be. Thanks to all of you for your pivotal role in helping us pay our mortgages!

Finally, we should acknowledge those who made it possible for us to get through the many months of writing. Bob first offers many thanks to Frank Banks, John Prendergast, and Dr. Steven Feig for keeping him ticking. Secondly, thanks to agent Carole McClendon of Waterside Productions for representing me in contractual matters. And finally, as always, thanks to friends and family who, even though used to seeing me disappear for months on end, let me back in the fold when it's over, especially Diane Zaremba, Hilary Abell, Kathy Geisler, Heidi Page, Kirsten Spalding, Jack Hoggatt, Anne Buchbinder, and Carol Christopher.

Brian adds thanks to Dave, Bryce, Frank, Todd, Bubba, and Lucy.

INTRODUCTION

WELCOME

Thank you for purchasing or considering the purchase of *Special Edition Using Microsoft Windows Vista* Second Edition. It's amazing the changes that 20 years can bring to a computer product such as Windows. When we wrote our first Windows book back in the mid-1980s, our publisher didn't even think the book would sell well enough to print more than 5,000 copies. Microsoft stock wasn't even a blip on most investors' radar screens. Boy, were they in the dark! Who could have imagined that a little more than a decade later, anyone who hoped to get hired for even a temp job in a small office would need to know how to use Microsoft Windows, Office, and a PC. Fifteen or so Windows books later, we're still finding new and exciting stuff to tell our readers.

Some people (including the U.S. Department of Justice) claim Microsoft's predominance on the PC operating system arena was won unethically through monopolistic practices. Whether or not this is true (we try, almost successfully, to stay out of the politics in this book), we believe that Windows has earned its position today through reasons other than having a stranglehold on the market. Consider that Windows NT 3.1 had 5 million lines of code. Windows Vista weighs in with about 50 million and takes up 4 or 5 gigabytes (sometimes more!) of disk space by itself. This represents a lot of work by anyone's accounting. Who could have imagined in 1985 that a mass-market operating system two decades later would have to include support for so many technologies, most of which didn't even exist at the time: DVD, DVD±RW, CD-R and CD-RW, Internet and intranet, MP3, MPEG, WMA, DV, USB, FireWire, APM, ACPI, RAID, UPS, PPOE, gigabit Ethernet, 802.11g, WPA2, IPv6, Teredo, fault tolerance, disk encryption and compression...? The list goes on. And that 4GB of disk space Vista occupies? It would have cost more than a quarter of a million dollars in 1985. Today, it costs a dollar or two.

Although rarely on the bleeding edge of technology, and often playing the role of the dictator with partner businesses and exterminator with competing businesses, Bill Gates has at least been benevolent from the users' point of view. In 1981, when we were building our first computers, the operating system (CP/M) had to be modified in assembly language and recompiled, and hardware parts had to be soldered together to make almost any new addition (such as a video display terminal) work. Virtually nothing was standardized, with the end result being that computers remained out of reach for average folks.

Together, Microsoft, Intel, and IBM changed all that. Today you can purchase a computer, a printer, a scanner, an external disk drive, a keyboard, a modem, a monitor, and a video card over the Internet, plug them in, install Windows, and they'll work together. The creation and adoption (and sometimes forcing) of hardware and software standards that have made the PC a household appliance the world over can largely be credited to Microsoft, like it or not. The unifying glue of this PC revolution has been Windows.

Yes, we all love to hate Windows, but it's here to stay. Linux and Mac OS X are formidable alternatives, but for most of us, at least for some time, Windows and Windows applications are "where it's at." And Windows Vista ushers in truly significant changes to the landscape. That's why we were excited to write this book.

Why This Book?

We all know this book will make an effective doorstop in a few years. You probably have a few already. (We've even written a few!) If you think it contains more information than you need, just remember how helpful a good reference can be when you need it at the 11th hour. And we all know that computer technology changes so fast that it's sometimes easier just to blink and ignore a phase than to study up on it. Windows Vista is definitely a significant upgrade in Windows's security and sophistication—one you're going to need to understand.

Windows Vista might seem similar to its predecessor, Windows XP, but it's a very different animal. Yes, the graphics and display elements are flashier, but it's the deeper changes that matter most. With its radically improved security systems, revamped Control Panel, friendlier network setup tools, new problem-tracking systems, improved support for mobile computers, and completely revamped networking and graphics software infrastructures, Vista leaves Windows XP in the dust. In all ways, it's superior to any operating system Microsoft has ever produced.

Is Windows Vista so easy to use that books are unnecessary? Unfortunately, no. True, as with other releases of Windows, online help is available. As has been the case ever since Windows 95, however, no printed documentation is available (to save Microsoft the cost), and the Help files are written by Microsoft employees and contractors. You won't find criticisms, complaints, workarounds, or suggestions that you use alternative software vendors, let alone explanations of *why* you have to do things a certain way. For that, you need this book! We will even show you tools and techniques that Microsoft's insiders didn't think were important enough to document at all.

You might know that Windows Vista comes in a bewildering array of versions, primarily Home Basic, Home Premium, Business, Enterprise, and Ultimate (not to mention Starter, which is sold only in emerging markets, and several extra versions sold in the European Union to comply with antitrust court-mandated restrictions). But Vista is Vista, and all that really distinguishes the versions is the availability of various features. *Most* of the differences matter only in the corporate world, where Vista will be managed by network administrators, so you don't need to worry about those yourself. For the remaining features, we tell you when certain features do or don't apply to your particular version of Windows Vista. (And we show you how to upgrade from one version to a better version, if you want the features your copy doesn't have!)

In this book's many pages, we focus not just on the gee-whiz side of the technology, but why you should care, what you can get from it, and what you can forget about. The lead author on this book has previously written 16 books about Windows, all in plain English (several bestsellers), designed for everyone from rank beginners to full-on system administrators deploying NT Server domains. The coauthor has designed software and networks for more than 20 years and has been writing about Windows for 10 years. We work with and write about various versions of Windows year in and year out. We have a clear understanding of what confuses users and system administrators about installing, configuring, or using Windows, as well as (we hope) how to best convey the solutions to our readers.

While writing this book, we tried to stay vigilant in following four cardinal rules:

- Keep it practical.
- Keep it accurate.
- Keep it concise.
- Keep it interesting, and even crack a joke or two.

We believe that you will find this to be the best and most comprehensive book available on Windows Vista for beginners through advanced users. And whether you use Windows Vista yourself or support others who do, we firmly believe this book will address your questions and needs.

Our book addresses both home and business computer users. We assume you probably are not an engineer, and we do our best to speak in plain English and not snow you with unexplained jargon. As we wrote, we imagined that you, our reader, are a friend or co-worker who's familiar enough with your computer to know what it's capable of, but might not know the details of how to make it all happen. So we show you, in a helpful, friendly, professional tone. In the process, we also hope to show you things that you might not have known, which will help make your life easier—your computing life, anyway. We spent months and months poking into Vista's darker corners so you wouldn't have to. And, if you're looking for power-user tips and some nitty-gritty details, we make sure you get those, too. We try to make clear what information is essential for you to understand and what is optional for just those of you who are especially interested.

We're also willing to tell you what we don't cover. No book can do it all. As the title implies, this book is about Windows Vista. We don't cover setting up the Server versions of this operating system called Windows 2000 Server, Windows Server 2003 Server, and the upcoming Windows Server code named "Longhorn." However, we do tell you how to connect to and interact with these servers, and even other operating systems, including Mac OS X, Linux, and older variants of Windows, over a local area network.

Because of space limitations, there is only one chapter devoted to coverage of Windows Vista's command-line utilities, batch file language, and Windows Script Host. For that (in spades!), you might want to check Brian's book *Windows XP Under the Hood*, which is still relevant to Vista.

Even when you've become a Windows Vista pro, we think you'll find this book to be a valuable source of reference information in the future. Both the table of contents and the very complete index will provide easy means for locating information when you need it quickly.

How Our Book Is Organized

Although this book advances logically from beginning to end, it's written so that you can jump in at any location, quickly get the information you need, and get out. You don't have to read it from start to finish, nor do you need to work through complex tutorials.

This book is broken down into six major parts. Here's the skinny on each one:

Part I, "Introducing Windows Vista," introduces Vista's new and improved features and shows you how to install it on a new computer or upgrade an older version of Windows to Vista. It also shows you how to apply Service Packs to keep your version of Vista up-to-date. Finally, we take you on a one-hour guided tour that shows you the best of Vista's features and walks you through making essential settings and adjustments that will help you get the most out of your computer.

In Part II, "Using Windows Vista," we cover the core parts of Vista, the parts you'll use no matter what else you do with your computer: managing documents and files, using the Windows desktop, starting and stopping applications, searching through your computer's contents, printing, and the new "Sidebar" desktop gadgets. Don't skip this section, even—or rather, *especially*—if you've used previous versions of Windows. Vista does many things differently, and you'll want to see how to take advantage of it!

Vista has great new tools for viewing, playing, creating, editing, and managing music, movies, and pictures. In Part III, "Multimedia and Imaging," we show you how to use the new Windows Media Player, purchase music online, burn CDs, extract and edit images from cameras and scanners, use Windows Movie Maker to edit video, and create DVDs. Finally, we show you how to use Windows Media Center, which lets you view all that stuff, and on a properly equipped computer, records and plays back your favorite TV shows. We even show you how to burn DVDs from your recorded shows and compress them for playback on other devices.

In Part IV, "Windows Vista and the Internet," we help you set up an Internet connection and then move on to Vista's Internet tools. We provide in-depth coverage of the new and improved (and safer!) Internet Explorer and the new and improved (and safer!) Windows Mail, which replaces the Outlook Express email and newsgroup reader provided with previous versions of Windows. The final two chapters show you how to set up your own web server and how to diagnose Internet connection problems.

Networks used to be found only in high-falutin' offices and corporate settings. Now, any home or office with two or more computers should have a network. A LAN is inexpensive, and with one you can share an Internet connection, copy and back up files, and use any printer from any computer. In Part V, "Networking," we give you a tour of Windows Vista's network features, walk you through setting up a network in your home or office, and show you how to take advantage of it in day-to-day use. We also show you how easy it is to share a DSL or cable Internet connection with all your computers at once, show you how to network with other operating systems, and finally, help you fix it when it all stops working.

Part VI, "Maintaining Windows Vista," covers system configuration and maintenance. We tell you how to work with the Control Panel and System Administration tools, provide tips and tricks for customizing the graphical user interface to maximize efficiency, manage your hard disk and other hardware, and describe a variety of ways to upgrade your hardware and software (including third-party programs) for maximum performance. We show you how to troubleshoot hardware and software problems, edit the Windows Registry, and for real power-users, show how to use the command-line interface.

When Windows was introduced nearly two decades ago, computer viruses, online fraud, and hacking were only starting to emerge as threats. Today (thanks in great part to *gaping* security holes in previous versions of Windows), computer threats are a worldwide problem, online and offline. In Part VII, "Security," we provide a 360-degree view of Windows Vista's substantial improvements in security. Here you'll find out both what Vista will do to help you, and what you must do for yourself. We cover protection against viruses and spyware, loss and theft, hackers and snoops, and fraud and spam—in that order.

Part VIII, "Windows on the Move," shows you how to get the most out of Windows Vista when either you or your computer, or both, are on the go. We show you how to use wireless networking safely, how to get the most out of your laptop, and how to connect to remote networks. We also show you how you and others can work together using your computers and Windows Meeting Space, and we finish up with a chapter that shows you how to use Remote Desktop to reach and use your own computer from anywhere in the world.

Appendix A, "Windows Programs and Services," lists all the programs and services provided with all the versions of Windows, so you can find out just what each of those things do that you see in the Task Manager and Control Panel.

Appendix B, "What's New in Service Pack 1," covers Service Pack 1 (SP-1) of Windows Vista, which shipped in the first half of 2008. There you can learn about the latest security and bug fixes and the few new added features in Service Pack 1.

Conventions Used in This Book

Special conventions are used throughout this book to help you get the most from the book and from Windows Vista.

Text Conventions

Various typefaces in this book identify terms and other special objects. These special typefaces include the following:

Type	Meaning
Italic	New terms or phrases when initially defined.
`Monospace`	Information that appears in code or onscreen.
`Bold monospace`	Information you type.

Words separated by commas—All Windows book publishers struggle with how to represent command sequences when menus and dialog boxes are involved. In this book, we separate commands using a comma. Yeah, we know it's confusing, but this is traditionally how the *Special Edition Using* book series does it, and traditions die hard. So, for example, the instruction "Choose Edit, Cut" means that you should open the Edit menu and choose Cut. Another, more complex example is "Click Start, Settings, Control Panel, System, Hardware, Device Manager."

Key combinations are represented with a plus sign. For example, if the text calls for you to press Ctrl+Alt+Delete, you would press the Ctrl, Alt, and Delete keys at the same time.

Tips from the Windows Pros

Ever wonder how the experts get their work done better and faster than anyone else? Ever wonder how they became experts in the first place? You'll find out in these special sections throughout the book. We've spent a lot of time under the Windows hood, so to speak, getting dirty and learning what makes Windows Vista tick. So, with the information we provide in these sections, you can roll up your shirt sleeves and dig in.

Special Elements

Throughout this book, you'll find Notes, Cautions, Sidebars, Cross-References, and Troubleshooting Tips. Often, you'll find just the tidbit you need to get through a rough day at the office or the one whiz-bang trick that will make you the office hero. You'll also find little nuggets of wisdom, humor, and lingo that you can use to amaze your friends and family, not to mention making you cocktail-party literate.

TIP
> We specially designed these tips to showcase the best of the best. Just because you get your work done doesn't mean you're doing it in the fastest, easiest way possible. We show you how to maximize your Windows experience. Don't miss these tips!

NOTE
> Notes point out items that you should be aware of, but you can skip them if you're in a hurry. Generally, we've added notes as a way to give you some extra information on a topic without weighing you down.

CAUTION
> Pay attention to cautions! They could save you precious hours in lost work.

We designed these elements to call attention to common pitfalls that you're likely to encounter. When you see a Troubleshooting Tip, you can flip to the end of the chapter to learn how to solve or avoid a problem.

CROSS-REFERENCES

Cross-references are designed to point you to other locations in this book (or other books in the Que family) that will provide supplemental or supporting information. Cross-references appear as follows:

→ For information on updating offline web pages, **see** "Browsing Offline," **p. 299**.

Sidebars
Sidebars are designed to provide information that is ancillary to the topic being discussed. Read this information if you want to learn more details about an application or task.

PART I

INTRODUCING WINDOWS VISTA

1 Introducing Windows Vista   3

2 Installing and Upgrading Windows Vista   41

3 The First Hour   77

CHAPTER 1

INTRODUCING WINDOWS VISTA

In this chapter

An Overview of Windows Vista   4

A Little Windows History   6

So What's New in Windows Vista?   8

Differences Among Versions of Vista   32

How Does Windows Vista Compare to UNIX and Linux?   35

Windows Vista on the Corporate Network   39

An Overview of Windows Vista

Windows Vista is the successor to Windows XP (Home and Professional). As such, it takes its place as the latest corporate desktop and workstation upgrade, and additionally sets its sights on the home office and even home entertainment/gaming console. That's quite a lot of product ambition under one hood. Perhaps that is why it has taken so many years to produce. Originally codenamed Longhorn, the "Long" part of the name turned out to be more prophetic than anyone could have known.

The goal Microsoft set for Windows Vista was so ambitious that it might explain the incredibly protracted time it took to get it to market. Vista came later than Godot. We've been waiting since 2003 (in 2000, Microsoft rumored Longhorn would arrive by then). To be more precise, at that time, Bill Gates promised a version of Windows that was more advanced even than Vista, dubbed Blackcomb. However, within 12 months of that announcement, Microsoft realized that this was not feasible and that a scaled-down version of Blackcomb (Longhorn) needed to be released to fill the gap. The market (and Microsoft) could not wait as long as Blackcomb would take to write.

As time passed, however, more and more features worked their way into Longhorn, and the project was becoming increasingly unwieldy. Despite attempts to control the size of this stopgap operating system, Longhorn was actually growing into the original vision of Blackcomb. The code was ballooning, and the process couldn't be stopped. The upshot was that this pushed out the delivery date of Longhorn, first to 2005, then to early 2006, and finally to late 2006.

Some talk circulated at Microsoft about delivering a stopgap version of Vista (which some called Shorthorn) between XP Service Pack 2 and Vista, but that idea was scrubbed. The upshot is that we have waited 5 years for a new operating system from Microsoft, and Microsoft execs have publicly sworn that nobody will ever have to wait this long for a Windows operating system upgrade. We have our doubts.

Anyway, let's move on to talk about what Vista is and is not.

Following in the footsteps of Windows XP Professional and Windows XP Home Edition, Windows Vista comes in five flavors (actually as many as seven, depending on how finely you split the hairs):

- Vista Home Basic
- Vista Home Premium
- Vista Business
- Vista Enterprise
- Vista Ultimate

In addition to these flavors, available at purchase, Vista lets you "roll your own" and upgrade its features to suit your computing needs and environment. This is a first for Microsoft, which previously steered users into one of two discrete camps, business or home. But as the definition of "workplace" has become increasingly sketchy (as in small office, home office, café office, multimedia office), computer and software makers have had to adapt their marketing strategies and product designs accordingly, building in a maximum of flexibility. Just like at Burger King, now you can have Vista your way.

Similar to Windows XP, which was the first Windows operating system to be erected upon a unified code base for both home and business users, Vista flavors benefit from being very much the same under the hood. Recall that between 1993 and the release of XP, there were very separate home-oriented (Windows 3.*x*/9*x*/Me) and corporate-oriented (Windows NT/2000) versions with drastically different internal designs. The common core of all the Vista versions makes program and device driver development much easier because device drivers and software programs need to be created just once rather than twice.

Admittedly, Vista's design mandate was ambitious: to create a more secure, flashy-looking, reliable, easy-to-use operating system with a functionality ranging from that of an excellent gaming and home entertainment platform all the way to a full-blown highly secure, mission-critical business networking machine. It needed to be more attractive, more capable, and much more robust than XP; incorporate all the latest technologies; and be far less susceptible to incursions from viruses, phishing attacks, spam, and the like. These malware infiltrations have kept legions of IT professionals in business, but they have grown nightmarish for all Windows-based IT departments.

Even though new technologies such as USB2, Bluetooth, TV recording (similar to TiVo), and ever-evolving versions of Windows Update, Windows Defender, and the like were being sort of Scotch-taped into XP through online downloads or later market-niche releases, these were really stopgap, piecemeal add-ins. Of course, Vista incorporates all these evolving technologies but goes further: The kernel of the operating system has been rewritten to correct inherent design flaws and vulnerabilities in the XP model that could not otherwise be addressed.

Vista also offered a seriously redesigned interface, while still being familiar enough for users upgrading from Windows 9*x* or Windows Me. Gone are many of the menus XP users have grown accustomed to, replaced by a much more web-like view of the computer, with phrase-like links that imply their function—for example, "See what happens when I press the Power button."

Windows XP was designed to provide application and hardware compatibility with products made for older versions of Windows, and even MS-DOS game and graphics applications. Vista carries over this same compatibility in its 32-bit versions, but Windows Vista 64-bit versions have abandoned those legacy programs. The time has come to put those old dogs to rest. There are ways around this, using Virtual PC, for example, so you don't have to jettison your favorite Windows 9*x* or DOS programs in Vista 64. We'll talk about Virtual PC in Chapter 2, "Installing and Upgrading Windows Vista."

A Little Windows History

First we review a little Windows history; then we get into what is and isn't in Windows Vista.

As you surely know, Windows is a *graphical user interface (GUI)* and *operating system (OS)* that is the heart and soul of your computer. Although Windows was once a toy (I remember when people bought Windows mainly because of the graphical word processor and paint program it included), it's now an essential element in nearly everyone's computing experience.

When Windows first hit the market in 1985, it actually was a shell that sat upon the increasingly shaky foundations of MS-DOS. Early versions were frequently used as menuing systems for launching MS-DOS programs because programs that required Windows were quite scarce for several years. In fact, to help promote Windows as a platform for programs, Microsoft distributed a "runtime" version of Windows with some of the early Windows-based programs, such as Aldus PageMaker (now an Adobe product). Users who didn't have a full version of Windows needed to install the runtime version before using the program. The runtime version of Windows was launched when the application (such as PageMaker) was started, and provided Windows menuing and print services; it closed when the application was closed. The original name for Windows was *Interface Manager*.

Windows didn't really take off until the introduction of Windows 3.0 in 1990 (it could multitask both DOS and Windows programs if you used a 386 or 486 processor) and Windows 3.1 in 1992, which introduced TrueType scalable fonts. Windows for Workgroups 3.1 (1992) and 3.11 (1994) pioneered the built-in networking features that typified all subsequent versions of Windows. Windows for Workgroups 3.11 was the last version of Windows to require that MS-DOS or a comparable text-based operating system be present at installation time.

In August 1995, Windows 95 was embraced with huge acclaim and excitement. Even people without computers queued up in long lines at midnight to buy it when it officially went on sale. Over a million copies sold in the first 4 days; about a million copies sold each day for a week.

Windows 98, Windows 98 Second Edition, and Windows Me followed Windows 95, but none of those releases could match the excitement generated by Windows 95, probably because they were only icing on the cake, adding a few features or new technologies to the same Windows 95 graphical user interface and code base.

Although Windows 95, Windows 98, and Windows Me made it appear as if MS-DOS wasn't being used, they were in fact deeply intertwined with and dependent on DOS to perform some functions. This dependence upon MS-DOS made for an increasingly unstable operating system because the management tricks necessary to keep MS-DOS, old 16-bit Windows applications, and new 32-bit Windows programs running on the same hardware at the same time led to frequent reboots and system lockups.

Although Windows XP retained and enhanced many of the features that Windows 9x and Windows Me pioneered, Windows XP was not a true descendent of DOS-based Windows. Instead, the Windows XP family was the latest descendent of the "business-class" Windows NT family, a family of Windows products that didn't use MS-DOS as its foundation. Microsoft's development of a non-DOS-based operating system goes back to 1987 and the joint development (with IBM) of a Windows replacement called OS/2. OS/2 was aimed squarely at the emerging corporate network world, then dominated by Novell and its NetWare network operating system.

Unlike NetWare, Microsoft and IBM's OS/2 was designed to handle both the server and the desktop side of network computing. Unfortunately for OS/2, the IBM-Microsoft partnership broke up in 1991 after a series of disagreements about the direction of OS/2. IBM kept OS/2, and Microsoft stuck with Windows. Microsoft had already begun the development of Windows NT in October 1988 with the hiring of Dave Cutler, who had developed the Virtual Memory System (VMS) operating system for the Digital Equipment (DEC) line of VAX multitasking and multiuser computers.

The development of Windows NT took several years: The first version to reach retail shelves, Windows NT 3.1, was introduced in mid-1993. Windows NT introduced several key features:

- Preemptive multitasking. The user doesn't need to wait for one task to finish before starting another one.
- Client/server model for computing. The operating system is divided into two parts, just as with mainframe systems.
- Dynamic disk caching/virtual memory. The operating system can use more than one drive as virtual memory (using disk space in place of RAM); desktop Windows versions up through Windows Me can use only one drive for virtual memory.
- Fault tolerance features. The capability to handle power outages and disk crashes.
- The capability to start and stop network services without rebooting.
- Fully 32-bit architecture. Windows NT and its successors are free of the limitations of 16-bit Windows (and MS-DOS!) instructions.
- Support for multiple file systems, including the old FAT16 file system used by MS-DOS and Windows 9x, and the NTFS file system developed for Windows NT, which supports advanced security features, long filenames, and automatic error correction.

Windows NT 4.0, introduced in mid-1996, was modeled after the Windows 95 user interface (instead of the Windows 3.1 user interface used by earlier Windows NT versions) and provided more effective crash protection than Windows 95. However, it lacked support for Plug and Play, the easy hardware-installation feature introduced by Windows 95, and many Windows 95–compatible hardware devices wouldn't work with Windows NT 4.0.

Windows 2000, introduced in early 2000, was originally called NT 5.0 during its prerelease period and began the NT family's move toward becoming user friendly. It had Plug and Play hardware support, ACPI power management, support for USB and IEEE-1394 ports and devices, AGP video, Internet Connection Sharing, and enhanced system management. Windows 2000 also improved drive support by adding support for FAT32, the file system introduced by Windows 95 OSR 2.*x* that solved the 2.1GB limit per drive letter imposed by FAT16. In addition, it introduced a more advanced version of the NT File System (NTFS) that supported file encryption, file compression, and support for mounting and dismounting drives, to allow them to be accessed through folders on another drive.

While Windows NT was being developed and improved, Microsoft was also advancing its Windows 9*x* product family, which culminated in the release of Windows Me in 2000. Like Windows 9*x*, Windows Me was a hybrid operating system with some features that it inherited from MS-DOS and 32-bit code, so its internal architecture was nothing like that of Windows XP. From the users' viewpoint, the most significant aspect was Windows Me's introduction of a variety of built-in multimedia and imaging features, including the Scanner and Camera Wizard, slideshows in the My Pictures folder, and Movie Maker. Another important feature Windows Me pioneered was System Restore, which enabled the user to get around tricky OS problems by resetting the system configuration to its state at a previous point in time.

Originally code-named Whistler, Windows XP was the product of a development process that began with a consumer operating system code-named Neptune in late 1999 and a separate business-oriented operating system code-named Odyssey, which was planned as a successor to Windows 2000. In January 2000, Microsoft decided to integrate Neptune and Odyssey into a single operating system family code-named Whistler, which you now know as Windows XP. Windows XP is a combination of the security, stability, and corporate networking features of Windows 2000, and the multimedia, entertainment, and error-handling features of Windows Me.

Windows XP was an "extensible" operating system built around a UNIX-like micro kernel derived from Windows 2000, featuring an object-oriented, modular design that enabled various types of services, file systems, and other subsystems to be attached to the core operating system, just as various types of hardware can be attached to a PC. Windows XP could emulate other operating systems and support applications originally designed for DOS, 16-bit Windows, older 32-bit Windows versions, and POSIX-compliant UNIX applications. Although Windows 2000 had a subsystem for OS/2, XP did not. Also, whereas Windows 2000 provided a "one-size-fits-all" approach to running older Windows programs, which didn't always work, Windows XP went beyond Windows 2000 by providing a customizable "compatibility mode" feature that enabled the user to select which version of Windows it should emulate to run a particular program.

So What's New in Windows Vista?

One of the questions people ask us as we write books about each new version of Windows is whether the new version is different enough to justify the hassle of upgrading. We don't always answer "yes." For example, Windows Me was not a major improvement over Windows 98. For that matter, Windows 98 wasn't much to write home about, either. In our opinion, it was much less stable than Win 95. By contrast, XP was a major upgrade from any previous version of Windows. Likewise, Vista is a major upgrade, in large part because of how long we had to wait for it. If you haven't taken the leap from Win 9*x* by now, you'd better think about it seriously: Microsoft no longer produces security fixes or provides any other support for Windows 95, 98, and Me.

> **NOTE**
>
> In this section, we discuss what is new in Vista. We don't bother telling you the boatloads of features and internals that Vista inherited from XP (and XP from Win 2000, NT, and so on). Please see our previous books for those dirty little details. (See *Special Edition Using Windows XP Professional* and *Platinum Edition Using Windows XP* for specifics about XP, *Using Windows 2000* for details about Windows 2000, and so on.) An Amazon search for "Cowart and Knittel" will fetch you the list of our almost 20 years of output as coauthors.

The jump from Windows XP to Vista, although more of an incremental leap (such as the jump from Windows 95 to 98), brings some significant improvements and many changes. Although Windows Vista is a much-improved version of the Windows XP family, preserving Windows XP's corporate networking and security features, it is also stacked with multimedia capabilities, including support for presentation projectors, slideshows, movie making, and DVD burning. Furthermore, in its Ultimate and Home versions, it includes Media Center capabilities.

How big a change is Windows Vista? Estimates are that by the time it was released, it contained about 55 million lines of code (see Table 1.1). That's about 20% more code than its immediate predecessor, Windows XP.

TABLE 1.1 LINES OF CODE COMPARISON

Operating System	Lines of Programming Code
Windows NT 3.1	3 million
Windows NT 3.5	10 million
Windows 95	10 million
Windows 98	13 million
NT 4	16.5 million
Windows 2000	~29 million
Windows 2000 Advanced Server	~33 million
Windows 2000 Datacenter	>40 million
Windows XP	45 million
Windows Server 2003	50 million
Windows Vista	~55 million

> **NOTE**
>
> Notice that approximately 10–15 million new lines of code were added in Vista, relative to XP. With a team of an estimated 2,000 developers working on Vista over 5 years, the average Vista developer was thus estimated to be producing only around 1,000 lines of code per year. Some estimates are that the average for software developers in the United States produces more on the order of 6,200 lines a year. It's anybody's guess why programmer output was slow at Microsoft, but some blogs have cited poor management issues.

Because Windows Vista offers so many improvements and new features compared to Windows XP, 9x, Me, and 2000, in this section, we highlight some of the new and improved features and what each feature does. Table 1.2 highlights some of the key improvements found in Windows Vista and points you to the chapter(s) in which each is covered. Most of them are at least introduced in this chapter.

TABLE 1.2   COVERAGE OF NEW AND IMPROVED WINDOWS VISTA FEATURES

New Vista Features	Covered in Chapters…
Setup:	
New Files and Settings Transfer Wizard	3
New interface:	
Aero	4, 26
Live task thumbnails	4
Flip and Flip 3D	4
Start "orb"	4
Welcome Center	3
Searching from the taskbar	5
New Explorers	4, 5
"Search folders"	5
Meta data editing	5, 8
Sidebar and Gadgets	7
Speech recognition	4
System security enhancements:	
User Account Control	3
Windows Defender	33
Better auto updater	29
Bidirectional firewall	35
Malicious Software Removal Tool (MSRT)	33

New Vista Features	Covered in Chapters...
Improved web browsing with IE 7:	
Tabbed browsing	15
Shrink-to-fit printing	15
RSS support	15
Tighter security	15, 33, 36
Data security enhancements:	
New Windows Backup	34, 35
"Previous Versions"	34
Volume Shadow Copy	34
Complete PC Backup	34
BitLocker	34
Performance:	
Windows SuperFetch	1
Windows ReadyBoost	1
Windows ReadyDrive	1
Restart Manager	1
Power management:	
Sleep mode	4, 25, 38
Mobility Center	25, 38
New or improved applications:	
Mail	16
Calendar	7
Windows Fax and Scan	10
Windows Meeting Space	39
Movie Maker	11
Media Player 11	8
Networking:	
New Network and Sharing Center	19, 20, 23
IPv6 support	19
Teredo IPv6 tunneling support	19
USB thumbdrive setup for workstations	37
Network Map display	1, 24

continues

Table 1.2   Continued

New Vista Features	Covered in Chapters...
Better wireless network security (WPA2)	19, 37
Network Location Awareness	19, 37
New network diagnostics tool	19, 37
Network speed optimization	19, 24
System management and stability:	
Less disruptive Windows Update	29
Reliability and Performance reports to detect impending hard-disk crash and other issues	28
Potential application crash warning	1
Startup Repair tool	28
Reliability Monitor	1
Productivity:	
Tablet PC support	41
Sync Center	38
XPS electronic document support	6
Entertainment:	
Enhanced new Media Center Edition, including HDTV and multiroom support	13
Family Safety Settings: parental controls for managing children's gaming and web activity	13, 15
Easy access Game folder	4
Miscellaneous	
Windows Ultimate Extras	29

Now on to a brief description of these new and/or improved features so you can get a sense of what the Vista hoopla is all about.

Interface Improvements

Hands down, Windows Vista really is the best-looking version of Windows ever. In fact, with the right display adapter, it's quite gorgeous and competes neck and neck with Apple's OS X. Of course, that is most certainly what Microsoft had in mind—keeping up with the Joneses. Even before you have time to check out all the improved functionality listed in Table 1.2, you'll notice the new look of Vista, called Aero. Vista takes advantage of features built into modern display adapter cards that until now mostly gamers have enjoyed. Modern display adapters offer gee-whiz capabilities that largely go underutilized by the Windows operating system (which is just one reason that games often work outside the operating system display software). We've grown used to a sort of pedestrian look of Windows and such oddities as windows that "tear" when you drag them across the screen too quickly, or windows that suddenly disappear behind others or down to the taskbar at the bottom of the screen if you accidentally click on the wrong object. In Vista, as with OS X, there are some visual cues as to where things have gone.

Aero and Glass

Even better, if your computer is running Home Premium, Ultimate, or one of the Business editions of Vista, that means it has a powerful enough display card to let Vista glam itself up by using the Aero interface. Aero gives you some slick eye candy, such as translucent title bars (called glass), live taskbar thumbnails, and Flip 3D. Figure 1.1 shows an example of Aero's glass. Notice that the close/minimize/restore buttons at the top-right corner of a window have also changed.

Figure 1.1
The new Aero, or "glass," look translucently reveals objects behind the front-most window.

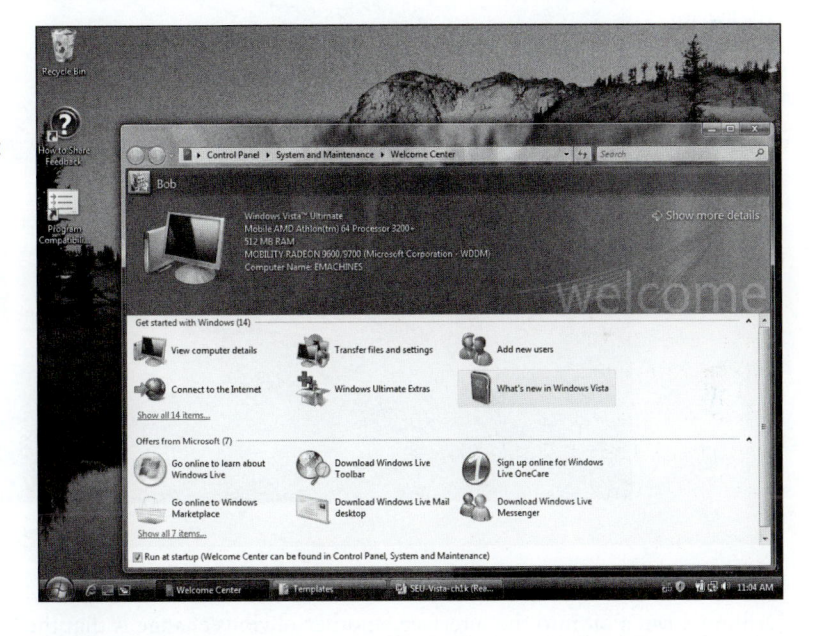

Ever lost track of what a button down on the taskbar is (that is, what application or document is minimized down there)? With Aero, you can just hover over a taskbar icon to see a live thumbnail appear above the button. Even if the application is playing a video or doing a slideshow, the thumbnail will accurately reflect what's going on because it's live. This is useful for tracking ongoing processes (such as video rendering, spreadsheet calculations, or file downloading), or just as a reminder of which window you want to restore to the screen. Figure 1.2 shows an example of a live thumbnail.

Thumbnails are fine, but they're a bit tiny. If you have Aero, a flashy new feature for task switching is called Flip 3D. It's like Alt+tabbing (which has been in Windows for a long time), only better. If you press Windows+Tab, you see live windows of each open application or document, stacked in 3D like on a Rolodex wheel. You can rotate through them with each key press and release when the one you want is up front, or click on the one you want anywhere in the stack. Even if a movie is playing in a window, it will be shown in tilted perspective, scaled properly, and will keep playing. Figure 1.3 shows an example of Flip 3D.

Figure 1.2
Just hover your pointer over a taskbar button, and Aero shows a live thumbnail of the application or document.

Figure 1.3
Flip 3D in the Aero interface lets you quickly cycle through your open apps and documents, just like Alt+tabbing, only with live windows.

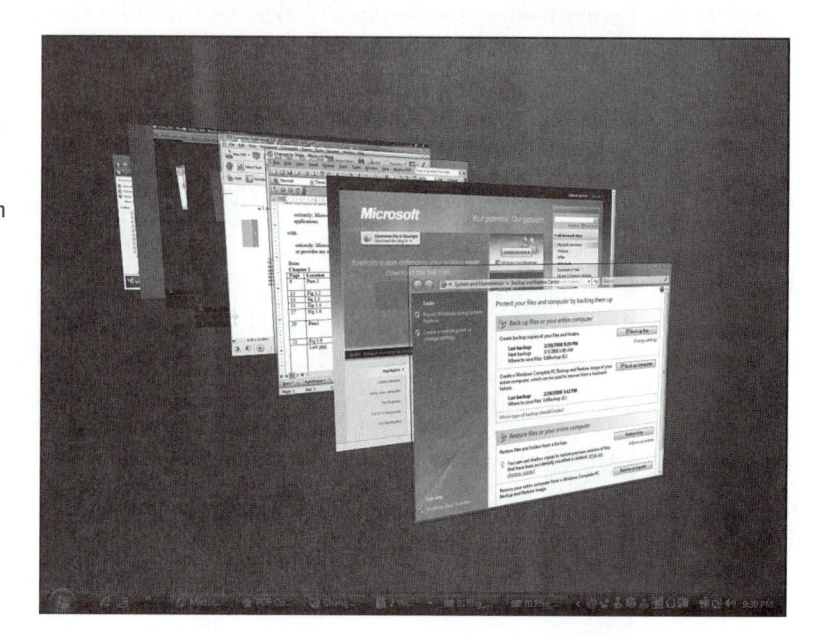

ORB AND SEARCH

Drilling down a bit into the interface, another obvious change is that the Start button has been replaced with a simple ball, or what some have dubbed "the orb." It was decided that clicking Start to shut down the computer was illogical. (Gee, I wonder who figured it out.)

The Start menu also has been seriously revised (see Figure 1.4).

On the Start menu is a search field. You can enter a local search right there, and very quickly a list of all the files, including emails and documents that meet the criteria, is displayed in a Search Folder. You can save the folder and use it later. If you created other files in the meantime that meet the search criteria, they appear in the Search Folder as well. If you've used Google's Desktop Search tool, you'll find this a welcome feature because in some ways it one-ups Google.

So What's New in Windows Vista? | 15

Figure 1.4
The new Start menu contains a local search field, along with some other improvements.

Instant Search Field

The Windows XP Search option is still in Vista, doing file, media, computer, Internet, and Help searches, but it includes email and is faster and more sophisticated. It uses the "as-you-type" approach, letting you refine the search as you type characters. In addition, every folder window now has a Search field at the bottom of it so you can quickly filter the contents of the window. If you've ever used iTunes, you know how "as you type" works: When you start typing in the Search field, the file listing decreases to show only items with those characters in the name. The new Windows Search Engine (WSE) is at work behind the scenes, and because WSE also searches through metatags (information embedded in files such as digital camera photos, Word documents, and MP3 files), you're likely to get more exact hits and be able to find that particular needle in the haystack.

START MENU

The Start menu has also changed. Outlook Express is now Mail, and links on the right side have been rearranged and renamed a bit. When you click on Programs, you don't see a huge cascade of multiple columns of programs that sometimes even exceed the size of the desktop. Instead, installed programs are shown one column at a time. You must scroll through the columns to move through your installed programs.

DESKTOP

The desktop has not changed much, although the supplied backgrounds are in beautiful colors because of the 32-bit graphics capabilities of Aero-capable computers. One feature that has improved is the desktop configuration dialog from the Control Panel. Figure 1.5 shows that dialog, which makes it much easier to set up your desktop background image.

METADATA EDITING

As mentioned earlier, Vista's search tool supports metadata, information about a file that goes beyond its filename and date. For example, a video file includes metadata about the aspect ratio (for example, 720×480), how long it runs (for example, 10 minutes), when it was shot, and so on. In XP, you could edit some metadata from Properties dialogs on the file.

Vista expands on this, to enable you to edit such information as author, rating, comments, and relevant file tags (this varies with file type—for example, it would involve genre, composer, and song information for MP3 files). Editing can be done from the folder window's preview pane using a supplied link; you don't have to open the Properties sheet.

Figure 1.5
The new Desktop Background chooser makes configuration a bit easier.

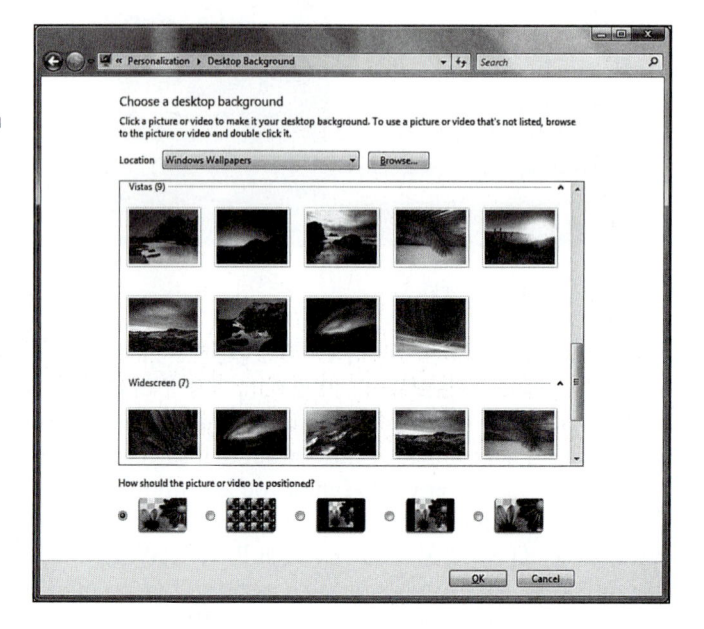

Again, the advantage of metadata is that you can easily search it, and Vista lets you use it to filter your searches in useful ways through Grouping, Stacking, and Filtering. Chapter 5, "Managing Files and Searching," covers this in more detail.

SIDEBAR AND GADGETS

Remember Active Desktop in previous versions of Windows? Microsoft promoted it greatly, but most users and critics maligned it because it was unstable and could crash your system. Those in the know turned off Active Desktop even though it was cool to use your home page as your desktop background, or put local weather maps or some other online data source like stock tickers on your desktop. Well, a form of AD is back in Windows, under a different name: Sidebar. It's much more stable—and much more useful—than its predecessor. Because most screens these days are wide, it makes sense to park some useful info such as a clock, weather, headlines, and CPU and RAM meters over there. The Sidebar holds these "Gadgets," which can be added or removed as you see fit. Figure 1.6 shows some of the supplied gadgets loaded into my Sidebar. Third-party software makers have created many more gadgets since Vista was introduced: There are more than 2,000 now available from Windows Live Gallery (http://gallery.live.com). Gadgets is certainly not a new idea, as a program called Konfabulator has been around for the PC and there are Widgets for the Mac.

Figure 1.6
The new Sidebar with some Gadgets installed.

NEW EXPLORERS

Windows Explorer is now much more useful for several reasons, thanks to a series of new Explorers, such as the Document Explorer.

- Instant Search is available on every window, as mentioned earlier, helping you to see only the items you are interested in. This works even in odd windows such as the Control Panel.
- Command bars on the left side change to offer only tasks that are relevant to the files at hand.
- Scalable live thumbnails of the files in the folder can be displayed. Thumbnails can be images, album art for songs, or even the first page of documents such as Word files, HTML web pages, or spreadsheets.
- Explorers have optional "reading panes" on the right side.
- The Internet-style address bar at the top of every window no longer shows the disk file pathname of the file being viewed (for example, C:\My Documents\jobs\application.doc), but instead uses a more natural language approach (for example, Bob > Documents). You can directly return to a previous location by clicking on it (such as on Bob) or via a drop-down list. This is much faster than clicking the "up folder" button multiple times. See Figure 1.7.

Figure 1.7
The new Explorer window is much more sophisticated than in XP.

Speech Recognition

Until now, speech recognition was available in Windows using third-party products such as Dragon (Scansoft) or Via Voice (IBM). Now Microsoft has jumped into the fray and included voice recognition right in the operating system. Time for another antitrust suit? Maybe. But in the meantime, you've got some voice recognition right inside Windows.

Windows Vista has a fully integrated speech engine that Microsoft says draws upon the latest in speech recognition and synthesis. Pundits criticized it during development, but it is actually on par with the competition, loads faster, and in some ways is easier to work with. The speech engine supports multiple languages, and its recognition accuracy improves with use as it adapts to your speaking style and vocabulary. A human-sounding synthesizer is included. You can dictate email and spreadsheets, and surf the Web all by voice. Whether you have a disability, you want to protect your hands from repetitive stress disorders like I do, or you're just lazy, Vista's speech input might do the job. (We've included a demo lesson on the CD-ROM in this book.)

System Security Enhancements

Certainly, the most often-heard beef about Windows (even XP) is that it's too fragile and vulnerable to malware and hackers. Some say it's simply not robust enough. Microsoft hears it, too, you can believe it. Imagine their support calls. So with each new iteration of Windows, they try to harden it against onslaught. (Of course, if it were not for the popularity of Windows, hacking it wouldn't be an issue, so the naysayers have a somewhat specious argument, in our opinion.) For each new and creative plan of attack, a counterattack or defense emerges. Thus, Vista has a new batch of security enhancements:

- **User Account Control (UAC)**—In XP, users often gave themselves administrative privileges, allowing malicious programs to run amok unexpectedly. Vista gives *everyone* the lowest level of privilege. The result is dialog boxes asking you (frequently!) to confirm that you want to run a program, install an applet, and so on. This helps prevent secretive programs from running without your knowledge, but it's a pain in the neck.
- **Windows Defender**—Although it's available for download into XP as well, Defender is Microsoft's answer to spyware detectors such as Ad-Aware. It's not an antivirus program, but it detects programs that sit in wait for you to enter passwords or other sensitive information, relaying them to the bad guys. The latest version of Defender is included in Vista and is updated regularly online, as any antivirus or spyware program is.
- **Better autoupdater**—Windows autoupdate has become more advanced and sophisticated. In Vista SP-1, Vista supports hotpatching, enabling most updates to be performed without the need to reboot the computer.
- **Bidirectional firewall**—Firewalls protect you from people trying to get direct access to your computer over the network, typically using unprotected "ports." Windows firewall in XP blocked incoming traffic (people trying to get in) but not weird stuff your computer might be doing against your will, such as spamming everyone in your email address book. The bidirectional firewall in Vista blocks such attempts.
- **Malicious Software Removal Tool (MSRT)**—The Malicious Software Removal Tool detects and removes high-profile viruses such as infections by specific, prevalent malicious software—including Blaster, Sasser, and Mydoom—and helps remove any infection found. It's not a real-time scanner, but runs periodically. Since the tool runs on all versions of Windows 2000 or later, it is not new with Vista, but its delivery to your system through Windows Live and auto updating is smoother.
- **Web security in IE 7**—Internet Explorer is now more robust because it runs in protected mode. Now given lower access rights to the operating system (for running hidden scripts on malicious web pages, for example), IE 7 has just enough user privilege to surf the Web effectively, but not much more. Additionally, a filter in IE looks for "phishing" expeditions (bogus websites that pretend to be what they are not, such as official banking sites where you're asked to input your bank account info) and warn you accordingly.
- **Windows Mail junk mail filter**—Outlook Express is now called Windows Mail. Overall, it hasn't been upgraded much, but it includes a filter that does its best to identify junk mail (spam) and move it to a junk mail folder, just as Outlook (part of Microsoft Office) does. It's not perfect, but it helps. Spammers are annoyingly persistent.
- **Service hardening**—Many internals to the operating system run as "services," and most users never see them unless they poke around with some management tools. Sometimes a service runs amok and crashes the operating system or gets caught in a loop and causes a slowdown. Vista services are given lower privileges than XP services were and are given only specific privileges. This limits their capacity to compromise the operating system.
- **BitLocker (Secure Startup)**—This is a biggie. Imagine that someone steals your computer and all your data. With BitLocker enabled, they won't be able to read it. A chip in some new computers, called a Trusted Platform Module (TPM) 1.2 chip, prevents it.

The chip offers protected storage of encryption keys, passwords, and digital certificates. Vista uses this capability to verify that a PC has not been tampered with when it starts up and to protect data through encryption. The TPM is typically part of the motherboard of the PC, although a USB thumb drive can be used as well. Because it is stored in hardware, the information is more secure from external software attacks such as viruses and worms and from physical theft. If you have to get data off a drive in a dead computer, the drive has to be moved to another computer, and that computer needs a key that you generated when you first set up the first computer and that you stored securely in another location. This feature is available only in Windows Vista Enterprise and Ultimate editions. In the original Vista Enterprise and Ultimate editions, BitLocker could encrypt only the system drive. However, Vista Enterprise and Ultimate SP-1 adds support for encrypting additional disk volumes.

- **Network access protection (NAP)**—If NAP is installed on a network server, it can inquire whether a computer asking to connect to the network is in "good health" (has the most recent virus inoculations, driver updates, security updates, and so on). If not, the workstation can be refused admission to the network until it is updated.

PERFORMANCE IMPROVEMENTS

Computers always seem to slow down over time, and no matter how fast the hardware gets, things seem to run at about the same speed. What we would have called a supercomputer a few years ago now must run word-processing and email apps about as fast as it did when the CPUs were a fraction of the speed. This is largely the result of programmer laziness: They know that the fast computers will run overly fat code just fine. It's also partly the result of added sizzle (more features—often unnecessary) to the programs and operating systems. In any case, some speed improvements in Vista are worth mentioning.

- **Startup**—As with Windows XP, Vista shortens the startup time by using a technique called *prefetching*, which loads major portions of the operating system at the same time that devices are being initialized rather than performing loading and device initialization in series. Vista now also uses asynchronous startup script and application launching. This means the core startup actions occur first and less important scripts execute as they can, without delaying the appearance of the desktop and giving the user control of the GUI. As with XP, Vista learns which hardware and software you use during the first few times you boot your system, and moves the files used by your hardware and software to the fastest parts of your drive, to further improve boot time.

- **Superfetch**—Vista introduces *superfetch*, a new kind of prefetching that predicts what you're up to when you use certain programs (time of day and day of the week) and preloads them into memory so the computer is more responsive. We've all noticed how if a virus scan is running and we return to the computer, it can take some time for responsiveness to return. The computer swaps out the antivirus program and data from memory and loads the application you want to use. Some people argue that SuperFetch was built in XP, but it wasn't.

- **ReadyBoost**—Here's a great new idea for upgrading performance. We all know that adding RAM can improve performance, but for many people, this is difficult to do and might violate a maintenance contract or annoy the IT people at a company. ReadyBoost lets users plug in a removable flash memory device, such as a USB thumb drive, to improve system performance without opening the computer box. The USB drive is used like more system memory, specifically for disk caching. ReadyBoost can handle someone yanking out the USB memory accidentally without any data loss. Also the data on it is protected by encryption to help prevent inappropriate access to data if the device is removed. Most recent USB flash drives of 1GB or higher capacity support ReadyBoost, but if the drive packaging does not identify the drive as ReadyBoost-compatible, it might not be fast enough to improve performance. See http://www.grantgibson.co.uk/misc/readyboost/ for test results for many brands of flash drives.

- **Sleep**—Vista introduces a new shutdown and startup type called Sleep. XP had Hibernate and Standby, but Sleep is something between these two. The problem with Standby was that if the computer's power was removed (laptop battery ran out or the desktop's AC power failed), you'd lose your work. Hibernate guarded against this but could be slow to stop and restart because it wrote and read a lot of data to and from the hard disk. Sleep is the best of both worlds: It works quickly (typically in just a few seconds), yet your work also survives a power loss. It does this by simultaneously employing both Standby and Hibernate. The Hibernate data stored to the hard disk is used if Standby power fails.

- **ReadyDrive**—Vista can take advantage of new "hybrid" disk drives designed for low-power situations such as laptops. To maximize battery life, some new mini hard drives now have large nonvolatile flash memory caches onboard. Vista PCs equipped with a hybrid hard disk boot up faster, resume from hibernate in less time, preserve battery power, and improve hard disk reliability because the drive is used less often.

- **Restart Manager**—How many times have you updated a program, only to be told you then had to reboot Windows? This is annoying when you have a lot of documents open. The Restart Manager tries to minimize this by keeping tabs on what behind-the-scenes system processes a program is running, shutting those down as necessary while the program is being updated, and then starting the services again, all without requiring a reboot. The upshot is that you have fewer reboot requests with Vista than with XP, even with the same applications.

- **Mobility Center**—Laptop users have had to fish about in XP for settings that affect battery life, such as screen brightness, volume, battery status, wireless networking, external display, syncing with external data devices, and giving presentations. A one-stop shop for this is now included in Vista. Figure 1.8 shows the Mobility Center.

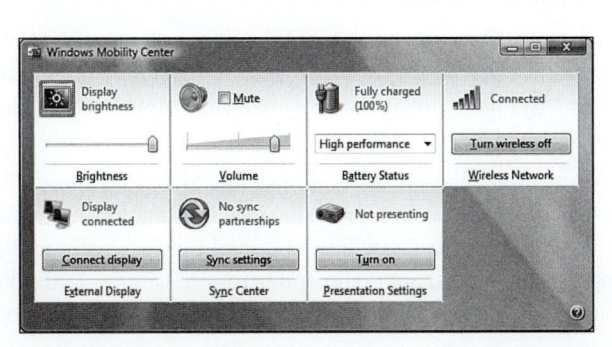

Figure 1.8
The Mobility Center is a convenient single dialog that enables users on the move to make changes that affect their laptops.

System Management and Stability Improvements

Stability is probably the most important issue when considering whether to upgrade to a new operating system or buy a computer with it installed. Early adopters have a choice about this, but when an operating system becomes ubiquitous and new PCs already have it installed, we just have to make peace with the thing. After the likes of Windows Me (we liked to call it Windows 666), the real question we always want to know the answer to is, "Does it crash less?" Vista has some pretty impressive anticrash technology. Think of them as antilock brakes and airbags for your computer:

- **Self-diagnostics to detect impending system failures**—With this important new feature, Vista can self-diagnose a number of common problems, including failing hard disks, memory leak problems, and networking issues. Windows Disk Diagnostics detect impending disk failures and guide users through data backup, disk replacement, and data restoration. This works using the Self-Monitoring and Reporting Technology (SMART) chips on many recent hard drives. Windows Memory Diagnostics work with Microsoft Online Crash Analysis to detect crashes possibly caused by failing memory, prompting the user to schedule a RAM test the next time the computer is restarted and providing guided support. In Active Directory domains, administrators can configure Built-in Diagnostics using Group Policy settings.

- **I/O cancellation**—Many crashes or slowdowns result when a program is waiting for you to type something, waiting for data to come in on a port, waiting for a hard disk to deliver data, or waiting for some other I/O (input/output) issue. Vista notices such thumb twiddling in the system and attempts to cooperate with any related programs, to terminate such a wait and return control of the computer without requiring a reboot or a rude three-key termination of the offending program.

- **Startup Repair Tool**—After an unsuccessful bootup, XP would try to recover but wasn't always successful. If you installed a new driver or application that hosed the system, you could be out of luck. Discovering the culprit and clearing the problem was the purview of serious Windows buffs and often took booting in safe mode (if you still could), and using tools such as the Windows Configuration Utility to turn off startup programs or Device Manager to remove new drivers, or the like. In Vista, the Startup Repair Tool (SRT) can be used to fix boot problems easily and automatically. It is launched by booting with the Windows Vista DVD or a special WinRE disc. After specifying language and location settings, select Repair My Computer on the next dialog to launch the Startup Repair Tool.

- **Service and system file recovery**—In XP, when a system service crashed or a system file got damaged, it often took down the operating system and required at least a reboot. Each service in Vista has a policy that governs what happens if it fails. In many cases, the service is restarted.

- **Reliability Monitor**—This Microsoft Management Console plug-in provides a system stability overview and trend analysis, with detailed information about individual events that might affect the system's overall stability. This might include software installations, operating system updates, rollbacks, uninstalls, and hardware failures. Reliability Monitor begins collecting data when you first install Vista on a machine. Figure 1.9 shows an example.

So What's New in Windows Vista?   23

- **Performance Monitors**—Another MMC plug-in, this monitor is a snap-in for the Microsoft Management Console. Using graphs, you can easily review system performance and spot trends based on data collected during system operation.

Figure 1.9
Reliability Monitor graphs system stability in various configurable views.

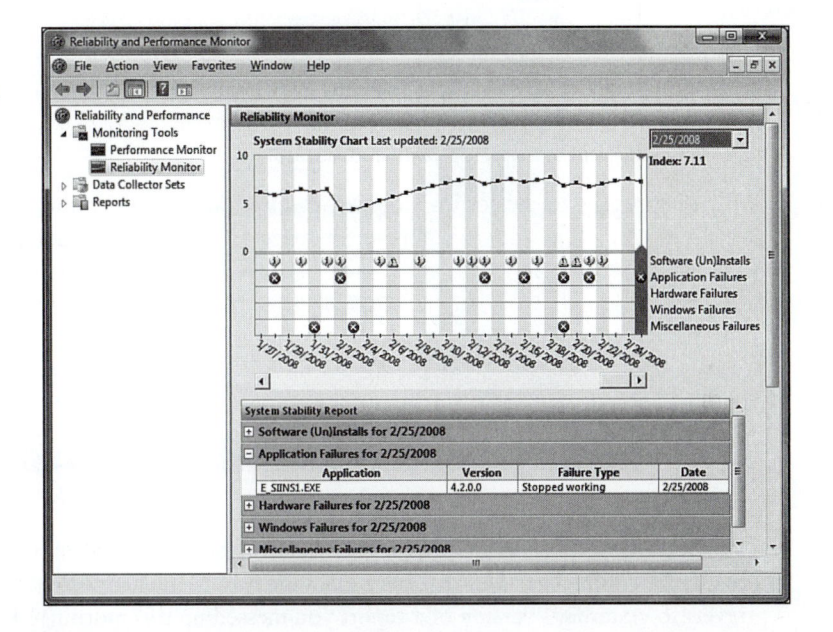

Data Security Enhancements

Maintaining data integrity on the PC is a constant job for IT people. Independent businesspeople without the aid of an IT professional worry about this just as much as the IT folks, if not more so, partly because they don't know what to do when things go south. In addition to the stability improvements listed earlier, there are two areas of significant improvement in data security (outlined here and in Part VII of this book).

- **Enhanced Windows Backup**—The backup program supplied with Vista is a complete departure from its predecessors. All Windows Vista editions include file/folder backup, while Business, Enterprise, and Ultimate editions also support a system image and disaster recovery backup feature known as Complete PC Backup. These features are presented in a single, unified Windows Backup and Restore Center. (See Figure 1.10.) Backup now supports writing to CD-ROM, DVD drives, USB, external drives (USB and 1394), and network drives. Backups can be automated on a schedule. A wizard helps you restore a file, folder, or disk image, if necessary. Advanced features let you restore files from another computer and restore with administrator privilege. Microsoft provides the Windows NT Backup - Restore Utility (available from www.microsoft.com/downloads) to enable you to restore backups made with Windows XP or Windows Server 2003. To use this utility, you must enable Removable Storage Management in Computer Management.

Figure 1.10
The Backup and Restore Center is the hub for backup and recovery.

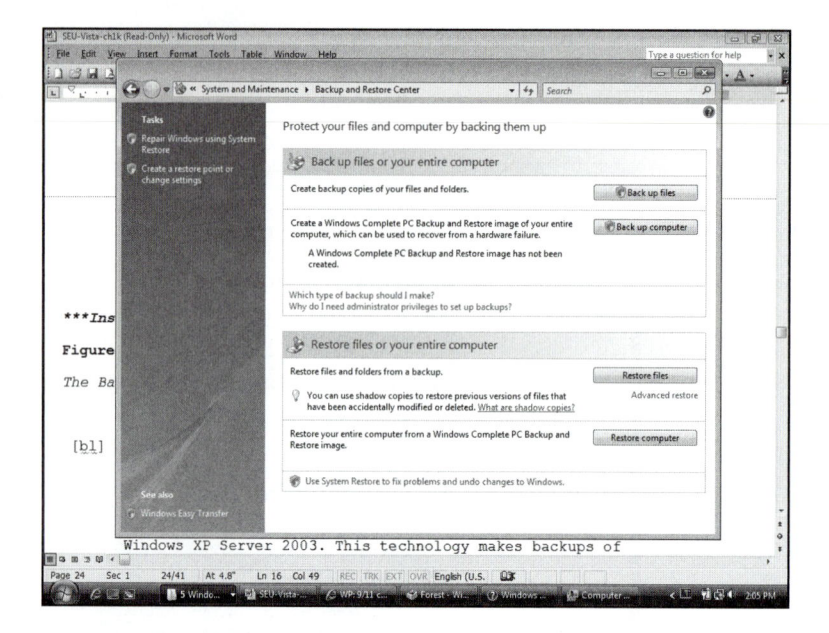

- **Previous Versions**—Vista's Ultimate, Business, and Enterprise editions have a feature that helps you recover files that have inadvertently been changed or deleted. Want to revert to yesterday's version of a report you messed up this morning? Just use Previous Versions. Vista incorporates this feature by default because it is based on Volume Shadow Copy technology, which first appeared in Windows Server 2003. This technology makes periodic automatic backups of all files that have changed. This is similar to a program called GoBack, by Roxio software, which we mentioned in our XP books, but this one is built into Vista; GoBack gave us problems, but Vista's Previous Versions feature works very well.

- **Complete PC Backup**—Windows Vista Business, Enterprise, and Ultimate editions include another backup system called Complete PC Backup. Like Previous Versions, it uses the Volume Shadow Copy service to periodically take a snapshot of the entire hard disk and sequesters a copy of all new and changed files on another disk or in a highly protected folder. The collection of snapshots can be used later on to reconstruct the entire contents of the disk.

New or Improved Accessories

Historically, Microsoft has packed ever increasing globs of accessories into Windows. In the olden days of Windows 1.0 you were lucky to get a clock and one game. Now it can be years before people discover all the accessories and playthings in a release of Windows. Here's what's new with the major accessories in Vista:

- **Mail**—Only a few things have been added to Outlook Express which, along with IE, are certainly the most-often used Windows accessories. First, Outlook Express has a new name—simply Windows Mail. This is probably to put an end to the eternal confusion between Outlook Express and Outlook. Not a bad idea. Next, you'll find a search box in the upper-right corner of the Mail window to help you quickly find mails, using the as-you-type approach. Very nice feature. A Junk mail filter, a la Outlook, also has been added to cull out the annoying emails, and a phishing filter to help you weed out malicious ones. Mail also stores individual messages as separate files, instead of folders that were actually corruption-prone database files.

- **Calendar**—This is a new application and one that was missing from Windows for a long time. (Actually, I'm happy even to see an analog clock reappear; we haven't had one since Windows 3.*x*. Calendar and clock are now both addable as gadgets to the Windows Sidebar, incidentally.) Calendar looks a bit like Outlook's calendar and is quite capable. Windows Calendar is fully compatible with the popular .iCalendar format, which lets you import and export calendar information to and from other applications and websites. Windows Calendar provides individual calendars for multiple people. This is especially helpful for families and other groups of people who share a single PC. The Calendar includes a task list with reminders, dates with alerts, and recurring appointments. Figure 1.11 shows the Calendar.

Figure 1.11
The new Vista Calendar program freebie.

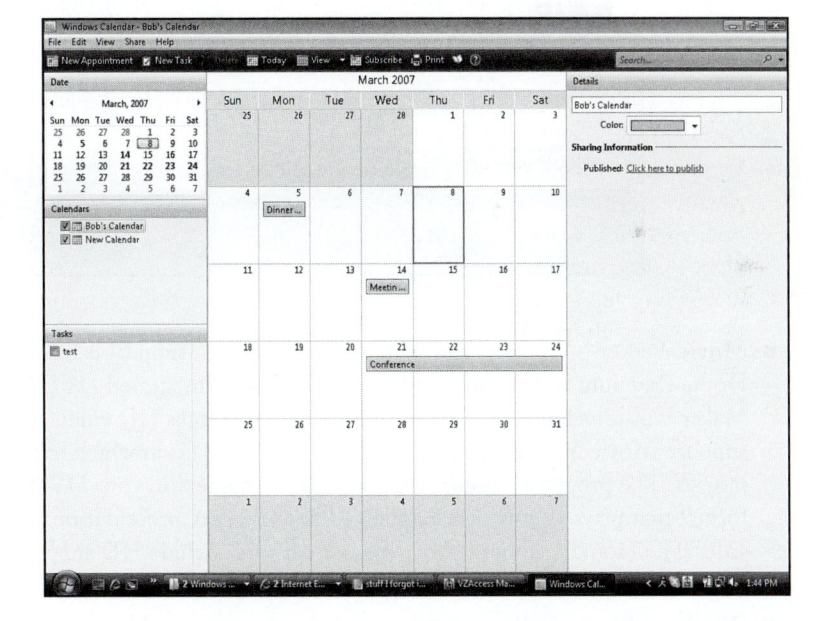

- **Windows Fax and Scan**—You can use this new application in Vista Business, Enterprise, and Ultimate editions to send, receive, store, organize, and view faxes. You can also scan documents and pictures, and use Windows Fax and Scan to view, store, and organize the scanned files. You can even use both features of Windows Fax and Scan together by scanning and then faxing a document in one fell swoop.

- **Windows Meeting Space**—Like the Netmeeting program that preceded it, this all-new application for Vista's Home Premium, Business, Enterprise, and Ultimate editions lets people in remote locations or offices work together. They can work on documents together, distribute "handouts," let one person demonstrate how a program works, let a remote person temporarily take control of someone's computer, let someone perform a *presentation* of some sort that everyone sees, connect to a network projector, or chat with each other using text. Up to 10 people can participate; all have to be running Vista. No special server is needed, and Vista can use your wireless network hardware to effortlessly and automatically connect to the other meeting participants. See Figure 1.12.

Figure 1.12
The new Windows Meeting Space program replaces Netmeeting.

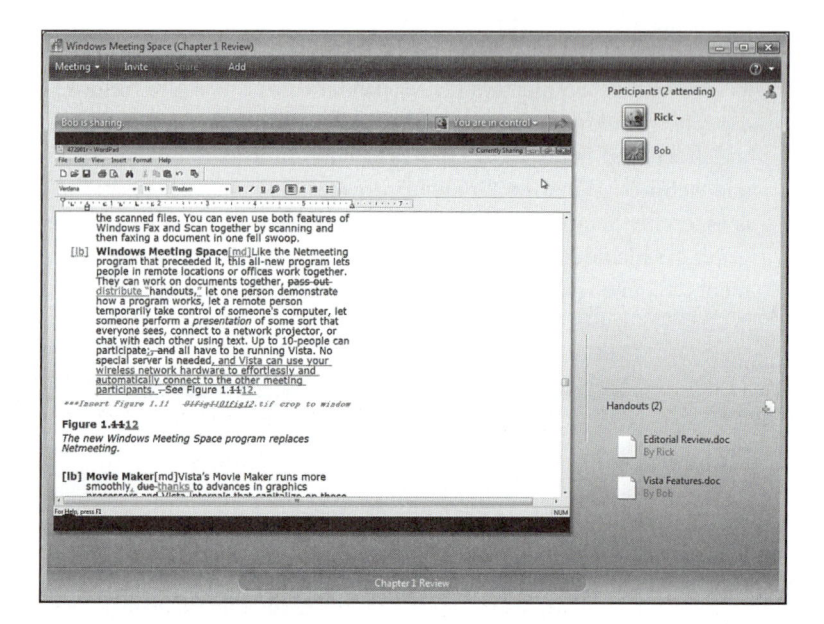

- **Movie Maker**—Vista's Movie Maker with HD video support is included in the Vista Home Premium and Ultimate editions, along with integrated DVD burning. Movie Maker is also included in Vista Home Basic, but it lacks HD video and DVD burning support. Movie Maker includes a wider variety of styles in which to publish your movies. The program automatically generates chapters in your DVD and exports in a format that plays as part of a Windows Photo Gallery presentation, mixing videos and stills. The Home Premium and Ultimate editions include HD support, while Home Basic does not. Movie Maker is not included in the Vista Business or Enterprise editions.

- **Windows Photo Gallery**—Given a run for their money by programs such as Adobe Album and Google Picasa, Microsoft got on the stick and developed its own photo-organizing tool. Photo Gallery meets most people's basic digital photo needs, short of editing. You can import from a camera (using the Vista Import Pictures Wizard), search, view, organize, rate, print, and share your photos (via email or burning on DVD or CD-ROM). Windows Live Photo Gallery, a part of Microsoft's Windows Live series of web-enabled utilities, is based on Windows Photo Gallery, but includes more editing options and includes web publishing support. I recommend downloading Windows Live Photo Gallery and using it in place of Windows Photo Gallery. Get it from http://get.live.com.

- **Media Player 11**—Media Player 11 is available for download for XP, but it comes standard with Vista. It has a slew of new features. The interface is cleaner and easier to figure out (thank goodness). It links to the URGE music store that Microsoft created in collaboration with MTV. Album art is displayed more prominently. A metadata editor is included. Searching via the as-you-type approach is supported, making it easy to find your media even in a huge collection. You can connect a Windows Media Center extender to your home theater system and play your music wirelessly through that. Portable music devices that display the PlaysForSure logo seamlessly connect to your Windows Vista–based PC as soon as you plug them in. There's no need to load any third-party software or drivers. You can access your Windows Media Player library from your Xbox 360 to enjoy your music in another room of your home or build game soundtracks. CD ripping is greatly improved, with many more options, including uncompressed WAV, VBR, and MP3. Burning is supported for both CD and DVD, and includes the option to "normalize" volume levels across the burned disk and disk spanning, to burn more than one disk at a time (if you have multiple drives). You can share your library across the local area network for use by other workstations. DVD movie playback has more sophisticated controls. See Figure 1.13.

Figure 1.13
Windows Media Player 11 is feature rich and better organized.

Networking

Vista networking includes a variety of new features. The Network Center is a single location that lets you easily perform common network tasks, much as the Mobility Center does for portable computers:

- Connect to a network
- Browse a network

- Create a network
- Diagnose network problems

Other new networking features include these:

- Support for the next-generation Internet Protocol, IPv6. IPv6 is currently used pretty much only in large corporate settings, but it will eventually be used on the global Internet, and Vista is ready.
- Teredo IPv6 Tunneling support lets applications that depend on IPv6 work effortlessly over IPv4 networks and the Internet, even if you use a shared Internet connection that includes Network Address Translation (NAT). One practical benefit of this is that Vista's Remote Assistance feature should now work even if you have a broadband connection sharing router.
- New and improved setup wizards for wireless, broadband, VPN, and dial-up connections. You can set up workstations in a preconfigured way quickly using USB thumbdrives.
- Services for native Macintosh and Novell NetWare networking have been removed.
- With the Network Map display, you can see the entire network you're connected to in a visual display, with icons that include routers. This makes the network make more sense, especially if you are troubleshooting.
- Wireless network security (WPA2) is better.
- TCP/IP window size autotuning supports faster throughput, which lets the network recover better from lost packets. TCP Receive Window Autotuning continually determines the optimal TCP Receive Window size on a per-connection basis by measuring the bandwidth-delay product (the bandwidth multiplied by the latency of the connection) and the application retrieve rate, and automatically adjusts the maximum TCP Receive Window size on an ongoing basis.
- Faster throughput is achieved via support for the latest network protocol, *Next-Generation TCP/IP Stack*.
- Network Location Awareness APIs enable applications to sense changes to the network to which the computer is connected, such as placing a laptop into standby mode at work and then opening it at a wireless hotspot. This enables Windows Vista to alert applications of network changes; these applications can then behave differently, to improve security and provide a seamless experience.
- Peer-to-Peer (P2P) communication and collaboration is networking that grants clients quicker communication and greater flexibility, such as deployment on disconnected or ad hoc networks. P2P is useful especially in interpersonal communication, content distribution, and home/office productivity. Vista includes new technologies to support P2P. For example, the new Windows Meeting Space application (aka Collaboration) uses P2P technology.
- With the Network Diagnostics Framework, Vista has built-in diagnostics to help users diagnose networking problems without having to call the IT guy. As an example, if the network cable or the wireless router goes down, Vista might sense the problem and tell you to reconnect the cable or check the router. In some cases, the problem can be solved automatically without even asking the user for assistance.

PRODUCTIVITY

Although certainly features such as Windows Meeting Space, junk mail filtering in the Mail program, improved networking speed, and the inclusion of a Calendar fall under the rubric of "Productivity," two areas fit more securely in that arena:

- **Tablet Vista**—Tablet PC Vista support is included with Business, Enterprise, Home Premium, and Ultimate. Tablet Vista is a whole chapter in and of itself, but suffice it to say that if you are the kind of computer user who doesn't like to type, and you grew up watching *Star Trek* episodes, Tablet Vista might just be your cup of tea. Most of the improvements discussed elsewhere in this chapter apply to Vista Tablet PC because a Tablet PC is essentially a PC without a keyboard and with some additional features to replace the keyboard, such as handwriting recognition. Some Tablet-specific improvements are a modified Tablet Input Panel (TIP), which can be moved off the screen until needed, password keys that are less easy for prying eyes to see, better visual feedback of when your pen is acting as a mouse and when you click, and better handwriting recognition, including automatic learning while you write. Using *flicks*, a quick flick of the pen can scroll a window up or down or navigate forward and backward on the Web. Flicks can also perform common actions, such as copy, paste, delete, and undo. Although you can install voice recognition on a Tablet PC (such as an XP-based one) using third-party software, Vista Tablet PC includes voice recognition natively. Together with better handwriting recognition, the keyboard phobic has this additional option for input. Finally, Home Premium and Ultimate versions of Vista include both Tablet PC and Media Center. This is cool because if you have the right hardware, you'll be able to do everything from listen to your favorite music to record your favorite television show right on your Tablet PC.

- **Sync Center**—Syncing various items to and from your PC has always involved using standalone programs such as Activesync (for Pocket PCs) or Media Center (for MP3 and portable movie players), or the desktop Briefcase folder, and so on. Each time you purchase a new gadget, such as a mobile phone or music player, it comes with its own sync program, and you have to hunt to find the applet or program to sync up. Because of the annoyance factor, people skip syncing and then it's too late—they have missed an appointment, lost a phone number, or lost an important file they could have backed up by doing a simple sync. The idea of the Sync Center, just like the Network Center and Mobility Center, is obvious: to provide one spot where all syncing chores collectively live. Syncing can be set up to be one-way or two-way. This enables you to update files on your computer and always have the latest versions copied to a server, where others can view them on the network or where you can store them for backup. You can also use Sync Center to copy files from the server to your computer so you always have the latest versions to work with, even when you lose your network connection to the server. The manufacturer of the gadget must support Sync Center for this to work, obviously, so it's not a panacea. At least for a while, we'll still be using standalone sync software, but that will likely change as the standard gels. Figure 1.14 shows the Sync Center.

Figure 1.14
Sync Center helps coordinate all Windows syncing in one place.

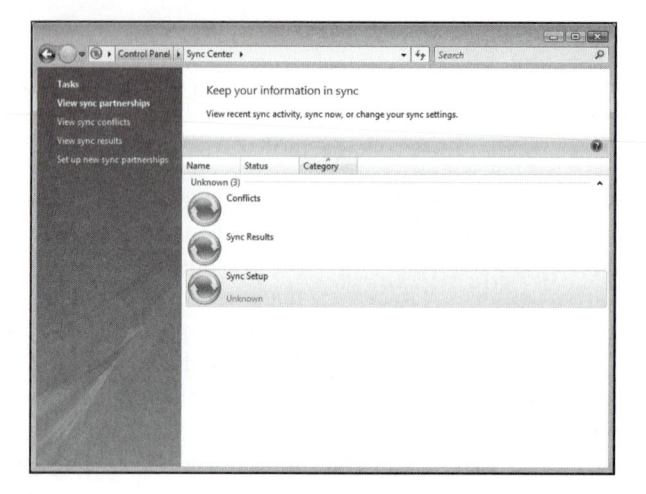

Internet Explorer 7

Internet browsing has probably become the most widely used application on the PC desktop. As such, it behooves Microsoft to make a constantly better browser. Ironically, Internet Explorer has been the bane of Microsoft's (and users') existence, constantly being one-upped by Netscape, Opera, Mozilla Firefox, and many others. IE is the constant target of hackers, so Windows Update is regularly doling out updates to harden IE; still, it's a game of catch-up, for the most part. As mentioned earlier in this chapter, Vista lowers the privilege level of IE now to help protect your PC. On the user end of things, IE 7 ups the bar on performance by keeping up with the Joneses again. Here are the perks for upgrading to IE 7 (regardless of your platform—Windows Server 2003, XP, or Vista).

- **Tabbed browsing!**—Finally, we get tabbed browsing in IE. Safari, Firefox, Opera, and some others have had tabbed browsing for eons already, and now IE catches up—and then some. As with other tab-enabled programs, each page opens on a new tab. But IE goes a bit further and offers a Quick Tabs view, in which you can see live thumbnails of all open pages. Click a tab, and the page returns. See Figure 1.15.
- **RSS feed support**—Many pages are now available as RSS feeds, meaning "push" technology is employed to update your computer with the latest version of the page, in case it changes (as news sites do). IE now supports this by noticing if a site has RSS and lets you subscribe and/or view it.
- **Favorites Center**—This is yet another new "Center," conglomerating your Favorites, History, and now RSS feeds so they are easier to get to.
- **Add-on management**—A dialog box helps you manage add-ons to IE, such as Active X components and toolbars. This is long overdue.
- **More than one home page**—You can specify multiple home pages, which doesn't make sense at first, but it will. Because you now have tabbed browsing, it can be useful. You can launch and load up to eight favorite pages when you run IE. It will take a little time to load them, of course.

- **Easy history deletion**—Want to cover your tracks? It's easier now than with IE 6. IE remembers passwords, past page addresses, and cookies; keeps temporary files of pages and images loaded; and more. You can clean house, removing each of these categories as you like, or all of them at once, from a simple dialog box.

Figure 1.15
Quick Tab view in IE 7 shows all open pages. Very spiffy.

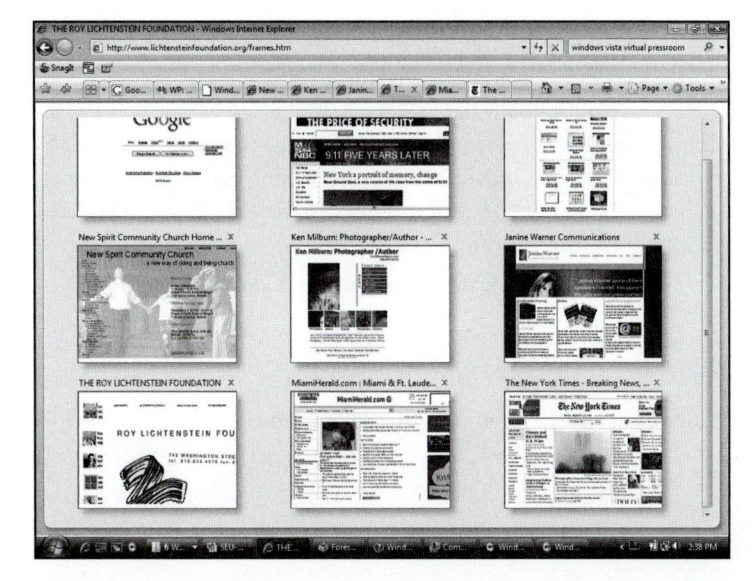

ENTERTAINMENT

A few odds and ends in the entertainment department are worth noting. Though this is not the full list, these are the notables:

- The Ultimate and Home Premium editions include the Media Center, including support for Media Center Extender and Media Center Games. Media Center previously was available only as a separate operating system (XP Media Center Edition) married to a specific kind of computer that met Media Center requirements (for example, enough RAM and typically a TV tuner card). Media Center PCs are designed with home entertainment in mind, are typically more quiet than normal PCs, and come with remote controls and other goodies. They can connect easily to projectors and TV sets so you can record and watch TV, see slick slideshows of your digital images, watch movies, listen to your MP3 songs, and so on, all using a hand-held remote control. Vista Media Center supports HDTV recording (if you have an HDTV source, that is) and multiroom broadcasting through Media Center Extenders. It has a better menuing system that is easier to navigate. You see notifications of incoming phone calls if your phone line is hooked up to the computer. This includes caller ID, if you have that feature. You can connect to a wireless network via Media Center remote control. Finally, the Media Center optimizes itself daily, so it doesn't bog down over time. If you have used MCE, you know this can happen and recorded TV can get skippy or choppy. Unfortunately, Media Center still records TV in *huge* files (ms-dvr) and should use today's CPU horsepower to compress video as an option, in DivX or Xvid, or even in WMV. Fortunately, you can use Windows Movie

Maker to convert ms-dvr files into smaller WMV files. Use the AutoMovie feature to make the conversion as easy as possible, or edit out commercials and other extraneous content manually.

- Media Center and Vista in general now has Family Safety Settings, parental controls for managing children's gaming and Web activity.
- With its easy-access Game Explorer, Vista makes it easier to get to your Games folder. In a clean system, there are nine games: FreeCell, Hearts, Minesweeper, Solitaire, Spider Solitaire, InkBall, Chess Titans, Mahjong Titans, and Purble Place. This is all in a single place, for all games shortcuts. Parental controls are available there, too, along with easily accessible metadata info such as publisher, date, version, and game ratings by the Entertainment Software Rating Board (ESRB). If game updates become available, a "game update" feature can be set to alert you of it.
- Each application in Vista that outputs sound gets it own volume control.

Differences Among Versions of Vista

Vista comes in five basic versions in the U.S. market:

- Vista Home Basic
- Vista Home Premium
- Vista Business
- Vista Enterprise
- Vista Ultimate

Although all versions contain the same integrated applications and many of the same multimedia features, the Business editions include greater security and emphasize the needs of the business sector. The Home versions emphasize the multimedia experience. For the buyer who has to have it all, the Ultimate version leaves nothing out. In addition to including all the features found in Home Premium and Business editions, Ultimate also features exclusive downloadable free utility and entertainment programs called Ultimate Extras. Unfortunately, very few Ultimate Extras have been released to date. Furthermore, 64-bit versions are available for all platforms. As of this writing, most users will be running the x86 code base because their computers have 32-bit processors. But as more 64-bit processors become available, that will change. The 64-bit CPUs, such as AMD's Athlon 64 and Opteron can take advantage of their speed and other enhancements. Also, it should be mentioned that there are limitations in the 64-bit versions. For example there is no longer Win16 or MS-DOS support, meaning you cannot run applications from the era of 16-bit Windows (3.x and 9x) or DOS apps. Also there is limited availability of 64-bit device drivers and ActiveX plugins for Internet Explorer for the 64-bit platform at present. Therefore, home/small office users should install the 32-bit version of Vista even if they have x64 processors. You should only use the 64-bit versions if you have to run specific 64-bit apps that have huge memory requirements.

NOTE

The N versions of the Home Basic and Business editions (available in Europe) are similar to the U.S. versions, but omit multimedia features such as Windows Media Player. Windows Vista Starter edition is available in 139 countries with emerging technology markets and leaves out some features found in Windows Vista Home Basic. This book does not cover these editions.

The 64-bit versions use an emulation layer called WOW64 to run Win32-based applications, although, for best performance, Microsoft recommends using 32-bit software on 32-bit Windows systems. The emulation feature enables organizations to use their Itanium-based systems with existing Windows applications until they create 64-bit versions created internally or purchase them from software vendors.

Table 1.3 compares the features in the various versions of Windows Vista.

TABLE 1.3 VARIOUS VERSIONS OF WINDOWS VISTA COMPARED

Feature	Home Basic	Home Premium	Business	Enterprise	Ultimate
Backup (scheduled)	—	✓	✓	✓	✓
Backup (network-based)	—	✓	✓	✓	✓
Shadow copy client	—	—	✓	✓	✓
Encrypted File System (EFS)	—	✓	✓	✓	✓
Supports migration from XP	✓	✓	✓	✓	✓
Desktop Window Manager (DWM)	✓	✓	✓	✓	✓
Aero glass, animations, visual effects	—	✓	✓	✓	✓
Productivity features (rolodex, tab previews, task bar previews)	—	✓	✓	✓	✓
Unlimited screen resolution support	✓	✓	✓	✓	✓
Fast User Switching (FUS)	✓	✓	✓	✓	✓
RDP/Remote Desktop	—	—	✓	✓	✓
Windows Meeting Space (ad hoc P2P meetings, people discovery, presentation broadcast)	—	—	✓	✓	✓
Windows Web Server (optional)	—	—	✓	✓	✓
Windows Fax client	—	—	✓ (Opt)	✓ (Opt)	✓ (Opt)

continues

Table 1.3 Continued

Feature	Home Basic	Home Premium	Business	Enterprise	Ultimate
DVD Video Authoring	—	✓	—	—	✓
Media Center (including Extender and games)	—	✓	—	—	✓
Number of remote Media Center sessions supported	n/a	5	n/a	n/a	5
Movie Maker HD (High Definition) Publishing	—	✓	—	—	✓
Advanced Photography features (e.g. fine-grain editing)	—	✓	✓ (Opt)	✓ (Opt)	✓ (Opt)
Premium Games (3D Chess, Shanghai Solitaire)	—	✓ (Opt)	✓ (Opt)	✓ (Opt)	✓ (Opt)
Windows Media Player 11 and related components	✓	✓	✓	✓	✓
Number of supported network connections	5	5	10	10	10
Domain join support	—	—	✓	✓	✓
1:1 Network Projector support	—	✓	✓	✓	✓
SNMP support	✓ (Opt)	✓ (Opt)	✓ (Opt)	✓ (Opt)	✓ (Opt)
Internet Connection Sharing (ICS)	✓	✓	✓	✓	✓
PC-to-PC Sync	—	✓	✓	✓	✓
Mobility Center	—	✓	✓	✓	✓
Tablet PC functionality	—	✓ (Opt)	✓ (Opt)	✓ (Opt)	✓ (Opt)
Auxiliary Display support	—	✓	✓	✓	✓
Ultimate Extras	—	—	—	—	✓
Offline folders with client-side caching	—	—	✓	✓	✓
Subsystem for UNIX-based Applications (SUA)	—	—	—	✓ (Opt)	✓ (Opt)
Secure Startup BitLocker	—	—	—	✓	✓ (Opt)
Multi-Language User Interface (MUI)	—	—	—	✓	✓ (Opt)
Supports 32-bit processors (x86)	✓	✓	✓	✓	✓
Amount of RAM supported on 32-bit systems	4GB	4GB	4GB	4GB	4GB
Supports 64-bit processors (x64)	✓	✓	✓	✓	✓

Feature	Home Basic	Home Premium	Business	Enterprise	Ultimate
Amount of RAM supported on x64 systems	8GB	16GB	128GB+	128GB+	128GB+
Number of physical CPUs supported	1	1	2	2	2

Some information in this table adapted from information found on Paul Thurrott's incredibly informative Windows Supersite (www.winsupersite.com).
(Opt) means "option," indicating that the feature is included with the edition but not installed, but can be installed at any time.

Table 1.4 outlines the upgrade options mapped to the different Windows Vista editions.

TABLE 1.4 WINDOWS VISTA UPGRADE PATHS

	Windows Vista Editions			
	Home Basic	*Home Premium*	*Business*	*Ultimate*
Windows XP Professional	1	1	2	2
Windows XP Home	2	2	2	2
Windows XP Media Center	1	2	1	2
Windows XP Tablet PC	1	1	2	2
Windows XP Professional x64	1	1	1	1
Windows 2000	1	1	1	1

Some information in this table adapted from information found on Paul Thurrott's incredibly informative Windows Supersite (www.winsupersite.com).
[1]Requires clean install.
[2]In-place installation option available.

How Does Windows Vista Compare to UNIX and Linux?

Like the Windows 2000 kernel, the Windows XP kernel has its roots in UNIX, a popular multitasking operating system developed at Bell Labs in the early 1970s. UNIX was designed by programmers for programmers. In fact, the language C was developed just to write UNIX. Even though UNIX has become a friendlier operating system with the addition of Windows-like interfaces such as MOTIF, it's still relatively user-unfriendly, requiring cryptic commands much like DOS.

UNIX

Because it is written in C, UNIX can run on nearly any computer that has a C compiler, making it quite portable. AT&T gave away the UNIX source code to universities and licensed it to several companies during its early years. AT&T no longer owns UNIX; OpenGroup now owns the UNIX trademark, although the Santa Cruz Operation (SCO) claims to own the source code; this is now in debate.

Unfortunately, to avoid paying licensing fees to AT&T, UNIX look-alikes sprung up over the years. Without the proper license, these versions could not call themselves UNIX—only "UNIX-like." As these clones proliferated, cross-compatibility became an issue. More than a handful of versions (dialects) of UNIX have appeared, the primary contenders being AT&T's own, known as System V, and another developed at the University of California at Berkeley, known as BSD4.*x* (with *x* being a number from 1 to 3). Other popular brands of UNIX these days are HP-UX from HP, AIX from IBM, Solaris from Sun, and SCO's version, UnixWare. Even Apple's Mac OS X operating system is actually a variant of UNIX!

In 1984, industry experts were brought together to create guidelines and standards for UNIX clones, in hopes of creating a more coherent market. The result was a single UNIX specification, which includes a requirement for POSIX (Portable Operating System Interface for UNIX) compliance. Accepted by the IEEE and ISO, POSIX is a standard that makes porting applications and other code among variants of UNIX as simple as recompiling the source code.

> **NOTE**
>
> Another popular version of UNIX that runs on the PC platform is called FreeBSD. Briefly, FreeBSD is a UNIX-like operating system based on U.C. Berkeley's 4.4BSD-lite release for the Intel 386 platform. It is also based indirectly on William Jolitz's port of U.C. Berkeley's Net/2 to the Intel 386, known as 386BSD, although very little of the 386BSD code remains. You can find a fuller description of what FreeBSD is and how it can work for you at www.freebsd.org.

UNIX has been the predominant operating system for workstations connected to servers, mostly because of its multiuser capabilities and its rock-solid performance. Windows NT and its successors, Windows 2000 and Windows XP, have been making inroads because of the extensive number of development tools and applications for the Windows platform.

Since so many networking and Internet application functions were developed on and continue to run on UNIX, Microsoft has produced a compatibility subsystem called the Subsystem for UNIX-Based Applications (SUA). This is a near-perfect UNIX operating system kernel that runs over the NT kernel and alongside Windows Vista. SUA is a free product included with Windows Vista Enterprise and Ultimate editions, and a full complement of UNIX programming tools is available for it. We'll discuss it in Chapter 21, "Mix and Match with Old Windows and Macs."

Also, you probably know that the free or low-cost UNIX variant called Linux is revitalizing UNIX across all platforms.

Linux

Linux is a UNIX look-alike. Linux isn't a port of a preexisting operating system. It was written from the ground up by Linus Torvalds, a Finnish-born computer scientist who wanted to develop a UNIX-like operating system for computer students to run on low-cost Intel computers. Torvalds wrote the kernel with the help of a handful of computer programmers. Like all variants of UNIX, Linux has many of the features of NT/Windows 2000/Windows XP/Vista, such as true multitasking, virtual memory, shared libraries, intelligent memory management, and TCP/IP networking. IT professionals willing to get under the hood and poke around and learn Linux's ways are impressed with its solidity. Although Linux is not commonly used as a business productivity workstation, some have embraced it for back-end web servers or transaction servers where reliability is a high priority.

Linux is an open system, and programmers worldwide are invited to participate in its building and refinement. Unlike other flavors of UNIX that were based on licensed source code, Linux is based on Minix, which mimics UNIX in a way that does not infringe on the UNIX license. That's why Linux distributions are practically free.

> **NOTE** Actually, the term *Linux* pertains only to the kernel. What people have come to refer to as Linux is actually a collection of separate pieces of code, the majority of which are GNU. It was not until Linux came together with GNU that the full power of the Linux OS (what GNU enthusiasts would called GNU Linux) crystallized.

The several popularly distributed Linux versions are differentiated mostly by the selection of tools and utilities bundled with them. The most popular package at this point is Ubuntu Linux. If you want to go it alone, you can acquire Linux for free, but buying some commercially bundled packages makes the job of installation and support easier because you get support. Technically, the distribution of the software must be free, in accordance with the GNU General Public License (GPL) agreement governing the distribution of Linux and the collected modules that accompany it.

Linux is now running on a wide variety of systems, including Sun JavaStations, the IBM RS/6000, and the Alpha chip originally developed by DEC and later sold by Compaq, MIPS, SPARC, Open VMS, Digital UNIX, and other platforms.

Windows Application Compatibility with Linux

As we mentioned, Microsoft has made it possible to compile and run UNIX applications on Windows. Not surprisingly, a lot of people are working to let applications move the other way, that is, to let Windows applications run on UNIX.

WINE, a DOS, Windows 3.1, and 32-bit Windows compatibility layer, is a popular program used by a number of vendors to move their Windows programs to the Linux platform. For more information, see the WINE website at www.winehq.org. However, even the most recent versions of WINE are limited, especially in their multimedia support. To get full

Linux and full Windows Vista support on a single system, set up a dual-boot system. The only reliable way to run Windows programs on a Linux system is to dual-boot.

→ To learn more about dual-booting Linux, **see** "Multibooting Windows Vista," **p. 66**.

Mainstream applications for Linux have taken a long time to arrive. Corel's WordPerfect Office for Linux and CorelDRAW for Linux were discontinued. Sun's StarOffice 8.x is a powerful office suite with many of the features of recent Microsoft Office releases. Of course, many downloadable freeware and shareware programs for Linux are available online.

Of course, until recently Microsoft didn't want to develop Linux versions of either its programming languages or applications such as Office, for obvious reasons. However, Microsoft will now officially support SUSE Linux in partnership with Novell. Whether this is a true partnership to help develop open source software or a divide-and-conquer strategy on Microsoft's part, only time will tell.

It seems surprising at first glance that Linux would be popular with entrepreneurs. However, many companies have found that they can make a profit providing services, support, and consulting for software they provide free. But because applications developers for the Linux environment are supposed to distribute their source code along with the applications, this is a daunting shift of worldview for a behemoth such as Microsoft, which works overtime to protect its intellectual property. The upshot is that you're out of luck if you want to run Word, Excel, Access, Internet Explorer, or any other Microsoft programs on a Linux box as a native application.

Windows Vista Versus Linux

Trying to compare Windows Vista and Linux is difficult, for several reasons:

- Windows Vista requires a relatively recent computer with at least 512MB of RAM just to function (and 1GB to work decently); Linux can run successfully on even 486-based systems, long obsolete for use with Windows.
- Windows Vista is available in just five versions; Linux is available in numerous distributions.
- Windows is primarily a GUI-based operating system; Linux is primarily command-line driven (although KDE and Gnome, the two most common GUIs, are increasingly popular).

Although Linux has made great strides in so-called "back end" uses, such as web servers, network servers, and embedded devices, Windows is a better choice for desktops, for several reasons:

- Compatibility testing and guarantees for the operating system and applications.
- Wide availability of commercial applications at retail and online stores.
- Long-term roadmap of operating system deployment plans.

- "Synchronous I/O," which allows smoother running in Windows Vista when multiple threads are being processed and waiting for input or output. It improves SMP scalability as well.
- Consistent GUI across all tools. Linux currently has no single standard GUI.
- A single version that can be installed for most major languages and countries.
- A dedicated support network, with close to a half-million Microsoft-certified trained professionals and engineers.

We believe that the entire Linux/Windows controversy comes down to this: Microsoft offers a lot of powerful stuff (which you can use to build very sophisticated software), from the C++ compiler, to the component-nature of Excel and other apps, to the ASP scripting language, to COM, and so on. These tools let you leverage everything Microsoft offers to make very powerful applications. As people said in the 1960s and '70s, nobody ever lost his job buying IBM. Now it's safe to say nobody ever lost his job buying Microsoft. True, you're locked into Windows because the stuff you build on Windows systems can't be ported to UNIX variants, but that's the price you pay for the tools, the user base, and the support and training. Although increasing support options are available for Linux, enterprise-level support for Linux is still not as widespread as for Windows. Still, it's interesting to note that IBM supports running Linux on its entire mainframe line, and Oracle Corporation provides enterprise Linux support. Microsoft officially supports SUSE Linux.

Linux might be a decent choice for the small-business owners or IS professionals who need to build low-cost servers for web, email, or file sharing. This operating system is designed for those uses, and the popular Red Hat and Ubuntu Linux packages make installation relatively painless (not as easy as Windows Vista, mind you). If you're thinking of using Linux on your desktop PC, beware—you might be biting off more than you can chew. The manuals that come with Linux—even the commercial versions—are dense. It is not always headache-free. But if you have a good understanding of computer technology and insist on switching from Windows to something more stable and more flexible, Linux might be the choice for you. If nothing else, using Linux will be a learning experience. However, for the foreseeable future, Linux will be primarily a server and embedded-device operating system instead of a desktop operating system.

Windows Vista on the Corporate Network

Because Windows Vista Business is designed as a replacement for Windows XP Professional, it is designed to work well on corporate networks. Thus, it contains all the network and security features of Windows XP Professional, including these:

- Support for IP Security (IPSec), to protect data being transmitted across VPNs
- Kerberos v5 support for authentication
- Group Policy settings for administering networks and users

- Roaming User Profiles to let users see their own files and preference settings on any computer
- Offline viewing of network data when not connected to the network
- Synchronization of local and network files
- Easy dial-up and VPN networking setup
- Support for Active Directory (Microsoft's directory service feature that helps manage users and resources on large networks)
- Disk quotas, to prevent a few storage-hog users from running the server out of space
- Internet Information Services, including FTP, World Wide Web service, and scriptable management interfaces
- Fax services for sending and receiving faxes
- Simple Network Management Protocol (SNMP) support
- Print services for UNIX

However, if you want to enjoy all these features plus the multimedia features of Home Premium, choose Vista Ultimate Edition. It is equally at home in corporate networks and as a part of a home entertainment system.

CHAPTER 2

INSTALLING AND UPGRADING WINDOWS VISTA

In this chapter

General Considerations for Windows Vista 42

Windows Vista Hardware Requirements 42

Performing a New Installation of Windows Vista 49

Upgrading Older Versions of Windows to Vista 62

Upgrading One Version of Vista to Another 65

Multibooting Windows Vista 66

Activating Windows Vista 70

The Virtual Machine Approach 73

Tips from the Windows Pros: Editing Your Windows Vista Boot Menu Entries 74

General Considerations for Windows Vista

You learned about the hype about Windows Vista, all its new features, and some of the details of its design and architecture in Chapter 1, "Introducing Windows Vista." The question at this point is, "Are you really going to install it?" If you are, you should go ahead and read this chapter and the next one. In this chapter, I coach you on preparing for the installation and checking your hardware and software requirements; then I discuss some compatibility issues that might affect your product-purchasing decisions. The next chapter covers post-installation issues, such as personalizing Windows Vista to suit you. I also walk you through the setup procedure.

Of course, if Windows Vista is already installed on your PC, you might be able to skip to Chapter 3, "The First Hour." However, you should at least take a brief look at this chapter because it includes some discussion that might affect your software and hardware installation decisions when using Windows Vista in the future. Understanding what you can do with and shouldn't expect from an operating system is always good background material when you use a tool as complex as a computer on a regular basis. Pay particular attention to the section about RAM and hard disk upgrades, and how to research hardware compatibility and find the Windows Vista–approved applications list on the Windows Catalog site.

As you'll learn later in this chapter, the Windows Vista Setup program automatically checks your hardware and software, and reports any potential conflicts. Using it is one way to find out whether your system is ready for prime time. It can be annoying; however, it is better than finding out something is amiss at midnight when you're doing an installation, especially when you could have purchased RAM or some other installation prerequisite the previous day when you were out at the computer store. Likewise, you don't want to be technically capable of running Windows Vista, only to experience disappointing performance. To help you prevent such calamity or surprise, the first part of this chapter covers hardware compatibility issues.

Windows Vista Hardware Requirements

Let's start with the basics. The principal (and minimal) hardware requirements for running Windows Vista are as follows:

With Windows Vista, Microsoft has defined two very different levels of minimum hardware requirements for the first time. In a sense, though, this is something that most power users were doing on their own. Microsoft defines the levels as Windows Vista Capable and Windows Vista Premium Ready. The Windows Vista Capable computer is one that meets the minimum requirements listed here. Although Windows Vista will run on a computer with these specifications, the experience will be less than optimal compared to running Windows Vista on a computer that meets the requirements of Windows Vista Premium Ready. The Windows Vista Capable hardware requirements are as follows:

- An 800MHz 32-bit (x86) or 64-bit (x64) processor
- 512MB of RAM

- A video card capable of at least 800×600 resolution and DirectX9
- A hard drive that is at least 20GB in total size, with at least 15GB of free space

These are Microsoft's suggested minimums, not necessarily what will provide satisfactory or exceptional performance. Some users have reported installing Vista on lesser machines. Microsoft tries to quote minimum requirements that will provide performance that the average user can live with. Although Microsoft doesn't specifically mention it, you'll also want at least 16MB of video RAM to allow your system to choose 24-bit and 32-bit color depths at 1024×768 resolutions, and a sound card to work with Windows Media Player.

In comparison, the Windows Vista Premium Ready specifications are as follows:

- A 1GHz (or faster) 32-bit (x86) or 64-bit (x64) processor
- A minimum of 1GB of RAM
- A video card that supports DirectX 9 graphics with a WDDM driver and has at least 128MB of graphics memory
- Video card support for Pixel Shader 2.0 and 32 bits per pixel
- A hard drive that is at least 40GB in total size, with at least 15GB of free space
- A DVD-ROM drive
- Audio output capability
- Internet connectivity for product activation

> **TIP**
> With the plummeting prices of CPUs and RAM these days, there's virtually no reason not to upgrade your CPU and motherboard, or just get a whole new system for Windows Vista. The price wars between Intel and AMD might be brutal on the corporate battlefield, but the consumer is clearly the winner. You'll find 2GHz–3GHz desktop computers with 150GB or larger hard disks and 2GB of RAM for around $500–$750 as of this writing.

Based on what you can get inexpensively these days, you shouldn't have much difficulty purchasing a machine that will run Windows Vista adequately. Despite the rapid de-escalation in prices and apparent exponential increase in computing speed, putting together a machine to run Windows Vista successfully for your needs might not be as easy as you think. Whenever I build a new system, I'm surprised by twists I hadn't considered, new hardware standards I didn't know even existed, and so on. In general, I believe that buying a complete, preconfigured system is smarter than building one from parts that you buy from separate manufacturers, unless you are a serious hardware geek. You probably know the story.

OPTION 1: USING WHAT YOU'VE GOT: ENSURING COMPATIBILITY VIA THE WINDOWS VISTA UPGRADE ADVISOR

If you have a fairly recent computer that meets the requirements listed earlier and you want to check compatibility before moving ahead with the Windows Vista installation, this is the option you'll likely want to choose. Microsoft has put together the Windows Vista Upgrade

CHAPTER 2 INSTALLING AND UPGRADING WINDOWS VISTA

Advisor for just this purpose. By downloading, installing, and running the Upgrade Advisor, you can create an easy-to-read report that lists all system and device compatibility issues with your current computer. Additionally, and perhaps most useful, the Upgrade Advisor recommends ways for you to resolve any discovered issues. Finally, the Upgrade Advisor helps you choose the correct version of Windows Vista for your needs.

To get started with the Windows Vista Upgrade Advisor, visit the Upgrade Advisor page at www.microsoft.com/windowsvista/getready/upgradeadvisor/ and download the Upgrade Advisor. After you've downloaded the Upgrade Advisor, follow these steps to get it installed and start using it:

> **NOTE**
> Depending on the software configuration of the computer you are running the Upgrade Advisor on, you may be prompted to install MSXML 6.0 and/or the .NET Framework before you will be able to use the Upgrade Advisor.

1. Locate the `VistaUpgradeAdvisor.msi` file and double-click it to start the installation process.
2. When prompted, click the Run button to start the installer.
3. On the opening dialog box of the Windows Vista Upgrade Advisor Wizard, click Next to continue.
4. On the License Agreement dialog box, select I Agree and then click Next to continue.
5. On the Select Installation Folder dialog box, shown in Figure 2.1, select the location where the Upgrade Advisor should be installed. Additionally, you need to specify who should be able to run the Upgrade Advisor after installation has completed. After making your selections, Click Next to continue.

Figure 2.1
You have the option to specify where the Upgrade Advisor is installed and who can run it.

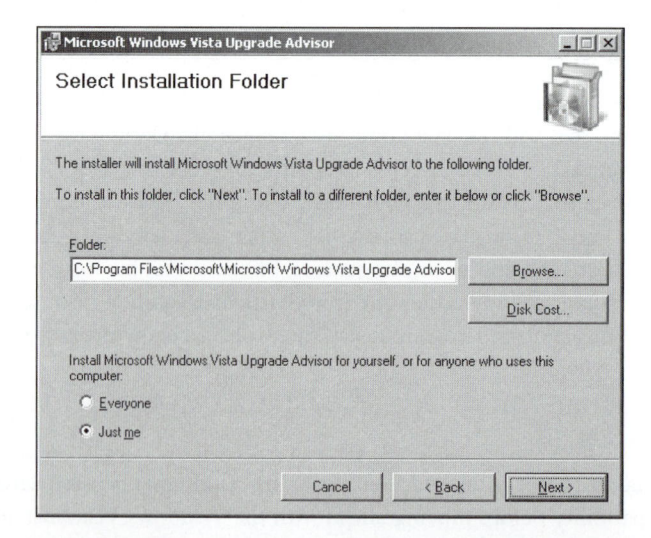

Windows Vista Hardware Requirements

6. On the Confirm Installation dialog box, click Next to start the installation.
7. On the Installation Complete dialog box, ensure that the Launch Microsoft Windows Vista Upgrade Advisor check box is selected and click Close. The Upgrade Advisor opens, as shown in Figure 2.2.

Figure 2.2
The Microsoft Windows Vista Upgrade Advisor scans your computer looking for upgrade and compatibility issues.

8. Click the Start Scan link to begin the scan process.
9. The Upgrade Advisor will spend some time scanning your computer. During this time, you can click on the various buttons on the bottom of the window, as seen in Figure 2.3, to view information about the different versions of Windows Vista.

Figure 2.3
You will need to wait a few minutes to allow the Upgrade Advisor to scan your computer.

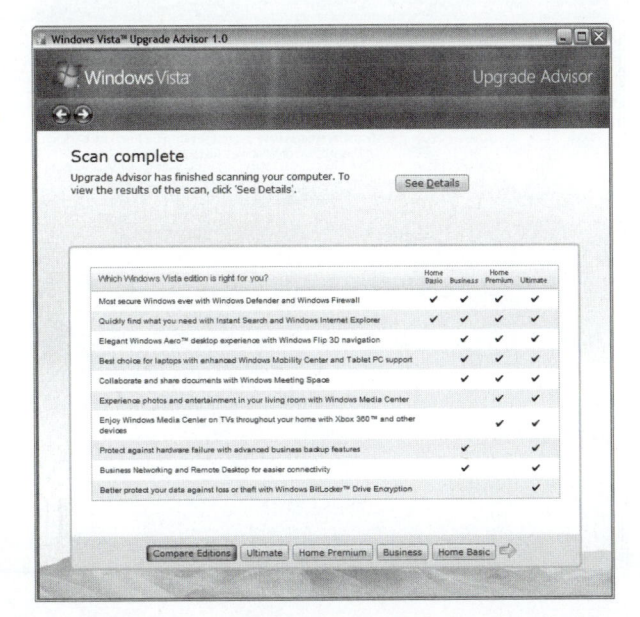

10. When the scan has completed, click the See Details button to continue You can quickly view the details of the scan and what each version of Windows Vista offers as seen in Figure 2.4.

Figure 2.4
The Microsoft Windows Vista Upgrade Advisor shows you what features are available in each version.

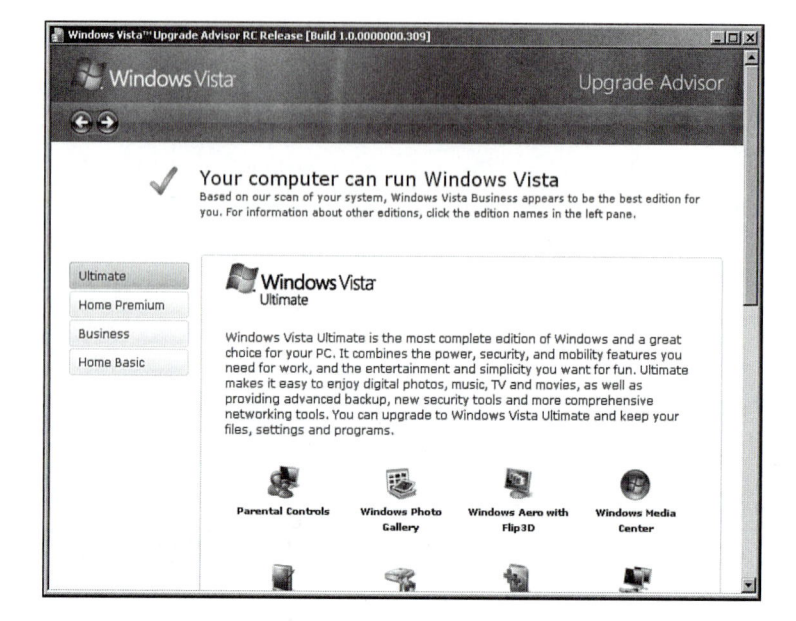

11. Scroll down to the bottom of the window to see what problems the Upgrade Advisor has identified for each version of Windows Vista, as seen in Figure 2.5.

Figure 2.5
You will be alerted to problems that must be addressed.

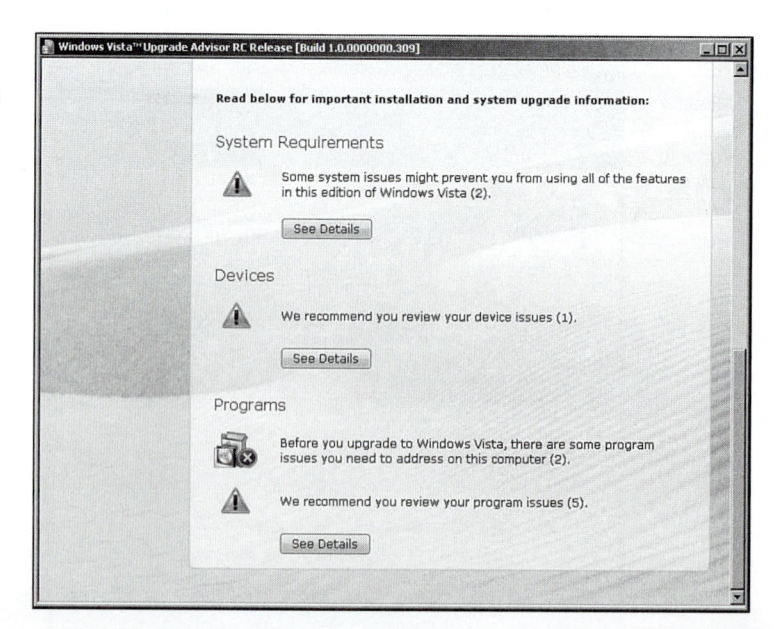

Windows Vista Hardware Requirements

12. Click the See Details button to view the report details as seen in Figure 2.6. On each tab you can view all items that need to be addressed in order to successfully install Windows Vista.

Figure 2.6
You will be given a detailed list of items to correct.

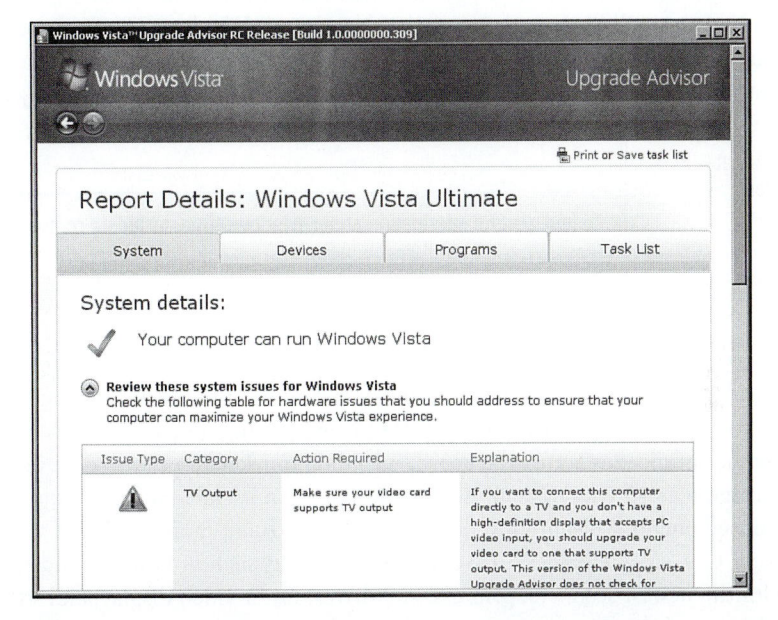

13. On the Task List tab of the report, shown in Figure 2.7, you will get a consolidated listing of all actions you must perform. Be sure to print or save your final report before closing the Upgrade Advisor.

Figure 2.7
The Task List tab provides a consolidated list of actions that need to be performed.

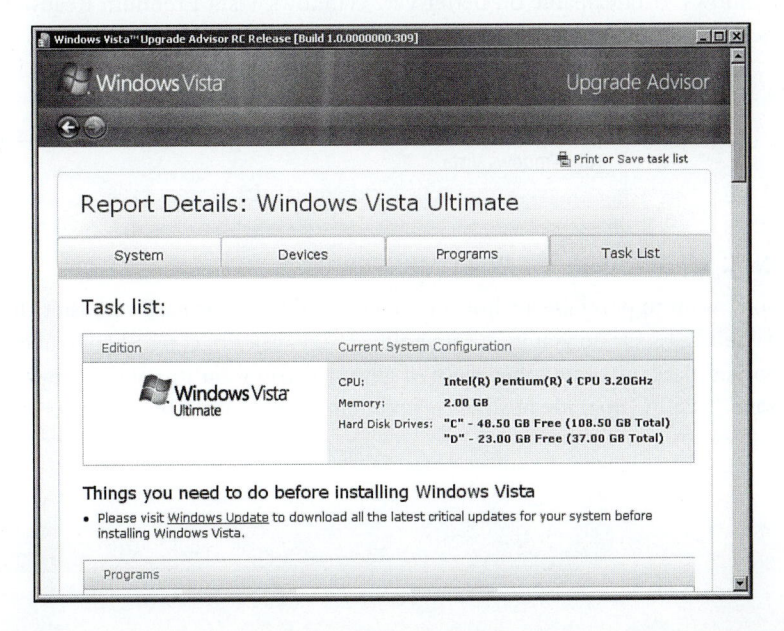

14. After you've printed and/or saved the final report, click the Close button at the bottom of the page.

Based on the results of the Upgrade Advisor scan, you should have a good idea of what, if any, issues you'll likely encounter when you install Windows Vista on your existing hardware. Of course, even if some areas of the report don't meet the requirements, such as the system seen in Figure 2.5 that doesn't support live TV, you can still enjoy many of the great new features of Windows Vista.

> **TIP**
>
> To find general information about Windows Vista, including compatibility, check out www.microsoft.com/windowsvista.

Option 2: Choosing a Windows Vista Premium Ready PC

It isn't a bad idea to just bite the bullet and shell out for a new machine about once every two or three years. When you upgrade to a new computer, you'll likely notice a significant number of niceties across the board, including quicker response; more inclusive power management so your system uses less power when it's idle (and cuts your utility bills); reduced energy consumption due to lower chip count; more hardware setting options; a faster CD-RW/DVD-RW drive; high-speed ports such as USB 2.0 and FireWire that work with the newest scanners, printers, and drives; faster video display; and so on.

If you have decided to start fresh and purchase new PCs for your personal or corporate arsenal, let me suggest an easier way to choose them than to research each piece separately. Visit the Windows Marketplace website, located at www.windowsmarketplace.com/Content.aspx?ctId=366, to browse all the desktop and portable computers that are either Windows Vista Capable or, better yet, Windows Vista Premium Ready. There's no shortage of systems there, so get ready to do a little head scratching.

> **TIP**
>
> If you happen to have a PC guaranteed to run Windows XP, chances are good that it will run Windows Vista.

Option 3: Upgrading Your Computer

Don't want to purchase a whole new computer, but your hardware isn't all on the Catalog or the HCL? Or do you have some old, stodgy disk drive, SCSI controller, video adapter, motherboard, or some other piece of gear that you want to upgrade anyway? You're not alone. The PC upgrade business is booming, as evidenced by the pages and pages of ads in the backs of computer rags and the popularity of computer "swap meets," where precious little swapping goes on except that of hardware components for the hard-earned green stuff.

> **TIP**
>
> If you plan to upgrade, see Scott Mueller's book *Upgrading and Repairing PCs* (Que, 2007; ISBN 0789736970) for the best (and most complete) information available on how to do the job right the first time. Also be sure to visit www.upgradingandrepairingpcs.com for regular updates to this perennial classic.

If you intend to upgrade your existing computer to support an installation of Windows Vista, you must not have any ISA devices installed. Windows Vista does not support ISA peripherals, so it seems that the time of ISA has finally gone by. Additionally, there have been many reports of incompatible motherboards despite all indications to the contrary. For example, the ASUS P5VDC-MX motherboard has been reported by many to have compatibility issues.

Performing a New Installation of Windows Vista

The three basic types of clean installation procedures are as follows:

- Install on a brand new disk or computer system
- Erase the disk, format it, and install
- Install into a new directory for dual-booting (see the multiboot discussion later in this chapter)

If you intend to use either of the first two methods, make sure you are equipped to boot your computer from the DVD-ROM. Most of today's computers support booting from the DVD-ROM drive. Doing so might require changing the drive boot order in the BIOS or CMOS, but try it first without doing this. With no floppy disk inserted and a clean hard disk, the DVD-ROM drive should be tried next. The Windows Vista DVD is bootable and should run the Setup program automatically.

Installation takes 15–90 minutes, depending on the speed of your machine. Refer to the following sections if you have questions about the steps of the process.

Typical Clean Setup Procedure

If you're installing into an empty partition and you can boot an operating system that is supported for the purpose of Setup (Windows 2000 or Windows XP), just boot up, insert the DVD, and choose Install Now from the resulting dialog box, shown in Figure 2.8. Then you can follow the installation step-by-step procedure.

Figure 2.8
Installing Windows Vista from an existing Windows installation is easy to start.

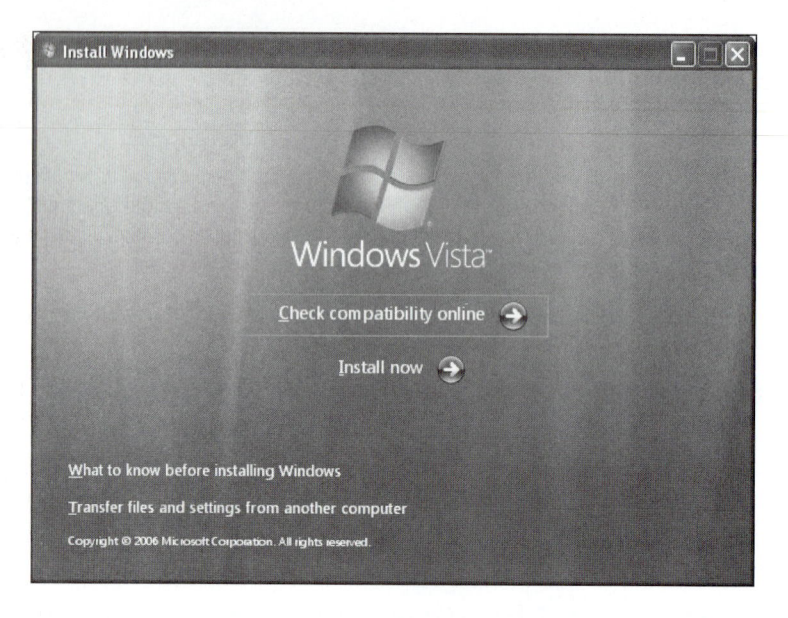

> **NOTE**
> Windows Vista will automatically format any disk it is installed on in a clean installation as NTFS.

If Windows doesn't automatically detect the DVD when you insert it, you must manually run the Setup program, setup.exe, from the Start, Run dialog box (after opening the Run dialog, type **D:/setup.exe**). You can find the setup.exe application located in the Sources directory on the DVD. After the Setup routine starts, you can follow the installation step-by-step procedure.

> **NOTE**
> When using the Run dialog box, substitute the actual letter for your DVD drive. We used D: in the example here, but yours might be different.

If your computer has a blank hard disk or your current operating system isn't supported, the process is different. You need to start the installation booting process from the Windows Vista DVD (this approach works only if your computer is newer and you can boot from the DVD-ROM drive). Setup automatically runs if you boot from the DVD.

Yet another setup-initiation method involves the network. To initiate a network installation, you must have a network share of the distribution DVD or a copy of the DVD on a hard drive. The destination system must have network access, and the user account must have at least read access to the installation files. Setup is initiated by executing setup.exe from the network share. For example, from the Start, Run command, type a path of `\\<servername>\<sharename>\sources\`. Setup recognizes an over-the-network installation and automatically copies all files from the network share to the local system before the first reboot.

The typical clean installation (on a blank hard disk) step-by-step procedure is as follows:

> **NOTE**
> All versions of Windows Vista, 32-bit or 64-bit, are included on the same DVD. The product key that you enter during setup determines what actual version of Windows Vista you end up with after the installation completes. Keep your Windows Vista DVD and product key in a safe location after you've performed your installation.

1. Insert the Windows Vista DVD into your computer's DVD-ROM drive, and restart the computer. Windows Vista setup should start automatically, as shown in Figure 2.9. If setup does not start automatically, ensure that your computer is configured to support booting from the DVD-ROM drive.

Figure 2.9
This screen is one of only two text-based setup screens you'll see in Windows Vista.

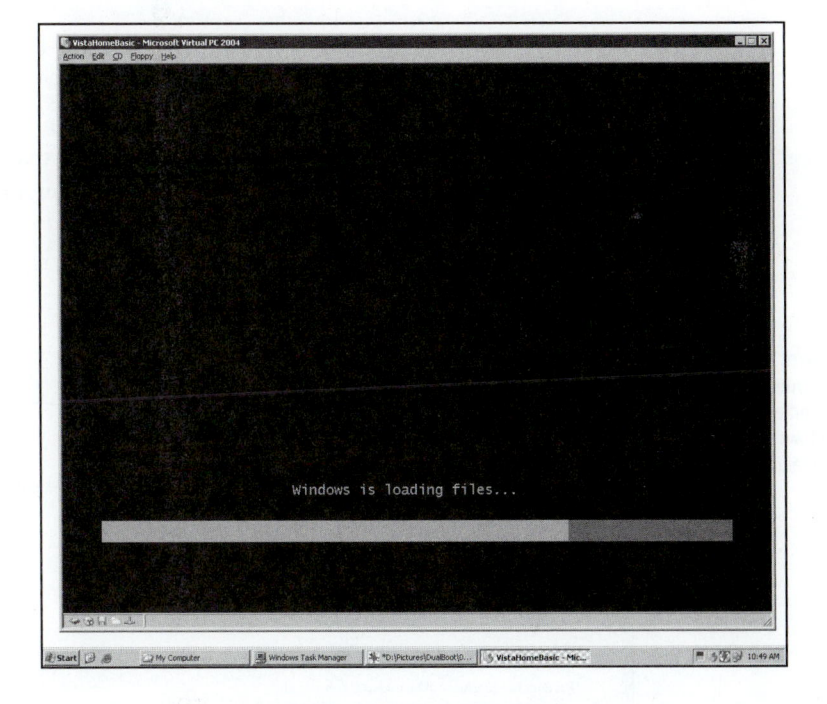

2. Next, you are asked to select the regional options for the Windows Vista installation, as shown in Figure 2.10. Make your selections and click Next to continue.

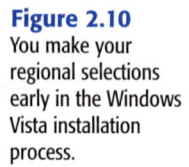

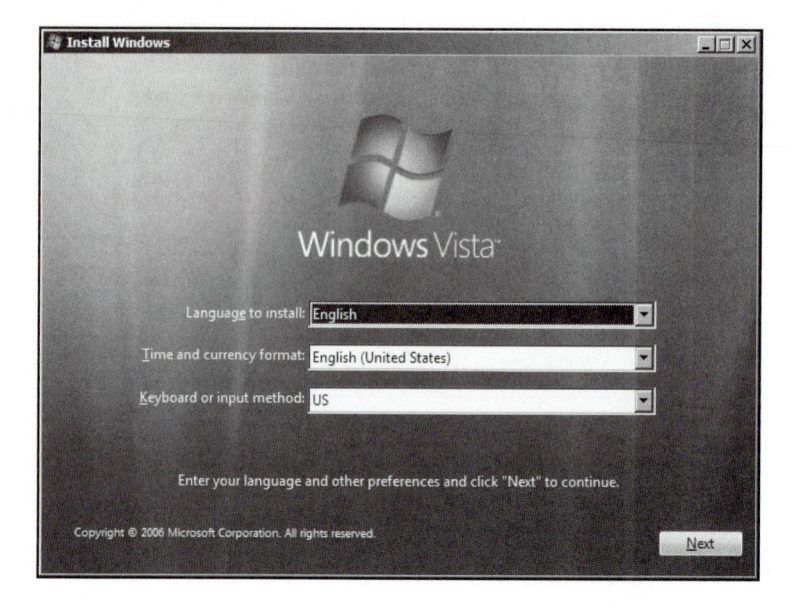

Figure 2.10
You make your regional selections early in the Windows Vista installation process.

3. On the next dialog box, you are prompted to start the installation. Click Install Now to begin the installation.

4. On the Type Your Product Key for Activation dialog box, shown in Figure 2.11, you are asked for your Windows Vista product key. Enter the product key that came with your Windows Vista DVD. It's also recommended that you leave the Automatically Activate Windows When I'm Online option checked to automatically take care of Windows Product Activation within the first 3 days following the Windows Vista installation. After entering your information, click Next to continue.

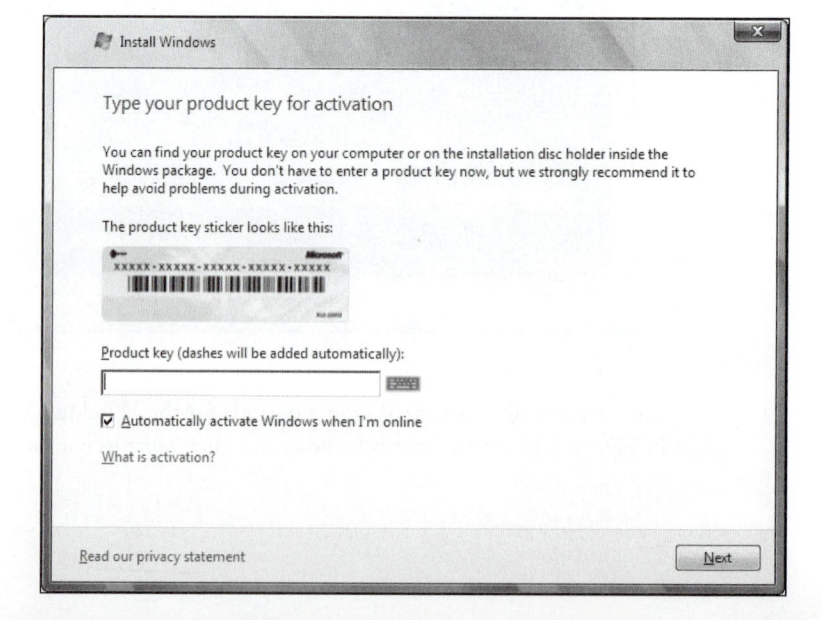

Figure 2.11
Enter your product key and ensure that Windows Vista can automatically activate itself.

You can also leave the Product Key box blank. If you do this, you'll be asked which version of Windows Vista you want to install, and you can select any version from Starter to Ultimate. You'll have to provide a valid product key, however, for whatever version you install within 30 days or Vista may stop working. (If you are installing a 'slipstreamed' copy of Vista Service Pack 1, or you use the Windows Update service to upgrade to SP-1, you'll simply be reminded to properly register rather than experiencing a crippled system.)

You can use the no-key method to play around with different versions of Vista, but be very careful if you select a version for which you don't have a key; you must perform a clean install every time you reinstall Vista, and you must eventually install a version for which you have a license, or erase it. You'll lose your applications and data every time you reinstall.

CAUTION

> You should definitely not play with alternate versions if you are performing an upgrade from an older version of Windows because you will have no way of going back and repeating the upgrade with your licensed version of Vista.

5. On the Please Read the License Terms dialog box, ensure that you read and understand the End User Licensing Agreement (EULA). When you're ready, select the I Accept the License Terms option and click Next to continue.

6. On the Which Type of Installation Do You Want? dialog box, shown in Figure 2.12, you are able to select only the select Custom (Advanced) option because you're performing a new installation on a blank hard disk. Click Custom (Advanced) to continue.

Figure 2.12
For new installations, only the Custom (Advanced) option is available.

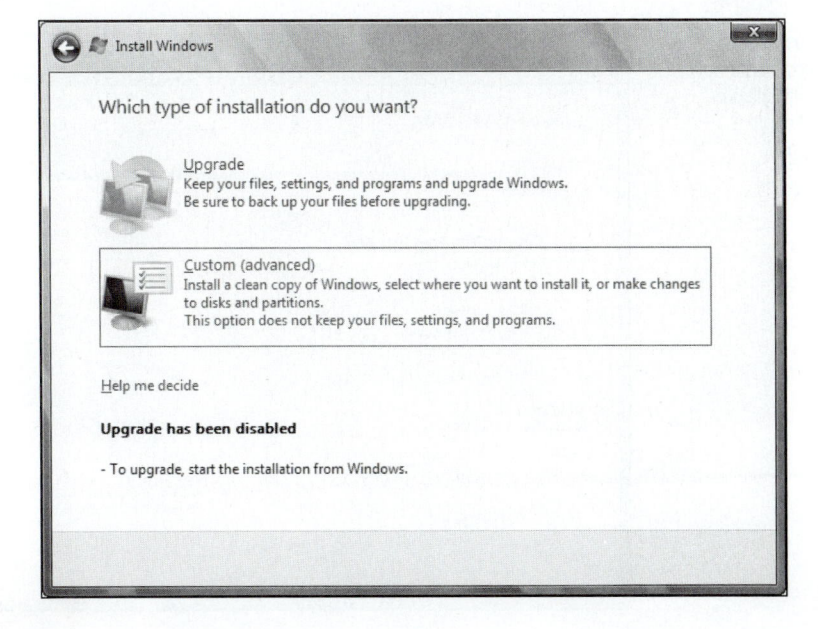

7. On the Where Do You Want to Install Windows? dialog box, shown in Figure 2.13, select the partition onto which you'll install Windows Vista. When you're ready to proceed, click Next. If you need to provide a RAID or SCSI driver, this is the time to do it.

Figure 2.13
You need to select an empty partition for the installation of Windows Vista.

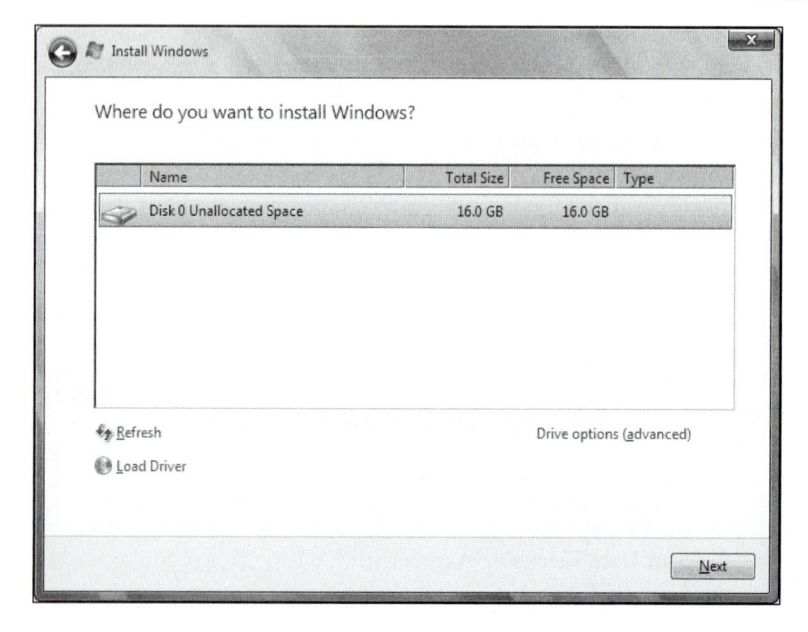

8. The Installing Windows dialog box appears, as shown in Figure 2.14, and gives you an updated status of the upgrade process.

Figure 2.14
Windows Vista now starts installation based on your selections.

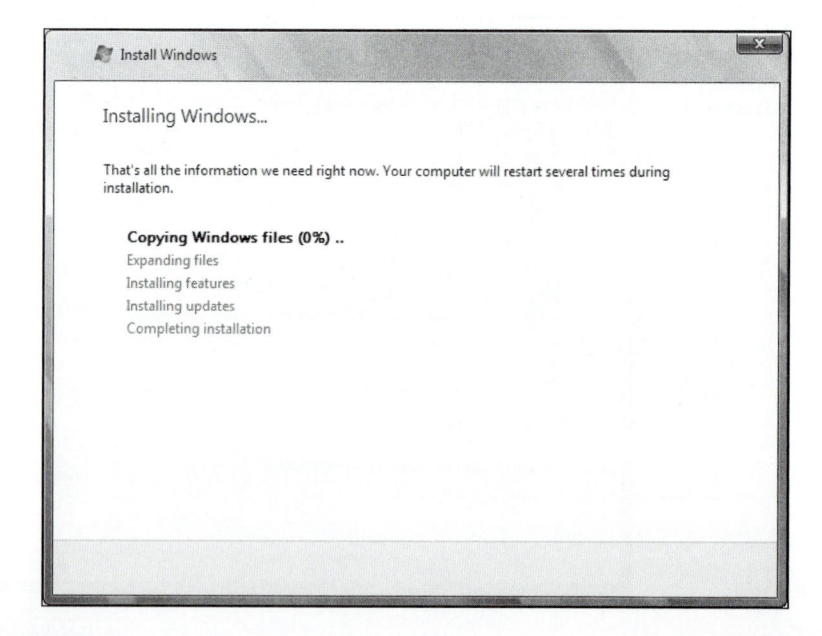

> **NOTE**
>
> If you are installing Windows Vista on a notebook computer and the screen goes black and stays black for several minutes at this point, try connecting an external monitor to the computer. A known bug in Vista setup can make this necessary.

9. After some time, your computer restarts and the newly installed Windows Vista loads. Windows Vista resumes the installation process. Windows typically restarts once more before it finally completes the installation process.

10. On the next restart, you'll see the screen in Figure 2.15 as Windows Vista prepares the new installation. Windows Vista moves back into a graphical display after a few minutes.

Figure 2.15
Windows Vista must prepare to start for the first time.

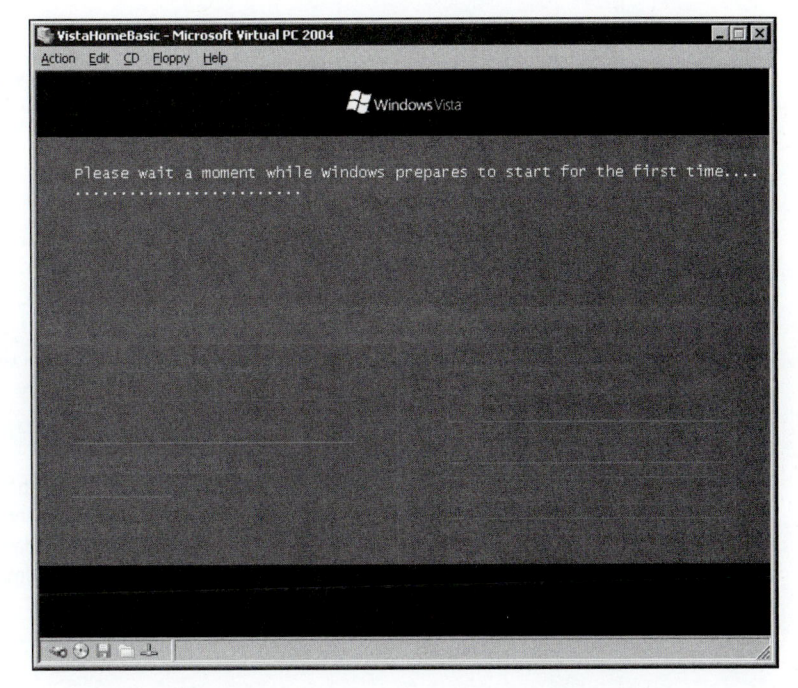

11. After completing the installation, Windows Vista asks you to provide a username and password for your account, as shown in Figure 2.16. You are required to enter your password twice, and you have the option to enter a password hint, if you want. Click Next to continue.

Figure 2.16
Be sure to pick a strong password for your user account.

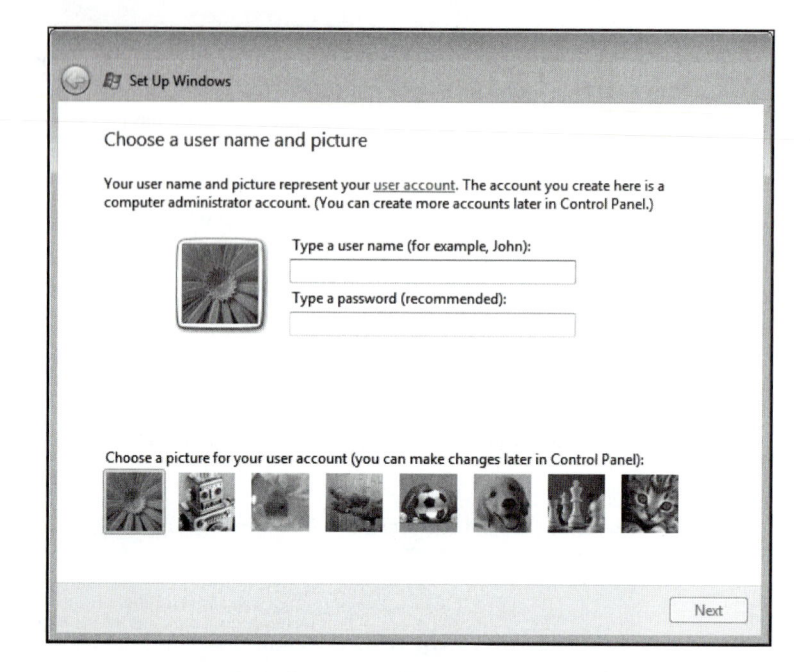

12. On the next dialog box, shown in Figure 2.17, you are asked to enter a name for your computer and choose a desktop background. After making your selections, click Next to continue.

> **NOTE**
>
> Choose a computer name that is unique. It must differ from any other computer, workgroup, or domain names on the network. You'll probably want to enter your name or a name of your own choice, although Setup supplies a recommendation for you. You might want to coordinate naming your computer with your LAN administrator, if you have one.

Figure 2.17
Be sure to choose a unique name for your computer.

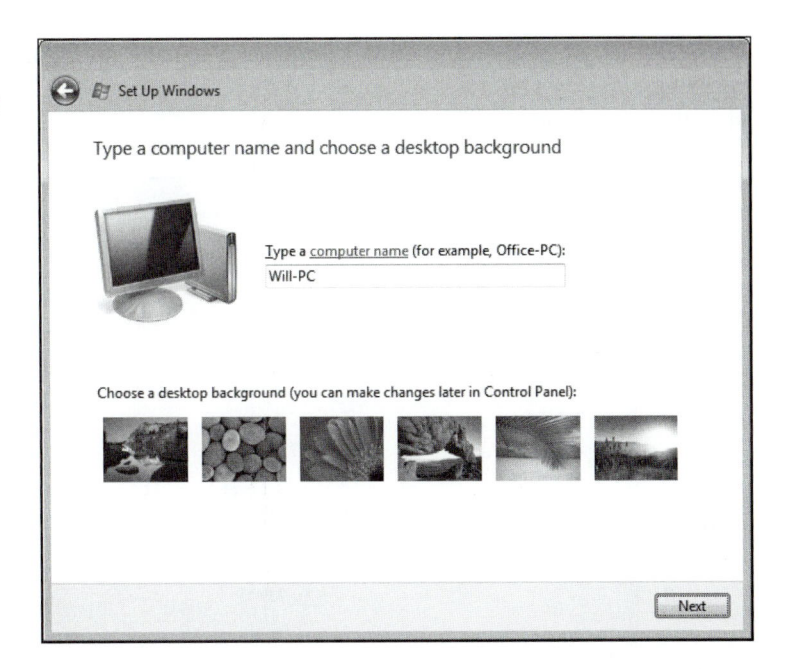

13. On the Help Protect Windows Automatically dialog box, shown in Figure 2.18, you are asked how to configure the base security for Windows Vista. In most cases, you should select Use Recommended Settings. Make your selection by clicking it.

Figure 2.18
Windows Vista encourages you to be secure upon installation.

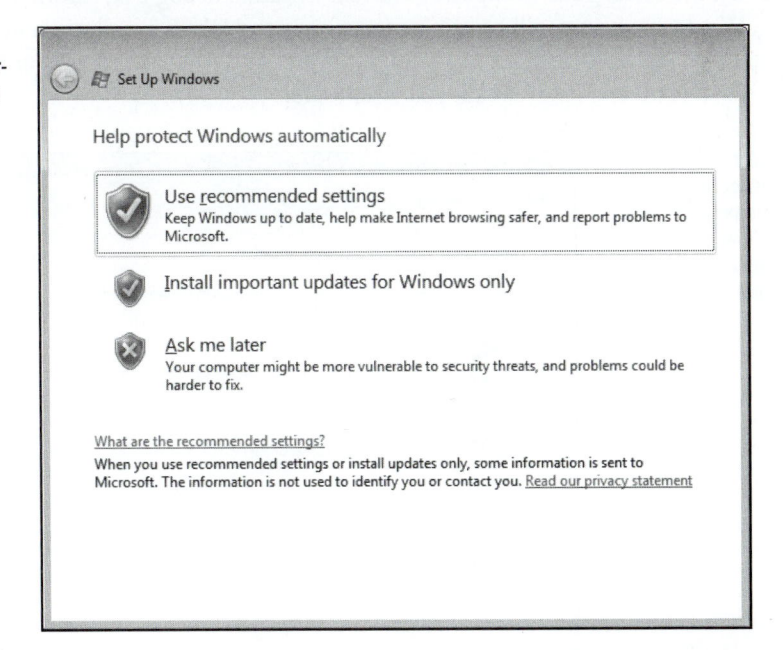

14. On the Review Your Time and Date Setting dialog box, shown in Figure 2.19, select your time zone, daylight savings option, and current date options. Click Finish to complete the upgrade process.

Figure 2.19
Be sure to set your location's current date and time information.

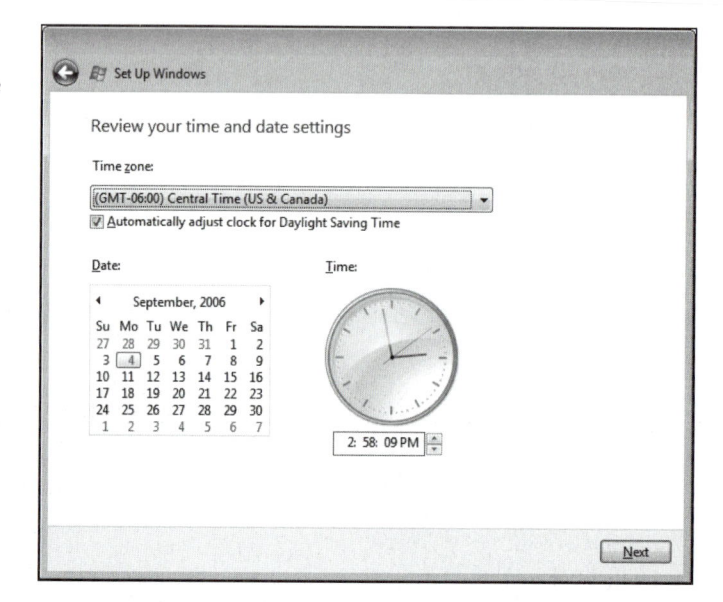

15. On the Select Your Computer's Current Location dialog box, shown in Figure 2.20, tell Windows where you'll be using your computer. Make your selection by clicking on it. Unlike previous versions of Windows, Windows Vista configures your network adapters for DHCP and does not ask you what to do.

Figure 2.20
The different location choices correspond to different levels of security on your Windows Vista computer.

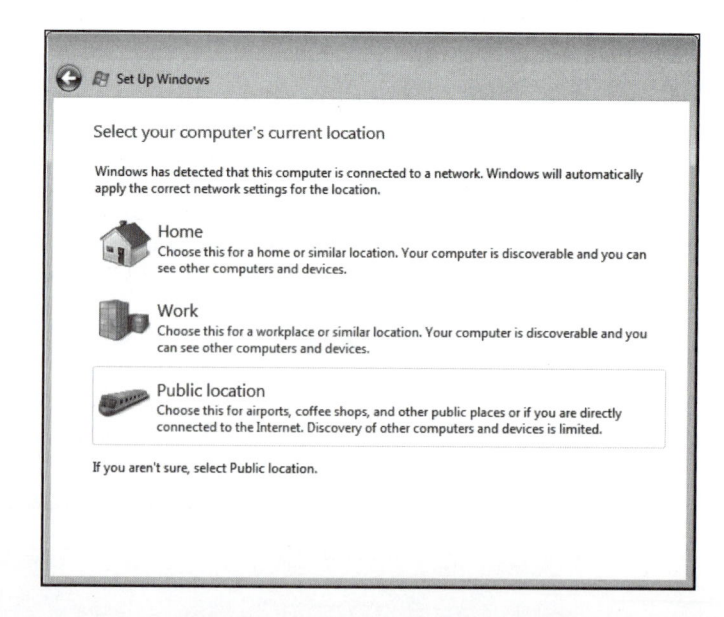

PERFORMING A NEW INSTALLATION OF WINDOWS VISTA | 59

16. Windows now prompts you one last time—after you click Start, you're finished with the installation.

17. After a few more minutes of waiting, you are finally presented with your brand new Windows Vista login screen, as shown in Figure 2.21. Congratulations, you've completed the installation of Windows Vista.

Figure 2.21
The Windows Vista login screen is much different than in previous versions.

If you initiate the setup routine from within an already installed instance of Windows 2000 or Windows XP, the step-by-step procedure is as follows:

> **NOTE**
> If you plan to perform a clean installation on your computer that is currently running Windows 2000 or Windows XP, be sure to get your data and other files off the computer beforehand. You can perform this process manually, or you can opt to use Windows Easy Transfer to automatically copy all your files and settings to an external hard drive or network location. After the clean installation of Windows Vista has completed, you can run Windows Easy Transfer again to reload your files and settings on the new installation of Windows Vista. Chapter 3 discusses using Windows Easy Transfer.

1. Insert the Windows Vista DVD into your computer's DVD-ROM drive. It should autoplay and present the Install Windows dialog box shown in Figure 2.22. If not, locate and double-click the `setup.exe` program in the Sources folder on the DVD.

Figure 2.22
You can start the upgrade process from within your currently installed Windows instance.

2. To download, install, and use the Windows Vista Upgrade Advisor, as detailed previously, click the Check Compatibility Online link. Otherwise, to begin the in-place upgrade to Windows Vista, click the Install Now link.

3. On the Get Important Updates for Installation dialog box, shown in Figure 2.23, you are asked whether you want to download updates to the Windows Vista install files. Typically, for computers that have an active Internet connection, you're better off getting the updates. Make your selection by clicking on it.

Figure 2.23
You should typically allow the Vista setup routine to download updates.

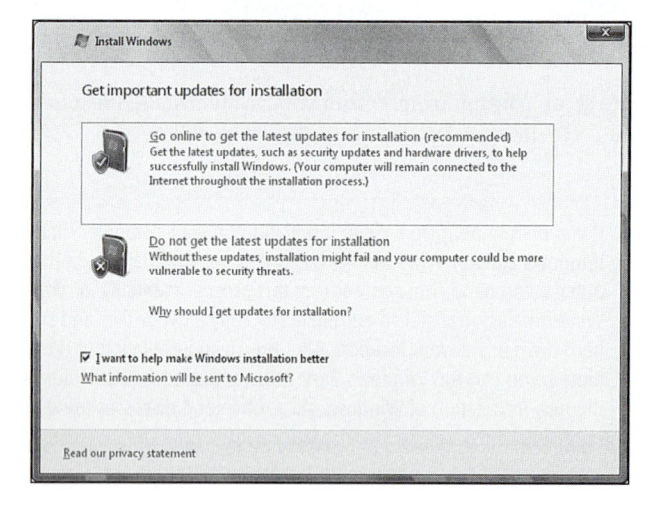

4. On the Type Your Product Key for Activation dialog box, you are asked to enter your Windows Vista product key. Enter the key and ensure that the Automatically Activate Windows When I'm Online option is checked, to enable Windows Product Activation. After entering the product key, click Next to continue.

5. On the Please Read the License Terms dialog box, ensure that you read and understand the End User Licensing Agreement (EULA). When you're ready, select the I Accept the License Terms option and click Next to continue.
6. On the Which Type of Installation Do You Want? dialog box, shown previously in Figure 2.12, select Custom (Advanced) because you're performing a clean installation here on top of an existing Windows XP installation.
7. On the Where Do You Want to Install Windows? dialog box, shown in Figure 2.24, select the partition onto which you'll install Windows Vista. When you're ready to proceed, click Next.

Figure 2.24
You need to select an existing partition for the installation of Windows Vista.

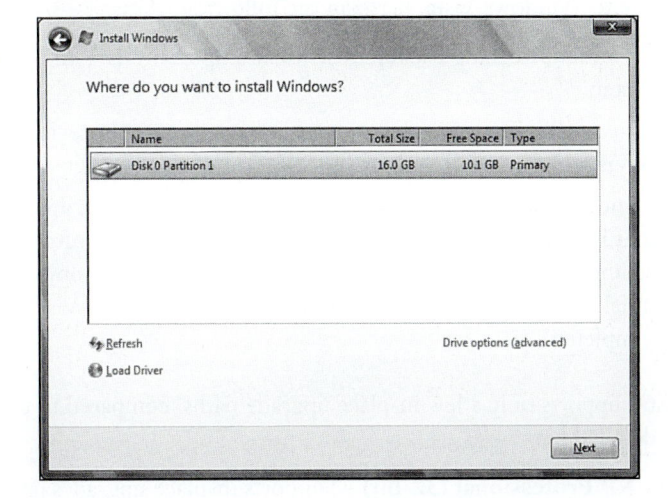

8. The setup application prompts you that the selected partition contains existing files from another Windows installation, as shown in Figure 2.25. After you read the information, click OK to continue.

Figure 2.25
Windows Vista setup moves all your existing Windows files to a new directory—you need to delete that directory later to reclaim that disk space.

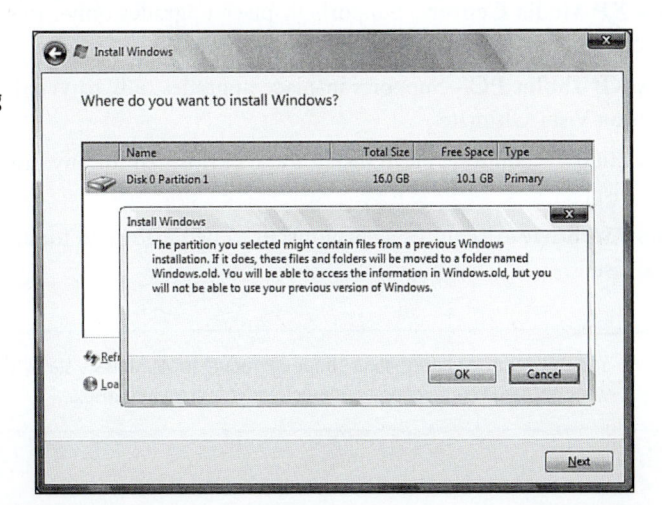

9. The Installing Windows dialog box appears, as shown previously in Figure 2.14, and gives you the updated status of the upgrade process.
10. From here, the rest of the process is similar to that detailed previously for a clean installation (on a blank hard disk), starting with Step 9.

Upgrading Older Versions of Windows to Vista

Although doing a new installation of Windows Vista is almost always the best plan, sometimes you'd rather perform an in-place upgrade on your computer. Before you attempt any in-place upgrade to Windows Vista, perform the following tasks:

- Ensure that a valid, working backup exists of all important data and other files stored on your computer.
- Ensure that your hardware meets the requirements discussed previously in the "Windows Vista Hardware Requirements" section of this chapter.
- Run the Windows Vista Upgrade Advisor to verify that your hardware and software environment is ready for an upgrade. Take special note of any software issues, such as drivers needing updates for Windows Vista. Be sure to print a copy of the Upgrade Advisor's final report so you'll have it handy after the Windows Vista upgrade installation has completed.

Windows Vista supports only a few in-place upgrade paths, compared to previous versions of Windows, as detailed here:

- **Windows XP Professional (32-bit)**—Supports in-place upgrades only to Windows Vista Business and Windows Vista Ultimate
- **Windows XP Professional (64-bit)**—Requires a clean install to be performed for any installation of Windows Vista
- **Windows XP Home**—Supports in-place upgrades to any version of Windows Vista
- **Windows XP Media Center**—Supports in-place upgrades only to Windows Vista Home Premium and Windows Vista Ultimate
- **Windows XP Tablet PC**—Supports in-place upgrades only to Windows Vista Business and Windows Vista Ultimate
- **Windows 2000**—Requires a clean install to be performed for any installation of Windows Vista
- **Windows 95/98/Me**—Requires a clean install to be performed for any installation of Windows Vista

> **NOTE**
>
> You can get more information about upgrading to Windows Vista by visiting www.microsoft.com/windowsvista/getready/upgradeinfo.mspx.

The process to perform an in-place upgrade from an already installed instance of Windows XP is as follows:

1. Insert the Windows Vista DVD into your computer's DVD-ROM drive. It should autoplay and present the Install Windows dialog box, shown previously in Figure 2.8. If not, locate the `setup.exe` program in the Sources folder on the DVD and double-click it.

2. To download, install, and use the Windows Vista Upgrade Advisor, as detailed previously, click the Check Compatibility Online link. Otherwise, to begin the in-place upgrade to Windows Vista, click the Install Now link.

3. On the Get Important Updates for Installation dialog box, shown previously in Figure 2.23, you are asked whether you want to download updates to the Windows Vista install files. Typically, for computers that have an active Internet connection, you're better off getting the updates. Make your selection by clicking on it.

4. On the Type Your Product Key for Activation dialog box, you are asked to enter your Windows Vista product key. Enter the key and ensure that the Automatically Activate Windows When I'm Online option is checked, to enable Windows Product Activation. After entering the product key, click Next to continue.

5. On the Please Read the License Terms dialog box, ensure that you read and understand the End User Licensing Agreement (EULA). When you're ready, select the I Accept the License Terms option, and click Next to continue.

6. On the Which Type of Installation Do You Want? dialog box, shown in Figure 2.26, select Upgrade because here you're performing an in-place upgrade of Windows XP.

Figure 2.26
In this instance, the Upgrade option is now available to select.

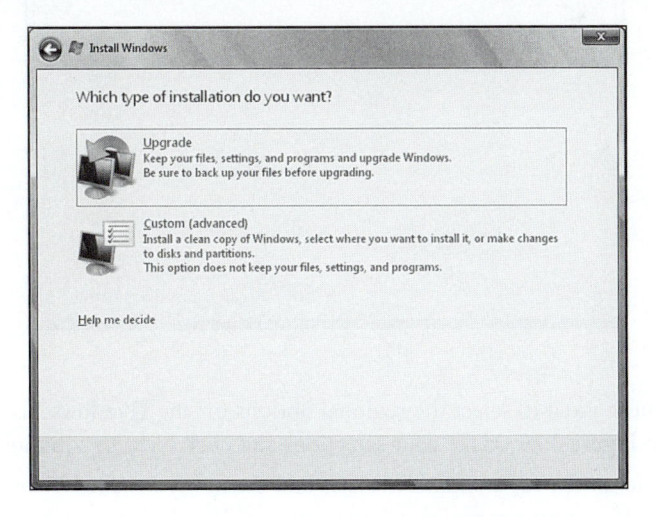

7. On the Compatibility Report dialog box, shown in Figure 2.27, note what items Vista setup flags as needing attention after the installation is complete. When you're ready to proceed, click Next.

Figure 2.27
You might need to upgrade some hardware drivers after the Vista upgrade has completed.

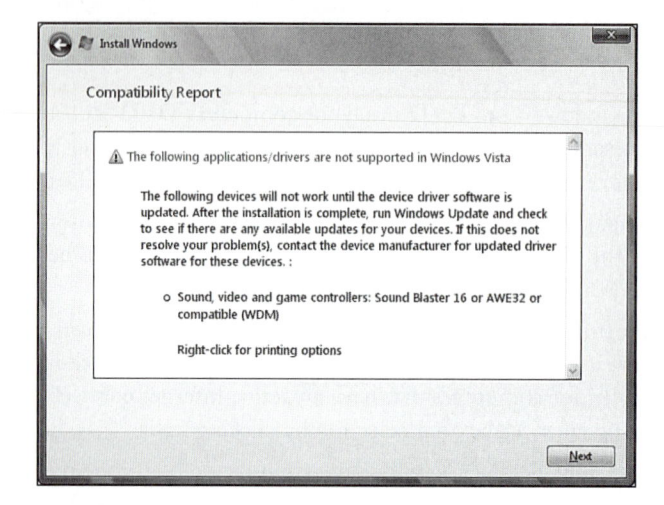

8. The Upgrading Windows dialog appears, as shown in Figure 2.28, and gives you an updated status of the upgrade process.

Figure 2.28
The upgrade process runs for some time.

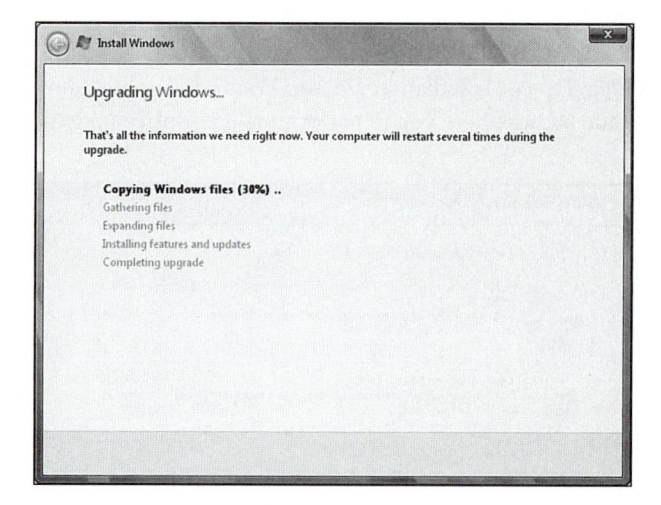

9. You are next asked to select the regional options for the Windows Vista installation, as shown in Figure 2.29. Make your selections and click Next to continue.
10. After some time, your computer restarts and the newly installed Windows Vista loads. Windows Vista resumes the installation process. Windows typically restarts once more before it finally completes the installation process.
11. On the Help Protect Windows Automatically dialog box, shown previously in Figure 2.18, you are asked how to configure the base security for Windows Vista. In most cases, you should select Use Recommended Settings. Make your selection by clicking it.

Figure 2.29
You need to select the regional preferences for your upgrade installation.

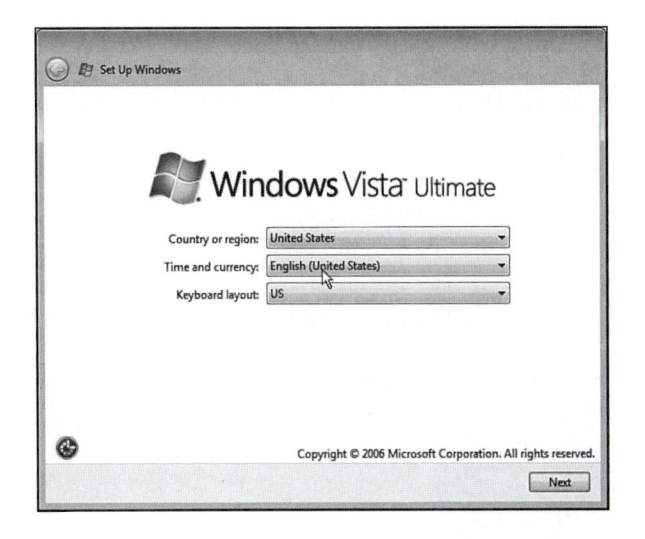

12. On the Review Your Time and Date Setting dialog box, shown previously in Figure 2.19, select your time zone, daylight savings option, and current date options. Click Finish to complete the upgrade process.

13. After a few more minutes of waiting, you are finally presented with your brand new Windows Vista login screen, shown previously in Figure 2.21. You've completed the upgrade to Windows Vista.

When your upgrade is complete, be sure to spend some time reading through Chapter 3.

> **NOTE**
> It's worth noting that an in-place upgrade of a new installation of Windows XP Professional SP2 to Windows Vista Ultimate uses approximately 8.5GB of disk space. Plan accordingly for your upgrades. Windows XP Service Pack 3 was due out shortly after this book was published, but was not yet available for testing. You can rest assured, however, that it will also take up a fair bit of disk space, so you will need to plan ahead.

Upgrading One Version of Vista to Another

If you want to upgrade from one version of Vista to another (for example, from the Home Basic version that came on a new computer to the Home Premium or Ultimate editions), you don't need to start over from scratch—you can simply purchase an upgrade kit and update the version of Vista with all your files, applications and settings intact.

When it was initially released, Microsoft offered a feature called Windows Anytime Upgrade that let you purchase a new product key over the Internet. With the new product key and your original Windows DVD in hand, you could be up and running with the new version an hour or so.

Microsoft no longer offers this instant upgrade service. You must now purchase an upgrade kit that includes a new Windows DVD from Microsoft's website or from a third-party seller. You can still use the Start menu to get to the Windows Anytime Upgrade website (see Figure 2.30) if you want to purchase the kit from Microsoft, but you'll have to wait for the DVD to arrive in the mail. It will include complete instructions for performing the upgrade.

Figure 2.30
Windows Anytime Update is located in the System and Maintenance option of the Control Panel.

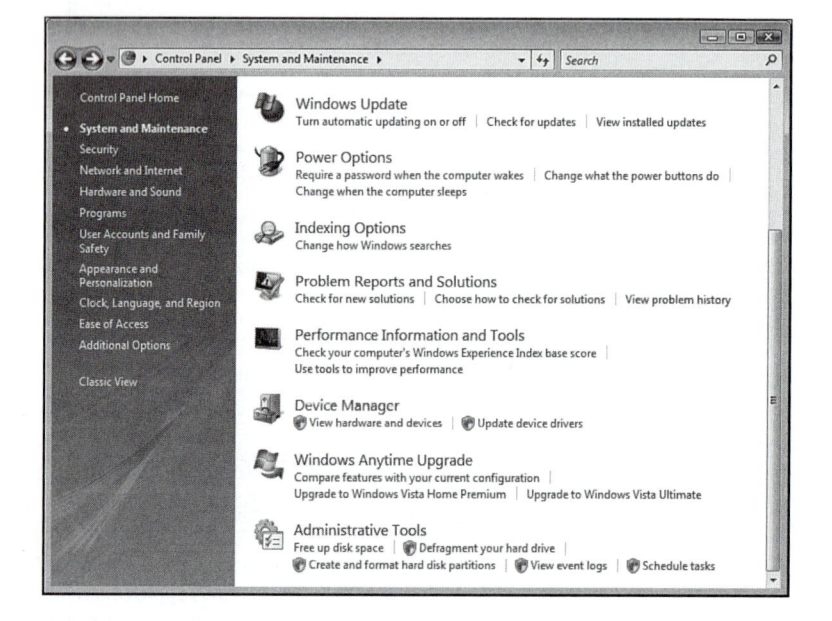

Multibooting Windows Vista

In today's world of advanced operating systems and low hard-disk prices, it certainly is not uncommon for many users to want to experiment with different operating systems. The world of consumer computing is ripe with many different options. Along with just plain curiosity and experimentation, some other good reasons exist for wanting to switch between operating systems:

- Many users use two or more operating systems because of application-compatibility issues. Hardware support issues arise, too: Windows 2000 and Windows XP might have drivers for older hardware that Windows Vista doesn't support.

- Some users want to run specific applications or games in the optimal environment.

- A developer might swap among Windows 2000 Professional, Windows XP Professional, and maybe even several different versions Windows Vista, to test application compatibility.
- Website developers need to use different OS versions to see how their pages look with the corresponding different web browser versions.

Other than buying multiple computers, you have two ways of accommodating these needs. You can multiboot (that is, select your desired operating system at bootup) or you can run another operating system in a "virtual" computer (that is, in a special application program that lets the alternate OS think it's running on a PC of its own). The "virtual" approach is useful; we cover it later in the chapter in the section titled "The Virtual Machine Approach."

One small wrench thrown into the multibooting works by Vista is that Vista uses a new boot scheme that's more complex and incompatible with the one used by previous versions of Windows. While Windows 2000 and XP let you set up a boot menu from which you could select any version of Windows, as well as other operating systems, Vista's boot menu only lets you select Vista versions, or "anything else," and the "anything else" selections have to be managed separately.

NOTE

Here's a rough sketch of what's changed: In the boot scheme used by the Intel x86 versions of Windows 2000 and XP, the boot partition's boot sector program loaded ntldr, which read the menu file boot.ini, and then loaded Windows. Aside from the boot sector, all of the stuff was in "super hidden" files (files marked with the system and hidden attributes), stored in the root directory. The Vista boot sector loads a file called bootmgr from the root directory, which loads a set of programs and DLLs in the \boot folder, which then reads the Boot Configuration Data (BCD) file (which is actually a Registry hive), and then loads Windows. The BCD hive is also loaded into and visible in the Windows Registry after bootup. In a Vista multiboot configuration, the root directory file bootsect.bak is a copy of the pre-Vista boot sector (XP's version of the boot sector). Choosing "Legacy" from the Vista boot menu loads and runs that original boot sector program, which then carries on as before.

The reason for making this change was to create a common boot system that would work on both BIOS-based computers and computers using the newer EFI configuration system. The impact of the new scheme is that the Vista boot menu can offer only Vista (and presumably also Longhorn Server) versions, and anything using the older boot loader is lumped under the "Legacy" entry. The boot.ini file is used *only* to list and load non-Vista operating systems.

As a result of the boot manager changes, if you want to set up a computer that can boot several different versions of Windows and/or other operating systems, you need to follow these guidelines:

- You must install each operating system into a separate disk volume (drive letter). To get these separate volumes, you can create multiple partitions on one disk drive, or use multiple disk drives, or a combination of the two.
- If you install multiple versions of Windows Vista on the same computer, the same rule applies: You must install each version in a separate disk volume.

  (If you do install multiple versions of Vista, see the Tips from the Windows Pros section at the end of this chapter to see how to make them distinguishable on the boot menu.)
- Install versions of Windows starting with the oldest and working toward the newest. For example, to set up a computer that can boot into Windows Me, Windows XP, and Windows Vista, install Me first, then XP, then Vista.

  You *must* install Windows Vista last!
- To install operating systems other than Windows, such as Linux, you may need a boot manager that is capable of recognizing the different operating systems. Linux offers a choice of several different boot managers. Their use is beyond the scope of this book, but you should be able to find instructions for multibooting Linux and Windows Vista on the Web.

To create a multiboot installation on a computer that already has Windows XP installed, use the following procedure. The steps are similar to the "clean install" procedure described earlier.

1. Insert the Windows Vista DVD into your computer's DVD-ROM drive. It should autoplay and present the Install Windows dialog box shown previously in Figure 2.22. If not, locate the `setup.exe` program in the Sources folder on the DVD, and double-click it.

   (Alternatively, you can restart your computer and boot from the DVD.)

2. To download, install, and use the Windows Vista Upgrade Advisor, as detailed previously, click the Check Compatibility Online link. Otherwise, to begin the in-place upgrade to Windows Vista, click the Install Now link.

3. On the Get Important Updates for Installation dialog box, shown previously in Figure 2.23, you are asked whether you want to download updates to the Windows Vista install files. Typically, for computers that have an active Internet connection, you are better off getting the updates. Make your selection by clicking on it.

4. On the Type Your Product Key for Activation dialog box, you are asked to enter your Windows Vista product key. Enter the key and ensure that the Automatically Activate

Windows When I'm Online option is checked, to enable Windows Product Activation. After entering the product key, click Next to continue.

5. On the Please Read the License Terms dialog box, ensure that you read and understand the End User Licensing Agreement (EULA). When you're ready, select the I Accept the License Terms option, and click Next to continue.

6. On the Which Type of Installation Do You Want? dialog box, shown previously in Figure 2.26, select **Custom (Advanced)** because here you're performing a clean, multi-boot installation of Windows Vista, not an upgrade.

7. On Where Do You Want to Install Windows? dialog box, shown in Figure 2.31, select the partition onto which you'll install Windows Vista. This must be a partition that does not already have a version of Windows installed on it. When you're ready to proceed, click Next.

Figure 2.31
You need to select an empty partition for the multiboot installation of Windows Vista.

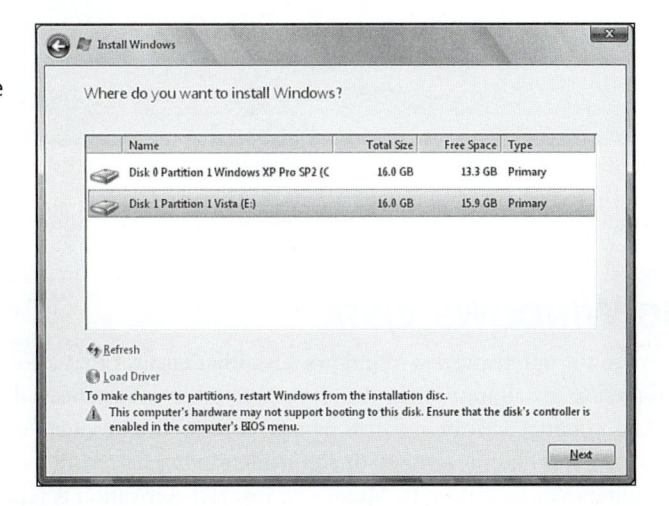

8. Follow the rest of the procedure described previously under "Typical Clean Setup Procedure," from steps 8 on through the end.

9. If you plan on installing another version of Windows Vista on this same computer, skip ahead to the Tips from the Windows Pros section at the end of this chapter to rename the current version's title in the boot menu.

10. You can check out the new Windows Vista boot menu, shown in Figure 2.32, on the next restart of your computer.

Figure 2.32
The Windows Vista boot menu has changed from Windows XP.

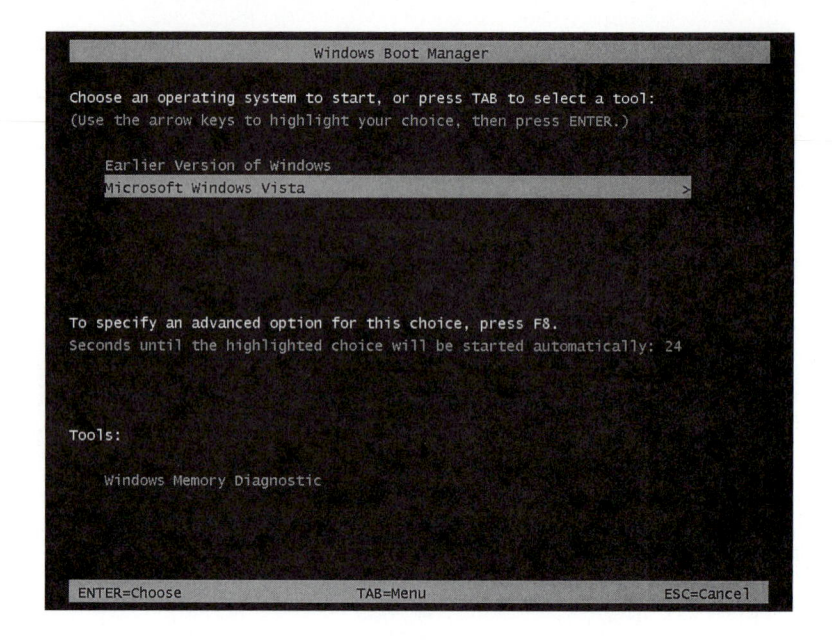

When your installation is complete, be sure to spend some time reading through Chapter 3.

Activating Windows Vista

Product Activation is one feature in Windows Vista that ensures that a software product key has not been used to install more than the allowed number of instances of that specific software. In general, product activation works by transmitting the product key used to perform the Windows Vista installation along with a non-identifying hardware hash that is generated from the computer's configuration to Microsoft. Product Activation is typically performed over the Internet, and occurs automatically in Windows Vista after 3 days, but you can opt to perform activation earlier if desired as we discuss next. It's important to understand that Product Activation is not intended to prevent you from reinstalling Windows Vista on the same computer more than once—instead it is intended to prevent you from installing Windows Vista on multiple computers that you are not licensed to perform the installation on. As such, you should typically not have any issue with reactivating your instance of Windows Vista on the same computer multiple times.

If you want to activate Windows Vista yourself, before it does so automatically after 3 days, you can do so by following the steps listed here:

1. Open My Computer, shown in Figure 2.33, by clicking Start, Computer.

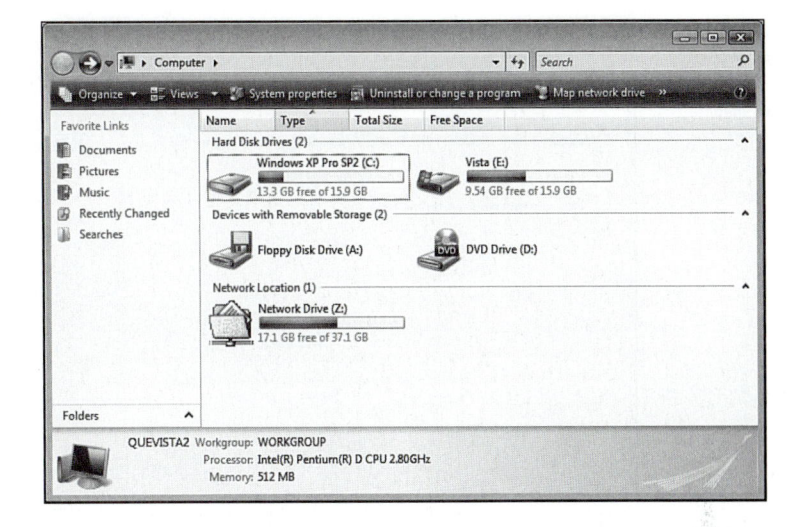

Figure 2.33
The My Computer look has been updated for Windows Vista.

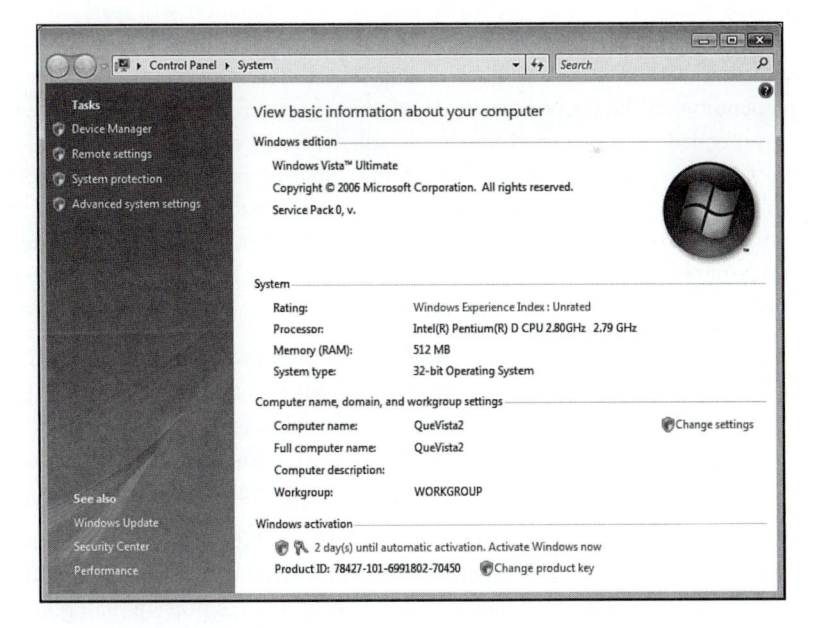

Figure 2.34
You can easily view basic properties of your Windows Vista computer.

2. In My Computer, click the System Properties button. The system properties are displayed, as shown in Figure 2.34.

3. At the bottom of the Properties dialog box, click the link to Activate Windows Now. The Activate Windows Now dialog box opens, as shown in Figure 2.35.
4. Click the Activate Windows Online Now link to start the activation process.

Figure 2.35
Windows Activation has been streamlined in Windows Vista.

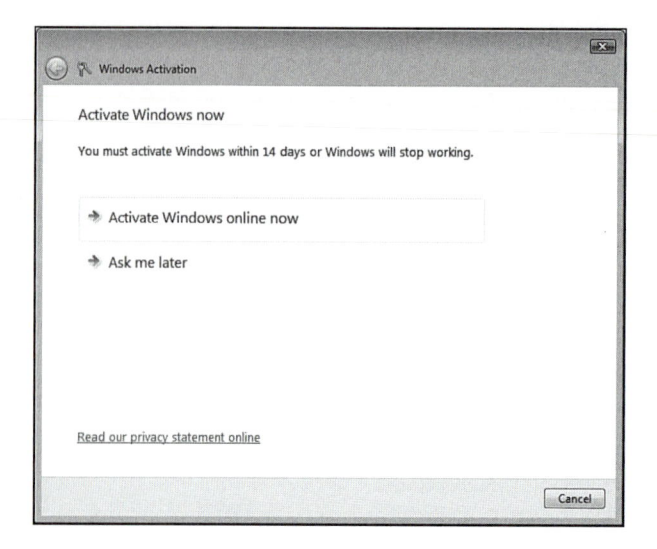

Note that you must activate Windows Vista within 30 days of installation, or (if you have not upgraded to SP-1) it will no longer function properly. Vista will go into Reduced Functionality Mode (RFM), where only Internet Explorer will work and it will prompt you to go online to activate, purchase a license, or make a phone call to Microsoft for activation assistance. Prior to Service Pack 1, illegitimate systems were subject to two different effects, depending on the circumstances. If you failed to activate Vista before the timeout period (30 days) ended, Vista reverted to what is called a Reduced Functionality Mode (RFM). You couldn't run programs, or even Windows Explorer, in this mode—you could only access the IE web browser, and even then for only an hour. After the 60 minutes passed, you were logged out. Alternatively, you could boot Vista Safe Mode to access your documents, but as you probably know, Safe Mode has major limitations, such as lower screen resolution and a limited set of device drivers.

A second reduced functionality mode known as Non-Genuine State (NGS) was activated if you attempted to download software from a Microsoft website (such as Windows Update) and Vista failed a web-based validation check. Vista isn't as crippled in NGS as it is in RFM, but some features, such as Windows Update, Windows Defender, Windows Aero, and ReadyBoost, were scaled down or rendered completely nonfunctional.

Beginning with SP-1, these two modes (RFM and NGS) are a thing of the past. Computers that fail the activation or validation tests will instead bug the user much the same way an XP system does when it fails validation. Upon logging in, a pop-up dialog box that can't be dismissed for 15 seconds appears, and reappears every hour by changing the desktop wallpaper or background to plain black and flashing activation and balloon help dialogs near the system tray. You can ignore the pop-ups and change the background back to your favorite photo, but it will all happen again in another hour. The good news is that as of SP-1, you won't lose any real functionality, as was the case with RFM and NGS. Microsoft heard users' complaints and had some mercy.

THE VIRTUAL MACHINE APPROACH

If you need access to multiple operating systems primarily for testing purposes rather than for long periods of work, there's a way to use multiple operating systems without any of the hassle of multiboot setups. In fact, you can even use multiple operating systems simultaneously on the same computer. It's done with a setup called a *virtual machine*. This is an old concept—IBM has used it on its mainframes since the 1970s—that's making a big comeback, thanks to today's fast processors and huge hard disks.

A virtual machine program emulates (simulates) in software all the hardware functions of a PC. It lets an entire operating system (called a *guest* operating system) run as an ordinary application program on a *host* operating system such as Windows Vista. Because all the hardware functions are emulated, the guest OS doesn't "know" it's not in complete control of a computer. When it attempts to physically access a hard disk, display card, network adapter, or serial port, the virtual machine program calls upon the host operating system to actually carry out the operation.

Even though, occasionally, the software might need to execute several hundred instructions to emulate one hardware operation, overall, the speed penalty is only 5%–10%. And if a guest OS crashes, it doesn't take down your system. You can simply click a Reset menu choice and "reboot" the virtual machine. Figure 2.36 shows a typical Virtual PC window.

Another advantage of the virtual machine programs currently on the market is that they don't allow the guest OS unfettered access to your real disk drives. Instead, you create a *virtual disk*, a single large file on your host operating system that contains what the virtual machine sees as a hard drive. With today's large hard drives, it's no big deal to create a 2GB–15GB file to serve as a virtual hard drive to host an older version of Windows or even Linux.

Figure 2.36
Virtual PC running Windows XP Professional in a virtual machine.

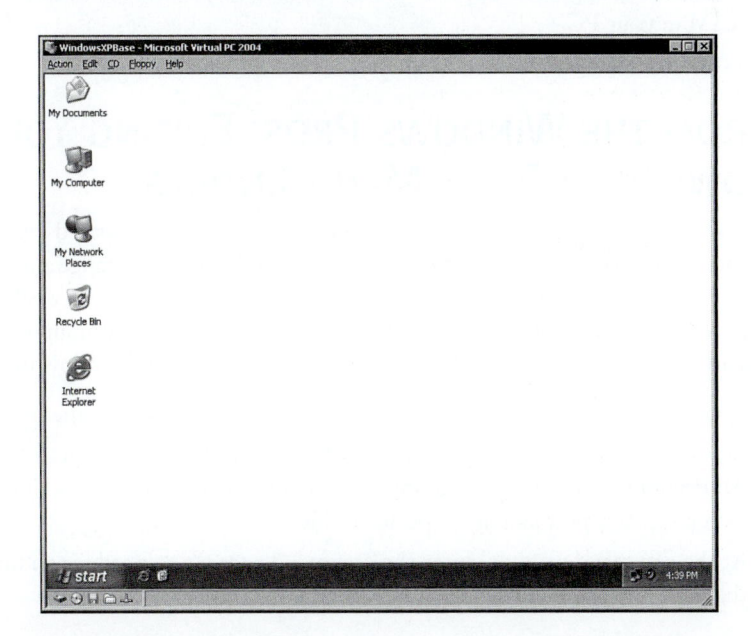

If you make a backup copy of the file after installing a guest operating system on one of these virtual disk drives, you can return the guest OS to its original, pristine state just by copying the backup over the virtual disk file. You can even boot up a guest OS, start a bunch of applications, and save the virtual machine in this exact state. When you want to use it again, you can just fire up the whole system starting right from this point. If you're a tester or experimenter, a virtual computer can save you hours of time installing, reinstalling, and rebooting.

Of course, you still need separate licenses for all the extra operating systems you install, but the virtual machine can let you run as many OSes and as many configurations of these OSes as you like, separately or simultaneously. And all this comes without the hassle of editing the Vista boot menu or worrying about partitions.

If this sounds interesting, you should check into two products:

- VMWare, now an EMC company, located at www.vmware.com. VMWare Workstation was the first commercial system to emulate a PC on a PC. It's the most "industrial-strength" PC emulator available. You can get a 30-day free trial of VMWare Workstation from the VMWare site. Or, you can use the free VMWare Player version to run virtual computers set up by others.

- Microsoft Virtual PC. Microsoft bought this program from Connectix Corporation. Versions are available for Windows and for the Mac; check out www.microsoft.com/virtualpc. The Windows version of Virtual PC 2007 is a free download that anyone can take advantage of. In general, the experience for non-Windows operating systems on Virtual PC is not as good as when using WMWare Workstation. However, it's free, so we can't complain that much. Be sure to download the Virtual PC extensions and give the Vista Virtual PC at least 1GB of memory (this is a setting in Virtual PC) for it to run with any appreciable speed. This requires that you have at least 1.5GB of physical RAM in your PC.

Tips from the Windows Pros: Editing Your Windows Vista Boot Menu Entries

If you're not exactly thrilled with the way Windows Vista has prepared your boot menu options for you, you can take matters into your own hands and change them. As if the rather plain entries, shown previously in Figure 2.32, aren't enough, you can easily get confused if you have multiple instances of Windows Vista installed on your computer in a multiboot scenario. To change boot menu entries in Windows Vista, simply follow these steps:

1. Boot into the first Windows Vista instance you want to change the boot menu entry for.
2. Open a command prompt by searching for `cmd` on the Start menu or by clicking Start, All Programs, Accessories, Command Prompt. You need to be working with Administrative permissions to perform this task.
3. At the command prompt, enter the command **bcdedit** to produce an output similar to that seen in Figure 2.37.

The Virtual Machine Approach | 75

Figure 2.37
The `bcdedit` command enables you to manage the Windows Vista boot menu.

4. Note that in the Windows Boot Loader section, you can see the name for the Windows Vista boot menu entry.
5. To change the boot menu entry displayed for this installation of Windows Vista, enter the following command as shown in Figure 2.38: **bcdedit /set description** "*New boot menu text*"

Figure 2.38
You can easily change one Windows Vista boot menu entry at a time using `bcdedit`.

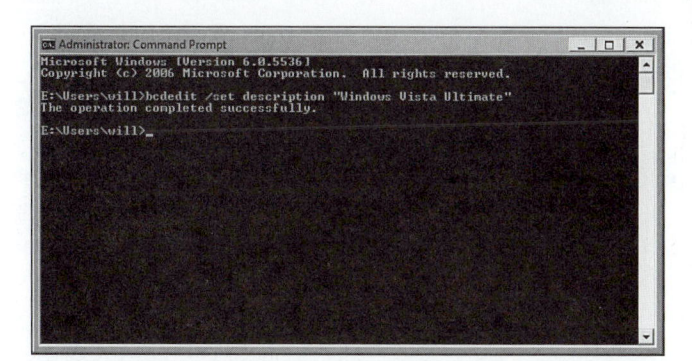

6. To continue renaming other Windows Vista installations on the computer, simply reboot into each installation and repeat Steps 2–4.

You should know that you cannot edit any other boot menu entries for any other operating systems using the `bcdedit` command. The boot menu entries for older versions of Windows that you have installed on the computer, as well as other operating systems (such as versions of Linux), are still managed through the Windows XP or Windows 2000 `boot.ini` file. When you select the Earlier Versions of Windows option on the Vista boot menu, you get another boot menu displayed using the information in the `boot.ini` file to help you select and launch any of the other operating systems installed on your computer.

One other thing: `bcdedit` isn't exactly a user-friendly program, and not surprisingly, people are developing better tools for editing Vista's boot configuration data. We've used and like Vista Boot Pro, available at www.vistabootpro.org.

CHAPTER 3

THE FIRST HOUR

In this chapter

The First Things to Do After Starting Windows Vista   78

A Quick Tour of Vista's Important Features   78

Windows Vista User Accounts   88

Set Up Internet Access   94

Download Critical Updates   95

Personalize Windows   95

Transfer Information from Your Old Computer   99

Log Off or Shut Down   104

More Than You Wanted to Know   105

Tips from the Windows Pros: Configuring the Default User Profile   116

The First Things to Do After Starting Windows Vista

If you just installed Windows Vista, or have just purchased a new computer that came with Vista already installed, you're probably itching to use it. This chapter is designed to help get you off to a good start. We're going to take you and your computer on a guided tour of Vista's new and unusual features, and walk you through making some important and useful changes to Vista's settings. Here's our itinerary:

- A quick tour of Vista's important features
- Setting up user accounts
- Personalizing Windows—changing system settings to make Vista more comfortable and effective
- Where's My Stuff?—or, an introduction to Vista's new file location scheme
- Transferring information from your old computer
- Setting up Internet access and automatic updates
- Logging off and shutting down

Our hope is that one hour invested in front of your computer following us through these topics will make you a happier Windows Vista user in the long run.

A Quick Tour of Vista's Important Features

Windows Vista is in many ways similar to its predecessors Windows 2000 and Windows XP. The differences that do exist range from fun to peculiar to irritating (at least, irritating at first). This section discusses some of the most important features and the most significant differences between Vista and Windows 2000 and XP. It would be best if you read this while seated in front of your computer and follow along. That way, when you run into these features and topics later in this book and in your work with Windows, you'll already have "been there, done that" at least once. We'll start with the Welcome screen, which appears after you finish installing Vista or when you turn on your computer for the first time (if Vista came preinstalled on your new PC).

> **NOTE** If you're using Windows Vista in a business setting and your computer was set up for you, some of the steps in this chapter won't be necessary, and they may not even be available to you. Don't worry—you can skip over any parts of this chapter that have already been taken care of, don't work, or don't interest you.

The Welcome Screen

When Windows starts, you see the Welcome screen, shown in Figure 3.1. (On your computer, of course, you see different usernames.)

Figure 3.1
The Welcome screen is the starting point for logging on.

> **NOTE**
>
> If you just purchased a new computer, the first screen you see might be from the tail end of the installation process described in the previous chapter. Your computer's manufacturer set it up this way so that you could choose settings, such as your local time zone and keyboard type. If you do see something other than the Welcome screen, scan back through Chapter 2, "Installing and Upgrading Windows Vista." If you recognize the screen you see in one of the chapter's illustrations, carry on from here.
>
> If Windows jumps right up to the Welcome Center (shown in Figure 3.2), your computer's manufacturer set up Windows not to require an initial logon. In that case, skip to the following section in this book. We show you how to fix this later on our tour.

The Welcome screen lists all the people (*users*, in computer parlance) who have been authorized to use the computer. Click your name, and if asked, enter the account's password. After you enter the password, press Enter, or click the right arrow button to complete the logon process.

The first time you log on, it may take a minute or two for Windows to prepare your *user profile*, the set of folders and files that hold your personal documents, email, pictures, preference settings, and so on. Logging on should take only a few seconds from the second time on. After the logon process is complete, Windows displays the desktop, and shortly after that, the Welcome Center window appears.

The Welcome Center

Each time you log on, Windows displays the Welcome Center, a feature that's new to Windows Vista, as shown in Figure 3.2. The Welcome Center contains icons that link to some setup and configuration tools, several of which we use in this chapter. It also contains links to extra services provided by or sold by Microsoft, and perhaps also your computer manufacturer.

Figure 3.2
The Welcome Center gives you shortcuts to Windows setup features and several marketing links.

Notice that the screen is more like a web page than the traditional Windows control panels and applications with which you may be familiar. Notice the underlined text that says Show All 14 Items, located under the icons in the Get Started with Windows section. This is just like a link on a web page. Click it and the list of icons expands.

Many of the Control Panel, setup, and management screens in Vista look and act like this. Instead of just the traditional buttons and check boxes, in Vista many of the words, titles, and lines of text on the page are links that make changes or bring you to other screens or options. It takes some getting used to because it's not always obvious that a particular word or phrase is meant to be clicked. They're usually underlined, but not always—sometimes, they're displayed in a larger typeface or a different color than other text on the screen.

Now, double-click the View Computer Details icon. This brings you to a screen that displays information about your computer's hardware, its name, and so on. Look at the upper-left corner of the screen, where there is a circular button with an arrow pointing to the left. This is another web browser-type feature you see all over Vista: the "back" button. Give it a click, and you'll be back at the Welcome Center. Click the right-arrow button that appears in the same region of the Welcome Center, and you go forward to the System screen again.

> **TIP**
>
> In a few days, after you become familiar with Windows Vista, you won't need or want the Welcome Center every time you log on. When you get to that point, uncheck Run at Startup and close the Welcome Center. You can always get back to it from the System and Maintenance section of the Control Panel.

To remove the Welcome Center, click its Close button (the X at the upper-right corner of the window). Similar visual clues and tools are used in Windows Explorer, which has a brand-new look in Windows Vista. We'll look at Windows Explorer right after we examine the Start menu.

THE NEW START MENU

As with every version of Windows since Windows 95, the route to Windows applications and functions is through the Start menu. To open it, click Start and…wait a minute. Start?

Here is a Windows Vista innovation: The Start button doesn't say Start on it. It's a round icon bearing the Windows logo, initially at the lower-left corner of the screen, as shown in Figure 3.3. While Vista was being developed, people tried to come up with more a appropriate name, such as the Windows Pearl or The Button Formerly Known as Start, but the old name stuck, so that's what we call it in this book.

Figure 3.3
The Start button doesn't say Start anymore.

The button formerly known as Start

Click the Start button. The Start menu appears as a large panel with a list of frequently used programs at the left and a list of locations and tools at the right. The items in the right list that were called My Computer, My Documents, and so on in previous versions of Windows are still present, but the names are now just Computer, Documents, and so on. (I'll show you later in this tour how to select which items appear in this list.)

Here is another new visual scheme used in Vista: Click All Programs, Accessories, and notice that the menus don't expand out in a series of pop-up panels as they did in former versions of Windows. In Vista, the idea was to reduce visual clutter. Instead, only one menu at a time is shown in its entirety. The "back" link that appears at the bottom of the list brings you back to the previous menu list. Try it, and watch how the menu display returns to the original Start menu.

The new Windows Search tool is also integrated into the Start menu. Under the words All Programs, notice the box that says Start Search. You can type a part of a filename or a phrase from a document into this box, and Windows attempts to locate the file or document. Results are displayed in the upper part of the Start menu panel.

A similar Search box appears in Windows Explorer, as you see in the next section.

THE NEW WINDOWS EXPLORER

To continue our tour, let's take a quick look at Windows Explorer. Click Start, Computer, and Windows displays the Windows Explorer file manager, shown in Figure 3.4.

Figure 3.4
Windows Explorer sports a new look in Vista.

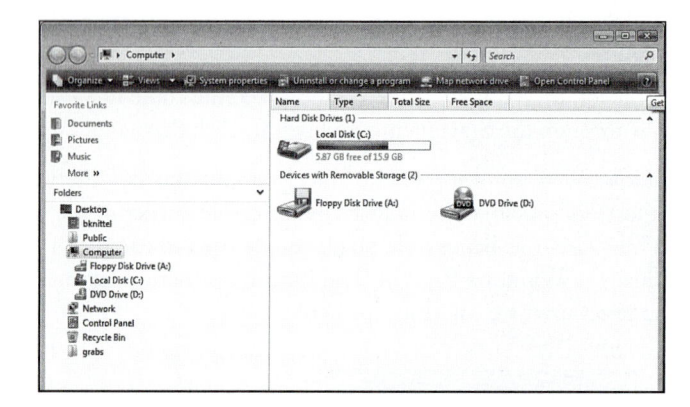

In the left pane, click Local Disk (C:), or whichever drive you used when you installed Windows. Then, click Users and select the folder name that corresponds to your user account. (This is usually the same name that you selected on the Welcome screen when you logged on to Windows.) Then, click on Documents.

Notice that as you dig into these folders on your hard disk, the path is displayed at the top of the window, like this: Computer . Local Disk (C:) . Users .*yourname* . Documents. In Vista, the names in this list are called *breadcrumbs*, after the breadcrumbs dropped by the children in the fairy tale *Hansel and Gretel*. (That trail of breadcrumbs, as you recall, led to their nearly being cooked and eaten by a witch. Why do we tell these gory stories to children?) Anyway, these breadcrumbs serve to show the way back through the path you took as you dug into the folders on your computer's disks. The important thing to remember is that you can always click any of the names in the list to immediately jump back to that particular folder.

We'll talk more about Windows Explorer in Chapter 5, "Managing Files and Searching." Close Windows Explorer now and we'll go on.

THE REDESIGNED CONTROL PANEL

The wordy "web page" layout used in Vista reaches its penultimate in the new Control Panel. Click Start, Control Panel, and you see the window shown in Figure 3.5.

Figure 3.5
The new Control Panel looks and acts a lot like a web page.

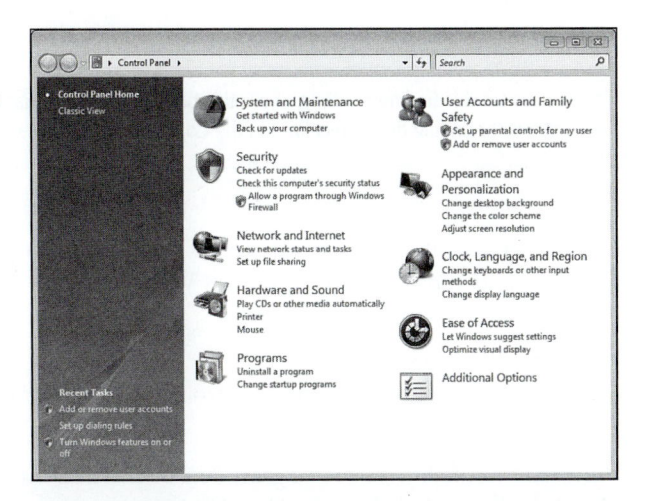

Whereas the old Control Panel model used icons that launched little configuration and control programs, the new Control Panel uses phrases—dozens and dozens of phrases—that describe various tasks. To see what I mean, click Classic View and check out the old scheme with icons; then click Control Panel Home to return to the text-based Vista model.

The major titles in large type, such as System and Maintenance, Security, and so on, are links to other pages with many subheadings and numerous tasks. The two or three tasks that appear under each title on the main Control Panel page, such as Back Up Your Computer under System and Maintenance, are there as convenient shortcuts, and they appear on the subpages as well.

Now, click the green title System and Maintenance. Notice that the trail of breadcrumbs at the top of the window shows the way back to the main Control Panel page, and the "back" button appears in the upper-left corner of the window as well, as we discussed previously. Notice that this System and Maintenance page has its own large list of headings, such as Welcome Center, Windows Update, and Power Options, and tasks under each heading.

On these pages, both the green headings *and* the task descriptions lead to various dialog boxes that let you configure and adjust Windows.

Personally, we think that the new Control Panel uses too many words. The tasks are arranged in categories that don't always make sense, some tasks appear more than once, and several tasks ultimately lead to the same dialog box and settings. It's more than a bit confusing, and it may take you some time to find things that you know should be there… somewhere.

> **TIP**
>
> If you have trouble finding a setting, check this book's index, and that should lead you to instructions for finding the correct links in the Control Panel or elsewhere.

Now, click Control Panel Home in the upper-left part of the Control Panel window. We're going to look at user accounts and security in Windows Vista.

User Account Control

We need to stop, at this point, to give you some background on the next feature that we'll show you.

One area where Microsoft justifiably received a great deal of criticism over the past decade or so was its handling of security. Windows 95, 98, and Me had no security scheme at all—any user could modify any file or program.

Windows NT, 2000, and XP did have the necessary structure to secure the operating system. The way Windows security works, any program that a user runs gains the privileges associated with the user's logon account; this determines what folders the user can save files in, what settings the user can change, and so on. Computer Administrator accounts, in particular, have the capability to change any system setting, change any file, or install any software.

Unfortunately, in Windows XP, *all* user accounts were by default created as Computer Administrator accounts, and it took a bit of effort and training to work with Windows any other way. So, for most home and small office users, Windows security was essentially bypassed. The consequences of this were, in turn

- Any program run by hundreds of millions of Windows 95, 98, Me, and XP Home users had complete access to the computer.
- When anyone was duped into running bad software downloaded from the Internet or received a bogus program by email, that software also had the complete run of the computer.
- Some tens of millions of Windows computers are, as a result, infected with spam-sending software, unbeknown to their owners.
- Criminals remotely control those computers and use them to send about 80% of the 130 billion or so spam emails (as of December 2007) that are sent every day.

So, the next time you clear out your email inbox, consider that most of the spam in there got there because Microsoft made no effort to make Windows secure "out of the box," meaning, as delivered to the owner. And few people knew how to take the complex steps needed to tighten things up.

Windows Vista changes that in a big way. Out of the box, Windows Vista enforces security through several means, including these:

- The disk on which Windows is installed uses the NTFS disk formatting system so that access to files and folders can be tightly controlled.
- As initially installed, the security system is actually used and ensures that users do not have the ability to randomly create, delete, or modify files in the Windows program folders. This protects Windows not only from accidents but also from rogue software.
- Programs and system control panels that can make changes that have security implications use a special feature called User Account Control to ensure that changes can't be made without your knowing it.

This latter part is what we want to talk about and show you now.

As mentioned earlier, Windows programs run with the permissions associated with a user account. Permissions include things such as the ability to create or modify files in each folder, change settings on features such as networking and hard disk management, install software and hardware device drivers, and so on. Computer Administrator accounts can do any of these things.

What's changed in Windows Vista is that programs run even by users with Administrator accounts *don't* automatically get all those privileges. The potential is there, but by default, all programs run with a reduced set of privileges that let them modify files in the user's own folders but *not* in the Windows folder or the Program Files folder. Likewise, by default, programs run even by a Computer Administrator cannot change networking settings, install applications, install device drivers, or change system software services.

Instead, you have to take a special step to run a program with *elevated privileges*, that is, with the full complement of Computer Administrator privileges. And, whenever you try to do this, Windows requires that you confirm that you actually do want to run that specific program with elevated privileges. Windows displays a dialog box, and you have to click a yes or no response before the program is allowed to run (or not).

What is important is that this "go or no go" dialog box is displayed by Windows in a secure way, from a deep, protected part of Windows, and there is no way for rogue software to bypass it or block it. Thus, there is no way for rogue software to install itself *without your consent*. This is called *User Account Control (UAC)*, and it's the most important distinction between Windows Vista and any of its predecessors.

Another important feature of User Account Control is this: If you logged on using a Computer Administrator account, Windows just asks you to consent to running the program. However, if you logged on using a "Standard" user account, Windows *can still run the administrative program*—the User Account Control prompt asks you to select the username and enter the password of a Computer Administrator account.

UAC makes Vista more secure *and* usable. It makes it safer to let people have and use Computer Administrator accounts. And, it is now reasonable to set up "Standard" user accounts for people whom you'd rather not be asked to judge which programs should run— for example, children or noncomputer-literate employees. Should they actually need to change some setting that brings up a User Account Control prompt, you can simply reach over their shoulders, type in a privileged account name and password, let them make the one change, and poof!—they're back to being a limited-privilege user.

Of course, this type of intervention is required only for programs that involve security-related settings. And this brings us to the reason that the Windows Vista Control Panel and other Windows management tools are so complex and fractured.

Microsoft went through all the Windows settings and adjustments and decided which ones could pose security risks and which were benign. For example, installing a device driver is a risky task, and selecting a desktop background picture is benign. Risky and benign settings had to be put into separate programs or Control Panel elements. The benign ones are packaged as nonprivileged programs so that they can be run by any user. The risky ones have been put into separate programs that are marked as requiring elevated privileges. So, Control Panel items that used to have dozens of settings on one dialog box had to be split into many smaller pieces.

A program can be run with elevated privileges in two ways:

- Some programs are "marked" by their developers as *requiring* elevated privileges. These programs display the User Account Control prompt whenever you try to run them.
- You can right-click *any* program's icon and select Run As Administrator. Generally, you need to do this only if you attempt some task and are told that you don't have permission. This can happen, for instance, if you try to delete some other user's document from the printer's queue.

So…that was a long explanation for something that can help you tremendously but in practice won't take up much of your time. Let's go on with the tour.

If you aren't looking at the Control Panel, now, click Start, Control Panel. Look under the Security and User Accounts and Family Safety headings, and notice that some of the tasks are shown with a small shield icon. This is the indication that a task requires elevated privileges. Click Add or Remove User Accounts. Windows dims the rest of the screen and displays one of the dialogs shown in Figure 3.6.

If you are currently logged on to a Computer Administrator account, you see dialog box (a) shown in Figure 3.6. The dialog shows the name and the origin of the program, if it can be determined. You can click Details to see more information about the program file, if any is available.

Figure 3.6
User Account Control asks for confirmation or asks you to provide an Administrator password.

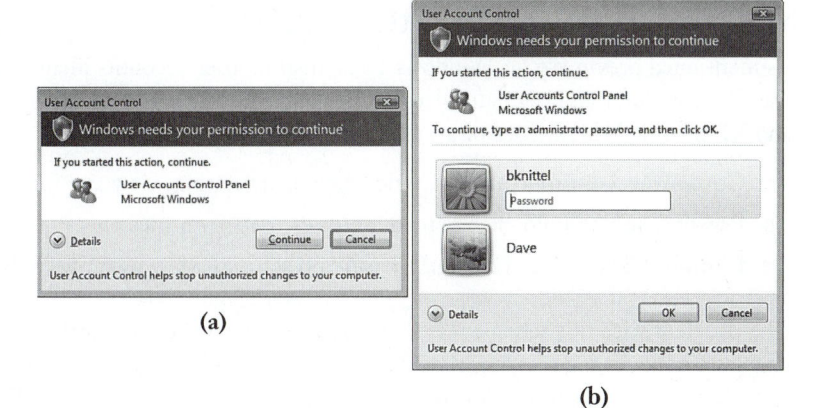

(a)

(b)

If you logged on to a Standard user account, Windows displays dialog box (b) shown in Figure 3.6. Here, you can also click Details to see more information about the program that caused the User Account Control pop-up. To proceed, you (or someone else) must select one of the Administrator account names and enter its password.

In either case, this is your chance to verify that you intended to run the program that caused the pop-up, and that you trust it to be safe to run.

CAUTION
> Don't get in the habit of just clicking Continue every time one of these dialogs appears. Read it and consider it every time.
>
> If you have any doubts about the program listed in the dialog, especially if a User Account Control pop-up appears when you didn't expect it, click Cancel.

NOTE
> Instead of displaying the dialogs in Figure 3.6, two other things could happen. If someone disabled User Account Control on your computer, Windows proceeds to the Manage Accounts panel. (We *strongly* discourage disabling User Account Control.) If you are on a domain network (as you probably are if you are using Vista in a corporate setting), you might not have the option of editing user accounts at all.

In this case, we did intend to run the User Accounts Control Panel, so either click Continue, or select an Administrator account and provide the password, as appropriate.

In the next part of our one-hour tour, we will help you set up user accounts for the people who will be using your computer.

Windows Vista User Accounts

As mentioned previously, in Windows Vista, distinct user accounts identify each person who uses the computer and regulate what settings and files the users can change. Windows 2000 and XP provided three types of user accounts:

- **Computer Administrator**—Could change any setting, view any file
- **Power User**—Could change many settings, view own files only
- **Limited User**—Could change virtually no settings, view own files only

The problem with this scheme was that Limited Users were constantly frustrated by being unable to make changes as trivial as choosing a screen saver. The Power User category was actually the right one to use for day-to-day use, but it wasn't available on Windows XP Home Edition, and even on XP Professional, it wasn't easy to create Power User accounts. The result was that most users were created as Computer Administrators, and we discussed earlier in this chapter what a disaster that has turned out to be.

On Vista, this situation has improved dramatically. First, the Limited category has now been renamed Standard, to reflect its "mainstream" role. Most settings that don't have security implications can now be changed by Standard Users. For instance, changing the screen resolution no longer requires Administrator privileges. Plugging in a new USB device used to require Administrator privileges, but in Vista, if a Microsoft-verified driver is pre-installed, a Standard user can add the device without any trouble. For any tasks that *do* require Administrator privileges, the User Account Control system makes it easy to perform the task without having to completely log off and log back on.

As a result, it's perfectly reasonable to use a Standard user account for your day-to-day work. And should you choose to use an Administrator account, even that is relatively safe now. So, although the Power User category is still present in Vista, it's not needed or useful.

So, at this point on our tour, let's add user accounts for the people who will be using your computer.

> **TIP**
>
> When you first installed Windows, Windows setup created a Computer Administrator account. I recommend that you create perhaps one additional Computer Administrator account, and that you create a Standard user account for yourself for day-to-day use. This gives you maximum protection against viruses and other malware.

> **NOTE**
>
> You don't need to worry about this now (or ever), but if you formerly used Windows 2000 or Windows XP Professional and wonder what happened to the user account that had the name Administrator, you'll read about it later in this chapter under "Accessing the Real Administrator Account."

CREATE NEW ACCOUNTS

If you aren't looking at the Manage Accounts screen now, click Start, Control Panel, and Add Or Change User Accounts under the heading User Accounts and Family Safety. You should see the window shown in Figure 3.7—of course, it shows your names instead of mine.

> **NOTE**
>
> If you plan on copying user accounts from an old computer to your new Vista computer using the Easy Transfer Wizard described later in this chapter, you can skip this section now, but be sure to come back to this step later to set a password for each transferred user account.

Figure 3.7
Manage Accounts lets you create or modify user accounts.

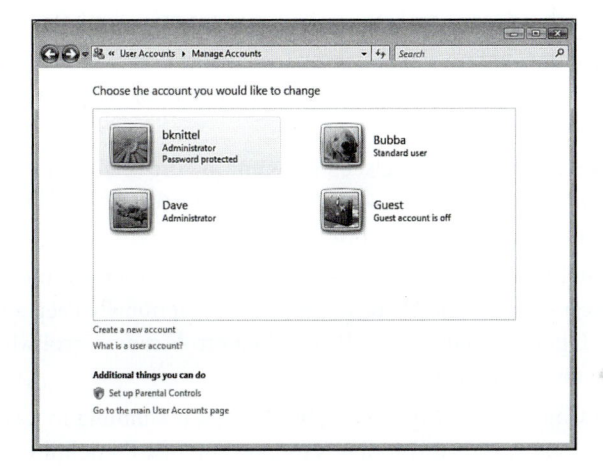

From the Manage Accounts screen, you can select an account to modify, or you can click Create a New Account. You'll find that it's best if each person who uses the computer has her own account so that each person's email can be kept separate, settings and preferences can be personalized, and so on.

To create a new user account, perform the following steps:

1. Click Create a New Account.
2. Type a name for the account. Use just letters, numbers, and optionally spaces or hyphens. I typically use each person's first initial and last name, but you can use any scheme you want.
3. If you want to create a Computer Administrator account, select Administrator; otherwise, leave the selection at Standard user. I recommend that you use Standard accounts for most users, and even for your own day-to-day use.
4. Click Create Account.

The new user appears in the Manage Accounts screen.

> **NOTE**
>
> Before logging on to any other accounts for the first time, see the "Tips from the Windows Pros: Configuring the Default User Profile" section at the end of this chapter.

Now, you can make adjustments to each account.

Change Account Settings

To change an account's settings, view the Manage Accounts screen, as shown in Figure 3.7, and click on an account name. The screen lists several tasks, including the following:

- **Change the Account Name**—Click to edit the account's username. (Note: If the user has already logged on, this won't actually change the name of his profile folder in the \users folder. If this doesn't make sense to you right now, don't worry about it.)

- **Set a Password** or **Change the Password**—Click to create or change the account's password. We *strongly* recommend that you set a password on every user account, or at the very least on *every* Administrator account.

- **Change the Picture**—Click to select a different picture to appear on the Start menu and the Welcome screen. You can select one of the pictures supplied by Microsoft or click Browse to locate one of your own images.

- **Set Up Parental Controls**—Click to control when this user can use the computer, what the user can view on the Web, and whether to optionally keep a record of the user's activity. Figure 3.8 shows how Parental Controls can control when a user is allowed to use the computer.

(The Parental Controls Activity Viewer, by the way, is stunning in its coverage of user activity. Take a look at it. If this tool was monitoring me, I'd definitely keep my nose clean!)

Figure 3.8
Parental Controls can keep a child off the computer except for weekends and after homework.

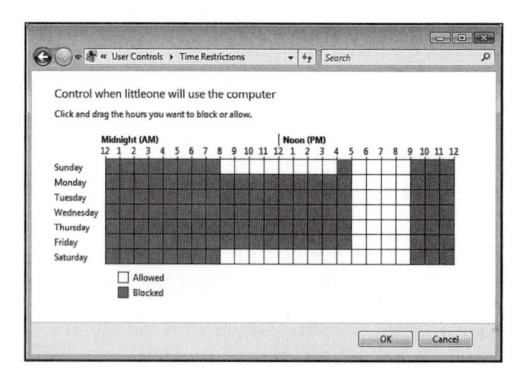

- **Change the Account Type**—Click to change the account type from Administrator to Standard user or *vice versa*.

- **Delete the Account**—Click to delete the account. You can elect to keep or delete the account's files (documents, pictures, and so on).

You can also select and enable the Guest account. The Guest account is a Standard user account that requires no password, and it should be enabled only if you want to provide a computer to guests in your home or office.

At this point on our tour of Windows Vista, we recommend that you take a moment now to add a user account for each person who will be using your computer. Definitely set a password on each Administrator account. We recommend that you set a password on each Standard user account as well.

> **TIP**
>
> Before logging on to other accounts for the first time, see "Tips from the Windows Pros: Configuring the Default User Profile" at the end of this chapter.

> **TIP**
>
> If you are in a home or small office environment, have more than one computer, and plan on setting up a local area network, we suggest that you create accounts for every one of your users on each of your computers, using the same name and same password for each person on each computer. This makes it possible for anyone to use any computer, and it makes it easier for you to manage security on your network.

After you add your user accounts, continue to the next section.

Before You Forget Your Password

If you forget your account's password, you could be in serious trouble. On a corporate domain network, you can ask your network administrator to save you. But, on a home computer, or in a small office, forgetting your password is serious. It can put your encrypted files at risk, and you could lose any passwords that you've stored for automatic use on websites. (Do you even remember them all?)

And if you can't remember the password to any Computer Administrator account, you'll really be stuck. You'll most likely have to reinstall Windows, and all of your applications, and you'll be *very* unhappy.

There is something you can do to prevent this disaster from happening to you. You can create a password reset disk *right now*, and put it away in a safe place. A password reset disk is linked to your account and lets you log in using data physically stored on the disk. It's like a physical key to your computer. Even if you later change your account's password between making the disk and forgetting the password, the reset disk will still work to unlock your account.

So…make a password reset disk now! Here's how. You need a blank, formatted floppy disk, recordable CD, removable USB thumb drive, or other such removable medium. Follow these steps:

1. Click Start, Control Panel, User Accounts and Family Safety; then click User Accounts at the top of the list.

2. In the Tasks list at the left side of the window, choose Create a Password Reset Disk.
3. When the wizard appears, click Next.
4. Select a removable disk drive from the list and click Next.
5. Enter your current password and click Next.
6. Follow the wizard's instructions. When the wizard finishes writing data, click Next and then click Finish.

The disk will now contain a file called `userkey.psw`, which is the key to your account. (You can copy this file to another medium, if you want.) Remove the disk, label it so that you'll remember what it is, and store it in a safe place.

> **CAUTION**
> A password reset disk, or rather the file `userkey.psw` that's on it, is as good as your password for gaining access to your computer, so store the reset disk in a safe, secure place.

You don't have to re-create the disk if you change your password in the future. The disk will still work regardless of your password at the time. However, a password disk works only to get into the account that created it, so each user should create one for himself.

> **NOTE**
> Be absolutely sure to create a password reset disk for at least one Computer Administrator account on your computer.

> **TIP**
> Each user should create his own Password Reset disk. In theory, a computer Administrator could always reset any other user's password, but that user would then lose his encrypted files and stored passwords. Better to have a Password Reset disk for *every* user account.

If you forget your password and can't log on, see "After You Forget Your Password" toward the end of this chapter.

ADJUST YOUR OWN USER ACCOUNT

Windows has a few settings that are set on a per-user basis, and some of them can be set in only one particular way, using the following steps. You don't necessarily need to do this now. If you want to, you can skip ahead to the next section.

To see the list of user account settings you can change, click Start, Control Panel, User Accounts and Family Safety; then click User Accounts at the top of the list.

The most common tasks are listed in the window's larger pane. These include options to change your password and the picture associated with your account, which we discussed earlier.

Look through the Tasks list on the left side of the screen. These selections appear only when you open the User Accounts control panel this particular way, and they have the following uses:

- **Create a Password Reset Disk**—Creates a disk that you can use to log on if you forget your password, as discussed in the previous section.

- **Manage Your Network Passwords**—Lets you add, delete, or change passwords that have been remembered by Windows for use on remote servers or websites. One useful feature here is that you can back up these passwords to a disk and copy them to your account on another computer.

- **Manage Your File Encryption Certificates**—Use this wizard to create, back up, or restore the certificates (keys) used to encrypt your files, on Windows Vista Business, Enterprise, or Ultimate editions only.

→ For more information on file encryption, **see** "Encrypted File System (EFS)," **p. 1173**.

- **Configure Advanced User Profile Properties**—If your computer is on a domain network, you can select whether your user profile should be copied back and forth to the file server (a roaming profile) or just kept on the computer in front of you (a local profile).

- **Change My Environment Variables**—You can customize environment variables for your account here. Environment variables tell Windows applications where to look for executable files, where to store temporary files, and so on.

→ For more information, **see** "Setting Environment Variables," **p. 1085**.

JUST ONE USER?

If you know that your computer will be used just by one user (you, perhaps?), there is a setting that you can use so that Windows starts up and goes directly to your desktop without asking you to log on. You may find that your computer does this anyway; some computer manufacturers turn on this setting before they ship the computer to you. Technically, a password is still used; it's just entered for you automatically.

We recommend that you don't use this automatic logon option. Without a password, your computer or your Internet connection could be abused by someone without your even knowing it. So, you probably want to skip ahead to the next section.

Still, there are some times it's reasonable to change this setting—for example, if your computer manufacturer set your computer up this way, you can disable it. Or you may want to use the feature in a computer that's used in a public place, or in an industrial control setting. To change the startup setting, follow these steps:

1. Click Start, and in the Search box, enter `control userpasswords2` and press Enter.

2. To require a logon, check Users Must Enter a Username and Password to Access This Computer, and click OK.

Alternately, to make Windows go to the desktop automatically, uncheck Users Must Enter a Username and Password to Access This Computer, and click OK. Then, type the username and password of the account that you want to log on automatically and click OK.

The change takes effect the next time Windows starts up.

Set Up Internet Access

Although you'll probably want to change a number of settings, you should start by making sure that your computer has a working Internet connection for two reasons. First, critical Windows security or device driver updates might have been released since your computer's copy of Windows was made. You definitely want to get those installed as quickly as possible. Second, at least one setting, which we're going to discuss later in this chapter, requires a functioning Internet connection.

If you have existing dial-up or broadband Internet service, or better still, if you have an existing network that you can just plug your computer into, this should be easy. We actually devote entire chapters in this book to the topic, but you might get on the air in just a few seconds, so let's give it a shot. Here's what to try:

1. If your home or office has a wired Ethernet network that provides Internet access, just plug in your computer. That's all you should need to do. Open Internet Explorer and see whether it works.

2. If you have a wireless network adapter in your computer and a wireless network available that provides Internet access, turn on your wireless adapter. Click Start, Network, and then select Network and Sharing Center. In the Tasks list at the left, click Connect To a Network.

    A list of available networks should appear. If your wireless network's name appears in the list, click the name and then click the Connect button. The Connection Wizard then walks you through establishing the connection.

3. If you have broadband cable or DSL service and you plan to connect your computer directly to the cable or DSL modem, connect your computer's network adapter to the modem now.

4. If you have cable Internet service, this might be enough to get your connection going... open Internet Explorer and see.

    If you have dial-up or DSL service, click Start, Network; then select Network and Sharing Center. In the Tasks list at the left, click Set Up a Connection or Network. Select Connect to the Internet and click Next. Then follow the wizard to set up a PPPoE (DSL) or dial-up connection.

If this seat-of-the-pants procedure doesn't work for you, jump ahead to Chapter 14, "Getting Connected," to get your connection working.

When your Internet connection is set up, you're ready to continue with the rest of this chapter.

Download Critical Updates

After your Internet connection is up and running, click Start, All Programs, Windows Update. In the left pane, click Check for Updates.

If no updates are available, and the screen says that Windows is up to date, you can close this window and skip ahead to the next section. If you use Windows Vista Ultimate Edition and there are Ultimate Extras available for download, make a mental note to come back later to get them, but again, skip ahead—we're only after critical updates right now.

If there are Windows updates to download, click Install Updates and wait for the process to complete before continuing the tour. And if your computer does not yet have Service Pack 1 installed, this is the time to get it. Windows Update will download and install the service pack for you. After installing the service pack, Windows will restart. Log on, and immediately return to Windows Update and see whether any *additional* updates are available. It's essential that you get any critical security fixes installed before proceeding.

Personalize Windows

For the next part of your first hour with Windows, we want to help you make changes to some settings that make Windows a bit easier to use, and a little easier to understand. So, let's tear through them.

As initially installed, Windows may set your screen's resolution to a lower resolution than your monitor supports. You might also want to change the screen background from the picture you chose during installation or set up a screen saver. Let's start personalizing Windows by adjusting these settings.

Personalize Screen Settings

Now we're ready to make a couple of quick selections to the settings that control Windows' appearance. To do this, right-click the desktop anywhere but on an icon and select Personalize. The window shown in Figure 3.9 appears.

Figure 3.9
Windows Vista's many display settings.

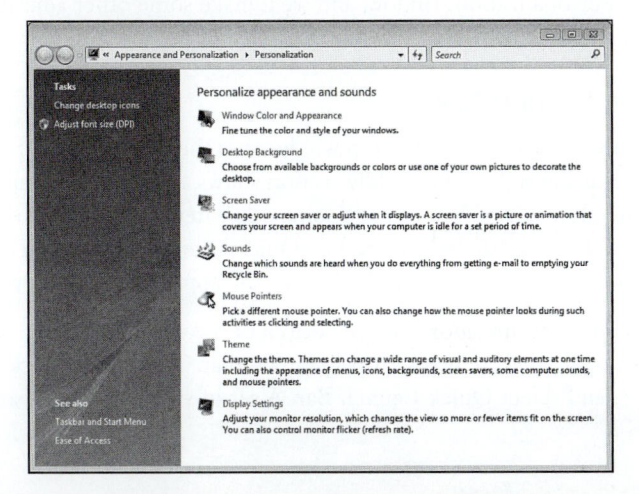

The important settings to hit now are

- **Desktop Background**—Click to select a different desktop picture. You can also change the Picture Location to Solid Colors to select a plain, uniform background, or click Browse to locate a favorite picture of your own.
- **Screen Saver**—Click to select a screen saver and set the timeout. If you want your computer to lock itself if you go away long enough for the screen saver to activate, check On Resume, Display Logon Screen.

> **NOTE**
>
> You can put those unused computer processor cycles to better use than making the Windows logo swim around your screen. Several worthy screen-saver alternatives actually might help find a cure for cancer or eavesdrop on ET phoning home. Our favorites can be found at boinc.berkeley.edu.

- **Display Settings**—Click to set the resolution of your monitor. If Windows looks a little blurry, especially on an LCD monitor, it could be that Windows guessed too low a resolution. Slide the resolution button to the right to set it to the exact native resolution of your LCD monitor; then click OK. (If the type is too small to read, don't worry; we'll get to that shortly.)

  Also, if you have two or more monitors attached to your computer, Windows should have offered you the option of extending your desktop onto all of them. If not, select the second monitor from the pull-down list and check Extend the Desktop onto This Monitor. Then, click Identify Monitors and move the two monitor icons in the dialog box so that they match the physical layout of your monitors. If you have more monitors, repeat this process with the third, and so on.
- **Adjust Font Size**—If you have trouble reading the type on the screen, select Adjust Font Size from the Tasks list at the left, and select either Larger Scale, or click Custom DPI and drag the ruler to set the type to a readable size. Click OK to close the dialog box.

Now, close the Personalization window, and we'll make some other adjustments to the desktop.

SET UP THE QUICK LAUNCH BAR

The taskbar at the bottom of the desktop window has the Start button at the left and the notification area at the right. The middle section shows a tab for each running application. By default, that's all it shows. You can add some other items to it, and we suggest that you enable the Quick Launch bar right now. The Quick Launch bar lets you add tiny icons to the taskbar that let you launch with a single click the applications you use most often.

To enable it, right-click the taskbar at the bottom of the screen, clicking somewhere where there are no icons or labels. Uncheck Lock the Taskbar. Then, right-click the taskbar again, select Toolbars, and select Quick Launch Bar. A set of small icons appear, as shown in

Figure 3.10. Make this new area of the taskbar a bit wider by dragging the separator part (which appears as a column of dots) to the right.

Now, click Start, All Programs, Accessories. Right-click Windows Explorer and, while holding down the right mouse button, drag the Windows Explorer icon down to the Quick Launch bar, just to the right of the existing icons. Release the mouse button and select Copy Here. Windows adds a new icon for Windows Explorer to the Quick Launch bar. You can use this button any time you want to copy or manage files.

Figure 3.10

If you use the Windows Command Prompt frequently, you'll want to do the same with the Command Prompt icon. Click Start, All Programs, Accessories; then right-drag Command Prompt to the Quick Launch bar, release, and select Copy Here.

Later, you may want to add icons for your favorite two or three applications as well. We suggest that you keep the Quick Launch bar small, five or six icons at most; otherwise, with such small icons, it is difficult to find the right one, and that defeats its purpose.

When you've added the icons, drag the divider back to the left to make the Quick Launch as small as possible while still showing all the icons. Then, right-click the taskbar and select Lock Taskbar.

Adjust the Explorers

You're probably familiar with Internet Explorer, Microsoft's web browser. The other Explorer you need to know about is Windows Explorer, the program behind the desktop, Start Menu, Computer, Documents, Music, and other file management windows. You're using Windows Explorer when you use any of those tools. You can also use it by itself to manage files. By default, though, it hides some information about files, and we want to give you the option of seeing it.

Disable Hide Extensions for Known File Types

By default, Windows Explorer hides the file extension at the end of most filenames: This is the .doc at the end of a Word document, the .xls at the end of an Excel spreadsheet, or the .exe at the end of an application program. Hiding the extension makes it more difficult for you to accidentally delete it when renaming the file, but we think it also makes it more difficult to tell what a given file is. It can also make it easier to fall for ruses, as when someone sends an email virus in a file named payroll.xls.exe. If Explorer hides the .exe part, you may fall for the trick and think the file is just an Excel spreadsheet.

To make Explorer show filenames in all their glory, follow these steps:

1. Start Windows Explorer using the Quick Launch button you just created, or click Start, Computer.

2. Click the Organize button at the top, left side of the window, and select Folder and Search Options.

3. Select the View tab. In the Advanced Settings list, find Hide Extensions for Known File Types and uncheck it.
4. This one is optional: If you're curious about Vista's internal files and folders, and plan on investigating them, also select Show Hidden Files and Folders. You can change this setting after you finish looking around.
5. Click OK.

Customize the Start Menu

There are some Windows maintenance tools that, for some reason, Microsoft doesn't put into the Start menu by default. We suggest that you enable them now so that you don't have to dig through the Control Panel to get to them. Here's how:

1. Right-click the Start button and select Properties.
2. Click the Customize button.
3. Scroll down through the list to find System Administrative Tools near the bottom. Select Display on the All Programs menu.
4. If you're interested, check out the rest of this list for other Start menu options. If you find that you *never* use the Music link, for example, you can remove it from the Start menu here.

    Or if you find that you miss the old Run option that lets you start programs by typing their name, you can enable it here. (Although, you should know that you can start a program by typing its name into the Vista search box on the Start menu, so Run isn't as necessary anymore. Still, the search Window can run only programs that are in the search path, so for hardcore command line users, the Run option is still useful.)
5. Click OK twice, closing both of the open dialog boxes in turn.

Set Internet Explorer's Home Page

By default, whenever you open Internet Explorer, it immediately displays a Microsoft website, or a website specified by your computer manufacturer. Personally, I prefer to have Internet Explorer open to a blank page because I rarely start my browsing in the same place twice. You may also prefer to select a different "home" page, one that *you* want to visit rather than one selected by some company's marketing department.

To take control of your Internet Explorer home page, take the following steps:

1. Click Start, Internet Explorer. (Or click the little e icon on the Quick Launch bar.)
2. To start IE with a blank page every time, in the upper-right corner of the window, click Tools, Internet Options. Then, click the Use Blank button.

    Or to select a page that you prefer to see each time IE starts, view that page now. Then, in the upper-right corner of the window, click Tools, Internet Options. Click the Use Current button.
3. Click OK to close the Internet Options dialog box.

If you prefer to use a different web browser entirely, FireFox and Opera are popular replacements for IE. For more information, see Chapter 15, "Using Internet Explorer 7."

Set Internet Explorer's Search Provider

Internet Explorer has a search tool built into the upper-right corner of the window. When you type something into this box and press Enter, IE sends the text to an Internet search engine and displays the result. This saves you having to open the search engine page first, type the search text, and then wait for the results.

However, by default IE sends you to Microsoft's own search engine, called Windows Live. Or your computer manufacturer may have specified a different default search engine. Again, we suggest that you take control and tell IE what search engine *you* want to use. You can use Windows Live, of course, but you can also select a different default site.

To change the default search site, follow these steps:

1. Internet Explorer should still be open from the previous section, but if it's not, click Start, Internet Explorer.
2. At the upper-right corner of the window, locate the little magnifying glass icon and click the small down-pointing arrow just to its right.
3. Select Find More Providers.
4. Click the name of one of the providers in the Web Search or Topic Search lists. When the Add Provider dialog appears, check Make This My Default Search Provider. Then, click Add Provider.
5. Test the new search tool: Type your name into the search box and press Enter.

That's the end of our list of "must-do" Windows settings. You can, of course, change hundreds of other things, which is why we went on to write Chapters 4 through 41.

> **NOTE**
>
> Normally, you have to go through most of these same setup steps for each user account on your computer. At the end of this chapter, under "Tips from the Windows Pros: Configuring the Default User Profile," we show you how you can do all of your setup, tweaking, and adjusting just once, and have your finely tuned setup be the default setup for all of your computer's user accounts.
>
> If that sounds interesting, skip ahead to the end of the chapter now, *before* you or anyone else logs on to any other account on your computer.

Transfer Information from Your Old Computer

If you have set up a new Vista computer rather than upgrading an old one, you probably have files and programs that you want to bring over to your new computer.

Windows Easy Transfer

The Windows Easy Transfer program lets you copy documents and preference settings from an older computer running Windows XP or Vista, to a new computer running Vista. You can use several different means to transfer the data. If you can plug both computers into the same Local Area Network (LAN), the transfer can occur directly over the network.

→ If you don't have a network but both of your computers have Ethernet network adapters, you can simply connect them using an Ethernet crossover cable. **See** "Connecting Just Two Computers," **p. 632**.

You can also connect the two computers using a special Easy Transfer USB cable, which you may have been provided when you purchased your new computer or which you can buy. Alternatively, you can elect to copy data on a Flash drive, card, a recordable DVD, or CD, although these media might not work if you have more data to transfer than will fit on a single drive, card, or disc.

Also, if your old computer runs Windows XP, you'll need a blank recordable CD or a USB flash drive to copy the transfer program over to your XP computer.

> **NOTE**
>
> There's no Back button in this wizard, so if you change your mind at any point, you have to cancel the process, and you may be forced to start over *on both computers*. Ugh!

Here is the procedure:

1. Start the process on your new Vista computer. If the Windows Welcome Center is displayed, click Transfer Files and Settings. Otherwise, click Start, All Programs, Accessories, System Tools, Windows Easy Transfer. When the window appears, click Next; then click My New Computer.

2. If you are going to use the special purpose Easy Transfer USB cable, click Yes, I Have an Easy Transfer Cable. Otherwise, click No, Show Me More Options.

3. If your old computer is running Windows Vista, select Yes My Old Computer Is Running Windows Vista, and proceed to step 4.

   Otherwise, if your old computer runs Windows XP, click No I Need to Install It Now; then select CD or USB Flash Drive, depending on the medium you have available. Click Next to copy the setup program to the selected removable drive.

   (You can also have the wizard copy the program to a shared network folder and install it on the XP computer from there, if you're comfortable with that method.)

4. Still on your new Vista computer, you may be asked to select whether you want to transfer your files and settings over a network connection or through recordable CD, DVD, or other removable media. Make the appropriate selection. In this example, I use the network option.

5. If you use a network connection, you need to let the Easy Transfer program unblock Windows Firewall. Then click No, I Need a Key. Windows displays a window with a string of letters and numerals. Leave this be and move to your old computer.

6. If your old computer is running Windows XP, log on as an Administrator and insert the Easy Transfer Wizard media or shared network folder copy you made in step 3. The transfer program should start automatically.

   If your old computer is running Vista, start the Easy Transfer program on that computer now, select the transfer means, and click My Old Computer.

7. Select the transfer method, allow the firewall to be unblocked if asked, and select Yes I Have a Key.

8. Enter or confirm the key code that's displayed by the transfer program on your new computer and click Next. Select the All Users transfer method. (The single user method is OK if you want to transfer only settings for the account you're currently using, but this method can't transfer files for non-Administrator XP accounts.)

9. Select the user accounts that you want to transfer, and select the files that you want to transfer from the old computer to the new, as shown in Figure 3.11. Be especially careful to scroll down to the Files in Other Locations entry and make your selections carefully; otherwise, you may find yourself transferring more data than you planned on. When you've selected files, click Next.

Figure 3.11
The Windows Easy Transfer wizard lets you select which accounts and folders to copy from your old computer to your new one.

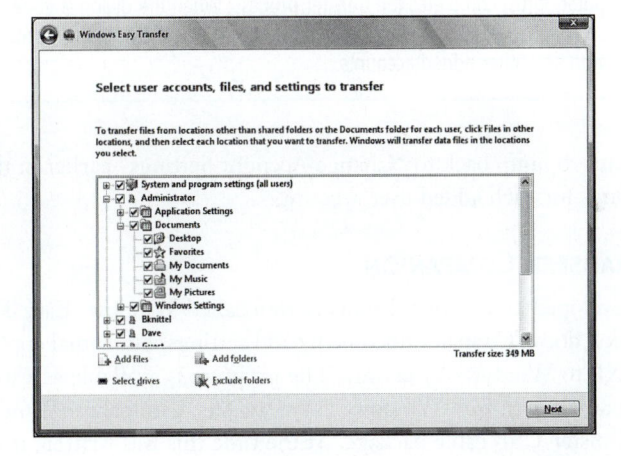

10. Select or enter the name of a new Vista user account to match up with each of the old computer accounts you're transferring, as shown in Figure 3.12. You must enter or select a user account name for each account you're transferring. Click Next when you finish.

11. Follow the wizard's prompts to create removable media, or wait while the data is collected and transferred over your network or Easy Transfer cable.

When the process is complete, you can close the program on the old computer. You need to restart the new computer.

Figure 3.12
Select or enter a username to use on Vista for each user account you're transferring.

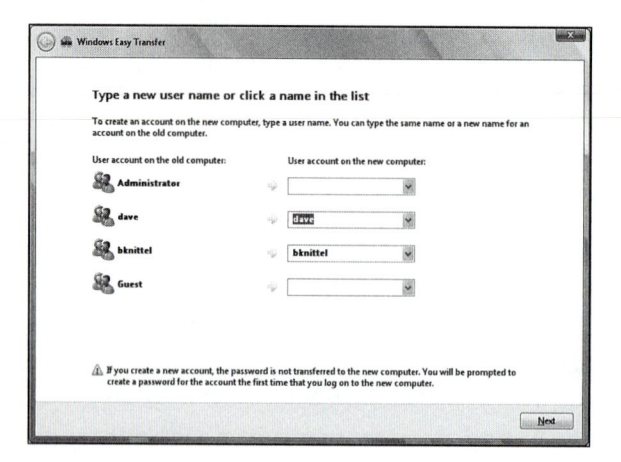

CAUTION

> The transfer process may have created new user accounts on your new Vista computer. For each account in turn, log on, and wait for a dialog box that asks you to enter the old computer's password. Note that this does *not* set the password on the new Vista computer, it just completes the transfer process. When the dialog is gone, press Ctrl+Alt+Del, select Change a Password, and set a password for the account. Then, log off and repeat with any other added accounts.

You may then want to jump back to "Change Account Settings" earlier in this chapter to tune up the settings for each added user account.

Windows Easy Transfer Companion

Microsoft has developed an additional transfer tool called Windows Easy Transfer Companion, which doesn't transfer documents and settings, but actual application software, from Windows XP to Windows Vista only. The program is available as a free download from microsoft.com (search for "Windows Easy Transfer Companion") and may be included with the Easy Transfer USB cable package. At the time this was written, it was still designated as a beta product, but it's been labeled that way for over a year, so we suspect that it's as finished as it's going to get. It can perform the transfer over either a network connection, with both computers on the same local area network, or an Easy Transfer USB cable.

NOTE

> Your new Vista computer must have the same number of hard drives and should have the same hard drive layout as your XP computer. For example, if your XP computer had two hard disk partitions named C: and D:, and Windows XP was installed on drive C:, the Easy Transfer Companion probably won't work unless your Vista computer has the same configuration.

NOTE

This procedure doesn't delete the transferred applications from your XP computer. But the license that you agreed to when you installed each application may forbid you from using it on more than one computer or even from transferring it from one to another. Check each application's license to be sure that it's okay for you to transfer the application. If a transfer is allowed but only one installation is permitted, after you've tested the application and are sure that you want to keep the copy on your Vista computer, you might be bound by the terms of your agreement to uninstall the copy on XP.

If you want to try this tool, you must download and install the Companion program on both your Windows XP computer and your Windows Vista computer. You must be logged on as a computer Administrator on both computers, with no one else logged on and no other applications running. Run the program on XP first and select the connection method. Then, run the program on Windows Vista.

To ensure privacy, the XP side of the connection displays a key number, as shown on the left side of Figure 3.13. Type this number into the Vista side. After a bit of chewing and thinking, the Vista side displays a list of programs that can be transferred, as shown on the right side of Figure 3.13. It also lists applications that it can't transfer, along with reasons why.

Figure 3.13
The Windows Easy Transfer Companion copies applications from Windows XP to Vista.

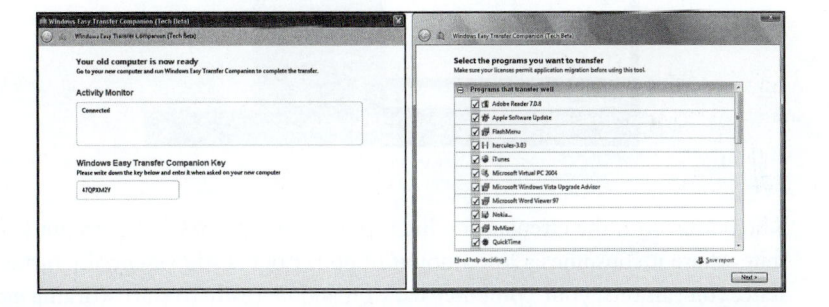

Uncheck any applications that you don't want to copy to your Vista computer and click Next. The program data will be copied over the network or USB link, your Vista computer will restart, and the applications should then be ready to use.

NOTE

If you're unhappy with the results, you can uninstall individual applications from the Control Panel, or you can undo the entire transfer. However, the undo procedure really rewinds your PC back to its state before the migration, so you'd lose changes even to documents that were unrelated to the transferred programs. If you're going to undo, decide to do it right away!

LOG OFF OR SHUT DOWN

We end our tour and setup hour by showing you how to log off and turn off your computer.

Windows Vista still requires you to stop by clicking the Start button—but at least it doesn't say Start anymore. So, click Start and look at the bottom of the Start menu, as indicated in Figure 3.14.

Figure 3.14
Sleep and other logoff and shutdown options on the Start menu.

The button with the circular graphic is the Sleep button. Click it to put your computer into state where it consumes a low amount of power but is still essentially turned on. In this state, you can turn your computer back on and be ready to start working again in a few seconds. But, if the computer loses power, Windows will not have a chance to shut down properly, and you could lose data if you hadn't saved your documents.

> **NOTE**
>
> If you leave the computer alone in this state for a certain amount of time, Windows will automatically turn the computer back on, save its memory to disk, and then really power itself off. This is called *hibernation*. When you turn the computer back on, it'll take longer to restart.

If you click the small right-pointing triangular arrow, Windows offers several other options. We discuss all of them in Chapter 4, "Using the Windows Vista Interface." The most important three are

- **Switch User**—Select this to stay logged in but let someone else use the computer for a while.
- **Log Off**—Select this to sign off from your account. The computer remains on so that someone else can use it.
- **Shut Down**—Select this to turn off your computer and shut it down. Always shut down Windows (or hibernate it) before unplugging it, or in the case of a laptop, storing it for more than a day or so.

This ends our tour. To close the book, so to speak, click the Start menu's Sleep button and watch Windows power off. When it's asleep, press your computer's power button briefly and see how fast it can power back up.

MORE THAN YOU WANTED TO KNOW

In the remainder of this chapter, I cover some more advanced topics that some of you may want to know about, and some of you won't. Feel free to skim the rest of the chapter and read just what interests you. You're probably itching to start poking around with Vista now anyway, and you can always come back to these items later on if the need arises.

Now, let's go on to learn where Vista stores your documents, music, and so on, and how this differs from previous versions of Windows.

WHERE'S MY STUFF, OR THE USER PROFILE STRUCTURE

Windows Vista stores your documents, music, and pictures in a different folder layout than did Windows XP and earlier versions of Windows.

In Vista, each user's personal files are stored in a folder with the same name as the user account inside folder \Users. (In some cases, Windows adds other letters or numbers to the username to create a unique folder name.)

This folder is called a *user profile*, and it contains not only your personal documents but also some hidden files that contain your personal Windows Registry data (which contains information used by Windows and application programs), temporary files used by Internet Explorer, and so on. Another folder inside \users is named Public, and this folder can be used by any of the computer's users. It's a place to put files that you want to share with anyone else.

In Windows Vista, you *can't* store files inside \Program Files, \Windows, or the root (top) folder of the drive on which Windows is installed, although you can create folders there and put files in the new folders.

The new directory structure looks like this:

```
C:\
   Windows
   Program Data
   Program Files
```

```
Users
    myname
    yourname
    ...
    Default
    Public
```

Here's a brief tour:

- The Windows and Program Files folders have the same purpose as preceding versions of Windows—to hold Windows and application programs, respectively.

- The Program Data folder is hidden, so you won't see it unless you elected to show hidden files earlier in the chapter in the section "Disable Hide Extensions for Known File Types." Its Start Menu subfolder contains Start Menu items that are displayed to all users. This was folder \Documents and Settings\All Users\Start Menu on Windows XP.

- The Users folder contains user profiles, the Public folder (which contains the rest of what was \Documents and Settings\All Users in Windows XP), and the Default user profile, which is discussed in "Tips from the Windows Pros: Configuring the Default User Profile" at the end of this chapter.

A User profile folder for a given account is created only when the user logs on for the first time. The hidden Default folder is used to create the new profile.

The user profile folder for the account named "myname" is c:\users\myname, the folder for the account named "yourname" is c:\users\yourname, and so on.

Inside each user's profile folder is a series of subfolders, which are listed in Table 3.1.

Table 3.1 Subfolders in a Vista User Profile

Folder Name	Purpose
AppData (hidden folder)	Per-user application data. Subfolders Local, LocalLow, and Roaming are used to separate data that will never leave this computer from data that should be copied back to a central server if the account is on a corporate network with roaming profiles.
Contacts	Address book data.
Desktop	Files and shortcuts that appear on the desktop.
Documents*	Personal documents. This folder is My Documents in Windows XP.
Downloads	Files downloaded from the Internet.
Favorites	Favorites links for Internet Explorer.
Links	Shortcuts to important Windows folders.
Music	Personal folder for music files.
Pictures	Personal folder for images.
Saved Games	Data saved by games.

Folder Name	Purpose
Searches	Saved search queries.
Videos	Personal folder for multimedia files.

* displayed in Windows Explorer as **My Documents** or **Username's Documents**
⁺ displayed in Windows Explorer as **Shared Documents**
† displayed in Windows Explorer as Public Desktop, Public Documents, etc.

Don't worry about having to know where these files are. Windows Explorer locates and displays them for you when you click Start, Computer. They appear in the file tree listing near Desktop under your account name.

> **NOTE**
> There is also a special hidden "virtual" folder named \Documents and Settings that is there to let old applications that assume the old Windows XP structure work correctly. It contains shortcuts to the new folder locations, but the folder itself isn't actually there, and you should just ignore it. We'll explain this "virtual folder" feature in the next section.

If you are familiar with the user profile folder structure used in Windows XP, you might want to look at Table 3.2, which compares the Vista and XP structures side by side.

TABLE 3.2 VISTA AND XP USER PROFILE STRUCTURES

Folder Structure in Windows Vista	Equivalent Folders in Windows XP
\Users	\Documents and Settings
Username	\Documents and Settings*Username*
AppData	
Local	\Documents and Settings*Username*\Local Settings
Temp	\Documents and Settings*Username*\Local Settings\Temp
VirtualStore	
LocalLow	
Roaming	\Documents and Settings*Username*\Application Data
Microsoft	
Windows	
Cookies	\Documents and Settings*Username*\Cookies
Network Shortcuts	\Documents and Settings*Username*\NetHood
Printer Shortcuts	\Documents and Settings*Username*\PrintHood
Recent	\Documents and Settings*Username*\My Recent Documents
SendTo	\Documents and Settings*Username*\SendTo
Start Menu	\Documents and Settings*Username*\Start Menu

continues

Table 3.2 Continued

Folder Structure in Windows Vista	Equivalent Folders in Windows XP
Templates	\Documents and Settings*Username*\Templates
Themes	
Contacts	
Desktop	\Documents and Settings*Username*\Desktop
Documents*	\Documents and Settings*Username*\My Documents*
Downloads	
Favorites	\Documents and Settings*Username*\Favorites
Links	
Music	\Documents and Settings*Username*\My Documents\My Music
Pictures	\Documents and Settings*Username*\My Documents\My Pictures
Saved Games	
Searches	
Videos	
Public	
Desktop†	\Documents and Settings\All Users\Desktop
Documents†	\Documents and Settings\All Users\Documents⁺
Downloads	
Favorites	\Documents and Settings\All Users\Favorites
Music	\Documents and Settings\All Users\Documents\My Music
Pictures	\Documents and Settings\All Users\Documents\My Pictures
Recorded TV	
Videos	\Documents and Settings\All Users\Documents\My Videos
Default (same subfolders as standard user)	\Documents and Settings\Default User (same subfolders as standard user)
\ProgramData	\Documents and Settings\All Users\Application Data
Microsoft	
Windows	
Start Menu	\Documents and Settings\All Users\Start Menu
Templates	\Documents and Settings\All Users\Templates

* displayed in Windows Explorer as **My Documents** or **Username's Documents**
⁺ displayed in Windows Explorer as **Shared Documents**
† displayed in Windows Explorer as Public Desktop, Public Documents, etc.

Correctly written application programs won't need to know about these differences; Windows has mechanisms to provide the paths to these various folders to programs based on their function, rather than their location. Still, for those applications whose programmers "wired-in" the old XP structure, Vista has a mechanism to let them run without problems, as I'll show you in the next section.

PROFILE COMPATIBILITY JUNCTION POINTS

Windows Vista setup creates *junction points* and *symbolic links* in the Windows drive that provide a measure of compatibility with applications that were hard-wired to expect the Windows XP user profile structure. Junction points and symbolic links are special "virtual" folders that point to other, real folders. When a program attempts to examine files in the virtual folder, Windows shows it the files in the real folder. This mechanism is used in Vista to support older applications; if they attempt to read from folder \Documents and Settings, for example, Windows shows them the contents of \Users. Table 3.3 lists the junction points and symbolic links that are installed in Windows Vista. You should ignore these folder names; don't delete them, and to the extent possible, forget that they exist. They are hidden system files by default, so you only see them, in fact, when you instruct Windows Explorer or the `dir` command line command to display hidden and system files.

TABLE 3.3 COMPATIBILITY JUNCTION POINTS AND SYMBOLIC LINKS

Junction or Link	Target Folder
\Documents and Settings	\Users
\Users	
Username	
Application Data	\Users*username*\AppData\Roaming
Cookies	\Users*username*\AppData\Roaming\Microsoft\Windows\Cookies
Local Settings	\Users*username*\AppData\Local
My Documents	\Users*username*\Documents
NetHood	\Users*username*\AppData\Roaming\Microsoft\Windows\ Network Shortcuts
PrintHood	\Users*username*\AppData\Roaming\Microsoft\Windows\ Printer Shortcuts
Recent	\Users*username*\AppData\Roaming\Microsoft\Windows\Recent
SendTo	\Users*username*\AppData\Roaming\Microsoft\Windows\SendTo
Templates	\Users*username*\AppData\Roaming\Microsoft\Windows\Templates
All Users	\ProgramData

continues

Table 3.3 Continued

Junction or Link	Target Folder
\ProgramData	
Application Data	\ProgramData
Desktop	\Users\Public\Desktop
Documents	\Users\Public\Documents
Favorites	\Users\Public\Favorites
Start Menu	\ProgramData\Microsoft\Windows\StartMenu
Templates	\ProgramData\Microsoft\Windows\Templates

Here is an example of how this set of junction points and links assists older applications. If an application attempts to access the contents of folder `\Documents and Settings\All Users\Start Menu`, the following folder name transformation takes place:

1. `\Documents and Settings` is translated to `\Users`, so the path becomes `\Users\All Users\Start Menu`
2. Next, `\Users\All` is translated to `\Program Data`, so the path becomes `\Program Data\Start Menu`
3. Finally, `\ProgramData\StartMenu` is translated to `\ProgramData\Microsoft\Windows\StartMenu`

The application is shown the contents of this final folder name. Thus, it sees the Start Menu items in the folder used by Vista, even though it used the path name used by XP.

Compatibility and Virtualization

In previous versions of Windows, applications could store files inside the \Program Files and \Windows folders, and they often took advantage of this to store common data that was shared among all users. The same was true for the Registry, a database of user and setup information—programs frequently stored information in the HKEY_LOCAL_MACHINE Registry section.

To make Vista more secure, user programs are no longer allowed to store files or Registry data in these areas unless their setup programs explicitly change Windows security settings to permit it. (And this has to happen while the program is being installed under elevated privileges.)

Most of the applications that ship with Windows are subject to these restrictions. Try it yourself—open Notepad, type a few words, and try to save a file in \Program Files. You can't. Any application that Windows deems as "modern" (or "should know better") is entirely blocked from saving information in these protected areas. (Technically, the presence of a manifest file tells Windows that the program is "modern.")

Older programs, however, expect to write in these privileged directories and Registry areas, and to maintain compatibility Vista gives them an assist called *file and Registry virtualization*. What happens is that if an older program attempts to create a file in one of the protected folders or Registry areas and access is blocked, and the program is not running with elevated permissions and the file doesn't have a manifest file, Vista stores the file or Registry data in an alternate, safer location. Whenever an older program tries to read a file or Registry data from a protected location, Vista first checks the alternate location to see whether it had been shunted there earlier and, if so, returns the data from that location.

Thus the application doesn't actually store information in the secure locations but thinks it has.

Why am I explaining this to you? There are two reasons:

- One consequence of virtualization is that programs that try to share data between users can't. Each user will see only his or her private copy of the files that should have been stored in a common place. For example, in the "high score" list in a game, each user may see only his or her own name and scores. This may also cause problems with programs that track licensing or registration.
- If you go searching for files in Windows Explorer or the command-line prompt, you won't see the files that got virtualized where you expected them to be because explorer.exe and cmd.exe have manifests—they don't get the virtualization treatment.

The first problem can't be helped; the older programs just have to be redesigned and replaced. Knowing that virtualization occurs, you can work around the second problem by knowing where to look.

Files intended for \Windows or \Program Files (or any of their subfolders) will be placed into \users*username*\AppData\Local\VirtualStore\Windows or ...\Program Files, respectively.

> **NOTE**
> If you view a folder in \Windows or \Program Files in Windows Explorer, a button appears on the Compatibility Files window. If you click this button, Explorer displays the corresponding subfolder in your VirtualStore folder. This is an easy way to examine your virtualized files.

Registry data intended for HKEY_LOCAL_MACHINE will be shunted to HKEY_CURRENT_USER\Software\Classes\VirtualStore\Machine. There is no quick-view button in the Registry editor, so to find this data, you have to browse to it.

> **NOTE**
> Some Registry keys are not virtualized in any case. For example, most keys under HKEY_LOCAL_MACHINE\Software\Microsoft\Windows will not be virtualized; attempts to write data in this key or most of its subkeys will simply fail. This prevents rogue applications from creating startup program Run entries.

Creating User Groups

Windows Vista takes full advantage of the Windows NTFS file system structure, which lets you and Windows control precisely which users are allowed to read or write each file and Windows Registry key.

If you want to adjust security settings on files, and if you have many users on your computer or network, you may find it tiresome to specify each individual who should be allowed to access specific files and folders. For example, in the workplace, you might want to let accounting and management have access to folders with payroll and accounting information but no one else.

Instead of adding each payroll and management staff member to the list of users allowed to access the payroll folders, you can create a *user group* with a list of usernames and set the folders' security so that the group can access them. This makes management simpler, and you can later change the list of people who can access the accounting folders by editing just the group list rather than every folder's security list.

To create a user group in Windows Vista, follow these steps:

1. Log on as a Computer Administrator. Click Start, right-click Computer, and select Manage.
2. In the left pane, open the Local Users and Groups item; then select the Groups item underneath it.
3. Right-click the white space in the right pane and select New Group.
4. Enter an appropriate name, such as Accounting. Then click Add.
5. Click Advanced; then click Find Now. Locate the logon name of a user whom you want to be in the group and double-click the name.
6. Repeat step 5 as many times as needed to add other usernames to the group.
7. Click OK, and the names should now appear in the new group list, as shown in Figure 3.15.
8. Finally, click Create and then click Close.

You can later return to this window and add or delete names from the group list.

When the group has been created, you can assign file access rights to the group, as shown in Figure 3.16. Setting file access permissions is discussed in more detail in Chapter 34, "Protecting Your Data from Loss and Theft."

After You Forget Your Password

Forgetting the password to your computer account is an unpleasant experience. It's definitely no fun to have your own computer thumb its proverbial nose at you and tell you it's not going to let you in to get your own files. If this happens to you, take a deep breath. You might recover from this. Here are the steps to try, in order of preference:

Figure 3.15
User groups can help you manage access to files and folders.

Figure 3.16
You can assign file access rights to a group just as easily as to a user.

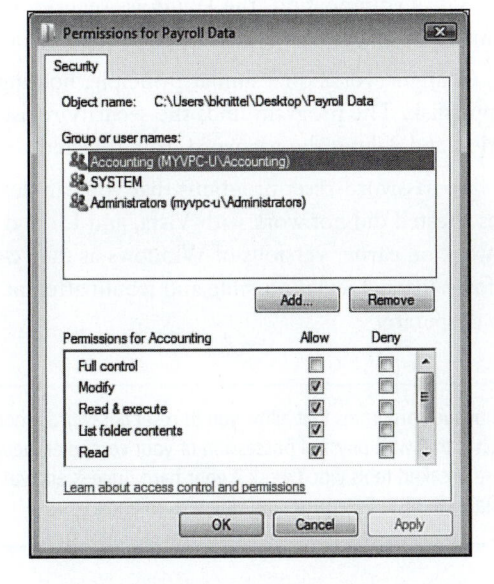

1. If you created a password reset disk, as described in earlier in the chapter in the section "Before You Forget Your Password," you're in good shape. Follow the instructions in the next section "Using a Password Recovery Disk."
2. If you are a member of a domain network, contact the network administrator to have her reset your password. The administrator *might* be able to recover any encrypted files you created.
3. Log on as a Computer Administrator user and use the User Accounts control panel to change your primary account's password.

> **CAUTION**
>
> If you have to resort to option number three (logging on as an administrator and changing your primary account's password), you will lose any stored website passwords linked to your account, and, worse, you will lose any files that you encrypted using Windows file encryption (a feature found on Vista Business, Enterprise, and Ultimate only). There will be absolutely *no way* to recover the encrypted files.

4. If you don't remember the password to any Administrator account, or you can't find someone else who does, you're in big trouble. Programs are available that can break into Windows and reset one of the Computer Administrator account's password. It's a gamble—there's a chance these programs might blow out your Windows installation. Still, if you're in this situation, you probably will want to risk it. Here are some programs you might look into:

   - Windows Key from LostPassword.com creates a Linux boot disk, which pokes through your NTFS disk volume, finds the Windows security Registry file, and replaces the administrator's password so that you can reboot and log on.

   - Active@ Password Changer works on a similar principle, booting up in Free-DOS from a CD or floppy disk. The program finds the security registry file on your Windows installation and deletes the password from selected accounts.

   - There are several free password-reset programs that you can download from the Internet. The ones I tested did not work with Vista, and I found that some of them didn't even work on earlier versions of Windows as they claimed to. I'd try to get one of the for-sale products if possible and would attempt a free program only if I was *really* desperate.

> **CAUTION**
>
> The existence of such programs that allow you to reset passwords should raise your eyebrows. The fact is that with physical possession of your computer, people can get into it. However, these break-in tools won't work if your hard drive is encrypted with BitLocker, a feature available in Vista Enterprise and Ultimate editions.

5. If you need to retrieve only files, you can remove the hard drive and install it in another Windows Vista, XP, or 2000 computer as a *secondary* drive. Boot it up, log on as an Administrator, and browse into the added drive. You probably need to take ownership of the drive's files to read them. (If the hard drive is encrypted with BitLocker, this technique won't work either).

6. If you get this far and are still stuck, things are pretty grim. You'll need to reinstall Windows using the Clean Install option, which will erase all your user settings. Then, as an Administrator, you can browse into the \users folder to retrieve files from the old user account folders.

If you are not a member of a domain network, I hope you avoid all this by creating a password reset disk ahead of time.

Using a Password Recovery Disk

If you have lost your password but have a password reset disk that you made earlier, you can use it to log on. Just attempt to sign on using the Welcome screen. When the logon fails, click Reset Password. Then, follow the Password Reset Wizard's instructions to change your password and store the password reset disk away for another rainy day. You don't need to remake the disk after using it.

Accessing the Real Administrator Account

In Windows NT, 2000, and XP, there was an account named Administrator that was, by definition, a Computer Administrator account. You may have noticed that it's nowhere to be seen in Windows Vista.

Actually, it's still there, but hidden. There's a good reason for this. It's disabled by default and hidden on the Welcome screen and even in Safe Mode. And it requires no password to log on. This was done to provide a way to recover if you somehow manage to delete the last (other) Computer Administrator account from your computer. In this case, Windows will automatically enable the Administrator account so that you can log on (without having to remember a password) and re-create one or more Computer Administrator accounts, or turn a Standard User into an Administrator. (You would then immediately log off and use the restored regular account.)

This is a good fail-safe scheme, and we recommend that you leave it set up this way. Still, if for some reason you want to set a password on the Administrator account or use it directly, here's how:

1. Click Start, right-click Computer, and select Manage.
2. Select Local Users and Groups, and open the Users list.
3. Right-click Administrator and select Properties. Uncheck Account Is Disabled and click OK.
4. Log off; then log on as Administrator (which now appears on the Welcome screen).
5. Press Ctrl+Alt+Del, and click Change a Password.
6. We strongly urge you to click Create a Password Reset Disk and make a password reset disk for the Administrator account, as described earlier in this chapter. Be sure to store it in a secure place.
7. Back at Change a Password, leave the old password field blank and enter a new password as requested. Press Enter when you finish.

Now, the Administrator account is accessible and secured.

CAUTION
> When you are logged on using the real Administrator account, User Account Control is bypassed, and all privileged programs run with elevated privileges.

If you're worried that this passwordless Administrator account is a security risk, remember that by default it can't be accessed unless all other administrator accounts have been deleted, and only an administrator user could manage to do that. So, a nonadministrator can't do anything by himself to get to Administrator. If you enable the Administrator account and hack the Registry to display it on the Welcome screen, then yes, you *must* set a password on the account.

Tips from the Windows Pros: Configuring the Default User Profile

As you saw in this chapter, it can take quite a bit of time to tune up a user account and set it up "just so." There are Quick Launch icons to add, things to change in Windows Explorer and Internet Explorer, and potentially dozens of other applications. It's bad enough doing this once, but if you have many accounts on your computer and you want them all to be set up more or less the same way (at least initially), you're looking at a *lot* of setup time.

Fortunately, you can do this just once and have Windows use your settings as the base settings for other accounts. You can set up one account as you want it and copy that account's profile to the Default user profile so that all future accounts start with a copy of your finely tuned setup. The trick is that you have to do this before other users have logged on to the computer for the first time.

To use this technique to set up nicely pretweaked accounts on your computer, follow these steps:

1. Log on to a Computer Administrator account and set it up just as you want all the accounts to look. (Of course, other users can change things after they log on; you're just setting up their account's initial look and feel.)

   In addition to setting preferences, you can add icons to the desktop and Quick Launch bar and add documents to the Documents folder and favorites to the Favorites list in Internet Explorer. You can also delete marketing junk installed by Microsoft or your computer manufacturer.

2. Create an additional user account. Name it xyz, create it as an Administrator account, and don't bother setting a password for it.

3. Log out and then log in using the new account xyz. Windows sets up its standard desktop and profile but don't bother making any changes.
4. Click Start, Computer. Click Organize, Folder, and Search Options. Select the View tab and select Show Hidden Files and Folders. Click OK; then close Computer.
5. Click Start, Control Panel, System and Maintenance, System; then in the left Tasks list, select Advanced System Settings.
6. In the middle User Profiles section, click Settings.
7. Select the entry for the account that you originally logged on to and set up. Click Copy To. Then click Browse.
8. In the Browse For Folder dialog box, open the drive that Windows is installed on, dig into Users, and select Default, as shown in Figure 3.17. Click OK to close the browse dialog box; then click OK to close the Copy To dialog.

Figure 3.17
Copy the tuned-up profile to \users\Default.

9. When prompted, click Yes to overwrite the original default profile.
10. When the copying finishes, close all the windows and log out.
11. Log back in to the original account.
12. Click Start, Control Panel, User Accounts and Family Safety, Add or Remove User Accounts.
13. Select account xyz and click Delete the Account. Click Delete Files; then click Delete Account.

Now, when any other user logs on for the first time, his user profile will be created from the copy you just created, with the settings, files, and icons exactly as you set them.

PART II

USING WINDOWS VISTA

4 Using the Windows Vista Interface   121

5 Managing Files and Searching   163

6 Printing   203

7 Sidebar and Other Supplied Accessories   233

CHAPTER 4

USING THE WINDOWS VISTA INTERFACE

In this chapter

Who Should Read This Chapter?   122

Logging In to Windows Vista   123

Using Windows Vista—The User Experience   124

The Taskbar, the Start Menu, and Other Tools   138

Running Your Applications   145

Using the Help System   153

Exiting Windows Gracefully   154

Dealing with a Crashed Application or Operating System   156

Troubleshooting   157

Tips from the Windows Pros: Working Efficiently   159

Who Should Read This Chapter?

Many might wonder why an advanced book such as this includes coverage of something as basic as the Windows user interface. This is a decision that was primarily driven by the knowledge that many users of Windows Vista will be upgrading from Windows 9*x*, NT, 2000, and even XP. For those users, savvy as they might be with Windows concepts, the Windows Vista interface is different enough that they'll need a roadmap to get started. When you are familiar with it, you'll wonder how you ever got around in those old clunky environments. In addition to just the new look of Windows Vista, many new functions are woven into the fabric of the new user interface (UI)—we don't want you to miss out on them. We've also included some UI tips and tricks that you might not know about. So even if you consider yourself a Windows veteran, at least take the time to skim through this chapter before you move on.

> **NOTE**
>
> Upgrading might not be just for the fun of it. Microsoft stopped offering support for MS-DOS, Windows 1.0-3.*x*, Windows for Workgroups, and Windows 95 on December 31, 2001. Support for Windows 98 (OSR2 and SE), Me, and Windows NT 4 Workstation was dropped on June 30, 2003. Support for Windows 2000 Professional ended on June 30, 2005. And support for Windows XP Service Pack 1 ended on October 10, 2006. When Microsoft says it will be dropping support, that means the Microsoft technical support system will not respond to calls or email with questions regarding these operating systems. In addition, and more importantly, Microsoft will no longer locate and fix security problems in these older operating systems. So upgrade or be left in the dust.

Don't just take our word for it. Experiment with the new user interface as you read this chapter. We've found that nothing can substitute for direct hands-on operation to get an understanding and a feel for the new user environment. Most of the information in this chapter is not of a level or type that can damage your system, but whenever caution is needed, we spell it out clearly.

We aren't able to cover everything about the new environment in this chapter, but we do a good job of covering the important aspects and those of interest to most readers. If you run across a button or command that you don't recognize, don't be afraid to explore the Windows Help service for details and instructions. The Vista Help system is much improved over its predecessors and actually includes meaningful content.

→ For those looking for ways to tweak and customize the new GUI, take a look at Chapter 26, "Tweaking the GUI," **p. 897**.

If at any time you want to put this book down and walk away from your system, jump to the "Exiting Windows Gracefully" section near the end of this chapter to find out how to log off with aplomb.

Logging In to Windows Vista

In Chapter 3, "The First Hour," we briefly showed you how to log on, and gave you a quick tour of the operating system. We'll cover the logon process and the Welcome screen in more detail in this section.

When Windows Vista starts up, you need to log on before you can start to work. There are three ways that this logon process can occur, depending on how your computer was set up:

- In most cases, you will see the Welcome screen, which displays a list of user account names and pictures. Locate and click your account name. If asked for a password, type in your password, then press Enter.

- If your computer is a member of a domain network (as is usually the case in a corporate setting), the screen may instruct you to press Ctrl+Alt+Del to log on. Hold down the Ctrl and Alt keys, and then strike the Del key. Then, when prompted, enter your logon information, as provided by your network administrator. This will include a username, password, and location, which is the network's domain name. To use a local account instead of a domain account, that is, a user account that is defined only in your computer, enter the name of your computer as the location.

- If your computer's bootup process takes you right to the Windows desktop, it's been set up to log on to an account automatically. You can leave it like this, if you want, and still use the Log Off or Switch Users feature to log on with other user accounts. Alternatively, you can disable the automatic logon feature and have Windows display the Welcome screen at startup.

→ For more information about automatic logons, **see** "Just One User?," **p. 93**.

By the way, it's likely that shortly after installing Windows, or upon booting the first time and logging in, you'll see a "balloon" notification at the bottom of your screen, warning you that your computer might be at risk because you do not have antivirus protection. Clicking on the balloon brings up the Windows Security Center. See the section "Windows Security Center" in Chapter 25, "Windows Management and Maintenance," for more about the Windows Security Center.

Logging On from the Welcome Screen

On most systems, you'll see the Welcome screen every time Windows starts up. You may also see it when another user has logged off, when someone has disconnected from Windows using Switch User, when the system has been locked, or after the screen saver has kicked in.

If you see the Welcome screen, just click on your user account to log on. The Welcome screen presents a list of available user accounts that can be used to access this system. If a password is associated with a selected account, you are prompted to provide it.

If you have forgotten your password, click the question mark. If there was a hint defined for your account, Windows will display the hint so that you might remember the password.

If you forget your password, and you previously created a password reset disk, you can use the reset disk to gain access to your account. If you don't have a password reset disk, you'll have to have another user log on using a Computer Administrator account and reset your account's password for you. This process could make you lose access to some information in your account, including website passwords that Windows remembered for you, and if you were using the Encrypted Files feature on Windows Vista Business, Enterprise or Ultimate edition, you could lose your encrypted files too. So, we strongly urge you to create a password reset disk for your account.

→ To learn how to create and use a password reset disk, **see** "Before Your Forget Your Password," **p. 91**.

After you've logged in, it's time to explore the user interface—or, as Microsoft likes to call it, the *user experience*.

USING WINDOWS VISTA—THE USER EXPERIENCE

Windows Vista has a familiar yet different user interface. Most of the visual aspects of the desktop environment have been updated, but you'll find most of the tools and applications you remember from Windows 9*x* and Windows 2000 right where you expect. The new interface or user experience is called Aero. Aero includes visual updates and improvements to all native dialog boxes, displays, windows, and interfaces. Most notably, these changes are seen on the Start menu, in navigability within and between windows, in Windows Explorer, and in the Control Panel. If you want the older stylings of previous Windows versions (mainly Windows 2000–era visual stylings), revert to the "classic" style. However, we highly recommend giving the new look and feel a try for a week or so before ditching it.

Microsoft's visual palette now has three different user styles to choose from:

- Windows Classic, which contains the same user interface as Windows 2000 and earlier versions, if you still prefer that interface.
- Vista Standard, which further refines the user interface updates in Windows XP with softer colors and a title bar that is integrated into the window frame.
- Aero, which provides a semitransparent "glass" look for the taskbars, menu bars, and window frames, as well as advanced features. Those features include Flip, which shows thumbnails of open programs when you move the mouse pointer over an application button in the button bar, animated windows when opening and closing windows, and Flip 3D for "flipping" between 3D representations of your windows. Aero is processor intensive and, therefore, needs a high-grade video graphics card installed on your computer to work.

But even with all the enhancements, everything still seems to have a similar function or placement to that of Windows 2000 and XP, and it's not too different from Windows 9*x* or Me. Thus, you'll easily leverage your existing experience and expertise in navigating and operating Windows Vista. After a few days, you'll soon forget how you got by without all these useful improvements.

> **NOTE**
>
> For a nearly exhaustive list of keyboard shortcuts for navigating and controlling aspects of Windows Vista, check out the "Windows Keyboard Shortcuts Overview" document, available through the Help and Support Center. Just click Start, Help and Support; type in the title in the Search field; and then click the blue magnifying glass. It should appear under Best 30 Results, so click on that link in the Search Results to get to it.

However, Windows is more than just an operating system and graphical user interface. Like other versions of Windows, Windows Vista includes a broad collection of useful programs, from a simple arithmetic calculator to a fancy system and network-management tools. This list also includes a word-processing program called WordPad, a drawing program called Paint, Internet Explorer for cruising the Web, Windows Mail for email, Windows Movie Maker for creating digital movies, Windows Meeting Space for video and telephone conferencing over the Internet, CD-burning software that lets you create your own CDs, DVD-burning and playback tools, utilities for keeping your hard disk in good working order, and a data-backup program—just to name a few.

PARTS OF THE WINDOWS VISTA SCREEN

At this point, you should be booted and signed in. After you've logged in, Windows Vista deposits you in its basic environment (called the *desktop*). You'll probably notice two things almost immediately: first, the taskbar at the bottom of the screen, and second, an empty (or nearly so) desktop (see Figure 4.1). The taskbar is the central control mechanism for the Windows Vista user experience. It hosts the Start menu, the Quick Launch bar, active program buttons, the notification area (previously called the system tray, in XP), and the clock. The only item that is present on your desktop is the Recycle Bin, although if you purchased a computer system with Vista preinstalled, you might see other icons as well. Notice that it's now located by default in the bottom-right corner. (That's awfully Macintosh-ish, don't you think?)

> **NOTE**
>
> If you or someone else has used your Windows Vista setup already, it's possible that some open windows will come up on the screen automatically when Windows boots (starts up). It's also possible that you'll see more icons on the desktop than what's shown in Figure 4.1, depending on the options chosen when Windows Vista was installed, whether other applications were loaded before upgrading, and whether custom shortcuts to the desktop have been defined.

Figure 4.1
The default desktop with the Start menu open.

You have three primary areas of the screen to explore: the desktop, icons, and the taskbar.

> **NOTE**
> You may also see some items on the right edge of your desktop such as a clock or calendar, or a news or stock ticker. These are clever desktop add-ons called Sidebar gadgets and are covered in Chapter 7, "Sidebar and Other Supplied Accessories."

All you really must know to use Windows Vista's interface are these essential building blocks and how to manipulate a window and its commands. If you've been using Windows 3.x, 9x, NT, 2000, or XP, you already know the latter. You just need to be brought up to speed on the advanced Vista interface specifics. As mentioned in the introduction, for the purposes of this book, we assume that you have basic Windows proficiency and have been using Windows 9x, NT, 2000, or XP. Therefore, we skip subjects such as how to click using the mouse, what double-clicking is, and how to scroll a window. (If you want a tutorial in Windows basics that covers topics like that, you might want to check out Shelley O'Hara's *Easy Microsoft Windows Vista* [Que, 2006; ISBN 0789735776].)

THE DESKTOP

Let's start with the desktop. This is your home base while doing your work in Windows. It is always on the screen as the backdrop (whether you see it or not) and you can deposit files and folders right on it for storage. It's analogous to a real desktop in this way. It also serves as a handy temporary holding area for files you might be copying from, say, a floppy disk to a hard disk folder. The *Recycle Bin* holds deleted work objects such as files and folders until you empty it (with caveats). Just as in previous versions of Windows (or the Mac for that matter, if you're coming from that background), you'll do all your work in Windows Vista using graphical representations of your files and applications (called *icons*).

All the desktop icons you are familiar with from Windows 9*x* and 2000 have been moved to the Start menu. (And if you upgraded from Windows XP, then the Windows Vista Start menu will look *very* familiar.) You can gain access to Computer, Documents, and Network with a simple click on the Start button. If you revert to the previous Windows 2000 Start menu (called classic), these items reappear on the desktop (see Chapter 26, "Tweaking the GUI"). In either case, you control which icons or shortcuts appear on your desktop. You can add icons and shortcuts to your desktop to your heart's content.

The Recycle Bin

The Recycle Bin acts a bit like the waste paper basket at the side of your desk. After you throw something into it, it's basically trash to be thrown out; however, you can still retrieve items from it if you get there before the cleaning staff takes it and throws it away for good. Within Windows Vista, the Recycle Bin holds those files you've deleted using Windows Explorer or Computer. It does not capture files deleted by third-party tools, files deleted from floppies or network drives, files removed with an uninstall program or from DOS boxes, and DOS files running in a DOS box.

The Recycle Bin has limited storage capacity. However, Windows Vista provides each user with a default amount of Recycle Bin space specified in megabytes. When the maximum size of the Recycle Bin is reached, the oldest files are permanently removed from the hard drive to make room for newly deleted files. The size of the Recycle Bin can be customized as a percentage across all drives or as a unique size on each individual volume. The Recycle Bin is customized through its Properties dialog box (see Figure 4.2). The configuration options are discussed in Chapter 26, but if you want to get there now, just right-click on the Recycle Bin icon and select Properties from the pop-up menu.

After a file is removed from the Recycle Bin, it cannot be recovered using native tools. You must restore the files from a backup, use a third-party recover tool (which often needs to be in place before the file is deleted), or live without the lost files. If you don't want your excess trash sitting around, you can also configure the system to bypass the Recycle Bin entirely so that it permanently deletes files immediately instead of granting you a recovery period.

To restore a file still retained in the Recycle Bin, double-click the desktop icon to open the Recycle Bin, locate and select the file to restore, and then click the Restore This Item button in the toolbar (see Figure 4.3). The file/folder(s) then are returned to the original location.

Figure 4.2
The Recycle Bin Properties dialog box.

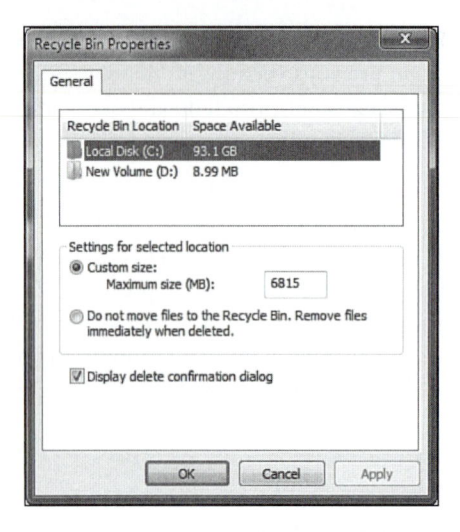

Figure 4.3
Restoring a file from the Recycle Bin.

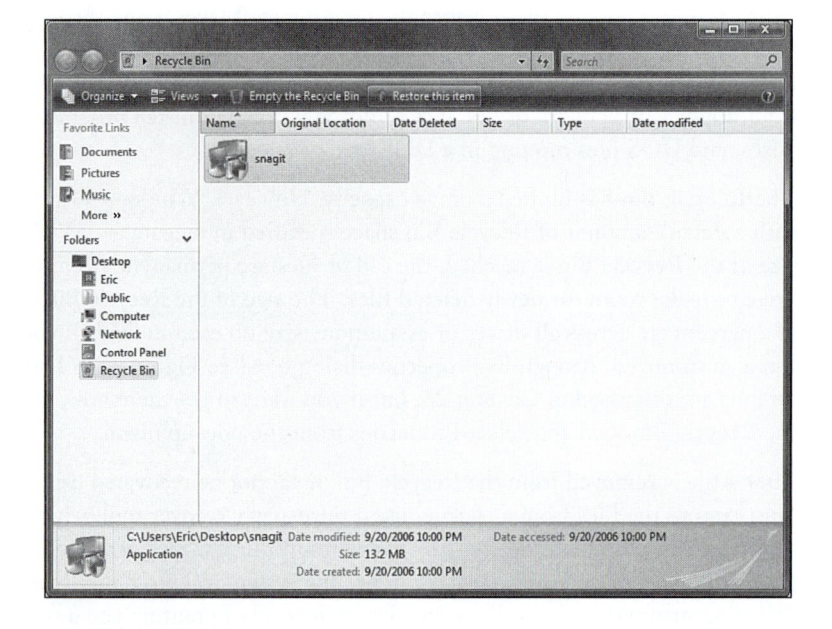

You can also manually empty the Recycle Bin. This is often a useful activity before defragmenting your hard drive or if you just want to permanently delete files and folders. The Empty Recycle Bin command, found in the right-click pop-up menu for the icon, the File menu (be sure no items are selected—otherwise, the File menu's context changes to file/folder restore operations), and the Recycle Bin Tasks list of the Recycle Bin interface, is used to clear out all files that are being retained.

CAUTION
> Don't try moving program files unless you know that they have not registered themselves with the operating system and they can harmlessly be moved between folders. If you must move applications, use a tool specifically designed for this.

CAUTION
> If you delete files in folders shared by other computers on a network, or delete files by typing commands into the Command Prompt window, the files are *not* moved to the Recycle Bin. They're deleted instantly and permanently.

Icons

As know, the small graphical representations of your programs and files are called *icons*. Windows Vista uses icons to represent folders, documents, programs, and groups of settings (such as dial-up connections). Graphically, icons got an Aero face-lift in Windows Vista, even when compared to their Windows XP counterparts. In most cases, the default icon displayed for an object somewhat represents the function of that object.

NOTE
> In recent versions of Windows, Microsoft has begun using the term *folder* instead of *directory*. They want to focus your thoughts toward the idea of your files being stored on the hard drive in a manner similar to that of a filing cabinet for manila folders. Although we think this analogy is helpful, we don't always stick to Microsoft-speak. So if you see *folder* or *directory* anywhere in this book, keep in mind that we consider them to be the same thing.

Icons are either objects themselves or shortcuts. A shortcut is a means to gain access to an object from multiple locations throughout the environment. Shortcuts are the preferred way to access the same object from multiple locations, to avoid having to make duplicate copies of the original object or application. Duplicating the object often causes version problems, such as never knowing which one has your most recent changes, and difficulties in upgrading or replacing applications. Shortcuts eliminate these issues and take up less space. You could have thousands of shortcuts pointing to the same application or document and still save drive space.

Additionally, a shortcut can define alternative launching parameters, such as default directories, command-line parameters, compatibility mode, and so on. To alter the settings of a shortcut, just right-click and select Properties from the pop-up menu.

NOTE

Compatibility mode is a nifty feature that enables Windows Vista to support a wider range of software products than Windows 95 and Windows NT combined. A compatibility mode is simply a designation for a software platform–emulation environment. In other words, when an application is launched with compatibility mode enabled, a virtual machine representing that application's native environment (Windows 9x, Windows NT, Windows 2000, or Windows XP) is created in such a way that the application is fooled into thinking that it is the only application present on the computer system running its preferred OS.

If you have installed a 64-bit version of Windows Vista (available in all editions except the Starter Edition), then you cannot run MS-DOS or Windows 16-bit (Windows 3.x) applications. However, if you have installed a 32-bit version of Windows Vista, MS-DOS or Windows 16-bit applications are automatically launched into their own virtual machine called WOW (Windows on Windows). That is discussed in Chapter 26.

Dialog Box Changes

The Open and Save dialog boxes (also known as file or browse dialog boxes) for most applications still offer the same shortcuts and controls as those of Windows 9x, Me, 2000, and XP. This typically includes a shortcut menu to History, Desktop, Documents, Computer, and Network. You'll also still find the Look In pull-down list, with quick selections for local drives, user home directories, shared folders, and more. Not all applications that function on Windows Vista offer a fully enhanced file dialog box.

Many dialog boxes have tabs. These often appear at the top of a dialog box, as the tabs for General and Security do (see Figure 4.4). Tabs are used to offer multiple pages or displays of controls within a single smaller window. Many of the configuration settings dialog boxes have tabs, so watch for them. To select another tab, just click on it. In some cases, tabs are easy to miss; the new color scheme and display enhancements don't always direct your eyes to tabs.

Figure 4.4
A properties dialog box containing tabs that you can click to see additional settings.

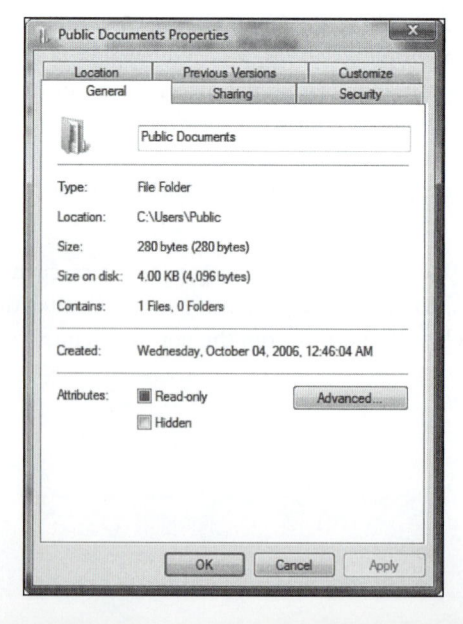

PUTTING ITEMS ON THE DESKTOP

The desktop is a convenient location for either permanent or temporary storage of items. Many folks use the desktop as a home for often-used documents and program shortcuts. I'm quite fond of using the desktop as an intermediary holding tank when moving items between drives or computers, or to and from floppy disks. It's particularly good for pulling found items out of a search window or other folder while awaiting final relocation elsewhere.

Here are some quick helpful notes about using the desktop. For starters, you can send a shortcut of an object to the desktop very easily by right-clicking it and choosing Send To, Desktop (thus creating the shortcut).

Second, remember that the desktop is nothing magical. Actually, it's just another folder with a few additional properties. Prime among them is the option to have live-active Internet-based information in the Windows Sidebar, such as stock tickers, weather, and the like. Also, each user on the machine can have his or her own desktop setup, with icons, background colors, screen saver, and such.

The major feature of the Desktop is that whatever you put on it is always available by minimizing or closing open windows, or more easily by clicking the Show Desktop button on the Quick Launch bar. Keep in mind that some items cannot be moved onto the desktop—only their shortcuts can. (For example, if you try to drag a Control Panel applet to the desktop, you'll see a message stating that you cannot copy or move the item to this location.)

If you must be able to access a Control Panel applet from the desktop, the answer is clear in this case because you don't really have a choice. Just create a shortcut to the applet and place it on the desktop. However, in other cases, when you're copying and moving items, particularly when using the right-click method, you'll be presented with the options of copying, moving, or creating a shortcut to the item. What's the best choice?

Here are a few reminders about shortcuts. Remember that they work just as well as the objects they point to (for example, the program or document file), yet they take up much less space on the hard disk. For this reason, they're generally a good idea. What's more, you can have as many shortcuts scattered about for a given object as you want. Therefore, for a program or folder you use a lot, put its shortcuts wherever you need them—put one on the desktop, one on the Quick Launch bar, one on the Start menu, and another in a folder of your favorite programs on the desktop.

Make up shortcuts for other objects you use a lot, such as folders, disk drives, network drives and printers, and web links. From Internet Explorer, for example, drag the little blue E icon that precedes a URL in the address bar to the desktop, to save it as a shortcut. Clicking it brings up the web page.

> **CAUTION**
>
> Remember that shortcuts are not the item they point to. They're aliases only. Therefore, copying a document's shortcut to a floppy or a network drive or adding it as an attachment to an email doesn't copy the document itself. If you want to send a document to some colleagues, don't make the mistake of sending them the shortcut unless it's something they'll have access to over the LAN or Web. If it's a shortcut to, say, a word-processing document or folder, they'll have nothing to open.

The link between shortcuts and the objects they point to can be broken. This happens typically when the true object is erased or moved. Clicking the shortcut can result in an error message. In Windows Vista, this problem is addressed in an ingenious way. Shortcuts automatically adjust when linked objects are moved. The operating system keeps track of all shortcuts and attempts to prevent breakage. Shortcut "healing" is built into Windows Vista for situations in which the automated recover mechanism fails.

If you're not sure about the nature of a given shortcut, try looking at its properties. Right-click the shortcut and choose Properties. Clicking on Find Target locates the object that the shortcut links to and displays it in a folder window.

> **TIP**
>
> To quickly bring up the Properties dialog box for most objects in the Windows GUI, you can highlight the object and press Alt+Enter.

SAVING FILES ON THE DESKTOP FROM A PROGRAM

Because the desktop is a convenient place to plop files and folders, Save As boxes in modern applications list the desktop as a destination option. Even if the app's dialog box doesn't have the desktop icon in the left pane, the drop-down list at the top of the box will have it.

> **NOTE**
>
> The location of the desktop folder for a user will not be on the local machine if *IntelliMirror* is being used on a network using Windows 2000 Server or Windows Server 2003 in such a way that the user's desktop will follow him or her from workstation to workstation. In this case, the desktop will be in a folder on the server and will be more difficult to locate from an old-style Save As dialog box. Just use another folder to save the file, and then move it to the desktop using Computer or Windows Explorer.

PROPERTIES AND THE RIGHT-CLICK

Ever since Windows 95, a common theme that unites items within Windows is the aspect called *properties*. Properties are pervasive throughout Windows 9*x*, NT 4, 2000, XP, and now Vista. The Properties dialog boxes provide a means of making changes to the behavior, appearance, security level, ownership, and other aspects of objects throughout the operating system. Object properties apply to everything from individual files to folders, printers, peripherals, screen appearance, the computer itself, or a network or workgroup. All these items have property sheets that enable you to easily change various settings. For example, you might want to alter whether a printer is the default printer or whether a folder on your hard disk is shared for use by co-workers on the LAN.

A typical set of properties is shown in Figure 4.5, which displays the properties for the D: drive (hard disk) on a computer. Notice that there are several tab pages on this dialog box. Some property dialogs have only a single page, whereas others have many.

Figure 4.5
A typical properties dialog box for a hard disk.

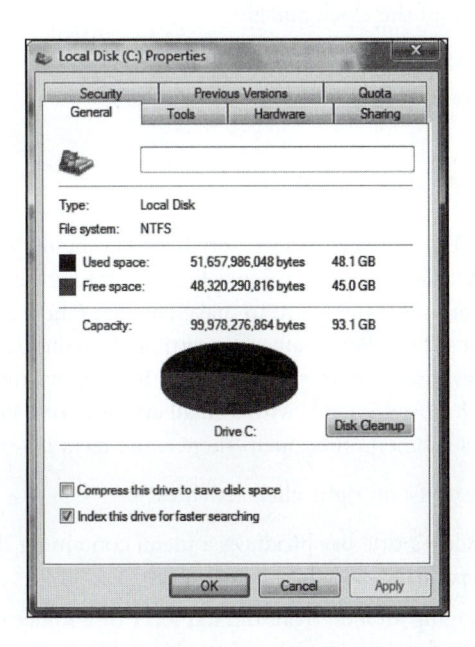

Property sheets are very useful and often serve as shortcuts for modifying settings that otherwise would take you into the Control Panel or through some other circuitous route. With some document files (for example, Word files), you can examine many settings that apply to the file, such as the creation date, author, editing history, and so forth. A typical printer's property sheet contains security, color management, location, name, and share status information. You can even change your screen colors, display resolution, screen savers, and more by right-clicking over the desktop and clicking Personalize from the pop-up menu. This opens the Personalization applet without having to traverse the Control Panel.

Although everyday users might not need property sheets, power users certainly do. As you use property sheets, you'll also become familiar with and accustomed to another aspect of the Windows Vista interface: the right-click. Until Windows 9x, the left (primary) mouse button was the one you did all your work with unless you were using a program that specifically used the other buttons, such as some art programs. However, Windows 9x instituted the use of the right-click to bring up various "context-sensitive" menus in programs and throughout the interface. These have been incorporated into Windows Vista.

Here are some typical uses of right-click context menus:

- Sharing a folder on the network
- Changing the name of your hard disk and checking its free space
- Changing a program's icon
- Creating a new folder
- Setting the desktop's colors, background, screen saver, and so on
- Adjusting the date and time of the clock quickly
- Closing an application by right-clicking on its icon in the taskbar and choosing Close
- Displaying a font's technical details
- Renaming an object
- Accessing an object's properties dialog box

As an example of the right-click, simply get to an empty place on the desktop and right-click on it. Right by the cursor, you'll see a menu that looks like the one shown in Figure 4.6. Notice that you can slide up and down the menu to make choices. Choose Personalize down at the bottom of the list. You'll see the Personalization settings for your desktop (as well as general video display, screen saver, and other related items). By the way, many menus (Start, menu bar, pop-up, and so on) have commands with a small arrow to one side. If you highlight one of these commands, a submenu flies open—hence, the term *fly-open menu*.

Here are some other examples of useful right-click activities:

- Right-clicking on any window's title bar produces a menu containing the Restore, Move, Size, Minimize, Maximize, and Close commands.
- Right-clicking on and dragging an icon from the Explorer or a folder onto the desktop reveals a pop-up menu with the options Copy Here, Move Here, Create Shortcuts Here, and Cancel.
- In many applications, selecting text and then right-clicking produces an edit menu at the cursor location that lets you choose Cut, Copy, or Paste.

Figure 4.6
An example of a right-click menu, this one from an empty location on the desktop. Notice that it contains fly-open menus.

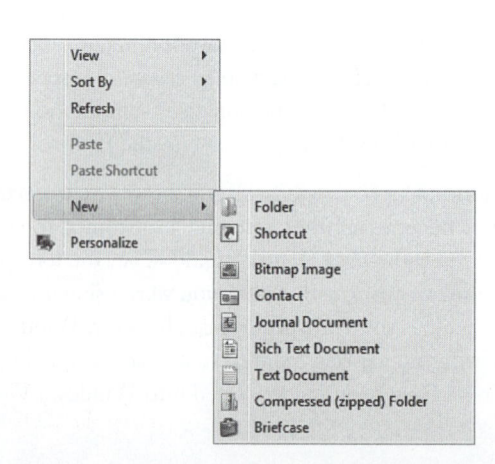

- Right-clicking an empty area of the taskbar gives you a menu that lets you manage the display of all the windows you have open. For example, you can tile all open windows or set the properties of the taskbar. (The taskbar is discussed in more detail later in this chapter.)

If you want to use Windows most efficiently, make a habit of right-clicking on objects to see what pops up. You might be surprised to see how much time you save with the resulting shortcuts.

> **NOTE**
> Starting with this chapter, we're going to assume that you understand the choice between single-click mode and double-click mode. Some of the figures in the book might have icons, files, or other object names underlined, whereas others might not, based on what mode the computer was set in when the screen shots were grabbed. Don't let it throw you. When we say "double-click something," we mean run it or open it by whatever technique is applicable based on your click setting. Also, when we say "click on it," that means select it. Remember that if you have single-clicking turned on, just hover the pointer over (that is, point to) the item to select it. Generally, we are working from the defaults set by Microsoft.

Using Windows Explorer

For a bird's-eye view of your computer, turning on the Folders bar is the way to go. It makes copying, moving, and examining all the contents of your computer easier than navigating up and down the directory tree through folders. If you're doing housekeeping, copying and moving items from one folder to another or across the network, or hopping back and forth between viewing web pages and your local hard disk, mastering this view will serve you well.

You probably remember that the folder view was introduced with Windows 95 in the form of Windows Explorer, and although it's still in Vista under that name, it's not featured as much as it used to be. This is because the functionality of Windows Explorer can be added to all folder windows (such as Computer) simply by clicking on the Folders button in the toolbar. The Folder View paradigm affords significant power and flexibility in file and folder control; Microsoft and other software makers have adopted it for other classes of programs. For example, right-click on Computer and choose Manage. The resulting application (Computer Management) uses the same approach, as do many web pages.

For everyday file and folder management, I prefer Folder view over the usual folder system, which can clutter your screen with numerous overlapping windows when you have lots of them open. Instead, with Folder view (call it Windows Explorer, if you want), you can examine the Control Panel, the local area network, the Internet, your hard disk, or the Recycle Bin—all done with a minimum of effort from the Explorer. Folder view also makes copying and moving files between far-flung folders and drives a snap.

To recap, you can get to Windows Explorer by clicking Start, All Programs, Accessories, Windows Explorer.

Figure 4.7 shows the folders that appear on my own computer in Folder view.

> **TIP**
>
> As an easy way into Windows Explorer, I always keep a shortcut to it on the Quick Launch bar or on the desktop (see Chapter 26 for how to use the Quick Launch bar). Another trick is to right-click the Start button and choose Explore. This brings up Windows Explorer, too.

Figure 4.7
The basic Windows Explorer screen, showing the computer's major components on the left and the contents on the right.

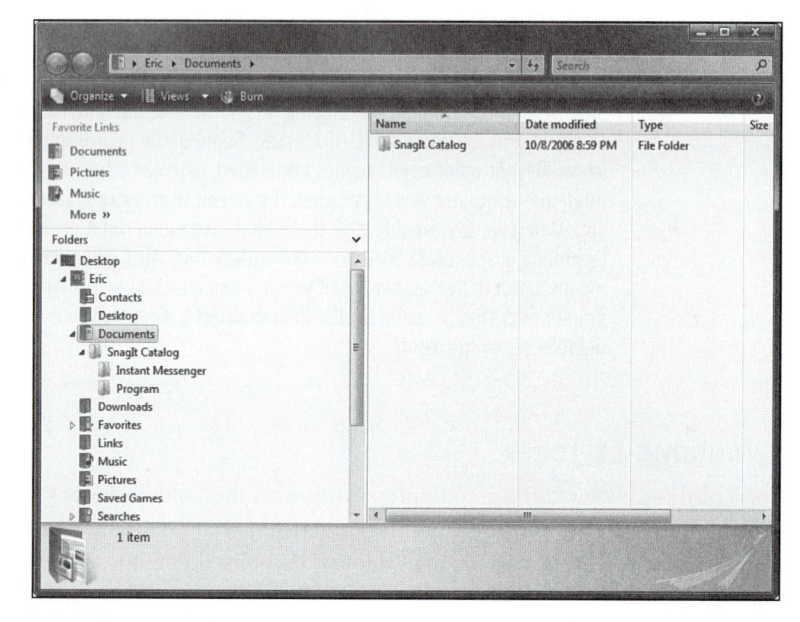

Displaying the Contents of Your Computer

When you use Folder view (or run Windows Explorer), all the objects constituting your computer appear in the list on the left. Some of those objects have a triangle pointing right next to them, which means the object is collapsed; it contains subitems that aren't currently showing.

Click an item in the left pane to see its contents in the right pane. If the item has a white triangle pointing to the right, click it to open the sublevels in the left pane, showing you the relationship of the folders and other items in a tree arrangement. In the figure, you can see that the Bob's Documents folder has been opened in this way. Notice that the triangle is no longer white and pointing to the right, but is now black and pointing downward, indicating that the object's display has been expanded. Clicking the black triangle causes that branch to collapse.

If you open a local disk drive or disk across the network, you can quickly get a graphical representation of the disk's folder layout. Then click a folder to see its contents. By right-clicking on disks, folders, or files, you can examine and set properties for them. The straight lines connecting folders indicate how they're related. If you have more folders than can be seen at one time, the window has a scrollbar that you can use to scroll the tree up and down.

Notice that there are two scrollbars—one for the left pane and one for the right. These scroll independently of one another, which can be very useful when you're copying items from one folder or drive to another.

WORKING WITH OBJECTS IN FOLDER VIEW

Working with folders and files in this view is simple. As explained previously, you just click an item in the left pane, and its contents appear in the right pane. Choose the view (Large Icons, Small Icons, and so on) for the right pane using the toolbar's View button. In Details view, you can sort the items by clicking the column headings.

When they're displayed, you can drag items to other destinations, such as a local hard disk, a floppy drive, or a networked drive. You can drag and drop files, run programs, open documents that have a program association, and use right-click menu options for various objects. For example, you can right-click files or folders and choose Send To, DVD RW Drive to copy items to a DVD disc. I use the Send To, Mail Recipient option all the time, to send attachments to people via email.

With a typical hard disk containing many files, when its folders are all listed in the left pane, some will be off-screen. Because the two panes have independent scrollbars, dragging items between distant folders is not a problem. Here's the game plan:

1. Be sure the source and destination folders are open and visible in the left pane, even if you have to scroll the pane up and down. For example, a network drive should be expanded, with its folders showing (using and mapping network drives is covered in Chapter 23, "Using a Windows Network").
2. Click the source folder in the left pane. Now its contents appear to the right.
3. Scroll the left pane up or down to expose the destination folder. (Click only the scrollbar, not a folder in the left pane; if you do, it changes the displayed items on the right side.)
4. In the right pane, locate and drag the items over to the left, landing on the destination folder. The folder must be highlighted; otherwise, you've aimed wrong.

This technique suffices most of the time. Sometimes it's too much of a nuisance to align everything for dragging. In that case, use the cut/copy-and-paste technique discussed earlier in the chapter. Remember, you can copy and paste across your home LAN as well as between your local drives.

Here are a few tips when selecting folders:

- Only one folder at a time can be selected in the left pane. If you want to select multiple folders, click the parent folder (such as the drive icon) and select the folders in the right pane. Use the same techniques described earlier for making multiple selections.
- When a folder is selected in the left pane, its name becomes highlighted. This is a reminder of which folder's contents are showing in the right pane.

- You can jump quickly to a folder's name by typing its first letter on the keyboard. If there's more than one folder with the same first letter, each press of the key advances to the next choice.
- The fastest way to collapse all the branches of a given drive is to click that drive's black triangle sign.
- You can quickly rearrange a drive's folder structure in the left pane by dragging folders. You can't drag disk drives, but you can create shortcuts for them (for example, a network drive) by dragging them to, say, the desktop.
- If a folder has subfolders, those appear in the right pane as folder icons. Clicking one of those opens it as though you had clicked that subfolder in the left pane.
- When dragging items to collapsed folders (ones with a plus sign), hovering the pointer over the folder for a second opens it.
- You can use the right-click-drag technique when dragging items if you want the option of clearly choosing Copy, Move, or Create Shortcut when you drop the item on the target.
- To create a new folder, in the left pane, click the folder under which you want to create the new folder. Right-click in the right pane and choose New, Folder.
- Delete a folder by right-clicking on it and choosing Delete. You're asked to confirm.

> **CAUTION**
>
> Although it's powerful, Folder view is also dangerous. It makes accidental rearrangement of your hard disk's folders extremely easy. When selecting folders, be careful to not accidentally drag them. The icons are small, and this is easy to do accidentally, especially in the left pane. A little flick of the wrist and a click of the mouse, and you've dragged one folder on top of another folder. This makes it a subfolder of the target. Remember, the left pane is "live," too. Rearranging the directory tree could make programs and files hard to find and even make some programs not work.

The Taskbar, the Start Menu, and Other Tools

The taskbar is the command center for your user environment under Windows Vista. With few or no desktop icons after initial setup, everything you do within Windows Vista has to start with the taskbar. The taskbar (refer to Figure 4.1) is host to several other highly useful tools, including the Start menu, the Quick Launch bar, the open application buttons, and the Notification Area.

The Start menu is the control center for Windows Vista. Most native applications and installed applications have an icon within the Start menu that is used to launch or access them. The Start menu has two columns of access elements. The left column includes Internet and email access on top and a list of most recently used applications on bottom. By default, it displays the most recently accessed applications. A fresh installation of Windows Vista includes prestocked items in this list, such as Windows Media Player,

Windows Movie Maker, and Welcome Center. This leaves room for only a single recently accessed application. These prestocked items eventually disappear, but that can take up to 60 days. You can forcibly remove them one at a time by issuing the Remove from This List command from the right-click pop-up menu.

At the bottom of the left column is All Programs, which is an access point to the rest of the Start menu. Those of you from Windows 9*x*/Me/NT/XP/2000 will recognize this as the Programs section of the Start menu. The Start menu's right column lists Documents, My Recent Documents, Pictures, Music, Games, Recent Items, Computer, Network (optionally), Connect To, Control Panel, Default Programs, and Help and Support. Below both columns are the Sleep and Lock buttons. Sleep is used to put the computer in a low-power state so you can quickly recover and continue working from where you left off. The Lock button locks the computer so no one else can access it without the proper password.

> **TIP** Pressing Ctrl+Esc or the Windows key opens the Start menu as though you clicked the Start button. You then can navigate using the arrow keys. Use the Enter key to launch or access the selected item.

It should be obvious that clicking on any of the items listed on the Start menu either launches an application or opens a new dialog box or menu. Most of the items on the top level of the Start menu are discussed later in this chapter. Clicking All Programs scrolls to second-page of programs, while leaving the quick links such as Control Panel still visible—a nice improvement of XP in which the fly-out menu of apps could cover your screen.

You can add new items to the Start menu by dragging an item from Computer or Windows Explorer over the Start menu button, then over All Programs, and then to the location where you want to drop it. You can even manipulate the Start menu as a set of files and shortcuts through Computer or Windows Explorer. You need to go to the system root (usually C:, but it could be anything on multiboot systems) and drill down to \Users*<username>*\Start Menu\Programs (where *<username>* is the name of the user account whose Start menu you want to modify).

The area immediately to the right of the Start menu is the Quick Launch bar. Microsoft sticks several quick launch links there by default: the Show Desktop tool, which minimizes all open windows; the Switch Between Windows tool, which opens a window that shows all active windows so you can choose the one to open; and the Internet Explorer icon for quickly launching IE. You can add your own link just by dragging and dropping an application icon over this area. Your Quick Launch Bar may not be enabled by default. To enable it, right click on an empty place on the taskbar and choose Toolbars and from the flyout menu, and choose Quick Launch to set its check box on.

To the far right on the taskbar is the *Notification Area*. Some services, OS functions, and applications place icons into this area. These icons provide both instant access to functions and settings, as well as status displays. For example, when you're working on a portable system, a battery appears in the Notification Area indicating how much juice is left. The clock is also located in the Notification Area.

Between the Quick Launch bar and the notification area are the active application buttons. These are grouped by similarity, not by order of launch. In addition, if the taskbar becomes crowded, multiple instances of similar applications are cascaded into a single button.

> **NOTE** You can reposition the taskbar on the right, left, or top of the screen. Just click any part of the taskbar other than a button and drag it to the edge of your choice. The Taskbar and Start Menu Properties dialog box includes a locking option to prevent the taskbar from being moved accidentally. Be sure to deselect this option before you attempt to relocate the taskbar (right-click the taskbar and clear the checkmark next to the Lock the Taskbar option).

You can further control and modify the taskbar and Start menu through their properties dialog boxes.

→ For more information on customizing the taskbar and the Start menu, **see** Chapter 26.

Uninstall or Change Programs

Unlike Windows XP and earlier versions of Windows dating back to Windows 9*x*, Windows Vista doesn't include an Add or Remove Programs applet. Instead, Windows Vista provides you with the Uninstall or Change a Program applet, which enables you to uninstall, change, or repair a program.

Uninstalling a program is analogous to what we called "removing" a program in earlier versions of Windows. *Changing* a program enables you to make changes to the functionality and features of the program, such as installing Microsoft Access from the Microsoft Office CD if you didn't install that program previously. *Repairing* a program enables you to repair any problems you're having with a program, such as a word processing program not saving files.

> **NOTE** In Windows XP and earlier versions, you could add Windows updates in the Add or Remove Programs applet. In Windows Vista, adding and viewing Windows Vista updates is in the System and Maintenance window. You'll learn more about updating Windows Vista in Chapter 25.

You've probably noticed that not all programs show up in the Uninstall or Change a Program applet. They don't appear because only programs that comply with the 32-bit Windows API standard for installation get their filenames and locations recorded in the system database, allowing them to be reliably erased without adversely affecting the operation of Windows. Many older or less-sophisticated applications simply install in their own way and don't bother registering with the operating system.

Most modern applications are written in compliance with the Microsoft Windows standards for installation and removal. Thus, you see them in your installed applications list in the Uninstall or Change a Program applet. This list is mainly the result of the PC software industry's response to kvetching from users and critics about tenacious programs that are hard to root out after they're installed. Some ambitious programs spread themselves out all over your hard disk like oil on your garage floor, with no easy way of reversing the process. Users complained about the loss of precious disk space, unexplained system slowdowns, and so forth.

This problem was the inspiration for such programs as Uninstaller, CleanSweep, and other utilities that monitor and keep a database of the files a program installs; they effectively wipe out these files when you decide to remove the program, also returning any modified Windows settings to their previous state, with any luck. I think this process is better relegated to those writing the operating system, and Microsoft rightly set up standards for the installation and removal of applications, overseen by this applet. Even if an application isn't installed via the Add or Remove Programs applet, per se, if it's well behaved, it should still make itself known to the operating system and register changes it makes, enabling you to make changes and/or uninstall it from there.

> **TIP**
> Never attempt to remove an application from your system by deleting its files from the \Program Files folders (or wherever). Actually, "never" might be too strong. Removal through manual deletion should be only a last resort. Always attempt to use the Uninstall or change a program applet or the uninstall utility from the application first.

What's more, the built-in uninstaller lets you make changes to applications, such as adding or removing suboptions (assuming that the application supports that feature).

> **TIP**
> Some programs, such as Microsoft Office, include service packs and other updates that help keep the programs running in top condition. However, these updates might cause Windows to run slowly and/or otherwise malfunction. If you suspect that a recently installed upgrade is the problem, you can view and uninstall updates by clicking the Uninstall a Program link and following the upcoming instructions starting with Step 3.

Using the uninstall feature of the applet is simple:

1. Click Start, Control Panel, click Programs, Programs and Features.
2. Check the list of installed applications. A typical list appears in Figure 4.8. Note that you can sort the applications by some interesting criteria in the sort box, such as frequency of use. (That one helps weed out stuff you almost never use.)

Figure 4.8
Choosing the program to uninstall or change.

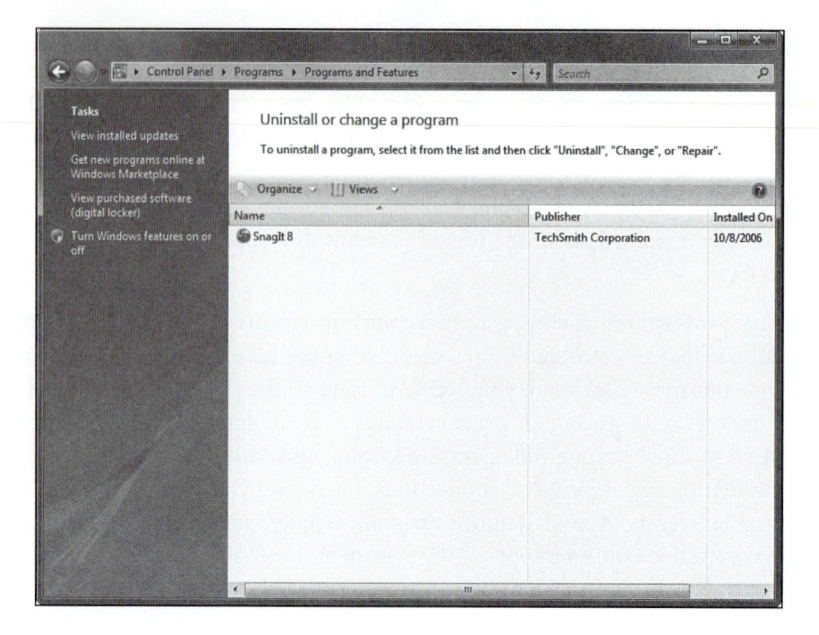

3. Select the program you want to change or uninstall.
4. Click the Uninstall button.
5. Answer any warnings about removing an application, as appropriate.

> **TIP**
>
> Obviously, removing an application can't easily be reversed by, say, restoring files from the Recycle Bin because settings from the Start menu and possibly the Registry are deleted.

Some applications (for example, Microsoft Office) prompt you to insert the program CD when you attempt to change or remove the app. These prompts can be annoying, but what can you do? The setup, change, and uninstall programs for some large suites are stored on their CDs, not on your hard disk. Just insert the disc when prompted.

> **NOTE**
>
> Incidentally, the Uninstall or Change a Program applet can be run only by users with Administrator credentials on their local computer. Although some applications can be installed or removed by nonadministrators, most require administrative privilege.

Add New Programs

So how do you install a program on a disc in your CD or DVD drive from the Control Panel in Windows Vista? You can't anymore as you did with Windows XP and earlier versions of Windows. Nearly all software written for Windows comes with an autoinstall program that runs when you insert the CD or DVD into the appropriate drive. Microsoft obviously believes that adding software from the Control Panel is now superfluous, but if you have a program that won't open the autoinstall program automatically, consult your software installation instructions or search for the autoinstall file on your CD using Computer or Windows Explorer. Autoinstall files usually have the name `setup.exe` or `install.exe`.

Using Older Programs

As I said at the beginning of the chapter, Microsoft is constantly moving people toward upgrading to the newest version of Windows. If you still have Windows 3.*x*, you will be dismayed to learn that Windows Vista 64-bit versions will not run DOS and Windows 3.*x* programs.

If you have programs written for Windows XP or earlier that worked correctly in those older operating systems but don't work well in Vista, Microsoft was kind enough to include the Program Compatibility Wizard in Vista so you can select and test compatibility settings that could identify the problem(s) and hopefully get your program working again.

Here's how you open the Program Compatibility Wizard:

1. Click Start, Control Panel, Programs.
2. Under the Programs and Features section at the top of the window, click the Use an Older Program with This Version of Windows link. The Program Compatibility Wizard window appears; you can use it to pinpoint the problem(s) with your application.

Windows Marketplace and Digital Locker

Microsoft has made it easy for you to find and install programs from Windows Marketplace. Windows Marketplace is an online source for you to download games, programs for your mobile (or handheld) computer, security software, music and video, and more. Windows Marketplace is obviously Microsoft's attempt to tie you in more closely with software that Microsoft produces and/or recommends, but you might be able to use it for some of your software needs. What's more, you can download trial versions of some programs on Windows Marketplace so you can try before you buy.

You can open Windows Marketplace by clicking the link Get New Programs Online at Windows Marketplace. The Internet Explorer 7 window opens and displays the Windows Marketplace home page, shown in Figure 4.9.

Figure 4.9
The Windows Marketplace home page.

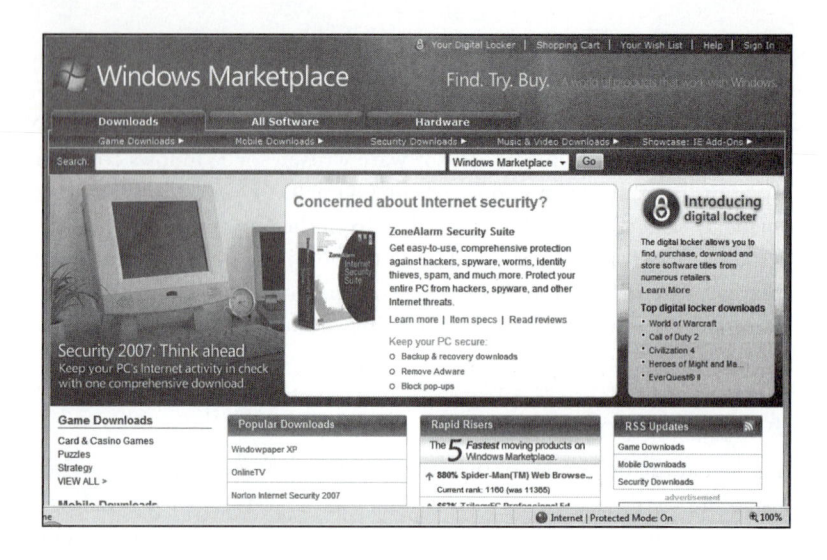

After you download a program from Windows Marketplace, Windows Vista places the software in a "digital locker" that shows all the purchased and trial software you've downloaded. You can view all the downloaded software by clicking the View Purchased Software (Digital Locker) link. The Digital Locker Assistant window appears (see Figure 4.10).

Figure 4.10
The Digital Locker Assistant window.

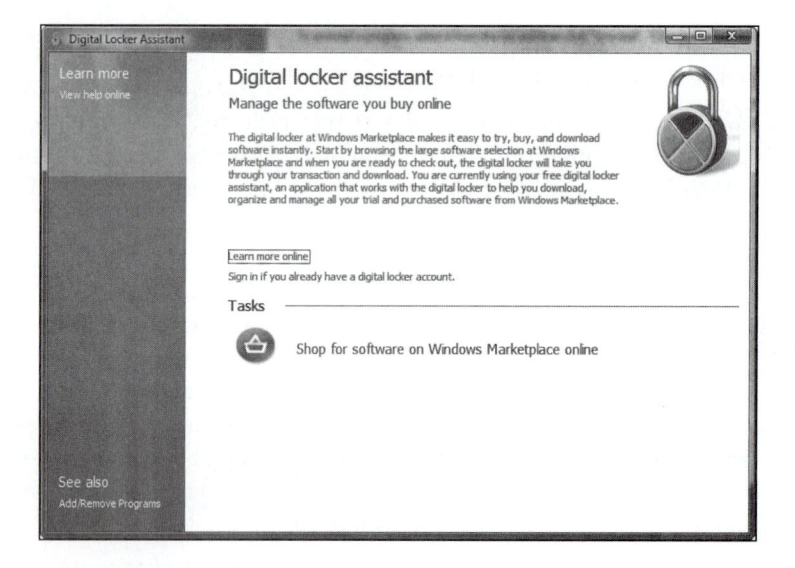

The Digital Locker assistant works with Microsoft Passport and Live ID to manage your personal information and purchase information. Live ID is the successor to Passport, but Live ID comes with a host of issues that you should be aware of. Chapter 15, "Using Internet Explorer 7," discusses those issues in greater detail.

Installing Programs from the Network

As you learned in Chapter 1, "Introducing Windows Vista," an administrator of a Windows 2000 or Windows Server 2003 domain can "publish" or "push" applications to workstations. When an application is published over the LAN, it usually is automatic. In other words, the software is installed without the knowledge of the user or the need for user input.

Push Technology Meets the LAN

You might have heard the term *push* used in relation to the Web over the past couple years. But how does this technology apply to the LAN and to applications? The idea of push is that it's a bit like television or radio. You turn on your TV, and there's the show. You don't have to do anything except choose the channel. Push technology on the Web works the same way. When you're connected, information is sent to your computer on a regular basis—for example, displaying stock prices in a ticker window on your desktop.

The push I'm talking about here with the LAN works much the same way, except that instead of being sent a web page or stock ticker, you're sent an entire application that gets installed automatically on your computer, according to your system administrator's wishes.

A server system's capability to push applications to clients is part of IntelliMirror. For more information on IntelliMirror and pushing applications to client systems, consult the Windows Vista Resource Kit and documentation on Windows 2000 Server or Windows Server 2003.

> **NOTE**
> In the case of "pushed" (or *assigned*) applications, when you log on to the machine or network, the applications assigned to you are automatically added to your machine across the network. In fact, if you accidentally or intentionally delete the application from your computer, it reinstalls itself.

Running Your Applications

If you're just upgrading from a previous Windows (such as 9x or XP), you already know how to run applications, how to switch between them, and how to manage them. But if you are new to Windows OSes, here is a quick how-to guide.

How to Launch Your Apps

Applications are launched under Windows Vista in a number of different ways, as is the case with many other things in Windows. You'll probably end up using the technique that best fits the occasion. To run an application, perform one of the following tasks (ranked in order of ease of use):

- Use the Start button to find the desired application from the resulting menus. Click All Programs if you don't see the one you want.
- Drag an application shortcut to the Quick Launch bar at the bottom of the screen and click it to run.

- Open Computer or Windows Explorer, browse through your folders to find the application's icon, and double-click it.
- Find the application by clicking Start and then typing the application name in the Start Search box. (The Search method works only for programs installed in a predefined list of folders called the search path, which is discussed in Chapter 32, "Command-Line and Automation Tools.")
- Customize the Start menu to include the Run command. Then, you can click Start, Run, and enter the command name. (Customizing the Start Menu is discussed in Chapter 26.)
- Enter command names from the command prompt (click Start, All Programs, Accessories, Command Prompt to open the Command Prompt window). For more information about using the Command Prompt window, see Chapter 32.
- Launch the Task Manager by pressing Ctrl+Alt+Del and then selecting Start Task Manager in the menu. Click on New Task and then type in the executable filename for the program (for example, `word.exe`).

An alternative approach is to open a document that's associated with a given application—this is a trick to open the application:

- Locate a document that was created with the application in question and double-click it. This runs the application and loads the document into it. With some applications, you can then close the document and open a new one, if you need to.
- Right-click on the desktop or in a folder and choose New. Then choose a document type from the resulting menu. This creates a new document of the type you want; when double-clicked, it runs the application.

Here's how to open an existing document in an application (ranked in order of ease of use):

- Click Start, Documents, and look among the most recently edited documents. Clicking one opens the document in the appropriate application. You can also click Start, Recent Items, and look among the most recently edited files.
- Click Start and then type the application name into the Start Search box. Depending on what Search tool you have installed (such as Google Desktop Search), you can also click the Start button, click Search, and then type the application name in the Search Results window. If you don't have a Search option on your Start menu, you can still access the Search window by tapping F3 or WinKey+F, by the way.
- Run the application that created the document and check the document's MRU (most recently used) list on the File menu. It might be there. If so, click it.

In the name of expediency, we don't cover all these options. When you get the hang of the most common approaches, you'll understand how to use the others. Notice that some of the approaches are "application-centric," whereas others are "document-centric." An application-centric person thinks, "I'll run Word so I can write up that trip expense report." A document-centric person thinks, "I have to work on that company manual. I'll look for it and double-click it."

Running Programs from the Start Button

The most popular way to run your applications is to use the Start button, which is located in the lower-left corner of your screen. When you install a new program, the program's name is usually added somewhere to the Start button's All Programs menu lists. If you've recently used an application, Windows Vista might list it in the recently used list on the top-level Start menu area. Sometimes you'll have to "drill down" a level or two to find a certain program because software makers sometimes like to store their applications under their company names (for example, RealNetworks creates a group called Real, which you have to open to run RealPlayer). Then you just find your way to the program's name and choose it, and the program runs. Suppose you want to run the calculator. Here are the steps to follow:

1. Click the Start button.
2. Click All Programs.
3. Click Accessories and then choose Calculator.

Note that all selections with an arrow pointing to the right of the name have submenus—that means they open when you click them or hover the pointer over them. Several levels of submenus might exist. For example, to see the System Tools submenu, you have to go through All Programs, Accessories, System Tools.

> **TIP**
>
> Sometimes spotting a program in a list is a visual hassle. Press the first letter of the program you're looking for, and the cursor jumps to it. If multiple items start with that letter, each keypress advances one item in the list. Also, pressing the right-arrow key opens a submenu. The Enter key executes the highlighted program. Items in the lists are ordered alphabetically, although folders appear first, in order, with programs after that.

Often you'll accidentally open a list that you don't want to look at (say, the Games submenu). Just move the pointer to the one you want and wait a second, or press the Esc key. Each press of Esc closes one level of any open lists. To close all open lists, just click anywhere else on the screen, such as on the desktop or another window. All open Start button lists go away.

If a shortcut on your Start menu doesn't work, **see** *"Shortcut Doesn't Work" in the "Troubleshooting" section at the end of this chapter.*

Running a Program from Computer or Windows Explorer

If you're a power user, chances are good that you'll be sleuthing around on your hard disk using either the Computer approach or Windows Explorer. I certainly have programs floating around on my hard disk that do not appear in my Start button program menus, and I have to execute them directly. In general, the rule for running programs without the Start menu is this: If you can find and display the program's icon, just double-click it. It should run.

TIP

Just as in Windows XP, 2000, and Me, the differences between Computer and Windows Explorer within Windows Vista are more cosmetic than functional. In fact, simply by changing the default view, you can obtain the same view (that is, the same layout, panes, and details) using either interface. To alter the views, use the View toolbar button.

TIP

Right-clicking Computer and choosing Manage launches a powerful computer manager program called Computer Management. This is covered in Chapter 25.

TIP

Network is a version of the Computer interface that is used to gain access to network resources. Overall, it's used in the same manner as Computer. The only difference is that you must be on a network and someone must grant you access to shared resources on other systems for this tool to be of any use. Thus, we've left the discussion of this tool to Part V, "Networking."

Getting to a program you want is often a little convoluted, but it's not too difficult to grasp. Plus, if you understand the DOS directory tree structure or you've used a Mac, you already know more about Vista than you think. Double-click a drive to open it, and then double-click a directory to open it. Then double-click the program you want to run. Figure 4.11 shows a typical directory listing for Computer.

Figure 4.11
A typical directory as shown in Computer.

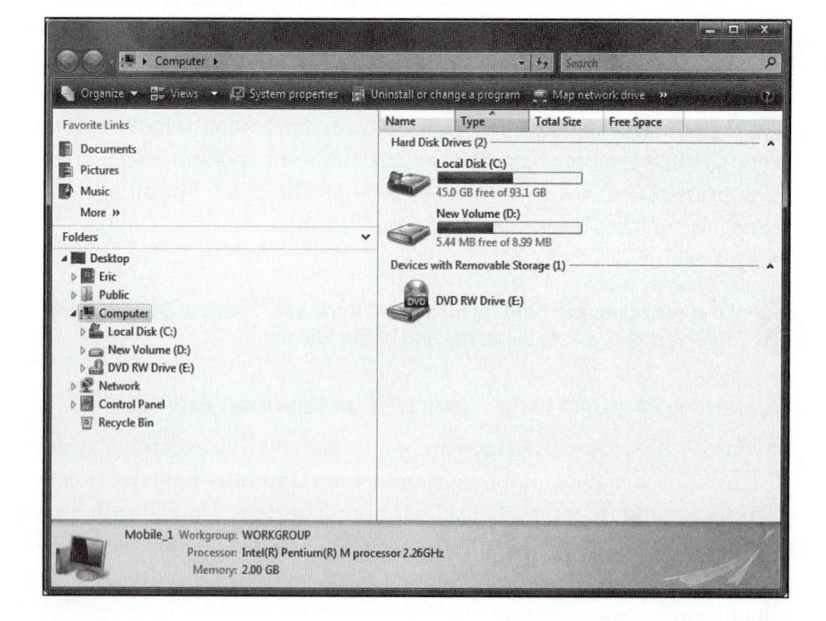

Here are some notes to remember:

- Get to the desktop quickly by clicking the Show Desktop icon in the Quick Launch bar (just to the right of the Start button).
- Folders are listed first, followed by files. Double-clicking a folder reveals its contents.
- If you want to see more folders on the screen at once to help in your search, you have several options. You can use the View button on the toolbar to change view options. The Small Icons view uses small icons with only the object name. The Medium Icons, Large Icons, and Extra Large Icons views display images extracted from the file objects themselves—this view is most useful for graphic files. The List view displays everything in a column by its object name only. The Details view offers the most comprehensive information about file system objects in a multicolumn display, with object names, object type, size, modified date, comments, and so on. The Tiles view provides an image with the object type and size.

> **TIP**
>
> Pressing Backspace while in any folder window moves you up one level in the directory tree. Also, the Back and Forward buttons work just like they do in a web browser–they move you forward and back through folders you've already visited.

Of course, many of the files you'll find in your folders are *not* programs; they're documents or support files. To easily find the applications, choose the Details view and then click the column head for Type. This sorts the listing by type, making it easy to find applications in the list (which carry an Application label).

> **NOTE**
>
> Applications, registered file types, and certain system files do not have their file extensions (a period and three-letter label that follows the filename) displayed by default. "Hidden" system files and directories are invisible, too. This choice was made to prevent cluttering the display with files that perform duties for the operating system but not directly for users. It also prevents you from meddling with files that could cripple applications and documents, or even the system at large. Personally, I like seeing as many details about files as possible, so when I first install a system, I change the default settings to show me every file on my system. You can do this through the View tab of the Folder Options applet, accessed through the Control Panel. You can also access the Folder Options applet quickly by typing **folder** in the Start menu Search box.

Using Documents, Pictures, and Music

Windows Vista is designed to help you focus on your creative tasks instead of the underlying OS, which supports the tools and files. Part of this includes the Documents, Pictures, and Music Start menu items. These links also appear on most file or browse windows, as well as within Computer and Windows Explorer. These three elements always link you back to a standard location where your personal data files are stored.

The Documents folder is the master folder for all your personal data files. This is the default storage location whenever you save a new document or data file. This is also where the Music and Pictures subfolders reside. These folders are provided to simplify the storage and retrieval of your most intimate file-stored creations. Clicking on one of these Start menu links opens a Computer window.

In Computer and Windows Explorer, the top of the left pane contains the Favorite Links section. When you click Documents in this section, the list of documents appears in the right pane.

> **TIP**
> Documents is not the same as Recent Items. Recent Items is a quick-access list of the 15 most recently accessed resources. This includes documents, music files, image files, archive files, and even (sometimes) programs.

PICTURES

The Pictures folder is to Windows Vista what the My Pictures folder was to Windows XP. You can store pictures in this folder and then view the pictures quickly from the Start menu (by clicking Start, Pictures) or from the Favorites Links section in Computer or Windows Explorer. A new installation of Windows Vista includes 12 high-quality sample pictures in the Sample Pictures subfolder.

MUSIC

The Music folder is to Windows Vista what the My Music folder was to Windows XP. You can store music files in this folder and then listening to the music files quickly from the Start menu (by clicking Start, Music) or from the Favorites Links section in Windows Explorer. A new installation of Windows Vista includes 11 high-quality sample music files in the Sample Music subfolder.

USING SPEECH RECOGNITION

Not everyone who uses Windows uses the keyboard. Some people are physically unable to use a keyboard, and others prefer voice commands to typing text whenever possible. With Speech Recognition, Windows Vista accommodates users who want to talk to their computer's Recognition.

Windows Vista interfaces with a keyboard and mouse (or mouse equivalent) by default. You can set up Speech Recognition by clicking Start, Control Panel, Ease of Access, Speech Recognition Options. The Speech Recognition Options window appears (see Figure 4.12).

Figure 4.12
The Speech Recognition Options window lets you configure your Speech Recognition settings.

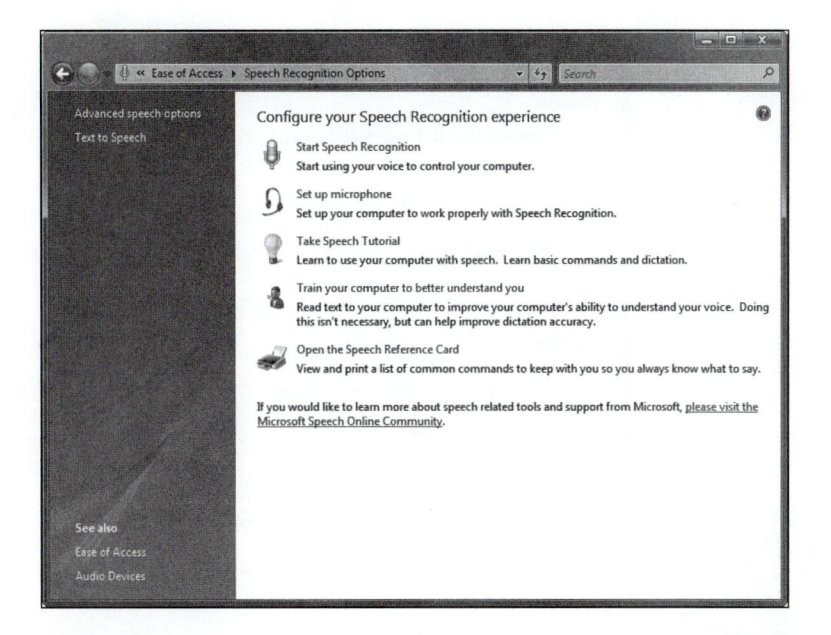

This window contains five links to choose from, but the link you want to click first to set up Speech Recognition is Start Speech Recognition. After you click this link, the Set Up Speech Recognition Wizard appears so you can set up the computer to recognize your voice. Tasks you complete in the wizard include setting up the microphone, taking a speech tutorial, and reading text to your computer to help your computer better translate your voice to text.

You can also view and print the Windows Speech Reference Card that contains a list of common voice commands that Windows Vista understands.

ADVANCED SPEECH OPTIONS

You can further configure Speech Recognition options by clicking the advanced speech options link in the Speech Recognition Options window. The Speech Properties window appears with the Speech Recognition tab open, as shown in Figure 4.13.

Figure 4.13
The Speech Properties window Speech Recognition tab.

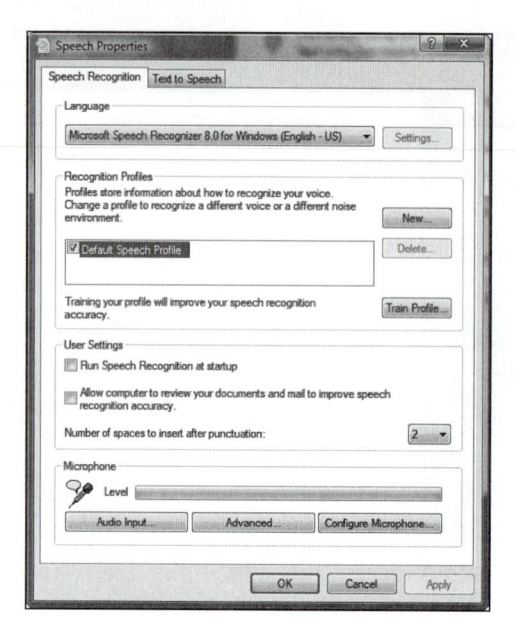

In this tab, you can select the Microsoft speech-recognition software for the type of English you're speaking—US English (which is the default) or UK English. (There's no mention of a requirement to speak the Queen's English.) You can also create a new Speech Recognition profile, determine whether you want to run Speech Recognition when Windows Vista starts, and specify how your computer will improve its speech-recognition accuracy. As part of that accuracy, you can also adjust your microphone input.

If you prefer Windows to read text aloud through your computer speakers, click the Text to Speech tab (see Figure 4.14).

Figure 4.14
The Speech Properties window Text to Speech tab.

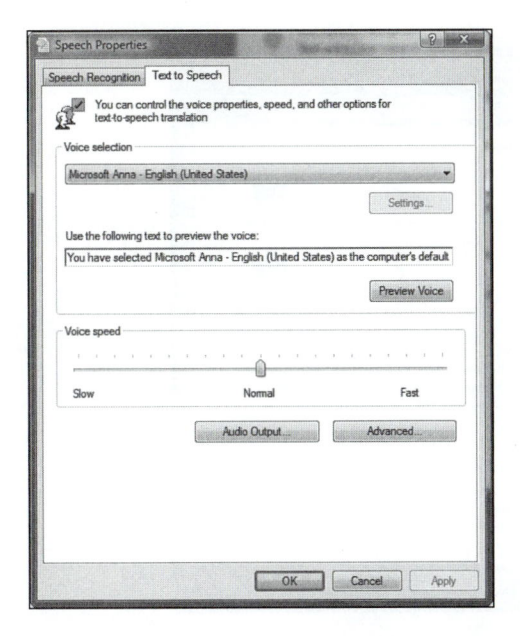

By default, only one voice is available in Windows Vista: Microsoft Anna, which is a pleasant female voice. You can preview Anna's voice by clicking Preview Voice. You can also control Anna's voice speed using the Voice speed slider bar. Enable Text to Speech by clicking OK.

Using the Help System

We haven't yet advanced our computing systems to the level displayed in *Star Trek*, where officers state an action verbally and the action takes place. When you want your computer to do something, you need to tell it what to do. Often you have to explain in great detail at every step exactly what actions to take or not to take. The Windows Vista Help system is designed to help you find out what everything within the environment can and cannot do, as well as teach you how to perform the activity you need for work or play.

You can access the Help system by clicking on the Help and Support item on the top level of the Start menu. The Help system offers a wide range of options, from a search routine, to topic-organized texts, to task-assisting walk-throughs, to Internet-updated dynamic content help (see Figure 4.15). The Help system also includes access to a full index, a history list, and a favorites list. It operates in much the same way as a web browser—using hyperlinks, Back and Forward buttons, and the capability to return to the start of the system using the Home button. When searching for material, you can use Boolean rules to fine-tune your keyword search phrases (AND, OR, NOT, and NEAR). This is definitely a tool that is worth exploring and consulting in times of trouble or confusion.

Figure 4.15
The Windows Help and Support interface.

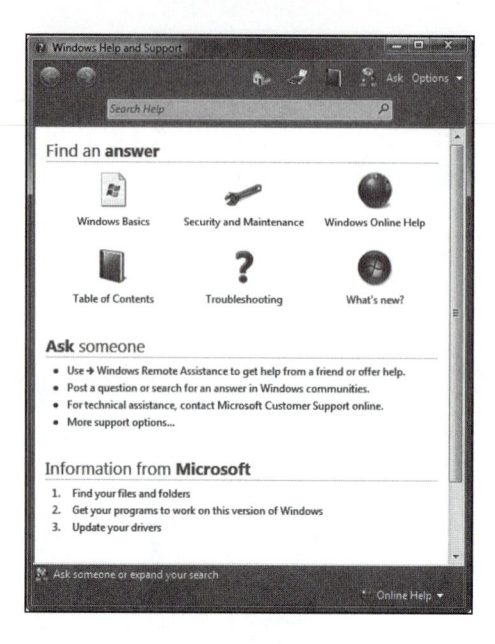

Exiting Windows Gracefully

When you've finished a Windows Vista session, you should properly shut down or log off to ensure that your work is saved and that no damage is done to the operating system. Shall we reiterate? Shutting down properly is very important. You can lose your work or otherwise foul up Windows settings if you don't shut down before turning off your computer. If multiple people share the computer, you should at least log off when you're finished so that others can log on. Logging off protects your work and settings from prying eyes. When you shut down, Windows does some housekeeping, closes all open files, prompts you to save any unsaved work files, and alerts the network that you and your shared resources are no longer available for consultation.

You can shut down the computer; all or only some of this information might apply to your machine. Newer machines have more shutdown features because they're likely to have advanced power management built into them via ACPI.

These are the steps for correctly exiting Windows:

1. Close any programs that you have running. (This can almost always be done from each program's File, Exit menu if the menu bar is active or by clicking the program's close button.) If you forget to close programs before issuing the Logout or Shut Down command, Windows attempts to close them for you. If you haven't saved your work, you're typically prompted to do so. You must close some programs, such as DOS programs, manually. Windows alerts you if it can't automatically close an open program. Quit the DOS program and type **exit** at the DOS prompt, if necessary. If you are just switching user context, your open application's status is saved so you can quickly return to it later.

2. Click Start, and then move the mouse over the right-arrow button to the right of the Lock button. You'll see the menu shown in Figure 4.16.

Figure 4.16
The Turn Off Computer selection menu.

3. Click on the desired option.

Consider these points:

- The Hibernate option records the current state of the system to disk and then shuts down the computer. When the power is turned back on, the system reboots. If you log back in as the same user who initiated the hibernation, the system returns to its exact state at the moment of hibernation.
- If you want to log off, select Log Off instead of Shut Down from the Start menu.
- If you attempt to shut down the computer while another user's desktop is still active (that is, Switch User was used and at least one other user is still logged on), you'll see a warning message stating that performing a shutdown could result in data loss, along with the options to continue with shutdown (Yes) or abort (No).

TIP
Logging off clears personal settings from memory and puts the computer in a neutral state, waiting for another user to log on. However, it doesn't bring the system to its knees. Logging off does not stop running services, which can include web services, file sharing, print sharing, UPS support, and scheduled tasks.

Sleep puts the computer in a suspended state, letting you quickly come right back to where you were working before you suspended the PC. This means you don't have to exit all your applications before turning off your computer. You only have to choose Sleep. This also saves energy because the hard drives, the CPU, the CPU fan, some internal electronics, and possibly the power supply and fan go into a low-power state. If your monitor is Energy Star compliant, it should also go into a frugal state of energy consumption. When you want to start up again, a quick press of the power switch (on some computers, a keypress on the keyboard or a jiggle of the mouse will do) should start up the system right where you left off. Be sure to press the power button for just a second or so. Anything more than 4 seconds on most modern computers in a Sleep state causes the computer to completely power down.

Be aware that Sleep holds your system state only as long as the computer has power. In XP, if the power failed, everything stored in the computer's RAM is lost. You'd end up doing a cold boot when the power is restored or, if it's a laptop with a dead battery, when you hook up your AC adapter to your laptop again. The good news is that in Vista, Sleep is more intelligent. When the battery level gets too low, the power management system in Vista switches into gear and inititiates Hibernation (which we'll discuss next). This is a very welcome new feature in Vista.

One of the more interesting features of recent versions of Windows, including Windows Vista, is *hibernation*. Like Sleep mode, hibernation lets you pause your work and resume later, without laboriously shutting down and reopening all your applications and files. But unlike Sleep, Hibernate isn't "volatile." If the AC power fails or batteries run flat, it doesn't matter because Hibernate stores the system state—that is, the contents of memory and the status of all hardware devices—on a portion of the hard disk, instead of keeping the system RAM alive in a low-power state. After storing the system state to the hard disk, the computer fully shuts down. When it's restarted, a little internal flag tells the boot loader that the system has been stored on disk, and it's reloaded into memory.

Hibernation requires as much free hard disk space as you have RAM in your PC. If you have 512MB of RAM, you'll need 512MB of free disk space for hibernation to work. When you choose Hibernate from the shutdown menu, Windows Vista has to create a fairly large file on disk. In my case, for example, it's 2GB in size. On a 3GHz Intel Pentium 4, the entire process takes about 15 seconds. Restarting takes about the same amount of time. Remember, if you're going to put a laptop running on batteries to sleep for more than a few hours, use Hibernate or just do a complete shutdown, closing your applications and documents. That way, if the batteries run out, you won't lose your work.

DEALING WITH A CRASHED APPLICATION OR OPERATING SYSTEM

Even though Windows Vista is fairly immune to crashing, the applications that run on it are not necessarily so robust. Not to be cynical, but many IS professionals don't consider any version of Windows worth their trouble until at least a service pack or two hit the streets, because they know that bugs tend to be prevalent in first-release software. Still, with an operating system as complex as Windows Vista, we bet there are a few gotchas lurking.

> *If your system is still stuck but you can get the Task Manager up,* **see** *"Forcing Your Computer to Shut Down" in the "Troubleshooting" section at the end of this chapter.*

> *If your laptop computer won't shut down no matter what you do,* **see** *"Ctrl+Alt+Delete Doesn't Work" in the "Troubleshooting" section at the end of this chapter.*

My point here is that you're going to bump into some unstable behavior from time to time. If you notice that a program isn't responding, you might have a crash on your hands. To gracefully survive a crash, possibly even without losing any of your data, try the following steps:

1. Try pressing Esc. Some programs get stuck in the middle of a process and Esc can sometimes get them back on track. For example, if you accidentally pressed Alt, this activates the menus. A press of Esc gets you out of that loop. If you've opened a menu, two presses of Esc or a click within the application's window might be required to return to normal operation.

2. Windows Vista has greatly improved application-management facilities. In most cases, even after an application has crashed, you should still be able to minimize, maximize, move, resize, and close its window.

3. Can you switch to the app to bring its window up front? First try clicking any portion of the window. If that doesn't work, click its button in the taskbar. Still no? Try using successive presses of Alt+Tab. If you get the window open and responding, try to save any unfinished work in the app and then try to close it by clicking the Close button or selecting File, Exit.

4. If that doesn't work, try right-clicking the program's button in the taskbar and choosing Close from the pop-up menu.

5. If that doesn't work, press Ctrl+Shift+Esc to launch the Task Manager. Notice the list of running applications. Does the one in question say "Not responding" next to it? If so, click it and then click End Task.

6. If Task Manager reports that you don't have sufficient access to terminate the task, you must reboot the system. First, attempt a graceful shutdown using the Turn Off Computer command. However, if that fails (that is, it hangs on the hung application or it never seems to complete the shutdown process), you need to resort to power-cycling. When the system reboots, you should be back to normal.

Troubleshooting

Shortcut Doesn't Work

I click a shortcut somewhere in my Start menu, and nothing happens or I get an error message.

Too much software overhead would be involved for the OS to keep track of all the shortcuts and update them as necessary when the files they point to are moved or deleted. A system that has been in use for some time will certainly have "dead" shortcuts, just as web pages have broken links floating around. When you click a shortcut icon anywhere in the system—be it in the Start menus, on the desktop, or in a folder—and you get an error message about the program file, click OK and let Windows take a stab at solving the problem by searching for the application. If it's found, Windows Vista "heals" the shortcut so that it will work again the next time you use it.

If that doesn't work, try searching yourself using Start, Search, or typing into the Search box above the Start button. (And recall that you can access the Search window by tapping F3 or WinKey+F.) See whether you can track down the runaway application. If you're successful, you're probably better off erasing the bad shortcut and creating a new one that points to the correct location. You can create a new shortcut by right-clicking the app's icon and choosing Create Shortcut. Then drag, copy, or move the shortcut to wherever you want, such as onto the Start button.

Another good trick to help you sort out a bad shortcut or to follow where its trail is leading is to right-click the icon and choose Properties, Find Target.

> **TIP**
>
> Remember, moving folders that contain applications (for example, Office might be in `C:\Program Files\MSOffice`) is a *really* bad idea. Once installed, many programs need to stay where they were put, unless you use a utility program specifically designed for the task. This is because application locations are recorded in the system registry and simply moving the program executable files around doesn't update the system registry.

Forcing Your Computer to Shut Down

The system is acting sluggish, nonresponsive, or otherwise weird.

If your system is really acting erratically or stuck in some serious way and you've already killed any unresponsive programs, press Ctrl+Alt+Delete. This should bring up the Windows Vista options menu. Click the red Shut Down button at the lower right-hand corner of the screen. If you get this far, there's hope for a graceful exit. You might have to wait a minute or so for the Turn Off command to take effect. If you're prompted to shut down some programs or save documents, do so. Hope for a speedy shutdown. Then reboot.

Ctrl+Alt+Delete Doesn't Work

Even Ctrl+Alt+Delete doesn't do anything.

If Turn Off doesn't work, it's time to power-cycle the computer. Press the power switch to turn off the machine. This might require holding in the power button for more than 4 seconds. You could lose some work, but what else are you going to do? Sometimes it happens. This is one good reason for saving your work regularly and looking for options in your programs that perform autosaving. As writers, we set our AutoSave function in Microsoft Word to save every 5 minutes. That way, we can recover from a system crash and lose only up to 5 minutes of work instead of everything.

Incidentally, although it's extremely rare, I've known laptops to not even respond to any form of command or power button when the operating system was fully hung. I've even had to remove any AC connection, fully remove the main battery, wait a few seconds, and then reinsert the battery and reboot. Removing the battery is important; otherwise, the battery keeps the computer in the same stuck state, thinking it's just in Sleep mode.

Tips from the Windows Pros: Working Efficiently

The interface is your portal into the operating system and, therefore, into your computer. You'll likely be using it every day, so it behooves you to "work the system" as effectively and efficiently as possible. As writers and programmers on deadlines, we're using our computers at breakneck speed most of the time. Cutting corners on how you control the system interface saves you literally hundreds of miles of mousing around on your desktop over the course of a few years. Here are our top time-saving and motion-saving tips for using Windows Vista:

- To get to the desktop (minimize all open windows), press the Windows key and M at the same time. To reverse the effect, press Shift+Windows+M. This is a real time-saver. If you prefer the mouse, click the Show Desktop button in the Quick Launch bar; it does the same thing.
- Change between applications by pressing Alt+Tab. Aiming for an application's little button on the taskbar is a hassle. You'll get tendonitis doing that all day. If you're using the Aero interface, you can also use Flip 3D to change between applications by pressing Windows+Tab as shown in Figure 4.17.

Figure 4.17
Flipping between applications using Flip 3D.

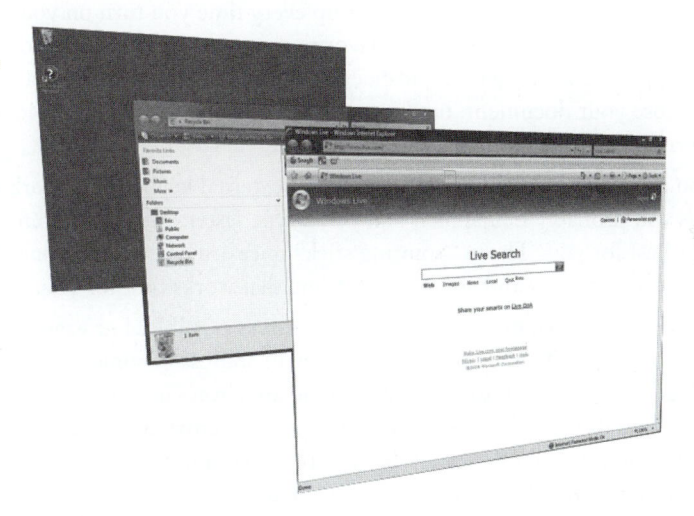

- Buy an ergonomic keyboard, split in the middle. Try not to rest your wrists on a hard surface. Cut a mouse pad in half and use Velcro, tape, or glue to affix it to the palm rest in front of the keys, if you're a "leaner."
- Double-click a window's title bar to make it go full screen. Editing in little windows on the screen is a hassle and requires unnecessary scrolling.
- To close a foreground program or window, press Alt+F4. It's that easy. Alternatively, right-click its button on the taskbar and choose Close. Aiming for that little X in the upper-right corner takes too much mouse movement.

- Put all your favorite applications, dial-up connections, folders, and documents on the Quick Launch bar. Forget about the Start button. You can put about 20 things on the Quick Launch bar for easy one-click access. Use it. When an item falls out of use, erase the shortcut. They're only shortcuts, so it doesn't matter if you erase them.

- If there are too many items within the Quick Launch bar to be displayed within the current area, two little arrows (>>) are displayed. This indicates that other Quick Launch icons are present but are currently hidden from view. To see the hidden icons, click on the double arrow to see a pop-up menu, or click and drag the edge of the main toolbar area (just to the right of the Quick Launch bar) to expand the space available for the Quick Launch bar.

- Those little double arrows appear in many locations throughout the user experience. You'll see them on the Quick Launch bar, the notification area, ends of toolbars, and more. They simply indicate that either more data is available but it's currently hidden from view, or all data is currently displayed but it can be hidden or reduced in size. In some cases, the double arrows are a toggle between minimum and expanded views; other times, the double arrows display the hidden items when clicked but return to their previous display after you make a selection or click somewhere else.

- Use Sleep and Hibernate. Don't boot up every time you turn on your computer; it's a waste of valuable time. Keep your favorite programs open: email, word processor, picture viewer, web browser, spreadsheet, whatever. Yes, do save your work and maybe even close your document, but leave the apps open and keep the machine in Sleep or Hibernate mode.

- If you use a laptop in the office, get a good external keyboard to work with it. Your hands will probably be happier, and you'll type faster. Also get a pointing device that works best for you. Those "pointing stick" mice are not for everyone. Try a few different pointing devices and come up with one that works best for you.

- Discover and use right-click shortcuts whenever possible. For example, in Windows Mail, you can easily copy the name and email address of someone from the Address Book and paste them into an email. People are always asking me for email addresses of mutual friends or colleagues. I click on a person's entry in the Address Book and press Ctrl+C (for copy); then I switch back to the email I'm writing and press Ctrl+V (paste). Then I press Ctrl+Enter, and the email is sent.

- Also in Windows Mail, you can reply to an email with Ctrl+R. Forward one with Ctrl+F. Send a message you've just written by pressing Ctrl+Enter. Send and receive all mail with Ctrl+M.

- In Internet Explorer, use the F11 toggle to go full screen. This gets all the other junk off the screen. Also, use the Search panel to do your web searches (opened by clicking the magnifying glass search toolbar button). You can easily check search results without having to use the Back button. And speaking of the Back button, don't bother moving the mouse up there to click Back. Just press Alt+left arrow. The left- and right-arrow buttons with Alt are the same as the Back and Forward buttons.

- In most Microsoft applications, including Windows Mail and Internet Explorer, F5 is the "refresh" key. In Windows Mail, for example, pressing F5 sends and receives all your mail, as long as the Inbox is highlighted. In IE, it refreshes the page. In Windows Explorer, it updates the listing in a window (to reflect the results of a file move, for example). Remember F5!
- In Word, Excel, and many other applications, Ctrl+F6 is the key that switches between open windows within the same app. No need to click on the Window menu in the application and choose the document in question. Just cycle through them with Ctrl+F6.
- In whatever applications you use most, look for shortcut keys or macros you can use or create to avoid unnecessary repetitious work. Most of us type the same words again and again. (See, there I go.) As writers, for example, we have macros programmed in Microsoft Word for common words such as *Windows Vista*, *Control Panel*, *desktop*, *folders*, and so on. Bob has created a slew of editing macros that perform tasks such as "delete to the end of line" (Ctrl+P), "delete line" (Ctrl+Y), and so on. In Word, press Alt+T+A and check out the AutoCorrect and AutoText features.

→ See Chapter 26 to add more time-saving tricks to your arsenal.

CHAPTER 5

MANAGING FILES AND SEARCHING

In this chapter

What's New in Windows Explorer   164

Buttons, Breadcrumbs, Toolbars, and More   170

Navigating the File System   177

Customizing File and Folder Views   185

Searching   189

Zipping and Packing Files   198

File and Folder Security   200

Troubleshooting   201

Tips from the Windows Pros: Using the Search Tool from the Start Menu   202

What's New in Windows Explorer

Chapter 4, "Using the Windows Vista Interface," touched on the two applications that allow you to view and manipulate files, folders, and other computer information: Computer and Windows Explorer. You may remember that Computer was dubbed My Computer in earlier versions of Windows, and both Computer and Windows Explorer are still present in Windows Vista with many of the same functions and features as in previous versions of Windows.

Yes, Windows Explorer is still hidden away in the Accessories area of the Start menu. Microsoft wants to draw your attention away from how files are managed on the hard drive and to direct your attention to how documents are arranged within your personal folders (such as Documents, Pictures, and so on). Computer and Windows Explorer are used to access the folder structure of your hard drives to locate files. Through these tools you can move, copy, delete, rename, create new, and more.

Indeed, Computer and Windows Explorer have the same interface and the same options. If you're in Windows Explorer, you can open the Computer folder to view your computer's media, and you can view other directories in the Computer window. The only difference is that when you open Computer from the Start menu, the Computer folder opens in the left pane and shows the current hard drives and removable drives installed on the computer, as shown in Figure 5.1.

Figure 5.1
The Computer window with the hard drives and removable drives in the right pane.

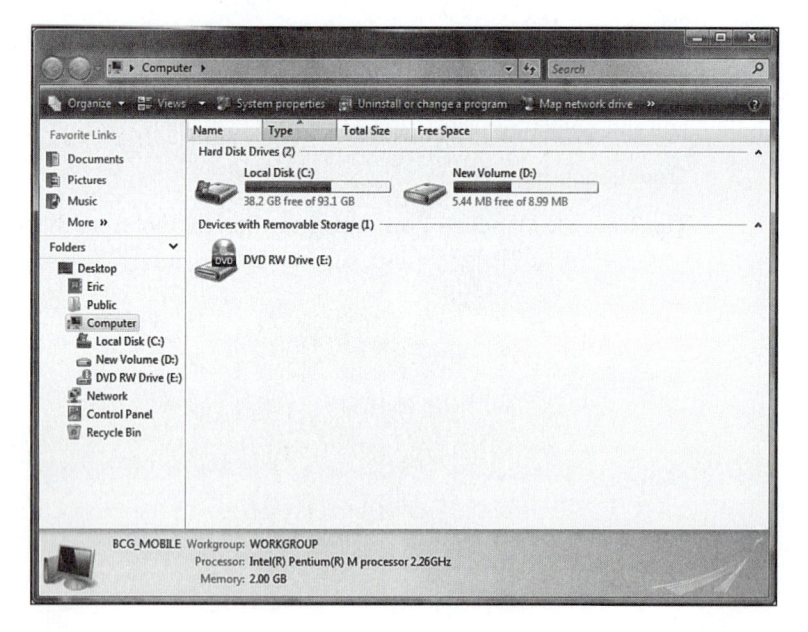

However, when you open Windows Explorer, Vista actually opens the Documents folder and displays the files and folders within the Documents folder as shown in Figure 5.2.

Figure 5.2
The Windows Explorer window with the contents of the Documents folder in the right pane.

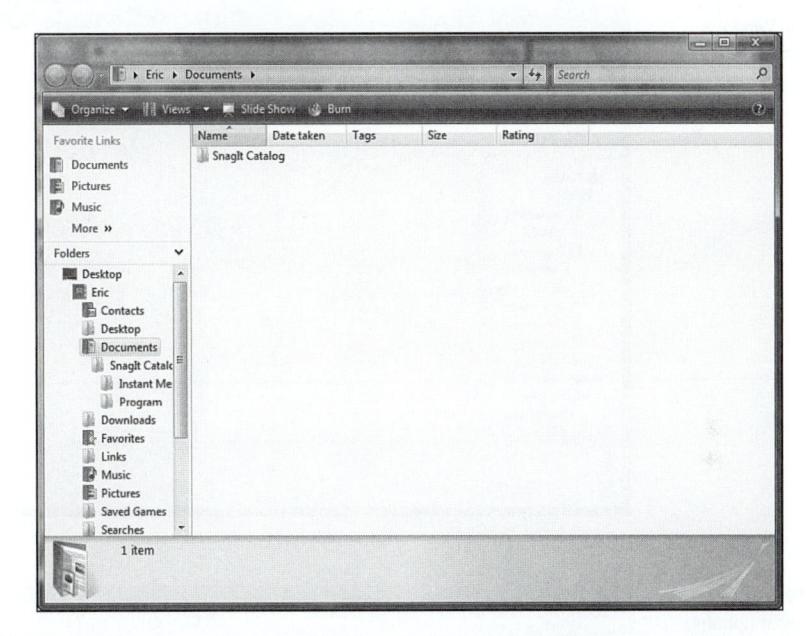

Though Computer and Windows Explorer have many of the same features as My Computer and Windows Explorer in older versions of Windows, there are significant changes as well:

- The menu bar at the top of the window is gone and is replaced with features closely aligned with the search and navigation tools in Internet Explorer. These include Back and Forward buttons, a box that shows *breadcrumbs* of where you are in relation to other windows, and the Search box replaces the Search pane in older versions of My Computer/Windows Explorer. (See more about breadcrumbs, below.)

- The toolbar has been combined with organizational features of the menu bar in older versions of My Computer/Windows Explorer; the options in the toolbar change to reflect the type of information you're viewing in the right pane so that you can perform tasks more quickly. For example, if you're viewing multimedia files in your Documents folder you may see toolbar options for burning a CD or creating a slideshow, as shown in Figure 5.3. If you're viewing your computer media in the Computer window you'll see toolbar options to view system properties, uninstall or change a program, map a network drive, and more as shown in Figure 5.4.

Figure 5.3
The toolbar options for the Documents folder in Windows Explorer.

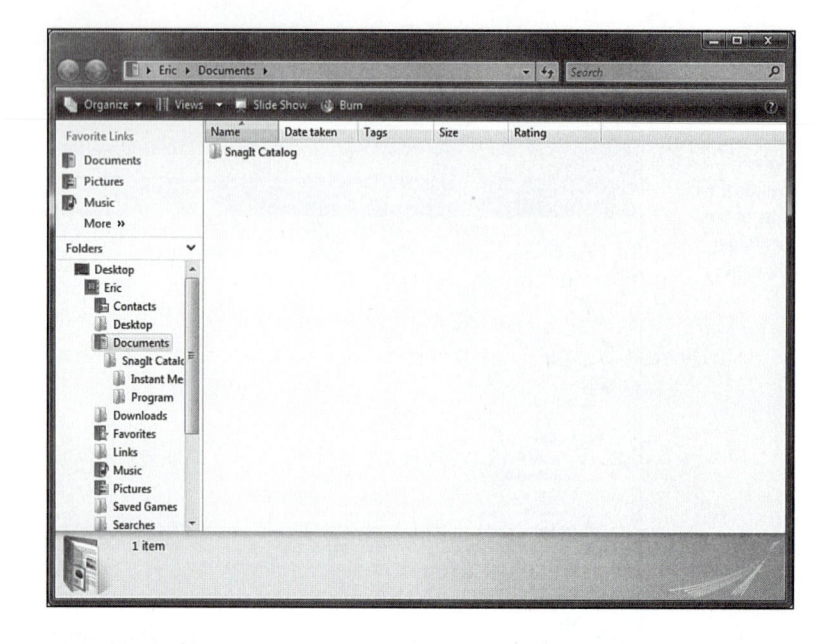

Figure 5.4
The toolbar options for the computer media listed in the Computer window.

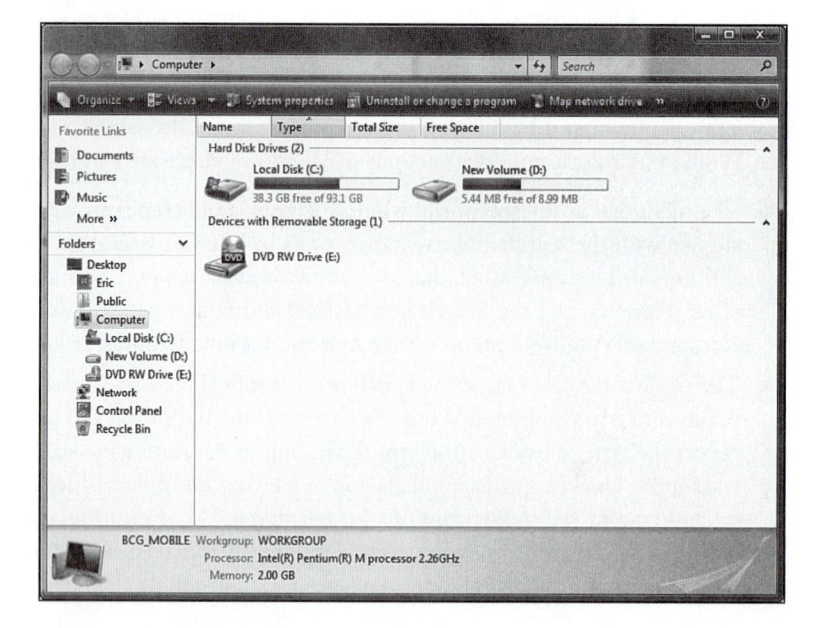

> **NOTE**
>
> If you have more toolbar options than the toolbar can hold, Windows Vista gives you a clue that more options are available by showing the double-arrow (>>) button to the right of the rightmost button in the toolbar. Figure 5.4 shows an example of this double-arrow button.

- You now have a wider variety of views when you look at objects in the Computer or Windows Explorer windows. You'll learn more about the different views available to you in the "Customizing File and Folder Views" section later in this chapter.

- Instead of clicking Help in the menu bar as you did in earlier versions of My Computer/Windows Explorer, the Computer and Windows Explorer window toolbars in Windows Vista include a Help button at the right side of the toolbars. When you click this button, the Help and Support Center window opens and displays the topic that is most germane to your current situation in the window.

- Though the list of folders appears in the left pane as with previous versions of My Computer/Windows Explorer, both Computer and Windows Explorer in Windows Vista include the Favorite Links section above the Folders list. The Favorite Links section lets you access the master folders for Documents, Pictures, and Music.

- The More button underneath Favorite Links contains the options Recently Changed and Searches, so you can see folders that contain recently changed files as well as the results of recent searches. You'll learn more about these and other "breadcrumbs" in the "Buttons, Breadcrumbs, Toolbars, and More" section later in this chapter.

- The Details pane appears at the bottom of the window that shows *metadata*, or information about the information in the computer (in the Computer window) or in the folder (in the Windows Explorer window). See "Viewing Meta-information" later in this chapter for more information.

THE LEGACY OF WEBVIEW

Windows XP included its WebView technology that attempted to make your local content integrate as seamlessly as possible with Internet-based content. This integration was designed to offer the benefits of more information displayed within the interface by default and quick access to common activities.

> **NOTE**
> The chapters in Part IV, "Windows Vista and the Internet," cover the ins and outs of getting connected, browsing the Web, using search engines, creating and serving web pages, and using email, newsgroups, and so forth. However, what's relevant here is how the Windows Vista WebView affects how you work with files and folders.

Microsoft ended WebView with Windows XP, but many features of WebView have been integrated into Windows Explorer and the Computer folder in Windows Explorer, and these features have been improved and refined in Windows Vista.

Figure 5.5 shows Windows Explorer in WebView. WebView gives you access to some common tasks related to files and folders in the toolbar above the left and right panes. The Details pane at the bottom of the window displays basic information about a selected item, such as

- The selected item's name and type (such as document, folder, application, and so on)

Figure 5.5
Windows Explorer in WebView.

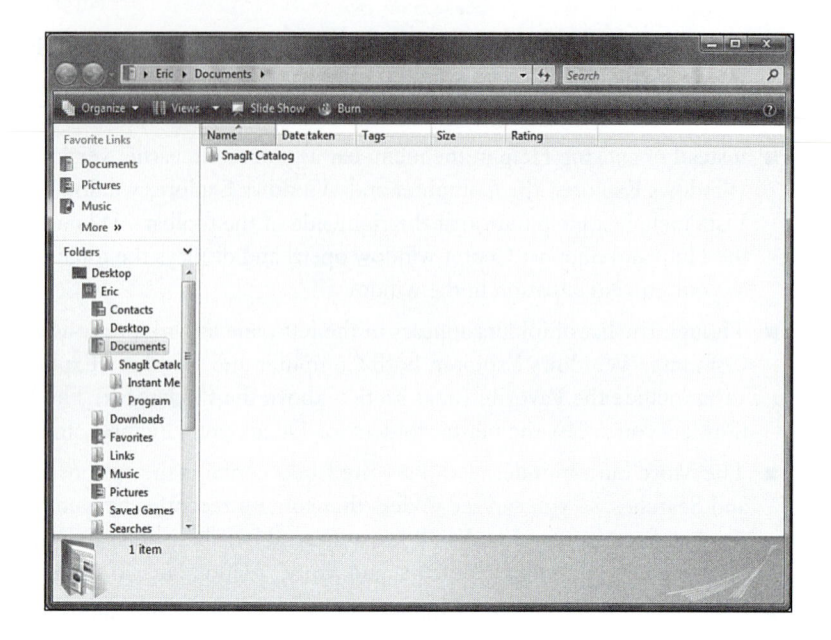

- The date on which it was most recently modified
- Its size, author, and other item-specific information

Much of this information also appears in a ToolTip when the mouse cursor is placed over an object.

Some key WebView effects have remained in Windows Vista such as the desktop Sidebar. Microsoft has worked hard to dovetail the interfaces of Internet Explorer and Computer/Windows Explorer more tightly than ever in Windows Vista. Some of the key WebView effects that have remained in Windows Vista include

- Computer and Windows Explorer have Back and Forward buttons, an Address bar, and a Search box just like Internet Explorer.
- The toolbars in folder and Windows Explorer windows are customizable and have address lines, just like a browser. You can type in a web address and press Enter (or click Go), and the Internet Explorer window will open and display the content. If you enter a web address, that page will display. If you enter a drive letter (C:, for example), its contents will be displayed.
- Windows Vista can navigate the contents of compressed archives, such as zip files, without a third-party utility. Archive files act like compressed folders. You'll learn more about zipping and packing files in "Zipping and Packing Files" later in this chapter.

There are many more features and options in the interface, but we'll get to those in the sections on customizing with the Control Panel, as well as in the Windows Explorer and Computer coverage. Also, Chapter 26, "Tweaking the GUI," covers even more ways to change the interface.

The WebView features are enabled by default on Windows Vista. But if you decide you would rather live without WebView features, it is not difficult to return to the Classic style of Windows 2000's interfaces. WebView is enabled and disabled through the Folder Options Control Panel applet by choosing Appearance and Personalization, Folder Options from the Control Panel window. As shown in Figure 5.6, WebView is enabled or disabled on the General tab of the Folder Options Control Panel applet by choosing either Show Preview and Filters or Use Windows Classic Folders. This is a systemwide change. After WebView is disabled, it is disabled on all Windows Explorer and Computer windows.

Figure 5.6
The General tab of the Folder Options Control Panel applet.

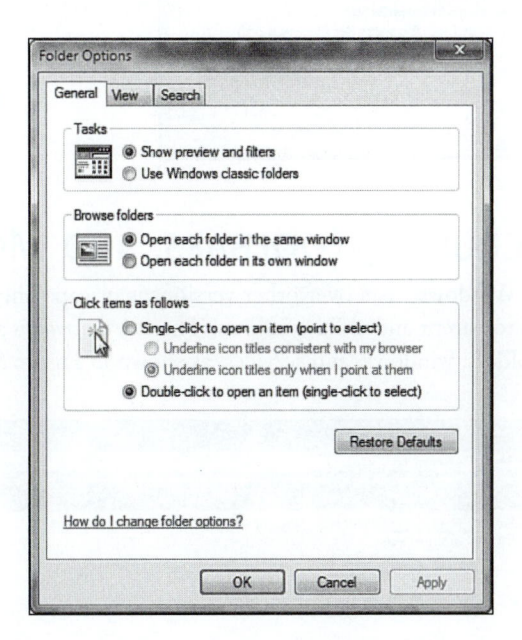

If you're the controlling type, you might want to fine-tune other aspects of your folders' behavior. Go back to the Folder Options applet and then select the View tab. You'll see a bevy of options that affect how folders and their contents are displayed, as shown in Figure 5.7. We'll discuss more of the settings in the View tab later in this chapter and check out most of the View tab options in Chapter 26.

Figure 5.7
The View tab of the Folder Options Control Panel applet.

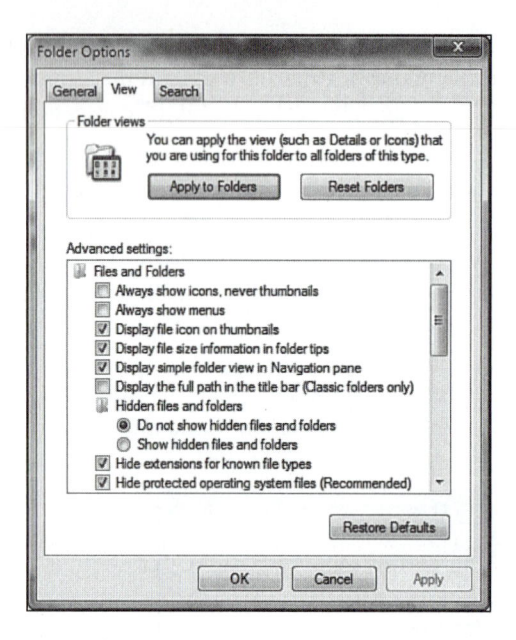

Buttons, Breadcrumbs, Toolbars, and More

One big improvement in Windows Vista over other versions is its capability to let you know where you are in relation to parent and child windows. These *breadcrumbs* appear as text and icon representations of folders, windows, and services, as shown in Figure 5.8.

Figure 5.8
Breadcrumbs in the Address bar.

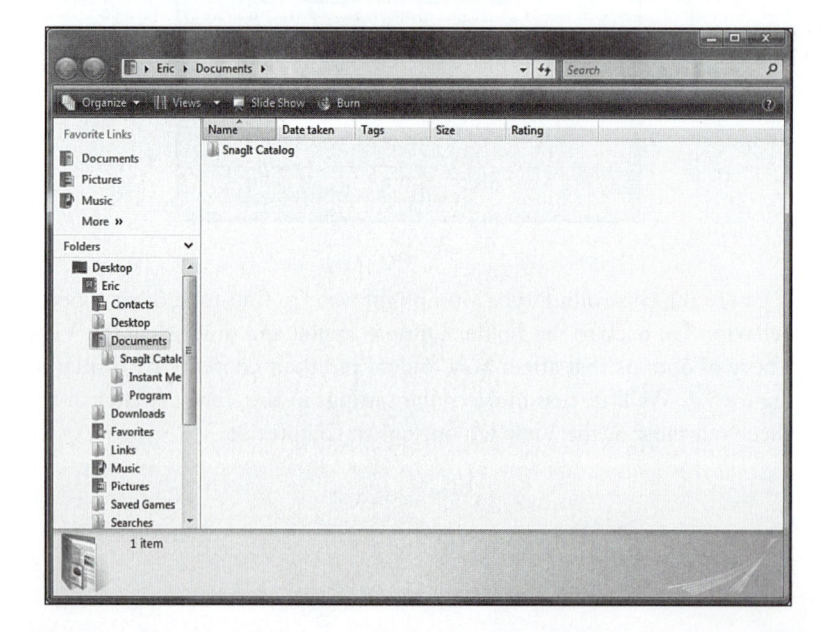

The Address bar displays your current *location*, which is any disk drive, folder, or other place where you can store files and folders. As you read the Address bar from left to right, the parent location appears at the far left of the box. Each child location appears directly to the right of its parent location, and the current location you're in appears without any child locations to its right. For example, in Figure 5.8, the current location is Documents because each breadcrumb is separated by an arrow pointing to the right.

> **NOTE**
>
> If there are no other child locations underneath the parent location, a right arrow will only appear to the right of the location name if that location has a submenu associated with it. Otherwise, no right arrow will appear next to the location name.

The breadcrumbs that appear depend on the folder you're in. What's more, the right arrow not only shows that the next window or service is the child of the current parent or service, but it also lets you select from a menu of related options. Let's take a look at examples of the breadcrumbs you see in the Computer window and Windows Explorer.

> **TIP**
>
> If you want to see the exact folder path you're in instead of the location, click on a blank area in the Address bar. The information in the Address bar changes to the exact folder path as shown in Figure 5.9. Return to the location view by clicking on a blank spot in the Folders tree or in the right pane.
>
> You can also type the exact folder path in the Address bar to open the folder instead of using location-based navigation.

Figure 5.9
The Address bar with the folder path.

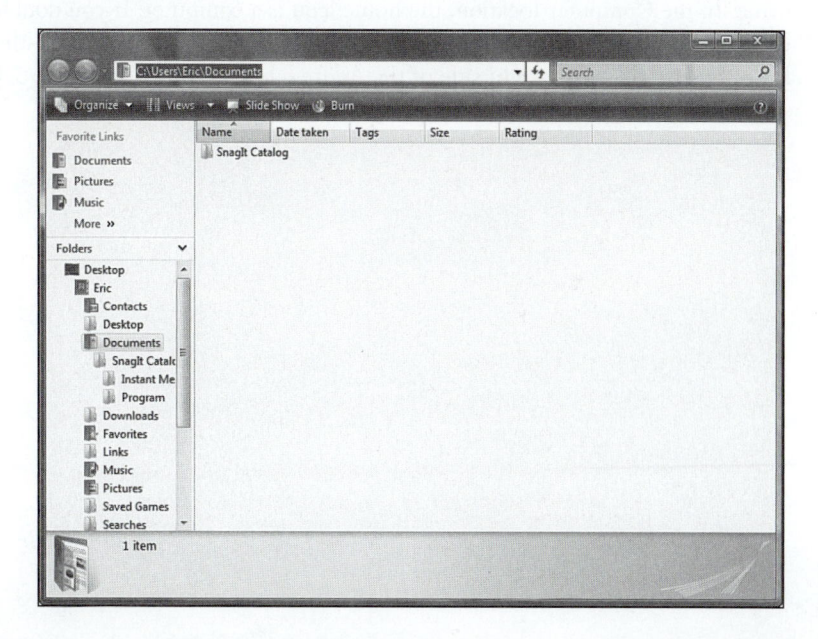

Breadcrumbs in the Computer Window

When you open the Computer window, the open Computer folder displays the computer media information in the right pane. In the Address bar, you see a computer icon and the location name Computer as shown in Figure 5.10.

Figure 5.10
The Computer window Address bar.

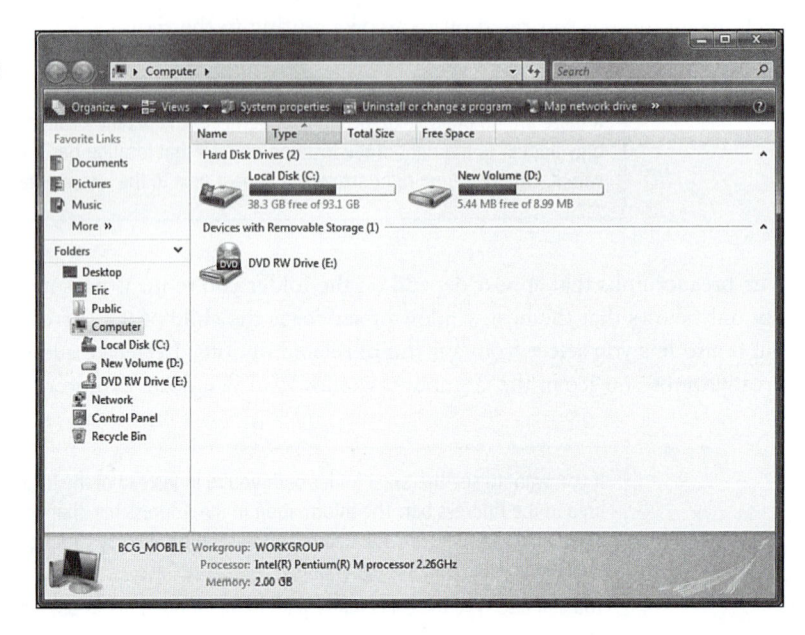

The home icon appears at the left side of the Address bar, followed by the Computer folder name. In the Computer location, the home icon is a computer. If you double-click on the C: drive in the right pane, the Address bar adds the name of your C: drive—the default name is Local Disk (C:)—to the right side of the Address bar, as shown in Figure 5.11.

Figure 5.11
The Computer window Address bar with the name of the C: drive added.

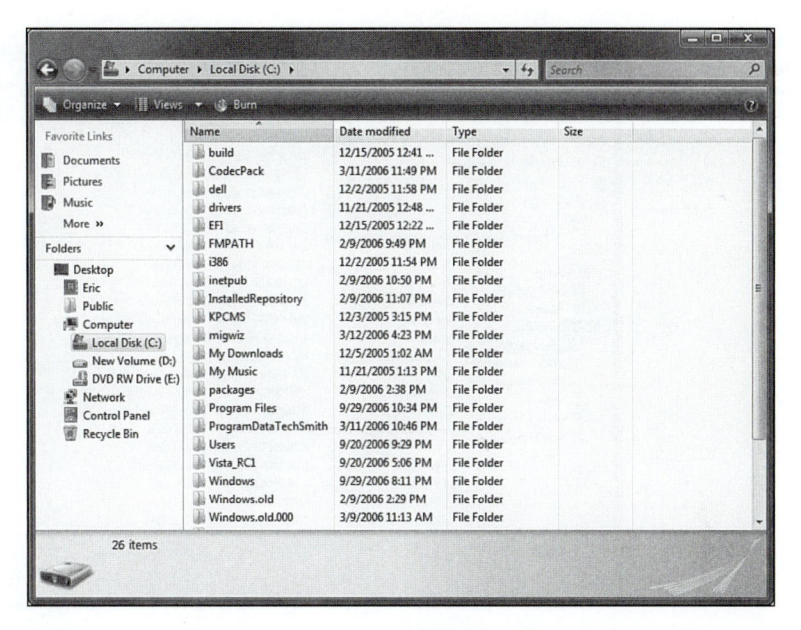

Note that the home icon has changed from a computer to a hard disk. The icon changes to reflect the location type. For example, if you open a folder in the C: drive, the icon in the Address bar changes to an open folder.

If there is a submenu underneath a location in the Address bar, you can open this submenu by clicking on the right arrow to the right of each location. When you click on the right arrow, the arrow changes to a button and the arrow points down toward the menu, which appears directly underneath the down arrow. Figures 5.12, 5.13, and 5.14 show the submenus for the home icon, the Computer location, and the Local Disk (C: drive), respectively.

Figure 5.12
The submenu for the home location.

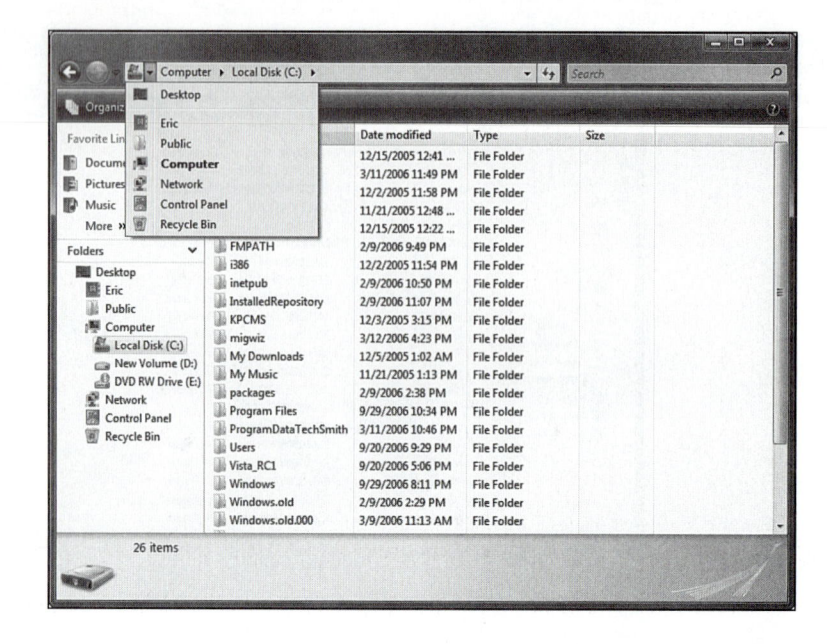

Figure 5.13
The submenu for the Computer location.

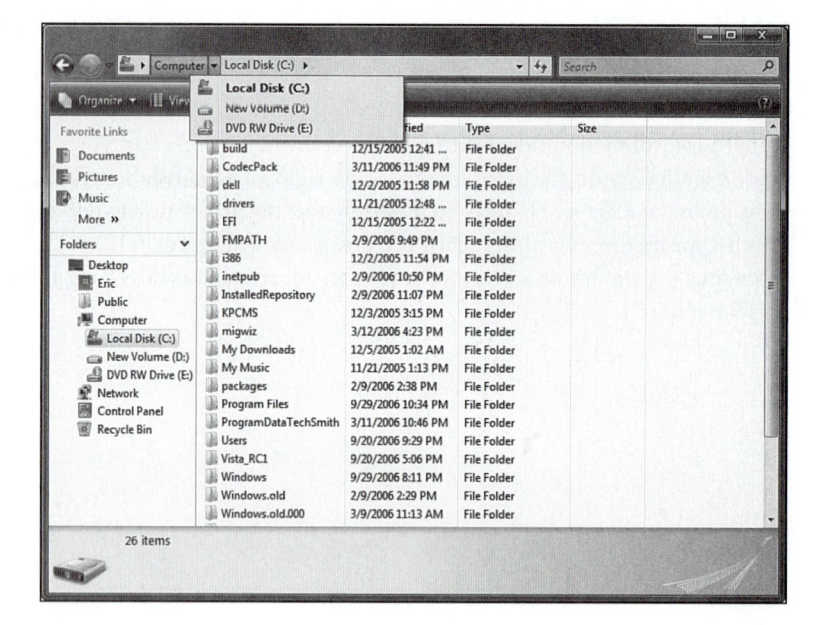

Figure 5.14
The submenu for the Local Disk (C:) location.

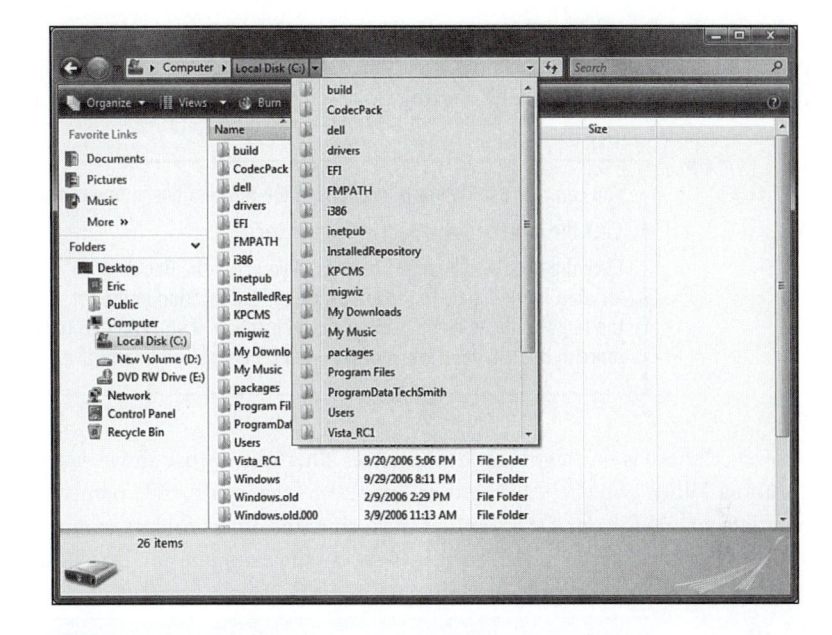

Menu options in bold text are locations that are currently open. If you click another location in the menu, the Address bar changes to reflect the new location to which you have moved.

Breadcrumbs in Windows Explorer

When you open Windows Explorer, the Documents folder opens by default. In the Address bar, you see that the Documents folder is your location as shown in Figure 5.15.

Figure 5.15
The Address bar for the Documents folder.

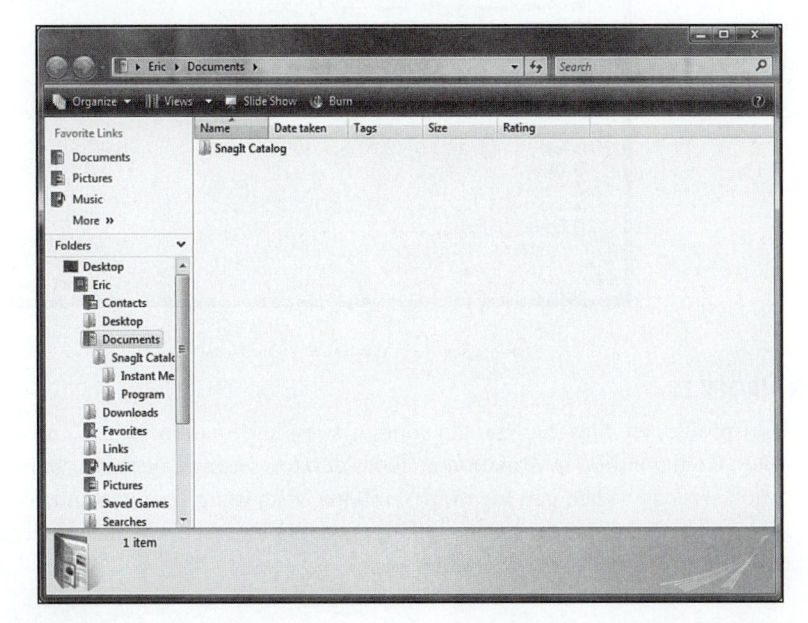

The functionality of the Address bar in Windows Explorer is the same as in the Computer window—you can move to a location by clicking on the location name in the Address bar, and you can also open submenus by clicking on the right arrow to the right of the location name.

> **TIP**
>
> You can move to different locations in the Address bar in one of two ways:
>
> Click the location name in the Address bar.
>
> Click the Back and Forward buttons. If you click the Back button, you go back to the location immediately to the left of the current location in the list. Click the Forward button to go to the current location's child location. If you can't go back and forward any more in the list, the Back and/or Forward buttons will be inactive.

However, there is one significant difference: The Address bar shows your user profile as a location. When you click the right arrow next to the user profile name a submenu appears that lets you open your Desktop files, Favorites and Links folders, contacts, games and media folders, and searches. Figure 5.16 shows the submenu for Eric's user profile.

Figure 5.16
The submenu for Eric's user profile.

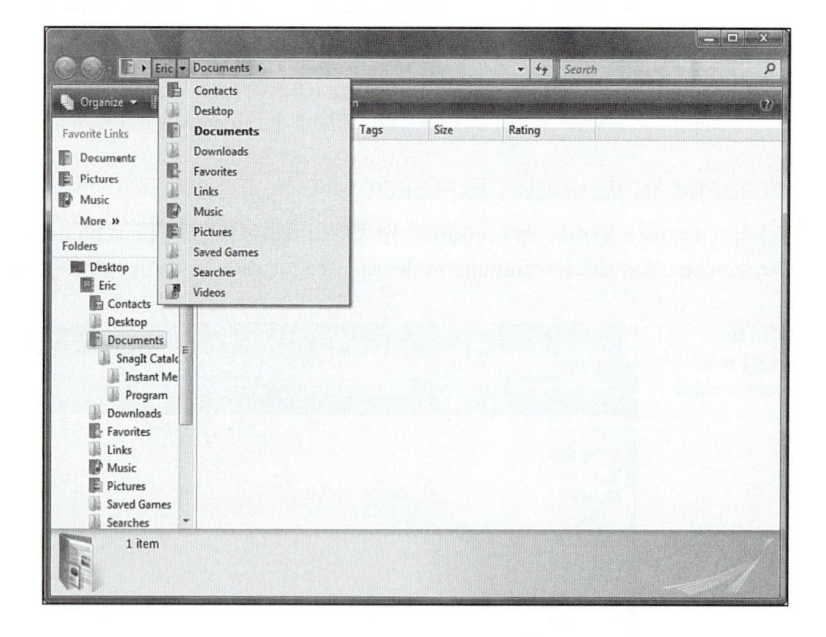

USER PROFILES

User profiles are files that contain configuration information for each user on your computer. Configuration information includes desktop settings, network connections, and application settings. When you log in to Windows Vista using your account, Windows reads this user profile and configures your desktop, network connections, and application settings so that everything works the way you expect.

A user profile is different from a user account. A user account contains information about what files and folders your account can access, the changes your account can make to your computer, and your user preferences such as your desktop background and color theme.

Windows Vista assigns the same number and type of directories shown in Figure 5.16 to each user profile. The user profile file also remembers which files go in which directory for that user. For example, if I have my own documents in my Documents directory and Lisa has her own documents in her Documents directory, I will see only my documents in my Documents folder.

Navigating the File System

Microsoft has refined file system navigation even further in Windows Vista. The biggest navigation change is the removal of the menu bar that was a staple in Windows XP and earlier versions of Windows. In Windows Vista, you now have a toolbar that changes every time you click on an object in the Computer window or Windows Explorer. These changes reflect what you can do with the file or folder. The menu bar still exists, however, and you can enable the menu bar as described in "Turning Panes On and Off" later in this chapter.

Figures 5.17 and 5.18 show two different examples of menu toolbar options available for two different objects. In Figure 5.17, the Windows Explorer window shows the Music folder with the four menu toolbar buttons showing what you can do with the files including Play All to play all the music files in the folder and Burn to burn a CD.

Figure 5.17
The Music folder menu toolbar options.

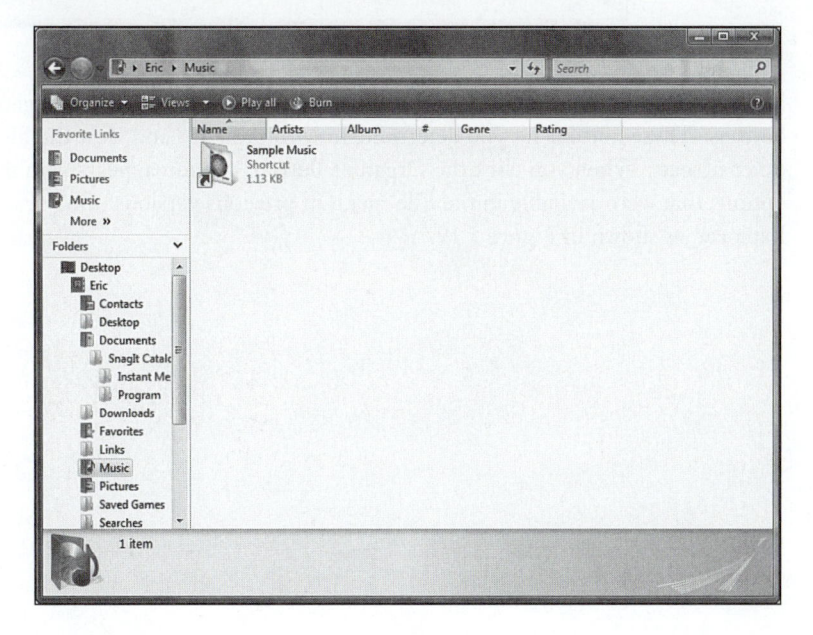

CHAPTER 5 MANAGING FILES AND SEARCHING

Figure 5.18 shows the Computer window with the computer's media listed. The menu toolbar buttons are different from those available for the Music folder. You can access system properties, uninstall or change a program, or map a network drive. So many toolbar buttons are available that they can't all fit on the toolbar. If you click on the double-arrow (>>) to the right of Map Network Drive you'll see a pop-up menu for opening the Control Panel.

Figure 5.18
The Computer menu toolbar options.

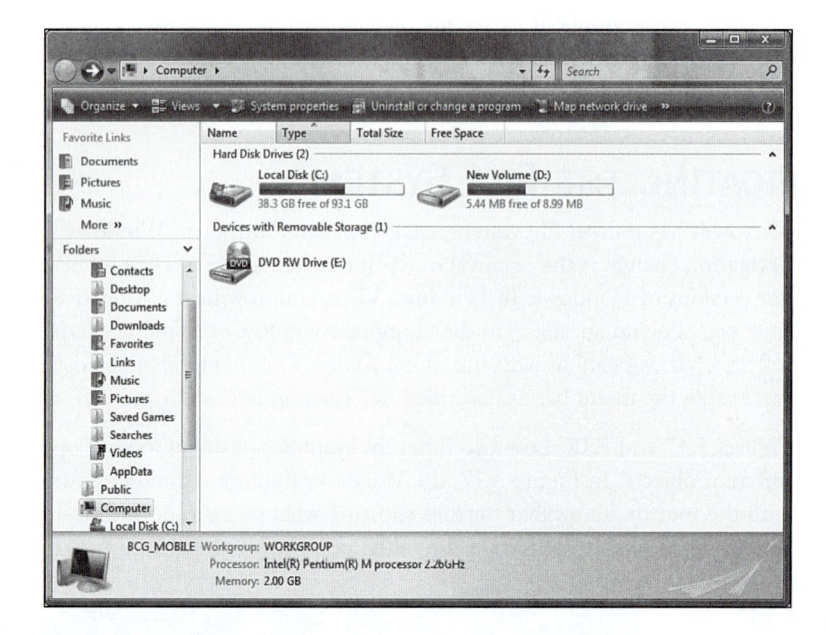

You probably noticed that one part of the toolbar never changes: the Organize and Views buttons. These buttons let you determine how to organize and view the files, folders, and other objects. When you click the Organize button, a menu appears with many of the same options that were available in the File menu in previous versions of My Computer/Windows Explorer, as shown in Figure 5.19.

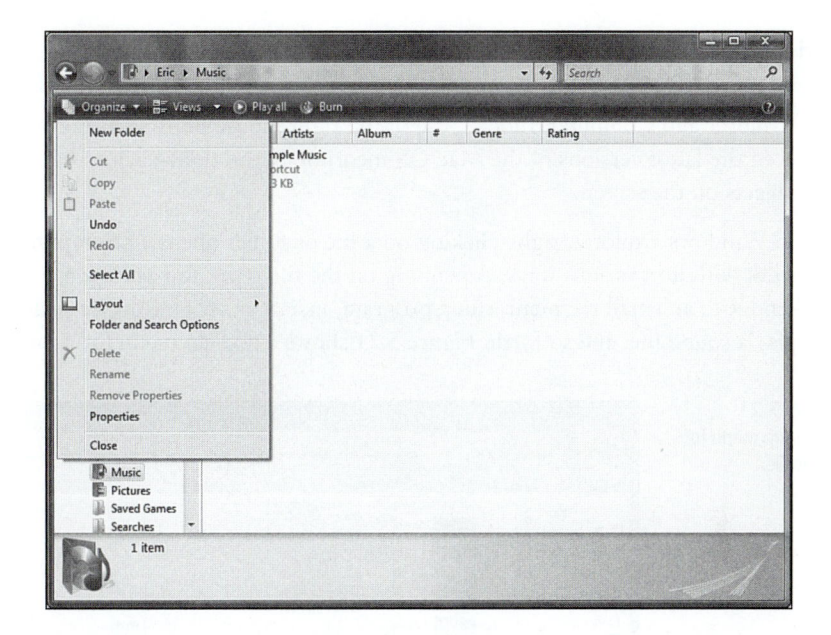

Figure 5.19
The Organize menu.

When you click the Views button, the Views menu appears as shown in Figure 5.20. The Views menu shows you the different ways of presenting information in the right pane of the window. You can select from seven different options using the slider bar, and the slider appears to the left of the selected view type. You will learn more about views in the "Customizing File and Folder Views" section later in this chapter.

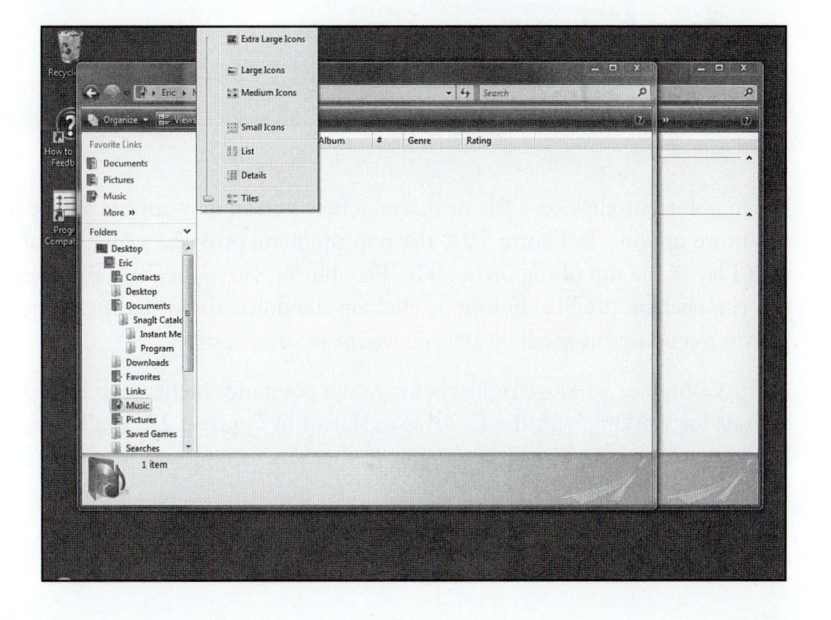

Figure 5.20
The Views menu.

Right-Clicking

Windows makes good use of the right mouse button to access information in Windows Explorer and Computer. Indeed, use of the right mouse button has become so prevalent that even the latest versions of the Mac OS incorporate the right-click to open and manipulate objects on the screen.

In Windows Explorer, right-clicking on a file or folder opens a pop-up menu so that you can work with it in various ways, depending on the file type. You can open a document or folder, send it to an email recipient, run a program, install or set up a utility such as a screen saver, play a sound file, and so forth. Figure 5.21 shows a pop-up menu for a music file.

Figure 5.21
The pop-up menu for a music file.

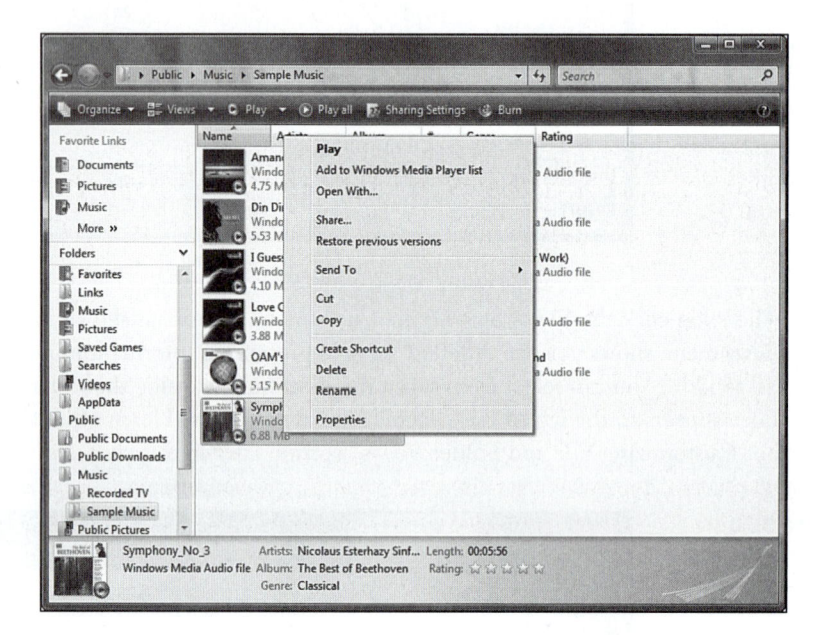

When you right-click on a file or folder, a new button may appear on the menu bar to give you more options. In Figure 5.21, the pop-up menu provides a number of choices starting with Play at the top of the menu. The Play button also appears in the menu toolbar so that you can click on the Play button or click on the down arrow button to the right of the Play button to choose the media player you want to use.

In the Computer window, right-clicking on a computer media icon brings up different options for working with the C: drive as shown in Figure 5.22. You'll also notice that the Properties button appears in the menu so that you can open up the Properties window for the C: drive.

Figure 5.22
The pop-up menu for a hard drive.

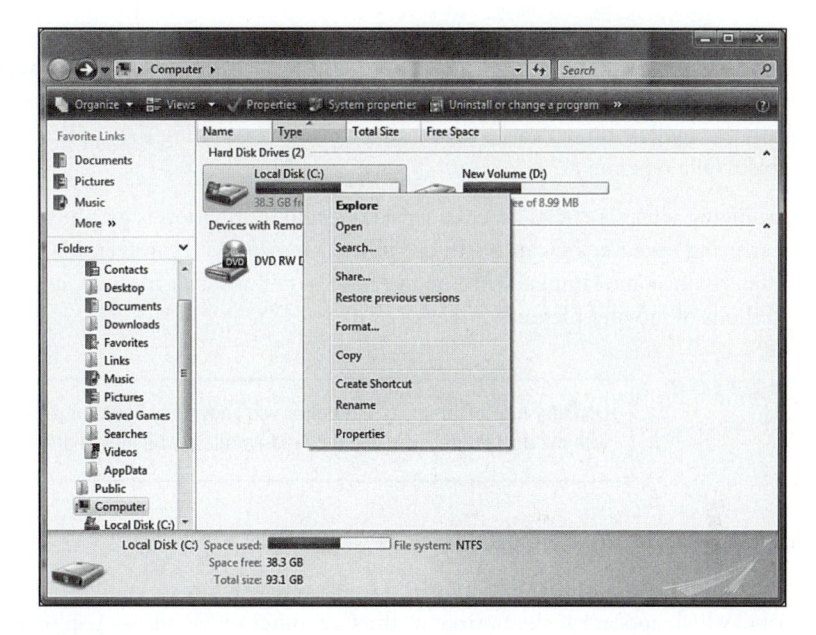

Selecting Several Items

On most lists, especially within Computer and Windows Explorer, not to mention the file and browser dialog boxes, you can select multiple items at once to save time. The normal rules of selection apply:

- Draw a box around them by clicking and holding over empty space near the first item amd then drag across and over the desired selections until all are highlighted and/or contained within the selection box; then release the mouse button.

- Select the first of the items, hold down the Ctrl key, and click to select each additional object you want to work with. Use this technique to select a number of noncontiguous items.

- Select the first of the items, hold down the Shift key, and click the last item. This selects the entire *range* of objects between the starting and ending points.

After several items are selected (they will be highlighted), right-clicking any one of the objects brings up the Cut, Copy, Paste menu. The option you choose applies to *all* the selected items. Also, clicking anywhere outside the selected items deselects them all, and Ctrl-clicking (or pointing) to one selected object deselects that object.

Drag-and-drop support is implemented uniformly across the Windows Vista interface. In general, if you want something placed somewhere else, you can drag it from the source to the destination. For example, you can drag items from the Search box into a folder or onto the desktop, or you can add a picture attachment to an email you're composing by dragging the picture file into the new email's window. Also, the destination folder does not have to be open in a window. Items dropped onto a closed folder icon are added to that folder. You can also drag and drop items via the taskbar by dragging an item over an application button and waiting a second for that application to be brought to the forefront. You can also drop items into the Start menu to add them to the listings, or drop items over desktop icons to open them with the application onto which you drop the item (assuming the application supports the object's file type).

Arranging your screen so you can see source and destination is graphically and intuitively reassuring because you can see the results of the process. However, it's not always the easiest. After you become familiar with the interface, you'll want to try the Cut, Copy, and Paste methods of moving files and folders.

> **CAUTION**
>
> Don't try moving program files unless you know they have not registered themselves with the operating system and they can harmlessly be moved around between folders.

Viewing Meta-Information

A feature in Computer and Windows Explorer that is new to Windows Vista is the Details pane, which appears at the bottom of the Computer or Windows Explorer window as shown in Figure 5.23.

Figure 5.23
The Details pane.

In Windows XP and older versions of Windows, Windows Explorer and My Computer only showed basic information about the selected object in the Status bar. This information is called *meta-information*, or information about the information contained in the file. For example, when you clicked on a Microsoft Word file you would see information about the type of file, the date and time the file was saved, and the size of the file all in small text that was squeezed onto one line in the Status bar.

As you can see in Figure 5.23, the Details pane provides more room for information about a selected object in a format that's much easier to read. Information in the details pane varies with the type of object you're viewing. In Figure 5.23, you see a music file that includes the following information:

- The icon associated with the file. In this case, it's a Beethoven album cover.
- The name of the file.
- The program the file is associated with, which is a Windows Media audio file.
- The name of the artist(s).
- The album name.
- The genre, which is classical.
- The length of the recording.
- The rating, which you can add in the music file properties. The rating can be from zero stars (which are all gray stars) to five gold stars.

The Details pane is different when you open the Computer window and click on the Local Disk (C:) icon. As shown in Figure 5.24, the Details pane shows a bar that denotes the amount of space used on the hard drive, the file system used, the amount of space free on the drive, and the total size of the drive.

Figure 5.24
The Details pane showing meta-information for Local Disk (C:).

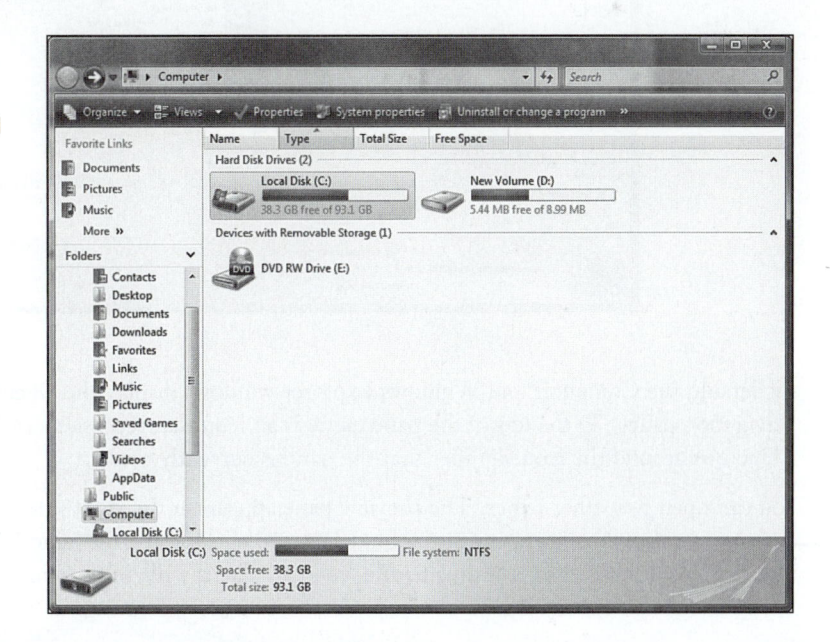

NOTE

If you don't select a file, folder, or other object in the right pane, the Details pane displays information about the current location. For example, if you haven't selected a file in the Music folder, the Details pane shows a folder icon with the number of items in the folder.

Turning Panes On and Off

The Computer and Windows Explorer windows have a total of four panes, and you can turn each one on and off to suit your needs. If you prefer to have a menu bar in the window, you can also display and use the menu bar.

View the panes and menu bar you have open by clicking the Organize button in the toolbar and then choosing Layout. The five options appear in the flyout menu as shown in Figure 5.25.

Figure 5.25
The Layout flyout menu.

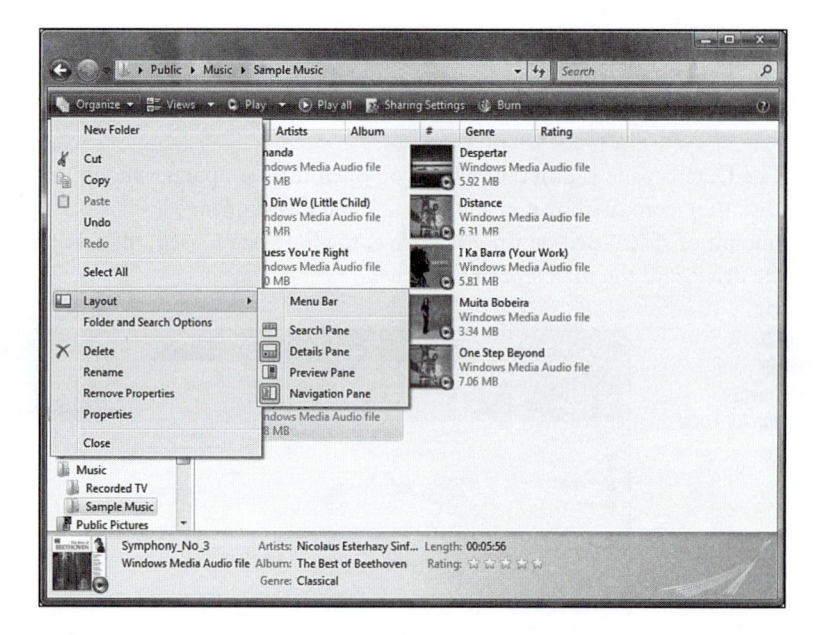

By default, the Computer and Windows Explorer windows display the Details and Navigation panes. To the left of the pane name is an icon that represents each pane, and a blue box around the icon signifies that the pane is currently active.

You can open two other panes. The preview pane appears at the right side of the window and shows a thumbnail preview of the file when you click on the filename, as shown in Figure 5.26. If the file is a multimedia file, you can play the file in the small window and see whether the file is something you want to play in Windows Media Player or your multimedia player of choice. If there is no file to preview, a message appears in the preview pane: "Select a file to preview."

Figure 5.26
The Preview pane.

NOTE The preview pane settings are specific to your current location. For example, if you enable the preview pane in the Music folder and then move to the Documents folder, you won't see the preview pane. However, if you go back to the Music folder the preview pane returns.

The other pane you can open is the Search pane, which you will learn about as part of a larger discussion about searching in the "Searching" section later in the chapter.

When you click on the Menu Bar in the Layout flyout menu, the menu bar you may be familiar with from earlier versions of Windows appears above the menu toolbar. This menu bar contains the well-known File, Edit, View, Tools, and Help menu options. Many features in these menus were brought over from Windows XP, and you can't get to these features without enabling the menu.

Customizing File and Folder Views

When you create a new user profile, Windows Vista automatically creates a personal folder that matches your username and places a number of subfolders within that master folder. These subfolders are categorized by name (including Documents, Photos, and Music) and allow you to put your files into them. What's more, these subfolders are private; no other user that uses your computer can view or open these subfolders. Yet what Microsoft gives you isn't uniquely you.

Windows Vista offers a wide range of options for customizing how files are displayed through the Computer and Windows Explorer utilities. The full set of options is available from the View menu, though you can access many of the options from the menu toolbar as well.

The View menu (see Figure 5.27) offers the following controls:

- **Toolbars**—This control is used to display any additional toolbars that you have installed on your computer. You can also lock the bars (so that stray clicks don't alter your layout) or fully customize the button toolbar.
- **Status Bar**—If you miss the Status bar at the bottom of the screen, this control enables the display of this information bar at the bottom of the window that shows object details, file size, free space, and so on.
- **Explorer Bar**—This control opens the Explorer bar at the bottom of the pane so that you can research a selected file in the list as well as discuss the file with others in the network.
- **Views**—This section allows quick change of the view used to display file objects: extra large icons, large icons, medium icons, small icons, list, details, and tiles.
- **Auto Arrange**—This command automatically arranges the files and folders in the list as Windows Vista sees fit.
- **Align to Grid**—This command automatically arranges the files and folders according to the Windows icon grid that you set up in Control Panel. See Chapter 26 for more information about tweaking the icon grid.
- **Sort By**—This menu allows you to determine the sort order for files and folders. For example, you could group music files by name and show the files in ascending order.
- **Group By**—This menu allows you to group files by a certain criteria, such as the filename.
- **Stack By**—This menu allows you to determine the stack order for a group of files. You'll learn more about stacking in the "Grouping and Stacking" section later in this chapter.
- **Choose Details**—This command sets the details that appear in ToolTips, details, and Tile view. The defaults are name, size, type, and modification date. Among the 33 options included are attributes, owner, subject, company, and file version.
- **Customize This Folder**—This command is used to define custom attributes for the selected folder (see the next section).
- **Go To**—This menu is used to navigate back, forward, up one level, to the home page, or to recently visited locations.
- **Refresh**—This command reloads the display of files and folders.

> **NOTE**
>
> Windows Vista remembers the view type you selected for each folder, but if a view type isn't specified, the default view type is Tiled.

Figure 5.27
The View menu of Windows Explorer.

Customize This Folder

If you have a complex organizational structure to your personal files, you might find this feature quite intriguing. Customizing folders allows you to select from five templates designed for a specific type of file (document, image, or music) or collection of files (all, one artist, one album). These templates set how the contents of these folders are displayed as well as the context for the menu commands. Additionally, you can define a custom image for thumbnails and a unique icon for the folder. All these customizations can help you keep track of what you've got stored where.

Setting Folder Options

Folder Options should be seen as more of a superset of controls over all folders on a system, whereas folder customization occurs on an individual or parent and subfolder basis. Folder Options is a Control Panel applet that you can access from Computer and Windows Explorer. This applet is used to set a wide range of file system features.

Open the Folder Options window by clicking the Organize button and then clicking Folder and Search Options. The Folder Options dialog box appears as shown in Figure 5.28.

Figure 5.28
The Folder Options dialog box.

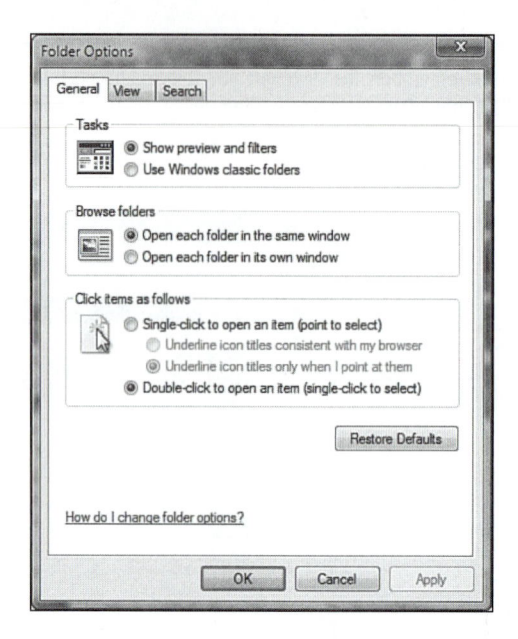

The General tab of the Folder Options dialog box defines whether common tasks are shown in folders or only classic Windows folders are displayed; whether folders are opened in the same or in a new window; and whether single-clicks or double-clicks are used to open items. If you make changes to this tab, you can always return to the default by clicking the Restore Defaults button.

The View tab (see Figure 5.29) performs two major functions—folder view management and advanced settings management. For folder view management, all folders can be reset to their default views, or the currently selected folder's view can be applied to all folders. Advanced settings management contains a long checklist of settings.

Figure 5.29
The View tab of Folder Options.

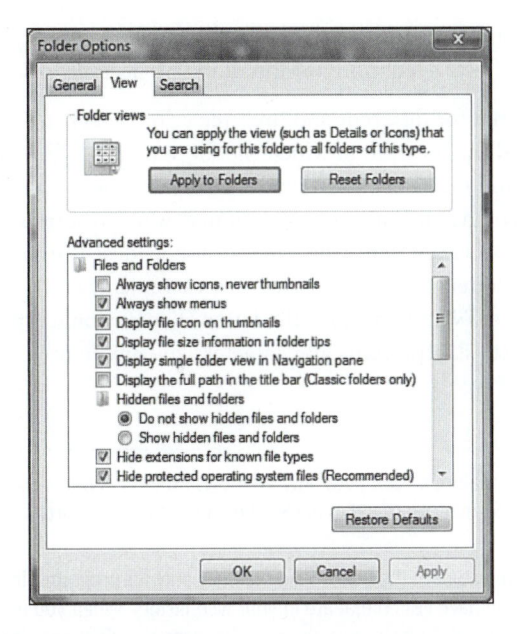

Because I like seeing every file on my system, I always enable Show Hidden Files and Folders and disable Hide Extensions for Known File Types and Hide Protected Operating System Files. You need to make your own choice on what you want the OS to show you and hide from you. If you want to return to the defaults, just click the Restore Defaults button.

> **NOTE**
>
> If you've tried to delete a folder that looked empty but an error message states that the folder still contains files, you are probably dealing with hidden files. To see what's not being shown, change the Hidden Files and Folders Advanced setting. I've run into this issue a few times with downloaded applications that must be extracted to a temporary folder before being installed. They sometimes include files premarked as hidden.

The other tab in the Folder Options window is the Search tab, which you learn more about in the next section.

SEARCHING

Windows Vista uses two different types of searching: intermediate and deep.

Intermediate searching uses an index to find objects with filenames that you type into the Search box in Windows as well as in the Start menu. Like the index of a book, Windows Vista stores information about files such as the filename, file date, and properties, including words in a document. As you type your search criteria into the Search box, the list of programs changes to show you files that meet that criteria based on what Windows Vista finds in the index. The big advantage to intermediate searching is that it's fast, but it only uses one criteria (the filename), so if you need more information you need deep searching.

Deep searching lets you search for different and multiple criteria such as the filename, the date the file was saved, and the location in which the file was saved. You can use Boolean arguments such as AND and OR as well as "greater than" and "less than" to help Windows Vista search for the files you need. For example, you may want to search for a file that was saved before (or less than) a certain date. You can also use wildcards in filenames to search for filenames that contain letters in certain places. For example, if you want to search for files that start with the letter N and end with the letter W, you would type **N*W** as the filename to search for; the asterisk represents all characters and any number of characters between N and W.

> **NOTE**
>
> The Search feature in Computer and Windows Explorer is not the same as the Search box or the Search command in the Start menu or the Live Search feature in Internet Explorer 7.
>
> The Search feature in the Start menu searches only for programs, Internet favorites, and websites you have visited that are in your web history. When you use the search engine in IE7 (be it the default Live Search or another search engine), that search engine searches the Web, not your computer.
>
> What's more, the Search feature doesn't exist in some Vista components (such as Windows Help and Support) as well as in many third-party programs, which include older programs such as Microsoft Office 2003.

CHANGING SEARCH AND INDEXING SETTINGS

Note while reading this section that we're describing here the built-in Windows Vista search features. As explained in Appendix B, your system might have a different search tool installed, such as Google Desktop Search, Yahoo Widgets, or some other brand—those tools will operate differently. You'll have to refer to those tools' help files or websites to learn how they work. However, you might want to know that you can choose which program will do your searching for you, and even switch back and forth between the programs you want to use as your default. Choose Start, Default Programs, Set Your Default Programs, and you'll see a screen that allows you to change which search tool to use by default. By default, Windows Vista indexes most common files on your computer including all the files in your personal folder, your email, and your offline files. Program files and system files are not indexed because Microsoft says those files are rarely searched.

That doesn't mean that Windows Vista won't search nonindexed files. Vista searches filenames and contents in indexed locations and only searches filenames in nonindexed files by default. You can change this default in the Folder Options window from Computer or Windows Explorer.

Open the Folder Options window by clicking the Organize button in the menu toolbar and then clicking Folder and Search Options. In the Folder Options dialog box that appears, click the Search tab. The Search tab appears as shown in Figure 5.30.

Figure 5.30
The Search tab of Folder Options.

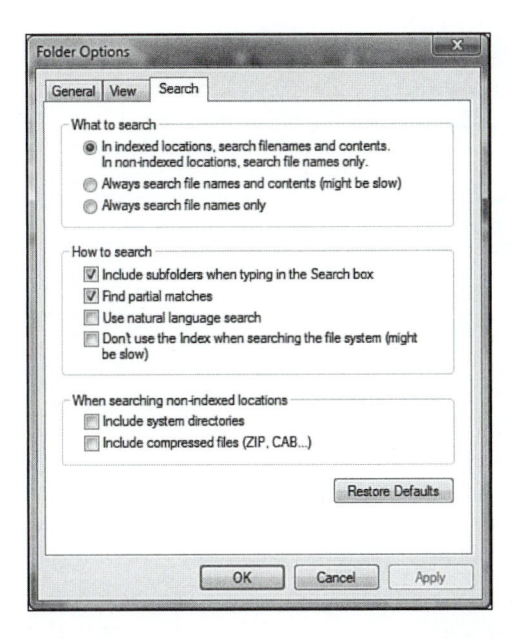

You can determine what to search in the What to Search area at the top of the tab. Other options in this area allow you to search filenames and contents in all files and always search filenames only. The former search type could be a lot slower than the latter depending on how many files you're searching. When you search nonindexed locations, you can also tell Windows Vista whether you want to include system directories and compressed files at the bottom of the tab.

In the How to Search area in the middle of the tab, the default search parameters are to search in subfolders as well as find partial matches. You can also decide how to search, including using natural language search (where you get to ask a question), and turn off the index. If you decide that you don't like your changes and want to revert back to the defaults, click Restore Defaults.

The Indexing Options applet in the Control Panel also lets you view the state of the index and make changes to the file types and folders you want to index. Open the Indexing Options applet by clicking Start, Control Panel, System and Maintenance, and then Indexing Options. The Indexing Options window appears as shown in Figure 5.31.

Figure 5.31
The Indexing Options window.

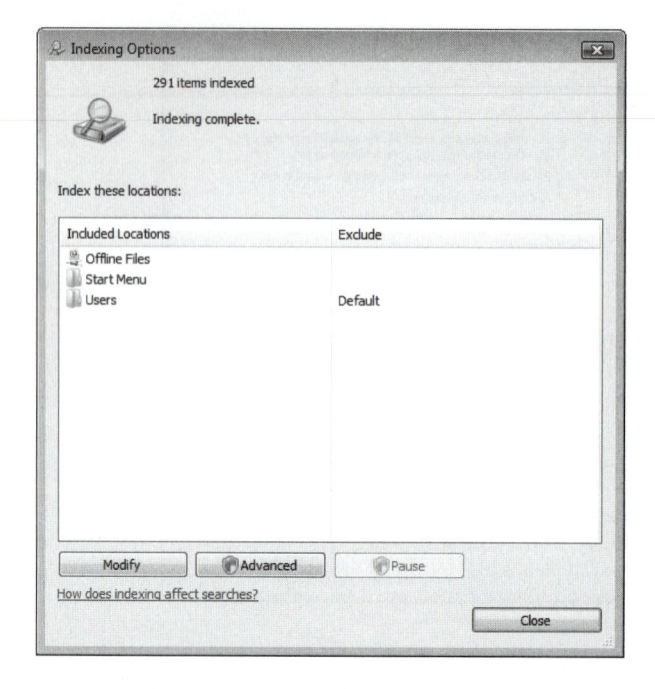

The Indexing Options window shows how many items are indexed and which folder locations have indexed files. You can modify the folder locations by clicking Modify. If you want to really drill down when configuring your index, click Advanced. The Advanced Options window appears so that you can rebuild your index, restore defaults, index encrypted files, and set the index location.

If you click the File Types tab as shown in Figure 5.32, you can scroll down the list and add and remove files to index categorized by file extension. You can also tell Windows Vista whether you want the file to be indexed by properties only or by properties and file contents. If you don't see the extension in the list, type the file extension in the text box at the bottom of the tab and then click Add New Extension.

Searching As You Type

You can search for files, folders, and even URLs as you type both in the Computer or Windows Explorer window as well as in the Start menu. You do this by typing characters in the Search box; Windows displays the matching results in the Search box.

> **TIP**
> When you type characters in the Search box, you can refine your search by prefacing the search characters with the object criteria name in which you want to search, followed by a colon and then your search criteria. For example, if you want to find a file with a name that starts with "b," type `filename:b` in the Search box. This searches for all files with a name starting with the letter "b." Other object criteria names include date and type.

Figure 5.32
The File Types tab in the Advanced Options window.

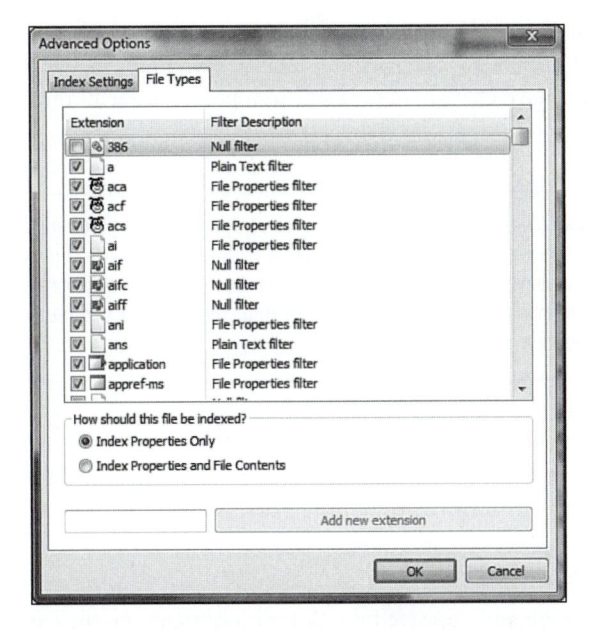

SEARCHING IN COMPUTER OR WINDOWS EXPLORER

Start searching by typing a character in the Search box. After you type the character, Windows automatically searches for files in the current location that match your criteria (see Figure 5.33). As you type more characters in the Search box, Windows Vista refines the search and culls the list of matches until you find the one match you need—or at least narrows it down to only a few matches so you can find the file you need quickly.

Figure 5.33
The list of search results in Windows Explorer.

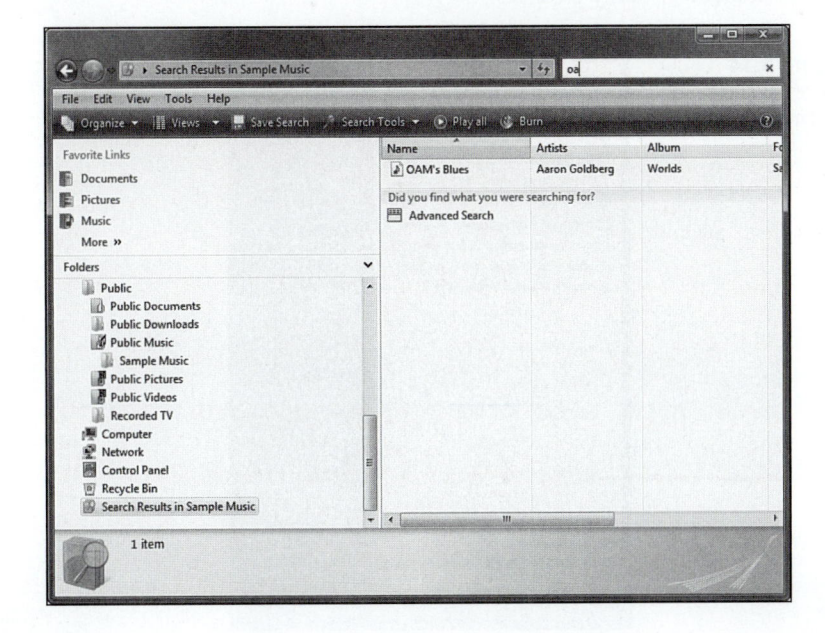

CHAPTER 5 MANAGING FILES AND SEARCHING

If the search can't find any files or folders that meet your search criteria, the right pane in the Computer or Windows Explorer window states, "No items match your search." You'll have to erase one or more characters in the Search box or erase all the characters in the Search box and start over.

> **TIP**
>
> After Windows Explorer (or Computer) starts a search, it opens a Search Results folder at the bottom of the Folders list. This folder contains search results in the locations you searched for in the past, and each Search Results folder name includes the location in which the search was performed. You can click this file to view the results in the right pane.

If you want to save the results of your search, click the Save Search button in the toolbar. Windows Vista asks you to name your search before you save it, and after you save the search file the file appears near the top of the Folders list.

SEARCHING IN THE START MENU

Windows Vista has kept and improved the Search tool that you can access from the Start menu, and you'll learn more about that program in the "Tips from the Windows Pros" section at the end of this chapter. However, if you want to perform a faster search to see what's on your computer that matches your search criteria, you can type search criteria in the Search box at the bottom of the Start menu.

As with typing in the Search box in Computer or Windows Explorer, type one character in the Search box and you will see the results as shown in Figure 5.34. (Yes, I have Baja Fresh as a member of my favorites.)

Figure 5.34
The results in the Start menu.

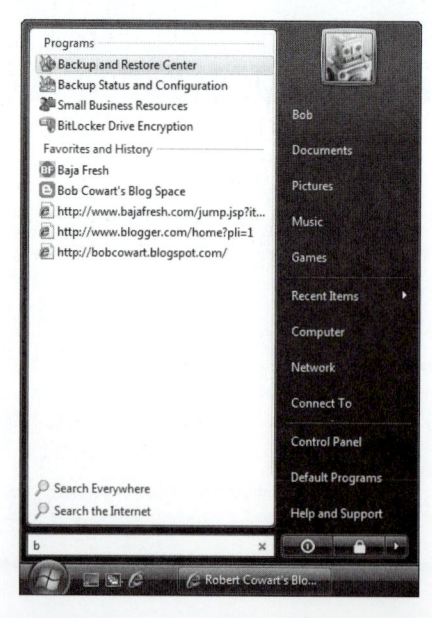

You can open the program or the website by clicking on the program or site in the list. If your search turns up no matches, the Start menu states, "No items match your search." You can expand your search by clicking the Search Everywhere link to show all files on your computer that match your search, or click Search the Internet for text on websites that match your search.

> **TIP**
>
> In the Start menu, you can see all results from the Start menu search by clicking the Search Everywhere link (this was previously the See All Results link prior to SP1) at the bottom of the search list. After you click the link, the Search Results in Indexed Locations window appears so that you can see all the search results in all indexed locations. If you have not installed another desktop search engine, this launches your search results in a Vista search window, called the Windows Vista Search Explorer. If you have changed it, for example, to Google Desktop Search, you'll see the results in that search tool's interface.

THE SEARCH PANE

If you need a deeper search than what the Search boxes in the Start menu and Computer or Windows Explorer provide, you can take advantage of Windows Vista's Advanced Search feature. After you search for your file or folder, a note appears at the bottom of the search results asking whether you found what you were searching for. If you haven't, click on the Advanced Search link to open the Advanced Search pane.

> **NOTE**
>
> You can also access the Advanced Search pane from the menu toolbar in one of two ways:
> Click Organize; then choose Layout and click Search Pane.
> Click Search Tools; then click Search Pane.

The Search pane appears above the menu toolbar as shown in Figure 5.35.

The Search pane consists of filters that you can apply to your search, such as email, documents, pictures, and music. You can also click Other if your file isn't in any one of these categories, such as a program file.

If you know the group where your wayward file resides, you can click on one of these filters and then type your search criteria in the Search box. However, if that doesn't work, you can expand your search by clicking the down arrow button to the right of the Advanced Search label. The pane expands downward to show the Advanced Search area as shown in Figure 5.36.

Here you can specify the location, date, size, filename, tags, and authors of the file. You can also search nonindexed, hidden, and system files.

Figure 5.35
The Search pane.

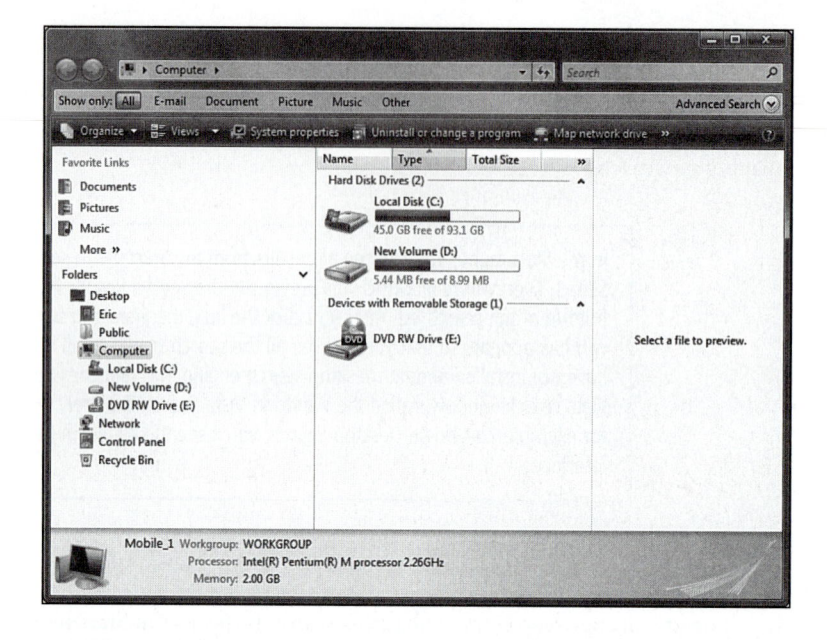

Figure 5.36
The Advanced Search area.

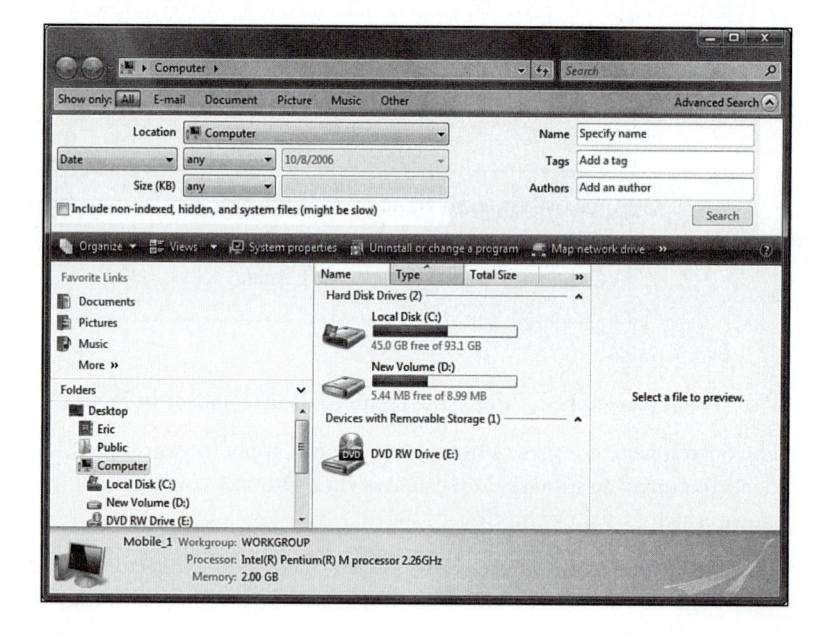

In the Date and Size criteria, you can select Boolean criteria from the drop-down lists that show any by default. You can also add Boolean operators to the Filename, Tags, and Authors fields, such as Bob AND Ross. When you finish setting your search criteria, click Search. The results appear in the right pane.

GROUPING AND STACKING

After you have searched for the file or folder (or website) Windows Vista not only comes with more powerful searching tools but more powerful organizational tools as well for sorting and filtering files in Computer or Windows Explorer.

The top of the right pane that contains a list of all files in your location includes five filter criteria that you can set to filter the files in the right pane. When you move the mouse pointer over the criteria name, a down arrow button appears to the right of the name. When you click on the button, filter information appears in a window underneath the button. Figure 5.37 shows an example.

Figure 5.37
The window for filtering files by a specific date.

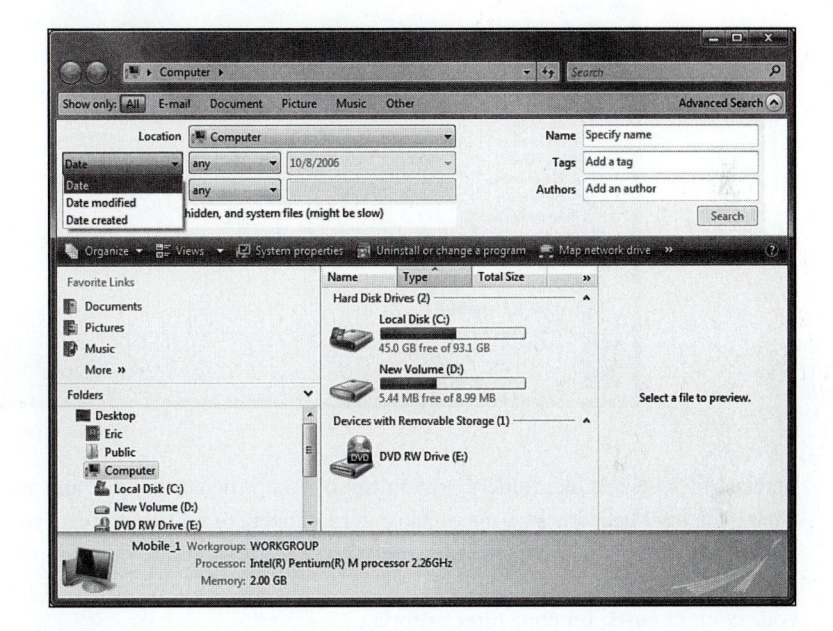

The filter criteria change depending on the location you're in. Some of the criteria you can sort by include

- Name, in three different categories (A-H, I-P, and Q-Z)
- Date taken, which lets you filter by a specific date you can select from a calendar as shown in Figure 5.37
- Artists
- Album
- Genre
- Tags
- Size
- Rating

These filtering windows also include two new views for browsing your files and folders. The Stack view reorganizes your files according to the stack criteria, such as pictures taken on a certain date. Then Windows Vista takes all these pictures and combines them into a stack, as shown in Figure 5.38.

Figure 5.38
Three stacked files organized by three groups of names.

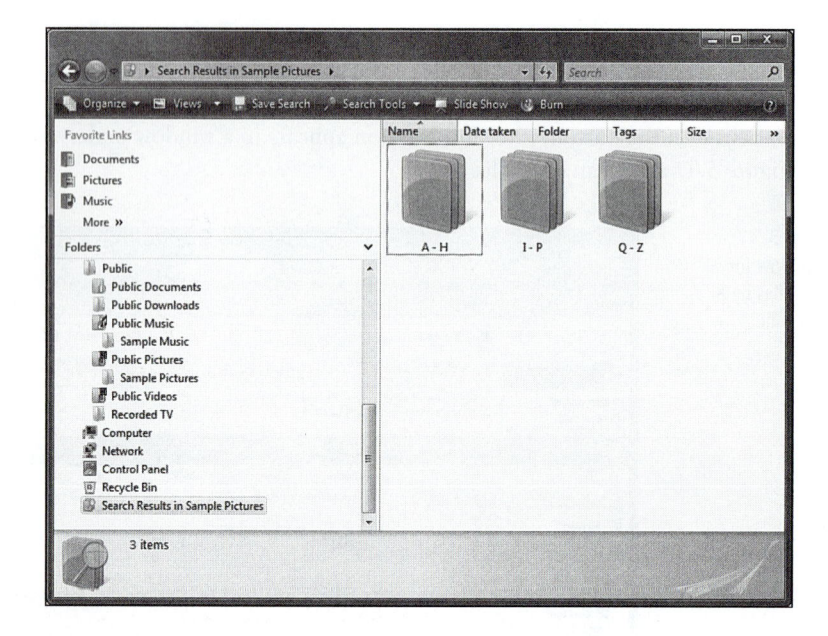

Stacked files behave like folders, so you can open up the stacked file and see what's inside. So what's the big deal? Stacks are a quick way to collect content that meets your criteria and put them all in one place. And stacks have no physical location on your computer, so they don't take up space on your computer as a folder does—stacks are just another representation of your content based on your filter criteria.

Windows Vista also allows you to group files by the criteria listed by the filter. For example, if you group files by name, Computer or Windows Explorer will group all the files by filename starting with the A-K group at the top, followed by the I-P group, and ending with the Q-Z group at the bottom. The grouping filter allows you to get a more granular view of which files belong to a particular group.

Zipping and Packing Files

In the 1980s as computer networking and sharing files through bulletin board systems became popular, it became important to make files as small as possible because transmission speeds in those days were slower than a snail's pace compared to today's speeds. (Of course, back then we thought 1200bps was blazing speed!)

Today we still send files back and forth through email, and computer server bandwidth has trouble handling it all, so compressing files to their minimum size is as relevant now as it was 20 years ago. In fact, it's become so relevant that Microsoft included built-in compression technology in Windows XP, and compression technology is also included in Windows Vista.

One of the most popular compression systems in the 1980s and 1990s was PKZip. Like Xerox and Google, whose brand names became synonymous with the products they perfected, compressing files soon became known as *zipping*. Today Windows Vista still refers to compressed files as zipped files.

Here's how you compress one or more files:

1. Select the file(s) you want to compress.
2. Right-click a selected filename.
3. In the pop-up menu choose Send To and then click Compressed (zipped) folder.

The compressed file appears in the same directory and takes on the name of the last file in the compression process, as shown in Figure 5.39. However, unlike Windows XP, Windows Vista selects the compressed file after you create it and highlights the filename so that you can delete it and give the compressed file its own name.

TIP
You can add new files to the compressed file by dragging the files to the compressed file.

Figure 5.39
A compressed, or zipped, file.

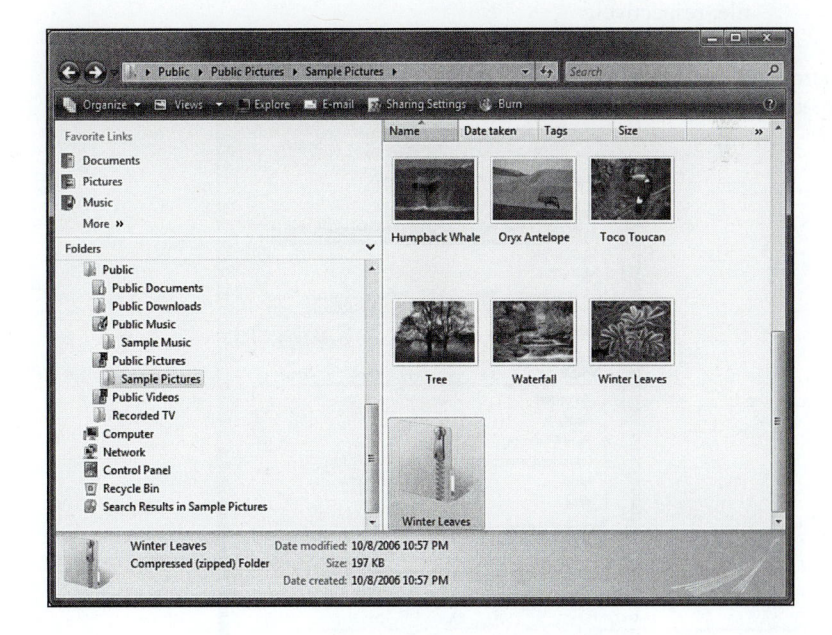

NOTE
You can't compress a file when you're viewing a stack or a group. If you do, a dialog box appears and asks whether you want to save the compressed file on the Desktop instead.

After you compress the file, you can extract files by right-clicking on the compressed file and then clicking Extract All in the menu. A dialog box appears and allows you to select a destination folder for the extracted files.

FILE AND FOLDER SECURITY

File and folder security is a necessary part of computing, especially in these days of always-on networking and multiple users and networks interacting with your computer. Therefore, security is an integral part of Windows Vista.

As Windows NT was developed in the 1990s, Microsoft realized that the standard File Allocation Table (FAT) file system could not provide security features users would need including permissions and editing to restrict user access to specific files. In response, Microsoft developed the NTFS file system. Today Microsoft recommends that computer users running Windows format their hard disks in NTFS primarily because NTFS-formatted files and folders provide better security.

You can access, view, and change security settings for folders and individual files. Here's how:

1. Right-click the file or folder.
2. Click Properties in the menu.
3. Click the Security tab. Figures 5.40 and 5.41 show the Security tabs for a folder and a file, respectively.

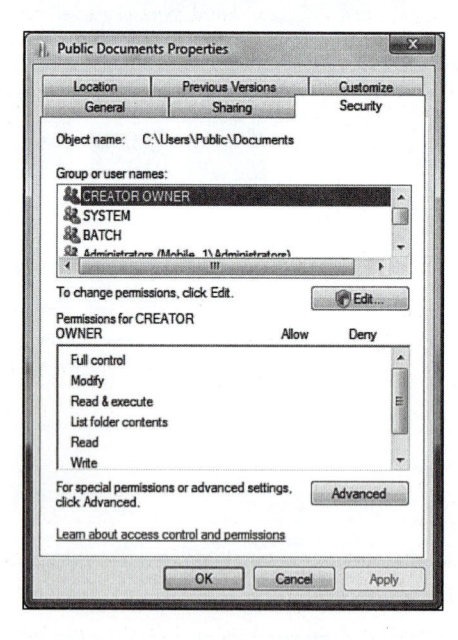

Figure 5.40
The Security tab for a folder.

Figure 5.41
The Security tab for a file.

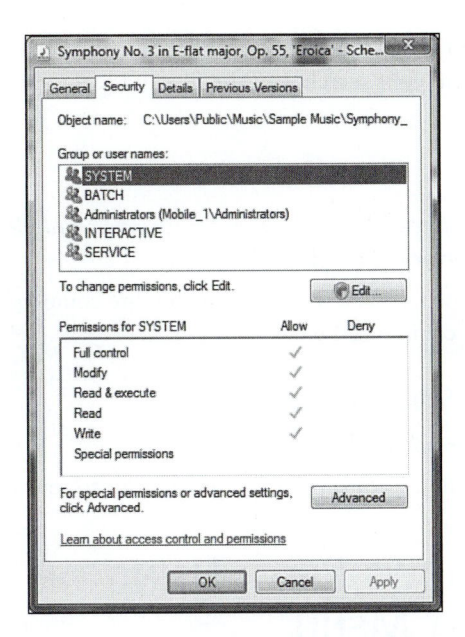

As you can see, there are only minor differences between the Security tab for a folder and the Security tab for a file. You can view the permissions for each group or username by clicking the group or username in the Group or User Names list. Change permissions for the selected group or user by clicking Edit. If you need to set special permissions or advanced settings, click Advanced.

→ To learn more about Windows Vista file security and other security features, **see** Chapter 34, "Protecting Your Data from Loss and Theft," **p. 1149**. You can also learn more about file management options including file and folder encryption and managing access and control by users and groups in Chapter 34.

Troubleshooting

Can't Find a File

I can't find a file on my computer despite all my efforts.

Your search may only be looking at indexed locations, and indexed locations aren't all the locations on your computer. To search your entire computer in an advanced search, select Everywhere from the Location list.

Can't Find Files That Belong to Other Users

My search results aren't returning files that belong to other users on my computer.

Windows Vista only searches your own files to index by default. However, you can add other users' files to your search results by opening the folder that contains the user's files. This is usually in the form of C:\Users\User, where *User* is the name of the person on your system with the files. (You may need to type the administrator password to get access to these files.) After this folder is open, perform your search, and the files in the directory are included in the search.

JPEG Files Not Compressing

When I put JPEG files into a compressed file, the total size of the compressed file is about the same size of the total size of the uncompressed JPEG files.

JPEG files are already compressed, so you won't see much more compression from those files when you place them in a compressed file.

Pressing Enter Required to Start a Search

In some searches I can't start the search until I press Enter.

When you search in nonindexed locations, you must press Enter to start a search.

Tips from the Windows Pros: Using the Search Tool from the Start Menu

The Search tool found at the top level of the Start menu is a fast way to access the powerful Search tool for locating files, folders, computers, people, and even Internet resources. Press F3 or Windows-F as shortcuts to the Search tool.

When you open the Search tool, it prompts you to type your search criteria in the Search box. The Search tool behaves the same way as the Search function in Computer or Windows Explorer. The difference is that the Search tool searches for all files and folders in all indexed locations, not just in your current location.

As with the Search function in Computer and Windows Explorer, the Search tool can use standard DOS-style wildcards in your searches for files. For example, the * character substitutes for a character string of any length, and ? replaces one character. After a list of possible suspects is returned, click on one to open it in its respective application.

After an item is listed in the search results, it is accessed by double-clicking on it. If it is an application, it will be launched. If it is a data file, it will be opened within its associated application. If it is a web URL, your web browser will be launched to view it. If it is a media file, the correct player will be launched to play back or display it. When using Search's All Files and Folders, be sure to pay attention to the Folder column so you can see where the file resides.

If you can't find the file using a simple search, you can start an advanced search by clicking the Advanced Search button.

CHAPTER 6

PRINTING

In this chapter

Windows Printing Primer   204

Installing and Configuring a Printer   206

Installing a Local Printer   208

Changing a Printer's Properties   214

Removing a Printer from the Printers Folder   219

Printing from Windows Applications   220

Printing from DOS Applications   222

Working with the Printer Queue   223

Viewing and Altering Print Document Properties   225

XPS Print Output   226

Print to Disk Option   227

Faxing   228

Troubleshooting   228

Tips from the Windows Pros: Does the Green Ink Have You Seeing Red?   230

Windows Printing Primer

In most cases, installing and using a printer in Windows Vista is nearly effortless. Just plugging the printer into your computer is usually enough. Installation and setup is automatic and silent. Add ink and paper, and within a few seconds you can start printing from whatever programs you use, without thinking any more about it.

Still, as a user of Windows Vista, you should know something about how Windows printing works, how to control your print jobs, how to print to network-based printers, and how to share your printer for others to use. This chapter covers these topics. In addition, we'll show you how to handle setting up a printer that *doesn't* simply start working the moment you plug it in.

It might help to first run through some of the terminology used to describe Windows printing features. You'll encounter these terms in this book and in Microsoft's printer help screens. When you print from an application, the application creates a list of the characters and graphics to be placed on each page and then hands it off to Windows. Windows passes the graphics description, which is called the *enhanced metafile format (EMF)*, through a *driver* program, which generates the specific codes and data that your particular brand of printer needs to *render*, or draw, the document. Driver programs are provided by the printer's manufacturer, and drivers for many common printers are preinstalled along with Windows. (Microsoft calls these *inbox* drivers, even though hardly anyone's copy of Windows comes in a literal box.)

Windows *spools* the printer instructions. Spooling is the process of temporarily stuffing onto the hard disk all the data to be transmitted to the printer, and then later reading it back at the relatively slow pace at which that printer can receive it. Spooling lets you get back to work with your program before printing has completed. Window can spool the device-independent EMF graphics descriptions—this is called *EMF spooling*—and later let the printer driver generate the codes for your printer, or Windows can run the EMF description through the printer driver first and spool the codes for your specific printer. This is called *raw* spooling. The raw codes are later read back from the disk and sent directly to the printer. This distinction will come up later when we get to network printing.

Either way, the spooled data is called a *print job*. Print jobs from your programs and possibly from other users (if you're sharing your printer on a network) are lined up in a *queue* and sent to the printer one complete job at a time. That way, if you have several applications print at the same time, or you and other users are printing documents at the same time, the pages won't get mixed together. Meanwhile, additional print jobs can continue to be added to a printer's queue, either from your computer or from users across the LAN, while a previous job is still printing.

The printer spooling system is called the Print Manager, and it manages all your printers. In cases of trouble (for example, ink or paper outage or paper jams), it also issues error messages or other appropriate warnings to print job originators. The graphical user interface to the Print Manager is the Printers folder.

The Printers Folder

Windows gives you control over the printing system through the Printers folder, shown in Figure 6.1. To get there, click Start, Control Panel, and then click the word Printers under Hardware and Sound.

> **TIP**
> If you use the Printers folder frequently, you will want to add it to your Start menu. Right-click the Start button and select Properties. Click Customize. Scroll down through the list of available items, and check Printers.

Figure 6.1 shows icons for four output devices:

- The Epson printer is shared by another computer on the network. The network cable in the icon indicates this.
- The HP LaserJet printer is the default printer. The checkmark indicates this.
- The Fax device and XPS Document Writer icons don't represent actual printers, but are options for faxing and creating portable XPS documents directly from within your applications. I'll discuss this more shortly.

Figure 6.1
The Printers folder is the starting point for printer setup and management. It's the graphical user interface to the Windows Print Manager.

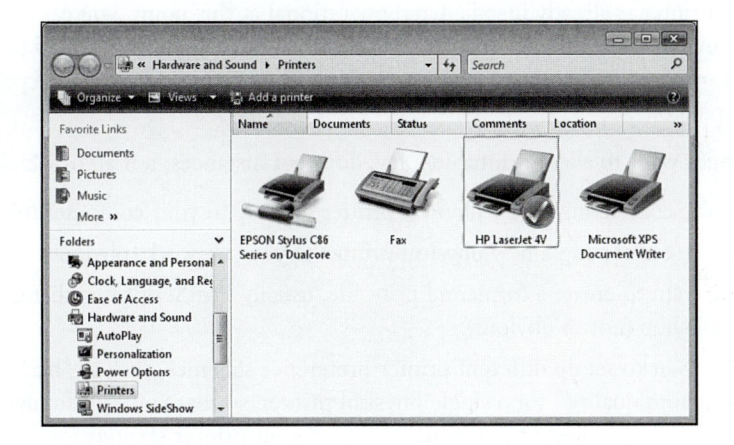

Initially, the task ribbon shows just one printer task: Add a Printer. If you click one of the printer icons, additional items appear: See What's Printing, Select Printing Preferences, and Delete This Printer.

You will probably find that when Windows was installed, one or more printer icons were installed for you. These may include any or all of the following:

- Icons for any printer(s) you have attached to your computer, which were detected by Windows and set up automatically.
- Icons for any printer(s) shared by computers attached to your network, which were installed for you by your network administrator (on a corporate network).

- Microsoft XPS Document Writer—This is not a printer in the physical sense. XPS is a type of electronic document format comparable to Adobe's Acrobat (PDF) format. It lets any computer view and/or print the document without having to have the application that created it.

    If you select the XPS Document Writer as the "printer" in any of your applications, the program's print function will create an XPS document file that you can then send to other people.

- Fax—If your computer has a modem with fax capability, or if your organization has a network fax server, the Fax printer lets you send faxes directly from your applications without having to first print a hard copy and then feed it through a fax machine or scanner. Instead, you simply select the Fax printer from inside your application and use the normal print function. (The Fax feature is not provided with Vista Home versions; you'll have to buy or download third-party software to send faxes from Home versions.)

In the next section I'll show you how to add icons for new printers that don't appear automatically. The subsequent sections will tell you how to manage your printers.

Installing and Configuring a Printer

If your printer is already installed and operational at this point, you can skip this section and skim ahead for others that may be of interest. However, if you need to install a new printer, modify or customize your current installation, or add additional printers to your setup, read on.

You might want to add a printer in a few different instances, not all of which are obvious:

- You're connecting a new physical printer directly to your computer (obvious).
- You're connecting a new physical printer to your network (obvious).
- You want to create a formatted print file, usually PostScript file, that can be sent to a print shop (not so obvious).
- You want to set up different printer preference schemes, such as "black and white only" or "photo quality," for a single physical printer, so that you can simply select a printer icon instead of having to manually change your printer settings for each print job (obscure but useful time-saving idea).

> **TIP**
>
> Before you buy a new piece of hardware, it's always a good idea to check Windows Catalog on the Web. You should at least check with the manufacturer or check the printer's manual to ensure that it's compatible with Windows Vista, XP, or 2000.
>
> You should know, though, that Windows Vista comes with preinstalled drivers for more printers than are listed in Windows Catalog. Before assuming that your old printer isn't supported, go through the manual installation procedure to see if your printer make and model is listed as an installation choice. If it's not, check the manufacturer's website for a downloadable driver.

The basic game plan for installing and configuring a printer is as follows:

- Read your printer's installation manual and follow the instructions for Windows Vista, or if there are none, the instructions for Windows XP or 2000.

> **TIP**
>
> Some printer manufacturers ask you to install their driver software *before* you plug in and turn on the printer for the first time. *Heed their advice!* If you plug the printer in first, Windows may install incorrect drivers.
>
> If this happens to you, unplug the printer, delete the printer icon, run the manufacturer's setup program, and follow their instructions from there.

- Plug in the printer. Many newer printers are detected when you plug them into the parallel or USB port. Your printer might be found and then configure itself automatically. If it does, you can skip on down to "Printing from Windows Applications," later in this chapter.
- If the printer doesn't configure itself, you can run the Add New Printer Wizard (or use a setup program, if one is supplied with your printer). We'll go over this procedure in detail in the next section.

At this point, you should have a functioning printer. You might want to make alterations and customizations to the printer setup, though. For example, you can do the following:

- Right-click the icon for the printer you'll be using most often and select the Default Printer option. This way, your printer will be preselected as the printer of choice when you use the Print function of Windows applications.
- Set job defaults pertaining to paper tray, two-sided printing, scaling, type of paper feed, halftone imaging, printer setup information (such as a PostScript "preamble"), ink color, and paper orientation. These will be the default print settings that every Windows application will start with when you select this printer.
- Check and possibly alter device-specific settings such as DPI (dots per inch), memory settings, and font substitution.
- Share the printer and specify its share name so that other network users can use your printer.
- If you are on a network and want to control who gets to use your printer, set permissions on the Security properties tab. (You must have Computer Administrator privileges to do this.)

> **NOTE**
>
> Printer security issues such as setting permissions, conducting printer access auditing, and setting ownership are covered in Chapter 23, "Using a Windows Network."

We'll discuss these topics in the following sections.

Adding a New Printer

How you go about adding a new printer depends on how you'll be connecting to it:

- If your printer is connected directly to your computer with a USB, parallel, or serial printer cable, you are installing a *local printer*. Installing a local printer is covered in the next section.

- If you want to use a printer that's physically attached to or controlled by another computer on your network, you still need to set up a printer icon on your own computer. This is called installing a *network printer*.

→ For detailed instructions on installing a network printer, **see** "Using Printers on the Network," **p. 757**.

- A printer that's physically connected to the network wiring itself and not cabled to another computer is called a "local printer on a network port," just to make things confusing. We'll cover the installation of these in Chapter 23 as well.

Installing a Local Printer

Installing a local printer can be a bit more complex than connecting to an existing network printer. For starters, unless Windows finds the printer automatically (via Plug and Play), you may have to specify the location where the printer is physically connected, what you want to name it, and a few other pieces of information.

The procedures vary, depending on how the printer is connected to your computer:

- Parallel printer port
- USB
- Serial port
- Infrared
- Bluetooth

Here's the basic game plan, which works with most printers. First, you must be logged on using a Computer Administrator account. Just follow these steps:

1. Read the printer's installation instructions for specific Windows Vista instructions, or if there are none, look for Windows XP or 2000 instructions. You may be instructed to install software *before* connecting the printer to your computer for the first time. This is especially important if your printer connects via USB.

2. Connect the printer to the appropriate port on your computer according to the printer manufacturer's instructions.

3. Locate the type of connection that your printer uses in the following list as directed:

Parallel Port — Connect the printer to your computer's parallel port. Windows might detect and install the printer. If it doesn't, open the Printers folder and select Add a Printer to start the wizard. Click Add a Local Printer. Select Use an Existing Port, and highlight the LPT port number that you used for the printer—this is usually LPT1. If Windows doesn't automatically detect your printer type, follow the remaining steps in this section to complete the installation.

> **NOTE** Many new computers have no parallel port. If you have a printer that has only a parallel port connector, but no parallel port on your computer, you can purchase an add-on parallel port card for your computer. Alternatively, you can get a network parallel print server device, or USB-to-parallel printer adapter, and connect to the printer through your network or a USB port.

USB — Install any driver programs provided by your manufacturer, and then connect the printer's USB cable to your computer. Windows will detect it and automatically start the Found New Hardware Wizard. Because USB is hot pluggable, you don't need to shut down or restart your computer. Simply follow the instructions on the screen to finish installing the printer.

Infrared — Be sure your printer is turned on and within range of your computer's infrared eye. Also, make sure your infrared service is installed properly. Windows should detect the printer automatically and create an icon for it.

Bluetooth or Wireless — If your computer and printer are Bluetooth and/or wireless capable, install any printer driver software provided by the printer's manufacturer. Then turn on the printer and enable your computer's Bluetooth or wireless adapter. (On some laptops, these are switched off by default to conserve power.) If the printer isn't detected automatically, open the Printers folder and select Add a Printer. Select Add a Network, Wireless, or Bluetooth printer. Windows will locate any available printer(s). Click the printer by name and click Next to proceed.

Serial Port — Some antique laser and daisywheel printers use a serial data connection. (If you're still using one of these, I like you already.) The next section describes how to setup a serial printer.

If Windows can't automatically detect the make and model of your printer, it will ask you to assist in selecting the appropriate type. If you can't find your printer's make and model in the list of choices, see Step 5 in the next section.

If the Printer Isn't Found or Is on a Serial (COM) Port

If your printer isn't found using the options in the preceding section, or if the printer is connected via a COM (serial) port, you have to fake out Plug and Play and go the manual route. To do so, follow these steps:

1. Open the Printers folder by clicking Start, Printer. If there's no Printer item on the Start Menu, click Control Panel. Under Hardware and Sound, click Printer. At the top of the Printers window, select Add a Printer.
2. Select Add a Local Printer.
3. Select the port to which the printer is connected. The choices are as follows:

Options	Notes
LPT1:, LPT2:, LPT3:	These are parallel port connections. Most computers have only one parallel port connection, LPT1. The higher numbered ports will still appear in the list even if your computer doesn't really have them—be careful.
COM1:, COM2:, COM3:, COM4:	If you know your printer is of the serial variety, it's probably connected to COM1 or COM2. If COM1 is tied up for use with some other device, such as a modem, use COM2. If you choose a COM port, you will have to configure the COM port in a subsequent step…keep reading.
File	This is for printing to a disk file instead of to the printer. When you later select and print to a printer set up for the File port, you will be prompted to enter a filename. (See the section "Print to Disk Option.")
XPS	The XPS port provides another "save to file" function. This port directs print output to an XPS sharable document format file.
Create a New Port	Create a New Port is used to make connections to printers that are directly connected to your LAN and are to be controlled by your computer. Its use is covered in Chapter 23.

After selecting the correct port, click Next.

4. Select the manufacturer and model of your printer in the next dialog box, as shown in Figure 6.2. You can quickly jump to a manufacturer's name by pressing the first letter of the name, such as H for HP. Then use the up- and down-arrow keys to home in on the correct one.

Figure 6.2
Choose the make and model of your printer here.

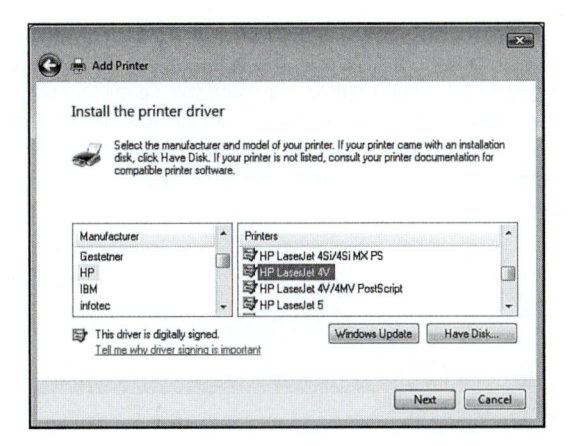

If you can't find the appropriate model, you have three choices:

- If you have an Internet connection, click Windows Update to see if Microsoft has a driver available (don't hold your breath, though).
- Get the manufacturer's driver on a floppy disk or CD-ROM or download it via the Internet, open or run the downloaded file to expand its files, and then click Have Disk. Locate the driver (look for an INF file, the standard type for driver setup programs) and click OK.
- Choose a similar, compatible model and risk getting less-than-perfect output. This option can often be successful with dot-matrix printers and *older* inkjet and laser printers, but is less likely to work with modern cheap inkjet or laser printers that have no internal "smarts."

→ For more information on dealing with unlisted printers, **see** the next section, "What to Do If Your Printer Isn't Listed."

If the wizard finds that the appropriate driver is already installed on your machine, you can elect to keep it or replace it. It's up to you. If you think the replacement will be better, go for it. By contrast, if no driver is listed on the machine, you may be prompted to install it or insert a disk from the vendor. On the whole, manufacturer-provided drivers tend to be newer and better than the default ones provided with Vista.

When you have selected a printer manufacturer and model, click Next.

5. Name the printer. The name will appear in LAN-based users' browse boxes if you decide to share this printer. Some computers have trouble with names longer than 31 characters, so if you intend to share the printer, keep the name short and sweet.

6. If you want this printer to be your default (primary) printer, check Set As the Default Printer.

Click Next. A User Account Control prompt may appear, confirming that you want to install the driver.

> **NOTE**
>
> If the driver software isn't "signed" with digital proof that it came from the manufacturer that it says it came from, Windows may warn you. Permit the software to be installed only if you *know* that it came directly from a reputable manufacturer. If it came from a website other than the manufacturer's, you probably do *not* want to trust it. On a corporate network you may be prevented from installing any unsigned drivers.

7. If you want be sure the printer is working, click Print a Test Page; otherwise, click Finish.

When you're finished, the icon for the printer appears in your Printers folder.

→ If you want to share the new printer with other users on your network, **see** "Sharing Printers," **p. 771**.
→ If you are going to share your printer, and some of the other computers on your network run older versions of Windows, **see** "Installing Extra Printer Drivers," **p. 772**.

If you have just set up a printer that's connected to a serial (COM) port, you have one additional series of setup steps:

1. Right-click the printer's icon and select Properties.
2. View the Ports tab, highlight the correct COM port line (which should be checked), and click Configure Port.
3. Select the proper data transfer rate in bits per second (Baud rate), data bits, parity, stop bits, and flow control. For *most* serial printers, these settings should be 9600, 8, None, 1, and Xon/Xoff, respectively.
4. Click OK to save the changes.

If your printer is set up and working now, you can skip ahead to the section titled "Changing a Printer's Properties."

What to Do If Your Printer Isn't Listed

If your printer isn't detected with Plug and Play and isn't listed in the printer manufacturer and model selection list discussed in the previous section, you'll have to find a driver elsewhere.

First, your printer probably came with a CD-ROM containing driver software. On the printer manufacturer selection dialog box, click Have Disk and then click Browse to find the Windows Vista driver files for your printer. Select the appropriate INF file and click OK.

If you can't find the disk or if it doesn't contain a Windows Vista driver, don't worry; there's still hope. Windows XP and Windows 2000 drivers are compatible, and your disk most likely has drivers for these operating systems. Virtually all printers manufactured since the late 1990s have XP or Windows 2000–compatible drivers, and many earlier printers are supported as well.

If your installation CD is missing, your next step should be to visit the printer manufacturer's website. Check out their Product Support section, and look for a way to locate and download drivers. If you can find an appropriate driver, follow the manufacturer's instructions for downloading it. It will probably come as a compressed or executable file that has to be expanded or run, and this will put the installation files into a folder on your hard drive. You can then use the "Have Disk" feature discussed earlier to point Windows to this folder.

If this fails, check Microsoft's download site page at `www.microsoft.com/downloads`. Click Drivers in the left column and search from there.

If neither Microsoft nor the manufacturer provides a driver, hope is fading. Still, some off-brand printers or models are designed to be compatible with one of the popular printer types, such as the Apple LaserWriters, Hewlett-Packard LaserJets, or one of the Epson series. Also, many printer models are very similar and can use the same driver (with mostly correct results). Check the product manual or manufacturer's website to see if your printer supports an *emulation mode*. This might help you identify an alternative printer model, and you can try its driver.

> **TIP**
>
> Use the Internet to see if other people have run into the same problem and have found a solution. For instance, you might use Google to search for `Windows Vista printer driver` *manufacturer model*, substituting in the manufacturer's name and model number. However, don't download a driver from some random site: It could be infected with a virus. Download drivers *only* from a credible corporate or institutional website.

Assuming that you have obtained a printer driver, follow these instructions to install it:

1. If you obtained a driver by downloading it from the Internet, run the downloaded file. This will either install the drivers directly or it will "expand" or "unzip" a set of files into a location on your hard disk. Take note of the location.
2. Follow Steps 1 through 4 in the preceding section.
3. Click the Have Disk button.
4. You're now prompted to insert a disk. Click the Browse button. If you downloaded the driver, locate the folder in which the driver files were expanded or unzipped. If you have a CD, insert the CD, wait a few moments, then browse to the driver files on the CD.

   The wizard is looking for a file with an `.INF` extension, which is the standard file extension the installer setup file provided with all drivers. You may have to hunt around a bit to find a folder with drivers for Windows Vista or XP.
5. When you have located the folder with .INF files, click OK. You might have to choose a printer model from a list if multiple options exist.
6. Continue through the wizard dialog boxes as explained in the previous section.

Changing a Printer's Properties

Each printer driver has a Properties sheet of associated settings (typically enough to choke a horse). The basic settings are covered in this chapter, whereas you'll find those relating to network printer sharing in Chapter 23.

Because different printers have different features, your printer's drivers will dictate the particular set of options that will be available on its Properties sheet. Because of the variations possible, the following sections describe the most general and common options. (In other words, your fancy new printer may have options we've never even heard of.)

The settings pertaining to a given printer are called properties preferences and printing defaults:

- **Printing Preferences**—The default page setup settings that each application will start with when you use the application's Print function. These include paper size, page orientation, and paper source. Although you should rely on your application's Print Setup commands to control an individual print job's settings, each application starts with the selections made in the printer's default Preferences.

    Preferences are *per user* settings. Each computer user can set his or her own Preferences.

    If you find yourself changing the printer settings for most print jobs, you can change the Preferences so that these settings will be the defaults every time you print.

- **Printing Defaults**—The initial Printing Preferences settings for each computer user. In other words, these are the base settings that each user can then customize using the Printing Preferences feature.

- **Properties**—Settings that apply to the printer itself, most of which tell Windows how to communicate with the printer, what capabilities and optional features it has, and so on.

When you add a printer, the wizard adds an icon for it in the Printers folder, and it's ready to go. At that point, you can start using it, or you can adjust its preferences and properties to suit your taste.

If you are logged on with Administrator privileges, or if the administrator has given you permission to manage the printer, you can then alter these settings as follows:

1. Open the Printers folder by clicking Start, Printers, or if Printers does not appear, by clicking Start, Control Panel, Printers.

    > **TIP**
    >
    > If you find yourself using the Printers folder frequently, you can add the Printers selection to the Start menu. Right-click the Start button and select Properties. Click Customize. Scroll down through the list of available items, and check Printers.

2. To adjust the Printing Preferences, select the printer and click Select Printing Preferences from the task ribbon at the top of the window, or right-click the icon and select Printing Preferences. I'll discuss Printing Preferences and Printing Defaults shortly.

3. To adjust the printer's Properties, right-click the printer icon and select Properties. The printer's Properties dialog box then appears, as shown in Figure 6.3.

Figure 6.3
A typical printer's Properties dialog box. The settings available vary among printers. Some have more or fewer tabs.

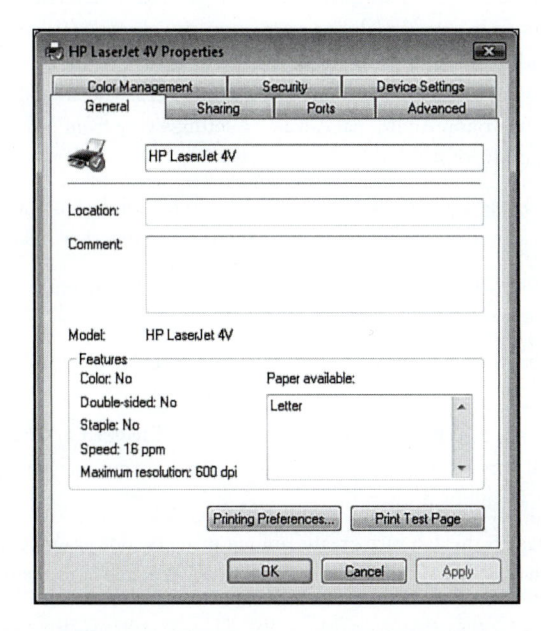

4. Change any of the entries as you see fit. Click OK to save the changes.

A printer's properties sheet can have as many as eight tabs: General, Sharing, Ports, Advanced, Color Management, Security, Device Settings, and Utilities. Table 6.1 shows the general breakdown. Again, the tabs you'll see may vary depending on the capabilities of your printer.

TABLE 6.1   PROPERTIES SHEET TABS

Tab	What It Controls
General	This tab lists the name, location, model number, and features of the printer. From this tab, you can print a test page. You also can set the default printing preferences from here. Some color printers may have settings for paper quality, color control, and buttons for maintenance functions on this tab.
Sharing	On this tab, you can alter whether the printer is shared and what the share name is. You also can provide drivers for users of other operating systems by clicking the Additional Drivers button. (See Chapter 23 for more.)
Ports	On this tab, you can select the printer's connection port, add and delete ports, set a time-out for LPT ports, and set baud rate, data bits, parity, stop bits, and flow control for serial ports. This tab also lets you set up additional ports for network-connected printers.

continues

Table 6.1	Continued
Tab	**What It Controls**
Advanced	This tab controls time availability, printer priority, driver file changes, spooling options, and advanced printing features such as booklet printing and page ordering. The first two settings are pertinent to larger networks and should be handled by a server administrator. Additional Advanced settings vary from printer to printer, depending on its capabilities. Booklet printing is worth looking into if you do lots of desktop publishing. Using this option, you can print pages laid out for stapling together small pamphlets. Also, the New Driver button on the Advanced tab lets you replace the current driver with a better one, should this be necessary.
Color Management	On this tab, you can set optional color profiles on color printers, if this capability is supported.
Security	If you have enabled Password Protected Sharing (discussed in Chapters 23 and 35), this tab will appear to let you set who has access to print, manage printers, or manage documents from this printer.
Device Settings	The settings on this tab vary greatly among printers. For example, you can set paper size in each tray, tell Windows how much RAM is installed in the printer, and substitute fonts.
Utilities	This tab, if present, will probably contain options for inkjet nozzle cleaning, head cleaning, head alignment, and so on.

We'll discuss the most important of the settings in more detail in the next section.

> **TIP**
> Each time you add a printer, Windows creates an icon for it in the Printers folder. Although each is called a printer, it is actually just a "pointer" to the printer, much the way a shortcut represents a document or application on the Windows desktop. A given *physical* printer can have multiple icons, each with different default settings. For example, one could be set to print in landscape orientation on legal-size paper, whereas another printer would default to portrait orientation with letter-size paper. Of course, you can always adjust these settings when you go to print a document, but that can get tedious. If you create multiple printer icons for the same printer, with different, descriptive names, you can choose a setup by selecting the appropriate printer icon.

→ For more details about printer sharing, printer pooling, and other server-related printing issues, **see** Chapter 23.

Comments About Various Settings

Table 6.2 describes the most common settings from the Properties dialog box for both PostScript and HP-compatible printers.

TABLE 6.2   OPTIONS IN THE PRINTER SETUP DIALOG BOX

Option	Description
2 Sides	This option enables or disables double-sided printing for printers that support this feature.
Default Datatype	This setting determines whether raw printer codes or EMF descriptive codes are spooled (that is, whether the print job is run through the printer driver before or after spooling). The default is RAW. Spooling EMF can result in faster transmission over slow networks (for example, VPN by modem).
Enable Advanced Printing Features	When this option is checked, options such as Page Order, Booklet Printing, and Pages Per Sheet may be available, depending on your printer. For normal printing, you should leave the advanced printing feature enabled. If compatibility problems occur, you can disable the feature.
Enable Bidirectional Support	This option lets the computer query the printer for settings and status information.
Font Substitution	The TrueType Font Substitution Table can be used to speed up printing on older PostScript printers by specifying that internal fonts should be used instead of downloading TrueType fonts.
Form-to-Tray Assignment	For this option, you click a source, such as a lower tray, and then choose a form name to match with the source. When you choose a form name (such as A4 Small) at print time, the printer driver tells the printer which tray to switch to and you don't have to think about it. You can repeat the process for each form name you want to set up.
Hold Mismatched Documents	This option is used mostly with dot-matrix forms printers, and directs the spooler to check the printer's current loaded form designation and match it to the document setup before sending documents to the print device. If the form type does not match, the document is held in the queue. A mismatched document in the queue does not prevent correctly matched documents from printing.
Keep Printed Documents	This option specifies that the spooler should not delete documents after they are printed. This way, a document can be resubmitted to the printer from the printer queue instead of from the program, which is faster.
New Driver	Use this button to install an updated driver for the printer. It runs the Add Printer Driver Wizard.
Orientation	This option sets the page orientation. Normal orientation is Portrait, which, like the portrait of the Mona Lisa, is taller than it is wide. Landscape, like a landscape painting, is the opposite. Rotated Landscape means a 90-degree counterclockwise rotation of the printout.

continues

Table 6.2 Continued

Option	Description
Page Order	This option determines the order in which documents are printed. Front to Back prints the document so that page 1 is on top of the stack. Back to Front prints the document so that page 1 is on the bottom of the stack.
Page Protect	If turned on, this option tells the printer to forcibly reserve enough memory to store a full page image; some intense graphics pages otherwise might not be able to print if the printer gives too much memory over to downloaded fonts and macros.
Print Directly to the Printer	This option prevents documents sent to the printer from being spooled. Thus, printing doesn't happen in the background; instead, the computer is tied up until the print job is completed. There's virtually no practical reason for tying up your computer this way, unless you are generating huge print jobs and your disk is nearly full. When a printer is shared over the network, this option isn't available.
Print Spooled Documents First	This option specifies that the spooler should favor documents that have completed spooling when deciding which document to print next, even if the completed documents are a lower priority than documents that are still spooling.
Printer Memory	This option tells Windows how much memory is installed in the printer.
Printing Defaults	You click this option to view or change the default document properties for all users of the selected printer. If you share your local printer, these settings are the default document properties for other users.
Resolution	Some printers can render graphics and images in more than one resolution. The higher the resolution, the longer printing takes, so you can save time by choosing a lower resolution. For finished, high-quality work, you should choose the highest resolution. On some printers, this choice is limited by the amount of memory in the printer.
Separator File	A preassigned file can be printed between jobs, usually to place an identification page listing the user, job ID, date, time, number of pages, and so forth. Files also can be used to switch a printer between PostScript and PCL (HP) mode for printers that can run in both modes.
Use Printer Halftoning	Halftoning is a process that converts pictures to printable patterns of black and white dots. Normally, Windows processes the halftoning of graphics printouts. Only printers that can do halftoning themselves offer halftone options.

> **TIP**
>
> You can access the Printing Defaults tab through two paths: one by choosing Printing Defaults from the Advanced tab and the other by choosing Printing Preferences from the General tab. What's the difference? Printing Defaults are the baseline settings offered to each user. Printing Preferences hold your own personal preferences, overriding the Printing Defaults (but are not forced on other users of this printer).
>
> Another set of properties is available for shared printers. To locate it, right-click an empty spot within the Printers folder and choose Server Properties. The Server Properties dialog lists ports and shows the collective list of all installed drivers in use. Here you can define forms and set events and notifications. The Server Properties dialog is covered in Chapter 23 because it's a network topic.

REMOVING A PRINTER FROM THE PRINTERS FOLDER

You might want to remove a printer setup for several reasons:

- The physical printer has been removed from service.
- You don't want to use a particular network printer anymore.
- You had several definitions of a physical printer using different default settings, and you want to remove one of them.
- You have a nonfunctioning or improperly functioning printer setup and want to remove it and start over by running the Add Printer Wizard.

In any of these cases, the approach is the same:

1. Be sure you are logged on with Administrator privileges.
2. Open the Printers folder.
3. Be sure nothing is in the print queue. You have to cancel all jobs in the printer's queue before deleting the printer. If you don't, Windows will try to delete all jobs in the queue for you, but it unfortunately isn't always successful.
4. Right-click the printer icon you want to kill, and choose Delete.
5. Windows will ask you to confirm that you want to delete the printer. Click Yes. The printer icon or window disappears from the Printers folder.

> **TIP**
>
> The removal process removes only the printer icon in the Printers folder. The related driver files and font files are *not* deleted from your hard disk. Therefore, if you ever want to re-create the printer, you don't have to insert disks or respond to prompts for the location of driver files. On the other hand, if you are having problems with the driver, deleting the icon and then reinstalling the printer won't delete the bad driver. Use the New Driver tool on the Advanced properties tab to solve the problem in this case.

Printing from Windows Applications

When you print from 16-bit or 32-bit Windows applications, the internal Print Manager kicks in and spools the print job for you, adding it to the queue for the selected printer. The spooler then feeds the file to the assigned printer(s), coordinating the flow of data and keeping you informed of the progress. Jobs are queued up and listed in the given printer's window, from which their status can be observed; they can be rearranged, deleted, and so forth. All the rights and privileges assigned to you, as the user, are applicable, potentially allowing you to alter the queue (as discussed later in this chapter), rearranging, deleting, pausing, or restarting print jobs.

If the application doesn't provide a way to select a specific printer (typically through a Print Setup dialog box), then the default printer is used. You can select the default printer from the Printers folder by right-clicking a printer and choosing Set As Default Printer.

Preprinting Checklist

To print from Windows applications, follow these steps:

1. Check to see that the printer and page settings are correct and the right printer is chosen for your output. Some applications provide a Printer Setup or other option on their File menu for this task. Recall that settings you make from such a box override the default settings made from the printer's Properties sheet. If the application has a Print Preview command, use it to check that the formatting of the document is acceptable.

2. Select File, Print from the application's window, and fill in whatever information is asked of you. Figure 6.4 shows the Print dialog for WordPad. (Print dialogs for other applications may differ.) Notice that you can just click a printer's icon to choose it. When you do, its printer driver kicks in, changing the options on the tabs. You can also find a printer on the LAN or print to a file, using their respective buttons. Two other tabs, Layout and Paper/Quality, could be useful. For advanced options such as halftoning and color matching, select the Layout tab and click Advanced.

3. Click OK (or otherwise confirm printing). The data is sent to the spooler, which writes it in a file and then begins printing it. If an error occurs—a port conflict, the printer is out of paper, or whatever—Windows will display a message indicating what the problem is.

You can attempt to fix the problem by checking the cable connection, the paper supply, and so forth. Then click Retry. If you run into more serious trouble, you can run the Troubleshooting Wizard from the Help menu.

For most users, following these steps is all you'll ever need to do to print. The remainder of this chapter deals mostly with how to work with the printer queues of your own workstation printer or of network printers, and how to alter, pause, delete, or restart print jobs.

> *If you receive printer errors when attempting to print a document,* **see** *"Printer Errors" in the "Troubleshooting" section at the end of this chapter.*
>
> *If nothing happens when you send a print job to the printer,* **see** *"Nothing Happens" in the "Troubleshooting" section at the end of this chapter.*

Figure 6.4
Preparing to print a typical file.

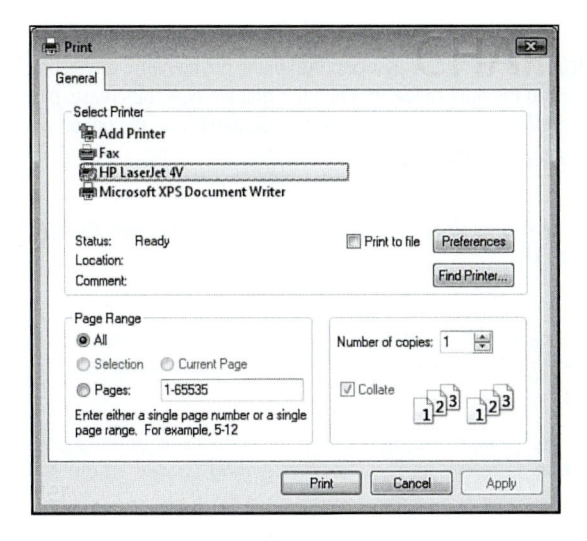

Printing by Dragging Files into the Print Manager

As a shortcut to printing a document, you can drag the icon of the document you want to print either onto an icon of a printer or into the printer's open window (from the Printers folder). You can drag the file from Explorer right onto the chosen printer's icon or open window to see it added to the print queue for that printer.

When you drop the document, Windows realizes you want to print it, and the file is loaded into the source application, the Print command is automatically executed, and the file is spooled to the Print Manager. Figure 6.5 shows an example of dropping a Word document on a PostScript printer.

Figure 6.5
You can print a document or a number of documents by dragging them onto a destination printer in the Printers folder. The files must have application associations.

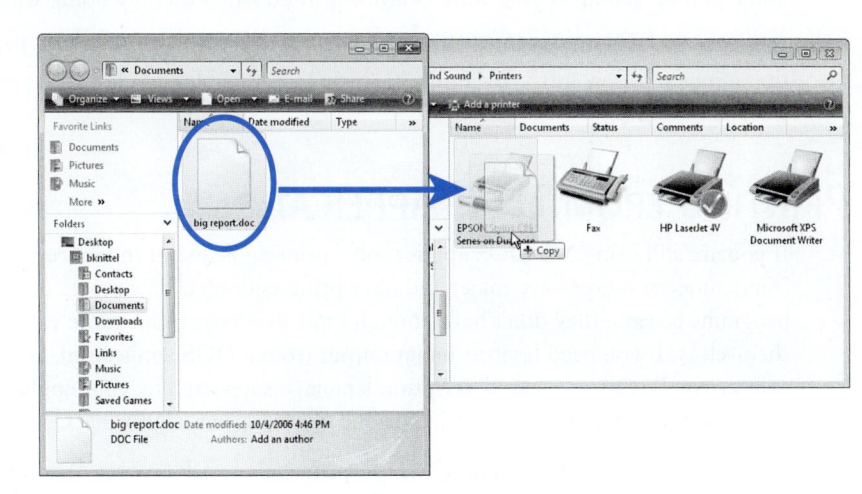

> **TIP**
>
> Documents must have associations linking the filename extension (for example, .doc or .bmp) to the application that handles that file type; otherwise, printing by dragging them to Print Manager doesn't work. Also, you don't have the option of setting printing options when you print this way. The defaults settings are used.

→ For more information about file associations, **see** "Setting Folder Options," **p. 187**.

If you're having trouble printing, if you're getting "garbage" printouts, or you're getting only partial pages, **see** "Printer Produces Garbled Text" in the "Troubleshooting" section at the end of this chapter.

If only half of the page prints correctly before the printer starts printing garbage text, **see** "Only Half of the Page Prints Correctly" in the "Troubleshooting" section at the end of this chapter.

PRINTING OFFLINE

If your printer is disconnected, you can still queue up documents for printing. You might want to do this while traveling, for instance, if you have a laptop and don't want to drag a 50-pound laser printer along in your carry-on luggage.

If you try this, however, you'll quickly find that the Print Manager will beep, pop up messages to tell you about the missing printer, and otherwise make your life miserable. You can silence it by right-clicking the printer's icon in the Printers folder and selecting Use Printer Offline. The printer's icon will turn a light gray color to show that it's been set for offline use.

Windows will now quietly and compliantly queue up anything you "print." (Just don't forget that you've done this or nothing will print even when you've reconnected your printer. You'll end up yelling at your unresponsive printer, when it's only doing what it was told.)

When you've reconnected the printer, right-click the icon and click Use Printer Online, and the output will flow forth. It's a nifty feature, but available only for local printers, not networked printers.

PRINTING FROM DOS APPLICATIONS

If you are still using MS-DOS applications, printing is one of the more problematic areas. Many modern inexpensive inkjet and laser printers don't even support output from DOS programs because they don't have enough built-in smarts to form the character images by themselves. If you need laser or inkjet output from a DOS application, be sure that any new printer you buy uses a page-description language supported by your application, such as PostScript, Hewlett-Packard's PCL, or one of the Epson text formats.

Furthermore, most DOS applications can print only to LPT ports. If you want to use a printer that is on a USB port or is out there somewhere on a LAN, nothing will come out! To direct a DOS program's output to a USB or network printer, share the printer (even if it's just attached to your own computer and you're not using a network), and then issue the command

```
net use lpt2: \\computername\sharename
```

from the Command Prompt window. Direct your DOS program to use LPT2. (You can use LPT1, LPT2 or LPT3, but you must select an LPT port number that does not have an associated physical LPT port in your computer.)

→ For more information about the net use command, **see** "Mapping Drives with net use," **p. 779**.

Working with the Printer Queue

After you or other users on the network have sent print jobs to a given printer, anyone with rights to manage the queue can work with it. If nothing else, it's often useful to observe the queue to check its progress. This way, you can better choose which printer to print to, or whether some intervention is necessary, such as adding more paper. By opening the Printers folder, you can see the basic state of each printer's queue, assuming you display the window contents in Details view.

For each printer, the window displays the status of the printer (in the title bar) and the documents that are queued up, including their sizes, status, owner, pages, date submitted, and so on.

> **TIP**
> You can drag a printer's icon from the Printers window to your desktop, for easy access. Click Yes when Windows asks if you want to create a shortcut.

Figure 6.6 shows a sample printer's folder with a print queue and related information.

Figure 6.6
A printer's folder showing two print jobs pending.

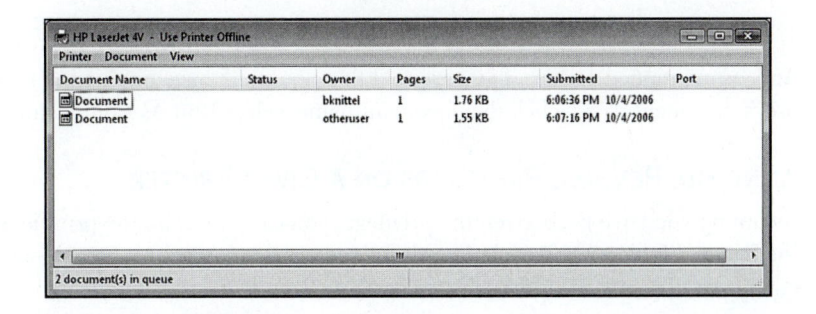

> **TIP**
> When print jobs are pending for a workstation, an icon appears in the notification area, near the clock. You can hover the mouse pointer over it to see the number of your documents waiting to print. Right-click it and select the printer's name to examine the queue.

For network printers, to keep network traffic down to a dull roar, Windows updates the queue display only every so often. If you are printing to a network printer and want to check the current state of affairs, choose View, Refresh, or press F5 to immediately update the queue information.

> **TIP**
> By default, all users can pause, resume, restart, and cancel printing of their own documents. However, to manage documents printed by other users, the printer's owner or the network administrator must give you the Manage Documents permission.
>
> If you find that Windows says you don't have permission to perform some function, such as deleting a document from the queue or changing printer settings, in most cases you can right-click the document, printer, or Printers window and select Run As Administrator to perform the operation with elevated privileges. From the pop-up menu, select the task that you were trying to perform, and try again.

Deleting a File from the Queue

After sending a document to the queue, you might reconsider printing it, or you might want to reedit the file and print it again later. If so, you can remove the file from the queue. To do so, right-click the document and choose Cancel, or choose Document, Cancel from the menu. The document is then removed from the printer's window.

If you're trying to delete the job that's currently printing, you might have some trouble. At the very least, the system might take some time to respond.

> **NOTE**
> Because print jobs are spooled to the hard disk, they can survive powering down Windows Vista. Any documents already in the queue when the system goes down, whether due to an intentional shutdown or a power outage, reappear in the queue when you power up.

And, as mentioned earlier, if you are told that you don't have permission to delete another user's document, right-click the document name, select Run As Administrator, and try again.

Canceling All Pending Print Jobs on a Given Printer

Assuming you have been given the privilege, you can cancel *all* the print jobs on a printer. In the Printers folder, right-click the printer and choose Cancel All Documents. A confirmation dialog box appears to confirm this action.

If you have a printer's queue window open, you can also select Printer, Cancel All Documents from that window's menu.

Pausing, Resuming, and Restarting the Printing Process

If you need to, you can pause the printing process for a particular printer or even just a single document print job. This capability can be useful in case you have second thoughts about a print job, want to give other jobs a chance to print first, or you just want to adjust or quiet the printer for some reason.

To pause a print job, right-click it and choose Pause. Pretty simple. The word Paused then appears on the document's line. The printing might not stop immediately because your printer might have a buffer that holds data in preparation for printing. The printing stops when the buffer is empty. When you're ready to resume printing, right-click the job in question, and choose Resume.

> **TIP**
>
> Pausing a document lets other documents later in the queue proceed to print, essentially moving them ahead in line.

In some situations, you might need to pause all the jobs on your printer so that you can add paper to it, alter the printer settings, or just quiet the printer for a bit while you take a phone call. To pause all jobs, open the Printer's window and choose Printer, Pause Printing. You have to choose the command again to resume printing, and the checkmark on the menu goes away.

Should you need to (because of a paper jam or other botch), you can restart a printing document from the beginning. Just right-click the document and choose Restart.

VIEWING AND ALTERING PRINT DOCUMENT PROPERTIES

Like everything in Windows, each document in the printer queue has its own properties. For a more detailed view of information pertaining to each document, you can open the Properties sheet for it by right-clicking it and choosing Properties. You can change only two settings from the resulting dialog box:

- The print priority. Documents with higher priority numbers get printed ahead of documents with lower numbers.
- The time of day when the document can be printed.

ADVANCED PRINTER MANAGEMENT

Windows Vista comes with a new printer management tool that's part of the Windows Management Console system. It's intended primarily for network administrators who sometimes have to manage dozens of printers spread around an office. I won't go into great detail on this tool here because it's fairly self-explanatory, but I'll show you how it works.

To run the tool, click Start and type `printmanagement.msc` into the Search box. When `printmanagement` appears in the search results list, press Enter. You will need to confirm the User Account Control prompt or enter an Administrator password, because this tool requires elevated privileges. The screen appears as shown in Figure 6.7.

Figure 6.7
The Print Management tool lets you view and manage all your printers at a glance.

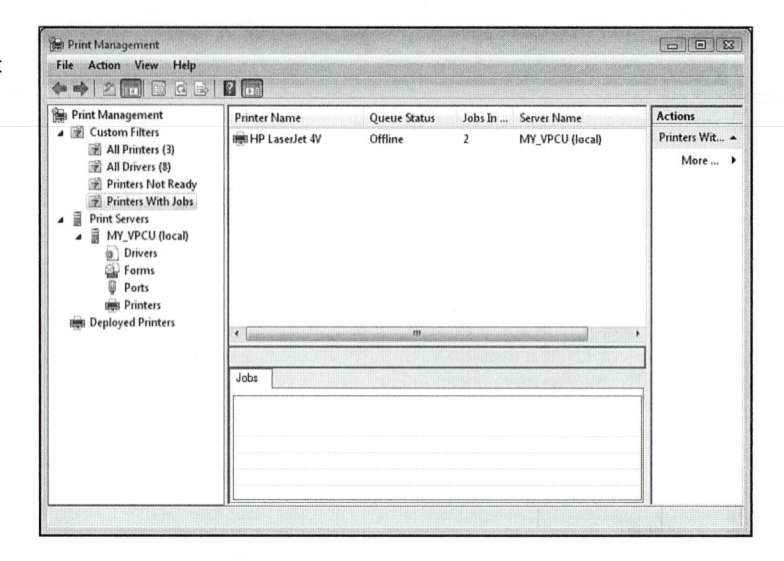

The left pane lets you choose views that include a lists of all of the printers installed on the local computer (or on a domain network), all printers that have documents pending, and so on. You can also create custom "filters" to select only printers with specific attributes.

Under the Print Servers section, the local computer is listed, and you can right-click the "Print Servers" title to add the names of other computers on your network (or named print server devices). You can use this feature to build a single panel that lists all your organization's printers. Print servers that you add to this list will remain in the list the next time you run the Printer Management tool.

XPS Print Output

Windows Vista includes support for a new document file type called XPS, which stands for XML Paper Specification. This is a file format that represents printed output electronically. The idea is that you can view an XPS file on any computer that has an XPS viewer program, without having to have a copy of the application that created the document. For example, you can view the XPS version of a Microsoft Word document without having to have a copy of Word. If this sounds suspiciously like Adobe's PDF file format, you're right. XPS is Microsoft's attempt to create a universal electronic document format. XPS has some advantages, but PDF is so widely used and understood that we suspect XPS doesn't stand a chance.

In any case, Vista does some with built-in support for XPS. You can generate XPS documents simply by following these steps:

1. Edit and format a document in one of your applications. Be sure to save the document in the application's native format, so that you can come back and change it later. You can't edit an XPS file.

2. Use the application's Print function to display the Windows print dialog. Select the Microsoft XPS Document Writer printer. Click Print.
3. When the Save the File As dialog appears, select a location and name for the XPS document.

You can now distribute the XPS document to others to view and print as desired.

Windows Vista has a built-in XPS document viewer. On Vista, just double-click an XPS file to open and view it.

Microsoft has created tools for viewing and creating XPS files on Windows XP, which you can get from www.microsoft.com/ whdc/xps/viewxps.mspx. These tools require the .NET Framework, so you may need to download and install that program as well. On other operating systems, you will need to download an XPS viewer program from some other source.

Print to Disk Option

Sometimes printing to a disk file rather than to a printer can be useful. What does printing to a disk file mean? It means that the same data that normally would be sent to the printer is shunted to a disk file, either locally or on the network. The file isn't a copy of the document you were printing; it contains all the special formatting codes that control the printer. Codes that change fonts, print graphics, set margins, break pages, and add attributes such as underline, bold, and so on are all included in this type of file. Print files destined for PostScript printers typically include a PostScript preamble, too.

The primary use of print-to-disk is to send formatted PostScript files to a service bureau for professional printing. You don't even need to own a PostScript printer to do this.

As we mentioned previously, Windows Vista includes support for a new document file type called XPS, which stands for XML Paper Specification. To make XPS output easier, Microsoft has given Vista an icon to make it easy to send XPS output to disk. To get PostScript or other output formats on disk, you'll probably have to set things up manually.

In some applications, a print to disk option is available in the Print dialog box. If it isn't, you will need to modify the printer's configuration to print to a file rather than to a port. Then, whenever you use that printer, it will use all the usual settings for the driver but send the data to a file of your choice instead of to the printer port. Just follow these steps:

1. In the Printers folder, right-click the printer's icon, and choose Properties.
2. Click Ports.
3. Set the port to File, and close the dialog box.

   The next time you or another local or network user prints to that printer, you'll be prompted to enter a filename. There will be no Browse button, so you will need to type in the full path along with the filename. Even if the printer is a network printer, the file will still be stored on the computer where you are running the printing application.

TIP

If you want to create an encapsulated PostScript file (.EPS), go through the Add New Printer procedure, select File as the port, and select an appropriate PostScript printer model suggested by your print service bureau. You don't actually need to have such a printer attached to your computer. Then, modify the properties of the printer via the Properties, Details, Job Defaults, Options dialog box to set an encapsulated PostScript filename.

FAXING

If your computer has a fax-capable modem installed, you can use it to send and receive faxes. Windows Vista Business, Enterprise, and Ultimate editions come with fax software built in.

To send a fax from Windows Vista, set up the Faxing service as described in Chapter 10, "Scanning and Faxing."

Then create a document using your favorite application, click Print, and select Fax as the printer. Windows will ask you for the fax phone number and make the call—no paper is involved. The fax service can even add a cover sheet to your document on the way out. To receive faxes, your modem can be set to answer calls. When a fax arrives, you can view its image onscreen or print it, or even have it printed automatically.

Third-party fax software such as Symantec's WinFax Pro has more bells and whistles, and can provide fax services for the whole network, but the basic version that comes with Windows will take care of most home and small office users' needs. Windows Vista faxing can't be shared among a number of users on the LAN the same way you can share regular printers, though. If you want to provide a shared fax modem for your LAN, you should look for a third-party product.

We'll talk more about faxing in Chapter 10.

TROUBLESHOOTING

PRINTER ERRORS

I receive error messages when I try to print. What's wrong?

When an error occurs during a print job, Windows tries to determine the cause. If the printer is out of paper, you might see a `Paper Out` pop-up balloon in the notification area. At other times, the message is ambiguous, and the word `Error` might appear in the status area. Check that the printer has paper; make sure that the printer is turned on, is online, and is correctly connected, and then make sure that the settings (particularly the driver) are correct for that printer.

Nothing Happens

I try to print, but nothing happens. How do I proceed?

If your print jobs never make it out the other end of the printer, open the Printers folder and work through this checklist:

- First, ask yourself whether you printed to the correct printer. Check to see whether your default printer is the one from which you are expecting output. If you're on a LAN, you can easily switch default printers and then forget that you made the switch.
- Right-click the printer and see if the option Use Printer Online appears. If it does, select this item.
- Next, check to see whether the printer you've chosen is actually powered up, online, and ready to roll.
- If you're using a network printer, is the station serving the printer powered up and ready to serve print jobs?
- Then check the cabling. Is it tight?
- Does the printer need ink, toner, or paper? Are any error lights or other indicators on the printer itself flashing or otherwise indicating an error, such as a paper jam?
- Are you printing from an MS-DOS application? You may need to use the `net use` command to redirect an LPT port to your Windows printer. See "Printing from DOS Applications" earlier in this chapter for more information.

Printer Produces Garbled Text

When I print, the printout contains a lot of garbled text.

If you're getting garbage characters in your printouts, check the following:

- You might have the wrong driver installed. Run the print test page and see whether it works. Open the Printers folder (by choosing Start, Control Panel, Printers), open the printer's Properties sheet, and print a test page. If that works, you're halfway home. If it doesn't, try removing the printer and reinstalling it. Right-click the printer icon in the Printers folder and choose Delete. Then add the printer again, and try printing.
- If the printer uses plug-in font cartridges, you also might have the wrong font cartridge installed in the printer, or your text might be formatted with the wrong font.
- Some printers have emulation modes that might conflict with one another. Check the manual. You may think you're printing to a PostScript printer, but the printer could be in an HP emulation mode; in this case, your driver is sending PostScript, and the printer is expecting PCL.

Only Half of the Page Prints Correctly

My printer prints about half of a page, and then it starts printing garbage.

This problem is a rare occurrence nowadays, but it's still possible if you're running a printer off a serial port. If your printer regularly prints about the same amount of text or graphics and then flips out, suspect a buffer-related problem. On serial printers, buffer problems can often be traced to cables that do not have all the serial-port conductors (wires), or a cable with wires that are not in the correct order. Make sure the cable is the correct kind for the printer.

Cannot Receive a Fax

My system can't receive a fax. What's wrong with it?

Here's a quick checklist of common stumbling blocks:

- Have you plugged in the phone line properly?
- Is your modem installed and working properly?
- Is it a true fax modem, not just a data modem?
- Did you enable fax reception via the Fax Configuration Wizard (the default setting is off)?
- Is another device (for example, an answering machine) picking up the phone before your fax modem is? Check the ring settings for the fax modem and/or answering machines. Consider using the option that lets you screen for a fax first and then activate it manually (see the faxing section earlier in the chapter).
- If your computer goes into standby mode and doesn't wake up to receive incoming faxes, you might need to turn on an option in the computer's BIOS to "wake on ring." This option wakes up the computer anytime it senses the ringer voltage on the phone line. If a fax is coming in, it takes the call. If it's not a fax, the computer goes back to sleep.

Tips from the Windows Pros: Does the Green Ink Have You Seeing Red?

If you're shopping for or currently use one of the giveaway or inexpensive color inkjet printers that are so popular these days, you might find that your pleasure over their low purchase price fades quickly when you find out how much the ink cartridges cost. This same argument goes for laser printers, too. There are monochrome laser printers on the market for as little as $100 now, but the cost of the toner cartridges can be as much as $70 each for only 3,000 pages! Ouch!

In the end it's the overall cost per page that matters most, and this can range from $.03 to $.25 per page for black-and-white printing, and *lots* more for color. If you print, for instance, an average of 10 pages per day, a printer that costs 5 cents per page less than a competing model will save you $180 a year. That can more than make up for a higher initial purchase price.

My advice is, when you're shopping for any printer, check out online reviews and estimate your actual cost of operation before you buy. You can find reviews at www.pcmag.com, www.zdnet.com, www.consumersearch.com, www.consumerreports.com (which requires a subscription), and many other sites. An hour or two invested in research now can save you a bundle later.

But suppose you already have a printer and find that it's been rated as the biggest ink-sucking pig on the market. If you use it heavily, consider trading it for a less-thirsty model. Remember, you might recoup the cost in short order. You also can look into using recycled, refilled ink or toner cartridges, or even get one of those fill-your-own kits on eBay. Using them might void your printer's warranty, but on a free-after-rebate printer, it's a worthwhile risk.

If you do a lot of printing, you should also consider getting a monochrome or color laser printer, or getting a monochrome laser printer for black-and-white output in addition to having an inkjet for color. Laser printers generally have a *much* lower cost per page and the print output generally looks more professional. And remember that if you have more than one computer, you can network them and share the printers with all of your computers.

And how about this for cheap: I have a clunky but tolerable Samsung laser printer I got on sale for $70, and whose cartridges should also cost $70 each. But, I'm still using the original cartridge that came with the printer, because I refill it once a year with a $15 bottle of toner from eBay—it's working out to about half a cent per page.

Finally, you might be able to tell your printer to go easy on the ink for all but keepsake photos and business correspondence. Try this: right-click the printer's icon in the Printers folder, click Properties, and look at the various properties tabs. Most color inkjet printers have a special settings page that lets you choose to print everything in black and white only, or to print in a "thrifty" mode that saves ink. Use the color and letter- or photo-quality output modes only when you really care about what you're printing.

CHAPTER 7

SIDEBAR AND OTHER SUPPLIED ACCESSORIES

In this chapter

Using Gadgets and the Sidebar   234

Calendar   247

The Other Accessories   252

Troubleshooting   254

Tips from the Windows Pros: Receiving Email on a Pocket PC or Blackberry   255

Using Gadgets and the Sidebar

As mentioned in Chapter 1, "Introducing Windows Vista," that old monster dubbed Active Desktop back in the Windows 98 days silently slipped away into oblivion and was dropped by Microsoft after we all realized that even the fastest computer could be brought to its knees when a few Active Desktop items were running. Add a weather map, stock sticker, and headline news ticker, and mysteriously, your computer would either lock up entirely or run so slowly that it might as well have. After you rebooted, you'd see a message like this:

```
Internet Explorer has experienced a problem or error. As a precaution, your Active
Desktop has temporarily been turned off. To start the Active Desktop again, use the
following troubleshooting tips
```

Remember that? Enabling Active Desktop actually set Internet Explorer to be the system shell. Rather than your desktop essentially being a Windows Explorer folder, it was now much more, tying closely into Internet Explorer. If IE crashed, the house of cards came crashing down, including your interface with the operating system. The problem had to do with Active Desktop being ravenous for system resources. Add more than a couple Active Desktop elements, and the system would starve for resources, disabling other applications you might want to open or have open.

Again the question was raised: Can't we do something useful with all that otherwise barren computer landscape especially now that screens are wider than they used to be? Apparently we have become enamored with the idea of our laptop computers being even better than video games or movie theaters in some ways. We can isolate ourselves now, with our own personal laptop wide-screen movie theaters. Give me a stack of movies and a pair of headphones, and I'm gone for days, despite my heated complaints about the demise of the taller screens. I mean what *are* computer makers and Microsoft and even Apple thinking? Do engineers think that most of us use computers to watch the latest Hollywood blockbusters that we've illegally downloaded from Bittorent? No, we're web browsing and writing documents in Office, such as PowerPoint presentations, Word docs, or Excel spreadsheets. These applications beg for taller not wider screens. If you're a writer, good luck finding a laptop with an old-fashioned 4:3 aspect ratio. Everything is now "wide," meaning also not as tall. Translate: more scrolling. (Incidentally, all the figure in this book are captured in 1024×768 resolution, which is a 4:3 ratio.)

But enough of my rant. In any case, we now have a generation of wide screen displays with gobs of extra unemployed pixels to both sides during most of the workday. That being the case, Microsoft was wise to exhume the concept of Active Desktop and give it another go, in the form of Gadgets and the Sidebar. The Gadgets are analogous to the Active Desktop add-ins or applets, and the Sidebar is the place on the screen (left or right side) where the Gadgets typically lodge themselves. You can actually pull most gadgets onto the desktop if you want to, but then they can become obscured by other windows. If you're familiar with the Mac OSX, perhaps you are thinking of Apple's Dashboard and Widgets right about now.

Hopefully, Sidebar and Gadgets will prove to be more stable than their predecessor Active Desktop. They should be, simply because they are built using either DHTML or the Windows Presentation Foundation.

Which gadgets you put in your Sidebar depends on your needs. Typically, you'll add a clock and a calendar, a CPU and RAM gauge (to see how maxed out your computer is, sort of like having a tachometer in your car), and a notepad. If you work with international money exchanging, or travel, the always up-to-date currency calculator is nice. The RSS feeds gadget connects to Internet Explorer and downloads headlines from your subscribed RSS feeds, displaying them in your Sidebar.

Figure 7.1 shows an example of a Sidebar setup using some of the gadgets supplied with Vista.

Figure 7.1
A typical Sidebar setup with several gadgets installed, including a local temperature gauge.

Running Sidebar

To run Sidebar, do the following:

1. Click Start, All Programs, Accessories, Windows Sidebar. Sidebar will appear on the right side of your screen.
2. To control settings such as which side of your screen the Sidebar appears on, right-click an empty area of the Sidebar and choose Properties. The dialog box shown in Figure 7.2 appears.

Figure 7.2
Use the Properties dialog box for customizing general Sidebar settings.

You can determine a number of settings from this box. Let's go through each one:

- **Start Sidebar When Windows Starts**—Check this box and the next time you boot up, Sidebar will start automatically.

- **Sidebar Is Always on Top of other Windows**—Choose whether Sidebar will push other windows to the side or whether the Sidebar will appear only when the desktop is showing and other windows are minimized. If you choose this setting, the bar will push all other windows off to the side, as though your overall work area is smaller. For widescreen monitors, this is usually acceptable, as you see in Figure 7.3.

- **Display Sidebar on This Side of Screen**—You can choose on which side of the screen Sidebar will appear. Most folks tend to keep their desktop icons on the left side of the screen, so putting the Sidebar on the right side makes sense. But it may not for you. You can reposition desktop icons elsewhere, or turn them off, freeing up space on the desktop, and then you could move the Sidebar to the left side.

Figure 7.3
On a wide-screen monitor, turning on the "on top of other windows" option keeps the Sidebar always visible.

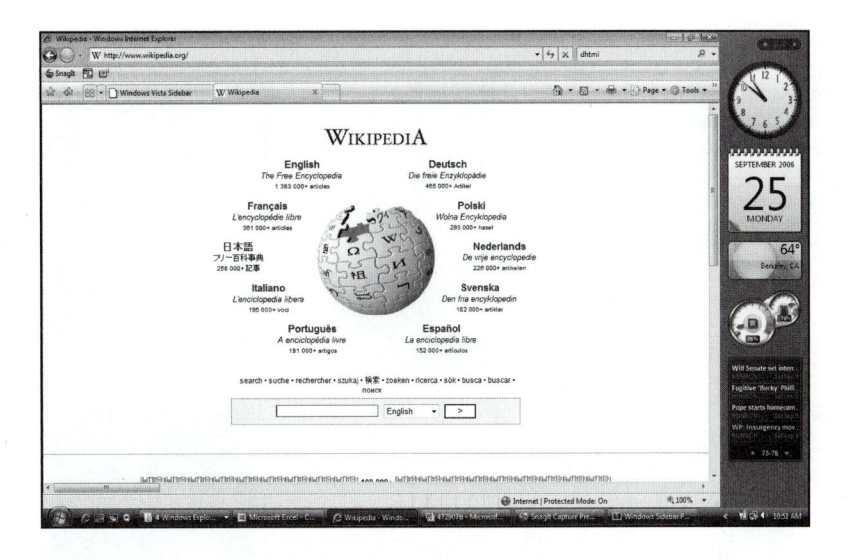

- **Display Sidebar on Monitor**—This is a great feature. If you have multiple monitors, you can set which one will display your Sidebar and gadgets. You can put the Sidebar and gadgets on a second monitor and maximize your primary monitor for use with your main applications. As you see later, you can even fill up the entire second monitor with gadgets by dragging them out of the Sidebar onto the desktop. (See more about dragging out gadgets later in this chapter.)

Figure 7.4 shows gadgets dragged onto my second monitor, which sits above my first monitor. To activate this setting, follow these steps:

1. Make sure that you have a second monitor installed.

→ To learn how to install a second monitor, **see** "Installing and Using Multiple Monitors," **p. 1019**.

2. In the Display Sidebar on Monitor option, choose the desired monitor from the drop-down list.
3. Click OK or Apply.

Figure 7.4
You can dedicate a second monitor to running your gadgets if you want. The upper half of this image is my second monitor.

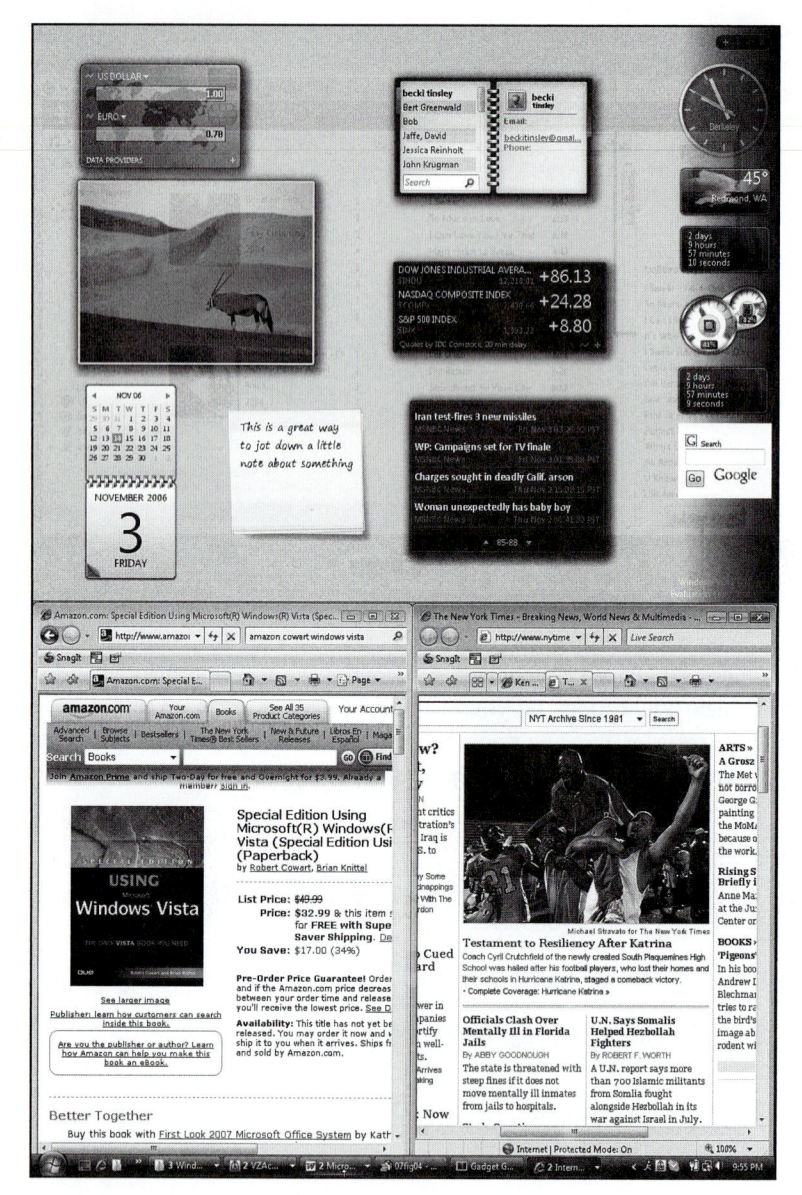

Adding new Gadgets

After you decide where to display your Sidebar, you need to determine what to put in it. Microsoft supplies a stock set of gadgets to choose from. It's self-explanatory and intuitive how to choose and organize them after you learn the basics:

USING GADGETS AND THE SIDEBAR | 239

1. Right-click anywhere in the Sidebar and choose Add Gadgets (or click the + sign at the top of the Sidebar). A dialog box with available gadgets appears, as shown in Figure 7.5.

Figure 7.5
Adding gadgets to your Sidebar is done through this dialog box.

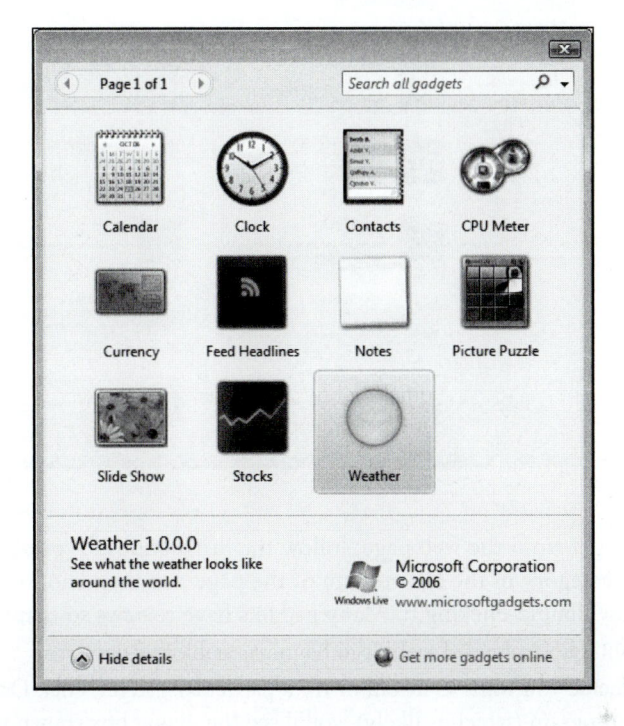

2. Click on Show Details to open the details for any gadget you click on. Depending on the gadget you may see a useful description.
3. Double-click a gadget to add it to your Sidebar. Alternatively, you can drag it to the sidebar and release it where you want it.

DOWNLOADING NEW GADGETS

Notice that as with all Explorer windows, there is an As-you-type search box in the upper-right corner to help you find the gadget you are looking for. If you can't find the tool for the job, try searching the Internet:

1. At the bottom of the Add New Gadgets dialog box, click Get More Gadgets Online. This will open an Internet Explorer window where you can download new gadgets, as you see in Figure 7.6.

Figure 7.6
You can download new gadgets as they become available from Microsoft or other venders.

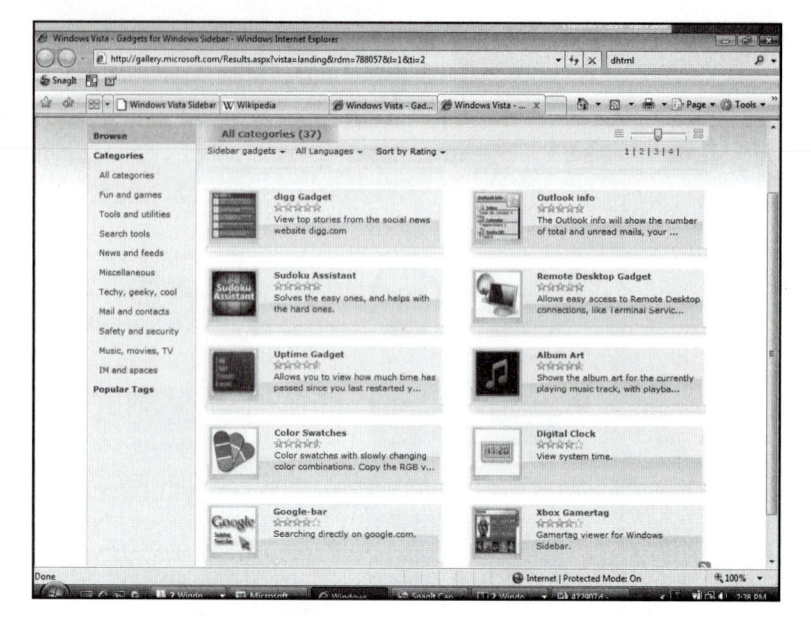

2. To add a gadget from the web page, follow the instructions. Typically the approach is to click a category in the left column of the page and then choose a gadget in the right pane by double-clicking it. Many gadgets have reviews so that you can read before trying.

3. After you decide you want to install or try a particular gadget, click Download. If it's a third-party program (which is likely), you'll see the dialog box shown in Figure 7.7.

Figure 7.7
You'll see a warning like this, even for gadgets posted on Microsoft's website.

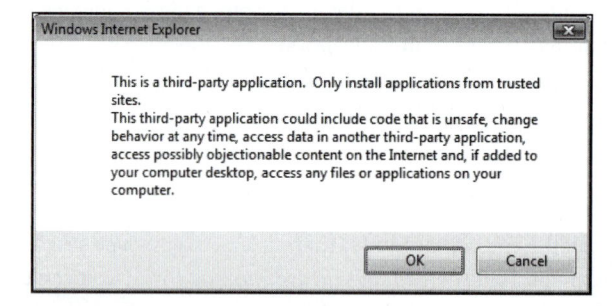

4. So, should you install the gadget? Consider the source. Microsoft no doubt will not post download gadgets that have not been tested and approved. I would not hesitate to install any gadgets found on the Microsoft web pages. Click OK to download the gadget.

5. When downloaded, click Open. You will see a dialog box asking whether you want to install the gadget, as you see in Figure 7.8.

Figure 7.8
Confirm whether you want to install the downloaded gadget.

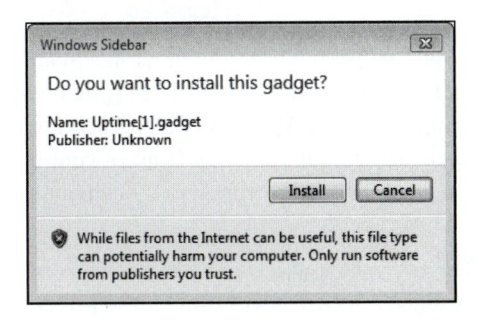

6. Click Install and the gadget is installed and added to your Sidebar automatically.

One gadget I find useful is called Uptime. This gadget allows you to see how much time has passed since you last restarted your computer. Even though Vista is stable, restarting once in a while is a good idea. I keep an eye on this gadget to help me keep track of when to reboot. I have made the mistake of letting my Vista or XP machine run for a month without rebooting and then wonder why it gets weird or slows down. The Notepad is another useful gadget, especially for jotting down phone numbers or other information when you're on the phone.

If there are more gadgets in the Sidebar than can display (the number depends on the resolution and size of your screen), they will be pushed off the screen. They are, however, still installed. If you drag one off to the desktop or remove it, an invisible but active gadget will pop up to fill the void. Also, if you click the little arrow at the top of the Sidebar it will scroll between columns of running gadgets.

> **TIP**
> MSN also offers gadgets that you can install on your Windows Live home page. Those gadgets won't install into Vista—they are a different animal. Those are Web gadgets as opposed to Sidebar gadgets.

HIDING THE SIDEBAR

If you want to hide the Sidebar to see your entire screen (for example, to view a photograph or large spreadsheet), do the following:

1. Right-click in the Sidebar area and choose Close Sidebar. The Sidebar is now minimized down into the system tray (next to the clock on the bottom line of your screen).

2. To revive the Sidebar, right-click the Sidebar icon in the system tray and choose Open, as shown in Figure 7.9.

Figure 7.9

If you pull your gadgets out of the sidebar and onto the desktop and are working on a document that obscures the gadgets, you might want to pop the gadgets forward to check the time, headlines, or whatever. Simply click the Windows Sidebar icon in the Notification Area (system tray) and the gadgets will pop into view, in front of your document. Then, click your document again and they will all disappear behind the document.

Adjusting a Gadget's Settings

If you move the cursor over a gadget, a little control panel for it will pop up. Most gadgets have settings that you can control in this way, as shown in Figure 7.10.

Figure 7.10
Most every gadget has these control buttons for closing them or adjusting settings. These buttons appear only when you hover the mouse pointer over them.

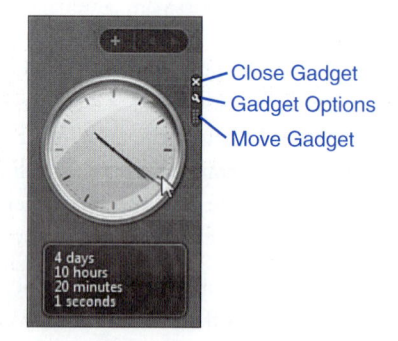

Here's how to adjust or close a gadget:

1. To close the gadget, click the X.
2. To adjust the settings for the gadget, click the wrench. Some gadgets don't have adjustments in a dialog box but may have settings on the gadget itself. See Figure 7.11 for an example of an adjustment dialog box.

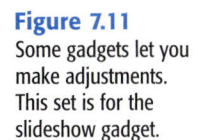

Figure 7.11
Some gadgets let you make adjustments. This set is for the slideshow gadget.

3. Adjust settings as necessary, and click OK.

MOVING GADGETS AROUND

Gadgets are flexible and can be moved all around the screen. They can be undocked, as mentioned before, and floated out on the screen or onto another monitor. Their order can be altered in the Sidebar, too.

To change the order of gadgets in the Sidebar, follow these steps:

1. Grab a gadget and drag it to the spot where you want it. To drag the gadget, click and drag the little Move Gadget button that looks like a grid. This shows up when you move the cursor over the gadget. (See Figure 7.11, referring to the Move Gadget button.) (With most gadgets, you can drag them from any spot on the gadget, but this is the official spot to avoid making other changes or clicking links on the gadget.)

2. Drop it where you want it. As you move a gadget up or down in the Sidebar, the other gadgets will adjust to make room for it in a graphically smooth way. This is the kind of high-def visual trick the Vista interface is good at doing.

To move a gadget onto the desktop, do the following:

1. First clear some space on the desktop.
2. You have to put the gadget in the Sidebar first, so add the gadget you want, using the steps outlined earlier.

3. Drag the gadget from the Sidebar to the desktop destination and drop it there. Often, the gadget will display a new characteristic when undocked, such as getting larger or opening up in some way. For example, the calendar shows not only the current day but also the entire month, and the Contacts list shows two pages of information instead of one.

4. Reposition any of the gadgets by dragging on the grid and dragging it around. Notice that gadgets can overlap one another on the desktop, even though they won't do that in the Sidebar.

> **TIP**
>
> You can also right-click a gadget and choose Detach from Sidebar to instantly drop a gadget somewhere on the desktop. Vista picks the location for you, so it could end up anywhere.

ADDING A GADGET MORE THAN ONCE

There is nothing to prevent you from adding a gadget to the Sidebar or to the desktop more than once. Want a pile of Notepads? Lots of slideshows running at the same time? A passel of stock tickers or news feeds all visible at once? No problem. Just add them, make the adjustments, and position them as you want.

If you deal with businesses or associates in multiple time zones, for example, it would be useful to have multiple clocks on your Sidebar, one for each time zone. Figure 7.12 shows an example. I named the clocks using the adjustment dialog for each one.

Figure 7.12
Adding gadgets more than once is possible. Here I have added four clocks set for different time zones.

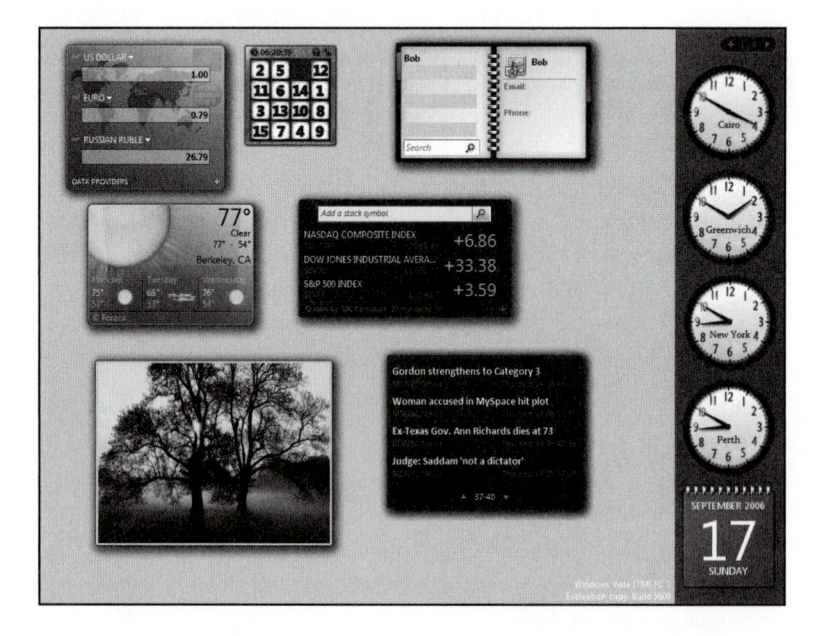

Changing Opacity of Gadgets

You may have noticed that when you right-click a gadget there is an Opacity option in the pop-up menu. This setting determines whether you can see through the object. This is a nifty feature, owing once again to the advanced Vista video architecture. What do you do with a transparent gadget? Well, suppose for example, that you don't want to relinquish screen real estate for the Sidebar, but you do want a clock always visible. Furthermore, suppose that you don't want the clock to obscure what's behind it. Opacity to the rescue—you can put a transparent clock on the desktop, as you see in Figure 7.13.

Figure 7.13
Use the Opacity setting to create transparent or semi-transparent gadgets such as this clock.

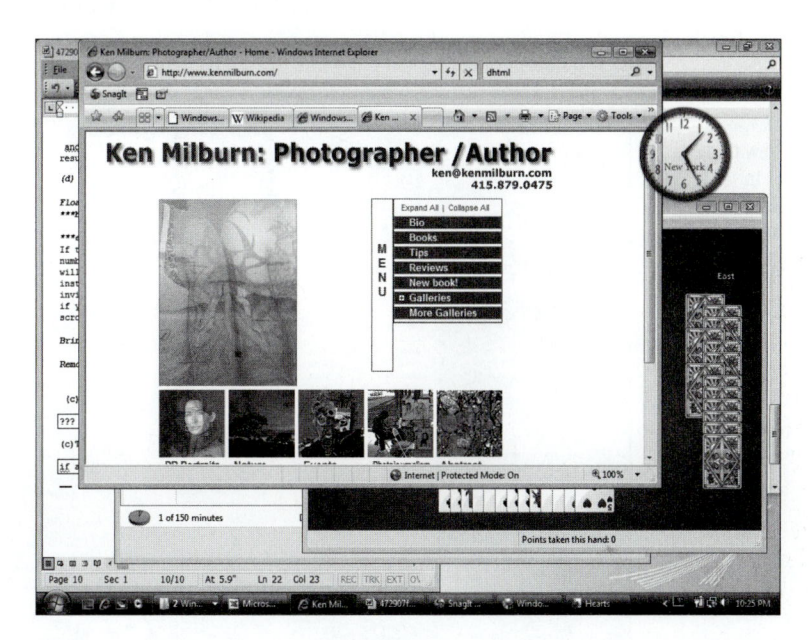

Note that even though a gadget is transparent, moving the cursor over the gadget makes it opaque, and you cannot click something behind it. You'll have to move the gadget first.

Bringing Gadgets to the Front

Sometimes, gadgets will be obscured by other windows if you don't have them set to always be on top. Open a few windows, and your clock and other gadgets are gone. They are not in the taskbar either, so how do you find them again? The quickest way to bring them all back into view is to right-click the Sidebar icon in the system tray and choose Bring Gadgets to Front.

Removing Gadgets

Gadgets you install will remain active until you close them and will persist on subsequent rerunning of Sidebar (which may be when you reboot your computer if you have the Start Sidebar When Windows Starts setting turned on). If you log off and log back on, likewise, they will be reloaded. If gadgets are so persistent, how do you turn them off?

As mentioned earlier, you can close an individual gadget by hovering over it and then clicking the X when its tool handle pops up. But for a more comprehensive approach that allows you to see all the currently running gadgets and quickly remove selected ones, do this:

1. Right-click the Sidebar or the Sidebar icon in the system tray.
2. Choose Properties.
3. In the Sidebar properties box, click View List of Running Gadgets. You'll see the dialog box shown in Figure 7.14.
4. Click the ones you want to stop running and click Remove. Close the box when you're finished.

Figure 7.14
Use the View Gadgets dialog box to see what gadgets are currently running and stop them if you want.

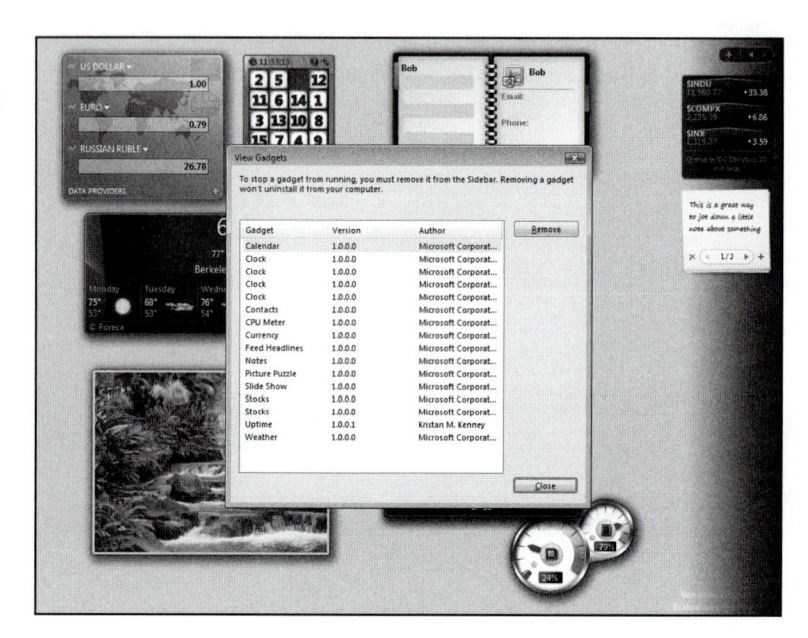

Even after you remove a gadget, it's not erased from your computer. It's still in the list of available gadgets, and clicking the + (add) button at the top of the Sidebar will reveal it, if you want to use it later. You can safely remove gadgets without fearing that you're obliterating them.

Installed gadgets do not appear in the Control Panel's Programs and Features applet, so you can't remove them from you hard disk that way.

> **TIP**
>
> The default gadget location is C:\Program Files\Windows Sidebar\Gadgets and a location that is specific for each user is C:\Users\user\AppData\Local\Microsoft\Windows Sidebar\Gadgets

> **TIP**
>
> If you are interested in making your own gadgets, visit http://microsoftgadgets.com/ or http://microsoftgadgets.com/Build/, or go to Google and search for "make build Vista gadgets."

CALENDAR

For the first time in a Windows product, Vista supplies an actually useful calendar. For Windows time immemorial, the system clock down at the bottom of the screen has afforded us the quick cheat of popping up a calendar if you double-clicked on it and messed around with the date (and then canceled the dialog so it didn't actually change the system clock). But now you actually have a calendar much like the one in Microsoft Outlook built in as a freebie in Windows. In addition to using Windows Calendar as your primary calendar, you can use it to organize your To-Do list (tasks) to subscribe to web calendars from any participating organization's website or to share your schedule with others.

To use Calendar, follow these steps:

1. Click Start, All Programs, Calendar. You'll see a window like that shown in Figure 7.15.

Figure 7.15
Windows Calendar's opening screen.

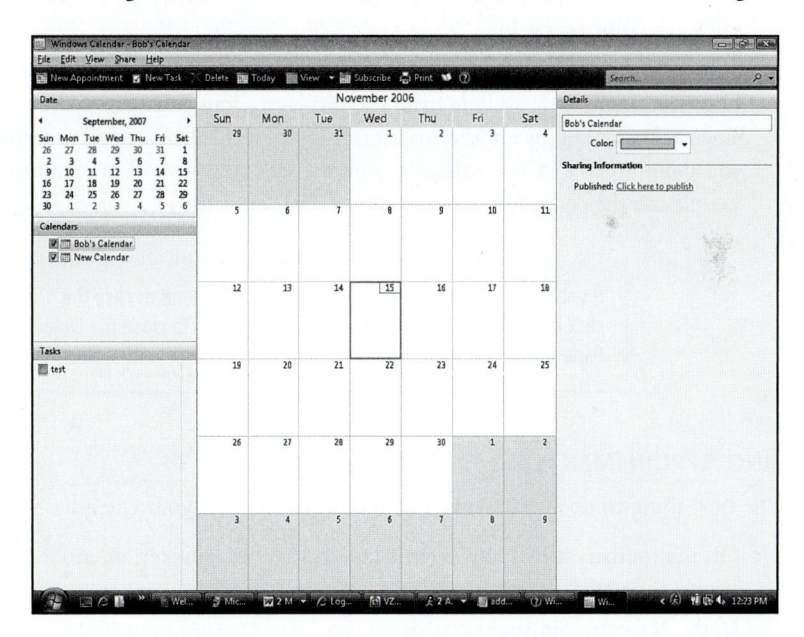

2. Figure 7.15 shows the calendar in month view, but you can view your calendar by day, work week, or week too. Just click View and then click the view you want. A check mark will appear next to the chosen view. You can also choose Today to see today's appointments (ever so useful for ensuring that you are not accidentally entering an appointment into the wrong week, month, or year) or go to a specific date that you can enter or choose from a little pop-up calendar.

> **TIP**
>
> You can also just click the Today button on the toolbar to get to today's schedule.

> **NOTE**
>
> Calendars are stored like this: C:\Users\Bob\AppData\Local\Microsoft\Windows Calendar\Calendars.

CREATING A CALENDAR

The first thing to do is create a new calendar for yourself. The calendar is saved in the Users file, making is specific to the user logged in. You can have separate calendars for different people who share the computer (or different purposes) and create appointments and tasks in each one. Each calendar gets a specific color of appointment assigned to it. To create a new calendar, perform the following steps:

1. Click the File menu; then click New Calendar.
2. In the New Calendar details box on the right side, type the name you want for the calendar.
3. To choose the color of your appointments, in the Details pane, click Color and then click the color you want.
4. In the left pane, the Navigation pane, you'll see the name of the new calendar. You can choose to include or exclude from the display various calendars stored on your computer. Each calendar you or another user creates gets a checkbox. Turn on the checkbox to see the appointments in that calendar overlaid with your own. This can be helpful if other people use the computer and you want to filter out their calendars.

> **TIP**
>
> If you can't see the details of a task, date, or calendar, click the View menu, and then click Details Pane so that a checkmark appears. To close the Details pane, click Details Pane again, so that the checkmark disappears.

ENTERING APPOINTMENTS

The next thing to do is start entering appointments into your calendar. Here's how:

1. On the toolbar, click New Appointment. Or even quicker, on any calendar view, double-click a time area.
2. In the New Appointment box or on the New Appointment highlight that appears where you clicked the calendar, type a description of the appointment. (You may have to select the words "New Appointment" and replace them with your description.)
3. In the Location box on the Details pane, type in the appointment's location if you want.
4. In the Calendar list, choose which calendar you want your appointment assigned to.
5. Next, choose the start and end times of the event or click All-Day Appointment if it's a full-day deal. If you're in any view other than month view, and you like the graphical mouse-based approach to setting the time, you can drag the bottom or top of the

appointment or drag the dark bar on the left of the appointment to change the start and stop times or even move the appointment from day to day or hour to hour.

6. Is this a recurring appointment? To make the appointment recur, in the Recurrence list, click the type of recurrence you want. It's normally set to None but can be set to daily, weekly, monthly, yearly, or for a specific number of times, or until a certain date, after which it will stop repeating.

7. You can set a reminder to alert you of the upcoming appointment if you like. In the Reminder list, click how long before the appointment you want to be reminded. A little alarm clock icon will appear in the appointment's box. A dialog box will pop up on your computer screen reminding you of your appointment and optionally playing a sound (see the Options dialog box explained later in this section).

8. Often you'll have to edit an appointment. You can double-click on it in any view and enter new information, drag it around, and edit information in the Details pane.

One great thing about Calendar is that you do not have to remember to save. Appointments are saved as soon as they are entered or edited.

> **TIP**
> You can easily invite someone to your appointment. In the Details pane, notice the Attendees area. Either click the button and choose one or more people from Contacts, or type in the email address of a person you want to invite and press Enter. Then click Invite.

SUBSCRIBING TO AND PUBLISHING CALENDARS

You may not know that TV and radio shows, schools, sports teams, and other institutions have online calendars that you can subscribe to. With a few clicks you can ensure that these organizations' events end up on your calendar without having to cruise to their website and copy and paste stuff into your calendar. The website or institution has to conform with the iCalendar format, however, for this to work. (iCalendars are stored in .ics files, incidentally.)

Follow these steps to see what's available:

1. Click Subscribe on the Toolbar. You'll see the dialog box shown in Figure 7.16.

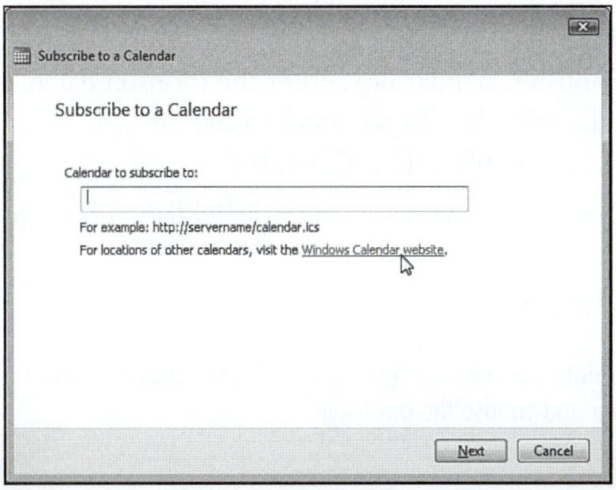

Figure 7.16
Subscribing to a public Calendar imports that calendar's events into yours.

2. Enter the calendar address, which you'll have to obtain from someone in the know, or a website. Alternatively, you can click the Windows Calendar Website link. This may take you to a list of public calendars you can subscribe to, though when we wrote this, it didn't show much.

Publishing a Calendar

Want to share a calendar of a public organization you work for or participate in so that others can view or subscribe to it, as explained previously? You could, of course, simply do what most organizations do—put up and maintain a website with a calendar or Coming Events page, but keeping the page up to date as your organization's schedule evolves is an expensive and time-consuming ritual. A better solution is to publish your Windows Calendar on the Internet through a web host so that others can easily see and share it, even as it evolves. Don't want to go that public? Perhaps you want to share your personal or office calendar for family members or your coworkers. You can require a password protection so that you can choose who can access and view your calendar. Follow these steps:

1. Click the Share menu; then click Publish. You'll see the dialog box shown in Figure 7.17.

Figure 7.17
Publishing a calendar for others to subscribe to.

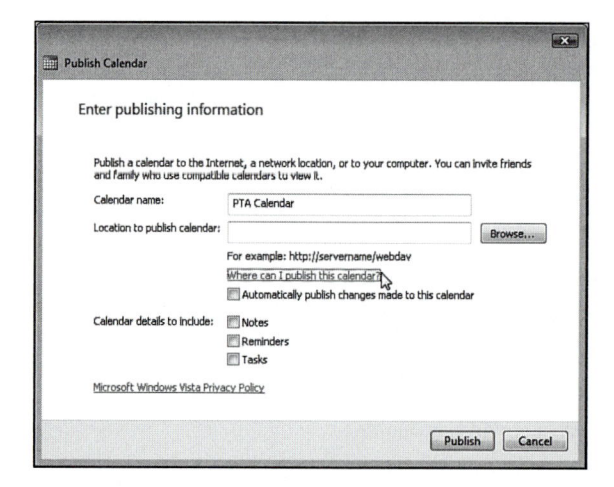

2. In the Calendar Name box, type the calendar name that you want to share.
3. In the Location to Publish Calendar box, enter the location (such as a website) where you want to publish the calendar. To see locations where you can publish your calendar online, click Where Can I Publish This Calendar?
4. Select any other options you want and then click Publish. The auto update feature is of particular note.

> **TIP**
>
> You can print your calendar by day, work week, week, or month. Simply click Print on the toolbar and choose the print style.

Setting Up Tasks

A task master is something everyone needs. I couldn't get through a week without my PDA and Outlook telling me where to go and when to do it. I used to miss appointments, but now I rarely do. Effective task management can also help you organize your time more efficiently. Enter tasks, give them due dates, set priorities, and even let the computer remind you to get into gear with task completion.

Here are the basic steps for setting up tasks:

1. On the toolbar, click New Task. "New Task" appears on the left side in the Navigation pane. If you don't see anything when you click New Task, it's because your Navigation pane is off. Click View, Navigation pane (or press Ctrl+I).
2. In the New Task box, type a description of the task.
3. In the Calendar list on the Details pane, click the calendar where you want the task to appear. If you don't see that, turn on your Details pane.
4. In the Priority list, click the priority you want: low, medium, or high.
5. Enter the start and due dates, whether you want a reminder, and any other notes you have about the task. I use the Notes field a lot to help me track what's developed around a task's completion, phone numbers of people, and so forth.
6. Click anywhere else on the calendar, and the task is recorded.

Setting Options

You can specify some important options for Calendar. Click File, Options, and you'll see the dialog box shown in Figure 7.18.

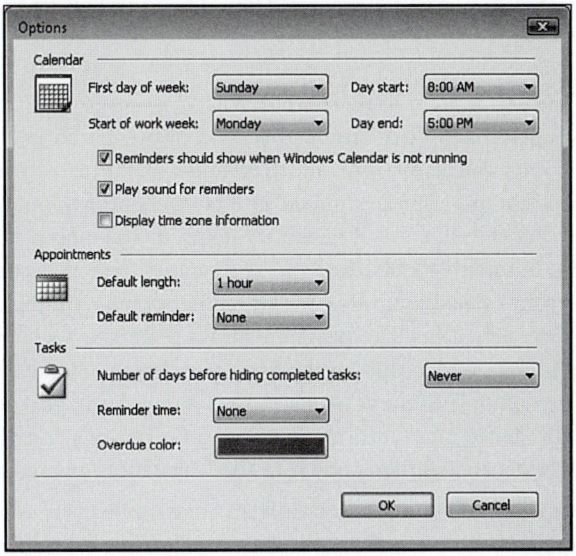

Figure 7.18
Windows Calendar has many useful options worth checking out.

Windows Calendar has many useful options worth checking out.

Of particular note is when your week starts (I like to start mine on Monday so that Saturday and Sunday show up adjacent as a weekend). Also, setting the beginning and end of the day are useful because that determines what hours show up onscreen in day and week views. The option Reminders Should Show When Windows Calendar Is Not Running is an important one. I suggest leaving this option box checked, or you will miss appointments if you forget to run Windows Calendar. You might want to add Calendar to your Startup group anyway. That's what I do, so that whenever I boot up, my calendar pops up onscreen too, always at the ready.

There isn't room here to discuss all the features of Calendar, but I encourage you to explore the other options in this dialog box as well as on the menus. The Share menu lets you send events to other people via email, and the Share, Sync All option lets you synchronize your calendar with Pocket PCs and other devices hooked up through the Sync Center. (Sync Center is covered in Chapter 38, "Hitting the Road," in the section "Sync Center.")

The Other Accessories

As you likely already know from using Windows in the past, a number of other freebie accessories come with Windows. Some are useful and some end up lying fallow for many PC users who never even know they exist. These little apps have been carried forward from generations of Windows going back to when I started writing about it with Windows 3.0. Because they are so well known by this point, we won't tie up book pages here with the kind of belabored descriptions used in our past books. It will suffice here to briefly tell you what each does. You reach Calculator, Notepad, Paint, and WordPad by clicking Start, All Programs, Accessories, and then choosing the program. To reach Character Map, click Start and in the Search box, type **Character Map**. Then in the list of results, double-click Character Map.

Here's a brief rundown of each program:

- **Calculator**—A quick-and-dirty onscreen version of two traditional pocket calculators: a standard no-brainer calculator and a more complex scientific calculator used by statisticians, engineers, computer programmers, and business professionals. They are good for adding up your lunch bill, a list of inventory items, or the mortgage payment on your office building. But neither calculator sports a running tape that you can use to backtrack through your calculations. You can switch between modes by choosing View, Standard or View, Scientific. The program always remembers which type was used last and comes up in that mode. Most of the operations on the Standard Calculator are self-explanatory, but a couple of them—square roots and percentages—are just a bit tricky. Check the Help file for more information. You can prepare a complex equation in a text editor such as Notepad and then copy it to the Calculator for execution.

- **Character Map**—A utility program that lets you examine every character in a given font and choose and easily insert into your documents special characters, such as trademark (™ and ®) and copyright symbols (©); foreign currency symbols, accented letters (such as ¥), and nonalphabetic symbols (such as fractions, $\tfrac{3}{4}$); DOS line-drawing characters (+), items from specialized fonts such as Symbol and Wingdings; or the common arrow symbols (←, →, ↑, and ↓). Some fonts include characters not mapped to the keyboard. Character Map lets you choose them, too, from its graphical display. The Program Map displays Unicode, DOS, and Windows fonts' characters. You can choose the character set, rearrange the items in a font (such as grouping all currency types together) to eliminate hunting, and search for a given character. Character Map works through the Windows Clipboard. You simply choose a character you want to use, click Copy, and it moves onto the Clipboard. Switch to your destination application (typically a word processing file), position the cursor, and choose Paste.

- **Paint**—A simple drawing program that creates and edits bitmapped images in a variety of formats. Using free-form drawing tools, text, and special effects, you can create projects such as invitations, maps, signs, and wallpaper for your desktop, and you can edit images linked into documents created by other programs. Paint is called a *bitmapped image editor*. Your computer's screen is divided into small dots (*pixels* or *pels*) that are controlled by the smallest division of computer information—*bits*. A *bitmap* is a collection of bits of information that creates an image when assigned (*mapped*) to dots on the screen. This bitmap is similar to one of those giant electronic billboards in Times Square, New York, that can display the score, a message, or even a picture by turning on and off specific light bulbs in the grid. Being a bitmapped drawing program, rather than an object-oriented drawing program such as Adobe Illustrator or CorelDraw, Paint has some significant limitations to keep in mind—also some advantages. After you paint a shape, you can't move it independently. You can use the computer to remove an area of the painting and place it somewhere else—as if you were cutting out a piece of the canvas and pasting it elsewhere. But all the dots in the area get moved, not just the ones in the shape you're interested in. Paint can store output in a variety of formats: .bmp, .jpg, .tif, .gif, .png.

- **Notepad**—A simple, no-frills text editor that does no fancy formatting (though it does enable you to change the display font) and is popular for composing "clean" ASCII (.txt) files. I use Notepad for jotting down quick notes. You could say Notepad is a *text editor*, whereas WordPad (see the following discussion of WordPad) is a *word processor*. Unlike WordPad, Notepad cannot view or edit Microsoft Word (.doc) or Rich Text Format (.rtf) files. It's a perfect tool to call up whenever you need to view a simple README.TXT file or fine-tune some program code (programmers like this tool). Although they're visually boring and lackluster, text files do have some important advantages over formatted text documents. Most importantly, they are the lowest common denominator for exchanging text between different programs and even between different types of computers. Literally any kind of word processor and many other types of programs, from email tools to databases, can share textual information using simple text files, regardless of computer type or operating system. To be sure your recipients using other kinds of computers can read a text email attachment or a text file on a disk, stick with the simple text files such as the ones Notepad creates. Windows recognizes any file with a .TXT extension as a text file and opens it in Notepad when you click it.

- **WordPad**—For more capable word processing than Notepad can accomplish, you can use WordPad. Many people think they need to purchase Microsoft Office to do word processing, and Microsoft would love you to do so, but it is not necessary. Though it's not Microsoft Word, this program works fine for most everyday writing chores. It includes most of the formatting tools people need for typical writing projects, and the price is right. You can edit documents of virtually any length, it supports drag-and-drop editing, and it can accept graphics pasted into it from the Windows Clipboard. WordPad does standard character formatting with font, style, and size; paragraph formatting with changing line spacing, indents and margins, bullets, justification, and right and left alignment; adjustable tab stops; search and replace; and headers and footers. It has pagination control, lets you insert and edit graphics, and has Undo and Print Preview. It doesn't do tables, columns, indexes, or master documents; it also doesn't have outline view or legal line numbering. Go get Word or WordPerfect if you have that level of word-processing needs. WordPad can open and save documents in Rich Text Format, text files such as Notepad creates, Unicode, Word for Windows (.doc), and Windows Write format (.wri). WordPad correctly opens even incorrectly named (wrong extension) RTF and Word 6 files if you select the All Documents option in the Files of Type area in the Open dialog box or type the document's full name. If WordPad doesn't detect a file's format, it opens it as a text-only file. Note that if a document contains formatting information created by another application, it will likely appear as garbage characters mixed with the document's normal text.

TROUBLESHOOTING

I CAN'T SEE MY GADGETS

I can't see the Gadgets even though I have turned them on.

If the Gadgets are contained within your Sidebar and you have not dragged them onto the desktop, your Sidebar is being obscured by the windows in front of it. Right-click the Sidebar icon in the Notification Area and choose Bring Gadgets to Front. That will work as a one-time fix. But if you want the Sidebar to always be in front of other windows, right-click the Sidebar icon and choose Properties. Then, choose Sidebar Is Always on Top of Other Windows.

MY TEXT IS CHOPPED OFF

I can't see all the text in a Notepad window. Where did it go?

You must manually turn on word wrap to get the text in a file to wrap around within the window. By default, word wrap is turned off, which can be annoying. The good news is that word wrap is now a persistent setting. After you turn it on and then close Notepad, it should be on the next time you run it. If you need to edit program code, be sure to turn off word wrap, or your program lines will wrap, making editing and analysis of code more confusing.

If you still can't see enough text, remember that Notepad now supports font changing for display. Change the display font from the Format menu. Choosing a monospaced font (for example, Courier) might help you line up columns. Choosing a smaller font and a proportional font (for example, Times) crams more text into the window.

ADDING AND MODIFYING TAB STOPS

Inserting and adjusting tab stops in WordPad is a pain. Is there an easy way?

You can easily insert and adjust tabs in WordPad by clicking in the ruler area. Choose View, Ruler to turn on the ruler. Then, click in the ruler area where you want to insert a tab stop. You can drag the cursor left and right to see a vertical rule to align the stop. To kill a tab stop, drag it out of the ruler area into the document.

TIPS FROM THE WINDOWS PROS: RECEIVING EMAIL ON A POCKET PC OR BLACKBERRY

Ever since I got stung by too many missed dentist appointments, I invested in a PDA. I have gone through several generations of Palms, including the first wireless Palm, the Palm VII. I eventually switched to the Pocket PC (PPC) format from Microsoft, mostly because I like the true multitasking that the PPC operating system has versus the single-tasking of the Palm operating systems. One of the best things about either the wireless Palm or PPC is that with the right device, I can be connected to my home PC and receive email and also get event reminders sent over the air (OTA). This requires, obviously, a *converged device* that has both a cellphone and a PDA in it, all tied together with software that communicates with my office computer. For this all to work, my cellphone service has to support it, of course. I use Sprint, but Verizon and other carriers have this service, too, as millions of Blackberry users know.

Here's how it works. When email comes into my office computer (which I have to leave on all the time), my PC uses software supplied by Sprint to relay my mail to my cellphone/PDA. This, of course, happens after spam filtering in my PC, so there isn't unnecessary spam in my PDA/cellphone. I can read and then compose email on my PDA and send it. It goes back up over the cell network and then back down onto the Internet and into my office PC. It then goes into my Outlook Outbox and is eventually sent out (I have Send/Receive set to activate every 5 minutes). The upshot it that I have mail in only one place, my office PC. It gets *mirrored* onto my PDA over the air, but the PDA is really acting a bit like a remote terminal.

The same approach is used for calendaring. I can make changes to my calendar on my PDA (perhaps I'm talking to a colleague at lunch and we make an appointment), and it goes up and over the cell network, onto the Internet, and into my PC's calendar program (Outlook). My secretary sees my new appointment and doesn't double-book me for a dentist appointment. Likewise, my secretary takes a phone call in the office and books me for a business lunch. It goes out to my PDA, and while I'm at lunch with my colleague, I realize I have just been booked for lunch next Tuesday at noon, so I don't accidentally double-book lunch with him.

All this depends on software that interfaces with Microsoft Exchange (and Microsoft Outlook complies with that standard), but no doubt we will see this kind of technology evolving to support Windows Mail and Windows Calendar. The popularity of handheld devices such as the Motorola Q, Blackberry, and Palm Treo will drive the industry into increasingly greater compliance with universal standards. For better or for worse, this will mean that we will be reachable and wired even in the middle of the Sahara Desert or atop the Half Dome in Yosemite National Park. (I have tested the latter already!).

PART III

MULTIMEDIA AND IMAGING

8 Windows Media Player   259

9 Windows Imaging Tools   287

10 Scanning and Faxing   307

11 Producing Videos with Windows Movie Maker   323

12 Sound Recorder, DVD Maker, and Other Multimedia Tools   349

13 Windows Media Center   361

CHAPTER 8

WINDOWS MEDIA PLAYER

In this chapter

Learning the Basics 260

Getting Music and Video on Your Computer 266

Taking Your Music and Video On the Go 272

Organizing Your Music Collection 279

Updating Media Information and Album Art 282

Tips from the Windows Pros: Playing Audio from Your Portable Device Through Your Car Stereo 285

Learning the Basics

Windows Media Player has grown into a pretty amazing application with multiple personalities. Its talents include playing music and video files from online sources or local drives (including DVDs), playing online radio and TV stations, displaying specialized web pages, organizing your music files (MP3s and WMAs), burning music CDs, copying and syncing to portable MP3 players, and providing a conduit to online media shopping sites.

Media Types Compatible with Media Player

Windows Media Player can play the file types shown in Table 8.1.

Table 8.1 Windows Media Player–Supported File Types

File Type	File Name Extension(s)
Music CD (CD audio)	.cda
Intel Indeo video	.ivf
Audio Interchange File Format (digitized sound)	.aif, .aifc, .aiff
Windows Media (audio and video)	.asf, .asx, .wax, .wm, .wma, .wmd, .wmv, .wvx, .wmp, .wmx, .wpl
Windows Media Center video	.dvr-ms
Windows video and audio	.avi, .wav
QuickTime content*	.mov, .qt
Windows Media Player skins	.wmz, .wms
MPEG (Motion Picture Experts Group) video	.mpeg, .mpg, .m1v, .mp2, .mpa, .mpe, .mp2v, .mp2
AU (UNIX audio)	.au, .snd
MP3 (digital audio)	.mp3, .m3u
MIDI (Musical Instrument Digital Interface)	.mid, .midi, .rmi
DVD video	.vob

Formats not supported: RealNetworks (.ra, .rm, .ram), iTunes (.m4p, .acc, .mp4)
* Only QuickTime files version 2.0 or earlier can be played in Windows Media Player. Later versions of QuickTime require the proprietary Apple QuickTime Player.

> **NOTE**
>
> Vista doesn't come from Microsoft with DVD playback capability, except in the editions containing Media Center—Vista Home Premium and Vista Ulimate. If your version of Vista does not contain Media Center and you want to play back DVD video and .mp2v files, you must first install a hardware or software DVD decoder on your system. If you insert a

LEARNING THE BASICS

DVD and it doesn't run, that's probably the problem. Installing a decoder is typically a simple software update you can download from the Web. To get a DVD decoder, search the Web for WinDVD or Power DVD. The decoder will cost you a few bucks, probably around $10. (Although current boxed editions of both players are around $50–$60.)

GETTING AROUND WINDOWS MEDIA PLAYER 11

Media Player 11 has a redesigned user interface, as shown in Figure 8.1, to make it easier for you to manage and enjoy your digital media. The classic menus have been replaced by an organized tab system, making managing and viewing your digital media easier than ever.

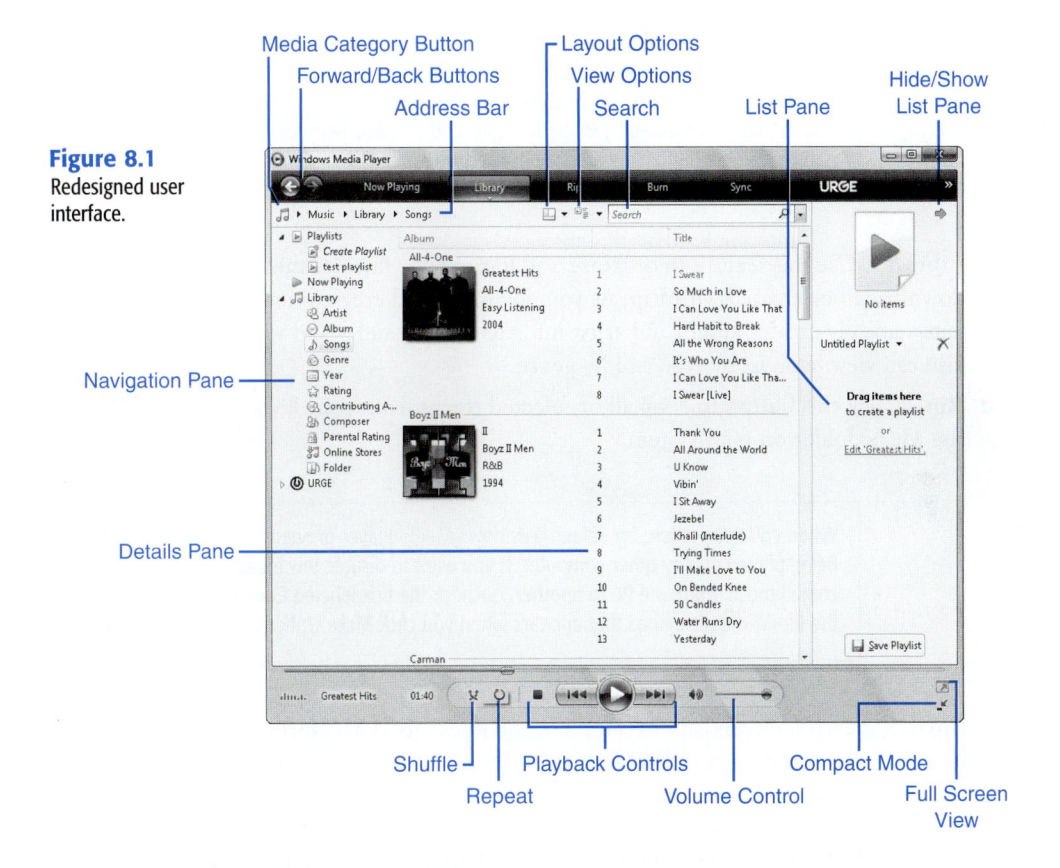

Figure 8.1
Redesigned user interface.

NAVIGATING MENU TABS

The tabs in Media Player 11, shown in Figure 8.2, provide a way to quickly focus on the task you want to perform.

Figure 8.2
New redesigned tabs in Media Player 11.

These tabs are accessed from the top of the Media Player 11 window and perform the following tasks:

- **Now Playing**—When you select online or locally stored content for playback, the Now Playing window displays a list of the content you're playing. An optional Visualizations feature can be used to display album art (when available) or various animated abstractions that change in response to the music.

> **TIP**
>
> Many visualizations are available online for use with Windows Media Player 11. A personal favorite of mine called PixelTrip can be obtained from the Windows Media Player website at http://www.wmplugins.com/ItemDetail.aspx?ItemID=881. *Another excellent visualization* is provided by Brian Spangler and is called TwistedPixel. You can download it from his website for free at www.visolu.com/TwistedPixel.

- **Library**—Use this feature to organize and locate your favorite media types you've downloaded or created with Rip. As you download and create music, Media Player automatically creates album and artist information for audio and video content. You also can view content by type and by genre.
- **Rip**—Click this button to copy all or selected tracks from your favorite music CDs to the Music folder on your system.

> **TIP**
>
> When you copy music, by default, Windows Media Player prevents copied tracks from being played on any other computer. If you want to disable this feature so you can move copied music from one PC to another, uncheck the box labeled Copy Protect Music in the Rip Music dialog box that appears when you click More Options in the Rip tab menu.

- **Burn**—After you download or convert music tracks to WMA format, use this feature to transfer your music mix to writable CDs (CD-R or CD-RW media).

> **TIP**
>
> Be sure you fill your CD with all the music you want to play; unlike conventional CD-mastering programs or Windows Vista's Copy to CD feature in other parts of the operating system, Windows Media Player's Copy to CD feature closes the CD (so it no longer can accept data) after you copy your selected music to it, even if you use only a small portion of the CD. Why? Standalone CD players are designed to handle single-session CDs and won't work if you add music later. If you want to create a CD for playback on your computer, use Windows Explorer's Copy to CD feature instead, which will allow you to copy music over several sessions.

- **Sync**—After you download or convert music tracks to WMA format, use this feature to transfer your music mix to PlaysForSure compatible portable audio players.
- **Media Guide/Online Stores**—This option enables you to purchase media online or select from a variety of online content.

The arrows below each tab provide quick access to setting and options relevant to the task of that tab. For instance, as shown in Figure 8.3, the arrow below the Now Playing tab provides the options for playback Enhancements as well as the capability to change the current Visualization.

> **TIP**
>
> To show the classic menus, right-click an empty area of the taskbar or an empty area around the playback controls and select Show Classic Menus or press Ctrl+M.

Figure 8.3
New tab menus for accessing options in Windows Media Player 11.

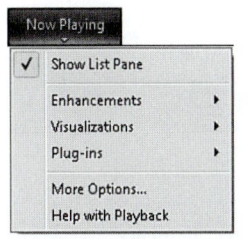

REDESIGNED BROWSING AND SEARCHING

The navigation of the music library is similar to that in Windows Explorer.

> **NOTE**
>
> For the best browsing and search experience, ensure that the media information is correct and up to date as described in the section "Updating Media Information and Album Art."

You can browse your media by performing the following steps:

1. Click the Select a Category button to choose the type of media to browse, as shown in Figure 8.4. Options include Music, Pictures, Video, Recorded TV, and Other Media.
2. Choose the desired view for your media. This includes Artist, Album, Songs, Genre, and more.
3. Narrow the items shown for the chosen view by clicking the arrow on the Address bar, as shown in Figure 8.5.

Figure 8.4
Select a media category.

Media Category

Navigation Views

TIP

More views can be found by right-clicking Library in the Navigation Pane and selecting Show More Views.

Figure 8.5
Narrow the items shown in the view by using the Address bar.

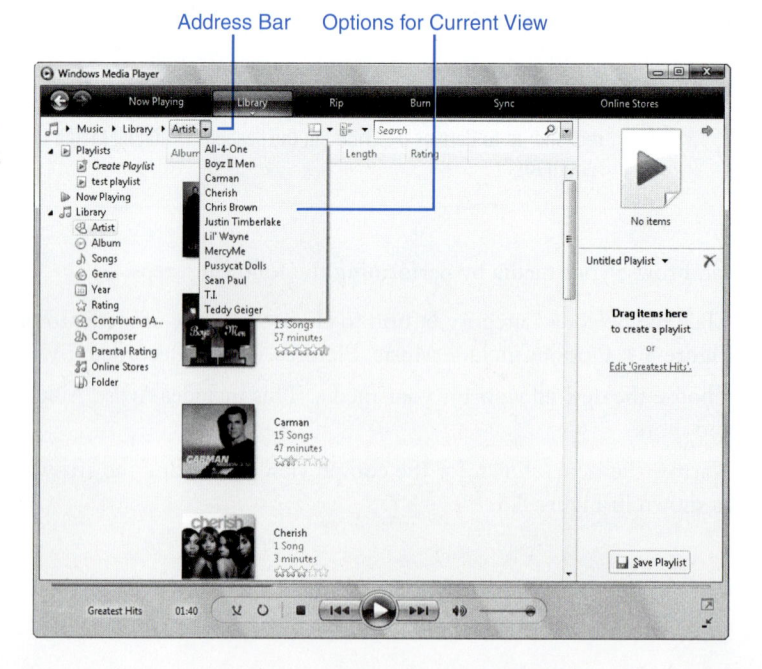

Address Bar *Options for Current View*

> **NOTE**
> To return to a higher level in the current view, click the desired level in the Address bar.

Searching can also be used to narrow the view of a chosen media category. After you have chosen a category as described in Step 1, enter your search term into the search box as shown in Figure 8.6.

Figure 8.6
Searching is a fast and easy way to narrow your media views.

PLAYING AUDIO AND VIDEO IN WINDOWS MEDIA PLAYER 11

There are three options for playing audio and video media in Windows Media Player 11. These include audio CDs and video DVDs, media stored on your hard disk, and media accessible over a home network.

PLAYING AN AUDIO CD OR DVD

To play an audio CD or DVD in Windows Media Player 11, follow these steps:

1. Insert the CD or DVD you want to play into your computer's CD-ROM or DVD-ROM drive.
2. Click the arrow below the Now Playing tab and select the drive that contains the disk you want to play, as shown in Figure 8.7.
3. While a disk is playing, you can use the Play/Pause, Previous, and Next buttons of the playback controls shown in Figure 8.1 to navigate the songs or chapters on the disk, or you can double-click the song or chapter in the List pane to play it immediately.

Figure 8.7
Select the CD you want to play from the Now Playing menu.

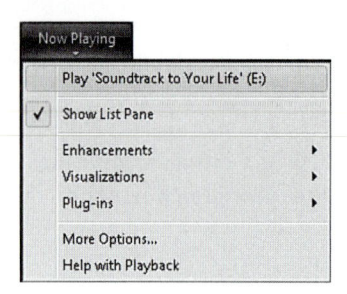

> **TIP**
> To play a DVD in full screen, click the View Full Screen button shown in Figure 8.1 or press Alt+Enter while the video is playing or paused.

Playing Media Stored on Your Hard Disk or Network Share

To play an item stored on your hard disk, add it to the library following the instructions in the section "Adding Items from Your Computer to Your Library." After the item is added to the library, you can select the media you want to view by double-clicking it in the Library view. If you want to add an item to the Now Playing list, right-click the item and select Add to Now Playing. Now Playing items can be navigated using the same playback controls described in the previous section.

→ To play media shared over your home network, see the section labeled "Sharing Media Throughout Your Home."

> **TIP**
> When playing large amounts of media from your library, you may want to have the player randomly choose the next song to play or shuffle your playback. To do this, click the Turn Shuffle On button shown in Figure 8.1.

Getting Music and Video on Your Computer

Media Player 11 offers many ways to add media to your media library. These methods include ripping music from CDs to your computer, purchasing media from online stores, and adding media items already stored on your computer to the library.

Ripping Songs from CDs onto Your Computer

The process of copying music from a CD to your computer and converting it to a format that Media Player understands is known as *ripping*. Songs ripped using Windows Media Player 11 automatically appear in the media library for playing.

GETTING MUSIC AND VIDEO ON YOUR COMPUTER | 267

NOTE
> For best results when ripping music, make sure your computer is connected to the Internet. When connected to the Internet, Media Player retrieves media information for inserted CDs and stores this information in the ripped media files. If the media information is incorrect or missing, you can add it or edit it after ripping. For information on how to add or edit media information, see "Updating Media Information and Album Art" later in this chapter. In addition, the filenames of the ripped music files can be set to use this media information in different ways. To do this, click the arrow below the Rip tab and select More Options. In this dialog box, you can change the rip music location by selecting Change under the Rip Music to This Location section. The ripped music filename is changed by selecting File Name from this same section and formatting the filename as desired. I choose to use Track Number followed by the Song Title with a space as the separator. I use this because it results in a very neat Music folder when organized as described in "Organizing Your Media Collection."

To rip music to your computer, complete the following steps:

1. Choose the desired format and bit rate for the file by clicking the arrow below the Rip tab, as shown in Figure 8.8. Select the desired options from the Format and Bit Rate commands. For more information on these options, see "Choosing a File Format" and "Choosing a Bit Rate" later in this section.

Figure 8.8
Change Format and Bit Rate in the Rip menu.

2. Insert a CD into the CD-ROM drive and click the Rip tab, as shown in Figure 8.9.

NOTE
> By default, Windows Media Player 11 begins ripping automatically when you are on the Rip tab and insert a new CD. Automatic ripping options can be changed by selecting More Options from the Rip tab menu.

3. After the player has started ripping the CD, you may choose to uncheck songs that you do not want Media Player to rip to your computer. You can also stop or start by clicking the Stop Rip or Start Rip buttons that appear in the Rip view.

Figure 8.9
The Rip tab used for copying from CDs to your computer.

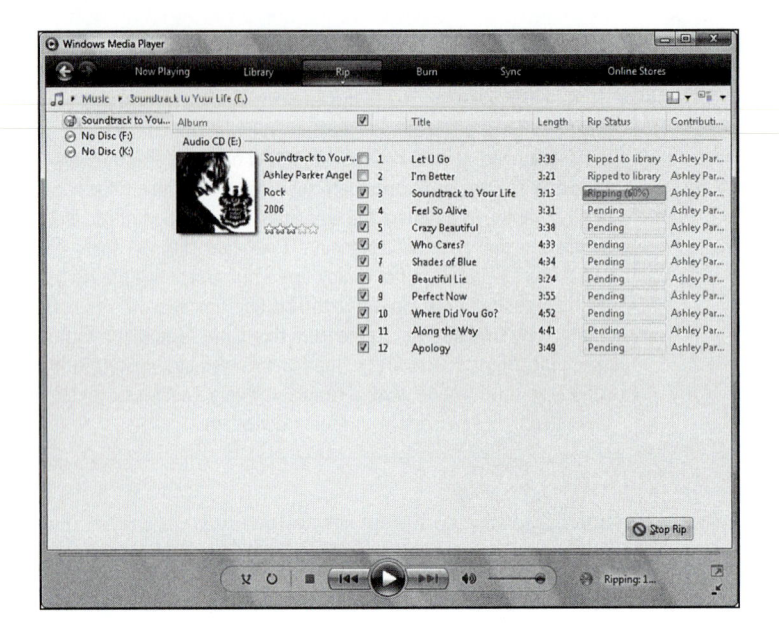

Choosing a File Format

By default, Windows Media Player 11 uses the Windows Media Audio Format. This format offers a balanced combination between sound quality and file size. Other available formats are

- **Windows Media Audio Pro**—Ideal for portable devices because of its higher sound quality at low bit rates.
- **Windows Media Audio Variable Bit Rate**—Results in smaller file size with the same audio quality.
- **Windows Media Audio Lossless**—Provides the best audio quality with the largest file size.
- **MP3**—Provides added flexibility with similar audio quality and a slightly larger file size than Windows Media Audio.
- **WAV**—Another lossless format providing added flexibility with high audio quality and large file size.

Choosing a Bit Rate

The bit rate determines the audio quality and file size of the resulting file. Typically, lower bit rates result in smaller file sizes that have lower audio quality. Alternatively, high bit rates result in high quality audio with very large file sizes.

You should choose a bit rate that balances quality and file size to meet your usage needs. A good bit rate is usually 96Kbps or 128Kbps if you plan to use your audio on portable devices with limited storage. Higher bit rates should be used for audio archiving on your PC where storage space is not an issue. True audiophiles won't be satisfied with MP3s ripped at anything under 192Kbps, however.

SHOPPING FOR MUSIC AND VIDEO FROM ONLINE STORES

Online stores provide a quick and easy way to legally download your favorite music or videos. Media Player 11 allows the browsing and purchasing of media from many online stores that are part of the PlaysForSure program. Although many stores are available, I will focus on the Napster service for buying songs and listening to online radio. Before October 2007, there was an online store called Urge, which was a partnership between Microsoft and MTV. It was fully integrated within Media Player and let you buy media directly from Library view, as shown in Figure 8.10. Unfortunately, this alliance ended, and MTV allied with the Rhapsody media service instead of Media Player.

Figure 8.10
The URGE music store was integrated directly into the library. Stores after SP-1 are not.

CHOOSING AN ONLINE STORE

The Online Stores tab displays the currently chosen online store, or might read Online Stores or Media Guide in the case that there is no store currently active. To choose an online store, click the arrow below the Online Stores tab, as shown in Figure 8.11, and select the desired store from the list. If you want to use a store not listed in the Online Stores menu, select Browse All Online Stores. Then you can choose Napster or whatever.

Figure 8.11
Use the Online Stores menu to choose your desired store.

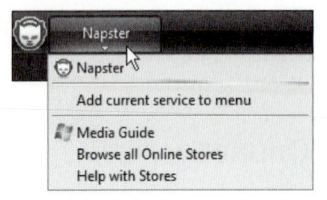

Setting Up an Account

Most online stores require a similar setup process of creating a username and password, entering your billing information, and choosing your account type. To set up an account for Napster, follow these steps:

1. Find Napster in the Browse Online Stores list, and read the instructions for downloading the Napster plugin for Media Player.
2. Select Create New Account in the dialog box that appears, as shown in Figure 8.12.

Figure 8.12
Napster store Sign In dialog box.

3. Enter your billing information and select an account type.

   Common account types are as follows:

   - **Purchase Only**—Standard account type that allows purchasing songs on an individual basis. Songs can usually be played on the computer, burned to a CD, or transferred to a portable device.
   - **Subscription with Streaming**—Subscription account that allows unlimited streaming of all content contained in the store's catalog. You must be connected to the Internet at all times to use this type of account.

Getting Music and Video on Your Computer

- **Subscription with Streaming and Download**—Subscription account that allows the download of music to your computer for playback when not connected to the Internet.
- **Subscription with Streaming, Download, and Sync**—Subscription account that allows you to download media and sync it to a PlaysForSure-compatible portable device.

Adding Items from Your Computer to Your Library

By default, Windows Media player 11 searches certain folders on your computer for media files and automatically adds these files to your library. If your media does not appear in the library automatically, it is located in a folder that is not monitored by Media Player. To change the folders that are monitored, perform the following steps:

1. Click the arrow below the Library tab and select Add to Library.
2. In the Add to Library dialog box, click Advanced Options.
3. As shown in Figure 8.13, you can Add or Remove monitored folders as well as change options for monitoring.

> **TIP**
>
> To add .m4a, .mp4, .m4p, or .aac files from iTunes to your Media Player 11 library, you must first convert the files to a compatible format such as Windows Media Audio or MP3. Many software programs convert media files, such as Xilisoft Audio Converter. To find one of these programs, search Google for "Audio Converter" and look for one that supports your desired source file type.

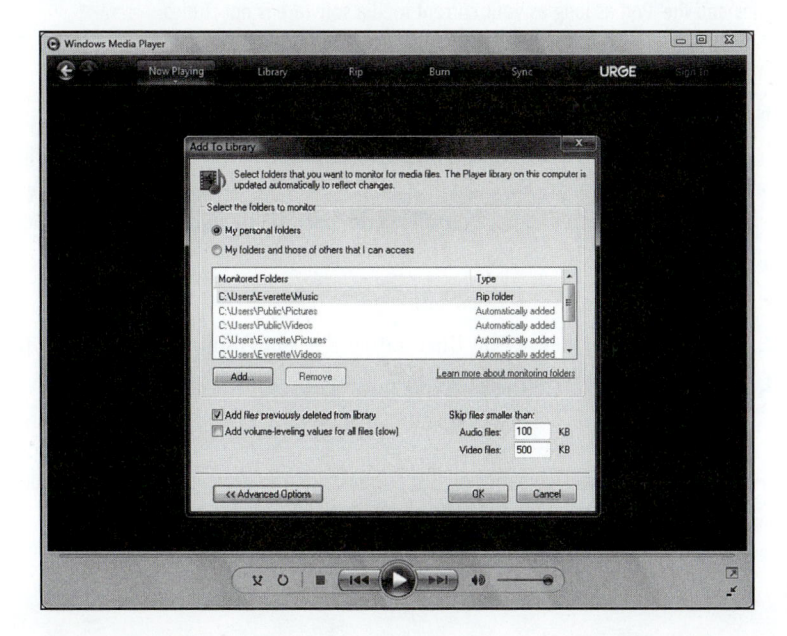

Figure 8.13
Add to Library options.

Taking Your Music and Video on the Go

Windows Media Player 11 provides many ways that make it easier than ever to take your music and video files with you. Media Player 11 has built-in functions for burning CDs, synchronizing files to your portable media player, and for sharing your media throughout your home network.

Media Player 11 and PlaysForSure Versus iTunes & iPod
One of the first questions that is asked is should I get an iPod or another type of MP3 player? Having used a large number of portable music players in the past, I would recommend one of the excellent, more featured alternative players. If you are choosing a new portable device, the first consideration is the software you currently use for your digital media. If you currently use iTunes for your digital media management and purchasing, then you should definitely choose the iPod since it would integrate with your current media system. However, if you currently use Windows Media Player or any other PC-based media software, I would recommend using Windows Media Player in conjunction with a PlaysForSure compatible device. Of the portable devices I have used, the Creative Zen Vision:M, found at www.creative.com, is by far a superior device. The device has an incredible screen offering 256,000 colors to view your video as well as extremely crisp audio provided by Creative's patented audio processors. The player also includes the ability to listen and record FM radio as well as support for TiVo-to-Go, both of which the iPod lacks. Other advantages over the iPod include the longer battery life of 4 hours of video or 14 hours of audio playback. The Zen provides a much larger number of formats, which is its main advantage over the iPod, in my opinion. Instead of being limited to a couple of audio and one video format, the Zen offers support for the WMA, MP3, and WAV audio formats as well as MPEG1/2/4-SP, WMV9, Motion-JPEG, DivX, and XviD, and Tivo-to-Go video support. All PlaysForSure devices also support the large number of online content providers available through Windows Media Player 11 instead of being restricted to only one provider, as iTunes/iPod are, the iTunes Store. Finally, with the newly redesigned Media Player 11, the benefits of the standardized PlaysForSure program offer far superior function to the proprietary iTunes software suite without the need to install another piece of software onto your system. For this reason, it is my recommendation to choose Windows Media Player 11 and a compatible PlaysForSure device over iTunes and the iPod as long as your current media software is not iTunes.

Burning Customized CDs

Media Player 11 provides the capability to create customized CDs for playing in your home or car CD player. Before you can burn a CD, you must first have a Windows Vista–compatible CD burner and a blank CD-R disc. To burn a custom CD, perform the following steps:

1. Begin by selecting the Burn tab.
2. Click the arrow below the Burn tab and select Audio CD, as shown in Figure 8.14.
3. Insert a blank CD into your CD burner drive.

> **NOTE**
>
> If you have multiple CD burners, you can change the destination burner by clicking Next Drive in the List pane of the Burn view, as shown in Figure 8.15.

TAKING YOUR MUSIC AND VIDEO ON THE GO | 273

Figure 8.14
Select Audio CD from the Burn menu.

4. Create the list of songs to burn by dragging items from the Details pane to the List pane to add those items to the burn list. To remove items from the list, right-click the item and choose Remove from List. Items can be rearranged by clicking and dragging the songs to match the order you desire for your CD.

Figure 8.15
Use the List pane to change the destination drive, set up the burn list, and start the burn.

> **NOTE**
>
> As you add items to the list, you will notice the time remaining, or free time on the disk, decrease to account for the newly added songs. If you choose more files than can fit on a single CD, you can choose to remove some items or have Media Player automatically split the list to burn two CDs.

5. At the bottom of the List pane, choose Start Burn, as shown in Figure 8.15. It is recommended that you not perform other tasks while the burn is in progress. The current progress can be viewed in the burn list.

SYNCING FILES TO YOUR PORTABLE MEDIA PLAYER

The first step to synchronizing your files with your portable media player is to choose a portable device. Many players will work with Windows Media Player 11, but for the best experience, you should look for a device that is PlaysForSure compatible.

Tivo-To-Go
For users with a Tivo Series 2 DVR, there is now a way to get those recorded episodes of *24* onto your portable player for watching on the go. This requires a PlaysForSure Video mobile device that states its support for Tivo-To-Go videos. An excellent player, and one I use quite often for this purpose, is Creative's Zen Vision:M. To use this feature, you must first have a Tivo that is connected to your home network. See your Tivo manual for how to do this. Secondly, you will need to download the free Tivo desktop software from Tivo's website at www.tivo.com/tivotogo. After it is installed, follow the instructions on Tivo's website or the Tivo desktop help file for how to transfer your recordings to your PC. After your recordings have transferred successfully to your PC, you can add them to your Media Player 11 Library, as described in "Adding Items from Your Computer to Your Library," and sync the files to your device either automatically or manually as described next.

PlaysForSure is a program between Microsoft and hardware vendors that ensures the best operation with Windows Media Player 11 without the need to install drivers or software for those devices. PlaysForSure is separated into many compatibilities that describe what services a device offers. To view a list of PlaysForSure devices, visit www.playsforsure.com. When shopping for your PlaysForSure device, look for the logos shown in Figure 8.16.

Figure 8.16
PlaysForSure logos indicate available services for the device.

After you have your device, open Media Player and connect the device to your computer. Media Player prompts you to choose either Automatic or Manual sync method. For a description of these methods, see the corresponding section that follows. If you decide later to change the sync method, click the arrow below the Sync tab, point to the device, and select Set Up Sync. You can then select or clear the Sync This Device Automatically check box.

Choosing What Syncs Automatically

If your device is set to sync automatically, the items selected to sync will be updated each time you connect your device to your computer. To select the items that will be synchronized, follow these steps:

1. Click the arrow below the Sync tab, point to the device name, and select Set Up Sync.
2. In the Device Setup dialog box, shown in Figure 8.17, you can choose the playlists that are synchronized with your device. Using the available playlists, select Add to sync the selected playlist with the device. To stop a playlist from synchronizing, select it in the Playlists to Sync list and choose Remove.

> **TIP**
>
> To make sure your favorite playlists sync in the event that your device runs out of storage space, make sure to use the priority arrows in the Device Setup dialog box to set the priority of the selected playlist.

Figure 8.17
The Device Setup dialog box allows you to choose the playlists to sync and their priority.

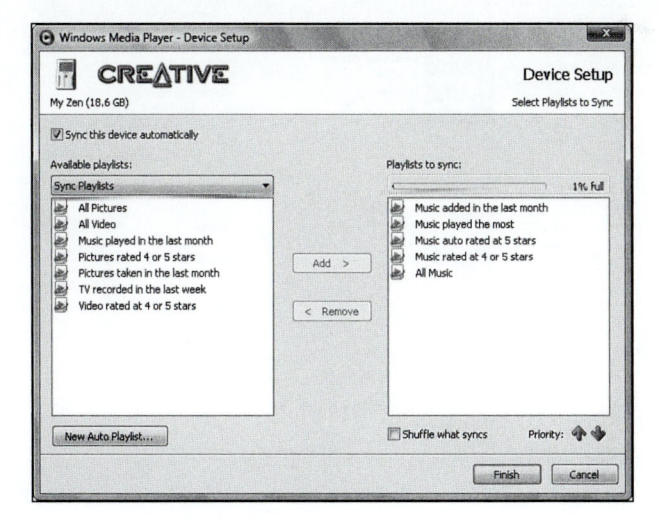

Selecting Item to Sync Manually

If your device is set to sync manually, each time you want to make changes to the files on your device, you must create a list of files to sync. To remove files from your device, navigate the device using the Navigation pane to find your file. Right-click the file and choose Delete. To set up a list of files to sync to the device, perform the following:

1. Select the Sync tab and clear the sync list by clicking the Clear List pane button as shown in Figure 8.18.

2. Find your media in your library and drag them to the List pane to add them to the Sync List as shown in Figure 8.18. To select multiple items, hold down the CTRL key while selecting your media. To remove items from the Sync List, right-click the item and select Remove from List.

> **TIP**
>
> To have Media Player automatically choose a set of random songs from your library, you can choose Click Here on the List pane when there are no items in the Sync List. After doing this, you can add or remove items from the list and click Shuffle Now.

3. After you have set up your Sync List, make sure that all the items will fit on your device by looking at the List pane. Remove any necessary items from the Sync List and click Start Sync.

Figure 8.18
Sync view allows you to manually set up your Sync List for your device.

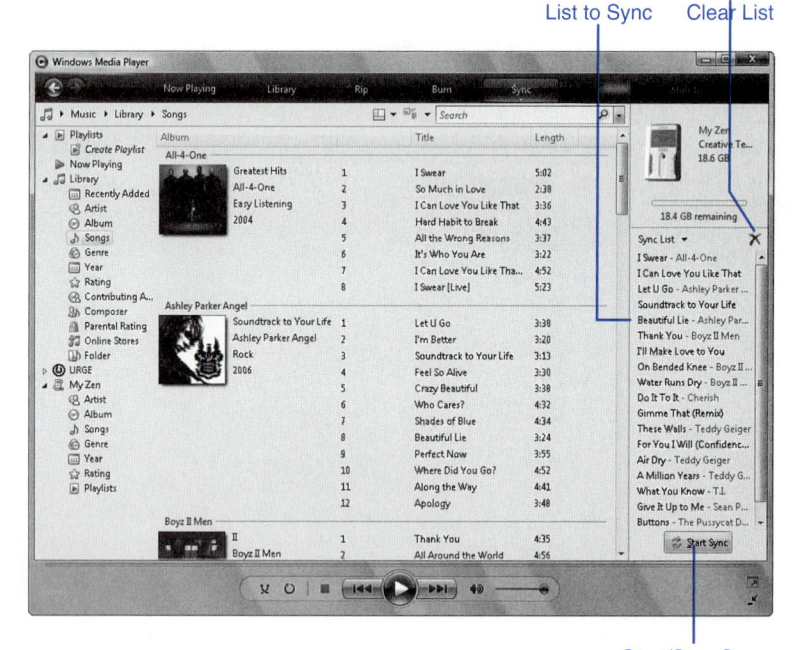

Sharing Media Throughout Your Home

Before you begin to set up media sharing throughout your home, you will need to make sure you have all the required equipment. To enable media sharing, you will need a home network and a networked digital media player. A networked digital media player, also known as a digital media receiver, is connected to your network and plays the content shared by Media Player on your Windows Vista machine. Suitable digital media receivers include other Windows Vista PCs and the Xbox 360, as well as a number of standalone units that can be found by visiting the PlaysForSure website at www.playsforsure.com.

To connect a digital media receiver to your network, you can use an ethernet cable or a wireless network adapter. Consult the documentation that comes with your device for more information on getting it connected to your home network. If you are connecting another Windows Vista PC as a digital media receiver or setting up a new home network, see Chapter 20, "Creating a Windows Network," later in this book.

After your device is connected to the network, turn it on and complete any configuration steps that may be needed to finalize the installation. If you are using another Windows Vista PC as your device, you must select the Find Media Others Are Sharing check box in the Media Sharing dialog box shown in Figure 8.19. After your device is fully connected and operational, complete the following steps to enable media sharing on your Windows Vista PC with your newly installed digital media receiver.

1. Click the arrow below the Library tab and select Media Sharing.
2. In the Media Sharing dialog box, enable media sharing by checking the Share My Media check box, as shown in Figure 8.19, and click OK.

Figure 8.19
The Media Sharing dialog box shown if media sharing is currently disabled.

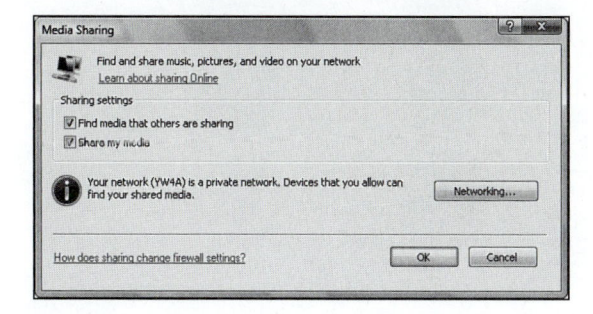

3. To allow sharing with your device, find the device in the list of devices in the Media Sharing dialog box and choose Allow, as shown in Figure 8.20. If you want to prevent access to a device, choose Deny.

> **TIP**
> To change what library items are shared with new devices by default, choose Settings in the Media Sharing dialog box. To change what library items are shared with a certain device, select that device from the device list and choose Customize.

Figure 8.20
The Media Sharing dialog box shown if media sharing is enabled. Notice the addition of the device list.

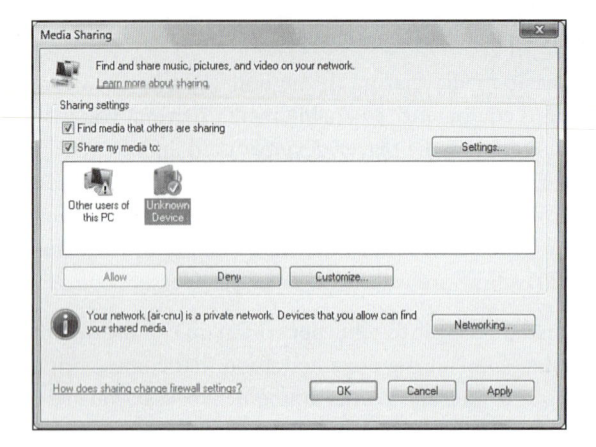

After you have sharing enabled, you are ready to play your media on your new digital media receiver. For information on how to do this, see the documentation that came with your device. If your digital media receiver is another Windows Vista PC, the shared media will appear in the Library view of Windows Media Player 11, as shown in Figure 8.21.

Figure 8.21
Accessible shared media appears in the Library view of Windows Media Player 11.

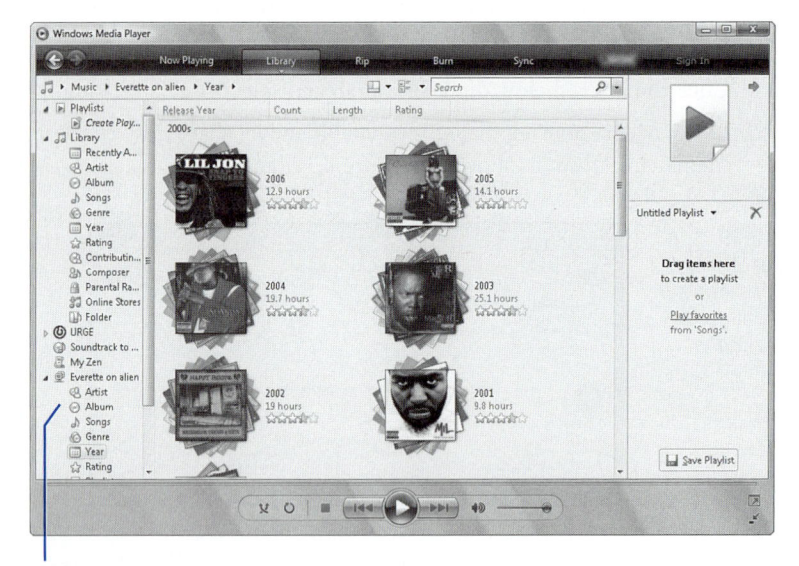

Shared Media on Your Network

CAUTION

Not all shared media will play back on your digital media receiver. Check your device's documentation for information on supported media types. Also note that media obtained from online stores may be supported only if purchased and might not be supported if obtained from a subscription service.

Organizing Your Music Collection

To keep track of all your media that you have added to your library, you must learn to organize your library and files for easy access of your favorites. Your media library can be set up to contain playlists that allow you to quickly play your favorite music. In addition, arranging the media files on your computer's hard disk in a neat fashion will greatly aid you in the event that you need to back up your media files for transfer to a new PC or for repair of your current PC.

Creating Your Own Custom Playlists

With Windows Media Player 11, it is easier than ever to create and edit custom playlists to contain your favorite media. With playlists, you can create the perfect layout of songs for any occasion. To create a new playlist, follow these instructions:

1. Open Windows Media Player 11 and select the Library tab. If you need to clear the List pane, click the Clear List pane button shown earlier in Figure 8.18.
2. To add media to your playlist, drag items from your media library onto the List pane, as shown in Figure 8.22. To rearrange items in the playlist, select and drag the item to the desired location. To remove items from the list, right-click the item, and select Remove from List.
3. When you are finished creating your playlist, select Save Playlist at the bottom of the List pane, as shown in Figure 8.22, and enter the name for your playlist.

> **NOTE**
>
> After your playlist is saved, you can play it by right-clicking it in the library Navigation pane and selecting play. In addition, the playlist may be edited anytime by selecting it from the Navigation pane and choosing Edit in List Pane. After it is opened in edit mode, make any changes to the playlist as described in Step 2 and select Save Playlist to save your changes.

Creating and Editing Auto Playlists

An auto playlist is a playlist that is set up with a set of filters. Using these filters, the content of these playlists is automatically updated to reflect changes to your media library. To create a new auto playlist, complete the following steps:

1. Click the arrow below the Library tab and select Create Auto Playlist.
2. Type the name of your new auto playlist into the Auto Playlist Name box.
3. In the bottom half of the window, set up your filters by selecting Click Here to Add Criteria, as shown in Figure 8.23. You can add as many filters as you would like to your auto playlist. To remove a filter, select it and choose Remove.

Figure 8.22
Drag items to the List pane to create a new playlist.

NOTE

To edit an existing auto playlist, right-click the playlist in the Navigation pane and select **Edit**.

Figure 8.23
Name your auto playlist and create filters.

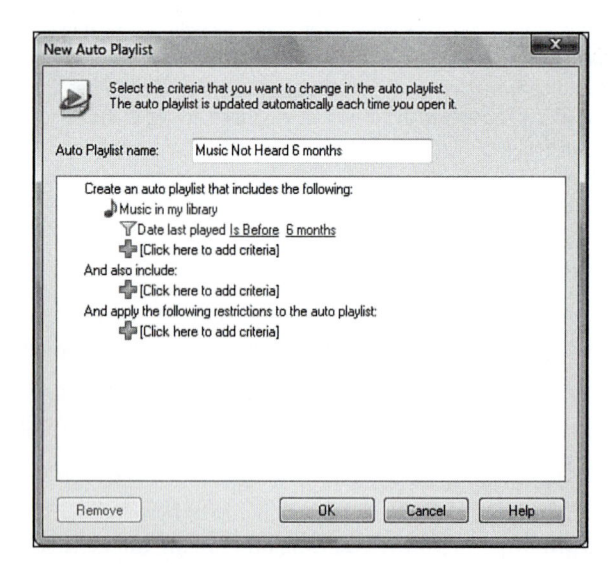

ORGANIZING YOUR MEDIA COLLECTION

Over time, your PC will have media files scattered all over the hard drive. This can make it difficult to find all your media files in the event that you want to create a backup. Your media library may also become cluttered with media files you no longer want or that you want to remove from your media library.

> **CAUTION**
>
> Before performing this next section, ensure that all your media has the correct media information as described in "Updating Media Information and Album Art." This will prevent the creation of incorrectly named folders and improperly grouped media.

To arrange your media files into an organized central location, perform the following:

1. Make sure your Rip music settings are set to use your Music folder and the filename is set up as described in the first note under "Ripping Songs from CDs onto Your Computer."
2. Click the arrow below the Library tab and select More Options.
3. Set up the Automatic Media Information Updates for Files section of the Library Options dialog box, as shown in Figure 8.24, and click OK.
4. Apply these changes to your media library files by clicking the arrow below the Library tab and selecting Apply Media Information Changes. The result will be a single Music folder, your rip music folder, arranged in folders by artist. Each Artist folder will contain Album folders that contain the songs that appear on that album.

> **TIP**
>
> When browsing your media files using Windows Explorer, you can set your view to any icon view to see the Album Art displayed for Album folders and a Collection of one or more Album Art images on Artist Folders. This provides a nice visual way to view your media files when you are not using Windows Media Player 11.

HOUSECLEANING FOR YOUR MEDIA LIBRARY

Although Media Player 11 automatically removes files from the library that are no longer present in the file system, you may at some point decide that you want to clean out your library. If you have tons of files that you no longer use and want to remove them from your library, you have two options:

First is to leave the file on your computer's hard drive and remove the file only from the library. This is a good choice if you think you might want to add the file back at a later time or if you just want to hold on to that file for sentimental reasons.

Figure 8.24
Settings to have your media files renamed and rearranged using your rip music settings.

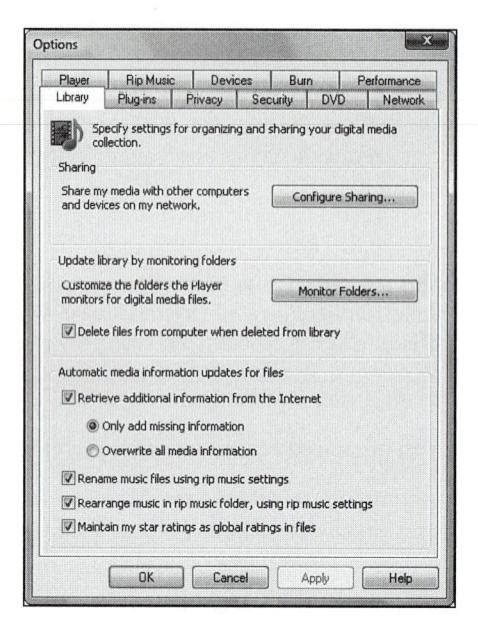

Second, you can have Media Player 11 remove the file from both your library and your PC. This results in the file being permanently lost and should be used only if you are sure you are never going to want the file again.

To remove media from your library, find the item in the Library view. Right-click the item and choose Delete. In the dialog box, choose the appropriate option for removal, as described previously.

Updating Media Information and Album Art

Most of the time, your media information will already be correct because it is downloaded when you rip a CD or it is embedded in the file when you buy music from an online store. However, on occasion, the media information that is downloaded for a file on your hard drive or for a CD is incorrect or missing. Incorrect or missing media information is a major problem when ripping CDs that are not well known or are a mix of different songs previously burned onto a CD.

> **TIP**
>
> To ensure your files stay organized and updated, make sure you update your media files after changing any media information or album art. To do this, click the arrow below the Library tab and select Apply Media Information Changes.

CAUTION

> Do not use the automatic Find Album Info features if the song was originally ripped as part of a mixed CD. This is because all files on that original CD are linked, and if you choose the album info for one file, all other files will be changed back to the album of the chosen file, thereby forcing you to redo the album info for every file in that mix CD. A word of advice—when in doubt, use the manual procedures for updating media info and album art.

Adding or Editing Media Information

In some cases, the media information of a file may be incomplete or missing. This inaccurate media information should be corrected immediately to ensure that your library and files remain neatly organized and easy to navigate and maintain. It is a lot easier to find your favorite song if it contains the correct media information than if its media information reads "Track 2, Unknown Album, Unknown Artist," along with about 400 other songs in your library. It may be tedious, but supplying your media library with correct information will make things much more enjoyable in the long run. You can enter media information into Windows Media Player 11 in several ways, including automatically from online databases, dragging items, and using the Advanced Tag Editor.

Automatically Get Media Information from an Online Database

Many albums have their information stored in online databases accessible to Windows Media Player 11. This is usually the easiest and fastest way to update your media information. To do this, complete the following steps:

1. Find the album you want to update in the Album view of the library.
2. Right-click the album and select Find Album Info.
3. Follow the instructions on the Find Album Information dialog box to search for the correct information and update the album.

If you are unable to find the album information in the online database, or if your media was originally part of a mix CD, you must use one of the manual options. The first of these is useful if you have at least one file in your library that has correct information for the album. Files with incorrect media information can be dragged on top of a file with the correct media information. Confirm the move and media information change to add the correct media information to the desired file. If this option is not possible, you must use the Advanced Tag Editor. This is the most powerful option for editing your media information and personally is my favorite because each file is edited independently and there is no chance you can mess up the media information you have already entered for other files. To use the Advanced Tag Editor, right-click a song in the library and select Advanced Tag Editor. Enter the correct media information in the boxes for the Track Info tab and the

Artist Info tab, as shown in Figure 8.25 and click OK. Although not all information will always be filled in, the essential fields are as follows:

- **Track Info tab** —Title, Genre, Track Number, Album
- **Artist Info tab**—Artist, Album Artist

> **TIP**
> To enter multiple artists in the Artist field, enter all artists separated by semicolons.

Figure 8.25
The Advanced Tag Editor is the most powerful way to modify a file's media information.

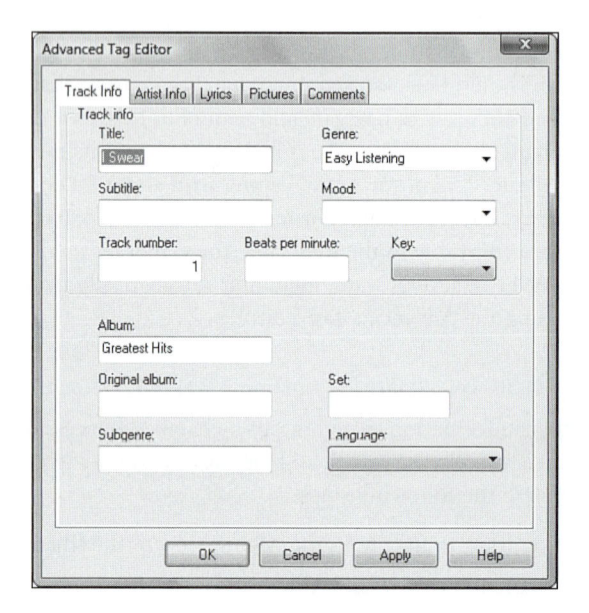

ADDING OR CHANGING ALBUM ART

The most common missing piece of media information is the album art. The album art provides a visual representation of every album in your media library and is displayed in the Expanded Tile view of your media library; it's used as well by many portable media players and digital media receivers.

> **TIP**
> Make sure all media information is correct before updating album art. This will reduce the risk of files being assigned incorrect album art.

To add or edit the album art, complete the following:

1. Click the Library tab and locate the album for which you want to add or change the album art.
2. To automatically find the album art, right-click the album and select Find Album Info. Search for the correct media information and click the correct entry.

If the media information found is correct, but there is a generic album art image or if the media information is not found at all, you must manually set the album art. The following steps describe how to manually add or change the album art.

1. Click the Library tab and locate the album for which you want to add or change the album art.
2. Find the image you would like to use on your computer or on the Internet. Good websites for finding album art are Google images, images.google.com, and albumart.org. When you find the desired album art, right-click the image and select Copy.
3. In Windows Media Player 11, right-click the album art box of the desired album and select Paste Album Art. The Album Art for all songs in that album is updated with the new album art.

Tips from the Windows Pros: Playing Audio from Your Portable Device Through Your Car Stereo

So now you know how to work Media Player and how to organize your media with complete media information and album art. You have synchronized your media to your portable device. The majority of music that people listen to during the day is in the car during the commute to and from work. Next, I explain the options you have for getting your newly stocked portable player connected to your car stereo so that you never have to carry a CD again.

To decide the best method to use, you need to know a little bit about your car stereo. If you have not already checked, see whether your stereo has an auxiliary input. This information can usually be found in the vehicle or stereo's manual, or you may need to call your local dealership. Another option to look into is whether your stereo supports a stereo Bluetooth link. After you know this information, review the following options, listed from best sound quality to worst, and choose the one that best suits your needs. In all cases, the portable media player's headphone jack is used as the audio source.

- **Auxiliary Input**—This is a direct connection to your stereo either through an auxiliary (front/rear) or an adapter connected to your specialized CD changer input. There is little interference with this type of connection and as a result, it is highly recommended over other methods.

- **Bluetooth Link**—If your stereo supports a Bluetooth link, you can get an adapter for your portable device that will allow a high-quality wireless direct connection with your stereo. Because the link is wireless, the Bluetooth link is subject to slightly more interference than the Auxiliary Input method.

- **Cassette Adapter**—This option offers quality similar to that of the FM options discussed next. However, because it is not bound to the FM spectrum, it is subject to less interference and noise. This device connects from your portable device directly into your car's cassette player.

- **Wired FM Transmitter**—This option does offer decreased sound quality to the previous option because of the limitations of the FM spectrum. A wired FM transmitter is a device installed in line with your stereo's FM antenna. While an audio source is connected to the device, the car's antenna is switched off and the audio signal is modulated to a set FM frequency, such as 88.9 FM. When there is no audio input source, the device switches the antenna back on to keep from interfering with FM radio reception.

- **Wireless FM Transmitter**—This is identical in operation to the wired FM transmitter, except that it modulates the audio to the FM frequency and then broadcasts it within a short range (usually 3–6 ft.) so that it can be picked up by your vehicle's antenna. Notice that this device does not switch off the vehicle's antenna, because it requires it for operation. Although most used, this option has the lowest audio quality because of the large amount of interference introduced by the wirelessly transmitted FM signals competing with other local FM stations.

CHAPTER 9

Windows Imaging Tools

In this chapter

Image Manipulation in Windows Vista   288

What's Built in to Windows Vista for Photographs?   288

Windows Photo Gallery   288

Working with Scanners and Cameras   290

Burning Your Pictures to CD   300

Troubleshooting   303

Tips from the Windows Pros: Archiving Your Company's History   305

Image Manipulation in Windows Vista

From the earliest versions of Microsoft Windows, there have been tools that helped you manage images on your PC. In the early days, when the technology we enjoy today was not as readily available, these programs were limited to creating a picture on your computer screen and printing it out—very limited, but then again, so was the hardware.

Now that the capability to take and manipulate digital pictures has hit the mainstream, it's not unusual for the average amateur videographer to have an array of hardware at his disposal. As items such as digital cameras (both still and video), scanners, and color photo-quality printers have come down in price, Microsoft has added and refined the tools built into Windows Vista to handle this massive influx of digital content. In this chapter, we discuss the many ways to get digital images into your computer, how to touch them up so they appear their best, and how to share these pictures with others whether in dead-tree or CD format.

What's Built in to Windows Vista for Photographs?

Like digital photography? Own a scanner? Windows Vista supports the immense popularity of digital photography and scanning with the following features:

- **Windows Photo Gallery**—New in Windows Vista, this is a powerful tool for viewing, editing, and organizing photos and movies.
- **Pictures folder**—Provides sorting, organizing, email, website publishing, slideshow, and screensaver options for your digital and scanned photos.

No matter where your digital images come from, these features can help you have more fun and get more use from your photographs. In the following sections, you learn how each of these features works.

Windows Photo Gallery

Windows Vista has many options for displaying photographs and movies, and many of these options can be accessed through the new Windows Photo Gallery included with Windows Vista. The Windows Photo Gallery, shown in Figure 9.1, can be found by choosing Start, All Programs, Windows Photo Gallery.

Figure 9.1
The Windows Photo Gallery main screen.

By default the Windows Photo Gallery shows all photos and videos that are in the Public folders, as well as the current user's Pictures folder. You easily can add individual photos or entire folders of photos and videos.

To add an individual photo or movie to Windows Photo Gallery, do the following:

1. Open Windows Photo Gallery.
2. Open the folder that contains the photo or video that you want to add to the Windows Photo Gallery.
3. Left-click and drag the photo from the folder that contains the photo or video to the Windows Photo Gallery.

That's it! After you drag the photo or video into the Windows Photo Gallery the file is copied to your Pictures folder and appears in the Gallery.

> **TIP**
> Only JPEG (.jpg) pictures will be displayed in Windows Photo Gallery. Pictures with other extensions such as .png or .gif will not be displayed.

You can filter the photos displayed in the main window by choosing one of the criteria listed in the left pane. To filter on multiple criteria (for example, photos that are landscapes) hold down the Ctrl key while selecting multiple criteria.

TIP

Can't quite make out what all those preview photos actually are in the main window? If you hover your mouse over a photo for a few seconds, Photo Gallery will show a larger preview of the photo, along with any tag or classification information associated with the photo.

IMPORTING FILES INTO WINDOWS PHOTO GALLERY

To add all the photos and movies from a specific folder (and every folder under that folder as well), choose File, Add Folder to Gallery, and browse to the desired folder. Windows Photo Gallery will scan the folder and add any photos and movies it finds to the Gallery window. A folder can be removed just as easily, by finding the folder under the Folders selection in the left pane, right-clicking it, and choosing Remove Folder. If the folder you are attempting to remove is a subfolder in the Folders view, it cannot be removed unless the parent folder is also removed.

CAUTION

Be careful which folder you choose to add to Windows Photo Gallery. If, for example, you were to add the Windows folder to the Gallery, your computer could become sluggish because Windows Photo Gallery attempts to get the file properties for every file in the Windows folder. For this reason, it is recommended that you add folders that are closer to the bottom of the folder structure.

ORGANIZING PHOTOS AND MOVIES IN WINDOWS PHOTO GALLERY

Once you have imported several photographs and movies into Windows Photo Gallery, your main gallery view can start to become a little crowded. To alleviate this problem, Windows Photo Gallery allows you to create custom categories called tags to group your videos and photos. You can create a tag by clicking on Create a New Tag in the left pane. When you do this, the words Create a New Tag turn into a text box, allowing you to enter a user-defined tag.

To use this tag to classify media in your collection, first press the Info button in the toolbar to get the information pane. Then select the media you wish to tag (you can select multiple pictures or movies by holding down Control or Shift as you click), and choosing Add Tags in the information pane to the right. You can type the name of an existing tag (Photo Gallery will try to help you out by auto-completing from the existing list of tags) or you can type a new tag into the box, and Photo Gallery will create the tag when it assigns it to the selected media.

WORKING WITH SCANNERS AND CAMERAS

With Windows Vista, Microsoft replaced the functionality of the Scanner and Camera Wizard with the Windows Photo Gallery. The Windows Photo Gallery allows you to scan images from a scanner, copy images from a digital still camera, or import a movie from a supported video camera. Almost any modern imaging device is supported by Windows Photo Gallery. If you have more than one imaging device supported by Windows Vista, you can import images from any of them from within the Windows Photo Gallery.

> **NOTE**
>
> If you have a choice between a USB-based scanner and other interface types such as SCSI and parallel, choose USB. Windows Fax and Scan automatically detects and uses many USB devices, but it might not work with other interface types unless specific Windows Vista–compatible drivers are available. If you set up other scanner types with Windows Vista drivers, you might need to use the scanner's own TWAIN interface to scan photos and other media. TWAIN is an older technology interface that is used for still image cameras and scanners only. TWAIN devices are accessed from the File, Acquire Image menu of most applications. Although TWAIN is not an official acronym, it is commonly referred to as Technology Without An Intelligent Name.

Using Windows Photo Gallery with a Scanner

To start the Windows Photo Gallery with your scanner, push the Scan button on your scanner, open Windows Photo Gallery, and choose File, Import from Camera or Scanner from the menu (refer to Figure 9.2). Or use the image acquisition feature from within your favorite photo editor or paint program. Image acquisition is located in the File menu of most applications.

When the wizard starts, follow this procedure to scan your pictures:

1. On the Choose Scanning Preferences screen, select the profile (which defaults to photo) and select Preview to prescan your picture with default settings. With some scanners, you might need to press the Scan button to perform the preview (see Figure 9.2).

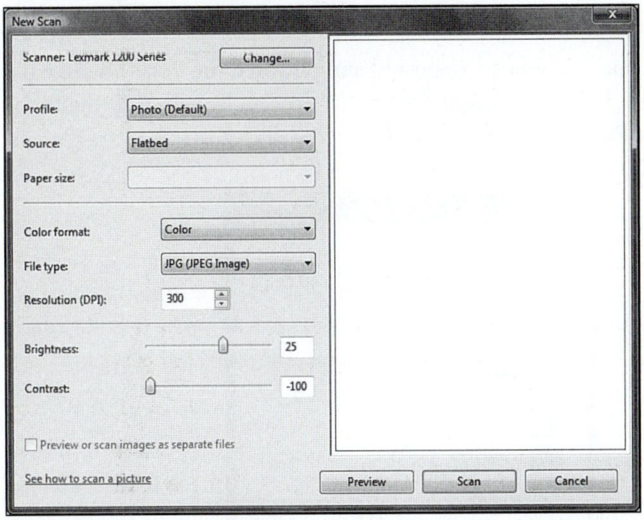

Figure 9.2
The New Scan pane, where you can set the scanning options.

> **TIP**
>
> If you place only one photo on your scanner, the wizard automatically selects it for you. Adjust the scan boundaries by dragging the corners only if you want to crop the photo during the scan. If you place more than one picture on the scanner, you will need to adjust the scan boundaries manually to scan each photo.

2. You can manually adjust the contrast, brightness, and resolution for the scan (I recommend 75dpi for scans you plan to use in slideshows and 150–300dpi for scans you want to print). After this is done, click Scan to acquire the picture from the scanner.

3. When scanning is complete, you will be prompted to tag the picture. This is optional but will make finding your scanned pictures easier after they are imported into Windows Photo Gallery. Click OK, and the picture is shown as it is imported into the Photo Gallery. You can then use the postprocessing commands mentioned elsewhere in the chapter to clean up the picture, if needed.

> **TIP**
>
> Which file format should you choose? The default, JPEG, creates small file sizes but does so by discarding fine image detail; it can be used on web pages. Unless you're short on disk space, I recommend TIF, which creates large file sizes but retains all picture detail. Use BMP if you're saving files for use on the Windows desktop. PNG files also can be used on web pages. If you save the file in one format and need to convert it into another later, retrieve the file into Windows Paint and save it in the format you need.

→ For details about the Pictures folder, **see** "Viewing Images," **p. 354**.

Using Windows Photo Gallery with a Digital Camera

Importing photographs from your digital camera is a simple process. The import process can be initiated in two ways:

1. When your camera is connected and powered on, you will see a dialog box similar to Figure 9.3. You can begin the import process by selecting the highlighted option, Import Pictures Using Windows.

Figure 9.3
The Autoplay menu for a digital camera.

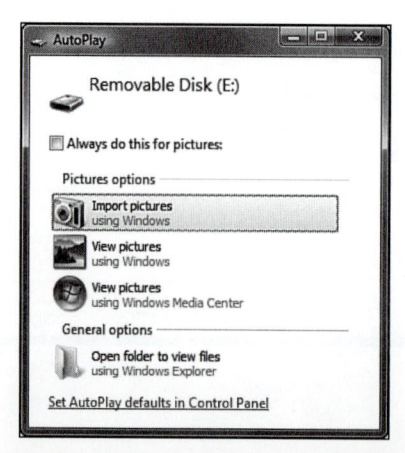

Working with Scanners and Cameras   293

> **NOTE**
> The first time you connect your digital camera to your computer, Windows Vista will need to load drivers specific for your camera. For most modern cameras, this is a transparent process that only takes a few seconds, but it might be a good idea to have any CDs or DVDs that came with the camera on hand, in case specialized drivers are required.

2. If your digital camera is already connected, you can import your photos inside Windows Photo Gallery by following these steps:
   1. Click Start, All Programs, Windows Photo Gallery.
   2. Choose File, Import from Camera or Scanner from the menu. This brings up the Import Pictures and Videos dialog. Choose the camera you want to import pictures from (it may be seen as a Removable Disk) and click Import (see Figure 9.4).

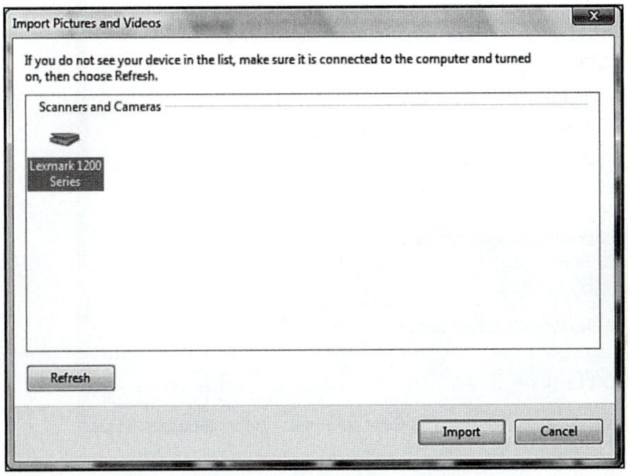

Figure 9.4
The Import Pictures and Videos screen allows you to select your camera or scanner.

Whichever way you choose to initiate the import process, you will end up at the dialog shown in Figure 9.5. From here, you can complete the import by following these steps:

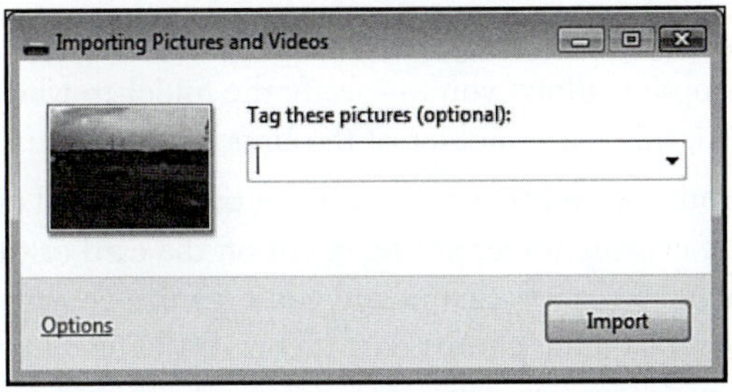

Figure 9.5
The beginning of the photo import process.

1. Windows quickly scans the camera and locates all the pictures and videos on the camera. After it does that, you can optionally choose to tag the photos with one of the tags from the Windows Photo Gallery for easy sorting and manipulation later. You can choose an existing tag or type one of your own. You can base the filenames of the imported photos on the tag name entered here.

2. To change the way Windows imports pictures, click the Options link. You will get the dialog shown in Figure 9.6. From here, you can change several options that will affect the way Windows imports the selected pictures:

Figure 9.6
The Options dialog allows you to modify import settings.

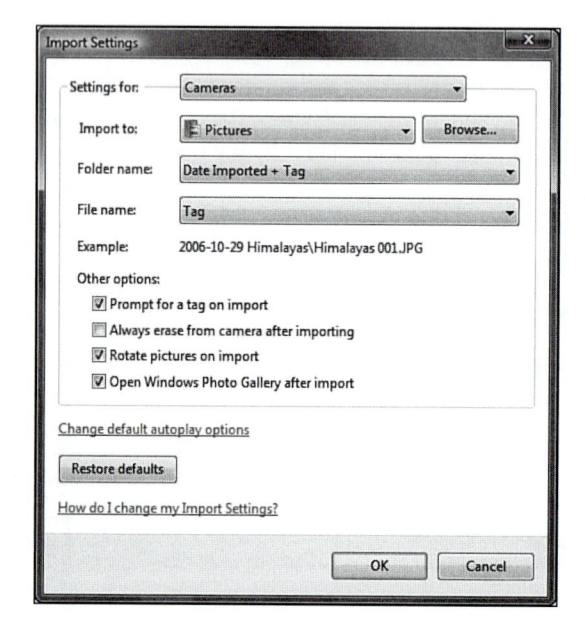

- **Settings for**—This allows you to select the default settings for scanners, cameras, or CDs/DVDs.
- **Import to**—Allows you to choose the top-level folder where the pictures are imported. A subfolder will be created for this import session, depending on the setting of the next option.
- **Folder name**—This option allows you to specify the folder to which the pictures will be imported. As stated, this is a subfolder of the Import To option.
- **File name**—The naming convention used to name the individual pictures. Preserve Folders means use the existing folder arrangement on the card or camera. You would use this option if you have a fancy camera and you organize your photos in your camera, or you had already organized the photos on a CD or DVD or removable camera card or USB flash drive using another program. More likely, you'll want to use the Tag setting for File Name.

Working with Scanners and Cameras   295

The Always Erase from Camera After Importing option is also worth mentioning. Choosing this option is generally a good idea, because unless you somehow erase the pictures from your camera, you will constantly re-import the photos from your camera, and have duplicate pictures all over the place.

Once you set the options to your liking, click the OK button, and choose Import at the Importing Pictures and Videos dialog.

3. The wizard displays each picture while it copies the selected pictures and provides a status display onscreen, shown in Figure 9.7.

Figure 9.7
The wizard displays the progress of the import task.

4. If you chose to delete the pictures from your imaging device, the wizard will also delete them and inform you of its progress.

→ For details about the Pictures folder, **see** "Viewing Images," **p. 354**.

Now the pictures are imported from your digital camera into the Windows Photo Gallery. You can view each of the pictures and, if needed, perform some basic manipulation on them, as outlined in the next section.

Manipulating Pictures in Windows Photo Gallery

Unless you are a perfect shot every time you click the shutter, there will inevitably be times where the photos you take with your digital camera can use some touching up—anything from removing red-eye to cropping out unnecessary portions of the photograph. Although previous versions of Windows did not include tools to do these types of things for you (requiring you to purchase third-party software), Windows Photo Gallery contains some tools that allow you to do basic image correction.

To fix a photo, double-click the photo inside Windows Photo Gallery. This will bring up the photo in the picture viewer and give you the following options to the right of the picture (see Figure 9.8):

Figure 9.8
Fixing a photograph in the Windows Photo Gallery.

- **Auto Adjust**—Automatically adjusts the Exposure and Color of the picture to give the best appearance
- **Adjust Exposure**—Gives you a submenu allowing you to change the Brightness and Contrast of the picture
- **Adjust Color**—Gives you a submenu allowing you to manually adjust the Color Temperature, Tint, and Saturation of the picture
- **Crop Picture**—Gives you a highlighted frame within the picture allowing you to "cut out" unnecessary picture elements
- **Fix Red Eye**—Allows you to select an area of the picture for the wizard to remove "red eye" (caused by the flash bouncing off the retina)

Any, changes made by the Auto Adjust option can be manually tweaked by selecting the options for Adjust Exposure or Adjust Color and moving the sliders within that submenu. Any changes made using the sliders under these options are reflected in real-time in the picture, so you can immediately see the results of your manipulation.

If you happen to get a little overzealous with the photograph manipulation tools, there is always the Undo button. Clicking this button will undo the last change made, and repeatedly clicking the Undo button will eventually take you all the way back to an unretouched photo. You can also press the down arrow next to the Undo button and choose to undo selected changes, or undo them all. If you have cropped the photograph, the option is also there to revert to the original. In case you ever need to redo a change, the Redo button works the same way.

TIP

When cropping a picture, you are initially given several standard photo sizes to select from, as well as the ability to customize the crop area to a different picture size. Although it might be easier to create a custom size to include all the areas you want in the photo, it is generally best to choose one of the standard sizes; you can then buy off-the-shelf frames to hold the photos you print.

Printing Your Masterpiece

Windows Vista's Slideshow feature can show you your digital photos immediately. How about instant prints from your digital photos? By printing the photos on your own color printer, you can have pictures as fast as your printer can produce them and get them in a variety of sizes.

You can print photos from either the toolbar in a photo folder or the pull-down menu in a photo folder. To make prints from the digital pictures stored on your computer, simply select the photos you want to print (use Ctrl+click or Shift+click to select individual photos from the folder, or you can use Ctrl+A to select all of them) and click the Print button. This brings up the Print Pictures dialog shown in Figure 9.9.

Figure 9.9
Options for printing a picture.

TIP

If you haven't used your inkjet printer for several days, or your printouts are of poor quality, click the Utilities tab (if available) and run your printer's head cleaning or nozzle test options with plain paper inserted in your printer (take out the photo paper until you're ready to print a good print). Head and nozzle clogs will ruin your printout and waste expensive photo paper, and most recent printers also offer a cleaning routine on this tab. If your printer doesn't have a menu option for head cleaning, check the instruction manual for the correct method to use. You might need to press buttons on the printer to activate a built-in head-cleaning routine.

From here, you can modify the options that control how and where the picture is printed. Above the picture you are printing, you can change the printer used, the paper size in the printer, and the print quality used. At the bottom, you can choose how many pictures are to be printed, as well as the option Fit Picture to Frame. If selected, this means that Windows will resize the picture so that it fills up the entire picture size selected on the right side of the window at the expense of cropping out some of the top and/or sides of the photograph. When deselected, it will print the original photograph in its entirety but will leave white space at the top and/or sides of the frame, where the photograph does not exactly fit the photograph size selected.

> **TIP**
>
> For best picture quality, it is generally recommended to leave the Fit Picture to Frame option selected. If you want exact control over what is displayed in the picture, you might want to use the crop picture options in the Windows Photo Gallery.

Along the right side of the Print Pictures window, you will see several options on how the printed photographs will fit on the paper selected. As you choose different finished photograph sizes on the right, the picture preview in the middle of the window will change to reflect how the photos should actually appear on the paper when printed, as reflected in Figure 9.10. If you choose fewer photographs than are available for the layout chosen, Windows will leave blank space on the photo sheet to conserve ink in your printer.

Figure 9.10
We are printing fewer pictures than are available in the format chosen, and Windows leaves blank spaces on the sheet.

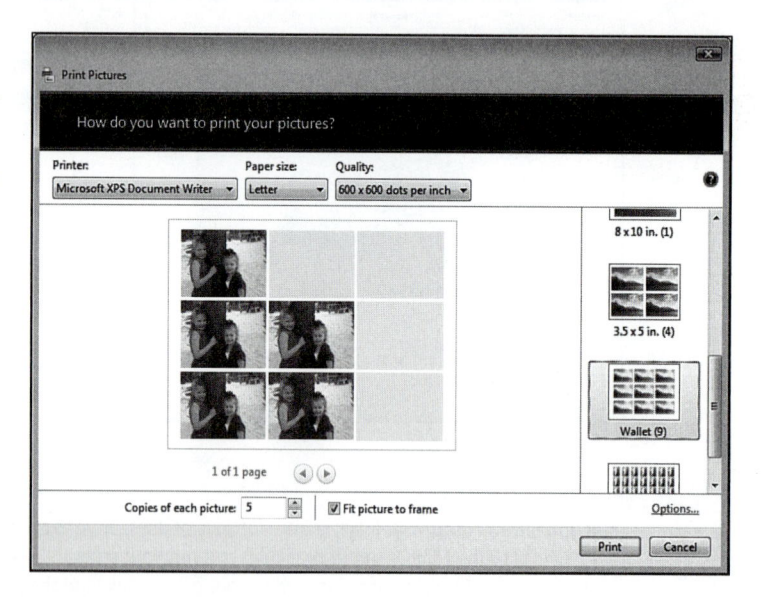

Sharing Your Photos with Others Electronically

Windows Photo Gallery supports two methods of sharing your photographs with others without having to print them out—emailing and burning them to CD/DVD. This section touches on the first of these methods. To learn more about creating a CD or DVD with Windows Photo Gallery, see the next section "Burning Your Pictures to CD."

Emailing photographs is straightforward; you select the pictures you want to email and choose E-mail from the toolbar at the top of the Photo Gallery main screen. You are then given the option of resizing the files to a lower resolution to make them smaller and therefore easier to send to someone as an email attachment. The Attach Files dialog defaults to 1024×768, which is a good standard size—however, you can size them to any resolution from 640×480 to 1280×1024, or choose to leave them at the same resolution as the source. Whichever resolution you choose, the Attach Files dialog will give you the size in megabytes of the attachments.

> **TIP**
>
> Resizing a picture to a lower resolution will definitely make it easier to manipulate as an email attachment, but as with everything there is a trade-off. Resizing a picture to a lower resolution will introduce visual artifacts into the photograph that will lessen the sharpness and detail. For this reason, it might be a good idea to leave the pictures at their source resolution if the email systems on both ends will support the attachment size.

After you have decided on a picture resolution, click the Attach button. Windows Photo Gallery will then resize each of the pictures and open a new email message in the default email program (which, by default, is Windows Mail) with each of the photos as a separate attachment to the email (see Figure 9.11 for an example). All that's left to do is address the email, edit the subject and text, and click Send.

Figure 9.11
An email with photograph attachments.

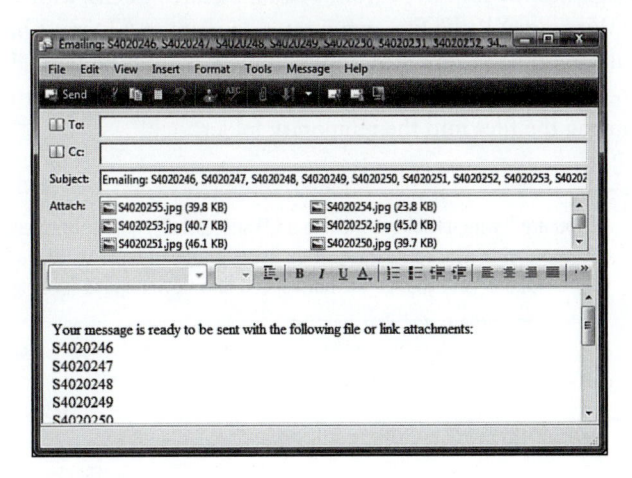

Burning Your Pictures to CD

There are times where you might think, "Having pictures on the computer is great, and I really like the printed photographs, but how can I keep my pictures in a more permanent format?" If you have a CD-R or CD-RW drive in your computer (most modern computers come with one by default), Windows Vista can help you create a photo CD so that you can keep your digital masterpieces safe from the hands of time, or the destructive power of the next big Internet worm.

You can get your digital memories out of your computer and onto a more stable format in two ways: You can use Windows Explorer (as in Windows XP), or you can use our new friend Windows Photo Gallery. We discuss both methods in this section and give the relative benefits of each.

Writing Photos to CD Using Windows Explorer

When Windows Vista detects a supported CD-RW, the toolbar in Windows Explorer gives Burn as an option. Here's how to use it:

1. If you want to copy only some of the pictures in your folder, select the pictures you want to copy and click Burn.
2. To copy all photos in the folder to CD, don't select any pictures first. Click Copy All Items to CD.
3. If the disc is currently blank, you will be prompted to name the disc. Do so and click Next.
4. The pictures are copied to the CD-RW.
5. Repeat steps 1–3 for other folders that contain pictures you want to add to the CD.

This process is significantly improved from writing pictures to CD with Windows XP—for example, under Windows XP, the files you wanted to write to CD must be copied and pasted into the CD-R device in My Computer, and then the CD must be burned as a separate step. This can lead to confusion if you are easily distracted like me, and forget to start the burn process after copying the files into the temporary folder.

> **TIP**
>
> If you are having problems making a CD successfully, adjust the speed used by your drive to record data. The easiest way to do this is to open Windows Media Player; choose Burn, More Options; and change the burn speed to a slower speed (see Figure 9.12).

Figure 9.12
Selecting a lower write speed on a CD-RW drive that lacks buffer-underrun protection.

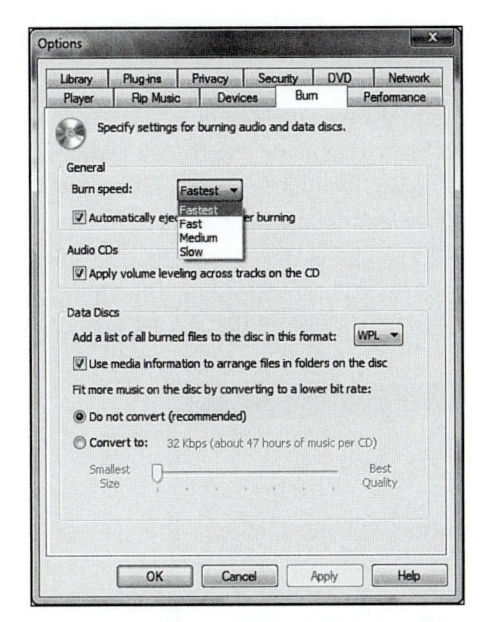

Your photo folders act as regular folders after they've been copied to the CD. If you want to use the special imaging features such as slideshow or photo printing discussed earlier in this chapter, select a file in the folder and choose File, Preview. The picture is loaded into the Windows Photo Gallery, which has buttons for photo printing, slideshows, image rotation, editing, and other imaging options.

> **TIP**
>
> If you start the copy-to-CD process and do not have a writable media in the drive, Windows Vista will prompt you to insert a writable CD into the drive. The Burn option in Windows Explorer only supports writable CDs, not DVDs—you will need to use the DVD Recorder functionality described in the next section or the Windows DVD Maker section of Chapter 12, "Sound Recorder, DVD Maker, and other Multimedia Tools," to burn your photos to a DVD.

MAKING CDS AND DVDS FROM WINDOWS PHOTO GALLERY

Writing picture CDs and DVDs from Windows Photo Gallery is significantly easier than writing them from Windows Explorer. From the Windows Photo Gallery main screen, simply select the photos you want to burn to recordable media and click the Burn button in the toolbar. When you click the Burn button, you are given two options—Data Disc and Video DVD.

Choosing Data Disc will write the selected files to a CD or DVD. If this is the first time you have used a CD with Windows Photo Gallery, you are given the screen shown in

Figure 9.13. This screen allows you to choose two different methods for storing files on the data CD:

- **Live File System**—This format is new with Windows Vista. Using this format will allow you to treat the CD-R much like a USB flash drive by allowing you to add/edit/delete files at will from the CD. However, Live File System CDs can only be read in computers using Windows XP or Windows Vista operating systems.

- **Mastered**—This option writes the files in the same manner as using Windows Explorer. Preparing the disc ensures that the CD is compatible with older versions of Windows and standalone hardware (CD/DVD players, MP3 players, and so on).

Figure 9.13
Choosing the type of file system for a blank data CD.

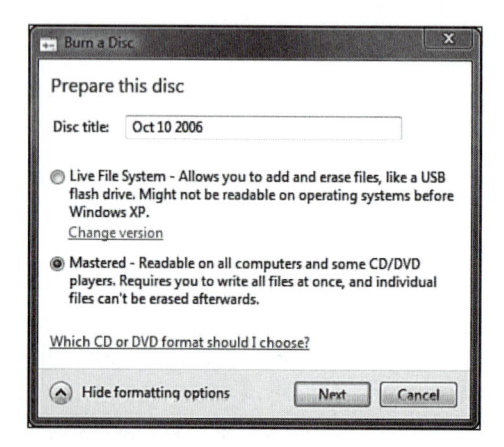

There are different versions of the Live File System format, and each of these different versions is compatible with different operating systems. You can change the version of the Live File System format by choosing the Change Version link under Live File System. Table 9.1 shows the version information for Live File System.

TABLE 9.1   LIVE FILE SYSTEM VERSIONS

Live File System Version	Best For
1.02	This format can be read on Windows 98 as well as many Apple computers. Use this version if you need to format DVD-RAM or MO (Magneto-optical) discs.
1.5	This format is compatible with Windows 2000, Windows XP, and Windows Server 2003. It might not be compatible with Windows 98 or Apple computers.
2.01	This format is compatible with Windows XP and Windows Server 2003. It might not be compatible with Windows 98, Windows 2000, or Apple computers.
2.5	This format is designed for Windows Vista and might not be compatible with earlier versions of Windows.

After you format a disc as a Live File System disc, it can be used just as you would use a floppy disc or USB flash drive.

You can also burn a Video DVD from the menu in Windows Photo Gallery. This is accomplished in much the same way as burning a Data CD:

1. Select the pictures or videos that you want to put on the Video DVD.
2. Choose Burn, Video DVD, and the files you selected are imported into Windows DVD maker.

There is one more option for making movies from Windows Photo Gallery—the Make a Movie button. Selecting photos and movies and clicking this button will import the media into Windows Movie Maker and use the AutoMovie option automatically. For more information on using Windows Movie Maker, see Chapter 11, "Producing Videos with Windows Movie Maker."

Which Output Option to Use

Obviously, you must choose the output option that best suits the intended audience. Who is the audience for your photo CD or DVD? Are you sending images to Granddad to play back on his DVD player in the living room, or are you preparing a slideshow for an important business meeting that will be played on a computer? Compatibility is the name of the game when it comes to sharing recordable CDs and DVDs, as you probably know. Target your audience and keep in mind that there are many firmware differences between different brands, models, and vintages of CD and DVD players that determine whether they can play back a disk. Send up a test balloon (send your colleague a couple example disks) and make sure your intended audience can read it. Few things are more disconcerting than having a crowd of people gather to see your show and all you have to share is a blank screen.

Troubleshooting

Poor Print Quality with Digital Photos

My digital photos look terrific onscreen but are poor quality when I print them.

Three major factors control digital photo quality:

- Camera settings
- Printer settings
- Paper type

Get any of these wrong, and you won't get the print quality you want.

Your digital camera should be set for its highest quality and resolution settings, especially if it's a two-megapixel or lower resolution camera. Highest quality uses less compression to avoid loss of fine detail (more space is used on the flash memory card per picture than with lower quality settings), and highest resolution uses all the pixels to make the picture (again, requiring more space on the flash memory card per picture). If you use your camera to create pictures for use on the Web, the lower-quality and lower-resolution settings are fine, but printed pictures need the best quality available. Remember that your monitor needs just 96 dots to make an inch, whereas most inkjet printers put 600 to 1,200 dots into the same inch. So, a picture that's just right to fit on the screen doesn't have enough detail to print well.

Similarly, the printer should be set for the best quality setting that matches the paper type. If you're planning to print "knock-em-dead" digital masterpieces, be sure to use photo-quality paper and set the printer's options accordingly. Just want a quick snapshot for the refrigerator? Use plain paper and set the printer for plain paper. Mismatch print type and paper type and you're sure to have problems because inkjet printers calculate how much ink to use and how to put it on the paper according to the options you select.

Remember, high-quality printing takes time; several minutes for an 8×10-inch enlargement on photo paper with high-quality settings is typical.

> **NOTE**
>
> If you've been using lower-quality and lower-resolution modes on your digital camera to jam more pictures into your flash memory card storage, that's false economy that leads to poor-quality pictures, especially for printing. With the explosion in the popularity of digital cameras, the per-MB price of flash memory cards is dropping. Camera vendors include small flash memory cards to hold down the selling price of the camera, but you can almost always use a much larger media size, and sizes continue to increase, almost exponentially it seems.
>
> Check your camera maker's website or a leading flash media website such as Lexar Media (www.lexarmedia.com) to find out what sizes of digital media you can use. If you're responsible for a prolonged shoot away from the office or home, consider picking up multiple memory cards (so you have plenty of digital "film" and don't run out) or the IBM Microdrive (now made by Hitachi) if your camera is compatible with it (find out at http://www.steves-digicams.com/microdrive.html). Another solution is a nifty gadget from I/O Magic. It's a small, portable, battery-powered hard drive and media card reader in one. Just insert your camera's card, press a button, and voilá—your pictures are copied to the device's high-capacity hard drive. See www.iomagic.com.

SCANNER NOT RECOGNIZED BY WINDOWS PHOTO GALLERY

My scanner was working fine with Windows XP, but Windows Vista won't list it in the Windows Photo Gallery. What do I do?

The Windows Photo Gallery is certainly a convenient way to use your scanner, but it's not the only way. Before you try the scanner again, be sure you install Windows Vista–compatible drivers for your scanner. You might be able to use Windows XP–compatible drivers if you can't get Windows Vista drivers yet. Install the latest drivers available (you might need to restart your computer afterward) and try the wizard again. Windows Update is a great way to get new drivers.

Next, see whether you can use the scanner with its own TWAIN or ISIS driver. If you can, you don't need to use Windows Photo Gallery. Remember to use the Scan button on the scanner if it has one; some scanners require you to push this button to start the scanning process.

Contact the scanner vendor for help if you're still unable to use the scanner with either the wizard or its own scanning software.

Tips from the Windows Pros: Archiving Your Company's History

If you've been chosen to create an archive of your company's history (or your family's, for that matter), you might need to add a few hardware and software tools to your system to do the job right.

Color photos in particular are frequently affected by fading and color shift as well as the usual photographic problems of poor cropping and exposure. You don't need to buy Adobe Photoshop to fix these kinds of problems. However, if you're not satisfied with the photo editor bundled with your scanner and you're on a budget, try Corel's Paint Shop Pro (www.corel.com). Paint Shop Pro (around $100–$110) is a powerful choice that will leave you some money for the rest of your gear.

As you saw earlier in this chapter, a CD-RW drive is a terrific way to store digital photos. Be sure the drive you buy has at least a 24x speed rating for writing CD-R media (a better choice for long-term storage than erasable CD-RW media) and has a buffer-underrun prevention feature such as BURNProof. If your computer has a free SATA port, you'll get the best throughput from this connector. Otherwise, you'll get better throughput from a USB 2.0 external drive than from IDE. Getting a USB 2.0 burner also gives you the added benefit of being able to easily move the burner between PCs. If you're planning to incorporate digital video into the mix, you might also want to consider an IEEE-1394–compatible CD-RW drive. It connects through the same port used by DV camcorders, and you can move it around to any machine with an IEEE-1394 card or port.

Until the 1970s, the most popular way to take color photos was 35mm slide film, and most flatbed scanners either can't scan slides or use clumsy adapters that don't provide high enough scanning resolution to pull fine detail from slides. If the boss hands you some Carousel trays of slides for the archive, you need a real slide scanner to do the job right.

A high-quality slide scanner should scan with a resolution of at least 2,700dpi to allow you to get great prints from the tiny 35mm slide. And, if black and white or color prints have gotten lost but you have the negatives, slide scanners can scan them as well. You can spend as little as $500 to as much as $1,000 or more for a slide scanner, but be sure the one you buy has a feature called Digital ICE (developed by Applied Science Fiction, Inc.—now owned by Kodak). Digital ICE removes dust and scratches from scans of less-than-perfect slides and negatives. Because most slides and negatives get dirty and scratched over time, Digital ICE is the way to go for scanners. It really works, and saves hours of retouching time (time you can't afford to spend anyway) afterward. Some of the better slide/negative scanners with Digital ICE on-board include

- Nikon Coolscan
- Canon CanoScan
- Minolta Dimage Scan Elite

> **NOTE** Before you buy *any* scanner, take a good look at the archival materials you're being asked to preserve. Use a flatbed scanner for black-and-white or color prints, and don't overlook the historical value of stock certificates, matchbook covers, postcards, personalized pens, and so on. You can scan anything that fits on the scanner, even if it's not completely flat.
>
> If your company history goes back far enough that some photos are actually large negatives (bigger than 35mm) or lantern slides, you need to buy a flatbed scanner with a special transparency adapter lid (which also can be added to some midrange or high-end scanners) or internal compartment. Some midline scanners can handle transparencies and negatives up to 4×5 inches, but if you have larger-format materials, you need a scanner that can scan up to 8×10 negatives. Some of the better choices with built-in transparency handling up to 8×10 size include Epson's E1680 Professional (www.epson.com—around $799) and Microtek's ScanMaker i800 Pro Design (www.microtekusa.com—around $450). These scanners can also handle normal prints, so you get two for the price of one.

Finally, you need a way to view and organize your pictures after you've scanned them. Although the Pictures folder has some built-in tricks (as described earlier in this chapter), third-party software can help you view and locate pictures stored in any folder and on any type of media. Here are a few programs that you should consider:

- MediaTracer (www.mediatracer.com)
- Adobe Photoshop Album (http://www.adobe.com/products/photoshopalbum/main.html)
- ACDSee (www.acdsystems.com)

CHAPTER 10

SCANNING AND FAXING

In this chapter

Introducing Windows Fax and Scan   308

Configuring the Fax Service   309

Sending Faxes from Windows Fax and Scan   313

Receiving Faxes   316

Scanning Documents with Windows Fax and Scan   316

Troubleshooting   320

Tips from the Windows Pros: Scanning and Faxing Slides and Transparencies   322

Introducing Windows Fax and Scan

Windows Fax and Scan (see Figure 10.1) lets you fax and scan documents with a single application, rather than using the combination of Fax Console and the Scanner and Camera Wizard that you had to use in Windows XP.

> **NOTE**
>
> Windows Fax and Scan is available on Windows Vista Business, Enterprise, and Ultimate Editions. If you have one of these versions but don't see Windows Fax and Scan in your Start Menu, go to the Control Panel, select Programs, and select Turn Windows Features On and Off. You should be able to enable it there.

Figure 10.1
Windows Fax and Scan lets you scan and/or fax documents.

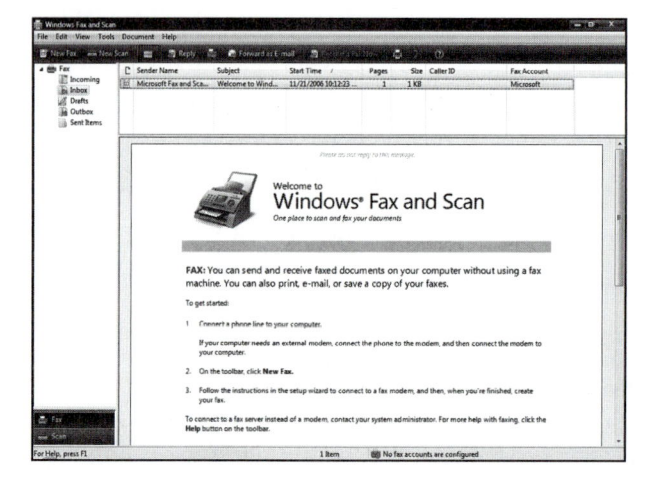

Windows Fax and Scan uses the following hardware:

- An image scanner for scanning documents or photos
- A fax device such as a modem

You don't actually need to have both a scanner and a fax modem to take advantage of Windows Fax and Scan. The program does help you use both together, but it can be useful even if you have just one or the other.

> **NOTE**
>
> If your computer has a dial-up (analog) modem, the modem probably includes fax capabilities.

> **NOTE**
>
> If your computer doesn't have a modem, you can easily install an inexpensive internal or USB external fax modem. If you have Internet-based telephone service, contact your phone service provider to see whether your line can carry fax signals. In a corporate setting, check to see if your organization uses digital telephone wiring before you try to hook up a dial-up modem. Digital phone lines can damage your modem.

The scanner and fax modem can be integrated into an all-in-one unit (print, scan, copy, fax), or you can use separate components. If you have a fax server or a multifunction (print, scan, copy, fax) device on your network, you can also use it with Windows Fax and Scan.

In this chapter, we'll show you how to set up the Windows Faxing service, how to send faxes from Windows Fax and Scan, and finally how to use the program to scan and store email and print documents.

> **NOTE**
>
> Windows Fax and Scan is designed primarily to make it easy to scan, store, and fax documents. Although you certainly can use it to scan pictures, if your primary goal is to scan your photograph library, you're better off using the Windows Photo Gallery tool, which is discussed under "Working with Scanners and Cameras" on page 290.

PREPARATIONS FOR USING WINDOWS FAX AND SCAN

If your scanner or fax device is not already installed, follow the manufacturer's recommendations to install the fax or scan hardware before you use Windows Fax and Scan. If you need to install a dial-up modem, you can use the Add Hardware applet in Control Panel to install most serial modems or USB modems that don't include special drivers. If your modem or scanner includes Vista drivers, install them as directed. Windows XP drivers may be used with some devices if Vista drivers are not provided by the vendor.

If you are given a choice between installing TWAIN or WIA drivers for your scanner, install WIA (Windows Imaging Architecture) drivers for use with Windows Fax and Scan. This is something to be especially careful of if you have a scanner that came with Windows XP drivers but not Windows Vista drivers. TWAIN drivers may support more advanced scanner features, such as transparency adapters or dust and scratch removal, found on some models, but they are not compatible with Windows Fax and Scan. Some scanner driver installations install both types of drivers.

→ To learn how to scan images that require TWAIN drivers (such as slides and negatives) and fax them, **see** the section "Tips from the Windows Pros: Scanning and Faxing Slides and Transparencies," **p. 322**.

CONFIGURING THE FAX SERVICE

To set up your system to send and receive faxes with a fax modem, make sure Fax view is selected: click Fax at the bottom of the left pane. Next, click the New Fax button on the toolbar (refer to Figure 10.1). The Fax Setup dialog box appears. Select Connect to a Fax

Modem. On the next screen, enter a name for the modem or keep the default name, Fax Modem. Click Next to continue.

CONFIGURING FAX-RECEIVING OPTIONS

On the next screen, choose how to receive faxes. Your options include the following:

- **Answer Automatically**—Choose this option if you have a dedicated fax line or a single phone line with a distinctive ring detection switch that automatically routes different types of calls to different devices.

- **Notify Me**—Choose this option if you have a single phone line but don't have a distinctive ring detection switch. The system will notify you of incoming calls, and you'll opt whether to answer them and receive incoming faxes.

- **I'll Choose Later**—Choose this option if you want to create a fax right away and prefer to delay setting up receiving faxes until later.

> **NOTE**
> You may see a Windows Security Alert indicating that Windows Firewall is blocking Windows Fax and Scan from receiving incoming network connections. If you want to use Windows Fax and Scan to send faxes originating on other systems, click Unblock.

A New Fax dialog box appears. If you don't want to send a fax now, close it.

→ To learn how to send faxes, **see** "Sending Faxes from Windows Fax and Scan," **p. 313**.

Each fax device you configure Windows Fax and Scan to use is a fax account. For example, if you have a fax modem and a fax server, you have two fax accounts.

SETTING UP SENDER INFORMATION

Click Tools, Sender Information to set up the information you want to place on the cover page. You can complete as much or as little (even none) of the dialog box as desired.

> **NOTE**
> If you are the only person who will use Windows Fax and Scan to send faxes, take time to complete Sender Information. When you create cover pages, this information will be placed there for you. If several people, especially in different departments, will be sending faxes, you may find it easier to have users provide sender information when they send their faxes.

CREATING A CUSTOMIZED COVER PAGE

To create a customized cover page, click Tools, Cover Pages. Existing cover pages (if any) are listed. Click New to open the Fax Cover Page Editor (see Figure 10.2). Use the Insert menu to place fields and field names as desired, along with simple shapes. Use the Format menu to align objects, adjust spacing, center the page, or change the order of overlapping objects. Use the View menu to show or hide menus and grid lines (grid lines are hidden by default, but can be useful in aligning design elements). Use the File menu to print or save your cover page. Cover pages are saved with the .cov file extension and are saved in your Personal CoverPages folder by default.

Figure 10.2
Creating a cover page with the Fax Cover Page Editor.

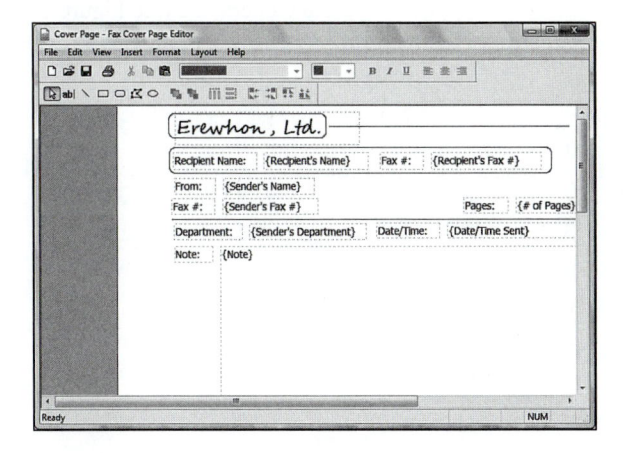

TIP   When you insert a field name and associated field, they're imported as a group. However, if you want to move them separately, click the background. To move several items, highlight them before dragging them.

To make your personalized cover page available to all users, you have to copy the cover page file to \ProgramData\Microsoft\Windows NT\MSFax\Common CoverPages*xx-xx*, where *xx-xx* is a code that specifies your geographic region and language. Moving the file there is a bit tricky. Follow these steps:

1. Create a cover page, and save the cover page file in your personal cover page folder. Test it by sending it in a fax to be sure that it looks the way you want it to. After you're sure that it's correct, proceed to the next step.

2. Click Start, Documents. Dig into Fax, then Personal CoverPages. Locate the cover page file, right-click it, and select Cut.

3. Browse to folder \ProgramData\Microsoft\Windows NT\MSFax\Common Coverpages. The uppermost folder, ProgramData, is usually hidden, so you will have to type **C:\ProgramData** into the Explorer window's address bar (just type it in where the breadcrumb path list is. If your copy of Windows is installed on a drive other than C:, type that drive letter instead of C:). Then dig into the lower-level folders. When you've gotten to Common Coverpages, dig into the regional folder, which is en-US for U.S. English, but may be different on your computer.

4. Right-click in the folder's contents pane and select Paste. You will have to go through a User Account Control prompt to get permission to paste the file into this folder.

The cover page will now be available to all users on your computer.

Configuring Fax Settings

To configure your fax, click Tools, Fax Settings. If prompted by UAC, click Continue if you are an administrator, or provide an administrator password if you are a standard user. A multi-tabbed Fax Settings dialog box appears. Use the General tab (see Figure 10.3) to specify whether the fax should send, receive, or send and receive faxes and how to answer incoming calls.

Figure 10.3
Configuring General fax settings.

1. Click the Tracking tab to adjust how to be notified about the status of a sent or received fax. By default, all notifications, fax monitor settings, and sound options are enabled. Clear check boxes to disable selected notifications.
2. Click the Advanced tab to view or move the location of the Fax Archive folder, disable the banner in sent faxes, adjust redialing settings, and specify when discount long-distance rates start and end.
3. Click the Security tab to specify which users and groups can send faxes or manage the fax service and fax documents.

Click Apply; then OK to save your changes and close the Fax Settings dialog.

Click Tools, Fax Accounts if you need to add or remove a fax modem or network fax server.

Click Tools, Options to bring up a multitabbed Fax Options dialog box. The General tab is used to enable (default) or disable playing a sound when new messages arrive. Click the Receipts tab to configure the sending of email delivery receipts (which can also include a copy of the sent fax). Click the Send tab if you want to enable the inclusion of an original message in a reply. Click Compose to change the default font used for faxes (10-pt. Arial Regular).

> **TIP**
> If you regularly send faxes to conventional fax machines (which usually have resolution of no more than 200dpi), a 10-pt. font is a little too small for easy reading. We recommend 12-pt. Arial instead.

Sending Faxes from Windows Fax and Scan

To send a fax with Windows Fax and Scan, click the New Fax button to open the New Fax dialog box shown in Figure 10.4.

Figure 10.4
The New Fax dialog box.

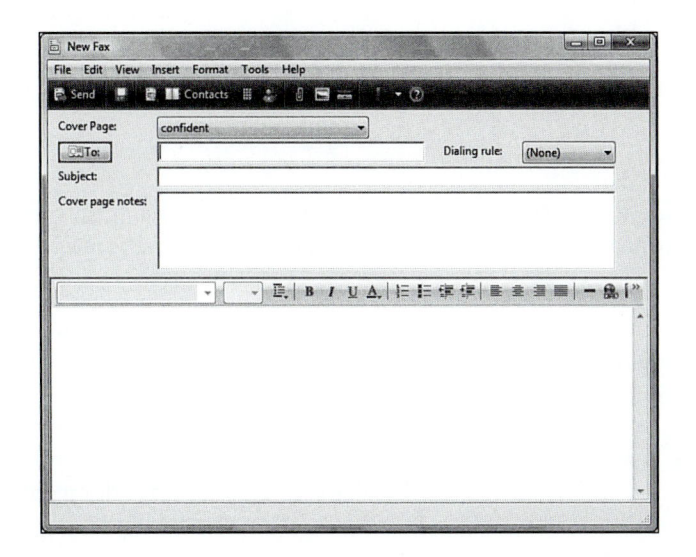

> If you are unable to send a fax, see "Fax Modem Doesn't Work" in the "Troubleshooting" section at the end of this chapter.

Selecting Recipients

To send a fax to a recipient not on your Contacts list, enter the fax number or numbers in the To field; use a semicolon to separate fax numbers. To send a fax to selected recipients on your Contacts list, or to create a new contact, click the To button to open the Select Recipients dialog box.

> If you are unable to send faxes to some contacts, see "Can't Fax to Specified Contacts" in the "Troubleshooting" section at the end of this chapter.

Entering Text

Enter the subject of the fax into the Subject field. If you are using a cover page and want to add notes to the cover page, enter note text into the Cover Page Notes field. The main text entry field is below a text-formatting toolbar (refer to Figure 10.4). Use this toolbar to change font, font size, select from predefined text and paragraph styles, insert bullet points or numbered steps, and align text.

Selecting a Cover Page

Windows Fax and Scan includes four optional cover pages: confident, fyi, generic, and urgent. To use one of these cover pages, or to select from a personal cover page, click the Cover Page pull-down menu and select the desired cover page.

Inserting Images, Text, and Files

To insert an existing image file, place the cursor where you'd like the image to go and click Insert, Picture. You can insert bitmap, JPEG, GIF, or PNG file types. Navigate to the picture location, select the image, and click Open. The picture is imported at the cursor location.

> **NOTE** The picture may appear to be too wide for the page, but Windows Fax and Scan scales it to fit on the page.

To insert a file attachment into the fax, click Insert, File Attachment. Navigate to the file and click Open. The file is converted to fax pages when the fax is received by a standard fax machine.

To insert text from a TXT or HTML file, place the cursor where you want to make the insertion. Click Insert, Text from File. Navigate to the file and click Open. The text is inserted at the file location.

> **TIP** Use the text-editing tools to delete any unwanted text or change text formatting.

Adding Scanned Pages

To add scanned pages to your fax, place the pages you want to scan into your scanner. Click Insert, Pages from Scanner. The pages are scanned automatically and show as an attachment. If your scanner does not have an ADF, remove the first page after scanning it, insert the next page, and repeat the process until all pages have been scanned. Each scanned page is inserted as a TIFF file.

If you are unable to scan, see "Scanner Doesn't Work" in the "Troubleshooting" section at the end of this chapter.

Previewing the Fax

After typing and inserting all the information needed into the fax, click View, Preview to see a preview of the fax. Attachments are converted into text or graphics, as appropriate. Figure 10.5 shows a typical fax in preview mode. Use the zoom pull-down menu to select a magnification for review.

Click View, Preview again to return to the normal fax-editing mode.

> **NOTE** You can edit text inserted into a fax, but not text in attached files.

Figure 10.5
Previewing a fax before sending it.

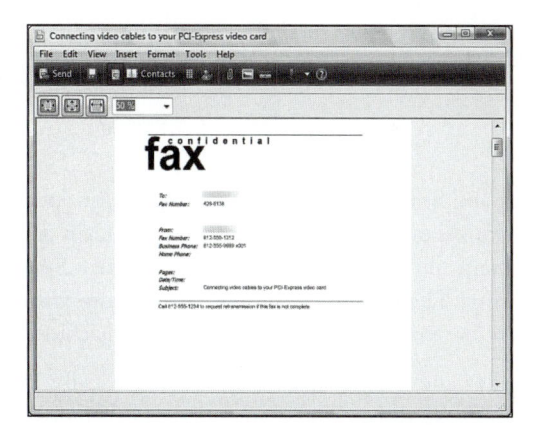

Setting Up Dialing Rules

If you need to specify a prefix for an outside line, click Dialing Rule, and select My Location to use the location information you set up when you installed your modem. If you are calling from a different location, select New Rule. When the Phone and Modem Options dialog is displayed, click New and provide the necessary information.

> For more information on dialing rules, see "Can Fax at Office or Home, but Not from Other Sites" in the "Troubleshooting" section at the end of this chapter.

Sending the Fax

To send the fax, click Send. The fax is placed in the Outbox folder until transmission is complete. After the fax is transmitted, the fax is placed in the Sent Items folder.

Monitoring Outgoing Faxes

A pop-up window (see Figure 10.6) appears, displaying the status of the current fax and previous fax events.

Figure 10.6
The Review Fax Status window appears when you send a fax.

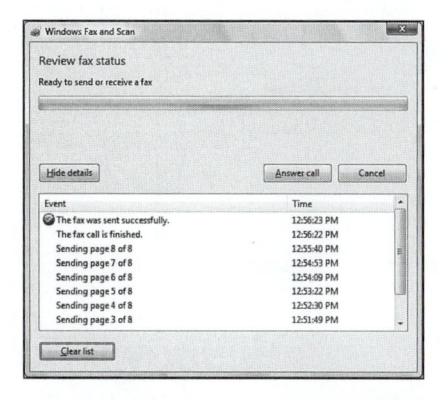

At the end of the fax transmission, a notification is also displayed over the system tray.

> *If the Fax Status window indicates there are problems sending the fax, see "Can't Detect a Dial Tone" in the "Troubleshooting" section at the end of this chapter.*

RECEIVING FAXES

To configure Windows Fax and Scan to receive a fax automatically, open Tools, Fax Settings, and make sure that the option Allow the Device to Receive Fax Calls is enabled (refer to Figure 10.3) and the Automatically Answer radio button is selected. Specify the number of rings to wait before answering. The computer will now answer any incoming call on the telephone line connected to its modem, just like a standard fax machine.

If you configure Windows Fax and Scan to receive a fax automatically, incoming faxes are received and saved to the Inbox automatically. If you configure Windows Fax and Scan to receive faxes manually (refer to Figure 10.3), a notification appears when an incoming call is detected. If the incoming call is from a fax device, click the notification to receive the fax.

During the reception, the Review Fax Status window displays the status of the incoming fax. Click Close to close the window after receiving the fax.

PRINTING RECEIVED FAXES AUTOMATICALLY

To print received faxes automatically, click Tools, Fax Settings. From the General tab, click More Options. In the When a Fax Is Received section, open the Print a Copy To pull-down menu and select a printer (see Figure 10.7). When you receive a fax, the fax will automatically be printed on the specified printer.

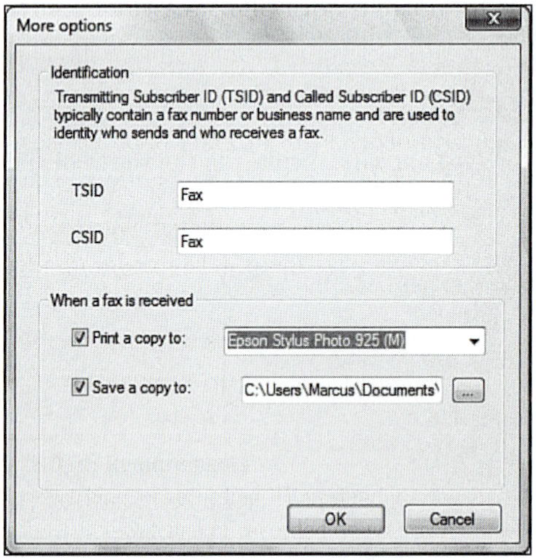

Figure 10.7
Specifying a printer and folder location for incoming faxes.

SCANNING DOCUMENTS WITH WINDOWS FAX AND SCAN

To start Windows Fax and Scan, click Start, All Programs, Windows Fax and Scan. When you open Windows Fax and Scan, the program opens to the Fax dialog box shown in Figure 10.1. Click the Scan button in the bottom of the left pane to switch to the Scan dialog box.

Scanning Documents with Windows Fax and Scan 317

To configure scan settings, click Tools, Scan Settings. The default settings, known as scan profiles, for a typical scanner are shown in Figure 10.8.

Figure 10.8
Default scan profiles for a typical scanner.

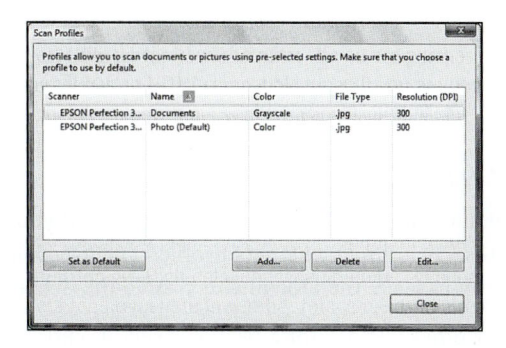

Scanning Images

To scan a photo with Windows Fax and Scan, insert the photo into your scanner. If the scanner is a flatbed design, insert the photo face down (photo against the cover glass). If the scanner includes an ADF or uses a sheet-fed design, see the documentation or markings on the scanner to determine whether photos are inserted face up or face down.

Click New Scan. Select the profile desired, and click Preview to see a preview scan. Click and drag the bounding boxes to the edges of the photo, or to crop the photo as desired. If the photo is too bright or too dark, adjust the brightness slider. Adjust the contrast slider if the photo is too flat (contrast too low) or too harsh (contrast too high). To see the results of the changes, click Preview again. When you are satisfied with scan quality, click Scan (see Figure 10.9).

If you are unable to scan, see "Scanner Doesn't Work" in the "Troubleshooting" section at the end of this chapter.

Figure 10.9
Preparing to scan a photo.

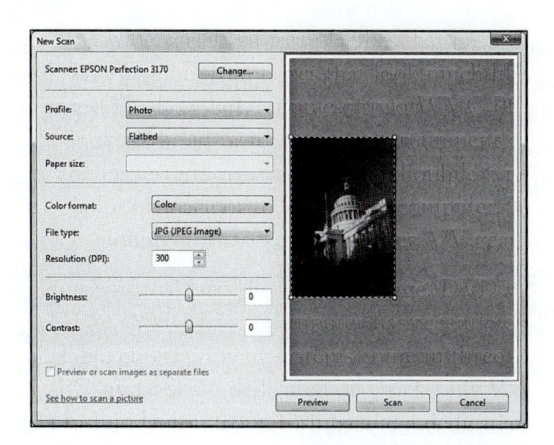

A scanning progress bar appears, and the scanned image is displayed in the workspace after being saved to disk.

NOTE

The default location for scanned documents is in your profile folder, under Documents. The full path is `C:\Users\`*`username`*`\Documents\Scanned Documents`.

If the scanner scans documents or images slowly, see "Slow Scanning Speed" in the "Troubleshooting" section at the end of this chapter.

EDITING SCAN PROFILE DEFAULTS

The Photo setting is the default scan profile (refer to Figure 10.8). If you plan to scan documents more often than photos, click the Documents profile name (second column), and then click the Set As Default button to make the Documents profile the default profile.

To edit the scan resolution or other settings for a profile, select it, and then click Edit. Figure 10.10 illustrates the settings for the Documents profile.

Figure 10.10
Editing the Documents scan profile.

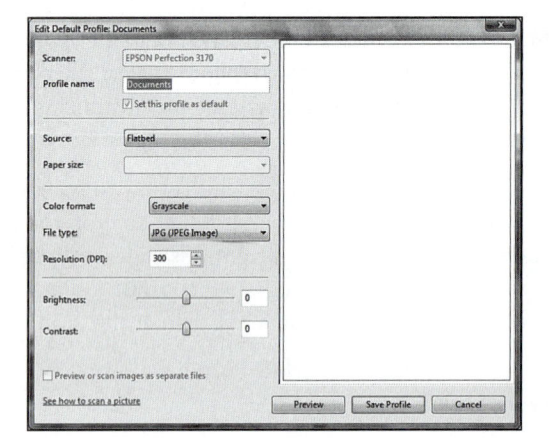

From this menu, you can select the scanner (if you have more than one installed), the name, the paper source (such as flatbed or automatic document feeder [ADF]), the paper size, the color format (black and white, grayscale, or color), the file type (JPEG, BMP, TIFF, or PNG), and the scan resolution, brightness, and color. Make the changes you want to the profile and click Save Profile to replace the current settings with your changes.

TIP

The default scan resolution for the Documents and Photo scan profiles is 300dpi (dots per inch). 300dpi matches the Very Fine (best quality) black and white document resolution setting supported by most recent fax machines. However, if you are transmitting a color document to a color fax machine, you may want to reduce the resolution to 200dpi. Fine and Photo fax settings in black and white mode are also 200dpi. Use a higher resolution, such as 600dpi, if you are scanning a photo for printing on a high-quality color inkjet or laser printer or for publishing use. See the printer documentation or the publisher's requirements for the recommended DPI.

> A TIFF file produces the best quality, but is rather large. If you want to save disk space, use JPEG or PNG. BMP can be used by applications that do not support other file types, but BMP files are also large.

CREATING A NEW SCAN PROFILE

To create a new profile, click Add in the Scan Profiles dialog box shown in Figure 10.8. The Add New Profile dialog box appears. Enter the profile name, select the paper source, and make other changes as needed. Click Save Profile to save the new scan profile.

> **TIP**
>
> The preset resolution for a new scan profile is 75dpi. This is far too low for any use other than creating an image to be viewed onscreen or to be emailed. To match the dpi of current Windows desktops, we recommend 96dpi for viewing or emailing. Use a resolution of at least 200dpi or more for profiles intended for printing or faxing. See the previous tip for specific resolution recommendations for different types of documents and destinations.

EMAILING SCANS

To email a scanned document or photo, open the Documents folder in Scan view. Select the item you want to email, and click Document, Forward As Email. Enter the recipient(s), message, and other information, and click Send to send the scan.

FAXING SCANS

To fax a scanned document or photo without switching to the Fax view, open the Documents folder in Scan view. Select the item you want to fax and click Document, Forward As Fax. The New Fax dialog box appears. Enter the fax number and other information and click Send to fax the scan.

→ For more information, **see** "Sending Faxes from Windows Fax and Scan," **p. 313**.

MANIPULATING SCANNED IMAGES

On a clean install of Windows Vista, scanned images are edited by Windows Photo Gallery by default. To edit a scanned image, click Start, Documents, Scanned Documents. Double-click the image to open it with the default photo editor. To choose a different photo editor, select the image you want to edit, and right-click Open With. Choose your preferred image editor from the context menu, or click Choose Default Program to select a different program from those listed.

> **NOTE**
>
> If you edit the image with a program that supports other image file formats, such as Adobe Photoshop or Adobe Photoshop Elements, make sure you save the edited image as a JPEG, TIFF, BMP, or PNG file if you want to be able to use it in Windows Fax and Scan.

Troubleshooting

Fax Modem Doesn't Work

If your fax modem doesn't work, check the following:

Testing the Fax Modem To make sure your modem is working properly, open Control Panel, click Phone and Modem Options, enter the location information, and click the Modems tab when it appears. Click Properties to open the properties sheet for your modem, and click the Diagnostics tab on the properties sheet. Click the Query Modem button to send test commands to the modem.

If the modem does not respond, check the modem listing in Device Manager; for an external modem connected to a serial (COM) port, you should also check the serial port section of Device Manager. If you see problems reported with the modem or the port, open the properties sheet to diagnose the problem.

→ For more information on Device Manager, **see** Chapter 28, "Troubleshooting and Repairing Problems," **p. 961**.

External Fax Modem Check the modem's power supply. If your modem is not connected to a working AC adapter, or if the AC adapter is not plugged in to a working AC outlet, your modem will not work. Some external modems have an on/off switch. Make sure the modem is turned on before use.

An external fax modem must be connected to a working COM or USB port. A COM (also known as RS-232 or Serial) port is a 9-pin male D-connector. The cable between the modem and the computer should be secured in place with the thumbscrews provided. Loose cables can cause the fax modem to not work reliably.

If you have disabled the COM ports in your system BIOS, you must reenable them before you can use an external modem. Check your system or motherboard documentation for details.

If you are using a COM-to-USB adapter, make sure the adapter works correctly. Problems with the adapter could cause your modem to appear to malfunction. Frankly, we advise you to use only USB or internal devices if you no longer have COM ports on your system.

If a USB external modem doesn't work, make sure the USB port is working. Attach a USB mouse to the port to check its operation.

Internal Fax Modem On a desktop PC, an internal fax modem slides into one of the available PCI expansion slots. If the card is not properly seated in the expansion slot, it may not work reliably.

Can't Detect a Dial Tone

If the fax modem doesn't detect a dial tone, it can't work. Make sure the RJ-11 telephone cable is properly connected to the fax modem and to the phone jack. Some fax modems use a pair of RJ-11 ports, one for the phone line and one to permit a telephone to piggyback on the modem to share a line when the modem is not in use. Make sure you use the correct port for each type of device if your modem marks the ports for different uses.

Replace damaged or suspect cables: If you're like us, you probably have a dozen or so unused RJ-11 cables lying around from various telephone, fax machine, and modem installations.

If the fax modem connects to a Y-splitter or other line-sharing device, try disconnecting the line-sharing device and plug it directly into the phone jack. A defective line-sharing device can cause the fax modem to malfunction.

Can't Fax to Specified Contacts

Windows Fax and Scan can fax to only contacts that have fax numbers in their contact information or to manually entered fax numbers. If you have contacts that do not have fax numbers listed, you will need to enter the fax numbers manually at faxing time or, better still, edit their contact information to supply the fax number.

If the contact has a fax number listed, you may need to add the area code or country code to the number to enable Windows Fax and Scan to make the call. Use the same information as you would provide for a standalone fax machine.

Can Fax at Office or Home, but Not from Other Sites

If you can fax from office or home with a particular dialing rule (My Location or a customized location), but you cannot fax from other locations, such as a meeting room or hotel, you should find out what is needed for a dialing rule and create a new one. If you will not be using that location again, you can also specify the phone number manually and add codes such as 9 (outside line) or a comma (each comma adds a one-second pause) as a prefix to the destination fax number.

Scanner Doesn't Work

If your scanner doesn't work, check the following:

Testing Scanner   To make sure your scanner is working properly, start Windows Photo Gallery, click File, and select Import from Camera or Scanner. Select the scanner, and click Import. The scanner application should appear.

Obtaining WIA Drivers   If the scanner does not respond, make sure you are using the correct drivers:

> Best: Windows Vista drivers with Windows Image Acquisition (WIA) support
>
> Acceptable: Windows XP drivers with WIA support
>
> Not Acceptable: Windows Vista or XP drivers with TWAIN support

Windows Fax and Scan and Windows Photo Gallery use WIA to interface with the scanner. With some types of scanners, the driver CD you receive with the scanner may include only

TWAIN drivers. TWAIN drivers can be used through third-party applications' Import menus, but they don't work with WIA applications.

Visit the scanner vendor's website to download and install WIA drivers if your scanner works with its own scanning application, but not with Windows Photo Gallery or Windows Fax and Scan. Note that some scanner vendors include both TWAIN and WIA in their default driver installation routine.

Slow Scanning Speed

If a USB 2.0–based scanner is very slow, make sure you have connected the scanner to a USB 2.0 (also known as Hi-Speed USB) port. Some front-mounted USB ports support only USB 1.1 speeds. If you have connected the scanner to an external USB hub, try connecting the scanner directly to a USB port on the computer.

Tips from the Windows Pros: Scanning and Faxing Slides and Transparencies

If you work with traditional photos, some of your photos might be slides or negatives, rather than prints. Most late-model flatbed scanners, including all-in-one units, include support for 35mm slides and negatives, and some also support larger sizes.

You must use the scanner vendor's own TWAIN drivers, not the WIA drivers supported by Windows Fax and Scan or Windows Photo Gallery, to gain access to slide and transparency adapters. Thus, if you want to fax a scan of a negative or slide, follow this procedure:

1. Run the scanner vendor's own scan program. This can be run directly from the Start menu, or from the File menu of most image-editing programs (look for an entry such as Import). Be sure to choose the TWAIN driver.
2. Select an appropriate resolution: 600dpi, although too low for slides or negatives, which must be enlarged a great deal to be printed, will provide adequate pixels for faxing.
3. Save the scanned image to the Scanned Documents folder under Documents.
4. Start Windows Fax and Scan and attach the scanned image to a fax.
5. Send the fax.

CHAPTER 11

PRODUCING VIDEOS WITH WINDOWS MOVIE MAKER

In this chapter

Multimedia, Imaging, and Windows   324

Video Capture and Editing with Microsoft Movie Maker 6   324

Capturing Your Video Clips   327

Troubleshooting   346

Tips from the Windows Pros: Adding Impact to Your Movies   346

Multimedia, Imaging, and Windows

When Windows was first developed in the mid-1980s, none of the hardware we use today to capture and transform still and video images was available. However, as time passed, still photographers and, more recently, videographers, have discovered the computer and its capability to edit, transform, organize, and store their work.

Whether you're a serious photographer with a portfolio that rivals Ansel Adams, a videographer inspired by Stanley Kubrick, or just a casual camera user who's looking for a way to organize company photos, Windows Vista contains built-in tools and features that are designed to make the marriage of images and pixels a happy one. Even if you plan to replace the multimedia and imaging tools in Windows Vista with higher-powered third-party solutions, Vista's architecture makes it easier to use the tools you want with the photos and video you love to create.

Some of the imaging and multimedia tools built into Windows Vista are improved versions of those released with Windows XP, and some of them, such as Photo Gallery and DVD Maker, are new with Vista. It used to be that the fun and games multimedia tools were thrown in only with the "home" versions of Windows, such as Windows Me. The business users running Windows 2000 did without. Since XP, and even more with Vista, there is no arbitrary division here. All the tools in this chapter are included in all flavors of Vista. You no longer need to sacrifice imaging and multimedia performance for the stability and security of a corporate operating system.

Surely the reasoning behind this development is that multimedia isn't just for fun anymore. Business and academic users are required to produce video and other kinds of multimedia documents simply to keep pace with an ever-growing hunger for multimedia-based information. Whether you're producing streaming video for your corporate, nonprofit, or academic website, you're giving a slide show at a business meeting, or you're conducting a multimedia Internet-based group conference call, Vista has many of the tools you will need.

In this chapter, we focus exclusively on video capture, editing, and output, using the freebie program called Movie Maker. The price is right, and it's actually quite capable.

Video Capture and Editing with Microsoft Movie Maker 6

If you thought you needed a Mac and Final Cut Pro, or at least iMovie or Adobe Premiere, to make a decent movie to post on YouTube, to wow your relatives with at the upcoming family reunion, or for that company pitch, you will be delightfully surprised by Movie Maker. Movie Maker has all the features of the iMovie program for the Mac (also a freebie) but that runs on the PC. I think of the two programs as roughly identical, after using them both and comparing their respective features. Being a professional video producer for instructional videos, I have my preferences for more powerful programs, but even then I find myself using Movie Maker because it's quick and dirty and makes it easy to get what I want. With the new DVD-authoring tool that comes with Vista, it's a complete package now, whereas in the past you had to do some fancy footwork to burn your movie onto a DVD.

STEPS OF MOVIE PRODUCTION WITH MOVIE MAKER

With Movie Maker, you go through roughly these steps in movie production:

1. Capture video to disk and save as clips.
2. Import clips and, optionally, photo stills, and music into your computer.
3. Place clips, stills, and music on your timeline.
4. Edit as you like by adding transitions such as fades, rearranging clips, and shorting clips.
5. Apply video effects to clips and stills, if desired, and add optional titles.
6. "Publish" your video (a.k.a. "render" it) to an output file, DVD, CD, email, or back to tape on your camcorder. If you output to a file on your hard disk, it can be played back through a software-based media program such as Windows Media Player.

The editing process that Windows Movie Maker and other digital video-editing programs use is often referred to as *nonlinear editing* because you can arrange different digital movie sources in any order, and you don't need to physically cut or damage video tape or film to edit your movies.

VIDEO FORMATS YOU CAN IMPORT

Previous versions of Windows Movie Maker program could capture video from the following sources:

- Web cameras
- DV camcorders
- Analog camcorders (with correct hardware)
- VHS and other video players (with correct hardware)

However, Movie Maker 6 captures only from a DV (digital video) camera.

If you want to import video from a VCR, analog video camera, or other analog video source and edit the video in Movie Maker, you can still do it. You need to have an analog video-capture device installed on your computer and then use software that enables you to import video from that analog capture device and store it in a file format that Movie Maker can read in—namely AVI or WMV (see next tip). For more information, check the documentation that came with your analog capture device or go to the manufacturer's website.

Many of today's crop of camcorder record directly to regular-sized or mini DVDs. You may be able to read the resulting files into the computer, depending on the camera and format of the files created. Refer to the camera's manual and supplied software to discover how you can import video files into the computer. Typically, you will import and save them on the hard disk, and then add them to the Movie Maker project. At the very least, you can import from these disks by capturing the analog stream as described next.

Some DV cameras have a "pass through" feature that enables you to connect them to an analog device, such as a VCR. When set to pass-through mode, the DV camera converts the video from the analog source into a digital video stream and delivers that to your computer via the Firewire cable. For more information, check the documentation that came with your DV camera or go to the manufacturer's website.

Connecting Your Camcorder

You can connect your DV camcorder to the computer in one of two ways. The first method is to use an IEEE 1394 (also known as Firewire, but that is an Apple term and you won't see Microsoft saying it) connection. In this case, one end of the IEEE 1394 cable is connected to the DV port on your camera, and the other end of the cable is plugged into an IEEE 1394 port on your computer. The other, less popular connection method is via a USB 2.0 cable. Some, but not many, cameras support this method. The camera has to support "streaming over USB" (also called a USB Video Class [UVC] camera).

> **TIP**
>
> To determine whether your DV camera supports USB streaming over DV, check Windows Device Manager and determine whether the camera appears as a USB Video Device, check the documentation that came with your DV camera, or go to the manufacturer's website.

You need a supported IEEE-1394 (Firewire) port or add-on card to capture video from a DV camcorder; Vista also must have support for the DV camcorder if you want to interface directly with Windows Movie Maker. Firewire and USB 2 are quite mature technologies at this point, so if you have a fairly recent camera, you are probably in good shape. I use a Sony VX-2000 DV camera, for example, and Vista knows what it is and how to control it and capture clips from it.

> **TIP**
>
> If Windows Movie Maker doesn't support your video hardware but your hardware can be used with third-party software, capture your data with third-party software and save it in a Windows Movie Maker–compatible format, such as .asf, .avi, .mpeg, .mpg, .m1v, .mp2, .mpa, .mpv2, .mpe, .wm, or .wmv. You can import these video types of files into Windows Movie Maker. Audio file types you can import are: aif, .aifc, .aiff .asf, .au, .mp2, .mp3, .mpa, .snd, .wav, and .wma. Picture files are .bmp, .dib, .emf, .gif, .jfif, .jpe, .jpeg, .jpg, .png, .tif, .tiff, and .wmf.

Capturing Your Video Clips

The first step in movie making is typically to capture some video from a camcorder or other video source. The first time you attach a supported DV camcorder to your Vista system and turn it on, Vista displays the menu shown in Figure 11.1. You can click Import Video or close the box and take no action. To make Import Video the default, highlight it and then check the Always Do This for This Device box.

Figure 11.1
When you plug in or turn on a video device, you will probably see this dialog box.

Typically, at this point, you just click Import Video. This brings up the Import Video Wizard and dialog box shown in Figure 11.2. You have three decisions to make at this point.

Figure 11.2
The Import Video dialog box asks some questions about importing your video.

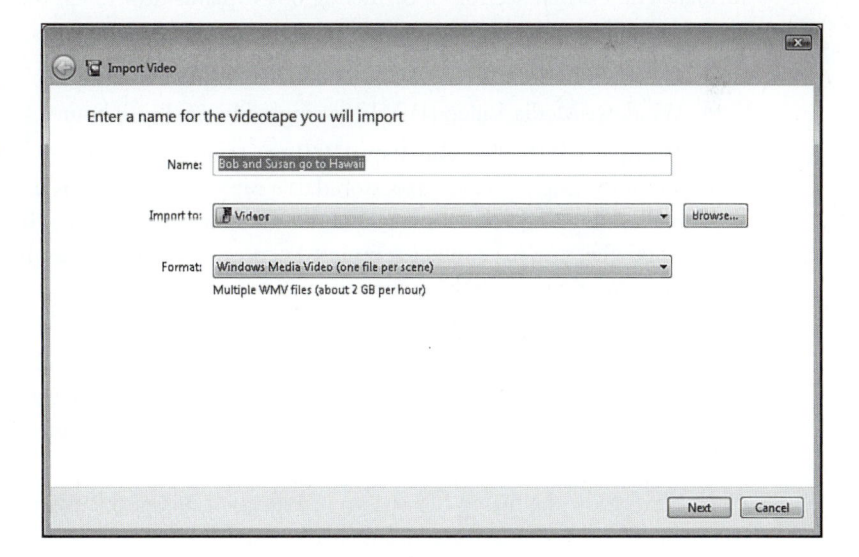

> **NOTE**
>
> You also can invoked this dialog box by clicking Import from Digital Video Camera in the Movie Maker task pane or by choosing File, Import from Digital Video Camera.

In general, importing from DV tape gives you very few options because they are not necessary. DV is a digital data stream, so it's a bit like copying data from one disk to another, except that, in this case, it's digital tape. But you do have several choices to make:

1. What do you want to call the video you're importing? This will be used as a filename. Name it something memorable so that you'll know what's in it when you want to arrange things on the timeline in your movie—for example, "Business meeting day 1" or "Trip to Blue Ridge Mountains."

2. Choose the folder where you want to store the video. By default, captured files go into `[username]/Videos`. Keep in mind that videos take a lot of space on your hard disk. People often buy an external USB or Firewire hard disk to store video files if they are going to do a lot of video work. Wherever you store your files, make sure that the hard disk has gobs of room if you're capturing from DV tape because, at the least compressed setting, they will consume 13GB per hour.

3. Choose the format of the captured video. Obviously, if your final output will be a low-resolution image (a postage stamp–size moving image small enough to email or send over the Web, for example), there is no need to capture it in a space-gobbling hi-def format. The Format section of the dialog box explains how much room each option consumes. These are the choices for DV tape capture:

   - AVI Audio Video Interleaved, a single file, 13GB per hour.
   - Windows Media Video (WMV), a single file, 2GB per hour.
   - Multiple WMV files, also about 2GB per hour. Each scene (as defined by pausing and restarting the camera) is stored as a separate file. This is useful because it makes dragging your clips around the timeline much simpler. If you save as only a single file, you have to cut it up into sections in Movie Maker before you can drag clips and reorganize the cuts in your movie.

   From the sizes reported (13GB per hour versus 2GB per hour), you can guess that WMV files are greatly compressed compared to AVI files. As a result of compression, there is some loss of quality. The files are not terrible-looking, but there will be a loss of quality; therefore, this is not recommended if you're planning to create a high-quality DVD for playback on a computer or TV.

4. Click Next. Now the dialog box shown in Figure 11.3 appears, asking whether you want to import the entire video tape or just parts of it.

Figure 11.3
Choosing whether to grab the entire tape or just sections of it.

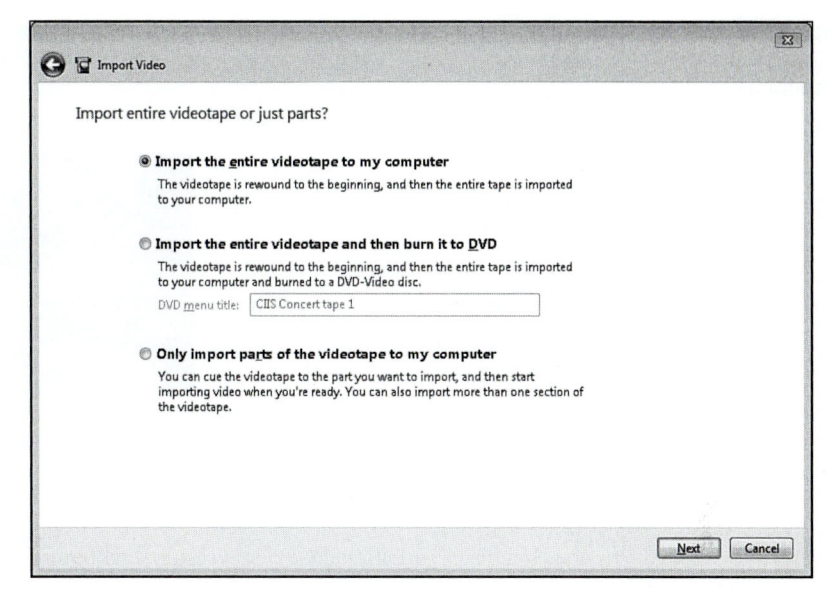

Here are your choices:

- You can import the entire tape. Vista will rewind the tape, capture the whole thing, and store it to a single file, using settings from the previous dialog box.
- A new addition in Vista allows you to burn directly to DVD. If all you want to do is copy your taped video onto a DVD so that folks can watch it on their DVD players, you're in business with this choice. If you do choose this, you can give the DVD a title so that when it is played, the title pops up on the TV before the video plays. (This option appears only if you have a DVD burner.)
- Import only parts of the tape. You're prompted to cue up the tape manually and then click Go to start the capture. You repeat this for each clip you want to grab.

While the capture is progressing, you see the dialog box shown in Figure 11.4.

Figure 11.4
While video is being imported, this dialog box appears.

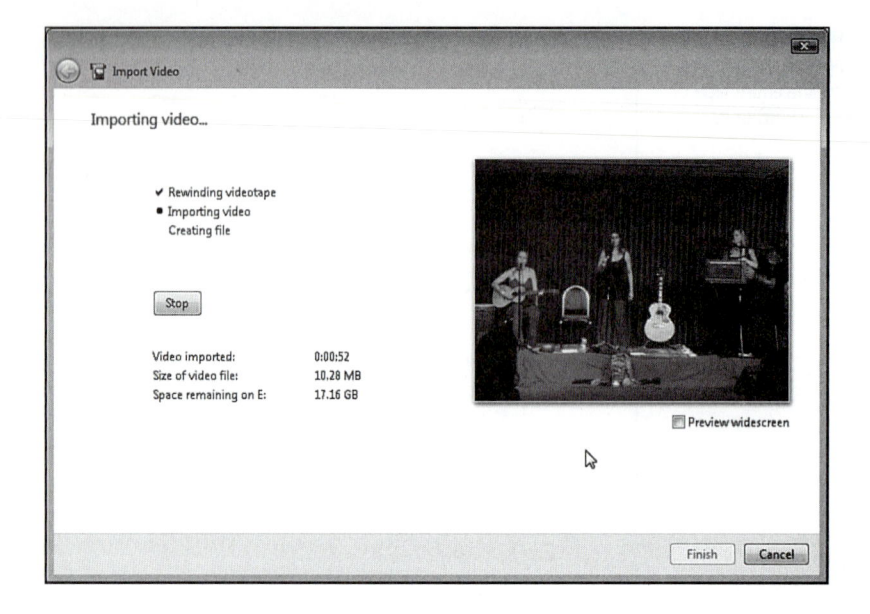

You can click Stop at any point to stop the import. The amount that you have imported up until then is saved to disk.

When the tape finishes (or you click Stop), Movie Maker does a heck of a lot of work saving the file to disk. Sometimes, it takes quite a while for the file to be created, especially if it's being converted to WMV format. Time for a coffee break; the CPU and HDD will likely be so tied up that your computer can't do much else. If the import is successful, a dialog box might report "Import has completed successfully." Then, click OK.

Manually Importing Video

If you chose to import only sections of the tape, follow these instructions:

1. First, you will see the dialog box shown in Figure 11.5.

Figure 11.5
Use the control buttons to import only specific sections of tape.

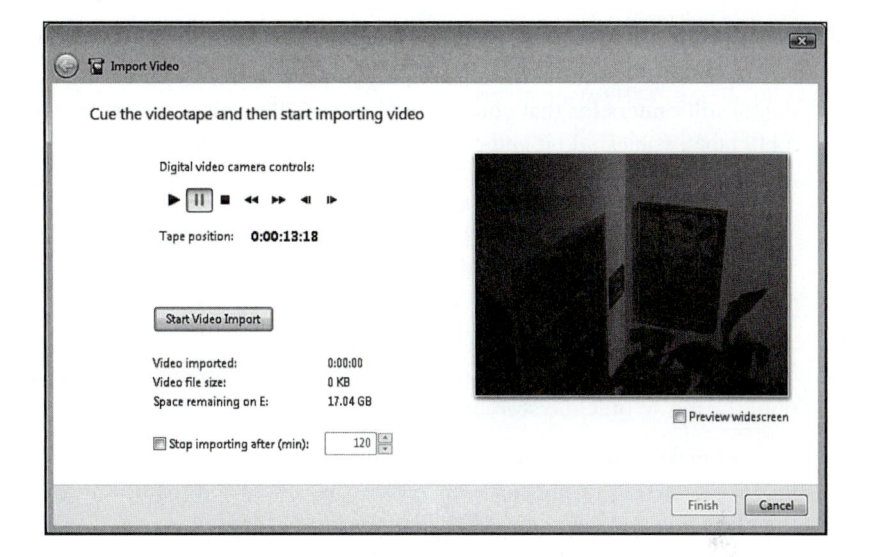

2. Use the controls in the dialog box to advance or rewind the tape to the desired point. Then, click Start Video Import.
3. Click the Stop button. This creates a clip.
4. Repeat for each section you want to capture. Each time you start and stop capture, a separate clip is created and is displayed in the work area, ready to be assigned to the storyboard.

Notice also that the dialog box reports the available disk space on the target drive. This is only somewhat useful because it doesn't tell you how many minutes of tape you can capture on that drive, using the selected quality. That depends on the capture settings you chose. You have to experiment to figure this out, unfortunately.

Each file that you save is referred to as a collection of one or more clips in Windows Movie Maker.

> **TIP**
>
> Got an event going on that you want to dump straight into the computer, while it's happening? You can skip the tape altogether. You can import live video from a digital video (DV) camera right to your computer's hard disk. Simply set up your camera to shoot as you normally would, but tethered to the computer's input (1394 or USB). Then set the camera mode to record live video (often labeled as Camera on a DV camera). The Import Video Wizard opens automatically. Choose to import. (You can do this, incidentally, from the Movie Maker program by clicking on Import from Digital Video Camera). The live video is encoded into a video file and saved to your computer's hard disk. After you import the live video, you can edit the resulting video file if you want, using Movie Maker or other software, or leave the file as is.

Importing Digital Still Camera Movies, Snaps, and Sound Files

As I mentioned earlier in the chapter, if you want to import videos that you shot on your digital still camera (or that you captured using other video-capture hardware, such as from VHS tape), you can do it and edit it into your movies. After this is imported, you can use it as the basis of your movie or to spice up your other imported video. Simply do this:

1. In the left (Tasks) pane of Movie Maker, under Import, click Videos.
2. Browse to and select the video files you want.
3. Click Import.

They are added to your working collection (work area) and are available for you to drag onto the movie timeline/storyboard.

When I make movies, I often want to pull in still images, too. Many folks have digital cameras these days, so images are easy to come by. These add richness to your productions. Use the preceding technique, but click Pictures instead of Videos.

You can import audio tracks, too, for spicing up your movies by adding theme songs, background music, speech, and so forth.

1. Under Import, click Audio or Music and browse to the file. Many popular sound file formats are supported (not QuickTime or RealMedia, but the oh-so-common MP3 is, at least).

> **TIP**
>
> I listed all the audio formats supported earlier in this chapter. If all else fails and you have an audio track on the computer that Movie Maker doesn't want to import, use another program to burn that to a standard audio CD; then import the track from the audio CD either directly or by ripping it to MP3 first.

2. Select the files and click Import (or just double-click the file). The files are added to the work collection for use as you construct your movie.

Organizing Your Clips

Now that you have chosen the basic materials from which your movie will be compiled, the next task is to start putting the pieces in order. After that, you fine-tune it and then output it. So now it's important to get organized. You'll want to get your video clips, stills, and audio into the same collection so that you can easily see them in the collection bin. This makes it simpler to pull them onto the timeline in the order you want.

1. Click the Show or Hide Collections button in the toolbar. The collections panel appears on the left. Alternatively, if you don't know which button that is, simply choose View, Collections from the menu bar.
2. Right-click Imported Media (in the left panel) and choose New Collection Folder. Give it a name, such as "Dan's Birthday Party."

3. Now, drag all your captured video clips, audio clips, and stills for this video production into this collection folder. (There are other ways to organize collections, such as keeping all video clips in one collection, audio in another, and so forth, but glomming them all together for a given project is the one I use most often.) Move objects around just as you do in Windows Explorer—that is, drag the thumbnails in the middle pane over to the destination collection in the left pane, or import them into a collection by highlighting the new collection name and then clicking on File, Import Media Items. You can also drag files from a Windows Explorer window, if you like. Figure 11.6 shows my collection setup for making my "Birthday Party" movie.

Figure 11.6
Getting your clips organized into a collection makes putting them on the timeline easier.

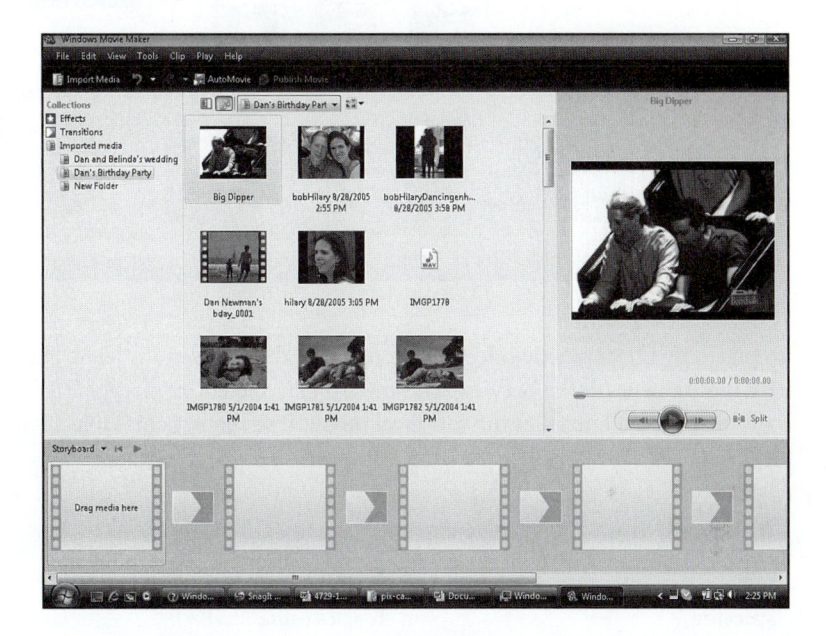

NOTE
You can resize the sections of the Movie Maker window, such as the Preview pane and Collections pane, by dragging the dividing lines.

Turning Your Video Clips into a Simple Movie

Next, start piecing together your movie by dragging your movie clips and still images into the Windows Movie Maker storyboard, which is the filmstrip-like area at the bottom of the screen. The clips you drag to the storyboard are positioned left to right. (You can change the order later.) The movie eventually plays starting with the leftmost clip and moves to the right, through all the clips in order.

Figure 11.7 shows the storyboard area after adding various clips from DV video that I captured while making a movie called "Dan's Birthday Party."

Figure 11.7
A simple movie built from various video clips displayed in Storyboard view.

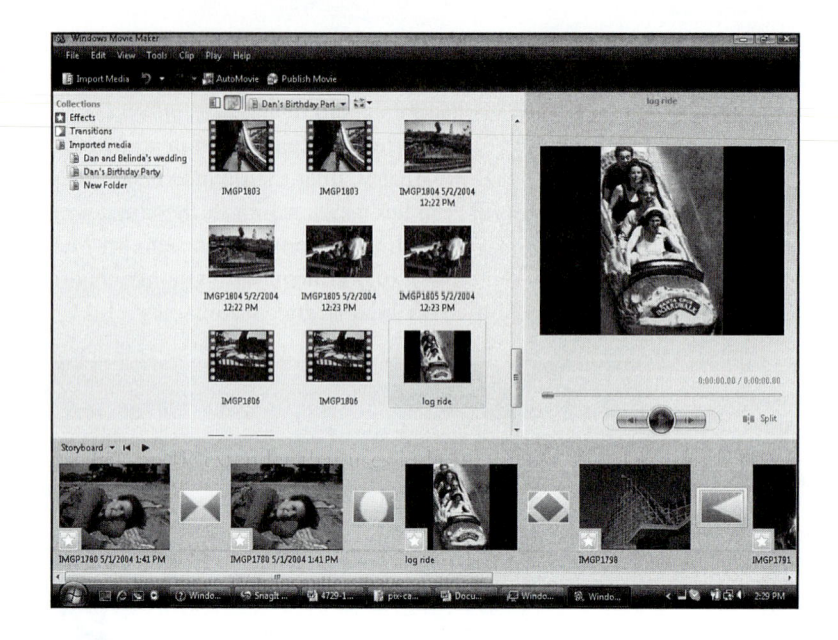

To play only the currently selected video clip in the Collections pane, click the triangular Play button beneath the preview window. To play the entire storyboard, click Play, Play Storyboard/Timeline from the top-level menu. Use the keys in Table 11.1 to control playback.

TABLE 11.1   WINDOWS MOVIE MAKER PLAYBACK CONTROL KEYS

Key	Action
Spacebar	Toggles pause/playback
Alt+Left arrow	Displays previous frame
Alt+Right arrow	Displays next frame
Alt+Ctrl+Left arrow	Moves to previous clip
Alt+Ctrl+Right arrow	Moves to next clip
Alt+Enter	Toggles full screen display

EDITING YOUR MOVIE

After you drag your clips and images to the storyboard, you can use the supplied tools to adjust the length of each clip, the order of your clips, and the transitions between each clip. I like to trim my clips at least roughly before I add transitions between them and add background music, credits, and so forth.

To change the length of each clip (called trimming), you must use Timeline view; click View, Timeline, or click the Show Timeline button just above the storyboard. The timeline replaces the storyboard at the bottom of your screen. To change the order of clips, it's best to be in Storyboard view; to edit and trim clips and adjust details of the timing of clips, use Timeline view.

When you have your clips in the basic order you want, you typically have to make adjustments such as these:

- Trim the beginning and ends of a clip.
- Split a clip into two or more clips so that you can move them around on the timeline independently, do transitions between the sections, or apply different effects to each portion.
- Combine two clips if you accidentally split them, or because it's easier to work with a smaller number of clips.

To adjust the length of each clip, follow these steps:

1. Switch to Timeline view, if necessary.
2. Click the + or – symbols just above the timeline, or choose View/Zoom commands to zoom in or out (making the clips appear larger or smaller). Zooming in makes it possible to accurately adjust the clip. You might have to scroll the timeline left and right a bit to find your clip. Use the scrollbar at the bottom of the Movie Maker window.
3. Click the clip in the timeline. Notice that if you hover the mouse pointer over the right or left edge of the clip, a red sizing arrow appears. Now, you can drag the clip.
4. To trim the start of a clip, move the trim handle at the left edge of the clip to the right, up to the point where you want the clip to start; to trim the end of a clip, drag the trim handle at the end of the clip over to the left until you reach the point where you want the clip to end.

TIP

If you're trying to shorten the end of a video clip, click the clip in the timeline and click the Play button to play the video clip from start to finish; then, play it again and stop it at the point where you want to cut it. A vertical line in the timeline shows the playback location. Now drag the trim handle at the end of the clip until it is lined up with the vertical line.

You can't make a video clip longer than its original length; you can only trim it. (Well, you can make it play in slow motion—see the section "Adding Video Effects (Filters) to Your Clips," later in this chapter.) However, still images (as opposed to video clips) can play as long as you want. Just drag the still image's edge down the timeline. By default, stills have a length of 5 seconds.

You can "scrub" across the timeline and see your movie play. Just position the pointer on the time area (looks like a ruler) of Timeline view. Then, click and drag. The video will play sort of jerkily. If you click a spot in the timeline ruler and then click the Play button in the preview window, the preview will start from that point. This is useful for working on a specific area of the movie.

To move a clip from one position to another, you can use either drag-and-drop or cut-and-paste. I prefer drag-and-drop if I can see the source clip and destination location at the same time. Otherwise, I use cut-and-paste. To use drag-and-drop, follow these steps:

1. Switch to Storyboard view (not required, but easier to use than Timeline view).
2. Drag the clip left or right on the timeline. A vertical blue line indicates where it will be inserted (always just *before* any clip you are hovering over).

To use cut-and-paste, follow these steps:

1. Switch to Storyboard view (not required, but easier to use than Timeline view).
2. Right-click the clip in the storyboard.
3. Choose Cut.
4. Click the clip in the timeline that will be *behind* the clip when you paste it.
5. Click Edit, Paste.

Adding Transitions Between Clips

Movie Maker comes with 63 different transition effects to use between clips. Transitions control how one clip blends into the next. The default transition is called a *flat cut*. Actually, most film and TV transitions are flat cuts. They happen so quickly we barely notice them. Transitions add life to your creations. As with fonts, though, it's easy to overuse transitions. However, an occasional transition is useful, especially between still images or for a special effect such as in a music video.

> **TIP**
>
> You can download more from various online sources such as www.microsoft.com/windowsxp/downloads/powertoys/mmcreate.mspx.

You can add transitions to your production in several ways. To create a transition effect from one scene to another, follow these steps:

1. Switch to Storyboard view. Zoom in as necessary. Notice that there is a little box between each clip. This is the placeholder for a transition.
2. In the Collections pane, click Transitions (or choose Transitions from the drop-down box at the top of the middle pane). A bunch of transitions appear in the middle pane. Double-click any one of them to see the effect played in the preview window. When you find the one you want, drag it to the little box between the two clips you're transitioning between. In Figure 11.8, I added a "Diagonal, Box Out" transition between two clips marked by the pointer.

> **TIP**
>
> You can drag transitions between transition placeholders on the timeline. You can remove a transition by right-clicking it and choosing Delete.

> **TIP**
>
> You can control the length of a *dissolve* (one clip fades into the next) by overlapping the clips on the timeline.

Figure 11.8
Transitions are dropped on the placeholders between clips in the storyboard.

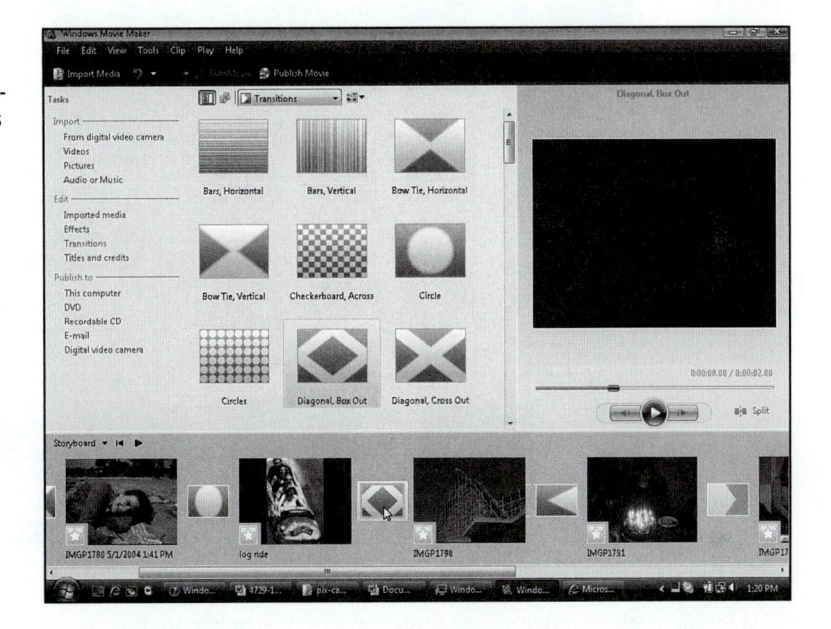

Adding Video Effects (Filters) to Your Clips

Video effects are fun to play with. If you've used Photoshop filters, you know what these are. They change the look of a clip, for example, from color to black and white. The nearly 50 different supplied effects run the gamut from painterly, to old-fashioned, to slow motion, even to psychedelic. For still shots, a few transitions add a sense of motion by panning left or right, or slowly zooming into a corner of the image. Professional documentaries often use this approach. Filters also exist for fading in and out, rotating clips, and increasing and decreasing brightness.

When you apply an effect, it alters the way the entire clip plays back. Transitions do not alter the actual clip file on your hard disk; they are just applied as the movie runs and to the final output file you'll create when you save the movie after editing. You can remove effects at any time, so don't hesitate to experiment. If you split the clip, both halves keep the effect.

To apply a video effect:

1. Switch to Storyboard view. (Timeline view works, but I think it's graphically easier to use Storyboard view.)
2. In the Collections pane, click Video Effects. The middle pane should show thumbnails of the available effects (see Figure 11.9). (You can choose View, Details to see descriptions of each effect instead of thumbnails.)

Figure 11.9
Applying effects to clips is easy. Just drag and drop the effect on the clip.

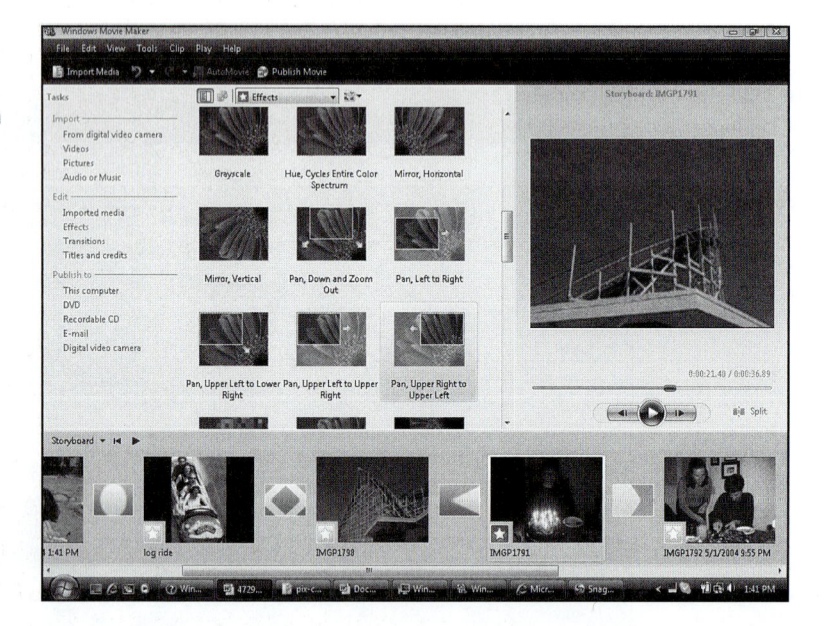

3. Double-click an effect to see how it works. If you like it, drag and drop it onto a clip and then click the Play button on the Preview pane to see the effect on the actual clip. If you don't like the effect, right-click the clip and choose Video Effects to bring up a dialog box. Click the effect you dislike and click Remove. When a clip has one or more effects on it, it displays a blue star on its thumbnail in the storyboard or timeline.
4. You can add multiple video effects to a single clip. Effects for that clip are processed in the order listed in the Video Effects dialog box.

Adding Narration to Your Movie

You can record narration for your movie when the movie is in Timeline view if you have a microphone attached to your computer. To record narration, follow these steps:

1. Select Timeline view.
2. Position the cursor somewhere on the timeline where there is no other audio track. (The Audio/Music track is visible below the video track.) Click Tools, Narrate Timeline.

3. The Record Narration Track pane appears (see Figure 11.10). Click Show More Options; you'll see the default audio device and input source, as shown in the figure. To change the defaults, use the drop-down lists.

Figure 11.10
The Record Narration pane, used to record a narration for your movie.

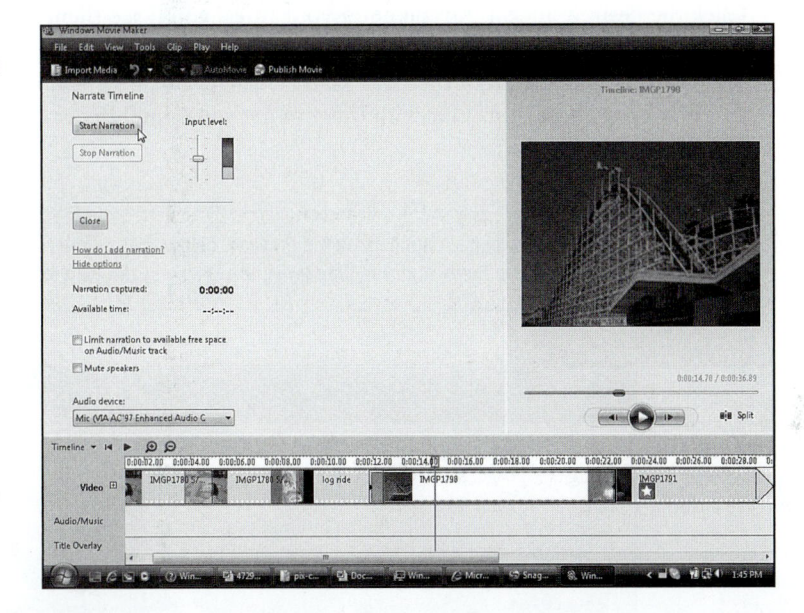

4. It's a good idea to click Mute Speakers if you have your sound turned up because it will prevent feedback between the speakers and the microphone.
5. Adjust the recording level as desired. (The level should be somewhere near the middle of the colorful Input Level meter.)
6. Click Start Narration to begin. Click Stop Narration when you're finished. You're asked to name the file. It's saved as a .wma (Windows Media audio) file and then automatically dropped into the timeline in exactly the place where you started narration.

ADDING TITLES TO YOUR MOVIE

Although Windows Movie Maker version 1 didn't have built-in titling features, titling was added as of version 2. Many titling styles are available at this point: You can have titles appear over the top of clips and stills, or as separate slides (like in an old silent movie). You can also create opening and closing animated titles and credits, just like in actual movies or TV shows. You can spend a few hours playing with the titling options, so I just point you in the right direction.

1. To add an opening title sequence, choose Tools, Titles and Credits. In a few seconds, the titler loads into the left pane.
2. Notice the options you have now. You can add a title in these places:
    - At the beginning of the movie
    - Before a selected clip

- On the selected clip
- At the end of the movie

3. Click the desired option. As you enter your titles, you'll see them immediately show up in the Preview pane as they will appear in your movie. The real key lies in the options near the bottom of the titler pane: Change the Title Animation, and Change the Text Font and Color. Play with these to get some fun effects. See Figure 11.11 for an example.

> **TIP**
> A Title Overlay track appears on the timeline, below the audio track. You can slide titles around down there, and trim their lengths, just as you can with stills and video clips.

Figure 11.11
The titler pane, for creating overlays and intro and ending credits, hosts myriad built-in animated title looks.

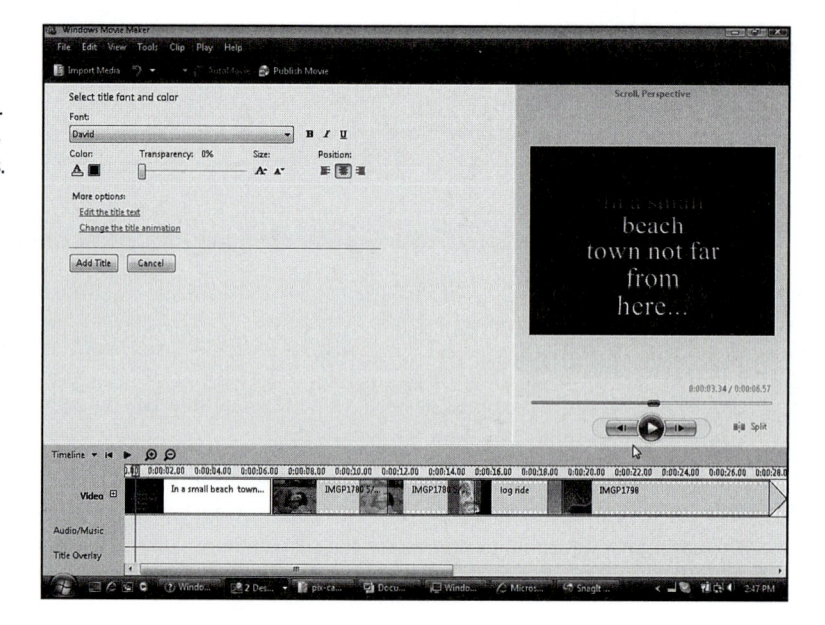

Saving Your Project and Saving Your Movie

You can save your work in Windows Movie Maker in two ways. To save the various parts of your movie (the clips on the timeline and the storyboard), click File, Save Project. By default, your Windows Movie Maker Project (.MSWMM) file is saved to the My Videos folder. Give your project a name and save it.

You should save your projects frequently during the creation and editing process. If you don't and a system lockup or power outage occurs, your clips will remain, but the structure and timing of your film will be lost, and it will be back to the digital "cutting room" to start over.

Here's how to save your movie:

1. Click File, Save Project.
2. Give it a name and location, and click Save.

Now your project is saved and safe. You can open it again and fine-tune the project, add to it as you capture more video, or whatever. You can close Movie Maker, if you want, and then open it and open the project. All the items in the collection should appear, as should the timeline and storyboard, just as it was when you saved it.

Next, you need to make sure you are happy with the movie. When you are, you *render* it, which means to output it in the desired format. This can take a little time, so be ready to take a coffee break while your computer chugs away. Because rendering takes time, it's best to do a dry run of your final movie. You can see it in the little preview window or full screen. Simply choose Play, Play Timeline. If you're happy with it, great. If not, edit as necessary. When you're satisfied with the movie, try outputting to the target medium and see how it looks.

1. The easiest way to render is to simply click Publish Movie in the command bar. A wizard begins, and you'll see the following choices: This computer, DVD, Recordable CD, Email, and Digital Video Camera.
2. Make one of those choices based on where your movie is headed. If you're going to view the movie only on your PC, just save it to This Computer. Use the DVD option if you have a DVD recorder and want to burn a DVD that will play on most DVD players (in a computer and standalone ones). Use Email to make a small version of the movie that is more easily sendable over email. (The image size will be small.) If you choose Digital Video Camera, the movie will be sent out the Firewire cable and back to the camera. Be sure to insert a blank tape in the camera (or one you want to record over), and be sure that the write-protect tab on the tape is not set to On). Click Next.
3. Depending on your choice, you're asked for additional details that pertain to your choice. For example, if you choose to send the movie over email, you'll watch as the movie is rendered and then dumped into a new email that you have to address. If you chose Save on a CD, you'll be prompted to insert a blank CD. If you choose DVD, you'll be told that the movie will render; then Windows DVD Maker runs and you burn the DVD from there. (See Chapter 12, "Sound Recorder, DVD Maker and other Multimedia Tools," for coverage of DVD Maker.) In some cases, you're be asked to make settings that affect the file size and movie quality (see Figure 11.12). Also reported are the size of the final file and how much space is left on your hard drive. (The hard disk is always used as the intermediary for rendering.) The file is written from the hard disk to the target destination.

Figure 11.12
The options for saving a movie to the hard disk.

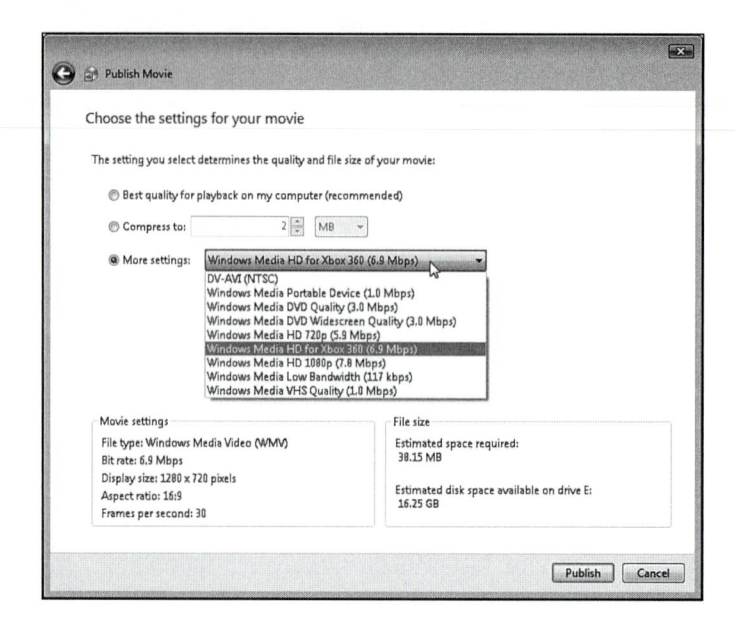

> **NOTE**
>
> Movies saved to a recordable CD are stored by using Microsoft HighMAT technology. A HighMAT (High-performance Media Access Technology) CD can contain audio, video, and pictures. HighMAT-compatible consumer electronic devices recognize how the content is organized on the CD and enable users to play content using the displayed menus. The recordable CD can be played back on a computer as well. Be aware that some older standalone DVD players won't recognize this format and will fail to play the movie. You'll have to experiment and do a little research. Newer consumer DVD players recognize more formats (such as rewriteable CDs and DVDs), but older ones don't.

Preparing Movie Maker Files for the Web

Movie Maker 2 had an option for publishing to the Web, with lots of options for output type and size. It must have been deemed too complicated for typical Movie Maker users. We agree that professional web video developers are probably using Final Cut Pro or Avid or Vegas Video, and all kinds of spiffy tools for preparing files for the Web, but we still think there should have been a Web output choice in Movie Maker 6, especially considering the popularity of YouTube. But no matter. You can post to sites such as YouTube with what Movie Maker renders. Just save to your hard disk after you check your favorite video site's requirements. When we wrote this, YouTube accepted only AVI, MOV, and MPG formats. They were not accepting WMV (Windows Media Video), though, so you have to choose AVI from the wizard settings, which you will notice is relatively uncompressed and creates large files. Next, click the Compress To button and set your maximum acceptable file size. (For example, the maximum file size YouTube allows (at the time of this writing) was 100MB. (But in today's world, such things don't stay constant for long.) Movie Maker does its best to compress your movie to your target size file.

Typically, for Web posting, you output several different versions and allow the viewer to choose among them, based on connection speed. You also need a Web server that can serve video. Services on the Web do this; check with your ISP or web server administrator. Numerous Web video hosting and sharing services exist now; just Google for them. As of this writing, 10 we found were Eyespot, Google Video, Grouper, Jumpcut, Ourmedia, Revver, Videoegg, Vimeo, vSocial, and YouTube.

4. A progress bar meter informs you of the process. After the movie is saved, click Yes to view it immediately. Windows Media Player loads the movie and plays it for you.

Regardless of the destination of your movie (such as in an email), you'll probably want to make a copy for safekeeping. Consider saving it on your computer or on a CD. You might also want to back up the project file and possibly the source files.

AutoMovie

Movie Maker 6 has a feature called AutoMovie that lets you relinquish control to Movie Maker for creating transitions and effects that suit a few preprogrammed genres. You might try playing with these to see what you think. It's a quick way to get something put together without having to drag in your transitions. If you don't like the quick movie it creates, you can just choose File, Undo Quick Movie and try another prefab setting.

Follow these steps for creating a quick AutoMovie:

1. Import your video from camera, videos, pictures, and audio.
2. Click that collection in the Collections pane, or Ctrl+click to select specific items in a collection to use only those items (videos, stills, music) in your movie. If you open a collection and don't select any specific items, all are used. Your selected elements must amount to at least 30 seconds of running time for AutoMovie to begin. (Stills are given 4 seconds each, by default, so 10 stills would equal 40 seconds.)
3. Click Tools, and then click AutoMovie.
4. On the Select an AutoMovie editing style page, select a style that sounds good to you. Each one has a description (see Figure 11.13). Try each one so you learn what they do. If you don't like the effect, click File, Undo AutoMovie, and try the next one.

Figure 11.13
Creating a quick movie with AutoMovie.

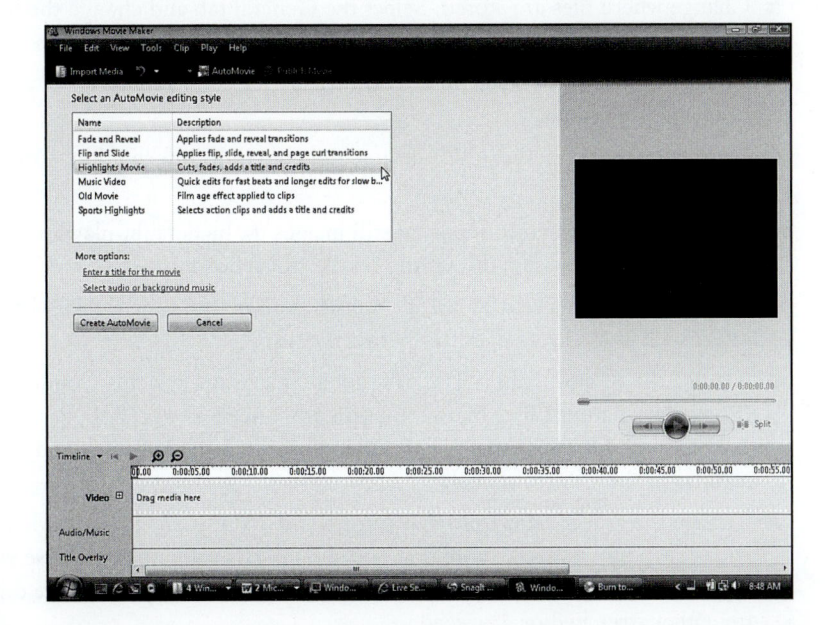

5. Under More options, click Enter a Title for the Movie. On the Enter Text for Title page, type the text that you want to use as the title.
6. If you want to add music to the AutoMovie, under More Options, click Select Audio or Background Music and browse to the file you want.
7. You can adjust the mix of audio on the Audio/Music track and the background audio from your video files and imported tapes. For example, you might want to have the background music quieter so that you can hear the people speaking on the video tape. Or for a music video you might want to totally mute the audio from the video tape you imported. To increase the volume of an audio clip on the Audio/Music track, drag the slider toward Audio/Music. To increase the volume of the audio on the Audio track that is part of a video clip, drag the slider toward Audio from Video.
8. Now that the style, titles, and sound options are set, click Create AutoMovie; wait for the clips in your movie to be added to the storyboard/timeline and for optional effects, titles, and music to be added.

How long this takes depends on the length of the movie and what is in it. After AutoMovie sets up the movie on the timeline, you can publish it or edit it just as you can any Movie Maker project. You'll likely want to move clips around a bit.

You might find that AutoMovie is a quick way to get a movie going, especially if the order of clips is not that important.

MOVIE MAKER ADVANCED SETTINGS

If you start using Movie Maker a lot, you'll want to dig into some of the more advanced settings. Click Tools, Options, and poke around. You might want to consider altering the following:

- Change where files are stored. Select the General tab and change the temporary storage area to a drive that has a lot of room on it.
- Change the AutoRecovery time. It's normally set to 10 minutes, but you might want it to be more frequent.
- You can turn off whether title, author, and copyright information is stored in the metadata of the file.
- You might want all your imported still images to, by default, play longer on the timeline than 5 seconds. Change the setting on the Advanced tab.
- Likewise, you can alter the default transition time (the time it takes for a transition effect such as a fade or dissolve) between clips.
- Change the output from NTSC (National Television Systems Committee) to PAL (Phase Alternating Line). Normally, you don't need to worry about the PAL versus NTSC setting because that is determined based on the Regional and Language Option settings in the Control Panel.
- Change the aspect ratio from 4:3 (normal old TV format) to 16:9 (what HDTV and widescreen movies use). Note that you should generally not try to use videos of both aspect ratios as sources in your movies. Some portions of your movie can end up looking either stretched or squeezed.

Beyond Windows Movie Maker

Windows Movie Maker provides an enjoyable and powerful way to experiment with digital movie making. Movie Maker 6 is actually powerful enough that I have started using it for small projects rather than using my favorite full-blown video editor. When you just want to suck in some pictures from your digital camera and "Ken Burns them" (Ken is a popular historical documentary maker shown on PBS a lot) with voiceover, or take those little video clips from your digital video camera or camcorder and quickly burn a DVD, Movie Maker is the freebie for the job. If you get hooked on video creation (which is likely to happen if you have the patience, the eye, and the disposition), you might want to try more powerful editing programs. Numerous video editors now work directly with DVD recorders and have fancy multitrack timelines for editing multicamera shoots, zillions of effects, color correction, industry-standard SMPTE time code, the capability to produce "edit decision lists (EDLs)," and all kinds of other stuff.

Some of the more popular low-priced video-editing programs on the market include Ulead's Video Studio, MGI's VideoWave, and Dazzle's DV-Editor SE. Some IEEE-1394 DV capture cards, TV capture cards, and VGA/TV capture cards might also include various video-editing programs, including the previously mentioned ones.

More powerful DV-editing programs that you might consider include Ulead Media Studio Pro, Sony Vegas Video (highly rated), and Adobe Premiere, which can be paired with Adobe AfterEffects for exciting special effects. Here's where to go for more information:

- Adobe Premiere: www.adobe.com
- Media Studio Pro, and Video Studio: www.ulead.com
- VideoWave: www.roxio.com
- Dazzle's lineup of digital video-editing programs and hardware: www.dazzle.com
- Keyspan 1394 Firewire desktop card: www.keyspan.com
- SIIG 1394 Firewire laptop card: www.siig.com
- External 1394 Firewire and USB hard drives: www.maxtor.com, www.iomega.com, www.seagate.com, and www.hammer-storage.com

Help Sites and Resources for Digital Video

In addition to the product websites listed in the previous section, check out these resources:

- ***Digital Video Magazine***—Look for the big "DV" on the cover for news, reviews, and tips for great digital video. The web companion to the magazine is located at www.dv.com.
- ***VideoMaker Magazine***—Get advice on good videographic techniques, as well as buyer's guides and reviews. The web companion to the magazine is located at www.videomaker.com.

Troubleshooting

You Can't Control the DV Camcorder in Windows Movie Maker

My DV camcorder is detected by Windows Movie Maker, but the only way I can capture video is by using the camera's own controls to advance the tape. What should I do?

Some DV camcorders work better with Movie Maker than others. If you can capture video by controlling the camera yourself but not with Movie Maker's onscreen buttons, check with the camera vendor for updated driver software. Otherwise, keep doing what you're doing. Remember that you can always cut extraneous information from a scene with the editing features in Movie Maker.

Windows Says You Don't Have the Privileges to Publish a Movie on a CD

If the Remove CD Burning Features setting in Group Policy is enabled by the system administrator, this prevents CD burning. Perhaps your system admin has set this protection for security purposes. (It makes it harder for people to lift large amounts of data from a PC.) To view and make changes in Group Policy, the account that you use to log on must have the appropriate Administrator privileges.

You Can't Publish Your Movie to the DV Camera

Not all cameras accept data input on the 1394 connector. Yours might not. Check the camera's manual.

The First Few Seconds of Your Movie Are Missing After You Publish to Tape

Some cameras start up too slowly, so when Movie Maker starts sending the data stream to the camera, data is lost at the beginning of the recording. Create a short 5-second or so title that is blank at the beginning of your movie. That will give the camera time to start up.

You Get an Error Message That the Temporary Files Exceed the 4GB FAT-32 File Size Limit

The FAT-32 file system has a file size limitation, and video files are often huge. This is one reason you should convert your data drive to NTFS; it has a much higher file size limit. You can use a nondestructive conversion program such as Acronis Disk Director Suite (works quite well at adjusting partition sizes as well) for this purpose (see www.acronis.com). Refer to Chapter 27, "Managing Hard Disks," for more information about file systems.

Tips from the Windows Pros: Adding Impact to Your Movies

Effects and Transitions Are Overrated

As with the use of excessive fonts in a printed document, fancy transitions and effects are overrated. Unless you are producing a sports video with instant replays and lots of statistics screens, and need to keep your audience on the edge of its chair, or perhaps if you're making a music video, you'll want to err on the side of being a tad conservative with your transitions and effects. Page tears, wipes, speckle-dissolves, flips, and the like should be reserved for occasional use or they lose their impact. They also distract viewers from your story, reminding them that they are watching a movie instead of letting them stay engaged in the magic of the moment. It's a little like an actor in a play speaking directly to the audience and breaking the "fourth wall." We suspend disbelief when we watch a movie, and that is just the point. If an effect works to advance the mood or the action, that's great. You have to decide whether it does that. For example, using a black-and-white filter on a clip or the entire timeline can certainly give your movie a serious feel—even make it seem like a period piece. (Of course, it helps if you can light your set like Alfred Hitchcock did and set up great scenes with stark contrasts and dramatic angles.) Still, I recommend using this classic effect cautiously. In general, put more attention on good audio and good background music that matches your scene, and keep most of your transitions to flat cuts.

COLOR AND EXPOSURE CORRECTION

The best video-editing programs make a science out of color correction because professional films need consistent coloring from scene to scene and from camera to camera (when multiple cameras are used on the same set). In real life, color balance changes depending on whether you are outside, inside under tungsten light, inside under halogen light, outside at sunset, outside at midday, or outside at dawn, and we don't notice it much. But on a screen in a movie, it can be unsettling if the color balance is off. Most of today's mini-DV cameras have "auto white balancing," to try to minimize variation between scenes you shoot. But if you are serious about movie making, turn off that feature, especially if you are moving the camera around and have different light sources at a shoot (for example, lamps in the room and also outdoor light coming in through a window); as you pan the room, the camera will change its white balance. This will change the color of people's faces, among other things.

Movie Maker doesn't have color correction built in, unfortunately, but it does have a brightness filter that can help fix a similar problem: mismatched clip brightness. With video cameras so sensitive these days due to efficient CCDs (the chips in the cameras that see the image and turn it into a digital signal, called Charge-Coupled Devices), many people shoot movies in low light, such as indoors. Often the results are decent enough, although it's not uncommon for the image to become "noisy" (grainy). This is because the electronics in the camera amplify the low signal, including parts of the digital signal where the chip can "see" just well enough, due to low light. The cameras try their best to eliminate this noise and, as a result, might give you a darker picture with less noise instead of a brighter one with more noise. The upshot is that you might have clips on your timeline that do not match in brightness. Preview your storyboard or click through your thumbnails, and notice if there is too much variation between your clips' brightness. If one is too dark or too light, adjust it with the Brightness, Decrease or Brightness, Increase effects. If one application of the setting isn't strong enough, add it again. You can add the same effect (any effect) more than once, for double or triple the effect.

Who's Zoomin' Who(m)?

Zoom is a great feature on a camera, whether it's a still camera or a video camera. Nature photographers love zoom because they can get closer to their subject than they ever could in person. When zoom is added to a video, it either can create desired emotional tension or, if used incorrectly, can become distracting. In the early days of "Wayne's World," the *Saturday Night Live* spoof of two guys making a cable TV show in their basement, Wayne and Garth regularly included "unnecessary zooms" as a tell-tale feature of their budget, low-brow videography. You can, too, if you want, and it is tempting. You might be taping your daughter's performance in the school play and you want to show the entire stage, the audience, close-ups of your daughter, how the principal is reacting, and so on. This all requires panning and, of course, zooming. In real TV, they use multiple cameras, each one trained on a particular person or angle, and the editor uses flat cuts to pull it all together. It looks natural and undistracting. And you will notice that when they do zoom, there is a very carefully choreographed zoom and usually a pan at the same time. This gives an added sense of motion. Instead of just zooming into the center of the established show, you pan up or down or to the side a bit while at the same zooming. A professional cameraman knows where she is headed and judiciously gets there. One trick to help you not miss your target is to keep one eye on your camera's screen (or eyepiece) and the other one open and looking into the room. Head slowly for your target and zoom *slowly*. Use a tripod if you must zoom in a lot. Turn on your image stabilizer feature. (Optical is best, but most cameras have at least a digital optical stabilizer.) This takes out some of the wiggles when you are zooming and zoomed in. Shaky zooms, quick zooms, and unnecessarily busy zooms are the hallmark of cheesy home movies.

Finally, when you do zoom in on faces, it's okay to have the top of their head cut off a bit. This is common in film and TV. Notice this in movies and in interview shows. Your target is the person's face and eyes; you don't have to include their entire head and hair.

CHAPTER 12

SOUND RECORDER, DVD MAKER, AND OTHER MULTIMEDIA TOOLS

In this chapter

Become a Recording Star   350

Windows Sound Recorder   350

Volume Control   351

Viewing Images   354

Recording to DVD   357

Troubleshooting   360

Become a Recording Star

As with past versions of Windows, Windows Vista comes with a simple tool to help you create and do basic modification of sound files—the Windows Sound Recorder. Although it is admittedly utilitarian in nature, this tool enables you to add audio notations to everything from word-processing documents to slideshows and enables you to create slideshows and photo CDs. This chapter covers the functionality of the Windows Sound Recorder, revisits the Windows Photo Gallery, and offers some troubleshooting tips for when things don't come out sounding exactly right.

This chapter also touches on the other multimedia utilities that come with Windows Vista. Because many of the accessory programs fall into discrete categories, such as communications, multimedia entertainment, or system tools, look to relevant sections of this book to find coverage of such tools. This chapter covers the more basic, yet still quite useful, tools that don't fit neatly into a pigeonhole.

Windows Sound Recorder

Windows Sound Recorder has been included with Windows since its earliest days. Windows Sound Recorder is not feature rich by any stretch of the imagination—in fact, it enables you only to record an audio file and save it to the hard drive on your computer. Whereas the older version of Windows Sound Recorder enabled you to record an audio file, change the speed of the recorded playback, and do basic editing and conversion of the saved output, this functionality is missing with Windows Vista. Windows Recorder can work with files that are in the Windows Media Audio (.wma) or Windows Wave (.wav) format.

> **NOTE**
> If you are using Windows Vista Home Basic or Windows Vista Business, your Sound Recorder files are saved as Windows Wave (.wav) files instead of Windows Media Audio (.wma) files.

To start Windows Recorder, click Start, All Programs, Accessories, Sound Recorder. This gives you the Sound Recorder interface, shown in Figure 12.1

Figure 12.1
The Windows Sound Recorder main interface.

Really only one option is available: Start Recording. Pressing this button enables you to record audio using your PC's microphone. When you have recorded all the information you need, press the Stop Recording button. When you stop recording, you get a Save As dialog box asking you where to save the recorded output, as shown in Figure 12.2.

Figure 12.2
The Save File As dialog box, which defaults to the Documents folder.

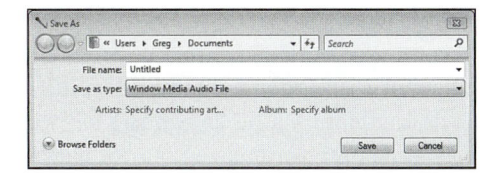

Here you need to enter a filename to save the file; you can optionally enter Artists and Album information (see Figure 12.3). If you enter the Artists and Album information, you can access this information inside Windows Media Player and the Documents folder later.

Figure 12.3
The Save File As dialog box, with optional tag information entered.

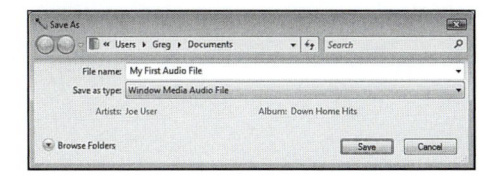

The file location defaults to the Documents folder, but you can change the location where the file is saved by clicking the Browse Folders button and browsing to the folder where you want to save the file.

If you saved the file in the default location, you can click Start, Documents and see the file that you just recorded; if you specified the artist and album information, it is displayed here as well (see Figure 12.4).

Figure 12.4
An audio file in the Documents folder. Notice the tag information that was entered earlier.

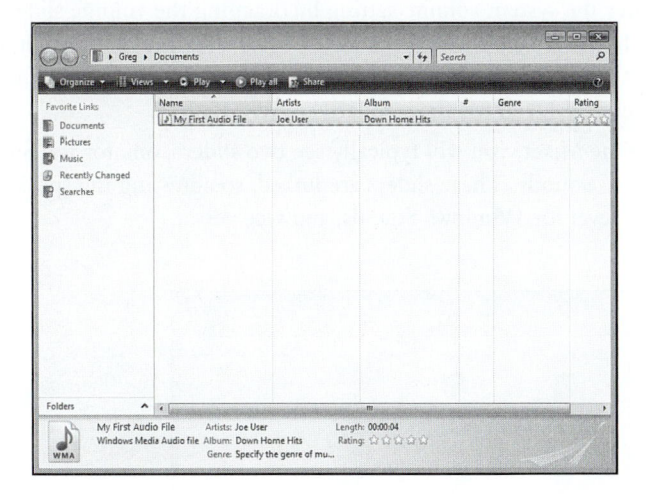

VOLUME CONTROL

The Volume Control accessory is basically a no-brainer. It provides a pop-up volume control sporting balance, mute, and other controls for your audio subsystem. Whether you're playing radio stations from the Web, playing CDs from your CD drive, listening to TV if you have a TV tuner card, or recording sound files, you need access to these controls from time to time. Of course, if you don't have a working sound card installed, this accessory isn't available—or, at least, it doesn't do anything. A little-known fact for many people is that this accessory has two sets of controls—one for recording and one for playback.

1. To open the standard volume controls, simply double-click the little speaker icon in the notification area on the Windows Vista taskbar (see Figure 12.5).

   You can alter the system volume setting by dragging the volume slider up or down. You can mute the output by clicking the picture of the speaker at the bottom of the column. If you want to see another volume control, you can select Mixer at the bottom of the column. Figure 12.6 shows the volume control exposed when you press the Mixer button.

Figure 12.5
The volume mixer, as seen when you click the speaker icon in the notification area.

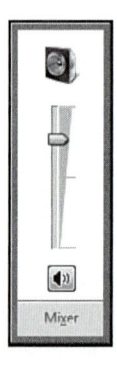

2. You can alter the system volume setting by dragging the volume slider up or down. You can mute the output by clicking the picture of the speaker at the bottom of the column. If you want to see another volume control, you can select Mixer at the bottom of the column. Figure 12.6 shows the standard volume control.

3. In the Volume Mixer, you will typically see two sliders, one for the Speakers and one for the Windows Sounds. These sliders are linked, so adjusting the speaker volume changes the volume level for Windows Sounds, and vice versa.

Figure 12.6
The basic volume control for setting playback volume.

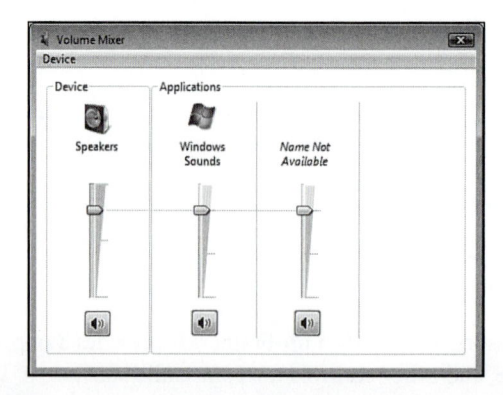

If you are doing any sound recording, be sure to view the recording controls, too. You can access both the playback and recording level controls as described next.

> **TIP**
>
> To quickly adjust or mute the sound output from your system, or to adjust the master volume level (useful when the phone rings), click the little speaker icon in the notification area, near the clock.

The controls you see by following these steps are a simplified version of the overall volume settings. To access the detailed volume settings, choose Start, Control Panel, Hardware and Sound, Manage Audio Devices; double-click the Speakers entry in the Playback tab in the Sound window; and choose the Levels tab. Your sound system's capabilities and possible changes that past users have made to the application's settings determine the format of the volume controls you see. On one of my computers, the controls look like what you see in Figure 12.7.

Figure 12.7
The detailed volume controls.

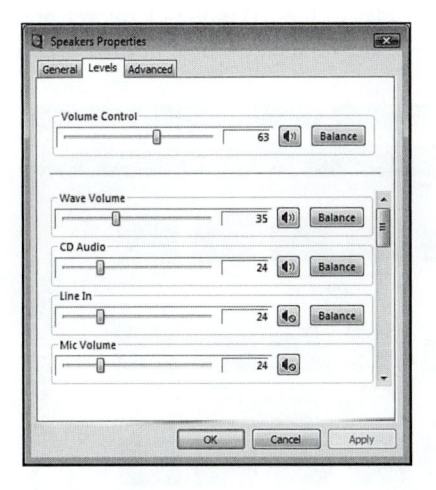

In this window, you can manually adjust the individual levels of the output elements. You can mute individual output elements by clicking the small speaker icon to the right of the volume sliders.

If your system suddenly doesn't have any sound, **see** *"No Sound" in the "Troubleshooting" section at the end of this chapter.*

If you are using a sound card with support for more than two speakers, you can also run basic diagnostics and choose the speaker configuration here by clicking the Speakers item in the Playback window and choosing the Configure button.

VIEWING IMAGES

Windows Vista gives you two ways to view your pictures:

- Through Windows Explorer
- As a slideshow

Which one is better for you? That depends on whether you're looking for immediate gratification or for long-term storage and enjoyment of your pictures. The following sections explain how to use both options.

USING WINDOWS EXPLORER TO VIEW YOUR PHOTOS

If you select the Windows Explorer option when you read the photos from your flash memory card, view pictures stored in the Pictures folder or a subfolder, or view the contents of a folder containing photos, Windows Explorer activates several special features designed to make working with your image files easier.

Instead of the normal large icons display of files, Windows Explorer presents you with a thumbnail display of all the photos in the folder, as shown in Figure 12.8.

Figure 12.8
Windows Vista automatically uses the thumbnail view when you view a folder that contains photos.

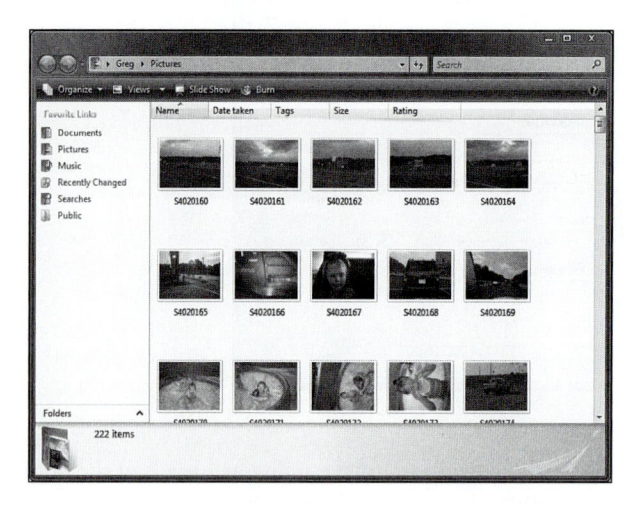

The File menu in Explorer also changes when you select a photo, providing the following options:

- **Edit**—Opens the photo in Windows Paint
- **Preview**—Opens the photo in the Windows Photo Gallery
- **Print**—Opens the Photo Printing Wizard
- **Rotate Clockwise/Counterclockwise**—Rotates the picture in 90-degree increments
- **Set As Desktop Background**—Puts your digital masterpiece on the Windows desktop

- **Open With**—Selects another program to open this picture
- **Send To**—Sends a photo to a compressed folder, a removable-media drive, or the Documents folder; creates a desktop shortcut; or provides other destinations
- **Properties**—Displays file properties

> **TIP**
> If you don't see the menu bar in Windows Explorer, you might need to choose Organize, Layout, and choose the Menu Bar option.

> **TIP**
> By default, the Edit menu in Explorer uses Windows Paint to edit photos. If you prefer another image editor (and who wouldn't?), right-click a photo and select Open With. Windows Vista displays Paint and Windows Picture and Fax Viewer, as well as Choose Program. Click Choose Program and select the program you want to use, if it's listed, or click Browse to locate the program you prefer. To keep this choice for all files of the same type, check the Always Use the Selected Program box. You also can search the Web for a suitable program. Click OK when you're finished.

USING A SLIDESHOW

Making a slideshow of your pictures once required you to fire up a program such as PowerPoint and click and paste your way through your digital stack of photos. If all you want to do is view your photos onscreen, you no longer need any third-party software: Just select the slideshow option when it's available within a folder.

The Windows Vista slideshow option is very simple: It sequences the images in a folder with 5 seconds per photo and continues to show the pictures in a loop until you press the Esc key on your keyboard. You can also use the slideshow controls at the bottom of the screen or the keyboard commands in Table 12.1 to control the show.

TABLE 12.1   SLIDESHOW CONTROL KEYS

Action Desired	Keys to Press
Go to the previous picture in the folder	Left arrow, up arrow, or Page Up
Go to the next picture in the folder	Right arrow, down arrow, or Page Down
Play or pause the slideshow	Spacebar (press once to pause, again to play)
Exit the show	Esc

If you leave the mouse still for 2 seconds, the slideshow controls disappear and you can see the entire picture. To get the controls back, simply move the mouse.

TIP

> If you don't want to display all the images in a folder during your slideshow, just select the ones you want to view with Ctrl+Click or Shift+Click, and then click the Slideshow button at the top of the screen. Only the slides you've selected are displayed. If only one picture is selected, the slideshow will not automatically advance—it will require you to use one of the keys in Table 12.1 to advance the slides.

When you get the slideshow sequenced exactly as you want, you can save the slideshow to burn to a DVD for playback later in a standard DVD player. To do this, choose the Make a Movie button in the toolbar. This opens Windows Movie Maker and imports the pictures selected from the Photo Gallery into a slideshow movie. From here, you can add music, modify transition effects, or change the order of the slides (see Figure 12.9).

You can find detailed instructions on the use of Windows Movie Maker in Chapter 11, "Producing Videos with Windows Movie Maker."

Figure 12.9
Windows Movie Maker imports the currently selected photos automatically.

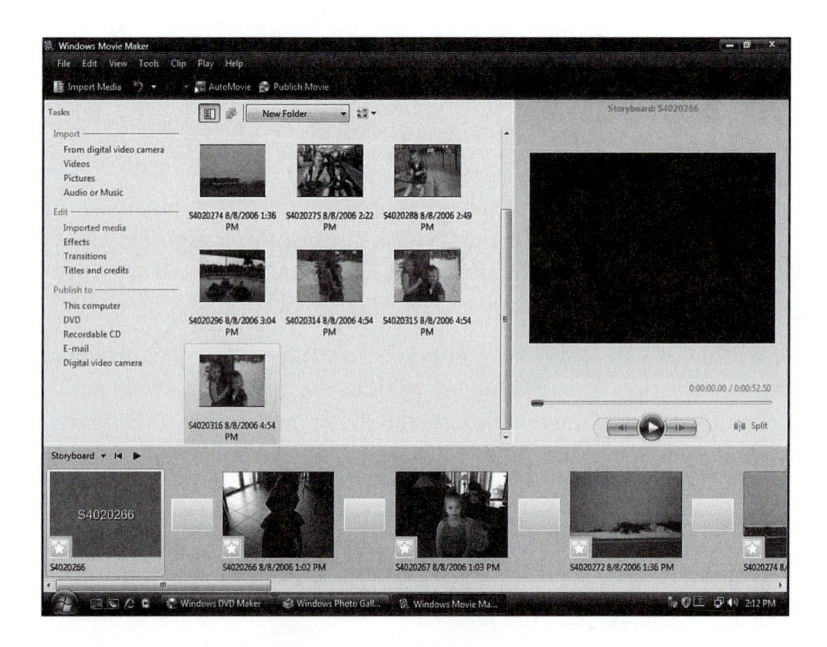

When the movie is set exactly as you like it, click the Publish Movie button in the toolbar. You then are prompted for where to publish the movie —if you have a DVD recorder, choose DVD to write the slideshow to a DVD and click Next. Windows opens the Windows DVD Maker, with the slideshow you've just created as the media to burn.

Using Your Own Photos as a Screen Saver

Want to show off the pictures of your spouse or kids, but you've run out of room on your desk? You can use the pictures you scan or copy from a digital camera to create a screen saver.

To set up your favorite pictures as a screen saver, create a folder with Windows Explorer and copy the pictures you want to use to that folder. Then open the Control Panel and choose Appearance and Personalization, Change Screen Saver. Select Photos, click Settings, and browse to the folder containing your pictures. You can change the speed at which the pictures are displayed and optionally shuffle the contents of the folder.

If you want even more control over the pictures displayed, you can choose to use all the photos in the Photo Gallery (discussed more in depth in Chapter 9, "Windows Imaging Tools") and narrow the selection using tags and ratings.

Recording to DVD

You might have turned here to learn how to publish your DVD movie from Movie Maker in Chapter 11, or you might want to burn a DVD for another reason, such as for committing a slideshow to disk for playing on Grandma's DVD player back home, or for safely storing and transporting more data than will fit on one (or several) CD-RWs. For these purposes, Windows Vista enables you to commit your content to DVD.

Unlike previous versions of Windows, Windows Vista comes with a DVD-burning application built into the operating system. You can open the DVD burner by choosing Start, All Programs, Windows DVD Maker (see Figure 12.10).

Figure 12.10
The Windows DVD Maker main screen.

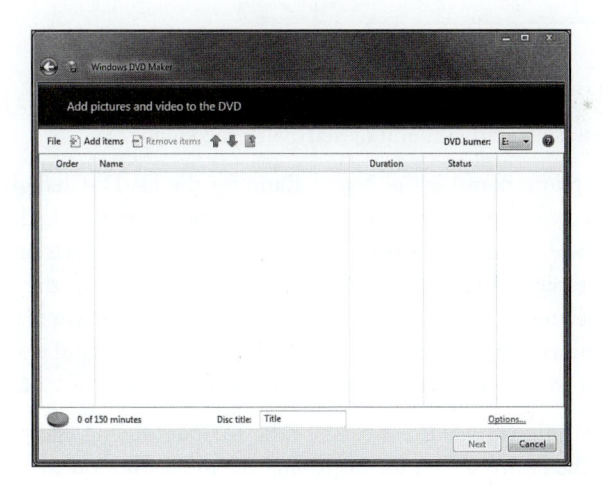

From this screen, you can click Add Items and browse for video files or still photographs. After you select the movie files or pictures, they appear in the main screen in the order they will be played on the DVD.

TIP

If you want to make a quick slideshow from pictures stored on your computer, click Add Items, and Ctrl+click any pictures you want to add. Windows DVD Creator makes a slide show out of the photos you selected; you can change the order the slides are presented in the main screen.

When you have the media elements in the correct order, you can change the advanced options for the DVD by clicking the Options link (see Figure 12.11).

Figure 12.11
Advanced DVD options.

The options in the first box control how you see the video after the DVD is put in the DVD player—whether you start with a menu or start with the video.

The second set of options controls the Aspect Ratio for the DVD. Changing this option to `16:9` enables you to create wide-screen DVDs suitable for playing on high-end television sets. Encoding a movie at the `16:9` aspect ratio on a wide-screen television, the DVD movie will take the entire screen. If you play a movie that was encoded with the `16:9` aspect ratio on a standard television set (`4:3`) the movie will be "letterboxed" (have black bars at the top and bottom of the movie). This is to allow standard television sets and computer displays to show all the content from a widescreen movie without losing any content.

The standard aspect ratio (`4:3`) is the inverse of the `16:9` setting—it allows standard television screens to use the entire screen for displaying the movie, but on wide-screen televisions the movie will be "pillar boxed" (have black bars on either side of the movie). The format you use depends mainly on your source media.

The options in the third box enable you to use either the National Television System(s) Committee (NTSC) or Phase-Alternating Line (PAL) format for the video. NTSC video is the format of choice for the Americas; PAL is used most everywhere else. Unless you need to play the movie you're creating on a PAL-compliant DVD player, it's generally best to leave the setting as NTSC.

You can also change the DVD burner speed. This should be set as high as you can without creating "coasters" (DVDs that had a failure during writing, rendering them useless).

When you finish on the main pane, click Next. You are presented with the Ready to Burn Disc dialog box, shown in Figure 12.12.

Figure 12.12
The Ready to Burn Disc dialog box, where you can change display options for the movie.

From this screen, you can change the style of the menus for the DVD movie, change the text and/or styles for the menu, or modify the settings for the slideshow in the movie. By clicking the Slide Show button in the toolbar, you can add audio to the slideshow or change the other settings for the slideshow (see Figure 12.13).

Figure 12.13
Slideshow options in the Windows DVD Maker.

After you add music to the slideshow, change the length of time between slides, and change the transitions, you can preview the slideshow by clicking the Preview button. When you're satisfied with the show, click the Change Slide Show button.

When everything is completely ready to go, click the Burn button. If you don't have a blank DVD in the drive, you're prompted to insert one. From here, make a cup of coffee and go to lunch; burning a DVD generally takes much longer than a CD, for two reasons:

1. The amount of data on a DVD is much greater than on a CD.
2. The write speed of most modern DVD writers is much slower than that of a CD writer.

The DVD Maker encodes the movie, which is very CPU intensive. After the movie is encoded, DVD Maker burns the DVD, ejects it, and gives you the option to burn another copy of the DVD you just created.

> **TIP**
>
> If you want to make multiple copies of the same movie, it is best to do it now; by burning multiple copies at once, you bypass the lengthy encoding phase.

TROUBLESHOOTING

NO SOUND

I'm adjusting the volume control from the notification area icon, but I don't get any sound.

Total loss of sound can be caused by myriad goofs, settings, hardware conflicts, or program malfunctions. As a result, troubleshooting your sound system isn't always easy. One tip is in order here: If you're using a laptop computer, ask yourself whether the sound stopped working after you hibernated or suspended the system. I've noticed this problem on several laptops, and this bug might not have been worked out of Windows Vista for your sound chip set. Try rebooting the computer, and see whether the sound comes back to life. Another thing to look for is a manual volume control on the computer. Many laptops have a control that you can turn or push, often found along the right or left side of the computer itself. Such settings override any settings within Windows. If you have a set of powered speakers attached to your computer, make sure they are plugged into power and are turned on. I often forget to do this and then wonder why I have no sound. For serious problems, you should consult other chapters in this book that deal with the Control Panel and the Device Manager. If none of these remedies works, you might have a bad sound card, or you might need a new device driver.

ERRORS BURNING DVDS

I constantly get errors when writing DVDs in the Windows DVD Maker, and the DVDs I create don't play in either a standalone DVD player or my computer.

Writing DVD files can sometimes be a tricky and resource-intensive task. Many modern DVD drives have more than enough file cache to prevent buffer underrun errors, but, as with CDs, sometimes problems happen. The best way to prevent underrun errors when burning a DVD is to choose a slower burning speed in the properties of the movie in DVD Maker.

CHAPTER 13

WINDOWS MEDIA CENTER

In this chapter

Windows Media Center—What's the Hubbub?   362

The WMC Hardware   364

The WMC Functions   370

Some Tricks of the Trade   378

Troubleshooting   387

Tips from the Windows Pros   388

Windows Media Center—What's the Hubbub?

Windows Media Center (or *WMC* as I'll refer to it from here on out) is included in Windows Vista Home Premium and Windows Vista Ultimate editions. All other versions of Vista do not include the WMC components. WMC is an outgrowth of Microsoft's interest in evolving the common PC into a multimedia entertainment center. Due to strict hardware requirements, which include a TV tuner capture card with built-in MPEG-2 video encoding and decoding, a high-end graphics card with a minimum of 64MB of video memory, DVD recording, a fast processor, and other goodies, this operating system is usually purchased as a preloaded component on a new PC. With the advent of the Vista Anywhere initiative, however, for the first time, users without media center compatible hardware can purchase the hardware separately, install it, then upgrade the operating system to an appropriate version of Vista and enjoy the Windows Media Center on their PC.

> **NOTE**
> Complete books have been written about Windows Media Center Edition (the predecessor to Windows Media Center equipped versions of Vista), and I expect new books will be written about WMC as well, although I believe that within a week's time of experimentation, a fairly savvy user can discover the ins and outs of WMC on her own. It certainly helps to have a bit of a primer, however, with some tips scattered throughout. That's what this chapter is.

WMC adds the capability to do the following with a large TV-like interface using a remote control:

- Display and record TV shows
- Listen to cable, broadcast, and Internet FM radio
- Rip and play music CDs
- Play DVDs
- Manage and display your digital photographs
- Record DVDs

Of course, as you know, you can rip music CDs, play DVDs, and display your digital photographs using Windows Media Player and Windows Photo Gallery, as described elsewhere in this book. WMC essentially puts a new skin on those functions and integrates them with TV viewing and a few other goodies.

As we know, Microsoft (often standing on the shoulders of innovative giants) has helped push the industry to new heights, or at least to take a deep breath on the technology ascent, by codifying standards. Whether through fostering cooperation among technology companies or by forcing its own agenda, it doesn't much matter. Progressive standards for such things as data CD recording, sound and video cards, high-resolution color displays, energy conservation, standardized I/O ports, Plug and Play interfaces, as well as greater overall computer performance have often been championed by Microsoft. Standards, of course, serve Microsoft because its bread and butter depend on selling operating systems that can run reliably on as many brands and models of PCs as possible.

WMC is an exciting milestone in the evolution of personal computer operating systems that began in earnest back when the first spec for a multimedia PC (MPC) was issued by Microsoft. I remember writing, even somewhat wistfully, about the MMPC in my earlier Windows books (3.11 and 95). At that time, it was a big deal to include in PCs the now-ubiquitous sound cards and CD-ROM drives. (I recall purchasing my first outboard SCSI-based CD-ROM drive from Toshiba for $600 and change.) The next step (learning from the woefully underpowered MPC spec) was the Entertainment PC 97 spec. The minimum system requirements for the Entertainment PC 97 are a 150MHz Pentium chip, a 256KB Level 2 cache, 32MB of memory, 3D audio, and the Universal Serial Bus. This spec was a subset of the Simply Interactive PC (SIPC) spec, to be technically accurate.

Of course, bloatware applications and the increasing speed demands of the now-gluttonous Windows itself also spurred the demand for quicker PCs. Unfortunately, this comes at some cost to the environment as well as our pocketbooks, as we feel obliged to continuously dispose of older computers and upgrade to newer ones. On the upside of this unceasing speed and size war (the belief that bigger and faster are always better) comes the likes of WMC. Were it not for lightning-fast CPUs, video cards, hard drives, front-side buses, DVD drives, and inexpensive color displays, PCs couldn't begin to tackle exotic, highly data-intensive tasks such as DVD playback and TV recording.

> **TIP**
>
> You'll find a lot of Media Center information at these URLs: www.xpmce.com and www.microsoft.com/windowsxp/using/mce/default.mspx

Following on the heels of the popular TiVo digital video recorder (DVR) and competing systems such as ShowStopper (from Panasonic) and ReplayTV (from ReplayTV), the WMC attraction to many is driven primarily by its capability to mimic a DVR. Although, as I mentioned, WMC also gives you MP3, CD, and DVD playback and digital photo slideshows, we could already do those with Windows Media Player and the Windows Picture and Fax viewer, respectively. The only difference in those departments is the delivery medium: WMC lets you control the show from the comfort of your armchair, using a remote control. The show itself plays on your TV or, preferably, through your TV projector in your home theater.

The idea of a computerized house—especially for entertainment delivery—is so appealing that home builders are beginning to build WMC machines, along with in-wall wiring and integrated large plasma screens into newly built homes. Some developers are doing this on a large-scale basis, in hundreds of homes. This helps housing developers differentiate themselves from the competition.

Speaking of competition, alternative hardware and software packages have been on the market for some time that do all that WMC does, but it's more of a mix-and-match approach to creating a home entertainment PC. For TV viewing and recording, you have to add hardware such as a TV tuner/video card to your PC, be sure that the sound card and TV tuner work together, and so on. You can record and play back TV and even do text searches through recorded captions, looking for hot words in, say, a newscast. A quick search on the Web reveals a few well-liked products, including

- Cyberlink PowerCinema
- SageTV
- Snapstream Beyond TV

Some of these programs have numerous features that WMC is missing, such as web-based control and media-server capability.

THE WMC HARDWARE

Suffice it to say that WMC machines have serious hardware requirements. At the most, an WMC machine has

- A remote infrared (IR) sensor that enables the remote control to communicate with the computer and that also controls the cable or satellite set-top box
- A fast graphics card for smoothly displaying moving images such as video and TV playback
- A TV tuner that captures the television signal from a cable, satellite, or antenna source
- A hardware encoder that enables you to record TV shows from cable, satellite, or antenna to your computer's hard disk in realtime
- A TV output jack so that you can display Media Center content on a television connected to your computer
- A digital audio output that allows you to integrate digital audio from your computer into an existing home entertainment system

Windows Media Center feature set can be read at www.microsoft.com/windowsvista/features/forhome/mediacenter.mspx.

High-Definition TV (HDTV) Requirements
WMC is not limited to watching, or recording, TV in standard definition format. High-definition TV shows, movies, and DVDs can also be watched or recorded on your computer. Unfortunately, you need different hardware to do so than the average WMC computer has available. So, just what will you need to achieve your goal of watching high-definition video? Well, at a minimum consider the following:

- A high-definition input source—This can be a cable box, satellite (I have a Hughes HR10-250 with DirectTV HD programming and TiVo software for DVR), or broadcast (over the airwaves) TV with an output your computer TV tuner can use as an HDTV input source.

At the time of this writing, the current crop of HDTV tuners for computers supports only broadcast (coaxial antenna) inputs. This means you can record only broadcast HDTV shows on your computer unless you are also fortunate enough to have an HD cable or satellite box with an HD Coax output that you can connect to your computer's HDTV tuner. Tuners with HDMI, DVI, or YPbPr aren't far away, in my opinion.

- A high-definition TV tuner for your computer—If you are purchasing a new Windows Media Center computer, make sure it has an HDTV-compatible tuner. If you are upgrading your existing computer or building your own, look for a new tuner with HD capabilities built in.
- A powerful video card—Video memory is used during the overlay process to display the output from your TV tuner. HDTV requires more video memory to display on your monitor without losing frames than standard definition TV (SDTV). Look for a video card with a minimum of 128MB, with 256MB recommended and 512MB preferred if you plan to use multiple output monitors.
- A vast amount of storage—High-definition video requires an enormous amount of disk storage. Video compression is also a requirement to lower the storage needs to a reasonable, cost-effective solution. To give you an idea for comparison, my TiVo box that uses MPEG2 video compression and has 500Gb of storage can record 515 hours of standard definition TV but only 77 hours of high-definition TV. Luckily, terabyte disk drives have recently become available at reasonable cost.
- An HDTV display—Although you can watch HDTV on your computer, you really will not get the most out of it without an HDTV display of 40 inches or more to view your HDTV shows.
- A significant budget—External terabyte disk drives as of this writing cost about $300 for a bare-bones model. Internal drives are available, but you can expect to pay a premium for them. Video cards with 512MB of video memory cost a couple of hundred dollars. The cost of HDTV displays, fast processors, fast RAM, and so on, all add up.

THE NEW WMC PC FORM FACTORS

As of this writing, numerous brand-name manufacturers provide complete ready-to-run systems running Media Center Edition 2005. If you can't find what you want in a brand-name system, you can have a local computer builder build the perfect system for you. If it meets the minimum requirements for Windows Vista Home Premium or Windows Vista Ultimate, it should be upgradable to the latest edition of WMC.

WMC PCs come in a wide variety of form factors that push the outside of the envelope of what we call a PC. They range from boxes that look much like PCs to those that most definitely do not. Figure 13.1 shows an example of two WMC PCs. As you can see, there's a trend to blend the look of the PC with home-entertainment gear such as a stereo receiver. This is becoming the preferred form factor for audiophile types who don't want their WMC machine to take up a lot of space or to look like a computer. This design also allows the computer to be rack-mounted or stacked with other A/V gear.

Due to the miniaturization of large hard disk storage, DVD writers, and bright wide-screen LCDs, another class of WMC-based computer has recently emerged: portables. These power-packed portable entertainment systems come in three flavors—a laptop computer on steroids, a Tablet PC, and a small dedicated playback-only WMC machine. Figure 13.2 shows an WMC Qosmio laptop from Toshiba and a dedicated, small WMC portable tablet device from Samsung. The Qosmio has a TV tuner card in it. However, some WMC laptops do not record TV, owing to the lack of a TV tuner card. Virtually all the small, portable WMC tablet-format devices are playback-only devices as well.

Figure 13.1
WMC PCs take major liberties with the physical appearance of a PC.

Figure 13.2
Laptops can run WMC, too, if they sport the necessary hardware. Dedicated tablet-format WMC machines are available as well.

As of this writing, you can find a list of WMC PC manufacturers at www.microsoft.com/windowsxp/mediacenter/evaluation/products.mspx.

Is Windows Media Center Based on Home or Business Versions?

Good question. I've had some debate with friends and colleagues about this. Media Center Edition 2004 was based on Windows XP Professional. It included the capability to join a domain and encrypt the file system. When Media Center 2005 came out, these features were no longer available, indicating that the 2005 version was based on the Home version of XP. This inability to join a domain handicapped business users and indicated that Microsoft's primary focus for MCE was the home user. That decision must have generated a lot of negative feedback to Microsoft because the current version of Media Center Edition is included in a home version (Windows Vista Home Premium) and a business-capable version (Windows Vista Ultimate).

Can I Upgrade My NonMedia Center PC to a Windows Media Center PC?

You might be wondering, "Can I install WMC on my own PC if I have the right hardware?"

You can if you have the right hardware and purchase a copy of Windows Vista Home Premium or Windows Vista Ultimate. Both of these versions include Media Center and support a wide range of hardware. You can purchase both of these versions as upgrades for previous Windows MCE computers; however, you do not need an WMC computer to use these products. You can also purchase a standard version and replace your current operating system. Some compatible video/TV cards are

- AVerMedia M150
- LEADTEK WinFast PVR2000 TV and FM Tuner Card
- HAUPPAUGE WinTV-PVR-250MCE
- NVIDIA DualTV
- ATI Technologies, Inc., HDTV Wonder
- ADS Tech Instant HDTV PCI

> **TIP**
> You'll find a lot of Media Center hardware information at the Microsoft Partner Directory at www.microsoft.com/windowsxp/mediacenter/partners/directory.mspx.

Microsoft makes a keyboard for WMC machines, which I suggest picking up. It has useful keys along the top edge to control movies, skipping commercials, and adjusting the system volume. Figure 13.3 shows a typical remote.

Figure 13.3
Example of an IR remote control designed for WMC.

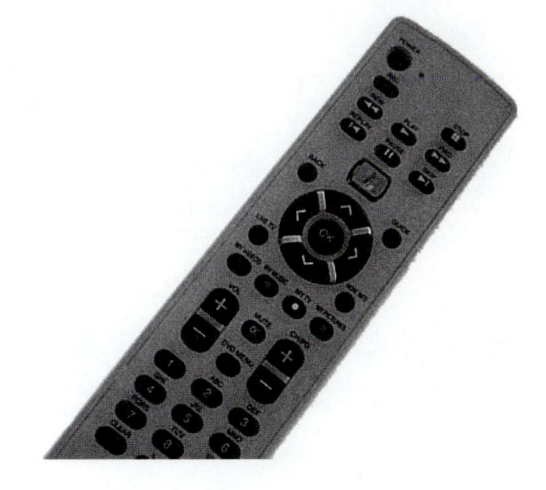

If you want to research how to upgrade to WMC or create a homebrew WMC box, you might want to do some web surfing. Here are some links that came up during a brief hunt:

   www.extremetech.com/article2/0,1697,1741030,00.asp

   http://en.wikipedia.org/wiki/Windows_Vista

   www.theosfiles.com/os_windows/ospg_Windows_Vista_Home.html

   www.theosfiles.com/os_windows/ospg_Windows_Vista_Business.html

   www.winsupersite.com/showcase/winvista_editions.asp

Basic WMC PC Hookup

If you've had the joy (or job) of setting up a home entertainment system or home theater, you know how convoluted the wiring can become. Assuming you have mastered the typical scenario with a TV or projector, an A/V switch, multiple video input devices, Dolby 5.1 (or 7.1) sound, and consolidating your remote controls, installing a WMC computer into your A/V arsenal is a relative no-brainer. Figure 13.4 displays a sample of the potpourri of gear you can integrate into an WMC setup.

Figure 13.4
A Vista WMC PC can serve as a creativity and entertainment center, integrating a mess of equipment.

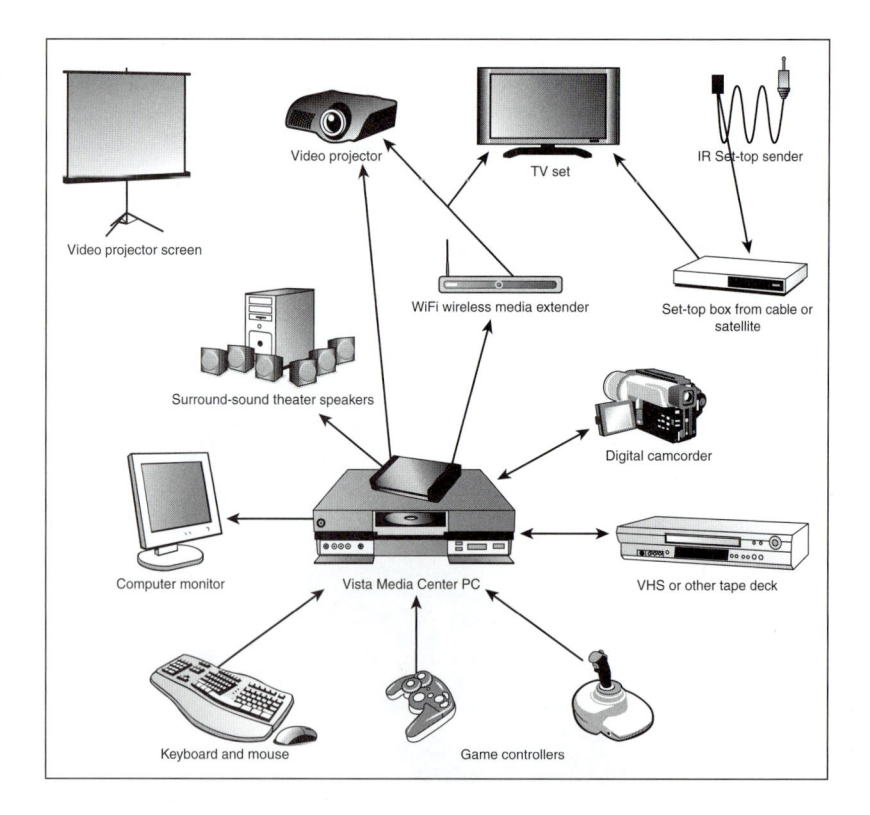

Leaving out the Cray computer, five digital high-def video dishes on the roof, and the four subwoofers you're likely to have accumulated over time if you're a home theater nut, Figure 13.5 shows a typical basic WMC hookup.

Figure 13.5
A typical WMC wiring diagram.

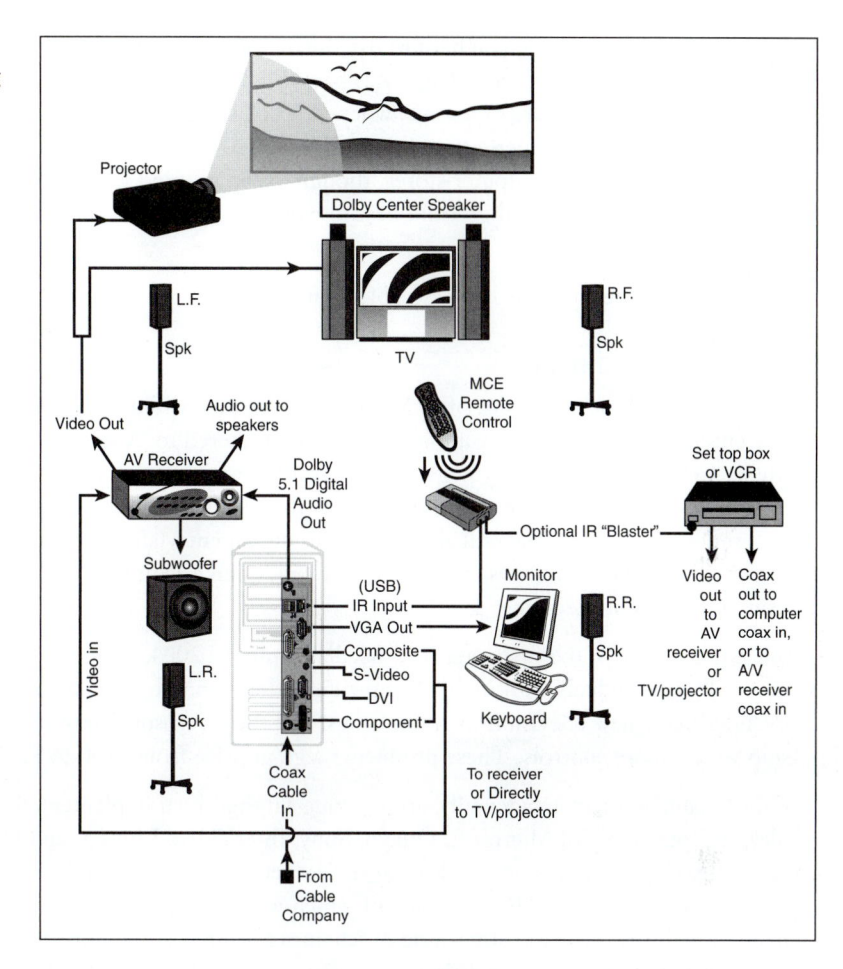

Notice in Figure 13.5 that a relationship exists between the cable or satellite box and the infrared blaster that connects to the IR receiver for the WMC remote control. This allows the single remote control to also control the cable/satellite box.

Also note that, depending on your computer's video card, you have more or fewer options for output to external display hardware (projectors, TV, and computer video displays). Most WMC computers have at least a composite video output with which to drive your TV or projection unit. For the cleanest image, though (especially if you are using a projector), you need a higher-resolution video connection. The next step up is an S-Video output. Obviously, your TV/projector must have an S-Video input for this to work. Moving up from there, many projectors have a VGA input, just like on the back of a computer monitor. I run a long VGA extension cable from my WMC machine to my projector using such a cable. I can run the projector in 1024×768 mode with a nice resolution and even do word processing or web surfing on my 10-foot screen, sitting in an easy chair with a wireless mouse and keyboard.

For the ultimate in clarity, you have to use the digital video interface (DVI) as your conduit to the projector. My projector (Sanyo Z2) has a DVI connector, as does my PC. The catch here is that DVI cables are expensive, whereas VGA cables are not, and S-Video and composite video cables are super cheap. Some sites online will sell you DVI cables at a fraction of what they charge at computer stores, though. Keep in mind when considering your connection type that clarity will go from best to worst, in this order: DVI, VGA, component, S-Video, composite.

An excellent cable source is www.csccable.com.

Media Center Extender

After folks catch onto the idea of WMC computers, they will not want to be trapped in the one entertainment room the computer is directly tethered to. A series of gadgets called the Media Center Extender lets you gain access to PC-based content for any connected (wired or wireless) TV or monitor within the house. To this aim, Microsoft is focusing on a new generation of products that will allow access to digital entertainment, such as live and recorded TV, photos, movies, and music that resides on a Windows Vista Media Center PC from any room in the home.

Since the release of the first version of Media Center in 2004, a variety of hardware makers have released products with Media Center Extender technology embedded in them. This includes many new televisions, set-top boxes, and the Microsoft Xbox 360. Set-top boxes ship with remote controls. These products range in price from $100 to $250.

Other manufacturers, incidentally, are working on their own implementations of this grand idea, independently of Microsoft. Onkyo, Sony, InterVideo, Linksys, and Hewlett-Packard are some of the manufacturers releasing similar hardware devices and systems, some of which will work with WMC and some of which will be for their own platforms. We're beginning to see many (mostly wireless) schemes for integrating more and more of the home with the computer-based entertainment system.

> **TIP**
> Here's a video about how to set up an Xbox 360 as an extender: www.microsoft.com/windowsxp/mediacenter/videos/Xbox360connection.asx.

> **TIP**
> Here's a good FAQ on Media Extenders: www.microsoft.com/windowsxp/mediacenter/extender/mcefaq.mspx.

The WMC Functions

As mentioned earlier in this chapter, WMC is simply a program that runs as a shell on top of Vista. The program path is %SystemRoot%\ehome\ehshell.exe.

> **NOTE**
>
> The "eh" means "electronic home," which is an overarching Microsoft initiative for developing the networked home of the future, based on Microsoft technology.

The shell has a large-print GUI that at first suggests it is designed for people with vision disabilities. It is certainly a boon to the visually impaired, but the thinking behind the interface was to make it easier to read on a TV screen. If you've ever used WebTV, you know what I mean—reading normal computer-sized text on a TV set can send you running to the optometrist for a checkup.

When you boot a WMC-enabled computer, it comes up looking like any normal Vista PC. Nothing notable happens until you run the Media Center program. Your desktop and Start menu sport a little green icon that launches the Media Center interface. Then, you see the WMC Start screen. When it appears, maximize the window; it then looks like the screen shown in Figure 13.6.

The number of options on the Start screen varies depending on the hardware in your computer. If you don't have an FM radio function on your TV card, for example, you won't see any radio functions (as is the case here).

Figure 13.6
A typical WMC Start screen.

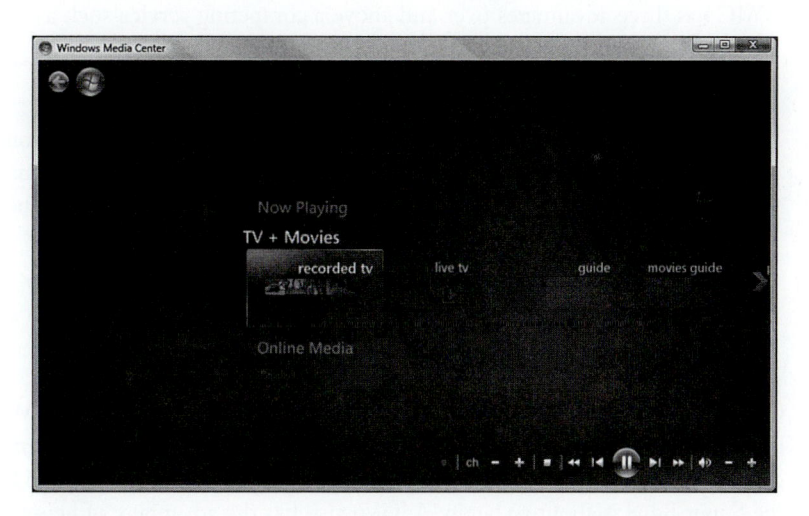

The following sections discuss the central features of WMC, but with emphasis on a few tricks for each one instead of telling you how to use them. Their use is actually straightforward, and you really don't need me to explain it to you. Suffice it to say, you engage each function of WMC by scrolling vertically to select the main function, or horizontally to select a subfunction, and then simply clicking the name (or alternatively using the remote control's up and down arrows to highlight the name) and pressing the Select button.

TV + Movies

Although it's novel that you can use your computer to watch TV, who cares? Personally, I never thought there was much worth watching on the tube anyway. Then again, I never have made a science out of TV program selection the way some people have. So, I end up channel surfing when I have some downtime, missing the beginning of a show I would have liked to see. Or maybe a friend tells me about an excellent program after the fact, when it's too late.

The electronic TV Guide in WMC has made a friend out of TV again and changed my watching habits. The Guide is your online TV programming guide, so you can see what is on TV and perform searches for programs you might want to see, prearrange recordings of upcoming programs, and so forth.

Using the Guide, I'm finding that there *are* some amazing shows from time to time—excellent documentaries, music programs, and old movies, for example. I can cull through two weeks' worth of upcoming programs using keyword searches and hone in on something I'd like to see. For example, recently I ran a keyword search on "music" and landed on a documentary about Joni Mitchell. I also set the DVR to record some weekly series, such as PBS's *Nova* and the daily broadcast of the BBC news. They stack up on my hard drive, and I can watch them whenever I get around to it.

WMC has three advantages over and above a competing service such as TiVo:

- I don't have to pay a monthly subscription charge (or lifetime charge) to access a TV programming guide.
- Nobody is keeping tabs on my viewing habits. (TiVo reports what you watch, and this data is used as input for various marketing databases.) Even if you can opt out of the data collection and the collection is anonymous, many people don't bother. In essence, many TiVo watchers' habits are being studied en masse.
- I don't need to rent or purchase another piece of hardware. I already have my computer, and it's a multifunction machine. It does a lot more than just tune in and play back TV shows.

On the downside, though, TiVo has some more-advanced features than WMC. For example, if you have both satellite and cable feeds, TiVo can combine both program guides into a single onscreen grid. And, because it's a simple machine, it's not likely to go haywire just when the Super Bowl is about to begin. A TiVo also has the advantage of being a dedicated device. For example, if your WMC machine is recording the latest episode of *America's Funniest Home Videos*, you're probably not going to be able to effectively play Doom 3.

Setting Up the Guide

Before you can benefit from the Guide, you have to make some settings:

1. Go to the Start page.
2. Click Tasks.
3. Click Settings.

4. Click TV.
5. Click Guide.

The Guide downloads new data at a time you choose on the Settings screen, keeping the listings up-to-date. It does this in the background while you're doing other work. Your computer has to be on, however.

The Guide displays channel and network information, titles and times of shows, and information about each show. You can drill down to check out an upcoming show to determine whether it's one you've seen, for example. You select a show and then click More Info/Details to do this.

> **TIP** To program WMC to record an upcoming show, highlight the show in the Guide and press the Record button on the remote or on the keyboard. One press records the individual show. Press it again to record the series.

When you're watching live TV, the DVR is at work in the background, even if you're not recording a previously scheduled show. It records what you are watching live, so you can press the Pause button (onscreen, on your keyboard, or on the remote) and go grab a snack. While you're gone, the recording continues, although the playback is paused. This way when you return, you just press the Play button, and you're back in the groove, right where you left off without missing any of the action. This is possible only because an WMC computer is fast enough to enable the DVR to record one thing and play back another simultaneously. Thus, it's writing to the hard drive and reading from it more or less at the same time.

WMC is interleaving the hard-disk reads and writes so intelligently that no recorded or played back frames are dropped. Caching of video data in separate RAM buffers helps make this possible. If you're not taxing the system heavily by doing other highly disk- or CPU-intensive computing in the background, this works flawlessly. WMC is given high priority by the operating system by default, and I haven't noticed dropped data, even with a large number of other tasks running.

> **TIP** If you want to record (and save) a program you're watching live, press the Record button on the remote or keyboard. Otherwise, the program isn't saved to disk.

Owing to this same slight of hand, you can also record a live show in the background and view a previously recorded one—a nice feature that other DVRs can perform. You cannot, however, watch one live show while recording another live show unless you have multiple TV tuners installed. This is because a TV tuner can tune to only one channel at a given time.

> **TIP**
>
> We all hate commercials, and DVRs let you skip them quite easily. If your WMC computer has a keyboard, it probably has a Skip Ahead key. So does your remote. This key jumps the playback ahead 29 seconds per press. Because commercials are typically 30 or 60 seconds long, one or two presses skips a commercial. I've gotten good at guessing the right number of presses to skip a spate of commercials in just a couple of seconds. If you get too aggressive, you'll need to back up. Each press of the Replay key on the remote backs you up 7 seconds.

Heavy Disk Consumption in Live TV

Unfortunately, the file format Microsoft used for the DVR (`<filename>.dvr-ms`) is not very efficient, especially if you use the highest-quality settings. They appear to be equivalent in size to the digital video files you would import from a DV camcorder. Figure about 3GB for a one-hour show. A half-hour show consumes about 1,576,600 bytes.

Microsoft's decision not to use a more compressed file format such as WMV or DivX isn't sensible, in our opinion.

One hour of Xvid or DivX consumes roughly 350MB—almost a factor of 10 difference! Even normal DVD data is smaller (about 2GB per hour). There are ways to convert Microsoft's format and store it as Xvid or DivX, but the couple of programs that are out there are still in beta stages as of this writing (for example, tvshowexport).

This flaw seriously limits the number of shows you can keep on the hard disk at any one time, especially at the highest-quality setting. You can choose a lower-quality setting as the default for all recordings, but you might not like the results. The four levels of record quality are fair, good, better, and best.

Table 13.1 shows the amount of hard disk space used for recording video, as well as the data rate used.

Table 13.1 Hard Disk Consumed Per Hour of Recording

Quality	Per Minute	Per Hour	Data Rate
Fair	20.48MB	1.2GB	2796Kbps
Good	24.06MB	1.41GB	3284Kbps
Better	34.82MB	2.04GB	4754Kbps
Best	45.57MB	2.67GB	6221Kbps

> **TIP**
>
> You can lower the quality level as a global default but still set the quality to a higher level for individual programs you intend to record. Use the Advanced Record settings for the program in question.

Particularly if you set the Guide to record a program on a regular basis, free disk space quickly evaporates. After you finish watching a recorded program, WMC asks whether you want to keep it or delete it—a nice feature that helps you keep house. If you continue to retain programs, or you record a slew of them without watching them, be prepared for the inevitable: You'll be out of space for recording more programs.

What's worse, the indirect effect can be doubly disappointing. Recorded shows you haven't watched yet or ones you wanted to keep until space becomes short can, under certain circumstances, be automatically deleted to free up room for new shows. I learned this the hard way when first using the DVR. I had been collecting *The Simpsons* episodes and documentaries. Then, I set up live TV to record the news. I went on a trip for a week, leaving the computer on to record the evening news each day. When I returned, *The Simpsons* episodes and the documentaries had vanished, and all I had on disk was a lot of old news.

The recorder has global settings that determine what happens when disk space is exhausted. The settings are reached as follows:

1. Go to the WMC Start page.
2. Select Tasks, Settings, TV, Recorder, Recording Defaults.
3. Change Quality using the mouse or +/- keys on the remote.

> **TIP**
>
> The Live TV DVR has a setting for the location of the hard disk volume and folder that will be used to store your recordings. If you don't have a large internal drive or don't want to tie up an internal drive, consider getting an external FireWire and USB 2.0 drive for that purpose. I use an external 250G FireWire drive for this purpose. You get to the setting by selecting Tasks, Settings, TV, Recorder, Recorder Storage. The drive you choose cannot be a network drive, and it needs a minimum of 5GB free space.

If you want to ensure that you don't lose a recording, set it to Keep Until I Delete. If you want to ensure that it's not erased before you watch it, tag it Keep Until I Watch. Similar archive settings can be applied to an ongoing series of recordings, as well. For example, I was recording three daily news programs (PBS, BBC, and ABC), and the shows were piling up, eventually preventing the DVR from recording any additional programs. Because old news isn't news, I decided I wanted to keep news shows for only one week. Figure 13.7 shows the screen for configuring such a setting.

> **TIP**
>
> To learn more about the format of .dvr-ms files and how they are recorded, check out this page: msdn.microsoft.com/library/default.asp?url=/library/en-us/dnwmt/html/dvrfilechanges.asp.

Figure 13.7
Each program or program series can have individual settings.

> **TIP**
>
> To play back a `.dvr-ms` file on an XP Home, Pro, or Tablet PC, you need the following: Windows XP Service Pack 2 and later; a Direct Show DVD decoder engine, such as Power DVD; Win DVD; or a DVD Playback Pack: www.microsoft.com/windowsxp/using/setup/expert/bridgman02april15.mspx.
>
> And you need the following hardware: Any Intel-compatible CPU running at 1GHz or higher, a video card with 32Mb, and onboard video RAM.

> **TIP**
>
> Read "Tips from the Windows Pros" at the end of this chapter if you want to learn a way to save your recorded videos in one-tenth the space and even remove commercials.

PICTURES + VIDEO

Pictures + Video is simply a slideshow presenter and video manager. You point the program to the directory (the default is Pictures) containing your digital photos, and you can step through the pictures manually or let the slideshow feature run automatically. Actually, the slideshow effect is quite pleasing because it does a cross-fade and some panning around in a bit of a random way to give a little more professional feel to your slideshow. (Some people call this the "Ken Burns" effect, after the documentary film maker Ken Burns who so often uses old still images in his productions.)

Personally, I have all my photos stored in my external FireWire drive because there are so many of them. So, I have to direct Pictures to find them there. You can do this by adding a folder to watch (Tasks, Settings, Library Setup) or creating a shortcut to the actual source of your files and putting that in Pictures:

1. Arrange Windows Explorer so that you can right-click and drag your photo folder into Pictures.
2. When the context menu pops up upon release of the left mouse button, select Create Shortcut Here.
3. When you go to Pictures in WMC, you'll now see a folder there with the name of your photo folder. Open that folder to see the pictures.

When you play your slideshow, it begins at the level of the open folder. If you have your photos arranged in folders like I do, first drill down into the folder to be included in the slideshow. Photos in the folders below the current level will not be displayed. You can use the remote control or keyboard to step through the slides.

If you just stick in a memory card from your camera, you can view those photos without even loading them onto the hard disk. Just do the following:

1. Insert a memory card.
2. When prompted by Autoplay, select View Pictures using Windows Media Center.
3. The Play Slide Show menu appears with the memory card selected. The name varies depending on the type of media inserted. For example, if your pictures are on a memory stick the media is called MEMORYSTICK. If you are using a SD memory card the media is called Microsoft WPD FileSystem driver.

You can add music to your slideshow (and even a playlist consisting of a number of files). This is a nice feature to spice up your slideshows. This way, even if you are boring your audience with endless pictures of your baby, at least they'll have some music to listen to. Do this:

1. From the WMC Start screen, go to Music and start your music playing first.
2. Return to the WMC Start screen and go to Pictures.
3. Click Tasks, Settings, Pictures to choose whether the song information shows onscreen while songs are being played.
4. Move back a page by clicking the Back button at the top of the WMC window. (It looks like a green left arrow.)
5. Start your slideshow by selecting Slide Show.

> **TIP**
> You can print a picture when stepping through images from WMC. When the picture you want to print is onscreen, press the More Info/Details button on the remote control. Then, choose Picture Details. Next, choose Print from the menu and Print once more when prompted to confirm your selection to print the image.

Music

This feature works in conjunction with Windows Media Player. WMC puts its interface (skin) on top of Media Player. You can play audio CDs, copy CD tracks to your music library, or play your library. When playing CDs or files from the library, song and album information (if available) is displayed onscreen. If you use another program—such as iTunes, MusicMatch, or WinAMP—to organize and play your MP3, WMA, or AAC files, you're out of luck unless you also import your files into Windows Media Player. But be careful that you don't rearrange your files in WMP and then mess up your song organization in your other player.

For dropping in a CD and playing it straight away, do the following:

1. Run WMC or press Start on the WMC remote.
2. Insert the CD. It should start to play.
3. If you want to copy the CD files into your music library, select Copy CD.

When your MP3 files are all organized using Media Player, run Music. You can play back tunes and view visualizations on your TV or computer monitor. You have to use Media Player to create playlists, manage your files, and modify ID3 tags (things like genre, artists' names, and so forth), however.

Click the Visualize button to switch the screen to a series of sometimes-lovely and mesmerizing motion graphics. WMC uses the same visualizations as Windows Media Player. You can find and install new ones by searching the Web for "visualization" and downloading ones designed for Windows Media Player.

Some Tricks of the Trade

For the most part, using the WMC is intuitive. Some areas, however, can use a bit more information to get the most out of the WMC. In this section, we look at a few of these items such as

- Playing DVDs and other video files
- Viewing TV on your HDTV or projector
- Broadcasting TV on your TV or projector
- Burning DVDs from recorded TV
- Setting Parental Controls

Playing DVDs and Other Video Files

After setting Windows Media Center as the default DVD player, simply inserting a DVD into a DVD-ROM drive should result in Media Center playing the DVD. To go to the DVD menu (where you can change scene selections, change languages, or choose your DVD's special features), press the DVD Menu button on the remote.

You can change the language, closed captioning, and remote control option defaults for all DVD playback in the main settings screen in WMC. (Go to the Start screen and select Tasks, Settings, DVD.)

Setting Media Center as the Default DVD Player

The first time you insert a DVD in the DVD-ROM drive, the AutoPlay Wizard will prompt you to select a default application, as shown in Figure 13.8. One choice is to play the DVD with Windows Media Player; another is to play it with WMC. If you have another DVD player, that might be an option, too.

Figure 13.8
Setting the default application for DVD playback.

> **TIP**
>
> If you want to change your default AutoPlay settings, you can do so in the Control Panel. Choose Hardware and Sound and then choose AutoPlay. For a quicker method, right-click the DVD drive icon in Windows Explorer and choose Open AutoPlay.

To make WMC the default application, just follow these steps:

1. Check the Always Do This for DVD Movies check box.
2. Click the Play DVD Movie item in the DVD Movie options. Your DVD will begin playing in Windows Media Center.

> **TIP**
>
> This sets the Media Center to play only DVDs by default. It doesn't apply to CDs. If you want to play CDs in WMC, you have to set that separately.

If the video doesn't look right on your screen due to some kind of distortion, you might have installed some third-party DVD player software. Remove the third-party software to correct the problem.

> **TIP**
>
> Vista includes the Microsoft VC1 decoder that will play back Blu-ray and HD-DVD titles. However, to handle the playback of Blu-ray and HD DVD titles, you will need a DVD drive that can read those formats and a third-party player, such as PowerDVD from Cyberlink. With a little work, you can even get Vista Media Center Edition to recognize when you have inserted a Blu-ray or HD-DVD disc and invoke the assigned program to run. As of SP1, MCE will not play hi-def DVDs in its own interface. Instead, it has to switch to another HD player.

Viewing TV Shows on Your HDTV or Projector

If you want to watch your recorded or live TV on something other than your computer screen, your computer must, obviously, have an output your TV can accept. I discussed this earlier in the chapter. Most high-definition TVs and many projectors have DVI or VGA connectors. These are the preferred methods to use to connect the display output of your WMC computer to your HDTV or projector.

The key to obtaining the best picture is to choose an output resolution that corresponds to your HDTV or projector display resolution. HDTV supports 480i/480p at 720×480, 720p at 1280×768, and 1080i/1080p at 1920×1024. If your projector is not an HDTV projector, you need to refer to your documentation to determine the best output resolution (usually 640×480, 800×600, or 1024×768) to use for your VGA connection.

The truly nice feature about using your HDTV, or projector, as the output of your WMC computer is that your HDTV becomes the primary display of your computer. If you use a wireless media center keyboard with built-in trackpad (mouse), you can operate your entire computer from your couch. This opens up many possibilities for family entertainment—from using your WMC computer as a digital video recorder (DVR), to playing music from your CD collection, watching DVD movies, playing video games, or even browsing the Internet.

If your WMC computer is in one room, and your HDTV or projector is in another room, one easy method to connect them is to use a Microsoft Xbox 360. To connect your WMC computer and Xbox 360 you need the following:

- WMC computer with a wired or wireless network connection
- Microsoft Xbox 360 with a wired connection, or the optional wireless network adapter
- Network hub for a wired connection, or wireless access point, router, or hub for a wireless network connection
- Optional Xbox 360 Universal remote control
- Standard TV with composite inputs or a high-definition TV with YPbPr inputs

After you have assembled the required hardware, the next step is to set it up, connect the various cables, and then configure the software. The basic process for a wireless network is as follows:

- Install the wireless network adapter to the Xbox 360.
- Connect the Xbox 360 AV HD adapter cable to the Xbox 360, set the Xbox 360 switch to HDTV, and connect the other end of the cable with three RCA male connectors color-coded green, red, and blue to your HDTV YPbPr inputs—green to green, red to red, and blue to blue. Then connect the audio inputs using the other set of color-coded connectors, yellow, red, and white, to your HDTV audio inputs—red to red and white to white. Leave the yellow connector unused.
- For a standard TV with composite inputs set the Xbox 360 switch to TV and connect the other end of the cable to your TV's composite inputs. Connect yellow to yellow (video), red to red (right audio), and white to white (left input). If your TV has one audio input, use the red one.

> **TIP**
> If you have a problem connecting your Xbox 360 to your TV/HDTV, check out the Xbox 360 support page at www.xbox.com/en-US/support/systemsetup/xbox360/console/tvhdtv.htm.

- Set your HDTV to use the YPbPr inputs. If you use a standard TV, set it to use the composite or monitor input.

> **NOTE**
> Optional Xbox AV cables are available with S-Video and VGA connectors.

- Boot the Xbox 360 and configure the wireless network card to match the settings in your wireless access point, router, or hub.
- Open the WMC and go to Start, Tasks, Add Extender, and step through the Extender Setup Wizard.

At this point, your Xbox 360 should be live and capable of accessing all the content on your WMC PC. You can use the Xbox 360 universal remote, or your WMC remote, to control the displayed Media Center Extender menus.

Broadcasting TV Shows to Your TV or Projector

Getting your TV signal to your TV can be a problem if your WMC computer is not in the same room as your TV or if you do not have a Microsoft Xbox 360. Your cleanest and clearest signal is over a DVI cable, but these are expensive—especially in any significant length. No matter which kind of cable you use (S-Video, composite, component, VGA, or DVI), you'll likely end up drilling holes into your house or apartment, or at least snaking the cable around the room and possibly tacking it around your baseboards. What a hassle.

If you're like me, you'll want a quick-and-dirty solution, at least as proof of concept, until you have that free Saturday to venture into the depths of your crawl space under the house and install the more permanent wiring. So trek down to your local electronics store (for example, RadioShack) and purchase a short-range A/V transmitter/receiver combo designed for this purpose. I bought a set (RCA brand) for about $100. These transmit and receive composite video and accompanying stereo audio. You connect the small transmitter box to the computer's video and audio outputs, and the other (receiver) module you connect to the TV or projector. The results, in my case, didn't look too bad, either. I was surprised. Check the specs on the package to see how far it can broadcast, and be sure you can return it if your walls turn out to be too thick; there is metal or some other signal blockage; too much video or audio noise is introduced by your microwave oven; or the TV and computer are too far away from each other for the product to work properly.

That leaves one additional issue: the remote control signal. I have my projector upstairs and my computer downstairs. I wanted to use the WMC remote. So, how was I going to get the IR signal to the IR receiver on my WMC computer? Again, the solution was found at the local electronics store—an IR extender that uses radio frequencies to transmit the IR signal between rooms.

> **TIP**
>
> Some short-range TV transmitters have an IR relay built in to them, so check that option first. The RCA job I bought did not.

So, I purchased an IR remote-control extender. Similar to the A/V transmitter, this gadget has two parts: a transmitter and a receiver. Set up the transmitter near your TV or projection screen. Put the receiver near your WMC machine with its IR blaster pointed toward the WMC IR receiver (what you'd normally point the remote control at). Now, you can use your remote from the comfort of your recliner. It will relay the signal back to the computer.

> **TIP**
>
> Don't confuse the IR blaster that comes with the WMC computer with the IR receiver that's typically built in to a little box that has a USB connector on it. Your little WMC remote control receiver box has two mini jacks on the back that you can plug IR blasters into. (A blaster typically has a long, skinny wire and a little IR module on the end.) You can use blasters to change the channel on external devices, such as set-top cable boxes or your VCR. Consult your computer's manual for how to position the blaster on your set-top box or VCR so that your remote control keypresses are passed through to those devices.
>
> I originally made the mistake of thinking these little IR pods were receivers. They are not. Point your remote at them, and they do nothing. All they do is repeat IR signals received by your IR receiver module along to another device. For tips about using the set-top box IR pods, read this URL: www.microsoft.com/windowsxp/mediacenter/using/setup/settop.mspx.

After you get the IR remote control working and the image coming through to your TV or projector, you might also have to reduce the size of the WMC window on your computer screen if you want to see the entire image on your TV or projector. This can take a little trial and error. The WMC window is completely sizable, just as any window is, and as you resize the window, the video image resizes accordingly.

On my system, I position the WMC window all the way into the upper-left corner of my computer monitor and then drag the window's lower-right corner diagonally until the window fills the projector's (or TV's) image. Because I have my projector in another room, I save myself the hassle of running back and forth between rooms by temporarily connecting a small TV monitor that sits beside my computer. I use that to make this adjustment. Then, I switch the output back to feed the projector.

> **TIP**
>
> If you don't like the WMC video player, the files the WMC DVR creates (they have the extension `.dvr-ms` and you can find them in the Recorded TV directory on the drive specified in the WMC Recorder settings) can also be played by Windows Media Player or other more feature-rich players such as bsplayer.

BURNING DVDs FROM RECORDED TV

An obvious trick you can perform is to create a DVD or VHS tape of shows recorded from TV + Movies. One reason is to keep the show for watching months or years from now, without tying up hard disk space in the meantime. (Be sure you are aware of copyright laws that pertain to the shows you want to copy, of course.) If your WMC computer includes a recordable DVD drive, you are already capable of creating your first DVD. It's a simple process with WMC. Just follow these steps:

1. Insert a blank recordable DVD in your DVD recorder.
2. Select Recorded TV in TV + Movies.
3. Select the TV show you want to record.
4. Click the Burn CD/DVD button.
5. Select the Video DVD radio button when prompted. Then, click the Next button to proceed.
6. Specify a name for the DVD when prompted. Then, click the Next button.
7. Click the Add More button to be prompted for additional TV shows to add to the DVD, the Clear All button to erase all shows from the recording process, or the Change Name button to change the name of a recorded show from the DVD menu. When you are ready to burn the DVD, click the Burn DVD button.

> **TIP**
>
> Next to each item to burn to the DVD is an up arrow, down arrow, and x. You can use the arrows to specify the order of TV shows in the main DVD menu, whereas the x will delete that show from the list of shows to record.

Now that you have recorded your first TV show to DVD, you may have noticed that it recorded everything that occurred during your recording. There is usually a couple of minutes of the previous show, commercials, and a few minutes of the following show. That's a lot of extra material that you probably don't want to watch, and it is certainly a lot of storage space you don't want to waste. So, what can you do about it? Quite a bit actually.

Windows Vista includes Windows Movie Maker. It's a basic application for merging video clips with simple transitions and creating an output file. The output file has several options—from playback on your computer as an AVI file to reducing it in resolution and compressing the file so that you can play it back on any Windows Mobile device, including your Windows Smartphone. It is also possible to burn the output file to DVD using Windows DVD Maker. Windows Movie Maker is covered in detail in Chapter 11, "Producing Videos with Windows Movie Maker."

Some key items to keep in mind with using Windows Movie Maker to edit and publish your recorded TV shows include

- Storage space and compression—High-quality video consumes a great deal of storage space on your disk. The WMC file format (DVR-MS) provides good quality video files, but a long-term storage conversion to a higher compression video format can lower your storage requirements significantly. Storing your files in high-quality DVD format can reduce the file size by two-thirds.
- Video quality—The better the quality of the video, the more space it requires on your disk. If you use a recorded TV show in standard definition TV (SDTV) format, use an output resolution of 720×480 as your highest-quality setting. Broadcast SDTV is as low as 320×240, whereas cable and satellite SDTV can be as high as 720×480. Using an output format higher than the input format generally does not produce a higher quality video. Instead, it usually just takes up more storage space on the disk.
- Back up your work—Editing is a time consuming process. Make frequent backups of your work in progress to avoid data loss in the event of a computer software/hardware glitch.
- Output/storage—Depending on the size of your video, you might output to a video CD (VCD). A VCD cannot store as much data as a DVD but is less expensive. A VCD also makes a good alternative for sending smaller files to relatives. If a file is too large to fit on a VCD, use a DVD. A single-sided DVD can store up to 2 hours of video in standard mode and 1 hour in high-quality mode.

> **TIP**
>
> To dub a show from your WMC machine to a VHS tape, connect the composite video output (or S-output if your VHS recorder accepts that as a video input source) to the recorder. Then, start playing back the show on the computer. Try a little sample at first, and play the tape back on a TV set to ensure that the entire image is making it onto the tape. On some computers, the entire video image is automatically scaled to fit into the NTSC analog output. On others, you have to manually size and position the playback window, as explained in the previous section.

Setting Parental Control Ratings

You might want to control what kinds of TV, movies, or DVDs are playable on your system. To prevent your children from watching inappropriate TV, follow these steps:

1. From the WMC Start screen, select Tasks.
2. Select Settings.
3. Select General.
4. Select Parental Controls.
5. When prompted, enter your four-digit code using the numeric keypad on the remote or keyboard. If this is the first time you have entered a code, confirm the code when prompted.
6. Select TV Ratings.
7. On the TV Ratings menu, you can make the selections shown in Table 13.2.
8. When finished specifying your ratings, click the Save button.

Table 13.2 TV Parental Controls

Control	Function
Turn on or turn off TV blocking.	Select or clear the check box next to Turn On TV Blocking. When the box is selected, TV programs that exceed the selected rating level are blocked.
Block or unblock unrated TV Programs.	Select or clear the check box next to Block Unrated TV programs. When the box is selected, TV programs that do not have a rating are blocked.
Set the maximum allowed TV rating.	Use the arrow buttons and the CH/PG+ and CH/PG- buttons to select the rating that cannot be exceeded for TV programs.

To prevent your children from seeing X-rated DVDs, follow these steps:

1. From the WMC Start screen, select Tasks.
2. Select Settings.
3. Select General.
4. Select Parental Controls.
5. When prompted, enter your four-digit code using the numeric keypad on the remote or keyboard. If this is the first time you entered your code, confirm the code when prompted.
6. Select Movie/DVD Ratings.
7. On the Movie/DVD Ratings menu, you can make the selections shown in Table 13.3.
8. When you finish specifying your ratings, click the Save button.

Table 13.3 Movie/DVD Parental Controls

Control	Function
Turn on or turn off movie blocking.	Select or clear the check box next to Turn On Movie Blocking. When the box is selected, Movies or DVDs that exceed the selected rating level are blocked.
Block or unblock unrated movies.	Select or clear the check box next to Block Unrated Movies. When the box is selected, Movies or DVDs that do not have a rating are blocked.
Set the maximum allowed movie rating.	Use the arrow buttons and the CH/PG+ and CH/PG- buttons to select the rating that cannot be exceeded for Movies or DVDs.

Table 13.4, shows the Keyboard Shortcuts for playing DVDs when you don't have the remote control available or are sitting at your PC.

Table 13.4 DVD Keyboard Shortcuts

To do this...	Press...
Go to the DVD menu	Ctrl+Shift+M
Play	Ctrl+Shift+P
Pause	Ctrl+P
Stop	Ctrl+Shift+S
Rewind	Ctrl+Shift+B
Fast forward	Ctrl+Shift+F
Skip back	Ctrl+B
Skip forward	Ctrl+F
Go to the previous chapter	Page Down
Go to the next chapter	Page Up
Change the DVD angle	Arrow keys
Change the DVD audio selection	Ctrl+Shift+A
Change the DVD subtitles selection	Ctrl+U

TROUBLESHOOTING

WMC was designed to make things easier for you as a consumer. That does not mean it is a perfect product, however, and from time to time, problems may occur that prevent you from enjoying your TV, music, or DVD movie. In this section we take a look at the most likely problems that may occur and provide solutions to resolve them.

MY TV TUNER IS NOT WORKING

WMC does not recognize my TV tuner.

This problem falls into two types of common problems: hardware and devices.

If you have a Media Center tuner that either is not supported by Windows Vista or does not work under Windows Vista, you can often resolve the problem by going to your manufacturer's website, downloading the latest Windows XP driver, and installing it. This worked for me on my Toshiba Satellite with an external USB TV Tuner. If you have supported hardware, but the driver fails to load you need to determine why. Some helpful troubleshooting device driver suggestions can be found in Chapter 29, "Keeping Windows and Other Software Up to Date."

NO VIDEO IN WMC

I am unable to see any live, or recorded, video in WMC.

If the device driver is loaded and functioning properly, it is time to look at signal-related issues. First, be sure the cables are connected properly. If you have another device, such as a portable TV, you can use to verify that the cables are connected properly and carrying a valid TV signal, do so. That way, you know that the cabling is not an issue. You may also find that the signal is not properly formatted for your TV tuner by using an external device.

> **TIP**
>
> My TV Tuner has coaxial and composite TV signal inputs. My signal provider is a DirectTV HD DVR with HDMI, composite, and YbPbR outputs. It is designed to provide high-definition signals to high-definition devices, but my TV tuner is a standard definition device. When I first connected it using the composite inputs, I could not figure out why I was not getting a picture. I was fairly confident that the cables were okay because I was getting sound. Then it dawned on me that I had my DVR set to provide an HD picture to my HDTV at 1080i. HDTV signals are output only on the HDMI and YbPbR outputs. To get a video signal output on the composite video outputs, I had to reconfigure the DVR to standard definition 480i mode.

If you get a good video signal and you still can't see any video in the WMC, perhaps WMC is not properly configured. The best way to test and verify your signal setup is to go to the Start page, select Tasks, Settings, TV, Set Up TV Signal and then manually configure your TV signal. When you get to the Automatic TV Signal Setup dialog box, choose the I Will Manually Configure My TV Signal radio button and click the Next button to proceed to the Select Your TV Signal dialog box. Verify your settings, or change them, to the correct signal provider. Use Cable for a TV signal from a cable set-top box, Satellite for a signal from a satellite provider (Dish, DirecTV, and so on), or Antenna from a public broadcast antenna or coaxial output from any type of signal provider. Then, move on to the Select a Working TV Signal dialog box. This is where you get the opportunity to select your TV Tuner's input signal. If you use a public broadcast (coaxial cable) signal, your input should be on channel 2, 3, or 4, with 3 being the most common. S-Video or composite video are more likely to be used by satellite and cable boxes, but some cable boxes also provide a coaxial output. If you use a cable box with a coaxial output, check the back of the box for a switch to set the channel to output the signal on. Usually, it is set to channel 3 with an alternative of channel 4. If you are unsure of your input channel, a simple test is to just try each input choice one at a time and see whether you get a signal in the preview window. After you obtain a signal, click Next and work your way through the rest of the dialog boxes until you complete the video setup.

Tips from the Windows Pros

Although I enjoy watching TV and movies, the biggest benefit of a digital video recorder, or personal video recorder as some like to call it, is choosing when to watch my TV shows or movies. Of course, choosing when to watch a TV show or movie first requires that you store it somewhere. In WMC, that means storing it on a hard drive, CD, or DVD. The key word in the previous phrase is *storing*. Specifically, I'm referring to how much storage space on your storage medium is used to store your TV shows or movies. That's where I can help by providing information on how to compress your video files using DivX for storing on your local hard disk or burning a DivX DVD.

Converting Your Videos to DivX to Save Disk Space

If you're like me, you're annoyed by how quickly you run out of space for recording TV. Sure, one solution is to run out to your local electronics store and buy a few hundred gigs of hard drive and then point MCE to that new drive as the storage spot for recording your TV shows. It almost looks like Microsoft has made a deal with hard drive makers to help sell more hardware. Why they don't offer the option of recording in DivX or Xvid is unknown to me, but I have developed a workaround for keeping many more shows on the computer and even for burning them to DVD. I can get about 8 hours of shows on a single-layer DVD this way. Here's the scheme:

1. Record TV shows as usual, using the Guide and MCE.
2. In MCE's recorder settings, note where you record your shows, and create a shortcut to that folder. Put the shortcut on the desktop or other handy location. I keep mine on the

Quick Launch bar. This makes it easy to open the folder and look at what is recorded and work with the files. You might want to turn on additional headings to display in your Explorer window, so you can see the metadata for the files, such as name of the show, time recorded, and so on. However, you can use a naming convention in the filenames that includes the time and date. Study the names a bit, and you'll figure it out. For example:

`South Park_COMEDYP_14_06_2006_23_59_00.dvr-ms`

This file is *South Park* recorded from Comedy Central on June 14, 2006, at 11:59 p.m.

3. Purchase VideoReDo, a program that reads and writes `dvr-ms` files (and other video formats as well). This program also searches quickly for commercials and helps you delete them if you want. It takes a little hand work but not much. It's the ultimate video file repair tool as well. An MCE recording that hangs or crashes in MCE can be fixed with this program. The URLs are www.VideoReDo.com and http://forums.VideoReDo.com.

4. Save the video file from VideoReDo, an MPG file. I usually just give it the same name and let VideoReDo change the extension. Then, I can see which recorded shows I have converted.

5. Download Auto Gordian Knot (AGK) for free conversion to DivX and XviD. It's kind of complicated to learn, but the price is right, and there are free tutorials in many languages supplied with it. The URL is www.autogk.me.uk.

6. If this is too hairy for you (and frankly I like a simpler approach), although it is less powerful, purchase the DivX Converter from www.divx.com/divx/windows/converter.

7. Whichever program you use doesn't matter, if you create a DivX file. You have to experiment with the settings more in Auto Gordian Knot than in DivX Converter, simply because you can! That is, DivX Converter has only a few compression options, whereas AGK has many.

8. The end result now is that after compression, which can take a little time, you will have a file (or files, because you can queue a mess of them up and let them run overnight) with `.divx` extensions. They will be roughly one-tenth the size of the original and look almost as good.

9. You need a means of playing back the DivX files. You must download the DivX CODEC (compressor/decompressor) from somewhere and install it to your PC. If you purchased DivX Converter, you received that automatically. The DivX player and CODEC are available free at www.divx.com. Either download just the CODEC and then use another video player, such as Windows Media Player, or download the entire DivX player. Now, when you click a DivX video file, it plays on your Vista computer.

Burn DivX to DVD

But what about burning and playing your shows on DVD, as mentioned earlier? No problem. The game plan goes like this:

1. Purchase a DivX-compatible DVD player. They are cheap. I got my Philips DivX-compatible player for $80 at Costco. Check the current list of compatible players on www.divx.com.

2. Use DVD Maker, Nero, or other DVD burning software to dump your DivX files from your hard disk onto a blank data DVD. Remember, don't burn a regular video DVD, record a data DVD. You're just dumping the DivX files onto the DVD as if copying files to another directory on your hard drive or to another drive. I like to put each DivX file into a separate folder on the DVD, but that is not necessary. The standalone DVD player finds the files and recognizes them as movies. Then use the DVD player's remote control to choose which file to play. You may want to shorten the filenames so that they display in some intelligible manner on the TV screen (for example, Simpsons S1E10) meaning Season 1, Episode 10) because the filename listing may be shortened by your DVD player when displayed on the TV screen. And remember, you can get a lot of DivX movies and TV on a single-layer DVD, and *really* a lot on a dual-layer. I think I have as many as eight full-length movies on a few of mine.

3. Now that you have stored your otherwise hard disk-greedy `.dvr-ms` files on DVD, you can go back and erase the shows you longer want hogging up your available recording time. Go into Recorded TV in MCE and delete the ones you have now effectively backed up.

> **TIP**
>
> I have had some trouble with recorded DVDs in general and would not count on them to be an eternally reliable backup medium. Some of the discs I have burned have worked fine for a while and then landed in my coaster collection. If a show is particularly important to your archive, I'd suggest making a duplicate backup and tucking it safely away for use if the first one fails. If the first one does fail, check that the second one works. If it does, duplicate it using a tool such as Nero.

PART IV

WINDOWS VISTA AND THE INTERNET

14 Getting Connected   393

15 Using Internet Explorer 7   423

16 Email and Newsgroups with Windows Mail   471

17 Troubleshooting Your Internet Connection   527

18 Hosting Web Pages with Internet Information Services   553

CHAPTER 14

GETTING CONNECTED

In this chapter

Going Worldwide   394

Connection Technologies   394

Choosing an Internet Service Provider   398

Choosing Equipment   400

Ordering the Service   401

Installing the Hardware   401

Configuring Your Internet Connection   406

Adjusting Dial-Up Connection Properties   409

Configuring a High-Speed Connection   411

Making and Ending a Dial-Up Connection   416

Changing the Default Connection   418

Managing Multiple Internet Connections   419

Troubleshooting   420

Tips from the Windows Pros: Staying Connected While Traveling Abroad   421

Going Worldwide

Hooking up to the Internet used to be a privilege afforded only to universities and corporations. Now it's an essential part of owning and using any PC, and it's available to virtually everyone.

In this chapter, you'll find information about choosing an Internet service provider (ISP), making the connection through a modem or other link, installing and configuring your system, and making your system safe and secure. This chapter tells how to select an Internet connection technology and connect a single computer to the Internet. However, this isn't your only option. You can take any one of several routes:

- If your computer is part of an existing local area network (LAN) with Internet access, you can skip this chapter entirely because Internet access comes as part and parcel of your LAN connection. In fact, if you are part of a corporate LAN, it is probably a violation of your company's security policy to establish your own independent connection. (If it's not, it should be!)

- If you are setting up a LAN for your home or office, you can provide Internet access to the entire LAN through one connection. You should read Chapter 22, "Connecting Your Network to the Internet," and decide whether you want to connect your LAN. Use the instructions in this chapter to set up the initial connection; Chapter 22 tells you how to share it with the rest of your workgroup.

- If you want to use your existing ISP account and connection technology, you can skip the introductory sections of this chapter and go right to "Installing a Modem in Windows Vista" or, for broadband connections, "Installing a Network Adapter."

- If you need to make a clean start with the Internet, read on!

Connection Technologies

Not long ago, you had one choice to make for your Internet connection: which brand of modem to buy. Now options abound, and you can choose among several technologies, speeds, and types of Internet service providers. A huge technology shift is taking place as high-speed digital (*broadband*) connection services are being deployed worldwide.

Let's take a look at the basic Internet connection technologies that are appropriate for an individual user or workgroup. After describing each one, I'll show you roughly what each costs to set up and use.

Analog Modem

Standard, tried-and-true dial-up modem service requires only a telephone line and a modem in your computer. The connection is made when your computer dials a local access number provided by your ISP. The downside is that this ties up a telephone line while you're online. Furthermore, if you have call waiting, the "beep" that occurs when someone calls while you're online can make the modem drop its connection. To avoid these hassles, many people order an additional phone line just for the modem, and this adds to the monthly expense.

NOTE

> Some modems and ISPs provide a service called Internet Call Waiting. The modem detects the call-waiting beep and notifies you via a pop-up window that a call is coming in; you can ignore it or suspend your Internet connection for a time while you take the call. This requires a modem that supports the V.92 standard and a participating ISP. The service costs more than $8 per month, if it's even available, so it's not a big win as far as I can see.

Modems transmit data at a top speed of 33Kbps and can receive data at up to 56Kbps (56 thousand bits per second). In real life, you will usually obtain download speeds of 40Kbps to 50Kbps. This speed is adequate for general Web surfing—that is, reading text and viewing pictures. However, you will find it woefully inadequate for viewing video or for voice communication. (In other words, forget about YouTube.)

To use standard dial-up Internet service, you need a modem and a telephone cable. Modems come in internal, external, USB, and PC card varieties from dozens of manufacturers. Most computers made for home use come with one preinstalled. On business computers, they're usually an extra-cost item.

ISDN

Integrated Services Digital Network (ISDN) is a special digital-only telephone service that can carry two independent voice or data conversations over one telephone wire. ISDN service is actually a different type of telephony; you can't plug an ordinary telephone into an ISDN line. ISDN modems can carry data at 64Kbps or 128Kbps, depending on whether you use one or two of its channels to connect to your ISP. Thanks to the worldwide spread of cable and DSL service, ISDN's star is fading rapidly. Still, ISDN is a good interim solution if you need higher speed than an analog modem can provide and if DSL and cable aren't yet available.

To use ISDN service, you need an internal or external ISDN modem, or an ISDN router device and a network adapter. Your ISP can help you choose compatible equipment. In addition, you need the special ISDN telephone line wired into your home or office.

DSL

Digital Subscriber Line (DSL) service sends a high-speed digital data signal over the same wires your telephone line uses while that line is simultaneously used for standard telephone service. This means that you can get DSL service installed without needing an extra telephone line. The most common DSL service is called *asymmetric*, or *ADSL*, because it receives data at 128Kbps to 6000Kbps but sends at a lower rate. (This is fine because most Web surfing involves sending a very small request and receiving a large amount of data.)

NOTE

> DSL varieties include asymmetric, symmetric, high-speed, and DSL over an ISDN line, so you'll see the acronyms *SDSL*, *ADSL*, *HDSL*, and *IDSL*, or the collective *xDSL*. For this chapter, these distinctions are unimportant, so I just call it DSL.

DSL service is not available everywhere yet, but it's spreading rapidly. However, DSL has at least one Achilles heel: Its availability is restricted by your distance from the telephone company's central office, and it isn't available when the distance is more than a couple miles (as the wires run, not as the crow flies). DSL's reach can be extended by optical fiber lines and special equipment, but this is expensive for the telephone companies to install. DSL might never make it into rural areas.

> **NOTE**
>
> U.S. readers can see reviews of various DSL providers and check for DSL service availability at www.dslreports.com.

DSL modems come in two varieties: External units connect to your computer through a network adapter or a USB cable. Internal units plug right into your computer. If your ISP uses external adapters, before you buy a network adapter, check with your DSL provider because often one is included in the installation kit. In addition, before you decide to pay extra to get service for multiple computers, read Chapter 22 to see how all your computers can share a single connection.

Cable Modem

Your local television cable company may provide cable modem Internet service, which sends high-speed data signals through the same distribution system it uses to carry high-quality TV signals.

Cable modem service has none of the distance limitations of ISDN or DSL. One criticism of cable service is that data speeds can drop during high-use times such as the early evening because everyone in a given neighborhood is sharing a single network "pipe." Surveys show, however, that cable subscribers usually get several times the download speed of DSL subscribers.

→ For more information on ISDN, xDSL, and cable modem service, **see** Chapter 22, **p. 701**. That chapter describes these technologies with a focus on using them to connect a LAN to the Internet, but you still might find the information helpful.

Cable modems generally are external devices that connect to your computer through a network adapter or a USB cable. Before you buy a network adapter, though, check with your ISP; one might be included in the installation kit. Some ISPs charge extra to lease the modem. The price of a cable modem has dropped to about $60 new and about $1 on eBay, so leasing one from your cable company isn't as good a deal as it once was. Also, before you decide to pay extra to get service for multiple computers, read Chapter 22 to see how all your computers can use a router to share a single connection. This is especially important for cable users. Multiple-computer cable service that doesn't use a router has some serious problems, as I discuss in Chapter 22.

Satellite Service

Satellite Internet service uses microwave signals and small (roughly 2-foot-diameter) dish antennas to connect to an orbiting communication satellite. Two types of satellite service are used: *unidirectional*, which receives high-speed data through the dish but transmits outgoing data by modem over a phone line, and *bidirectional*, which uses the satellite dish for both sending and receiving. Bidirectional service is the way to go. It's currently available in most parts of the world.

Satellite's big advantage is that it's available wherever there's a good view of either the southern sky in the Northern Hemisphere, or the northern sky in the Southern Hemisphere. The disadvantages are that installation requires the abilities of both a rocket scientist and a carpenter, the equipment and service plans can be expensive, and the system suffers from the same slowdowns that affect cable service. In addition, heavy rain or snow can interfere with the signal, so service may be interrupted or degraded during storms.

> **NOTE** In the U.S., check out www.starband.com and www.hughesnet.com. In Australia, check www.telstra.com. In Europe, Southern Africa, the Middle East, the Indian subcontinent, and Southeast Asia, see www.intelsat.com. Satellite services are often resold through regional companies.

Satellite service requires you to purchase a receiving dish antenna, a receiver, and a USB or network adapter to connect the setup to your computer. Your ISP should furnish these devices. For unidirectional satellite service, you also need to have a phone line near your computer.

Wireless

Wireless Internet service is available in most major metropolitan areas. Cellphone companies are getting into this in a big way, and its popularity has spread rapidly over the past few years. The wireless modem connects to a small whip or dish antenna, and data-transfer rates typically are more than 1Mbps using setups with fixed antennae.

> **NOTE** Check www.sprintbroadband.com for more information.

Wireless is similar to satellite service. You have to purchase a receiving antenna, a receiver, and a USB or network adapter to connect the setup to your computer. Your ISP should furnish these devices. You'll also have to pay for professional installation.

Choosing a Technology

With all the options potentially available to Windows users for Internet access, making a choice that fits your needs and limitations can become a bit confusing. Research the options that local and national ISPs provide, and then start narrowing them. Table 14.1 summarizes the costs and speeds of the different ways for a single computer user to access the Internet. The prices shown are typical costs for the service in question after applying the usual discounts and special offers.

TABLE 14.1 INTERNET CONNECTION OPTIONS FOR THE INDIVIDUAL USER

Method	Approximate Cost, $ per Month	Approximate Setup and Equipment Cost	Time Limits in Hours (per month)	Availability	Download Speed
Analog Modem	$0*–$25	$50	10 to unlimited	Worldwide	33Kbps–56Kbps
ISDN	$40 plus ISDN toll charges	$300	10 to unlimited	Limited, unlikely to expand	64Kbps–128Kbps
DSL	$30 and up	$100	Unlimited	Limited but growing	312Kbps–6Mbps
Cable Modem	$30–$50	$100	Unlimited	Limited but growing	1Mbps–10Mbps
Satellite	$50–$150	$200–$800	25 and up	Almost worldwide	400Kbps

Some ISPs are "free"; I discuss them later in this chapter.

Remember that you have three or four costs to factor in:

- The cost of hardware required to make the connection
- The cost of installation and setup
- The monthly ISP cost for Internet service
- The cost of telephone or ISDN lines, if you order a separate line just for Internet access

Try to estimate how long you'll keep the service, and amortize the startup and equipment costs over that time frame when comparing technologies. If several computers will share the connection, if you plan to download lots of large files, or if you will be playing games online, a faster service might make more sense, even if it's a bit more expensive.

CHOOSING AN INTERNET SERVICE PROVIDER

Several different kinds of businesses offer Internet connections, including large companies with access points in many cities, smaller local or regional Internet service providers, and online information services that provide TCP/IP connections to the Internet along with their own proprietary information sources (I'm talking about AOL here, of course).

You might notice that Windows Vista can refer you to Microsoft's MSN service if you don't have an ISP, but you don't have to use Microsoft as your Internet service provider. Windows has all the software it needs to connect to any ISP. Do your own research to find the best fit for you.

Consider the following points when choosing an ISP:

- Does the ISP offer the connection technology you want?
- Can you have multiple email accounts for family members or employees? If so, how many?
- Does the ISP provide you with a news server so you can interact with Internet newsgroups?

→ To learn more about newsgroups, **see** Chapter 16, "Email and Newsgroups with Windows Mail," **p. 471**.

- What is the charge for connection time? Some ISPs offer unlimited use per day. Others charge by the hour or have a limit on continuous connection time.
- Does the ISP have local (that is, free) phone numbers in the areas you live, work, and visit? If not, factor in the toll charges when you're comparing prices.
- Can you get a discount by signing up for a year or longer-term contract?

If you have access to the Web, check www.thelist.com. You'll learn a lot about comparative pricing and features that ISPs offer, along with links to their pages for opening an account. Another good site is www.lightreading.com.

Finally, you should know that some ISPs give you free dial-up Internet access. These providers install software on your computer that displays a small window of advertising the entire time you're connected. If you're pinching pennies, this isn't a terrible way to go. You might check out www.freedomlist.com/ for a list of free (and cheap) ISPs in your area.

> **TIP**
>
> In my opinion, getting good customer service is more important than saving a few dollars a month. As you narrow your list of potential ISPs, call their customer support telephone number and see how long it takes to get to talk to a human being. This experience can be very illuminating.

Travel Considerations

If you're a frequent traveler and have a laptop or other device with which you want to connect to the Internet while on the road, remember that broadband service is wired into place. In other words, it doesn't provide for access when you travel or roam about town, unlike many national dial-up ISPs that offer roaming. However, some broadband ISPs include a standard modem dial-up account at no extra charge just to compensate for this factor.

If you want Internet connectivity when you travel, consider these options:

- For occasional or personal travel, you can forgo national access. Just find an Internet cafe or get Internet access at your hotel. Wireless hotspots are appearing everywhere, so you might do well just to buy a wireless network adapter.

- If you want to use your own computer for occasional travel, you can always place a long-distance call to your own ISP. Subtract your expected monthly toll charges from the money you might save by using a less expensive local ISP, versus the higher prices of a national ISP, to see which solution is best.

- If you travel frequently, choose a national ISP with local access numbers in the places you visit frequently, or an ISP that offers toll-free access with an acceptable surcharge.

At the end of this chapter, I'll give you some advice about getting Internet access while traveling overseas.

Choosing Equipment

You need to purchase equipment that is compatible with the particular type of Internet service you'll be using. If you will use dial-up service, your computer probably came with a modem preinstalled, so you don't have any choices to make. If you will buy new connection hardware, here are some points to consider:

- Most broadband services require specific hardware that your ISP provides (you can sometimes buy a DSL or cable modem independently, but be sure it will be compatible with the equipment your ISP uses). In addition, broadband modems connect via USB or through an Ethernet network adapter. If your service needs a network adapter, and your computer doesn't already have an Ethernet adapter, be sure to get one that's compatible with Windows Vista.

- If you will want to share your Internet connection with other computers via a LAN, read Chapter 22 before making any hardware purchases; you'll find information on some special hardware setups.

- Above all, be sure any hardware that you have to plug directly into the computer (modem or LAN adapter) appears in the Windows Tested Products list (http://testedproducts.windowsmarketplace.com). This is important because Windows Vista has not been around long, and not every vendor has had time to (or even plans to) produce compatible drivers for all of their products. Therefore, check the list before you make any purchases.

- For dial-up service, choose a modem that is compatible with the fastest service level your ISP provides. Your ISP should be using V.90 modems for 56Kbps service. If your ISP still uses X2 or K6Flex modems, it's way behind the times. Some ISPs support the V.92 call-waiting protocol. If you have a modem that supports this feature, ask prospective ISPs whether they support it and whether there's an additional charge.

Ordering the Service

Ordering standard dial-up modem Internet service is really quite simple. Just call the ISP, talk to the sales department, and ask the sales representative to mail or fax you instructions for configuring Windows Vista. In fact, it's easy enough that they might just talk you through it over the phone.

Ordering ISDN service is quite a different matter. The most difficult part is getting the ISDN telephone line ordered and installed correctly because ISDN service has a bewildering number of options, all specified in telephone company–ese. What you probably want is standard "2B+D, two data and voice" service with no extra-cost features.

> **TIP**
>
> Your best bet is to have your ISP order an ISDN line for you. If your ISP won't do it, some ISDN modem manufacturers—for example, 3COM—will order your ISDN service for you.

Ordering cable, DSL, or satellite service is also quite easy because the ISP takes care of all the details. The provider first checks to see whether your neighborhood qualifies for the service. Then a rep calls you back with the news and either sends you a self-installation kit or schedules an installation appointment. (Getting DSL installers to actually show up can be a nightmare—but don't let me discourage you from trying. The service is really nice.)

When the service is installed, you're ready to configure your Windows Vista computer. I'll discuss modems first and then cover broadband equipment setup.

Installing the Hardware

No matter what kind of Internet connection you'll be using, you need a modem, a network adapter, or some other sort of connection hardware. If you're lucky, your computer came with this preinstalled and you can just skip ahead to "Configuring Your Internet Connection."

Otherwise, you'll be adding some hardware. For most types of high-speed service, your ISP either installs everything for you or gives you detailed instructions. For the basic service types, I'll give you some generic installation instructions in the next few sections. Your connection hardware might come with detailed instructions. If it does, by all means follow those.

Installing a Modem in Windows Vista

Installing a modem is a pretty painless process these days. If you had to undergo the experience in the mid-1990s, you might remember worrying about experiencing interrupt conflicts, having to set jumpers, and needing to navigate the computer's setup screen. Plug and

Play has pretty much eliminated this mess. Your modem should come with straightforward installation instructions; follow those, and you'll be online in no time.

For an internal modem, you'll pop open your PC's case and insert the modem card into a free expansion slot inside the computer. For an external modem, it's a more simple matter of cabling it to a USB or serial port on your PC. (Don't forget to connect the power supply and turn it on.) A PC card modem simply plugs into your portable computer.

→ For more information about installing new hardware, **see** Chapter 30, "Installing and Replacing Hardware," **p. 1009**.

From that point, here's what you need to do. These procedures apply to analog modems as well as external ISDN modems.

If your modem is Plug and Play (PnP) compatible, Windows Vista should automatically detect it when you turn on your computer and log in.

If Windows cannot find a set of drivers that match your brand and model of modem, you might be asked to insert a CD or floppy disk that the modem manufacturer should have provided with your modem.

If you're using an older modem, you might need to add it to the configuration manually by following these steps:

1. Log in with an Administrator user account. Choose Start, Control Panel, Hardware and Sound, Phone and Modem Options.

2. Select the Modems tab, shown in Figure 14.1.

Figure 14.1
The Modems tab identifies the modems currently installed in your system.

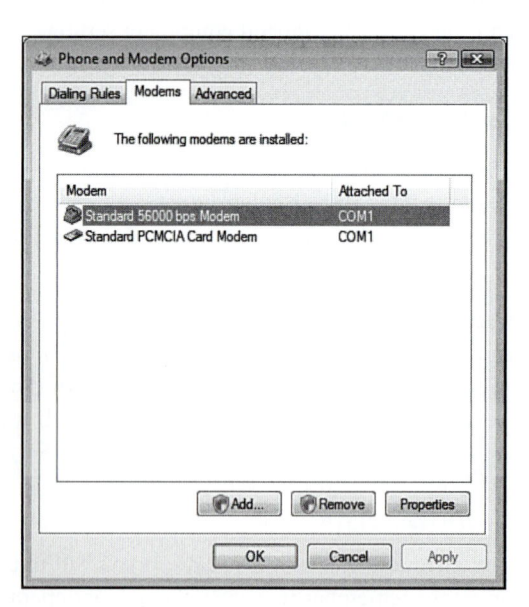

3. If Windows has already detected your modem, its name appears in the Modems tab. If the correct modem type is listed, skip to Step 8. If the wrong modem type is listed, skip down to the next section, "Changing the Modem Type."

   If no modem is listed, click the Add button to run the Add Hardware Wizard.

4. Click Next. Windows locates the COM port and determines the type of modem you have. If this is successful, Windows tells you. In this case, continue with Step 7.

5. If Windows detects your modem incorrectly and doesn't offer you the chance to correct the mistake, skip to Step 7 and then correct the problem using the instructions in the next section. If you are given the opportunity to correct the problem, click Change and locate the manufacturer and model of your modem in the dialog box. If you find the correct make and model, select them and click OK. If your modem came with a driver disk for Windows Vista, click Have Disk and locate the installation file for the modem.

   If your modem isn't listed, try to download the proper driver from Windows Update or from the modem manufacturer (using another computer, of course). You also might try selecting a similar model by the same manufacturer.

6. After you select the modem type, click OK and then Next.

7. Click Finish to complete the installation. The modem then appears in the list of installed modems in the Phone and Modem Options dialog box.

8. Select the Dialing Rules tab.

9. Select My Location and click Edit.

10. Enter the General tab information for your current location, as shown in Figure 14.2.

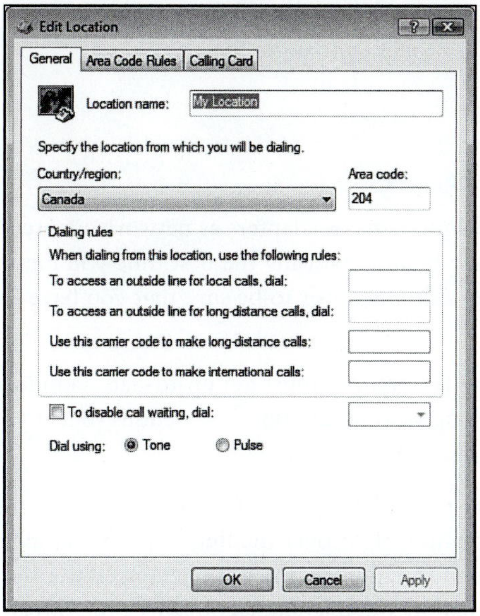

Figure 14.2
In the Edit Location dialog box, you can record the dialing instructions for your current location. The important settings are Country/Region, Area Code Access for an outside line, and Disable Call Waiting.

11. Enter a name for your location—for example, home, the name of your city, or another name to distinguish the current telephone dialing properties. Set the country, area code, and dialing rules information.

    For example, if your telephone system requires you to dial a 9 to make an outside local call, enter **9** in the box labeled To Access an Outside Line for Local Calls, Dial. Make a corresponding entry for long-distance access.

    If your telephone line has call waiting, check To Disable Call Waiting, Dial and choose the appropriate disable code.

    I assume here that your ISP access number is a local call in the same area code. If this is not the case, you might want to fill in the Area Code Rules table for the ISP access number. (If you don't know the number yet, don't worry; you can come back and fix it later.)

12. Click OK.

Now your modem is installed and you can continue with "Configuring Your Internet Connection," later in this chapter.

Changing the Modem Type

If Windows incorrectly determines your modem type, you can change it by selecting the appropriate modem in the Modem list (see Figure 14.1) and clicking Properties. Then follow these steps:

1. Select the Driver tab and click Update Driver.
2. Select Browse My Computer for Driver Software.
3. Click Browse to locate the proper `.inf` setup file.
4. Click Finish.

Installing Internal ISDN Adapters

Windows treats internal ISDN modems or adapters as network adapters, not modems. Plug and Play adapters should be set up automatically the first time you log in after installing the adapter. Log in as a Computer Administrator to be sure that you have sufficient privileges to install hardware drivers.

For older non–Plug and Play adapters, you must get up-to-date Windows Vista drivers from the manufacturer's website, along with installation instructions (but if your ISDN adapter is that old, don't count on finding any).

Modern ISDN driver software might be capable of getting the ISDN line's telephone number and other necessary information right over the line from the phone company, but you might be prompted for setup information. In this case, you need the service profile identification (SPID, a number assigned by the telephone company), the directory number, and switch-type information provided by your telephone company.

Installing a Network Adapter

Some DSL and cable modems use a USB connection and can just be plugged into your computer this way.

However, most DSL and cable service providers require an Ethernet network adapter for use by their modems. If you're lucky, they'll supply and install this for you. You won't have to lift a finger, in fact, as long as the installer is familiar with Windows Vista. You just need to log in using an Administrator account and supervise while the installer does his or her stuff.

> **TIP**
>
> If a professional installer configures your computer or adds software to it, be sure to take thorough notes of what he or she does. Don't hesitate to ask questions—you have a right to know exactly what the installer is doing. Be sure to test the setup before the installer leaves.

If you want to purchase or install the network adapter yourself, install it according to the manufacturer's instructions. This process should involve no more than inserting the card into your computer, powering up, and logging on. The Plug and Play system should take care of the rest for you.

After installation, confirm that the network adapter is installed and functioning by following these steps:

1. Click Start, right-click Computer, and then select Manage.
2. Select the Device Manager in the left pane. The list in the right pane should show only "first-level" items. Under Network Adapters, you should see no items listed with an exclamation mark icon superimposed.

If the network adapter appears and is marked with a yellow exclamation point, follow the network card troubleshooting instructions in Chapter 24, "Troubleshooting Your Network."

For DSL service with self-installation, you will be provided with filters, devices that plug into your telephone jacks and block the DSL signal from reaching your telephones and answering machines. You need to identify every phone jack that is connected to the line your DSL service uses, and install a filter on every jack but the one that plugs into your DSL modem. If you need to plug a phone into the same jack that the DSL modem uses, use a dual jack adapter, with a filter on the side that connects to the phone.

Alternatively, the service installer might connect your telephone line to a device called a *splitter* outside the house and will install a separate cable to bring the DSL signal to your computer. These devices separate the high-frequency DSL carrier signal from the normal telephone signal. The phone line will be connected to a DSL modem, which then plugs into a USB port or a LAN adapter on your computer.

> **CAUTION**
>
> After a LAN adapter or USB connection is made, you *must* be sure that the Windows Firewall is enabled to protect your computer against hackers. I mention this again later in the chapter. You can read more about firewalls and network security in Chapter 35, "Protecting Your Network from Hackers and Snoops."

INSTALLING A SATELLITE OR WIRELESS CONNECTION

Installing satellite or wireless modems is not terribly tricky, but the procedure is specific to the type of hardware you're using. Unfortunately, I have to leave you at the mercy of the manufacturer's instruction manual.

One bit of advice I can give: Installing a satellite dish is difficult, and it's best to hire a professional dish installer for this task. (Our executive editor, Rick Kughen, didn't have the benefit of this sage advice when he installed his, and his conclusion is, "About halfway through the ordeal, I decided that I really wished I had paid the $199 installation fee.")

> **CAUTION**
>
> After your satellite connection is set up, you *must* be sure that the Windows Firewall is enabled to protect your computer against hackers. I mention this again later in the chapter. You can read more about firewalls and network security in Chapter 35.

CONFIGURING YOUR INTERNET CONNECTION

Now that your modem is installed and ready to go, it's time to head off to see the wizard—the Connect to the Internet Wizard, that is.

> **TIP**
>
> Have your Windows Vista Installation DVD handy. It's not likely, but the wizard might need to install some Windows files to set up your Internet connection.

The Connect to the Internet Wizard runs the first time you try to open Internet Explorer. You can also fire it up at any time by clicking Start, Connect To and selecting Set Up a Connection or Network. Select Connect to the Internet and click Next. You'll then see the wizard screen shown in Figure 14.3.

Figure 14.3
The Connect to the Internet Wizard has ways to set up a new Internet connection.

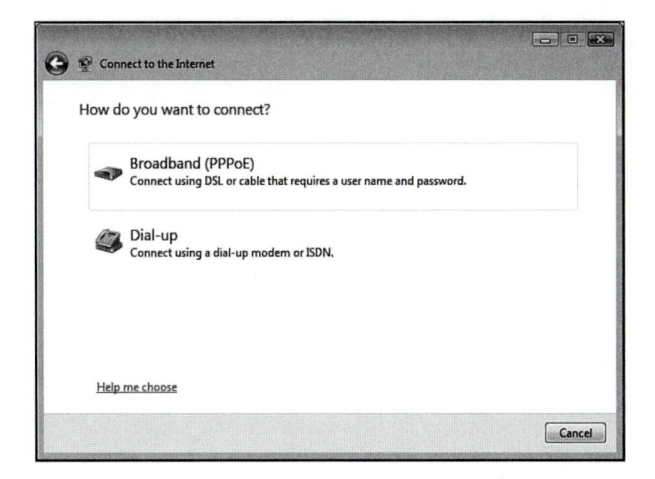

The first alternative is for DSL and cable connections. If you want to take this route, go on to "Configuring a High-Speed Connection," later in this chapter.

The second alternative is to create a dial-up connection using a dial-up modem or ISDN. When you click this option, you are prompted for ISP information.

Configuring an ISP Account

If you already have an ISP account, you need to fill in the information provided by your ISP when prompted.

The first field asks for the local access telephone number for your ISP. Enter the local number, optionally preceded by any other codes needed to dial the call. For instance, in the U.S., I enter **1** followed by the area code, as shown in Figure 14.4. You can enter dashes (-) between the parts of the number, if you want; the modem ignores them.

> **TIP**
>
> If your phone line has call waiting, you might want to precede the telephone number with the code you use to disable call waiting so that your online session won't be disrupted. For many areas, the code is *70. Add a comma after this to make the modem pause. The combined entry might be something like this: *70, 1-510-555-4999.
>
> However, a better way to handle the area-code and call-waiting settings is to edit the connection's properties after the wizard has finished. I mention this again later in "Adjusting Dial-Up Connection Properties."

Figure 14.4
When prompted, enter the local access number for your ISP.

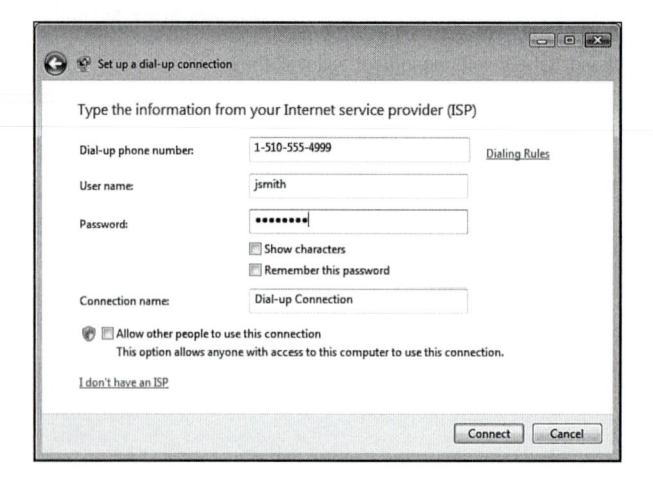

> **CAUTION**
>
> Be sure to use a local number. Your ISP will not help pay your phone bill if you choose a toll number by mistake.

The two preceding fields ask for your ISP username and password, as shown in Figure 14.4. If you select the Show Characters option, the password field displays the characters in your password instead of the black circles. This can be useful if you need to verify that you are typing in the correct password. If you turn on this option for this reason, I recommend turning it off again when you are done; it could be a potential security risk because your password is then visible to prying eyes.

If you want to have the password for your ISP account remembered so you don't need to type it in each time you connect to the Internet, select the Remember This Password option.

The last field asks for a connection name. Type in a name that will help you identify what the connection is used for. Using the name of the ISP is always good.

The last option, Allow Other People to Use This Connection, is not enabled by default. Select this option if you want the Internet account information to be useable by anyone who uses the computer. Uncheck this if you don't want other users to connect to the Internet with your dial-up account.

Click Connect. Windows Vista immediately dials your ISP.

That's it; your connection is ready to use. If you have no other LAN or dial-up connections, you can simply start Internet Explorer to automatically dial. You can choose Start, Control Panel, Network and Internet, Network and Sharing Center, and then Manage Network Connections under the list of tasks to modify your dial-up configuration at any time.

If you have several ISP accounts, ISP access numbers for different cities, or both personal and business dial-up connections, you can add connections by repeating the Connect to the Internet Wizard process for each access telephone number or account.

> **TIP**
> If you find yourself frequently having to dig into Network Connections to get to a connection icon, you can make a desktop or quick-launch shortcut for it. Click and drag the connection icon from Network Connections to the desktop or Quick Launch bar. The shortcut is created when you release the mouse button.

> **TIP**
> For maximum protection against hackers, I suggest that you read Chapter 35, on network security. At the very least, follow the steps in the next section to be sure that Windows Firewall is enabled. It ought to be enabled by default, but you should check just to be safe.

ADJUSTING DIAL-UP CONNECTION PROPERTIES

As configured by the wizard, your dial-up connection is properly set up for most Internet service providers. The wizard doesn't do a good job of setting up the area-code and call-waiting settings, so you might want to manually adjust these. You won't likely need to change any of the other settings, but just in case (and because I know you're curious), I walk you through the various settings and properties that are part of a dial-up connection. (I explain dial-up connection properties in more detail in Chapter 37, "Wireless Networking.")

You can view a connection's properties by selecting Start, Control Panel, Network and Internet Connections, Network and Sharing Center, and clicking Manage Network Connections. This displays all dial-up connections you've configured (see Figure 14.5). Right-click the icon for your dial-up connection and select Properties. You'll see four tabs, shown in Figure 14.6, which I will run through in the order in which they appear. Only a few settings ever need to be changed for an ISP connection. These do matter:

- The General tab contains modem properties and the ISP telephone number. If you travel with your computer, check Use Dialing Rules, be sure the area code is set correctly and is not entered in the Phone Number field, and click Dialing Rules if you want to enable call-waiting control.

- If you have multiple modems, you can choose at the top of this page which of one or more of these modems will be used for this particular connection.

- Using the Configure button for the modem, you can set the maximum speed used to communicate from the computer to the modem. For *external* modems connected via a COM port, if you don't have a special-purpose high-speed serial port, you might want to reduce this speed from the default 115200 to 57600.

Figure 14.5
Network Connections shows icons for each of your dial-up accounts and high-speed links.

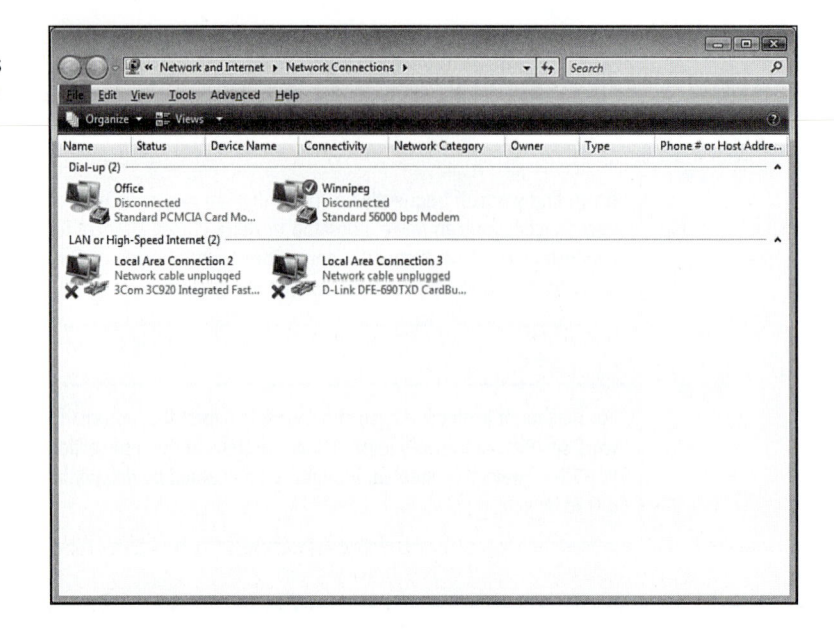

Figure 14.6
A dial-up connection's properties page lets you change dialing rules, set network parameters, and manage the security options.

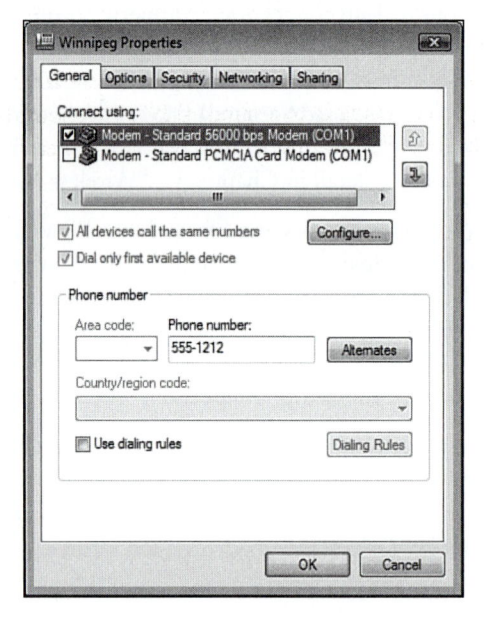

- Using the Alternates button for the telephone number, you can add multiple telephone numbers for your ISP, which will be automatically tried, in turn, if the first doesn't answer.

- On the Options tab, you can configure dialing and redialing options.
    - Select the Display Progress While Connecting option to have progress information displayed during the connection process.
    - Select the Prompt for Name and Password, Certificate, etc. option to have Windows Vista prompt you for your dial-up username and password each time you connect. You can also use dial-up networking to log on to your Windows domain. Don't check this option if you use a commercial ISP; that's only for connections to corporate networks.
    - You can select to have Windows Vista prompt you for the phone number of your ISP each time you connect.
    - You can select a time to wait before hanging up the line when no activity occurs. By doing so, you can help cut costs if you pay an hourly rate to your ISP by having your computer disconnect itself from the Internet if it detects that you've not been using your connection for a set amount of time.
    - To maintain a permanent or *nailed-up* dial-up connection, check Redial If Line Is Dropped and set the disconnect time to Never. (Do this only with the consent of your ISP.)
- The Security tab controls whether your password can be sent in unencrypted form. It's okay to send your ISP password unsecured.
- The Networking tab determines which network components are accessible to the Internet connection. If you're dialing in to a standard ISP, you should leave File and Printer Sharing unchecked; you'll learn more about that in Chapter 22.

Click OK to save your changes.

Configuring a High-Speed Connection

If you're using an Ethernet network adapter to connect your computer to a DSL or cable Internet service, the installer might set up your computer for you. "Self-install" providers give you a set of instructions specific to your service. In the next several sections, I give you a general idea of what's required.

You start by installing and configuring a network adapter to connect to the modem, or plugging in a USB-based modem, and then setting up the connection with the Connect to the Internet Wizard. Configuring the network adapter goes something like this:

1. If your computer has a built-in Ethernet network adapter that you're not already using for a home or office LAN, you can use the built-in adapter to connect to your broadband modem, so you can skip ahead to Step 3. Otherwise, you have to install an additional plug-in Ethernet adapter. Your ISP might provide this, or you might have to purchase one.

2. For an internal adapter, shut down the computer, insert the card, turn the computer back on, and log on as a Computer Administrator. In most cases, Windows automatically installs and configures drivers for the adapter. For an external or PCMCIA (PC Card) adapter, just log on as a Computer Administrator and plug it in.

3. Configure the network adapter according to the instructions your ISP gave you. In most cases, you can leave it with all the default settings, although in some cases you might need to configure a specific IP address, as described in the later section "Setting Up Dynamic IP Addressing (DHCP)."

> **CAUTION**
>
> If your broadband service uses a network adapter (that is, an Ethernet adapter) to connect to a cable or DSL modem, you *must* take these additional steps to secure your computer from hackers.
>
> 1. Open the Network Connections window. You can get to this from the Control Panel by clicking Network and Internet, Network and Sharing Center, Manage Network Connections.
> 2. Locate the icon that corresponds to the network adapter that connects to your DSL or cable modem—it's probably labeled Local Area Connection. Right-click it and select Properties.
> 3. Under This Connection Uses the Following Items, only QoS Packet Scheduler and Internet Protocol (TCP/IP) should be checked. If any other entries have checkmarks, click the checkmarks to remove them.
> 4. Double-check to be sure that neither Client for Microsoft Networks nor File and Printer Sharing for Microsoft Networks is checked.
> 5. Click OK and then close Network Connections.
>
> Although I strongly recommend that you read the Windows Firewall section in Chapter 22, if you don't, at least be sure to take these steps.

After the adapter has been configured and attached to the DSL or cable modem with a network cable, you configure the connection. The procedure depends on whether your ISP uses PPPoE or an always-on connection. The next two sections describe these procedures.

Configuring a PPPoE Broadband Connection

Most DSL and some cable Internet providers use a connection scheme called *Point-to-Point Protocol over Ethernet (PPPoE)*. This technology works a lot like a standard dial-up connection, but the "call" takes place through the DSL circuit or TV cable instead of over a voice connection. Windows Vista has PPPoE software built in, but the setup process varies from provider to provider; yours should give you clear instructions.

> **NOTE**
>
> Some Internet service providers give you a CD-ROM with installation software that does the next setup procedure for you. I intensely dislike this practice: Who knows what other software—including adware and "customer support" spyware—they're installing? Personally, I lie to them, tell them I'm installing the connection on a Macintosh or Linux computer that can't use their software, and ask for the information needed to perform the setup manually. Sometimes this works, and sometimes it makes life very difficult. For instance, one major ISP I've worked with requires you to set up the service account through a special website, so if you want to shun their software, you need Internet access to set up your Internet access.

If you perform the procedure manually, the steps should look like this:

1. Open the Network Connections window by clicking Start, Control Panel, Network and Internet, and Network and Sharing Center.
2. Click Set Up a Connection or Network. Select Connect to the Internet and click Next. If necessary, click No.
4. Select Broadband.
5. Enter the username and password assigned by your ISP.
6. Enter your ISP's name and click Connect.

At this point, you're prompted to sign on. The procedure for signing on and off is the same as for dial-up Internet service and is described later in this chapter under "Making and Ending a Dial-Up Connection."

> **NOTE**
>
> Installing a network adapter to connect to a broadband modem doesn't give you a local area network—it's just a way of connecting to the modem. If you want to set up a LAN in addition to an Internet connection, see Chapter 20, "Creating a Windows Network," and Chapter 22, "Connecting Your Network to the Internet."

SETTING UP DYNAMIC IP ADDRESSING (DHCP)

In most cases, your ISP will use the DHCP protocol to configure client network adapters. This is the default setting for all new network adapters. To confirm the setting, follow these steps:

1. Log on using an Administrator account. Open the Network Connections window, for example, from Start, Control Panel, Network and Internet, Network and Sharing Center, Manage Network Connections.
2. Right-click the icon for the local area connection that corresponds to the adapter connected to your DSL or cable modem, and select Properties.
3. Highlight Internet Protocol (TCP/IP) and click Properties.

4. Ensure that Obtain an IP Address Automatically and Obtain DNS Server Address Automatically are selected.

Some ISPs require you to give them the *MAC address* of your network adapter. This is an identification number built into the hardware that uniquely identifies your particular network adapter. To find this number, follow these steps:

1. Open a command prompt window by clicking Start, All Programs, Accessories, Command Prompt.
2. Type `ipconfig /all` and press Enter.
3. You might need to scroll back, but find the title that reads something similar to Ethernet Adapter Local Area Connection. Look for the name of the adapter that goes to your broadband modem. This might be Local Area Connection 2, if you've installed an extra adapter. Ignore any entries that mention the word *Miniport*. If you have multiple adapters and can't tell which is which, unplug the network cable from all but the one that goes to the modem and type the command again.
4. Find the line titled Physical Address. It will be followed by six pairs of numbers and letters, as in 00-03-FF-B9-0E-14. This is the information to give to your ISP.

Alternatively, you might be instructed to set your computer's name to a name that your ISP provides. To do this, follow these steps:

1. Log on using an Administrator account. Click Start and right-click Computer. Select Properties.
2. Under Computer Name, Domain, and Workgroup Setting, click Change Settings. On the Computer Name tab, click the Change button.
3. Enter the computer name as supplied by your ISP, as shown in Figure 14.7.

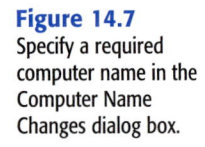

Figure 14.7
Specify a required computer name in the Computer Name Changes dialog box.

Configuring a High-Speed Connection

4. Click More and enter the domain name specified by your ISP, as shown in Figure 14.8.

Figure 14.8
Enter your ISP's full domain name in the DNS Suffix dialog box.

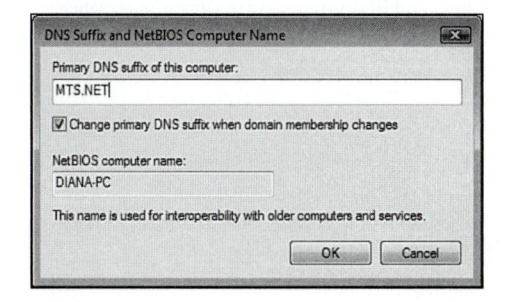

When you close all these dialog boxes by clicking OK, you need to let Windows restart. When it restarts, your Internet connection should be up and running.

Setting Up a Fixed IP Address

In some cases, your ISP will require you to set your LAN adapter to a fixed IP address. This might be required with either PPPoE or "always-on" service. To set the address, follow these steps:

1. Log on as a Computer Administrator. Open the Network Connections window, for example, from Start, Control Panel, Network and Internet, Network and Sharing Center, and Manage Network Connections.
2. Right-click the Local Area Connection icon and select Properties.
3. Select Internet Protocol and click the Properties button.
4. Select Use the Following IP Address, and enter the IP address, subnet mask, and default gateway information provided by your ISP, as shown in Figure 14.9.

Figure 14.9
Here you can add the network address, subnet mask, and DNS information supplied by your ISP.

> **TIP**
> If you use your computer at work and at home, and have a fixed IP address at home, leave the IP address and DNS settings set to Obtain Automatically for work, and make the fixed IP address entries for home on the Alternate Configuration tab that appears when Obtain Automatically is selected.

> **TIP**
> When you're entering TCP/IP dotted-decimal numbers such as 1.2.3.4, the spacebar advances the cursor across the periods. This technique is much easier than using the mouse to change fields.

5. Select Use the Following DNS Server Addresses, and enter the two DNS addresses provided by your ISP.
6. Click OK to return to the Local Area Connection Properties dialog box.

When you have completed this procedure, return to the PPPoE setup steps, or, if you have always-on service, open Internet Explorer to test-drive your new connection.

Making and Ending a Dial-Up Connection

If you use a dial-up connection with an analog modem or ISDN line, after you've set up an icon for your ISP, making the connection is a snap. You use this same procedure if you use a broadband connection with PPPoE that requires you to log on:

1. Click Start and click Connect To.
2. Select the appropriate connection from the list and click Connect.
3. When Windows displays a connection dialog box (see Figure 14.10), enter the password assigned by your ISP. If you're not the only one using the PC and you want to allow others to connect with your account (or you don't care who uses your account), check Save This Username and Password for the Following Users and click Anyone Who Uses This Computer.

> **TIP**
> If you use the Classic Start menu, you can put your dial-up connections on your Start menu for quick access. To do this, first right-click the Start button and click Properties. Then click Customize. Click the Expand Network Connections option from the list of Advanced Start Menu Options. Click OK.

Figure 14.10
When you want to initiate a dial-up connection, enter your user ID and password, and check Save Password to simplify connecting in the future.

4. For a dial-up connection only, check that the phone number is correct, including area code and any required prefix numbers. You might need to correct your current location (Dialing From) and/or the Dialing Rules if the prefix or area code isn't correct; to do this, click Properties and then, optionally, Dialing Rules.

5. Click Dial to make the connection.

Windows then dials your ISP and establishes the connection; if it works, a connection icon appears in the notification area with a temporary note indicating the connection speed.

If your modem doesn't attempt to connect to your ISP, **see** *"Modem Didn't Dial ISP" in the "Troubleshooting" section at the end of this chapter.*

If the connection fails, Windows displays a (usually) sensible message explaining why: There was no dial tone because your modem is unplugged, there was no answer at the ISP or the line is busy, or your user ID and password failed. In the last case, you get three tries to enter the correct information before Windows hangs up the phone.

If the modem dials but fails to establish a connection, **see** *"Modem Dialed ISP but the Connection Failed" in the "Troubleshooting" section at the end of this chapter.*

(Of course, if you use a dedicated, always-on Internet connection, you won't have to fool with dialing and hanging up connections. To be honest, I don't know which I like more about my DSL connection, its lickety-split speed or the fact that I don't have to wait for a modem connection to be made.)

When your connection is made, you should be able to browse websites, check your email, and so on.

> *If your Internet connection seems to be working but you can't view any web pages,* **see** *"Can't Reach Any Websites" in the "Troubleshooting" section at the end of this chapter.*

Checking the Connection Status

The notification area connection icon shows two tiny computer screens, which are normally black. They flicker when data activity occurs on the dial-up connection, momentarily turning green to show that the modem is active. The two indicators represent data you're sending and data returned from your ISP, respectively. This icon is actually a decent troubleshooting tool because you can immediately see whether modem activity is taking place.

If you let your mouse cursor hover over the connection icon, a small pop-up window shows the number of bytes transmitted and received over the current connection.

> **NOTE**
> The network connections icon should appear in the notification area by default. If it is not there, check that it has not mistakenly been disabled. Right-click the Start menu and click Properties. Select the Notification Area tab. Verify that there is a check beside the Network option.

Hanging Up a Dial-Up Connection

When you finish with your Internet connection, simply right-click the connection icon in your task tray and select Disconnect. Windows hangs up the dial-up connection and removes the icon from the Notification Area in a few seconds.

Changing the Default Connection

If you don't establish a connection manually before using an Internet program such as Internet Explorer, Windows dials your ISP automatically when you start these programs. If you don't want Windows to dial automatically, or if you have defined multiple dial-up connections, you can tell Windows which, if any, of the connections you want it to dial automatically.

To change the default settings, follow these steps:

1. Open the Control Panel, select Network and Internet, and click Internet Options. Alternatively, within Internet Explorer, you can choose Tools, Internet Options.
2. Select the Connections tab and highlight the dial-up connection you want to use for Internet browsing (see Figure 14.11).

Figure 14.11
In the Internet Properties dialog box, you can specify which dial-up connection to use automatically when an Internet application is started.

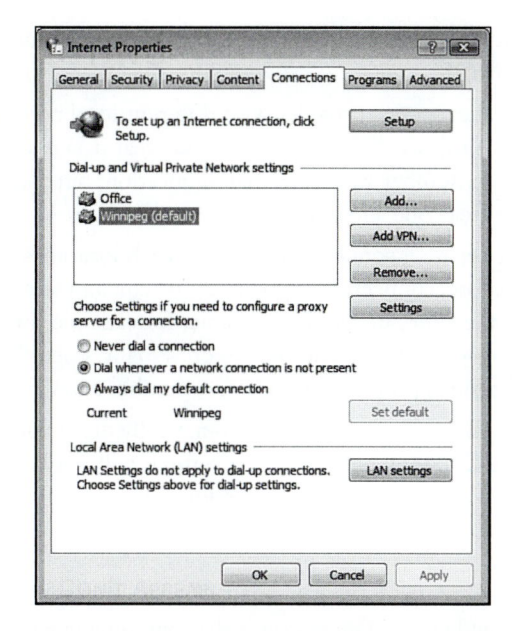

3. If you use a standalone computer or a portable computer that sometimes has Internet access via a LAN, select Dial Whenever a Network Connection Is Not Present.

   If you want to use the modem connection even while you're connected to a LAN, you can select Always Dial My Default Connection.

   Finally, if you don't want Windows to dial automatically and you prefer to make your connection manually, you can choose Never Dial a Connection.

4. If you have actually changed the default dial-up connection, click Set Default.
5. Click OK.

Managing Multiple Internet Connections

Life would be so simple if computers and people just stayed put, but that's not the way the world works anymore. Portable computers now account for more than half of the computers sold in the United States. Managing Internet connections from multiple locations can be a little tricky.

I talk a bit more about the ins and outs of traveling with your computer in Chapter 37, "Wireless Networking," and Chapter 38, "Hitting the Road," where the topics are wireless and remote networking.

The issue comes up with plain Internet connectivity as well, so let me share some tips:

- If you use a LAN Internet connection in the office and a modem connection elsewhere, bring up the Connections tab of the Internet Properties dialog box and choose Dial Whenever a Network Connection Is Not Present, as I discussed in the previous section, "Changing the Default Connection."

- If you use different LAN connections in different locations, see "Multiple LAN Connections," in Chapter 38.
- If you use a dial-up Internet service provider with different local access numbers in different locations, life is a bit more difficult. It would be great if Windows would let you associate a distinct dial-up number with each dialing location, but it doesn't—dialing locations just adjust the area code and dialing prefixes.

   The solution is to make separate connection icons for each location's access number. After you set up and test one connection, right-click its icon and select Create Copy. Rename the icon using the alternate city in the name; for example, I might name my icons My ISP Berkeley, My ISP Freestone, and so on. Finally, open the properties page for the new icon and set the appropriate local access number and dialing location.

   In this case, it's best to tell Windows never to automatically dial a connection (as shown earlier in "Changing the Default Connection") because it will not know which of several connections is the right one to use; it might dial a long-distance number without you noticing.

Moving around from one network to another or one ISP to another can also cause major headaches when you try to send email. The reason is that outgoing email has to be sent from your email program to a mail server called an SMTP server. These servers are set up to reject incoming email from any unidentified user who is not directly connected to or dialed up to their own network. For example, if you have Windows Mail set up to send email through your company's mail server and you try to send mail from home, your company's server will see that you're connected from a foreign network—that is, your ISP's network—and might reject the message, calling it an "attempt to relay mail."

Likewise, you might experience the same problem if you are set up to send through your ISP's mail server and then try to send mail from a wireless connection at an Internet café.

Troubleshooting

Modem Didn't Dial ISP

When I attempted to make a connection to my ISP, the modem didn't make an audible attempt to connect.

Four possible problems are involved here:

- Your phone line might not be correctly plugged into the modem. Be sure the phone cable is plugged into the correct jack on the modem.
- The phone line might not be working. Try an extension phone in the same wall jack to see if there's a dial tone.

- The modem might be working, but its speaker volume might be turned down. (This has fooled me more than once!) Some external modems have volume knobs. You can set the volume on an internal modem by opening Control Panel, Hardware and Sound, and Phone and Modem Options. View the Modems tab and select Properties. Select the Modem tab and adjust the volume control.

- The modem might have a hardware problem. Open the modem properties, as described in the previous paragraph. View the Diagnostics tab and click Query Modem. After 5–15 seconds, you should see some entries in the Command/Response list. If an error message appears instead, your modem is not working properly. If it's an external modem, be sure it's powered up. If it's an internal modem, see Chapter 30. Try to update the modem's driver software.

MODEM DIALED ISP BUT THE CONNECTION FAILED

When I attempted to make a connection to my ISP, the modem made the call, but the Internet connection still failed.

Windows should indicate what sort of problem was encountered. You might have typed your account name and password incorrectly. Try one or two more times. If it still doesn't work, a call to your ISP is the best next step. Your ISP might require you to enter the account name information in an unintuitive way. (Earthlink, for example, requires you put ELN\ before your account name.) Your ISP's customer support people can help you straighten this out.

CAN'T REACH ANY WEBSITES

My Internet connection seems to be established correctly, but I can't reach any websites.

Troubleshooting connection problems is such a large topic that an entire chapter is devoted to it. If you're having trouble, turn to Chapter 24, "Troubleshooting Your Network," for the nitty-gritty details.

TIPS FROM THE WINDOWS PROS: STAYING CONNECTED WHILE TRAVELING ABROAD

As I said earlier, you can choose an ISP with regional local access numbers to let you connect without toll charges wherever you roam in your home country. But what about when you travel overseas?

Actually, you usually don't have to go far to find an Internet terminal. You can rent PCs with Internet connections for roughly $1–$10 per hour almost anywhere. Listings of Internet cafés and computer parlors are now a required element in guidebooks (such as the fantastic *Rough Guide* series), and tourism information centers in most towns can direct you to the nearest rental centers.

If you want to connect your own computer, however, connecting is a bit more difficult. The following are some tips I've picked up in travels through Mexico, Australia, and Europe:

- Do your research before you leave. Search the Internet to find at least one Internet location and/or ISP in each area you'll be visiting. Print these pages and bring them along, being sure to get the local address and telephone number. You might find a more convenient location or better service after you arrive, but this way you have a place to start.

- Most Internet cafés won't let you hook up your own computer. Some will. You can find Kinko's Copy centers, for example, in many large cities in North America, Europe, and Asia; they're outfitted with fast computers, fast connections, and at least one bay with an Ethernet cable that you can use to connect your own laptop. If your laptop doesn't have a built-in Ethernet adapter, be sure to bring along a PCMCIA (PC card) Ethernet card. (You have to configure it using the Local Area Connection icon in Network Connections, as you'll learn in Chapter 20, using the settings the rental center provides.)

- Bring some formatted floppy disks and a USB thumb drive with you. If you need to transfer files and can't hook up your own computer, you can at least use these removable disks.

- If you normally receive email through a POP mail server at your ISP, use one of the free email services such as Hotmail or Yahoo! Mail to view your home email via the Web while you're traveling. Use a different password, not your regular password, for the free account. Set up the free service to fetch mail from your ISP, using what is called *external* or POP mail. Set the mail service to "leave mail on the server" so you can filter through your mail the normal way when you get home. Delete the free account or change its password when you return home.

  These steps let you read your mail from virtually any Internet terminal in the world and protect your real mail password from unscrupulous types who might be monitoring the network traffic in the places you visit.

- If you're staying a reasonable length of time in one country, you can sign up for a month of Internet service. For example, in Australia, I used ozemail.com, which gave me local access numbers all over the Australian continent. A month's service cost only $17, with no setup fee. Once I found an adapter for Australia's curious telephone jacks, I was all set.

- If you do use a foreign ISP, configure your email software to use the foreign ISP's outgoing mail (SMTP) server, but keep your incoming POP server pointed to your home ISP. (This step is important because most ISPs' mail servers won't accept mail from dial-up users outside their own networks. You need to use *their* SMTP server to *send* mail, and your home POP server to *pick up* mail.)

- Get power plug adapters and telephone plug adapters from a travel store, telephone accessory store, or international appliance store before you leave, if you can.

CHAPTER 15

Using Internet Explorer 7

In this chapter

Origins and Development of the World Wide Web   424

What's New in Internet Explorer 7?   425

Internet Explorer 7 Quick Tour   426

Using Multimedia Browsing and Downloading   435

Customizing the Browser and Setting Internet Options   448

Effectively Searching the Web   462

Safer Alternatives to IE   464

Getting a Microsoft Live ID   465

Troubleshooting   467

Tips from the Windows Pros: Finding and Using PDF Documents on the World Wide Web   468

Origins and Development of the World Wide Web

The World Wide Web (also called WWW or the Web) has worked its way into virtually every aspect of modern life. That's an astounding fact, considering that just a short 20 years ago, it was nothing more than an idea living inside a computer scientist's head. That scientist was Tim Berners-Lee. While working at the European Laboratory for Particle Physics (or CERN, from its original name, *Conseil Européen pour la Recherche Nucléaire*), Berners-Lee needed to devise a way in which scientific data could easily be shared simultaneously with physicists around the world. Along with Robert Cailliau, Berners-Lee designed the first web browser in 1990, to allow scientists to access information remotely without having to reformat the data.

This new communications technology that Berners-Lee and Cailliau developed transmitted data to viewers via the Internet, which by the early 1990s already existed as a global network, linking numerous educational and government institutions worldwide. The Internet served for decades as a means of exchanging electronic mail (email), transferring files, and holding virtual conversations in newsgroups, although data shared online was typically static and text only. The new technology provided data in hypertext format, which made it easier for far-removed scientists to view the electronic library at CERN's information server. The hypertext data could even incorporate graphics and other file formats, a practice virtually unknown to Internet users of the time.

Despite a relatively small initial audience, the hypertext concept quickly caught on, and by 1993, more than 50 hypertext information servers were available on the Internet. That year also saw the development of Mosaic, the first modern and truly user-friendly hypertext browser. Mosaic was produced by the National Center for Supercomputing Applications (NCSA) at the University of Illinois with versions for the X Window System, PC, and Macintosh. Mosaic served as the basis for a number of browsers produced by commercial software developers, with Netscape Navigator and Microsoft Internet Explorer eventually becoming Mosaic's best-known offspring.

The world was eager when the first commercial websites began appearing in 1994. President Bill Clinton and Vice President Al Gore had already popularized the idea of an "information superhighway" during their 1992 political campaign, and by the next year, it seemed that everyone wanted to get online and see what this new World Wide Web of information had to offer. A high level of media coverage meant that, by 1995, most of the general public knew what the World Wide Web was and wanted to be part of it.

The rest, as they say, is history. In its current form, the Web exists on hundreds of thousands of servers around the world. The system of naming and addressing websites is implemented by a number of private registrars contracted by the United States government. Today you can go shopping, play games, conduct research, download tax forms, check the status of a shipment, find directions to a new restaurant, get advice, or just plain goof off on the World Wide Web.

The hypertext concept has grown as well, even outside the confines of the Internet. These days, Microsoft structures much of the Windows interface in a Hypertext Markup Language (HTML) format. This makes interfacing with the Web more seamless and enables you to use the same program—in this case, Internet Explorer 7—to browse the World Wide Web, your company's intranet, the contents of your own computer, the online Help system, the Control Panel, and other network resources.

What's New in Internet Explorer 7?

If you have used Internet Explorer 5 or 6, IE7 will be familiar to you. Some of its new features are behind the scenes—not readily apparent, but designed to make IE run more smoothly. Others are enhancements that you will see, including these:

- The interface is streamlined; the menu and links are no longer visible by default (although you can still activate them, if you want).
- The Search Companion in Internet Explorer 6 is gone; it was replaced by the Live Search box at the upper-right corner of the window (underneath the Minimize, Maximize, and Close buttons). The Live Search box makes it faster and easier for you to search for items on the Web.
- The toolbar appears below the Address box, and Internet Explorer presents web pages in tabs. You can open a new page in your current tab, or you can open a new tab and have any number of web pages open at one time, all contained within a single browser window. You just click on tabs to switch between each web page. The Favorites and Add Favorites buttons appear to the left of the tab.
- The right side of the toolbar contains easily accessible task menus, including the capability to obtain RSS feeds automatically from sites that IE7 recognizes as having them available.

> **TIP**
>
> When you open a website, IE7 automatically looks for web feeds that are available on the page. A *web feed* is content that is published frequently by a website. That content can include text, graphics, audio, and video. You may have heard of RSS, or Really Simple Syndication, which is the leading system for creating and delivering web feeds. If IE7 finds a web feed on the page, the Web Feed button changes color from gray (no web feed) to orange (web feed available) so you can download and view and/or listen to the content as well as subscribe to the feed so you can receive new content from the website automatically.

- As with IE6, playback support for Flash and Shockwave files is built into IE7.

> **NOTE**
>
> The Department of Justice Consent Decree has caused some changes in the way that middleware applications are handled. You can configure your computer to show only Microsoft middleware applications (Windows Mail, Internet Explorer, and so on) to show only non-Microsoft middleware applications (Netscape Navigator, Eudora, and so forth), or to show some combination of both. See Chapter 26, "Tweaking and Customizing Windows," for more information on how to make these changes to your Windows Vista computer.

Internet Explorer 7 Quick Tour

Web browsers have become so ubiquitous that we assume you are already comfortable with the basics of web browsing. And because many Windows Vista elements such as Windows Explorer, the Control Panel, and Network use the background code of IE6, you are probably already familiar with the location of common toolbar buttons, menus, and other screen elements.

Still, IE7 does have some new features, so I provide an overview of how to use some of them here. This overview will be especially useful if you are switching from an even earlier version of Internet Explorer or another web browser, such as Netscape Navigator.

→ You must have a connection to the Internet configured on your computer before you can connect to the Web. **See** "Getting Connected," **p. 393**.

You can begin browsing the Internet by launching Internet Explorer from the Start menu.

If you connect to the Internet via a dial-up connection, you might be prompted to connect. When the connection is established, Internet Explorer probably opens by default to the Windows Live home page, as shown in Figure 15.1, so you can search the Web. Some PC manufacturers, such as Compaq, customize IE before delivery so that you see their home page instead.

→ To change the home page so that you see a personal favorite when IE opens, **see** "Tweaking the GUI," **p. 897**.

> *Did a web page freeze your browser?* **See** *"Internet Explorer Crashes on Certain Web Pages" in the "Troubleshooting" section, later in this chapter.*

Web pages change frequently, so the page you see will probably look different than Figure 15.1. The general layout of the IE7 window might also be different from what is shown here, although if you have performed a standard installation of Windows Vista and have not done any customizations, it should look like this.

> **TIP**
>
> Want even more space to view web pages? Press F11 to change the view and remove some screen elements to make more room for web documents. If you don't like what you see, press F11 again to toggle back.

Figure 15.1
Internet Explorer opens with Windows Live, the default home page, displayed.

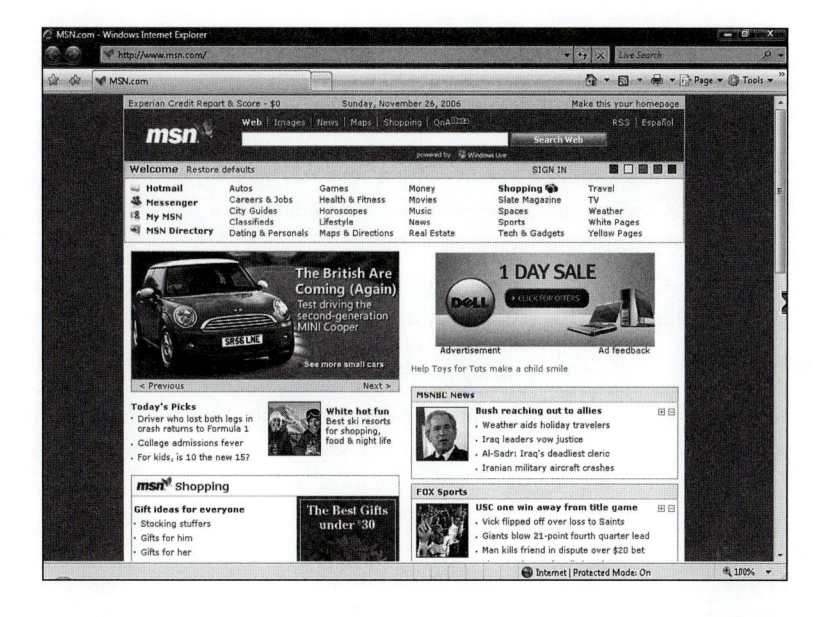

Consider creating buttons on the Links bar for the web pages you visit most frequently. To see the Links bar, right-click on an empty area of the toolbar and then click Links from the pop-up menu. The Links bar appears, as shown in Figure 15.2. Before you customize the Links bar, keep these tips in mind:

- The Customize Links button merely takes you to a Microsoft-hosted web page that provides instructions on how to do what is already described here. Consider removing that button to make room for your own favorites.

Figure 15.2
The Links bar is a handy place to store your most frequently visited websites.

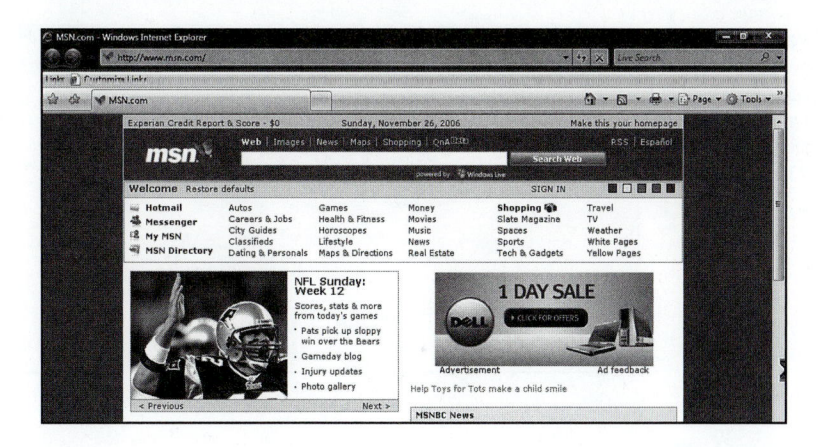

- You can remove unwanted Links buttons by right-clicking them and choosing Delete from the menu that appears.

- Make space for more Links by right-clicking an existing Links button and choosing Rename from the menu that appears. Type in a shorter name or abbreviation and then click OK.
- To create more room, reduce the length of your Address box and move it to share a "line" with another toolbar. (The main toolbar, on the top line, is a good place for the Address box.) Experiment with the placement of all toolbars so that you have as much space as possible to view web pages.
- The easiest way to add a web page to the Links bar is to drag the icon for the page from the Address box and drop it onto the Links bar. Figure 15.2 demonstrates this technique.

You can navigate around the Internet by typing web addresses into the Address box or by clicking hyperlinks on a page. The mouse pointer changes from an arrow into a hand whenever it is located over a link. Among the most useful features of the IE7 interface are the Back and Forward buttons. When you click the Back button, you return to the previously visited page. Clicking Forward moves you ahead once again. (To move around even faster, Alt+back arrow and Alt+forward arrow produce the back and forward functions; if you have a new mouse, it might also have special Back and Forward buttons on it.)

> Are you frustrated because Internet Explorer tells you that a site you frequently visit is unavailable? See "What Happened to the 'Website?" in the "Troubleshooting" section later in this chapter.

Notice that next to both the Back and Forward buttons are downward-pointing arrows. If you have been browsing several web pages, click the Recent Pages button, which is the button with the down arrow next to the Forward button. A menu similar to that shown in Figure 15.3 should appear, showing a backward progression of the web pages you have visited. Click a listing to move back several pages simultaneously instead of one at a time.

Figure 15.3
To move back several web pages instead of to the previous one, click the Recent Pages button next to the Forward button.

Entering URLs

Every web document you view in IE7 is identified by a unique address called a uniform resource locator (URL). When you visit a web page, for example, the URL for that page appears in the Address box of Internet Explorer. URLs for links usually also appear in the status bar when you place the mouse pointer over a hyperlink, although website designers are sometimes creating scripts so that an advertisement or other message appears in the status bar instead of the URL.

URLs are broken down into three main components. To illustrate, consider these URLs:

http://www.quepublishing.com/

http://www.irs.treas.gov/formspubs/index.html

http://smallbusiness.yahoo.com/

Each of the listed addresses conforms to this scheme:

`protocol://domain/path`

The protocol for all World Wide Web documents is `http`, short for Hypertext Transfer Protocol. The protocol is followed by a colon, two forward slashes, and the domain name. The domain often—but not always—starts with `www`. Following the domain is the path to a specific document file. You might notice that the first URL listed does not actually show a path; this is usually okay because Internet Explorer automatically looks for a file called `default.htm`, `index.htm`, `home.html`, or something along those lines in the root directory of the domain.

> **TIP**
> If you get an error message when trying to visit a URL, remove the path from the address and try again. Although the exact link might have changed, it's quite possible that the main page for the site still exists and that you will be able to find your information there.

When you type a URL into the IE Address box, a built-in feature automatically reviews your browsing history and presents possible matches. A list appears directly under the Address box and shrinks as you type more characters, narrowing the search. If you see a desired URL appear in the list, click it to go directly to that page. This feature, called AutoComplete, can save keystrokes, but it can also be incriminating if others use your computer and user profile. Do you really want your boss or a coworker to know you visited howtomakebandanasfrombananas.com? AutoComplete works with web form data as well, which means that others could see your user IDs, passwords, and other sensitive data for various sites.

If you are concerned about others viewing your data, disable AutoComplete by doing the following:

1. Click the Tools button in the toolbar and then click Internet Options.
2. Click the Content tab to bring it to the front, and in the AutoComplete area, click Settings.
3. Remove check marks next to the items that you do not want affected by AutoComplete.

4. To prevent existing URLs from being compromised, select the General tab in the Internet Options dialog box and, in the Browsing history area, click Delete. Click OK to finish.

> **NOTE**
>
> If no one else has access to your Windows Vista user profile or you really don't care who sees where you've been browsing, AutoComplete doesn't present a security problem. In this case, you should be able to safely leave the feature enabled.

Browsing in Tabbed Pages

If you open several different pages at once and you don't want multiple Internet Explorer buttons to clog your taskbar, you can view multiple pages from within the Internet Explorer 7 window by creating new tabbed pages and then opening a new website in each page. Tabbed pages have been around for a long time in other web browsers such as Firefox and add-ons to IE such as Avant Browser, but now Microsoft has finally caught up with the times, thank goodness.

When you open Internet Explorer 7, your home page appears in the default tab. As mentioned earlier, the default home page is Windows Live, as shown in Figure 15.4.

Figure 15.4
The Internet Explorer window that displays the Windows Live page in the Windows Live tab.

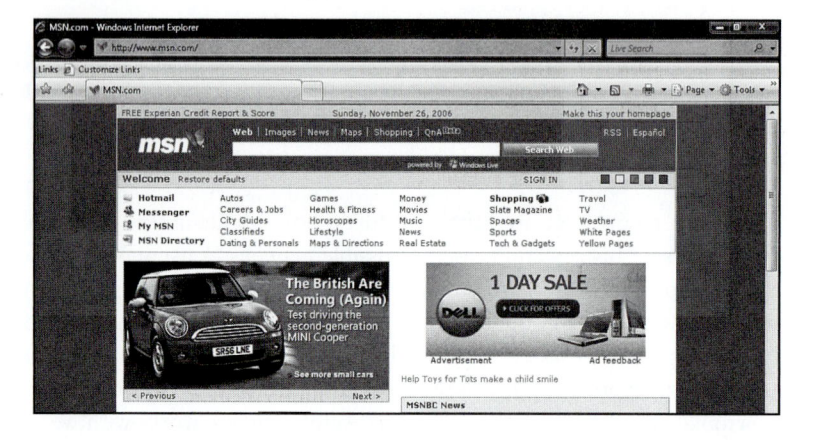

The name of the page appears in the tab. Next to the tab is a second, smaller tab. When you click this tab, a new tabbed page appears to the right of the first tab and displays the Welcome to Tabbed Browsing page, as shown in Figure 15.5.

The Welcome to Tabbed Browsing page provides information about how to get started with tabbed browsing and to learn more about tabs. The tab at the top of the window (with the title "Welcome to Tabbed Browsing") is raised and appears in a different color, to let you know that the tabbed page is the one you're viewing. Now that the new tabbed page is open, you can open a website in the page by typing the URL in the Address box.

Figure 15.5
The Welcome to Tabbed Browsing page.

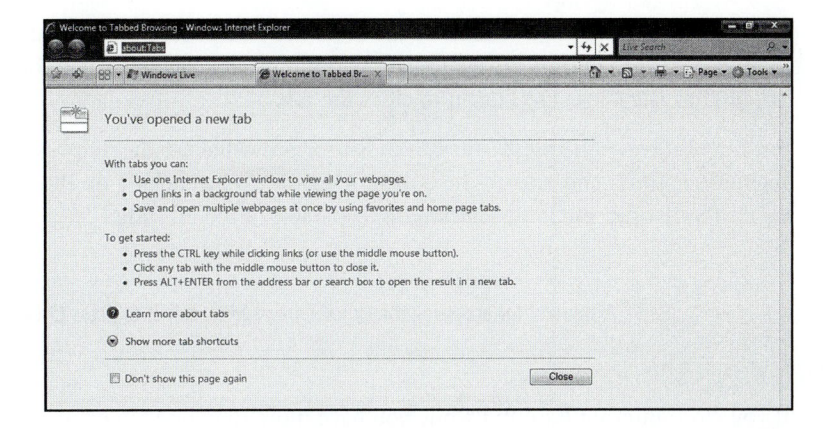

You can create a new tab by clicking on the small tab to the right of the new tab you just created. If you want to close your current tab, click the X to the right of the tab title.

> **TIP**
>
> Tabs also have pop-up menus that you can access by right-clicking on a tab that has a web page. This pop-up menu lets you close the current tab, close all other tabs except for the current one, refresh the page in the tab, refresh the pages in all tabs, and create a new tab.

Each tab has a set width, and all the tabs must fit between the Add Favorites button and the buttons on the right side of the toolbar. If the page title in the tab is too long to fit in the width of the tab, the title is truncated with ellipses at the right side of the title. You can view the entire name by moving the mouse pointer over the tab; about a half-second later, a pop-up menu appears that displays the full name of the tab. Unless the name of the page is extremely long, the full name appears in the Internet Explorer title bar as well.

When you create more than one tab, two small tabs appear to the left of the first tab. When you click the Quick Tabs tab, a list of all your open web pages in tabs appears in the Quick Tabs page, as shown in Figure 15.6.

Figure 15.6
The Quick Tabs page.

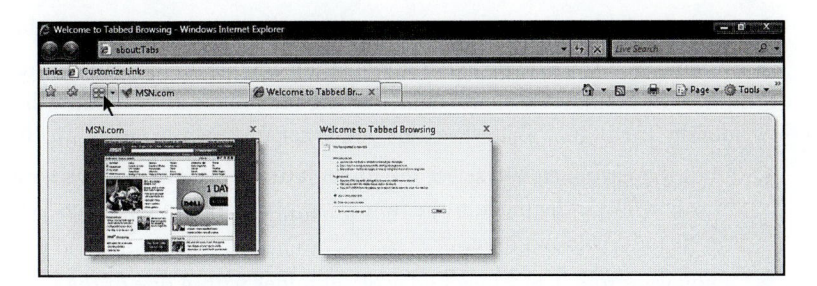

The Quick Tabs page shows thumbnails of all the web pages in all the tabs. The page titles and the Close (X) button appear above the thumbnails. Click on a thumbnail to open the tab, or click the Close (X) button to close the tab.

You can also view a list of all the tabs in list form by clicking the Tab List button. A list of open tabs appears underneath the button. Open a tab by clicking on the tab name in the list; the currently open tab has a checkmark to the left of the tab title.

> **NOTE**
>
> A shortcut for accessing the Quick Tabs page quickly is to press Ctrl+Q.

If you close Internet Explorer while you have more than one tab open, a dialog box appears and asks if you want to close all tabs. When you click the Close Tabs button, IE7 closes and only one tab appears the next time you open IE7. You can click the Show Options button to tell IE7 to reopen all the currently open tabs the next time you open Internet Explorer, and then click the Close Tabs button to close IE7.

> **TIP**
>
> Some other tabbed-browser programs give you more extensive tabbing features, such as setting up favorite groups of websites as related tabs that you can open up all at once—a great feature for doing research on specific topics where you have a load of web pages open at once. Check out Avant Browser or FireFox.

Adding Sites to Your Favorites

It's very inefficient (not to mention annoying) to type the URL in the Address box every time you want to access your favorite site. It's also difficult, if not impossible, to remember all your favorites. Fortunately, IE7 lets you add, save, and categorize your favorites so you can access them in the Favorites pane.

The process of adding a favorite is fairly simple. Your first step is to browse to the website you want to make one of your favorites. For best results, open the main or index page of the website first. Now try the following:

1. Click the Add to Favorites button in the toolbar, and then click Add to Favorites.
2. In the Add a Favorite dialog box, type the name of the favorite in the Name box, as shown in Figure 15.7. You can also change the name so that you will be able to easily identify the page. Whatever name you enter is shown in your Favorites list.
3. From the Create In list, select the folder where you want to save the favorite. IE7 contains five folders by default: the home (Favorites) directory, Links, Microsoft websites, MSN, and Windows Live.
4. If you want to create a new folder or subfolder within one of the current folders, click the New Folder button. The Create a Folder window appears, as shown in Figure 15.8.

Figure 15.7
The Add a Favorite dialog box.

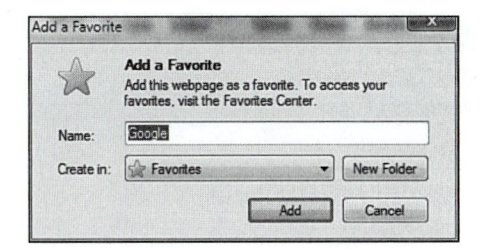

Figure 15.8
The Create a Folder window.

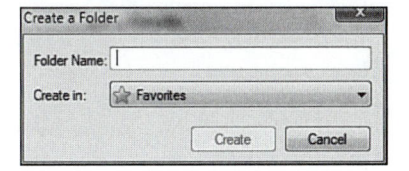

5. Type the folder name in the Folder Name box.
6. From the Create In list, select the folder where you want to create the new folder. The default is the home (Favorites) directory.
7. Click OK. The new folder you created appears in the Create In list.
8. Click Add. IE7 adds your favorite to the list.

Now that you've added a favorite to the list, you can view the favorite by opening the Favorites Center pane. Here's how:

1. Click the Favorites button in the toolbar. The Favorites Center pane appears on the left side of the window, as shown in Figure 15.9. Notice that the Favorite pane overlaps the web page you're viewing.
2. Click the folder that contains the favorite. The favorite appears underneath the folder name.
3. Click the favorite name to open the web page in the right pane.
4. Close the Favorites Center pane by clicking the Favorites button.

Working Offline

Many websites have Flash components that update automatically with new messages. However, if you have a slow dial-up connection, the constant changes can slow your connection to a crawl. This can prevent you from doing work on the website, such as reading text on the page.

Windows Vista makes it easy for you to turn off your connection by clicking the Tools button in the toolbar and then clicking Work Offline. When you're working offline, hyperlinks won't work and other active content (such as Flash components) won't update automatically. If you click on a hyperlink or a piece of active content, a dialog box appears and asks you whether you want to connect to the site or stay offline.

Figure 15.9
The Favorites pane.

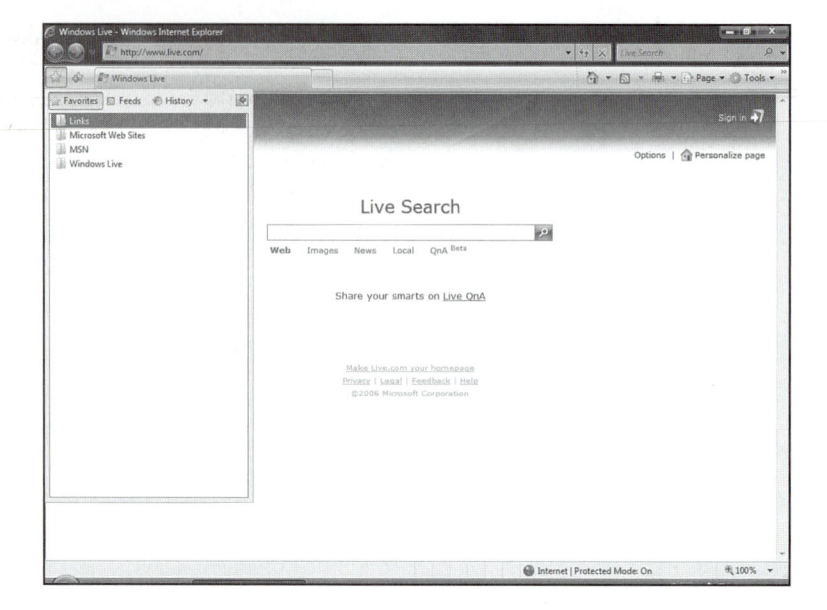

If you want to browse online again, click the Tools button in the toolbar and click Work Offline again.

> **NOTE**
>
> So what happened to viewing your favorite sites offline as you could in Internet Explorer 6? Apparently, Microsoft believes that because a majority of web surfers have broadband, always-on connections instead of dial-up, saving and viewing a page offline is no longer necessary. If you use a dial-up connection to access the Web, you need to be online to view the site.

SAVING A SINGLE WEB PAGE FOR LATER VIEWING

Sometimes you might want to save only a single web page, not a whole site, for offline viewing. Say you want to just reference a page, defer reading a page, save a page that shows proof of an online purchase, or print a page later, when you're offline. Here's how:

1. In IE, click the Page button in the toolbar and then click Save As.
2. In the Save As Type section of the dialog box, choose Web Page, Complete.
3. Then choose the folder, name the file, and click Save.

What happens now depends on your page content. The web page itself (the HTML file) will be stored in the folder you specified. If images, scripts, and other supporting files exist on the page, IE creates a folder just *under* the target folder and puts those items in it. Then IE modifies the HTML code in the HTML page to point to that subfolder instead of across the Web. This lets you open the web page without being online, and it should still look correct.

It's important to understand that, by default, the HTML file and its subfolder are linked and act as a single entity. Moving one or the other will move both of them. This prevents the entity from becoming nonfunctional if you move them separately.

If you have Microsoft Office installed, you have three options for altering this linkage behavior:

1. Open the Control Panel window and choose Appearance and Personalization, Folder Options.
2. Click the View tab.
3. Scroll down to Managing Pairs of Web Pages and Folders. Double-click it if it's not showing the three options below. The options are:
   - Show and Manage the Pair As a Single File (default setting)
   - Show Both Parts and Manage Them Independently
   - Show Both Parts But Manage Them As a Single File

NOTE If you try to change the name of either the HTML page or the underlying subfolder containing the associated files, you'll be warned that this will break the page.

Using Multimedia Browsing and Downloading

When the World Wide Web first debuted as a method for sharing scientific data among physicists, the hypertext format of the data was specifically chosen to enable sharing information in many different formats. For early Internet users, the ability to download pictures and other graphics in conjunction with web pages was both exciting and profound.

Today web pages containing pictures are common. Web developers continue to push the multimedia horizon, with many sites now featuring audio and video. You can even listen to radio stations and watch other broadcasts live over the Web.

In addition to multimedia-rich websites, you'll find that the Web is a good place to download software. You can find many places to download freeware, shareware, and software updates, and sites to purchase and download full versions of programs.

Images

Believe it or not, graphics-rich websites were once controversial. Some people believed that graphics would put too much strain on the bandwidth capacity of the Internet, but those gloom-and-doom predictions have not become a reality. Backbone improvements have helped the Net keep pace with the ever-growing appetite for multimedia on the Web, and images are now both common and expected.

Internet Explorer supports three basic graphics formats used in web pages:

- **JPEG**—Short for Joint Photographic Experts Group, this format enables pictures to be significantly compressed (reducing download time and bandwidth, but also image quality), so this is often used for photos on web pages.
- **GIF**—Short for Graphical Interchange Format, this format is often used for buttons and other simple icons used on web pages.
- **PNG**—Short for Portable Networking Graphics, this format was developed to help images load faster and keep them looking the same on different platforms.

The exact format used for each image is not apparent when you view the page. Normally, the specific format used is not important unless you plan to copy the graphics and use them for some other purpose. For web use, the formats are essentially interchangeable.

By default, IE7 displays graphics used in web pages. Although the idea of disabling this feature to enable speedier downloads might seem appealing, many web pages now rely so heavily on graphics that they do not include text links. This means you cannot navigate the site without the images. Don't disable this feature unless you deem it absolutely necessary.

> What if some graphics on a page open, but others don't? **See** "Some Graphics Don't Appear" in the "Troubleshooting" section, later in this chapter.

You can do a variety of things with online graphics. You will notice a new feature in IE7: When you mouse over a graphic, a pop-up window appears. Click the appropriate icon if you want to save the image to your hard drive, print it, email it, or just open the Pictures folder. If you find this toolbar annoying, disable it by clicking on the Tools button in the toolbar and then clicking Internet Options. Under the Advanced tab, scroll down to Multimedia and deselect Enable Image Toolbar. Click OK to save and close the window.

You'll also notice a little square with four arrows on it, in the lower-right corner of some pictures. This happens only on pictures that, if shown full size, wouldn't fit on the screen. IE7 thoughtfully autosizes such pictures so that you can see the whole image at once. Click on the little box; the image scales up to its full size, in higher resolution. When it's full size, click the little box again; the image you're viewing returns to the compressed size.

> **CAUTION**
>
> Before you use any graphics you find on the Web, check the website for a copyright statement or other information about terms of use. You should obtain permission before you use any copyrighted material.

Audio and Video

A growing number of websites offer audio or video content in addition to standard text and graphics. When used in conjunction with web content, the terms *audio* and *video* can mean a few different things:

- Basic audio files, such as MIDI music files, that play in the background while you view a web page.
- Video files on websites that download and play automatically or play when you click a Play button.
- Video media that plays using the Windows Media Player.
- Animated GIFs that give the appearance of a video signal but with a significantly reduced bandwidth requirement. They display a series of static GIF frames that simulate video and are often used in logos.
- Flash movies that also appear to be video but are actually vector-based instructions requiring very little bandwidth. "Vector-based" simply means that they have small mathematical descriptions (much the same way fonts do in Windows) that can be manipulated to animate the objects.
- Streaming audio or video that you choose to open and listen to or watch.

You might have noticed that when you visit certain websites, a song starts to play while you read the page. Audio isn't nearly as common as graphics in web pages because some people find it annoying. If you come across a web page that contains a song you would rather not hear, the most obvious solution is to turn down your speaker volume or mute the Windows volume control. If you're listening to music on your computer (such as from a CD or MP3 file) and you don't want to end your entire audio experience by turning off the speakers, see the following note.

> **NOTE**
> To disable audio, video, or other multimedia from automatically downloading when you visit a website, see Chapter 26. By disabling these "features," you also might notice that web pages will load faster. Note that some web pages use media-playback programs that IE settings won't control. For example, if a page has a RealMedia or QuickTime sound or video file in it, autoplayback of those files will commence regardless of IE settings.

Likewise, some websites contain video files and animations set to download and play automatically. MPEG and AVI video files are usually very large; if you have restricted bandwidth capacity, you might want to consider disabling them.

Web-based video seems to be improving almost daily, but most broadcasts are still lower in quality than that produced by a plain old television set. Whereas a broadcast TV signal typically delivers about 30 frames per second (fps), typical web-based streaming videos provide just 5–15fps. In contrast to streaming, many sites give you the option of downloading a video clip before playing it. Usually the clip in this format is much larger and of a higher quality than the streaming video. After the entire clip has been downloaded, it can be played and might appear as a high-quality image, depending on how it was produced. Playback typically is in Windows Media Player, QuickTime Player, or RealPlayer. The ranges of file sizes, frame sizes, and compression techniques—all of which affect the quality of the picture—abounds. Unlike the TV standard we are all accustomed to, the Web is the wild, wild West of video nonstandards.

→ To learn more about using the Windows Vista audio controls, **see** "Sound Recorder, DVD Maker, and other Multimedia Tools," **p. 349**.

MPEG, AVI, AND WMV VIDEOS

By default, MPEG, AVI, and WMV (Windows Media Video) files are played using Windows Media Player. Windows Media formats are sort of the new kid on the block and are Microsoft's attempt to be a big player in the Internet multimedia market. Just as movies encoded in Apple's QuickTime format or RealNetworks' RealPlayer format require those companies' proprietary player, Microsoft's proprietary format plays only in the Microsoft player.

→ Windows Media Player is covered in depth in Chapter 8, "Windows Media Player," but because how you deal with online video is relevant to mastering web browsing, I briefly mention its use in this context. Be sure to check Chapter 8 for more information about the Media Player, **p. 259**.

Snarfed Media Associations

When you install players such as RealPlayer, the programs want to alter your file associations. Each of the popular media players (QuickTime player, RealPlayer, and Windows Media Player) is engaged in a war of kidnapping your filename associations and wants to become your player of choice. They do this in hopes of garnering your business (that is, your money) one way or another. They do this either by selling you upgrades to the fancier model of the player or by selling advertisements that show up in their content—or both. These incentives behoove them to offer a quick means to reclaim any file associations that another player has hijacked. You don't have to play their game, though. You can always change those associations back to the player of your choice.

The easiest way to reset media file association is through the Preferences dialog box for the media player in question. However, unlike earlier versions of Windows and Windows Media Player, Windows Vista now requires you to change the default file type associated with a specific program. You do this in Windows Vista by opening the Control Panel, then clicking Programs, and then clicking Default Programs. In the Default Programs window, set a program (such as Windows Media Player) as the default by clicking the Set Your Default Programs link. In the Set Default Programs window, you can set the Windows Media Player as the program to open all applicable file types and protocols.

Some players try to reclaim associations each time you run them, which can be really annoying. Be aware, though, that not all players can play all the popular file formats. You need RealPlayer for Real format and QuickTime for QuickTime Windows. However, Media Player plays the greatest number of audio and video formats. If you have an Apple iPod and use Apple's insanely popular iTunes software, be aware that any songs or video downloaded with iTunes will not play in other software. Try as you might to avoid using multiple media applications, even if you are a middle-of-the-road media fan, you will likely need to switch among various media applications because there is no one-size-fits-all solution.

Most web pages that feature videos online give you links for RealPlayer, QuickTime, or Media Player, and let you choose your preference. Some sites give you links for downloading MPEG or AVI files. These don't stream, so you must first download them. Depending on your connection speed, downloading could take a while because these files tend to be very large. Just be prepared for a long download, especially if using a dial-up connection.

You might notice that Media Player opens as soon as you click the link. Earlier versions of Media Player (prior to version 8) remained blank until the entire file was downloaded. Now, with some types of files such as WMV (Windows Media Video) files, movies can start playing more quickly even though they are not technically streaming. (See the next section to read about streaming.) Instead, they are doing a progressive download. This is less reliable than streaming, but at least you don't have to wait until the movie is completely downloaded before you start seeing it. The download might stop a few times, though, if your connection speed is slow. QuickTime movies have had this feature for some time; now Media Player does, too.

If you click on the Media button in the toolbar, a miniature version of the Media Player opens in the left pane of your IE window, along with links for supposedly interesting media. When you click on a web page link for an audio or video file, you are asked whether you want it to play in this tiny Media Player or open in a regular Media Player window. The choice is up to you. The advantage of opening in the small window is that it lets you neatly play some tunes, movie trailers, or whatever in the left pane while you continue your web surfing.

Streaming Broadcasts

As mentioned earlier, another type of sound or video that you might play over the Internet is *streaming audio* or *streaming video*. Streaming audio/video is a format in which a signal "plays" over your Internet connection, starting a few seconds after you click, instead of playing from a file that was first downloaded to your hard drive.

When you first click a streaming signal, a portion of the signal is buffered in RAM on your computer. This buffer helps provide a steady feed if connection quality wavers. If the signal is received faster than it can be played, the additional data is buffered. However, if your connection deteriorates significantly, the video might not play smoothly. Streaming broadcasts are not written to the disk, so retrieving the signal later from your own PC will be impossible.

Although the minimum requirement of many streaming audio signals is typically 56K, a quicker connection is desirable. A lower speed delivers a lower-quality broadcast, skipping and jumping of video, or stopping altogether.

Streaming audio signals are often used to play various types of audio signals over the Web. For example, most online music retailers offer you the capability to listen to sample audio tracks from many of the CDs they sell. In addition, you can listen to many radio stations and programs—such as those on National Public Radio (www.npr.org)—over your Internet connection instead of a radio.

A number of information providers use streaming video to send newscasts and other broadcasts across the Web. You can watch news stories online through many news sites, such as www.cnn.com. You'll notice that you can continue to surf the Web while a current audio or video is playing.

MSN (www.msn.com) provides links to a number of online video resources, streaming and otherwise.

To access streaming audio or video signals, you need to have an appropriate plug-in program for IE7, such as the RealPlayer from Real Broadcast Network (www.real.com), QuickTime from Apple (www.apple.com/quicktime/), or Windows Media Player, included with Windows Vista. After you have downloaded and installed the appropriate streaming player (following the installation instructions provided by the player's publisher), you can access the streaming signals over the Web.

Although the Windows Media Player can handle many formats, most broadcasts require a specific player. Check the website that hosts the streaming media you want to play for specific requirements. Some websites offer a choice of player formats, and often the website will have a convenient link for downloading the necessary freeware. RealPlayer is a common application used for streaming audio, and many streaming video providers use QuickTime. Although the look might be different because of custom "skins" used on flashier sites, the basic functions are similar. If you look closely, you can tell whether it's Windows Media Player, RealPlayer, QuickTime, or another player.

Sometimes you need to wait for the file to download; other times it streams right away. QuickTime gives you the choice to download the entire file first so you can avoid glitches when you watch it. Notice that the play slider can go at a different rate than the progress bar, which indicates how much of the file has been downloaded. When it's downloaded, you can easily replay the clip without interruption. Note that the Windows Media Player can be encoded right into a web page, so the video might begin playing when you hit a particular URL.

→ To learn about downloading programs from the Web, **see** "Downloading Programs," **p. 442**.

To use a streaming media player, follow these steps:

1. Locate a link to an audio clip or video signal that you want to access, and click it.
2. Your streaming media player should open automatically. RealPlayer, Windows Media Player, and Apple QuickTime include standard Play, Pause, and Stop buttons.
3. When you are finished listening to the streaming signal, click the Close (X) button for the player.

When you access a streaming signal from the Web, notice the bandwidth requirements. Many signal providers provide scaling of signals from as low as 14.4Kbps to 300Kbps and higher. Choosing a signal that is scaled higher provides a higher-quality broadcast only if your connection can handle it. If you choose a larger signal than you have bandwidth for, the signal will arrive too fragmented to use. For example, suppose you use a dial-up connection that typically runs at 24Kbps–26Kbps, and the broadcaster offers signals in either 14.4 or 28.8 flavors. Although you might be tempted to opt for the 28.8Kbps signal because your connection is *almost* up to it, you will probably find that the 14.4Kbps broadcast provides a more usable signal.

MP3 Audio

MP3 is an audio file format whose name refers to files using MPEG Audio Layer 3, an encoding scheme for audio tracks. MP3 files are small (about $\frac{1}{12}$ the size of CD audio tracks), but they maintain a high sound quality. A minute of CD-quality MP3 music requires only 1MB of storage space.

Controversy has surrounded MP3 since its introduction. The small size of MP3 files makes it easier for people to slide behind copyright laws, pirate music, and illegally distribute them over the Internet. Authorities are currently working on ways to prevent these actions. However, this has only led to Napster spin-offs that are harder to control and much more difficult to track down or prosecute. It will be interesting to see how the Justice Department handles the impending and unavoidable new age of intellectual property protection.

The bottom line is this: Distributing or downloading MP3 files from any artist without permission is technically a violation of the law. Although some artists (particularly new ones) willingly provide audio tracks for free download as a means of building a fan base, many MP3 sites contain audio files that have been pirated. If you have questions about the legality of MP3 files you find on the Internet, you need to be the judge. Probably the most ethical approach is not to download them, but I don't want to sound like a prude. As I said, it's a brave new world out there in copyright protection. I believe that free music on the Web probably drives the purchase of new CDs and concert ticket sales. I'm a musician myself, and although I would want my music (and my books) protected, I also wouldn't mind more people becoming acquainted with my works—it could pay off in the long run. In any case, you might want to be careful sharing your MP3s of other people's music on the Web because it could be deemed illegal.

The MP3 format has become extremely popular, with tiny portable players (such as the iPod from Apple) available that can store endless hours of music. It is possible to load all your music into your computer and create your very own jukebox. Software for recording and organizing your music is available at www.real.com/player/, www.itunes.com, www.winamp.com, and www.musicmatch.com, to name a few. Many different applications can download MP3 files, including Windows Media Player, RealPlayer, and QuickTime. A number of consumer electronics companies are also now producing devices that allow you to play MP3 files away from your computer. Samsung makes a single device (called a Digimax) that functions as three: a digital camera, a PC camera to use for video conferencing, and an MP3 player. A wide variety of MP3 players are available, with varying storage capacities—some units as small as a pen. You can transfer MP3 files to the player's storage via a Universal Serial Bus (USB) or a parallel or serial port connection.

For a good resource and free downloads, and to learn a bit more about the MP3 format, go to www.mp3.com. After you have downloaded an MP3 file, you can play it using the Windows Media Player, RealPlayer, QuickTime, or any other MP3-compatible player.

> **TIP**
>
> Sound quality is affected not only by your hardware, but also by the player application. Experiment with several different programs to find the one that works best for you.

When you click a web page link for an MP3 file, your default MP3 application will probably open, which might not be the application you want to use. In addition, the MP3 file will be inconveniently saved in IE's cache. You can exercise more control over the process by following these steps:

1. When you see a link for an MP3 file, right-click the link and choose Save Target As.
2. Select the location where you want to save the file download.
3. When the download is complete, open the desired player application manually and choose File, Open to listen to the file. If you click Open in the File Download dialog box, your default MP3 player opens.

> **NOTE**
>
> Another new product called MP3 Pro is an audio format that uses half the storage space per minute, allegedly without reducing quality. You can learn more about MP3 Pro at http://www.mp3prozone.com/.

Downloading Programs

Although the World Wide Web is most often thought of as a source of information and entertainment, it is also an excellent place to obtain new software or updates for existing programs.

You can find numerous excellent resources for downloading free or trial versions of software. Good sources are www.tucows.com and www.download.com. Follow the specific instructions for installation provided by the software publisher (and offered on most download sites), but when you're downloading, these general rules apply:

- Some websites require you to choose from a number of "mirror sites" for your download. Mirror sites are servers in different parts of the world that have the same files on them. The redundancy prevents traffic jams on a single server when many people access it for the same program downloads. You are asked to select a location that is geographically close to you, but you're usually free to choose any site you want. The closer ones are sometimes faster, but not always. Sometimes I get quicker downloads from a mirror site in another country whose citizens are likely sleeping.

- To begin the download, typically you click on a link that says something similar to "Download Now." This should open a dialog box asking you if you want to open or save the file. Choose to save. Select a location that you will remember for saving the download files—it is a good idea to create a "downloads" folder. Within the Downloads file, I create a new folder with the name of the program and then switch to that folder and save the program there. This way, all my downloads are organized.

- At the office, check with your network administrator before you install any new software to find out what your company policies are. In fact, if you are in a corporate environment, you probably won't be able to install new programs unless you are one of the lucky few with administrator privileges. Most corporations limit users installing software, for obvious security reasons.
- Scan all downloads with virus-scanning software before you install them.
- Many downloads come in a compressed `.zip` format. If you download such a file, you can run it easily in Vista because ZIP files are supported without needing to install a Zip program such as WinZIP or TurboZIP. Just double-click the Zip file, and it will open in a folder window. Then examine the contents. You probably need to double-click the installer or Setup program to begin installing the program into Vista.

> **TIP**
> Downloads are fastest when Internet traffic is low, such as late at night. If you are given a choice of mirror sites for a download, keep in mind the local time for each site and choose a server located where current traffic is likely to be lower.

During the download process, a window appears showing the download progress and the estimated time remaining. The estimates are helpful, but thanks to fluctuating transfer speeds, these estimates also can be extremely unreliable. You might want to watch the window for a moment to see if the estimate changes in your favor. If you can't wait that long, click Cancel and try again later.

In addition to downloading new software, you can download updates to software you already own. Check the manufacturer's website occasionally to see whether new updates, patches, or bug fixes are available (this is especially important for entertainment software).

> **TIP**
> Create a Software folder in your Favorites list, and add to it the manufacturers' websites for software you own. Doing so will make it easier to periodically check for updates.

Protecting Against Bad Downloaded Programs

IE helps protect your computer from potentially malicious software. When you use Internet Explorer to download a file, a message might appear in the information bar just below the Address box saying this:

> To help protect your security, Internet Explorer blocked this site from downloading files to your computer. Click here for options.

Clicking on the information bar opens a drop-down list of options (see Figure 15.10).

Figure 15.10
IE offers to block downloads from the particular page.

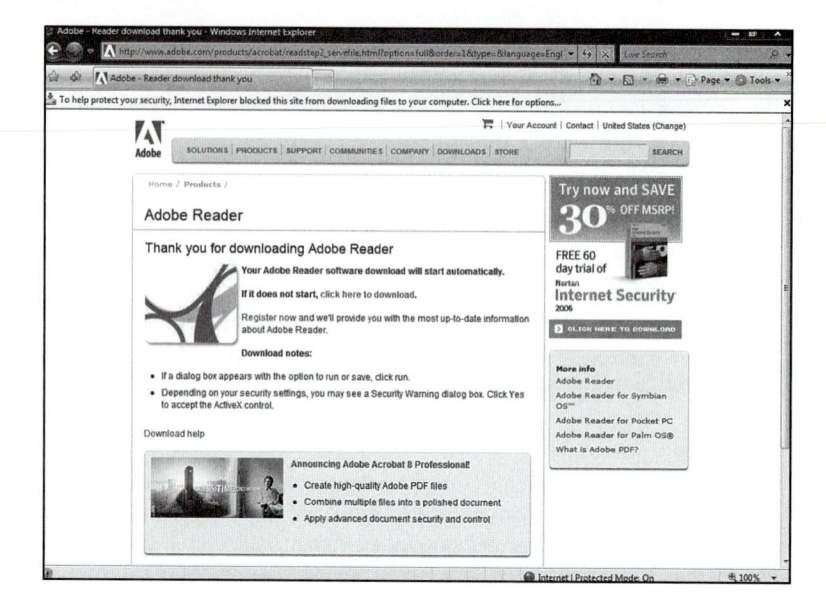

If you choose to allow the page to download a program, you'll see another dialog box warning you about downloaded programs and asking whether you want to run the program from its remote location across the Web or save it to your hard disk, as shown in Figure 15.11.

Figure 15.11
If you decide to accept downloads from that page, you'll see another warning and some options at the bottom of the dialog box.

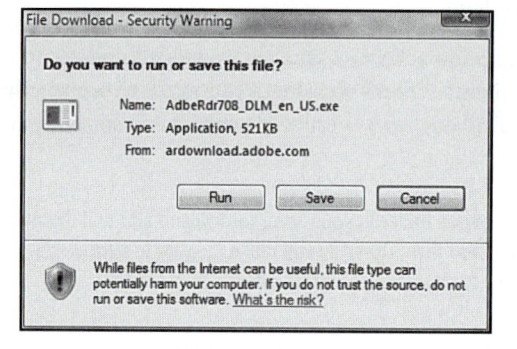

If you choose to run the program from the site rather than save it, you'll likely see the dialog box shown in Figure 15.12. All executable files that are downloaded are checked for publisher information using a scheme called Authenticode. Authenticode checks the digital signature of the file against a database of known good software publishers, and gives you some advice about the file. After being presented with the information, you can make a more informed decision about running the file.

Figure 15.12
If a publisher is not verified, you will be prompted if you try to run the program from the web page.

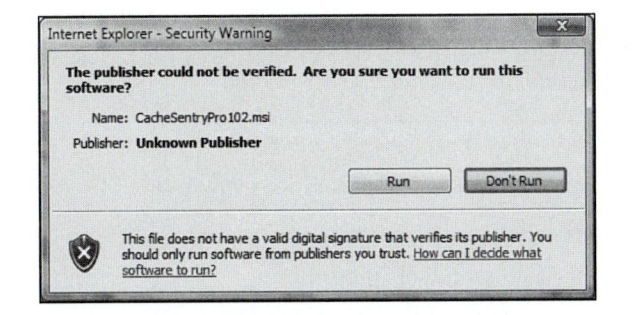

Some program publishers have been "black listed," and Windows Vista prevents them from running in your PC under Windows Vista. Executable files with blocked publishers are not allowed to run.

> **TIP**
>
> You can unblock a publisher by using Manage Add-Ons in Internet Explorer. This is explained later in this chapter, in the section "Viewing and Managing Your IE Add-Ons."

PROTECTING AGAINST "DRIVE-BY" DOWNLOADS OF IE ADD-ONS

A recurring cause of instability in Windows machines is attributable to what's sometimes called "drive-by" downloads from the Web. How many times have you visited a website only to see a pop-up dialog box saying you need to install software for the website to work on your browser? Sometimes it's clearly stated why this is necessary (for playing a video, a proprietary sound file, or Flash animation, for example), and other times, the reason is not so clear. All you know is that you are faced with the decision of letting some (typically) unknown source install software on your computer so you can enjoy the web page, or opting out and moving on. Maybe you assume it can do no harm because it's only an addition to IE and not to your operating system. But because IE is often the back door through which viruses, adware, spyware, Trojan horses, and other malware infect your computer, being cautious at this juncture is extremely important.

These spur-of-the-moment additions that websites can push at you are called *IE add-ons*, and they are typically ActiveX controls (although not all are). ActiveX controls and active script (sometimes called script or JavaScript) are small programs used extensively on the Internet. Without scripts, websites would be much more static and boring. Script and ActiveX controls allow all sorts of animation and other entertaining features on the Internet. Websites become more interactive by offering customized content based on information about your computer, your browser, and so on. Common add-ons include extra toolbars, animated mouse pointers, stock tickers, and pop-up ad blockers.

> **TIP**
>
> IE now has its own pop-up blocker. See "Blocking Pop-Ups and Pop-Unders," later in this chapter.

Add-ons can be installed from a variety of locations and in several ways, including these:

- Download and installation while viewing web pages
- User installation via an executable program
- As preinstalled components of the operating system
- As preinstalled add-ons that come with the operating system

A risk of add-ons is that these programs can also be used to collect information from your computer for harmful purposes. After 6 months or a year of surfing the Web with IE, many users don't recall what add-ons they authorized and don't know what those add-ons might be doing to compromise the stability of their systems.

You could unknowingly have many add-ons installed. This can happen if you previously gave permission for all downloads from a particular website, or because the add-on was part of another program that you installed. Some add-ons are installed with Microsoft Windows.

You'll sometimes be given more information about potentially damaging add-ons so you can make an informed decision about installing one. Some add-ons have digital signatures that verify who wrote them. This is called a *certificate*. IE verifies a signature and can tell you if it's valid. If a signature is reported as invalid, you definitely shouldn't trust the publisher as asserting a truthful identity. Allowing installation of ActiveX controls that have invalid signatures obviously is not recommended and introduces additional risk to your computer.

Internet Explorer blocks file downloads in these circumstances when you are using the default security settings:

- When a file has an invalid signature on its certificate
- When a file has no signature on its certificate
- When you or someone else who uses your computer has blocked the source of the file

Even if an add-on has a legitimate certificate, it doesn't mean the program won't mess up your computer. In the end, it is your decision whether to install an add-on. Make the decision based on whether you know the source to be trustworthy. After installing an add-on, if your system or IE becomes unstable, use the information in the following section to track and remove the add-on.

> **NOTE**
>
> Certificates are explained in more detail in the section "Using Encryption," later in this chapter.

Allowing Add-Ons with Invalid Signatures

Some add-ons are known to be bad; Microsoft has blocked these intentionally. You can't install or run add-ons from blocked publishers on the computer. If you really want to, you can force the use of an add-on that has an invalid signature:

1. In Internet Explorer, click the Tools button in the toolbar, then click Internet Options, and then click the Security tab.
2. In the Security level for this zone box, click Custom Level.
3. Scroll down to Download Unsigned ActiveX Controls and choose Enable or Prompt.

Another approach is to unblock a *specific* publisher. This is a safer approach because it doesn't open you up to all invalid signatures. To do this, follow these steps:

1. Click the Tools button in the toolbar, then click Manage Add-Ons, and then click Enable or Disable Add-Ons.
2. Select the publisher you want to unblock and then click Enable.

Viewing and Managing Your IE Add-Ons

You can review all your add-ons, update selected ones, choose ones to remove, and, if you've been having IE crashes, potentially see which one was responsible for your last IE crash. (Crashing can happen if the add-on was poorly built or created for an earlier version of IE.) You work with your add-ons using the IE Add-On Manager. The Add-On Manager even shows some add-ons that were not previously shown and could be very difficult to detect.

To see all add-ons for Internet Explorer, follow these steps:

1. Click the Tools button in the toolbar, then click Manage Add-Ons, and then click Enable or Disable Add-Ons. You'll see the Manage Add-Ons window, shown in Figure 15.13.
2. In the Show list, select the set of add-ons you want to see.

Add-ons are sorted into two groups in the Show list. Installed add-ons are a complete list and include all the add-ons that reside on your computer. Loaded add-ons are only those that were needed for the current web page or a recently viewed web page.

Some add-ons can crash your IE session. If you experience a system crash after you've installed an add-on, you have two options:

- **Disable it**—If an add-on causes repeated problems, you can disable the add-on. Click the add-on you want to disable and then click Disable. Some web pages, or Internet Explorer, might not display properly if an add-on is disabled. It is recommended that you disable an add-on only if it repeatedly causes Internet Explorer to close. Add-ons can be disabled but not easily removed.

Figure 15.13
The Manage Add-Ons window lets you see and control the IE add-ons you've either wittingly or unwittingly downloaded and installed.

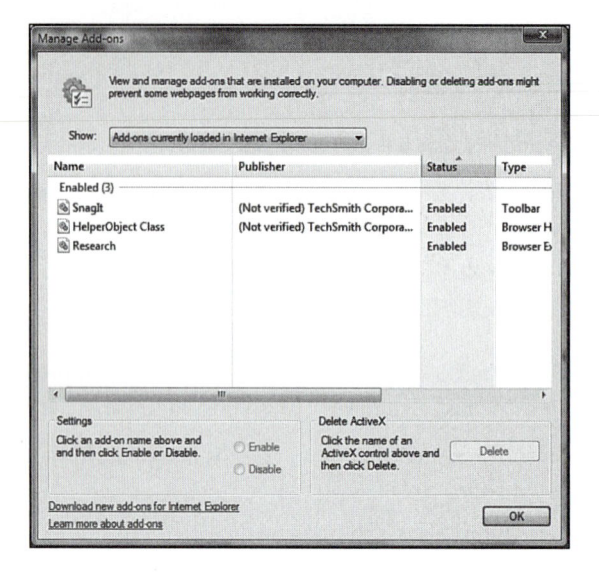

> **NOTE**
>
> If you disable an add-on and then realize it was needed, click the add-on you want to enable and then click Enable.

- **Report it**—When prompted, you might want to report the glitch to Microsoft. This is completely anonymous and requires nothing from you but your permission. Microsoft claims the info is used improve its products and to encourage other companies to update and improve theirs.

Internet Explorer Add-On Crash Detection attempts to detect crashes in Internet Explorer that are related to an add-on. If IE identifies the faulty add-on, you'll be informed. You then have the option of disabling add-ons to diagnose crashes and improve the overall stability of IE.

> **TIP**
>
> You can turn off notifications about browser add-ons if you don't want to be bugged about them. Choose Tools, Internet Options and click the Advanced tab. Under Browsing, clear the Notify When Add-Ons Disabled check box.

Customizing the Browser and Setting Internet Options

One of the most important features of Internet Explorer is the capability to tailor it to your specific needs. Every user sets up IE differently based on programs used, favorite websites, bandwidth capability, security needs, and so on.

Customizing the Browser and Setting Internet Options

You can make most customizations in the Internet Options dialog box, which you can access either through the Windows Control Panel or by clicking on the Tools button in the toolbar and then clicking Internet Options. The dialog box contains seven tabs, each holding a number of unique preference settings. Figure 15.14 shows the General tab.

Figure 15.14
On the General tab, you can set general preferences for your home page, temporary cache files, history, and browser view options.

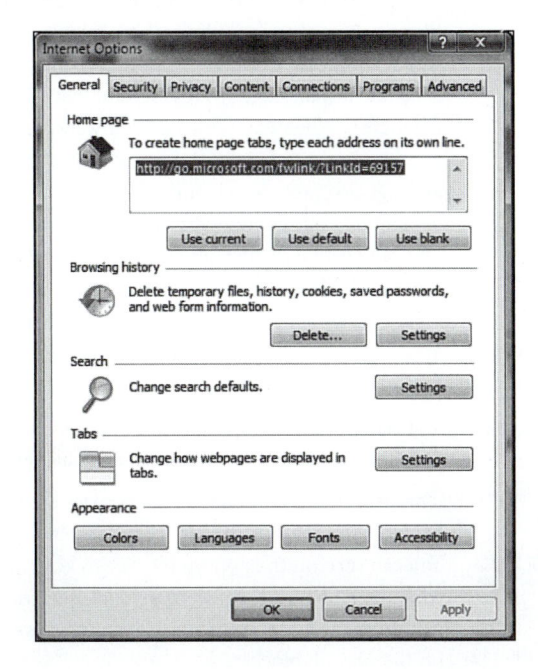

Check each tab in the dialog box to customize your own IE7 settings. Table 15.1 describes some of the key preference settings you can change.

TABLE 15.1 IMPORTANT INTERNET OPTIONS

Tab	Option	Description
General	Home Page	The home page is the first page that appears when you open Internet Explorer. It is probably set to Windows Live or has been customized by your PC's manufacturer. Consider changing this page to your company's home page or something else you find more useful.
	Temporary Internet Files	When you view a web page, the files for the page are saved on your hard drive as Temporary Internet Files (also called the cache). You can clear all files from the cache or change the amount of disk space they are allowed to consume.

continues

TABLE 15.1 CONTINUED

Tab	Option	Description
	Browsing History	IE7 maintains a record of the websites you have visited. You can change the length of time these records are kept or clear the history altogether, including all cookies, saved passwords, and web form information. A cookie is a message from a website that IE7 stores on your computer. When you return to that website, IE7 sends the message in the cookie to the site so that it loads more quickly and can also provide customized web searches. If you don't want cookies on your computer, you can delete them.
	Search Tabs	You can change the default search provider for IE7. You can tell IE7 whether you want to have tabbed web pages and how to open pop-ups and links from other programs.
	Colors, Fonts, and so on	You can customize default colors, fonts, and languages, and set accessibility options here.
Security	Zones and Levels	You can set security options for IE7. See "Setting Security and Privacy Preferences," later in this chapter.
Privacy	Settings	This area defines how and when cookies are sent. See "Setting Security and Privacy Preferences," later in this chapter.
	Pop-Up Blocker	You can turn on the pop-up blocker to keep most pop-up windows generated by a website from appearing and annoying you. If you want to see these pop-up windows you can also turn off the pop-up blocker.
Content	Content Advisor	You can set ratings for each website you visit to control which users can see that content on your computer. See "Controlling Objectionable Content," later in this chapter.
	Certificates	When a web page tries to run a script or install a piece of software on your computer, you can accept certificates from the publisher to authenticate their identity and trustworthiness. See "Setting Security and Privacy Preferences," later in this chapter.
	AutoComplete	You can enable or disable AutoComplete when typing web URLs, email addresses, or form data.
	Feeds	You can specify how often you receive a web feed from a website.
Connections		You can set up preferences for your Internet connection, whether it be through a dial-up or network connection.
Programs		You can select default programs for various actions. See "Setting Default Mail, News, and HTML Editor Programs," later in this chapter.
Advanced		You can set various (but obscure) options for browsing, multimedia, web page printing, searches from the address bar, and security. You can also enable and disable automatic downloading of graphics, videos, audio, and more.

Setting Default Mail, News, and HTML Editor Programs

Windows Vista has consolidated much of this information for setting defaults in the Set Default Programs window, which you can access through the Control Panel. You can also access the default program settings in the Programs tab of the Internet Options dialog box.

The Programs tab still lets you set your preferred HTML editor for editing HTML files. If you have not installed any other Internet-related software packages, such as Microsoft Word, you probably won't have many choices here, but if you use different programs, these options can be useful. Figure 15.15 shows the default program settings you can make on the Programs tab, and Table 15.2 describes the various options you can set.

Figure 15.15
On the Programs tab, you can choose the default HTML editor.

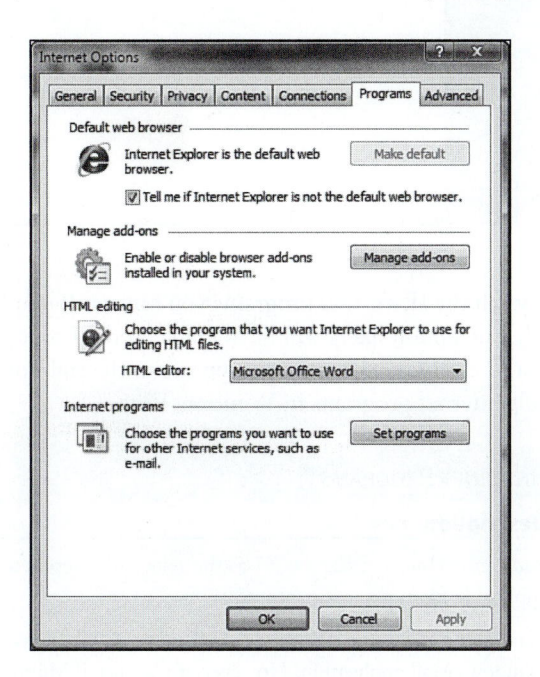

If you are a web developer, make sure the correct editor is listed here. This will simplify editing during your testing process. The list might include Word, Notepad, FrontPage, or another installed editor.

If you want to view and change Internet programs, click Set Programs. In the Default Programs window, click Set Your Default Programs. The Set Default Programs window then appears, as shown in Figure 15.16.

Figure 15.16
The Set Default Programs window.

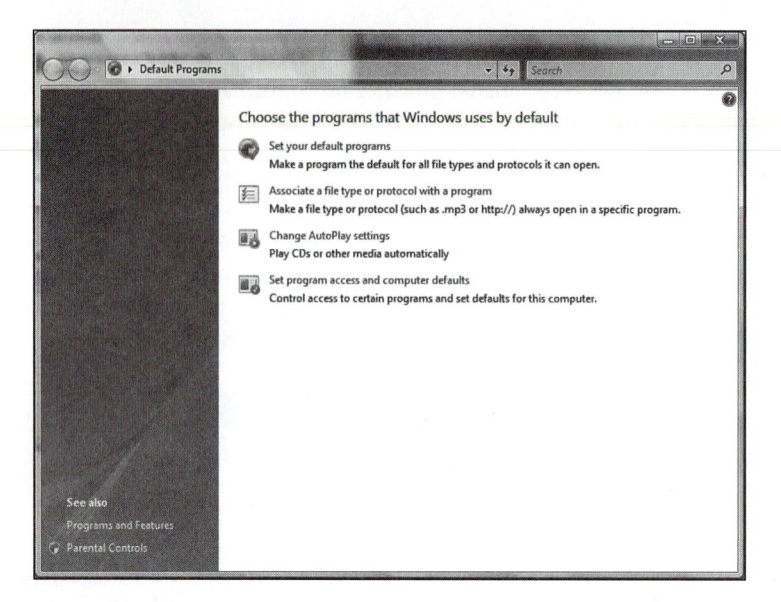

The Programs list displays all the IE-related programs you can set. If you haven't installed very many programs, only one option likely will be available in the Programs list. After you click a Program in the list, the program description appears to the right of the Programs list. Table 15.2 lists the default Internet programs in Windows Vista.

TABLE 15.2   DEFAULT INTERNET PROGRAMS

Program	Description
Internet Explorer	You can set Internet Explorer 7 as the selected program to open all applicable file types and protocols.
Windows Calendar	Windows Calendar is the standard calendar for Windows Vista and the Windows Mail application. However, if you install Microsoft Outlook, Outlook will have a separate calendar file.
Windows Contacts	Windows Contacts is your default address book (and was previously called Address Book).
Windows Mail	This program opens when you send a page or link by email from the Page button in the IE7 toolbar, or when you click an email link on a web page.
Windows Mail (News)	If you link to or open a newsgroup URL, the Windows Mail newsreader opens.
Windows Media Center	You can set this program to open DVR files by default. DVR files are the standard format for Windows-recorded video. The Windows Media Center is available only in the Home Premium and Ultimate editions of Windows Vista.
Windows Media Player	You can set this program to open all popular music and video file types (such as AVI video, MPEG video, and MP3) in Windows Media Player.
Windows Photo Gallery	You can choose Windows Photo Gallery to open all applicable image formats, including GIF, JPG, PNG, and TIF.

You can set the program as the default for all the file types and protocols it can open by clicking the Set This Program As Default link. You can also choose which file types and protocols the selected program opens by default by clicking the Choose Defaults for This Program link.

> Email links in web pages can cause many frustrations. **See** "Email Link Troubles" in the "Troubleshooting" section, later in this chapter.

SETTING SECURITY AND PRIVACY PREFERENCES

In many ways, the World Wide Web is a safer place than the "real" world, but it does present its own unique dangers. The greatest hazards involve sensitive and private information about you or your company being compromised, or having your computer infected with a software virus. IE7 incorporates a number of security features to protect you from these hazards, and you can customize those features to suit your own needs, browsing habits, and company policies.

Begin by clicking the Tools button in the toolbar and then opening the Internet Options dialog box from the IE7 Tools menu. Click the Security tab to bring it to the front. Click Default Level in the lower-right corner of the dialog box to show the slider that allows you to set a security level for each zone, as shown in Figure 15.17.

Figure 15.17
On the Security tab, you can customize security settings for various web zones.

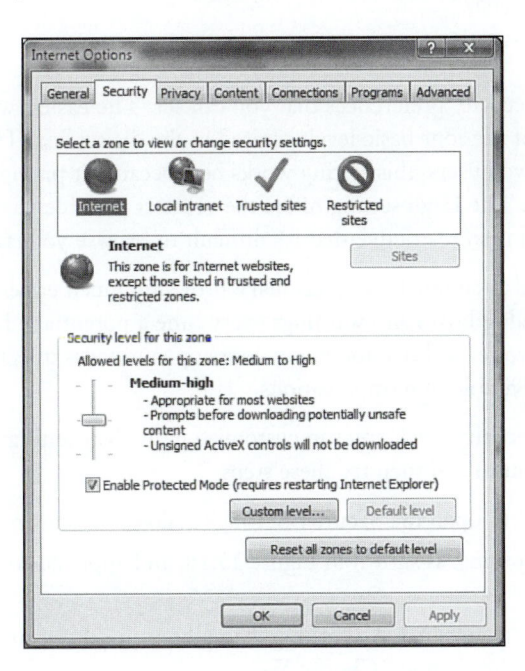

You first need to select a zone for which you want to customize settings. Figure 15.17 shows the four zones.

Internet
: This zone applies to all resources outside your LAN or intranet.

Local Intranet
: This zone applies to pages available on your company's intranet. These pages are usually more trustworthy and can justify less restrictive settings.

Trusted Sites
: You manually designate these sites as trusted. To designate a trusted site, browse to the site, open this dialog box, select the Trusted Sites zone, and click Sites. Here you can add the site to your Trusted Sites zone list. Trusted sites usually allow lighter security.

Restricted Sites
: Designated in the same manner as Trusted Sites, websites listed here are ones you specifically find untrustworthy. They should have the strictest security settings.

> **CAUTION**
>
> Before you designate a web page as trusted, remember that even the most diligently maintained sites can be compromised. Recent "hacker" attacks at websites of the FBI, U.S. Army, and others might make you question the practice of designating any website as "trustworthy."

Each zone has its own security preferences that you can set. The easiest way to set preferences is to choose one of the four basic levels offered in the dialog box. The default level is Medium, and for most web users, this setting works best because it provides a good balance of security and usability. The High setting offers the greatest possible security, but you might find that the level is so restrictive that it's difficult to browse your favorite websites.

In contrast, the Low and Medium-Low levels make browsing much easier because you aren't presented with dialog boxes and warnings every time a potentially hazardous activity begins. Because these two levels leave too many doors open to virus infection and other dangers, they are not advisable in most situations.

Besides setting a basic security level, you can customize individual settings. First, choose a basic level (such as Medium) and then try these steps:

1. Click Custom Level to open the Security Settings dialog box, shown in Figure 15.17.
2. Browse the list of options, as shown in Figure 15.18, and apply custom settings as you see fit.
3. Click OK when you're finished. A Warning dialog box appears, asking whether you really want to apply the changes. Choose Yes.

Figure 15.18
You can scroll through this list to make custom security setting changes.

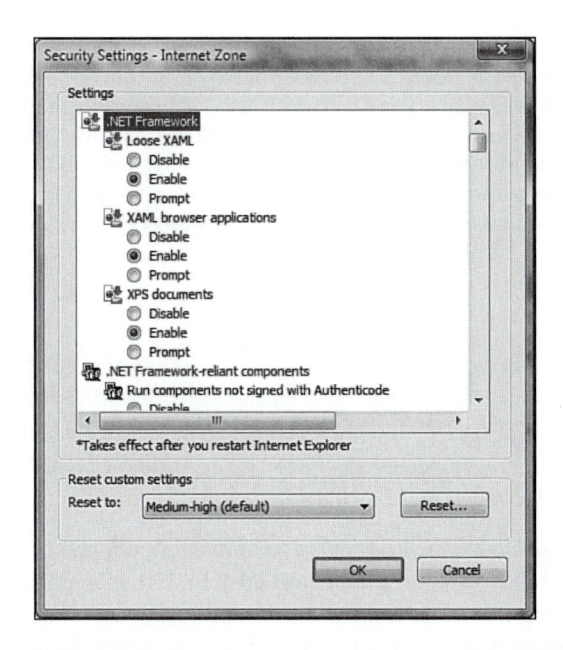

Review the items in the Security Settings dialog box that pertain to ActiveX controls and Java applets. Assess these settings carefully, especially those for ActiveX controls, because of the unique hazards they can present. The ActiveX standard contains loopholes, so unsigned controls can run virtually any OLE-compliant operation on your system. Java, on the other hand, is relatively—but not entirely—secure.

You should also consider your desired level of cookie security. Because cookies are text only, they cannot contain a virus or other harmful content. However, they can contain personal information, such as a record of web pages you have visited, how long you spent at a page, how many times you have visited, personal preferences for a web page, and even user IDs and passwords. For these reasons, many people regard cookies as an invasion of privacy.

You can disable cookies, or you can choose to have IE prompt you every time a site attempts to leave a cookie in your cache. However, keep in mind that some websites make such heavy use of cookies that you could find it difficult—if not impossible—to browse the Web normally.

To set your cookie preferences, click on the Tools button in the toolbar, then click Internet Options, and then click on the Privacy tab. The Settings area enables you to determine how and when cookies are sent. Choose a level you are comfortable with, or click the Advanced button to always accept, block, or prompt you before enabling first-party or third-party cookies. (For more on first-party and third-party cookies, see "Getting a Microsoft Live ID," later in this chapter.)

You might want to override your normal cookies settings for certain websites. If so, go to the Websites area of the Privacy tab and click the Edit button. In the text box, enter a complete website address. Then click the Block or Allow button to specify websites for which you want to never or always allow cookies.

> **TIP**
>
> A major security hole in IE involves the option Allow Paste Operations via Script, which is enabled in all security levels but High. It allows any website to see the contents of your Windows Clipboard via a scripted Paste operation. If you have been working with sensitive information in another program and used a Copy or Cut command, that information could be compromised by unscrupulous webmasters. To be on the safe side, change this setting to Disable or Prompt, no matter which security level you use.

Using Encryption

The Advanced tab of the Internet Options dialog box has a number of other security settings that deserve your attention. In particular, most of the security settings deal with *certificates*. Certificates can be saved on your computer and serve to authenticate your identity or the identity of the server you are connected to. They also provide for secure encrypted communication over secure web connections.

IE supports *Secure Socket Layer (SSL) encryption* technology developed by Netscape. It supports 128-bit encrypted SSL sessions, the highest level of data encryption available in the online world. SSL encryption works using a pair of encryption keys, one public and one private. One key is needed to decrypt the other. Certificates facilitate this process by including the following information:

- The issuing authority, such as VeriSign
- The identity of the person or organization for which the certificate is issued
- The public key
- Time stamps

The certificate provides and authenticates the basis for an encrypted session. The identity is reverified, the private key is shared, and encryption is enabled.

Another encryption protocol that IE supports is *Private Communication Technology (PCT)*, developed by Microsoft. PCT is similar to SSL encryption, except that it uses a separate key for identity authentication and data encryption. Thus, in theory, PCT should provide slightly enhanced security versus SSL.

Again, encryption protocols can be enabled or disabled on the Advanced tab of the Internet Options dialog box. If you disable a protocol, any page you try to access on a secure server that uses that protocol will not open in IE.

→ Learn how to obtain a digital certificate for yourself in "Protecting Yourself from Fraud and Spam," **p. 1243**.

Stopping Phishers

The term *phishing* refers to the practice of nefarious people gathering your sensitive personal information, such as your credit card number(s) and Social Security number, by masquerading as a reputable company.

For example, a company might send you email that purports to be from an officer of your bank or credit card company, and tells you that there has been an error with their database system. The email demands that, to protect your records, you must click on the link in the email and submit your sensitive information. Then the unwitting submitter is astonished to find that his or her bank account has been drained—or worse.

Internet Explorer 7 includes a default built-in Phishing Filter that checks each site you visit for telltale signs of a phisher site. You can learn more about phishing and how IE7 protects you in Chapter 36, "Protecting Yourself from Fraud and Spam."

BLOCKING POP-UPS AND POP-UNDERS

Pop-up windows are an intrusive means for advertisers on the Web to ensure that you see their plug. We've all seen pop-up windows that appear unexpectedly, sometimes blaring music or flashing to catch our attention. Usually they pop up when you've clicked a link to go to another page. A less intrusive, though a little more insidious, window is called the pop-under window. You don't discover it until you close the window you're looking at. This way, it's harder to tell which site actually spawned the pop-under, so you don't know who to blame.

Many power users have figured out ways to prevent pop-ups, such as by installing the Google toolbar or one of the many add-ins, or installing some other browser, such as Opera, that blocks pop-ups. AOL's browser does this, as do Netscape and Mozilla's Firefox. Oddly enough, 70% or more of web surfing is done with IE, even though prior versions didn't contain the modern nicety of pop-up blocking. The good news is that IE7 has a pop-up blocker built in.

> **TIP**
>
> You can stop the pop-ups dead in their tracks with this quick solution: Turn off Active Scripting (JavaScript). This works because pop-up windows require Active Scripting to launch. Even though other browser functions need Active Scripting, you can surf quite effectively on most sites without it. You can turn off Active Scripting by clicking on the Tools button in the toolbar and then clicking Internet Options. Then select the Security tab, change your Internet security level to High, and click OK. Five quick steps, no pop-ups, and you haven't spent a dime on a blocker or upgraded to the latest version of IE. Of course, using the latest IE is a better idea because of the improved security features and add-in management.

IE's pop-up blocker is turned on by default. When a pop-up window tries to launch, you'll receive notification in the IE yellow information bar (just below the Address box). It will inform you that that a pop-up has been blocked and list steps you can take to show the pop-up, if you want. Click on the information bar to see the options (see Figure 15.19).

Figure 15.19
IE7 blocks pop-ups. When a pop-up is blocked, you can click on the information bar for options.

Sometimes it's useful to see blocked pop-ups. Just follow these steps:

1. Click on the information bar.
2. From the menu, choose Show Blocked Pop-ups.

Some sites won't work properly with pop-ups disabled, such as shopping sites. If you want to always allow pop-ups from one or more specific sites, you can authorize this by adding those sites to an exception list:

1. Click on the Tools button in the toolbar, choose Pop-Up Blocker, and then choose Pop-Up Blocker Settings.
2. In the Pop-Up Blocker Settings window, type the URL of the website and then click Add.
3. Repeat Step 2 for as many sites as you want to add. When you're finished, click Close.

A FEW NOTES ABOUT POP-UP EXCEPTIONS

Sometimes the pop-up blocker won't be able to preclude a pop-up from appearing, for several possible reasons. First, you might have software on your computer that is launching pop-ups. To stop these pop-ups, you have to identify the software and remove it or change its settings. Try installing an adware and spyware sleuthing program such as Spybot Search and Destroy or Ad-Aware.

Second, some pop-ups are written cleverly enough that they can circumnavigate the IE pop-up blocker.

Third, Internet Explorer will not block pop-ups from websites that are in your Intranet or Trusted Sites zones. If you want to specifically remove such a site from your trusted zone, you can do that from the IE Settings dialog boxes:

1. In IE, click on the Tools button in the toolbar, click Internet Options, and then click Security.
2. Click the zone from which you want to remove a website, and then click Sites.
3. Skip this step unless you chose the Intranet zone in the last step. Click Advanced and then go to Step 4.
4. In the Websites box, click the website you want to remove, and then click Remove.

Controlling Objectionable Content

The World Wide Web holds the most diverse range of information and content of any library in the world. That diverse range includes a great deal of material that you might deem objectionable, and there is no perfect way of protecting yourself from it—short of never going online. However, Internet Explorer incorporates two features, called Parental Controls and the Content Advisor, to help you screen out many of the things you or the other people using your computer would rather not see.

Parental Controls

Parental Controls is a new feature in Internet Explorer 7. If your children often use your computer and you don't want them seeing some material on the Web, or even using a certain program, you can set up Parental Controls to block access to those websites.

You must set up a System Recovery Account password before you can use Parental Controls. The System Recovery Account is an administrator account that is built into Windows Vista, in case problems arise with your account. You'll learn more about the System Recovery Account for recovery purposes in Chapter 28, "Troubleshooting and Repairing Problems." However, this account password serves a second purpose: You can use the password to disable Parental Controls. Without this password, any user on your computer can disable Parental Controls.

After you set up the System Recovery Account password, click the user picture or name in the list to set up Parental Controls for that user. The User Controls window allows you to enable Parental Controls, as shown in Figure 15.20.

In this window, you can also collect information about the user's activity on your computer; determine the websites, games, and other programs you don't want the user to access; and control how long the user can use the computer.

The Content Advisor

The Content Advisor evaluates web content based on a rating system. The included rating system was developed by RSACi (Recreational Software Advisory Council on the Internet), but you can add others, if you want.

Figure 15.20
Set parental controls for the selected user in the User Controls window.

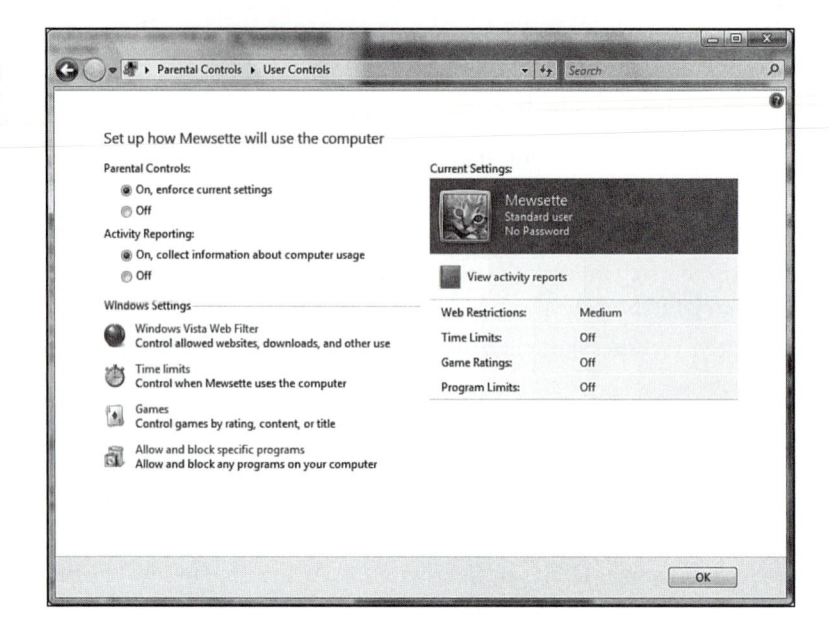

You must manually enable the Content Advisor, but after it is set up, you can password-protect the Advisor so that only you can adjust the settings. To enable the Content Advisor, open the Internet Options dialog box and do the following:

1. Click the Content tab to bring it to the front, and click Enable to open the Content Advisor dialog box. (You may be asked to allow this operation via the familiar User Account Control dialog box.)

2. The Content Advisor dialog box contains four tabs, as shown in Figure 15.21. On the Ratings tab, you can move the slider to set a rating level in each of the four categories presented.

3. Click the Approved Sites tab to bring it to the front. List specific websites here to control access to them. Click Always to make it easily acceptable, or click Never to restrict access.

4. On the General tab, choose whether unrated sites can be viewed. Keep in mind that many objectionable sites will not be rated. You can also set a password to let users view unrated or restricted sites on a case-by-case basis, or you can add another rating system here.

5. Click the Advanced tab. If you plan to use a ratings bureau or PICSRules file that you obtain from the Internet, your ISP, or another source, add it here. Click OK when you're finished.

Figure 15.21
On the Ratings tab, you can move the slider to change the rating level.

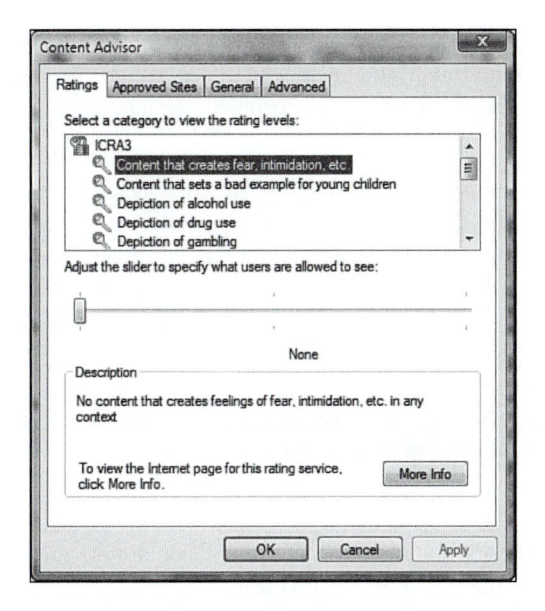

RSACi and other organizations provide content-rating systems based on the Platform for Internet Content Selection (PICS) system developed by the World Wide Web Consortium, or W3C (www.w3.org/PICS/). They work using metatags in the code of a web page. The tags are usually generated by the rating organization after a site developer follows a brief rating procedure. Developers can then place the PICS metatag in the header of their HTML code, where it is identified by IE's Content Advisor when you try to open the page. The tag identifies the types and levels of content contained in the site, and the Content Advisor allows or disallows the site based on the content settings you have chosen. If you want to screen websites using a system other than RSACi's, you must install an appropriate PICSRules file provided by the rating organization.

Of course, rating is voluntary. Developers set the rating levels in the metatags based on their own evaluation of the site content, so you don't get a surefire guarantee that the tag accurately represents the site. RSACi periodically audits rated sites, and web developers generally *try* to rate their sites as accurately as possible. Because it is a voluntary system, providing inaccurate ratings defeats the purpose.

OTHER INTERNET SETTINGS

Several other settings also deserve your attention. On the Content tab of the Internet Options dialog box, click the Settings button in the AutoComplete area to open the AutoComplete Settings dialog box, and make sure it does not contain information that you don't want compromised. AutoComplete makes it easier to fill in data fields on forms and URLs in the Address box, but if other people use your user identity, these settings could reveal your personal information.

One setting you probably should *not* enable is the Print Background Colors and Images option. If a web page uses anything but a plain white background, a printed copy of it will waste a considerable amount of printer ink and probably be harder to read.

Review the Search settings on the Advanced tab. In earlier versions of Internet Explorer, if you wanted to visit a website with a fairly simple URL such as www.quepublishing.com, you could just type `quepublishing` and press Enter. Internet Explorer would assume the missing `www.` and `.com` and fill it in for you. But now, if you type only `quepublishing` in the Address box, IE7 opens a Search window in the Explorer bar. In theory, this is supposed to make searching easier, but if you've been using IE for a while, you might find it annoying.

> **TIP**
>
> If you press Ctrl+Enter after typing a word in the Address box, IE7 assumes that it is preceded by `www.` and followed by `.com` to create a URL.

You cannot completely restore the previous function of "assuming" the missing bits of the URL, but you can modify the way in which this feature works by altering settings under the Advanced tab. The different search options have the following results:

- **Do not search from the Address box**—No search is made of any kind. Typing a single word in the Address box will generally result in a "Page not available" error.
- **Just display the results in the main window**—No attempt is made to find a close match, nor is the Explorer bar opened. A search engine opens in the main window.

Under Security, check Empty Temporary Internet Files Folder When Browser Is Closed to discard cache files you don't want others to see. This setting can also be useful if disk space is limited, but you shouldn't use it if you want to be able to view pages in offline mode later.

Effectively Searching the Web

You've probably heard that you can find virtually anything on the Web, and if you've spent much time online, you might be left wondering where it all is. Finding information on the World Wide Web is a fine art, but Internet Explorer 7 makes the process much simpler than before.

Internet Explorer 7 has streamlined the search approach by dropping the Search Companion in IE6 and replacing it with the Search box to the right of the Address box, as shown in Figure 15.22.

Figure 15.22
The Search box enables you to search for several different kinds of information.

If you haven't typed anything in the Search box, the name of the search engine appears in the box. By default, the search engine name is Live Search, Microsoft's search engine. To begin searching, enter a word, phrase, or even question in the Live Search box, and then click the Search button. Your results will appear in the Live Search page, with nine links appearing on each page. If you type a single word—such as "antiques"—the search will probably yield a list of results too big to be useful. Using more words, and more descriptive words, will narrow your search. You probably will get better results by searching for "antique furniture" or "antique French furniture" instead. You can click directly on a search result to link to that site, or you can click Next to see the next 15 results.

To start a new search, type another word, phrase, or question in the Live Search box. If you want to go back to the results from a previous search, click the Back button.

You can also refine and expand your search using the Live Search box. Click the down arrow button to the right of the Search button to open the Search menu. This menu enables you to modify your search in three ways:

- Find on This Page opens the Find dialog box so you can find a word or phrase in the current web page.
- Find More Providers opens the Add Search Providers to Internet Explorer 7 page on the Microsoft website so you can add a search engine to the Search menu. When you search in the Live Search box, you can open the Search menu and select the search engine you want to use.
- Change Search Defaults opens the Change Search Defaults dialog box so you can set one of the search providers you have added as the default search engine.

When you're finished searching, close the Search Companion. To revisit a previous search, click on the History button on the IE toolbar and go to the Search folders. Depending on the search engines you used, you could find information in folders labeled `search.msn`, `search.yahoo`, and `northernlight`. Another way to find previous search results is by clicking the Search button at the top of the History pane and entering a word to search among the pages you've visited recently.

As helpful as the Search box in IE7 can be, when you've become familiar with the Internet, you are likely to discover your own favorite search engine. You could add it to your Links bar for easy access. Many search engines have advanced options that enable you to perform a more directed search.

Try these helpful search engines by entering them directly from a web page:

- www.hotbot.com (includes a drop-down list for more effective searching)
- www.google.com (has a Web Directory that works much like Yellow Pages do in a phone book, and Google Groups, which searches newsgroups)
- www.northernlight.com (categorizes search results into folders to help refine your search)

Safer Alternatives to IE

With more than 70% (some say as much as 90%) of web surfing done with IE, Microsoft's browser has become the obvious target for hackers everywhere. Because a large proportion of viruses and other malware can enter your computer through websites (typically through exploitation of Microsoft ActiveX controls), switching to a different browser might not be a crazy suggestion your propeller-head Linux evangelist friends push on you. It might be a necessity.

Even though ActiveX was meant to extend the capability of IE in exciting ways, such as into the area of multimedia, it has instead become an enticing target for hackers. Because of this, the U.S. Computer Emergency Readiness Team (US-CERT), a partnership between the tech industry and the Department of Homeland Security, recently began advising computer users to consider switching browsers. Whether or not you do, US-CERT advises upping your Internet Explorer security settings.

It might take a little work to get a non-IE browser to properly display all the sites you want to view, but it might be worth it. For example, you'll probably need to reinstall plug-ins for some sites and install Sun's Java engine for viewing Java-powered sites.

In general, make sure you're switching to a browser that isn't simply a shell on top of IE—that will still leave you vulnerable. You'll want an entirely new browser, such as Firefox, Opera, or Maxthon.

For more information about browser security, visit www.us-cert.gov/.

Getting a Microsoft Live ID

In past years, Microsoft required the use of Microsoft Passport to access several of their sites and services. With the release of Windows Vista and 2007 upgrades to other Microsoft products (such as Microsoft Money) and Web services (such as Windows Marketplace), Microsoft is rolling out the upgrade and replacement for Passport: Live ID. If you already have a Hotmail or MSN email address, you already have a Live ID. If not, you can get a Microsoft Live ID simply by signing up for a free Hotmail address at www.hotmail.com.

As with Live ID's predecessor, Microsoft Passport, some might be understandably concerned that Live ID is yet another way Microsoft is trying to invade our space and privacy to increase its profits. You can minimize the effect by entering the bare minimum of personal information when you sign up for a Live ID. We were able to sign up using a single letter for a first name and last name. You also must enter a birth year and a ZIP Code, but the Microsoft stormtroopers are not going to knock down your door in the middle of the night if you don't enter it truthfully.

Hey, Who's Afraid of Microsoft Live ID?

The Microsoft Live ID makes it easy to sign on and purchase items and services from a growing number of sites affiliated with (read: "owned by") Microsoft. Because people struggle to remember all their passwords, the idea of using a simple Live ID that stores your username, password, credit card info, and so forth, and promises to effortlessly log you on to all kinds of websites and services, might sound pretty alluring. I mean, I forget my passwords all the time, don't you? In fact, I keep a Notepad file on my computer of nothing but my passwords. If I don't have access to this file when I'm traveling and I want to purchase a plane ticket, I'm out of luck because I can't remember how to log in to Travelocity. (Of course, I keep this file in an encrypted file folder running under Windows Vista, so it's not going to be easy for someone to liquidate my IRA. After the "substantial penalty for early withdrawal," it's not going to amount to that much anyway.)

However, Live ID isn't all it's cracked up to be. In fact, it's a lot less. If you were concerned about cookies, you'll really be scared of Live ID. As mentioned earlier, cookies are small text files stored locally on your computer that contain information about you. When you go to a website that uses cookies, the web server and your computer agree to exchange information based on what you do on the website. Suppose you set up an account at Jack's Pizza with your name and address, or just that you like pepperoni pizza. The information you give to that site, along with possibly when you viewed the site, what you purchased, and what server you were coming from, will be stored in the cookie. The idea is to make it easier for the site to recognize you the next time you visit. This is why you can go to some sites and the web page says "Hi Karen!" It simply looks in your cookie directory on your hard disk (the cookie jar) and looks for the one it stored there. It opens the cookie, sees that your name is Karen (because you typed that into its site the last time you visited), and then displays it. It also knows that last time you bought an extra-large pepperoni pizza and a bag of fries. This time it automatically suggests an extra-large pepperoni pizza and fries. Neat. Convenient. It's like going into your favorite restaurant, and the waiter knows what you like.

The important point to remember is this: The agreement is that this information is transacted only between you and the website you're visiting. You have some privacy of information. Jack's Pizza's web server is not talking to Jill's Soda Pop Company's web server and then generating email to you trying to sell you a soda to wash your pizza down with. (Okay, maybe you want a soda with your pizza, so it's not a bad idea. But it can get out of hand. Keep reading.)

The idea of Live ID is totally different. Although it contends otherwise, I don't think Microsoft is just trying to offer a better user experience on the Web by offering you a Live ID to keep your passwords and other information all tidy. With Live ID, you sign on in one place—essentially, Microsoft—even if you're clicking the Sign In Through Live ID link on your favorite website. Really, you're signing in at Microsoft's Live ID, which, in turn, links you back to the site you wanted. Then you start hopping around among sites. Although most of the Live ID sites are now MS sites such as Hotmail, they hope to entice other vendors to become Live ID enabled. (With any luck on Microsoft's site, Jack and Jill will both fall down this slippery slope.) When that happens, the web servers are linked to one another. Garnering lots of valuable customer information (such as your buying patterns, net worth, geographical location, age, sex, hobbies, medical history, and other such private info) can be easily aggregated into one large database. Do you think that kind of information is valuable? You bet it is, and Microsoft knows it!

Let's consider some examples. Log in to the MSN Money site (moneycentral.msn.com/home.asp) and look in the upper-right corner. There's a Sign In link for Live ID. Suppose you're buying a house, refinancing your current one, or buying a new car through a Live ID–affiliated site. It is possible, using today's technology, that the selling agent can determine your net worth by checking your portfolio on Investor.com and bargain harder with you. I'm not saying this is currently happening, but it's possible. In fact, this kind of thing actually happened with Amazon, which raised its DVD prices for people who regularly bought DVDs from them. The practice was based only on cookies (and was stopped after customers discovered what was going on).

If you want to read that story, here's a brief quote and URL: "Amazon charging different prices on some DVDs."
www.computerworld.com/industrytopics/retail/story/0,10801,49569,00.html

In essence, the idea of cookies being private is being circumnavigated by Live ID. What's particularly scary about all this is that there is one entry point (or gatekeeper) to all Live ID sites—Microsoft. Over time, look to see more sites (and even IE itself) incorporating Live ID. I think we should be wary of the aggregation of information about us and should not allow that information to be passed around freely among corporations. Even umpteen-page-long privacy statements can't protect you when a web company goes bankrupt and the court orders sale of its valuable database with your buying patterns or other private information in it.

Troubleshooting

Web Page Errors

An error occurs when I try to visit a specific web page.

Try clicking the Refresh button to reload the page. If you still don't have any luck, remove the path information (that would be everything after the domain name) from the URL in the Address box, and press Enter.

Email Link Troubles

When I click an email link, Windows Mail opens, but I prefer a different email program.

Click the Tools button in the toolbar, click Internet Options to open the Internet Options dialog box, and then change the default mail program on the Programs tab. You should be able to select any installed email client (such as Outlook, Windows Mail, Eudora, Netscape Mail, and so on) here.

Some Graphics Don't Appear

Some pictures on a page don't open.

If the web page contains many pictures—say, a dozen or more—the graphics at the bottom of the page often do not open. Right-click the placeholder boxes for the images that didn't download, and choose Show Picture from the menu that appears.

Internet Explorer Crashes on Certain Web Pages

A web page freezes Internet Explorer.

Scripts that try to detect the brand and version of your browser frequently cause this problem. Click the Stop button on the IE toolbar, and close and reopen the program, if necessary. You can try disabling most scripting operations in the Security Settings dialog box, but doing so might cause the offending web page not to display properly. Read the section in this chapter called "Viewing and Managing Your IE Add-Ons" to deactivate specific scripts.

What Happened to the Website?

I get a lot of "Page not available" errors, even on major commercial sites.

The most obvious suggestion is to check your Internet connection. Your server might also be having a temporary problem, or high Internet traffic might be preventing your access. Another thing to consider is whether the page you are trying to visit is on a secure web server. Click on the Tools button in the toolbar, click Internet Options, and then click the Advanced tab to bring it to the front. Scroll down to the group of security settings and see whether any of the encryption protocols supported by IE are disabled. For example, if you are trying to visit a page that uses PCT encryption but Use PCT 1.0 is disabled, that page will not open.

Tips from the Windows Pros: Finding and Using PDF Documents on the World Wide Web

Perhaps you saw the photograph on the cover of *Time* magazine a few years ago of Bill Gates in a forest, sitting atop a tree-size stack of papers while holding a single compact disk in his hand, suggesting that digital information storage could save trees. It can, but it isn't easy.

The problem with digital documents is that, even with the best available technology, they are still not as easy to read as a paper book. Computer monitors put considerably more strain on your eyes, and even laptop PCs can be too bulky or clumsy to carry with you to a comfortable reading location. Furthermore, current digital storage technologies have a shorter shelf life than paper. Most CDs begin to deteriorate and lose their data after 10–20 years, but properly stored paper can last for centuries.

Still, digital documents have many advantages. First and foremost is cost: A single compact disc can contain hundreds of books yet cost less than $1 to manufacture. Printing the same amount of data on paper would cost hundreds, if not thousands, of dollars. Electronic books can be searched quickly, efficiently, and more thoroughly than printed ones. And, of course, digital documents are much easier to distribute.

One of the most popular methods for producing and distributing electronic books online is via PDF (Portable Document Format) files. PDF documents can be read using the Adobe Acrobat Reader, a free program offered by Adobe Systems, Inc. (www.adobe.com). PDF books can have the appearance and properties of a paper book, but without the paper. They also have the advantage of being compatible across many platforms, with versions of the Reader software available for Windows, Macintosh, Linux, and various incarnations of UNIX. A PDF document link on a web page is usually identified by the PDF icon.

PDF is used for a wide range of documents:

- It is used for government documents such as tax forms and educational materials.
- Technology companies, such as Intel, distribute technical documents and white papers in PDF.
- Private and commercial publishers produce and distribute electronic libraries of PDF books, both on CD and on the Web.
- News agencies produce PDF weather maps and other news material.

You can obtain the Acrobat Reader from many sources. If you own any other Adobe software—such as Photoshop or PhotoDeluxe—the Reader is probably already installed on your computer. Look for a program group called Adobe or Adobe Acrobat in your Start menu. You can also download it for free from the Adobe website.

Even if you find Adobe Acrobat on your computer, it's best to download the latest version of the Acrobat Reader. Later versions integrate nicely with Internet Explorer to read PDF documents directly over the Web, and include the Find feature. When you're choosing the version to download, click the box next to Include Option for Searching PDF Files and

Tips from the Windows Pros: Finding and Using PDF Documents on the World Wide Web 469

Accessibility Support. The file size is just a little larger, but the additional features are well worth it. Some features are dependent on the writer of the PDF file. For example, "bookmarks" work only with PDF documents that have been indexed.

Acrobat Reader works as a plug-in for Internet Explorer. When you click a link for a PDF document, it opens Acrobat Reader within IE, but the toolbars and menu will change, as shown in Figure 15.23. Just click the Back button to bring you back to the web page you were viewing.

Figure 15.23
PDF files can be viewed within a web page.

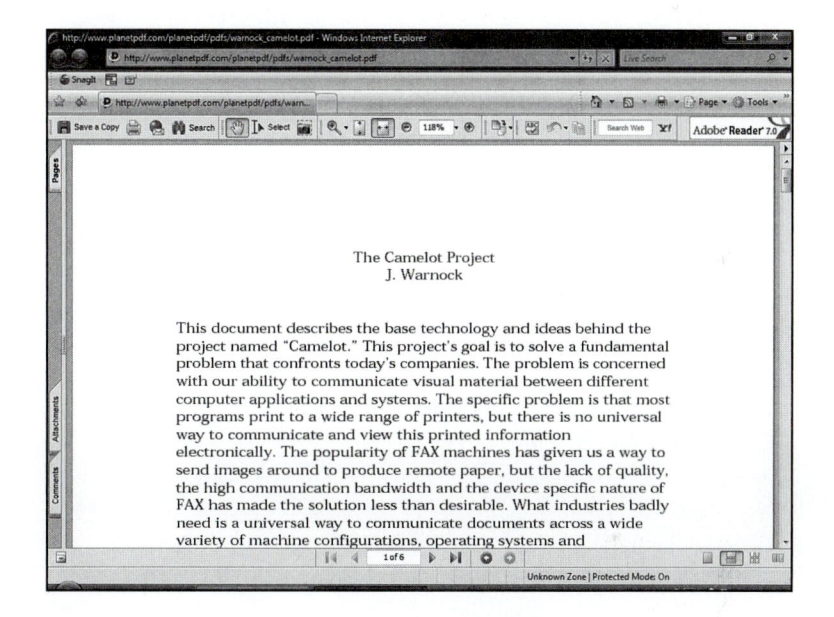

It is not uncommon to have problems with this whole procedure, although it does run more smoothly with the latest version. If you have trouble reading PDF documents over the Web, first save the PDF document to your hard drive. Instead of clicking the PDF link to open the file in a browser, right-click it and choose Save Target As from the shortcut menu that appears. After saving the document to the location you choose, open it manually using Acrobat Reader outside the IE session. Saving the PDF document in this manner has the added advantage of making the document easily available to you for future reference and available offline.

CHAPTER 16

EMAIL AND NEWSGROUPS WITH WINDOWS MAIL

In this chapter

Choosing an Email Client   472

Windows Mail Quick Tour   476

Creating and Sending New Mail   483

Using the Windows Contacts Address Book   492

Handling Unique Mail Situations   495

Additional Security Features in Windows Mail   496

Newsgroups and the Internet   509

Setting Up a Newsgroup Account in Windows Mail   512

Finding and Reading Newsgroups   513

Troubleshooting Email   519

Troubleshooting Newsgroups   521

Tips from the Windows Pros: Creating Formatted Email   523

Tips from the Windows Pros: Newsgroups—For More Than Just News   524

Choosing an Email Client

From the start, the Internet has been touted as a means for enhancing human communications, and among the many communication tools available in the online world, few have had the impact of electronic mail (email).

To fully understand the nature of email, keep in mind that, at its most basic level, it is simply a way for users to send messages to each other over a network. This network could be a local area network (LAN) run by your company using MS Exchange Server software. In this situation, the network server manages all message traffic. The server can also act as a gateway to other servers, allowing you to send mail beyond the local network. If you have an email account with an Internet service provider (ISP) or other Internet-based service, the provider's server acts as your gateway to other mail servers across the Internet.

Email has been criticized by some as diminishing the art of written communication by making letter writing into a less formal exchange. You may or may not agree, but if your daily work requires you to use a computer, chances are you are also expected to use email for much of your business communication.

Given that email is here to stay, you must decide which email client you plan to use for reading, composing, and sending messages. A number of options are available to you, and which one you ultimately choose will depend not only on your personal preferences but also on professional needs.

Windows Vista includes an excellent email client called Windows Mail, which is actually the update to Outlook Express 6 from Windows XP and renamed Windows Mail 7. No doubt the new name was chosen to minimize the confusion between Outlook (which is part of Microsoft Office) and Outlook Express (the freebie mail program supplied with Windows). When I'm troubleshooting email problems, I can't tell you how many times I have had to ask friends and clients to specify whether they were using Outlook Express or Outlook proper. (I call them "Outlook Express" and "Outlook-Outlook" just to underscore the difference.) They usually have absolutely no idea what I'm talking about or that these are two very different animals.

Windows Mail is a multifeatured program designed to appeal to a variety of email users, but it isn't for everyone, especially if you work in a corporation that requires tight integration of email with its communications infrastructure (for example, mobile communications devices such as Blackberrys, PocketPCs, and Palm Treos). Windows Mail can also function as a newsgroup client, making it a "one-stop" program if you routinely communicate via email and use newsgroups.

Windows Mail includes some important improvements over its predecessor, Outlook Express, although it is essentially an update of the same program. Some of these upgrades will be described more in-depth later, and some of these points are technical, but we decided to put them right up front in this chapter so that you can quickly see what's new in Vista Windows Mail:

- Instant as-you-type searching, which includes a full index search of subject and message text. Even though the Vista file system (the shell) has all the emails indexed for searching from the Start button, Windows Mail is actually faster for displaying things such as read or unread mail, flags, and so on, because searching is based on an internal, indexed Windows Mail database.
- Intelligent spam filtering, inherited from Hotmail. The filter is kept updated via Windows Update. The algorithms come from the huge database of Hotmail users rather than just from the individual's preferences or training of his email program.
- Phishing filter to help users recognize when someone unscrupulous is trying to get you to send passwords, bank account info, and so on to them.
- Windows Mail now stores emails differently on the hard disk. Instead of one .dbx file for each mail folder, we now have a separate .eml data file for each email. All folders in the Mail system are stored in corresponding folders on hard disk. Newsgroup messages are stored as .nws files. All .eml files have special properties in the operating system shell, allowing you to right-click on them and choose Reply, Reply All, Forward, Previous Versions, and so on.
- The data format is more reliable, so your emails are better protected against calamity. If the system stops with a message only half written to the hard disk, such as during a power outage, the operating system will see that the record is half written and will roll it back to the previous state. If the database is corrupted for some reason, Windows Mail will sense that and examine all the emails again and re-create the database. For further protection, there are always two backups of the database, so if the first one is lost, the backup one is loaded.
- Backup is easier. You can back up your entire mail folder by copying the folder to a CD or other media. (Mail is stored in a directory called Windows Mail, a subfolder of the user's Desktop folder, though you will have to drill down to [*user name*]/AppData/Local/ Microsoft/Windows Mail/ Local Folders.)
- Enhancements have been made for newsgroups. The name of the default news server, msnews@microsoft.com, has been changed to Microsoft Communities. Now you can look up products by Microsoft product name and join the groups. You can then post your questions or comments. Each class of message is assigned a different icon. For example, a question gets a question mark. If a question gets fully answered to the poster's satisfaction, it gets a check mark icon. Readers of a thread can then also rate it the answer. If a person posts many good answers, she will be tagged as a gold, silver, or bronze poster, depending on how many readers thought the posts were useful, so that readers will know how much weight to give a posting.

- The new Windows Contacts application interfaces with Windows Mail to provide a more comprehensive address list for mail, much like Outlook has. In Outlook Express, contacts were stored in a .wab (Windows Address Book) file. The .wab file has been around since Windows 98 and is clumsy. The new Contacts program creates a separate file for each contact (using a .contacts extension). It is a simple XML file now that other programs can easily access. The shell stores the contacts database now. You can back up your Address Book by copying the directory. To move Vista Contacts to XP, save them as .vcf files and import them. Likewise, to import XP Outlook Express contacts to Windows Mail, save them as .vcf files and import them.
- All the Windows Mail account information (POP server information, for example) is stored in XML files in the Windows Mail folder, not in the Registry. This is much simpler. Simply point Windows Mail to the new store folder, and it picks up all the account information (with the exception of the password, which is encrypted).

→ To learn more about using Windows Mail to read newsgroups, **see** "Finding and Reading Newsgroups," **p. 513**.

Windows Mail is relatively compact as Windows applications go. If you want an efficient program that can handle your email needs without a lot of extra fluff, Windows Mail is a pretty good choice. However, it does lack a few features that you might want or need, so read the next couple of sections to find out whether you should be using a different client.

> **NOTE**
>
> This discussion assumes you have a choice in email clients. If you're using Windows Vista in an office environment, check with your company's Information Systems (IS) manager to find out whether you must use one specific client.

What If You Like Outlook 97, 98, 2000, 2003, or 2007?

If you use Microsoft's Office suite, you're probably familiar with Outlook. Outlook is the primary communications tool included in the Office package, and many professional PC users like it. However, don't be misled by the fact that Outlook and Windows Mail are both from Microsoft. Windows Mail is not a "lite" version of Outlook; as mentioned previously, these two applications are actually quite different. Outlook includes many features that Windows Mail does not, such as the following:

- A personal calendar
- An electronic journal
- Fax capability
- Compatibility with Microsoft Exchange Server
- You can use Microsoft Word to compose and edit emails

In addition, Outlook's system of managing personal contacts is far more advanced than that of Windows Mail (however, the new Contacts program included in Vista improves things a bit over Outlook Express). See "Using the Windows Contact Address Book" later in this chapter. If the ability to tightly integrate a heavy email load with your personal scheduler on a daily basis is important to you, Outlook is the better choice. If you are already using Outlook and like the Calendar and Journal, stick with it. Vista now comes with a calendaring program that was swiped from Outlook (see Chapter 7 for coverage of Windows Calendar), but it is not as sophisticated or as tightly connected with other personal management features as is Outlook's calendaring. Furthermore, if your company's network or workgroup uses Exchange Server for mail services, Outlook is the only fully compatible upgrade to that system. Outlook is also Messaging Application Programming Interface (MAPI) capable, which means it can share mail with other MAPI-capable programs on your system. Windows Mail is not MAPI-capable. Because Outlook is bigger than Windows Mail, it requires more disk space, more RAM, and slightly more patience on the part of the user because it is so feature rich. If you find that you don't use Outlook for anything but email, you will likely be better served by Windows Mail.

Other Email Clients

Microsoft isn't the only company producing high-quality email clients. One of the most popular alternatives is Eudora from Qualcomm (www.eudora.com). Eudora offers an excellent package of mail management and filtering features, as well as compatibility with the latest Internet mail standards. Like Windows Mail, it is considerably more compact than Outlook, but it does not incorporate a newsgroup reader. Some unique Eudora features include the following:

- Very fast searching
- "Mood watch" to check for incendiary language (flaming)
- Virus protection
- Built-in compression agent to shorten download times on slow dial-up connections
- Inline spell checking as you type
- Encryption
- Remote access to email

A free version of Eudora called Eudora Light is available, but it lacks so many of the features available in the identically priced Windows Mail that, at this point, it isn't worth your consideration. An ad-based version of Eudora packs more features but displays advertisements within its interface and mail.

Numerous other email clients exist. A simple search on the Web or of www.download.com will flush them out. Of course, many people avoid the hassle of having an email "client" program on their computer altogether by using web-based, online mail clients such as those offered by Yahoo, Hotmail, and Google. These are called Web-mail or HTML mail services. Features vary between companies and are continually changing, so we won't try to summarize them here. You learn more about interfacing Windows Mail with web-based HTML mail later in this chapter.

Windows Mail Quick Tour

Because covering the many different email clients available would be beyond the scope of this book, we will assume that you have chosen Windows Mail. It comes free with Windows Vista and will meet many of your electronic mail needs.

Windows Mail is installed during a clean installation of Windows Vista, so it should be ready to open. You can launch it by clicking the Windows Mail icon near the top of the Start menu, labeled E-mail.

> **NOTE**
>
> In Windows, there is something called your "default email program." This is the program used to generate email from other programs. For example, it will be used if you click a link in IE to send an email to someone. As installed, Windows Vista assumes that Windows Mail is your default email program. If you upgraded your previous version of Windows to XP and had been using another email program such as Outlook or Eudora for email, that program will be your default email program instead. Still, this does not mean it will necessarily appear at the top of the Start menu next to E-mail. This setting should automatically show your default email client. If not, you can simply change it by right-clicking the Start button; choosing Properties, Start Menu, and the Customize button; and then changing the E-mail drop-down list to the program of your choice. If you don't see the program you expected, it's not installed into Vista.

→ If you have not yet set up an Internet connection, you will need to do so. The New Connection Wizard will pop up to guide you through the process. **See** Chapter 14, "Getting Connected" **p. 393**.

If you are online and you already have an email account set up, Windows Mail automatically checks for new mail when you open the program. If you don't yet have an account set up, when you open Windows Mail for the first time a wizard opens to help you set up a mail account. For now, click Cancel to close this screen and take a look at Windows Mail. I'll talk about setting up your account(s) in the next section, "Setting Up an Email Account." For now, see Figure 16.1.

→ If you haven't yet set up an account, **see** "Setting Up an Email Account," **p. 478**.

If this is the first time you've opened Windows Mail, notice that you have one unread mail message. Click the link to go to your Inbox and read the message, which is actually just a welcome letter from Microsoft.

When the Inbox opens, as shown in Figure 16.1, you'll see that the right side of the window is divided. The upper half is a list of messages in your Inbox, with unread messages shown in boldface. The lower half is the preview pane, which shows a preview of whichever message is selected above. You can use the scrollbar to read more of the message.

Figure 16.1
Windows Mail opens with the Inbox selected. The Inbox includes a list of new messages and a preview pane that you can use to read them.

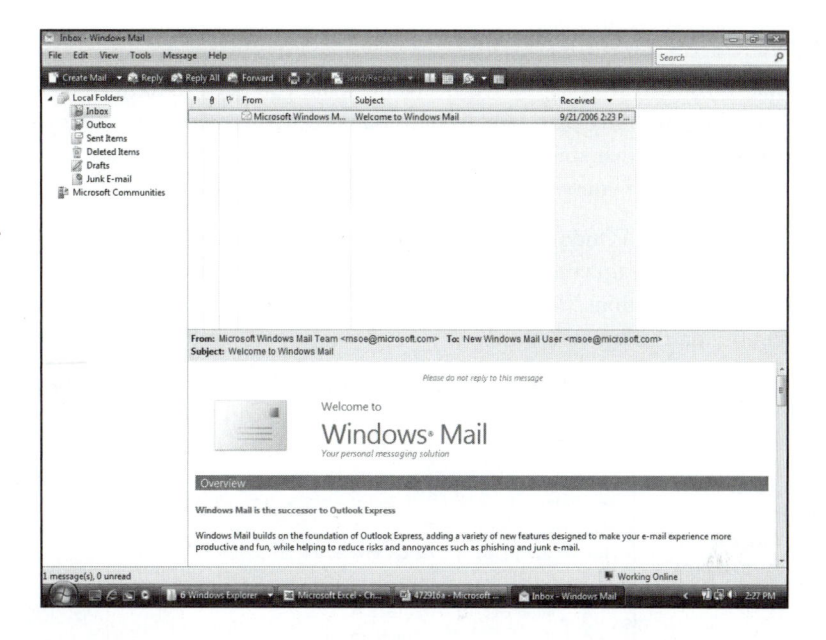

The preview pane is useful, but some people don't like it because it crowds the message headers a bit. Before Windows XP SP2, the preview pane came with some security risks, potentially alerting spammers that you were reading their mail, or even running malicious code. But as of SP2 and now in Vista, you can safely read messages in the preview pane. If you want to hide the preview pane to make more room to view the list of Inbox messages, you can. To hide that pane or make a variety of other adjustments to the Windows Mail interface, follow these steps:

1. Choose View, Layout.
2. In the Window Layout Properties dialog, select or deselect the screen elements you want to show or hide. Deselect the preview pane if you don't plan to use it.
3. Experiment with the settings, and click OK when you have Windows Mail looking the way you want it.

Take a look at the other screen elements. Having the Folders List turned on, as shown in Figure 16.2, is handy because you can use it to quickly jump to any part of Windows Mail, including newsgroups if you have an account set up. You just click on a folder in the left pane to select it.

> Does Windows Mail always seem to check for new mail at the wrong time? **See** "Making Windows Mail Less Automated" in the "Troubleshooting" section at the end of the chapter.

Setting Up an Email Account

Before you can send or receive electronic mail, you need to have an email account. There is a good possibility that your account has already been configured by your company's IS department or that some software from your ISP took care of it for you. Otherwise, you'll have to set it up yourself.

When you run Windows Mail the first time, the New Account Wizard will run to walk you through setting up your account, but in case you canceled it, you can start it again, using the following directions. These steps also work for setting up a second or third account or mail identity on the same machine:

1. In Windows Mail, choose Tools, Accounts. You'll see the dialog box shown in Figure 16.2.

Figure 16.2
Starting the New Account Wizard to set up your email account.

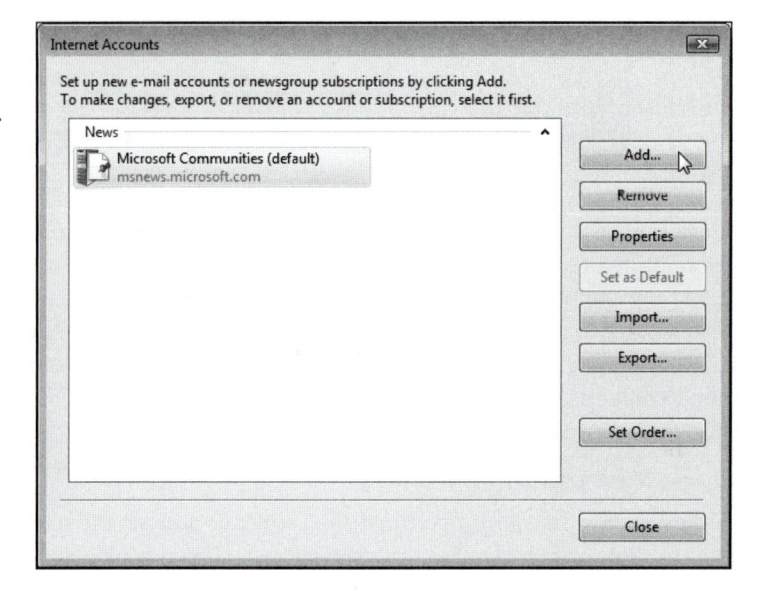

2. Click Add, then select E-mail Account, and click Next.
3. You are asked for your "display name." This is the name that other people will see when you send them mail, such as Benjamin Franklin, so choose carefully. Click Next after you've entered a name.
4. The next wizard box asks for your email account address, which should have been provided by your company or ISP (see Figure 16.3). Click Next.

Figure 16.3
Enter your email address here. It should have been supplied by your ISP or other email provider.

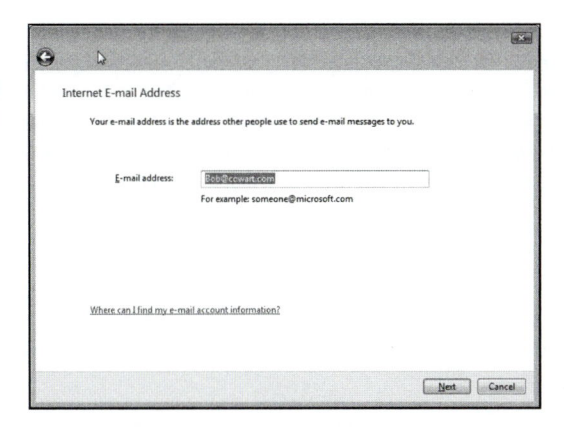

5. You must enter the types and names of your incoming and outgoing email servers in the next dialog, which is shown in Figure 16.4. Again, this information is provided by your company or ISP (often, you can find this information on your ISP's FAQ page). Your incoming email type is probably POP3. (See the next section for an explanation of the different server types.) Check the Outgoing Server Requires Authentication check box only if your ISP informed you that this should be turned on. Click Next.

Figure 16.4
Enter the types and names of your email servers.

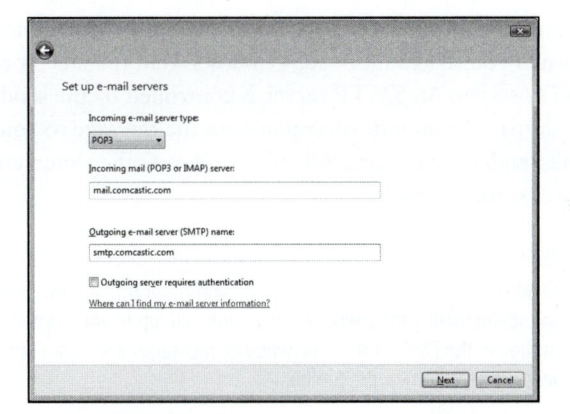

6. The next dialog asks for your login name and password. Again, this is information from your ISP or network administrator. Do not check the option Remember Password if other people have access to your computer account and you don't want them to be allowed to check your email. (If other people have their own Vista system logon and account, they will not have access to your mail, so don't worry about it when that's the case.)

7. Click Next. You'll see the Congratulations dialog box. Click Finish. Your new account should now be listed in the Internet Accounts dialog. Unless you checked Do Not Check My Email Immediately, Windows Mail will now check for any new mail that is on your mail server. If either your password or your username doesn't work right, you'll see a dialog box asking you to verify those again. Otherwise, mail will start flowing in if there is any waiting for you.

> **NOTE**
>
> Secure Password Authentication (SPA) is used by some email services to prevent unauthorized users from getting or sending your email. When you attempt to receive your mail in Windows Mail, a screen will pop up asking for you to enter a username and password. Both Windows Mail and MS Outlook have this feature. Most email (POP) servers do not use this feature, so you should probably leave it turned off.

The only other piece of information that Windows Mail may need to ask is which network or dial-up connection it should use when sending and receiving mail. You probably don't need to select this connection because Windows Mail automatically assigns your default connection to all mail accounts.

→ If you don't have a connection set up, **see** "Getting Connected," **p. 393**.

> If you routinely encounter server errors when sending or receiving mail, **see** "Missing Mail Servers" in the "Troubleshooting" section at the end of the chapter.

What Are POP, IMAP, SMTP, and HTTP?

You've probably noticed the veritable alphabet soup of acronyms that exist for the many different kinds of email servers. Unlike so many other cryptic terms thrown around in the PC world, these acronyms are actually worth remembering.

First, a basic understanding of how email flows across networks (including the Internet) is important. Usually, when you send a message, Windows Mail transfers it to a *Simple Mail Transfer Protocol (SMTP)* server. An SMTP server is controlled by the sender, meaning that it waits for you to push mail through it. After you send the message to your SMTP server using Windows Mail's Send/Recv or Send All command, no other interaction is required to deliver the message to its final destination.

> **NOTE**
>
> The Send command must be used in the main program, not just in an individual email. Otherwise, the mail you've written will simply pile up in your Outbox. You can click on the Outbox in the Folder list to see whether messages are waiting to be sent. If so, click the Send/Recv button on the toolbar.

Mail sent to your computer doesn't just go from the sender to your PC. Because your PC is likely not always online, and certainly not always ready to receive email, messages must go to an interim server (usually maintained through your Internet service provider). To receive mail, you probably use either a *Post Office Protocol (POP)* or *Internet Message Access Protocol (IMAP)* server. POP and IMAP differ in that POP servers forward all messages directly to your local machine, whereas IMAP servers maintain the messages on the server until you delete them. When you check for mail on an IMAP server, a list of message headers is downloaded, but the actual message bodies stay on the server (like newsgroup messages, as explained later in this chapter). An IMAP server comes in handy if you travel a lot and want to be able to check messages on the road with your laptop or PDA but don't want to remove them from the server until you can download the mail to a more permanent location on your home desktop. IMAP servers let you work with email messages without downloading them to your computer first. You can preview, delete, and organize messages directly on the email server, and copies are stored on the server until you choose to delete them. IMAP is commonly used for business email accounts.

Another type of email server is a *Hypertext Transfer Protocol (HTTP)* server, such as those offered by Yahoo!, Hotmail (Microsoft), Gmail (Google), and others. An HTTP mail account is useful for those who want to travel light because it is not necessary to take a computer or software with you. You can access your HTTP account using a web browser on any computer with access to the Internet, and generally the only information you will need to provide is your login name and password. Windows Mail can also be used to read and send mail using an HTTP account.

> **NOTE**
>
> Outlook Express supported HTTP accounts, but Windows Mail does not. This is a drag, but someone at Microsoft decided it was for the better.

Having trouble with a stubborn account password dialog? **See** *"Password Trouble" in the "Troubleshooting" section at the end of the chapter.*

READING AND PROCESSING INCOMING MESSAGES

After you have an account set up, you are ready to begin downloading and reading mail. To get started, open Windows Mail, and go to the Inbox. By default, Windows Mail automatically checks for new mail when it first opens. If your installation is configured otherwise, click the Send/Recv button on the toolbar. As your mail is coming in, a dialog box appears indicating which account is being checked and shows the progress of the sending and receiving. It will also tell you how many messages are being transferred. New messages will then appear in your inbox, as shown in Figure 16.5.

Figure 16.5
The Inbox has five new messages.

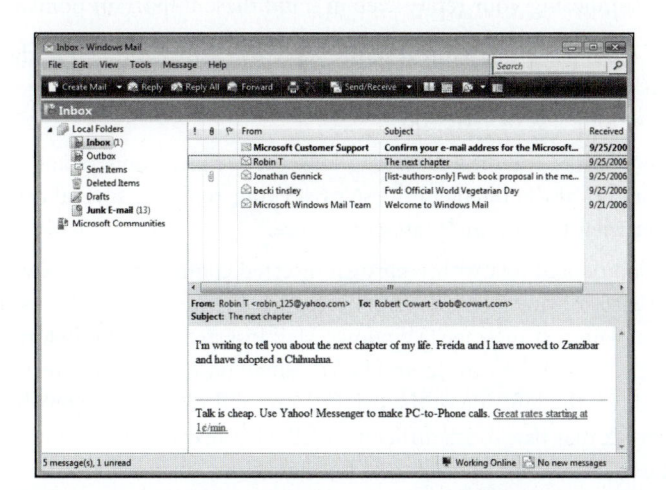

> **TIP**
>
> If you receive a message from someone you plan to communicate with regularly, right-click his or her name in the message header, and choose Add Sender to Address Book. By doing so, you add the person to your contacts list so that sending him or her mail in the future will be easier. Note that when you save a contact in this way, it may not store them in a way you can recognize later. It will store them under the name in the "From" column. Unfortunately, many people fail to set up their email accounts with their proper name as their email identity. So you receive emails from people such as jpjones@aol.com. This is a pretty useless entry in your contacts list, unless you think of your friend as jpjones and not John Paul Jones. So, after saving a contact in this way (which only has the advantage of saving you the hassle and potential mistyping of their email address), you may want to edit the contact and enter the correct first name and last name. More Contacts management is covered later in this chapter.

When you reply to a message, you need to be wary of a few things. First, note that if the incoming message was sent to a group of people, clicking the Reply button will send your message to the single person who sent it to you; clicking Reply All will send your message to the entire list of people who received the original message. Although this can be a helpful tool when communicating with a group of people, it could get you in trouble if you think you are writing to a specific person and accidentally click the Reply All button. Before you send any message, make sure the correct person or persons are listed in the To: and Cc: fields. Anyone listed in those two fields will receive a copy of the message as well as a list of the other recipients and their email addresses, so make sure you aren't airing your dirty laundry more publicly than you intended. The section "Creating and Sending New Mail" later in this chapter discusses addressing messages more thoroughly.

The rest of the reply process is straightforward. You just type in your own text and click Send on the toolbar when you are ready to deliver the message. By default, Windows Mail automatically places the text of the original message in the reply.

When you're composing your reply, keep in mind these important points:

- Consider editing the quoted text in the reply by cutting it down to the text you actually intend to respond to. Most people don't appreciate reading four pages of quoted text followed at long last by "Me too."

- Include enough of the original text to help the recipient understand exactly what you are replying to. If the recipient doesn't read your reply for several days, he might not remember what the original statements were.

- Breaking up quoted text with your own inserted comments is usually acceptable, but make sure it is obvious which words are yours. Figure 16.6 illustrates this reply technique in a plain text message. Windows Mail inserts the > sign before each line of the email you're responding to. In an HTML email (also called rich text), a solid vertical bar runs down the left side of the original text and writing new text between paragraphs doesn't break that bar, so it's difficult to tell what text is newly written. In that case, use colored text or another font (choose Format, Font).

Figure 16.6
Quoted text and reply text are interspersed throughout the message, but there is little doubt as to who wrote what.

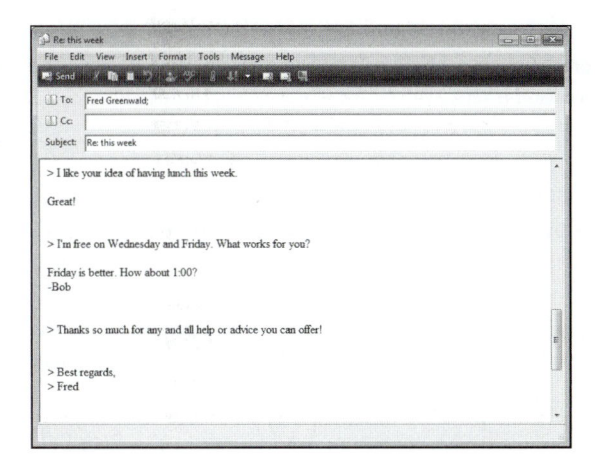

Deleting Messages

How and when messages are deleted depends on what kind of mail server you use. If you receive mail from a POP server, deleted messages remain in the Windows Mail Deleted Items folder indefinitely, similar to "deleted" files in the Windows Recycle Bin.

You can permanently delete messages by right-clicking the Deleted Items folder and choosing Empty 'Deleted Items' Folder from the shortcut menu that appears. If you have an IMAP mail server, the Deleted Items folder is emptied automatically when you log off the mail server.

You can change the way Windows Mail handles items in the Deleted Items folder. To do so, choose Tools, Options, and select the Maintenance tab to customize when and how mail messages are deleted.

Creating and Sending New Mail

The process of creating and sending new mail is almost as easy as receiving it. To open a New Message composition window, click the Create Mail button on the Windows Mail toolbar.

> **TIP**
>
> In Outlook Express you had to install Microsoft Word to have a spell-checking option when composing mail. In Windows Mail, spell checking is built in. Click the Spelling icon in the message window when composing a message. Adjust your spelling options by going to Tools, Options, and clicking on the Spelling tab.

Addressing messages properly is important. A single misplaced character, or an extra one, in an email address can send the message to the wrong person or to no one at all. A typical email address looks like this:

bob@pearsoneducation.com

> **TIP**
>
> Some mail servers are case sensitive. If you're not sure, just type the whole address in lowercase letters.

Notice that Windows Mail has two address fields that appear by default, To: and Cc:. Cc: is short for Carbon Copy or, these days when that messy blue paper is nearly extinct, Courtesy Copy. The address field is the only required field when sending email; all the others, including the subject and even the message body, can be blank. The To: field usually contains the email address of the primary recipient, although it can contain more than one address, as shown in Figure 16.7. You separate multiple addresses with a semicolon (;).

To send email to several people without allowing its recipients to see the names or email addresses of others who also received it, enter addresses in the Bcc: field (Blind Carbon/Courtesy Copy). In an email window, choose View, All Headers. The Bcc: field will now appear in the email window.

> **TIP**
>
> It is a good idea to use the BCC field when you are sending an email to a large audience. This hides the addresses from prying eyes and potential spammers who might then pick up the addresses. Use the CC line if you are corresponding with a few people on a project and want everyone in the loop and give them all the ability see everyone's address. This also allows any recipient to click Reply All and send a response to the group, whereas BCC does not.

Figure 16.7
A new message with an attachment has been addressed to several people.

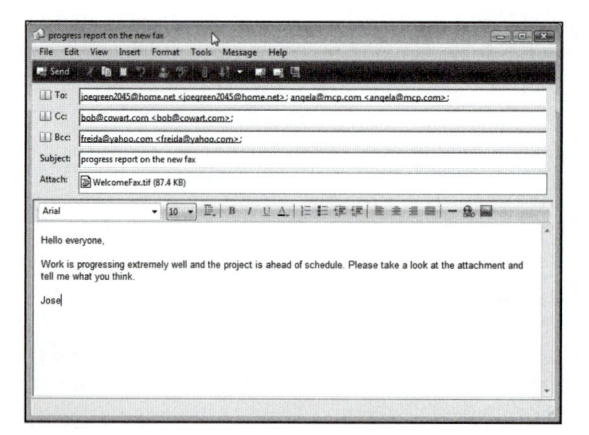

When you are finished composing the message, just click Send on the toolbar. If you do not want your message sent right away, choose File, Send Later. The message is then sent to the Outbox folder and will be sent to your mail server the next time the Send command is given. If you want to save the message for later editing, and not send it yet, click File, Save. The file is then saved in your Drafts folder where you can open it again later, edit it, and send it.

If you don't like the name that is being assigned to your outgoing mail, **see** *"Identity Crisis" in the "Troubleshooting" section at the end of the chapter.*

SENDING AND RECEIVING ATTACHMENTS

Of the many features that make email a versatile method for communication, perhaps the most useful is the capability to send files along with an email message. You can attach any electronic file stored on disk to an email message in Windows Mail and then send it to someone else.

> **NOTE**
>
> Some email accounts do not allow you to send or receive file attachments with messages. Others, particularly HTTP accounts, limit the number and size of attachments allowed. Check with your account provider to find out whether you have this capability. Also, make sure that the recipient has the capability to receive attachments.

Attaching a file to an outgoing message is easy. In the message composition window, click the Attach button on the toolbar and locate the file you want to send in the Insert Attachment dialog. After you have selected the file, click Attach. The file attachment should appear in the header information, as shown earlier in Figure 16.7.

Before you send any attached files, consider the bandwidth it will require. Even if you have a fast network or Internet connection, if the recipient connects to the Internet via a dial-up modem, downloading the attachment could take a long time. In general, you should avoid sending any attachments that are larger than one or two megabytes unless you are sure the recipient can handle them or knows in advance that they're about to receive some rather large files. It's best to ask your recipient first. Many mail servers (especially web-based accounts) limit the total amount of space a person can use, and many also set a limit to the size of attachments allowed (often capping the attachment size at 1 or 2MB, though some high-speed servers such as Comcast cap it at 10MB at the time we wrote this).

One more thing: If you or the recipient uses a 56Kbps or slower Internet connection, it is usually a good idea to compress large attachments before you send them. Simply right-click on the document(s) you wish to send, choose Send To, and then Compressed (zipped) Folder. Attach the compressed version to your email.

To open an attachment in a message you receive, right-click the attachment (listed in the header) and choose Save As to save it to disk, or simply open it. If the attachment is a picture file, it often appears in the body of the message as well.

> **TIP**
>
> Here is a tip that can save you a significant amount of cash. You can view and print Microsoft Word, Excel, PowerPoint, and Visio attachments without having to purchase Microsoft Office. You can't edit the documents, but you can view and print them. All you need to do is download the free Word, Excel, and PowerPoint viewer programs from Microsoft.com. Go to http://www.microsoft.com/downloads/ and search for Office viewers.

Guarding Yourself Against Email Viruses

Computer viruses often propagate themselves through email attachments. Hackers seem to get their jollies out of slowing down the Internet or bringing corporate business to a crawl. One way to do this seems to be targeting the most popular email programs, such as Outlook and Windows Mail. As a result, the bulk of email-borne contagion exists in the form of attachments whose payloads sneak through weaknesses in those two programs. Personally, I think that both these programs are excellent email clients, so I don't suggest changing your email program just to avoid the onslaughts of malicious Internet hackers.

As you might suspect, Microsoft doesn't want to lose customers either, so it makes a point of looking for viruses and posting critical updates to its site for easy download. A good approach is to run a Windows System Update regularly. Automatic Updates are turned on for just this reason.

In addition, security has been improved in Windows Mail to specifically combat this problem. By going to Tools, Options and clicking the Security tab, you'll notice the options for Virus Protection. By default, Windows Mail will warn you if another program attempts to send a message to contacts in your address book. As you may be aware, this is a common way for viruses to spread. I recommend that you keep this option selected.

There is also an option that deals with potential threats from incoming email attachments. If you click the box next to Do Not Allow Attachments to Be Saved or Opened That Could Potentially Be a Virus, you'll be more protected, but your ability to access any attachment to email in Windows Mail will be limited. If you're diligent about it, a better way of dealing with the possibility of attachment-borne viruses is to carefully look over your incoming email before opening any attachment by following the tips presented a little later in this section. I've found that when enabling the automatic feature in Windows Mail, even the most innocuous attachments are prevented from opening. (You can regain access to these attachments simply by returning to the Security dialog box and deselecting this option.)

Yet another option is to download and use one of many available antivirus programs. A reliable source is http://www.mcafee.com, and its website is another good place to check for the latest discovered viruses and how to protect your computer from them. I like a freebie called Avast (http://www.avast.com) and have had good luck with it for several years.

→ For help dealing with junk mail and spam and phishing emails, and for information on protecting your computer from viruses, adware, malware, Trojans, and all other manner of invasive mischief, **see** Chapter 33, "Protecting Windows from Viruses and Spyware," **p. 1131**, and Chapter 36, "Protecting Yourself from Fraud and Spam," **p. 1243**.

Contrary to popular belief, simply downloading an infected attachment virtually never harms your computer. With few exceptions, it is only if you open an attached executable file that there could be dire consequences. If possible, save the file attachment on a separate disk and then scan it with antivirus software.

Be especially wary of the following:

- Attachments you weren't expecting (even from people you know). If in doubt, write back to the sender and ask whether they intended to send you the attachment. Their computer may have a virus they are unaware of. Ask whether the attachment is safe and whether they've run it on their computer.

- Executable attachments (filenames ending in .exe, .vbs, or .js). Be aware that sometimes filenames are misleading on purpose. For example, you might see an attachment such as party.jpg.vbs. This is not a picture. The final extension is the one that counts.

- Emails with cryptic or odd subjects and messages, such as "I Luv U," "Here's that document you requested," or "CHECK THIS OUT!!!"

- Anything that comes from a source you are unfamiliar with.

→ For further discussion of this important topic and about the phishing filter, **see** "Additional Security Features in Windows Mail," **p. 496**.

SETTING UP A SIGNATURE

If you use email for much of your personal and business communication, you may like to "sign" outgoing messages with an electronic signature file. These signatures frequently include additional information about you, such as an address, title, phone number, company name, web URL, or a witty quote. Windows Mail makes it easy to set up a standard signature that will be included in every message you compose. You can configure your own signature by following these steps:

1. Choose Tools, Options. Click the Signatures tab to bring it to the front.
2. Click New to begin typing a new signature. Type your signature information as shown in Figure 16.8.
3. If you have multiple email accounts, click Advanced and select the account or accounts you want this signature to be used with.
4. Place a checkmark next to Add Signatures to All Outgoing Messages to enable this feature. Notice that, by default, your signatures will not be added to replies and forwards. Click OK when you're finished.

> **TIP**
>
> Consider creating several signatures, with varying levels of personal information. You can then choose a signature in the message window by selecting Insert, Signature.

Figure 16.8
You can create a standard signature for your outgoing messages here.

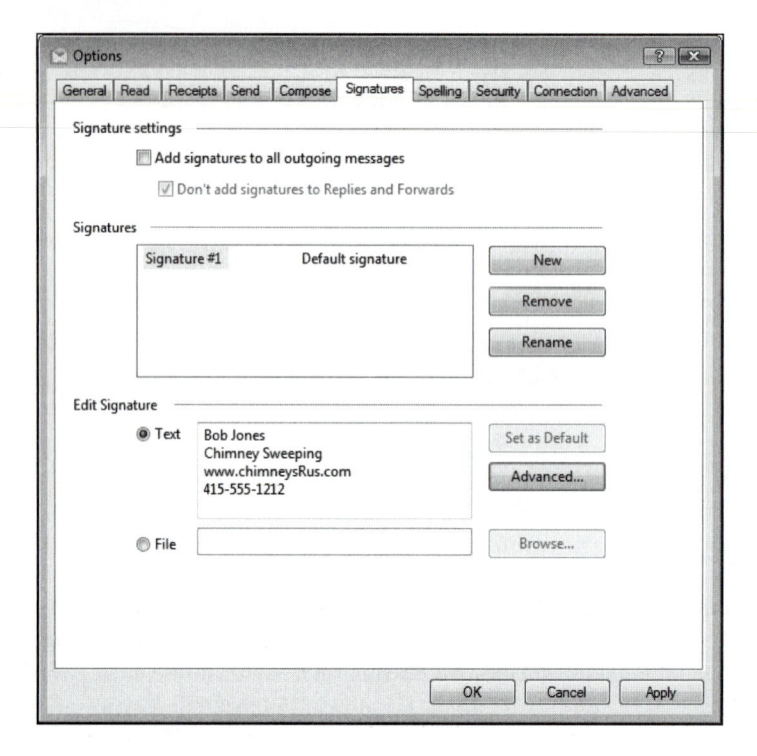

REQUESTING RECEIPTS

It is possible for Windows Mail to send a request along with email you send, asking the recipient to simply click a box to notify you that your email message has been read. This is called a *read receipt*. When typing a message, go to Tools, Request Read Receipt. If there is not already a checkmark next to it, click on Request Read Receipt.

Note that this is a request only: The recipient has the option of refusing to send the receipt. Still, it is a helpful tool: If you don't get a receipt, you can follow up with another email or a phone call. Some people feel that read receipts are an invasion of their privacy and will not respond to them for that reason alone.

If you intend to request a read receipt every time you send email, you can change your settings to make it simple. In Windows Mail, go to Tools, Options, and click on the Receipts tab. Click the box at the top of the window that says Request a Read Receipt for All Sent Messages. Consider this carefully; your Inbox could get filled quickly with read receipts, and the significance of receipts could be diluted (and recipients irritated) if a request is attached even to the messages of minor importance that you send. In addition, this window allows you to select your preference for returning read receipts. If you find the pop-up windows to be annoying, choose an option to Never or Always send a receipt when requested.

FORMATTING OPTIONS FOR MAIL

A simple way to enrich email is to apply message formatting using HTML code, the same type of code used to construct web pages. HTML is the default format for new messages you create in Windows Mail, although replies are typically formatted in whatever manner they were originally sent to you.

Applying special formatting to HTML messages is easy. Windows Mail provides a formatting toolbar similar to what you would see in a word processing program, where you can choose such formatting options as bold, italic, and so on. You also can give HTML messages graphic backgrounds by choosing one of several varieties of "stationery" provided by Windows Mail. To do this, choose Format, Apply Stationery. You can even generate email that looks much like a web page, complete with pictures (and, heaven forbid, banner ads), as well as links.

→ For details on how to create web-page-like HTML email, **see** "Tips from the Windows Pros: Creating Formatted Email," **p. 523**.

> **CAUTION**
>
> Although you don't have to worry about accidentally generating malicious HTML-formatted email, you might want to know that HTML email can carry scripts that might damage your system or invade your privacy. Some viruses (such as the infamous bubbleboy virus) have used HTML mail to propagate. Also, HTML emails can be used to track how people view their email. For example, some emails have links to pictures in them that automatically download from the Internet when you click on the message. These links can be used by advertisers (if they care to notice) to track when you've opened an email. They can also track how often you read that email. Some people consider this a breach of privacy.

One problem with HTML messages is that not all modern email clients can view them properly, or some people turn off the HTML capabilities of their email client programs as a protective strategy against malware. HTML messages viewed in a plain text window often appear with a huge quantity of gibberish at the end of the message. Likewise, mailing lists usually cannot handle HTML formatting in messages that are sent to them.

Two types of plain text message formatting are available. Until a few years ago, all email was formatted as simple text, with no special characters or fancy formatting. These early emails utilized a message format called *uuencode*, short for UNIX-to-UNIX encode. You don't need to be running UNIX to read uuencoded messages, though; virtually any email client you are likely to encounter—including Windows Mail—can read and send messages in this format.

To address the shortcomings of ASCII-based uuencode email, the *Multipurpose Internet Mail Extensions (MIME)* specification was developed. MIME, which is supported by most modern email clients, allows the use of graphics, file attachments, and some special non-ASCII characters in email messages.

Most mailing lists and users in general can handle MIME messages. To change the default sending formats for outgoing messages, open the Options dialog in Windows Mail. On the Send tab, choose HTML or Plain Text. If you choose Plain Text, your default message format will actually be MIME. If you want to change to uuencode, click the Plain Text Settings button and choose the appropriate options in the dialog that appears.

> **TIP**
>
> If you happen to know that your recipient is using some truly ancient technology to download and read email, such as Telnet and a text reader, send messages to that person uuencoded.

Is the formatting of your outgoing messages creating discontent among your recipients? **See** *"Recipients Don't Like My Mail Formatting" in the "Troubleshooting" section at the end of the chapter.*

SENDING AND RECEIVING SECURE MESSAGES

Email has fast become an essential method of communication, but for some uses, it might not be secure enough. Hiding or falsifying one's identity on the Internet is easy enough that some unscrupulous person could be masquerading as you or one of your associates. To combat this problem, several companies offer *digital IDs* that help verify the identity of the sender.

Another threat to the privacy of email is the possibility that messages will be intercepted and read by others (think digital wiretapping). Sending *encrypted* email will prevent your mail from being read by anyone on the way to your intended recipient.

A digital ID is made up of a private key, a public key, and a digital signature. When you digitally sign a message, two of these three things are added to your email: a public key and your digital signature. This is called a *certificate*. The private key stays with you.

When you send secure mail, recipients use your digital signature to verify your identity. They use your public key to send encrypted email to you. When you receive the encrypted email, you use your private key to decrypt the message.

The mechanics of how this works are elaborate and a topic that can entertain the most advanced cryptologists and software engineers. What's important is that to send or receive secure mail, you will need to have a digital ID. To encrypt messages you send, your Address Book must contain a digital ID for each recipient.

You can obtain a digital ID for yourself by following these steps:

1. In Windows Mail, choose Tools, Options.
2. On the Security tab, click Get Digital ID, as shown in Figure 16.9. Choosing this option will launch your browser and automatically go to a Microsoft web page that contains links to various certification authorities. Among those listed are VeriSign, GeoTrust, Avoco secure2trust, and Comodo Certification.

Figure 16.9
Get a Digital ID and adjust your security preferences on the Security tab of the Options dialog box.

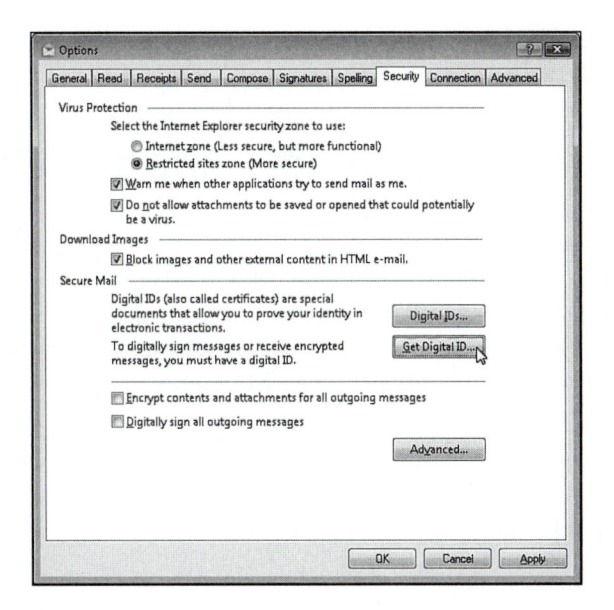

3. Select one of these companies and go to its website. Follow the instructions provided there to obtain and install a digital ID.

When you have a digital ID, it is simple to add it to a message. To do so, perform the following steps:

1. Open Windows Mail and click Create Mail.
2. In the new mail window, go to Tools and click Digitally Sign.
3. Compose and send your message.

Windows Mail will automatically add your digital ID to your email account when you send your first digitally signed message by searching your computer for a valid digital ID that matches the email address from which you are sending. If more than one valid digital ID is found, you must choose which ID to add to that email account. Also note that if you have more than one email account, you will need to have a different digital ID for each account from which you want to send secure email.

> **NOTE**
> When sending secure email, your reply address must match the account from which you send digitally signed email. If you have set up a different reply address (on the General tab of your account properties dialog box), message recipients won't be able to use your ID to reply with encrypted email.

When others send digitally signed email to you, messages are marked with a red seal in the message header. Windows Mail shows you an explanatory message about digital signatures before displaying the message. If you are online, you can check the validity of the digital ID of the sending party. To do this, choose Tools, Options, Security tab, Advanced, Check for Revoked Digital IDs, Only When Online.

Using the Windows Contacts Address Book

You don't have to communicate via email for long before you mistype someone's address. Suddenly, spelling has become more important than ever before. Your local mail carrier can direct your parcel to you when the label is misspelled, tattered, and torn, but email with a misspelled address just gets bounced back to you. Email addresses can also be cryptic and long, and some are even case sensitive. The Windows Contacts list (previously called Address Book in Outlook Express and Windows XP) feature in Windows Mail is a big help with all of this.

Before going through the inner workings of the Address Book, keep in mind that this single feature goes by two different names within Windows Mail. Sometimes it is called the Address Book, and other times it is called the Contacts list. We'll use the terms here interchangeably.

You can open the Address Book in its own window by choosing Tools, Windows Contacts, or by clicking the Contacts icon in the toolbar.

> *If you have too many unwanted entries in your Address Book,* **see** *"Thinning Your Contacts List" in the "Troubleshooting" section at the end of the chapter.*

Adding, Editing, and Removing Entries

By default, Windows Mail adds an entry to your Address Book whenever you reply to an email you've received. This is an easy way to fatten up your contacts list quickly. Before your address book grows to an unmanageable size, you may want to turn off that feature (see the "Troubleshooting" section at the end of this chapter). If you do this, you'll need to know how to add contacts in other ways. A foolproof way to add someone to your Address Book is by doing the following:

1. Open a message sent to you by someone you want to add to the Address Book.
2. Right-click the individual's name or email address in the message header and choose Add to Contacts.
3. A Properties sheet opens for the entry as shown in Figure 16.10, but don't close it yet. Click the Name tab to bring it to the front. If the person uses a nickname, you might need to edit the name entries on this tab so that they are displayed correctly in your Contacts list, especially the Preferred setting on the Name and E-mail tab. This determines which email address will be used for that person by default. Because many people now have multiple email addresses, this can be a time-saver.

Figure 16.10
Go through all the tabs on the Properties sheet and enter any information about this contact you feel appropriate.

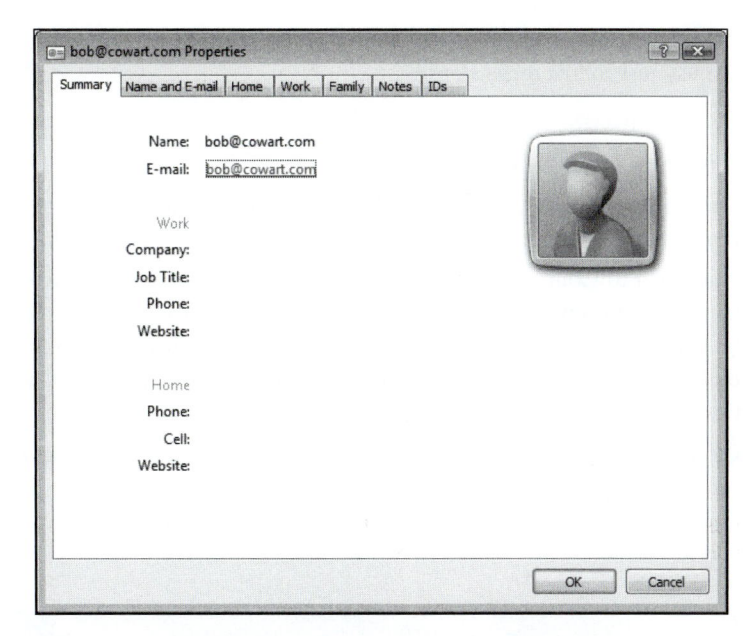

4. Review all the other tabs in the Properties sheet, and enter any other information about this person you feel appropriate. Click OK when you're finished.

You also can add someone to your Address Book the old-fashioned way—that is, manually from a business card or other source. In Windows Mail, click on the Contacts icon. This will open up the Contacts list. Click on the New Contact icon and select New Contact. The Properties window, described previously, will open for you to enter information.

To edit a contact later, click on the Addresses icon to open the Address Book. Select the contact that you want to edit by double-clicking that person's name. The Properties window will now open with a summary of that person's contact information. To change or add information, you need to click on one of the other tabs along the top of the window—the information cannot be changed on the Summary tab.

You might find duplicate listings or unwanted contacts in your Address Book. Deleting a contact is simple: Just highlight the entry and click Delete (on the toolbar). Be certain you've selected the correct contact because this action cannot be undone.

CREATING DISTRIBUTION LISTS

Sending a single email message to several people is not unusual. However, entering multiple addresses can get tiresome, especially if you frequently send messages to the same group of people.

To simplify this task, you can create *distribution lists* in the Contacts list. You can group many people into a single list, and when you want to send a message to the group, you simply choose the distribution listing from your Address Book. Distribution lists can be created for co-workers, customers, friends, and family, or any other group you communicate with. To create a list, just follow these steps:

1. Open Contacts.
2. Click New Contact Group in the menu bar.
3. On the Contact Group tab of the Properties dialog that opens, type a descriptive name. For example, consider using the name of your department at work.
4. Click Add to Contact Group. In the Add Members to Contact Group dialog, pick a name or names from your Contacts, and click Add. You can select a range of contacts by shift-clicking or dragging across the range. You can select noncontiguous contacts by Ctrl+clicking. Repeat until you have selected all the names you want in the distribution list.
5. Click OK when you are finished selecting names from the Address Book. As you can see in Figure 16.11, each member is listed in the box. Check the Contact Group Details tab to see whether you should enter any information there, and click OK when you're finished.

Figure 16.11
A distribution list has been created for sending group emails.

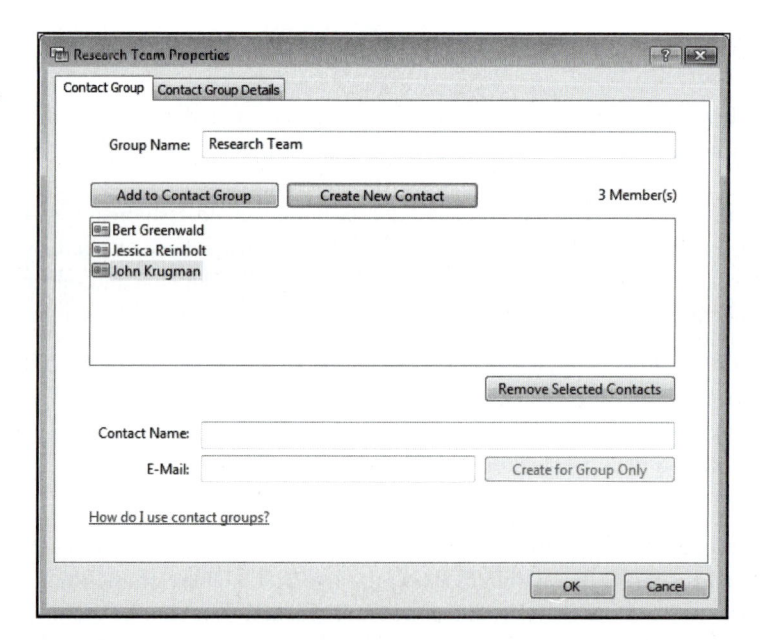

A listing for the group then appears in your Contacts. When you are composing email for the group, simply select the group name from your Contacts to automatically send the message to all group members. To delete a group, highlight the group name in Contacts and click Delete. Note that this deletes the group, but not the group's members, from your Contacts.

Finding People Who Aren't in Your Address Book

Outlook Express used to have a search engine built into it for looking up people on the Internet, making it easy for you to search for people and add them to your Contacts list. This has been dropped in Windows Mail.

However, you can sometimes find an email address on the Internet if you poke around. Try using www.switchboard.com, or do a Google search for "email directory," and you'll find scads of links. Another source is www.theultimates.com/email, which lists Yahoo!, WhoWhere, IAF, InfoSpace, Bigfoot, and Switchboard on one screen.

> **TIP**
>
> No matter how obscure a name may seem, you would be amazed at how many other people in the world share it. When you locate someone in an online directory, first send that person an email inquiry to confirm that he or she is indeed the person you are seeking *before* you share any sensitive information with her. Unfortunately, you'll also find that the information given by some online directories is frustratingly out of date. (So much for the speed of the Internet.) If you suspect the information is not current, try a different search engine.

Handling Unique Mail Situations

Windows Mail has features that go well beyond the most common email-related tasks of reading and composing mail, addressing and sending messages, or using the Contacts list. For example, you may have more than one email account. You can set preferences for these accounts, choose to keep them separate, or to bring them all into the same Windows Mail Inbox. You'll also learn ways to organize and filter your mail, check your mail while traveling, and how to make an alternate backup location for the mail you want to save and protect. In this section, we'll describe these more advanced situations and capabilities. Even if you don't intend to use these features, skim through the sections just so you know what features are available. After you know what features are built in, you might want to come back and try them out later.

Modifying an Existing Email Account

After setting up an email account or two, you may find that you want to change a few things, such as the server name, password, connection preference, and more. To do this, go to Tools, Accounts; click a mail account; and click Properties. Poke around in here to see all the characteristics that you can change.

Under the General tab, you can change how your name will appear on outgoing mail. Whatever you enter in the Name box will be what the recipient sees. Think about whether you want your email to be listed in recipients' inboxes in a casual or formal way, or even with your business name instead. (In other words, enter `Bob Cowart` or `Mr. Robert Cowart` or `Bob's Car Care`.)

You might want to send mail from one email address but have replies go to a different email address (when recipients click Reply). To do this, enter the outgoing email address in the Email address box, and the alternate email address in the Reply address box.

Some email accounts (University accounts, for example) require you to connect to the Internet using a specific connection to access your email. If you need to change the connection used for an account, open the Internet Accounts dialog and follow these steps:

1. Click the account you want to change. Click the Properties button on the right side of the dialog.
2. Click the Connection tab. If you need to use a specific connection, place a checkmark next to Always Connect to This Account Using, and select a connection from the drop-down menu.
3. Click OK and Close to exit all the open dialogs.

Additional Security Features in Windows Mail

As of Service Pack 2, Outlook Express (and now Windows Mail) included a couple of security features worth knowing about. The post SP2 version deals with two essential problems: spam and unsafe email attachments.

Of course, one way around most viruses and other intrusive malware (uninvited programs that do harm to your computer) is to switch to the Mac and Linux operating system and/or hardware. The degree to which hackers are interested in writing malicious code for a platform is directly proportional to the size of the installed base of a platform, and Windows wins that competition by a long shot. However, if, like us, you really enjoy the broad base of applications and utilities available for the Windows platform, switching to a Mac or Linux system simply to avoid viruses seems self-defeating. Better to understand how to protect yourself from malware's ravages by taking reasonable security measures. Spam is another issue, one that affects most anyone who uses email.

Limiting Spam

Some estimate that spam (unsolicited email) constitutes as much as 60% of all Internet traffic. This is an unbelievable waste of bandwidth that could be better used. Then again, look at how much paper "spam" we get in our physical mailboxes every week, and that consumes trees. Don't get me started!

Spammers are clever about distinguishing between live addresses and dead ones. Spammers often use programs that generate thousands of potentially accurate email addresses, based on known domain names (such as AOL.com, Mindspring.com, or other domains in the publicly viewable domain registries). As explained earlier, one way of "mining" a real address is to send out an email that has image links in it. You may not know that email images can be sent in two different ways: Stored in the email itself or pointed to by placeholders in the email that direct the email reading program (in this case, Windows Mail) to download the images from a server on the Internet. The former is a good way of ensuring that recipients can see the images even if they are not online at the time they read the email. However, this approach slows down the transmission of the emails because the images increase the file size of the emails. Pumping out spam in this way takes too much time, so spammers use the second method, with an additional benefit. When the recipient views an email (assuming they are online), the links download the images from the spammer's web server. At that point, the spammer's server notes who is downloading the images and then updates its spam database, marking that address as live.

One way around this problem is to use a less popular email "client" (program), such as Eudora, Pegasus, or a web-based client such as Yahoo! mail or Hotmail. But I have found incompatibilities of various kinds that I prefer not to deal with. Again, I'd prefer to buttress my defenses and continue to use the industry standard Outlook or Windows Mail. Outlook 2003 already had a defense against this image downloading issue, and it has migrated into Windows Mail. Here's how to use it:

1. In Windows Mail, open Tools, Options. Click on the Security tab.
2. Make sure that the Block Images and Other External Content in HTML E-mail check box is selected (see Figure 16.12).
3. When you receive an email with images in it, the images will be blank and will indicate that you can right-click on the image and choose Download images after you have determined that you can trust the sender of the email. The images are downloaded and stored with the email on your computer and can be viewed later.

Figure 16.12
Turning off auto-downloading of external images and other HTML items helps decrease spam.

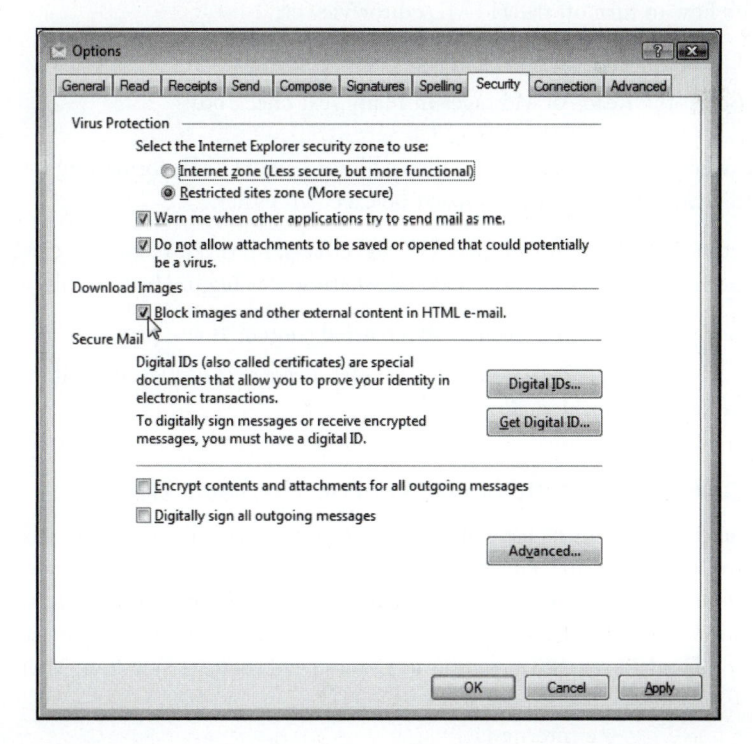

Another advantage of this arrangement pertains to folks using dial-up connections to the Internet. In some previous Outlook Express versions, viewing an HTML email with external images (that download from a server) would cause the computer to begin a dial-up session. This was annoying.

More spam-battling techniques are described later in this chapter, in the section "Dealing with Spam."

Protecting Against HTML Scripts

Email programs that can read and execute HTML-formatted email are potential targets for virus authors because HTML email can include scripts. These scripts are little programs that can run when the email is viewed. Microsoft attempts to thwart such vulnerabilities in Internet Explorer and Windows Mail via security patches and system updates disseminated via the Windows Update site, but people don't check it as often as they could, and there is often a delay between the outbreak of a virus across the Internet and the availability of a fix. However, a more failsafe approach is to turn off Windows Mail's capability to execute HTML email altogether.

Windows Mail can do this via a setting that causes emails to be read using a *rich text* editor instead of the HTML editor. This turns off the part of Windows Mail that would execute malicious HTML code (typically code stored in the *HTML header*). You won't see images or things such as font styles, sizes, and color, but you can still read the text just fine.

Here's how to turn off the HTML editor/viewer:

1. Choose Tools, Options. Then click the Read tab.
2. Select the Read All Messages in Plain Text check box.

Now whenever you read emails, they will not have HTML formatting displayed, but potential malicious HTML headers won't be executed either.

Sometimes you'll want to display HTML effects, however, because it can be easier to read the message when it's all prettified and whatnot. No biggie. Just do this:

1. Ask yourself: Is this email from a trusted source? If yes, proceed.
2. Choose View, Message in HTML. The message is displayed in all its glory. (This can't be reversed, incidentally.)

Handling Multiple Email Accounts for the Same User

Increasingly, individuals have more than one email account. Windows Mail can be configured to handle multiple email accounts, even if they are on separate servers. For example, I have four email accounts, one from each of my Internet service providers. I can pull all my email into one inbox by setting up the various accounts under a single user identity. When I click on Send/Receive Mail on the Windows Mail toolbar, Windows Mail goes out and pulls in all the new mail from all four accounts automatically. It's just that simple. How do you set up your system so it can do this? Read on.

Each email account needs to be set up and configured in Windows Mail as explained earlier in this chapter. Simply set up an account for each email address and server you have, using the information provided by each ISP (or email account, if a single ISP has given you multiple email accounts).

> **NOTE** While you can check multiple accounts at once, it's not possible (or at least not easily so) to do the same if one or more of those accounts is on a corporate Microsoft Exchange server. Don't get too hopeful that you'll be able to get your work email at home if you work for a major corporation. Typically, corporations strictly prohibit you from using their equipment to check your personal email through any other means than a WebMail interface. Check with your friendly company IT person to see if it's possible to set up a Windows Mail account that works with your company email.

Normally, Windows Mail checks all accounts when looking for new mail, even if they use different servers. Sending and receiving email from different accounts will normally happen automatically and without impediments. You connect to the Internet (whether by dial-up service or over your LAN or cable/DSL modem), click Send/Receive, and Windows Mail will try to access each server one after another, using the currently active Internet connection. However, there are a couple instances where this gets more complicated:

- If you have specified that an account must use a specific connection, you will see a dialog box when you try to use that account on another connection. Here, you must decide whether you want to switch connections or try to locate the server on the current connection.

- Some services require that you be actually dialed in to their Internet connection service before you can send email through their SMTP (mail sending) service. This is to prevent "spoofing" or "spamming" by nonpaying users who jam up SMTP servers sending their unwelcome advertisements. It's sort of like hijacking the U.S. Postal Service to send free bulk mail. Such services check to see that you are connected to the Internet through them and logged in. When you are, you can send mail through that account. Sometimes such services will let you *receive* mail regardless of how you are connected to the Net, because that doesn't infringe on their services. It is typically only the *sending* that is restricted. If a unique connection is needed for a given email account, you must specify this in the account's properties dialogs. Click on the Connection tab and choose the Always Connect to This Account Using option. Then choose which connection the account in question should use.

You can set up an unlimited number of email accounts in Windows Mail. You can even set up multiple accounts using the same email address and server information. Each account can serve as a separate identity for you.

When you compose a new mail message, it is automatically addressed for your default mail account. The default account can be set in the Internet Accounts dialog. You can change the account used for an individual message manually, as follows:

1. Click Create Mail in Windows Mail to begin composing a new message.
2. In the New Message window, select an identity from the drop-down menu next to From: in the header, as shown in Figure 16.13. The identity used here appears on your outgoing mail and also determines the Reply to: address used if the recipient replies. (Note that the From box appears only if you have created two or more email accounts.)

Figure 16.13
You can choose an identity for your new message here.

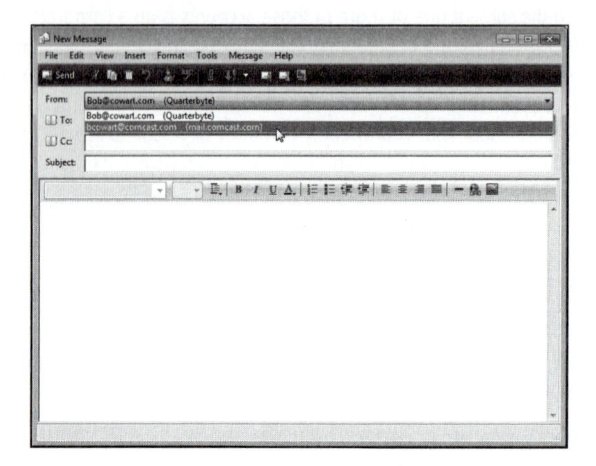

Does Windows Mail check for new mail in some of your accounts but not in others? **See** "Checking Mail in Multiple Accounts" in the "Troubleshooting" section at the end of the chapter.

Organizing Your Mail

You don't have to receive much mail to realize that your Inbox can get cluttered in a hurry. The best way to save important mail and stay organized is to organize your mail into folders, just like files are organized on your hard drive.

The process of creating folders and storing messages in them is simple:

1. Right-click the Inbox in the Windows Mail Folder list and choose New Folder. The Create Folder dialog opens.
2. Type a descriptive name for your folder under Folder Name. Look at the folder list in the lower half of the dialog to make sure that the correct parent folder is selected.
3. Click OK to create the folder.

The new folder appears in the Windows Mail Folder list under the parent folder. You can simply drag and drop messages from the message list to the designated storage or project folder.

Compacting Your Mail Folder

If you send many emails, with time your Windows Mail folder may become overly large. This calls for either culling out old emails or letting Windows Mail compress your email folders automatically. Recall that Windows Mail stores each email as a separate file, unlike Outlook Express which saved all the emails in a given mail folder in a .dbx file with that folder's name (inbox.dbx, sent.dbx, and so on). Used to be that letting Outlook Express compress your email files in the background was not a good idea because the files could get corrupted if the power when out during compaction. Thus, that feature has been removed in Windows Mail. The additional precaution against file corruption designed into Windows Mail is that each email is stored in a separate file. So even if a file is corrupted, it doesn't mess up, say, your entire Inbox.

As a default, Windows Mail is set to compact the email database every 100 times you run the program. If you want to change this, you do so by choosing Tools, Options, Advanced. Then click Maintenance and change the number. Notice here that you can also turn on Empty Messages from the Deleted Items Folder on Exit. This can help clear up disk space as well. Be cautious about the Clean Up Now button. A few wrong clicks and you can remove all of your emails.

Unlike in previous versions of Windows Mail, you cannot manually choose to compact the database.

Filtering Your Mail

Many email users—especially those who subscribe to mailing lists—receive dozens or even hundreds of messages per day. Wading through all this mail for the really important stuff can be challenging (to say the least), so Windows Mail includes a mail filtering feature similar to Outlook's Inbox Rules that helps you direct certain kinds of mail to specific locations. For example, you might want to direct all mail from a list you are subscribed to into a special folder where it can be read later.

You can even use mail filters to delete mail you don't want to see at all. Mail can be filtered by content, subject, or sender information. If you are frequently being bothered by someone, you can simply set up Windows Mail to send all messages from that person to the Deleted Items folder.

To set up a filter, follow these steps:

1. In Windows Mail, choose Tools and select Message Rules, Mail. You will see the window shown in Figure 16.14. If one or more Mail Rules are already set up, the Message Rules dialog opens first. In that case, click New to get to the New Mail Rule window, or click Modify to change an existing rule.

2. Select a condition from box 1 of the New Mail Rule dialog. Place a checkmark next to the condition or conditions you want to apply.

3. Select an action in box 2. This action will happen if the condition specified in box 1 is met.

4. Follow the instructions in box 3. They will be specific to the conditions and actions you set in boxes 1 and 2. You have to click on the links that appear in box 3 to state the conditions.

   As you can see in Figure 16.14, we have set up a rule that automatically files certain incoming messages in a specific folder. The reply states that we are away from the office until a certain date.

5. Check the description in box 3 to make sure the correct action will take place. Name the rule in box 4, and click OK when you are finished.

The rule then appears in the Message Rules dialog with a checkmark next to it. You can open this dialog at any time to edit, disable (by clearing the check box), or remove any rules. You can also change the order in which the rules are applied to your incoming emails. If you have many rules, the order of execution could alter the results.

You can easily create a rule for a given message you have received, too. Just select the message header and click Message, Create Rule from Message. Typically, you'll want to set up a rule to move all messages from that sender into another folder, and this makes it easy to set that up. If what you want to do is delete any mail coming from that source, you'll want to use the Junk Mail filter described later in this chapter, under the topic "Dealing with Spam."

Figure 16.14
You can create mail rules to filter your mail and automate certain tasks.

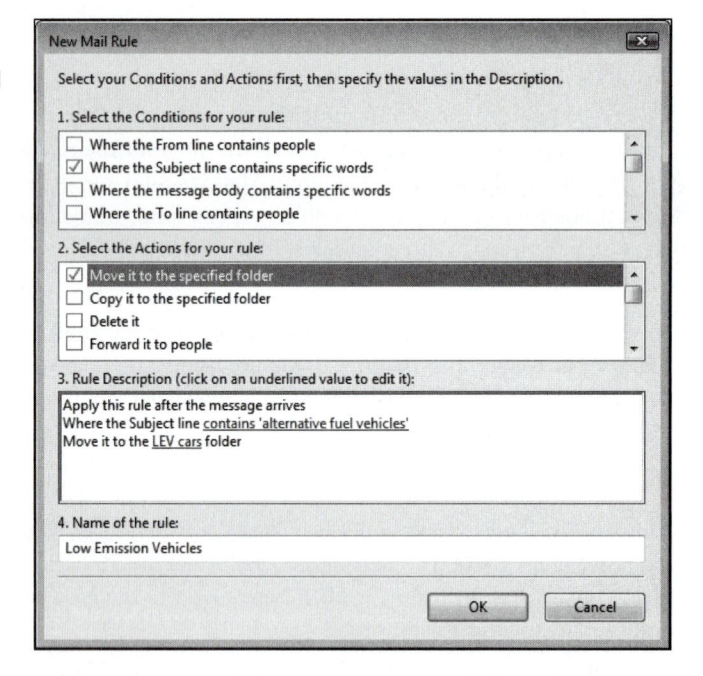

> **TIP**
>
> An "out of office" auto reply rule can be created in mail rules to automatically respond to all incoming messages, stating that we are away from the office until a certain date. Although this can be useful, do not enable such a rule if you are subscribed to any mailing lists.

→ For more on mailing lists, **see** "What About Mailing Lists?," **p. 510**.

CHECKING YOUR MESSAGES WHILE TRAVELING

Before leaving on a trip, consider setting up a message rule in Windows Mail to forward all incoming messages to your HTTP mail account (such as Hotmail or Yahoo!). That way, you can read all of your mail on the road, regardless of which address your messages are sent to. Of course, for this method to work, your computer must remain on while you are away, and Windows Mail must be set to check for new messages regularly. This is not the best idea, environmentally speaking, but there are conditions where it will work with no wasted energy, such as if your office computer will be in use by others in your absence.

A better way to check email while away from your computer is to set up POP mail in your HTTP mail account. At your HTTP account online, go to options (or something similar) to enter your POP server settings. Some servers let you differentiate between different mail accounts with color coding of messages. After this is set up, simply click on the online Inbox or, in some cases, Check Other Mail.

ALL YOUR MAIL IS IN A LAPTOP

If you're like me, though, you'll want to keep all your mail in the same computer, not scattered around in places such as Hotmail, Yahoo! Mail, and Google Mail as well as in your laptop or desktop in Outlook or Windows Mail. I have two "ultimate" solutions to this, depending on how you work.

If all your work is on a laptop and that is your primary computer, all you have to do when traveling is to make sure you have an email account that lets you *send out* mail from the road, using the various connections you'll find along the way (typically WiFi connections in airports, hotels, and cafes). Although WiFi *hotspots* are becoming ubiquitous, the gotcha is when you try to send out mail on your usual email account and you find out (usually much to your chagrin), that it won't go. Why is this? It's because many ISPs, in an attempt to thwart spammers, won't let just anyone use their SMTP (outgoing mail) server. You have to be connected directly to their server to do so.

For example, I have cable at home, using Comcast. Until recently, I couldn't send email out through Comcast unless I was actually communicating through the cable connection. This was a bummer because I like to work in cafes. But cafes usually don't have SMTP servers available. Why? Because spammers would sit in cafes and deluge the cafe's SMTP server with outgoing spam. Sad but true. When on the road, I have two options. I checked with

Comcast and found that they now have an "authenticated SMTP" server. I went into the account settings for my email (Tools, Accounts, Mail tab, Servers) and made the appropriate settings, turning on authenticated SMTP. This allows me to send outgoing mail through Comcast's server even when I'm connected to the Internet through another ISP such as a WiFi hotspot. You may want to ask your ISP or your SMTP administrator whether authenticated SMTP is supported for dealing with such circumstances.

My backup solution, when authenticated SMTP isn't available, is to maintain a dial-up connection I can use from hotels and friends' houses. The trick here is that I must have a separate Windows Mail email account for that server. In my case, it's Earthlink. So, using the techniques explained earlier in this chapter (in "Handling Multiple Email Accounts for the Same User"), I created an Earthlink account. When I write an email, it's automatically set to be sent by the default mail account, which is usually Comcast for me. I have to make a point of either changing the default email account or manually choosing the account I'm going to send each new email with. If you have multiple email accounts, you'll have a drop-down list on the From field in your new emails. Click open the list and choose the email account that has the SMTP server that corresponds to your current Internet connection at the time of sending the message(s).

ALL YOUR WORK IS IN YOUR DESKTOP

My other and newer solution is this. I have so much work on my desktop computer that I decided to leave it all there and not worry about taking some email folders with me on the road. I'm doing video editing and have all my MP3s and photos on my desktop. It's too much to carry with me. Transferring stuff onto my laptop prior to a trip was always a last-minute hassle. What's more, I'm running beta operating systems on the desktop using Virtual PC and don't want that to potentially confuse things on my laptop. So here's what I do (and no, I'm not getting paid for this shameless advertising):

1. I subscribed to GoToMyPC.com. It's about $20 a month; no biggie for the convenience it affords me. An alternative is LogMeIn.com (and that one is free, for a somewhat limited account).

2. I leave my desktop at home on and running. I make sure it's not going to power down (check the Control Panel's Power Options). (The desktop computer has to be connected to the Internet with a cable or DSL connection for this to work reasonably fast enough, by the way.)

3. When I'm on the road, I get online (preferably on a high-speed connection such as in a cafe) and then go to www.gotomypc.com (or www.logmein.com) and log in. In a few seconds, my desktop computer screen comes up on my laptop, and I'm working as though I'm at home, only a tad slower. The speed degradation is not too bad if both computers have DSL, cable, T1, and so on. It's livable.

Of course, you can achieve similar results using Remote Desktop (see Chapter 40, "Remote Desktop") but with a little more elbow grease to get it working. Notably, with Remote Desktop, routers get in the way and have to be set up carefully to allow the signal to pass through. But once set up, it's free. Remote Desktop will also connect the COM ports, printer ports, disk drives, and sound cards of the host computer to the remote computer. However, for a simple, easy-to-connect solution to remote email needs we're addressing here, my vote is for GoToMyPC or LogMeIn, partly because virtually any web-browser-enabled computer will function as the remote machine. Caught without your laptop but need to check your mail? I have logged onto my desktop PC from both Macs and PCs in libraries, for example.

> **NOTE**
>
> Other remote control programs such as pcAnywhere (Symantec) offer similar functionality. VNC is another similar (though somewhat crippled) tool. But it's free. Timbuktu is another remote control program. You can find all of these on the Web.

BACKING UP WINDOWS MAIL DATA

One of the unique aspects of electronic mail is that it can serve as a permanent record of your communications. Mail that seems insignificant now may be invaluable in the future, and many people back up all their correspondence on a regular basis to ensure that a record is kept for all time. You can save copies of individual messages by choosing File, Save As from the menu in the message window. Choosing this option opens a standard Windows Save dialog, where you can choose a location and name for the file. It is saved with the .eml extension.

In addition, you might want to use a backup procedure regularly to store messages elsewhere and remove them from Windows Mail. If you receive and send thousands of messages a year, removing them and storing them elsewhere (yearly or quarterly) will help keep Windows Mail running efficiently and will free up space on your hard drive.

BACKING UP ALL YOUR WINDOWS MAIL MESSAGES

The easiest and perhaps safest way to back up your mail is to make a backup copy of your entire Windows Mail email message files. Because in Windows Mail, emails are just files dumped into a hard disk folder that has the same name as the email folder, this is really easy. As mentioned at the top of this chapter, all you have to do is burn the mail folder to a CD or copy it to an external hard disk or across the network, and you're finished.

However, it's a little complicated to find the Mail folder, but there is a shortcut built into Windows Mail for accomplishing the task.

1. In Windows Mail, click File, Export, Messages.
2. Choose the message format you want to export to, most likely Microsoft Windows Mail (so that you can later import the messages should you have to), and click Next.
3. Choose the Store folder you want to place the backup into. Browse to that location. The folder must be empty or the wizard will stop. (If you want to burn to a CD, you'll have to create a folder first, such as on the desktop, and then burn from there.) Click Select Folder.
4. Click Next.

5. Select the folders you want to back up. Typically just leave the All Folders button selected, but you can select from the list if you want. To select multiple folders, Shift+click or Ctrl+click.

6. Click Next and the messages are backed up. A progress bar reports each folder's progress, as you see in Figure 16.15. When finished, you should see the message "Your messages were exported in Windows Mail format."

> **TIP**
> You might want to make one backup folder on your hard drive and another on a CD-R or other media, just to have a double back up.

Figure 16.15
Backing up email to another folder.

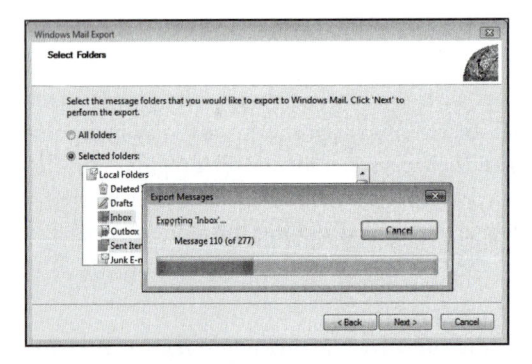

TO RESTORE MAIL DATA FROM A BACKUP

Restoring mail from a backup is easy. This procedure also works for importing mail from another computer, from a CD, across the LAN, and so on. Perform the following steps:

1. In Windows Mail choose File, Import, Messages.
2. In the resulting dialog box choose the Microsoft Windows Mail format.
3. Browse to the source folder where the backed up messages are.
4. Click Next.
5. Choose the folders you want to import, or click the All Folders button.
6. Click Next.

BACKING UP THE WINDOWS MAIL ADDRESS BOOK

The next thing you'll want to back up is your all-important Contacts list (Address Book). If you have a significant number of addresses, and especially mailing-list groups, losing your Address Book due to a reinstallation of Windows or a hard disk crash would be unfortunate. You'll be glad you have a backup.

In XP, backing up contacts was a hassle, requiring that you sleuth out the location of the single .wab (Windows Address Book) file used by Windows Mail for each user that logs on to an XP system and then back up the file somewhere safe. You could export addresses using the File command, but then they were not in the native .wab format. You exported in comma-separated value (CSV) format, typically. But importing in that format wasn't so easy.

In Vista there are two ways to back up. One is by finding the Contacts folder and backing up the whole thing or individual files somewhere safe. The folder that stores the Contacts files (there is one file for each person in the contacts database), has a path like this:

C:\users\bob\contacts

Each user will have a file in the folder. This is the most complete way to back up contacts because the files contain a lot of special metadata such as photos, family information, and notes.

However, if you don't have a lot of notes, family info, and photos in your contacts, it's easier to use the File, Export command like this:

1. In Windows Mail choose File, Export, Windows Contacts.
2. Choose the export format: CSV or vCards. I would suggest vCards because vCards contain more information. (Use CSV only when you are trying to export to a spreadsheet or a text file, or for use in some other database or email program. Many programs can import CSV files.)
3. Choose the destination folder.

> **TIP**
>
> To convert just a single contact to the vCard format and send it to someone, right-click the contact and then click Send Contact. The contact will be converted and then attached to an email message in Windows Mail.

To restore backed-up Contacts data into Windows Mail, you have two options, depending on how you backed up:

- If you backed up the actual Contacts files, simply copy the saved Contacts back to your Contacts folder. You can freely copy contacts in and out of your Contacts folder. Each time you open Contacts the database is reconstructed, so it doesn't matter what you do with it in this regard. Copy, move, delete—it's all fine. This is a much more free-form approach than with the previous .wab file format. Likewise, friends or colleagues can send you contacts as files in email, across the LAN, on CD, or whatever, and you can add them to your Contacts by dragging them in.
- If you saved the contacts as CSV or vCard, you can use the File, Import, Contacts command in Windows Mail, choose the format you're importing, and click Import. You'll have to browse to the source of the files. This is a good way to import contacts from Outlook Express because one of the options is Outlook Express format (.wab), or from vCard (which you may have received from an Outlook user.

To Send Someone a vCard or Contact   Often people will ask you to send them contact information for someone in your Contacts. You can send a single contact as a vCard (.vcf file) or Windows Contact (.contacts file). Follow these steps:

1. Start an email to the person making the request (New or Reply).
2. Open the Contacts list and adjust the windows so that you can drag from Contacts into the body of the email.
3. Drag the contact(s) you want to send and drop it into the body of the email. You'll be asked whether you want to send a vCard or a Windows Contacts file.

> **TIP**
>
> Here's a shortcut for sending a contact: Right-click on the contact(s) in question and choose Send To, Mail Recipient.

Backing Up and Restoring Mail and Newsgroup Account Information

After you have your mail and newsgroup settings (server names, usernames, passwords, and related settings) established and working, it is a royal pain to have to re-create them. Thankfully the programmers of Windows Mail made it easy to import and export these settings.

To back up or restore your Windows Mail mail accounts, do the following:

1. In Windows Mail, choose Tools, click Accounts.
2. Choose the Mail or Newsgroup account in question and select the Export or Import tab (as desired).
3. Point to or name the .iaf file you want to import or export to.

Dealing with Spam

A hot topic in email circles today is the subject of commercial advertisements mass delivered via electronic mail. This type of unsolicited mail is generally referred to as *spam*, a name attributed in Internet lore to a Monty Python musical skit pertaining to the pink meat product of the same name. This type of mail is so offensive to some people that a few states have even enacted laws against it.

Some groups are also working with the United States federal government to ban unsolicited electronic mail and place identification requirements on people and organizations who send advertisements via email. Countless antispam organizations exist, with one of the foremost being CAUCE, the Coalition Against Unsolicited Commercial Email (www.cauce.org).

The real problem with spam is that scam operations are rampant and difficult to detect. Spam also has an impact on Internet traffic, requiring a considerable amount of bandwidth that many people feel would be better used for other purposes.

If you have been online for more than an hour, you've almost certainly received some spam yourself. Windows Mail now has a Junk Mail filter inherited from Outlook that uses massive amounts of data collected by Microsoft's Hotmail service to help differentiate junk mail from real mail. As a default, it is turned on. Before mail comes into your Inbox, it is analyzed by the Junk Mail filter using the latest information supplied by Microsoft through online updates. It then moves suspected junk mail into the Junk Mail folder for you to examine later. I do recommend that you visually scan the Junk Mail box once a day until you become convinced that it's not eating up real emails that you would otherwise miss. If an email has been mistaken as spam, right click it, choose Mark As Not Junk. It will be moved to the Inbox. If you want to prevent the next email from this sender from going into Junk Mail again, right click on the email and choose Add Sender to Safe Sender's list. This puts them in your "white list" of valid senders.

NEWSGROUPS AND THE INTERNET

With the overwhelming and still growing popularity of the World Wide Web since its inception in the early 1990s, you might easily forget that the Internet was around for more than two decades before the first web page saw the light of a cathode ray tube. Before the inception of the Web, people used the Internet to access newsgroups. Newsgroups began in 1979 as a forum in which UNIX users could communicate with each other, and the concept grew steadily from there into what is now a global assemblage of people sharing information on virtually every topic imaginable.

Originally, news servers exchanged articles using UNIX-to-UNIX Copy Protocol (UUCP), which involves direct modem dial-up over long-distance phone lines. In 1986, the Network News Transport Protocol (NNTP) was released, allowing news to be transported via TCP/IP connection over the Internet. Most modern newsgroups use the NNTP protocol, and it is the only news protocol supported by Windows Mail.

Newsgroups are scattered on servers around the world, and the rough network used to carry newsgroup bandwidth is generally referred to as *Usenet*. We're not implying, however, that some authority provides oversight of Usenet. "Usenet is not a democracy" is one of the first statements you will read in virtually any primer or Frequently Asked Questions (FAQ) list on the subject, alluding to the virtual anarchy in which this medium exists. Usenet has become so large and diverse that a simple definition cannot possibly do it justice.

What we can do, however, is roughly describe the types of newsgroups and news servers that you can access using Windows Mail. Basically, the administrator of your news server determines which news feeds you will have access to. Feeds are passed along to the server from adjacent servers, providing a decidedly decentralized structure to Usenet. Each server maintains a list of message IDs to ensure that new articles are received at a given server only once. An individual server can control which feeds it propagates, although the interconnectivity of Usenet servers ensures that a lone server has little or no control of the overall distribution. Thus, the authority of a news server is generally limited to what clients (that would be you) can access and what kind of material those clients can post. Likewise, the decentralization of servers means that an article you post may take hours—or even days—to circulate among all other news servers.

A free alternative to commercial news servers is a web-based news service, such as the one created by deja.com. An advantage of using a web-based news service is that a search brings back results from many newsgroups, not only one. It's a terrific way to find expert postings on just about anything from open-heart surgery, to child adoption, to what people think of the new car you're considering buying. However, messages are not brought into your news client program (such as Windows Mail) for reference offline. Deja was bought out and redesigned by Google a while back, so until recently, you couldn't post new messages to Usenet, but now you can again. Just go to http://www.google.com and click the Groups link.

But many folks still use newsgroups and want a decent reader and newsgroup message composer that works more like an email program. As mentioned at the top of this chapter, it's also noteworthy that Microsoft has rethought newsgroups a bit and has some useful offerings in the way of help information on all its products, by way of Microsoft Communities, a set of super newsgroups with new features.

> **NOTE**
> The terms *newsgroup* and *Usenet* are used almost interchangeably in today's online world, but it is useful to know that *newsgroup* refers to individual groups, whereas *Usenet* refers to the entire network of groups as a whole.

WHAT ABOUT MAILING LISTS?

Are newsgroups the same as mailing lists, or *listservs*, as some people call them? No. So here's a little digression about those, just to make the distinction. The openness that makes newsgroups desirable has its drawbacks: privacy and security are almost nonexistent. Mailing list posts are less public because usually the only people who can read them are other list members, and lists are generally less susceptible to spam and objectionable material. Furthermore, mailing list traffic comes into your email reader (your Inbox in Windows Mail), making lists easier to deal with for some people.

Mailing lists are simple; you send a message to the list address, which is then forwarded to every other list member. Every time another member posts a message to the list, you receive a copy. The list is managed by a list administrator who often, but not always, works directly with the mail server hosting the list. Often the administrator can be reached via the email address listproc or majordomo followed by @ and the name of the domain server.

Virtually any topic imaginable has a mailing list. If you want to find one to join, a good place to start would be CataList, available online at http://www.lsoft.com/lists/listref.html.

Locating News Servers

Many ISPs and companies provide news server accounts to their Internet users, but you still might find yourself looking for a server on your own. This might be the case even if you have a news account available to you; some service providers censor the news content that is available, and if you want uncensored news, you must rely on a different source.

Censorship, Big Brother, and NNTP Servers

News feeds are censored for a variety of reasons. For example, your company's server might restrict feeds from `alt.`, `rec.`, and `talk.` groups to reduce the number of work hours lost to employee abuse or simply to reduce bandwidth. Many other servers restrict feeds that contain pornographic content for both legal and moral reasons.

Even if your news server provides a relatively unrestricted news feed, you should exercise care when deciding which articles you download from the server. Virtually all servers maintain logs of the activities of each login account. This means that your service provider can track which articles you download, and in most cases these logs can be subpoenaed and used against you in court.

In other words, Big Brother might be watching you download porn, bomb-making instructions, and bootleg copies of the latest Hollywood blockbuster. Be especially paranoid if you access a company news server; hours spent receiving otherwise legal content such as fruit cake recipes, Bill Gates jokes, and the like could still land you in hot water if the boss is monitoring your online activities.

Many news servers are available through virtually any Internet connection, but you'll pay for that connection. Typically, monthly charges for a personal news server account range from $10 to $20 per month and get higher for corporate or higher bandwidth accounts. If you plan to use newsgroups frequently, you might want to factor in this cost when you're shopping for an ISP. You can find a good list of commercial news servers at http://freenews.maxbaud.net/forfee.html.

However, if you have an Internet connection and simply want a different news server, you can find a list of free news servers available online at http://freenews.maxbaud.net/newspage.html?date=today. The list of free servers can change daily.

If Windows Mail has trouble locating your news server, **see** *"No News Server Connection" in the "Troubleshooting" section at the end of this chapter.*

Web-based news servers at the time of this writing could be found at http://newsguy.com/news.asp.

If you cannot locate a particular newsgroup on your news server, **see** *"Newsgroup Isn't Available on News Server" in the "Troubleshooting" section at the end of this chapter.*

Setting Up a Newsgroup Account in Windows Mail

Before using newsgroups, you have to set up a news account in Windows Mail. Windows Mail actually comes with a newsgroup already set up, called Microsoft Communities, but it only has groups that pertain to Microsoft products, so you can write in for support on Vista, Office, and any other products. For real newsgroup reading you have to configure a regular newsgroup account. Before you can configure your news account, you need to obtain a news server address, which should look something like news.domainname.com.

Your company might also have a news server account with a commercial provider. You can configure multiple server accounts in Windows Mail, just as you can set up multiple email accounts.

As mentioned earlier, a news server provides you with news feeds from other news servers. Which feeds are available to you depends on decisions made by your server's administrator. For example, some news servers restrict feeds for all alt. (alternative) newsgroups because some of them contain highly objectionable material.

→ If you do not have a news server you can access, **see** "Locating News Servers," **p. 510**.

To set up your account in Windows Mail, follow these steps:

1. Open Windows Mail, and choose Tools, Accounts to open the Internet Accounts dialog.
2. Click Add, choose Newsgroup Account, and click Next.
3. Follow the instructions in the Internet Connection Wizard for inputting your display name and email address (the wizard may provide this information for you).
4. Type the name of your news (NNTP) server. If you don't know the NNTP server name, contact your ISP or check its web page.
5. (optional) You may have to log on to your news server with a password. If your ISP says you do, click that option in the box before clicking Next. You'll be prompted to enter your username and password.
6. Click Finish. This finalizes your setup.

Downloading the Newsgroup List

After you have set up the news account, your next step is to download a list of newsgroups from the server. Depending on how many groups the server allows access to, this list could contain more than 75,000 newsgroups. In reality, most servers list less than half that number.

Why aren't they all listed? As you've already seen, some content might be censored by the server's administrator. In many cases, though, it is a much more practical matter: New groups are created so frequently that your server simply might not be aware of them. If you become aware of a newsgroup you want to join, but it is not currently available on your server, try dropping an email message to the administrator and asking for the group to be added. Assuming the group falls within the administrator's guidelines for acceptable content, adding the group will take only a few seconds.

To begin downloading your server's list, follow these steps:

1. Click the listing for your news account in the Windows Mail Folders list.
2. A message appears stating that you are not currently subscribed to any newsgroups and asking whether you want to view the list, as shown in Figure 16.16.

Figure 16.16
Downloading the list of newsgroups.

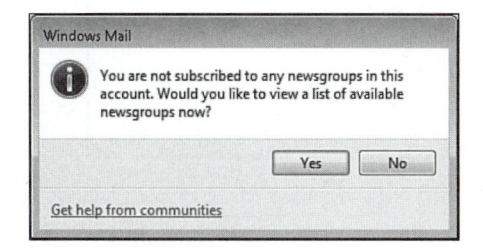

Depending on the size of the list and the speed of your connection, downloading could take several minutes. You probably have time to go get another cup of coffee. When the process is finished, the list is downloaded, and you are ready to locate and subscribe to newsgroups. If your news server required a password and it was incorrect, you will be prompted again to enter it.

> **TIP**
>
> Although new newsgroups are created daily, the list that has been downloaded to your computer is static and doesn't show new groups. The next time you click on a newsgroup server in the left pane, you'll probably see a dialog box telling you that there have been new groups added since your last session, giving you the option of updating your list. To make sure you have a current list, right-click on a newsgroup server name in the left pane and choose Reset List.

FINDING AND READING NEWSGROUPS

Usually, when you read a newsgroup, you must first subscribe to it. A subscription simply means you've placed a bookmark of sorts in Windows Mail for that group, making it easy to return to and follow conversations whenever you are using Windows Mail.

Before you can subscribe to a newsgroup, you need to find one that piques your interest. Searching for a group in your downloaded list is fairly simple in Windows Mail (see Figure 16.17). If the list isn't already open, you can open it by clicking your news account in folders pane, or by simply clicking the Newsgroups button up on the toolbar.

As you type a word in the Display Newsgroups That Contain field (see Figure 16.17), the list of newsgroups shrinks. You can experiment by typing a keyword you are interested in and pausing after each keystroke.

Figure 16.17
You can begin typing a word to search the newsgroup list. The list automatically gets smaller as you type, showing only those groups with names that match what you typed.

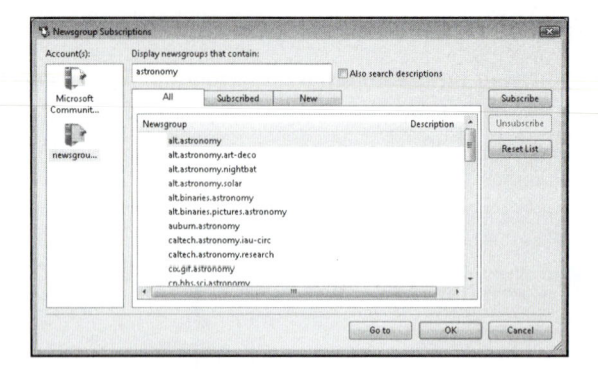

Newsgroups are usually—but not always—named descriptively. In Figure 16.17, you can see the option to search newsgroup descriptions as well as their names, but few groups actually have descriptions listed in this window.

> **TIP**
>
> If you don't find a newsgroup that interests you, try a search at http://groups.google.com/ or another web source to see whether other groups not currently available on your news server exist. There is no such thing as a "complete" list of newsgroups, so a search of several different resources will yield the best results.

Subscribing to Newsgroups

Windows Mail does not require you to subscribe to a group to view its contents. You can simply select a group from the list and click Go To to see messages posted to the group, but you might find it easier to manage the process by simply subscribing anyway. Subscribing to a newsgroup does not require any great level of commitment on your part because you can always unsubscribe with just two mouse clicks.

When you find a newsgroup you want to subscribe to, do the following:

1. Click once on the newsgroup name to select it and then click the Subscribe button. An icon should appear next to the group name, as shown in Figure 16.18.
2. Click Go To at the bottom of the Newsgroup Subscriptions window. The window closes, and the 300 most recent posts are downloaded to your computer.

Actually, only the message headers are downloaded, and they appear listed in the window. The message contents are not downloaded until you choose to view a specific message.

Figure 16.18
You can select a newsgroup and subscribe to it here. When you click Go To, this window automatically closes.

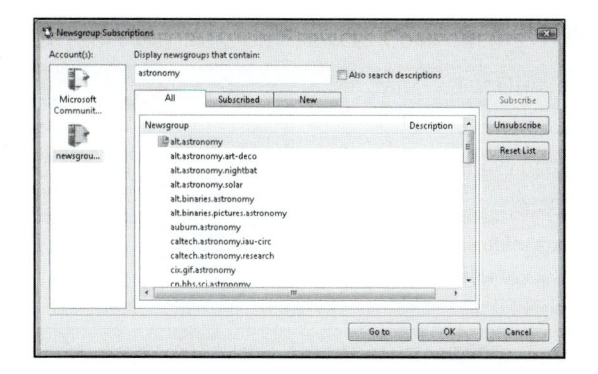

If you decide that you don't want to remain subscribed to a group, unsubscribing is easy. Just right-click the group's listing in the left pane, and choose Unsubscribe from the context menu that appears. Alternatively, click the Newsgroups icon in the toolbar, choose the news server in question, and click on the Subscribed tab. This will list all the groups you are subscribed to. Click a group, and then click Subscribe or Unsubscribe.

READING AND POSTING MESSAGES TO A NEWSGROUP

When you first access a newsgroup only the first 300 message headers are downloaded. You can download additional headers by clicking Tools, Get Next 300 Headers.

If you want to read a message, you need to manually open it. If you are using the preview pane, all you have to do is click once on the message header to cause it to download. If you are not using the preview pane, you can double-click a message to open it in a separate message window.

> **TIP**
> Turn on and off the preview pane by clicking View, Layout.

As you peruse the list of messages in the group, you need to understand the concept of *discussion threads*. A thread occurs when someone responds to a message. Others respond to the response, and this conversation becomes its own discussion thread. Messages that are part of a thread have a plus (+) sign next to them, and you can click this icon to expand a list of other messages in the thread. Figure 16.19 shows several expanded threads.

Figure 16.19
Threaded messages.

Posting messages to a newsgroup is simple. Perhaps the easiest way to post is to reply to an existing message. This process works much the same as replying to regular email, except that you must take extra care to ensure that your reply is going to the right place. Notice that the toolbar has a new button—the Reply Group button—as shown in Figure 16.20.

Figure 16.20
You must choose your reply mode carefully.

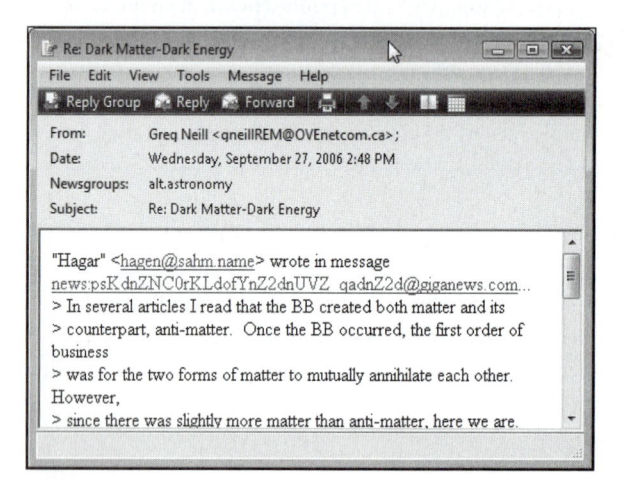

Each reply button serves a unique purpose:

Reply Group	Sends a reply back to the group
Reply	Sends a reply only to the original sender
Forward	Forwards the message to a third party

One aspect to watch carefully is that messages you post to a newsgroup are relevant. If the newsgroup is moderated, someone reviews all posts and removes posts deemed inappropriate. Look for a newsgroup FAQ (Frequently Asked Questions) for more information on netiquette and any rules that might apply to the groups you are subscribed to.

CAUTION
> Information posted in newsgroups can be viewed by anyone, and we do mean *anyone*! Never post personal or sensitive information in a newsgroup.

NOTE
> The default news message format is Plain Text. You should maintain this setting to ensure that your message can be read by other news readers.

Managing Messages

By default, Windows Mail deletes messages from your computer five days after you download them, but you can change this option easily. Likewise, you can also set up Windows Mail to delete read messages every time you leave the group. You can review these settings by choosing Tools, Options. In the Options dialog, click the Advanced tab to bring it to the front, and then click the Maintenance button. The resulting dialog box is shown in Figure 16.21.

> *If a message you read earlier becomes unavailable,* **see** *"Message No Longer Available" in the "Troubleshooting" section at the end of this chapter.*

> *If you're not sure which messages have been read and which haven't,* **see** *"Which Ones Are New?" in the "Troubleshooting" section at the end of the chapter.*

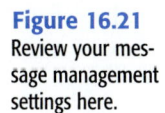

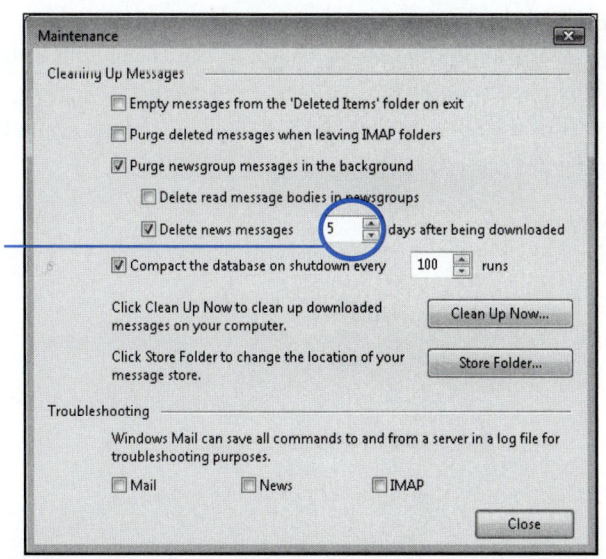

Figure 16.21
Review your message management settings here.

Adjust the length of time read messages are saved

If you want to maintain a record of the messages in your newsgroup, remove the checkmarks next to each Delete option shown in Figure 16.21. Messages remain in Windows Mail indefinitely if you deselect both of these options, but keep in mind that if the group has high traffic, these messages could eventually eat up a lot of disk space.

The better option is to save individual messages that you want to maintain. To do so, create a new folder for storing news messages under Local Folders in the Windows Mail Folders list, and then drag any messages you want to save into the folder. You can also drag and drop newsgroup messages to any of your email folders, but you might find it easier to keep newsgroup and email correspondence separate.

Reading News Offline

In Chapter 15, "Using Internet Explorer 7," you learned that you can download web pages for offline viewing. You can do the same with newsgroup messages, a capability that makes especially good sense if you must limit your Internet connection time or will be traveling with your laptop. Windows Mail calls this feature *synchronizing*.

> **CAUTION**
>
> Before you synchronize a newsgroup for offline viewing, check the size of the messages you will download. Some people post pictures and other large files into newsgroups, and they can add significantly to download time.

To begin downloading a newsgroup for offline viewing, click your news server account in the Folders list (the left pane of Windows Mail). A list of the groups you are subscribed to then appears, as shown in Figure 16.22. Now follow these steps:

1. Select the newsgroup you want to synchronize, and review the synchronization settings by right-clicking on the newsgroup name choosing Synchronization Settings. By default, only new messages will be synchronized, but you can change this setting by choosing another option.

2. Place a dot next to the relevant Synchronization setting, as shown in Figure 16.22. You can only choose one option.

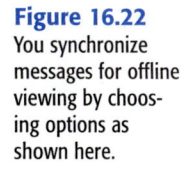

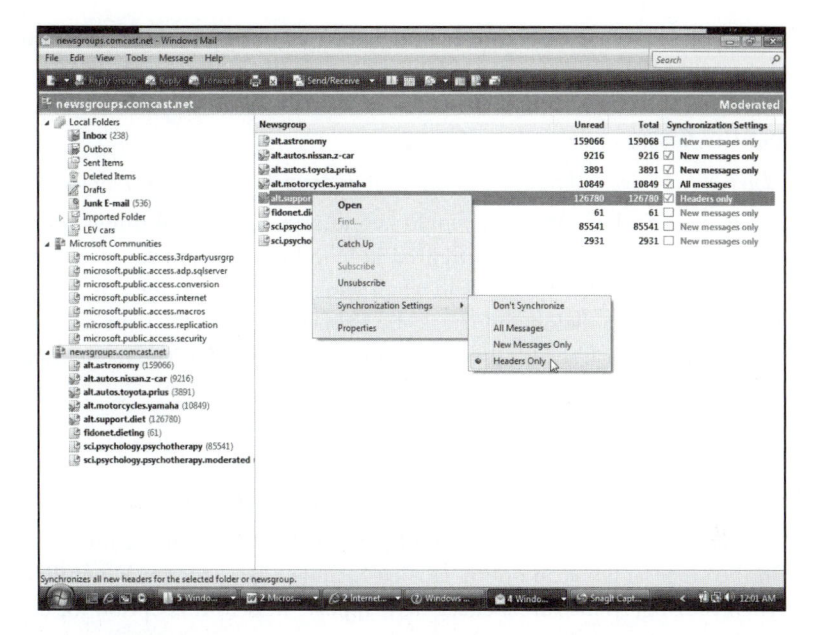

Figure 16.22
You synchronize messages for offline viewing by choosing options as shown here.

3. Choose Tools, Synchronize Newgroup. Messages are downloaded based on the synchronization settings you choose. Keep in mind that if you choose to synchronize all messages, the download could take a while.

When the download is complete, you can get offline to read the downloaded messages. If you try to open a message that isn't available offline, a warning advises you of this fact.

If, after you synchronize a newsgroup, some messages are not available, **see** *"Some Messages Are Unavailable After Synchronizing" in the "Troubleshooting" section at the end of this chapter.*

You also can select individual messages for offline reading. Choosing particular messages may be a better course of action, especially if the newsgroup has thousands of messages and you want to download only the first few. Select several message headers in the newsgroup by Ctrl+clicking or Shift+clicking. Then right-click the selection and choose Download Message Later from the menu that appears. When you later synchronize the account, only the selected messages are downloaded. Note that if you select to download all messages in your synchronization settings, all messages will be downloaded, not only the ones you selected.

Troubleshooting Email

Password Trouble

The server will not accept my password.

Many email servers are case sensitive. If the Caps Lock key on your keyboard is on, it could cause the password to be entered in the wrong case. Sometimes an inadvertent space can be the culprit as well. This is true even if you have configured Windows Mail to remember your email address so that you don't have to type it in every time you check mail.

IDENTITY CRISIS

I don't like the name Windows Mail is using to identify me in outgoing messages.

The name Windows Mail uses could be indicative of several things. First, if you have multiple accounts or identities configured in Windows Mail, make sure that you are selecting the desired one in the From: field when you send the messages. You can also open the Internet Accounts dialog and check the Properties sheet for your email address(es). The Name field under User Information on the General tab is the name used to identify you on outgoing mail.

CHECKING MAIL IN MULTIPLE ACCOUNTS

I have several mail accounts, but Windows Mail doesn't check all of them when I click Send/Recv.

Open the Properties sheet for each of your mail accounts in the Internet Accounts dialog. On the General tab is an option labeled Include This Account When Receiving Mail or Synchronizing. Make sure a checkmark appears next to this option for each of your mail accounts.

THINNING YOUR CONTACTS LIST

Several people in my Contacts list shouldn't be there, including spammers.

By default, Windows Mail adds an entry to the Address Book for every source to which you reply. You can disable this feature by opening the Options dialog in the Tools menu. On the Send tab, disable the option labeled Automatically Put People I Reply to in My Contacts List. Then, to remove unwanted entries from your Address Book, highlight the contact and click Delete.

RECIPIENTS DON'T LIKE MY MAIL FORMATTING

People on my mailing list are sending me hate mail because of machine characters or strange attachments that accompany each of my posts.

HTML messages are not compatible with most electronic mailing lists. Change your default mail-sending format to Plain Text on the Send tab of the Windows Mail Options dialog.

Alternatively, you can have Windows Mail remind you of specific people in your Address Book who request Plain Text messages. Open the Contacts list and click on the name of a person who requests Plain Text mail. Click on the Name tab, and put a check mark in the box next to Send E-Mail Using Plain Text Only. When you try to send HTML email to this person, a reminder window will pop up asking whether you want Windows Mail to reformat the email to Plain Text.

Missing Mail Servers

When I try to go online and check mail, an error occurs stating that the server could not be found.

Assuming that the server information for your account is correct, you probably have a problem with your connection. Windows Mail should automatically dial a connection if one is not present, but if it doesn't, open the Internet Properties icon in the Windows Control Panel. On the Connection tab, select the option Dial Whenever a Network Connection Is Not Present, and click OK to close the dialog.

Making Windows Mail Less Automated

I want/don't want Windows Mail to automatically check for mail periodically.

Go to the General tab of the Options dialog. If the option Check for New Messages Every XX Minutes is checked, Windows Mail automatically checks for new mail at the specified interval. Just below that option, you can also specify whether you want Windows Mail to automatically dial a connection at this time.

Missing Windows Mail Folders

My Windows Mail folders seem to have disappeared.

They might be still on disk, just not in Windows Mail anymore. Use these steps:

1. In Windows Mail, choose Tools, Options, Advanced tab, Maintenance button, and click Store Folder to locate the store folder. Select the whole path of the store location and press Ctrl+C to copy it.
2. Click Start, Run, and then press Ctrl+V to paste in the name of the store file location. This opens a window with all your message store files in it.
3. Rename the folders.dbx file to folders.xxx. (You might need system administrator privileges to do this.)
4. Restart Windows Mail. Your folders should reappear, but all folders will now be on the same level instead of appearing as subfolders. Reorganize the folder structure by dragging and dropping. Check your message rules for any rules that move messages into folders to be certain that the destination folder is correct. Also, check other settings such as your Identities, Signatures, and Newsgroup Synchronization.

Troubleshooting Newsgroups

Newsgroup Isn't Available on News Server

A newsgroup I want to access isn't available on my server.

Click Reset List in the Newsgroup Subscriptions window. The newsgroup may be new and simply not shown in your current list. If the group still isn't there, try contacting the ISP or other service that hosts the list and ask that service to add it. Often new groups simply go unnoticed because so many of them are out there. Many news servers are willing to respond to such a request, unless they have a rule restricting or censoring the particular group.

Try paying for an alternative dedicated news server that does carry the newsgroup you're interested in.

Some Messages Are Unavailable After Synchronizing

I tried to synchronize the group, but some messages I click aren't available.

Obviously, you should first check that the settings for the group are correct. If the group isn't set to All Messages, and the Synchronize check box isn't checked, this could easily explain the missing message bodies. Another possibility is that the message was removed from the host server sometime after the header list was distributed. It can take up to 72 hours after a message is physically removed before it disappears from the header list.

News servers only have so much disk space. To allow them to continually add incoming files to their lists, they must continually discard old files. If your server is missing a few articles you may "ask" for a repost of the incomplete files, but while the poster is expected to service reasonable repost requests there is no requirement to do so. Sometimes a regular poster might not service repost requests at all, but will instead indicate an FTP, ICQ, or IRQ service where you can pick up missing files. And in many cases a repost request will be answered by a person who just happens to have downloaded the same file set and is willing to help support the group.

Finally, if you are doing everything right and your server is not gathering all the articles that were posted, consider informing your ISP's support desk of the problem. It does not do any good to complain to everyone else in the newsgroup if you are not telling the few people who are actually paid to help you. Servers and the connecting routers are sensitive electronic equipment, and their only guarantee is that they will fail at some point. Help your ISP monitor the network.

If your server is poorly connected and misses a lot of articles, as stated previously, consider hiring a dedicated news service as a secondary server.

Message No Longer Available

A message I read earlier is no longer available.

The default settings in Windows Mail delete read messages five days after you have downloaded them. You can change this option on the Advanced Tab, Maintenance button of the Windows Mail Options dialog.

Which Ones Are New?

I can't tell which messages are new.

Open the Options dialog by choosing Tools, Options. On the Read tab, place a checkmark next to Mark All Messages As Read When Exiting a Newsgroup.

No News Server Connection

Windows Mail cannot locate my news server.

Do you need to use a separate Internet connection to access the news server? If so, choose Tools, Accounts, and then click the News Account in question. Click Properties and select the Connection tab. Place a checkmark next to Always Connect to This Account Using, and select the appropriate connection from the drop-down list.

Tips from the Windows Pros: Creating Formatted Email

So you know a lot about email. What about the fancy-looking messages you get in your Inbox—the ones that look like web pages? This type of email is created with HTML formatting.

And how do you create fancy HTML email messages, anyway? In its simplest form, HTML mail lets you format the font and other goodies such as color and background. We already talked about stationery, so you know that this is HTML mail. You can also use the Insert Picture button on the Windows Mail toolbar to insert an image. But your ability to design a document with much control is still limited.

If you want to create more elaborate email, with tables, text that wraps around pictures, and many links in it, you'll probably want to use a web design program such as FrontPage or Dreamweaver. After you've designed a page there, follow these steps:

1. Start a new email in Windows Mail.
2. Select and copy the new page you designed in your web design program and paste into the new email you're constructing. As you paste in the text and images, they should appear in your email.
3. Adjust as necessary.

Test the look of the email you created by sending the sample mail to yourself; see how it looks when you open it. Make sure to test it by sending it to another computer, too, or to a friend or colleague. Ask them to report to you whether it looks correct or not. That way you can determine whether there are any missing images. Your test can be deceptive if you send and receive from the same computer because the images you use are already on the source computer. If the images are missing from the email, they are still likely to show up if you use the source computer for testing it, simply because they are being called up from your local hard drive.

Another way to create formatted email is by using a program dedicated to this purpose. A web search will lead you to current products.

To keep your email easy to read, keep the page fairly narrow. Also, don't expect your message to display as predictably as it does in a web browser because HTML-capable email programs just aren't as polished in their capability to render HTML. It's a good idea to check your mail in various email clients first to get an idea of how it will look to a variety of readers.

Much spam HTML email only downloads the HTML code and the text portion into Windows Mail. The rest of the images are not loaded in until you look at the mail (assuming you are online at the time). When you click on the mail to read it, the images stream in because the HTML code in the message "points" to the image sources, which are out on web servers somewhere across the Internet. This is an acceptable way to construct your HTML mail, but it assumes your readers are online. If you want to be sure people can read your mail offline, you should include the images in the email itself. However, this does make the file larger and can slow down the transfer time. Make sure to keep your images relatively small and compressed (as a rule, your images shouldn't exceed about 25KB). Use a program such as Fireworks, FrontPage, or Photoshop to optimize photos and other images for transmission over the Web.

> **TIP**
>
> Some programs cannot read HTML mail. In the subject line of HTML mail, I like to include the words *HTML version* so that people will know not to bother reading it if their email program isn't HTML-savvy. Then I send another message that is plain text, with a subject line that includes the words *Plain text version*.

Tips from the Windows Pros: Newsgroups—For More Than Just News

Newsgroups began innocently enough as forums for university, government, and science research folks to find and offer various kinds of support and share information over the precursor to the Internet. However, it didn't take long for Usenet to explode as a means of online recreation. Today, no matter how obscure you think your hobby or personal interest may be, a newsgroup is probably already dedicated to it. And one of the great advantages of newsgroups is the fact that files can be easily attached to posts. Attachments can be in the form of pictures, sound files, movies, text documents, programs, or anything else imaginable. In this respect, newsgroups really shine when compared to mailing lists; most mailing lists strictly forbid attachments, but in Usenet they are welcome.

Newsgroups with the word *binaries* in their address are good places to find attachments. The word *binary* refers to a nontext attachment, some kind of a data or program file. Naturally, you need to exercise some care before you download any messages with large attachments. First, ask yourself whether you have enough bandwidth to download the message. The message list tells you the size of each individual message, in the right column.

After you have determined that you can handle the message download, you should also keep virus safety in mind. If the attachment is a standard multimedia format, such as JPEG, WAV, GIF, MP3, or AVI, it should be safe. But if the attachment is an unknown format or is an executable program (.exe and .vbs are common extensions for these), you should follow your standard antivirus procedures.

Large news attachments are posted as multipart files, to get around the message-size limitations of news servers. These postings break up the large attachment over several consecutive posts. You can usually identify these types of posts by the Subject field, which identifies the message as part of a series. For example, you might see something like, "xfiles.avi (1/3), xfiles.avi (2/3)...," and so on.

Multipart attachments open properly only if downloaded and then combined together. Your first step is to identify each part of the series; if you miss even one portion of the series, it will not open properly. Use Ctrl+click and/or Shift+click to select each member of the series. After you've selected all of them, right-click the series, and choose Combine and Decode from the shortcut menu, as shown in Figure 16.23.

Figure 16.23
You must be sure you select every member of a multipart attachment series before attempting the download.

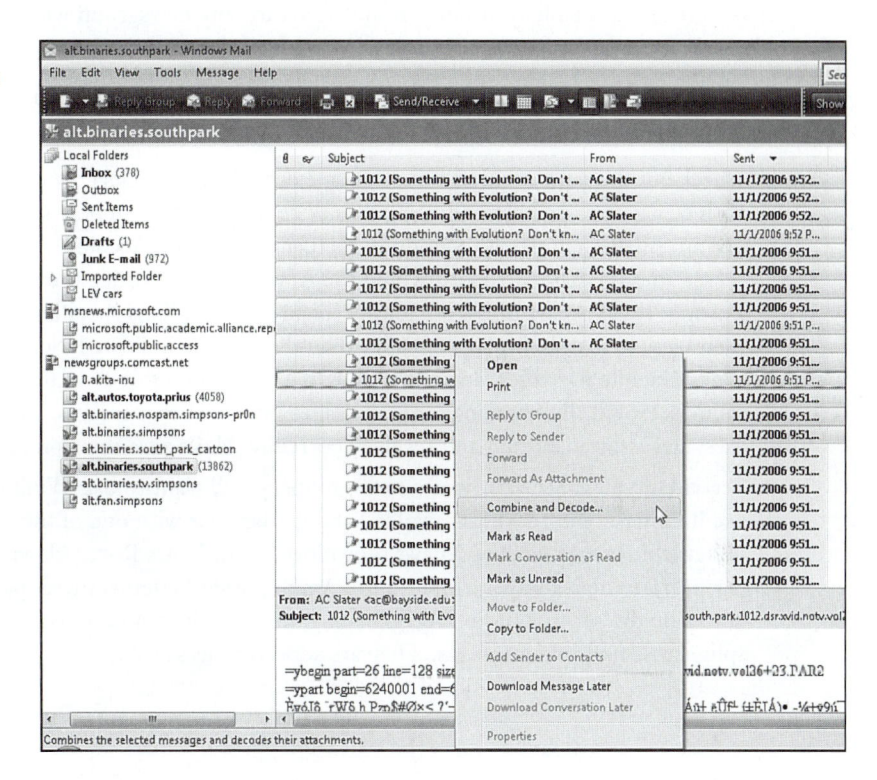

You are next presented with a dialog box asking you to put the series members in order. They should be in numeric order, starting with part one at the top of the list. Use the Move Up and Move Down buttons to place them in the correct order. Depending on the size of the multipart attachment, the download may take some time. When it is complete, a message window opens with a single attachment listed. This doesn't make much sense because it looks as though you're going to send the file to someone. But typically you want to save it to your hard disk. So just right-click on that file icon in the attachment line, and choose Save As. Then save the file with the name and location you want.

Multimedia attachments in Usenet can be a lot of fun. For example, the group alt.binaries.tv.simpsons usually contains WAV and AVI files of popular sound bites and catchphrases—or even an entire episode—from the television series *The Simpsons*. If you save downloaded WAV files in the \WINNT\Media folder of your hard drive, you can later assign those sounds to various Windows events. Wouldn't Windows be more enjoyable if each critical stop were accompanied by Bart Simpson's "Aye Carumba" rather than the monotonous Chord.wav?

Another gem to be on the lookout for in Usenet is MP3 music. MP3 files offer CD-quality music, but because they use about one-twelfth the storage space, they can be transported efficiently over the Internet. You probably know about MP3s from all the hoopla about MP3 players such as the iPod and the old Napster court case, but you may not have known that MP3s were also available over newsgroups. Look for any newsgroup with *mp3* in the address, but watch out for those bootlegs!

If you become a serious newsgroup junkie, especially if you're into downloading (or uploading) large files, you'll have some boning up to do:

- Check out the news stuff at groups.google.com (formerly Deja.com) and correspond with heavy news posters on your group of choice. When you post large files, split them up into smaller chunks. In Windows Mail, choose Tools, Accounts. Choose the news server you use. Click Properties, and the Advanced tab. Notice the setting there for Posting: Break Apart Messages Larger Than ____KB. This specifies to break up large messages, so that each part is smaller than the file size indicated. Some older servers cannot handle messages larger than 64KB. More commonly as of this writing the maximum is 256KB. By breaking large messages into smaller messages, you ensure that the messages are transmitted and received correctly. Make sure this option is selected.

- Second, if you are seriously into newsgroups, you'll want to bag Windows Mail and use it only for your email. Download and get familiar with one of the serious programs designed for news, such as Xnews (download.com), News Rover (download.com), or Agent (forteinc.com/agent/index.php). Among other benefits, these specialized products automate the process of finding, grouping, downloading, and decoding file attachments split across multiple messages. They are serious time-savers.

CHAPTER 17

TROUBLESHOOTING YOUR INTERNET CONNECTION

In this chapter

It's Great When It Works, but... 528

Before You Run into Trouble 528

Troubleshooting Step by Step 531

Identifying Software-Configuration Problems 535

Identifying Network Hardware Problems 539

Troubleshooting Internet Problems with Windows TCP/IP Utilities 543

Third-Party Utilities 549

Tips from the Windows Pros: Pinging with Larger Packets 551

It's Great When It Works, but...

Browsing the Internet is great fun and very useful. In fact, watch as I instantly transfer millions of dollars from my secret Swiss bank account to…. Wait a minute, what's a "404 Server Not Found Error"? What's going on? Did the modem disconnect? Is the IRS closing in on me? Help! Where's my money?

If you've used the Internet for any length of time, this scene might seem all too familiar—except for the bit about the Swiss bank account. (A guy can dream, can't he?) Connecting to the Internet and using the Web is an amazingly user-friendly experience, yet we can't escape that it's a staggeringly complex system. If something goes wrong at any step along the way between your fingertips and a server in cyberspace, the whole system comes to a crashing halt. Where do you begin to find and fix the problem?

In this chapter, I'll show you the basic strategies to use when tracking down Internet problems, and I'll briefly discuss some of the diagnostic tools available to help you pinpoint the trouble.

> **TIP**
>
> Experiment with the diagnostic tools that we'll be discussing in this chapter when your network and Internet connection are operating correctly, to learn how the programs work and what output you should expect. This way, if you run into trouble later, you can compare the results to what you saw when things were working.

Before You Run Into Trouble

The best tool to have on hand when you're diagnosing Internet problems is information about what you should expect when your connection is *working*. If you collect this information in advance of running into trouble, you'll save yourself a lot of time, trouble and grief.

For starters, gather the information that your ISP provided when you set up your Internet connection. This might include the following information:

- The customer support telephone number for your ISP.
- The type of service you're using: dial-up modem, DSL, cable modem, satellite, or other type of service.
- For dial-up service, the dial-in telephone number(s) for your area, and the URL of the web page that you can use to find other dial-up numbers in other areas.
- For DSL or cable service, the make and model of the DSL or cable modem that you were given.
- The login name and password that is used to connect to the service. (This usually does not apply to cable Internet service; your provider will tell you if it does.)
- The usernames and passwords used to access the email accounts you have with your ISP.

- The names or IP addresses of any servers provided by your ISP, including outgoing mail (SMTP server), incoming mail (POP3 server), and news reader (NNTP server).
- If your service provides you with a static IP address, you need to know your IP address, your network mask, your gateway address, and two or more DNS server addresses.

I suggest that you collect and type all this information, and store it in a handy place near your computer. You can use WordPad (click Start, All Programs, Accessories, WordPad) or your favorite word processor. The important part is to *print the information* so it's available even if your computer is acting up. Keep the printout in a manila file folder labeled "Internet Connection Information."

It's also helpful to collect the correct output of the TCP/IP diagnostic programs (whose use I'll describe later in the chapter), and store copies of the output in your file folder for reference. You can use the PrntScrn key to take snapshots of the output and setup windows, and then paste the pictures into a WordPad document. Again, it really helps to have this information available when trouble occurs—but you have to prepare it in advance.

Here are some things to record:

- The output of the `tracert` command-line program showing the results for a sample website. The `tracert` tool records all the intermediate steps that Internet data passes through between your computer and a site on the Net. Knowing what the route looks like when things are working can later help tell whether a problem is in your computer or out on the Internet, beyond your control.

    To record this output, open a command prompt window (click Start, All Programs, Accessories, Command Prompt) and type this command:

    `tracert www.sonic.net`

    This command might take about 30 seconds to display several lines of text, ending with "Trace complete." If it does run successfully, type this command:

    `tracert www.sonic.net > goodtracert.txt`

    This time, you will not see any output, but the command is running. After the same 30 seconds, the command prompt returns. Now type this:

    `notepad goodtracert.txt`

    This is the saved output of the successful `tracert` command, which you can now print and put into your Internet Connection Information folder.

- The output of the command-line command `ipconfig /all`, run on each of your computers while you're successfully connected to the Internet. `ipconfig` lists all your networking settings, so you can check for mistakes.

    To record this output, type these commands:

    `ipconfig /all > ipconfig.txt`
    `notepad ipconfig.txt`

    As before, you should print and file the results.

- The Network Hardware and Protocol Configuration dialog boxes in Network Connections, as pictures snapped with PrntScrn. If you have a network or a network adapter that you use for a broadband cable or DSL Internet connection, it's handy to record the setup information in case you need to re-enter it later. For example, you might need to do that if you replace your network adapter. To document these settings, follow these steps:

  1. Open WordPad (click Start, All Programs, Accessories, WordPad) or your favorite word processor.
  2. Open the Network Connections window (click Start, Control Panel, Network and Internet, Network and Sharing Center, Manage Network Connections).
  3. Right-click the icon that corresponds to your Internet connection (a dial-up, broadband, or LAN connection, depending on your Internet connection type). Select Properties.

  NOTE
  The User Account Control warning may pop up at various points during this procedure. If it does, click Continue, or supply an Administrator account name and password to proceed.

  4. Select the first tab. Press Alt+PrtScrn. Click the cursor in the WordPad window, and press Ctrl+V to paste in the picture.
  5. Return to the Properties dialog box and select the next tab. Again, press Alt+PrtScrn to capture a picture of the dialog box; then select WordPad and press Ctrl+V to paste in the picture. Repeat this process for every tab in the dialog box.
  6. Close the Connection Properties dialog box. Repeat steps 3 through 5 for any other connection icons in the Network Connections window.
  7. Print the WordPad document and store it in your file folder.

- The configuration of any routers or network connection equipment. If you have an Internet connection sharing router, it's a *very* good idea to record its correct settings, in case they are accidentally changed or you update or replace the device. You can do this by printing each of its setup screens from your web browser.

- The settings for any dial-up connections used. Many ISPs talk you through their setup process or provide you with "wizard" software that does the work for you, and it's important to record the setup information in case you need to reconstruct it someday. The information you need is the telephone number, login name, and password.

- Diagrams showing network cabling, hubs, routers, and computers. If your 3-year-old is a budding network installer and rewires your computer, it's handy to have a diagram of the correct setup to help you get all the wiring spaghetti back in order.

> **TIP**
>
> In a business setting, documenting your LAN configuration is a "due diligence" issue—it's not optional. Be sure to keep it up-to-date, too. If you use an outside contractor to set up your business's computers, network, or Internet connection, be sure that your contract specifies that good documentation will be provided.

With this documentation at hand, you'll be armed with supportive information if a problem does occur.

TROUBLESHOOTING STEP BY STEP

A functioning Internet connection depends on an entire chain of hardware and software components that reach all the way from your keyboard to a computer that might be halfway around the world. Troubleshooting is a real detective's art, and it's based more on methodical tracking down of potential suspect problems than intuition. If something goes wrong, you have to go through each component, asking "Is *this* the one that's causing the problem?"

Windows Vista comes with new network–troubleshooting capabilities that, in *some* cases, can identify and repair problems automatically. If you encounter Internet connection problems—especially problems using high-speed broadband Internet service—try these steps:

1. Click Start, Control Panel, View Network Status (under Network and Internet), Tasks. If there is a problem with your Internet connection, Windows displays a red X, as shown in Figure 17.1.

Figure 17.1
Windows displays a red X on the map, showing that your Internet connection is not working.

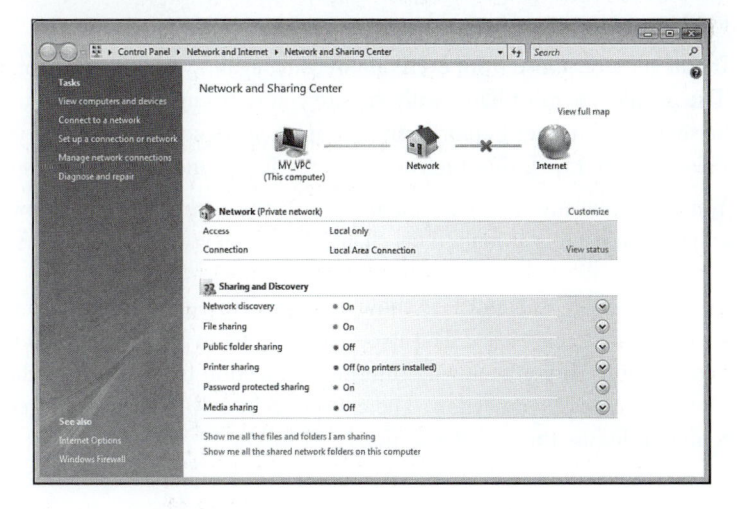

2. In the Tasks list, click Diagnose and Repair.
3. If Windows displays a message indicating that it might be able to repair the problem, click Repair.

If the problem occurred because your computer failed to obtain its network settings from a router, this procedure will often work. However, in my testing, I've found that the Diagnose and Repair Wizard is not terribly useful. For example, I get my Internet connection through a DSL modem and a separate router that shares the Internet connection. I unplugged the DSL modem, leaving the router turned on. Windows' conclusion was, "There might be a problem with your domain name server (DNS) configuration." It got one of the symptoms right, but it failed to consider that the router (which Windows knows about) couldn't reach the Internet. This is a real shortcoming on the part of Vista's diagnostic tools, because this modem-plus-sharing router setup is used in hundreds of thousands of homes and small offices, and a failed connection is a very common problem.

In many cases, you need to locate the problem yourself, using good old-fashioned Sherlock Holmes–style deductive reasoning. Here's how it goes. Let's assume that you are having trouble using a certain website. It could be that...

- You can view some of its pages but not others, or you see text displayed but not the streaming video or sound.

    In this case, you know that your Internet connection itself is fine because something does appear. The problem, then, is that the video or sound application isn't working. You might want to check the index to see if we discuss the application in this book. You might also check the application's built-in help pages. If the application was one that you downloaded or purchased, check the manufacturer's website for support information or an updated software version.

- Nothing on this particular site is responding. In this case, see if you can view any other website. Try www.google.com, www.quepublishing.com, your ISP's website, or your local newspaper's website.

    If you get a response from even one website, again, your Internet connection is fine. The problem is most likely with the site you're trying to use or with your ISP. Check to be sure that Internet Explorer isn't set up to block access to the site you're interested in. (See Chapter 15, "Using Internet Explorer 7," for more help on this topic.)

- You can't view any web pages on any site. If this is the case, you know that your Internet connection itself is at fault. This chapter can help you find out what's wrong.

To that end, Figures 17.2 and 17.3 show flowcharts to help direct you to the source of the problem. The first chart is for dial-up connections to an ISP; the second is for broadband or LAN connections. If you're having Internet connection trouble, follow the appropriate flowchart for your type of connection. The endpoints in each flowchart suggest places to look for trouble. I discuss these in the sections that follow.

TROUBLESHOOTING STEP BY STEP

Figure 17.2
Flowchart for diagnosing dial-up Internet connection problems.

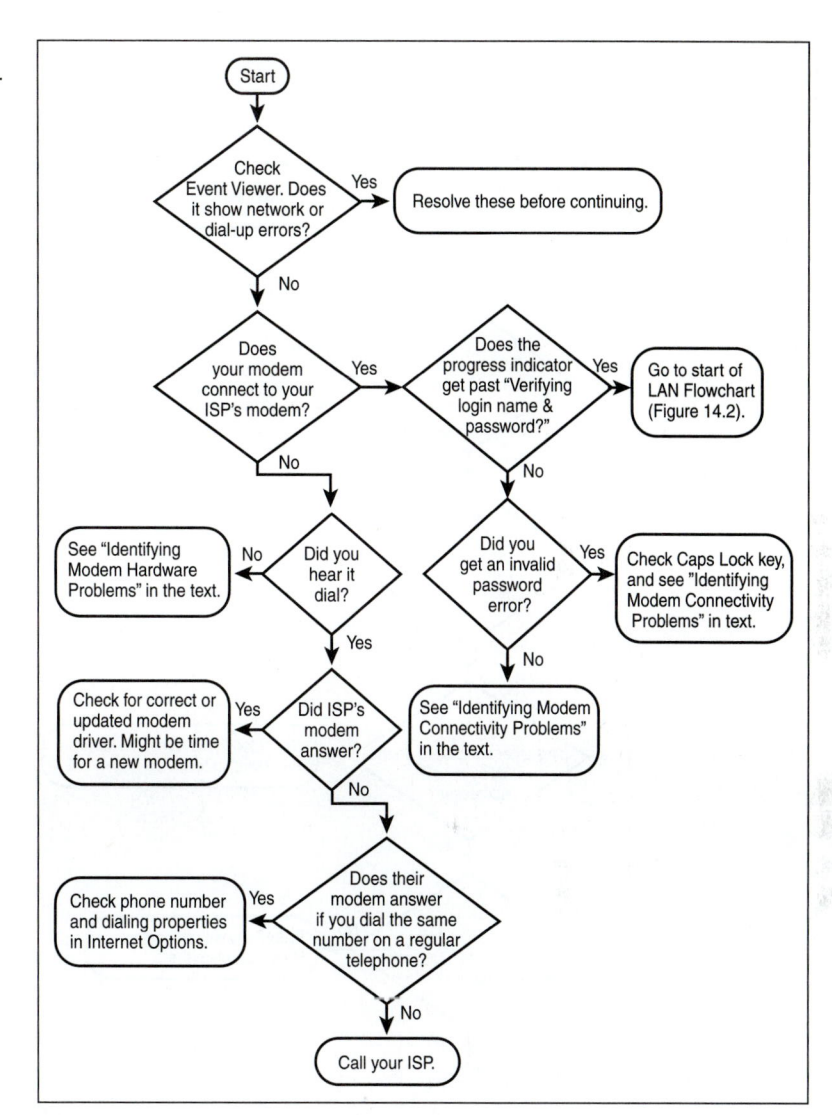

Figure 17.3
Flowchart for diagnosing broadband or LAN-based Internet connection problems.

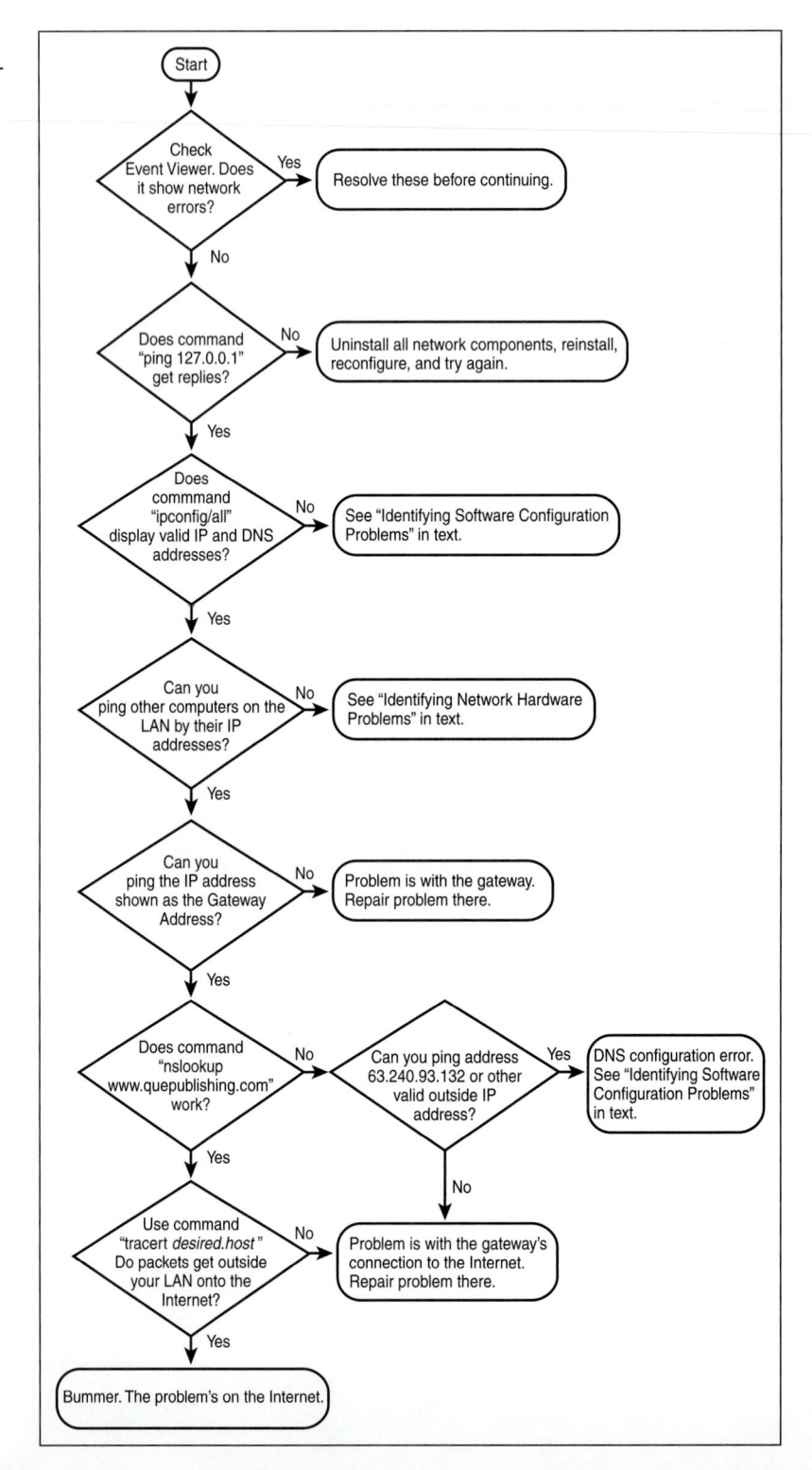

Identifying Software-Configuration Problems

Software-configuration problems can easily be the cause of Internet connection problems, and it's fairly simple to determine that this is the problem—you can't make any Internet connection whatsoever, although the Device Manager says your network card or modem seems to be working correctly. The potential problems depend on the type of Internet connection you use.

Troubleshooting a Dial-Up Connection

If your modem appears to connect to your ISP but you still can't access any web pages or Internet services, here are some steps you can take:

1. In Internet Explorer, select Tools, Internet Options. Select the Connections tab. Be sure you have selected the correct dial-up connection. Click LAN Settings and be sure that Use a Proxy Server is not checked, as shown in Figure 17.4. (The exception to this rule is if you are using a third-party connection speed–enhancement program; in this case, the software manufacturer might specify proxy settings.)

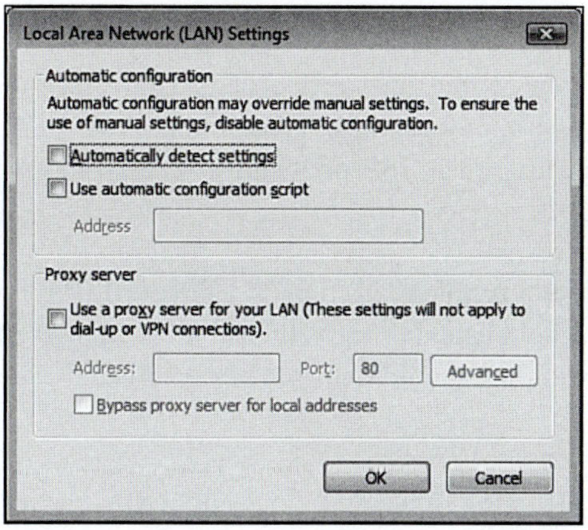

Figure 17.4
For a dial-up Internet connection, Proxy Server should not be checked, except as noted in the text.

2. Click Start, Connect To, and right-click your dial-up connection. Select Properties and view the Networking tab. Under Components Used by This Connection, only the Internet Protocol entries and QoS Packet Scheduler should be checked, as shown in Figure 17.5.

Figure 17.5
For a dial-up Internet connection, only the Internet Protocol and QoS Packet Scheduler items should be checked.

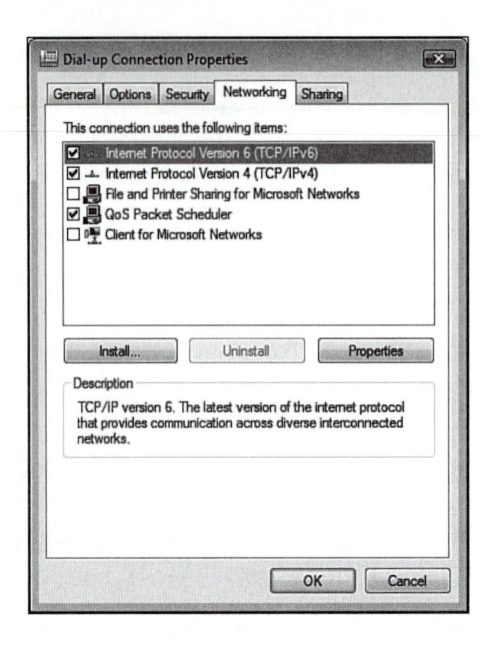

3. On the Security tab of your connection's properties sheet (refer to Step 2), look at the Verify My Identity As Follows settings. This should be set to Allow Unsecured Password if you're connecting to an ISP, or Require Secured Password if you're connecting to your office LAN.

If none of these steps identifies a problem, it's time to call your ISP for assistance. You might have to spend a half-hour on hold listening to really bad music, but at this point, it's their job to help you get online, and they should help you cheerfully and expertly. (Otherwise, you should get a new ISP.)

TROUBLESHOOTING A CABLE OR DSL MODEM CONNECTION

If your computer connects directly to a cable or DSL modem, you might have one or two network cards installed in your computer, depending on whether you're sharing the high-speed connection on your LAN.

> **NOTE**
> If you have DSL or cable service, but your computer connects to a connection-sharing router and the *router* connects to the modem, don't follow these instructions. Instead, see "Identifying Network Hardware Problems" later in this chapter.

To check for the proper settings, follow these steps:

1. In a command prompt window (click Start, All Programs, Accessories, Command Prompt), type `ipconfig /all` and press Enter. Be sure that the IP address and DNS

information for the network card that connects to your high-speed modem is accurate. Your ISP's tech support people can help you confirm this.

2. If your DSL provider requires you to "sign on" before using the Internet, you'll be using a sort of "dial-up" connection, except that the connection is made digitally over the DSL network. (This is called Point to Point Protocol over Ethernet, or PPPoE.) You set up this connection using the Broadband (PPPoE) option, as described in Chapter 8, "Windows Media Player."

    If this is the case, and if you use a LAN adapter to connect to your DSL modem, the IP address displayed for the LAN adapter itself will have an IP address that is used only to communicate with your DSL modem. Be sure to check with your ISP to be certain that this computer-to-modem connection is configured correctly; if it's not, you won't be able to make the connection to your ISP.

    Use the Connection icon to connect to your ISP. You can get to it quickly using Start, Connect To.

    When the logon process has completed, `ipconfig /all` should show a dial-up connection with a different IP address. This is your real, public Internet address for the duration of the connection.

3. If you're sharing your computer's high-speed connection with your home or office LAN using two network cards in your computer, be sure that you've enabled sharing on the correct connection. The connection to check as "shared" is the one that connects to your high-speed DSL or cable modem. The LAN-side connection is not the shared connection and should have an IP address of 192.168.0.1. Internet Connection Sharing is described in Chapter 22, "Connecting Your Network to the Internet."

TROUBLESHOOTING A LAN CONNECTION

If you connect to the Internet via a wired or wireless connection on your LAN, the first question is, can you communicate with other computers on your LAN? To test this, you should use the `ping` command.

Open a command prompt window (click Start, All Programs, Accessories, Command Prompt) and type the command **ipconfig**. The output of `ipconfig` lists a number called a gateway address. To test the connection to your gateway, type **ping** followed by the gateway address, and then press Enter. For example:

ping 192.168.0.1

This tests the connection to the computer or router that is sharing its Internet connection. If `ping` says "Request timed out" or "Transmit failed" instead of listing four successful replies, you have a LAN problem that you need to fix first.

If you are using a wireless network connection, be sure that your wireless connection is working correctly, that you are connected to the correct wireless network, and that you have the correct network key entered. Chapter 24, "Troubleshooting Your Network," is devoted to LAN troubleshooting.

> **TIP**
>
> Windows has a diagnostic and repair function that resets all the software components of a LAN connection, including the DHCP address assignment. This often solves LAN problems. To use it, open the Network Connections page, find your LAN or wireless connection, right-click it, and select Diagnose. If a problem is identified, follow the instructions or select the Reset option.

If you can communicate with other computers on the LAN but not the Internet, can anyone else on your LAN access the Internet? If no one can, the problem is in your LAN's connection to the Net. If your LAN uses Internet Connection Sharing, go to the sharing computer and start diagnosing the problem there. Otherwise, follow these steps:

1. Open a command prompt window and type `ipconfig /all` to view your TCP/IP settings. The output appears similar to that shown in Listing 17.1. (The Tunnel Adapter entries are not important here and are not shown.)

LISTING 17.1 OUTPUT FROM THE `ipconfig /all` COMMAND

```
Windows IP Configuration
    Host Name . . . . . . . . . . . . : MyComputer
    Primary Dns Suffix  . . . . . . . :
    Node Type . . . . . . . . . . . . : Hybrid
    IP Routing Enabled. . . . . . . . : No
    WINS Proxy Enabled. . . . . . . . : No
Ethernet adapter Local Area Connection:
    Connection-specific DNS Suffix  . :
    Description . . . . . . . . . . . : Intel PCI Fast Ethernet Adapter
    Physical Address. . . . . . . . . : 00-03-FF-D0-CA-5F
    DHCP Enabled. . . . . . . . . . . : Yes
    Autoconfiguration Enabled . . . . : Yes
    Link-local IPv6 Address . . . . . : fe80::8014:cfc7:9a98:cdfe%10(Preferred)
    IPv4 Address. . . . . . . . . . . : 192.168.15.106(Preferred)
    Subnet Mask . . . . . . . . . . . : 255.255.255.0
    Lease Obtained. . . . . . . . . . : Sunday, September 17, 2006 7:22:23 PM
    Lease Expires . . . . . . . . . . : Sunday, September 24, 2006 7:22:22 PM
    Default Gateway . . . . . . . . . : 192.168.15.1
    DHCP Server . . . . . . . . . . . : 192.168.15.1
    DHCPv6 IAID . . . . . . . . . . . : 167773183
    DNS Servers . . . . . . . . . . . : 192.168.15.1
    NetBIOS over Tcpip. . . . . . . . : Enabled
```

Within the output, check the following:

- The DNS suffix search list and the connection-specific DNS suffix should be set correctly for your ISP's domain name or your company's domain name. (This is helpful but not crucial.) It can also be left blank.

- The IP address should be appropriate for your LAN. If you're using Internet Connection Sharing, the number will be 192.168.0.*xxx*. If you're using a hardware connection sharing device, the number might be different.

- If your IP address appears to be 169.254.*xxx.yyy*, the sharing computer or router was not running the connection-sharing service when you booted up your computer, or it is no longer set up to share its connection. Get the sharing computer or router restarted and then skip to Step 2.

- The default gateway address should be the IP address of your router or sharing computer, usually something similar to 192.168.0.1 or 192.168.1.1.

- The default gateway address and your IP address should be identical for the first few sets of numbers, corresponding to those parts of the subnet mask that are set to 255. That is, both might start with 192.168.0 or 192.168.1.

- If your computer gets its IP address information automatically, DHCP Enabled should be set to Yes. If your computer has its IP address information entered manually, no DHCP server should be listed.

- If you're using connection sharing, the DNS server address will be 192.168.0.1. Otherwise, the DNS server numbers should be those provided by your ISP or network administrator.

- If your computer gets its settings automatically or uses a shared connection, continue with the next two steps.

2. Be sure the master router or sharing computer is running. Then, in the Network Connections window, right-click your Local Area Connection icon and select Diagnose. This might lead you through solving the problem. Alternately, view the Network and Sharing Center, and select Diagnose and Repair from the task list.

3. Repeat the `ipconfig` command and see whether the correct information appears now. If it does, you're all set. If not, the master computer or the router is not supplying the information that I described previously and needs to be set correctly before you can proceed.

These steps should take care of any software-configuration problems. If none of these steps indicates or solves the problem, check that your network or modem hardware is functioning correctly.

IDENTIFYING NETWORK HARDWARE PROBLEMS

If you suspect hardware as the source of your Internet connection problems, check the following:

- Log on using an account with Administrator privileges. On the Start menu, right-click Computer and select Manage to open the Computer Management. Select Device Manager. Look for any yellow exclamation point (!) icons in the device list. If your network adapter is marked with this trouble indicator, you have to solve the hardware problem before continuing. Double-click the line that's marked with the exclamation point and click the Check For Solutions button to get troubleshooting assistance. If the device needs an updated driver, see "Updating Drivers" in Chapter 30, "Installing and Replacing Hardware," for more information.

- Also within Computer Management, check the Event Viewer for any potentially informative error messages that might indicate a hardware problem.

- Use `ipconfig` on each of your computers to check that all the computers on your LAN have the same gateway and network mask values, and similar but distinct IP addresses.
- If your LAN has indicator lights on the network cards and hubs, open a command prompt window and type

  `ping -t x.x.x.x`

  where `x.x.x.x` is your network's default gateway address. (This might be something similar to 192.168.0.1.) This forces your computer to transmit data once per second. Confirm that the indicator lights blink on your LAN adapter and the hub, if you have one. This test might point out a cabling problem.
- If your hub or LAN card's indicator doesn't flash, you might have a bad LAN adapter, the wrong driver might be installed, or you might have configured the card incorrectly. You can stop the `ping` test by pressing Ctrl+C when you're finished checking.

If you use a hardware connection-sharing router for a broadband (DSL or cable) connection, your router might provide further assistance. To access the router, follow these steps:

1. Open a command prompt window (click Start, All Programs, Accessories, Command Prompt).
2. Type the command `ipconfig` and press Enter.
3. Note the gateway address. It will be something along the lines of 192.168.0.1.
4. Open Internet Explorer. In the address bar, type the address `//192.168.0.1`, but enter the gateway address that you noted in the previous step.
5. You are prompted to enter the administrative username and password for your router. Each manufacturer has a default name and password, which you can find in the router's user's manual. You might also have changed it when you installed it.
6. Most routers have a Status menu item that displays the status of the router's Internet connection. If it says that it can't connect, you might have an incorrect PPPoE username or password entered. Or it might have dropped the connection. In this case, there might be a Connect button you can press, or you might want to just power off and then power on the router.

If you use a dial-up Internet connection, the next section can help you diagnose modem problems.

Identifying Modem Hardware Problems

Modems can have a greater variety of problems than network adapters. You can take a few steps to determine what the problem might be:

1. Before getting too frustrated, check the obvious one more time: Is a functioning telephone line connected to the right socket on the modem? Unless you're using an ISDN modem, it also doesn't hurt to plug in an extension phone and listen as the modem dials and your ISP answers. You must somehow put the extension on the "line" side of the

Identifying Network Hardware Problems   541

modem, though, because most modems disable the "telephone" jack when dialing. A duplex telephone jack can help with this.

If dialing was actually taking place but you couldn't hear it, run the Phone and Modem Options (open the Control Panel and click Hardware and Sound; then, Phone and Modem Options). Select the Modems tab, highlight the Modem, and click Properties. Click Change Settings and then click Continue. Select the Modem tab and move the volume slider up to its rightmost position. Click OK to save the change.

If you have a voicemail system that uses a stutter dial tone to indicate that you have messages waiting, your modem might not dial when the stutter is active. If this is the case, go to the Modem tab within the Control Panel dialog box and disable the Wait for Dial Tone Before Dialing option, as shown in Figure 17.6.

Figure 17.6
Uncheck the Wait for Dial Tone Before Dialing option if your voicemail notification interferes with dialing.

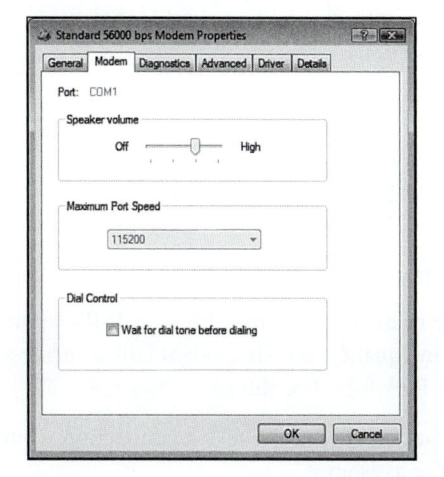

2. If you have an external analog or ISDN modem, be sure that it's plugged in and turned on. When you attempt to make a connection, watch for flickering in the Send Data LEDs. If you don't see flickering, your modem cable might not be installed correctly.

3. Check the Event Viewer for informative error messages that might indicate a hardware problem.

4. In the Start menu, right-click Computer, select Manage, and select Device Manager. Look for any yellow exclamation point (!) icons in the device list; if a modem or port is marked with this trouble indicator, you need to solve the hardware problem before continuing. Double-click the line that's marked with the exclamation point and click the Check For Solutions button to get troubleshooting assistance. If the device needs an updated driver, see "Updating Drivers" in Chapter 30 for more information.

> **NOTE**
> If you'd like to learn more about troubleshooting hardware and resolving device conflicts, I recommend that you pick up a copy of Scott Mueller's *Upgrading and Repairing PCs*, published by Que.

5. In the Dial-Up Connection Properties dialog box's Options tab, check Prompt for Phone Number and try to make the connection. This shows you the actual number being dialed. Verify that the call-waiting code, outside line-access codes, and area code are correct. These are set on the connection's General tab and in the Phone and Modem Options Control Panel (on the Dialing Rules dialog box, select the proper location and click Edit).

6. If you have an analog or ISDN modem and dialing is taking place but no connection is made, in the Device Manager or Control Panel Phone and Modem Properties, view the modem's Properties dialog box. On the General tab, click Change Settings and then click Continue. Select the Diagnostics tab and check Append to Log. Close the dialog box and try to make the connection again. Go back to the Properties dialog box and select View Log. This log might indicate what is happening with the modem. Be sure to uncheck Append to Log when you're finished, or the file that stores this information could grow to enormous proportions.

7. Try reducing the Maximum Port Speed (computer-to-modem connection speed) setting in Modem Properties to 19200. If this solves your problem, you need a new modem or, if you have an external serial modem, a higher-quality serial port card. However, with modems less than 10 years old, this should not be a problem.

Identifying Modem Connectivity Problems

Modem problems are usually due to incompatibility with your ISP's equipment compatibility problems, or to poor telephone line quality. If your modem fails to make a connection or disconnects by itself, you need to look for a few things:

- If the ISP's modem answers but you don't establish a connection, your modem might be incompatible; call your ISP for assistance.

- If your modem disconnects and you are told that there was a problem with your username or password, try to connect again and check these entries carefully. If you try two or three times and still can't connect, contact your ISP for help. Sometimes, ISPs get bought by other companies, and the format of the required sign-on username can change as a result.

- Create and view a log file of modem activity and look for error messages indicating a protocol-negotiation error. Your ISP can assist with this as well.

- If your modem makes screeching sounds for approximately 15 seconds and hangs up, your modem is probably incompatible with the equipment used at your ISP, and you needs an updated modem. Before you buy a new one, note that some modems can be updated via software. Check the manufacturer's website for information.

- If your connection works but the modem disconnects after a certain amount of time, there are two possible causes. If your connection was sitting idle, you might have run into the Windows inactivity timer. Click Start, Connect To; right-click your dial-up entry and select Properties; and then click Continue. View the Options tab. Check the entry Idle Time Before Hanging Up. Increase the time. If this problem recurs, you might enable the modem log and see whether it provides an explanation. Your ISP might also have set up its equipment to disconnect after a certain period of inactivity.

- If you don't think that idle time was the cause, your connection might have been interrupted by call waiting. On the connection's General tab, check Use Dialing Rules, click the Dialing Rules button, and then click Edit. Verify that you've chosen to disable call waiting and have selected the proper call-waiting turn-off setting (for example, *70). Some newer modems can cope with call waiting and even alert you to a call coming in. If you rely on call waiting, it might be time for an upgrade. In this case, however, you're probably better suited switching to a cable or DSL connection, if one is available to you.

- If none of these is the cause, you might simply have a scratchy telephone line or a flagging older modem. This is an annoying problem that is difficult to diagnose. Try changing modems.

If your modem is making contact with your ISP but, despite a solid modem connection, you still can't use the Internet, see the next section for tips on diagnosing Internet connectivity problems.

TROUBLESHOOTING INTERNET PROBLEMS WITH WINDOWS TCP/IP UTILITIES

If you think you are connected to your ISP but you still can't communicate, you can use some of the command-line tools provided with Windows to trace TCP/IP problems. (TCP/IP is the network language or protocol used by the Internet; see Chapter 19, "Overview of Windows Networking," for an introduction to networking and protocols.)

To run the command-line utilities, open a command prompt box with Start, All Programs, Accessories, Command Prompt. Then, type in the commands as I describe them later. If you're not familiar with command-line utilities, you can launch Windows Help (Start, Help and Support) and search for the command names, such as `ping` and `tracert`. You can also open a command prompt window and type the command name followed by /?, as in this example:

`Ping /?`

Now, let's go through some of the TCP/IP diagnostic and command-line utilities provided with Windows.

> **NOTE**
> If you're a UNIX devotee, you'll find these utilities familiar, if not identical, to their UNIX counterparts. If you're new to TCP/IP networking or debugging, you might find these utilities a little unfriendly. (Welcome to the world of networking.)

IPCONFIG

`ipconfig` is one of the most useful command-line utilities provided with Windows, because it displays the current IP address information for each of your computer's network adapters and active dial-up connections. On networks that assign addresses automatically, `ipconfig` can tell you what your computer's IP address is, if you ever need to know it.

After opening a command prompt window, typing the command

`ipconfig`

returns the following information (of course the IP, subnet, and gateway information `ipconfig` provides will be different for your computer, and you might see a dial-up connection listed instead of a LAN adapter):

```
Windows IP Configuration

Ethernet adapter Local Area Connection:
   Connection-specific DNS Suffix  . :
   Link-local IPv6 Address . . . . . : fe80::8014:cfc7:9a98:cdfe%10
   IPv4 Address. . . . . . . . . . . : 192.168.15.106
   Subnet Mask . . . . . . . . . . . : 255.255.255.0
   Default Gateway . . . . . . . . . : 192.168.15.1
```

(You can ignore the Tunnel adapter information; this is part of the Version 6 Internet Protocol system, which is used only on large, managed corporate networks.)

If you type the command

`Ipconfig /all`

Windows displays additional information about your DNS settings, including the following:

Host Name	**The Name You Gave Your Computer**
Primary DNS suffix	The Internet domain to which your computer belongs. (You might temporarily belong to others as well while using a dial-up connection.) This might be blank; it is not a problem.
Node type	The method that Windows uses to locate other computers on your LAN when you use Windows Networking. This usually is Hybrid or Broadcast.
DNS suffix search list	Alternative domain names used if you type just part of a host name and the default domain does not provide a match.
Connection-specific	The domain name for this particular DNS suffix connection. This is most applicable to dial-up connections.
DHCP enabled	If set to Yes, this adapter is set to receive its IP address automatically. If set to No, the address was set manually.
DNS servers	IP addresses of domain name servers.

`ipconfig` displays most of the information that can be set in the Network and Dial-Up Connection Properties dialog box, but it shows their real-world values. This makes it an invaluable "first stop" when troubleshooting any network problem. If you determine that an Internet connection problem lies in your equipment somewhere (because you cannot access any Internet destinations), typing **`ipconfig /all`** can tell you whether your network setup is correct. You need this information at hand before calling your ISP for assistance.

PING

If you try to browse the Internet or share files with other computers on your LAN and get no response, it could be because the other computer isn't receiving your data or isn't responding. After `ipconfig`, `ping` is the most useful tool to determine where your Internet connection or your network has stopped working.

> **TIP**
>
> You can type `ping x.x.x.x`, replacing `x.x.x.x` with the default gateway address or the address of any other operational computer on the Internet or your network (if applicable), and in an instant, you will know whether your dial-up or high-speed modem, computer, network hardware, and cabling are operating properly. If echoes come back, the physical part of your network is functioning properly. If they don't, you can use `tracert` and other tools explained later in this chapter to see why.

Here's how it works:

1. The `ping` command sends a few packets of data to any computer you specify.
2. The other computer should immediately send these packets back to you.
3. `ping` lets you know whether the packets come back.

Therefore, `ping` tests the low-level communication between two computers. If `ping` works, you know that your network wiring, TCP/IP software, and any routers in between you and the other computer are working. `ping` takes several options that can customize the type and amount of output it reports back to you. Three especially useful variations of these options exist; the first two are

`C:\> ping hostname`

where *hostname* is the name of one of the computers on your network, and

`C:\> ping nnn.nnn.nnn.nnn`

where *nnn.nnn.nnn.nnn* is a computer's numeric IP address, as discovered by `ipconfig`. These variations transmit four packets to the host or IP address you specify and tell you whether they return. This command returns the following information:

```
C:\> ping www.mycompany.com
Pinging sumatra.mycompany.com [202.222.132.163] with 32 bytes of data:
Reply from 202.222.132.163: bytes=32 time<10ms TTL=32
Reply from 202.222.132.163: bytes=32 time<10ms TTL=32
Reply from 202.222.132.163: bytes=32 time<10ms TTL=32
Reply from 202.222.132.163: bytes=32 time<10ms TTL=32
```

In this example, the fact that the packets returned tells us that the computer can communicate with www.mycompany.com. It also tells us that everything in between is working.

> **NOTE**
>
> It's not uncommon for one packet of the four to be lost; when the Internet gets congested, sometimes `ping` packets are discarded as unimportant. If any come back, the intervening networks are working.

The third useful variation is to add the `-t` option. This makes `ping` run endlessly once per second until you press Ctrl+C. This is especially helpful if you're looking at indicator lights on your network hub, changing cables, and so on. The endless testing lets you just watch the screen to see whether any changes you make cause a difference.

`ping` is a great quick test of connectivity to any location. If the `ping` test fails, use `tracert` or `pathping` to tell you where the problem is. `ping` is a good, quick tool to use to discover whether an Internet site is alive. (However, some large companies have made their servers not respond to `ping` tests. `ping www.microsoft.com` doesn't work ever, even with a good Internet connection. It's not just that Microsoft got tired of being the first site everyone thought of to test their Internet connections; malicious people also can use `ping` to suck up all of a company's Internet bandwidth).

TRACERT

`tracert` is similar to `ping`: It sends packets to a remote host and sees whether packets return. However, `tracert` adds a wrinkle: It checks the connectivity to each individual router in the path between you and the remote host. (Routers are the devices that connect one network to another. The Internet itself is the conglomeration of a few million networks all connected by routers.) If your computer and Internet connection are working but you still can't reach some or all Internet sites, `tracert` can help you find the blockage.

In the output of `tracert`, the address it tests first is your local network's gateway (if you connect to the Internet via a high-speed connection or a LAN) or the modem-answering equipment at your ISP's office (if you're using a dial-up connection). If this first address responds, you know that your modem, LAN, or broadband connection is working. If the connection stops after two or three routers, the problem is in your ISP's network. If the problem occurs farther out, there might be an Internet outage somewhere else in the country.

Here's an example that shows the route between my network and the fictitious web server www.fictitious.net. Typing

```
C:\> tracert www.fictitious.net
```

returns the following:

```
Tracing route to www.fictitious.com [204.179.107.3]
over a maximum of 30 hops:

  1    <10 ms    <10 ms    <10 ms  190.mycompany.com [202.201.200.190]
  2    <10 ms    <10 ms     10 ms  129.mycompany.com [202.201.200.129]
```

```
3     20 ms    20 ms    20 ms    w001.z216112073.sjc-ca.dsl.cnc.net [216.112.73.1]
4     10 ms    10 ms    10 ms    206.83.66.153
5     10 ms    10 ms    10 ms    rt001f0801.sjc-ca.concentric.net [206.83.90.161]
6     10 ms    20 ms    20 ms    us-ca-sjc-core2-f5-0.rtr.concentric.net [205.158.11.133]
7     10 ms    20 ms    10 ms    us-ca-sjc-core1-g4-0-0.rtr.concentric.net [205.158.10.2]
8     10 ms    20 ms    20 ms    us-ca-pa-core1-a9-0d1.rtr.concentric.net [205.158.11.14]
9     10 ms    20 ms    20 ms    ATM2-0-0.br2.pao1.ALTER.NET [137.39.23.189]
10    10 ms    20 ms    20 ms    125.ATM3-0.XR1.PAO1.ALTER.NET [152.63.49.170]
11    10 ms    10 ms    20 ms    289.at-1-0-0.XR3.SCL1.ALTER.NET [152.63.49.98]
12    20 ms    20 ms    20 ms    295.ATM8-0-0.GW2.SCL1.ALTER.NET [152.63.48.113]
13    20 ms    20 ms    20 ms    2250-gw.customer.ALTER.NET [157.130.193.14]
14    41 ms    30 ms    20 ms    www.fictitious.com [204.179.107.3]
Trace complete.
```

You can see that between my computer and this web server, data passes through 13 intermediate routers owned by two ISPs.

> **TIP**
>
> As I mentioned at the start of the chapter, when your Internet connection is working, run `tracert` to trace the path between your computer and a few Internet hosts. Print and save the listings. Someday when you're having Internet problems, you can use these listings as a baseline reference. It's very helpful to know whether packets are stopping in your LAN, in your ISP's network, or beyond when you pick up the phone to yell about it.

I should point out a couple of `tracert` oddities. First, notice in the example that on the command line I typed www.fictitious.net, but `tracert` printed www.fictitious.com. That's not unusual. Web servers sometimes have alternative names. `tracert` starts with a reverse name lookup to find the *canonical* (primary) name for a given IP address.

You might run into another glitch as well. For security reasons, many organizations use firewall software or devices, which block `tracert` packets at the firewall between their LAN and the Internet. In these instances, `tracert` will never reach its intended destination, even when regular communications are working correctly. Instead, you'll see an endless list that looks similar to this:

```
14     *        *        *     Request timed out.
15     *        *        *     Request timed out.
16     *        *        *     Request timed out.
```

This continues up to the `tracert` limit of 30 probes. If this happens, just press Ctrl+C to cancel the test. If `tracert` could reach routers outside your own LAN or PC, your equipment and Internet connection are fine—and that's all you can directly control.

PATHPING

`pathping` is relatively new to the Windows toolkit, having first appeared in Windows 2000. It provides the function of `tracert` and adds a more intensive network traffic test. `pathping` performs the route-tracing function faster than `tracert` because it sends only one test packet per hop, compared to `tracert`'s three.

After determining the route, `pathping` does a punishing test of network traffic at each router by sending 100 `ping` packets to each router in the path between you and the host you're testing. It measures the number of lost packets and the average round-trip time for each hop, and it displays the results in a table.

The results tell you which routers are experiencing congestion because they cannot return every echo packet they're sent, and they might take some time to do it. Performing the `pathping` test can take quite awhile. Fortunately, you can cancel the test by pressing Ctrl+C, or you can specify command-line options to shorten the test. A reasonably quick test of the path to a site—say, www.quepublishing.com—can be performed using just 10 queries instead of the default 100 using this command:

```
pathping -q 10 www.quepublishing.com
```

You can type

pathping /?

to get a full description of the command-line options.

ROUTE

Most of us have no more than one modem or one LAN adapter through which we make our Internet and other network connections, but Windows Networking components are sophisticated enough to handle multiple LAN and dial-up adapters in one computer. When multiple connections are made, Windows has to know which connections to use to speak with another remote computer. For the TCP/IP or Internet Protocol (IP) data, this information comes from the routing table. This table stores lists of IP addresses and subnets (blocks of IP addresses) and also indicates which adapter (or interface) Windows used to reach each of them.

Now, this is getting into some hardcore networking that only a few readers will be interested in. Please don't think that you need to know about this tool; there will be no quiz next Friday. I'm discussing this only to cover the details for those few people who have a complex network setup and need to know how to go to this information. You don't have to worry about routing unless one of the following scenarios is true:

- You use a dial-up connection and a LAN adapter simultaneously.
- You use multiple LAN adapters.
- You use virtual private networking (VPN) connections, as discussed in Chapter 38, "Hitting the Road."

If you have trouble reaching an Internet destination and fall into any of these three categories, type **route** at the command line. You're shown a table that looks similar to this:

```
===========================================================================
Interface List
 10 ...00 03 ff d0 ca 5f ...... Intel 21140-Based PCI Fast Ethernet Adapter
  1 ........................... Software Loopback Interface 1
 13 ...00 00 00 00 00 00 00 e0  isatap.{3C3E0C23-191B-4E11-9713-97D239EA2995}
 11 ...02 00 54 55 4e 01 ...... Teredo Tunneling Pseudo-Interface
===========================================================================
```

```
IPv4 Route Table
===========================================================================
Active Routes:
Network Destination        Netmask          Gateway       Interface  Metric
          0.0.0.0          0.0.0.0     192.168.15.1  192.168.15.106      20
        127.0.0.0        255.0.0.0          On-link       127.0.0.1     306
        127.0.0.1  255.255.255.255          On-link       127.0.0.1     306
  127.255.255.255  255.255.255.255          On-link       127.0.0.1     306
     192.168.15.0    255.255.255.0          On-link  192.168.15.106     276
   192.168.15.106  255.255.255.255          On-link  192.168.15.106     276
   192.168.15.255  255.255.255.255          On-link  192.168.15.106     276
        224.0.0.0        240.0.0.0          On-link       127.0.0.1     306
        224.0.0.0        240.0.0.0          On-link  192.168.15.106     276
  255.255.255.255  255.255.255.255          On-link       127.0.0.1     306
  255.255.255.255  255.255.255.255          On-link  192.168.15.106     276
===========================================================================
Persistent Routes:
  None

IPv6 Route Table
...
```

(You can ignore the IPv6 section for now.)

There's a lot of information here, but for our purpose, we can boil it down to this: The entry for network destination 0.0.0.0 is the effective gateway address for general Internet destinations. This can be different from your LAN's specified default gateway, especially while a dial-up or VPN connection is active. That, in turn, might mean that you can't get to the Internet. If you have multiple LAN adapters, the issues are more complicated. Contact your network administrator for assistance.

→ If the gateway address is incorrect after you've made a dial-up connection, see "Routing Issues," **p. 1296**.

Third-Party Utilities

In addition to the utilities provided with Windows, you can use some third-party tools to help diagnose your connection and gather Internet information. I describe three web-based utilities and one commercial software package.

Speed Check

Ever wondered how to find the real-world transfer rate of your Internet connection? Intel Corporation has a nifty web-based program to measure transfer speeds using an Adobe (formerly Shockwave) Flash applet. Check out www.intel.com/personal/digital-life/broadband. (Every time I put this URL into print, Intel seems to feel the need to change it. If you get a "Page not found" error, search the Intel site for "broadband speed test.")

You can find other speed test sites at www.dslreports.com. Click on Tools and then Speed Tests.

whois Database

Anyone registering an Internet domain name is required to file contact information with a domain registry. This is public information, and you can use it to find out how to contact the owners of a domain whose customers have sent spam mail or with whom you have other concerns.

Finding the registrar for a given domain name can be cumbersome. You can find the registrar information for any .aero, .arpa, .biz, .com, .coop, .edu, .info, .int, .museum, .net, or .org domain via the following web page:

www.internic.net/whois.html

The search results from this page indicate the URL of the whois lookup page for the associated domain registrar. Enter the domain name again on that page, and you should see the contact information.

It's a bit harder to find the registrar associated with two-letter country code domains ending in, for example, .au, .de, .it, and so on. The InterNIC site recommends searching through www.uwhois.com.

You can find the owner of an IP address through a similar lookup at www.arin.net/whois. Enter an IP address to find the owner of the block of IP addresses from which the specific address was allocated. This is usually an ISP or, in some cases, an organization that has had IP addresses assigned to it directly.

Reverse tracert

As I discussed earlier, the tracert program investigates the path that data you send through the Internet takes to reach another location. Interestingly, data coming back to you can take a different path. Users of some satellite Internet service know this already because their outbound data goes through a modem, although incoming data arrives by satellite. This can happen even with standard Internet service, depending on the way your ISP has set up its own internal network.

It's handy to know the path data takes coming to you. If you record this information while your Internet connection is working, if you run into trouble, you can have a friend perform a tracert to you. (You need to give him your IP address, which you can find using the ipconfig command.) If the results differ, you might be able to tell whether the problem is with your computer, your ISP, or the Internet.

You can visit www.traceroute.org for a list of hundreds of web servers that can perform a traceroute test from their site to you. Don't be surprised if the test results take a while to appear; these tests typically take a minute or longer.

WS_Ping Pro Pack

If you want to be well equipped to handle Internet and general networking problems, you can buy third-party utilities that are much easier to use than the standard ones built into Windows. I like WS_Ping ProPack from Ipswitch Software (www.ipswitch.com). This one utility packs almost all the TCP/IP tools into one graphical interface and adds other features such as `whois` for domain-registration lookups, SNMP probing, and network scanning. The program can be used for free for 30 days, after which the registration fee is $44.95 U.S. for a single-user license. I rarely use third-party add-ons such as this, but this particular program is on my "must have" list.

Tips from the Windows Pros: Pinging with Larger Packets

I have a DSL connection in my office, and one night it appeared that my Internet connection had stopped working. After a closer look, I saw that only downstream communication was affected, meaning that my browser could contact websites, but information from the Web wasn't reaching my computer.

I first tried `pinging` my ISP at the gateway address of my DSL modem. It worked just fine. In fact, I could `ping` any site in the entire Internet but still could not view a single web page. I called my Internet service provider, and they found out that `pings` from their network into my LAN worked, too. The guy I spoke to suggested that I must have a software problem.

That didn't make sense to me, especially because everything had been working perfectly just minutes before. Then I had a hunch. By default, `ping` sends very small packets: 32 bytes each, plus a few bytes of IP packet packaging. Requests for web pages are very small, too (maybe 100 bytes). However, responses from web servers are big and come in the largest packets possible—about 1,500 bytes each. Perhaps, the problem wasn't with the direction the data was going. Instead, the size of the data could be causing the problem: If there were a lot of interference on my DSL line, small packets might have made it through between bursts of electrical interference, but larger packets might have been garbled.

I vaguely remembered that `ping` has a bunch of command-line options, so I looked up "ping" in Windows Help and saw that I could increase the size of its packets with the `-l` option. Typing

```
ping -l 300 www.someplace.com
```

tells `ping` to send 300-byte packets. Aha! I found that only about 50% of these packets made the roundtrip. When I sent 500-byte packets, the success rate dropped to 10%. When I called tech support with this news, the guy at my ISP tried the same test, and got the same result when he tried to `ping` my computer from his network. Now we knew that there was a physical problem that the ISP was responsible for fixing.

That problem was eventually fixed, but still every month or so my Internet connection seems to bog down. Usually, this lasts only a minute or two because of random Internet happenings, but sometimes it slows down and stays slow. When this happens, I `ping` the gateway address to see what the round-trip time is. For my connection, this is normally about 20ms. For reasons I still don't understand, occasionally this jumps to more than 4,000ms (more than 4 seconds) and stays there. I have to power-cycle my DSL modem to return to normal response times.

The moral of this story is that it pays to be familiar with your friendly neighborhood command-line utilities.

CHAPTER 18

HOSTING WEB PAGES WITH INTERNET INFORMATION SERVICES

In this chapter

Overview of Internet Information Services 7.0   554

IIS Services and Requirements   558

Installing IIS   562

Setting Up a Simple Website   567

Managing Your Site with the Computer Management Console   569

Managing the FTP Server   575

Log Files   580

Making the Site Available on the Internet   580

Security Issues for Internet Services   582

Troubleshooting   584

Tips from the Windows Pros: Scripting for Interactive Sites   585

Overview of Internet Information Services 7.0

Internet Information Services (IIS) 7.0 is a collection of programs and services that make up Microsoft's industrial-strength IIS web server platform. Besides acting as a web (HTTP) server, it includes a File Transfer Protocol (FTP) server, the ASP script processor, management tools, and support for sophisticated web-based services. Microsoft primarily makes IIS available on Windows Vista for software developers to use as a test and development platform, but you can also use IIS to host a website for your business or family, for a private or public audience.

IIS is unusual among Vista's many optional features, in that it's available on almost all versions of Windows Vista, but in varying levels of completeness. Table 18.1 shows the breakdown.

Table 18.1 IIS Availability in Windows Vista Versions

Vista Version	IIS Availability
Starter, Home Basic	Some IIS components are present, but not enough to run a stand-alone web server. The components that are present are there only to support future advanced software applications. If you have Home Basic or the Starter edition, this chapter doesn't apply to you. (Windows Vista Starter is sold only in emerging markets.)
Home Premium	Enough of IIS is available to run a small web server. Some advanced features are not available. I'll discuss these features shortly.
Ultimate Business Enterprise	All IIS components are available. Connection restrictions still exist, as noted shortly.

In the Home Basic and Starter versions, the core server components that deliver static and dynamic web pages are missing; all that is present are the parts that enable .NET applications to be activated and operated through a web-based network connection.

On Windows Vista Home Premium, the most significant missing component is the FTP server. This means that you have to copy your website's content (HTML files and pictures) into the web server's "shared" folder on your computer manually instead of transferring it using the FTP network service that editor programs such as Microsoft FrontPage usually use. This should be a relatively minor inconvenience.

On Windows Vista Ultimate and the business versions, all IIS components are present. However, limitations still govern the number of visitors you are allowed to host, as I'll discuss later in the chapter under "IIS Services and Requirements."

> **CAUTION**
>
> If you are part of a corporate network, before you go any further, check with your network administrators; policies might prohibit you from setting up a website on your own. Many legitimate security concerns are involved, and in some companies, you could be fired for violating established security policies. Check first if you're not sure what's permitted. You might also find that your company's network administrator has locked access to the Windows Components or Windows Firewall control panels, so you might not be able to install IIS.

While I'm on the subject of warnings, one more is important enough that I repeat it later in the chapter:

> **CAUTION**
>
> Installing Internet Information Services might sound like fun, but don't install it unless you're really sure you need it and are willing to keep up with its frequent bug fixes and maintenance alerts. IIS has been one of Microsoft's biggest sources of strange and dangerous security flaws. All sophisticated services come with a measure of risk, and IIS is *very* sophisticated.
>
> Microsoft has produced some tools to help you keep up-to-date on IIS security; visit www.microsoft.com/technet/security. Be sure to sign up for the security bulletin service.
>
> Also be sure to visit www.microsoft.com/technet/iis to get up-to-date information about IIS security and management techniques.

Now I take you on a brief tour of what a web server actually does. If you already are familiar with the function of web servers, you can skip ahead to "IIS Services and Requirements."

What Does a Web Server Do?

In the most basic sense, a web server works like a call desk librarian: When you request a book by name, the librarian looks up the book's location, fetches the desired tome, passes it across the counter, and goes on to the next patron as quickly as possible. If the desired book is not in the shelves, the librarian says so and again goes on to the next client. The interactions are brief and involve no interpretation of the content—that is, the content of the book—passing back and forth.

The roles of a web server and a web browser are very similar. A web browser sends a short request message to a web server. The request is a text string, mostly just the uniform resource locator (URL) that you typed in or clicked. The server turns this "virtual" filename into the real, physical name of a file stored on its disk and passes the appropriate HTML, image, or other type of file back across the Internet. When the URL refers to an executable program or a script file, instead of returning the file itself, a web server runs the program and passes back whatever the program generates as its response. The web browser displays the result.

A Directory by Any Other Name...

The translation of a URL filename into a physical filename is generally straightforward. When you set up your website, you specify which directory (folder) contains the documents that you want to publish. The website has a *home directory*, which is the starting point for the translation of URL names into filenames. For example, if the home directory is `C:\inetpub\wwwroot`, the URL filename

`/index.html`

returns this file:

`C:\inetpub\wwwroot\index.html`

Any file or folder inside the home directory is available to web browsers. For example, the URL

`/sales/catalog.html`

would return this file:

`C:\inetpub\wwwroot\sales\catalog.html`

You can add other folders on your computer to this mapping, even if they aren't below the home directory or its subfolders. They are called *virtual directories* because, to web visitors, they *appear* to be part of the home directory structure, but they aren't physically. You could instruct IIS to share the folder `C:\partlist` with the virtual URL name of `/parts` so that the URL

`/parts/index.html`

would return the file

`C:\partlist\index.html`

instead of this:

`C:\inetpub\wwwroot\parts\index.html`

Web servers can also use a process called *redirection*, in which the server is told to make a virtual directory whose content is stored on another web server. When a web browser requests a file in a redirected virtual directory, the web server tells the browser program to fetch the file from the other server (or an alternate location on the same server). Redirection is useful when you rearrange your site—you can let visitors that are using old URLs obtained from a search engine retrieve the pages they want, even though they're now stored in a new location.

Default Documents

In Web-speak, a *home page* is a URL that lists a server name but no filename, as in www.ibm1130.org. So what does an empty or home page URL map to? For example, what file does www.ibm1130.org refer to? You might guess that it corresponds to the name of the server's home directory:

`C:\inetpub\wwwroot`

Indeed, it does, but this doesn't specify a filename, so the server has no content to return. By tradition, in this case web servers look inside the named folder for a *default document*, using a predetermined name or list of names. IIS 7.0 looks first for a file named `default.htm`. If that file exists, it's returned as the URL's content. If `default.htm` doesn't exist, IIS looks for `default.asp`, `index.htm`, `index.html`, `iisstart.htm`, and finally `default.aspx`, in turn. If a file by one of these names is found, it's returned as the content for the URL. The order is important to know: If you put files named `index.html` and `default.html` in your web directory, web visitors will see the content of `index.html`, not `default.html`. (Of course, you can change this list or its order after you've installed IIS.) You can imagine that many web authors have spent hours wondering why the changes they're making to their website aren't seen when viewed in a web browser—it's because they're updating the wrong default document file.

If no default document can be found, by default, IIS gives up and returns an error message to the visitor. However, you can enable a feature called *directory browsing* on a folder-by-folder basis. When directory browsing is enabled, IIS returns a listing of all the files in the folder. This can be very useful if you're setting up a website folder as a file repository; just putting files in the folders makes them available to visitors.

MIMEs Make It Happen

Web browsers must be told how to interpret the content returned by the server. They don't know in advance whether they're going to get HTML text, a Microsoft Word document, an image, or something else. Windows determines a file's type from the end of its filename—for example, `.doc` or `.html`, but this system isn't universally used by other operating systems, and the Web was designed specifically to encourage cooperation among different computers and operating systems. A standardized naming scheme thus was developed for the Web. Web servers tell web browsers how to interpret content using a name called a *MIME type*. MIME stands for Multipurpose Internet Mail Extensions.

MIME type names are agreed-upon Internet standards, and it's the web server's job to know how to label each of the files it shares. When it's sending files, IIS uses the Windows File Types Registry to map file types such as `.doc` and `.html` into the corresponding MIME types, and you can add to the list any special types of files you share.

To Run or Not to Run

When a URL refers to a program file, a web server can send you the program file itself, as it does with all other content files, so you can save or run it on your computer. This happens every time you download a program or software update.

However, the web server can also run the program on *its* side and return the program's output to you. This second option produces what is called *dynamic web content*. Whereas web pages stored in HTML files are *static* and change only when their owner edits them, *dynamic* web pages are generated from scratch every time they're viewed and thus can contain interactive, up-to-the minute information. Programs on the server's side can do virtually anything: search libraries, access your bank account, buy airline tickets or music, fetch email, or move robots on the moon, and then return the results to you as a web page. In fact, this flexibility is *the* crucial feature that made the World Wide Web grow from a scientific document library system into, well, a worldwide phenomenon.

These page-generating programs are generically called *Common Gateway Interface (CGI)* programs, or *server-side scripts*, if they're written in a language such as Perl, JavaScript, VBScript, or another interpreted language. Useful CGI programs and scripts can be created with programming know-how, or can be purchased or downloaded.

For IIS, the distinction between "send the program file itself" and "run the program and return the output" is made by changing a web folder's `Read`, `Script`, and `Execute` attributes. Folders with the `Read` attribute treat scripts and executable programs as data to be returned directly. With the `Script` or `Execute` attributes set, scripts and programs, respectively, are run by the server, and their output is sent back to the person visiting your site.

Just to reassure you, you don't need to take advantage of all this complexity if you just want to publish some simple web pages and make files available to web visitors. IIS can publish web pages out-of-the box with no programming.

IIS Services and Requirements

Some parts of IIS 7.0 are included with all version of Windows. However, as discussed earlier, only Windows Vista Home Premium, Business, Enterprise, and Ultimate editions have enough of IIS to function as a useful web server. Vista Home Basic and Starter editions do have some components of IIS—notably, the Windows Process Activation Service—but they're there to provide support for yet-to-be-developed web-based peer-to-peer application software, not to act as a standalone web server.

IIS 7.0 has significant additions and improvements over versions 5.1 and 6.0, which shipped with earlier Windows products. The principal components of IIS 7.0 fall into several categories:

- World Wide Web Services, the core web server component that delivers static web page files. Several standard web server features can be enabled or disabled independently.
- Application Development Features, which delivers dynamic content. Options include support for CGI programs, scripting, and .NET web applications.
- Health and Diagnostics, which provides monitoring, tracing, logging, and debugging tools.
- Security, which provides various means for website visitors to prove that they're authorized to view restricted content. (Security features are limited on Vista Home Premium.)
- Performance Features, which provides means of compressing text and image data to improve delivery speeds and save on bandwidth use.
- Web Management Tools, various means of controlling and configuring the web server.

- FTP Publishing Service, which enables you and others to copy files and website content to your web server via the Internet-standard File Transfer Protocol. (The FTP Service is not available on Home Premium.)
- Windows Process Activation Service, which lets software applications on one computer start and communicate with applications on your computer via the Web's HTTP protocol.

These components are divided into more than 40 individually installable features. Such fine control makes it easy to block features that aren't ever used, thus reducing potential openings for hackers.

These features are the same as those provided with IIS on Microsoft's Windows Server products–based brethren, but the license agreement for Windows Vista restricts the use of your computer and any services it hosts, to a maximum of 10 concurrent connections. Microsoft's current interpretation of this limitation is that a website hosted by Windows Vista can handle, at most, 10 simultaneous requests.

The version of IIS software supplied with Windows Vista can also support multiple, separate websites with different names, called multiple *virtual domains*, which formerly was forbidden on all but Windows Server versions. This is an advanced feature that we don't cover here.

The bottom line is that it's legal to use Vista only for a low-volume site. Practically speaking, unless you're selling Viagra online or you get listed on slashdot, you probably don't have to worry about these limitations.

Do You *Really* Want to Do This?

Before going any further, consider this one more time: If you can get the hosting services you need from your Internet service provider (ISP), your corporate IS department, or just about anyone else, you probably don't want to bother with setting up your own web server. There's no glory in hosting your own website, just hard work. Web servers at an ISP have faster connections to the Internet, they're probably backed up every night, *and* some poor soul with a pager tied around his neck is probably on call 24×7 in case something goes wrong with the server. With low-volume websites to be had for as little as $5 U.S. a month, including domain name service (DNS), mailboxes, FTP, and FrontPage support, taking on this project yourself hardly seems worthwhile.

In addition, hosting a public World Wide Web site requires domain name service, which Windows Vista alone doesn't provide. Therefore, if you want your site to be accessible with a URL such as www.mysite.com, you still need someone else or an add-on product to provide DNS support. This support alone can cost nearly as much as a full-service website package, although there are free and discounted DNS services, too.

On the other hand, you might want to install IIS if you…

- Want to host in-house communication within your company or workgroup.
- Want to share files over the Internet using Web Sharing.

- Develop custom web programs or scripts, or use CGI programs that an ISP can't or won't provide.
- Want to write and preview web pages and applications before deploying them to an online site.
- Think that a chance to participate in this global Internet thing is just too cool to pass by, no matter how much work it is. (I have to admit that this was the initial reason *I* set up a web server, but that was more than 10 years ago, and I have no valid excuse now.)

Whatever your reason, IIS installed in all its glory gives you plenty to chew on.

Before You Get Started

Before you start to set up IIS itself, you have to take care of some requirements.

First of all, IIS consumes a fair bit of memory. Don't even think of installing it on your computer unless you have 1GB of RAM or more.

In addition, the folder or folders that hold the files that your web server will display must be located on an NTFS-formatted disk or disks so that Windows can use its file security features to protect both your programs and your web data. Otherwise, if you make the slightest mistake configuring IIS, it's quite possible for an outsider to take control of your computer and use it for nefarious purposes: sending spam, phishing for credit card numbers, or worse. Trust me on this—people are scanning the Internet constantly, using software that hunts for vulnerable computers. Don't be their next victim!

> **CAUTION**
>
> *Do not* install IIS unless the drive that holds Windows and the drive that holds your web content (which will be the same drive, in most cases) are formatted with NTFS.

Finally, you need adequate connectivity. If you only want to make web pages available to others in your own home or office, your computer just needs to be connected to a local area network. However, if you want to publish web pages on the Internet at large—that is, be part of the World Wide Web—you need an always-on Internet connection as well. After all, if your site is available only a few hours a day while you're dialed in to your ISP, few people will ever be able to see it. Full-time, dedicated service is much less expensive today than it was only a few years ago, and it can be had in most areas of the U.S. for less than $50 a month. (You can read about Internet connectivity in Chapter 14, "Getting Connected," and Chapter 22, "Connecting Your Network to the Internet.") For global availability, you also need domain name service, which I discuss in the next section.

Name Service

If you plan to use IIS just to develop and test web pages, or if you want to share pages on a home, office, or corporate network, you don't have to worry about your computer being visible to the Internet at large. But if you want to host a public website with Windows Vista, you need to arrange for an entry in the Internet's domain name service so that people can find your site using a standard name such as www.myfamouswebsite.com. This is the link between your website's name and the public IP address of your web server. Getting this set up is beyond the scope of this book, but here are a few tips:

- If your network has a Windows 200*x* Server, your network administrator can set up domain name service for you because a DNS server is included with these Server versions. Your site can use your company's domain name, or your company might be willing to host an alternative domain name for you. (This might happen if, say, you own the company. Otherwise, don't hold your breath.)

- If you use an always-on broadband Internet connection such as cable, DSL, satellite, or other dedicated link, you might want to see if you can get a permanent, static IP address from your Internet provider. (Some providers won't do this, some will, and some levy an additional charge.) A static address makes your life easier because the link between your domain name and your IP address can be set once and then left alone.

    Given a static address, your ISP might provide you with domain name service, or you might be able to buy this type of service from a commercial website provider for about $5 a month. Or, if you have the technical know-how, you might want to do a Google search for "free DNS service" and check out some of the listed providers.

- If you use a dial-up connection, DSL service that requires a username and password to connect, or DHCP-based cable Internet service, your IP address changes with each connection and you have to use a *dynamic DNS* service that automatically updates the link between your site's name and IP address every time the address changes. Dynamic DNS service is a little less convenient and reliable, which is why a static IP address is much more desirable. Still, you can check out dynamic DNS providers such as www.dyndns.org or www.tzo.com, or others listed at www.technopagan.org/dynamic. You'll need to install a Dynamic DNS Update Client program on your computer so that your computer's DNS name entry will be updated every time your IP address changes. Dyndns.org provides a free program called the Dynamic DNS Updater that will do this for you. It runs as a Windows service.

    In addition, some broadband-sharing routers have dynamic DNS capability built in. It usually appears in the Advanced setup menus and is sometimes listed under the name DDNS. The router can be told to send an update to one of several free DDNS providers whenever it gets assigned a new address. However, my experience has been that the software in the routers doesn't work as well as add-on software such as dyndns.org's Updater service.

- Unless you use a host and domain name provided by one of the dynamic DNS providers (which can get you a free domain name along the lines of brian.is-a-geek.com, or a custom domain name for a small annual fee), you also have to *register* a domain name with an Internet registry service. The original Internet registrar www.networksolutions.com charges about $35 per year. However, several other registry services (such as www.stargateinc.com and www.godaddy.com) charge $10 per year or less, with free (static) DNS included, so it pays to shop around. The only worry about working with any ultracheap registrars is that there's no telling if they will still be online next year. If they shut down, you might have a big problem getting your domain name transferred to another registrar; pick one that has been in business for a while.

Finally, if you use a shared Internet connection or a broadband router, you need to configure the sharing software or router to direct incoming website requests to the computer that's actually running IIS. I'll discuss this later in the chapter in the section "Making the Site Available on the Internet."

INSTALLING IIS

IIS has more than 40 optional components. However, many management and debugging options are of use only to web software developers and IT managers, so you don't need all the components. Describing them all and showing how to configure and use them would fill up most of this book, so instead I show you only what to do to set up a basic website with some scripting capability.

To install IIS, log on with an Administrator-level account. Then follow these steps:

1. Click Start, Control Panel, Programs, Turn Windows Features On or Off.
2. Scroll down the list of features and view Internet Information Services, as shown in Figure 18.1. Click the + signs to open the contents. You'll see many subcomponents, and most are not checked by default. Table 18.2 shows the list of components, with a description of what they're used for. For a basic website with scripting capability, check the exact list of items shown checked in the table.

Figure 18.1
Use Table 18.2 to select Internet Information Services components to install.

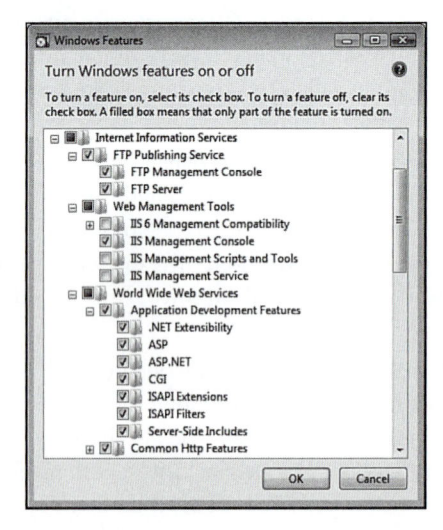

Table 18.2 Internet Information Services Components

Component	Install?	Function
FTP Publishing Service*	✓	See note following table.
FTP Management Console*	✓	Plug-in for Computer Management that manages the FTP service.
FTP Server*	✓	Enables you and/or others to transfer files to and from your computer using the FTP protocol.
Web Management Tools	∎	(∎ means that only some of the category's components will be installed.)
IIS 6 Management Compatibility		Enables you to manage IIS 7.0 using tools and scripts developed for IIS 6.0. Install this only if you have such tools that you don't want to give up.
IIS 6 Management Console		Computer Management snap-in, IIS 6 version.
IIS 6 Scripting Tools		IIS management scripting interfaces.
IIS 6 WMI Compatibility		WMI scripting interfaces.
IIS Metabase and IIS 6 Configuration Compatibility		IIS metabase (configuration file) compatibility. IIS 7 is configured using plain-text XML files.
IIS Management Console	✓	Computer Management snap-in, IIS 7 version.
IIS Management Scripts and Tools		Scripts and programs used to manage IIS from the command line.
IIS Management Service		IIS remote management support service.
World Wide Web Services	∎	
Application Development Features	✓	
.NET Extensibility	✓	Lets server host .NET Framework application.
ASP	✓	Lets server run ASP scripts.
ASP.NET	✓	Lets server run ASP.NET script applications.
CGI	✓	Lets server run CGI programs (`.exe` files).
ISAPI Extensions	✓	Lets server run ISAPI CGI programs (`.dll` files).

continues

Table 18.2 Continued

Component	Install?	Function
ISAPI Filters	✓	Lets server run ISAPI filter programs.
Server-Side Includes	✓	Lets server process `.shtml` files for limited dynamic content.
Common HTTP Features	✓	The basic parts of the web server, with several optional components:
Default Document	✓	Lets IIS search for `default.html` or `index.html`, for example, when only a folder name is passed in the URL.
Directory Browsing	✓	Lets you instruct IIS to list directory contents when no default document is found.
HTTP Errors	✓	Lets IIS return customizable documents to describe errors.
HTTP Redirection	✓	Lets IIS redirect requests to alternate URLs.
Static Content	✓	Lets IIS return static files (for example, HTML files).
Health and Diagnostics	■	
Custom Logging		Enables you to develop custom formats to log requests.
HTTP Logging	✓	Enables standard IIS log file format.
Logging Tools	✓	Installs IIS 7.0 logging tools and scripts.
ODBC Logging*		Lets IIS write logs to an ODBC database.
Request Monitor	✓	Provides debugging support.
Tracing		Enables logging of internal flow of information.
Performance Features	■	
HTTP Compression Dynamic		Enables compression of dynamically generated content.
Static Content Compression	✓	Enables compression of static (file-based) content. For bulky text files, this can speed transmission and lower bandwidth usage.

Component	Install?	Function
Security	■	
Basic Authentication		Permits use of unencrypted usernames and passwords. Not recommended.
Client Certificate Mapping Authentication		Used only on corporate (domain) networks.
Digest Authentication*		Lets IIS use Windows usernames/passwords and NTFS permissions over the Internet on Windows domain computers.
IIS Client Certificate Mapping Authentication*		Used only on corporate (domain) networks.
IP Security		Lets IIS permit or deny access based on IP address.
Request Filtering	✓	Lets IIS use rules to selectively permit or deny requests.
URL Authorization		Lets IIS define user-based access to URLs.
Windows Authentication*	✓	Lets IIS use Windows domain usernames/passwords and NTFS file permissions to control access to content over the local network.

*Feature not available in Windows Vista Home Premium Edition.

NOTE

> FTP enables you and/or remote users to retrieve or deliver files to your computer. FTP has some serious security implications. If you will be copying your web content into the home folder on your own computer directly, you don't need FTP. If you use a web page editor such as FrontPage, you might want to install FTP so that it can copy the files into the web folder for you. However, be sure to read the configuration notes in the section titled 'Managing the FTP Server" later in this chapter.

3. After you've selected all the desired IIS components, click OK.

When the installation procedure is finished—and this is the most important step—click Start, All Programs, Windows Update, and have Windows Update install any available critical security fixes for IIS.

Opening the Firewall

After you've installed IIS, you can check to see whether it has been installed correctly by opening Internet Explorer and typing this URL into the address bar: //localhost. This tells IE to look for the website hosted on your own computer. You should see a picture that says "Welcome" in several languages. If you click it, you're taken to Microsoft's website.

At this point, however, your web server is functional but isn't reachable by anyone else; oddly enough, the IIS installation procedure doesn't create an exception in Windows Firewall. You need to do this manually by following these steps:

1. Log on as a Computer Administrator user.
2. Click Start, Control Panel, Allow a Program Through Windows Firewall.
3. Click Continue when User Account Control pops up.
4. Click Add Port.
5. For Name, type `Web Server`. For Port Number, type `80`.
6. If you want your site to (eventually) be accessible to the Internet at large, or if you are on a large corporate network and the entire company should have access, skip to Step 8.
7. If your website is just for use in your own home or small office, click Change Scope and select My Subnet (Network) Only; then click OK.
8. Click OK to close the Add a Port dialog box.
9. If you have installed the FTP service and want to make it available as well, repeat Steps 4 through 8 twice more. Type `FTP Server` for the name both times. For the port, enter `20` the first time and `21` the second time.
10. Click OK to close the Firewall dialog box.

Check to be sure that other users on your network can view your website by going to another computer, opening Internet Explorer, and viewing the URL http://*machinename*, where *machinename* is the name you assigned to your computer. On a corporate LAN, your network manager will set up the necessary DNS information so that your computer can be viewed using a URL such as the previous one, or using a more standard http://*name.domain* format. Later in the chapter, in the section titled "Making the Site Available on the Internet," I'll talk about making the site available to the Internet at large.

> **TIP**
>
> To find your computer's name, right-click Computer and select Properties. The computer name is shown under the title Computer Name, Domain and Workgroup Settings.

If other computer users can't view your web page, see "Other Computers Can't Reach the Site," in the "Troubleshooting" section at the end of this chapter.

Setting File Permissions

One last step is needed. By default, the home directory for your website is the folder `C:\inetpub\wwwroot`. (The drive letter might be different if you installed Windows onto a drive other than `C:`). This folder is protected by permissions that permit only an Administrator user to create files in it. The problem with this is that when only Administrators can write files, the files must be written by a program running with elevated privileges; that is, the program must have been run with Run As Administrator. For example, you can locate Windows Explorer, right-click it, and select Run As Administrator. Then you can drag or copy files from another location into `\inetpub\wwwroot`.

This can quickly get tedious. Although it does diminish security somewhat, on Windows Vista Ultimate, Business, and Enterprise, you can set the home directory's permissions so that you have permission to read and write files in this folder. Follow these steps while logged on as a Computer Administrator:

1. Click Start, All Programs, Accessories, Windows Explorer.
2. Browse to `C:\inetpub`.
3. Right-click wwwroot and select Properties.
4. Select the Security tab.
5. Click Edit; when the UAC dialog box appears, click Continue.
6. Click Add, then Advanced, then Find Now.
7. Locate your account name and double-click it.
8. Click OK.
9. In the Permissions section, click Full Control and then click OK.

(On Windows Vista Home Premium, you cannot perform these steps unless you boot the computer in Safe Mode, so you might as well just use the privileged Explorer technique I mentioned earlier.)

Setting Up a Simple Website

As installed in the previous section, IIS is ready to serve up static web pages and images.

If you have files from an existing website, or if you can create and edit HTML files yourself, you can simply copy them into the home directory `C:\inetpub\wwwroot` and any subfolders you want to create. As discussed earlier under "Default Documents," the default page filename is `default.htm`, so give this name to your home page file and delete the file `\inetpub\wwwroot\iisstart.htm` that the installation procedure put there.

You might want to use a web page–editing program such as FrontPage or Dreamweaver. Microsoft might also decide to produce a photo slideshow–publishing wizard for Windows Vista, similar to the one that was distributed as one of the Windows XP PowerToys. If you use one of these tools, by all means, use them; they're a great way to create visually pleasing website content. Microsoft Word can also create web pages (using a Save As HTML or Publish to Web option), but the pages tend to be poorly formatted and tend to display correctly only when viewed in Internet Explorer.

The tricky part with any of these tools is that, for the most part, these programs expect to edit the website's files on a computer that's separate from the web server. That is, they store the HTML files in files and folders on your hard disk, and expect you to copy the content to a web server using a "publish" feature that uses the File Transfer Protocol (FTP) or Microsoft's WebDAV protocol to reach the server computer.

When the content files are being edited, the links between web pages and from web pages to pictures can be stored with these hard disk locations "hard-coded" into the files. The editor program expects to be able to fix up the links as it copies the files during the Publish procedure. If you copy the edited files to \inetpub\wwwroot manually, the links *might* not work, depending on the way that your web page editor works. Getting around this problem might be a bit tricky, depending on what version of Windows Vista you have:

- If you have Windows Vista Ultimate, Business, or Enterprise, you may have installed the FTP service in the previous section. Later in this chapter under "Managing the FTP Server," I show you how to configure the FTP service to enable you to copy your web pages using your editor's normal Publish procedure.

- If you have Windows Vista Home Premium, no FTP service was provided with Windows. Therefore, you have to copy the files to your web server folder manually. I recommend that you instruct your web page editor to create its files in \inetpub\wwwroot to begin with. This is the easiest way to go. You'll be editing your site "live," and people who visit it while you're in the middle of making changes might get broken links. But this shouldn't be a significant problem for a small site.

If you're the impatient type, as I am, you might want to create a quick-and-dirty web page to see your web server get into action right away, just to prove to yourself that you really do have a web server up and running. If you want to try this, follow these steps:

1. Select Start, All Programs, Accessories.
2. Right-click Notepad and select Run As Administrator. Click Continue when the UAC dialog box appears.
3. Type the following text:
```
<HTML>
<HEAD>
<TITLE>This is My Home Page</TITLE>
</HEAD>
<BODY>
Welcome to my completely spiffy new website, hosted by Windows Vista!
</BODY>
</HTML>
```
Be especially careful to get the angle brackets (< and >) right and to use the forward slash (/), not the backslash (\).

4. Select File, Save As, and enter `C:\inetpub\wwwroot\default.htm` as the filename. Click OK.

5. View http://localhost in Internet Explorer.

You have produced your very own home page. It's not much to look at, but you can now honestly say you've coded a web page by hand. This will impress people.

Finally, remember that IIS can deliver more than static web pages. I talk about dynamic web pages and scripting in the next section, and in the "Tips from the Windows Pros" section at the end of this chapter.

Managing Your Site with the Computer Management Console

You manage your web server with the Internet Information Services management plug-in. You can get to it in two easy ways:

- Click Start, right-click Computer, and select Manage. Look under Services and Applications for the entry titled Internet Information Services (IIS) Manager. This item manages the web server. If you installed the FTP service, there will also be an entry titled Internet Information Services (IIS) 6.0 Manager. This item manages the FTP server.

- If you've customized your Start menu so that it displays Administrative Tools, just click Start, All Programs, Administrative Tools. The Internet Information Services item(s) will be available here.

I discuss the web server manager in this section and the FTP server manager in the following section.

> **TIP**
>
> The Internet Information Services (IIS) Manager is rather strangely laid out. To use it effectively, your screen resolution should be set to at least 1024×768, and preferably greater. Maximize the window. If you are viewing it in the Computer Management window, it also helps to click the Show/Hide Console Tree button, fourth from the left in the toolbar, and the Show/Hide Action Pane button (rightmost in the toolbar). This removes some of the clutter. You can get a bit more display space if you click View, Customize and uncheck Action Pane. Then drag the vertical pane dividers left and right as necessary to make the contents readable.

Figure 18.2 shows the manager window after arranging it as described in the preceding tip.

Figure 18.2
The Internet Information Services (IIS) Manager contains icons or all the installed IIS 7.0 web server components.

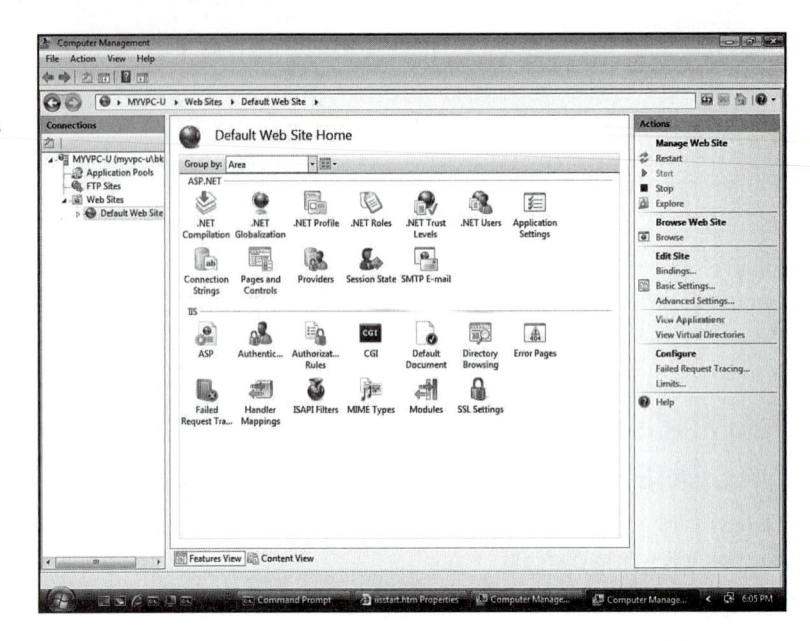

In this Control Panel–like view of the IIS components, you can take complete control of IIS's behavior, down to its treatment of individual files.

Important IIS Settings and Components

Most of the components in the Internet Information Service (IIS) Manager are of interest only to application developers and corporate web server managers. For a simple web server, you might not need to make any changes.

At the bottom of the window are tabs labeled Features View and Content View. With Content View selected, the center pane shows the contents of folders selected in the left pane. Features View lets you set properties that apply to whatever item was most recently selected in Content View or the left "tree" pane.

Many of the icons that control IIS properties can be edited not only for the web server as a whole, but for individual files or subfolders. When you select a server, a folder, or a file, you can set properties for that item and all items it contains, unless you make further changes to any lower-level items. Selecting individual files also can be sort of tricky. Here's how to adjust the settings for various scopes:

- To set a property for your entire website, select Default Website in the Connections pane at the left. Then, using the Features View, double-click the desired component icon.
- To set a property for a folder and its contents, locate it in the Connections Pane under Default Website. Then, using Features View, double-click the desired icon.
- To set a property for a single file, select Content View. Locate and select the desired file. Switch to Features View, and double-click the desired icon.

> **TIP**
> When you've finished viewing or changing the information for one of the component icons, click the *circular* left arrow (Back) button in the upper-left corner of the window to get back to the list of icons.

The following sections cover the most important settings and components. In most cases, when you have entered new information, you need to click Apply in the rightmost Actions pane to save the changes.

Physical Path

The folder that the web server publishes by default is `\inetpub\wwwroot`, on the drive on which Windows is installed. This is called the web server's *physical path*. Only contents of wwwroot and any of its subdirectories, along with any virtual directories that you designate, are made available to web browsers.

If you need to change this "starting" folder, right-click Default Website in the left Connections pane and select Advanced Settings. You can enter a different physical path in the Advanced Settings dialog box.

> **CAUTION**
> If you change the physical path, be *sure* to check the file access permissions set on the new folder so that you are sure that remote visitors cannot write any changes to the website content.

Authentication

If you want to be able to restrict what files or subfolders visitors can see on your web server, double-click Authentication. Right-click Windows Authentication and select Enable. Now you can set NTFS (file) permissions on the files in `\inetpub\wwwroot` to restrict viewing to authorized users only. (For this to work, you must make sure that Everyone does not have read permission on the files. This should be the case already, but if you upgraded a copy of Windows 2000 or XP that had IIS installed, you might need to modify these permissions.)

> **CAUTION**
> If you've set up your web server to exclude people from accessing certain files or other content, *always* test it immediately afterward by trying to view the secured content from another computer, using someone else's user account, if necessary. Always prove to yourself that what you think can't happen really can't happen.
>
> Remember, if someone can't access something they need to, they'll tell you about it right away. But if someone can access something they're not supposed to, you won't hear about it until it's too late.

If *anonymous access* is enabled in the web or FTP server, these servers can grant access to users who provide no username or password. Anonymous access is the most common form of website access, and it's enabled by default for the web service. You have to explicitly enable it for the FTP service. (That turns out to be a complex topic, which we'll discuss later in the chapter under "Managing the FTP Server."

If anonymous web access is enabled, by default, site visitors who provide no user credentials are assigned to the built-in account named IUSR, which is implicitly a member of the pre-defined Users group. (You can change the user account that is used for anonymous access, but that's beyond the scope of this book.)

Thus, to grant access to a folder or file to anonymous web browsers, it must have read access by user IUSR or group Users. By default, all files in \inetpub\wwwroot are given read permission by Users and are thus readable by anyone in the world. To block anonymous access, then, you can disable anonymous access by editing the web server's propreties, or you can edit the security properties of specific files and folders, and either remove the read permissions for group Users or add a "deny read" access entry for IUSR.

If you enable anonymous access in the FTP server, anonymous access is performed using an account named IUSR_*machinename*, where *machinename* is the name of your computer, which is created when you install the FTP service. Files that are marked as readable by user IUSR_*machinename* are thus readable via FTP by anyone in the world. By default IUSR_*machinename* is not granted rights to any folder, so you have to explicitly grant permission to IUSR_*machinename* to grant anonymous access to files via FTP.

> **NOTE**
>
> If Microsoft upgrades the FTP server that is provided with Windows Vista from the IIS 6 version to the IIS 7 version, then the FTP service will no longer use IUSR_*machinename*, but will use account IUSR and group IIS_IUSRS just as the IIS 7 web server does. It's a shame that this is so complex, but IIS 7 was still being developed when Microsoft "locked down" Vista for release, and the IIS 7 FTP server wasn't Internet ready. As of Vista Service Pack 1, the FTP component still has not been upgraded.

Default Document

If you want to change the order or names of the files that IIS searches to find the default document when a URL names a folder, edit this component. The default list is `default.htm`, `default.asp`, `index.htm`, `index.html`, `iisstart.htm`, and `default.aspx`.

Directory Browsing

This component determines what IIS does if a URL specifies the name of a folder but no default document is present in the folder. If directory browsing is disabled, IIS displays an error message. If directory browsing is enabled, IIS displays to the visitor a listing of all the files in the folder.

In general, you should enable directory browsing only on specific directories that you *know* you want visitors to see the contents of. If you're setting up a folder to act as a file repository—for example, to hold a bunch of commonly used documents that you want to share with your office—directory browsing is great: Just add a new file to the folder, and visitors will be able to find it. Without browsing, you'd have to edit an HTML document and add a link for every document you wanted to make visible.

To enable directory browsing, expand the Websites item in the left Connections pane, expand Default Website, and dig down to the folder that you want to expose. Select it and double-click Directory Browsing. In the right Action pane, click Enable.

Scripting

By default, the `.asp` script file can be placed in any folder in the website; IIS executes and interprets these files when they are viewed by a site visitor. By default, CGI programs (`.exe` files) and ISAPI programs (`.dll` files) are disabled.

If you want to let people retrieve `.asp` files from a folder on your website without interpretation, you need to disable ASP scripting in that folder. Likewise, to have `.exe` files run as CGI programs instead of being themselves delivered to the site visitor, you must enable CGI or ISAPI for a selected folder or file.

To enable or disable script and execute settings, navigate to the folder or to a specific file under the Default Website item. Select it and double-click Handler Mappings. Select one of the following entries, right-click, and choose Edit Handler Permissions:

- **ASP-classic**—Check Script to enable scripting; uncheck to deliver `.asp` files intact.
- **CGI-exe**—Check Execute to enable CGI execution; uncheck to deliver `.exe` files intact.
- **ISAPI-dll**—Check Execute to enable ISAPI extensions execution; uncheck to deliver `.dll` files intact.

I suggest that you create a specific folder for scripts or CGI applications, and enable Script and/or Execute only on that folder.

MIME Mappings

MIME mappings are used to determine what MIME type the web server should assign to each file that it sends to a visiting web browser. (MIME types were discussed earlier in the chapter, in the section "MIMEs Make It Happen.") IIS uses MIME mapping settings to determine each file's MIME type from its file type. For example, MIME mappings tell IIS that files with names ending in `.html` have a MIME type of text/html.

If you are distributing files with uncommon file types, you might need to add other MIME mappings so that IIS can tell web browsers what sort of content they are receiving. To view or edit the MIME type mappings, select Default Web Site in the Connections pane; then double-click the MIME Types icon. The MIME Types editor will display a list of filename extensions and their associated MIME types. For example, if you scroll down the list you can see that `.mp3` is associated with MIME type `audio/mpeg`. If you are serving files with an extension that is not listed, click Add in the Actions pane. Enter the file extension (including the initial period), and the correct MIME type name. Then, click OK to save the new mapping.

> **NOTE**
>
> If you don't know what the correct MIME type is for a particular type of file that you're linking to on your website, check www.iana.org/assignments/media-types, which is the official list.

If your web browser launches the wrong viewer application when you download a file from your website, see "Hyperlinks Return Gibberish" in the Troubleshooting section at the end of this chapter.

VIRTUAL DIRECTORIES

As I mentioned earlier in the chapter, a *virtual directory* is a folder that is treated as if it were part of the directory structure inside your website but is actually located elsewhere. IIS can grant web visitors access to a folder on your hard drive or one shared by another computer over the network.

To add a virtual directory, follow these steps:

1. Browse underneath Default Website in the left Connections pane, and select the folder that you want to appear to contain the virtual folder. Select the Default Website entry itself if you want the virtual folder to appear to be under the site's home folder.
2. Right-click the folder name and select Add Virtual Directory.
3. In the Alias field, enter the name that you want to give the virtual directory in your website's directory structure. For example, if you add a virtual directory to the Default Website (main folder) and give it the alias `bigfolder`, then `http://computername/bigfolder` gives you the contents of the virtual folder, regardless of what the folder's real name is.
4. In the Physical Path field, enter the path to the folder that you want to graft into your website structure. You can click the ... button to locate the folder graphically.

SMTP SERVER

If you plan to use the `system.net.mail` object to send email from ASP.NET scripts and web forms, you need to specify information about your ISP's or company's mail server. In the ASP.NET group, double-click the SMTP Server icon and enter the following information:

Email Address	Enter the email address that you want to use as the return address for outgoing email.
Deliver Email to SMTP Server	Check this item.

Use Localhost	Uncheck this item.
SMTP Server	Enter the hostname of your ISP's or company's outgoing mail server, usually something such as `smtp.myisp.net`.
Port	Usually 25.
Authentication Setting	Most mail servers require no authentication for outgoing mail. If yours does, check Specify Credentials and then click Set.

After you have entered the information, click Apply in the rightmost Actions pane.

Managing the FTP Server

If you have installed the FTP service, open the Internet Information Services (IIS) 6.0 Manager using one of the following methods:

- Click Start, right-click Computer, and select Manage. Look under Services and Applications for the entry titled Internet Information Services (IIS) 6.0 Manager. This item manages the FTP server.

- If you've customized your Start menu so that it displays Administrative Tools, just click Start, All Programs, Administrative Tools. The Internet Information Services 6.0 Manager item is available here.

Figure 18.3 shows this tool.

Figure 18.3
The IIS Version 6 Manager, used for the FTP Service.

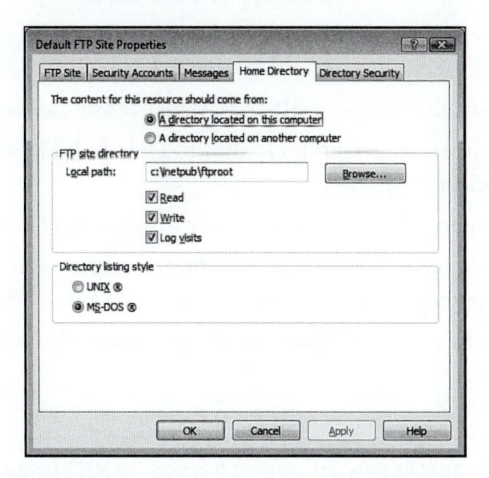

Now, FTP is sort of a bag of worms. The problem is that FTP is an old protocol from a happier time, when network hacking was not really a concern, and it requires sending your username and password through the network with no encryption. This means that it's dangerous to use FTP to reach your computer over the Internet. And although FTP is a handy way to let other people send large files to you (no problems with extra large email attachments), it's also risky to let other people put arbitrarily large files directly onto your computer, especially when you have no control over what those files contain.

For the purposes of this book, I'll show you two ways that you can use FTP in *relative* safety:

- As a means of publishing website content to your own web server from a web page editor on the same computer or elsewhere on your local network *only*
- As a means of exchanging files with clients over the Internet

> **CAUTION**
>
> These two uses are mutually exclusive! To avoid creating an FTP server that is subject to abuse, you must pick just one of the two scenarios.

The FTP Service is not available on Windows Vista Home editions.

Using the FTP Service to Publish Website Content

If you use a website-editing program that uses FTP to publish or copy the edited website content to the web server, you can configure the FTP service to help you do this. I give you a step-by-step procedure shortly, but the basics are this:

- Set the FTP server root folder to be the same as the web server's.
- Set permissions that allow only you to write to the files in the website folder.
- Set permissions on the FTP server so that only you can use it.

Here is the procedure. To configure the FTP server, make the following settings:

1. Open the Internet Information Services (IIS) 6.0 Manager as described previously.
2. Navigate through the left pane through FTP Sites to Default FTP Site. Right-click Default FTP Site and select Properties.
3. Select the Security Accounts tab and uncheck Allow Anonymous Connections.
4. Select the Home Directory tab. Click the Browse button and navigate to the folder that holds the web server's content, usually `C:\inetpub\wwwroot`. Click OK.
5. Check Write. Read, Write, and Log Visits should all be checked, as shown in Figure 18.3. Click OK.

> **CAUTION**
>
> The FTP folder *must* be on a disk partition that uses the NTFS format.

Now you can connect to the FTP service and copy files into the web server's directory structure. Make sure that your user account has permission to read and write files in `-\inetpub\wwwroot`. You use your account name and password when connecting with FTP.

To avoid sending your password over the Internet in plain-text form, take the following precautions:

- Never connect to your computer's FTP service over the Internet—that is, from a computer that's not on your own office or home network.
- If you can get by running your website editor only on the same computer that is running your web server, don't open ports 20 and 21 in Windows Firewall. Just tell the FTP transfer program that the hostname is `localhost`. This way, your password never leaves your own computer.
- If you need to transfer files from another computer on your home or office network, you need to open ports 20 and 21 in Windows Firewall. This is described earlier in the chapter.

Using the FTP Service to Exchange Files

If your computer has a public Internet connection, you can use the FTP service to let off-site clients or others transfer files to and from your computer. For example, you might want to do this if you have clients that routinely send you large files or need to pick up large files from you.

> **CAUTION**
> This is something that you should do only if you *completely* trust the other users; otherwise, you might find that your computer is being used to distribute pirated music, movies, or porn.
> In addition, your computer's hard disk *must* be formatted with the NTFS file format.

To set up this kind of file transfer system, you must set up folders for each such remote user *very carefully* so that that they can't see other people's files.

> **TIP**
> You might want to install a separate hard drive and format it with the NTFS file system, to hold the folders you'll expose using FTP. This way, if someone sends huge amounts of data, they won't fill up the hard disk you use for day-to-day work.

When you've made your preparations, follow these steps:

1. If you are on a Windows Domain network, skip ahead to Step 2.

   If your computer is not part of a domain network, create a standard (not Administrator) user account for each of the people with whom you want to exchange files—a different account for each person. Give each account a simple name with no spaces, using the person's first and last names. For example, for me, you might use the name `knittelb`.

   Create good strong passwords for each of the accounts.

> **CAUTION**
>
> If you will make your computer available over the Internet, you *must* assign complex passwords to all accounts that will have permissions to write in any of the folders reachable by FTP. This means you have to set passwords with uppercase letters *and* lowercase letters *and* numbers or punctuation. It's become increasingly common for Internet hackers to set up automatic searches for FTP servers, which they then attack with thousands of attempts to guess passwords. It helps that the Administrator account is disabled under normal conditions on Windows Vista because this is the primary target username.

2. Use Windows Explorer to view the folder `\inetpub\ftproot`. (If you've installed a separate drive, put the folder on that drive.) Create a new folder within `ftproot` named `LocalUser`.

   Inside `LocalUser`, for each of the new accounts, create a new folder for each of the user accounts, giving each folder the same name as the account. For me, you'd create the folder `\inetpub\ftproot\LocalUser\knittelb`.

   (If you are on a Windows Domain network, instead of creating a folder named `LocalUser`, use the name of your Windows domain instead. Then create the user folders inside that, using domain login account names.)

3. Open the Internet Information Services (IIS) 6.0 Manager as described previously.

4. Navigate in the left pane to the Default FTP Site item. Right-click it and delete it.

5. Right-click FTP Sites and select New, FTP Site. Click Next.

6. For the name, enter User Isolated FTP Site and click Next.

7. Leave the default IP settings as is and click Next.

8. Check Isolate Users and click Next.

9. For the path, click Browse and locate the `ftproot` folder graphically (not the LocalUser folder). It might be on a different drive than Windows, if you installed a new drive for this purpose. When you've located the `ftproot` folder, click Next.

10. If you want to let the remote users only pick up files from you, leave Write unchecked. Otherwise, be sure both Read and Write are checked. Click Next, then Finish.

11. In the left pane, right-click User Isolated FTP Site and select Properties.

12. Select the Security Accounts tab and uncheck Allow Anonymous Connections. Click OK.

13. Select the Messages tab. Under Welcome, enter something along these lines:

    ```
    All access to this server is logged. Access to this server is
    allowed by permission only and unauthorized use will be prosecuted.
    ```

14. In the left pane, right-click User Isolated FTP Site and select Start.

In addition you must take pretty much the same steps to make your FTP server publicly available as you do to make a web server available:

- You need to add exceptions to ports 20 and 21 in the Windows Firewall, as discussed earlier in the chapter under "Opening the Firewall."
- If you use an Internet Connection Sharing router or service, you must forward ports 20 and 21 to your computer, as discussed later in the chapter.
- You must register a domain and set up domain name service so that your clients can locate your computer by name.

You should be able to use Windows Explorer to view all the folders yourself so that you can pick up files they've sent and can drop files into their folders for others to pick up.

> **NOTE** If you can't write in the folders, right-click the folder in Explorer, select Properties, select the Security tab, click Edit, and add yourself to the list with the Modify permission.

It's a fair bit of work, but when you're finished, your FTP server is set up so that each of the users for whom you created folders can connect using FTP, and can send and receive files from their folders only. It's much easier than sending email attachments, and it can look more professional.

Managing FTP Connections

You can view and disconnect current FTP site visitors from the FTP Site tab of the Default FTP Properties dialog box by clicking Current Sessions. You can use Disconnect to remove any of them if you need to terminate their activity on your computer.

> **NOTE** The version of the FTP Service that is shipped with the initial release of Windows Vista is based on IIS 6.0. At a future date, Microsoft might substitute the version of FTP that goes with IIS 7.0. Its management scheme differs from the one described here, and it should provide security enhancements that include encryption of passwords and data. This more advanced FTP service might also be made available as a download that you could obtain from Microsoft. If you use the FTP service, it's worth checking to see if you can upgrade it to version 7.

Log Files

By default, IIS services create log files in the Windows directory, usually in `\inetpub\logs\LogFiles`. The web service log files are in the subfolder `W3SVC1` and are named `exyymmdd.log`, where *yymmdd* consists of digits that indicate the current date. By default, a new log file is created on any day on which web server activity occurs.

> **NOTE**
>
> By default, the date and time zone used in the logs is UTC, so U.S. users see a new log file appear sometime in the afternoon or evening rather than their local midnight. Use of UTC is a convention on web servers. For example, it helps when you're reporting abuse of your server to an ISP in some other part of the world because it's easier to translate the UTC times to local times to help identify the perpetrator.

The FTP service follows a similar format, but because the FTP server provided with Windows Vista is the IIS 6.0 version, it stores its log files in `\Windows\System32\LogFiles\MSFTPSVC1`.

You can change the period for changing log files from daily to hourly, weekly, or monthly, or you can base this change on the log file growing to a certain size. To do so, you use the Default Web or FTP Site Properties dialog boxes. Just locate the Enable Logging check box and click the Properties button next to it.

The log files are plain ASCII text files that contain a line for each file or page retrieved from the web server. Each line contains the time, the browser's IP address, the HTTP method used (usually `GET`), and the URL requested.

If you are interested in analyzing the use of your website, several free or shareware analysis tools are available. You also might want to adjust the list of fields recorded in the log file. Of course, you can hire hugely expensive consultants for intense analysis of your web server activity logs for marketing research, but this in-depth analysis is probably more than you want. If you're a Windows Script Host pro, you can also take advantage of the MSWC.IISLog object to parse through IIS log files.

Making the Site Available on the Internet

If your computer is on a corporate LAN, your network managers are responsible for making your site available to the Internet at large, if this is permitted.

On a home or small office network, as I said earlier, you need to arrange for DNS service so that people can type `www.yourwonderfulwebsite.org` and their web browser can figure out how to send the request to your computer. This process consists of five parts:

- Unless you're willing to live with the silly domain names provided for free by Dynamic DNS providers, you must register a domain name with a domain name registrar. You have to pay for this—no way around it—and it costs around $10 to $35 per year, depending on which registrar you use.

- You need always-on Internet service, usually cable or DSL. If you can get a static IP address, it will help.
- You must have domain name service (DNS), which maps your domain name to the IP address of your computer. This service can be free. If you have a static IP address, you can enter it once and forget it.

  You must provide your registrar with the names or IP addresses of the name servers. Your DNS provider can give you this information.
- If your Internet service assigns addresses dynamically, you need to set up a dynamic DNS update client to update your DNS provider whenever your IP address changes. Some broadband routers can do this for you as a built-in feature. I prefer to use dyndns.org as the Dynamic DNS provider, and to install its Dynamic DNS Updater service to keep the IP address information up to date. For a small fee, you can purchase their "Custom DNS" service, which lets you register a domain name of your own choosing for a reasonable price.
- If you are using a shared Internet connection (that is, a router or Windows Internet Connection Sharing), you have to configure your sharing device or software to direct incoming HTTP requests to the computer that's running IIS. Otherwise, these requests will stop at the router or the connection-sharing computer because they won't know which computer they're intended for. For each of the services you've installed *and* want to make publicly available, you need to forward the port(s) listed in Table 18.3 from the sharing service or router to the IIS computer.

→ The last step, connection forwarding, is described in "Making Services Available," **p. 728**.

TABLE 18.3   PORTS TO FORWARD FOR IIS SERVICES

Service	Port
HTTP (web)	TCP 80
HTTPS (secure web)	TCP 443
FTP	TCP 20–21

With Microsoft's Internet Connection Sharing service on a computer running Windows XP or Windows Vista, you can simply specify your computer's name as the target of the forwarded requests. If you use a connection-sharing router device, unless it supports Universal Plug and Play (UPNP), you have to enter the IIS computer's IP address. This, in turn, means that you can't use automatic IP address assignment (DHCP) for the IIS computer because its address could change from day to day, and the forwarded requests would end up going to the wrong computer. You must assign a fixed IP address to the IIS computer.

You can read more about configuring IP address information in Chapter 20, "Creating a Windows Network."

> **NOTE**
>
> At this point, using a hosting service for $5 per month is probably starting to sound like a good deal, isn't it?

Security Issues for Internet Services

Simply stated, if your computer is connected to the Internet, it's exposed to millions of people who can reach it in milliseconds from anywhere in the world, many of whom very much want to break into your computer. They're highly motivated because they make big money using other people's computers to send spam, sell drugs, collect people's credit card numbers as part of fraud operations, crack passwords on government computers, and, well, who knows what else. Thanks in large part to Microsoft's past cavalier attitude toward security, these criminals have harnessed hundreds of thousands of computers running older versions of Windows to do their dirty work, and—no joke—they're trying to get yours right now, as you read this. Having a web server running on your computer makes you that much more inviting of a target. So consider your connection to the Internet like the door to your house, and it's in a rough neighborhood. Never leave the door unlocked, and let's talk about putting bars on the windows.

Dealing with security is a little bit scary, but you can take a few steps to ensure your safety.

→ For a more detailed discussion of keeping your network safe from prying eyes, **see** "It's a Cold, Cruel World" **p. 1206**.

Keeping Up-to-Date

First and foremost, you need to keep up on bug fixes and security updates that Microsoft releases. Because IIS has access to your computer *and* is in contact with the rest of the world, it's critical that you keep it up-to-date. You should be sure that your computer is set up to receive and automatically install Automatic Updates from Microsoft. You also need to subscribe to the Microsoft security bulletin service so that you hear about problems as soon as they're discovered. Sometimes they describe interim precautionary measures you can take before bug fixes are released. You can sign up at www.microsoft.com/security/bulletins. On the right side, click on Sign Up Now.

> **NOTE**
>
> Microsoft rearranges its website constantly, so if those instructions don't work, poke around or search microsoft.com for "sign up security bulletins."

> **NOTE**
>
> There are professional security auditing services that will periodically scan your web server for known security problems. You'd be well advised to use one of these services!

→ For more information, **see** the "Tips from the Windows Pros" section at the end of Chapter 35, **p. 1242**.

File Security

Your server's file system contributes to the security of data on it. You can do the following:

- Use NTFS for any drives that contain folders containing files that IIS shares. This is not just a suggestion; it's essential.
- By default, Windows puts the web and FTP data directories on the same drive as Windows. For maximum safety, set up a separate NTFS-formatted drive or partition and use that for your IIS data. You can change the location of the web and FTP home directories using the Internet Information Services management tools that I described earlier in the chapter.
- Carefully review and adjust the permission settings in your \inetpub folder and all its subfolders. Examine any folders that you create under the \inetpub folder to be sure that only authorized users can read and write files there. As discussed previously under "Authentication," the username IUSR is used for anonymous web users, and IUSR is a member of group Users. The username IUSR_*machinename*, where *machinename* is your computer's name, is used for anonymous FTP access. Thus, group Users or user IUSR_*machinename* needs read permission in any folder that contains pages or files that you want to make available to anyone via the web or FTP servers, respectively. You should not grant write permission to IUSR, Users, IUSR_*machinename*, or Everyone in any of these folders.
- Store executable and script files in a separate folder from web pages, and enable the `CGI-exe`, `ASP-classic`, and `ISAPI-dll` handlers only for that one folder. See the "Scripting" section earlier in the chapter for instructions.
- Enable auditing of access failures and privilege violations.

→ For instructions on auditing access failures, **see** "Tightening Local Security Policy," **p. 1227**.

For additional security, take these measures:

- Back up your system frequently.
- Run virus checks regularly.
- Be sure that your computer is behind a firewall (Windows Firewall will do) *and* that you use a connection-sharing router or Windows Internet Connection Sharing. These services help block incoming attacks.
- Keep track of the services that should be running on your computer, and watch for unknown services that might have been installed by rogue software or unauthorized users.
- Scan your log files regularly for evidence of attacks. The FTP service, in particular, is one that you have to watch out for. I regularly see periods in which someone makes several thousand attempts to guess the Administrator password. Luckily, on Windows Vista, there should be no functioning account named Administrator.

Troubleshooting

Check to See Whether IIS Is Working

I cannot access my IIS server from another computer.

Go to the computer running IIS, start Internet Explorer, and view the address http://localhost. If you see a web page, IIS is functioning. If you don't, try restarting it following the instructions in the next troubleshooting tip.

Server Doesn't Respond to Requests

A web browser appears to connect to my computer, but the status stays at "Contacting Server" or "Waiting for Response." No web page is returned.

First, make sure that you opened port 80 in the Windows Firewall on the computer running IIS, as shown. This is described earlier in the chapter in the section "Opening the Firewall." If you are attempting to connect using a URL starting with `ftp://` and you are running the FTP service, there should be exceptions for TCP ports 20 and 21 as well.

If that doesn't fix the problem, use the Internet Services Manager to stop and restart the IIS Server.

Other Computers Can't Reach the Site

The IIS computer can view the web pages it's serving, but other computers can't.

In this case, you most likely have a problem with DNS or with the naming service used on your network. On a home/small office LAN, `http://machinename` might not work if there is a conflict with the Browser service (a Windows name-resolving service that has nothing to do with web browsing), and this is a common problem. Wait 15 minutes and try again; if that doesn't help, shut all the computers down, boot up the IIS computer, and then boot up the others.

If you can't get to the IIS site through the Internet, your DNS entries could be wrong, or the forwarding entries on your router or on the computer that is sharing your Internet connection could be wrong. To check, have someone with an Internet connection open a command prompt window on any version of Windows and type `ping www.yourdomain.com`, putting your domain name after the `ping` command. Have that person tell you what IP address the `ping` command is using. If it's not your site's public IP address, you have a DNS problem.

If the address is correct, your router or Internet Connection Sharing could be forwarding TCP port 80 requests to the wrong computer. Check your IIS computer's IP address (type `ipconfig` in a command prompt window to see what it is), and check that against the network's forwarding setup screen.

If all that checks out, be sure that Windows Firewall is not blocking the incoming requests, as discussed in a previous troubleshooting note.

Hyperlinks Return Gibberish

When I click on a document or data file that is linked in my website, my browser shows a screen full of random letters and numbers; or the wrong application is launched, and the application doesn't know what to do with the file.

Check the file type to MIME type mappings on the web server and the MIME type to application viewer mappings on your browser. In the browser, choose File, Save As to save the seemingly senseless information to a file with the appropriate name (for example, xxxx.gif if you think you have downloaded a GIF file) and try to view it by double-clicking the file in Explorer. If it displays correctly there, the only problem is the MIME type mapping. If the MIME type mapping is correct on the server, check your browser's application association for that MIME type.

You first need to determine the correct MIME type for the file type you are sending. You can find the official list of MIME types at www.iana.org/assignments/media-types.

For information on setting MIME type mappings, see "MIME Mappings," earlier in the chapter.

Browser Doesn't Show Modified Web Page

I have modified a file on my website, but the browser still gets the old version.

Click Refresh on the browser. If that trick doesn't work, shut down the browser, restart it, and try again. It's usually the browser's fault. If you still get the wrong version, confirm that you are viewing the correct virtual directory. In addition, if you're looking at a default page (that is, you are using a URL that names a folder but not a specific file), be sure that you're editing the right file. If the folder contains, for example, files named `index.html` and `default.html`, IIS is returning the latter, not the former. The search order is discussed earlier in the chapter under "Default Documents." The search order might have been changed, so check the IIS management tool to see what the current list looks like.

Tips from the Windows Pros: Scripting for Interactive Sites

As I said earlier in the chapter, the idea of using programs to generate web pages on the fly was the real spark that turned the Web into a global phenomenon.

The original server-side programs were complex and difficult to write and debug, however, until bright people developed scripting languages for web servers. Scripting systems put most of the complex stuff into one program that was provided with the web server. Then users could write short, easy-to-manage programs, or scripts, that leverage the power in the main program to do all sorts of interesting and interactive things.

The most common scripting language is Perl, which is very popular in the UNIX and Linux world. Perl can be added to IIS so that you can take advantage of the huge pool of already-written Perl programs that are available for free on the Internet. If you know Perl or want to learn, you can download a free Windows version at www.activestate.com. These folks give away Windows versions of Python and TCL as well, two other popular scripting programs, and have a huge library of documentation and free scripts.

Microsoft came up with a scripting system called ASP, which stands for Active Server Pages. (Everything at Microsoft was "Active-something-or-other" for a while there. Now it's .NET this and .NET that.) You can choose what programming language you want to use inside: The default is a dialect of Visual Basic, but you can also use JavaScript, Perl, or other languages, if you install the appropriate interpreter programs.

The cool thing about ASP is that you can mix HTML and your chosen script language in the same file. You can use HTML to manage the formatting and static part of the page, and scripting to generate the dynamic part, and it's all there in one place.

ASP scripts can take full advantage of Microsoft COM and ActiveX programming objects. These objects provide a way for scripts to perform very complex functions, such as manipulating databases and sending email. You can find loads of useful prewritten ASP scripts on the Internet. For example, check out www.asp-pro.com and click on ASP on the left side. Also take a look at the Microsoft Developer's website at msdn.microsoft.com/code; on the left side, select Code Samples by Topic, ASP.

As an example of what ASP scripting can do, use Notepad to create a file named `time.asp` in `C:\inetpub\wwwroot`, with this inside:

```
<HTML>
<HEAD>
<TITLE>What time is it?</TITLE>
</head>
<BODY>
You viewed this web page at
<% response.write time() %>,
<% response.write date() %>.
</BODY>
</HTML>
```

Then view `http://localhost/time.asp` in Internet Explorer.

Here's what's happening: IIS copies most of the file literally. But stuff in between `<%` and `%>` is treated as *script* code, which consists of commands written in VBScript or JavaScript. In this case, VBScript commands insert the time and date into the HTML file before it's sent to your browser. To see what I mean, right-click the displayed page in Internet Explorer and select View Source. You'll see what the ASP script generated and sent to you. Notice that the scripting code is not present; the replacement happened in the server.

> **CAUTION**
>
> Dozens of websites have libraries of scripts that you can download and use. *Be very careful* when you use a script obtained from these sources. Remember, scripts run as programs on your computer, and they can do a lot of damage if they're poorly written or have nefarious stuff built in. For example, several widely used but poorly written scripts that are used to send the contents of HTML forms via email can easily be exploited by spammers to send any message they want to anybody they want. You could find one day that your computer has spent the last week or so sending a few million Herbal Viagra ads. The recipients of those emails won't be happy with you. Do your research and check out the bug history and credibility of any script you download.

PART V

NETWORKING

- **19** Overview of Windows Networking   589
- **20** Creating a Windows Network   611
- **21** Mix and Match with Old Windows and Macs   663
- **22** Connecting Your Network to the Internet   701
- **23** Using a Windows Network   739
- **24** Troubleshooting Your Network   785

CHAPTER 19

OVERVIEW OF WINDOWS NETWORKING

In this chapter

Networking for Everybody   590

Windows Vista's Network Personalities   591

Network Hardware Options   593

Network Terminology   598

Windows Vista Network Services   600

Tips from the Windows Pros: Becoming a Networking Professional   610

Networking for Everybody

It's strange to realize that a scant 25 years ago, having the computers in an office connected to each other through a network was an expensive proposition handled by highly trained technicians—and networks in homes were nonexistent.

Today networks aren't limited to just the work environment. Many homes that start out with one computer quickly end up with two or more, and it's incredibly useful to tie them together through networking. Networking lets you share printers, Internet connections, music and video, and other files. And it's inexpensive: Most computers today come with networking hardware built in, so you just need to add some cables and a small box that together cost less than a single family outing to the movie theater. So even if you don't have a network now, a network is probably in your future.

In this chapter, we give you an overview of the network features that Windows Vista provides and offer an introduction to the terminology, hardware, and software you'll run into. But don't let the complexity of the technology scare you off—you could skip this chapter and still set up and start using a network at home in less than an hour, as we show you in the chapters that follow.

Why You Really Need a Network

I probably don't have to convince you of the value of tying your computers together with a network, even if you have only two. But in case you aren't sold on the idea, here goes. With a network, you can do the following:

- Use any printer attached to any computer.
- Share files—that is, from one computer, access files stored on another computer. At home, having this capability might mean that you can finish that letter you were writing yesterday using your kids' computer because they're now using yours to manage their stock portfolios. In the office, a network lets workers share information quickly and facilitates the creation of a centralized documentation system.
- Share CD-ROMs.
- Back up networked computers with one common backup system—for example, a tape drive or a large hard disk.
- Use network-enabled application software, such as databases, workgroup scheduling and calendar programs, and email. Network-enabled software is designed to give multiple users simultaneous access to information that is updated in real time.
- Share a single dial-up, DSL, or cable Internet connection among several computers, saving on telephone lines and connection costs.
- Play multiuser games within your home or office, or across the Internet.

A network can justify its cost with printer or Internet connection sharing alone.

What does it cost to set one up? Roughly $10 to $50 per computer, depending on whether you want to set up a wireless (radio-based) network or use cables to connect the computers, and whether your computers already have network adapters built in.

NOTE
> The technical terms for these two types of network are *Ethernet* for wired networks and *802.11* for wireless. Each comes in various flavors, as we'll discuss shortly.

Why It Won't Cost Much

Luckily, most new computers have networking hardware built in. The few items that you will still need to purchase are very inexpensive. Here's the breakdown. If you use wired networking equipment, you need the following items:

- Most recent computers have an Ethernet network adapter built in. If any of your computers don't, they need one. As I was writing this, I found adapters for desktops and laptops for $3 and $12 each, respectively, at newegg.com.

- If you want to connect your DSL or cable Internet service to the network, you need a small box called a router; models for home or small office use cost about $20. Otherwise, you need a small box called a hub or switch, which also costs $20 or more, depending on the number of computers it's designed to connect.

- You need a cable to reach from each computer to the router or hub, at a cost of about $5 to $20 each, depending on the length. (Shop online—name-brand network cables from the big computer store chains are usually *way* overpriced.)

For a wireless network, figure on these costs:

- Some laptops and even some desktop computers have wireless 802.11g networking built in. For any computer that doesn't have wireless capability, you need to add an adapter for about $20 to $40 per computer.

- You need one small box called a wireless router or access point. These cost about $40 also.

In the following sections, I give you an overview of the hardware choices and names.

Windows Vista's Network Personalities

Vista can assume several personalities, depending on the type of network that you have. Your computer might fit into one of the following roles:

- A standalone computer that lets you log on *after* making a connection to a network via a modem or through the Internet. An example is a laptop computer that uses a modem to connect to an office network. Windows Vista also has support for securely connecting to an office network through the Internet via *virtual private networking*. Such a computer can be called a *remote workstation*.

- A computer in a small network of computers with no central "server." This is called a *workgroup computer* on a *workgroup* or *peer-to-peer* network. No one computer has an intrinsically special role in making the network work. Most home and small-office networks are workgroup networks.

- A member of a group of computers—from tens to thousands in numbers—working under the stewardship of one or more central computers running a Windows Server operating system. The central server(s) manage a centralized list of usernames and passwords information. In this situation, the Windows Vista computer is called a *domain member* or *member computer* on a *domain* network.

- A member of a client/server network that is, in turn, connected to other networks. An example is a computer in a branch office of a large company. This computer is a *domain member* of an *enterprise network*, where special consideration is made to management, security, and the allocation of resources of many, many computers and people spread out over a wide geographical area.

Some versions of Windows Vista can work in any of these ways; other versions are limited to just a few. Table 19.1 lists the capabilities of each Windows Vista version.

TABLE 19.1 POSSIBLE WORKSTATION TYPES FOR WINDOWS VISTA

Vista Version	Workstation Type			
	Remote (VPN)	Workgroup	Domain	Enterprise
Home Basic		✓		
Home Premium		✓		
Business	✓	✓	✓	✓
Enterprise	✓	✓	✓	✓
Ultimate	✓	✓	✓	✓

One thing Vista can't do is take the central, or server, role of a domain or enterprise network. For that, you need at least one computer running one of the Windows Server versions or one of its more upscale varieties: Advanced Server, Enterprise Server, or Data Center.

> **NOTE**
>
> Microsoft cleverly named the successor to Windows 2000 Server as Windows Server 2003. Why they had to rearrange the name, we don't know. The newest version is Windows Server 2008. To keep things simple in our text, we just use the name Windows 200x Server when we don't have to make a distinction among the various versions.

In addition, the Windows Vista file-sharing service can make a network connection with, at most, 5 to 10 other computers: 5 for the Vista Home versions, and 10 for the Business, Enterprise and Ultimate versions. If you need to share a network resource (such as a printer or file folder) with more than 10 computers at once, you need one of the Windows Server versions.

In the next few chapters, you learn how to configure and tune up Windows Vista in each of these environments. If you are already familiar with networks, you can skip ahead to "Windows Vista Network Services," later in this chapter. If not, check out the following sections for an introduction to the equipment, concepts, and terms you will want to be familiar with.

Network Hardware Options

The signals transmitted across a LAN are generated and interpreted by electronics in each computer. Some computers have built-in network interfaces; otherwise, each computer in a LAN needs a *network interface card*, or *NIC*. I also refer to them as *network cards* or *network adapters*.

These electrical signals have to be carried from computer to computer somehow. For the average home or small-office network, there are two options: wired and wireless.

Wired Ethernet Networks

Wired or *Ethernet* networks send data over cables that are run from each computer to one or more central points, called *hubs* or *switches*. Figure 19.1 shows a typical Ethernet setup for a home or small office.

> **NOTE**
> The plug that's used at the ends of Ethernet network cables is commonly called an RJ-45 connector. It looks like a wider version of a telephone modular plug. To be absolutely precise, the connector that we use for networking is called an 8P8C connector. The "true" RJ-45 is used by the telephone industry and it's physically slightly different. However, almost everyone outside the telephone industry uses the term RJ-45 when talking about the computer version, so we'll stick with that name in this book.

Figure 19.1
Typical Ethernet network.

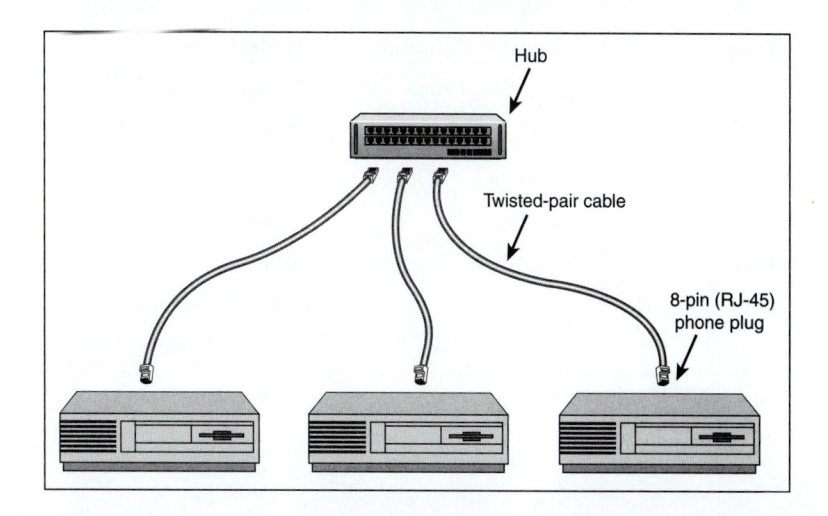

Ethernet networks can transfer data at one of three rates: 10Mbps (million bits per second), 100Mbps, or 1000Mbps. These three speeds are often called *Standard Ethernet*, *Fast Ethernet*, and *Gigabit Ethernet*, respectively. They are also sometimes called 10BASE-T, 100BASE-T, and 1000BASE-T.

Most networking hardware manufactured in this century is designed to work at more than one of these rates and automatically runs at the maximum speed of the other equipment to which it's connected. Thus, most network adapters you'll see are labeled as 10/100, meaning that they can run at 10Mbps or 100Mbps, or 10/100/1000, meaning that they can run at 10Mbps, 100Mbps, or 1000Mbps.

In most cases, 100Mbps is fast enough for office work and Internet downloads. 1000MBps makes a noticeable difference only when you are transferring very large files (video files, for instance) from one computer to another within your own network. Because 1000Mbps equipment is more expensive, you can base your purchasing decisions on that activity. We talk more about this in the next chapter.

UNSHIELDED TWISTED-PAIR (UTP) CABLE

The cable used to connect computers to hubs in an Ethernet network is called *unshielded twisted pair*, or *UTP*. UTP is so called because like-colored pairs of wires inside the cable are gently twisted together for better immunity to electrical interference from fluorescent lights, radio signals, and so on. This inexpensive type of cable is also used for telephone connections, although the network variety is of a higher quality and is certified for its capability to carry high data rates. UTP cables are terminated with eight-wire RJ-45 connectors, which are wider versions of the familiar modular telephone connectors.

UTP cable quality is categorized by the highest data rate it has been designed and certified to carry reliably. Table 19.2 shows the most common UTP cable rating categories.

TABLE 19.2   UTP CABLE CATEGORIES

Designation	Highest Data Rate	Application
CAT-1	Less than 1Mbps	Telephone (voice)
CAT-2	4Mbps	IBM 4Mbps Token Ring
CAT-3	16Mbps	10Mbps Ethernet (10BASE-T)
CAT-4	20Mbps	16Mbps Token Ring
CAT-5	100Mbps	100Mbps Ethernet (100BASE-T), ATM, others
CAT-5E or -5X	250Mbps	Gigabit Ethernet* (1000BASE-T)
CAT-6	250Mbps	Gigabit Ethernet*

Gigabit Ethernet uses four pairs of wire, each carrying 250Mbps, providing an aggregate speed of 1000Mbps.

Remember that you can't use just any old wiring you find in your walls to carry a network signal: You have to look for the appropriate "CAT-something" designation, which is printed on the cable jacket every foot or so. If you are using 10/100 Ethernet equipment, you must use CAT-5 or better cabling and connectors. If you are using Gigabit Ethernet equipment, you must use CAT-5E, CAT-5X, or CAT-6 cabling and connectors.

> **TIP**
>
> CAT-5E, -5X, or -6 cable and connectors are more expensive, but putting in one type of cable now and replacing it later is even more expensive. If you will use 10/100Mbps networking now but think that you might eventually want to upgrade to Gigabit Ethernet, go ahead and get the higher-rated cable now.

> **NOTE**
>
> The longest allowable single run of UTP cable in an Ethernet network is 100 meters, or 328 feet. If you need to place a computer more than 100 meters from a hub, you need to use more than one hub, or use a wireless or fiber-optic cable connection. We talk more about this in Chapter 20, "Creating a Windows Network."

WIRELESS NETWORKS

Wireless networks use radio signals to transmit the network data. The most common wireless equipment used in homes and offices uses frequencies in the 2.4GHz and 5GHz bands, which are shared with some cordless telephones and microwave ovens. In addition to its use for file-sharing networks, wireless is commonly used to provide Internet access in cafes, hotels, conference centers, airports, hospitals, and other public sites. Some cities are even setting up free city-wide wireless coverage for the public. Figure 19.2 shows a home or office wireless network that uses both wired and wireless connections.

Figure 19.2
A network that includes both wireless and wired connections.

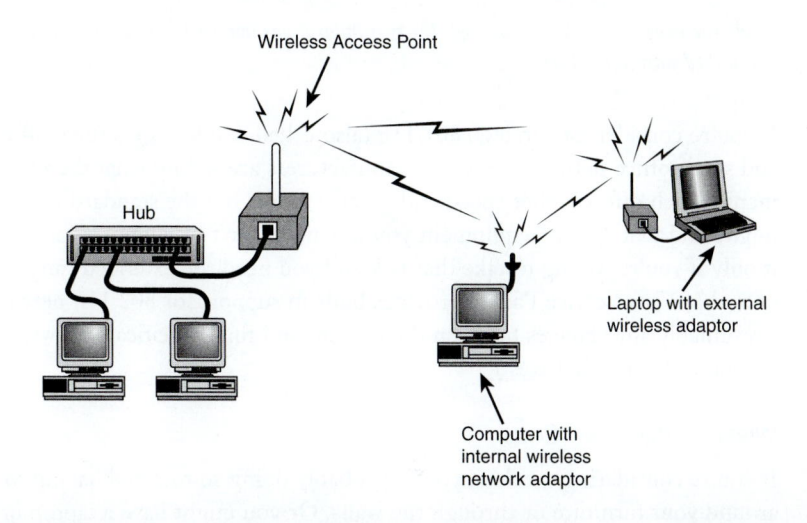

NOTE

> The wireless network manufacturer's organization is called the Wi-Fi Alliance. *Wi-Fi* stands for wireless fidelity and, in a loose way, *Wi-Fi* is used to refer to wireless networking. However, the technical term most commonly used is *802.11* followed by a letter, as I explain shortly.

One thing you have to watch out for is that there are currently three official wireless standards, named 802.11a, 802.11b, and 802.11g, and one soon-to-be-standard called 802.11*n*. The "standard" refers to the fact that the technology is governed by an international committee, to ensure that equipment made by one manufacturer *should* work correctly with equipment made by another.

Equipment designed for one standard won't necessarily work with equipment designed for a different standard, as shown in Table 19.3. 802.11a equipment can communicate only with other 802.11a devices. 802.11b and 802.11g equipment can interoperate, but only at the lowest-common-denominator speed. Although the *-n* version hasn't been finalized, it's expected that 802.11*n* devices will be capable of interoperating with 802.11a and g hardware.

TABLE 19.3   WIRELESS NETWORKING STANDARDS

Wireless Standard	Data Rate[1]	Compatible with
802.11a	Up to 54Mbps	802.11a only
802.11b	Up to 11Mbps	802.11g
802.11g	Up to 54Mbps	801.11b and n[2]
802.11n[2]	Up to 540Mbps	802.11a and g

[1] *Some manufacturers have tweaked their wireless devices to let them communicate at twice the standard's maximum speed, but only when connected to equipment by the same manufacturer.*

[2] *At the time this book was printed, the* n *standard was not yet finalized, and it was not expected to be finalized until late 2008.*

If you're considering wireless, 801.11g (also called wireless-g) is the stuff to get for home and small-office networks. Several manufacturers are selling what they call "pre-*n*" equipment, which offers higher speed and greater range, but the standard isn't finalized, so you might find that "pre-*n*" equipment you buy now won't be supported in the future. Consider it only if you're willing to take that risk and you need the extended range. (It's interesting to note that Vista Service Pack 1 provides built-in support for 802.11n networking devices. Presumably any changes between the current and final specifications will be addressed with Windows Update hotfixes.)

WIRELESS PROS AND CONS

If you're considering wireless, you're probably doing so to avoid having to snake cables around your furniture or through the walls. Or you might have a laptop or palm-sized computer that you want carry to around while checking email and surfing the Internet. These are great reasons to use it.

However, wireless has some downsides. First, a wireless network is not as reliable as a wired network. In my experience and that of many friends, it simply stops working at random intervals—sometimes once a day, sometimes once a week. It might start working again by itself after a few seconds or minutes or hours, or you might have to restart your computers and wireless router to get it back on the air. In contrast, unless someone trips over a cable and yanks off the connector, a wired Ethernet network should run for years without a glitch.

Second, the wireless signal loses strength passing through walls, floors, and ceilings, so if you're in a very large house or are spread out in a concrete-and-steel office building, wireless might not work well for you (at least, not without adding some moderately expensive add-ons). In any case, the greatest actual data-transfer rate you'll achieve is about half the rated maximum, under the best signal conditions; it goes downhill from there.

Third, and most important, unless you take explicit steps to secure it, a wireless network is "open to the public," and it's a trivial matter for random passersby to browse your shared files and borrow your Internet connection. Making a wireless network secure takes some effort. It's sold as being easy, but to be frank, I've found that it can be difficult and confusing even for networking pros, let alone for the technologically challenged. As a result, many people skip the security step just to get their network working and end up getting their computers hacked into.

> **TIP**
>
> If your computers are close enough together that running the wires isn't a big problem, and you don't have any mobile devices that *need* wireless, I recommend that you put in a wired network. It has greater reliability, greater security, and easier setup. You can always add a wireless access device later, if you want to.

POWERLINE AND PHONELINE

Network data can also be transmitted as radio signals through your existing telephone lines or electrical wiring. Meant primarily for home use, powerline networking equipment (called HomePlug by its manufacturers' association) and phoneline networking (called HomePNA) send data at up to 10Mbps. They have the advantage of being very easy to install—an adapter plugs into a wall socket or phone jack, and connects to your computer or Internet connection-sharing router with an Ethernet cable. No other wiring or setup is involved.

I soundly derided this equipment when it first came out, but the technology has improved considerably and the prices have fallen to the point that it makes perfect sense to use it in the average home. Powerline Ethernet, in particular, is a great way to create or extend a network, whether or not it includes existing wired computers. Powerline Ethernet adapters should cost about $30 each.

Network Terminology

Here are a few terms that you might encounter if you're setting up or working with networks. We define some terms here. We introduce some other terms later, when we cover the various network services provided by Windows Vista.

- *AppleTalk* and its Ethernet-based counterpart, *LocalTalk*, are used in Apple Macintosh networking. Windows 2000 Professional and Server versions provided LocalTalk to facilitate using LAN-connected Apple printers, but Microsoft omitted support for it in Windows Vista and Windows XP.

- *Point-to-Point Protocol*, or *PPP*, is used to carry Internet Protocol data packets across a dial-up modem connection. This protocol is used for dial-up Internet connections.

- *Point-to-Point Protocol over Ethernet*, or *PPPoE*, is used by most DSL and some cable Internet service providers to link your computer to the ISP's routing equipment. PPPoE is built into Windows as part of its broadband Internet connection support.

- A network *protocol* is a scheme that allows computers to organize and regulate the information they send to each other. Do you remember how the police and astronauts always used to say "over" every time they were finished talking to the command center? That's an example of a protocol. It was necessary because, with those old radios, you couldn't hear the other party if you were holding down your own "talk" button, and you would miss something if you started talking before the other person finished. (And neither of you would know it had even happened because they wouldn't hear you, either.) So the "over" protocol was used to make sure each party understood that the roles of talker and listener were being switched.

   Protocols on computer networks serve the same purpose, from link-level protocols that regulate when computers can transmit data (just as "over" did on radios), to higher-level protocols that determine the organization of the data.

   The most commonly known network protocol these days is Transmission Control Protocol/Internet Protocol (TCP/IP). TCP/IP lets computers transmit data across networks such as the Internet. The IP part of the name refers to the standard way that data is formatted for transmission, and TCP to a method used to account for problems such as network delays and data lost along the way.

- *Wired Equivalent Privacy*, or *WEP*, is an encryption protocol that wireless networks use to protect data from being intercepted by eavesdroppers and to prevent random passersby from being able to connect to and use the network without permission. In urban areas, it's now common to find that your computer can pick up a half-dozen or more wireless network signals. That means that a half-dozen or more random other people can pick up *your* wireless signal, and you don't want them poking into your files. WEP was intended to help prevent that. Unfortunately, it turns out that WEP is not unbreakable—a hacker with a laptop can park in front of your house or office for a few hours and eventually be able to get on your network. Another encryption standard thus was developed, and is becoming more common….

- *Wi-Fi Protected Access*, or *WPA*, is an improved encryption scheme for wireless networking that was intended to provide something better than WEP until a more powerful formally standardized security scheme could be developed (see WPA2, the next entry).

  Windows Vista includes WPA support. Most wireless equipment vendors now support it as well. However, if you have existing equipment, you might have to download upgraded software to get it.

- *WPA2* or *802.11i* is an improved finalized version of WPA. This is the preferred security scheme for wireless networks. It's supported by Windows Vista. (For Windows XP, you must have Service Pack 3, or Service Pack 2 *and* the hotfix described in Microsoft Knowledge Base Article KB893357.)

> **TIP**
>
> When you are setting up a wireless network's access point or router, you must use a security scheme that's supported by *all* the devices and computers that will be using the network. This means that if you have even one device that supports WEP but not WPA or WPA2, and you need to use that device, you will be forced to use WEP on the network. Before you settle for this, try to upgrade your wireless adapters, drivers, and/or routers to support WPA2 or at least WPA.

- *Point-to-Point Tunneling Protocol*, or *PPTP*, is used to create *virtual private networks*, or *VPN*s. PPTP repackages data destined for a private, remote network for transmission across the Internet. At the other end, it unpackages the data to be released into the private, protected network. I go into greater detail explaining VPNs in Chapter 38, "Hitting the Road."

- In these network chapters, a *resource* is a file, folder, or printer on someone else's computer that you can access through the LAN.

- *Layer 2 Tunneling Protocol* (*L2TP*) is another protocol used to create VPN connections. Windows Vista comes with built-in support for both PPTP and L2TC. It is always used along with IPSec for encryption.

- *Secure Socket Tunneling Protocol (SSTP)* is<$SSTP (Secure Socket Tunneling Protocol> yet another VPN technology, and it has a much easier time passing through corporate firewalls and home Internet connection sharing routers than PPTP or L2TP. SSTP support is added to Vista by Service Pack 1 and currently can connect only to Windows Server 2008.

- *Internet Protocol Security (IPSec)* is a protocol that provides very strong encryption of data sent through a TCP/IP network. On Windows Vista, IPSec is supported on domain networks.

- *IPv6*, for *Internet Protocol Version 6*, is a new version of TCP/IP. It's sort of TCP/IP on steroids. Today's ubiquitous TCP/IP protocol is technically Version 5. Versions 1 through 3 came and went before the Internet as most of us know it today existed. Vista supports IPv6, although it's not yet widely used.

  IPv6 is designed primarily to get around the most serious limitation of IPv4, which is its limited number of unique IP addresses—the Internet's equivalent of telephone numbers. The current IPv4 Internet addressing scheme can accommodate only about four billion addresses. Not every one of them can actually be used, for much the same reason that telephone numbers such as 000-0000 can't be used, so the global Internet is actually running short of addresses for new subscribers and services. IPv6 solves that problem and would enable us to assign a unique network address to just about every particle of dirt on the planet.

Now let's look at Vista's new and improved networking features.

Windows Vista Network Services

Besides file and printer sharing, Windows Vista provides many other network services. You might never interact with some of these services directly, but their presence makes Windows the amazing application platform it is.

Let's take a tour of Windows network services. First, I point out what makes networking in Windows Vista different than in Windows XP. Then I describe each of Vista's networking services, explain why they're useful, and tell where to find out how to install, configure, or use them, if appropriate.

What's Changed in Vista

If you were familiar with networking services in Windows XP, Vista has a few changes that you should know about. I describe these first before going on to describe Vista's services in more detail. If you're new to Vista or networking, this list might not make much sense. If that's the case, just skip on ahead to the next section.

Microsoft started with Windows XP when they created Vista, but they made quite a few changes to the networking components. To be honest, most of the visible differences in the setup and management screens are fairly superficial—new ways of viewing old things. The more significant changes are deeper, and some are invisible—you'll just experience greater performance and reliabilty. Here are some of the major differences between Vista and XP networking:

- Vista has new graphical interfaces for network setup and diagnostics. The new Network and Sharing Center lets you quickly adjust network features and security settings. My Network Places is now called simply Network and includes a graphical map of your network's devices and an improved diagnostic and repair feature. The Network Connections folder has a new look but still holds an icon for each configured connection and network adapter.

- Support for the NetBEUI and IPX/SPX protocols has been dropped; at least, none is provided by Microsoft. This means that networks that include computers running older versions of Windows (Windows Me and earlier) might have to be reconfigured to use the TCP/IP protocol throughout. I'll talk more about this in Chapter 21, "Mix and Match with Old Windows and Macs."

- Native support for Novell NetWare file servers has been dropped. Microsoft no longer provides the Client Services for Network component. However, Novell Corporation did finally release a version of its NetWare client for Windows Vista in August 2007. It is available in x86 and x64 versions, but does not support connections to NetWare 5.0 or earlier, nor many older NetWare functions, such as NDPS printing.

- Internet Protocol Version 6 (IPv6) is now installed by default. Although IPv6 is not yet commonly used outside large enterprises, its use will eventually become widespread and Vista will be ready. Vista also includes two technologies for letting IPv6 network data travel over IPv4 networks such as the Internet: Teredo and 6to4. Whereas 6to4 requires specialized software in Internet routers, Teredo works out of the box to let IPv6 applications talk to each other locally and across the Internet.

- Teredo provides a way for computers with standard IPv4 Internet and network connections to communicate with each other using the more advanced IPv6 network protocol. Teredo is installed by default on Windows Vista, so application software that requires IPv6 should simply work transparently. Teredo has another important benefit: It lets computers communicate with each other even if they are on separate networks that use shared Internet connections. Teredo automatically routes data through the Network Address Translation (NAT) scheme used by connection-sharing routers, with no manual configuration required. Remote Assistance on Windows Vista takes advantage of this, and it *should* work through NAT routers.

> **NOTE**
>
> For more information about Teredo, see en.wikipedia.org/wiki/Teredo_tunneling or www.microsoft.com/technet/network/ipv6/teredo.mspx. The Microsoft.com article is *amazingly* dense, so I recommend starting with the Wikipedia article.

- Simple File Sharing has been changed and renamed. The option is now called Password Protected File Sharing, and the sense of it is reversed: Enabling Vista's Password Protected File Sharing is like turning off XP's Simple File Sharing. Also, whereas the Windows XP Home Edition had Simple File Sharing forced on, Password Protected File Sharing is a settable option on all Vista versions, including the Home versions. The bottom line is that you now have the choice of using or not using passwords to protect folders you share on the network.

- The Windows Firewall now has a means of filtering outbound connections as well as inbound connections. By default, only inbound filtering is performed, but a new configuration interface enables advanced users or network administrators to set up outbound filtering, if desired.

- Windows Vista understands that not all network connections are equally safe or dangerous. On Vista, you can designate each identified wireless connection, dialup connection, and local area network connection as either Public (dangerous), Work (safe), or Home (moderately safe); Windows enables or disables risky features such as file sharing and LLTD discovery accordingly.

- Support for Wireless Protected Access Version 2 (WPA2) is now provided by default. On XP, WPA2 had to be downloaded as a hotfix from Microsoft's support website.

- The Remote Desktop system supports remote access to more devices. XP's version let the host computer use the client computer's disk, COM ports, and sound. When you're connecting to a Windows Vista host, the host can use the client computer's smart card devices and some additional USB devices. The new Remote Desktop client can also use multiple monitors.

- Vista's TCP/IP software (called the *TCP/IP stack*) has been rewritten from scratch to improve performance. The new TCP/IP stack monitors network speed and latency (data travel time), and adjust a parameter called the *receive window* on the fly. Microsoft claims that transfers of large files across Internet and especially LAN connections will occur up to several times faster than before and that the faster the LAN connection is, the greater the improvement will be. On the other hand, XP's networking software had more than five years of field-testing and bug fixes under its proverbial belt, and security experts warn that that a brand-new, relatively untested network stack means that Vista could be more vulnerable to network denial-of-service attacks than was XP.

- Link Layer Topology Discovery Protocol (LLTD) support has been added, which lets Vista construct a graphical map of your network. LLTD support can be downloaded and added to XP, but not earlier versions of Windows, so they'll be literally "off the map."

- On a corporate network, Network Access Protection (NAP) lets network administrators set the conditions under which a computer is allowed to connect to the network. The conditions include the ability to require an up-to-date antivirus program, active firewall, and so on.

Now let's take a look at Vista's networking features, old and new.

File and Printer Sharing

Networking software was originally developed to share and transfer files between computers. (Instant Messaging came later, if you can believe that!) Windows Vista comes with the following services and features:

- Client for Microsoft Networks, which gives access to files and printers that other Windows computers share.

- File and Printer Sharing for Microsoft Networks, which lets Windows share files and printers with users of those same operating systems. Windows Vista Starter and Home Basic editions are limited to 5 simultaneous connections from other computers. All other versions of Vista are limited to 10 simultaneous connections. The Server version is required for larger LANs.

- Although Windows doesn't provide support for Apple file-sharing protocols, Macintosh computers running OS X can use Windows file-sharing protocols. So any version of Windows Vista can share files and printers with Macs, and vice versa.

- LPR and LPD Print Services let you use and share printers with UNIX and Linux computers using the UNIX operating system's LPR protocol.

- Windows Vista Enterprise and Ultimate editions can use files shared by UNIX computers using the Network File Sharing (NFS) protocol.

→ For information about installing, configuring, and using Microsoft network software, **see** Chapters 20, **p. 611** and 23, **p. 739**.

→ For information about interacting with UNIX and Mac computers, **see** Chapter 21, **p. 663**.

Link Layer Discovery Protocol (LLDP)

LLDP is a network protocol that lets computers and network devices broadcast (advertise) their presence and capabilities to each other. Windows Vista uses LLTD to create the Network Map display that shows how your computer is connected to routers, computers, hubs, gateways, and other networks.

Vista supports LLTD out of the box. You can download an LLTD driver for Windows XP so that XP computers will show up correctly in Vista's network map.

Although it's a nifty feature even for home networks, LLTD will really bear fruit on corporate networks, where it should be able to let network management software not only automatically survey and map out every piece of network hardware and all of their interconnections, but also identify them using serial numbers and asset ids.

Roaming User Profiles

When Windows Vista Business, Enterprise, or Ultimate Edition is connected to a Windows Server domain, besides simply validating usernames and passwords, Server can manage the member computer's user profile folders.

A profile is a set of folders that contains a user's personal files, application settings, and Windows settings. The profile includes files for the following:

- Desktop icons and shortcuts
- The contents of your Documents and other personal folders
- Your configuration and preference settings for all the software you use, from your Word preferences to your choice of screen savers
- Management settings that control, for example, whether you are allowed to change Control Panel entries

On a domain network, a *roaming profile* can let you see the same desktop, settings, and personal files, no matter which physical computer you use. When you log on, Vista copies your files from the network server; when you log out, it copies any changed files back to the server. This way, no matter which computer you use, you'll see the same files, settings, and so on.

Distributed Applications

Windows Vista provides network protocols that let software application developers write programs that interact across a network. You will probably never have to install, configure, or even know such protocols exist; you'll just use the programs that use them and happily go about your business. But someone might mention them, so you should be familiar with their names: RPC, COM+, and Peer to Peer.

RPC

Microsoft's Remote Procedure Call (RPC) network protocol allows software to be split into pieces that run on different computers and interact across a network. For instance, the RPC mechanism is used when a user on one Windows computer pauses print spooling on another. It's the basis of most of Windows's remote management capabilities; these are more sophisticated things than the authors of the basic file-sharing protocols made allowances for.

COM+ (Formerly COM and DCOM)

The former Component Object Model (COM) and Distributed COM (DCOM) services have been combined in Windows Vista, XP, and 2000 to the upgraded COM+ service. COM+ provides software developers tools to build highly modular software in a variety of languages. The "+" and "Distributed" parts refer to the service's capability to let software communicate across the network with software running on other computers. For example, Windows Management Instrumentation (WMI) uses COM+ to provide a means of remotely monitoring and managing networked computers.

> **NOTE**
>
> By default, Windows Firewall blocks incoming RPC and DCOM requests, all of which initially use TCP Port 135. This port must be opened to allow remote computers to access RPC/DCOM services on your computer. In addition, Windows Firewall must be told which applications are allowed to receive the incoming connections. If you or your company has developed RPC or DCOM applications, configuration or programming changes will probably be necessary to make them work on Windows Vista, or on Windows XP with SP2. (On a corporate network, this is done through Group Policy.)

To learn more about COM and DCOM, pick up a copy of *COM/DCOM Unleashed* (Sams, 1999; ISBN 0672313529). For information about the changes to RPC and DCOM on Windows Vista and XP SP2, visit www.microsoft.com/technet and search for "dcom rpc developer sp2."

Peer-to-Peer Networking and Windows Communication Foundation

With an unfortunate and confusing name, the Peer-to-Peer networking service has nothing to do with the peer-to-peer workgroup network type we discussed earlier in this chapter. Windows Peer-to-Peer Networking is a new service that lets software developers write applications that run on multiple computers. The potential applications include number-crunching tools that can take advantage of unused processing power on other people's computers, file- and media-sharing tools (think Napster), and discussion/collaboration/communication tools. Vista's Windows Meeting Space and People Near Me application use this service.

Windows Vista includes a new software platform called Windows Communication Foundation that makes it easy for software developers to create new types of interactive software.

.NET

The .NET (pronounced "dot net") initiative is Microsoft's most recent replacement for COM, DCOM, and RPC. .NET is an entire software framework for Internet-enabled software application development. While the .NET Framework was an optional download on Windows XP, Windows Vista ships with .NET Framework 3.0 pre-installed. Again, it's something that you will probably never interact with directly, but it will make possible a whole new generation of software applications.

Virtual Private Networking

All editions of Windows Vista can connect to remote LANs through the Internet using *virtual private networking (VPN)*. This very secure technology makes it safe to use Microsoft networking over the public, insecure Internet. Vista supports NAT connections using the Point to Point Tunneling Protocol (PPTP) and Layer 2 Tunneling Protocol (L2TP) support. Vista Service Pack 1 adds support for VPNs based on the Secure Socket Tunneling Protocol (SSTP), which simplifies making connections when the VPN client or server's Internet connection uses Network Address Translation (NAT).

→ If you're interested in learning more about virtual private networking, **see** "Virtual Private Networking," **p. 1287**.

Remote Access Service (RAS)

If you travel with a laptop or often work from a location outside your physical LAN, you can still use Remote Access Service (RAS, also called *dial-up networking*) to interact with people and files on your network.

→ For more detailed information about RAS, **see** "VPN and Dial-Up Networking," **p. 1286**.

Remote Access by Modem and VPN

Windows Vista allows you to reach your own computer via modem or VPN. You can provide access to your home or office LAN, for example, so that you can retrieve files at your office while you are at home or in the field. At most two incoming connections are permitted at once.

→ To configure Remote Access, **see** "Setting Up VPN and Dial-Up Networking," **p. 1288**.

Remote Desktop and Windows Terminal Services

Both Windows Vista and Windows 200*x* Server provide a sort of remote-control system called, variously, Windows Terminal Services, Remote Desktop, Remote Assistance, and Windows Meeting Space. Terminal Services lets you use a computer remotely. Your applications run on one computer, which you view and control using another computer's display, keyboard, and mouse. Four names exist for what is basically the same piece of software because it's used four different ways:

- **Terminal Services**—A Windows 200*x* Server can be set up to host applications used by remote clients. For example, one beefy computer can run complex software, while the remote computers, which only need to provide a display and keyboard, can be relative lightweights. Terminal Services is also great for remote administration of a server—a manager can sit in front of one computer but can control and configure servers anywhere in the world.

    Although the service is provided only by Windows 200*x* Server, the client software is available for Windows Vista, XP, 2000, 9*x*, and NT.

- **Remote Desktop**—Windows Vista Business, Enterprise, and Ultimate editions have a Remote Desktop feature, which is actually a copy of the Terminal Services server limited to *one* incoming connection. For example, it's intended to enable an employee to access his or her computer at the office from home. You can also use it to access your home computer from just about anywhere in the world, as long as you have Vista Ultimate at home. This is without a doubt my favorite feature in Windows.

- **Remote Assistance**—Windows Vista's Remote Assistance feature is based on—you guessed it—Terminal Services again. It's intended to let a remote user see the Vista user's screen and control his or her keyboard to collaborate on a project or solve a problem. The remote connection can occur only when the computer owner emails the remote user an electronic invitation, which is good for one connection only. This makes the service useless for general remote employee–type work but handy for one-time assistance from a friend or from tech support staff.
- **Windows Meeting Space** is the fourth use of the Terminal Services system. Windows Meeting Space is similar to Remote Assistance, except that it lets a group of two or more people work together with applications on a common desktop.

→ To enable Remote Desktop access to your computer, **see** Chapter 40, "Remote Desktop," **p. 1329**.
→ To see how to connect to another computer using Remote Desktop Connection, **see** "Connecting to Other Computers with Remote Desktop, " **p. 1342**.
→ To learn how to use Remote Assistance, **see** "Remote Assistance, " **p. 1322**.
→ To see how to use Windows Meeting Space, **see** "Windows Meeting Space," **p. 1315**.

Internet Connection Sharing

Windows Vista has a handy feature called Internet Connection Sharing, which lets one computer with a modem or high-speed Internet connection provide Internet access to all users of a LAN. This access is somewhat limited, however. It's not suitable for larger networks because Windows takes over the job of managing network addressing for the entire network. It also requires that the computer with the modem or high-speed connection be left turned on all the time.

Chapter 22, "Connecting Your Network to the Internet," describes connection sharing in more detail.

Windows Firewall

Starting with Windows XP Service Pack 2, Microsoft finally provided Windows with significantly beefed-up Internet security features. Windows Vista takes this several steps forward with an advanced firewall feature that can block both unwanted incoming and outgoing network connections. Windows Firewall is discussed in Chapter 22 and Chapter 35, "Protecting Your Network from Hackers and Snoops."

Universal Plug and Play

Windows Vista includes support for Universal Plug and Play (UPnP), a network protocol that lets "smart" networked devices advertise their presence on the network. For instance, many of the inexpensive Internet Connection Sharing routers on the market support UPnP, although you usually have to turn on the feature using the devices' setup screens. Windows automatically detects the router's presence and, to a limited extent, can enable you to configure them through the Windows interface. More important, UPnP lets network-dependent application software such as Windows Live Messenger function correctly across an Internet router; UPnP provides a means for the application and the router to talk to each other.

Chapters 22 and 35 include some discussion of UPnP.

NOTE

> UPnP and LLTD are similar, in that both let computers and network devices automatically gather information about each other. LLTD is the newer technique, and it provides additional information about physical connections that UPnP doesn't. UPnP has wider support among routers and other network devices.

ACTIVE DIRECTORY

Windows Vista Business, Enterprise, or Ultimate editions on a domain network can take advantage of a service called *Active Directory (AD)*. Active Directory combines a name/address directory, management and security services, and wide-area replicated database technologies to provide a foundation for all Windows networking functions. If your network is managed by a Windows 200*x* Server with AD installed, this service is automatically and transparently made available to you.

→ To learn how to use Active Directory services, **see** "Exploring and Searching the Network," **p. 748**.

Active Directory is a *distributed database*. *Distributed* means that information about separate parts of a geographically dispersed network are automatically copied from region to region, from server to server, so that the same information is available at all locations. Any of the information can be managed from any location, and the changes made automatically propagate throughout the network. This might not matter or make sense to the user of an eight-person network, but to the manager of a corporate network that spans several continents, the ability to manage a given computer just as easily from Canada as from Canberra is *very* appealing indeed.

Active Directory is a true database: It can store any sort of information. Out of the box, it's used to store usernames, passwords, group membership, privileges and other security information, and feature-limiting controls called Group Policies, as well as the names and locations of computers and network printers. But software developers also can use it to store arbitrary information about software applications, such as the location and names of the nearest database servers—anything that would be useful to have spread throughout an organization's network.

The most significant part of AD is that it's hierarchical: It arranges information in user-defined groups called *containers*, which can be nested to any depth. The purpose of this hierarchy is to let AD represent the real structure of an organization. AD lets a network manager define groups by geographical region, department, workgroup, function, or whatever categories make sense to the organization. Each grouping can contain other groups, until finally actual users and/or their computers, printers, and other resources are entered.

The purpose of this feature is to enable network managers to assign usage and management privileges, such as the right to access certain files or the right to manage user accounts to these containers at appropriate levels instead of to individuals. Therefore, a network manager can grant access to users based on the organization's own structure instead of on a user-by-user basis or through "flat" enterprise-wide groups.

For example, let's say a company has East Coast and West Coast divisions and an accounting department in each (see Figure 19.3).

Figure 19.3
Active Directory lets network managers define groups based on actual organizational structure. These groupings model the organization's chains of command. The resulting structure can then be used to sensibly control access privileges and to delegate management rights.

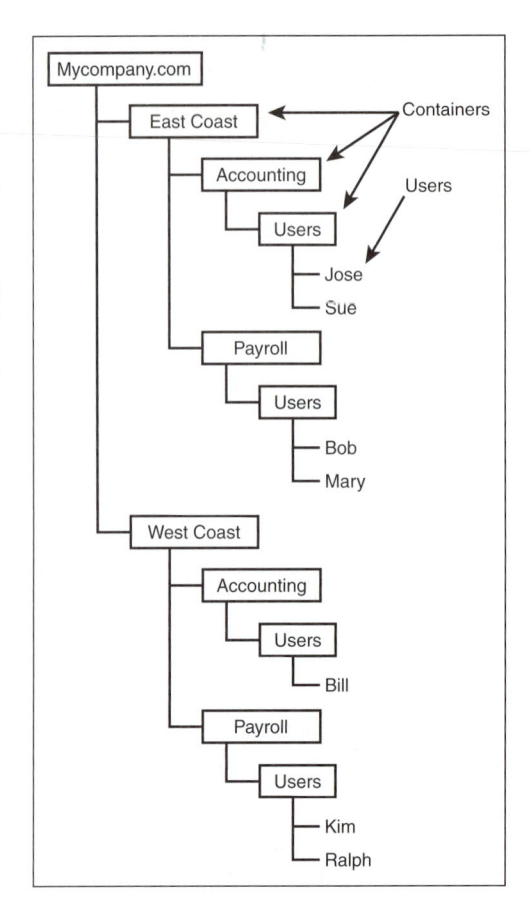

```
Mycompany.com
├── East Coast                    ← Containers
│   ├── Accounting                  Users
│   │   └── Users
│   │       ├── Jose
│   │       └── Sue
│   └── Payroll
│       └── Users
│           ├── Bob
│           └── Mary
└── West Coast
    ├── Accounting
    │   └── Users
    │       └── Bill
    └── Payroll
        └── Users
            ├── Kim
            └── Ralph
```

If the network manager grants read and write privileges to a shared network folder to the East Coast container, all users anywhere in the East Coast structure (Jose, Sue, Bob, and Mary) get access rights to the folder. If Jose is granted "manager" rights to the East Coast Accounting group, he can control the user accounts for Sue and himself.

Management of all East Coast printers could be granted to a network manager by granting him management rights to the East Coast container. He then would get the right to manage any printers within the entire container, across all its subdivisions.

Active Directory can be integrated into the domain name system for a company's network so that, for example, a computer in the East Coast accounting division could be named bigbox.accounting.eastcoast.mycompany.com.

Active Directory is used internally by Windows tools such as Explorer and the Print Manager. User-written programs can get access to the directory's contents through a programming interface called Active Directory Services Interface (ADSI) or more generally through an Internet protocol called Lightweight Directory Access Protocol (LDAP), which is an industry standard for directory queries and responses.

IntelliMirror

You might hear the term *IntelliMirror* and wonder what sort of network feature it is. IntelliMirror actually is just Microsoft's name for several features and services provided by its domain networks based on Active Directory:

- **Remote Installation**—Windows Vista can be installed from scratch onto an empty hard drive over a network.
- **Roaming User Profiles**—Your Documents folder and your preferences settings are stored on the network servers and copied to the computers you use, so they're available anywhere on your enterprise network.
- **Group Policy**—Windows's capability to "force" preferences settings and restrict access to system configuration dialog boxes is based on Registry entries defined by the network administrators and copied to your computer when you log in.
- **Application Publication**—Application software such as Word and Excel can be installed automatically across the network, based again on Group Policy settings.

Together these features let network administrators give you the experience of walking up to any computer in your organization and having it be "your" computer, with all your files, settings, and applications. In theory, you should even be able to log off, throw your computer out the window, and replace it with a brand new, empty one, and in short order pick up your work where you left off. In theory, anyway.

Intranet/Internet Services and Tools

Windows Vista comes with a set of applications and tools that Internet and UNIX users expect on a TCP/IP-based computer. They're not part of Windows Networking, technically speaking, because they don't use the Networking Clients. They communicate with other computers using TCP/IP directly. These tools include the following:

- Internet Explorer (Web browser)
- SNMP agents
- `telnet`
- `ping`
- FTP
- `nslookup`
- `pathping`
- `tracert`
- Windows Mail (SMTP/POP mail client)
- Internet Information Server (web server)

These programs are discussed in Part IV, "Windows Vista and the Internet."

Security

Finally, when Vista Business, Enterprise, or Ultimate editions act as members of a Windows Server–based network, they support the use of two very sophisticated network security systems to encrypt network traffic and to communicate passwords and information about user rights between computers:

- **IPSec**—The IPSec TCP/IP data-encryption standard provides a means by which each of the data packets sent across a network can be encrypted—scrambled—so that an eavesdropper with a wiretapping device can't glean passwords or other sensitive information from your data while it flows through the wires of your building, through airwaves in a wireless network, or across the Internet.

- **Kerberos**—The Kerberos network authentication protocol was developed at the Massachusetts Institute of Technology (MIT) and is now widely used in secure distributed network operating systems. Kerberos manages the identification of computer users on a network to eliminate many network security risks, such as the recording and playback of passwords. Kerberos also makes possible the "single sign-on" feature that enables you to log on to one computer and then be recognized as a legitimate user by other computers on a network, without having to re-enter your password.

> **TIP**
>
> Both IPSec TCP/IP data encryption and the Kerberos network authentication protocol are activated under the control of the administrator of Windows 200x Server and are invisible to you as a Windows Vista user.

Tips from the Windows Pros: Becoming a Networking Professional

I've found that modern network software works perfectly the first time about 99% of the time. When things go wrong, however, you quickly find that even Windows Vista's pretty diagnostic tools are nowhere near as sophisticated, automated, or helpful as the installation tools. You need a more complete understanding of network technology and structure to diagnose a broken network than you do to install one. More to the point, you need a more complete understanding than I can give you in a general-purpose book like this.

So the big tip for this chapter is this: If you're planning to set up a network for more than a few computers, or if you're setting up a network in a business situation, you should have some pretty solid expertise on hand for the times when problems arise. You might have a consultant install and maintain your network, or you might at least establish a relationship with a consultant or technician whom you can call if you run into trouble.

If you want to become a networking professional yourself, I recommend the following books as places to continue your training:

> *Upgrading and Repairing Networks*, Fourth Edition (Que, 2003; ISBN 0789728176)
>
> *Networking with Windows Vista* (Que, 2008, ISBN 0789737779)

CHAPTER 20

Creating a Windows Network

In this chapter

Creating or Joining a Network   612

Planning Your Network   612

Choosing a Network and Cabling System   617

Installing Network Adapters   625

Installing Network Wiring   628

Configuring a Peer-to-Peer Network   642

Joining a Windows Domain Network   653

Network Security   655

Checking Out the Neighborhood   655

Installing and Configuring Backup Software   656

Bridging Two Network Types with Windows Vista   658

Troubleshooting   659

Tips from the Windows Pros: Grassroots Networking   661

Creating or Joining a Network

In the previous chapter, I discussed the benefits of having a network, whether it's between two computers in your home, ten in your office, or thousands spanning the globe. In this chapter, I show you what you'll need to buy to install your own home or small-office network using Windows Vista. Later in the chapter, I cover the actual network installation.

This chapter is directed primarily toward a small group of users, at home or at work, who want to set up a LAN for themselves. This type of LAN is called a *peer-to-peer network* because no one computer has a central role in managing the network. This type of network doesn't take full advantage of all Windows Vista's networking capabilities, but unless you have more than 10 computers to network, you probably don't need all those capabilities. For you, a peer-to-peer network is just the thing to let you share files and printers with your co-workers or housemates. Creating a speedy, useful network isn't nearly as hard or expensive as you might think. In fact, once you've done the planning and shopping, you should be able to get a network up and running in an hour or two.

If you're adding a computer to an existing network, you can skip ahead to the section titled "Installing Network Adapters." If you're on a corporate network, you probably won't need to handle any of the installation details yourself—your end-user support department will likely take care of all of this for you, and you can just skip ahead to the next chapter.

> **NOTE**
>
> If you are part of a Windows 200x domain network, or if your company uses Remote Installation Services and Management features, you probably won't need to (and might not even be able to) view or change any of the network settings or control panels described in this chapter.

If you're setting up a new network, though, read on. This chapter should give you all the information you need.

By the way, when I say "Windows 200x Server" I mean Windows 2000 Server, Windows Server 2003, or its successors.

Planning Your Network

You must plan your network around your own particular needs. What do you expect from a network? The following tasks are some you might want your network to perform:

- Share printers, files, and optical drives
- Share an Internet connection
- Receive faxes directly in one computer and print or route them to individuals

- Provide access to a wide area network (WAN) or other remote site
- Provide access to your LAN via a modem or the Internet from remote locations
- Host a website
- Operate a database server
- Play multiuser games

You should make a list of your network goals. You need to provide adequate capacity to meet these and future needs, but you also don't need to overbuild.

Instant Networking

If your goal is to share printers, files, and maybe an Internet connection among a few computers that are fairly close together and you don't want to make any decisions, here's a recipe for instant networking. Get the following items at your local computer store, or at an online shop such as www.buy.com. Chain computer or office supply stores are also a good bet if a sale or rebate offer is available.

- One 10/100BASE-T network adapter for each computer that doesn't already have a network interface. These cost $5–$15 for internal PCI cards, and $40 for PCMCIA or USB adapters. (The buy.com category is Computers–Networking–NIC Cards, PC Cards [for laptops], or USB Networks. Choose one of the featured or sale items.)
- A 10/100BASE-T hub with four or more ports for $10–$40, *or* a DSL/cable-sharing or dial-up gateway router with a built-in four-switch/hub, for $20–$90. (The buy.com category is Computers–Networking–Hubs or Cable/DSL.) I recommend using a router even if you aren't setting up a shared Internet connection.
- One CAT-5 patch cable for each computer. You'll place the hub next to one of the computers, so you'll need one short four-foot cable. The other cables need to be long enough to reach from the other computers to the hub. (The buy.com category is Computers–Accessories–Cables.)

When you have these parts, skip ahead to the "Installing Network Adapters" section, later in this chapter. By the way, I'm not getting a kickback from buy.com! I've just found that buying from them is a no-brainer. Their prices are low enough that it's hardly worth the time to shop around and, more important, their service is ultra-reliable and fast.

On the other hand, if you want to use wireless networking, need access to large databases, want fast Internet connectivity, or require centralized backup of all workstations, you need to plan and invest more carefully. I discuss some of the issues you should consider in the next section.

Are You Being Served?

If you're planning a network of more than a few computers, you need to make a big decision: whether to use Windows 200*x* Server. The Server versions provide a raft of networking services that Vista doesn't have, but you must learn how to configure and support them.

Table 20.1 lists the primary trade-offs between Vista and Server.

TABLE 20.1 PRIMARY DIFFERENCES BETWEEN WINDOWS VISTA AND WINDOWS 200X SERVER

Network with Windows Vista Only	Network with Windows 200x Server
This network provides up to 10 connections to other computers, but only up to 5 connections for the Home versions of Windows Vista.	Connections to the server are unlimited (subject to client licensing fees).
The cost is low.	This network costs a few hundred dollars more, plus additional fees for Client Access Licenses.
Configuration is simple (relatively, anyway).	This network is complex to configure and administer.
Each machine must be administered independently.	Administration is centralized.
Rudimentary remote access, connection sharing, and WAN support are provided.	The features are more sophisticated.
Managing file security is difficult when you have more than one user per computer.	Centralized user management eases the task of managing security.

For me, the five or ten-connection limit with Windows Vista is the main dividing line. You can work around the limit by not having a "main machine" that all users look to for shared files. But this is exactly what you'll find you need as your network grows to this size or larger. So if you have a network of more than ten computers, I recommend using at least one copy of Windows 200x Server.

NOTE

If you are running either of the Windows Vista Home editions, your computer will be limited to a maximum of five user connections. All other versions support a maximum of ten.

You can certainly use Server with smaller networks, too. Reasons for doing so include these:

- You want to connect your LAN through a WAN or through the Internet to another LAN at another location; that is, you want to join your network to a Server domain somewhere else.

- You want to support multiple simultaneous remote dial-in or virtual private network (VPN) users. (Of course, you can buy inexpensive VPN routers to handle this.)

- You want to exercise strict security controls, restrict your users' ability to change system settings, or use automatic application installation.

- You want to take advantage of advanced services such as DHCP, DNS, WINS, and so on.

If you decide you need or want Windows 200x Server, you should get a book dedicated to that OS and a big box of Alka Seltzer before you go any further.

When to Hire a Professional

You've probably heard this old adage: "If you want something done right, do it yourself!" It is true, to a point. Sometimes, though, the benefit of hiring someone else outweighs the pleasure of doing it yourself.

For a home network, you should definitely try to set it up yourself. Call it a learning experience, get friends to help and, if things still don't work, treat yourself to a truly humbling experience and watch a high-school-aged neighbor get it all working in 15 minutes. As long as you don't have to run wires through the wall or construct your own cables, you should be able to manage this job even with no prior networking experience. When something is called "Plug and Play" now, it really is.

However, the balance tips the other way for a business. If you depend on your computers to get your work done, getting them set up should be your first concern, but keeping them working should be your second, third, and fourth. If you have solid experience in network installation, installing a Windows Vista network will be a snap. But your business is hanging in the balance, and you should consider the cost of computer failure when you're deciding whether it's worth spending money on setup and installation. Hiring a good consultant and/or contractor will give you the following:

- An established relationship. If something goes wrong, you'll already know whom to call, and that person will already know the details of your system.
- A professional installation job.
- The benefit of full-time experience in network and system design without needing to pay a full-time salary.
- Time to spend doing something more productive than installing a network.

If you do want to hire someone, it's important to choose your consultant or contractor very carefully. Some tips include these:

- Ask friends and business associates for referrals before you go to Craigslist or the Yellow Pages.
- Ask a consultant or contractor for references, and check them out.
- Find out what the contractor's guaranteed response time is, if problems or failures occur in the future.
- Be sure that documentation is one of the contractor's "deliverables." You should get written documentation describing your system's installation, setup, and configuration, as well as written procedures for routine maintenance, such as making backups, adding users, and so on.

Even if you do hire someone else to build your network, you should stay involved in the process and understand the choices and decisions that are made.

Planning for Adequate Capacity

After you've looked at your requirements and considered your work habits, make a diagram of your office or home showing computer locations, and indicate where you want to place your computers and special shared resources, such as modems, printers, and so on. Remember that shared resources and the computers they're attached to need to be *turned on* to be used. For example, your main printer should probably be connected to a computer that will be on and accessible when it's needed by others. Likewise, if you use Internet Connection Sharing (ICS), the computer that makes your Internet connection needs to be turned on for others to access the Internet. It might make sense to designate one computer to be your "main machine," leave it turned on, and locate most of your shared resources there.

You can use your designated "main machine" as an ordinary workstation, but it should be one of your fastest computers with lots of memory. If you're planning to have this computer host a website using Internet Information Services (IIS), it should have *at least* 1GB of memory. If you don't want to have to leave one particular computer turned on all the time, you could get a network-ready printer and a network disk storage box.

Printers

You can share any printer connected to any of your Windows computers, and use it from any of your other computers. The printer cable will force you to locate the printer within 6–10 feet from the computer to which it's connected.

For an office network, remember that you can purchase printers that connect directly to your network so that they can be located farther away from your workstations. You'll pay up to several hundred dollars extra for this capability, but you'll get added flexibility and printing speed. Networked printers still need to use a Windows computer as a "print spooler," so you'll still need to leave their controlling computer on all the time. On the other hand, one Windows Vista computer can manage quite a few networked printers.

Backup System

You must include at least one backup system on your network if it's for business use. You can use magnetic tape or external, removable hard disks, but whatever medium you choose, your backup system should ideally be large enough to back up the entire hard drive of your "main machine" on one disk or tape. For home use, a large external hard disk should suffice. For business use, I recommend getting a Travan tape storage system and third-party tape backup program.

Some backup software can be configured to back up not only the machine with the tape drive, but also other machines, via your network. This type of backup works only when the computers remain turned on, but it can be a real boon in a business environment. A system that performs automatic daily backups of every computer in the office is a valuable insurance policy. I've used Computer Associates' Arcserve for this purpose; it's rather difficult to install and set up, but it's really a first-class system. Veritas Software's Backup Exec is another good bet.

> **NOTE**
>
> Windows Vista Home edition does not support scheduled backups or network-based backups. If you plan to use either of these, you'll either have to upgrade your version of Windows Vista, or use third-party backup software.

→ To learn more about network backups, **see** "Installing and Configuring Backup Software," **p. 656**.

Power Surprise

One of the last things people think about when planning a network is the fact that every computer and external device has to be powered. You might be surprised how often people plan a network and get all their hardware together, only to realize that they have no power outlet near their computer or have placed 10 devices next to one outlet. The result can be a tangle of extension cords and a reprimand from the fire marshal.

Furthermore, your file server(s) or "main machine(s)" should be protected with an uninterruptible power supply, or UPS. These devices contain rechargeable batteries and instantly step in if the AC power to your building fails. When a power failure occurs during the exact instant that your computer is writing data to its hard disk, without a UPS, you're almost guaranteed some sort of data corruption: lost data, missing files, corrupted database index files, or worse—fried motherboards and dead hard drives.

> **TIP**
>
> I find it helpful to plug a power strip into a UPS when connecting several low-consumption devices such as modems or hub power supplies. I write "UPS" all over these power strips with a red marker so that nobody uses them for laser printers or other devices that should not be plugged into the UPS.

Finally, in an office situation, if you clump your server or "central" computer, laser printers, office copiers, and fax machine together (as many people do), call in an electrician to ensure that you have adequate power circuits to run all these energy-sucking devices.

Choosing a Network and Cabling System

For a simple home or small office network, you can choose among four types of network connections:

- 10/100BASE-T (Fast Ethernet) over high-quality CAT-5 UTP wiring
- 1000MB (gigabit) Ethernet over CAT-5E wiring
- Phone line or power line networking
- 802.11g wireless networking

I described these systems in Chapter 19, "Overview of Windows Networking." The 1000Mbps wired option is the fastest option, but for the average small office or home network, any of these four options will provide perfectly adequate performance. In the next sections, I go over the pros and cons of each type.

> **TIP**
>
> If your network is small and/or temporary, you can run network cables along walls and desks. Otherwise, you probably should keep them out of the way and protect them from accidental damage by installing them in the walls of your home or office. As you survey your site and plan your network, consider how the network cabling is to be routed.

If you can't or aren't allowed to drill through your location's walls, see "Can't Drill Through Walls or Ceilings" in the "Troubleshooting" section later in this chapter.

10/100BASE-T Ethernet

10/100BASE-T Ethernet networks use unshielded twisted-pair (commonly called UTP), twisted-pair, or phone wire cabling. This last name is a little dangerous because I'm not talking about the thin, flat, ribbonlike cable used to connect a phone to a wall jack, nor is it likely that phone wires installed in the 1930s will work. The "10/100" part of the name means that the equipment can run at 100Mbps, but it can automatically slow down to 10Mbps if it's connected to older 10BASE-T equipment.

These networks require that you use cable and connectors designated "CAT-5" or better. You can buy premade network cables in lengths of 3–50 feet, or you can buy bulk cable and attach the connectors yourself. I discuss this more in the "Installing Network Wiring" section later in this chapter.

→ To learn more about UTP wiring, **see** "Unshielded Twisted Pair (UTP) Cable," **p. 594**.

A cable is run from each computer to a hub, which is a small connecting box that routes the signals between each computer. You need to get a hub that has at least as many ports (sockets) as you have computers, plus a spare or two. 10/100BASE-T hubs cost roughly $5–$10 per port. A typical setup is shown in Figure 20.1.

> **TIP**
>
> Multiple hubs can be connected if your network grows beyond the capacity of your first hub. You can add on instead of replacing your original equipment.

> **TIP**
>
> If you have DSL or cable broadband Internet service, see Chapter 22, "Connecting Your Network to the Internet," for some advice about hardware connection-sharing devices before you make any decisions about your network. Some connection-sharing router devices have a built-in hub, sparing you the expense of buying a separate one.

Figure 20.1
A 10/100BASE-T network connects each computer to a hub with UTP cabling. It sounds sophisticated, but remember, you can buy this stuff at most office supply stores.

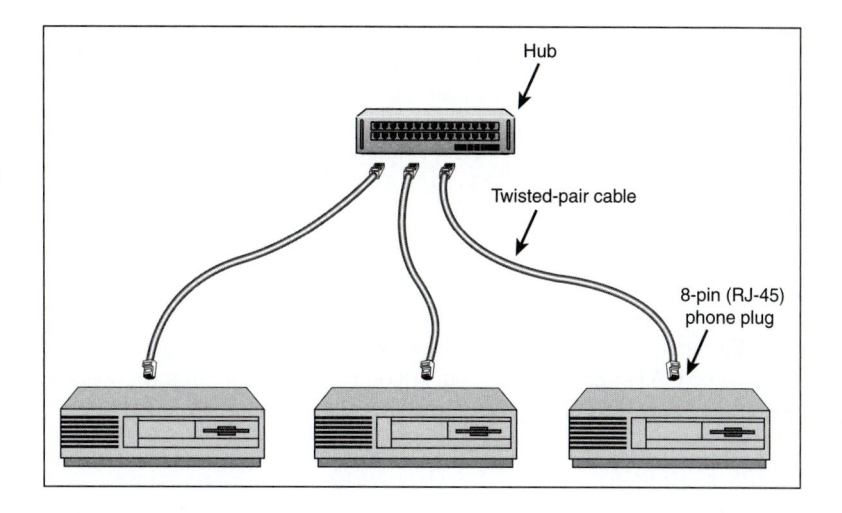

10/100BASE-T network interface cards (NICs) are available for as little as $5 each (if you catch a sale) and are made by companies such as Intel, 3COM, NetGear, Farallon, SMC, Kingston, D-Link, Linksys, Boca, and Cnet. Most "nameless" cheapo cards are based on one of a handful of standard chipsets, so they'll usually work even if they're not listed in the Windows Catalog at www.windowsmarketplace.com or www.microsoft.com/whdc/hcl/default.mspx.

> **NOTE**
> Adapters come in three styles: external adapters that you connect with a USB cable; thin, credit card–size PCMCIA (PC card) adapters for laptops; and internal PCI cards for desktop computers. If your computer is so old that it has only ISA slots, you'll need to get a 10BASE-T ISA adapter.

Remember, if you want to use existing in-wall wiring for your network, you should ensure that it's at least CAT-5 certified.

When you're shopping for a hub, you might see devices called switches. *Switches* are hubs on steroids. Whereas a hub is a simple repeater that forwards received data to every device on the LAN, a switch can route data among several pairs of computers simultaneously, if all are transmitting at once. Switches used to be more expensive than hubs, but the circuitry inside is now mass-produced and cheap enough that a price difference no longer exists. Get the switch type, if you can.

> **TIP**
>
> Even if you're not going to set up a shared broadband Internet connection, I recommend that you buy an Internet Connection Sharing router instead of a plain hub to use as your network's hub, just to get the DHCP service it provides (more on that later in the chapter). On sale, these routers cost no more than a plain hub. In fact, as I write this, today's newspaper has an ad for a router for $20 with a $20 mail-in rebate.

Overall, 10/100BASE-T networking is as inexpensive as it gets—hooking up three computers should set you back less than $75. It's easy to set up, and it's very reliable. On the down side, though, you do need to run those wires around, and any connectors and wall data jacks need to be CAT-5 certified as well. If you use in-wall wiring, the work should be done by someone with professional-level skills.

1000Mbps Ethernet (Gigabit Ethernet)

Ultra-high-speed Gigabit Ethernet networking is probably overkill for most home and small office networks, but it's making an appearance in the corporate world and in some fields such as medical imaging and digital movie production. The cost is so low now that some new PCs and Macs now come with 10/100/1000Gb Ethernet adapters as standard equipment.

If you want to use Gigabit Ethernet, you need to use CAT-5E- or CAT-6-certified connectors and cabling. You should use only commercially manufactured patch cables or professionally installed wiring. If you want, you can use a 10/100/1000Mbps hub or switch to connect your computers so that not all of your computers need to use the more expensive cabling and adapters.

> **NOTE**
>
> Most cable/DSL–sharing routers have 10/100Mbps switching hubs built in. Your Gigabit adapters will run at only 100Mbps if plugged into such a device. If you want a full-speed Gigabit network with a shared broadband connection, plug your computers into a 10/100/1000MBps (Gigabit) switch using CAT-6 cables and then connect the switch's "cascade" port to your Cable/DSL–sharing router.

Phone Line and Power Line Networking

HomePNA (Home Phoneline Networking Association) devices send network data by transmitting radio signals over your existing telephone wiring, using a network adapter that plugs into a telephone jack (see Figure 20.2). These devices don't interfere with the normal operation of your telephones; the extra signal just hitchhikes along the wires.

Figure 20.2
Phone line networking uses existing household telephone wiring to carry a radio frequency signal between networked computers.

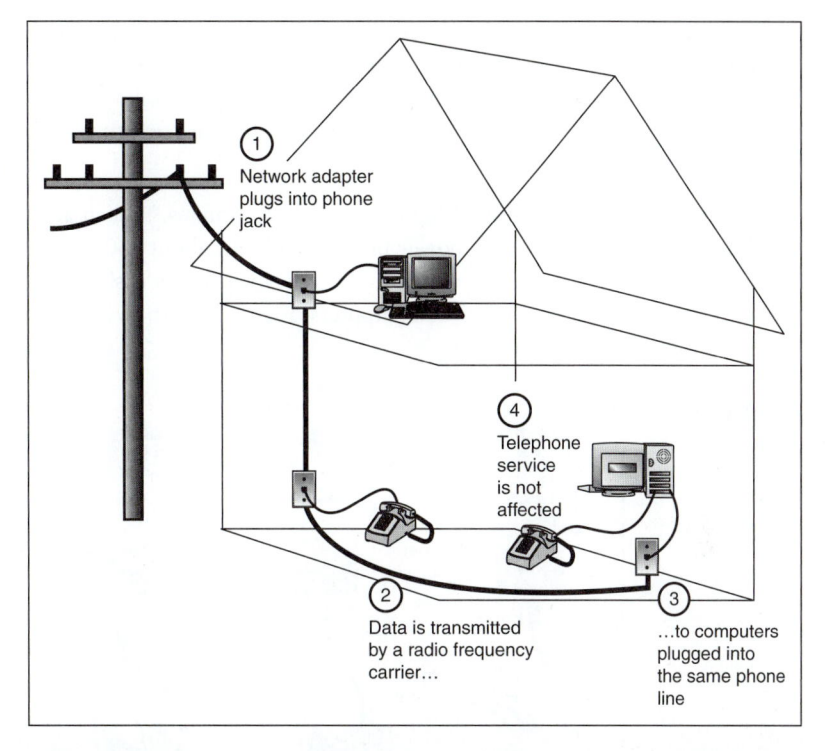

1. Network adapter plugs into phone jack
2. Data is transmitted by a radio frequency carrier…
3. …to computers plugged into the same phone line
4. Telephone service is not affected

> **TIP**
>
> If you use phone line networking, be certain to get only HPNA 2.0–compatible adapters or better. This will ensure that your equipment will operate at least at 10Mbps and will work with other manufacturers' products. Don't get any device that connects through your computer's parallel port: It's too slow.

Phone line networking is intended primarily for home use. The products are relatively inexpensive—about $70 per computer—and don't require you to string cables around the house. However, they have some disadvantages:

- All your adapters must be plugged into the same telephone line. So the same extension must be present at a phone outlet near each of your computers. If you need to call in a wiring contractor to add a phone extension, you haven't saved much over a wired network.
- "Access Point" devices, used to link a standard wired-networked computer to your phone line network, are relatively rare.

Without a hardware access point, it's difficult to use a hardware Internet Connection Sharing device or to add standard wired computers to your network. However, Windows Vista can manage it in software, if necessary. I discuss this later in this chapter under "Bridging Two Network Types with Windows Vista."

HomePlug (HomePlug Powerline Alliance) adapters work in a similar fashion, sending signals through your electrical wiring, and are plugged into a wall socket. These also provide 10MBps performance, and they are more flexible than the phone line system because you don't need to worry about having a phone jack near your computers—just a nearby electrical outlet.

In addition, you can get HomePlug devices called "bridges," which are specifically designed to link a wired network to the power line network, for about $60—the Linksys Powerline EtherFast 10/100 Bridge is an example. This means you can easily add a shared Internet connection router or mix in wired computers. Figure 20.3 shows how this would look in a typical home network.

Figure 20.3
Typical power line networking setup, showing HomePlug adapters and bridges.

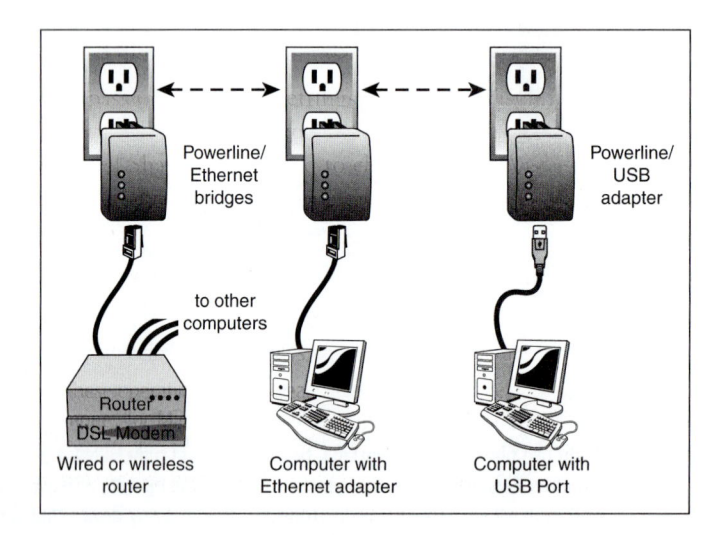

802.11G Wireless Networking

One way to build a network without hubs, cables, connectors, drills, swearing, tools, or outside contractors is to go wireless. Blocks of radio frequencies in the 2.4GHz (802.11b) and 5GHz (802.11a) bands are reserved for close-range data communications, and standardized products from cordless telephones to computer networks are now available to take advantage of this. Prices have fallen to the point that wireless connectivity is now competitive with wired networks, even before the installation cost savings are factored in.

Today's high-speed 802.11g equipment operates at up to 54Mbps and is compatible with older 802.11b (11MBps) equipment. Some manufacturers offer Wireless-G equipment that operates at up to 108Mbps. This is great, but you should know that you'll get the speed boost only if you buy all your equipment from the same manufacturer (and even then, you need to read the packaging carefully to see if the double-speed function will work with the particular parts you're buying). You might also read about 802.11a equipment. "Wireless A" is used mainly in corporate environments and is much more expensive than the more modern "Wireless G" equipment that I am recommending.

CHOOSING A NETWORK AND CABLING SYSTEM | 623

NOTE
> You might also come across "Pre-N" wireless equipment. These devices are based on the new, yet to be approved, 802.11n standard. This means that such devices do not conform to any standard at this point. When the 802.11n standard is released in a few years, there is no guarantee that existing Pre-N devices will conform to it.

Wireless networking products typically

- Give actual throughput of about half the advertised speed.
- Can transmit data about 100 feet indoors and up to 300 feet outdoors.
- Are available for both desktop and laptop computers, in PCI, PCMCIA (PC card), or USB formats.
- Cost $25–$70 per adapter.
- Can be bridged to a wired LAN through an optional device called an access point, router, bridge, or base unit, costing $40 and up. (That's not a typo: $40, if you catch a good sale.)
- Don't work well between floors of a multistory building.

TIP
> Whether or not you decide to set up a shared Internet connection, you'll save time and money by using a wireless Internet Connection Sharing router as your network's access point. A router includes a DHCP server (more on that later) that simplifies setting up your network.

Figure 20.4 shows a typical family of wireless products: a wireless access point (Ethernet bridge), a wireless router that can also share a DSL or Internet connection, an internal wireless network adapter for desktop computers, and a PCMCIA adapter for laptops.

Figure 20.4
Typical wireless networking equipment. Clockwise from upper left: access point, router with Internet Connection Sharing capability, PCI adapter, PCMCIA adapter. (Photo used by permission of D-Link.)

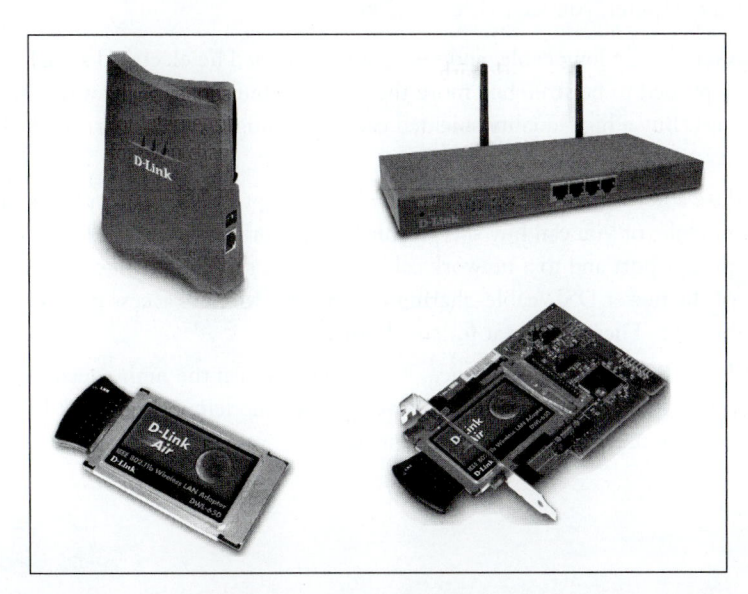

Mixed Networking

If you are updating an existing network or are connecting two separate types of networks, you should consider several things.

If you have some existing 10Mbps-only devices and want to add new 100Mbps devices without upgrading the old, you can buy a new dual-speed (10/100) hub, which connects to each computer at the maximum speed it permits. But you should be wary of some so-called autosensing 10/100Mbps hubs, which purport to let you connect both 10Mbps and 100Mbps devices. Some of these hubs force the entire network to run at 10Mbps if any one device runs this lower speed. Read the specifications carefully. You want a hub that's labeled either "N-way autosensing" or "switching."

> **TIP**
>
> To speed up a 10Mbps network, instead of replacing all the wiring and network cards in all your computers, upgrade just the network card in your file server to a 100Mbps device. Get a 10/100 switching hub to connect the server to the workstations, and use a CAT-5 cable to connect the server to the new hub. This effectively gives every computer its own full 10Mbps channel to the file server at a minimal cost.

Finally, if you want to mix standard Ethernet or wireless devices on your network, you can use the Bridge feature built into Windows Vista, or you'll need one of the bridges or access points I mentioned earlier. I discuss bridging in the section "Bridging Two Network Types with Windows Vista," later in this chapter.

Printing and Faxing

Shared printers simply need to be connected to their host Windows Vista computers with a standard USB or parallel printer cable. If the printer needs to be farther than 10 feet away from a computer, you have three choices:

1. Get a really long cable, and take your chances. The electrical signal for printers is not supposed to be stretched more then 10 feet, but I've gotten away with 25 feet in the past. Buy a high-quality shielded cable. You might get data errors (bad printed characters) with this approach.

2. Use a network-capable printer. Or, for some printers, you can buy a network printer module, or you can buy special third-party "print server" modules, which connect to the printer port and to a network cable. Network supply catalogs list myriad devices. Some of the newer DSL/cable–sharing routers and wireless access points have a print server built in. These are great for small offices.

3. Use a printer-extender device. These devices turn the high-speed parallel data signal into a serial data connection, somewhat as a modem does. I don't like these devices because they result in very slow printing.

If your network includes Windows 95, 98, NT 3 or 4, or Windows 3.1 computers, take the time to collect the CDs or floppy disks containing the printer drivers for all the operating systems you use, for each of your printers. Windows Vista lets you load in the printer drivers for the older operating systems and lets these computers automatically download the proper printer driver when they use the shared printer. We cover this slick feature in Chapter 23, "Using a Windows Network."

Providing Internet Connectivity

You'll probably want to have Internet access on your LAN. It's far less expensive, and far safer security-wise, to have one connection to the Net for the entire LAN than to let each user fend for himself or herself.

Windows Vista has a built-in Internet Connection Sharing feature that lets a single computer use a dial-up, cable, or DSL modem and make the connection on behalf of any user on your LAN. You can also use an inexpensive hardware device called a router to make the connection. I strongly prefer the hardware devices over Windows Internet Connection Sharing. This topic is important enough that it gets its own chapter. I recommend that you read Chapter 22 before you buy any equipment.

You should also study Chapter 35, "Protecting Your Network from Hackers and Snoops," and pay close attention to the section titled "Network Security Basics" to build in proper safeguards against hacking and abuse. This is especially important with full-time cable/DSL connections.

Providing Remote Access

You also can provide connectivity to your network from the outside world, either through the Internet or via a modem. This connectivity enables you to access your LAN resources from home or out in the field, with full assurance that your network is safe from outside attacks. Chapter 38, "Hitting The Road" covers dial-up and VPN network access, and Chapter 40 covers Remote Desktop.

If you need to access your network from outside and you aren't planning to have a permanent direct Internet connection, you might want to plan for the installation of a telephone line near one of your Windows Vista computers so that you can set up a dedicated modem line for incoming access.

Installing Network Adapters

If you're installing a new network adapter, follow the manufacturer's instructions for installing with Windows Vista (if applicable). Even if it does not come with specific Windows Vista instructions, the installation should be a snap. Just follow these steps:

1. If you have purchased an internal card, shut down Windows, shut off the computer, unplug it, open the case, install the card in an empty slot, close the case, and restart Windows.

> **TIP**
>
> If you've never worked inside your computer, jump ahead to Chapter 30, "Installing and Replacing Hardware," for advice and handy tips.

If you are adding a PCMCIA or USB adapter, be sure you're logged on with a Computer Administrator account, and then plug it in while Windows is running.

2. When you're back at the Windows login screen, log in as a Computer Administrator. Windows displays the New Hardware Detected dialog box when you log in.

3. The New Hardware Detected dialog box might instruct you to insert your Windows Vista DVD. If Windows cannot find a suitable driver for your adapter from this DVD, it might ask you to insert a driver disk that your network card's manufacturer should have provided (either a CD-ROM or a floppy disk).

   If you are asked, insert the manufacturer's disk and click OK. If Windows says that it cannot locate an appropriate device driver, try again, and this time click the Browse button. Locate a folder named Windows Vista (or some reasonable approximation) and click OK.

> **NOTE**
>
> The exact name of the folder containing your device driver varies from vendor to vendor. You might have to poke around a little on the disk to find it.

4. After Windows has installed the card's driver software, it automatically configures and uses the card. Check the Device Manager to see whether the card is installed and functioning. Then you can proceed to "Installing Network Wiring," later in this chapter.

→ For more detailed instructions about installing drivers, see Chapter 30.

Checking Existing Adapters

If your adapter was already installed when you set up Windows Vista, it should be ready to go. In this case, you can skip this section and jump down to "Installing Network Wiring." Follow these steps to see whether the adapter is already set up:

1. Click Start, right-click Computer, and select Manage.

2. Select Device Manager in the left pane, and open the Network Adapters list in the right pane.

3. Look for an entry for your network card. If it appears and does not have a yellow exclamation point (!) icon to the left of its name, the card is installed and correctly configured. In this case, you can skip ahead to "Installing Network Wiring."

   If an entry appears but has a yellow exclamation point icon by its name, the card is not correctly configured.

4. If no entry exists for the card, the adapter is not fully plugged into the motherboard, it's broken, or it is not Plug and Play capable. Be sure the card is installed correctly. If the card is broken or not Plug-and-Play, you should replace it. Check out Chapter 30 for troubleshooting tips.

> **NOTE** If you see an exclamation point icon in the Network Adapters list, skip ahead to Chapter 38, "Troubleshooting And Repairing Problems," for tips on getting the card to work before you proceed. Here's an additional tip: Network adapters are really inexpensive. If you're having trouble with an old adapter, just go get a new one.

INSTALLING MULTIPLE NETWORK ADAPTERS

You might want to install multiple network adapters in your computer in these situations:

- You simultaneously connect to two or more different networks with different IP addresses or protocols. You'd use a separate adapter to connect to each network.
- You want to share a broadband cable or DSL Internet connection with your LAN without using a hardware-sharing router. I strongly recommend using a hardware router, as I discuss in Chapter 22, but you can also do it using one adapter to connect to your LAN and another to connect to your cable or DSL modem.
- You have two different network types, such as phone line and Ethernet, and you want the computers on both LAN types to be able to communicate. You could use a hardware access point, but you could also install both types of adapters in one of your computers and use the Bridging feature to connect the networks. I discuss bridging later in this chapter.

I suggest that you use the following procedure to install multiple adapters:

1. Install and configure the first adapter. If you're doing this to share an Internet connection, install and configure the one you'll use for the Internet connection first. Configure and test the Internet connection as well.
2. Click Start, Control Panel, Network and Internet, Network and Sharing Center. Click Manage Network Connections from the task list on the left side of the window. Select the icon named Local Area Connection and choose Rename This Connection in Network Tasks. (Or, right-click the icon and select Rename.) Change the connection's name to something that indicates what it's used for, such as "Connection to Cable Modem" or "Office Ethernet Network."
3. Write the name on a piece of tape or a sticky label and apply it to the back of your computer above the network adapter, or to the edge plate of the network card.
4. Install the second adapter. Configure it and repeat Steps 2 and 3 with the new Local Area Connection icon. Name this connection appropriately—for example, "LAN" or "Wireless Net"—and put a tape or paper label on the computer, too.

If you follow these steps, you'll be able to easily distinguish the two connections instead of needing to remember which Local Area Connection icon is which.

Installing Network Wiring

When your network adapters are installed, the next step is to get your computers connected. Installing the wiring can be the most difficult task of setting up a network. How you proceed depends on the type of networking adapters you have:

- If you're using wireless adapters, of course, you don't need to worry about wiring. You can just skip ahead to "Installing a Wireless Network," later in this chapter.

- If you're using phone line networking, plug a standard modular telephone cable into each phone line network adapter and connect them to the appropriate wall jacks. The adapter must be plugged directly into the wall jack, and then additional devices such as modems, telephones, and answering machines can be connected to the adapter. Remember that each of the phone jacks must be wired to the same telephone line. Then skip ahead to the "Configuring a Peer-to-Peer Network" section, later in the chapter.

- If you're using a power line networking adapter, follow the manufacturer's installation instructions. If you're using a power line bridge, plug the bridge into a wall socket and connect it to your computer or other networked device with a CAT-5 patch cable. Follow the manufacturer's instructions for configuring the adapter's security features. You should enable encryption if it's available. Then skip ahead to the "Configuring a Peer-to-Peer Network" section, later in the chapter.

If you're using UTP Ethernet adapters, you need to decide how to route your wiring and what type of cables to use. The remainder of this section discusses UTP wiring.

Cabling for Ethernet Networks

If your computers are close together, you can use prebuilt patch cables to connect your computers to a hub. (The term *patch cable* originated in the telephone industry—in the old days, switchboard operators used patch cables to temporarily connect, or patch, one phone circuit to another. In networking, the term refers to cables that are simply plugged in and not permanently wired.) You can run these cables through the habitable area of your home or office by routing them behind furniture, around partitions, and so on. Just don't put them where they'll be crushed, walked on, tripped over, or run over by desk chair wheels.

If the cables need to run through walls or stretch long distances, you should consider having them installed inside the walls with plug-in jacks, just like your telephone wiring. I discuss this topic later in this section. Hardware stores sell special cable covers that you can use if you need to run a cable where it's exposed to foot traffic, as well as covers for wires that need to run up walls or over doorways.

TIP
> As you install each network card and plug it into the cables running to your hub, you should see a green light come on at the hub and on the network adapter. These lights indicate that the network wiring is correct.

If you don't get green lights, stop immediately and get the wiring fixed. Check out "Hub Lights Do Not Come On" in the "Troubleshooting" section, later in this chapter.

GENERAL CABLING TIPS

You can determine how much cable you need by measuring the distance between computers and your hub location(s). Remember to account for vertical distances, too, where cables run from the floor up to a desktop, or go up and over a partition or wall.

CAUTION
> If you need to run cables through the ceiling space of an office building, you should check with your building management to see whether the ceiling is listed as a plenum or air-conditioning air return. You might be required by law to use certified plenum cable and follow all applicable electrical codes. Plenum cable is specially formulated not to emit toxic smoke in a fire.

Keep in mind the following points:

- Existing household telephone wire probably won't work. If the wires are red, green, black, and yellow: no way. The cable jacket must have CAT-5 (or higher) printed on it. It must have color-matched twisted pairs of wires; usually each pair has one wire in a solid color and the other white with colored stripes.

- You must use CAT-5-quality wiring and components throughout, and not just the cables. Any jacks, plugs, connectors, terminal blocks, patch cables, and so on also must be CAT-5 certified.

- If you're installing in-wall wiring, follow professional CAT-5 wiring practices throughout. Be sure not to untwist more than half an inch of any pair of wires when attaching cables to connectors. Don't solder or splice the wires.

- When you're installing cables, be gentle. Don't pull, kink, or stretch them. Don't bend them sharply around corners; you should allow at least a 1-inch radius for bends. Don't staple or crimp them. To attach cables to a wall or baseboard, use rigid cable clips that don't squeeze the cable, as shown in Figure 20.5. Your local electronics store can sell you the right kind of clips.

- Keep network cables away from AC power wiring and away from electrically noisy devices such as arc welders, diathermy machines, and the like.

Figure 20.5
Use rigid cable clips or staples that don't squeeze the cable if you nail it to a wall or baseboard.

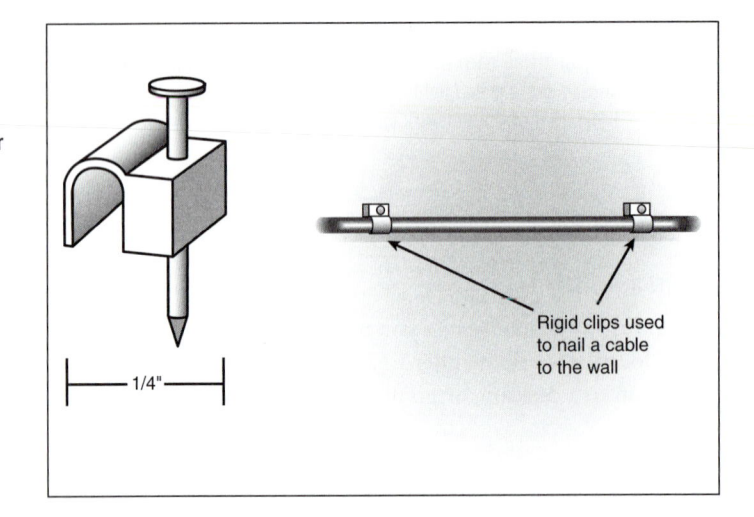

[Figure shows a rigid cable clip with a nail, 1/4" wide, and rigid clips used to nail a cable to the wall.]

NOTE

> If you really want to get into the nuts and bolts, so to speak, of pulling your own cable, a good starting point is Frank Derfler and Les Freed's *Practical Network Cabling* (Que, 1999; ISBN 078972247X), which will help you roll up your shirt sleeves and get dirty (literally, if you need to crawl around through your attic or wrestle with dust bunnies under too many desks at the office).

Wiring with Patch Cables

If your computers are close together and you can simply run prefabricated cables between your computers and hub, you've got it made. Buy CAT-5 cables of the appropriate length online or at your local computer store. Just plug (click) in, and you're finished. Figure 20.1 shows how to connect your computers to the hub.

If you have the desire and patience, you can build custom-length cables from crimp-on connectors and bulk cable stock. Making your own cables requires about $75 worth of tools, though, and more detailed instructions than I can give here. Making just a few cables certainly doesn't make buying the tools worthwhile. Factory-assembled cables are also more reliable than homemade ones because the connectors are attached by machine. They're worth the extra few dollars.

For the ambitious or parsimonious reader, Figure 20.6 shows the correct way to order the wires in the connector.

Figure 20.6
Standard wiring order for UTP network cables.

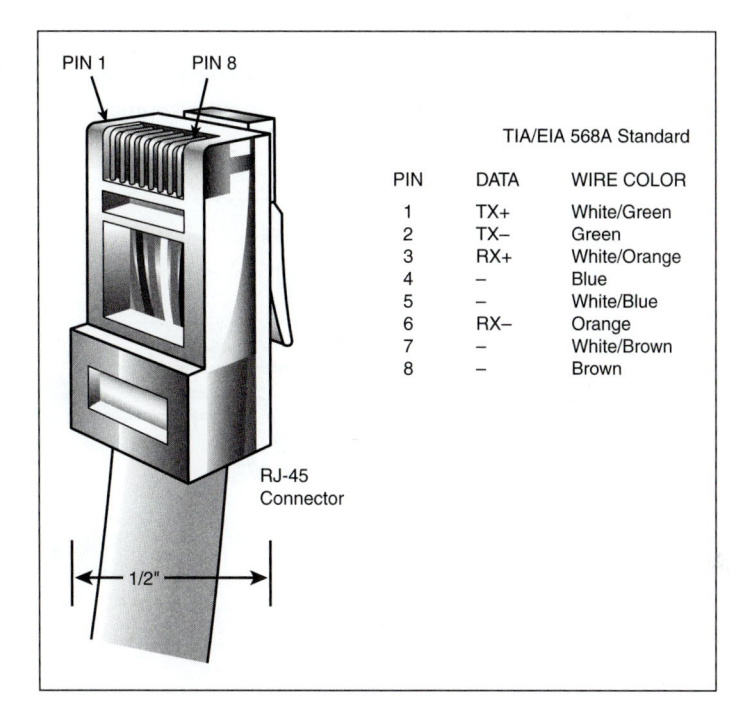

PIN	DATA	WIRE COLOR
1	TX+	White/Green
2	TX–	Green
3	RX+	White/Orange
4	–	Blue
5	–	White/Blue
6	RX–	Orange
7	–	White/Brown
8	–	Brown

TIA/EIA 568A Standard

INSTALLING IN-WALL WIRING

In-wall wiring is the most professional and permanent way to go. However, this often involves climbing around in the attic or under a building, drilling through walls, or working in an office telephone closet. If this is the case, calling in a professional is probably best. Personally, I find it a frustrating task and one I would rather watch someone else do. Hiring someone to get the job done might cost $30–$75 per computer, but you'll get a professional job, and if you consider that the price of network cards has gone down at least this much in the last few years, you can pretend that you're getting the wiring thrown in for free.

TIP

Look in the Yellow Pages under "Telephone Wiring," and ask the contractors you call whether they have experience with network wiring. The following are some points to check out when you shop for a wiring contractor:

- Ask for references, and check them out.
- Ask for billing details up front: Do they charge by the hour or at a fixed rate? Do they sell equipment themselves, or do you need to supply cables, connectors, and so on?
- Ask for prices for parts and labor separately so that you know whether you're getting a good deal and can comparison-shop.
- Find out what their guaranteed response time is, if problems or failures occur in the future.
- Ask what the warranty terms are. How long are parts and labor covered?

In-wall wiring is brought out to special network-style modular jacks mounted to the baseboard of your wall. These RJ-45 jacks look similar to telephone modular jacks but are wider. You need patch cables to connect the jacks to your computers and hub, as shown in Figure 20.7.

Figure 20.7
Connect your computers and hub to the network jacks using short patch cables.

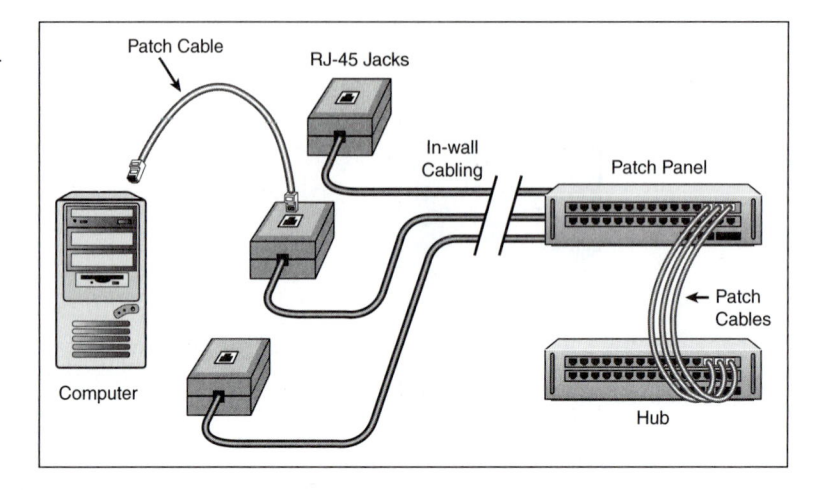

> **NOTE**
>
> To pick a technical nit here, the modular connector used in networking is really called an 8P8C connector. The "true telephone RJ45" connector is slightly different, and not compatible. If you're buying RJ45 connectors, just make sure that the package says that the connectors are for networking use.

OUT OF THE (PHONE) CLOSET

If you're wiring an office, running all your network wiring alongside the office's phone system wiring to a central location—the phone closet—might be most sensible. You might be able to put your hub near the phone equipment in this case. Your building might even already have CAT-5 wiring in place.

In most office buildings, telephone and data wiring are run to a central location on each floor or in each office suite. Connector blocks called *punchdown blocks* are bolted to the wall, where your individual telephone extension wires are joined to thick distribution cables maintained by the phone company or the building management.

These commercial wiring systems are a little bit daunting, and if you aren't familiar with them, it's best to hire a wiring contractor to install your network wiring.

CONNECTING JUST TWO COMPUTERS

If you're making a network of just two computers, you might be able to take a shortcut and eliminate the need for a network hub or additional special hardware. If you want to add on to your network later, you can always add the extra gear then.

If you are connecting two computers with Ethernet, yours is the second-easiest-possible network installation: Simply run a special cable called a *crossover cable* from one computer's network adapter to the other, and you're finished. This special type of cable reverses the send and receive signals between the two ends and eliminates the need for a hub. You can purchase a crossover cable from a computer store or network supply shop, or you can make one, as shown in Figure 20.8.

> **TIP**
>
> Be sure that your crossover cable is labeled as such. It won't work to connect a computer to a hub, and you'll go nuts wondering what's wrong if you try. Factory-made models usually have yellow ends. When I make them myself, I draw three rings around each end of the cable with a permanent-ink marker.

> **NOTE**
>
> Microsoft is encouraging the use of a special USB Cable for use by the Windows Easy Transfer program, for people who don't have a network. But, you can just as easily (and much less expensively) use an Ethernet crossover cable.

Figure 20.8
Wiring for a UTP crossover cable. The cable reverses the send and receive wires so that two network cards can be directly connected without a hub. Note that the green pair and orange pair are reversed across the cable.

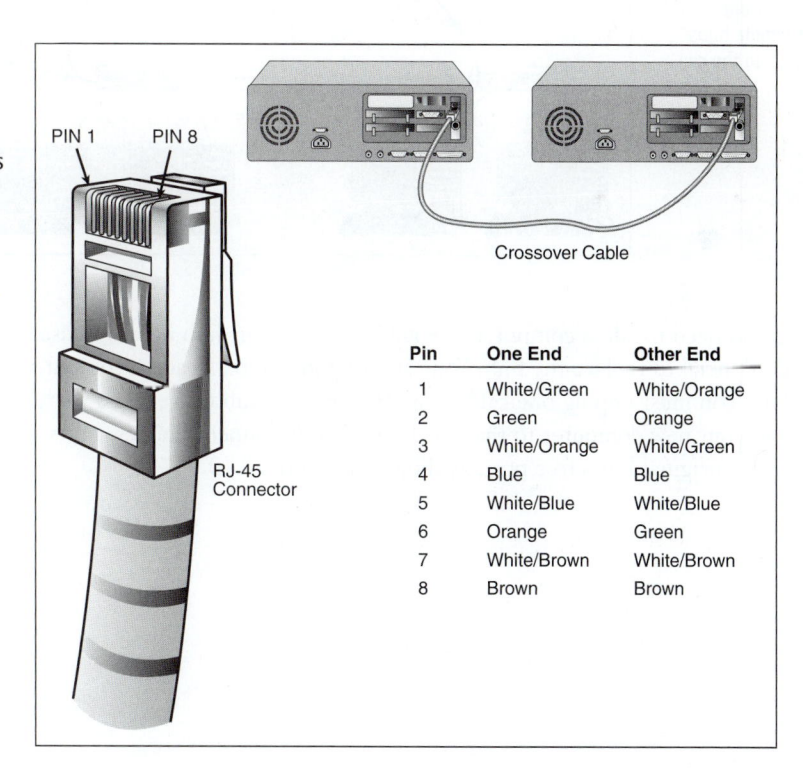

Pin	One End	Other End
1	White/Green	White/Orange
2	Green	Orange
3	White/Orange	White/Green
4	Blue	Blue
5	White/Blue	White/Blue
6	Orange	Green
7	White/Brown	White/Brown
8	Brown	Brown

CONNECTING MULTIPLE HUBS

You might want to use more than one hub to reduce the number of long network cables you need if you have groups of computers in two or more locations. For example, you can connect the computers on each "end" of the network to the nearest hub, and then connect the hubs to a main hub. Figure 20.9 shows a typical arrangement using this technique.

> **NOTE**
>
> A *cascade port* is a hub connector designed to be connected to another hub. Some hubs have a separate connector for this purpose, whereas others make one of the hub's regular ports do double-duty by providing a switch that turns the last hub port into a cascade port. Refer to your hub's manual to see what to do with your particular hardware.

Figure 20.9
You can connect groups of computers with multiple hubs to reduce the number of long cables needed. Use the cascade port on the remote hubs to connect to the central hub.

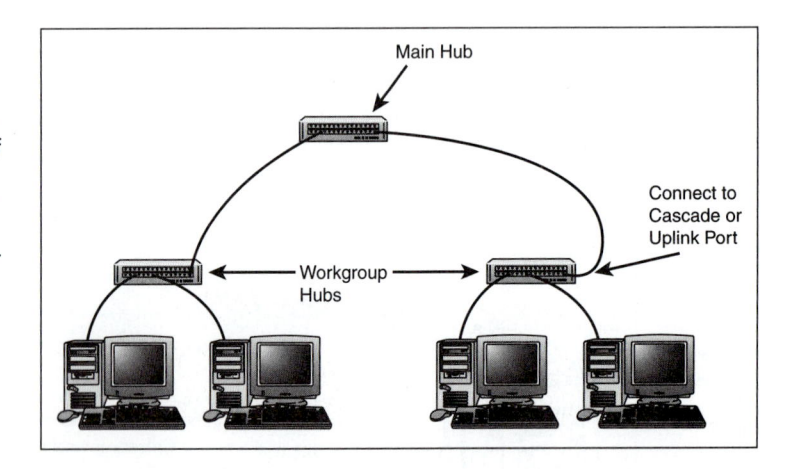

If you need to add a computer to your LAN and your hub has no unused connectors, you don't need to replace the hub. You can just add a hub. To add a computer to a fully loaded hub, you must unplug one cable from the original hub to free up a port. Connect this cable and your new computer to the new hub. Finally, connect the new hub's *cascade* or *uplink port* to the original hub's free port, as shown in Figure 20.10.

Figure 20.10
You can expand your network by cascading hubs. The instructions included with your hub describe how to connect two hubs using a patch cable. Some hubs have a dedicated uplink port, whereas others have a switch that turns a regular port into an uplink port.

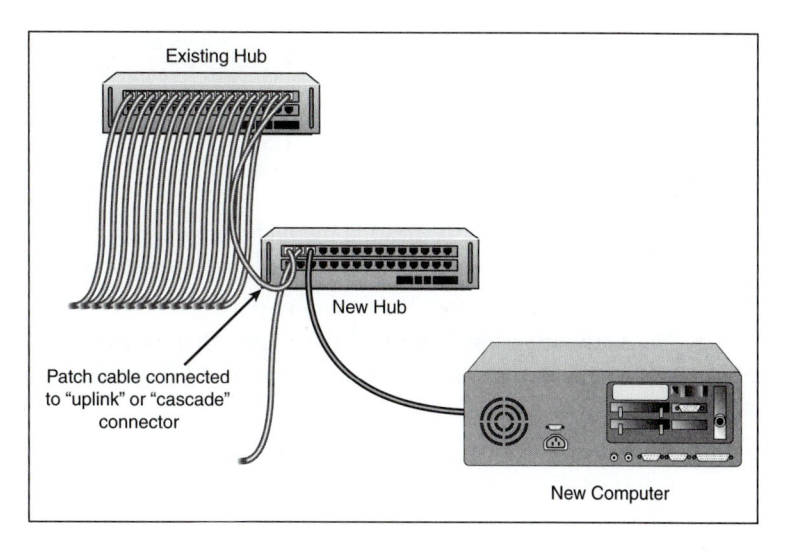

INSTALLING A WIRELESS NETWORK

If you are installing a wireless network, you need to configure wireless security and networking options after installing your network adapters.

> **NOTE**
> This section tells how to set up a wireless network in a home or small office. On a corporate wireless network, your network administrator will most likely be the one to configure the wireless adapter and security settings.

> **CAUTION**
> If you want to use file and printer sharing on your Wireless network, you must make the network secure by assigning a cryptographic "key" to the network. Otherwise, random people will be able to get at your computer.
>
> If you want to set up an "open" wireless hotspot to share your Internet connection with friends, neighbors, or the world, that's great, but you must not use file and printer sharing on the same network. See Chapter 19 for safer options.

Here's the scoop: It can easily happen that separate groups of people with wireless network gear set up within radio range of each other. In my office, I can pick up signals from four separate wireless networks: mine, the office next door's, a friend's from nearly a block away, and one other (I can't tell whose it is). Even in the suburbs, it's not uncommon to find that you can receive signals from several neighbors. And people do actually drive around with laptops in their car, looking for free Internet access. To protect against both freeloaders and hackers, one or two protection tecniques are used: *encryption*, which scrambles data, and *authentication*, which certifies that a given computer should be allowed to connect to the network. You can use either encryption alone, or both encryption and authentication.

To be able to distinguish your network's signal from others and to secure your network, you must make the following choices when you set up a wireless network:

- **An SSID (Service Set Identifier)**—A short name that you give your network, up to 32 characters in length. This could be your last name, your company name, your pet's name, or whatever makes sense to you.
- **A security type**—The authentication method that your network uses to determine whether or not a given computer should be allowed to connect. The choices are as follows, in order of increasing security:
  - **No Authentication (open)**—No authentication is performed; any computer can connect to the network. Networks that use WEP encryption should use this option.
  - **Shared**—All devices on the network are configured with a common passphrase (which is a fancy name for a password). Any device that knows the passphrase is allowed to connect to the network. This option actually creates additional security risks and should not be used.
  - **802.1X**—An older authentication method that uses a network server, software certificate, or smart card to authenticate computers. This method is used on some corporate networks along with WEP encryption.
  - **WPA-Personal**—An improved authentication method that uses a passphrase to validate each computer's membership in the network. The passphrase also serves as an encryption key.
  - **WPA2-Personal**—An improved version of WPA-Personal.
  - **WPA-Enterprise**—A version of WPA that uses a network server, smart card, or software certificate to validate network membership, used on corporate networks.
  - **WPA2-Enterprise**—An improved version of WPA-Enterprise.
- **An encryption type**—The encryption method used to secure network data against eavesdropping. The options that are available depend on the security (authentication) type that was selected. The choices, in increasing order of security, are:
  - **None**—No data encryption is performed. This option is available only when the security type is set to No Authentication.
  - **WEP**—Data is encrypted using the WEP protocol, using a 40-bit, 128-bit or 256-bit key. WEP is available only when the Security Type is set to No Authentication, Shared Authentication, or 802.1X.
  - **TKIP**—An encryption method that can be used with any of the WPA security types.
  - **AES**—An improved encryption method that can be used with any of the WPA security types.
- **An encryption key**—The key used to encrypt and decrypt data sent over the network. The different encryption methods use keys of different lengths.

For WEP encryption, you must enter the key as a string of 26 hexadecimal digits—that is, the numerals 0 through 9 and the letters A through F. (Windows Vista supports only

128-bit WEP encryption. 40-bit encryption is not supported. Previous versions of Windows also let you enter the WEP key as a text phrase, but the text method was pretty much guaranteed not to work when entered into wireless routers and access points, so it's been abandoned.)

For WPA or WPA encryption, enter a passphrase, a word, or phrase using any letters or characters, of 8 or more letters—the more the better, up to 63. The passphrase is case sensitive and can contain spaces, but must not begin or end with a space.

The encryption key should be kept secret because with it, someone can connect to your network, and from there get to your data and your shared files.

- **A channel number**—Selects the frequency used to transmit your network's data. In the U.S., this is a number between 1 and 11; the numbers might be different in other countries. The most common channels used are 1, 6, and 11. Start with channel 6.

Why so many different security methods? Because thieves, like rust, never sleep, and it seems that as soon as a new, safer method is standardized, someone figures out a way to break it. WEP stands for Wired-Equivalent Privacy but it turned out to be an overly optimistic name. It was found shortly after its release that a determined interloper can break WEP security in as little as a few hours. WPA (which stands for Wi-Fi Protected Access) has an improved encrypting scheme and is strong enough to prevent most attacks. WPA2 is a further improvement upon that, and it's the best option we have at present. It should deter even the most determined hacker but I wouldn't want to bet that it would keep the National Security Agency scratching its collective head for too long, if you know what I mean.

Which method should you use? On a corporate network, your network manager will configure your network or will give you setup instructions. On a home or small office network, you're limited by the least-capable of the devices on your network. So, select the best security method that is supported by *all* of your network gear, including any access points or routers.

Here are the options you should consider, in *decreasing* order of security. Use the first one that your equipment supports:

- If all of your equipment supports WPA2, use WPA2-Personal security with AES encryption.
- If all of your equipment supports WPA, use WPA-Personal with AES encryption.
- If the best method that is supported by all of your equipment is WEP, use No Authentication (open) security with WEP encryption. You must use the 128-bit WEP option; Vista doesn't let you create a 40-bit WEP network.
- If you want to run an open network that anyone can use without any security at all, use No Authentication and no encryption. This is definitely not a good idea if you also have computers that use file or printer sharing on the same network. (We'll talk about that more in Chapter 22.)

> **NOTE**
>
> Windows Vista provides WPA2 support "out of the box." If your router doesn't support WPA2 or WPA, you might be able to install updated firmware to get it. You would also need to download updated driver software to get WPA2 or WPA support for older versions of Windows. If you have computers running Windows XP, you can update them to support WPA2 by downloading and installing a hotfix from Microsoft. For more information, visit support.microsoft.com and search for KB893357. It's likely that XP Service Pack 3 will install WPA2 support as well, although it was not available for testing at the time this book was being written.

Finally, one more bit of nomenclature: If you have a router or access point, you are setting up what is called an *infrastructure network*. Windows Vista has a wizard to help you choose the correct settings. We'll go through this in the next section.

> **NOTE**
>
> If you don't use a router, you are creating an *ad hoc* network. We focus on infrastructure networks here because using a router makes it easier to network with wired-in computers and also to share an Internet connection. Ad hoc networks are discussed in Chapter 39, "Meetings, Conferencing, and Collaboration."

SETTING UP A NEW WIRELESS NETWORK

As I mentioned in the previous section, you need to select five things to set up a wireless network: an SSID (name), security type encryption type, encryption key, and channel number. If you're using a wireless access point or router, you can make all of these settings manually. You can also use the Wireless Network Setup wizard to help you select the settings. It can also copy them to each computer on your network and even to your router. However, you must have a USB removable flash drive (sometimes called a thumb drive) in order to use the wizard provided with Windows Vista.

> **NOTE**
>
> If you just want to add a computer to an existing wireless network, see the later section "Joining an Existing Wireless Network."

To set up a new wireless network using the wizard, follow this procedure:

1. Log on with a Computer Administrator-type account. Click Start and then Connect To. Click Set Up a Connection or Network and then select Set Up a Wireless Router or Access Point. Click Next twice to continue. Windows Vista detects your network hardware and settings.
2. Click Create Wireless Network Settings and Save to USB Flash Drive.
3. In the first screen (see Figure 20.11), enter a name for your wireless network. Click Next.

Figure 20.11
The first page of the Wireless Network Setup Wizard lets you select a network name.

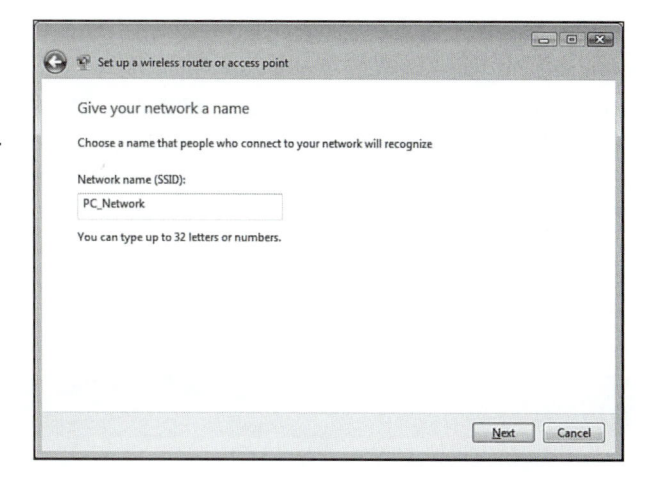

4. By default, Windows will assume you want to use WPA-Personal security. If you can use WPA2, or need to use WEP or no security at all, click Show Advanced Network Security Options, and use the drop-down arrow to change the Security method.

   Windows will create a random WPA passphrase or WEP key for you (see Figure 20.12), which you can keep, or you can enter your own. Optionally, you can click Create a Different Security Key or Passphrase For Me to have Windows generate a new one. If you're concerned that someone is peeking over your shoulder, uncheck Display Characters.

5. Write the selected passphrase or key down before you proceed. Then, click Next.

Figure 20.12
If you're entering a key manually, check Display Characters so you can see what you're typing.

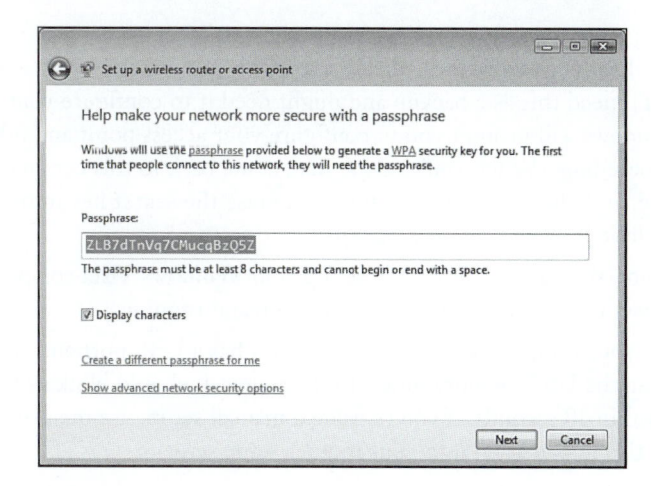

6. Choose file and printer sharing options. The default is Allow Sharing with Anyone with a User Account and Password for This Computer. Click Next.

7. Now for the clever part (see Figure 20.13). Insert a USB-based keychain Flash memory device, or attach a USB-connected digital camera or memory card reader that presents the memory cards as disk drives on your computer. Windows will copy to this device a file containing the wireless settings and an "autoplay" program that will load the settings when you plug the card into other computers.

After you connect the removable memory device, select its name from the list, and click Next.

Figure 20.13
Choose a removable drive to use to copy the wireless settings.

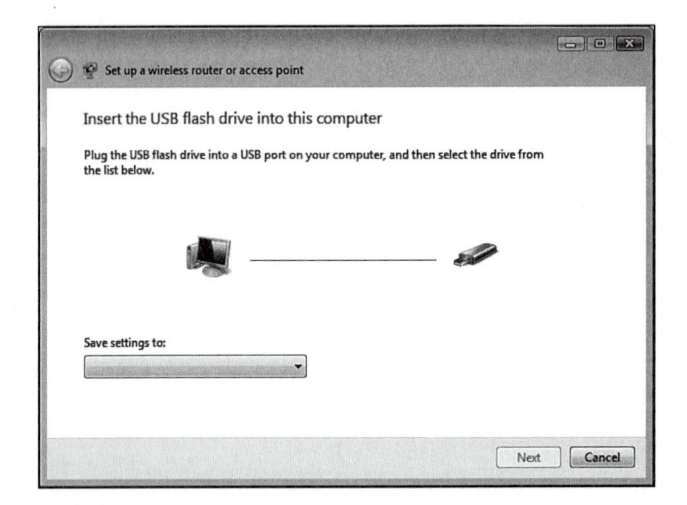

8. After Windows copies the files, click Print Network Settings to get a copy of the settings. You'll need this as a backup and might need it to configure your router. Click Next. Windows will prompt you to configure your access point and other computers before proceeding. (When you've done that, come back to this computer, reinsert the USB drive, and click Next so Windows can erase the secret key information from the USB drive.)

9. At this point, the wizard has already set up your Windows Vista computer to automatically connect to your new network when it's up and running.

10. Configure your router or access point next. If it has a USB port and you're using a USB device, plug the USB memory unit into the router. It should blink its lights and load the settings within 30 seconds. If you're using a manual setup, use the printed list of settings and enter this information into your router's setup screens.

11. Finally, configure the other computers on your network using one of these methods:
    - If you're using a USB device, plug the device into the computer. Setup should run automatically and add the computer to the wireless network.
    - If you're adding computers manually, go to each computer. Use the printed sheet of setup information to add the computer to the network. I cover this procedure in the next section.
12. Go back to the first computer when you're finished with the other computers and reinsert the disk. Click Next on the screen remaining from when you first ran the wizard. This erases the sensitive key information from the removable drive.

If you later need to add more computers to the network, you can rerun this process on the computer you started with, and it will walk you through the process of reinstalling the setup software on your USB drive or reprinting the instruction sheet. Or, you can follow the procedure in the next section to join them to the network manually.

When all your computers have joined the wireless network, skip the next section and continue with "Configuring a Peer-to-Peer Network."

JOINING AN EXISTING WIRELESS NETWORK

If you are using a wireless connection on a corporate network, your wireless configuration can and should be managed by your network administrators. Your administrator will most likely install a security "certificate" file that will identify your computer as one authorized to use the wireless network. It's also likely that you won't need to make any manual settings to use the network.

However, if your home or small office wireless network has already been configured and you're just adding a new computer, or if you are taking your computer into someone's work or home and want to use that person's wireless network, you will need to take some steps to be able to use the network. You can use the Wireless Network Setup Wizard, discussed in the previous section, or you can connect to and use the network by following this manual procedure:

1. In the notification area at the bottom corner of your screen, locate the Wireless Connection icon and double-click it.
2. Windows displays a list of the names (SSIDs) of the wireless networks that it "hears." Click on the network you want to use and then click Connect.

> **NOTE**
>
> If the network you want to use doesn't appear, it could be because the signal is too weak. Also, some people prevent their router from broadcasting the SSID name over the airwaves. (This doesn't really provide much extra security because hackers can find the network anyway.) If the network you want to use isn't broadcasting its SSID, you need to enter the information manually.

3. Windows determines what type of security the network is using. If the network is encrypted, it prompts you to enter the network key. Enter the 10- or 26-digit key that was used to set up the network to begin with.

→ We talk more about managing connections to multiple wireless networks in Chapter 37, "Wireless Networking."

After the wireless connections are made, you can continue setting up the rest of your network, as described in the following sections.

Configuring a Peer-to-Peer Network

When you're sure that the physical connection between your computers is set up correctly, you're ready to configure Windows Vista. With today's Plug and Play network cards and with all the needed software built into Windows, this configuration is a snap.

> **NOTE**
>
> As you can see from the heading, this section is dedicated to setting up a peer-to-peer network. Reference has been made in earlier sections to Windows Vista's support for wireless networking. Chapter 37 provides more details about wireless networking.

If your computer is part of a Windows Server domain network, which is often the case in a corporate setting, skip ahead to "Joining a Windows Domain Network."

Adding Network Clients, Services, and Protocols

When your network card and its drivers are installed, Windows knows the card is there but doesn't have any networking software attached to it. Follow these steps to attach the networking protocols and services you'll need.

Log on using a Computer Administrator-type account. Choose Start, Control Panel, Network and Internet, Network and Sharing Center and then Manage Network Connections in the Tasks list. Right-click Local Area Connection and select Properties. You should see a Properties dialog box with your network card named at the top under Connect Using. The list below This Connection Uses the Following Items will probably contain at least the items shown in Figure 20.14.

Figure 20.14
Default network components installed with Windows Vista.

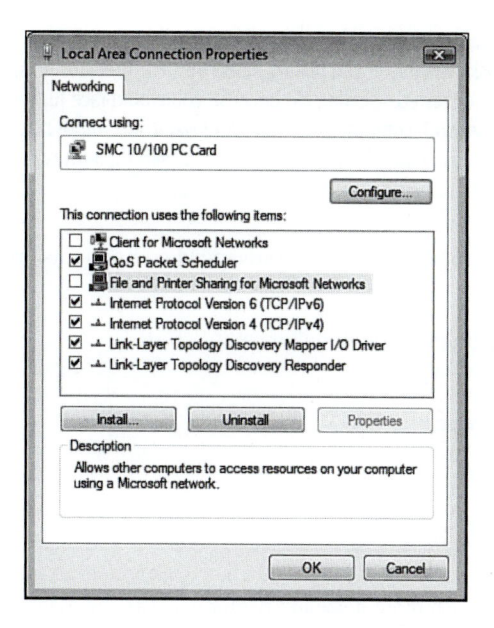

These components will suffice for most home or office LANs:

- **Client for Microsoft Networks** lets your computer use files and printers shared by other computers.

- **File and Printer Sharing for Microsoft Networks** lets your computer share files or printers with others. (If you definitely don't need to share files or printers from this computer, you can uncheck this item—this will help protect your computer from unwanted visitors.)

- **QoS Packet Scheduler** is used on some networks to assign varying priorities for different type of network traffic. (It's not necessary for small networks, but it doesn't hurt to leave it in.)

- **Internet Protocol (TCP/IP)** is the basic network protocol used for all Internet services, and usually for Microsoft file and printer sharing as well. You will likely see two versions of the protocol listed: Version 4 and Version 6. Microsoft TCP/IP Version 6 provides support for IPV6, the "Next Generation Internet" protocol that is starting to be used on large corporate and university networks.

If you need to add any components beyond those listed, or if any were inadvertently removed, use this procedure to add them:

1. Click Install. From the list shown in the Select Network Feature Type dialog box, choose Client, Service, or Protocol, and then click Add. (You might need to search through the list of components under each of these three categories to find the component you're seeking.)

2. From the list of Network Clients, Services, or Protocols, select the desired entry and click OK.

> **TIP**
>
> If Windows asks whether it can restart, select Yes. For previous versions of Windows, I would have suggested selecting No because you would face further restarts as you added other network components. With Windows Vista, you're rarely asked to restart more than once, so you might as well get it over with right away.

In addition to these standard components, some advanced components are available through Windows Setup:

- Simple Network Management Protocol
- WMI SNMP Provider
- Internet Information Services
- RIP Listener
- Simple TCP/IP Services
- LPD Print Service

→ These services are discussed in much more detail in Chapter 21, "Mix and Match with Old Windows and Macs."

In general, you need these advanced components only if your network is large and your network manager tells you that they are required, or if you have an Internet Connection Sharing router that supports Universal Plug and Play. (We discuss this in more detail in Chapter 22.) It's best not to install any components unless you're sure you need them. If any are required on your network, perform the following steps:

1. Open the Control Panel and click Programs.
2. Click Turn Windows Features On or Off.
3. Check the box(es) next to the desired component(s)—for example, Simple TCP/IP Services—and click OK.

Configuring the TCP/IP Protocol

After your network adapters are all installed—and, if you're using a wired network, cabled together—you need to ensure that each computer is assigned an *IP address*. This is a number that uniquely identifies the computer on the network. These numbers are assigned in three ways:

- If the network has a computer that uses Windows Internet Connection Sharing to share an Internet connection, if there is a hardware Internet sharing router, or if you are on a corporate LAN running Windows 200*x* Server, each computer should be assigned an IP address automatically—they're doled out by the Dynamic Host Configuration Protocol (DHCP) service that runs on the sharing computer or in the router. This is why I recommend using a router even if you aren't setting up a shared Internet connection.

- Each computer can be given an address manually, which is called a *static address* as opposed to a dynamic (automatic) one.
- If no static settings are made but no DHCP server exists on the network, Windows automatically assigns IP addresses anyway. Although the network will work, this is not an ideal situation and can slow Windows.

If you're setting up a new computer on an existing network, use whatever scheme the existing computers use; check their settings and follow suit with your new one. If you're setting up a new computer, follow these steps to ensure that the network is set up correctly:

1. Log on using a Computer Administrator-type account. Open the Network and Sharing Center and click Manage Network Connections. Right-click the Local Area Connection or Wireless Connection icon that corresponds to your LAN connection and select Properties.
2. Highlight Internet Protocol Version 4 (TCP/IP) and click Properties.
3. Configure the appropriate settings in the Properties page, as shown in Figure 20.15.

Figure 20.15
Make IP address settings within Internet Protocol (TCP/IP) Version 4 Properties.

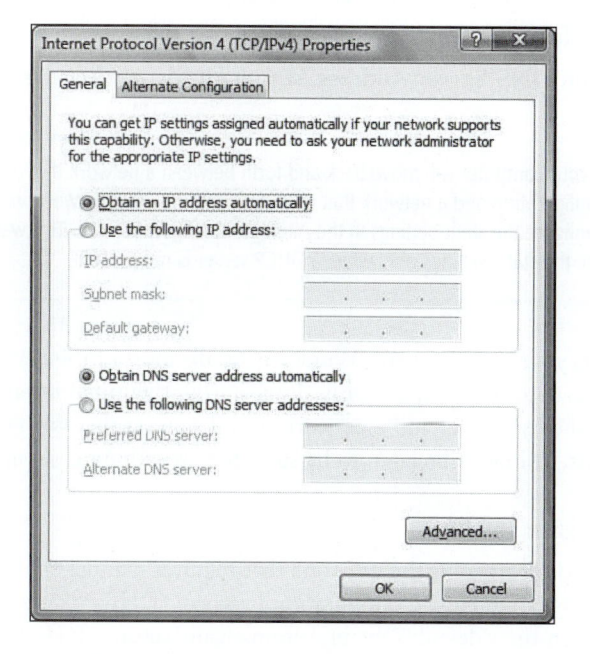

- If you will use Windows Internet Connection Sharing, first set up the one computer that will be sharing its connection, as described in Chapter 22.

    All the computers, including the one sharing its Internet connection, should be set to Obtain an IP Address Automatically, as shown in Figure 20.15.

- If you will use a hardware router, configure the router first, following the manufacturer's instructions. Enable its DHCP feature. Set the starting DHCP IP address to 100 so that numbers from 2 to 99 can be used for computers with static settings. Also, if your ISP has provided you with static IP address settings, be sure to enter your ISP's DNS server addresses in the router's setup screens so it can pass them to the computers that rely on the router for their IP setup. (For more information about configuring a shared Internet connection, see Chapter 22.) Then all your computers should be set as shown in Figure 20.15.

- If you will not have a shared Internet connection, you should configure your network with static IP address information. Assign a unique number to each of your computers, starting with 2 and counting up. Open the Internet Protocol Properties page, shown in Figure 20.15, and make the following settings:

    - **Use the Following IP Address**—Select this item.
    - **IP Address**—Enter `192.168.0.x`, replacing *x* with the number you chose for this particular computer.
    - **Subnet Mask**—Enter `255.255.255.0`.
    - **Default Gateway**—Leave this blank.
    - **Obtain DNS Server Address Automatically**—Select this item.

> **TIP**
>
> If your computer will move back and forth between a network that uses automatic configuration and a network that uses static settings—say, between work and home—configure the static settings in the Alternate Configuration tab. This way, Windows will use the static settings only when a DHCP server is not present.

When it first detects your network card, Windows installs most of the necessary network software components automatically. This can occur during the initial installation of Windows Vista or when you later add a network card. I suggest that you go through the installed components, as I describe later, to be sure that everything is set up correctly.

Manually Configuring TCP/IP

Normally, the TCP/IP protocol is the only one that requires manual configuration. If your network provides a Dynamic Host Configuration Protocol (DHCP) server, you can leave the TCP/IP parameters on their default Obtain Automatically setting. DHCP service is provided by most Internet routers, connection-sharing devices, and Windows computers that provide Internet Connection Sharing.

If you have a small network with no DHCP server and you're not using Internet Connection Sharing or a hardware connection-sharing device, you can still leave the TCP/IP settings alone and Windows will choose appropriate automatic-configuration values.

> **TIP**
>
> As I discuss in the sidebar, if computers are set up for automatic (dynamic) addressing but no DHCP server is found on the network, Windows uses Automatic Private IP Addressing to make the network operational. You can force Windows to use static addressing as its fallback option on the Internet Protocol (TCP/IP) Properties Alternate Configuration tab. This is helpful if you carry your computer between a network that has DHCP and one that doesn't. On the Alternate Configuration tab, you can set up static addressing for your home network, for example, and still leave Windows set up to try dynamic addressing first so that it will also work on your office network.

If your computer is part of a network with predetermined IP addresses (such as a corporate LAN or a LAN with routed Internet service), you might need to manually enter IP information. You'll need the following information from your network manager or your Internet service provider:

- IP address
- Subnet mask
- Default gateway
- DNS domain name
- Preferred DNS servers

Automatic Configuration Without DHCP

Dynamic Host Configuration Protocol, or DHCP, is a network service that lets computers receive their TCP/IP configuration automatically over the network. It's great because a network administrator can make all the settings within a DHCP server configuration program instead of having to manage individual setups for tens, hundreds, or even thousands of computers. DHCP service can be provided by Windows Vista, 200*x*, and NT Server; UNIX servers; and many network and Internet gateway routers. Computers running Windows Internet Connection Sharing also provide DHCP service for their LAN.

If a computer is set for automatic configuration, it broadcasts a message on the LAN when it boots, basically saying, "Help! Who am I?" The LAN's DHCP server responds, assigns an IP address to the computer, and sends other information, such as DNS server addresses, the domain name, and so on.

What's interesting is that a Windows TCP/IP network will still work even without a DHCP server.

Here's what happens: When each computer on the LAN is booted up, during its startup, it cries "Help!" as usual. But this time, there's no answer. The computer repeats the request a couple times, to no avail. So it picks an IP address at random from the range 169.254.0.1 through 169.254.0.254. (These addresses were reserved by Microsoft for this purpose and will never conflict with other computers on the Internet.) The computer sends a broadcast to the LAN asking whether any other computer is using this address. If none answers, the computer continues on its merry way. If the address is already in use, the computer tries others until it finds one that is unclaimed. This scheme is called *Automatic Private IP Addressing (APIPA)*.

Each computer on the LAN is capable of obtaining an IP address this way, but not network gateways, domain names, or DNS server information. But because this system is for only the simplest of LANs with no server and no permanent outside connections, that's fine. The other information comes if and when these computers dial out to the Internet independently.

Just to be on the safe side, each computer bleats its "Help!" request every 5 minutes, in the hope that there really was a DHCP server that had just been temporarily indisposed. If a DHCP server actually does come online later (perhaps the server computer had been turned off while the others booted up), the Windows computers discard their made-up IP configurations for the real thing. This makes the network "self-healing," but at a cost: The continual checks for a DHCP server can significantly slow Windows.

When Internet Connection Sharing is in use, the picture is a little different. The sharing computer acts as a DHCP server because it needs to give the others its own IP address as the gateway and DNS server address for the LAN. This topic is covered in Chapter 22.

If you are setting up a shared LAN connection to the Internet, see Chapter 19 for a discussion of TCP/IP configuration.

If you need to join your computer to an existing TCP/IP network, you might need to do a little more work. Contact the network manager to obtain instructions for assigning the TCP/IP parameters. If your network has a DHCP server, or if your other computers are already set up for automatic configuration, you can leave the TCP/IP settings on Automatic, and your computer will obtain all its network settings from the DHCP server. (This is so slick!)

Otherwise, your network manager will give you the required settings for the five parameters listed previously.

To configure settings for the TCP/IP protocol, log on using a Computer Administrator–type account and follow these steps:

1. In Local Area Connection Properties, select the Internet Protocol (TCP/IP) and click Properties to open the dialog box shown in Figure 20.15.
2. Select Use the Following IP Address, and enter the required IP address, subnet mask, and default gateway address, as shown in Figure 20.16. (Of course, you need to enter *your* IP address information, not the information in the figure.)

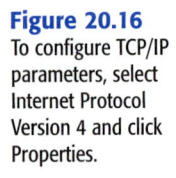

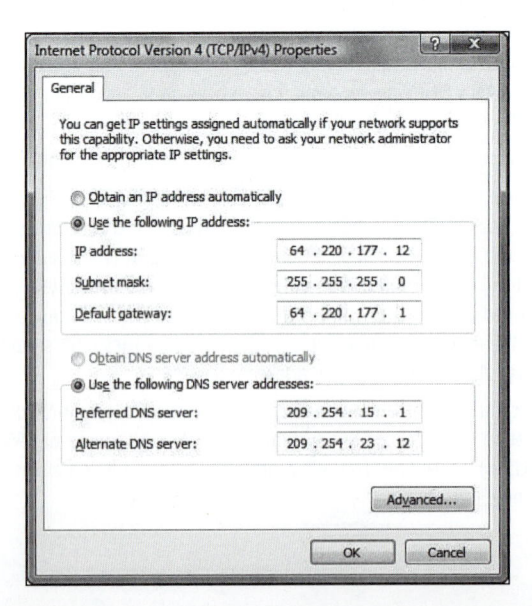

Figure 20.16
To configure TCP/IP parameters, select Internet Protocol Version 4 and click Properties.

> **TIP**
>
> When you're entering IP addresses, if you enter 3 digits, the cursor automatically moves to the next part of the address field. If you enter 1 or 2 digits, press the period (.) or spacebar to move to the next address field.

3. Select Use the Following DNS Server Addresses and enter one or two DNS server addresses.

4. If your LAN is not connected to the Internet, you're finished, so just click OK. Otherwise, if your LAN has access to the Internet via a direct connection or Connection Sharing, click the Advanced button and select the DNS tab, as shown in Figure 20.17.

5. Be sure that Append Primary and Connection-Specific DNS Suffixes is selected and that Append Parent Suffixes of the Primary DNS Suffix is not checked.

6. Under DNS Suffix for This Connection, enter your company's registered domain name or use your Internet provider's domain. This setting is used only if you use a computer name without a domain name in your web browser, so it's not terribly important. But this setting is helpful, for example, if you want to refer to your mail server as mail instead of mail.myisp.com. (In a corporate environment, this technique often can be used to automatically reach the nearest mail server on the local connection's domain.)

7. Click OK after you've made all the required entries.

The other TCP/IP parameters are used only on larger corporate networks, and when they're appropriate, the network manager will take care of the settings for you—in fact, you probably won't be able to change or even view them.

Choosing Your Network Location

The first time you connect to a network, Windows Vista will prompt you to choose a network location. The type of network you select determines the firewall settings that are applied. This way, you can be sure that the appropriate level of security is being applied for the type of network you are connecting to. As an example, a higher level of security is required when you connect to the Internet from an airport as opposed to from your home office.

You can choose from three different locations: Home, Work, and Public. You can select Home or Work when you are connecting to a trusted network. Network discovery is enabled with both of these locations, which makes your computer visible to others on the network.

Select Public when you are connecting your computer to an untrusted network, such as a network in a café, hotel, airport, school, or the office of a client or competitor. This network location is the most secure. Network Discovery is disabled so your computer is not visible to others, and access to your shared files is blocked.

When you move your computer from one network to another, Windows will usually detect the change and prompt you to select a new network location.

> **CAUTION**
>
> If you connect to a wireless or wired network that you've never used before and Windows doesn't prompt you to select the network location type, change the location manually, using the following procedure.

To change your network location manually, follow these steps:

1. Click Start, Network, then click Network and Sharing Center.
2. Click the Customize option at the right side of the window, to the right of the name of the network. You should see the dialog shown in Figure 20.17.
3. Select Public if the network to which you are connected is not trustworthy; that is, if you don't know and trust the other users who are connected to the network. This is the choice to make in an airport, hotel, school, café and so on.

    Select Private if the network to which you're connected can be trusted to use your shared files safely.
4. Click Next. You may have to approve a User Account Control prompt. Finally, click Close.

Yes, it's a bit strange that the first time you select a network location your choices are Home, Work, and Private, and if you want to change it the choices are Public and Private. The important thing to remember is that if you are working in an untrustworthy place, the location shown on the Network and Sharing Center must be Public.

Figure 20.17
You can change the Network Location within the Network and Sharing Center.

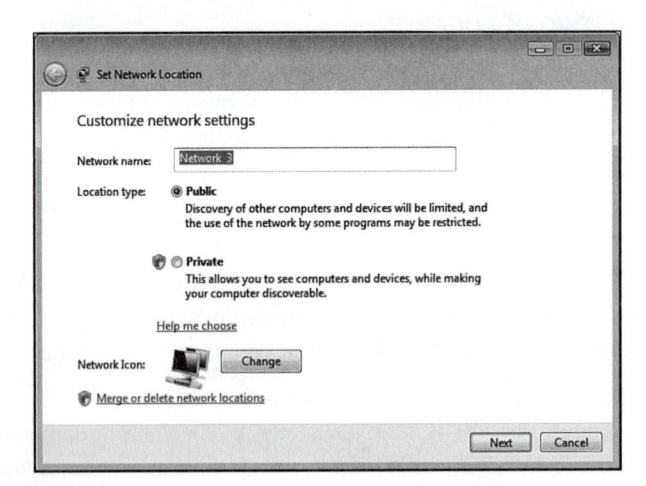

Setting Your Computer Identification

After you've configured your network, the next step is to make sure that each of the computers on your network is a member of the same domain or workgroup.

If you are part of a Windows domain–type network, your system administrator will give you the information you need to set your computer identification.

> **NOTE**
> Your domain administrator must know about your new computer and create a computer account for it before you try to add your computer to the domain. Just as you have a username and password, so does your computer. Refer to Chapter 2, "Installing and Upgrading Windows Vista," for more details.

If you are setting up your own network of Windows computers without Windows $200x$ Server, click Start, right-click Computer, and select Properties. Click Change Settings in the Computer Name, Domain, and Workgroup settings area. Check each of the Windows computers on your network. Do they each have a different full computer name and the same workgroup name? If so, you're all set. If not, click the Network ID button and prepare to answer the wizard's questions.

Click Next on the wizard's first screen. You are asked to select the option that best describes your computer:

- This Computer Is Part of a Business Network; I Use It to Connect to Other Computers at Work.
- This Computer Is a Home Computer; It's Not Part of a Business Network.

Which one you choose makes a significant difference. If you choose the "Home Use" option, the wizard sets up your computer for peer-to-peer networking with the workgroup name WORKGROUP and finishes.

> **NOTE**
> If you use the Home Use option, be sure that all your computers are set up the same way, with the workgroup name WORKGROUP. Otherwise, you'll have trouble working with the other computers on your network.

If you choose the "business" route, Windows configures your computer for a higher standard of security than it will for home use. This choice is described in Chapter 2.

The wizard next asks you to choose from one of the following responses:

- My Company Uses a Network With a Domain
- My Company Uses a Network Without a Domain

If you are joining an existing network with a Windows 200x Server, check With a Domain, but you should consult your network manager first.

Otherwise, if you are building your own network as described in this chapter, select Without a Domain and click Next.

The last question asks for a name for the network workgroup. Enter a cute name for your network (using only letters and numbers), such as ACCOUNTING or HOCKEYTOWN, or leave the default setting WORKGROUP in place.

Click Next and then click Finish to complete the setup. You need to let Windows restart your computer if you changed the Workgroup setting.

CAUTION

You must be sure that every computer on your network uses the same workgroup name if you want them to be able to share files and printers.

Configuring Windows Firewall

It is a good idea to check that the Windows Firewall is set up correctly; otherwise, you could end up exposed to Internet hacking, or you could find that your network is so locked down that you can't use file and printer sharing. Windows Firewall is discussed in detail in Chapter 35.

If your Windows Vista computer is connected to a domain network, your network manager can and should configure your computer so that it uses a correctly configured firewall "profile" when you are connected to the corporate network. You won't be able to change these settings. These administrators will also probably configure another "default" profile to protect you when you are disconnected from the corporate network, such as when you are traveling or using your computer at home.

In this section, I assume that you are managing your own computer and that your network is not protected by a professionally installed firewall. Home and small office users should go through this quick checklist of steps to confirm that your network will function safely. The critical points are highlighted in bold.

1. Log on using a Computer Administrator–type account. Open the Windows Firewall window. You can get there from Start, Control Panel, Security, Windows Firewall. Click Change Settings.
2. **On the General tab, be sure that On (Recommended) is selected.** The Block All Incoming Connections option should normally be unchecked to use your LAN for file and printer sharing.
3. On the Exceptions tab, be sure that the File and Printer Sharing entry is checked.
4. **On the Advanced tab, every connection name should have a checkmark next to it.** Check any that are missing.

5. Click OK to close the Windows Firewall dialog box and the Security Center window.
6. If your computer connects to the Internet only via the LAN—that is, through a connection shared by a router or some other computer on your network—you can stop here. Otherwise, continue.

   If your computer connects directly to the Internet via a modem or a network adapter that connects to a broadband modem, **Windows Firewall is not sufficient to protect you from hacking by other people who use your same Internet service provider.** You should take the following steps to protect yourself:
7. Open the Network and Sharing Center Window; click Start, Control Panel, Network and Internet, and Network and Sharing Center.
8. Verify that the network location is set to Public Network. This disables all file and printer sharing and Network Discovery. Refer to the earlier section titled "Choosing Your Network Location" for steps on how to change the network location.

This completes the procedure for setting up Windows networking on one Windows Vista computer. Repeat the procedures on your other computers, and you'll be able to start using your network.

If you have other computers that are running a version of Windows earlier than Vista or other operating systems entirely, refer to Chapter 21.

Advanced Features

Windows Vista has some additional advanced networking features that you might want to take advantage of, and they're covered in other chapters. See Chapter 38 for instructions on enabling incoming access to your computer via dial-up modem or Virtual Private Networking (VPN) connections. See Chapter 21 for information about networking with Macintosh, UNIX, Linux, and older versions of Windows, as well as advanced networking services like SNMP.

Joining a Windows Domain Network

This section describes how to add your computer to a domain network run by Windows NT Server, Windows 2000 Server, or Windows Server 2003. If you're lucky, your network administrator will take care of this for you. Alternatively, she or he might give you custom-tailored instructions for your network. By all means, use those instructions instead of the generic plan in this section.

Most Windows Vista installations will work "out of the box" without the need to install or configure any network components. If your network uses Novell servers, though, you need to add either the Microsoft Client for Novell Networks or the Novell Networks Client software—and, unfortunately, only your network administrator can tell you which is appropriate for your organization. Installing additional network components is described earlier in this chapter, in the section "Adding Network Clients, Services, and Protocols."

At the very least, your network administrator will give you four pieces of information:

- The name to be given to your computer.
- The domain name for your network.
- Your network logon name and password.
- Any specific configuration information for the Internet Protocol (TCP/IP). In most cases, it is not necessary to make any changes in the default settings of Windows.

If your computer was connected to the network when you installed Windows Vista and you entered this information then, your network setup is already complete and you can skip ahead to Chapter 23.

When you know that the network configuration is correct, use the following procedure to make your computer a member of your network domain:

1. Log on to Windows with a Computer Administrator-type account.
2. Click Start, right-click Computer, and select Properties. On the Properties dialog box, select Change Settings in the Computer Name, Domain, and Workgroup settings area. Verify that the Computer Name tab is active.
3. Click the Network ID button.
4. Select This Computer Is Part of a Business Network; I Use It to Connect to Other Computers at Work, and then click Next.
5. Select My Company Uses a Network with a Domain, and then click Next twice.
6. Enter your network login name, password, and the network domain name, as shown in Figure 20.18. This information will have been supplied by your network administrator. Then click Next.

Figure 20.18
To join a domain network, you must enter a domain login name, a password, and the domain name.

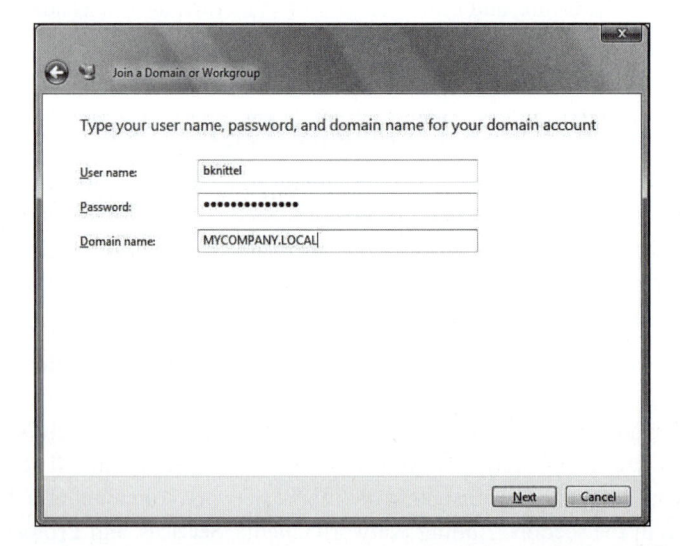

7. You might be asked to enter your computer's name and its domain name. This information will also have been supplied by your network administrator. If you're asked, enter the computer and domain names provided, and then click Next.

   You also might be prompted for a domain Administrator account name and password. If this occurs, the network administrator will have to assist you.

8. You should finally get the message "Welcome to the *xxx* domain." Close the Properties dialog box and allow Windows to restart.

   If an error message appears instead, click Details to view the detailed explanation of the problem. Report this information to your network administrator for resolution. The problem could be in your computer or in the network itself.

When your computer has been joined to the domain and restarted, the Windows Vista Welcome screen no longer appears and you need to use the old-style logon system to sign on. To log on, press Ctrl+Alt+Del and then enter your account name, password, and domain name. You can specify an alternative domain name by entering your username and account together this way: `myaccount@domain`.

> **NOTE**
>
> If your computer is disconnected from the network or you want to install new hardware, you can log on using a local account. Select the computer's name instead of your network domain name, and log on using the Administrator account or another local Computer administrator account.

NETWORK SECURITY

Now that you have a LAN—even if it's just a simple peer-to-peer LAN—you should be worried about network security and hackers. Why? Because you'll certainly be connecting to the Internet, even if only intermittently, and when you do, you risk exposing your network to the entire world. These risks are not as far-fetched as you might think.

Refer to Chapter 35 to find out what risks you'll be exposed to and what you can do to protect your LAN. If you use Internet Connection Sharing or a connection-sharing router, you're in pretty good shape. But in any case, go through Chapter 35 very carefully—it is very important.

CHECKING OUT THE NEIGHBORHOOD

Your network is finally ready to go. After you have configured, connected, and perhaps restarted each of your computers, click Network on your Start menu. The Network folder provides access to computers on your network. From here, you can locate shared folders and network devices such as printers.

If your network is up and running, and Network Discovery is enabled, you should see one icon for every computer you've connected.

> *If you don't see other computers in the Network window, see "Network Shows No Other Computers" in the "Troubleshooting" section, later in this chapter, and read Chapter 24, "Troubleshooting Your Network."*

Congratulations, your network is up and running! But before you continue to Chapter 21, there's one unpleasant task left: backups. I suggest doing this now.

INSTALLING AND CONFIGURING BACKUP SOFTWARE

If you are using your LAN for business purposes, you should have a good backup system to protect your business data and your investment in setup and configuration. As my friend Richard Katz says, "If you don't back up, you may have to back up a long way."

If you don't already have one, install a tape backup unit and, preferably, a good commercial backup software package on at least one main computer on your network. Follow the instructions on the software to configure it to perform automatic backups. Or, use an external disk drive connected through a USB 2.0 adapter; in this case, the backup software can be told to save the backup set in a single file stored on the external drive.

The Backup function included with Windows Vista lets you back up to DVD-ROM, CD-ROM, internal hard disk or external hard disk, and a network share. Folders and files can be backed up daily, weekly, or monthly.

> **NOTE**
> The graphical backup tool on Windows Vista Home Basic Edition does not let you back up to a network share. You can only backup to hard disk or CD/DVD. The command-line program wbadmin does let you back up to a network share on any version of Windows Vista.

→ For more information about wbadmin, **see** "WBADMIN Command-Line System Backup and Restore" on **p. 1162**.

The Backup function included in Windows Vista is very limited in its capabilities. This limited functionality is likely fine for home users; it's discussed some here, and in greater detail in Chapter 34, "Protecting Your Data from Loss and Theft."

However, in a business setting, the built-in Windows backup function doesn't give you the protection you need, and due diligence requires getting a third-party backup solution.

Backups should ideally be made automatically every day.

Rotate your backup media so that the most recent full backup set is kept offsite.

Configure the backup software to exclude certain files, if you can:

~*.*	Any file starting with a tilde
*.tmp	Any file with extension .tmp
*.bak	Any backup file
.ff	Fast-find index files

`*.ci*`	IIS Index Server index files
`\pagefile.sys`	Windows virtual memory page file
`\hiberfil.sys`	Windows Hibernation save file

Be sure to test your backup system at least once a month by viewing a tape directory or by restoring a single file from the tape. This not only will ensure that your backup system is functioning properly, but it also will maintain your skill in operating the backup-and-restore software.

> **CAUTION**
>
> If you use the encrypted file feature on Vista Business, Enterprise, or Ultimate, be *sure* to test your backup scheme's ability to back up and successfully restore encrypted files.

FILE AND FOLDER BACKUP

Windows Vista makes it easy for you to back up your files and folders. Windows Vista now presents the entire backup and restore functions in a single window. Click Start, Control Panel, System and Maintenance, and select Backup and Restore Center.

> **NOTE**
>
> If you have already run a backup, you might need to use the Change Backup Settings option. The settings you configured previously are retained and when the Backup Files button is selected, it attempts to utilize previous settings without presenting the options described below.

When you open the Backup and Restore Center, one of the options you will see is Use the File and Folder Backup Wizard to make copies of your files and folders. Click the Set Up Backup button to launch the wizard.

The wizard prompts you to select a location to save your backup. As I mentioned earlier, you have a number of options, including DVD drives and network locations. Choose your backup location(s) and click Next. Now you can choose the files and folders that you want to back up, the frequency of the backup (such as daily), and the time of day when the backup should run. A general rule of thumb is to run your backups when your computer is not being used. Complete the wizard by clicking Save Settings and Start Backup.

SYSTEM BACKUP

You can also perform a complete system backup from within the Backup and Restore Center. The CompletePC Backup that is provided with Vista Business, Enterprise, and Ultimate editions makes a backup image of your entire hard disk. In the event of a hardware failure, such as a hard drive failure, you can use the image backup to restore your system. The image backup includes applications, system settings, and files. The procedure includes a backup of your boot volume and system volume.

To perform a system backup, click the Back Up Computer button within the Backup and Restore Center window. Choose the backup location and click Next. Click Save Settings and Start Backup.

> **TIP**
>
> It is important to understand that the purpose of a system backup is not to back up your personal folders and files. Its purpose is to restore your operating system in the event of failure. Use the File and Folder Backup Wizard to back up your personal folders and files.

BRIDGING TWO NETWORK TYPES WITH WINDOWS VISTA

Windows Vista provides the capability to connect or bridge two different network types through software. This can eliminate the need to buy a hardware device to connect two disparate networks. Figure 20.19 shows an example of what bridging can do. In the figure, one Windows Vista computer serves as a bridge between an Ethernet LAN and a phone line LAN.

Figure 20.19
Bridging a phone line and Ethernet network with Windows Vista. Computers on either network can communicate as if they were directly connected.

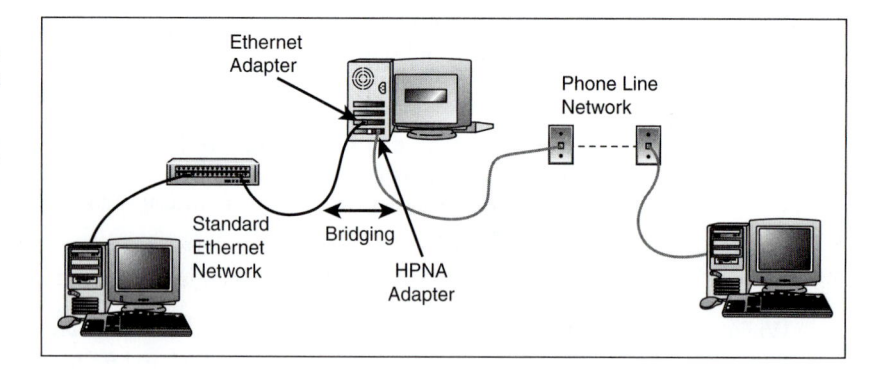

Bridging is similar to routing, but it's more appropriate for small LANs because it's easier to configure and doesn't require different sets of IP addresses on each network segment. Technically, bridging occurs at the physical level of the network protocol stack. Windows forwards network traffic, including broadcasts and packets of all protocol types received on either adapter to the other. In effect, it creates one larger network.

To enable bridging in your Windows Vista computer, install and configure two or more network adapters, as described under "Installing Multiple Network Adapters," earlier in this chapter. However, don't worry about setting up the Internet Protocol (TCP/IP) parameters for either of the adapters. Then do the following:

1. View the connection icons by clicking Start, Control Panel, Network and Internet, Network and Sharing Center, Manage Network Connections.

2. Select the icons you want to bridge by clicking on the first, holding down the Shift key, and clicking on the second.

3. Right-click on one of the icons and select Bridge Connections.

4. A new icon appears. Select the new bridge icon and, if you want, rename it appropriately—for example "Ethernet to Phoneline."

5. Double-click the bridge icon. Select Internet Protocol (TCP/IP) and configure your computer's TCP/IP settings. You must do this because any TCP/IP settings for the original two adapters are lost.

When you've created a bridge, your two network adapters function as one and share one IP address, so Microsoft disables the "network properties" of the individual network adapters. You must configure your computer's network properties with the bridge's icon.

Remember that the connection between the two networks depends on the computer with the bridge being powered on.

You can remove the bridge later by right-clicking the network bridge and clicking Delete.

Troubleshooting

Can't Drill Through Walls or Ceilings

My lease or the physical limitations of my building prevent me from drilling through walls or the ceiling to install network cabling.

In this case, you can install wires along baseboards, around doors, and so on. It's not as pretty, but because network wiring is low voltage, it's not as risky to do so as it would be with power wiring. (My office has a cable shamefully strung through a skylight, across the ceiling, and into a closet.) You also can use products called wiring channels to conceal the wires run along baseboards and rubber guards to protect them where they might be trod upon. You can find these products in the hardware store or in business product catalogs. Of course, you can also consider using a wireless network.

Hub Lights Do Not Come On

One or more UTP hub link lights do not come on when the associated computers are connected.

The problem lies in one of the cables between the computer and the hub. Which one is it? To find out, do the following:

1. Move the computer right next to the hub. You can leave the keyboard, mouse, and monitor behind. Just plug in the computer, turn it on, and use a commercially manufactured or known-to-be-working patch cable to connect the computer to the hub. If the light doesn't come on regardless of which hub connection socket you use, you probably have a bad network card.

2. If you were using any patch cables when you first tried to get the computer connected, test them using the same computer and hub socket. This trick might identify a bad cable.

3. If the LAN card, hub, and patch cables are all working, the problem is in whatever is left, which would be your in-wall wiring. Check the connectors for proper crimping and check that the wire pairs are correctly wired end to end. You might need to use a cable

analyzer if you can't spot the problem by eye. These devices cost about $75. You connect a "transmitter" box to one end of your cabling, and a "receiver" at the other. The receiver has four LEDs that blink in a 1-2-3-4 sequence if your wiring is correct.

Network Shows No Other Computers

The Network window doesn't show any other computers when I boot up.

One of the first things you should check is that Network Discovery is not blocking access. If Network Discovery is disabled on your computer, it will not appear to other computers within the Network folder.

If you've eliminated the network card and any UTP wiring as the source of the problem, you can use the Windows built-in diagnostic tools to help. Here's how:

1. The first thing to check is whether the LAN hardware itself is working. Check the Device Manager to be sure that your network card is operating properly. Be sure that you're using an approved network card and that you have up-to-date drivers for it. If the Device Manager gives you a message that reads "The Card Is Not Functioning," you almost certainly have the wrong drivers. Check with the vendor to see whether up-to-date Windows Vista drivers are available for you to download over the Internet.

2. If you have a UTP LAN, make sure all the expected indicators on your hub are lit.

3. On each computer, start a command prompt. Then type the command `ipconfig`.

4. When you see IP addresses listed, be sure each computer has a different IP address. They should all be similar but different. For example, they might look similar to `209.203.104.x`, where the *x* is different for each computer. If not, check the Internet Protocol properties on each computer to be sure each was correctly configured.

5. Type `ping x.x.x.x`, where *x.x.x.x* is the computer's own IP address. It should have four "replies," which look like this:
   `Reply from x.x.x.x: bytes=32 time<10msec TTL=128`

   If not, remove, reinstall, and reconfigure the TCP/IP protocol.

6. Type `ping x.x.x.y`, where *x.x.x.y* is one of the IP addresses of the other computers on your LAN. If the replies don't come back, your network hardware is at fault. Check the wiring as follows:

   On a 10BASE-T or 100BASE-T LAN, see whether an "activity" LED flashes on your network card when you type a `ping` command. If it doesn't, the problem is your network card. If it does, you might need to get a cable-testing device to find out what's wrong with the wiring. (A professional installer will have one—it's time to call for help.)

   Another possibility with combination 10/100BASE-T network cards is that the cards might not have decided to use the correct speed. You can force them to use a speed in the Device Manager by viewing the network card's Properties page and selecting the Advanced tab. This tab usually has a Link Speed/Duplex Mode property. Set all the cards to the appropriate value for the type of hub you are using.

7. If the ping commands work between computers, be sure that each computer's Network Identification has the same workgroup name. This information is on the System Properties page.
8. If none of these steps helps, see whether the Event Log has any helpful error messages. To do so, right-click Computer, select Manage, and view the logs under the System Tool Event Viewer.
9. Finally, you can use a diagnostic provided with Windows. Click Start, Control Panel, Network and Internet, Network and Sharing Center. In the task list, click Diagnose and Repair.

For more troubleshooting tips, see Chapter 24, "Troubleshooting Your Network."

Tips from the Windows Pros: Grassroots Networking

Despite the fact that they've become so inexpensive and simple to install, networks are extremely complex systems under the hood. It's hard enough to solve the problems that creep up from time to time in an existing, functional LAN, but new LANs are worse because *everything* is untested, and a little problem in any one part can mess up the whole thing. Where do you start looking for the problem?

The answer is an exercise in delayed gratification. It's exciting to see all the new equipment, parts, and cables all over the place, but as much as I'd like to hook it all up and see what happens when I turn on the switch for the first time, I've found that it's best to start small.

Whenever I build a new network, I put two computers side by side on one desk. They can be two regular computers for a peer-to-peer network, or a Windows 200*x* Server and a regular workstation for a server-based network. I wire them together in the simplest possible way, usually with two short patch cables and a hub.

This technique gives me the smallest, least complex system possible to start with. It's much easier to solve a networking problem when you can see both computers' screens at the same time.

When I have these two computers completely configured and tested, I start adding components one at a time: a network printer, an Internet connection, a tape backup system, an uninterruptible power supply, and so on.

When something goes wrong during this technique, I know it must have something to do with the last component I added, and I'm not searching for a needle in a haystack.

Finally, when I have all the parts working, I take the two computers to their final locations and see whether they still work with the real-world wiring. Then I add workstations to the network one at a time. Attaching them this way is not as much fun as assembling the whole thing at once, but I've found that staying up all night diagnosing problems on a new network is even less fun.

CHAPTER 21

Mix and Match with Old Windows and Macs

In this chapter

Networking with Other Operating Systems   664

Internetworking with Windows XP and Windows 2000   665

Internetworking with Windows 95, 98, and Me   670

Internetworking with UNIX and Linux   672

Internetworking with Macintosh   683

Advanced Networking Services   690

Troubleshooting   696

Tips from the Windows Pros: The Hosts File   699

Networking with Other Operating Systems

In the previous chapters, you learned about basic peer-to-peer and Active Directory networking, but these chapters considered only "vanilla" Windows networks. Real-life networks are seldom so simple, even at home. Often networks have a mix of operating systems, and Windows must get along with them. Also, some optional networking components are not necessary in most environments, but some network managers use them for maintenance and monitoring. This chapter covers internetworking and these more obscure parts of the Windows network puzzle.

On a real-life LAN with multiple operating systems, it's not enough that computers be capable of coexisting on the same network cable at the same time. They need to actually *work* with each other, or *internetwork*, so that users of these various systems can share files and printers. At best, this sharing should occur without anyone even knowing that alternative platforms are involved. Achieving this kind of seamlessness can range from effortless to excruciating.

> **TIP**
>
> One way to avoid *most* of the hassles of internetworking is to buy a *network appliance*, also called *network-attached storage*: a small server computer that "speaks" all the networking languages you need—Windows, UNIX, Macintosh, or whatever. These devices can cost as little as $200 and can put several hundred gigabytes of storage on your network that anyone can access. They tend to be very easy to set up, and a few even provide Internet Connection Sharing, wireless connectivity, an email server, a firewall, and a web server all in the same box. Products for the home and small office are made by Axentra (www.axentra.com), Seagate Mirra (www.mirra.com), GreenComputer (www.greencomputer.com), Linksys (www.linksys.com), DLink (www.dlink.com), Buffalo Technology (ww.buffalotech.com), and several other companies.
>
> However, if you're shopping for such a network appliance, be very careful to check what format it uses on its disks and what maximum file size it supports. Some devices support a maximum file size of only 2GB or 4GB, depending on the disk format and internal operating system used. Such a device might be okay for storing documents and photos, but it will be incapable of storing complete movies and computer backup files, many of which run 6GB in size or more—often way more.

If a network appliance isn't in the cards, you need to get your computers to interoperate directly. This chapter shows you how to get computers running Windows, Macintosh OS X, UNIX, and Linux to play together nicely.

As we discussed in Chapter 19, "Overview of Windows Networking," some new features have been added to Windows Vista networking, and support for some old features has been removed. With respect to internetworking, this list provides a summary of the most significant changes:

- The NetBEUI network protocol is not available under Windows Vista. This could impact you if your network includes computers running Windows Me, 98, or earlier versions. I'll discuss this in more detail when we talk about networking with older versions of Windows later in this chapter.

- The Link Level Discovery Protocol (LLDP) has been added to Windows Vista. LLDP lets Vista eke out a map of the connections between your computers and the other hardware on your network. LLDP support is currently available only for Windows Vista, XP (via a download), Server 2003, and Server 2008. Computers running older versions of Windows won't appear on the network map. Computers running Linux and Mac OS X probably won't appear, either—LLDP support was not available at the time this book was written, but I suspect that it will eventually be provided in a future Mac or Linux version or update. An Open Source effort to bring LLDP to Linux and the Mac was underway at the time this was written (see openLLDP.sourceforge.net) and some commercial network mapping applications (such as LanSurveyor at www.SolarWinds.com) also have a Mac LLDP responder.

- Microsoft does not provide out-of-the-box support for Novell NetWare (an industrial-strength corporate networking system) with Windows. Novell Corporation has finally released a NetWare client for Vista, but its installation and use is beyond the scope of this book.

However, although some things change, other things stay the same. You probably won't be surprised to learn that the Network Browser service (the relatively obscure software component responsible for collecting the list of names of the computers on your network, the list upon which the old Network Neighborhood display was based) is still present, and it still doesn't work worth a darn.

In addition to covering internetworking issues, this chapter discusses some of the advanced and optional networking features provided with Windows Vista. These features are not needed for "vanilla" Windows networks, but they are used for the more complex networks found in corporate environments.

INTERNETWORKING WITH WINDOWS XP AND WINDOWS 2000

Windows Vista's file- and printer-sharing services work quite well with Windows XP and Windows 2000 Professional. Both operating systems were developed during the Internet era, and they were intended from the start to work well with the TCP/IP network protocol favored by Windows Vista.

If your network has computers running Windows XP and/or Windows 2000 Professional, the differences in operating systems show up in three areas:

- **Default Networking Protocols**—You might have configured older computers to use the NetBIOS or SPX/IPX protocols as the primary networking protocol. Vista requires that you use only TCP/IP.

- **LLDP Mapping**—By default, Windows XP and Windows 2000 computers did not come with support for the Link Level Discovery Protocol (LLDP); without LLDP, these computers will not appear on the network map display. You can download and install an LLDP add-on for Windows XP, but not for Windows 2000.

- **Password Protection and Simple File Sharing**—Windows Vista, XP, and 2000 can provide username/password security for shared files and folders. Windows XP and Vista have a passwordless option that Windows 2000 doesn't have. You might need to work around this.

We cover these topics in the next three sections.

Setting TCP/IP As the Default Network Protocol

When installed, Windows 2000 and XP were set up to use the TCP/IP network protocol for file and printer sharing. If your network previously included Windows 95, 98, or Me computers, you might have changed the network protocols to simplify internetworking with the older operating systems.

Because Windows Vista supports only TCP/IP, you need to make sure that TCP/IP is enabled on your Windows 2000 and XP computers. Also, Windows networking works much more reliably when every computer on the network has the exact same set of protocols installed. So if your home or small office network no longer includes Windows 95, 98, or Me computers, you need to make sure that TCP/IP is the *only* installed network protocol.

> **NOTE**
>
> These instructions don't apply if your computer is part of a corporate network, especially one that uses Novell NetWare servers. If your computer is connected to a corporate network, your network administrator will make all necessary changes for you.

Follow these steps on all your computers that run Windows 2000 Professional, XP Home Edition, or XP Professional:

1. On Windows XP, log on using a Computer Administrator account.

   On Windows 2000, log on using the Administrator account.

2. On Windows XP, click Start, Control Panel, Network and Internet Connections; then click the Network Connections icon.

   On Windows 2000, click Start, Settings, Network and Dial-Up Connections.

3. Right-click the Local Area Connection icon and select Properties.

4. Look in the list of installed components and make sure that Internet Protocol (TCP/IP) is listed. If not, click Install, select Protocols, click Add, and select Internet Protocol (TCP/IP). If your network uses manually assigned (static) IP addresses, configure the Internet Protocol entry just as you configured your Windows Vista computers.

5. Look in the list of installed components for the NWLink IPX/SPX or NetBEUI protocols. If your network does not include Windows 95, 98, or Me computers, select these entries and click Uninstall.

6. Click OK to close the Local Area Connection Properties dialog box.

7. From the menu in the main window (Network Connections on Windows XP, Network and Dial-Up Connections on Windows 2000), select Advanced, Advanced Settings. Select the Adapters and Bindings tab.
8. In the top list, select Local Area Connection. In the lower list, make sure that Internet Protocol (TCP/IP) is checked under both File and Printer Sharing for Microsoft Networks and Client for Microsoft Networks.
9. Click OK to close the dialog box.

After checking all your computers, restart *all* your computers, including those running Windows Vista, if you had to make changes on *any* of them.

INSTALLING THE LLDP RESPONDER FOR WINDOWS XP

Windows Vista includes a graphical network map feature that's pretty and might even be useful. The problem is that it diagrams only Windows Vista computers and most, but not all, network hardware devices such as routers, switches, and hubs.

Computers and network appliances that offer Windows file sharing and are part of the same workgroup as your Windows Vista computers also show up on the display, but they appear as disconnected icons at the bottom of the map. You can't do anything about this for Windows 2000 computers, but Microsoft did create an add-on to Windows XP called the LLDP Responder for Windows XP that lets XP computers appear on the network wiring diagram.

To download the software, search microsoft.com or Google for "Link Layer Topology Discovery (LLTD) Responder." You need to install it on each of your XP computers while logged on as a Computer Administrator. After you install it, it starts to work immediately—no configuration steps are needed.

If some Windows computers are missing from the network map, **see** *"Some Computers Are Missing from Network Map" in the "Troubleshooting" section later in this chapter.*

PASSWORD PROTECTION AND SIMPLE FILE SHARING

On small Windows networks (that is, networks that aren't managed by a Windows Server computer using the Domain security model), each computer is separately responsible for managing usernames and passwords. Before Windows XP, this made it difficult to securely share files across the network—you had to create accounts for each of your users on every one of your computers, using the same password for each user on each computer.

Windows XP introduced a concept called Simple File Sharing; when enabled, it entirely eliminated security for file sharing. Essentially, anyone with physical access to your network could access any shared file. This made it much easier for other people in your home and office to get to each other's files. (Horrifyingly, it was enabled by default, and there was no

Windows Firewall when XP first came out—so everyone on the Internet also could get to your files, until Windows XP Service Pack 2 was released. But I digress.)

Windows Vista also includes Simple File Sharing, although on Vista it's called Password Protected Sharing. And, the effect of disabling and enabling the features is reversed on the two operating systems. Table 21.1 shows the settings and the results.

TABLE 21.1 FILE SHARING SETTINGS ON WINDOWS XP AND VISTA

Windows Vista: Password Protected Sharing	XP Professional: Simple File Sharing	…Means Account and Password Is
On	Unchecked	Required
Off	Checked	Not required

To make things even more complex, the settings are not always changeable, as shown in Table 21.2.

TABLE 21.2 SHARE PASSWORD REQUIREMENTS BY WINDOWS VERSION

Windows Version	Network Type	Passwords Required?
2000 Professional	Any	Always
XP Home Edition	Workgroup (only)	Never
XP Professional	Workgroup	Adjustable
	Domain	Always
Vista Home versions	Workgroup (only)	Adjustable
Vista Business, Enterprise, and Ultimate	Workgroup	Adjustable
	Domain	Always

I know this has probably given you a headache by now. But it can be pretty easy to decide how to set things up, based on how concerned you need to be about security. Decide which of the following three categories best describes your environment:

1. **My computer is part of a corporate domain network.**

   In this case: Accounts and passwords are always required. Your network administrator sets these up. Use the Security tab on any folder that you share to select the users and groups to which you want to grant access.

2. **Ease of use is my priority, and network security is not a great concern.** Nobody can plug their computer into my network, or if they do, I don't care what they can access. If I have a wireless network, it has WEP or WPA security enabled.

   In this case: Turn off Password Protected Sharing on Vista, and enable Simple File Sharing on Windows XP Professional. This lets anyone on the network access any shared folder.

However, you *must* make sure that a firewall is set up to block File and Printer Sharing access over your Internet connection. Use a connection-sharing router, Windows Firewall, or a third-party firewall program to do this.

If you have Windows 2000 computers on your network, see if you can get by without sharing any printers or folders from those computers—let them use resources shared by your XP and Vista computers. If you must share resources from a Windows 2000 computer, you need to create an account on that computer for each user who needs access to the resources. For each user, create an account with the same name and the same password as on that user's own computer.

3. **Network security is important to me.** I don't want visitors who manage to plug into my wired network to access my shared files. Or, I have a wireless network that is not secured with a WPA or WEP key.

   In this case: turn on Password Protected Sharing on Vista and disable Simple File Sharing on XP Professional. Do not share resources from any computer that runs Windows XP Home Edition (or do not use XP Home Edition at all).

   On every computer that does share sensitive folders or printers with the network, you need to create an account for every user who needs access to the shared folders or printers. For each user, be sure to create an account with the same name and the same password as on that user's own computer.

And, of course, no matter what, use a different password for each separate user.

> **NOTE**
> If you change your password on any computer, it's a good idea to make the same change on every computer where you have an account. This way, you won't be asked to supply your password whenever you use network resources.

To change the Simple File Sharing setting on Windows XP Professional, follow these steps:

1. Log on as a Computer Administrator.
2. Click Start, My Computer.
3. From the menu, select Tools, Folder Options, and then select the View tab.
4. Scroll to the bottom of the Advanced Settings list. Simple File Sharing is the last entry in the list.

More discussion of Simple File Sharing and password arrangements is found in Chapter 20, "Creating a Windows Network," and in Chapter 35, "Protecting Your Network from Hackers and Snoops."

INTERNETWORKING WITH WINDOWS 95, 98, AND ME

Internetworking between Windows Vista and Windows 95, 98, or Me requires some additional setup work that previous versions of Windows did not require.

First, Microsoft has dropped support for the NetBEUI network transport protocol that older versions of Windows, MS-DOS, and OS/2 used. If you still need to use computers running Windows 95, 98, or Me on your network, you must configure them to use TCP/IP as their networking protocol.

In practice, Windows computers have difficulty "seeing" each other if you don't have the exact same set of networking protocols installed on every computer on the network. You need to ensure that every Windows 95, 98, and Me computer has the TCP/IP protocol installed, and you also must uninstall the NetBEUI and IPX/SPX protocols from them.

Second, the default password security settings used when Vista is installed make Vista harder for a network hacker (or hardware hacker) to break your Vista passwords. Unless you turn off Password Protected Sharing, you need to change one of Vista's security settings. This significantly increases the risk that someone could break into your computer.

> **CAUTION**
>
> Microsoft no longer creates security updates for Windows 95, 98, or Me. Furthermore, to be able to access resources shared by Windows Vista from Windows 9*x* or Me, you might need to reduce Vista's security level considerably.
>
> These operating systems really should no longer be used. I'm not trying to make more money for Microsoft; it's simply not safe to continue to use these operating systems in any situation where Internet access also exists. If you must continue to use these operating systems to run specific applications, consider running them within Microsoft Virtual PC or VMWare instead, with their networking functions disabled.

If you really must use Windows 95, 98, or Me on your network, you most likely need to change the protocol settings on the older computers, using the following steps. You might be asked to insert your Windows installation CD, unless your computer manufacturer copied its entire contents to your hard drive.

1. Click Start, Control Panel, and then open the Network icon.
2. In the components list, select entries whose names start with "NetBEUI" or "IPX/SPX Compatible Protocol," and click Remove. Repeat for any additional entries.
3. Make sure that Client for Microsoft Networks appears in the list. If it does not, click Add, Client, and select Client for Microsoft Networks. Click OK as necessary to return to the Network control panel dialog box.
4. If your Windows 9*x*/Me computer is a member of a corporate domain network, view the Access Control tab and select User-Level Access Control. Enter the name of a domain controller computer. (Your network administrator will help with this.)

   On home or small-office networks, view the Access Control tab and make sure that Share-Level Access Control is selected.

5. Click OK to close the dialog boxes. You might be prompted to insert your Windows installation CD if you had to add the Client for Microsoft Networks in Step 3.
6. Let Windows restart.

If you need to share printers or folders from your Windows 9*x* or Me computers for use by computers running Windows 2000, XP, or Vista, do not set a password for the shared folder. These newer versions of Windows cannot supply a password in the way that Windows 9*x* or Me expects. The only security option you have is whether to select Read-Only or Full on the Sharing tab of the folders you select to share.

A completely separate issue arises if you need to access folders or printers shared by computers running Windows Vista from computers running Windows 9*x* or Me. These older versions of Windows use an older, easily broken encryption scheme called LMHash when storing your password on the hard disk and when sending your password over the network. By default, Windows Vista has LMHash disabled. To access resources shared by Vista from computers running Windows 9*x* or Me, you must do one of the following two things:

- You can turn off Password Protected Sharing from Vista's Network and Sharing Center. If you turn off Password Protected Sharing, anyone with access to your network can access any of your shared folders and printers without a password. Password Protected Sharing was discussed earlier in the chapter under "Password Protection and Simple File Sharing."
- If you need to protect your shared folders with passwords, you must change a Vista security policy setting so that the weak LMHash encryption technique is used to store your passwords on Vista.

CAUTION

Enabling LMHash password storage makes it *very* easy for hackers who tap into your network or steal your computer to crack your password. If they get your password, they get anything your password gives them: documents, encrypted documents, stored passwords for Internet sites, and so on. Be *very* sure you understand and want to take this risk before you change this setting.

To enable LMHash password storage on Vista, follow these steps:
1. Click Start, Control Panel, System and Maintenance, Administrative Tools.
2. In the right pane, double-click Local Security Policy and confirm the User Account Control prompt.
3. In the left pane, open Local Policies, then Security Options.
4. In the right pane, double-click Network Security: Do Not Store LAN Manager Hash Value on Next Password Change.
5. Select Disabled. Click OK and then close all the windows.

6. You must now reset the password on every account that accesses shared folders or printers from Windows 9x and Me.

   To do this, log on to each account on Vista. Press Ctrl+Alt+Del and then select Change Passwords. Then log off and do the same with each remaining account.

Only after you change each account's password is an LMHash version of the password stored by Windows Vista. The LMHash version of the password is necessary before Windows 9x or Me can access shared resources using the associated account.

> **NOTE**
>
> On corporate domain networks, Password Protected Sharing cannot be disabled, and most network managers lock Vista's security settings using Group Policy so that the LMHash setting cannot be disabled. Thus, either way, you probably cannot use Windows 9*x* or Me computers on the network.

If you attempt to access a resource shared by Windows Vista from a Windows 9x/Me computer, **see** *"Windows 98/Me Cannot Access Resources Shared by Vista" in the "Troubleshooting" section later in this chapter.*

INTERNETWORKING WITH UNIX AND LINUX

The UNIX operating system, originally developed in the 1970s at AT&T's Bell Laboratories as a platform for internal software development and as a "workbench" for programmers, is still evolving and growing. In its early days, UNIX was distributed at no cost to academic institutions, and as a result, an entire generation of programmers and computer scientists learned their art on UNIX systems in college. (I'm part of this generation. Most of us have little hair left now, but that's not UNIX's fault.)

Most of the Internet software you're familiar with today was originally developed on UNIX systems, and UNIX is still one of the most common operating systems for corporate web servers and high-end graphics and engineering workstations. The open source phenomenon (which is by no means new but is certainly resurgent) has also produced the no-cost NetBSD, GNU, and Linux UNIX clones, ensuring that a new generation of programmers will continue the traditions of openness, collaboration, and sharing that typify the UNIX community. The Linux operating system in particular has developed a large following in the business community, as evidenced by Microsoft's agreement to work with Novell Corporation on smoothing the road for Windows/Linux interoperation.

> **NOTE**
>
> Linux isn't used just on Internet servers and workstations—it's used internally in many hardware devices, such as the inexpensive routers and network disk storage boxes that many of us use in our homes and small offices. Even some consumer products like the TiVo digital video recorder use Linux.

This section looks at ways to network Windows Vista with UNIX-type operating systems. Although many of the examples involve Linux, most of the examples can be translated to almost any UNIX-type operating system.

The SMB/CIFS Protocol

The Server Message Block (SMB) protocol is the high-level network protocol used for Windows and LAN Manager file and printer sharing. To promote interoperation, Microsoft, the Santa Cruz Operation (SCO), Intel, and other companies began the Common Internet File System (CIFS) initiative to extend SMB networking to other operating systems. CIFS-compatible software packages can be obtained for many varieties of UNIX and Linux. For this chapter, I concentrate on just one: the Samba package.

Samba

Certainly the most popular UNIX-to-Windows networking package, Samba can be a life-saver for integrated networks. Samba is an open source (free) software suite based on the SMB/CIFS protocol. The Samba server program makes it possible for UNIX/Linux computers to share folders and printers that Windows users can access, and the Samba client tools let UNIX/Linux users access folders and printers shared by Windows computers. (Samba is included with Apple's OS X, by the way, which is how Macs get their Windows file-sharing capability.) And because typing "UNIX/Linux" is already getting tiresome, I just write UNIX from now on, but for the purposes of this discussion, I mean "UNIX and/or Linux and/or Mac OS X."

> **NOTE**
>
> You can get more information about Samba and download a version for your UNIX system from www.samba.org. Most Linux distributions include a version of Samba and install it by default. For a good Samba introduction and reference, check out *The Official Samba-3 HOWTO and Reference Guide* (Prentice Hall, 2003, 0131453556).

Samba Client Tools

To access file services on a Windows server from UNIX, you must know exactly what resources are available from a given host on the network. Samba includes a command-line program called `smbclient` for just that purpose. This application enables you to list available Windows shares and printers from within UNIX. For example, the command

`smbclient -L \\lombok`

lists all the folders and printers shared by the computer named lombok.

When you know the name of the desired shared folder, the `smbmount` command enables you to mount the Windows share on the local Linux file system. The command

`smbmount //lombok/shareddocs /mnt/winshare -U brian`

mounts the SharedDocs folder on the computer lombok to the local directory `/mnt/winshare`. The `-U` switch tells `smbclient` what username to use when trying to mount the share. You are prompted for a password.

> **NOTE**
>
> If the Windows computer is running Windows Vista with Password Protected Sharing turned off or Windows XP with Simple File Sharing enabled, you can use any username and password. With Simple File Sharing, all network access is made using Guest credentials.
>
> Password Protected sharing is discussed earlier in the chapter under "Password Protection and Simple File Sharing."

You also can use a Windows printer from a UNIX client. The easiest way to configure a Windows printer on a Red Hat Linux system is to use the Red Hat GUI–based print tool while logged on as root. This way, you can set up an SMB-based printer with a minimal amount of hassle. If you are not using Red Hat Linux, you must edit your `/etc/printcap` file manually. The number of options involved are beyond the scope of this chapter. I recommend that you give the SMB How-To, available from http://en.tldp.org/HOWTO/SMB-HOWTO.html, a thorough reading.

Samba Server Tools

Samba also includes tools and servers to make your UNIX system look just like a Windows-based network server; this capability lets your Windows computers use files and printers shared by UNIX systems.

The parameters for configuring Samba in a server capacity are contained in the file `/etc/smb.conf` on the UNIX host. The default file included with Samba has comments for every parameter to explain each one. Configuring the Samba server is beyond the scope of this book. However, I can offer a few pointers:

- Samba is complex. You should read the documentation and FAQs for your Samba version before starting the setup procedure. A good place to start is http://en.tldp.org/HOWTO/SMB-HOWTO.html.

- Configure Samba for user-specific passwords with the `security` option. You need to set up UNIX user accounts for each of your Windows users. Alternatively, you could set up a single UNIX account that all Windows will share; Windows users need to supply the username and password when they use the UNIX share.

    Either way, set `encrypt passwords = yes` in `smb.conf`. You also need to set up a user and password file for Samba's use, which is usually specified with the `smb.conf` entry `smb passwd file = /etc/smbpasswd`. Your Samba documentation explains how to do this.

- Alternatively, you can use share-level security without a password. This makes Samba behave similar to Windows Vista with Password Protected File Sharing disabled. However, in this case, you *must* take care to prevent SMB access to your UNIX computer from the Internet.

When you have finished editing the `smb.conf` file, you can test to see that the syntax is correct by using the Samba program `testparm`. `testparm` checks `smb.conf` for internal "correctness" before you actually use it in a production environment. By running

```
/usr/bin/testparm
```

you get a printout similar to the following, if all goes well:

```
Load smb config files from /etc/smb.conf
Processing section "[homes]"
Processing section "[printers]"
Processing section "[storage]"
Loaded services file OK.
Press enter to see a dump of your service definitions
```

You can press Enter to see a dump of all the parameters the server uses to configure itself. When the configuration file is complete and correct, you must stop and restart the `smbd` service to make the changes take effect.

PRINTING TO UNIX QUEUES FROM WINDOWS

You can configure Samba to offer standard Windows shared printer service. As an alternative, Windows Vista has built-in support to send output to UNIX-based printers using the `lpr` protocol. You can install a standard Windows printer whose output is directed to a UNIX system and can use this printer just as you would any local or networked Windows printer.

→ For instruction on connecting to an `lpr`-based printer, **see** "Using UNIX and LPR Printers," **p. 764**.

PRINTING TO WINDOWS PRINTERS FROM UNIX

You can also install an LPD server on Windows Vista to let UNIX users print to any local printers shared by your computer.

To install this service, log on as a Computer Administrator and follow these steps:

1. Click Start, Control Panel, Programs, Turn Windows Features On or Off. Confirm the User Account Control prompt.
2. Scroll through the list of features and open Print Services.
3. Check LPD Print Service, and then click OK.

> **NOTE**
> Windows automatically creates an exception in the Windows Firewall titled "TCP/IP Print Server," which passes TCP port 515. You must leave this exception enabled for UNIX users to send print jobs.

Now UNIX users can send print jobs to your computer by using the command

```
lpr -S computername -P sharename
```

where *computername* is the DNS name or IP address of your computer, and *sharename* is the share name of any of the shared printers attached to your computer.

> **TIP**
>
> By default, Windows treats incoming print jobs as ASCII text that must be formatted and printed. If the UNIX machine is sending, say, a PostScript file, Windows prints the PostScript source code instead of the document the file represents. UNIX users must use the appropriate -o option to send a "binary" print job in this case. For example, you can enter the following:
>
> `lpr -S ambon -P Laserjet -o l filename.ps`

If text files are printed with line feeds inserted where just carriage returns were expected, **see** *"Carriage Returns and Line Feeds Are Mangled" in the "Troubleshooting" section later in this chapter.*

TELNET

The `telnet` command is perhaps one of the most well-known UNIX network tools. Telnet provides a remote terminal function; on a UNIX system, it lets you use a shell or command prompt environment on a remote system across a LAN or the Internet. Windows Vista includes a Telnet client for connecting to other systems running a Telnet server. However, unlike previous versions of Windows, it's not installed by default. If you need to use Telnet in your environment, you can install it using the following steps:

1. Click Start, Control Panel, Programs, Turn Windows Features On or Off. Confirm the User Account Control prompt.
2. Scroll through the list of features and check Telnet Client.
3. Click OK.

This Telnet client is a Windows console program, meaning that it looks similar to a command prompt window rather than a regular graphical Windows program. It also supports built-in NTLM authentication, so it can securely connect to the Telnet host service provided with Windows Vista, XP Professional, and Server. To connect to a remote server with Telnet—for example, `amber.somewhere.edu`—, open a command prompt window, and type this:

telnet amber.somewhere.edu

Alternatively, you can simply run the Telnet program without naming a remote host to start it in its "prompt" mode. Type **help** in prompt mode to see the list of valid commands.

To terminate a Telnet session, you can press Ctrl+] and enter the **quit** command, or simply close the Telnet console window.

> **TIP**
>
> Microsoft's Telnet client is less than wonderful. You might want to download a GUI-based, free SSH (secure shell)–capable Telnet client from www.chiark.greenend.org.uk/~sgtatham/putty or www.ssh.com. Commercial SSH clients are available as well–see, for example, www.ssh.com.
>
> These alternatives don't support NTLM encryption, so they're not secure for connecting to Windows Telnet hosts over the Internet, but the SSH clients are essential for connecting to UNIX hosts over the Internet.

THE TELNET HOST SERVICE

Windows Vista comes equipped with a Telnet server as well as a client. Having both a server and a client sounds like a boon for network managers because it theoretically lets a remote user connect to and run programs on your Windows Vista computer. It could conceivably also let a UNIX user connect to and run programs on a Windows computer. This could provide access to industrial-strength command-line management tools, including `cscript` (Windows Script Host) and `netsh` (Network Shell). It's limited to two simultaneous incoming connections.

However, I don't recommend using the Telnet Host Service. As I've mentioned, Telnet is an insecure protocol. The Windows Vista Telnet server does use the NTLM password-encryption protocol to authenticate users, but this feature can be disabled. In the end, using it is more of a risk than a benefit, and you can accomplish the same results by using Windows graphical interface management tools, such as Remote Desktop.

If you *really* want to try it, you must install and activate it manually using these steps:

1. Click Start, Control Panel, Programs, Turn Windows Features On or Off. Confirm the User Account Control prompt.
2. Scroll through the list of features and check Telnet Server.
3. Click OK. This installs the Telnet service and opens an exception in Windows Firewall, but it does not activate the service.
4. Open an Administrator command prompt window. To do this, click Start and type `cmd` in the Search box. In the search results list, right-click `cmd` and select Run As Administrator. Confirm the User Account Control prompt.
5. Type the command `tlntadmn` to view the current Telnet server settings, and `tlntadmn -?` to view the list of configuration options. Unless you *must* access the Telnet server from UNIX clients, you should at least enter the command `tlntadmn config sec -passwd` to disable acceptance of unencrypted passwords; this allows only NTLM authentication.
6. Click Start and right-click Computer, and then select Manage.
7. Open Services and Applications, and select Services.
8. Locate Telnet in the right pane and double-click it.
9. The service is disabled by default. If you want to run it just occasionally, change the Startup type to Manual. If you want the service to run whenever you start Windows, change the Startup Type to Automatic.
10. Click Start, then OK.
11. By default, no one is permitted to sign on via Telnet. To allow users to log on, you must add users to the TelnetClients local security group.

> **TIP**
>
> On the Windows Vista Home versions, you can't access the Local Users and Groups tool. However, you can use the `net` command-line tool to do the job. Open an Administrator-level command prompt window and type the folllowing command to add a specific user to the TelnetClients group:
>
> `net localgroup TelnetClients `*`username`*` /add`
>
> Here, *username* is the desired logon name. Or, you can enter this to remove an account:
>
> `net localgroup TelnetClients `*`username`*` /delete`

12. Test the service by opening a command prompt window and typing the commands **telnet**, **set ntlm**, and **open localhost**.
13. Type **exit** to disconnect. If you want to stop the service, go back to the Services Manager, right-click Telnet, and select Stop.

> **CAUTION**
>
> If you enable Telnet, I *really* caution you against permitting connections to the Telnet service from the Internet. You should block incoming connections on TCP port 23 at your router. Telnet is a prime target of network scanners and hackers, and dictionary attacks on key accounts such as Administrator are common. The Administrator account is disabled by default on Windows Vista, but you should still block Telnet at the border of your network.

SERVICES FOR NFS

Windows Vista Ultimate and Enterprise editions come with client support for the network file system (NFS) file-sharing system used on many UNIX systems. By "client support," I mean that Windows Vista Ultimate and Enterprise editions can use files and folders shared by NFS file servers, but they cannot share files to the network using NFS. It's an optional component and is not installed by default.

To install client support NFS file resources, follow these steps:

1. Log on as a Computer Administrator user.
2. Install Services for NFS by clicking Start, Control Panel, Programs, Turn Windows Features On or Off, and check Services for NFS. Click OK to complete the installation.
3. Click Start, Control Panel, System and Maintenance, Administrative Tools.
4. In the tool list, double-click Services for Network File System (NFS). Confirm the User Account Control prompt.

This displays the Services for Network File System management tool, shown in Figure 21.1. The tool is not put together in the usual way. The right pane contains only help information. It's useful, though; click on any of the links to display the Windows Help pages for NFS. The management functions are found in the left pane.

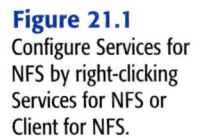

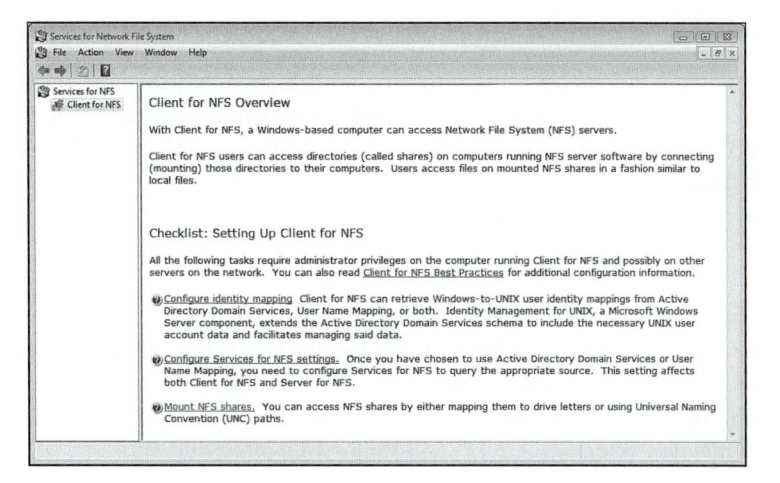

Figure 21.1
Configure Services for NFS by right-clicking Services for NFS or Client for NFS.

To configure the client, follow these steps:

1. To select the method that NFS should use to map Windows logon names to UNIX logon names, right-click Services for NFS and select Properties. If your network provides UNIX name-mapping information through Active Directory, check Active Directory and enter the name of the Windows domain. If a User Name Mapping Service server exists on the network, check Use Name Mapping and enter the host name of the mapping server. Either way, your network administrator should provide you with this information.

   If you select neither Active Directory nor User Name Mapping, the NFS client will access shares anonymously. The NFS server might restrict or reject anonymous access.

2. To select whether to use "hard" or "soft" mounts, right-click Client for NFS and select Properties. This setting determines how many times the client service will attempt to reconnect to a server that goes offline or becomes unreachable. Microsoft recommends using soft mounts, although your network administrator might advise otherwise.

   This Properties page also lets you determine whether the client uses TCP, UDP, or TCP and UDP for NFS access. You should be able to use the default TCP/UDP setting.

3. To set the UNIX access mask that the client should use when creating new files or folders in an NFS share, right-click Client for NFS, select Properties, and view the Permissions tab. Check the boxes corresponding to the permissions that you want to grant on new files that you might create. (This setting corresponds to the umask setting in a UNIX shell; the default Client settings correspond to a umask of 755.)

To start or stop the client service, right-click Client for NFS and select Start Service or Stop Service. Normally, it should start immediately on installation and whenever you start Windows.

The Berkeley "r" Commands

Although Windows XP came with versions of a set of UNIX-derived utilities called the Berkeley "r" commands (`rsh`, `rexec`, and `rcp`), Windows Vista does not include them. On Windows Vista Ultimate and Enterprise editions, you can get them by installing the Subsystem for UNIX-Based Applications and then downloading the Utilities and SDK package, as described in the next section.

Subsystem for UNIX-Based Applications

With Windows Vista Ultimate and Enterprise editions, Microsoft offers a free set of tools called the Subsystem for UNIX-Based Applications (SUA). SUA replaces the earlier Services for UNIX product that was available for Windows XP Professional and Windows Server 2003. SUA provides almost all the utilities you need to seamlessly glue together a network that includes Windows, UNIX, and Linux computers and services.

> **NOTE**
> SUA is available only on Windows Vista Ultimate and Enterprise Editions. It is not available on any other Vista versions.

The "Subsystem" part of the name is significant. The Windows NT kernel on which Windows Vista is based was designed to allow direct support of other operating system models in addition to Windows. SUA is actually a full-fledged UNIX operating system environment that runs *in parallel* to Windows, not "over" it. SUA runs UNIX executable files directly and provides a mostly POSIX-compatible environment with complete case-sensitive filenames, `fork()` and `pthreads` support, a single-root file system, and so on.

When the optional Software Development Kit component (SDK) is downloaded and installed, a full UNIX toolkit is available. With the SDK installed, the major components of SUA are as follows:

- Korn and C shells.
- Telnet and FTP clients—SUA offers full-featured versions of these and many other standard TCP/IP applications.
- Utilities including the vi editor, the GCC C/C++ compiler, the GNU SDK, `make`, `rcs`, `yacc`, `lex`, and more than 300 other standard UNIX programs.
- Support for debugging UNIX programs within Microsoft Visual Studio.
- Windows versions of the vi editor and about 30 UNIX file-management utilities so that these tools are available in Windows command prompt windows as well as UNIX shell windows. (Support also exists for accessing more than 140 Windows applications and utilities from within the UNIX shell environment. For example, `wmore` runs the Windows version of the `more` utility.)
- Several X Window System applications. (X Window System is the graphical user interface platform used on UNIX systems.) However, although SUA includes several X Window System client programs and support for developing X applications, no X Window System server is included with the package. An X server program is required to actually use X applications on Windows Vista.

To install SUA on Vista Ultimate or Enterprise, follow these steps:

1. Click Start, Control Panel, Programs, Turn Windows Features On or Off, and check Subsystem for UNIX-Based Applications. Click OK to perform the installation.

   If you need to run only a few specific UNIX applications that you already possess, you can stop at this point.

   If you want to install the full complement of UNIX utilities and development tools and/or the X Window System environment, proceed to Step 2.

2. Click Start, All Programs, Subsystem for UNIX-Based Applications, and select Download Utilities for Subsystem for UNIX-Based Applications. Download and save the installation package to a temporary location.

3. Right-click the downloaded file and select Run As Administrator. If you want to install the package on only one computer, take note of the temporary file location displayed in the Unzip to Folder field, and then click Unzip. This unzips the files to the temporary folder and automatically runs the setup program. Then proceed to Step 4.

   If you want to install the package on several computers, follow these additional steps:

   a. Uncheck the option When Done Unzipping Open Setup.exe.
   b. Create a folder named SUA SDK Setup on a network-shared folder.
   c. Set the Unzip to Folder path to this new folder. Then click Unzip to unzip the setup files.
   d. To install the utilities and SDK programs on a given computer, locate and open the SUA SDK Setup folder. Right-click `setup.exe` and select Run As Administrator.

4. Click Next to start the installation wizard. Successive wizard pages ask you to enter your name and organization, and approve the license agreement. In the fourth page, you are asked whether to perform a standard or custom installation. The standard installation installs the base SUA utilities (a set of BSD UNIX programs) and base SDK components (mostly standard includes files, libraries, and build utilities).

   If you select custom installation, you can additionally elect to install the SVR-5 utilities (a set of programs deriving from UNIX SVR-5), GNU compilers and utilities, the GNU SDK, Perl, and a Visual-Studio debugger add-in. Figure 21.2 shows the selection screen. To select a component, click the red X and select Will Be Installed on Local Hard Drive.

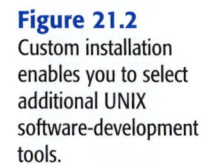

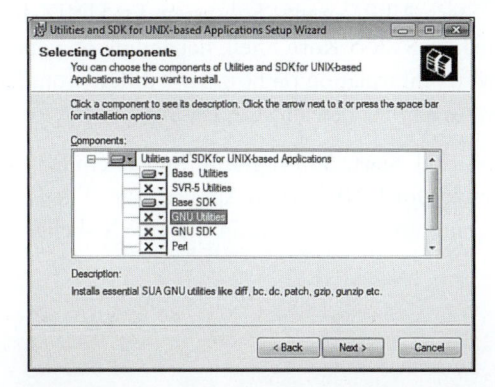

Figure 21.2
Custom installation enables you to select additional UNIX software-development tools.

In most cases, you probably want to select the custom installation and install all components.

5. Click Next until you reach the Security Settings page. Here, you can enable `setuid` behavior and case sensitivity for filenames and system objects.

   With `setuid`, you can mark a program so that when anyone runs it, it runs with the security context of the program's owner. In Windows terms, it automatically uses "run as" whenever it's run, and the user doesn't need to enter a password. Case sensitivity lets the Windows file system treat upper- and lowercase letters as distinct; for example, `Note.txt` and `NOTE.TXT` are considered to be different filenames, and both can exist in the same folder. UNIX applications treat them as different files. (However, Windows applications do not and just open a file arbitrarily.)

   Both `setuid` and case sensitivity are the norm on UNIX systems. Some UNIX programs require them, but they are foreign concepts to most Windows users, and they have both positive and negative security implications. Microsoft recommends disabling `setuid` unless you are sure that your UNIX applications or daemons (services) require it. Case sensitivity is usually required for correct operation of UNIX software-development tools (makefiles).

   For more information, you should open and read `install.htm`, which was unzipped into the temporary folder or network shared folder in Step 3. Also remember that you can change these settings after installation by editing the Windows Registry and rebooting, as noted in `install.htm`.

6. After the installer finishes, if you enabled case sensitivity or `setuid`, restart Windows. When Windows is back up again, log on as a Computer Administrator.

7. Click Start, All Programs, Subsystem for UNIX-Based Applications, Check for Critical Updates. This takes you to a Microsoft web page that lets you check for security updates to the utilities.

   Although updates for the UNIX Subsystem itself are delivered through Windows Update and Automatic Updates, security fixes for the downloaded utilities are not. You need to remember to periodically use this menu selection to check for security updates to the utilities.

When the Utilities and SDK have been installed, you can start a UNIX shell (command prompt window) by clicking Start, All Programs, Subsystem for UNIX-Based Applications, and either C Shell, Korn Shell, or SVR-5 Korn Shell, depending on your preference. The What's New menu item provides information on how SUA differs from the Windows XP Services for UNIX and provides an overview of SUA features.

For detailed help information, click Start, All Programs, Subsystem for UNIX-Based Applications, Help for Subsystem for UNIX-Based Applications. The UNIX `man`, `apropos`, and other standard help programs are available within the UNIX shells.

Internetworking with Macintosh

The Apple Macintosh is arguably *the* computer of choice in the music, graphic arts, design, and publishing worlds. Apple has even moved to the Intel processor platform, and you can run Windows Vista on a Mac, if you want to. But if you're a Mac fan, you probably don't want to.

Although Macs used to live pretty much in a world apart, it's common now for both Macs and Windows computers to need to coexist on the same network. However, Macintoshes normally use a proprietary file-sharing system called AppleTalk File Protocol (AFP).

To link Macs and PCs on a network, either the Macs must learn to "speak" SMB or the Windows computers must speak AFP. Both solutions are possible. On a corporate network based on Windows Server, your network administrator can install a component called Services for Macintosh (SFM), which speaks AFP to make Windows-based resources visible to Macs, and resources shared by Macs visible to Windows users. The process of installing and configuring SFM is not complicated, but it needs to be done by the administrator of a Windows Server computer; as such, it's beyond the scope of this book.

Microsoft appears to have lost interest in providing support for Mac users in the home and small office. Fortunately, Apple has stepped up and provided Windows-compatible networking support as a standard part of OS X. You can also add Windows networking support to older Mac OS computers. We cover these options in the next several sections. First, though, let's talk about other issues that come up when Windows and Macs need to work together.

Planning for Compatibility

Before getting to the details of *how* to share files between Macintosh and Windows computers, let's look at what you must do to be sure that the files—however shared—will make sense to both platforms.

Big Forking Deal

One surprising property of Macintosh files is that they actually consist of two separate parts, called *forks*:

- The data fork, which contains data, document text, program code, and so on.
- The resource fork, which in applications contains language-specific strings and dialog box layouts for programs, and in documents contains the association information that links a document to the application that created it.

The two parts can be read and written to completely independently. It's as if each file is composed of two bundled but separate files.

Windows actually supports this concept on disks that are formatted with the NTFS file system. On Windows, the separate file sections are called *streams*. (Windows uses streams to support several basic features, such as file encryption, attribute tagging, and "trustworthiness" history for downloaded program files.) However, either Windows doesn't provide stream support across the network or Macs don't take advantage of it. Whatever the reason, when a Mac file is copied to a Windows shared folder, the resource fork data is stored in a separate hidden file. If the Mac file is named `special.doc`, the resource fork file on Windows is named `._special.doc`. And it's invisible, unless you enable the display of hidden files in Windows Explorer.

The problem is that if you move, edit, or rename the main document or application file in Windows, the resource file might be left behind or end up with the wrong name. Then, on the Mac side, the Mac will no longer know what application to use to open the document, or, in the case of an application program, the application will not run. Thus, it's best not to store Mac applications on Windows shares if they will be renamed or moved.

> If Macintosh users discover that the Finder can't find the correct application to open a document that a Windows user has edited or moved, **see** *"Macintosh Files Have Lost Application Associations"* in the "Troubleshooting" section later in this chapter.

FILENAME COMPATIBILITY

On older versions of the Mac OS, filenames could not exceed 31 characters, including the extension (for example, `.doc`). A second-generation disk formatting system called HFS+ is available for users of Mac OS 8 or higher. With HFS+, filenames can have up to 255 characters. Mac filenames can contain any character except the colon (:).

Windows permits filenames up to 256 characters in length but has a longer list of unacceptable characters: the colon (:), backslash (\), forward slash (/), question mark (?), asterisk (*), quotation mark ("), greater-than symbol (>), less-than symbol (<), and pipe symbol (|).

Therefore, you must be careful when naming files that are to be visible to users in both camps. It's best to stick with shorter names that use characters that are legal on *both* operating systems.

FILE AND VOLUME SIZE LIMITATIONS

Macintosh computers running the Mac operating system (Mac OS) versions earlier than 7.6.1 can't see further than 2GB into any disk drive, local or networked. If your Windows network shares files from disk volumes larger than 2GB, your Macs must run OS 7.6.1 or higher. OS X doesn't have this limitation.

OS COMPATIBILITY

Some Macintosh applications don't properly install themselves when they're installed into a Windows shared folder. An error occurs when more than one user tries to run the application at the same time.

> *If Macintosh users get a network error when more than one Mac accesses an application, see "Can't Run Macintosh Application Concurrently" in the "Troubleshooting" section later in this chapter.*

Working with Mac OS X

Mac's OS X comes with Windows-compatible Server Message Block (SMB) networking support built-in, via the `smbclient` and Samba software mentioned earlier in the chapter. This means that Macs running OS X can connect directly to drives and folders shared by Windows computers right out of the box. You don't even need to use the command line; the Mac GUI manages `smbclient` and Samba sharing for you.

> **NOTE** This section shows you how to use Windows shared files from your Mac, and how to share files from your Mac for use by Windows. To see how to set up file sharing on Windows, see Chapter 23, "Using a Windows Network."

Using Windows Shared Files on the Mac

To connect to a shared Windows folder from the Mac, select the Finder and choose Go, Connect to Server. The dialog box shown in Figure 21.3 appears.

Figure 21.3
The Connect to Server dialog box lets a Mac OS X computer connect directly to a folder shared by Windows. Click Browse or enter **smb:** followed by the share's UNC path.

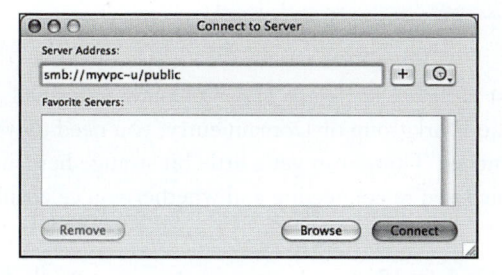

If you want, you can enter the UNC name of the shared folder directly, in the format `smb://computername/sharename`, where *computername* is the name of the Windows computer or its IP address, and *sharename* is the name of the shared folder. For example, the Public folder on a computer named Daves would be entered as `smb://daves/public` or using an IP address, as in `smb://192.168.0.12/public`. Click OK to proceed.

You can also click the + button to add the path to the Favorites list.

On OX 10.3 (Panther) and later versions, there is an additional, easier way to connect to shared folders. Click the Browse button, and you can select from a list of detected Mac and Windows computers, as shown in Figure 21.4. Macs appear if you click the Servers entry. For Windows computers, click the computer name and then click Connect.

Figure 21.4
The Mac server browser lets you select and connect to a Mac or Windows computer.

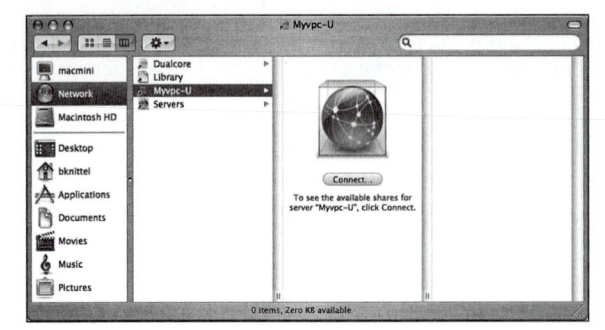

Figure 21.5
The login dialog box appears when you connect to a Windows computer.

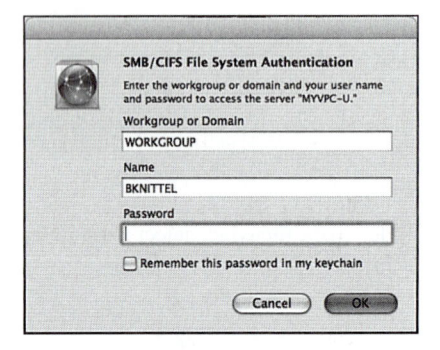

A login dialog box appears, as shown in Figure 21.5. On a home or small office workgroup network, you can ignore the Workgroup or Domain entry; you need to worry about only the Name and Password entries. Things can get a little bit strange here, depending on the version of Windows to which you're connecting and whether you've enabled Password Protected Sharing:

If you're connecting to a Windows Vista computer on a home or small office network, the following applies:

- You can enter a username and password that is valid on the Windows Vista computer. You will connect with the file and folder access rights associated with this account.

- If you have not enabled Password Protected Sharing, you also have the option of entering the username Guest with no password. (Actually, you can enter any *invalid* username, with any password.) This gives you the file and folder access rights granted to "Everyone." In most cases, this means that you will have access to the Public folder but no other shared folders, unless the person who shared the other folders explicitly granted rights to Everyone.

If you're connecting to Windows XP Home Edition or to Windows XP Professional with Simple File Sharing enabled, you shouldn't need to enter any account information. Just click OK.

If you are connecting to a computer on a Windows domain network, or Windows XP Pro with Simple File Sharing disabled, enter a username and password.

The Mac then asks you which shared folder to use, as shown in Figure 21.6. Select one of the names from the drop-down list (Public has been selected in the figure) and click OK.

Figure 21.6
Select the shared folder you want to use from the drop-down list.

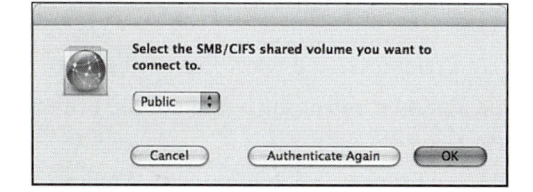

When the Mac has made the network connection, the shared folder appears as a drive icon on the Mac desktop. If you open it, you'll see the Windows files and folders in the Finder display, as shown in Figure 21.7.

Figure 21.7
The Windows computer's files and folders appear in a standard Finder window.

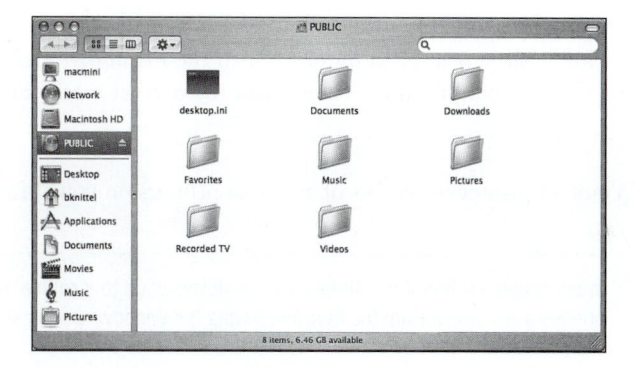

To disconnect from the network share, drag the shared folder desktop icon to the trash, or locate it in the Finder and click the Eject button.

Now, remember the point I made earlier about Mac files having two parts or forks. If you copy a file from a Mac to a shared Windows folder, Windows might create an extra hidden file to contain the resource information for the file. The resource file's name will consist of a period and an underscore followed by the name of the main file, as shown in Figure 21.7. Windows users need to move and rename these files together; otherwise, Mac users will receive errors when they try to access the files.

Also, as you can see in Figure 21.7, when a Mac user opens a Window share, the Finder creates a file named .DS_Store and sometimes also one named ._.DS_Store to hold Mac desktop information. Windows users should ignore these files, just as Mac users should ignore the file desktop.ini.

Using Windows Printers on the Mac

If you are using a Mac, to use a printer that is shared by a Windows computer, follow these steps:

1. On the Windows computer, when you share the printer, be sure to use a share name that's no more than 12 letters long. If you use a longer name, the printer will not appear in the list of printers on the Mac.
2. On the Mac, open System Preferences and select Print & Fax.
3. Click the + button to add a printer, and at the bottom of the Printer Browser dialog box, click More Printers.
4. At the top of the next Printer Browser dialog box, select Windows Printing at the top and, underneath, select the appropriate Windows workgroup name (or select Network Neighborhood and choose the desired workgroup). In the computer list, choose the name of the computer that is sharing the printer you want to use.
5. In the Connect To dialog box, enter a username and password that is valid on the Windows computer. (If you unchecked Password Protecting on Windows Vista, you should be able to enter username Guest with no password.)
6. Select the desired shared printer in the list. Open the Printer Model list and select the correct printer manufacturer name. Then select the correct model number. Finally, click Add.

This adds the Windows printer to the list of available printers on your Mac.

> **NOTE**
> In our testing we found that there could be delays of up to a couple of minutes between printing a document from the Mac and having the Windows printer start up.

Using Mac Shared Files on Windows

You can also share folders and printers from Mac OS X computers to the network, using the free, built-in Samba file server software.

To enable Windows-compatible file sharing on the Mac, follow these steps. The following instructions are for OS X 10.4:

1. Open System Preferences and select Sharing. Check Windows Sharing, as shown in Figure 21.8. This automatically enables an exception (opening) for Windows file sharing in the Firewall tab.

Figure 21.8
Enable Windows-compatible file sharing from the Sharing page in System Preferences.

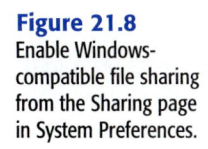

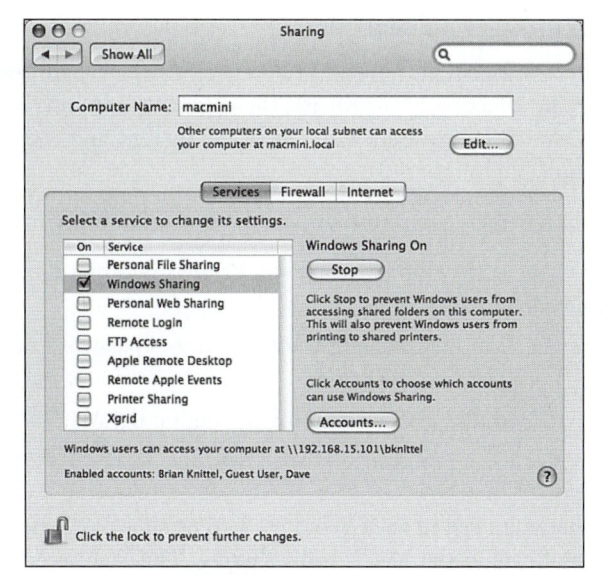

2. Click the Accounts button and check the names of the accounts that you want to permit to be used for Windows sharing connections. That is, you can use any of these account names when connecting from Windows to the Mac.

> **TIP**
>
> To save yourself a world of pain, create user accounts on your Mac and Windows computers using the same account names (short names, in Mac parlance) and passwords on both types of computers.
>
> From the Windows side, you cannot use or even see a list of the folders or printers shared by the Mac unless you are using a Windows account that matches up with one on the Mac and that has been enabled on the Sharing page.

3. Click Show All and select Accounts.

On Windows, you can use Mac shared folders just as you use folders shared from any Windows computer. Macs appear in the list of available computers in the Network folder, and you can open the shared folders from those icons, or you can use a Mac shared folder directly using a UNC pathname such as `//maccomputername/username`, where *username* is a Mac user account name—the Mac shares just users' home directories.

> **NOTE**
>
> When you open the Mac icon or use the `net view` command to view the items shared by the Mac, you see only printers (if any are shared) and the home directory share corresponding to your own account. You do not see the folders for other user accounts. This is how OS X 10.4 works, anyway.

Using Mac Shared Printers on Windows

After enabling Windows Sharing in System Preferences, you can share your Mac's printer(s) with Windows users by selecting Show All and then clicking Print and Fax. View the Sharing tab, click Share These Printers with Other Computers, and check the printers that you want to make available to others.

To use a printer shared from a Macintosh on Windows, the following must be true:

1. You must have enabled Windows Sharing and Printer Sharing on the Sharing System Preferences page.
2. You must be using a Windows account whose name and password matches an account on the Mac.
3. You must have enabled that user account for sharing on the Mac.
4. You must follow a strange procedure, which I describe next.

The strange bit is that you need to trick Windows into using a PostScript printer driver, no matter what type of printer the Mac is really sharing. The Mac accepts only PostScript printer codes and converts the PostScript to the appropriate codes for its installed printer.

To connect to the Mac printer from Windows, follow these steps:

1. Open the Printers control panel and select Add a Printer.
2. Click Add a Network, Wireless, or Bluetooth Printer.
3. Wait for the desired Mac printer to appear in the list. Double-click it. (If requirements 1 or 2 from the earlier list aren't met, the printer won't appear.)

   It also won't appear if the Mac is on a different subnet than the Windows computer. In this case, you probably need to manually enter the printer share name as `\\ipaddress\sharename`, where `ipaddress` is the IP address of the Mac and `sharename` is the name of the Mac printer.
4. When the message "The server for the printer does not have the correct printer driver installed" appears, click OK.
5. In the Manufacturer list, select HP. In the Printers list, if the Mac printer is a color printer, select HP Color LaserJet 8550 PS. If the Mac printer is a black-and-white printer, select HP LaserJet 5000 Series PS. Then click OK.

Advanced Networking Services

Several Windows networking options and settings are difficult to categorize. These topics must be covered somewhere, so I've collected them here.

Setting Network Bindings

Windows lets you specify how network components are connected. A network uses many layers of components. *Bindings* are the connections between these components. Through bindings, you can control whether the file- and printer-sharing service can be reached by each installed protocol and through which network and/or dial-up adapters.

You'll find step-by-step instructions for setting bindings elsewhere in this book where necessary. Let me give you the general picture here, in case you're arriving at this topic through the index.

To set network bindings, open the Network Connections window and then press and release the Alt key. Then, select Advanced, Advanced Settings from the menu. Select the Adapters and Bindings tab, as shown in Figure 21.9.

Select a network adapter (such as Local Area Connection) in the upper part of the dialog box. In the bottom, you can check and uncheck services and individual transport protocols to connect or disconnect these services from the selected network adapter.

To set bindings for dial-up connections, you must view the Properties pages of the individual dial-up connections. On the Networking tab, you can check which services and protocols are to be used across the connection.

Figure 21.9
On the Adapters and Bindings tab, you can sever the connection between specific network components.

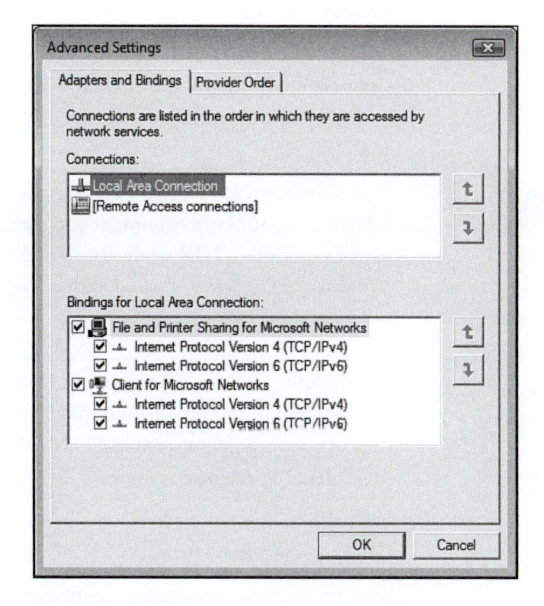

Installing Optional Network Components

Windows Vista comes with some networking features or services that are not used in most networks but can be essential in others. I don't cover these features in great detail because your network manager will probably install them for you if they're used on your LAN.

Table 21.3 describes the optional features. Not every component is available on every version of Windows Vista. Table 21.4 summarizes their availability.

To enable any of the components, click Start, Control Panel, Programs, Turn Windows Features On or Off. Check the box next to each desired feature, and then click OK.

TABLE 21.3 WINDOWS VISTA OPTIONAL NETWORKING FEATURES

Category/Component	Description
Web and Application Services	
Internet Information Services (IIS)	IIS is a full-featured web server. See Chapter 18, "Hosting Web Pages with Internet Information Services," for information on installing and using it. IIS can also be used by software developers as a platform for a new generation of peer-to-peer application software, which is why certain IIS components are provided with all versions of Windows Vista. If you install an application that requires IIS, the application's installer will most likely configure it for you.
Windows Communication Foundation HTTP Activation	The HTTP Activation system can be used by .NET application software to run services on demand. This component is enabled by the application program(s) as needed. (This selection is located under Microsoft .NET Framework 3.0).
Microsoft Message Queue (MSMQ) Server	MSMQ Server is a tool used primarily in distributed database applications. It is provided with Vista primarily for use by software developers who are writing and testing such applications.
Subsystem for UNIX-Based Applications (SUA)	The Subsystem for UNIX-Based Applications provides a UNIX-compatible environment and toolkit that can be used to migrate UNIX applications and services to Windows. SUA was discussed earlier in this chapter.
Management and Monitoring Tools	
SNMP Feature	The Simple Network Management Protocol (SNMP) is a remote monitoring and measurement tool used by some network-management systems. This protocol is discussed in more detail in the next section.
WMI SNMP Provider	This allows Windows Management Instrumentation (WMI) applications to access SNMP data.
Telnet Client	This enables you to connect computers and network devices using a command-line interface. Telnet was discussed earlier in this chapter.
Telnet Server	This enables you or an administrator to log on to your computer remotely using only a command-line interface. Telnet was discussed earlier in this chapter.
TFTP Client	The TFTP Client can be used to retrieve files from a TFTP server. This tool is used primarily to test network boot servers or to retrieve network device firmware.

Category/Component	Description
Networking Services	
Internet Printing Client	The Internet Printing Client provides support for network- or Internet-hosted printers or printing services using the Internet Printing Protocol (IPP).
LPD Print Service	This service lets UNIX computers send print output to your Windows computer's shared printers.
LPR Port Monitor	This enables you to send print output to network-connected printers or UNIX servers.
RIP Listener	This service is used to listen for network routing information in large networks. Your network manager will indicate whether you need to install it. Don't install it unless it's required.
Services for NFS	This enables you to use files shared by NFS file servers (typically UNIX file servers).
Simple TCP/IP services	This suite of services performs simple functions for testing purposes, such as echoing data to a remote computer or generating a stream of data. Don't install these services unless you're instructed to do so by a network manager. They don't do anything particularly useful, but hackers can use them to tie up your network with pointless traffic.

Table 21.4 shows the availability of these optional networking features on the primary versions of Windows Vista. In the table, "●" indicates a feature that is enabled by default, "○" indicates a feature that is available but must be enabled, and "–" indicates a feature that is not available on the particular version of Windows.

TABLE 21.4 AVAILABILITY OF OPTIONAL NETWORKING COMPONENTS ON WINDOWS VISTA VERSIONS

	Home Basic	Home Premium	Business	Enterprise	Ultimate
Internet Information Services	○	○	○	○	○
Microsoft .NET Framework 3.0 Windows Communication Foundation HTTP Activation	○	○	○	○	○
Microsoft Message Queue (MSMQ) Server	○	○	○	○	○
Print Services	●	●	●	●	●

continues

Table 21.4 Continued

	Home Basic	Home Premium	Business	Enterprise	Ultimate
Internet Printing Client	●	●	●	●	●
LPD Print Service	○	○	○	○	○
LPR Port Monitor	○	○	○	○	○
RIP Listener	○	○	○	○	○
Services for NFS	–	–	–	○	○
Simple TCP/IP Services	○	○	○	○	○
SNMP Feature	○	○	○	○	○
WMI SNMP Provider	○	○	○	○	○
Subsystem for UNIX-Based Applications	–	–	–	○	○
Telnet Client	○	○	○	○	○
Telnet Server	○	○	○	○	○
TFTP Client	○	○	○	○	○

The SNMP service requires special consideration, as you'll see in the next section.

SNMP

The Simple Network Management Protocol, or SNMP, is used on large corporate networks to monitor, measure, test, and configure network equipment from a central location. For example, monitoring software can use it to detect whether servers or WAN connections have gone offline, to alert staff or sound an alarm.

Windows Vista doesn't come with a tool to actually *use* the information SNMP can reveal, but it does come with an optional networking component that lets an SNMP-based monitoring system measure network activity in your computer.

SNMP should not be installed unless your network administrator requires its use because some security risks are attached to it. SNMP requires remote users to supply a *community name*, which is essentially a password, before they can view or change your computer's network setup. Unlike previous versions of Windows, the Windows Vista SNMP service, as initially installed, is given a very secure setup: No default community name exists, and the service will not accept connections from other computers.

Your network administrators will probably configure one or more community names when they install the service. If you need to add a name manually, follow these steps:

1. Click Start, right-click Computer, and select Manage. Confirm the User Account Control prompt.
2. Open Services and Applications, select Services, and locate SNMP Service in the right pane. Double-click it to open its Properties page.

3. Select the Security tab, shown in Figure 21.10. Click Add, enter a community name, and select one of the permission levels from the drop-down list. Then click OK. You can add more than one community name. It's common to create one community name with READ ONLY permission and a separate one with WRITE-CREATE permission.

Figure 21.10
Configure community names and trusted hosts on the SNMP Service's Security tab.

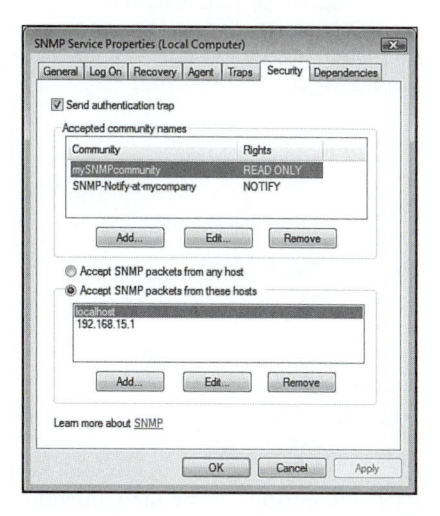

4. To allow another computer to use your computer's SNMP service, click Add and enter the computer's IP address. Alternatively, you can select Accept SNMP Packets from any Computer, but if you do this, you must be sure that your network is properly protected by a firewall that will block SNMP traffic from the Internet.

> **CAUTION**
>
> SNMP can be a security risk because it reveals the names of user accounts on your computer, as well as your computer's network routing information. A community name with RFAD-WRITE or WRITE-CREATE permission can alter network routing tables. For this reason, SNMP (UDP ports 161 and 162) should be blocked by your network's firewall, and you should *not* install it unless it's necessary.

5. An SNMP trap is a message that notifies an SNMP-based network health-monitoring system of a network problem or other event of interest. If your network uses a trap-monitoring system, select the Traps tab, type a community name into the drop-down box, and click Add to List. Then click the Add button and enter the IP address of your network's SNMP trap receiver.

> **TIP**
>
> If you're a network manager and use SNMP to monitor equipment health, you might find it valuable to know that Windows Vista, XP, and 2000 come with a utility that can turn specified Windows Event Log entries into SNMP traps (messages) as they happen. This feature is configured by the poorly documented program `evntwin`, which edits and saves a list of event-to-trap mappings to a file. Another command, `evntcmd`, installs this mapping on computers, and it can even do it remotely. These two tools are installed when you install SNMP. Google "Windows evntwin" and "Windows evntcmd" for links to Microsoft and other documentation.

TROUBLESHOOTING

SOME COMPUTERS ARE MISSING FROM NETWORK MAP

The list of computers is incomplete in the Network window or the Network Map window.

If computer names are missing, the network has elected a browser master that doesn't have all the protocols used by Windows networking computers on your LAN. This is a random selection, so be sure to install and bind the same set of protocols on every workstation in your LAN.

If a Windows XP computer appears at the bottom of the map, download and install the LLTD Responder for Windows XP. Visit support.microsoft.com for downloading instructions.

If you have a network router, hub, switch, or other device that does not appear correctly on the network map, visit the manufacturer's website to see if they can provide a firmware update that includes LLTD support.

> **CAUTION**
>
> Be careful to print copies of any network device's configuration screens before updating its firmware. You might also see if the device includes a "save configuration to disk" option. But don't forgo the screen printouts. Often, after a firmware upgrade, network devices revert to their original factory settings and, in some cases, don't accept previously saved configuration files—you'll need to reconfigure them entirely by hand.

WINDOWS 98/ME CANNOT ACCESS RESOURCES SHARED BY VISTA

When I try to access a folder shared by Windows Vista from Windows 9x or Me, I get a network error, or the folder never opens.

You shouldn't be using Windows 98 or Me anymore. Microsoft has stopped providing security updates for these versions of Windows, leaving you vulnerable to what is probably by now a terrifying number of known but unpatched bugs.

But you are still using it. Okay. Well, this is going to be a longer answer than you wanted, but you're just going to need to read it. When asking another computer for access to shared files, Windows sends your password over the network in an encrypted form, where it's compared to an identically encrypted copy of your password stored on the remote computer.

The problem is that the encryption format used by Windows 98 and Me is very poor, and it's a big security risk letting Windows keep copies of poorly encrypted copies of passwords. A hacker with access to your computer can fairly quickly decode the passwords and then use them to break into other computers on your network.

To mitigate against this, by default, Microsoft by default prevents Vista from storing a weakly encrypted copy of your password in its security database (it does store a copy encrypted with a much stronger method). Thus, it can't validate the weakly encrypted password sent by Windows 9*x* or Me, so you can't access the shared files. This happens even if Password Protected Sharing is turned off.

If you *absolutely* need to let Vista share files with Windows 98 or Me, you need to tell Vista to store a weakly encrypted copy of your passwords. To do this, follow the procedure for editing the local security policy, as described earlier in this chapter under "Internetworking with Windows 95, 98, and Me."

CARRIAGE RETURNS AND LINE FEEDS ARE MANGLED

When plain-text files are sent from UNIX machines to my printers using `lpr` *and Print Services for UNIX, carriage returns and line feeds are mangled. Line feeds are inserted where just carriage returns were present.*

When it's receiving plain ASCII text for printing, the TCP/IP Print Server replaces both LF (line feed or newline) and CR (carriage return) characters with a carriage return/line feed pair. This messes up print jobs that wanted to overprint lines using just a carriage return.

You can disable the translation of both newlines and carriage returns, or just carriage returns, by adding a value to the Registry.

→ For instructions and warnings about using the Registry Editor, **see** "Using Regedit," **p. 1054**.

Use the Registry Editor called Regedit to find the key `HKEY_LOCAL_MACHINE\System\CurrentControlSet\Control\Print\Printers\`*printername*`\PrinterDriverData`, where *printername* is the name of the shared printer the UNIX user is using.

To prevent the TCP/IP Print Server from replacing either CR or LF with CR+LF, follow these steps:

1. Select the key `PrinterDriverData` and choose Edit, New, DWORD Value. Enter the name `Winprint_TextNoTranslation`, and set the value to 1.

2. To prevent the server from replacing CR with CR+LF but still have it replace LF with CR+LF, add the DWORD value `Winprint_TextNoCRTranslation` with the value 1.

3. After making either of these additions, go to Computer Management, view Services, right-click TCP/IP Print Server, and select Restart.

Some Windows printer drivers do not correctly implement overprinted lines. You might find that the lines are now correctly stacked on top of each other, but only the text from the topmost line is visible. You might need to use the binary mode flag (-o 1) in your `lpr` command and add a form feed to the end of your file.

If you later decide to undo the Registry change, you can remove the value item or set its value to 0 and then restart the service.

CAN'T RUN MACINTOSH APPLICATION CONCURRENTLY

When a Macintosh application is installed on a shared folder stored on a Windows computer, an "Unable to Open File" error occurs on Macintoshes when more than one Macintosh user attempts to run the application concurrently.

Some Macintosh programs fail to open their application executable files in the proper file-sharing mode. You can patch the problem by using a resource editor program on the Macintosh; just follow these steps:

1. Obtain a copy of ResEdit. In the past we recommended that you download it from ResExcellence (www.resexcellence.com), which was a terrific resource (pun intended) for all things resource related. As of this writing, the site is not active, but we hope that they get their act together to get it back on the air. For novice users, a better resource editor program is FileBuddy, from SkyTag (www.skytag.com).
2. Start ResEdit or FileBuddy. Select Get Info from the File menu. In the dialog box that appears, you can select the application.
3. Put a check in the Shared check box.
4. If you're using ResEdit, quit the application and choose Yes to save the changes. In FileBuddy, click OK.

> **CAUTION**
>
> Resource editing on a Macintosh is as risky as Registry editing in Windows. Always make a copy of whatever file you're going to edit before making changes, and *never* throw out an original, even if it seems that your modified version works like a charm.

MACINTOSH FILES HAVE LOST APPLICATION ASSOCIATIONS

After a Windows user edits a shared file and a Macintosh user tries to open the file, the Macintosh Finder says it can't find the application required to open the document.

The file's resource fork was stripped out when the file was edited in Windows, so the file's Type and Creator codes are missing. The Macintosh user can drag and drop the file onto the application's icon or manually locate the application. When the Macintosh user saves the file, the association will be restored for future edits.

The Type and Creator codes can also be set using a Macintosh resource editor, as described previously. However, resource editing is tricky and best not done unless it's an emergency.

> **NOTE**
>
> Type and Creator codes are case sensitive. MSWD is not the same as MsWd or mswd. Case can often cause confusion if you must restore the codes after they were stripped on a trip through Windows or DOS.

Tips from the Windows Pros: The Hosts File

If you have an office LAN, especially one with mixed and matched computers, you probably, like me, have a chart of computer names and IP addresses posted on your wall—not just computers, but routers, firewalls, monitored devices, and all manner of devices. Who knows? Soon the espresso machine might be wired in, too.

On a corporate or enterprise LAN, the LAN administrators will probably enter each device into the organization's DNS system under your own default domain so that you can type a command such as `ping firewall` instead of needing to type `ping firewall.mycompany.com` or, worse, something like `ping 192.168.56.102`.

On a home or small office LAN, though, you probably don't have your own domain name server, or your network manager hasn't entered names for the networked devices you use most frequently (for example, your new Linksys "Wireless-Z Router and Espresso Maker"—don't tell me you don't have one yet). On a heterogeneous network, your Macintosh and testbed Linux machines probably aren't in any domain name list.

The hosts file is the answer to this annoying situation. You can add entries to the file `\windows\system32\drivers\etc\hosts` to associate names with IP addresses. The Windows domain name–lookup system looks first in the hosts file before consulting the network, so you can add entries for your own workgroup's computers and devices, regardless of operating system.

The format is simple, but editing it is a bit tricky. The hosts file has become a target for adware hackers, who put fake entries in it to hijack your web browser.

To edit it, click Start, All Programs, Accessories, and right-click Notepad. Select Run As Administrator and confirm the User Account Control prompt. Then, when the Notepad window opens, open `\windows\system32\driver\etc\hosts`.

Add lines to the file, listing IP addresses at the left margin, followed by some whitespace (tabs or spaces), followed by one or more names. You can enter simple names or full domain names. Simple names are assumed to belong to your own domain.

My hosts file looks like this:

```
127.0.0.0      localhost lh
192.168.56.1   firewall fw
192.168.56.45  macmini
```

The first entry is the default entry shipped with Windows. `localhost` stands for "my own computer" and is used for internal testing of the network software. I've added a second name, `lh`, because I'm lazy and would rather type `ping lh` than `ping localhost`.

I added the second entry myself to give a name to my network's firewall. I can now configure the firewall by typing `telnet firewall` or, better yet, `telnet fw` instead of needing to look up at that sheet on the wall and type a bunch of numbers.

Finally, there's an entry for my Macintosh computer, `macmini`. This way, I can view its web server's home page from Internet Explorer using http://macmini instead of needing to remember its IP address.

This file also serves as a sort of documentation of my network because it records important IP addresses. One thing you must watch out for, though, is that Windows checks this file before using the real DNS system to look up names. If you put a name in your LAN's (or the Internet's) DNS system and the computer's IP address later changes, your hosts file will be incorrect. It's best to use this file only for machines that are in nobody's DNS system.

CHAPTER 22

CONNECTING YOUR NETWORK TO THE INTERNET

In this chapter

It's a Great Time to Connect Your LAN to the Internet   702

The Nuts and Bolts of the Connection   702

Configuring Your LAN   713

Making Services Available   728

Troubleshooting   736

Tips from the Windows Pros: Speeding Up Vista?   737

It's a Great Time to Connect Your LAN to the Internet

Because you now have your computers tied together with a nifty local area network (LAN), it seems silly that each user should have to use a modem to gain Internet access individually. No worries: You have a host of options for shared Internet connections. You can use a high-speed connection to serve the entire LAN, or you can share a modem connection made from one designated Windows Vista computer. Either way, shared access makes online life simpler *and safer* for everyone on the network.

A shared Internet connection can actually provide better protection against hackers than an individual connection. In this chapter, I'll show you why. I'll also cover your Internet connection options and discuss the pros and cons of each.

> **TIP**
>
> You should also read Chapter 35, "Protecting Your Network from Hackers and Snoops," for more details on protecting your network from hacking.

The Nuts and Bolts of the Connection

You're probably familiar with using a modem to connect your own PC to an Internet service provider and, hence, to the Internet. When you're connecting an entire network of computers, the process is a little more involved. We address five main issues, starting with the physical connection itself. We discuss the pros and cons of each of the most common and reasonable alternatives.

The Need for Speed

Of the several connection technologies, each has advantages and disadvantages in reliability, speed, and cost.

Speed is everything on the Internet now, and the need for raw speed will become even more important in the future. Remember that everyone on your LAN is sharing a single connection, so you have to consider the speed requirements for the applications you'll be using over the network and multiply that requirement by the number of *simultaneous* users you'll want to support at that speed. If you have eight users checking email and occasionally browsing the Web, your speed requirements might be met by a single modem, but if you have just two users who want to use voice and videoconferencing at the same time, you might need a very high-speed connection.

If you can get it, high-speed DSL, cable, or satellite service will provide a much better experience than a dial-up setup. It costs a bit more per month, but if you take into the account that one shared broadband connection can replace several dial-up accounts and free up several phone lines, it might turn out to be the least expensive alternative—as well as the most fun.

Ways to Make the Connection

When you're using a single computer, you use its analog modem or a broadband cable, DSL, or satellite modem to connect to your ISP as needed. When you share your Internet connection on a network, either you designate one computer running Windows Vista or XP to make the connection, or you use an inexpensive hardware device called a *connection-sharing router* or *residential gateway* to serve as a bridge between your network and a dial-up, cable, or DSL modem. Whichever method you choose, the designated computer or router automatically sets up the connection any time anybody on your network needs it.

As an overview, Figure 22.1 shows six ways you can hook up your LAN to an Internet service provider:

1. **Microsoft Internet Connection Sharing (ICS) with an analog or ISDN dial-up connection**—In this scenario, the built-in software in Windows automatically dials your ISP from one computer whenever anyone on the LAN wants to connect to the Internet. This is called *demand-dialing*. (By the way, the modem doesn't have to be an external one; it can be an internal modem. I just wanted it to show up in the figure.)

2. **ICS with a broadband DSL or cable modem**—The computer that hosts the shared connection uses a second LAN adapter to connect to a broadband modem. This type of connection might be always-on, or, if your ISP uses a connection-based setup called PPPoE, Windows will establish the link whenever anyone wants to use the Internet.

→ To learn more about PPPoE, **see** "Configuring a High-Speed Connection," **p. 411**.

3. **Connection-sharing router with a broadband, analog, or ISDN modem**—You can use a small hardware device that costs about $20–$100 to do the same job as Internet Connection Sharing. The advantage of this is that you don't have to leave a particular Windows computer turned on for other users to reach the Internet. It is also more secure because a separate device is shielding Windows from the Internet.

Figure 22.1
Six ways to connect your LAN to the Internet.

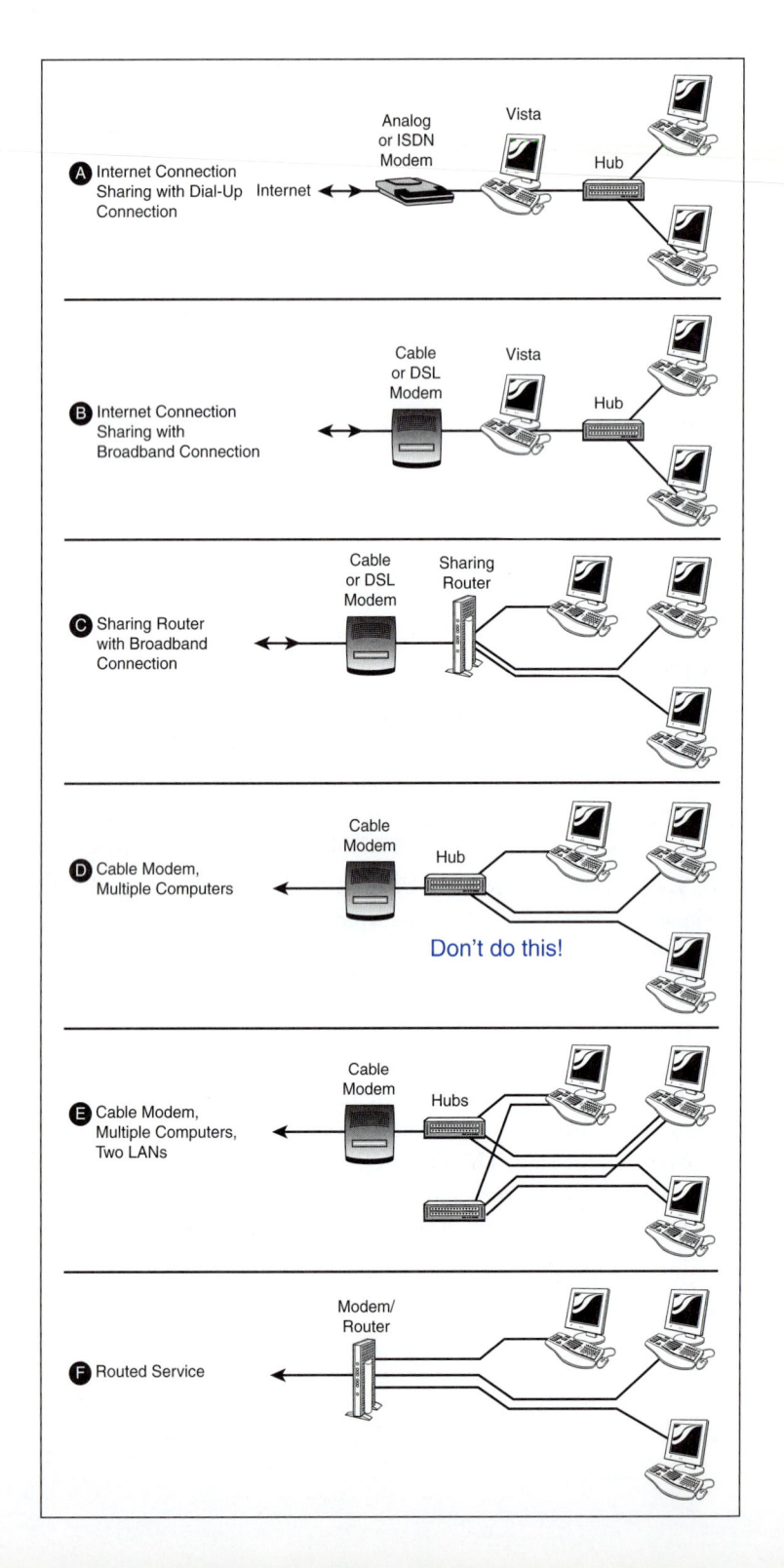

A — Internet Connection Sharing with Dial-Up Connection

B — Internet Connection Sharing with Broadband Connection

C — Sharing Router with Broadband Connection

D — Cable Modem, Multiple Computers

Don't do this!

E — Cable Modem, Multiple Computers, Two LANs

F — Routed Service

4. **Cable service with multiple directly connected computers**—This is the setup that some cable Internet providers recommend for a home with more than one computer, but it is a *bad idea*. You can't use this method and also use file and printer sharing. Use schemes 2, 3, or 5 instead. See "Special Notes for Cable Service," later in this chapter, for more information.

5. **Cable service with multiple directly connected computers and a separate LAN for file and printer sharing**—If you don't use connection sharing (schemes 2 and 3), this is the only safe way to share files and printers *and* have an "unfiltered" broadband Internet connection.

6. **Routed service with a router**—Some ISPs provide *routed* Internet service through DSL, cable, Frame Relay, or other technologies. There's usually an extra charge for this type of service because it provides a separate public IP address to each computer on the LAN. This has some advantages that I discuss later, but it also incurs a risk of exposing your network to hackers, unless you're vigilant in setting it up.

I discussed the pros and cons of dial-up, ISDN, and broadband connections themselves in Chapter 14, "Getting Connected," so I won't repeat that discussion here. Instead, I'll discuss the costs and benefits of these six connection-sharing strategies.

> **NOTE**
>
> Although I really prefer using the shared connection strategies—the first three schemes in Figure 22.1—they have a drawback: It's more difficult to enable incoming access to your computer. In particular, it makes it hard to reach your computer with Remote Desktop, and it can be difficult for someone (tech support personnel, for example) to work with Windows XP users using Remote Assistance. I show you how to make these strategies work at the end of the chapter, under "Making Services Available."

Now let's look at the issues involved in having a single ISP connection serve multiple computers.

Managing IP Addresses

Connecting a LAN to the Internet requires you to delve into some issues about how computers are identified on your LAN and on the Internet. Each computer on your LAN uses a unique network identification number called an *IP address* that is used to route data to the correct computer. As long as the data stays on your LAN, it doesn't matter what numbers are used; your LAN is essentially a private affair. In fact, on LANs with no shared Internet connection, Windows just makes up random IP address numbers for each computer, and that's good enough.

When you connect to the Internet, though, those random numbers can't be used to direct data to you; your ISP has to assign *public* IP addresses to you so that other computers on the Internet can properly route data to your ISP and then to you.

Now, when you establish a solo dial-up connection from your computer to the Internet, this isn't a big problem. When you dial up, your ISP assigns your connection a temporary public IP address. Any computer on the entire Internet can send data to you using this address. When you want to connect a LAN, though, it's not quite as easy. Two approaches are used:

- You can get a valid public IP address for each of your computers so they can each participate in the Internet at large.
- You can use *one* public IP address and share it among all the users of your LAN.

The first approach is called *routed* Internet service because your ISP assigns a fixed block of IP addresses for your LAN—one for each of your computers—and routes all data for these addresses to your site. The second approach uses a technique called *Network Address Translation*, or NAT, in which all the computers on your LAN share one IP address and connection.

NAT and Internet Connection Sharing

Microsoft's Internet Connection Sharing system and the popular devices called *residential gateways* or *connection-sharing routers* use Network Address Translation to establish all Internet connections using one public IP address. The computer or device running the NAT service mediates all connections between computers on your LAN and the Internet (see Figure 22.2).

To explain NAT, it's helpful to make an analogy to postal mail service. Normally, mail is delivered to each house according to its address, and the postal worker stops at each separate house on a given block. This is analogous to routed Internet service, in which each of your computers has its own public IP address. Data is routed to your LAN and then delivered to each computer independently.

Figure 22.2
A NAT device or program carries out all Internet communications using one IP address. NAT keeps track of outgoing data from your LAN to determine where to send responses from the outside.

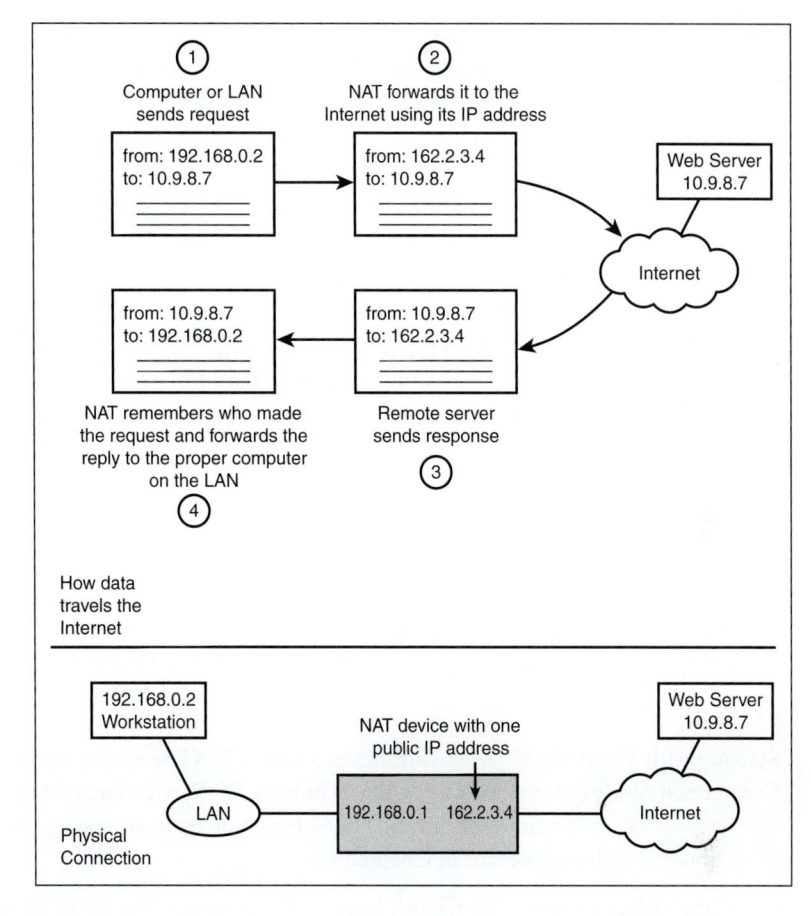

① Computer or LAN sends request
from: 192.168.0.2
to: 10.9.8.7

② NAT forwards it to the Internet using its IP address
from: 162.2.3.4
to: 10.9.8.7

Web Server 10.9.8.7

Internet

from: 10.9.8.7
to: 192.168.0.2

from: 10.9.8.7
to: 162.2.3.4

④ NAT remembers who made the request and forwards the reply to the proper computer on the LAN

③ Remote server sends response

How data travels the Internet

192.168.0.2 Workstation

NAT device with one public IP address

Web Server 10.9.8.7

LAN — 192.168.0.1 162.2.3.4 — Internet

Physical Connection

NAT works more like a large commercial office building, where there's one address for many people. Mail is delivered to the mail room, which sorts it and delivers it internally to the correct recipient. With NAT, you are assigned one public IP address, and all communication between your LAN and the Internet uses this address. The NAT service takes care of changing or translating the IP addresses in data packets from the private, internal IP addresses used on your LAN to the one public address used on the Internet.

Using NAT has several significant consequences:

- You can hook up as many computers on your LAN as you want. Your ISP won't care, or even know, that more than one computer is using the connection. You will save money because you need to pay for only a single-user connection.

- You can assign IP addresses inside your LAN however you want. In fact, all the NAT setups I've seen provide DHCP, an automatic IP address service, so virtually no manual configuration is needed on the computers you add to your LAN.

- If you want to host a website, VPN, or other service on your LAN and make it available from the Internet, you have some additional setup work to do. When you contact a remote website, NAT knows to send the returned data back to you, but when an unsolicited request comes from outside, NAT has to be told where to send the incoming connection. I'll discuss this later in the chapter.

- NAT serves as an additional firewall to protect your LAN from probing by Internet hackers. Incoming requests, such as those to read your shared folders, are simply ignored if you haven't specifically set up your connection-sharing service to forward requests to a particular computer.

- Some network services can't be made to work with NAT. For example, you might not be able to use audio and video chat with Windows Live Messenger and NetMeeting. These programs expect that the IP address of the computer on which they're running is a public address. Windows Internet Connection Sharing and some hardware-sharing routers can work around this problem using the Universal Plug and Play protocol, which I'll discuss later in the chapter.

- A hardware connection-sharing router might provide you with better security than Windows Internet Connection Sharing because, as special-purpose devices, their software is simpler and less likely to be buggy than Windows. Also, when used with Windows Firewall, you have *two* separate lines of defense against hackers instead of just one.

Starting with Windows 98, Microsoft has provided a NAT service through its Internet Connection Sharing feature. In addition, Windows XP Service Pack 2 introduced Windows Firewall, a security feature that prevents outside people from accessing your LAN. I talk more about Windows Firewall in Chapter 35.

Given the choice between Microsoft's Internet Connection Sharing (ICS) service and an external hardware router, I recommend that you use a router, for two reasons:

- First, to use ICS, you have to leave one of your Windows computers turned on so that other computers can reach the Internet. Connection-sharing routers have to be left on, too, but they consume very little power compared to what a PC sucks up.

- More important, connection-sharing routers provide better security than Windows. These little boxes have very little going on inside them, so it's more likely that any security flaws have been noticed and fixed. Windows, on the other hand, is hugely complex, and Microsoft finds security flaws at the rate of one or two a week. If you use ICS and host a website on the connection-sharing computer, you're inviting outside people to run complex software on the same computer that's protecting your network. If they find a way to circumvent NAT or the Windows Firewall, they're already inside your computer. With the hardware router, they have to break through the router and then break into Windows.

I won't go so far as to say that you shouldn't trust ICS, and later I show you how to hook up your LAN using all of the methods I described earlier. I just put in as my final word on this issue that I use DSL/cable–sharing routers at my own home and office.

If you decide to use a router, look at the products made by Linksys, D-Link, SMC, and Netgear. You can find them at computer stores, office supply stores, and online (check www.buy.com), and on sale you can pick one up for $20 or less. Wireless versions that include an 802.11g wireless networking base station as well as a hub for wired Ethernet connections don't cost that much more—I'm looking at the ads in my Sunday paper right now and see prices ranging from $40 to $60.

More advanced (and expensive) versions include additional features such as a built-in print server or virtual private networking (VPN) service. For example, the D-Link DI-713P Wireless Broadband Router provides NAT (connection sharing), a three-port switching Ethernet hub, a print server, and a wireless access point, all in one box. But although combination devices might be less expensive when you look at the total cost of getting separate devices, separate units give you more flexibility in where you locate the devices, and if one device fails, you don't lose all the functions at once.

NOTE
> Although most connection-sharing routers on the market are designed for use with cable or DSL Internet service, some can connect with an analog or ISDN modem. If you use dial-up service, you're not left out. Netgear and SMC make devices that can be hooked up to a modem.

RUNNING YOUR OWN WEB SERVERS

If you want to host your own public web or email servers on your LAN, or if you want to reach your LAN through Remote Desktop or a VPN connection, you need to have an always-on connection so that the network can always be reached from the outside. A demand-dialing modem connection is not a good choice for this use because the connection is established only when you try to reach out. Many years ago, it was cost-effective to use a permanently connected dial-up service, but it's no longer cost-effective. Broadband is really the only way to go. Routed Internet service is a big advantage here because each computer gets a fixed, public, always-on IP address, but you can get by with a shared connection, too.

You'll probably also want to be able to reach your website or computers by typing in a standard domain name, such as www.mysitename.com. For this, you need to register a domain name, and you need domain name service (DNS) to give the Internet the means of finding your computer's public IP address. You can have your ISP provide domain name service, but it will probably cost you an extra $5–$20 a month. You also might check out the free public DNS services hosted by www.dyndns.org and others (do a Google search for "free DNS service" and check out the sponsored links).

Whether you use NAT or a routed Internet service, it's best if you can get your ISP to assign you a permanent, or *static*, IP address so that your computers' IP addresses don't change from day to day, as a dial-up connection's does. This way, your DNS information can be set up once, and it will work as long as you keep your ISP. Static IP addressing is not available with every connection technology or ISP, though, so you have to ask when shopping for your service provider.

If you have dial-up, cable, or nonstatic DSL service, you'll have to get "dynamic DNS" service because your network's public IP address will change every time your connection is reestablished. Check out www.dyndns.org for more information about dynamic DNS, or do a Google search for "free DNS service" and check the sponsored links. Many hardware-sharing routers support dynamic DNS. Dyndns.org also provides a software dynamic DNS client that runs as a Windows service. You can use this software if your router can't or doesn't reliably handle dynamic DNS or if you use Windows Internet Connection Sharing.

Chapter 18, "Hosting Web Pages with Internet Information Services," includes more information about port forwarding, including a detailed example.

Inverse DNS

If you go for dedicated Internet access and your ISP assigns you a block of IP fixed addresses, you might want to ask your ISP to enter *inverse DNS* information for you as well as register your domain name.

The domain name service (DNS) is called into play whenever you use an Internet address, such as www.microsoft.com. DNS looks up this name in a directory and returns some computer's IP address—for example, 207.46.131.137. The DNS system can also work in reverse and return the name of a computer given its IP address. For example, the name 4.3.2.1 turns out to be durham2-001.dsl.gtei.net.

When you get routed Internet access, the "inverse" lookup names for the IP addresses assigned to you either are left undefined or are set to some generic names, such as cust137.dsl131.someISP.com. If you ask, your ISP can set up names that identify your computers and domain so that anyone on the Internet to whom you connect can find out the name of your computer.

Using inverse DNS has some pros and cons. One pro is that some email servers on the Internet don't accept email from systems without a valid inverse DNS entry. If you run an email server on your network, at least that computer should have an inverse DNS entry. One con is that website managers can tell the name of your computer and domain when you visit websites, so you give up some privacy.

The choice is yours. If you want to register your computers, talk to your ISP.

The next two sections discuss issues that are important to business users. If you're setting up an Internet for your home, you can skip ahead.

A Warning for Business Users

My enthusiasm notwithstanding, cable and DSL Internet service are based on newer technologies, and the businesses delivering them are new and growing extremely rapidly. I can tell you from direct experience that they can give you a painful, bumpy ride. Some DSL ISPs (two of mine, for example) have already gone bankrupt and stranded their customers.

Customer support ranges from okay to incredibly bad, installation appointments are routinely missed, and even billing can be a terrible mess. If you ask a provider for a service-level agreement (a guaranteed percentage of uptime and throughput), the likely reply will be hysterical laughter. If your business truly depends on your Internet connection for survival, DSL and cable are probably not for you.

It costs a lot more in the short term to set up Frame Relay or dedicated ISDN service, but if you lose business when your connection fails, you probably can't afford the risks that come with consumer-class DSL and cable Internet access. If you do want to use cable or DSL, it's worth paying extra for "business class" service.

Frame Relay

I talked about dial-up, DSL, cable, ISDN, wireless, and satellite Internet connectivity in Chapter 14. For serious business use, Frame Relay is one more option to consider. Frame Relay is an older technology that was primarily designed for private, dedicated, long-distance connections for the corporate world. It's connected using hardware very similar to DSL, but it requires its own dedicated telephone line from your office to the phone company and some expensive equipment.

Although installing and setting up Frame Relay Internet hardware is tough, after the equipment is in, it just plugs into your LAN and virtually no setup is involved with Windows itself. (In Figure 22.1, it falls into the last category, routed service.)

Frame Relay connections are extremely reliable and run at data rates similar to DSL, but they have a severe disadvantage in price. Table 22.1 compares the costs for 128Kbps Frame Relay to those for DSL service.

Table 22.1   128Kbps Frame Relay Versus 128Kbps DSL

	128Kbps Frame Relay	128Kbps DSL
Installation by telephone company	$1,000	$0–100
Set up by ISP	$400	0
Required hardware (modem and so on)	$1,200–1,800	$0–400
Monthly data line fee	$325	$40
Monthly Internet service provider fee	$400	$10

It's pricey, but Frame Relay users can expect service interruptions of no more than 3 minutes per month versus perhaps 3 hours per month with DSL service. If this sounds worthwhile to you, contact a telecommunications consultant or a networking pro for more information.

Special Notes for Wireless Networking

If you're setting up a wireless network, you *must* enable WEP or WPA encryption to protect your network from unexpected use by random strangers. People connecting to your wireless network appear to Windows to be part of your own LAN and are trusted accordingly.

If you really want to provide free access to your broadband connection as a public service, provide it using a second, unsecured wireless router plugged into your network, as shown in Figure 22.3. Use a different channel number and SSID from the ones set up for your own wireless LAN. Set up filtering in this router to prevent Windows file-sharing queries from penetrating into your own network. See "Scheme F—Routed Service Using a Router," later in this chapter, for the list of ports that you must block.

(And remember that someone might use your connection to send spam or attack other networks. If the FBI knocks on your door some day, don't say I didn't warn you.)

Figure 22.3
If you want to provide unsecured, free wireless Internet access to strangers, use a second wireless router to protect your own LAN.

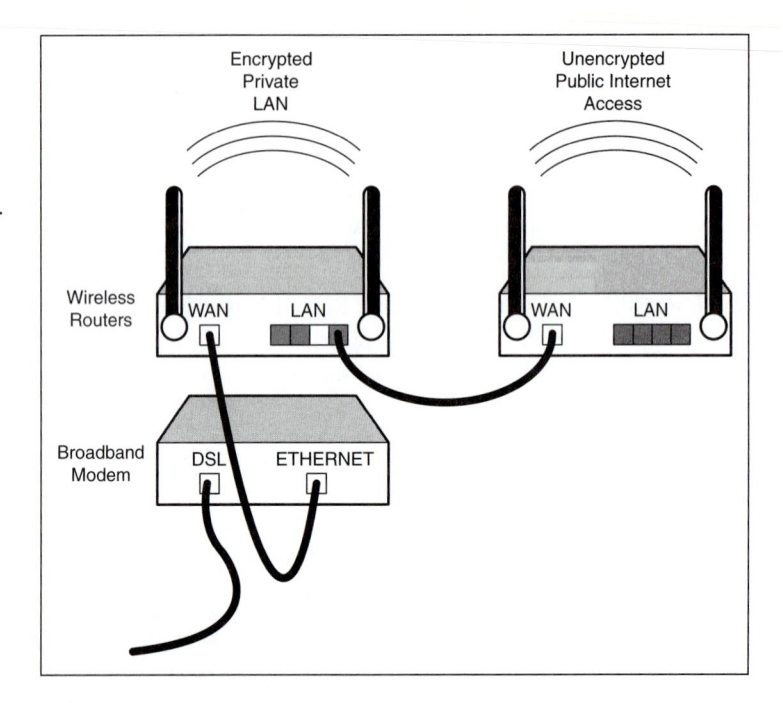

SPECIAL NOTES FOR CABLE SERVICE

Some cable Internet providers can provide you with multiple IP addresses so you can connect multiple computers directly to your cable modem. However, I strongly urge you *not* to use this type of service.

This type of setup requires you to connect your cable modem directly to your LAN, without any firewall protection between the Internet and your computers. You would *have* to disable file and printer sharing on each computer. If you didn't, you would expose all your computers to a *severe security risk*.

CAUTION

Do not connect a cable modem directly to your LAN without a router, gateway, or firewall in between. Anyone on the Internet would be able to read and change your shared files and folders, and could possibly infect your computer with viruses and other nasty software.

If you don't care about file and printer sharing, this isn't a big loss. But if you want the full advantage of having a LAN in your home or office, you can solve this dilemma in either of two ways.

- You could set up two separate networks, one to connect each computer to the cable modem and the other to connect the computers for file sharing (see Figure 22.1, E). With Ethernet network adapters costing as little as $5 each, this isn't a bad solution. You would have to take great care to configure the two networks correctly. I'll discuss this shortly.
- Or you could use Internet Connection Sharing (Figure 22.1B) or an inexpensive connection sharing router (Figure 22.1C).

Some cable ISPs don't want you to use a router, but I think it provides superior protection against hacking, and that needs to be your first priority. You can always pay your ISP for the extra computers and use just the one, safe connection to provide service to your other computers.

SPECIAL NOTES FOR ISDN SERVICE

If you are ordering ISDN service, you should know what kind of ISDN modem or router you will be using before you order an ISDN line from the phone company. ISDN provisioning is complex, and most telephone companies can determine the options you need if you tell them the brand of equipment you're using. Also, your ISDN equipment manual might list a special "quick order" code to give your telephone company. You will probably order "2B+D, Data and voice, 64K data" service with no special call functions.

When your ISDN line is installed, be sure to ask the installer for the following information:

- Switch type
- SPID (Service Profile Identifiers) numbers
- Directory numbers

You'll need these when you install your ISDN modem.

CONFIGURING YOUR LAN

You waited weeks for installation day, and the installer finally came. Now all you can think of is all those bits, just waiting to blast their way onto your network. Hang on; we're almost done.

You now need to set up your network's TCP/IP software to let your computers talk through the Internet connection in a coordinated way. This step depends not so much on the connection type you choose, but on the sharing system and the IP address system you'll use.

In the following sections, I describe how to set up each of the connection schemes diagrammed in Figure 22.1. If you're still in the planning stages for your network, you might want to read all the sections to see what's involved; this might help you decide what configuration you want to use. If your LAN is already set up and your Internet service is ready to go now, just skip ahead to the appropriate section.

Scheme A—Microsoft Internet Connection Sharing with a Dial-Up Connection

This section shows how to set up the Internet connection method illustrated in Figure 22.1, A.

The Internet Connection Sharing feature provided with Windows Vista can share modem, ISDN, or broadband connections that require a sign-on procedure. The connection is made automatically whenever any user on the network tries to access the Internet; this is called demand-dialing. The following section describes how to set it up.

Setting Up the Shared Connection

To set up a shared connection, first install and test your modem and ISP information on the computer that will be used to share the connection. To do this, set up a standard dial-up connection using the procedure described in Chapter 14. Be sure that you can access the Internet properly by viewing at least one web page. When you know this is working, you're ready to set up Internet Connection Sharing. To set up Internet Connection Sharing, follow these steps:

1. Click Start, Network, and select Network and Sharing Center. Select Manage Network Connections. Right-click the icon for the connection to your ISP and select Properties.
2. Choose the Sharing tab. Check all the boxes, as shown in Figure 22.4.
3. Select the Options tab. Uncheck Prompt for Name and Password and also Prompt for Phone Number. This allows the connection to start up without user intervention.
4. If you want a dedicated, always-on 24×7 connection, use these settings: Check Redial If Line Is Dropped, set the number of Redial Attempts to 99, set Time Between Redial Attempts to 10 Seconds, and set Idle Time Before Hanging Up to Never. Be aware that if you pay per-minute charges, this can result in an astounding phone bill!

Figure 22.4
On the computer that will share its connection, enable Internet Connection Sharing.

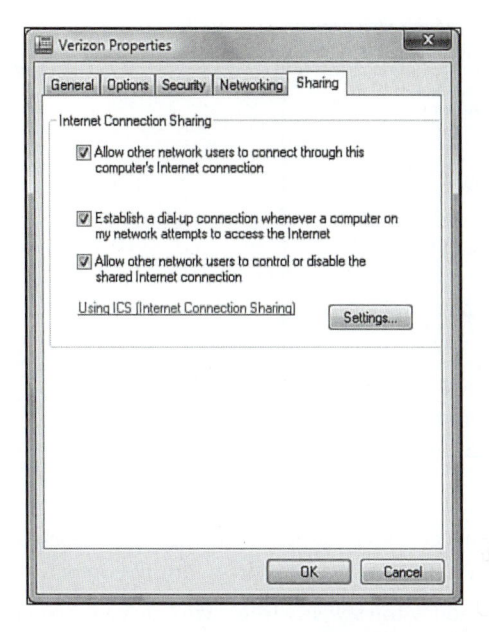

Usually, though, you'll want a demand-dialing connection. Use these settings: Uncheck Redial If Line Is Dropped. Set the number of Redial Attempts to 10, set Time Between Redial Attempts to 10 Seconds, and set Idle Time Before Hanging Up to 10 Minutes. (I recommend using 10 minutes; you can increase it later if you find that the line disconnects too frequently while you're working.)

> **CAUTION**
>
> The following step is a crucial part of protecting your computer and LAN from hacking over the Internet. Omitting this step could make your computer vulnerable to hacking.

5. Select the Networking tab. In the list of components used by the connection, be sure that *only* Internet Protocol Version 6 (TCP/IPv6), Internet Protocol Version 4 (TCP/IPv4), and QoS Packet Scheduler are checked, as shown in Figure 22.5. This will prevent file sharing from being exposed to the Internet. The Firewall will do that, too, but it doesn't hurt to be extra safe.

Figure 22.5
Be *sure* that on your Internet connection, the Client and Sharing components are not checked.

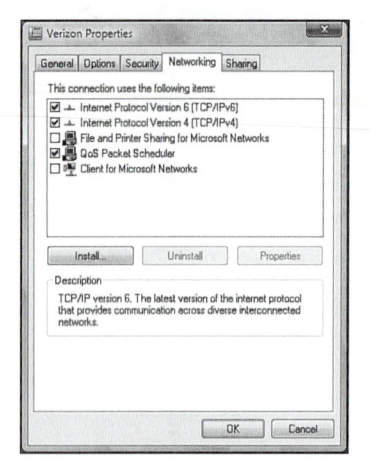

6. Click OK. Windows then warns you that it is changing the network address of your LAN adapter to 192.168.0.1. This is now the IP address for this computer on your LAN.

7. Restart your computer and try to view any web page (such as www.google.com). Your computer should automatically dial your ISP. If the web page appears, proceed to "Configuring the Rest of the Network." If it doesn't, you'll have to resolve the problem before continuing.

If your modem doesn't dial up when you try to view a web page, **see** *"Shared Connection Doesn't Happen" in the "Troubleshooting" section at the end of this chapter.*

Configuring the Rest of the Network

When the shared connection is set up, configuring the rest of your LAN should be easy. The computer sharing its Internet connection is now running the Internet Connection Sharing service, which makes it

- A DHCP server, which parcels out IP addresses and setup information.
- The network gateway, which forwards to the Internet any network traffic that isn't directed at local computers.
- A DNS server, which assists the other computers in converting domain names into IP addresses.

Its IP address is 192.168.0.1, and all your other computers simply refer to it for network services.

NOTE
To enable File and Printer sharing throughout your LAN without exposing your network to the Internet, ensure that your Internet connection is set up as in Step 5 in the previous section, and set up sharing for your LAN as described in Chapter 23, "Using a Windows Network."

On each of your *other* computers (all except the connections-sharing computer), follow these steps:

1. Open Network and Sharing Center and select Manage Network Connections. Open Local Area Connection's Properties. On versions of Windows other than Vista, you might have to use different selections to get to your network adapter's settings; check online help or your copy of the corresponding *Special Edition Using* book.
2. Select Internet Protocol Version 6 (TCP/IPv6) and then select Properties.
3. Check Obtain an IP Address Automatically and Obtain DNS Server Address Automatically.
4. Click OK. The computer should reconfigure itself with a new IP address obtained from the computer with the shared dial-up connection.
5. Repeat Steps 2–4 for Internet Protocol Version 4 (TCP/IPv4).
6. When finished, you might want to restart your computer. Then you should be able to open Internet Explorer and view a website. When you try, the connection-sharing computer should dial out.

> **NOTE**
>
> When you're using a shared dial-up connection, it takes a while for the dialer to go through its paces if the connection wasn't already up. Before it can finish, you might get an error from Internet Explorer saying that it can't open the page. If this happens, just wait a few seconds and click Refresh to try again.

If you are using Microsoft Internet Connection Sharing or a connection-sharing router that supports Universal Plug and Play (UPnP), the Network window of all the other computers on your network should have an icon that represents the shared Internet connection, as shown in Figure 22.6. Windows automatically establishes and drops the shared connection as needed.

Figure 22.6
The other computers on your network can view the shared connection from their Network window.

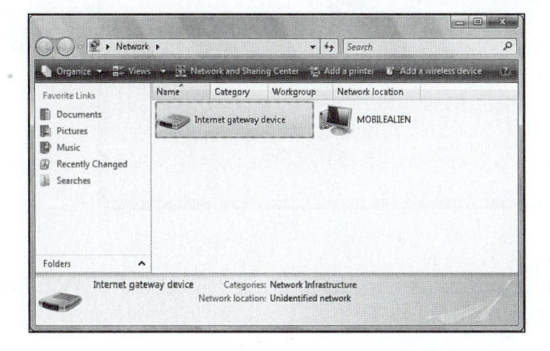

> If the computer can't browse web pages, **see** "Can't Access a Shared Modem Connection from the LAN" in the "Troubleshooting" section at the end of this chapter.

→ If you want to make services available to the Internet, continue with "Making Services Available," later in this chapter.

Scheme B—Microsoft Internet Connection Sharing with a Broadband Connection

This section shows how to set up the Internet connection method illustrated in Figure 22.1, B.

The procedure for configuring a shared high-speed cable or DSL Internet connection with Microsoft ICS is very similar to that for setting up a shared dial-up connection. To prepare, be sure to install and test your DSL or cable connection on the computer you'll use to host the shared connection, as described in Chapter 14. It's essential that you have this working before you proceed to set up your LAN and the shared connection.

TIP

> If your broadband service uses a LAN adapter instead of a USB to connect your computer to the DSL or cable modem, you'll be installing two LAN adapters in this computer: one for the LAN and one for the modem. I suggest that you install them one at a time. Install the one that you'll use for your broadband connection first. View the adapter's icon in Network Connections, right-click it, and rename it DSL Connection or Internet Connection, or some other name that indicates what it's used for, as shown in Figure 22.7. Configure and test the Internet connection. Then install the network adapter that you'll use to connect to your LAN. Rename this connection LAN Connection or leave it as Local Area Connection. This will help you later in the setup process, when you need to know which connection goes to your ISP.

Figure 22.7
Install and rename your network adapters one at a time, indicating what purpose they'll serve. "DSL Connection" or "Internet Connection" is much more informative than "Local Area Connection #2."

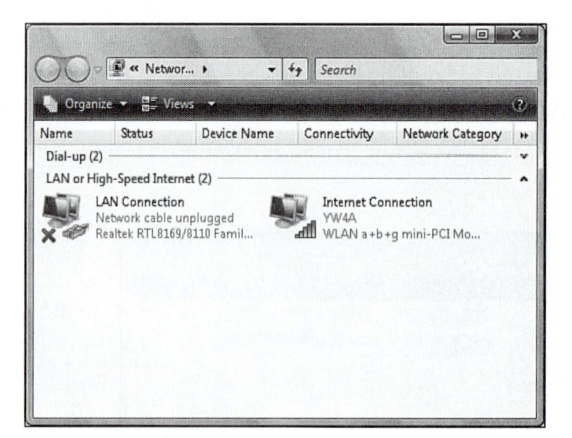

Verify that the broadband Internet connection is not connected to Windows file and printer sharing. To do this, follow these steps:

1. Open the Network Connections window by clicking Start, Network, Network and Sharing Center, and selecting Manage Network Connections.

2. Right-click the icon that corresponds to your broadband connection and select Properties. Be sure that *only* QoS Packet Scheduler, Internet Protocol Version 6 (TCP/IPv6), and Internet Protocol Version 4 (TCP/IPv4) are checked, as shown in Figure 22.5.

When your broadband connection is configured correctly and is working, follow these steps:

1. Locate the icon for the adapter that goes to your broadband modem in Network Connections. Right-click it and select Properties.
2. Choose the Sharing tab. Check all the boxes, as shown in Figure 22.4.
3. Select the Networking tab. In the list of components used by the connection, be sure that *only* QoS Packet Scheduler, Internet Protocol Version 6 (TCP/IPv6), and Internet Protocol Version 4 (TCP/IPv4) are checked. (This will prevent file sharing from being exposed to the Internet. Windows Firewall will do that, too, but it doesn't hurt to be extra safe.)
4. Click OK. Windows then warns you that it is changing the network address of your LAN adapter to `192.168.0.1`. This is now the IP address for this computer on your LAN.
5. Select Windows Firewall from Network and Sharing. In the Windows Firewall window, select Change Settings. Make sure the Windows Firewall is On and that Block All Incoming Connections is unchecked.
6. Restart Windows and try to view any web page (such as www.google.com). If it appears, proceed to Step 7. If it doesn't, you'll have to resolve the problem before proceeding. You should check the appropriate connection icon to be sure it's still configured correctly for your ISP.

→. When Connection Sharing has been set up, follow the instructions under "Configuring the Rest of the Network," on **p. 716**.

Scheme C—Sharing Router with a Broadband or Dial-Up Connection

This section shows how to set up the Internet connection method illustrated in Figure 22.1, C.

Your router's manufacturer will provide instructions for installing and configuring it. If you're using cable or DSL Internet service, you'll connect your broadband modem to the router using a short Ethernet patch cable. If you're using a dial-up or ISDN account, you'll need to set up the router and a modem. Then you'll connect the router to your LAN using one of the two methods shown in Figure 22.8.

Figure 22.8
Connecting a connection-sharing router to your LAN.

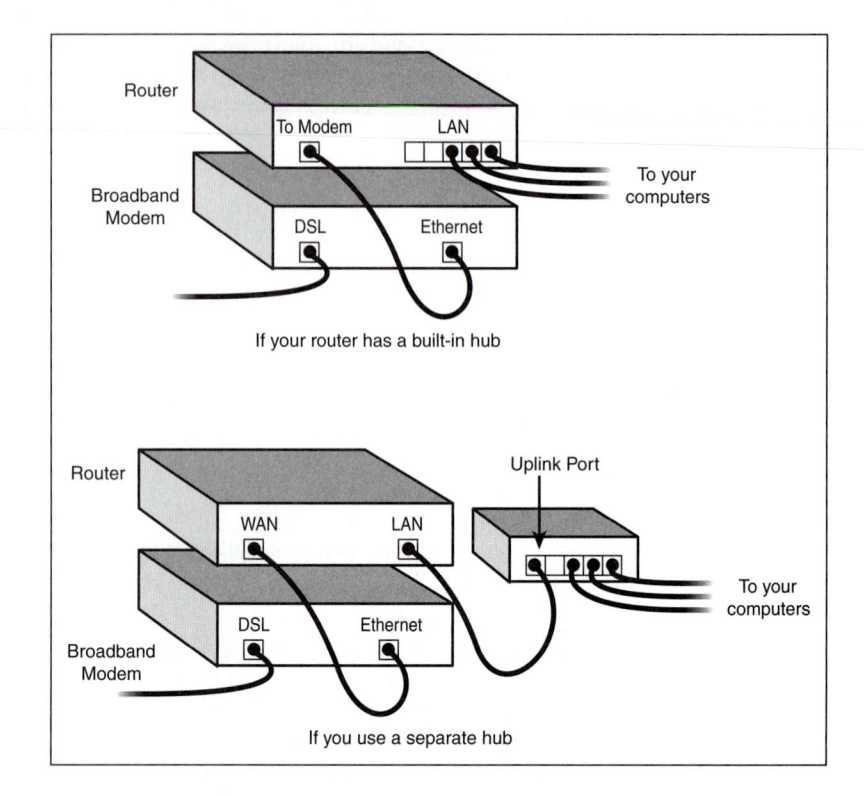

If your router has a built-in hub

If you use a separate hub

If you connect your router to a separate hub, be sure that the link indicators come on at both the hub and the router. If they don't, you might need to switch the hub end of the cable from a regular port to an uplink port or *vice versa*.

You then configure the router, telling it how to contact your ISP and what range of IP addresses to serve up to your LAN. Every device will use a different procedure, but I can show you the basic steps used by the Linksys Cable/DSL Sharing Routers that I have been so happy with.

The procedure goes something like this: When the router is attached to your network, you set up one of your computers' LAN adapters to obtain its IP address information automatically. Then you use Internet Explorer to connect to the router by viewing `http://192.168.1.1`. (The address might be different for your router.) A password is required; on my router, the factory default value was `admin`. (On some routers, you have to enter both a username and a password.)

You fill in your ISP's IP and sign-on information, if any, on a web page similar to the one shown in Figure 22.9.

You might need to enter a static IP address, if your ISP assigned one to you. If your ISP uses DHCP to assign IP addresses dynamically, the router might need to be assigned the host and domain name expected by your provider. This is common with cable Internet setups.

If your ISP uses PPPoE to establish a connection, you need to enable PPPoE and enter your logon and password. Most DSL service works this way. If your DSL provider does use PPPoE, you should enable the router's auto-sign-on feature, and you can optionally set up a "keepalive" value that will tell the modem to periodically send network traffic even if you don't, to keep your connection active all the time. (This might violate your service agreement with the DSL provider—better check before you do this.)

If you use cable Internet service and your ISP didn't provide you with a special host name that you had to give to your computer, your ISP probably identifies you by your network adapter's MAC (hardware) address. You'll probably find that your Internet connection won't work when you set up the router. One of your router's setup pages should show you its MAC address. You can either call your ISP's customer service line and tell them that this is your new adapter's MAC address, or configure the router to "clone" your computer's MAC address—that is, copy the address from the computer you originally used to set up your cable connection. Your router's setup manual should tell you how to do this.

C A U T I O N

Be sure to change the factory-supplied password of your router after you install it. (And write the password somewhere in the router's manual.) Also, be sure to disable outside (Internet) access to the router's management screens.

As you are configuring your router, you might want to enable Universal Plug and Play (UPnP). I discuss this later in this chapter.

You might also opt for even better hacker protection by having your router filter (block) Microsoft file and printer sharing data. This is usually done on an advanced setup screen labeled Filtering. See "Scheme F—Routed Service Using a Router," later in this chapter, for the list of ports that you must block.

→ When the router has been set up, go to each of your computers and follow the instructions under "Configuring the Rest of the Network," on **p. 716**.

Figure 22.9
Sample setup page for a cable/DSL connection-sharing router.

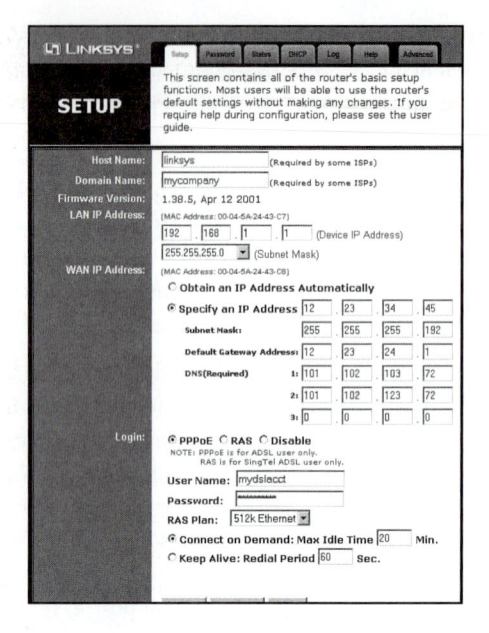

Using Universal Plug and Play

If you use a hardware connection-sharing router, you might want to consider enabling a feature called Universal Plug and Play (UPnP). UPnP provides a way for software running on your computer to communicate with the router. Here's what UPnP can do:

- It provides a means for the router to tell software on your computer that it is separated from the Internet by Network Address Translation. Some software—the video and audio parts of most instant messaging programs, in particular—asks the computer on the other end of the connection to establish a connection back to your IP address. On a network with a shared connection, however, the IP address that the computer sees is not the public IP address that the shared Internet connection uses. UPnP lets application software find out what the public IP address is. It also provides a way for the router to suggest alternate port numbers if several computers on the network want to provide the same service (for example, if several users try to establish videoconferences).

- It provides a means for software running on the network to tell the router to forward expected incoming connections to the correct computer. Again, Windows Live Messenger is a good example. When the computer on the other end of the connection starts sending data, the router would not know to send it to your computer. UPnP lets UPnP-aware application programs automatically set up forwarding in the router.

- UPnP provides a means for other types of as-yet-undeveloped hardware devices to announce their presence on the network so that Windows can automatically take advantage of the services they provide.

UPnP has a downside, however—it has no built-in security mechanism, so any program on any computer on your network could potentially take control of the router and open "holes" for incoming connections. However, Windows Firewall still provides some protection and warns you if an undesired program attempts to receive incoming network connections, so this is not yet a serious problem. If you use videoconferencing, the benefits that UPnP provides probably outweighs the risks.

To use UPnP, you must enable the feature in your router. It's usually disabled by default. If your router doesn't currently support UPnP, you might have to download and install a firmware upgrade from the manufacturer. Most routers now do support UPnP.

By default, Windows Vista provides support for detecting UPnP-enabled routers. If you have a UPnP router or Windows Internet Connection Sharing running on your network, the Network window should display an icon for the router, as shown in Figure 22.10.

Figure 22.10
If your router supports UPnP, a router icon should appear in the Network Window.

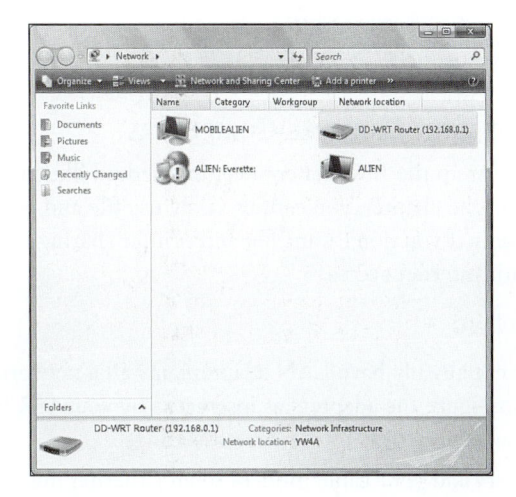

NOTE

If the icon doesn't appear, be sure that Network Discovery is turned on in the Network and Sharing Center.

If you right-click the router icon, select Properties, and select the Network Device tab, you'll see a dialog similar to the one shown in Figure 22.11, displaying information about your router.

Click Settings on the General tab to display a list of network services for which the router is forwarding incoming connections to computers on your network. This list shows only forwarding settings made via UPnP. Services forwarded by the setup screens on your router, a process discussed later in this chapter under "Making Services Available," do not appear here and new settings need not be made here—they might disappear when the router is reset.

Figure 22.11
Router information displayed via UPnP.

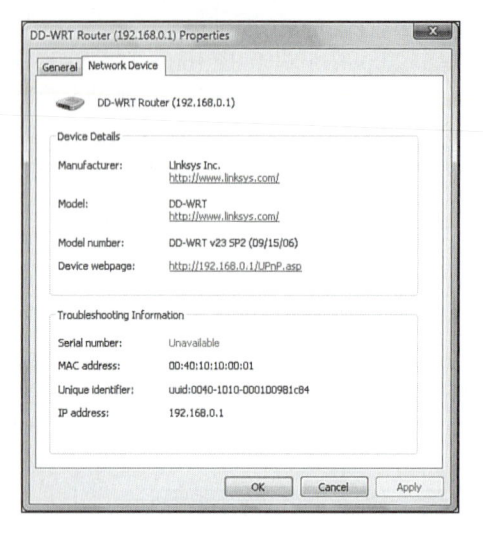

Scheme D—Cable Internet with Multiple Computers

This section shows how to set up the Internet connection method illustrated in Figure 22.1, D. As I mentioned earlier in the chapter, you cannot safely use file and printer sharing with this setup. Use this setup only if you don't want file and printer sharing and just want to have several computers with Internet access.

This is the procedure to follow:

1. If your computers do not already have LAN adapters, install a network adapter in each of your computers. Configure the adapters as instructed by your ISP. In most cases, you won't need to make any adjustments to the default settings.

2. Connect your computers and your cable modem to an Ethernet hub. Chapter 20, "Creating a Windows Network," provides details on installing network wiring.

3. Open Network and Sharing Center and select Manage Network Connections. Open Local Area Connection's properties. On versions of Windows other than Vista, you might have to use different selections to get to your network adapter's settings; check online help or your copy of the corresponding *Special Edition Using* book.

4. Select Internet Protocol Version 6 (TCP/IPv6), and then select Properties.

5. Check Obtain an IP Address Automatically and Obtain DNS Server Address Automatically.

6. Click OK. The computer should reconfigure itself with a new IP address obtained from the computer with the shared dial-up connection.

7. Repeat Steps 2–4 for Internet Protocol Version 4 (TCP/IPv4).

→ If your ISP has given you a specific name to use with each computer, set it as described in the section "Setting Your Computer Identification," on **p. 651**.

9. Disable File and Printer Sharing by opening the Network Connections window, right-clicking the Local Area Connection icon, and clicking properties. In the Network tab, uncheck the Client and Sharing items, as shown in Figure 22.5. Click OK and then restart Windows.

> **NOTE**
>
> To make sure that your Network is not exposed to the Internet, turn off all Sharing and Discovery options in the Network and Sharing Center.

If you later decide that you want to use file and printer sharing, *do not* simply enable the Client and Sharing items. Instead, set up a shared connection using schemes B or C, or install a second LAN, as described in the next section.

Scheme E—Cable Internet with Multiple Computers and a Separate LAN

This section shows how to set up the Internet connection method illustrated in Figure 22.1, E. If you want to have file and printer sharing *and* have multiple computers on a cable Internet connection, but for some reason do not want to use a connection-sharing setup, you ***must*** set up a second, private network for file sharing that is physically separate from the network used for the Internet connection.

To do this, set up and test the LAN for the cable service as described in the previous section. Then, on each of the computers that is to participate in file and printer sharing, perform the following steps:

1. View the Network Connections screen, right-click the icon that corresponds to the network adapter, and select Rename. Change the name to Internet Connection.

2. Shut down the computer and install a second network adapter. Connect this adapter to a *separate* network hub.

3. On the Network Connections window, right click the Internet Connection icon, select Properties, and be sure that it is still configured as shown in Figure 22.5.

4. Right-click the Local Area Connection icon (which corresponds to your new, second network), select Properties, and be sure that all the component items are checked.

   You also might want to assign each computer a static IP address. To do this, select Internet Protocol Version 4 (TCP/IPv4) and click Properties. Click Use the Following IP Address. For the first computer, enter `192.168.0.1`. Set the Network Mask to `255.255.255.0` and leave the Default Gateway address blank. Leave the DNS setting on automatic. For the second computer, enter address `192.168.0.2`, and so on.

> **CAUTION**
>
> To prevent a security breach caused by crosstalk between your two networks, make sure the IP Addresses you choose for your local LAN are on a different subnet than your Internet connection. For example, if your Internet connection IP address is in the subnet 192.168.1, you should set your LAN IP Addresses to be of the subnet 192.168.x, where "x" can be any number from 0 to 255 except 1.

5. In the Network and Sharing Center, select Windows Firewall. Be sure the firewall is set On.

6. Select Allow a Program Through Windows Firewall and confirm the User Account Control prompt. Check File and Printer Sharing. Click OK to close the dialog box.

Now file and printer sharing will use your second, private LAN, while the first LAN is used only for Internet service.

Scheme F—Routed Service Using a Router

This section shows how to set up the Internet connection method illustrated in Figure 22.1, F.

Some Internet service providers will sell you service that provides multiple, fixed IP addresses. This is the case for all Frame Relay service and, in some cases, higher-priced business-class DSL service. You should really have a good reason for going this way, beyond just wanting to connect multiple computers—it's not as secure as a single shared connection. Good reasons might be that you want the reliability of Frame Relay service or you need fixed IP addresses to host web, email, or other Internet-based services on several different computers.

For this type of service, if you are using a cable, DSL, satellite, or Frame Relay modem with a built-in router, your ISP will help you configure your network. In this setup, you will be provided with a fixed set of IP addresses, which you'll have to parcel out to your computers. Your ISP should help you install all of this, but I can give you some pointers.

First of all, it is *absolutely essential* that your router be set up to protect your network. You must ensure that at least these three items are taken care of:

1. The router must be set up with filters to prevent Microsoft file-sharing service (NetBIOS and NetBT) packets from entering or leaving your LAN. In technical terms, the router must be set up to block TCP and UDP on port 137, UDP on port 138, and TCP on ports 139 and 445. It should "drop" rather than "reject" packets, if possible. This helps prevent hackers from discovering that these services are present but blocked. Better to let them think they're not there at all.

2. Be *absolutely* sure to change your router's administrative password from the factory default value to something hard to guess, with uppercase letters, lowercase letters, numbers, and punctuation. Don't let your ISP talk you out of this, but you should let them know what the new password is so they can get into the router from their end, if needed.

3. Disable SNMP access, or change the SNMP read and read-write "community names" to something other than the default. Again, use something with letters, numbers, and punctuation.

Configuring Your LAN   727

CAUTION

> If your router is not properly configured to filter out NetBIOS traffic, your network will be exposed to hackers. This is absolutely unacceptable. If you're in doubt, have your ISP help you configure the router. Also, after setting things up, visit http://www.grc.com and use the "Shields Up!" pages there to be sure your computers are properly protected.
>
> For more information about network security, see Chapter 35.

Second, you need to manually set up a fixed IP address for each computer that is to host a service reachable from the "outside." You can make address settings manually in all your computers or just the ones that are hosting services, with your router providing DHCP service to configure the other computers.

Make a list showing the name of each computer that is to get a static IP address, and the IP address you want to assign. On each of these computers, you also have to manually enter the network mask, gateway IP address, and DNS server addresses supplied by your ISP.

Follow these steps on each computer that is to get manual settings:

 1. View the Network and Sharing Center and select Manage Network Connections.
 2. Right-click the Local Area Connection icon and select Properties.
 3. Select the Networking tab, select Internet Protocol Version 4 (TCP/IPv4), and then click Properties.
 4. Enter an IP address and other assigned information. Figure 22.12 shows an example; you have to use the information provided by your ISP.

NOTE

> If your ISP supplies you with Internet Protocol Version 6 (TCP/IPv6) Settings, repeat the previous steps, except select Internet Protocol Version 6 (TCP/IPv6) in Step 3.

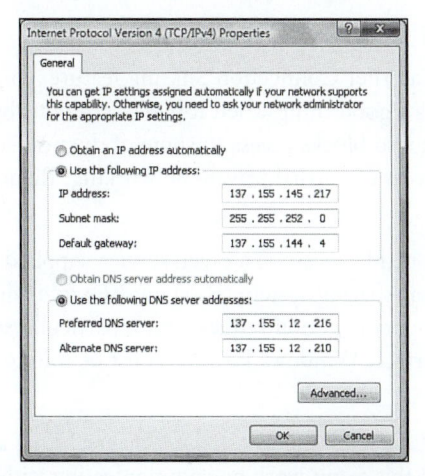

Figure 22.12
Setting up static assigned IP address information.

> **CAUTION**
>
> Make sure that Windows Firewall is turned on, to protect your network form hackers. For more information on network security, see Chapter 35.

Making Services Available

You might want to make some internal network services available to the outside world through your Internet connection. You would want to do this in these situations:

- You want to host a Web server using Internet Information Services
- You want to enable incoming VPN access to your LAN so you can securely connect from home or afield
- You want to enable incoming Remote Desktop access to your computer

If you have set up routed Internet service with a router (as in the fourth setup in Figure 22.1), you don't have to worry about this because your network connection is wide open and doesn't use Network Address Translation. As long as the outside users know the IP address of the computer hosting your service—or its DNS name, if you have set up DNS service—you're on the air already.

Otherwise, you have either Windows Firewall, Network Address Translation, or both in the way of incoming access. To make specific services accessible, you need to follow one of the sets of specific instructions in the next few sections, depending on the type of Internet connection setup you've used. Skip ahead to the appropriate section.

> **NOTE**
>
> If you're interested in being able to reach your computer over the Internet using Remote Desktop, see Chapter 40, "Remote Desktop," which is entirely devoted to the subject.

Enabling Access with Internet Connection Sharing

When you are using Microsoft's Internet Connection Sharing feature, your network is protected from outside access. This is a good thing when it blocks attempts by hackers to get to your shared files and folders. It also blocks access to some of the neat services you might *want* the outside world to have access to: virtual private networking, Remote Desktop, web and FTP service, and so on.

Two steps are needed to provide outside access to a given service supplied by a computer on your network. First, the connection-sharing system (ICS) must be told which computer on your network is to receive incoming connection requests for a particular service. Then, on the computer that provides the service, Windows Firewall must be told to let these requests through.

Some services, such as Windows Live Messenger, use the Universal Plug and Play (UPnP) protocol to automatically perform this setup work by communicating with the computer that is sharing its connection. So when you are using ICS to share your network connection, these services simply work.

However, most server-type functions, such as Remote Desktop and Internet Information Services, require manual setup. On the computer that is providing the service itself, you must tell Windows Firewall to allow incoming connections to the service by following these steps:

1. Open the Windows Firewall screen by clicking Windows Firewall in the Network and Sharing Center.
2. Click Allow a Program Through Windows Firewall. See if the service this computer is providing is already listed and checked. If so, you can proceed to configure the computer that is sharing its Internet connection.
3. If the service isn't already listed, click Add Port, enter the service name and port number, and select TCP or UDP, as shown in Figure 22.13. Table 22.2 lists common service numbers and protocols. (For the FTP and DNS services, you have to make two entries.)
4. Click Change Scope and select Any Computer (Including Those on the Internet). Click OK, and then click OK again.

Figure 22.13
Add a service's port number and protocol type to the Windows Firewall on the computer that is running the service.

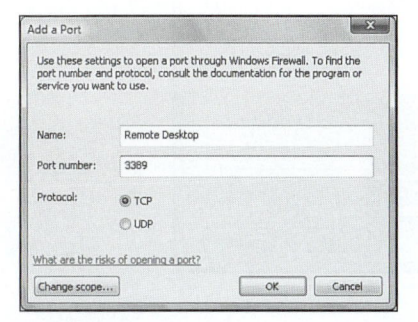

TABLE 22.2   COMMON SERVICES AND PORT NUMBERS

Protocol	Port	Associated Service
TCP	20 and 21	File Transfer Protocol (FTP)
TCP	23	Telnet
TCP	25	Simple Mail Transfer Protocol (SMTP)
TCP and UDP	53	Domain name service (DNS)
TCP	80	HTTP—World Wide Web
TCP	110	Post Office Protocol (POP3)
TCP	3389	Remote Desktop
TCP and UDP	5631 5632	Symantec PCAnywhere

Then you must instruct the computer that is sharing its Internet connection to forward incoming requests to the designated computer. On the computer that physically connects to the Internet, follow these steps:

1. Click Start, select Network, click Network and Sharing Center, and then select Manage Network Connections.
2. Right-click the icon for the shared Internet connection and select Properties. View the Sharing tab and, under Internet Connection Sharing, click Settings.
3. On the Advanced Settings dialog box, view the Services tab (shown in Figure 22.14).

Figure 22.14
The Services tab lets you specify which services are to be forwarded by Internet Connection Sharing.

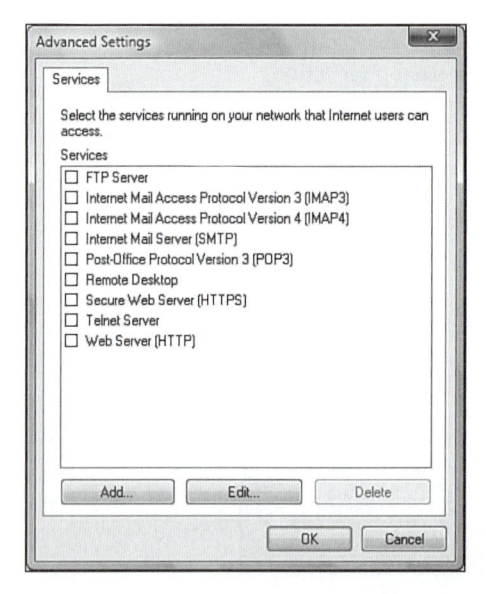

4. Check the Service entry for each service for which you want to permit access and for which you have servers on your LAN. The most common ones to select are Remote Desktop and FTP Server and Web Server, if you have set up IIS.
5. When you select a check box, a dialog box appears, as shown in Figure 22.15.

Figure 22.15
The Service Settings dialog box lets you specify the name or IP address of the computer that is to handle incoming connections for a particular service.

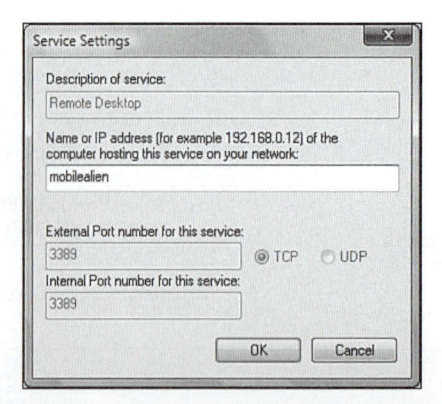

6. Enter the IP address of the computer that is hosting this service, if your LAN uses fixed IP addresses. If your LAN uses automatically assigned addresses from Internet Connection Sharing, you can enter the computer's name, and the software will locate the correct computer.

7. If you want to use an incoming VPN connection, you must set it up on the computer that hosts the Internet Connection Sharing or Firewall service. You can't forward VPN connections to other computers.

8. If the service you want to use isn't listed, you need to find out what TCP and/or UDP ports the service communicates with. You have to search through the service software's documentation or the Internet to find these port values. For example, Symantec PCAnywhere uses TCP Port 5631 and UDP Port 5632.

To add an unlisted service, click Add. Enter the name of the service, the IP address or host name of the computer that is running this service, and the port number, as shown in Figure 22.16. Generally, you'll want to use the same number for the port number the public sees (external port) and the port number used on the LAN (internal port). Check TCP or UDP, and then click OK.

In the PCAnywhere example I'm using, after creating an entry for TCP Port 5631, I have to add a second entry to forward UDP port 5632.

When you've enabled the desired services, incoming requests using the selected service ports will be forwarded to the appropriate computer on your LAN. Windows Firewall will know to let these services through.

Figure 22.16
Enter port information for a new service in this dialog box.

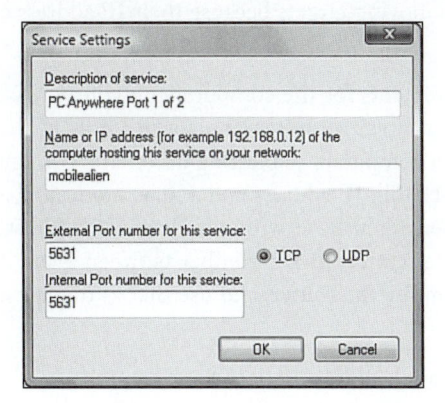

CAUTION

With the exception of incoming VPN connection service, I suggest that you don't run any other services on the computer that manages your firewall and/or Internet Connection Sharing, especially IIS. There's too great a risk that a security flaw in the service might let hackers compromise the firewall.

> **TIP**
>
> If you're not sure which port a given service uses, you can use the Windows Firewall logging feature to find out what ports are used. To do this, click Start, select Control Panel, and click System and Maintenance. Click Administrative Tools and select Windows Firewall with Advanced Security. Choose Windows Firewall Properties in the Overview section. Choose the tab corresponding to the Networking profile used for your connection—you can determine this by looking at the Network and Sharing Center. In the Logging section, select Customize. Change Log Dropped Packets to Yes and click OK. Then attempt to connect to the sharing computer from outside on the Internet using the service of interest. View the log file (by default, `C:\Windows\system32\LogFiles\Firewall\pfirewall.log`). The eighth column in this file lists the "destination port" that you tried to use. This is the port your service needs to have forwarded.

ENABLING ACCESS WITH A SHARING ROUTER

If you use a connection-sharing router on your LAN, you need to follow a somewhat different procedure to enable outside access to services on your network.

You must still open the Windows firewall on the computer(s) providing services, as described in the first four-step procedure in the previous section.

Then you must use a manufacturer-specific procedure to set up forwarding for services that you want to expose to the Internet.

One difficulty with these devices is that you must forward services by IP address, not by computer name, and, normally, you set up computers to obtain their IP addresses automatically. This makes the computers moving targets because their IP address could change from day to day.

You have to make special arrangements for the computers on your LAN that you want to use to host services. On your router's setup screens, make a note of the range of IP addresses that it will hand out to computers requesting automatic configuration. Most routers have a place to enter a starting IP address and a maximum number of addresses. For instance, the starting number might be 2, with a limit of 100 addresses. For each computer that will provide an outside service, pick a number between 2 and 254 that is *not* in the range of addresses handed out by the router, and use that as the last number in the computer's IP address.

To configure the computer's network address, follow these steps:

1. View its Network Connections window, right-click the icon that corresponds to its network adapter, and select Properties.
2. Select Internet Protocol Version 4 (TCP/IPv4) and click Properties.
3. Check Use the Following IP Address.
4. Enter the selected IP address. For the first three numbers, use the same numbers set up in the router (usually `192.168.0` or `192.168.1`), and follow it with the fixed number you selected for this computer. The final result might be something like `192.168.0.250`.

5. For the network mask, enter `255.255.255.0`.
6. For the Default Gateway, enter `192.168.0.1` or `192.168.1.1`, again using the same first three numbers set up on the router.
7. Leave the DNS setting on Automatic.
8. Click OK and then OK again to close the dialog boxes.

> **NOTE**
>
> If your router's IP address is different than the standard `192.168.0.1` or `192.168.1.1`, make sure the default gateway is set to use the IP address of your router.
>
> Also note that if you are using an Internet Protocol Version 6 (TCP/IPv6) network, you must change the properties of this protocol instead, as set up in your router.

Then you need to use the router's setup screens to set up forwarding to this computer. You can set up forwarding in two ways. One is appropriate for services that use standard, well-known TCP or UDP protocol ports (such as a web server or Remote Desktop); the other is appropriate for access to services that use nonstandard protocols (such as Microsoft VPN connections).

FORWARDING STANDARD TCP AND UDP SERVICES

For standard services with a known TCP or UDP port number, view the Forwarding setup page on your router's internal configuration screen. Enter the appropriate port number, protocol type, and target IP address. For example, Figure 22.17 shows a router set up to forward a whole slew of services into computers on my LAN. Table 22.3 shows what is being forwarded here. Of course, your gateway router might use different configuration screens—check its documentation for examples appropriate for your setup.

Figure 22.17
Service Forwarding configuration for a typical connection-sharing router.

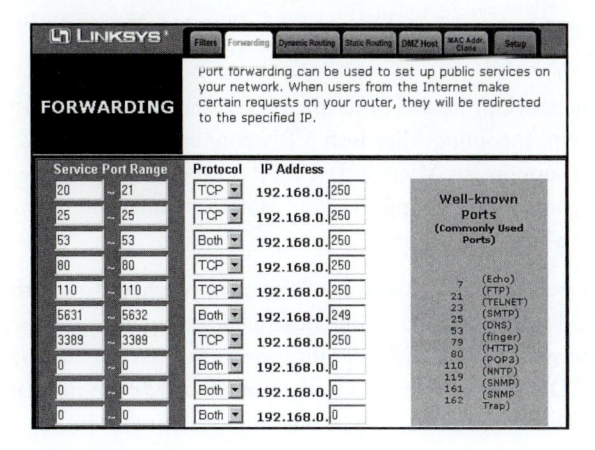

Table 22.3 Services Being Forwarded in Figure 22.17

Port	Service
20–21	File Transfer Protocol (FTP)
25	Simple Mail Transfer Protocol (SMTP)
53	Domain name service (DNS)
80	HTTP (web server)
110	POP3 (mailbox server)
3389	Remote Desktop
5631–5632	Symantec PC Anywhere

> **TIP**
>
> You can set up Remote Desktop forwarding to more than one computer by a making a separate entry for each computer. Each must have a different "external" port number. For example, I use port number 3389 for the first computer, 3390 for the second, and so on. The "internal" port number must be 3389 in each case. Then when I use the Remote Desktop Client to connect to my network from the Internet, I enter the URL `mycompany.com:3389` to get to the first computer, `mycompany.com:3390` to get to the second, and so on.

Forwarding Nonstandard Services

For services that use TCP/UDP in unpredictable ways, you must use another approach to forwarding on your LAN. Some services, such as Windows Live Messenger, communicate their *private*, internal IP address to the computer on the other end of the connection; when the other computer tries to send data to this private address, it fails. To use these services with a hardware router, you must enable Universal Plug and Play (UPnP), as described earlier in the chapter.

Other services use network protocols other than TCP and UDP, and most routers can't be set up to forward them. Incoming Microsoft VPN connections fall into this category. Some routers have built-in support for Microsoft's PPTP protocol, which is the basis of virtual private networking. If yours has this support, your router's manual will tell you how to forward VPN connections to a host computer.

Otherwise, to support nonstandard services of this sort, you have to tell the router to forward *all* unrecognized incoming data to one designated computer. In effect, this exposes that computer to the Internet, so it's a fairly significant security risk. In fact, most routers call this targeted computer a DMZ host, referring to the notorious Korean no-man's-land called the Demilitarized Zone and the peculiar danger one faces standing in it.

To enable a DMZ host, you want to use a fixed IP address on the designated computer, as described in the previous section. Use your router's configuration screen to specify this selected IP address as the DMZ host. The configuration screen for my particular router is shown in Figure 22.18; yours might differ.

Figure 22.18
Enabling a DMZ host to receive all unrecognized incoming connection requests

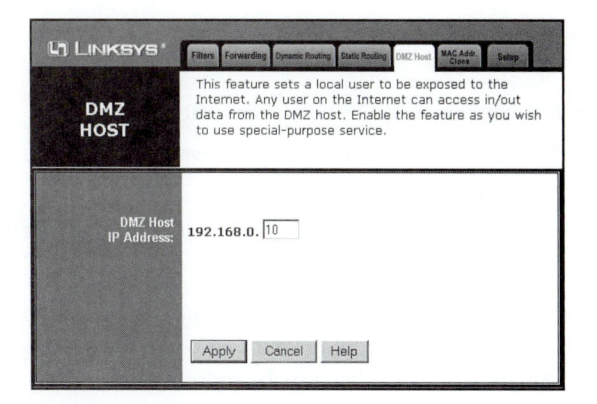

Now, designating a DMZ host means that this computer is fully exposed to the Internet, so you must protect it with a firewall of some sort. You can enable Windows Firewall on this computer's LAN connection, but you must also block access to Windows file and printer sharing. You could disable these services on this computer by disconnecting them from the network adapter, as shown in Figure 22.5. You should also set up filtering in your router to block ports 137–139 and 445. Figure 22.19 shows how this is done on my Linksys router; your router might use a different method.

> **TIP**
>
> It's not a bad idea to enable filtering for these ports even if you're not using a DMZ host. It's *essential* to do this if you set up a DMZ host.

Figure 22.19
Configuring filters to block Microsoft file-sharing services

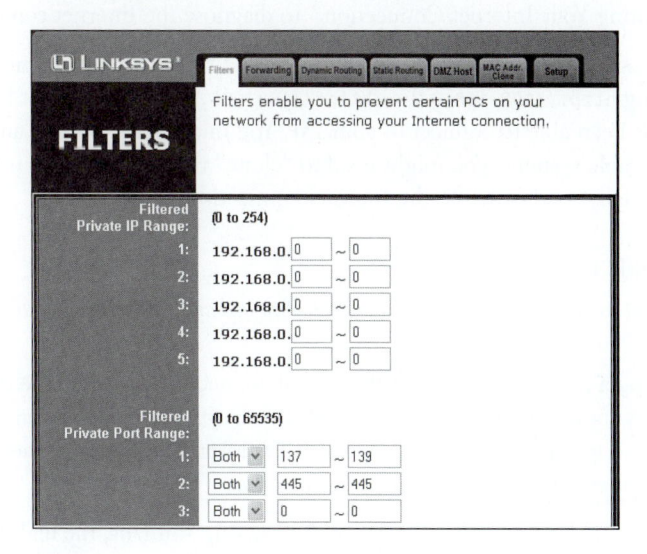

Troubleshooting

Can't Access a Shared Modem Connection from the LAN

When I attempt to view an Internet page from a LAN computer, my web browser doesn't get past "Looking up host www.somewhere.com."

A delay of 30 seconds or so is normal while the dial-up connection is established when you first start using the Internet.

If the connection doesn't progress after 30 seconds, be sure of the following: The sharing computer was turned on when you booted up your computer, the sharing computer is logged in, and your computer is set to obtain its IP address automatically.

Try to make the connection from the sharing computer to be sure the modem is connecting properly. If it's not, see the "Troubleshooting" section at the end of Chapter 14 to diagnose the dial-up connection problem.

Can't Access a Shared DSL or Cable Connection from the LAN

When I attempt to view an Internet page from a LAN computer, my web browser doesn't get past "Looking up host www.somewhere.com."

Be sure that the sharing computer was turned on when you booted up your computer, that the connection to the DSL or cable modem is the one marked as shared, and that your computer is set to obtain its IP address automatically.

Try to view web pages from the sharing computer to be sure the high-speed connection is functioning. If it's not, see the "Troubleshooting" section at the end of Chapter 17, "Troubleshooting Your Internet Connection," to diagnose the Internet connectivity problem.

If you are using a connection-sharing router, view the router's built-in Status web page (usually by viewing http://192.168.0.1 or http://192.168.1.1 with Internet Explorer). See if the router has been able to connect to your ISP. You might have entered an incorrect password, or, for cable systems, you might need to "clone" the MAC address of the computer that you originally used to set up the Internet connection.

Shared Connection Doesn't Happen

When I attempt to view a web page on a network with a shared connection, no Internet connection is established.

If you are using a modem to establish the shared connection, listen to the modem to see whether it's trying to establish the connection. If it is, you might just need to wait a bit and try to view the page again. Sometimes Internet Explorer gives an error message before the modem has had enough time to make the connection.

If the modem is making a connection but web browsing still fails, the dial-up connection on the shared computer might not be set up with a saved password. On that computer, open the Network and Sharing Center, select Manage Network Connections, and attempt to make the connection manually. Be sure that you've checked Save This Username and Password and selected Anyone Who Uses This Computer.

→ If the modem isn't attempting to make the connection at all, try following the steps to set up Internet Connection Sharing again, as described in "Setting Up the Shared Connection," on **p. 714**.

Tips from the Windows Pros: Speeding Up Vista?

You might run across websites, books, "tune-up" software, friends, or consultants that tell you that you can speed up your Internet connection, or even Windows Vista itself, by making settings in the Windows Registry that Microsoft didn't bother to make for you (or, in other versions of the tale, is trying to keep secret). In fact, our Special Edition books that cover Windows XP and Windows 2000 Professional contain exactly this sort of advice in the chapters that correspond to this one, to help you get the most out of your shared Internet connection. But when it comes to Vista, our advice is *don't bother*.

Here's the scoop. Some of these tips really were valid for previous versions of Windows, but they're *not* helpful on Vista. Other tips we've seen are just plain ineffective. Harmless, usually, but ineffective. And some of the "tune-up" programs out there deliberately make things worse, and then they pop up advertisements for "fix it" software sold by the same people. (Be especially wary of advertisements that are made to look like Windows dialog boxes and say things such as "Registry clean-up recommended.")

What you need to know is that Vista's built-in networking software isn't based on the stuff used in older versions of Windows but was completely rewritten to take advantage of today's high-speed Internet and LAN connections. It automatically measures your network and Internet connection speed and timing (latency) characteristics and tunes itself to get the highest possible throughput every time you transfer data. It takes advantage of some newly developed and standardized methods (algorithms) for improving network transfer rates. And Vista Service Pack 1 includes further significant improvements that are especially helpful when you're transferring large files over the Internet and between computers running Vista (for example, when you're making backups and or moving video).

So our advice here is to leave Vista alone. It'll do a terrific job all by itself, without any help or hindrance from us or any other "experts" out there.

CHAPTER 23

USING A WINDOWS NETWORK

In this chapter

Windows Vista Was Made to Network   740

File Sharing in Windows Vista   742

The Network and Sharing Center in Windows Vista   744

Using Shared Folders   747

Exploring and Searching the Network   748

Using Printers on the Network   757

Using Network Resources Effectively   766

Sharing Resources   767

Sharing Folders and Drives   768

Sharing Printers   771

Managing Network Use of Your Computer   778

Managing Network Resources Using the Command Line   778

Troubleshooting   781

Tips from the Windows Pros: Using Command-Line Utilities   782

Windows Vista Was Made to Network

Aside from finally finding a use for the right button on the mouse, almost all the advancements in the Windows platform over the last 15 years have been made in the area of networking. Back in Windows Version 3.1, network software was an expensive add-on product—an afterthought—cumbersome to install and manage. Not so anymore! Networking is built right into the heart of Windows Vista so that Windows is hardly even *happy* without a network attached.

Okay, I'm exaggerating. But the truth is, Windows Vista's personality does change for the better when it's connected to a network, and the change depends on the type of network to which it's attached. In this chapter, I show you how to use Windows Vista networking and share tips for making the most of whatever type of network you have.

In Windows Vista, using files and printers on the network is exactly the same as using files and printers on your own hard drive. The "look and feel" are identical. The only new tasks you have to learn are how to find resources shared by others and how to make your own computer's resources available to others on the network. Windows Vista also adds security enhancements that make the process of connecting to and using other resources more secure.

I'll use the word *resource* frequently in this chapter. When I say *resource*, I mean a shared folder or printer on someone else's computer, which you can access through the LAN or the Internet. *The American Heritage Dictionary* defines a resource as "an available supply that can be drawn upon when needed." That's actually a perfect description of a network resource: It's there for you to use—provided that you can find it and that you have permission.

The ways of finding resources and managing permissions change depending on the type of network you have. I talked about these network models in detail in Chapter 19, "Overview of Windows Networking," but here's a quick review:

- **Workgroup network (peer to peer)**—A workgroup network, also called a peer-to-peer network, does not have a central server computer to perform user/password verification. On this network, each computer manages its own user list and security system. Home users and small offices usually use workgroup networks. Networks that mix Windows computers with Macintosh, Linux, and UNIX computers also fall into this category.

- **Domain network**—A domain-based network uses one or more computers running a version of Windows Server 2008, Windows Server 2003, Windows 2000 Server, or even Windows NT Server to provide a centralized user security database. All computers on the network look to a *domain controller*, or primary server, for usernames, group memberships, and passwords.

> **NOTE**
>
> From now on, I'll write "Windows 200*x* Server" when I'm referring to one of the Windows Server operating systems.

- **Active Directory Network**—Active Directory (AD) adds a distributed, global user directory to a domain network. It not only provides a user and password database, but it also provides a way for management permissions to be delegated and controlled; this capability is very important in large, spread-out organizations.

- **Remote Network**—All the editions of Windows Vista function very well on a stand-alone computer, but some editions, such as Business and Ultimate, also let you connect to and disconnect from networks, or get remote access by modem, wide area network (WAN), or the Internet. Windows provides special services to help you deal with this "on again/off again" network relationship.

Most network functions are identical, regardless of your network type. The following are some notable differences:

- On a domain network, the administrator can set up *roaming profiles* so that your settings, preferences, Documents folder, and so on are centrally stored on the network and are available to you on any computer on your LAN or even at other network sites.

- Active Directory (AD) gives you added search functions to find users and printers on your network. These search functions appear as added icons and menu choices that non-AD network computers don't have.

- In a domain or Active Directory network, the network administrator might use *policy* functions to restrict the network-management features you can use. For example, you might not have the option to map network drives or add network protocols in such a strictly controlled LAN. Rather than rouse up a protest for computer freedom, though, be thankful that you'll have less maintenance and futzing to do yourself.

> **NOTE**
>
> I'm already tired of typing *Active Directory* over and over, so from here on, I'll usually abbreviate it as *AD*.

Members of a Windows network with AD have some options—menu choices and buttons in dialog boxes, for example—that workgroup network users don't have. If you are using a workgroup network, don't feel left out. Because a workgroup typically has fewer than 10 computers, the searching and corporate-style management functions provided by AD simply aren't necessary.

In this chapter, I try to point out the differences you might encounter, depending on your network type. But it's difficult to generalize about AD networks because AD's policy-based restrictions mean that some options might not appear where I say they will. If you are on a domain or Active Directory network and can't find an option I show you, call your network manager to see whether its use has been restricted.

Workgroup Versus Domain Networking

On a Windows domain-based network (that is, a network managed by a Windows $200x$ Server), user accounts are set up on the domain servers. Domain users are known by every computer on the network. When you and the network managers are establishing who can and can't have access to files, you can choose users and groups from the entire list of all users in your organization. You can grant access to specific individuals, departments, sites, or other groupings, even though those users might be scattered around the globe.

In a workgroup network, which is what you'll have in most homes and small offices, it's a different story. Each computer in the workgroup has its own separate list of usernames. This makes it more difficult to be sure that a user on one computer can be granted access to another. To make network file sharing managable for you and understandable for the network's users, you should choose one of the following two schemes:

- If you want to make shared files available to everyone on your network, and don't need to make distinctions about who can access which shared files and folders, turn off Password Projected Sharing on every Windows Vista computer, and enable Simple File Sharing on every Windows XP computer. Have each user put the files they want to share into their computer's Public folder (This is called the Shared Documents folder on XP). This way, anyone who logs on to any computer on your network can use the shared files. This makes it all very simple.

  It's also somewhat riskier: Your files can be accessed by anyone who logs on to a Guest account, or connects to your wireless or wired network. If you use wireless networking, and you don't use Wireless security (that is, you don't require the use of a WEP or WPA key), then you must not use this no-password option!

- If you want to secure your shared files and folders, so that you can specify which user or users can access each shared folder, then you must do the following things: Enable Password Protected Sharing on each Vista computer that is going to share files. Create the same set of user accounts on every computer, with the same name and the same password for each user. This scheme is much more secure, but it's a bit harder to set up. And if any user changes her password on one computer, she'll need to go to the other computers and change her password on them as well.

File Sharing in Windows Vista

Windows Vista enables sharing of files and folders in several ways. The primary two means of sharing files and folders are to share them directly or to move them into the Public Folder. Either way, users within your network can see the files and, if you set up permissions as such, can access the files just as they would any other file or folder.

File and folder shares are accessed via Universal Naming Convention (UNC) names with Windows Vista, just as in previous versions of Windows.

What's in a Name?

Virtually the only difference you'll notice between local and networked files is their names. If you've found the use of the backslash character to be an annoying and peculiar convention, you'd better hang on to your hat because slashes of all persuasions are in your future in a big way.

Let's look at the names of shared network folders and files. Each computer on your network (or on an intranet or the Internet) has a name, and every folder or printer that is offered up for shared use on the network must be given a share name as well. For example, if I want to give officemates the use of my business documents, I might share my hard disk's folder C:\documents and give that folder the share name of docs.

> **NOTE**
>
> It might seem confusing to use a different name for the share name than for the folder. The reason for this is that whereas folder names can be very long and can contain spaces, share names should be limited to 12 characters or less and should have no spaces. This isn't very user-friendly, but it's the way it is.

My computer is named Ambon, so other users can use this folder by its network name `\\ambon\docs`.

The UNC Naming Convention

To continue the preceding example, I can specify the location of a file on my hard drive with a drive and pathname, like this:

`C:\documents\roofing bids.xls`

A user on another computer can refer to this same file using a syntax called the *Universal Naming Convention*, or *UNC*:

`\\ambon\docs\roofing bids.xls`

The double backslash indicates that ambon is the name of a computer on the LAN instead of the name of a folder in the top directory of the local hard disk. docs is the share name of the folder, and everything past that specifies the path and file relative to that shared folder.

If the computer whose files you want to use is on a corporate LAN using Active Directory or is part of a distant company network, you can also specify the remote computer name more completely, as in the following:

`\\ambon.mycompany.com\docs\roofing bids.xls`

Or, if you know only the remote computer's IP network address (such as if you're connecting to the remote computer with Dial-Up Networking), you can even use a notation like this:

`\\192.168.0.10\docs\roofing bids.xls`

No matter which way you specify the remote computer, Windows finds it and locates its shared folder docs.

> **NOTE**
>
> Elsewhere in this chapter, I use UNC names such as ***server******folder*** as a generic sort of name. By "*server*," I mean the name of the computer that's sharing *folder*. It doesn't have to be a Windows 200x Server—on a peer-to-peer network, there usually won't even be one. It can be any computer on your network. You need to use your network's actual computer names and shared folder names.

Shared printers are also given share names and are specified by their UNC path. For example, if I share my HP LaserJet 4V printer, I might give it the share name **HPLaser**, and it will be known on the network as \\ambon\HPLaser. Here, it's not a folder, but rather a printer, and Windows keeps track of the type of resource.

The Network and Sharing Center in Windows Vista

The Network and Sharing Center in Windows Vista is central to working with network settings. Within the Network and Sharing Center, shown in Figure 23.1, you'll find things such as the current network status, details about the network, and a current summary of the computer's settings as they relate to networking.

Figure 23.1
The Network and Sharing Center is an important and useful management application for quickly checking network status and configuring settings.

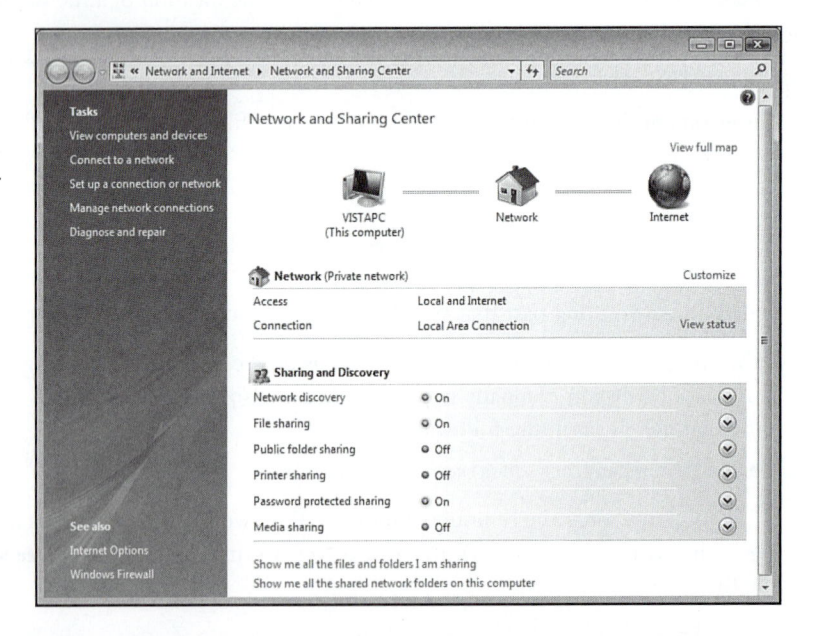

You can access the Network and Sharing Center through the Control Panel or through the Network Center. To access the Network and Sharing Center from the Control Panel, click on Start, select Control Panel and then Network and Internet, and then select Network and Sharing Center. To access the Network and Sharing Center from the Network Center, click on Start and select Network and then Network and Sharing Center. (You can also customize the Start menu to display the Network item. It's one click from Network to the Network and Sharing Center.)

The Major Components of the Network and Sharing Center

The Network and Sharing Center has three main areas:

- **Network Map**—Provides a graphical overview of the computer's location in relation to the network and, if applicable, the Internet
- **Status**—Provides additional detail of the current network configuration
- **Sharing and Discovery**—Provides details about settings related to sharing and network discovery

Finding Network Shares

How do you find the folders and printers floating around out there somewhere in the network Twilight Zone? If you've been using Windows for any length of time, you might have guessed by now that you can do the job in several ways. The most straightforward way is through the Network Explorer display.

The Network Explorer view gives you a way to browse, search, and select "favorite" network resources, including shared folders, web pages, FTP sites, and so on. To open the Network Explorer view, click Start and then select Network.

> **TIP**
>
> If you find yourself using the Network Explorer view frequently, you might benefit from timely use of a right-click. A fairly common task is to map a network drive so that it can be accessed like another drive letter–based resource on your computer. Instead of left-clicking on Network in the Start menu, simply right-click to see options for mapping a shared network drive.

When you select Network from the Start menu, you get a view of the Network Explorer view similar to that in Figure 23.2.

The Network Explorer view is meant to be a place to collect shortcuts to commonly used remote network resources such as shared folders, web folders, FTP sites, shared Windows Media libraries, and the like. When you first install Windows, the Network Explorer doesn't have any of your personalized shortcuts, of course. On a workgroup network, by default, it displays an icon for each computer on your network.

Figure 23.2
The Network Explorer view is the starting point for searching and opening network resources.

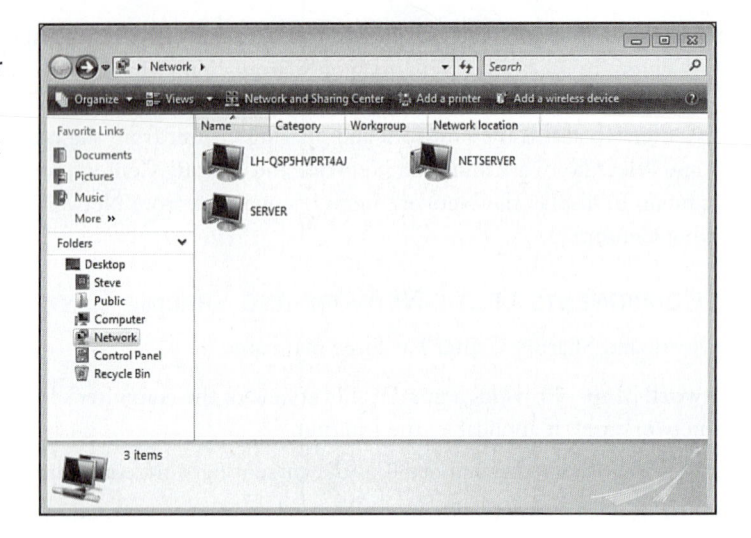

On a domain network, you have to browse through the network or ask your network administrator to identify shared network folders for you. I'll show you how to browse later in this chapter under "Exploring and Searching the Network."

The Network Explorer view organizes your network resource shortcuts and lists several commonly used tasks:

- **Add a Printer**—Opens a wizard to connect to a printer, either locally or a printer shared on a network through another means
- **Add a Wireless Device**—Opens a wizard to assist in adding a wireless device such as a wireless network card

Additional tasks can be performed from within the Network and Sharing Center:

- **View Computers and Devices**—Shows the computers and devices found or seen by this computer on the network
- **Connect to a Network**—Either connect to a computer or another network
- **Setup a Connection or Network**—Starts a wizard to connect to other types of networks
- **Manage Network Connections**—Opens another applet that shows the physical network devices, such as network cards that are installed in this computer
- **Diagnose and Repair**—Invokes the Windows Network Diagnostics Framework to help find causes for common network problems

I suggest that you browse the Network Explorer and Network and Sharing Center to check out the computers and resources on your network.

Using Shared Folders

File sharing lets users on a network browse and use files and folders, no matter which computer's hard drive the files actually reside on. The "look and feel" is exactly the same.

Let's say I want to share a folder named C:\bookstuff. I have to select users on this computer who will have permission on this share and give it a *share name* by which it'll be known on the network. For its share name, I might give the folder the share name book, as shown in Figure 23.3.

Figure 23.3
Sharing a folder on my computer.

When other network users browse their Network Explorer display, they will see that Book is a shared folder attached to my computer. It looks like any folder on their own computers.

If they open it, they'll see the same folders and file listings I see in C:\bookstuff. The information about filenames, dates, and contents is sent over the network. If anyone drags a file into this folder, all other users will see it appear there. If anyone edits a file in this shared folder, the next time another user opens the file, that user will get the changed version.

That's network file sharing in a nutshell; the rest is just a matter of details.

On home and small office workgroup networks, you might not even need to go to the trouble to set up shared folders; you can rather simply drag files and folders into the Public Folder structure. Doing so saves the step of having to create users on the local computer and grant rights to the share to those users. "Public Folder" is a folder that's created and shared by default when you install Vista.

> **TIP**
>
> If you put files into your Public Folders hierarchy, not only will other users of your computer be able to view and use these files, but so will other users on your network.
>
> This is a pretty intuitive way to organize things, and you might not need to set up or use any other shared folders.

Exploring and Searching the Network

Of course, before you can use a network resource, you have to know where to find it. I suggest that you take a moment right now to get familiar with your network.

If you are a member of a workgroup or home network, you can look through your network for shared folders and printers by exploring the following areas in turn:

- View Documents and select Network in the Folders list. On a workgroup network, by default, Windows automatically displays an icon for each computer on the network. You can expand these icons to view and use these folders just like the folders on your own hard drive.

- On a workgroup network, you can select Network from the Start menu to peruse all the computers with the same workgroup name as yours. Opening the computer icons displays any folders and printers they're sharing.

If you're on a domain-type network with Active Directory Network, you have an additional item in Network Tasks called Search Active Directory.

I'll discuss searching later in this chapter. The network searching tool can help you locate printers, computers, people, and files anywhere in your organization.

A Look at Shared Resources

If you do a bit of poking around, you might find that some computers share folders that don't make much sense. In particular, server computers on a domain network offer some network resources to member computers that are used by automatic services or are used for maintenance. Table 23.1 shows some of the shared resources you might see and describes what they do.

TABLE 23.1 TYPICAL ADMINISTRATIVE FOLDERS SHARED ON A WINDOWS 200X SERVER

Folder	Description
CertEnroll	Contains data used to provide security certificates to member computers, if your network has its own Certificate Authority. This share is used only by the Certificate Wizard.
NETLOGON	Used only by the domain login system.

Folder	Description
Published	Contains installation packages for published and assigned application software, which can be available to or forced into your computer. When using the Add/Remove Software Control Panel via the network, files are automatically retrieved from the Published folder.
SYSVOL	Used only by the domain login system.
Printers	Mirrors the computer's Printers folder; can be used by an administrator to install or control printers across the LAN.
Scheduled Tasks	Mirrors the computer's Scheduled Task list; can be used by an administrator for remote maintenance.
ADMIN$	Used by remote-administration software.
IPC$	Used for remote procedure calls, a network software system built into Windows.
print$	Shared folder containing print drivers for the computer's shared printers.
FxsSrvCp$	Shared fax service data.
C$, D$, and so on	Entire hard drives, shared for administrators' use. These shares can only be used by the actual Administrator account, and so are really useful only on domain type networks.

NOTE Share names that end in $ are hidden from display in Explorer's browsing lists.

Of these folders, only Printers and Scheduled Tasks are of interest, and then only to administrators. The operating system uses the others, which should not be modified.

If Public Folder Sharing is enabled in the Network and Sharing Center, then there will also be a share named Public. This is the Public user profile, and inside it you will find the public Documents folder, Pictures folder, and so on. On Windows XP, Shared Documents serves the same function as the Public \Documents folder on Windows Vista.

Any other folders that appear were explicitly shared by the computer's users or managers.

SEARCHING THE NETWORK

You can locate shared folders or printers by exploring the Network Center. Users with Active Directory at their disposal have more searching choices than those without Active Directory.

The Search functions let Windows explore resources on your network just as efficiently as it searches your hard disk.

Searching for Printers

Active Directory networks provide a very powerful printer search tool. In a large corporate network, hundreds or thousands of network printers might be scattered over a large area. Search for Printers lets an AD network user find just the right type of printer using a powerful query form, which I show you in "Searching for Printers in Active Directory," later in this chapter.

Searching for Computers

From within the Network Center, you can search simply by using the search textbox. You can enter either the full computer name or a fragment of its name. Windows lists the matching computers, as shown in Figure 23.4.

Figure 23.4
When you're searching for computers by their network names, you can enter full or partial names. Select one of the matching computer icons to explore its shared contents.

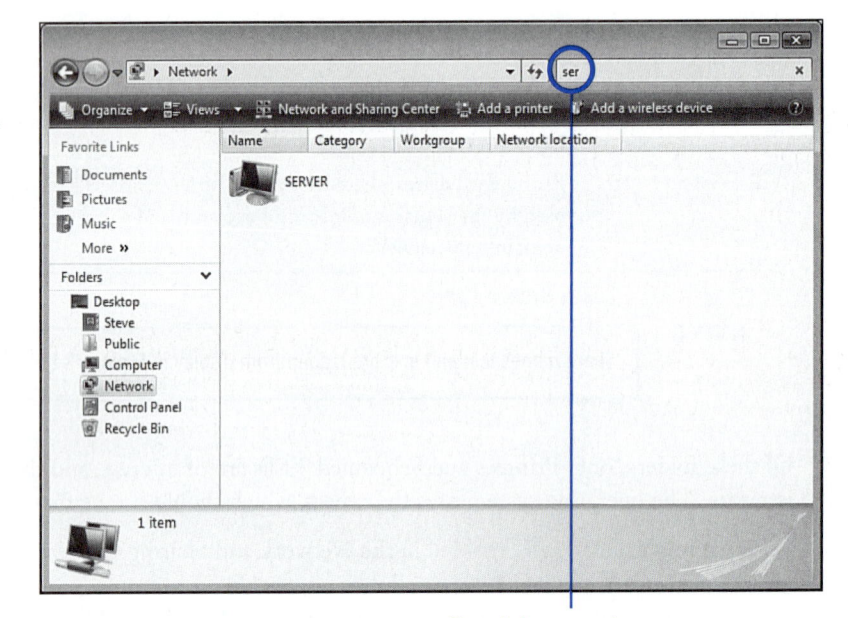

Search by computer name

You can explore any of the listed computers to view its shared folders or printers; if you delve into the shared folders, you can open or copy the available files as you find them.

Searching for Files or Folders

When you use Windows Search to look for files and folders, you can tell Windows to look on the network as well as on your own computer.

When entering your search request, expand Advanced Search. In the Location drop-down box, select Everywhere. You can select simply Everywhere if you want Windows to scan every shared folder on every computer of your network. You also can dig down to a specific computer or shared folder to narrow things. (On the other hand, if you don't know where to look, it's nice to know that Windows can do the schlepping for you.)

As Windows finds matching files, it displays them along with the name of the computer where the file was found, as shown in Figure 23.5.

You can view or open the files you've found on the network just as you can files you've found on your own computer.

On an Active Directory network, the domain administrator can choose to list, or *publish*, some shared folders in the directory; they might contain important resources that the company wants to make widely accessible and easy to find. See "Advanced Active Directory Searching," later in the chapter, for more information. If you are trying to find a particular shared folder but it has not been explicitly published in the directory, you're out of luck; there's no other way to find it besides browsing.

Figure 23.5
Use the Advanced Search option and set the location to Everywhere to search for files across your network.

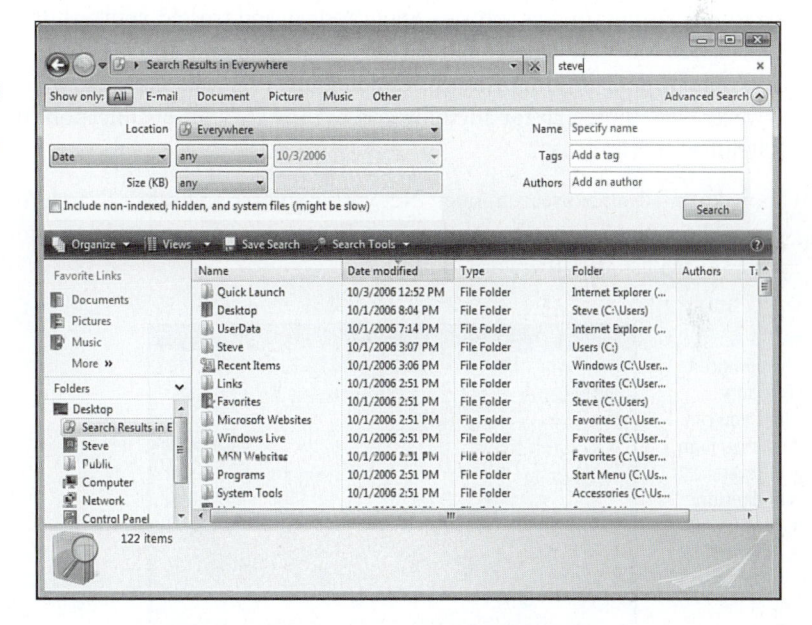

TIP

If you have administrative privileges on a network computer (that is, you are logged in as Administrator or an equivalent account, and your administrator credentials are valid on the remote computer), you can have Explorer view the special shared folder C$. C$ displays the entire contents of the computer's hard drive. Windows automatically shares a network computer's entire hard disk for use by administrators. However, the default "full drive" shares do not work when the remote computer is on a workgroup network and has Password Protected Sharing disabled.

What can you do with the contents of shared folders, assuming that you have the appropriate access rights? Just as with folders on your system, you can do the following:

- Cut, copy, and paste files and subfolders
- Open documents for viewing, printing, and editing
- Create shortcuts to files and documents on the remote drive or other remote drives

Remember, using Windows Vista's Search tools and specifying what you're looking for can be much faster than simply browsing to the location you need, especially if you're not certain where the file or folder is located.

Advanced Active Directory Searching

Active Directory contains information on many more objects than just users, computers, and printers. It includes shared folders, organizational units, certificate templates, containers (business groupings), foreign security principals, remote storage services, RPC services (used for advanced client/server software applications), and trusted domains. It can also contain information for other objects defined by your own organization. Most of this information is used only by domain administrators to configure Windows networks over vast distances; however, you can search for anything and can specify your qualifications based on more than 100 different criteria.

To make an advanced search, open Network Explorer and select Search Active Directory. The AD search tool appears, as shown in Figure 23.6. You can select various search categories in the list after the word "Find."

Figure 23.6
Using the advanced Active Directory search tool, you can use a simplified form for any of several categories of directory objects, or you can use the Advanced tab to construct queries using any of the objects fields.

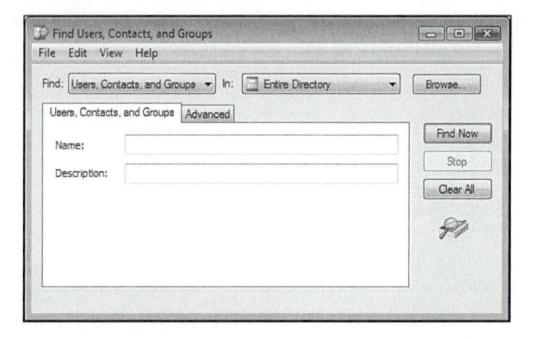

Using the advanced search tool, you can use a quick form-based search for any of the most useful objects, similar to the forms you saw when you searched for users. You can also use the Advanced tab to build specific queries such as "Last Name Starts with *xxx*." But this is the full-blown search system, and here you have 53 fields to choose from when searching for users, everything from Assistant to ZIP Code: A to Z, if you need it.

If you choose Custom Search, you have the whole gamut of fields to choose from, and in the Advanced tab, you can enter Lightweight Directory Access Protocol (LDAP) queries directly for submission to the AD service, as shown in Figure 23.7. This is the native query syntax for Active Directory, and it's available here mostly for system debugging.

> **NOTE**
>
> Strangely, in Custom Search, any qualifiers set in the form-based search are applied along with a manually entered LDAP query; you should be sure to clear the form if you are going to enter an LDAP query directly.

Figure 23.7
Querying the Active Directory Server directly with its native LDAP query syntax.

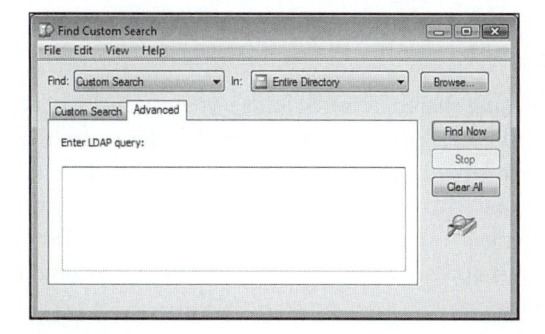

Using a Shared Disk Drive

Shared folders don't have to be subfolders. Computer owners can share the *root folder* of their disk drives, making the entire drive available over the network. This is especially useful with DVD, CD, floppy, and USB disk drives. For example, an entire CD-ROM drive is shared, you can access the entire CD from any computer on the network.

Just so you know, Windows automatically shares your entire hard drive with the special name C$. (Any other hard drives would also be shared as D$, E$, and so on.) These shares don't show up when you browse the network—the dollar sign at the end tells Windows to keep the name hidden. But you can enter the share name directly, as in \\ambon\c$, in Explorer or other programs, to view the entire drive. (You must have Administrator rights on the remote machine to use this feature. Also, on a workgroup network with Password Protected Sharing disabled, these administrative shares are never accessible because all network users are treated as Guest.)

> **TIP**
>
> If you need to install CD-ROM-based software on a computer with a broken CD-ROM drive but a good network connection, you can put the CD-ROM in another computer's drive and share the entire drive. See the section "Mapping Drive Letters," later in this chapter, to see how to access the CD from the disabled computer.

Using Internet-Based File Storage Services

Starting with Windows XP, Microsoft added the capability to make shortcuts to commercial services that provide file storage space over the Internet. To use these services, you must first visit the provider's website to obtain a username and password (and to take care of small details such as payment). When your account is set up, you can use the Add a Network Place Wizard to create a shortcut to the services.

When you're online, you can easily move files to and from your personal folder on the provider's network simply by opening the service's icon.

Mapping Drive Letters

If you frequently use the same shared network folder, you can make it a "permanent house-guest" of your computer by *mapping* the network shared folder to an unused drive letter on your computer—one of the letters after your hard drive's "C:" and the CD-ROM drive's "D:" (assuming you have one hard drive and one CD-ROM drive and have not already changed your drive mappings). You can give the shared folder \\server\shared the drive letter I:, for example, so that it appears that your computer has a new disk drive I:, whose contents are those of the shared folder.

Mapping gives you several benefits:

- The mapped drive appears along with your computer's other real, physical drives in the Computer view for quick browsing, opening, and saving of files.
- Access to the shared folder is faster because Windows maintains an open connection to the sharing computer.
- MS-DOS applications can use the shared folder through its assigned letter. Most legacy DOS applications can't accept UNC-formatted names such as \\server\shared\subfolder\file, but they can use I:\subfolder\file.
- If you need to, you can map a shared folder using an alternative username and password to gain access rights that you might not have with your current Windows login name.

If you've used Novell or older Windows networks in the past, this might be the only way you've ever used a network. Good news: You still can.

To map a drive, follow these steps:

1. Right-click on Network in the Start menu and select Map Network Drive. You can also access Map Network Drive through a right-click in several Explorer views, such as Computer and Network, when right-clicking on a network resource.

2. Next, select an unused drive letter from the drop-down list, as shown in Figure 23.8. If possible, pick a drive letter that has some association for you with the resource you'll be using: E for Editorial, S for Sales—whatever makes sense to you.

Figure 23.8
You can select an unused drive letter to use for the drive mapping.

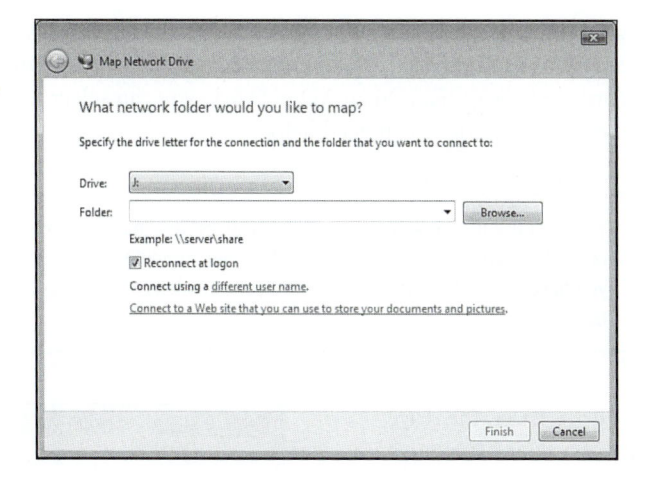

3. Then select the name of the shared folder you want to assign to the drive letter. You can type the UNC-formatted name, if you know it already—for example, *servername**sharename*—or you can click Browse to poke through your network's resources and select the shared folder.
4. Find the desired shared folder in the expandable list of workgroups, computers, and share names, shown in Figure 23.9, and click OK.

Figure 23.9
Browsing for a shared folder. You can open the list view to see network types, workgroups, computers, and shared folders.

5. After you select the shared folder and click OK, the folder name appears in the dialog box. You have two options:
    - If you want this mapping to reappear every time you log in, check Reconnect at Logon. If you don't check this box, the mapping disappears when you log off.
    - If your current Windows username and password don't give you sufficient permissions to use the shared resource, or if your username won't be recognized at the other computer because your account name is different there, select Connect

Using a Different Username. Choosing this option displays a Connect As dialog box, as shown in Figure 23.10. Here, you can enter the alternative username and password, and click OK. (On an AD network, you can select Browse to view valid usernames by location if you need help.)

> **NOTE**
>
> You must use the same username for *all* connections to a given computer. If you have other drive letters already mapped to the other computer with your original username, you have to unmap those drives before you can make a drive mapping with a different username.

After you map a drive letter, the drive appears in your Computer list along with your local disk drives. You might notice a couple of funny things with these drives:

- If you haven't accessed the network drive for 20 minutes or so, it might turn gray, indicating that the network connection to the remote computer has been disconnected. When you use the drive again, it will reconnect and turn black.

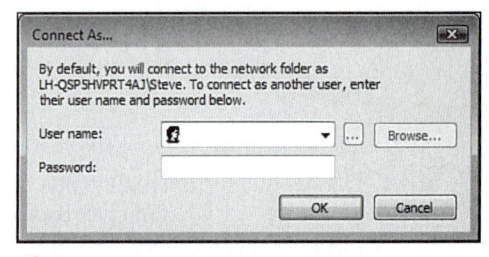

Figure 23.10
Connecting with credentials different than those of the currently logged-in user.

- If the remote computer (or you) really goes offline, a red X appears through the drive.

If you enjoy the more esoteric aspects of networking, you'll be interested in a couple of nifty features—mapping a drive to a subfolder and mapping shared folders with no drive letter.

Mapping a Drive to a Subfolder

When you're setting up a mapped drive and you browse to find a shared folder, notice that Windows lets you delve into the shared folders themselves. If you drill down into a subfolder and select it as the location to use in mapping a drive letter, you'll find that the mapped drive starts at the subfolder. The subfolder becomes the mapped drive's "root directory," and you can't explore upward into the shared folder that contains it.

NetWare users call this the *map root* function. See Figure 23.11, in which I've selected the subfolder Documents\2006 from the shared folder \\server\data. If I map drive Z: to that folder, drive Z: will contain the contents of folder \\server\data\Documents\2006, and it can't be made to see up into \\server\data\Documents or higher. The root, or top-level, directory of Z: will be the images folder.

> **TIP**
>
> This feature is most useful for administrators in setting up scripts to map drives based on a user's login name. For example, mail might be stored in subfolders of `\\server\mail` according to username. Mapping drive M: to the folder `\\server\mail\%username%` would let users get at their mail (directly) via drive M: and discourage users from poking around in other people's mail folders.
>
> Once administrators have configured the drive mapping, users can configure their mail programs to get mail from drive M:, and the same configuration will work for everyone.

Figure 23.11
By delving into a shared folder, you can map the root directory of a drive letter to a deeper point in the share.

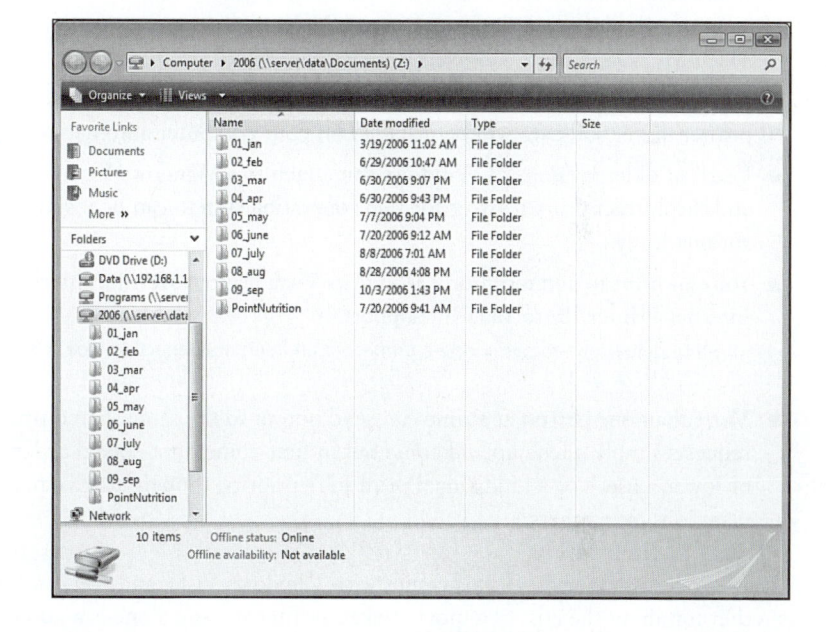

Mapping a subfolder can be a good thing because it makes any program that uses the mapped drive letter see just that subfolder as the drive's root directory.

Mapping a Shared Folder Without a Drive Letter

You can make an established connection to a shared folder, keeping it readily available for quick response without assigning it a drive letter. Within the Search box on the Start menu, simply type the server name followed by the share, as in `\\server\data`. This opens the folder in Explorer directly.

Using Printers on the Network

Whether you're part of a large corporation or a small workgroup, or even if you're a home user with just two computers, network printing is a great time and money saver. Why connect a printer to each computer when it will spend most of its time idle? By not having to buy a printer for each user, you can spend the money you save more constructively on faster, higher-quality, and more interesting printers. You might add a color photo-quality printer or a transparency maker to give your network users more output choices.

Windows Vista really excels at network printing. Here are some of the neat features of Windows Vista network printing:

- Windows can print to any of hundreds of printer models, whether they're attached to a computer or connected directly to the LAN.
- It can send printer output to other operating systems. OS/2 and Linux/UNIX printer support is built in to Windows. Linux/UNIX users can access your shared printers, and Macintosh OS X users can print to Windows shared printers.
- If you select a printer shared by a computer running Windows Vista, the necessary printer driver software will be installed on your computer automatically.
- Users of older versions of Windows can attach to a Windows Vista network printer, and the correct printer driver for their operating system can be installed for them automatically.
- You can print to and monitor a Windows Vista printer over the Internet with new Internet Printer Protocol (IPP) support.

→ To learn more details about monitoring a printer via an Internet connection, **see** "Using Printers over the Internet with IPP," **p. 762**.

- More than one person at a time can send output to the same shared printer; their print requests simply queue up and come out in first-come, first-served order. (You can raise or lower a user's or an individual print job's priority, though, to give preference to some print jobs over others.)

Because the oftware to do all this comes with Windows Vista, and you can hook computers together for about the cost of a movie ticket, printer sharing alone is a good enough reason to install a network.

The best part is that, from the user's standpoint, using a network printer is no different than using a local printer. Everything you learned about printing in Chapter 6, "Printing," applies to network printers; the only difference is in the one-time step of adding the printer to Windows. Later in the chapter, I'll describe how to share a printer attached to your computer; right now, let's look at using a printer that has already been shared elsewhere on the network.

Windows can directly attach to printers shared by any computer that supports Microsoft Networking services, whether it's running Windows Vista, XP, 2000, NT, 95, or 98; Windows for Workgroups; OS/2, or even the Samba service from UNIX. Windows can also connect to networked printers that use the LPR or other TCP/IP protocols.

Installing Network Printers

To use any networked printer, you have to set up an icon for the printer in your Printers window. One way to do this is to browse or search your network for shared printers. If you locate an appropriate printer, right-click its icon and select Open to set it up for your computer.

However, a more straightforward way to prepare to use network printers is to use the Add Printer Wizard. Unlike Windows XP, there is no Printers and Faxes applet on the Start menu.

To invoke the Add Printer Wizard, follow these steps:

1. You can invoke the wizard in the Network Explorer view by clicking on the aptly titled Add a Printer icon. This wizard walks you through locating and installing the printer.
2. Select Add a Network, Wireless, or Bluetooth Printer instead of Add a Local Printer.
3. Now you have to identify the shared printer. Windows Vista displays a list of printers that it knows about, such as ones that it finds shared within the same workgroup. If the printer that you want to connect to isn't listed, click on The Printer That I Want Isn't Listed button.
4. You're then presented with another dialog box, where you can type the location and name of the printer to which you want to connect.
5. If you know its network name already, click Select a Shared Printer By Name and enter the share name into the Name box in UNC format—for example, `\\san\LaserJet`, as shown in Figure 23.12.

Figure 23.12
You can enter a UNC shared printer name, if you know it, or you can leave the Name field blank and choose Next to browse the network for a shared printer.

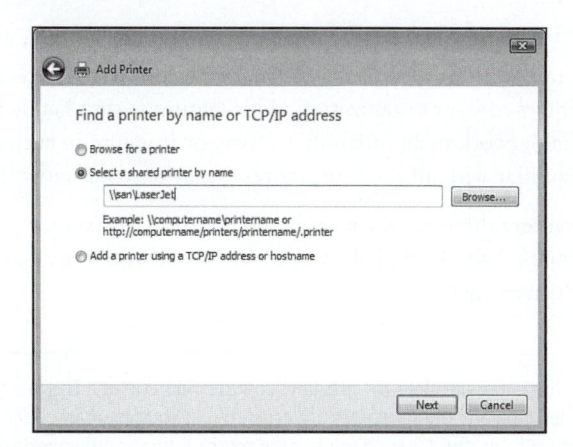

6. After you've identified the shared printer, click Next to finish installing it. From this point, the installation process proceeds much like the installation of a local printer, as described in Chapter 6.

Browsing for a Suitable Printer

If you don't know the name of the printer you want to use, you can browse through the network. In this case, choose Browse for a Printer and click Next.

The network display appears, as shown in Figure 23.13, to let you probe into domains or workgroups, computers, and their shared printers.

Figure 23.13
You can browse your workgroup network for shared printers by opening the list view of networks, domains, workgroups, and computers. Shared printers are found listed under each computer. It helps that the list includes only computers with shared printers.

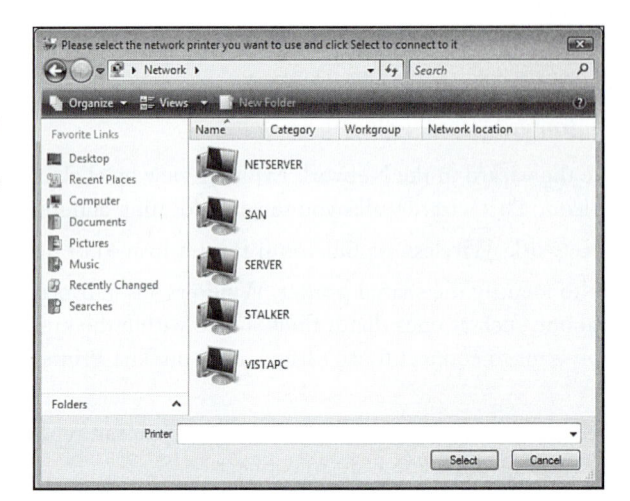

From here, just select the printer you want and click Next to finish the installation.

Searching for Printers in Active Directory

If your computer is connected to a domain-type network, the Active Directory can help you locate networked printers in your organization. This feature is very handy if you're a business traveler using the network in an unfamiliar office, or if you're in such a large office setting that you aren't familiar with all the printing resources on your network.

You can search for printers three ways: by name and location, by printer capabilities, or by more advanced attributes. You can find all the printers in the directory by entering no information in the Find Printers dialog box.

> **TIP**
>
> View the entire directory the first time you use Find Printers. This will give you an idea of how location and printer names are organized in your company. If too many names are listed, you can click Clear All to clear the search listing and then restrict your search using a location name that makes sense for your network. For example, if your company has put floor and room numbers like "10-123" in the Location column, you might restrict your search to printers on the 10th floor by searching for "10-" in Location.

Finishing the Installation

When you've chosen a printer, Windows automatically looks to the computer sharing that printer for the correct software driver for Windows Vista. If it finds the driver, that driver is instantly downloaded to your PC, and the installation completes without your having to look up the printer's model number, hunt for the right driver disks, or otherwise lift a finger.

You might hit a snag, though, if the sharing computer doesn't have the correct Windows Vista printer driver for you. You might have this problem if the remote computer isn't running Windows Vista. In this case, Windows pops up a message reading, "The server on which the printer resides does not have the correct printer driver installed. If you want to install the driver on your local computer, click OK."

If you want to use the printer, well, now you have to lift a finger. Click OK, and Windows displays the Add Printer Wizard with its list of known printer manufacturers and models, as discussed in Chapter 6. Choose the correct make and model from the list and then click OK.

→ If you can't locate the correct printer model in this list and need more detailed instructions on installing printer drivers, **see** "What to Do If Your Printer Isn't Listed," **p. 212**.

If you are adding a second or subsequent printer, after the printer driver has been downloaded or installed, Windows asks whether you want this newly installed printer to be set as your default printer. You can choose Yes or No, as you like; then select Next. You can always change your choice of default printer later by right-clicking a printer icon and selecting Set As Default.

When you click Finish, the wizard adds the printer to your list of printer choices, and you're finished. The network printer is ready to use in any application. The whole process usually takes about 15 seconds from start to finish.

> **NOTE**
>
> When the new printer appears in your printer window, you might want to verify that you can actually use the printer and that its output is correct. To do so, right-click the printer icon and select Properties. Select Print a Test Page to ensure that the network printer is working correctly.

Using a Network Printer

When the network printer is set up, you can use it in exactly the same way that you use a locally attached printer, so the printer-management discussion in Chapter 6 applies to network printers, too. The only difference is that the remote computer's administrator might not have given you management privileges for the printer, so you might not be able to change the printer's properties.

It's probably best that you don't have that capability anyway: It's considered bad form to change the hardware setup of someone else's printer without permission. If you connect to a computer that doesn't use Simple File Sharing (such as a computer on a domain network, or

Windows 200x Server), view the printer's Properties page, and have access to all the usual printer configuration tabs—Sharing, Ports, Advanced, Security, and Device Settings—don't make any changes without the permission of the printer's owner. Changing the port, for example, will certainly make the printer stop working, and the remote user probably won't figure out why for quite some time (when he or she does, leave town).

You can view and manage the printer's list of pending documents by double-clicking the printer icon. However, you can't cancel or alter the properties of anyone's print jobs but your own unless you have been granted Manage Documents rights.

Using Printers over the Internet with IPP

A fairly new feature in Windows is the capability to connect to and print to a shared printer through the Internet as easily as you can through a LAN. The Internet Printing Protocol (IPP) was developed by a group of network and printer technology companies at the initiative of Novell Corporation and Xerox Corporation. They saw the need for a standardized way to provide reliable, secure, and full-featured print spooling functions over the Internet.

The idea is that business travelers should be able to send reports back to their home offices via the Internet and use the same technology to print reports or presentations in a hotel's business center or a commercial copy service center. I use it myself to print to my office's laser printer from home. IPP is based on the Hypertext Transfer Protocol (HTTP), which runs the World Wide Web, so it's simple and it passes safely through network firewalls. In Windows, IPP uses Windows's own safely encrypted username and password security, so your printers are protected from abuse by anonymous outsiders.

As with all the shared resources I'm discussing, using and providing these services are really separate things. You can use IPP to reach a printer without providing the service yourself, and vice versa. In this section, I talk about *using* the service.

The blessing of IPP is that after you've installed the printer icon, you can use the remote printer in exactly the same way that you use any Windows printer. The printer queue, management tools, and other operations are all exactly the same, as long as you're connected to the Internet or the appropriate intranet LAN.

Selecting an IPP Printer By Its URL

You can connect to a remote printer via IPP in two ways.

If you know the URL of the IPP-connected printer, you can use the Add Printer Wizard, as I discussed earlier in this chapter. Your network administrator should supply you with the URL if the printer is on your company's intranet, or by a hotel or service bureau after they've gotten your credit card number.

1. Follow the instructions from the section "Installing Network Printers" earlier in this chapter.
2. When you are asked to enter the printer name, choose Connect to a Printer on the Internet or on a Home or Office Network instead of browsing the network.

3. Enter the URL provided by your administrator or the service you are using, and click Next.

4. You might be prompted for a username and password. If so, enter the name and password supplied by the vendor or, if the printer is on your own network, your network username and password.

5. Continue with the installation procedure described earlier; you might need to select a print driver if the remote print server doesn't provide it automatically.

When the new printer icon is installed, you have a fully functional Windows printer. You can view the pending jobs and set your print and page preferences as usual, as long as you're connected to the Internet (or the LAN, in a service establishment).

> **TIP**
>
> If you use a printing service, remember to delete the printer from your Printers folder when you leave town; you don't want to accidentally print reports in Katmandu after you've returned home.
>
> Also, if you are printing to a different brand and model than you normally do, you should select the remote printer and scroll through your document to check for changes in page breaks or other options that could affect your output. If your document's layout has changed because you're about to use a different printer, save your document under a different name before you print it.

SELECTING AN IPP PRINTER VIA THE WEB

If you can reach the website of a service bureau or a Windows computer that sports both Internet Information Services (IIS) and a shared printer, Internet printing is a snap. If you run into trouble, take a look at the "Installing Network Printers" section earlier in this chapter or read through the following section on using other IPP Printers. In most cases, Windows computers sharing a printer and running IIS should make the process of connecting to and using their shared printer very easy, though.

USING OTHER IPP PRINTERS

You can buy an IPP-capable printer and plug it directly into your LAN. An IPP-capable printer will probably provide web-based management and status, which is a great way to monitor its health from across the country (or across the room).

In a workgroup, an IPP-capable printer might not get a registered host name, so you might need to refer to it by its assigned IP address, as in `http://192.168.0.24/hplaser4`. The installation instructions for the printer tell you what URL to use.

When you know the URL for the intranet- or Internet-accessible printer, follow the instructions in the section "Installing Network Printers," earlier in this chapter. You don't have to search for the printer, though. You can simply enter the URL and then go on installing the printer as instructed earlier.

When it is set up, you can use the printer as if it were directly connected to your PC.

> **TIP**
>
> I recommend that you connect to the printer this way with just *one* of your Windows Vista computers. Then share the printer from that computer with the rest of your LAN. This way, you make installation easier for everyone else.

USING UNIX AND LPR PRINTERS

In the UNIX world, most shared printers use a protocol called LPR/LPD, which was developed at the University of California at Berkeley during the early years of UNIX and the TCP/IP protocol.

> **NOTE**
>
> If you have a UNIX background, you might be happy to know that the familiar `lpr` and `lpq` utilities are available as command-line programs in Windows Vista once LPR support has been installed. Read on in this section to find instructions for installing LPR support.

→ For more information about UNIX printing, **see** "Internetworking with UNIX and Linux," **p. 672**.

Manufacturers such as Hewlett-Packard make direct network-connected printers that accept the LPR protocol, and many companies sell small LPR-based print server devices that can attach to your printer as well. You can connect one of these printers to your LAN, configure its TCP/IP settings to match your LAN, and immediately print without running a cable from a computer to the printer. This way, you can place a printer in a more convenient place than can be reached by a 10-foot printer cable. Better yet, you can use these networked printers without requiring a Windows computer to be left turned on to manage it.

You can install a Windows printer that directs its output to an LPR print queue or device as easily as you can install a directly connected printer. Follow these steps:

1. For the first LPR-based printer you use, you have to install LPR support. To do this, open Network Connections by clicking Start, Control Panel, Programs, Turn Windows Features On or Off. Confirm the User Account Control prompt. Scroll down through the list of features and open Print Services. Check LPR Port Monitor and click OK.

2. View Printers and Faxes and select Add a Printer.

3. Select Local Printer. (You choose Local because Network connects only to Windows and IPP shared printers.) Uncheck Automatically Detect and Install My Plug and Play Printer, and click Next.

4. Select the Create a New Port option. In the Type of Port box, choose LPR Port and click Next.

5. In the Add LPR Compatible Printer dialog box, enter the IP address or host name of the UNIX or print server, and the name of the print queue on that server, as shown in Figure 23.14.

Figure 23.14
In this dialog box, enter the IP address or host name of the LPR print server and the queue or printer name.

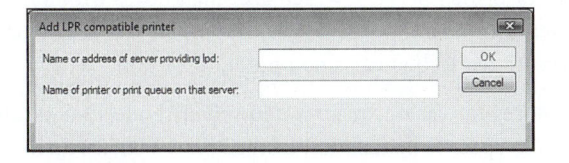

6. Select the manufacturer and printer model as usual, and proceed with the rest of the printer installation.

> **NOTE**
> If you enter the wrong IP address, host name, or print queue name, Windows will not let you change this information. To correct the problem, bring up the printer's Properties page, select the Ports tab, highlight the LPR port, and select Configure Port. If Windows doesn't display a dialog box to let you change the IP information, uncheck the LPR port. Delete the port and add a new LPR port with the correct information. Then check the port to connect your Windows printer to the LPR server.

USING APPLETALK PRINTERS

If your network has AppleTalk printers attached, you probably have Macintosh users on your LAN. If you want to share files with Macintosh users, you need to have Windows 200x Server on your network because it includes File and Printer Services for Macintosh Networks. These services let Macintosh and Windows users access shared printers and folders on each others' networks as if they were their own.

Windows Vista doesn't provide such services, so without the Server version, you can't directly use AppleTalk-based printers. Regrettably, Windows Vista doesn't come with the AppleTalk Protocol and AppleTalk Printer port monitor components that were provided with previous versions of Windows. However, Mac OS X users can use printers shared by Windows computers, and with some work, Vista users can print to printers shared by Macs running OS X.

→ To learn more details about internetworking with Macintosh computers, **see** "Internetworking with Macintosh," **p. 683**.

> **NOTE**
> Before giving up, however, check the documentation on your networked printer. Some printers support access via all three standard protocols: AppleTalk, NetBIOS (SMB), and TCP/IP.

Using Other Network-Connected Printers

Windows Vista can use other types of network-connected printers as well. Some printer models come with a built-in network connection, and others have a network adapter option. You can also buy network printer servers, which are small boxes with a network connector and one to three printer-connection ports. These devices let you locate printers in a convenient area, which doesn't need to be near a computer.

The installation procedures for various printer and server models vary. Your networked printer or print server has specific installation instructions. When you install it, you have a choice about how the printer will be shared on your network:

- You can install the network-to-printer connection software on *one* of your Windows computers and then use standard Windows printer sharing to make the printer available to the other computers on your network.

- You can install the printer's connection software on *each* of your computers.

With the first method, you guarantee that print jobs will be run first come, first served (or you can set priorities for print jobs, if you want) because one computer will provide a queue for the printer. Another plus is that you have to do the software setup only once; it's much easier to set up the other workstations to use the standard Windows shared printer. The one computer must be left on for others to use the printer, however.

With the second method, each computer contacts the printer independently, so there could be contention for the printer. However, no computers need to be left on because each workstation contacts the printer directly.

You can use either method. The first one is simplest and is best suited for a busy office. The second method is probably more convenient for home networks and small offices.

Using Network Resources Effectively

Tips are scattered throughout this chapter, but I want to collect a few of the best ones here, for easy reference. The following tips and strategies help you make the most of your LAN.

Use Network Explorer

The Network Explorer not only serves as a convenient place to collect shortcuts to network resources, but it also appears when you open or save files in any application. This feature can save you lots of time when you use the same network folders repeatedly.

You can make shortcuts in Network Explorer for the handful of the network shared folders that you use most frequently.

If you find that you always have to drill your way into the main shared folder to get to the folder you actually want, you can add the names of subfolders when you make these shortcuts.

Make Folder Shortcuts

You can drag the icon that appears in the address field from any shared folder view to your desktop, to Network Explorer, or to any other convenient place for reuse later. (The Address Bar might not appear on your Explorer windows. You might need to right-click the toolbar and check Address Bar. You also might need to uncheck Lock the Toolbars to drag it into a visible position.)

I like to organize projects into folders on my desktop and put related network resources in each. For example, I might have three project folders on my desktop and, in each one, three shortcuts to related shared folders.

Because shortcuts aren't the "real thing," you can have shortcuts to the same network places wherever you need them.

Use Offline Network Folders

If you use network resources from a portable computer or a computer with an intermittent network connection (by design or by accident), you can use the Offline Folders feature to keep local copies of important network folders in your own computer for use when the network is unavailable.

→ If you want to learn more details about Offline Folders, **see** "Offline Folders," **p. 1301**.

Put Tools and Documentation Online

Administrators and power users should put management batch files, Registry installation and setup files, special program utilities, and documentation in a shared network folder for convenient access from any computer on the network. Your network's users don't need to know it's there unless you want them to.

Organize Your Network to Fit Your Users

You should organize shared folders to fit the way users actually work. For example, if your organization frequently passes documents back and forth between users, you could make a shared folder named Inbox that contains a subfolder for each user. Co-workers could deliver documents to each other by dropping them into the appropriate network Inbox. Users could each have a shortcut to their inboxes on their desktops for quick access.

Sharing Resources

On a large corporate LAN, most important network resources, shared folders, and printers are set up and tightly controlled by network managers. You might not even be able to share resources from your own computer. This helps control the cost of maintaining and managing the network, but it doesn't help you and your co-workers if you want to share files for a project among yourselves. You might have to plead with your network manager to prepare a common shared folder for you.

On the other hand, you might be able to set up the file sharing yourself. In a workgroup network, it's almost certain you can. Administrators and members of the Administrators and Power Users groups can manage file and printer sharing.

Before you decide to share resources, you should give some thought to just what you want to share, how you want to organize it, and who should have permission to see, use, or change files you've published in the shared folders.

Sharing Folders and Drives

Windows Vista provides two primary methods for sharing files and folders: through Public folders or via standard, traditional sharing. Furthermore, you can change the way people access shares with the use of Password Protected Sharing. Regardless of how you want to share files and folders, the Network and Sharing Center provides the central place from which you can manage file share settings in Windows Vista.

The procedure for sharing files and folders has some slight differences, depending on the type of network you have and the method you choose. If you're using a workgroup-type network with Public folder sharing enabled, follow the procedure in the next section.

> **NOTE**
>
> As you start to select folders to share, you might notice that Windows has automatically already shared your entire hard drive with the name C$. Leave this share alone; it lets network Administrators manage your computer. The default C$ share is only available to users of the Administrators group while a share that you create might have wider permissions and allow more users to have access. It's essentially usable only on a Windows domain network. You can choose an additional, different name if you want to share an entire hard drive—for example, cdrive or cdrive$, although Microsoft discourages sharing entire hard disk drives. If you do set up a share for an entire drive, it is important that you only allow as much access as necessary so as to prevent someone from inadvertently (or intentionally) deleting important operating system or program files from your C drive and rendering your computer unusable.

Sharing Folders on a Workgroup or Domain Network

On workgroup networks, Microsoft provides a simplified user interface and security system for file sharing using the Public folder and the option of disabling Password Protected Sharing. If you've disabled the Public folder, skip ahead to the next section. But if you are on a workgroup network and Public folder sharing is enabled, heed this warning:

> **CAUTION**
>
> When you share folders on a computer that has Public folder sharing enabled, *anybody* can see the files. If you choose to enable changes, anybody can change the files within the Public folder structure as well.

For Public folder sharing to work, it must be enabled. You can enable it through the Network and Sharing Center by selecting Public Folder Sharing from the Sharing and Discovery section. From within the Network and Sharing Center, select Public Folder Sharing, which expands to show options for configuring the behavior of Public folder shares. As illustrated in Figure 23.15, when this is expanded, you can choose to turn on sharing to let people see files in the Public folders, you can turn on sharing and let people see and also change files, or you can turn off Public folder sharing entirely.

Figure 23.15
Selecting an option for Public folder sharing through the Network and Sharing Center.

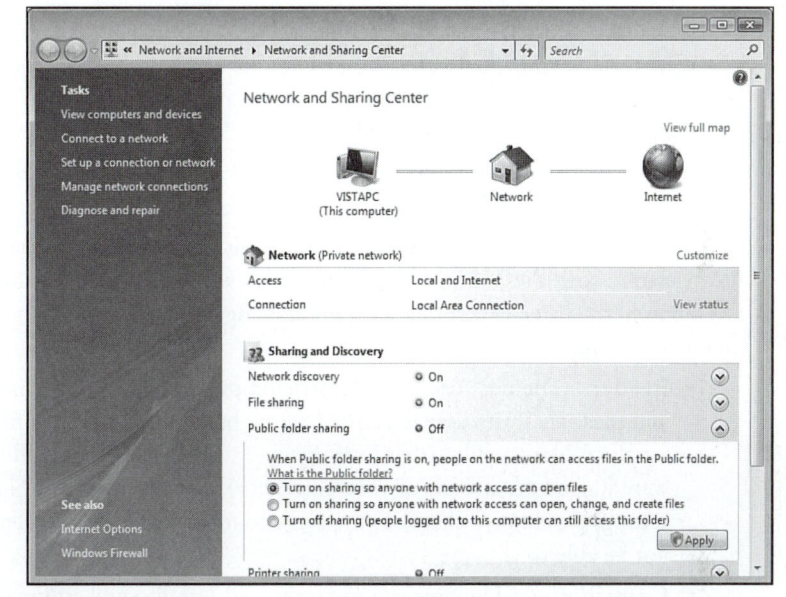

When this is enabled, you must then share files through the Public folder structure. To share a file or folder with Public folder sharing, drag the file or folder to the C:\Users\Public folder structure:

1. Select a folder or file to share from Explorer.

2. Use the mouse to drag the file to C:\Users\Public or one of the subfolders within C:\Users\Public. If you want to *move* your files to the Public folder, just drag and drop them there.

   If you want to *copy* files to the Public folder and leave your original versions intact, press and hold the Shift key while you drop the files into the Public folder. Don't release the mouse button until you see a + sign appear next to the cursor.

To share a folder with standard file sharing, follow these steps:

1. Select a folder in Explorer, or select the name of the CD-ROM, floppy, USB or hard drive itself at the top of the Explorer view, if you want to share the entire disk.

2. Right-click the folder, and choose Share. This invokes the File Sharing Wizard; the first step is to select people to share with. This dialog box is shown in Figure 23.16.

3. You must now determine who can access the shared folder and what they can do with its contents. If Password Protected Sharing is enabled on the Network and Sharing Center page, then you need to add individual user account names. You can also enter the name Everyone to set the rights for *anyone* with a user account. To add a name or group, select the arrow to drop down a list of available users on this computer, or type a name into the box and click Add.

   If Password Protected Sharing is disabled, then the only name that makes sense to add is Everyone, since individual user accounts are not recognized. Everyone in this case means "anyone at all, whether they have an account or not." To add "Everyone," type the name **Everyone** into the box and click Add.

4. After entering or selecting a name, select one of the three permissions levels: Reader, Contributor, or Co-Owner.

   Here's how the permission levels work: If the disk drive on which the shared file resides is formatted with the NTFS file system (which will be the case for the drive that holds Windows), the three categories set the following access restrictions for the listed user name or group:

   - **Reader**—The network user is restricted to read access only, and can view folders and files *only* if the user is granted access based on the NTFS file security settings for the folders or files (that is, if the user would be able to read the files if she were logged on directly at your computer). However, even if NTFS permission settings would give that user the right to modify, create, or delete files, she will not be able to.

   - **Contributor**—The user can not only view but also add and make changes (including delete) to the files that she has added, subject to any restrictions set by NTFS file permissions.

   - **Co-Owner**—Like Contributor, but the user can delete or modify files created by other users as well, again, subject to NTFS permission restrictions.

   If the disk on which the shared folder resides is formatted with the older FAT file system (which would be the case for extra drives or partitions that were formatted by earlier versions of Windows), the settings set the following restrictions:

   - **Reader**—Restricts network users to read access only. A network user will be able to read any file, but not create, modify, or delete files.

   - **Contributor** or **Co-Owner**—A network user can create, modify, or delete any file at will.

5. If Password Protected Sharing is enabled, you can add additional users. It might make sense, for example, to give group Everyone "Reader" permission, and then add specific individuals with Contributor or Co-Owner permission. Or, you could give Everyone Contributor permission, and specific individuals Co-Owner permission.

6. When you're done selecting users, click on Share. This shares the folder.

Figure 23.16
Selecting users for permissions in the File Sharing Wizard.

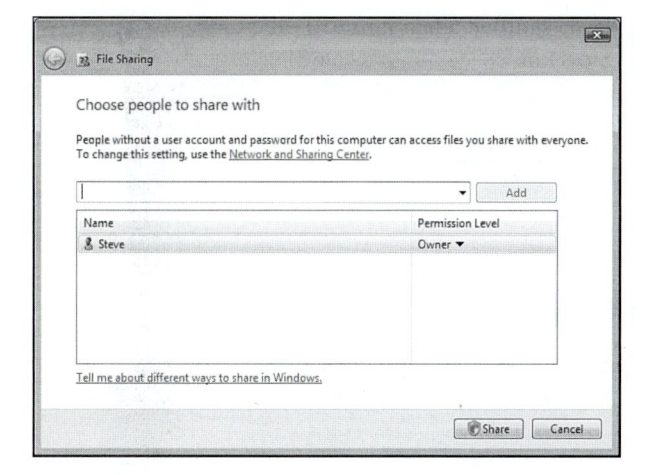

> **TIP**
>
> You can prevent other users from seeing your shared folder when they browse the network by adding a dollar sign to the end of the share name, as in mystuff$. They must know to type this name to use the shared folder. However, this convention alone does *not* prevent them from seeing your files if they know the share name.

Sharing Printers

You can share any local printer on your computer. This can be a printer directly cabled to your computer or one connected via the network using LPR or other network protocols.

To enable printer sharing, do the following:

1. Choose Start and select Network, and then select Network and Sharing Center.
2. From within the Network and Sharing Center, select Printer Sharing from the Sharing and Discovery section. Enable printer sharing by selecting Turn On Printer Sharing and click Apply.
3. Select Share This Printer and enter a network name for the printer, as shown in Figure 23.17. Enter up to 14 characters, using letters, numbers, and hyphens.
4. If your network has only Windows Vista, XP, and 2000 computers, click OK, and you're finished. Other network users can now use the shared printer.

Otherwise, continue to the next section to add extra printer drivers for other operating systems.

> **NOTE**
>
> If you invoke the Sharing or Properties tab of a printer without using the Run As Administrator option, you'll need to click on the Change Sharing Options button before the sharing options will become available.

Figure 23.17
Enabling sharing for a printer.

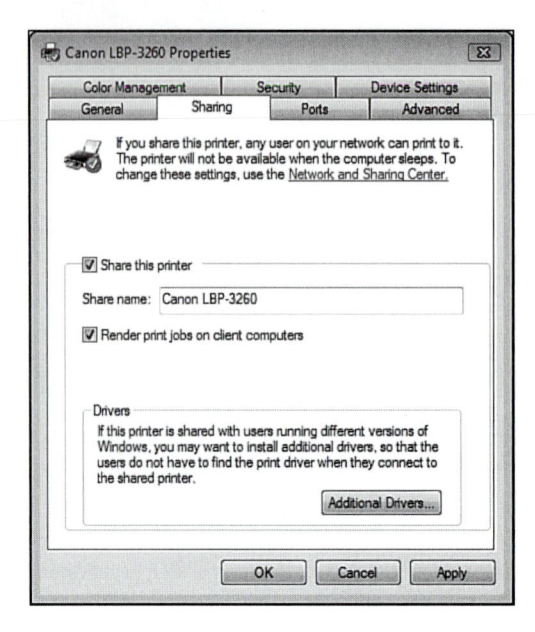

Installing Extra Printer Drivers

If you have computers running other versions of Windows or other CPU types, you can load the appropriate printer drivers for those operating systems now, and network users will receive them automatically when they connect to your printer. This step is optional, but it's the friendly thing to do.

View the Sharing tab in your printer's Properties dialog box and select the Additional Drivers button. Windows displays a list of supported operating systems and CPU types, as shown in Figure 23.18.

Figure 23.18
You can install drivers for additional operating systems or CPUs to make it easy for network users to attach to your printer.

Check the boxes for the CPUs and operating systems you want to support, and click OK. Windows then goes through any additional operating systems that you chose one by one; it might ask for either your Windows Vista installation media or other operating system installation disks to locate the appropriate drivers.

> **NOTE**
>
> A Type 3 (user mode) x86 driver will work for any computer running a 32-bit version of Windows Vista, XP, or 2000. An x64 driver will work for Windows Vista 64-bit versions and Windows XP Professional 64-bit Edition for x64. An Itanium (IA-64) driver will work on Windows XP Professional 64-bit Edition for IA-64 and the IA-64 Windows Server versions. Vista doesn't let you load drivers for Windows 98/Me clients.

You can find these drivers on the original installation disks for the alternative operating system or often on disks provided with the printer, which might contain support for many operating systems on the same disk.

When installed, the alternative drivers are sequestered in your Windows folder and delivered to users of the other operating systems when necessary.

> If one of your network printers stops working, your users have output waiting to print, and you have an alternative printer available, **see** "Network Printer Has Stopped Working" in the "Troubleshooting" section at the end of this chapter.

Setting Printer Permissions

If you have a peer-to-peer network and have disabled Password Protected Sharing, you don't need to worry about setting permissions for Printers. If you're on a domain network or have chosen to use detailed user-level permissions on your peer-to-peer network, you can control access to your shared printers with three security attributes that can be assigned to users or groups, as shown in Figure 23.19:

Permission	Lets User or Group...
Print	Send output to the printer
Manage Printers	Change printer configuration settings, and share or unshare a printer
Manage Documents	Cancel or suspend other users' print jobs

You can use the Security tab in the printer's Properties dialog box to alter the groups and users assigned to each of these permissions.

The CREATOR OWNER name applies to the user who submitted a given print job.

You probably don't have to change the default permission settings unless you want to limit use of the printer by outside users in a domain environment only. In this case, delete Everyone and add specific groups with Print permission.

Tracking Printer Users

If you want to track usage patterns of your printer, you can instruct Windows to record print job completion and maintenance alerts in the System Event Log, through settings on the Print Server Properties dialog box. Here's how:

1. Open the Printers and Faxes window.
2. Choose File, Server Properties. It may be necessary to right-click in an empty area in Printers in order to get to the Properties.

Figure 23.19
The Security tab lets you assign printer-management permissions for users, groups, and the creator of a networked printer.

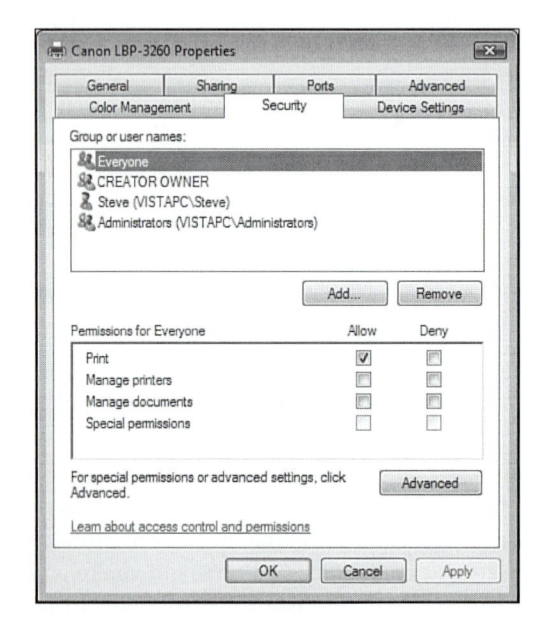

3. Select the Advanced tab.
4. Check Log events to record the degree of login required:

    Log Spooler Error Events records the most severe printer errors.

    Log Spooler Warning Events records less severe errors.

    Log Spooler Information Events records successful print job completion.
5. Click OK.

I generally disable Log Spooler Information Events to prevent the system log from recording print activity, which I don't care to keep track of.

If you do care, though, more detailed recording of printer use and management activity is available through Auditing. Auditing provides a way to record printer activity in the Windows Event Security Log.

The Windows Auditing feature records an event when a specified permission has been either granted or denied. The granting or denying of permission implies that someone completed, or tried to complete, the action that the permission controls.

This situation sounds a little more complex than it is. In practical terms, if you audit success *and* failure of the Print permission, you'll see who submitted print jobs, and who tried and was denied. If you audit just failure of the Manage Documents permission, you'll see who tried to delete another user's document and was prohibited.

You can add permissions in the Auditing tab by viewing a printer's Security properties using the Run As Administrator properties, clicking Security and then Advanced, and selecting the Auditing tab. Select Add, choose a user or group of users to select for auditing, and then choose permissions and outcomes to audit, as shown in Figure 23.20.

Figure 23.20
Adding an Audit entry to record when Printing permission has been granted or denied to anyone.

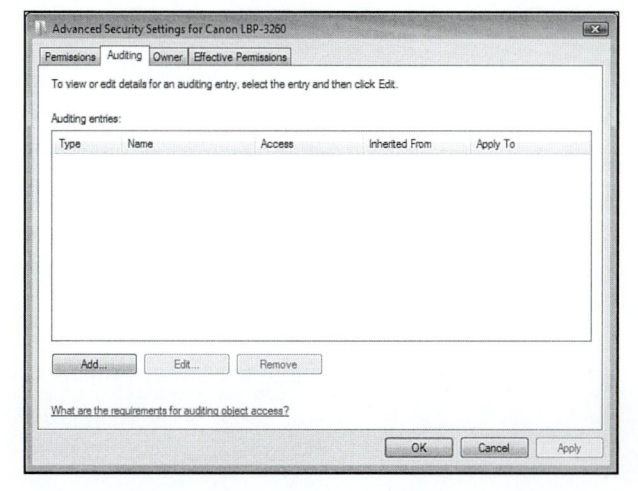

Finally, click OK to add the permission to the Audit list, and add more, if desired.

CHANGING THE LOCATION OF THE SPOOL DIRECTORY

When jobs are queued up to print, Windows stores the data it has prepared for the printer in a folder on the computer that's sharing the printer. Data for your own print jobs and for any network users will all end up on your hard drive temporarily. If the drive holding your Windows directory is getting full and you'd rather house this print data on another drive, you can change the location of the spool directory.

To change the location of the Windows print spooler folder, follow these steps:

1. Select Printers from the Hardware and Sound section of the Control Panel.
2. Right-click within the Printers view; select Run As Administrator and then Server Properties.
3. Click on the Advanced tab.
4. Enter a new location for the Spool Folder and click OK.

Printer Pooling

If your network involves heavy-duty printing, you might find that your printers are the bottleneck in getting your work done. One solution is to get faster printers, and another is to add multiple printers.

If you have two printers shared separately, you have to choose one for your printing. You'll probably encounter bank-line syndrome: The other line always seems to move faster.

The way around this problem is to use printer pooling. You can set up one shared printer queue that sends its output to multiple printers. The documents line up in one list, and multiple printers take jobs from the front of the line, first come, first served.

To set up pooled printers, follow these steps:

1. Buy identical printers—they must at least be identical from the software point of view.
2. Set up and test one printer, and configure network sharing for it.
3. Install the extra printer(s) on the same computer as the first. If you use network-connected printers, you need to add the necessary additional network ports.
4. View the printer's properties and select the Ports tab. Mark Enable Printer Pooling and mark the ports for the additional printers.

That's all there is to it; Windows passes print jobs to as many printers as you select on the Ports pages.

Separator Pages

Windows Vista has a feature that lets you add a cover page to each print job sent to a given printer. The cover page can be configured to show the name of the user who sent the print job, his or her computer name, and so on. On a network with dozens of users sharing a given printer, these cover pages can be very helpful in sorting out whose printouts are whose. On the other hand, using cover pages wastes paper and isn't a good "green" practice unless the confusion around your printers is really significant.

Separator pages have another very important use: They can be used to switch "multiple personality" printers into one language mode. For example, some Hewlett-Packard printers accept input in both the PostScript and PCL page-description languages. These printers normally detect which format is being used and adjust automatically. They don't always, however, so setup information stored in separator page files can be used to force the issue.

You can set up the pages like this: Create two Windows shared printer icons in the Printers folder, both pointing to the same physical printer on the same LPT port. Configure one with the PostScript driver and the other with the standard PCL driver. Name the printers appropriately—for example, LaserJet-PS and LaserJet-PCL. Configure each printer with a separator page that forces the printer into the correct mode. This way, you can select the printer driver you want, and the printer will never mistake the language being used. This is really handy if UNIX or Macintosh users are sending output to your printers.

Windows ships with four predefined separator files:

`pcl.sep`	Forces a LaserJet printer into PCL mode and prints a separator page
`sysprint.sep`	Forces a LaserJet printer into PostScript mode and prints a separator page
`pscript.sep`	Forces a LaserJet printer into PostScript mode but doesn't print a separator page
`sysprtj.sep`	Contains a Japanese font version of `sysprint.sep`

Separator files are stored in your `\Windows\System32` folder. You can use one of the predefined files, or you can create one of your own. You can edit these plain-text files with Notepad. To assign a separator page to a given printer, follow these steps:

1. Open the printer's Properties box using the Run As Administrator method, and select the Advanced tab.
2. Click the Separator Page button and enter the desired filename, or click Browse to find the file manually.
3. Click OK.

The first line of a `*.sep` file contains only one character, which sets the "escape character" for the rest of the file. Subsequent lines are sent to the printer. Sequences that start with the escape character are interpreted as substitution commands; the sequence is replaced with other text before being sent to the printer. Table 23.2 shows the command substitutions. In the table, I assume that backslash (\) is the escape character.

TABLE 23.2   SEPARATOR PAGE SUBSTITUTIONS

Sequence	Is Replaced With…
\N	Name of the user who submitted the print job.
\I	Print job number.
\D	Date the job was printed.
\T	Time the job was printed.
\L*xxxxxx*	Text *xxxxxx*, up to the next escape.
\F*filename*	Contents of the file *filename*. This file is copied literally, with no substitution. It can be used for a "message of the day."
\H*xx*	Hexadecimal value *xx*. Particularly useful is \H1B, which emits the ASCII `<esc>` character used in printer control commands.
\W*nn*	Limits the width of the page to *nn* columns.

You can create or modify separator page files using the predefined files as examples. Table 23.2 can help you interpret these files.

> **TIP**
>
> If you have a two-bin printer, you can put colored paper in the second bin and print the separator pages on it so they really stand out. To do so, add the appropriate printer-control sequences to the `.sep` file. At the beginning of the file, have the sep file reset the printer and switch to bin 2, print the separator page stuff, and then switch back to bin 1.

Managing Network Use of Your Computer

If you've shared folders on your LAN, you might want to know who's using them. For example, you might need to know this information if someone were editing a file in your shared folder. If you tried to edit the same file, you'd be told by your word processor that the file was "in use by another." But by whom?

Computer Management can help you. Open the Start menu, right-click Computer, select Manage, and open the Shared Folders system tool. It displays the shared folders that your computer offers and the number of users attached to them.

You can add new shared folders using the Shares tool with a right-click.

You can also view the current users (sessions) and the files they have in use with the Sessions and Open Files views. This lets you know whom to ask to close a file, or, in an emergency, you can disconnect a user or close an open file with the Delete key. (This is a drastic measure and is sure to mess up the remote user, so use it only when absolutely necessary.)

Managing Network Resources Using the Command Line

If you find yourself repeating certain network and file operations day after day, it makes sense to try to automate the processes. You might get so used to the graphical interface that you forget the command line, but it's still there, and you can perform drive mappings and printer selections with the command line almost as easily as from the GUI. Batch files, which were so familiar in the old DOS days, are still around and are a great way to perform repetitive administrative tasks.

I use batch files to perform simple computer-to-computer backups of important files. Let's say I want to back up the folder C:\book on my computer to a shared folder of the same name on another computer named abalone. Here's how a batch file to do this might look:

```
@echo off
net use q: /delete 1>nul 2>nul
net use q: \\abalone\book
xcopy c:\book q: /e /r /c /y
net use q: /delete
exit
```

Of course, I could bring up Explorer, locate my C:\book folder and the abalone book folder, drag the folder from one computer to the other, and repeat this process every time I want to make a copy of my files. But a shortcut to the previous batch file on my desktop will do the same job with a double-click. It's smart enough to copy only files that have changed, and I can add the batch file as a Scheduled Task to run automatically every night. *Now* which seems more convenient—that nifty GUI or the humble command-line batch file? Knowing the net utilities gives you an extra set of tools to work with, and their ancient origins shouldn't make them seem less worthy!

The net command comes to us virtually unchanged since the original PC network software developed by Microsoft and IBM debuted in 1984. There are so many variations of the net command that I think of them as separate commands: net view, net use, net *whatever*. Each net command contains a word that selects a subcommand or operation type.

You can get online help listing all the net subcommands by typing **net /?**, and detailed help by typing **net *command* /?**, where *command* is any one of the net subcommands.

MAPPING DRIVES WITH net use

The net use command is the most useful of the command-line network functions. net use makes and disconnects drive mappings, and establishes printer redirection for command-line programs. The basic command is as follows:

```
net use drive sharename
```

The following example maps drive letter q to the shared folder \\abalone\book:

```
net use q: \\abalone\book
```

You can't replace the shared folder attached to an already mapped drive, so it's best to place commands in the batch file to delete any previous mapping before trying to make a new one:

```
net use q: /delete
net use q: \\abalone\book
```

The /delete command prints an error message if there was no previous message. An elegant solution to this is to redirect the output of the first net command to NUL, which discards any output. I usually redirect both standard output and standard error output with

```
net use q: /delete 1>nul 2>nul
```

to ensure that this command will do its work silently.

You can add the /persistent:yes option to a net use command to make the drive mapping return when you log off and back on, matching the function of the Reconnect at Login check box in the graphical drive-mapping tool.

You can also map a drive to a subfolder of a shared folder, mimicking the "map root" function familiar to Novell NetWare veterans. Subfolder mapping lets you run legacy DOS applications that require certain files or directories to be placed in the root directory of a hard disk. You can fool them into running with data on a shared network folder. I like to do this because it lets me store data in a centralized place where it will get backed up regularly.

For example, suppose the hypothetical program runit needs to see its data files in the current root directory and runs from directory \startdir. I want all the files to reside in a shared network folder, in a subdirectory oldprog of a shared folder named \\server\officedata. This batch file does the trick:

```
@echo off
net use e: /delete 1>nul 2>nul
net use e: \\server\officedata\oldprog
e:
cd \startdir
runit
c:
net use e: /delete
exit
```

Creating a shortcut to this batch file in Windows Vista lets me run the old program with a double-click.

`net use` also maps network printers to the legacy DOS printer devices LPT1, LPT2, and LPT3. The `capture` printer setting found in Windows 9x is not available, and the only way to redirect DOS program output to a network printer is through `net use`.

The following command directs DOS application LPT1 printer output to the network printer:

`net use lpt1: \\server\printername`

The following command cancels it:

`net use lpt1: /delete`

Figure 23.21
The Distributed File System lets a Windows 200x Server administrator graft shared folders from elsewhere in the network into the server's own file system, building one virtual file system from several computers.

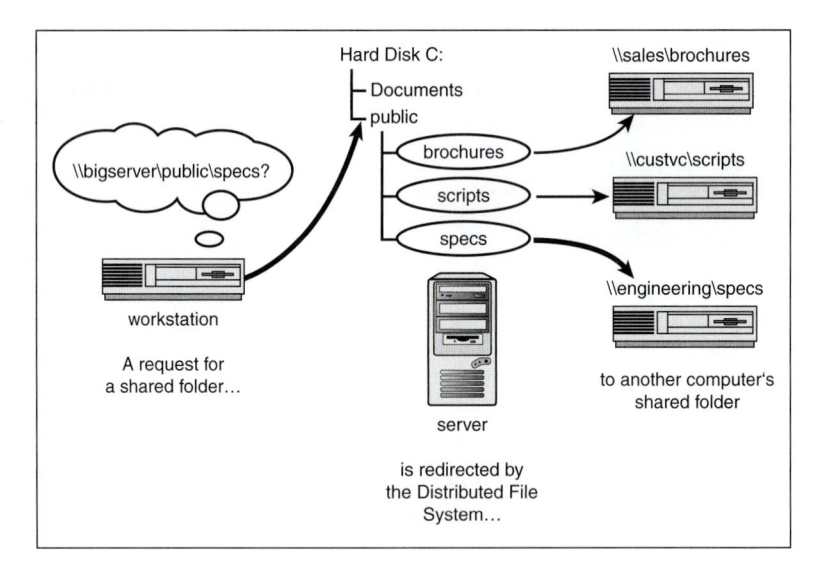

Troubleshooting

Can't Find Any Printers in Active Directory

When I use Find Printers, no printers appear in the results list.

You might have selected criteria that no printers match, or you might be specifying the criteria too closely and missing some near but inexact matches. Remove a criterion or two and repeat the search. If your search reveals more printers than you want to look at, try narrowing the search more slowly. Instead of specifying Postscript Level 2 as a printer language, for example, try searching for "Post." You might be missing a printer that was entered as PostScript Lvl 2.

Network Printer Has Stopped Working

Documents are waiting to be printed on a networked printer, but the printer has stopped working.

If a shared network printer stops working with important documents in its queue, you still might be able to get the documents out by redirecting the output of a stalled printer queue to another printer of the same make and model.

To do this, at the computer sharing the printer, log on as a Computer Administrator. Open the Printers applet from the Control Panel, right-click the disabled printer, and select Properties. View the Ports tab. Here, you can direct the queued print output to one of these printers:

- **A printer on a different port on the same computer**—Check the alternative LPT or USB port name.

- **A printer on a different network server**—Click Add Port, select Local Port, and enter the alternative printer's share name in UNC format, such as `\\sumatra\laserjet`.

This sends output to the alternative printer, and network users won't have to make any changes to their printer setup. However, this works only when the alternative printer is completely compatible with the original.

File Is in Use By Another

When I attempt to edit a file in a folder I've shared on the network, I receive an error message indicating that the file is in use by another user.

You can find out which remote user has the file open by using the Shared Folder tool in Computer Management, as I described earlier in this chapter under "Managing Network Use of Your Computer."

You can wait for the remote user to finish using your file, or you can ask that person to quit. Only in a dire emergency should you use the Shared Folder tool to disconnect the remote user or close the file. The only reasons I can think of to do this are that the remote user's computer has crashed but your computer thinks the connection is still established, or that the remote user is an intruder.

Tips from the Windows Pros: Using Command-Line Utilities

Setting up a new network can be a grueling task. If you've ever set up a dozen computers in a day, you know what I mean. Think how long it took you to set up Windows, install applications, set up printers and network information, and get the desktop just so. Then multiply that work by 10 or more. Then repeat the process anytime a new computer is installed or repaired and reformatted.

Network managers do anything they can to minimize the amount of work they need to do to set up and maintain computers. Windows 200*x* Server offers a remote installation service that can set up a completely outfitted Windows Vista workstation in a virgin computer over the LAN without laying a finger on it. This is a blessing for them, but what about those of us with peer-to-peer workgroup LANs?

The rest of us rely on whatever handy labor-saving tricks we can find to minimize the amount of work needed. Batch files can go a long way to ease the pain of installing, and they have two other benefits: They let you make more consistent installations, and they serve as a sort of documentation of whatever configuration they're performing.

My first tip to a workgroup manager is to learn the Windows Vista command-line utilities; you can set up batch files to make some consistent settings on new computers. It doesn't hurt to learn how to use Windows Scripting Host. Chapter 32, "Command-Line and Automation Tools," introduces you to these valuable environments. If Microsoft produces a resource kit, as they have for previous operating systems, it will likely offer a big pile of extra command-line utilities. Every network manager should have a copy of the resource kit.

Put any batch files and scripts you develop in a shared network folder, and you'll have an installation and configuration toolkit. If a user accidentally disconnects a mapped network drive, that person can visit your folder of handy icons and click MAPDRIVES to have everything reset. This can be done with `net use` commands in a batch file.

You can also install printers with the command line. The entire functionality of the Install Printer Wizard is available at the command line; you can pop up graphical utilities such as the queue manager, and you even can perform installations and configure printers in a batch file.

Type the following at the command prompt for a full listing of the printer configuration utility's commands:

```
rundll32 printui.dll,PrintUIEntry /?
```

Scroll to the bottom of the list for an eye-popping list of examples. (I warn you, it's ugly. Some experimentation is required to get some of the commands to work, even with the examples given here.)

One really handy use of this command is to install a connection to a network shared printer. This example sets up the local computer to use the shared printer \\bali\laserjet:

```
rundll32 printui.dll,PrintUIEntry /n "\\bali\laserjet" /in
rundll32 printui.dll,PrintUIEntry /n "\\bali\laserjet" /y
```

The first command installs the printer, and the second makes it the default printer.

If you put commands such as these in a batch file (using your network's printer names, of course) and put the batch file in a shared network folder, you can add the printer(s) to any computer just by double-clicking the batch file icon. This capability can be a real time-saver when you're configuring many workstations. You could also put these commands in a common login script batch file on your network so that they are executed when your users log in.

CHAPTER 24

TROUBLESHOOTING YOUR NETWORK

In this chapter

When Good Networks Go Bad   786

Getting Started   786

Diagnostic Tools   788

Testing Network Cables   794

Checking Network Configuration   795

Testing Network Connectivity   797

Diagnosing File and Printer Sharing Problems   799

Tips from the Windows Pros: Monitoring Your LAN   799

When Good Networks Go Bad

As a part of my software consulting work, I end up doing a fair bit of network support for my clients. And every time I get a call from a client with a network problem, I cringe. I never know whether it's going to take 10 minutes or a week to fix. Sometimes the problem isn't so bad; I've fixed more than one "broken" computer by turning it on. If such an easy fix doesn't present itself immediately, though, a bit of a cold sweat breaks out on my forehead. The problem could be anything. How do you even start to find a nasty problem in the maze of cards, wires, drivers, and hidden, inexplicable system services? And it's difficult enough debugging the stuff that belongs there. What if viruses, adware, or rootkits are messing up the works?

Well, if you work for a corporation with a network support staff, of course, the answer to any of these questions is "Call the Help Desk!" or "Call Bob!" or call whoever or whatever is responsible for network problems in your organization and then take a refreshing walk around the block while someone else sweats over your network. It's great if you can get that kind of support. If you want to or have to go it alone, though, the good news is that some tools provided with Windows can help you find the problem. After discussing troubleshooting in general, this chapter shows you how to use these tools.

In reading this chapter, you probably won't find the solution to any particular network problem you're having. I can't really help you solve any one specific problem here, but I can show you some of the tools available to help you identify the source of a problem you might have.

Getting Started

As a consultant, I've spent many years helping clients with hardware, software, and network problems. One thing I've noticed is that the most common—and most frustrating—way people report a problem is to say "I can't…" or "The computer won't…". Unfortunately, knowing what *doesn't* happen isn't helpful at all. I always have to ask "What happens when you try…?" The answer to that question usually gets me well on the way to solving the problem. The original report usually leaves out important error messages and symptoms that might immediately identify the problem. So, start by trying to express whatever problem you're having in terms of what *is* happening, not what isn't.

And extending that principle, as you work on a problem, pay as much attention to what *does* work as to what doesn't. Knowing what isn't broken lets you eliminate whole categories of problems. For example, check to see whether a problem affects just one computer or all the computers on your local area network (LAN). If other computers can manage the task that one computer is having trouble with, you know that the problem is located *in that one computer*, or in its connection to the others.

The following are some other questions I always ask:

- Does the problem occur all the time or just sometimes?
- Can you reproduce the problem consistently? If you can define a procedure to reproduce the problem, can you reduce it to the shortest, most direct procedure possible?
- Has the system ever worked, even once? If so, when did it stop working, and what happened just before that? What changed?

These questions can help you determine whether the problem is fundamental (for example, due to a nonfunctioning network card) or interactive (that is, due to a conflict with other users, with new software, or confined to a particular subsystem of the network). You might be able to spot the problem right off the bat if you look at the scene this way. If you can't, you can use some tools to help narrow down the problem.

Generally, network problems fall into one or more of these categories:

- Application software
- Network clients
- Name-resolving services
- Network protocols
- Addressing and network configuration
- Driver software
- Network cards and hardware configuration
- Wiring/hubs

If you can determine which category a problem falls in, you're halfway there. At that point, diagnostic tools and good, old-fashioned deductive reasoning come into play.

You might be able to eliminate one or more categories right away. For example, if your computer can communicate with some other computers but not all of them, and your network uses a central hub, you can deduce that at least your computer's network card and the wiring from your computer to the hub are working properly.

Windows comes with some diagnostic tools to further help you narrow down the cause of a network problem. In the rest of this chapter, I outline these tools and suggest how to use them.

> **TIP**
>
> You might also peruse Chapter 17, "Troubleshooting Your Internet Connection," for tips on diagnosing network problems specific to the Internet (TCP/IP) protocol.

Diagnostic Tools

Each diagnostic tool described in this section serves to test the operation of one or more of the categories mentioned in the preceding section. The tools are discussed in roughly the order you should try them.

Some tools can be used to find problems in any of the many networking components. These tools quickly identify many problems.

The Network Window

You might not think of the Network window as a diagnostic tool, but it can be one. It will quickly tell you whether your computer's network discovery and file sharing features are turned on and whether your computer can communicate with any other computers on your LAN using Windows's file and printer sharing client services. If at least one other computer is visible and online, you can be pretty sure that your computer's network card and cabling are okay.

To use it, click Start, Network. The window that appears should look something like Figure 24.1, except that the names of the computers on your network will be different. My network also includes a router device, which also appears in this display because its Universal Plug and Play (UPnP) feature has been enabled.

Figure 24.1
The Network window shows whether your computer is communicating with other computers.

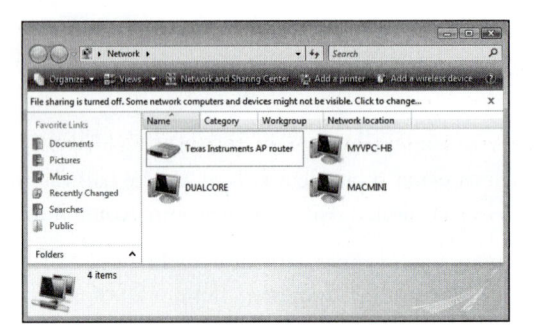

If you see at least one other computer besides your own displayed here, your computer's network cabling, network adapter, and drivers are working correctly.

An informational bar just above the list of icons may provide additional information about possible limitations to Windows networking. The bar is present in Figure 24.1, but if there is nothing to report, it won't appear on your computer. Here are some of the messages that might appear:

- **Network Discovery Is Turned Off**—This means the service that locates other computers is disabled, or that all incoming connections have been disabled in Windows Firewall. Either way, icons for other computers won't be shown, and if you really did want network discovery turned off or the firewall completely blocked, their absence on this screen doesn't mean that there is a problem. If you are connected to a safe network (for instance, a network in your home or office but *not* a public Internet café) and you want to be able to share files, click the message bar and then click Turn On Network Discovery and File Sharing. This will turn on both functions and open Windows Firewall. If you only want to use others' shared files, click Open Network and Sharing Center and enable just network discovery.

After you change the settings, view the Network window again and press the F5 key to refresh the display. Other computers should now appear.

- **File Sharing Is Turned Off**—This means that Windows file sharing is disabled on your computer. You can still use files and printers shared by other computers, but others cannot use files or printers shared by your computer. This isn't necessarily a problem, unless you do want to enable sharing. To do so, click the message bar and select Turn On Network Discovery and File Sharing.

- **This Computer Is Not Connected to a Network**—Your computer's network cable is disconnected, or your wireless connection isn't connected, or there may be a problem with your computer's network drivers. This is a fundamental problem: Your computer can't talk to any other computers.

Other messages could also appear. Click on the message to see what diagnostic and repair options Windows might offer.

If other computers still don't appear, and you know that network discovery is turned on and that Windows Firewall is open, it's possible that the network browser function, which is a behind-the-scenes service that Windows uses to locate other computers, is not working. This is a common problem. To investigate it, try these procedures:

- Wait 20 minutes and press the F5 key. Other computers may appear this time.
- Check each of the computers in your workgroup and make sure that each computer is set to use the same workgroup name and that each computer has the same set of network protocols installed. In particular, because Vista supports only TCP/IP, your other Windows computers should be reconfigured to use only TCP/IP and not IPX/SPX or NetBEUI.

→ For more information about networking with older versions of Windows, **see** "Networking with Other Operating Systems," **p. 664**.

The next step is to check the Network and Sharing Center to be sure that the network is enabled.

NETWORK AND SHARING CENTER

If other users can't use resources shared by your computer, the problem may be that the sharing services aren't enabled. You can get an overview of the networking services that Windows is providing from the Network and Sharing Center. To view it, click Start, Network. At the top of the Network window, click Network and Sharing Center. Figure 24.2 shows this window.

Figure 24.2
The Network and Sharing Center shows which networking services have been enabled.

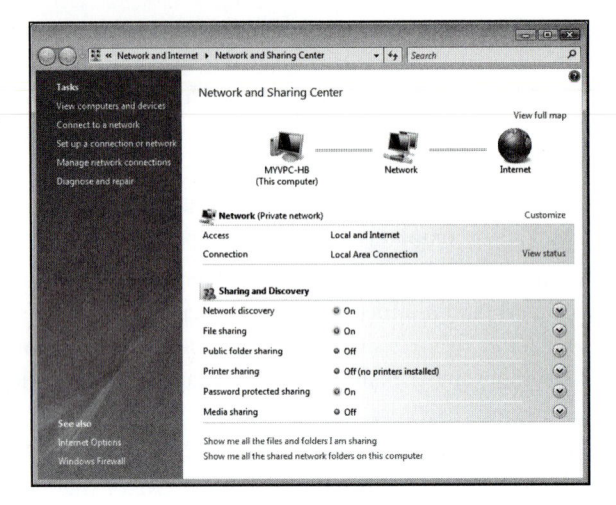

Check the list features at the bottom of the window to be sure that the features turned on are what you expect and want. The features are as follows:

Feature	If Set to On
Network Discovery	Your computer will appear in other computers' Network folders, and other computers will appear in yours.
File Sharing	You can share files from your computer with other computers.
Public Folder Sharing	Your computer's Public profile folder will be shared on the network.
Printer Sharing	You can share your computer's printers with other computers.
Password Protected Sharing	Users of other computers will have to provide the name of an account that's been set up on your computer, and the corresponding password, before they can use your shared files or printers. If set to Off, anyone on your network can see your shared files and use your shared printers.
Media Sharing	Your computer's shared media (music and video) can be played by other computers and by media player devices on the network.

These first two windows covered the basics. If there's still a problem, it's time to let Windows have a crack at solving it.

NETWORK DIAGNOSTICS

Windows Vista features a new network repair tool called Network Diagnostics that is said (by Microsoft) to be capable of recognizing and diagnosing more than 100 network problems. Windows Vista Service Pack 1 is said to improve the capabilities of Network Diagnostics even further. I'm skeptical of claims like this, but, on the other hand, it takes only a few seconds to let Network Diagnostics examine your network and offer whatever advice it can, so it's absolutely worth a crack.

To run the Network Diagnostics tool, click Start, Network. At the top of the Network window, click Network and Sharing Center to display the window shown in Figure 24.2. Then, in the task list at left, click Diagnose and Repair.

Windows will display a box that says "Identifying the problem..." and will then display a results window that explains what was found to be wrong, what Windows did about it (if anything), what the outcome was, and where to go for more assistance. Figure 24.3 shows a typical diagnosis result.

Figure 24.3
Network Diagnostics tries to present an explanation and a solution.

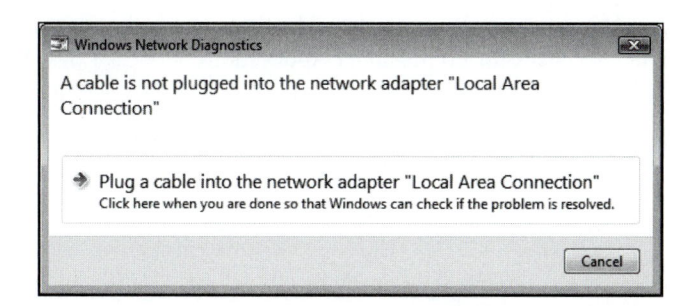

If the diagnostics tool doesn't solve your network problem, check Windows Firewall to be sure it isn't blocking a desired network service.

WINDOWS FIREWALL

Another configuration setting that could prevent file and printer sharing from working correctly is the Windows Firewall. To ensure that file and printer sharing isn't blocked, open the Windows Firewall window by clicking Start, Control Panel, Security, Windows Firewall. Then, click Change Settings and confirm the User Account Control prompt.

On the General tab, be sure that Windows Firewall is enabled (On is checked), and that Block All Incoming Connections is *not* checked. (This is unlikely to be the problem, however, because the Network window would have caught this, as discussed earlier in the section "The Network Window.")

> **NOTE**
> On Windows Vista, you do not have to set up an exception for file and printer sharing, and in fact sharing doesn't even appear on the Exceptions tab. Windows automatically opens an exception for file and printer sharing whenever you enable sharing in the Network and Sharing Center.

→ For more information about configuring the firewall, **see** "Configuring Windows Firewall," **p. 1230**.

If the firewall settings appear to be correct, the next step is to check the Windows Event Viewer, to see whether Windows has left a record of any network problems there.

Event Viewer

The Event Viewer is another important diagnostic tool and one of the first to check because Windows often silently records useful information about problems with hardware and software in its Event Log. To display the Event Log, click Start, right-click Computer, select Manage, confirm the User Account Control Prompt, and then select the Event Viewer system tool. Select Windows Logs, and examine the System, Application, and Security logs in turn. You might also check for events under Applications Services Logs, Microsoft, Windows.

The Event Viewer displays Event Log entries, most recent first, on the right (see Figure 24.4).

Figure 24.4
The Event Viewer might display important diagnostic information when you have network problems. View the System, Application, and Security logs in turn.

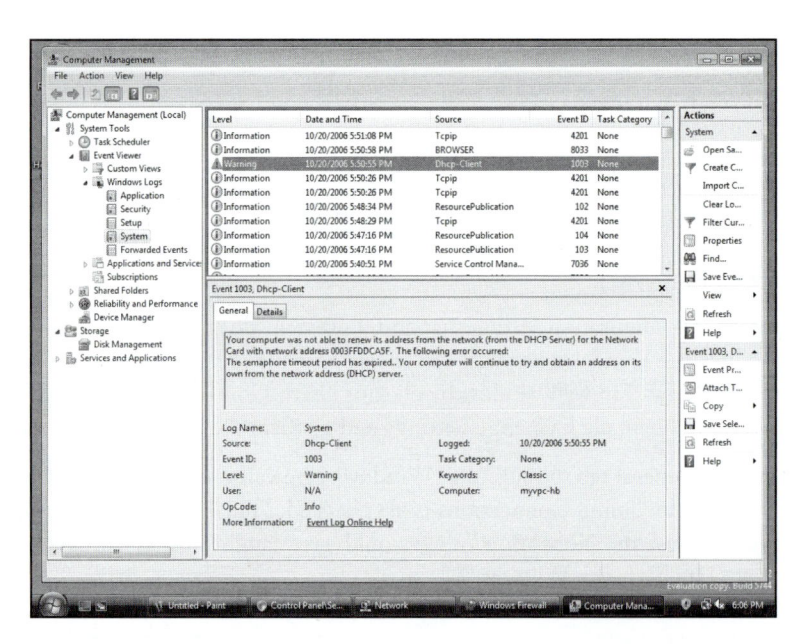

Log entries for serious errors are displayed with a red X in a circle; warnings appear with a yellow ! in a triangle. Informational entries (marked with a blue *i*) usually don't relate to problems. Double-click any error or warning entries in the log to view the detailed description and any associated data recorded with the entry. The Error entry in Figure 24.4 indicates that my computer couldn't acquire a network address in a reasonable amount of time. It turns out that my router had come unplugged.

These messages are usually significant and informative to help diagnose network problems; they may indicate that a network card is malfunctioning, that a domain controller for authentication or a DHCP server for configuration can't be found, and so on. The Source column in the error log indicates which Windows component or service recorded the event.

These names are usually fairly cryptic. Table 24.1 lists a few of the more common nonobvious ones.

TABLE 24.1 NETWORK SOURCES OF EVENT LOG ENTRIES

Source	Description
NetBT	Client for Microsoft Networks
MrxSmb	Client for Microsoft Networks
Browser	Name resolution system for Client for Microsoft Networks
Application Popup	(Can come from any system utility; these warning messages are usually significant.)
RemoteAccess	Dial-up networking
W32Time	Computer clock synchronization service
Dnsapi	DNS client component
Dnscache	DNS client component
atapi	IDE hard disk/CD-ROM controller

If you're at a loss to solve the problem even with the information given, check the configuration of the indicated component, or remove and reinstall it to see whether you can clear up the problem.

→ To learn more details about the Event Log, **see** "Event Viewer," **p. 876**.

> **TIP**
> A problem with one network system usually causes other problems. Therefore, the oldest error message in a closely timed sequence of errors is usually the most significant; subsequent errors are just a result of the first failure. Because the Event Log is ordered most-recent-first, you might get the most useful information down a bit from the top of the list.

> **TIP**
> The real cause of your problem might reveal itself at system startup time rather than when you observe the problem. Reboot your system, and note the time. Then reproduce the problem. Check the Event Log for messages starting at the reboot time.

DEVICE MANAGER

Hardware problems with your network card will most likely be recorded in the Event Log. If you suspect that your network card is the culprit, and nothing is recorded in the Event Log, check the Device Manager.

To use it, click Start, right-click Computer, select Manage, confirm the User Account Control prompt, and choose the Device Manager system tool. Any devices with detectable hardware problems or configuration conflicts appear with a yellow ! icon when you display the Device Manager. If no yellow icons appear, you don't have a *detected* hardware problem. This doesn't mean that you don't have a problem, but the odds are slim that your network card is the problem.

If devices are shown with ! icons, double-click the device name to see the Windows explanation of the device status and any problems. A device that you've told Windows not to use (disabled) will have a red X on it; this is generally not a problem.

→ For more detailed instructions and tips on device troubleshooting, **see** Chapter 28, "Troubleshooting and Repairing Problems," **p. 961**.

Testing Network Cables

If your computer can't communicate with any other on your LAN, and the Device Manager doesn't indicate a faulty network card, you *might* have a wiring problem. Wiring problems can be the most difficult to solve because it's difficult to prove that data is leaving one computer but not arriving at another. The `ping` program, discussed later in this chapter, can help with this problem.

→ To learn how you can use the `ping` command to diagnose Internet-related problems, as opposed to LAN problems, **see** "ping," **p. 545**.

If your computer is not properly wired into the LAN, in many cases, Windows displays an offline icon right on the system tray and indicates that your network card is disconnected. It might not, though, so you shouldn't take a lack of this kind of message to mean that no wiring problems exist.

If your network uses UTP cabling plugged in to a hub, there's usually a green LED indicator on each network card and at each port on the hub. Be sure that the lights are on at each end of your network cable and those for the other computers on your LAN.

You also can use inexpensive (about $75) cable test devices that check for continuity and correct pin-to-pin wiring order for UTP wiring. They come as a set of two boxes. One gets plugged in to each end of a given cable run, and a set of blinking lights tells you whether all four wire pairs are connected and in the correct order. (If you install your own network cabling and/or make your own patch cables, these tools are handy to have to check your work.)

> **NOTE**
>
> If you really want to get into the guts of your network cabling or are planning a major installation and want to learn more details so that you can oversee a professional installation, I recommend that you read *Networking with Microsoft Windows Vista* by Paul McFedries, published by Que.

Checking Network Configuration

If hardware isn't at fault, you may have a fundamental network configuration problem. Often the Event Log or Device Manager gives these problems away, but if they don't, you can use another batch of tools to check the computer's network configuration.

ipconfig

If your computer can't communicate with others on your LAN, after you check the Event Log and Device Manager, use the `ipconfig` command-line utility to see whether your computer has a valid IP address. Check other computers on the LAN, too, to ensure that they do as well.

At the command prompt (which you open by choosing Start, All Programs, Accessories, Command Prompt), type the following command:

`ipconfig /all`

The results should look something like this:

```
Windows IP Configuration
    Host Name . . . . . . . . . . . . : myvpc-hb
    Primary Dns Suffix  . . . . . . . : mycompany.com
    Node Type . . . . . . . . . . . . : Hybrid
    IP Routing Enabled. . . . . . . . : Yes
    WINS Proxy Enabled. . . . . . . . : No

Ethernet adapter Local Area Connection:
    Connection-specific DNS Suffix  . :
    Description . . . . . . . . . . . : Intel 21140-Based PCI Fast Ethernet Adapter
    Physical Address. . . . . . . . . : 00-03-FF-DD-CA-5F
    DHCP Enabled. . . . . . . . . . . : Yes
    Autoconfiguration Enabled . . . . : Yes
    Link-local IPv6 Address . . . . . : fe80::ed10:dff9:693c:803d%8(Preferred)
    IPv4 Address. . . . . . . . . . . : 192.168.15.108(Preferred)
    Subnet Mask . . . . . . . . . . . : 255.255.255.0
    Lease Obtained. . . . . . . . . . : Friday, October 20, 2006 5:55:11 PM
    Lease Expires . . . . . . . . . . : Friday, October 27, 2006 5:55:23 PM
    Default Gateway . . . . . . . . . : 192.168.15.1
    DHCP Server . . . . . . . . . . . : 192.168.15.1
    DHCPv6 IAID . . . . . . . . . . . : 201327615
    DNS Servers . . . . . . . . . . . : 192.168.15.1
    NetBIOS over Tcpip. . . . . . . . : Enabled
```

(Unless you're troubleshooting IPv6 Teredo connections, ignore the parts that mention Tunnel adapters.)

The most important items to look for are the following:

- **Host name**—This should be set to the desired name for each computer. If you can correspond with some computers but not others, be sure that the ones that don't work are turned on and correctly named. Make sure that you don't have two computers with the same name, and that none of the computer names is the same as the workgroup name.

- **IP address**—This should be set appropriately for your network. If your LAN uses Internet Connection Sharing, the address will be a number in the range 192.168.0.1

through 192.168.0.254. If your LAN uses DHCP for automatic configuration, your network manager can tell you whether the IP address is correct. Networks with cable/DSL sharing routers *usually* use numbers starting with 192.168.x where x is a number from 0 to 15.

If you see a number in the range 169.254.0.1 through 169.254.255.254, your computer is set for automatic configuration, but no DHCP server was found, so Windows has chosen an IP address by itself. This is fine if your LAN uses this automatic configuration system. However, if there should have been a DHCP server, or if you use Internet Connection Sharing or a hardware Internet Connection router, this is a problem. Restart the ICS computer or the router, and then restart your computer and try again.

- **Network mask**—This usually looks like 255.255.255.0, but other settings are possible. At the least, all computers on the same LAN should have the same network mask.

Each computer on the same LAN should have a similar valid IP address and the same network mask. If they don't, check your network configuration. The built-in Windows "Repair" function may also be used to help fix problems with DHCP-based (automatic) IP address assignment.

> **NOTE**
>
> To learn more about IP addressing, network masks, and configuration, visit support.microsoft.com and search for article number 164015, which is titled "Understanding TCP/IP Addressing and Subnetting Basics."

COMPUTER

You can check your computer's identification and workgroup or domain membership setup from the Computer window. To do so, click Start, Computer. Look in the Details pane at the bottom of the screen for the computer name and domain or workgroup name, as shown in Figure 24.5.

Figure 24.5
Your computer's name and workgroup or domain membership is displayed at the bottom of the Computer window.

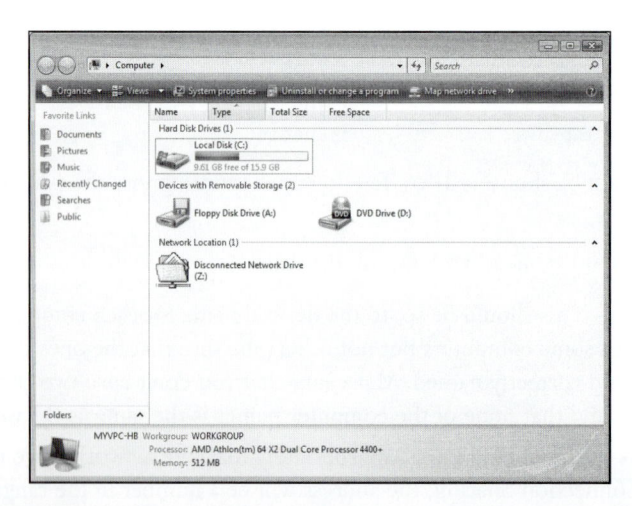

On a Windows Workgroup network, the workgroup name should be the same on all computers on your workgroup LAN. All of the computer names *must* be different from each other.

> **NOTE**
> None of your computers can use the workgroup or domain name as its computer name. For example, if your workgroup is MSHOME, you can't also name a computer MSHOME. If you find this on one of your computers, change that computer's name.

On a Windows domain network, you should see your computer's name displayed as part of a Windows domain name (for example, my computer named `myvpc-hb` would be called `myvpc-hb.mycompany.com` on a domain network) and the domain name. Your domain name might not include `.com`. It might say `.local` instead, or may use a different ending. In any case, be sure that your computer is actually a domain member. If the word "workgroup" appears instead, your computer is not a domain member and will not be able to use domain logins or some domain resources.

Network Connections

You can manually check all installed network protocols and services and their configuration by viewing Network Connections and viewing the properties for Local Area Connection. To view this screen, click Start, Network. At the top of the Network window, click Network and Sharing Center. In the left pane of that window, click Manage Network Settings. Then, right-click your Local Area Connection icon (or the appropriate wireless connection icon) and select Properties.

Confirm that each required protocol is installed and correctly configured. In general, the settings on each computer on your LAN should match, except that the IP address differs (usually only in the last of its four dot-separated numbers). If your LAN uses Automatic IP address configuration, you need to use the `ipconfig` command, described earlier, to check the settings.

Testing Network Connectivity

A few tools can help you determine whether the network can send data between computers; these tools test the network protocols as well as low-level network hardware layers.

ping

`ping` is a fundamental tool for testing TCP/IP network connectivity. Because most networks today use the Internet (TCP/IP) protocol for file and printer sharing services, as well as for Internet access, most Windows users can use the `ping` test to confirm that their network cabling, hardware, and the TCP/IP protocol are all functioning correctly. Ping sends several data packets to a specified computer and waits for the other computer to send the packets back. By default, it sends four packets and prints the results of the four tests.

To see whether the network can carry data between a pair of computers, use the `ipconfig` command (described previously) to find the IP address of the two computers. Then, on one computer, open a command prompt window by choosing Start, All Programs, Accessories, Command Prompt.

Next, type the following command:

ping 127.0.0.1

This command tests the networking software of the computer itself by sending packets to the special internal IP address 127.0.0.1. This test has the computer send data to itself. It should print the following:

```
Reply from 127.0.0.1: bytes=32 time<10ms TTL=128
Reply from 127.0.0.1: bytes=32 time<10ms TTL=128
Reply from 127.0.0.1: bytes=32 time<10ms TTL=128
Reply from 127.0.0.1: bytes=32 time<10ms TTL=128
```

If it doesn't, the TCP/IP protocol itself is incorrectly installed or configured; check the computer's IP address configuration, or, if that seems correct, remove and reinstall the Internet Protocol from Local Area Connection in Network Connections. (I have to say, in more than 10 years of working with PC networks, I've never seen this test fail.)

If your computer can send data to itself, try another computer on your LAN. Find its IP address by running `ipconfig` on that computer and then issue the `ping` command again on the first computer, as in this example:

ping 192.168.0.23

Of course, you should use the other computer's real IP address in place of 192.168.0.23. You should get four replies as before:

```
Reply from 192.168.0.23: bytes=32 time<10ms TTL=32
Reply from 192.168.0.23: bytes=32 time<10ms TTL=32
Reply from 192.168.0.23: bytes=32 time<10ms TTL=32
Reply from 192.168.0.23: bytes=32 time<10ms TTL=32
```

These replies indicate that you have successfully sent data to the other machine and received it back.

If, on the other hand, the `ping` command returns `Request timed out`, the packets either didn't make it to the other computer or they were not returned. In either case, you have a problem with your cabling, network adapter, or the TCP/IP protocol setup.

You can use `ping` to determine which computers can send to which other computers on your LAN or across wide area networks (WANs) or the Internet. `ping` works when given a computer's IP address or its network name.

> **NOTE**
>
> If you enter a computer name, and `ping` can't determine the computer's IP address, the problem isn't necessarily a wiring problem—it could be that the DNS or WINS name lookup systems are not working correctly. Try using an IP address with `ping` in this case to help determine what the problem really is.

Diagnosing File and Printer Sharing Problems

If the tests in the previous section don't point to a problem—that is, if basic network connectivity is fine but you're still having problems with file or printer sharing, the next step depends on whether you have a workgroup or domain-type network.

If you're on a domain network, it's time to call your network administrator for assistance. They've had more training and experience in network troubleshooting than I can impart in the space allowed here.

If you're on a home or small office workgroup network, there are a few things you might try. Here are some tips:

- Did you make sure that file sharing is enabled on each of your computers?
- If you use Internet Connection Sharing, restart the computer that's sharing your Internet connection and wait a minute or two after it's booted up. Then, restart your other computers. This may help. The ICS computer needs to be up and running *before* any other computers on your LAN start up.
- If you don't see other computers in the Network window, wait 10 to 20 minutes (really) and then select View, Refresh or press F5. Sometimes it takes up to 20 minutes for the list of online computers to be updated.

Tips from the Windows Pros: Monitoring Your LAN

As businesses increasingly rely on computers by the thousands, flung far and wide around the globe, the job of managing them—that is, monitoring, identifying, and correcting problems—has become an industry of its own. *Enterprise management* is a hot expression in the computer industry. *Very* pricey software systems have been developed to centrally monitor computers, networks, hubs, routing hardware, UPSes, and even computer room fire alarms. These systems detect problems and can notify staff via pager, email, and printouts.

The purpose of these systems is to catch problems as they develop, and with any luck, before they disrupt people trying to do their work. Instrumentation is the key here: Equipment has to be designed to be monitored. A TCP/IP-based protocol called Simple Network Management Protocol (SNMP) has been around for years, and "managed" network equipment is capable of being probed and reconfigured via SNMP. The Link Layer Discovery Protocol (LLDP) included with Windows Vista is another effort in this direction. Along with this capability comes a hefty price tag, but the net cost of maintaining and dispatching staff to fix problems is much greater.

My small LAN with four users and a handful of development and online servers doesn't need a $20,000 management system, managed hubs, and the like. But, even in my little office, I find myself constantly checking to make sure that the servers are up, that they have plenty of disk space, and that the Internet connection is working. What I really want is something to check these things periodically and let me know whether something's amiss.

I guess plenty of other people do, too. Free enterprise is a wonderful thing. I searched the Web and found a handful of packages targeted for small LANs just like mine. If you have a LAN you depend on for your business, you might want to check them out. Hearing about a problem from your pager is a lot nicer than hearing about it from a client or an employee!

Using these products, you can specify a series of computers or devices to be periodically tested. The tests can include `ping`, SNMP, file sharing services, Windows Service activity, disk space availability, server responsiveness, and so on. Failures can be announced to a list of alert recipients via pager, email, or printout. (Different problems may call for different announcement methods, of course. If your LAN is down, an email alert won't get delivered.) Some products can even send announcements to selected employees based on their work schedules.

Using these tools, you can enter a list of your most important network servers and other resources, and rest assured that if something goes wrong with any of them, you'll be notified immediately.

The following are a few products worth investigating. These programs or services can detect whether a remote server is active, test various types of network services (for example, file sharing, web services, and so on), and send an email or a pager message if a failure occurs:

- **PA Server Monitor**—www.poweradmin.com/ServerMonitor (Pro, Lite and Free versions available)
- **IPSentry**—www.ipsentry.com
- **Servers Alive**—www.woodstone.nu/salive/

It's best, if possible, to use a monitoring program that runs as a Windows service so that it can do its job even while nobody is logged in to the monitoring computer.

These products are not quite as sophisticated or well designed as their $20,000 cousins, but they might be just the ticket for a small business.

PART **VI**

MAINTAINING WINDOWS VISTA

25 Windows Management and Maintenance   803

26 Tweaking the GUI   897

27 Managing Hard Disks   929

28 Troubleshooting and Repairing Problems   961

29 Keeping Windows and Other Software Up To Date   985

30 Installing and Replacing Hardware   1009

31 Editing the Registry   1037

32 Command-Line and Automation Tools   1069

CHAPTER 25

WINDOWS MANAGEMENT AND MAINTENANCE

In this chapter

Overview   804

The Windows Vista Control Panel   804

AutoPlay   820

Date and Time   821

Default Programs   823

Device Manager   825

Understanding and Resolving Hardware Conflicts   827

Ease of Access Center   837

Fonts   841

Game Controllers   846

Keyboard   847

Mouse   847

Performance Information and Tools   850

Reliability and Performance Monitor   857

System Diagnostics Report   860

Power Options   860

Programs and Features   861

Regional and Language Options   867

System   868

Windows SideShow   872

Administrative Tools   872

Computer Management   874

Services   880

Task Scheduler   881

System Configuration   881

Task Manager   883

System Information   889

Adjust Visual Effects and Performance Options   890

Using the iSCSI Initiator   891

System Tools Folder in Start Menu   892

Troubleshooting   895

Tips from the Windows Pros: Creating and Using Shortcuts to Your Favorite Control Panel Applets   895

Overview

Windows Vista incorporates the most powerful set of management and diagnostic utilities yet seen in a desktop version of Windows. Although Windows Vista offers many new and improved tools, they work in (mostly) familiar ways. In Vista, there's as much emphasis on helping you use familiar tools in better ways as on the creation of new tools. The emphasis on a new and improved interface for a mix of familiar and new tools begins with the Control Panel, which is where many (although not all) management and maintenance tasks are performed.

In addition to the Control Panel, however, Vista's management and diagnostic tools can also be found in the following locations:

- Administrative tools
- System tools
- Command-line programs
- Maintenance
- Computer Management
- Registry Editor

In this chapter, we give you a tour of all of these management tools, except the Registry Editor, which is the sole topic of Chapter 31, "Editing the Registry." Many of the other tools we show you are discussed in more detail in other chapters; we point this out as we go.

The Windows Vista Control Panel

Just as with previous Windows versions, the Control Panel is the central location for making systemwide modifications to everything from accessibility options to user profiles. And although the Category view introduced in Windows XP was merely annoying, in Vista, Microsoft somehow found a way to make it—in addition—disorienting, obtuse, and nearly incomprehensible. The Vista Control Panel is organized as a very wordy web page, with links to access virtually every individual Conrol Panel applet from one or more (mostly) logical categories that also include shortcuts to the most commonly used utilities. To help you make sense of and navigate through this "new and improved" Category view, see Table 25.1 in the next section.

As with previous versions of Control Panel, some items are simply a shortcut to operations you can perform in other ways. For example, you can adjust display and audio properties settings by right-clicking the desktop and selecting Personalize, or you can use the Appearance and Personalization category in the Control Panel. However, Control Panel is also the home of applets that are not available elsewhere, such as the new iSCSI Initiator and new Parental Controls.

As with previous versions, the preference settings you make via the Control Panel applets are stored in the Registry. Some are systemwide, whereas others are made on a per-user basis and go into effect the next time you log in.

Keep in mind that you must have administrator-level access to modify many of the settings in the Control Panel. User-level settings such as display appearances are not a big deal. However, systemwide settings such as the addition and removal of hardware are governed by the security monitor, and you must have the requisite permissions to successfully make modifications. As you use the Control Panel, expect to see the User Account Control (UAC) dialog box appear frequently.

→ For more information on User Account Control, **see** "User Account Control (UAC)," **p. 1144**.

> **TIP**
>
> By default, the Control Panel displays as a window when you click Start and select the Control Panel. However, you can also configure the Control Panel to display as a fly-out menu from the Start menu (a huge time-saver if you ask us). To make this your default setting, right-click the Start menu and select Properties. In the dialog box that appears, click Customize; then select the Display As a Menu radio button under the Control Panel in the list of Start menu items. Control Panel items are displayed individually, as in Classic mode.
>
> If you use a particular applet a lot, you can drag it into the Start menu or the Quick Launch bar for even faster access. Dragging an applet to the Start menu or Quick Launch bar doesn't actually move the applet. Rather, it creates a shortcut.

Not all Control Panel settings are discussed in detail in this chapter. Because a few Control Panel options pertain to other topics, such as networking or printing, or fall under the umbrella of system management, performance tweaking, or system applications, you'll find them in later chapters. Table 25.1, in the next section, lists each applet and where to look in this book for coverage of those not discussed here. Also, I won't bore you by covering each and every option in the dialog boxes. Many settings are intuitively obvious.

BREAKING DOWN THE CATEGORY VIEW

Although Windows Vista, like Windows XP, defaults to the Category view, the categories and their contents are much different in Vista than in its predecessor.

There are 10 standard categories in the Category view on a desktop computer, and 11 on a mobile PC (such as a laptop or Tablet PC). One of these categories, Additional Options, appears only when you install some third-party programs that add applets to the Control Panel, such as Apple's QuickTime, Sun's Java, and so forth. (Some third-party applets are installed instead into one of the standard categories.) The Mobile PC category is not present on desktop computers. Virtually every Control Panel applet in Windows Vista can be accessed from one or more categories.

> **NOTE**
>
> If you need to access a Control Panel option that's available only in Classic view (such as Add Hardware), or if you just plain prefer the Classic view, you can get to Classic view by opening the Control Panel and clicking Classic View (see Figure 25.1).

Tables 25.1 through 25.8 list the tasks for each category. These are listed in the order of appearance, from top left to bottom right, not alphabetically. Figures 25.1 through 25.11 show each Control Panel category view.

In the tables, the **NEW** icon indicates that the item is new in Windows Vista. In the Control Panel screens, items featuring the Windows Vista Security shield indicate that the item is protected by User Account Control; standard users must provide a password from an administrator account to open these items.

Figure 25.1
The Control Panel in the default Category view (top) and in the Classic view (bottom).

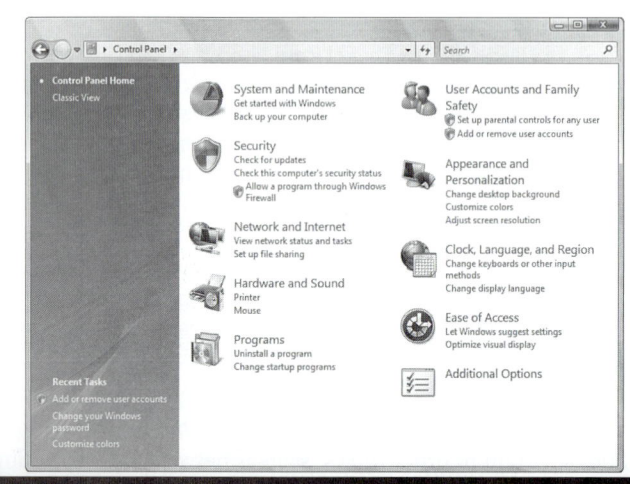

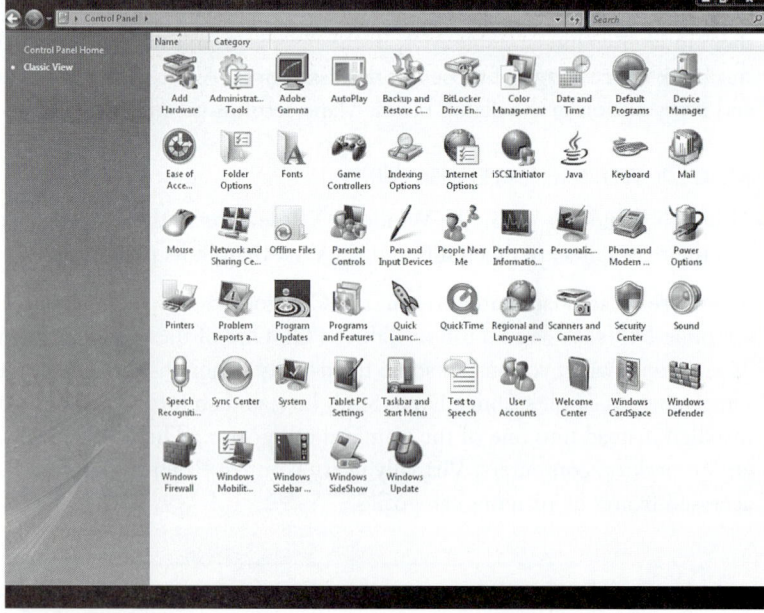

The Windows Vista Control Panel

Table 25.1 System and Maintenance Category View

Applet or Subcategory	Tasks
Welcome Center **NEW**	Welcomes users to Windows, provides shortcuts to common tasks for new users and offers from Microsoft
Backup and Restore Center **NEW**	File backup/restore services; Business and Ultimate versions also offer Complete PC (disaster recovery) backup/restore
System	Displays processor speed, Windows Experience Index, remote access, other system properties
Windows Update	Configures delivery and installation of updates to Windows and Microsoft applications
Power Options	Manages power settings for laptop and desktop systems
Indexing Options **NEW**	Configures Windows search and index settings
Problem Reports and Solutions **NEW**	Configures Windows problem and solution service
Performance Information and Tools **NEW**	Displays Windows Experience score and provides tips for improving performance
Device Manager	Manage onboard and connected hardware and drivers
Administrative Tools	Tools for managing advanced features and diagnosing system problems

Figure 25.2
Clicking the System and Maintenance category takes you to this screen.

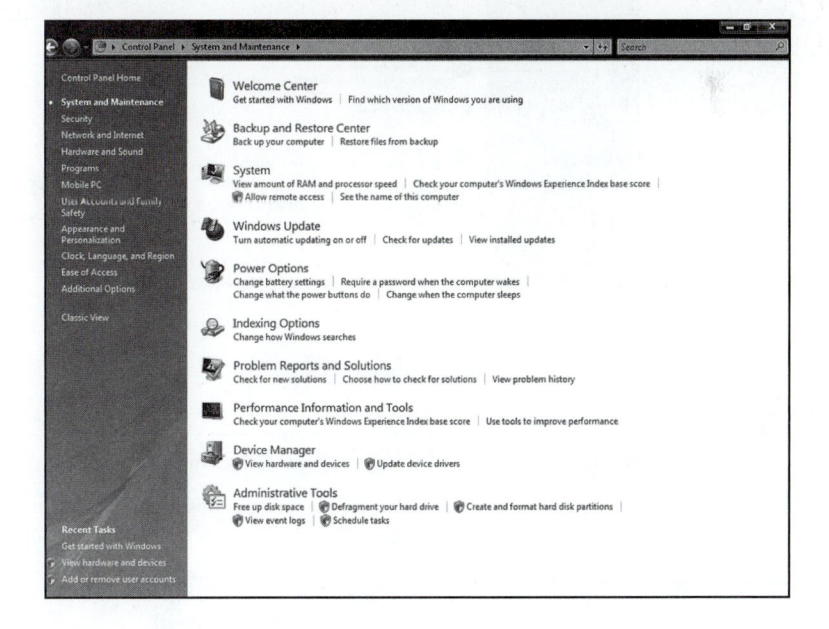

Table 25.2 Security Category View[1]

Applet or Subcategory	Tasks
Security Center	Displays security settings (firewall, antivirus, others)
Windows Firewall	Configures Windows Firewall
Windows Update	Configures update settings
Windows Defender NEW	Integrated antispyware application
Internet Options	Configures security, connection, and other settings for Internet Explorer 7 and other MS applications
Parental Controls NEW	Configures parental control features
BitLocker Drive Encryption NEW	Encrypts drive's contents to protect against unauthorized use (available in Ultimate and Enterprise only)

[1] Windows Ultimate users who have installed the BitLocker and EFS Enhancements Ultimate Extra will also see an additional item, Secure Online Key Backup. This stores BitLocker recovery key or EFS certificates in a secure online location.

Figure 25.3
Clicking the Security category takes you to this screen.

Table 25.3 Network and Internet Category

Applet or Subcategory	Tasks
Network and Sharing Center NEW	Displays and configures network status and settings
Internet Options	Configures security, connection, and other settings for Internet Explorer 7 and other MS applications
Offline Files	Configures offline file settings
Windows Firewall	Configures Windows Firewall
People Near Me NEW	Locates other network users for use with Windows Collaboration
Sync Center NEW	Synchronizes files with other computers and devices

Figure 25.4
Clicking the Network and Internet category takes you to this screen.

TABLE 25.4 HARDWARE AND SOUND CATEGORY

Major Features	Description
Printers	Adds and configures printers and fax devices
AutoPlay NEW	Configures AutoPlay settings for supported devices
Sound	Configures audio hardware and system sounds
Mouse	Configures pointers, mouse performance, and other features
Power Options	Configures power plans, power buttons
Personalization NEW	Adjust visual effects, display settings, and sound effects
Scanners and Cameras	Displays connected imaging devices
Keyboard	Configures keyboard hardware
Device Manager	Displays devices and their resource usage, updates or rolls back drivers
Phone and Modem Options	Configures phone and modem dialing rules and devices
Game Controllers	Configures USB-based game controllers
Windows SideShow NEW	Sets up PocketPC or other devices as secondary displays for Windows SideShow
Pen and Input Devices NEW	Configures tablet and pen devices
Color Management	Color calibration for display and output devices
Tablet PC Settings NEW	Configures Tablet PC screen and input devices

Figure 25.5
Clicking the Hardware and Sound category takes you to this screen.

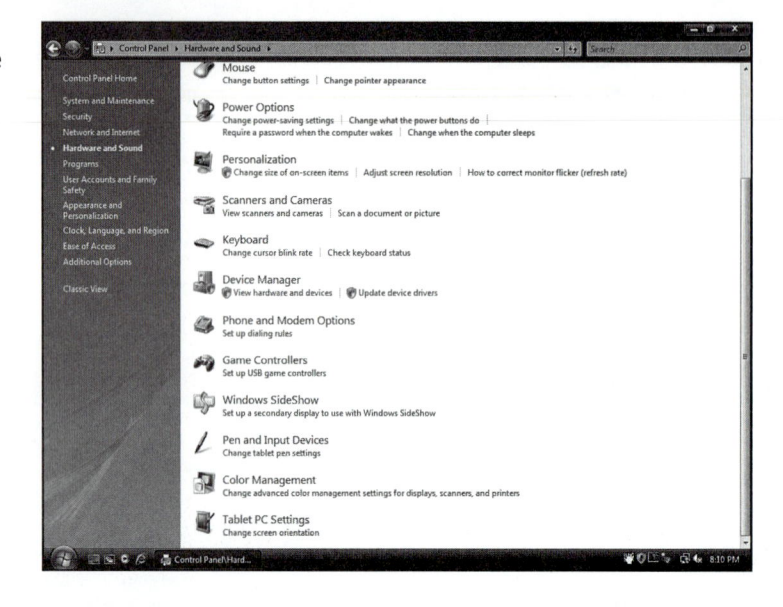

Table 25.5 Programs Category View

Major Features	Description
Programs and Features	Installs, enables, and removes Windows features and applications
Windows Defender	Integrated antispyware application
Default Programs	Configures startup and default programs and file types
Windows SideShow **NEW**	Configures Windows SideShow, which uses a secondary display to display email, media, or other information
Windows Sidebar Properties **NEW**	Configures Windows Sidebar and installs gadgets for Sidebar
Get Programs Online	Purchases and manages purchased programs online at Windows Marketplace

Figure 25.6
Clicking the Programs category takes you to this screen.

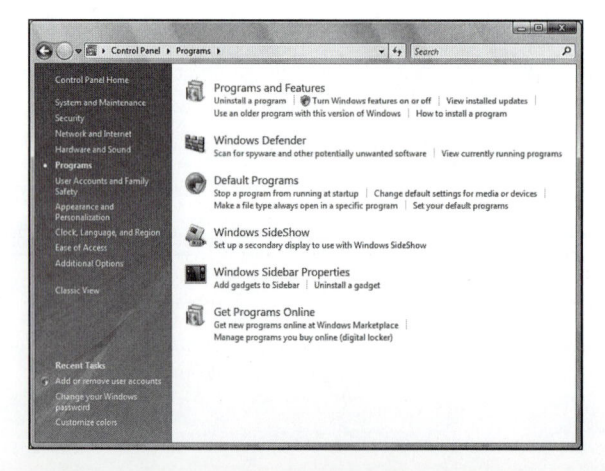

The Windows Vista Control Panel

TABLE 25.6 MOBILE PC CATEGORY VIEW

Major Features	Description
Windows Mobility Center NEW	Configures power, audio, network, synchronization, presentation, and other settings for laptops and Tablet PCs
Power Options	Configures power management and power buttons
Personalization NEW	Configures display and audio settings
Tablet PC Settings NEW	Configures handwriting recognition, screen orientation, and other settings for Tablet PCs
Pen and Input Devices NEW	Configures Tablet PC pen settings
Sync Center NEW	Configures synchronization settings

Figure 25.7
On a laptop or Tablet PC, clicking the Mobile PC category takes you to this screen.

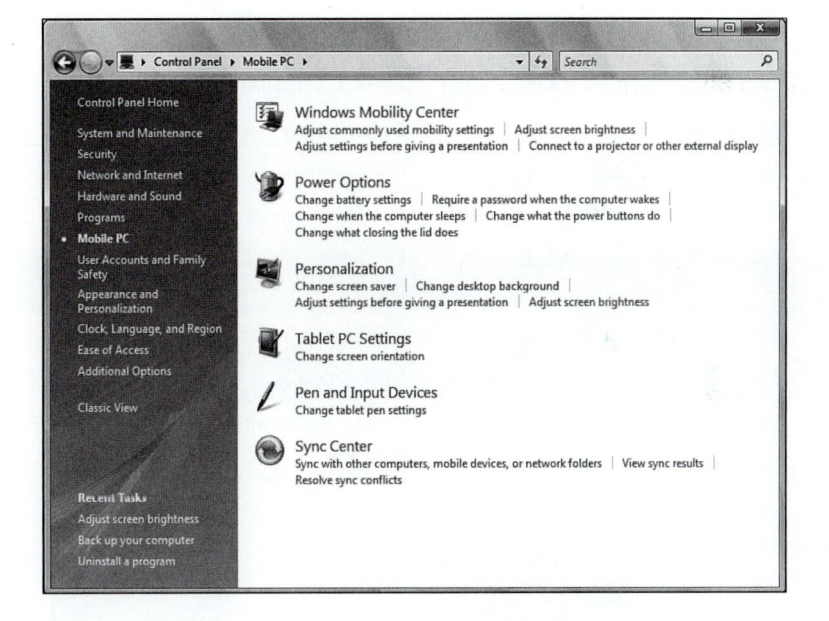

TABLE 25.7 USER ACCOUNTS AND FAMILY SAFETY CATEGORY[1]

Major Features	Description
User Accounts	Creates and configures user accounts and passwords
Parental Controls NEW	Configures parental controls and displays reports
Windows CardSpace NEW (previously called Digital Identities)	Creates and configures Information Cards for logging in to password-protected sites

[1]Systems running Microsoft Office 2003 may also display a Mail applet in this category; it is used to configure Microsoft Outlook. This applet is not part of Windows Vista.

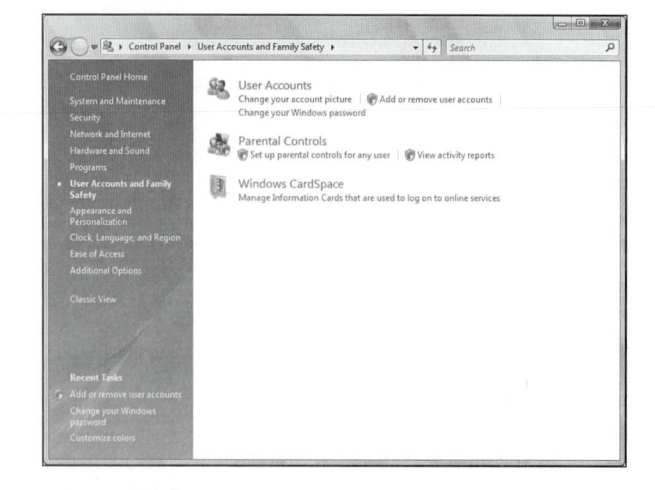

Figure 25.8
Clicking the User Accounts and Family Safety category takes you to this screen.

TABLE 25.8   APPEARANCE AND PERSONALIZATION CATEGORY

Major Features	Description
Personalization NEW	Configures visual effects, display settings, and sound effects
Taskbar and Start Menu	Configures appearance of taskbar and Start menu
Ease of Access Center NEW	Configures user interface for users with limited vision or hearing
Folder Options	Configures folder settings
Fonts	Views, installs, removes fonts
Windows Sidebar Properties NEW	Configures Windows Sidebar and installs gadgets for Sidebar

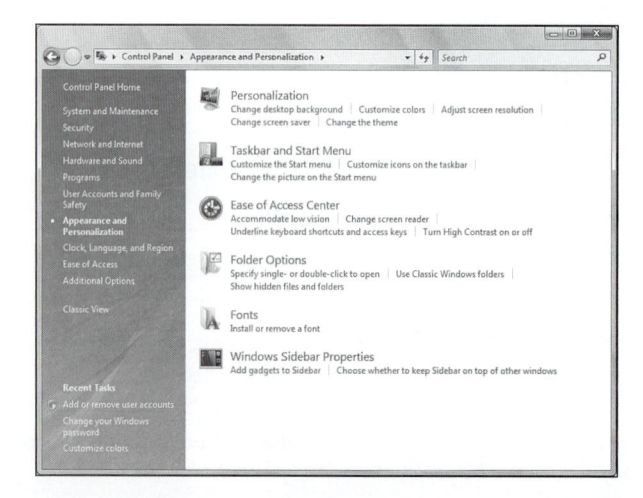

Figure 25.9
Clicking the Appearance and Personalization category takes you to this screen.

THE WINDOWS VISTA CONTROL PANEL | 813

TABLE 25.9   CLOCK, LANGUAGE, AND REGION CATEGORY

Major Features	Description
Date and Time	Sets date, time, time zone; adds additional clocks; time synchronization
Regional and Language Options	Selects default language, location, keyboard settings

Figure 25.10
Clicking the Clock, Language, and Region category takes you to this screen.

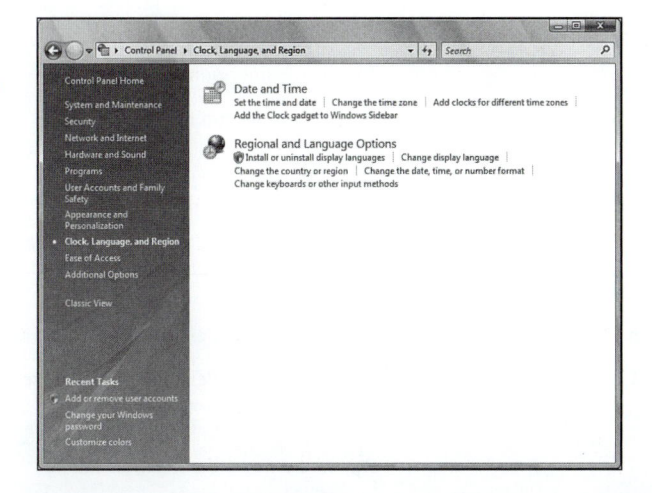

TABLE 25.10   EASE OF ACCESS CATEGORY

Major Features	Description
Ease of Access Center	Configures user interface for users with limited vision or hearing
Speech Recognition Options	Configures speech recognition and microphone

Figure 25.11
Clicking the Ease of Access category takes you to this screen.

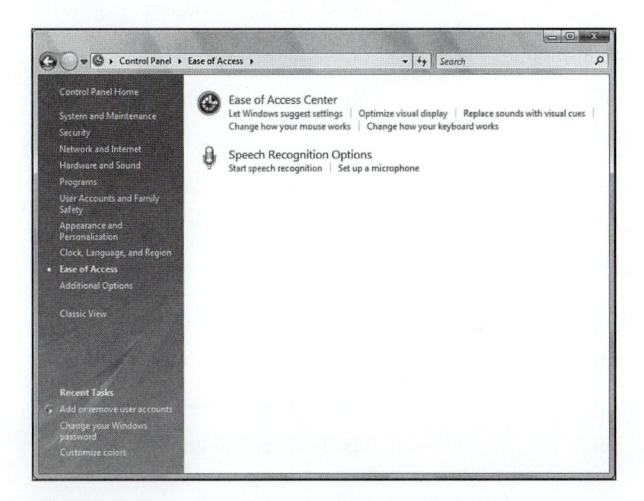

25

Virtually every Control Panel Classic view applet can be accessed from one or more categories. However, a few can be accessed only from Classic view. Classic view applets are listed and cross-referenced to their respective categories in Table 25.11.

TABLE 25.11 Control Panel Classic Mode Applets and Categories

Applet	Also Found in This Category
Add Hardware	—
Administrative Tools	System and Maintenance
AutoPlay	Hardware and Sound
Backup and Restore Center	System and Maintenance
BitLocker Drive Encryption	Security
Color Management	Hardware and Sound
Date and Time	Clock, Language, and Region
Default Programs	Programs
Device Manager	System and Maintenance, Hardware and Sound
Ease of Access Center	Appearance and Personalization, Ease of Access
Folder Options	Appearance and Personalization
Fonts	Appearance and Personalization
Game Controllers	Hardware and Sound
Indexing Options	System and Maintenance
Internet Options	Security, Network, and Internet
iSCSI Initiator	Administrative Tools submenu of System and Maintenance
Keyboard	Hardware and Sound
Mouse	Hardware and Sound
Network and Sharing Center	Network and Internet
Offline Files	Network and Internet
Parental Controls	User Accounts and Family Safety
Pen and Input Devices	Hardware and Sound
People Near Me	Network and Internet
Performance Information and Tools	System and Maintenance
Personalization	Appearance and Personalization
Phone and Modem Options	Hardware and Sound
Power Options	Hardware and Sound
Printers	Hardware and Sound

TABLE 25.11 CONTINUED	
Applet	**Also Found in This Category**
Problem Reports and Solutions	System and Maintenance
Programs and Features	Programs
Regional and Language Options	Clock, Language, and Region
Scanners and Cameras	Hardware and Sound
Security Center	Security
Sound	Hardware and Sound
Speech Recognition Options	Ease of Access
Sync Center	Network and Internet
System	System and Maintenance
Tablet PC Settings	Hardware and Sound
Taskbar and Start Menu	Appearance and Personalization
Text to Speech	Ease of Access Speech Recognition Options (task)
User Accounts	User Accounts and Family Safety
Welcome Center	System and Maintenance
Windows CardSpace	User Accounts and Family Safety
Windows Defender	Programs
Windows Firewall	Security
Windows Sidebar	Appearance and Personalization
Windows SideShow	Hardware and Sound
Windows Update	System and Maintenance

You can use either the Category view or the Classic view to access virtually every feature of the Control Panel. If you prefer the Classic view, click Classic view from the Quick List in the Control Panel's opening view. To revert to the Category view, click Control Panel Home from the Quick List (refer to Figure 25.1).

> **TIP**
> As with previous versions of Windows, there are usually several ways to get to the same place. For example, if you right-click Computer on the Start menu and select Properties, you get the System control panel, just as if you went through Control Panel under System and Maintenance. This is fine; you'll eventually decide that one way or the other is easier for you to remember and faster to use.
>
> However, one thing that you might find confusing about Vista is that to improve security, functions that require Administrator privileges have been separated from functions that don't. Features that used to live together in the same Control Panel dialog in previous

continues

continued

> versions of Windows might not be together on Vista, or worse, access to them might be blocked if you don't get to the Control Panel item in just the right way. (This is the "disorienting" part that we mentioned earlier). We've done our best to tell you about these issues throughout this book, which leads us to this important advice: When you need to change a Windows setting that you know exists but can't seem to find, look it up by name in the index of this book. Chances are that it will point you to specific instructions for finding the setting on Vista.

What Should You Use?

Working with the Control Panel in Category view simplifies access to both common and less-commonly used configuration controls. However, some applets are referenced by more than one category, and the Add Hardware applet can be accessed only in Classic view. Consequently, to provide an exhaustive discussion of the applets, this chapter focuses on reviewing each applet as listed in the Classic view. If you want to use the Category view, refer to Tables 25.1 to 25.10.

Table 25.12 shows a list of all the standard Control Panel applets and what they accomplish. Your Control Panel may include other applets that are installed by other products from Microsoft and third parties.

TABLE 25.12   CONTROL PANEL CLASSIC MODE APPLETS

Applet	Function
Add Hardware Wizard	Installs or troubleshoots a wide variety of non-PnP hardware devices such as sound, video, CD-ROM, hard and floppy disk controllers, SCSI controllers, display adapters, keyboard, mouse, and ports. PnP devices are detected and installed automatically by Windows Vista. Installation of printers is covered in Chapter 6, "Printing." Installation of other hardware is covered in Chapter 30, "Installing and Replacing Hardware."
Administrative Tools	Provides shortcuts to these administrative tools—Computer Management, Data Sources (ODBC) settings, Event Viewer, iSCSI Initiator NEW, Local Security Policy, Memory Diagnostics NEW, Print Management, Reliability and Performance Monitor, Services, System Configuration, Task Scheduler, and Windows Firewall with Advanced Security. These tools are discussed later in this chapter.
AutoPlay NEW	Configures Auto Play options for different types of storage media and multimedia files.
Backup and Restore Center NEW	Provides file backup and restore and system restore (Ultimate and Business also provide image backup and restore). See Chapter 34, "Protecting Your Data from Loss and Theft," for details.

TABLE 25.12 CONTINUED

Applet	Function
BitLocker Drive Encryption	Configures and manages full-drive encryption (Ultimate and Business versions only). See Chapter 34 for details.
Color Management NEW	Configures color management settings for displays and printers. To learn more about Color Management, see Chapter 6.
Date and Time	Sets the current date, time, and time zone for the computer. It can also synchronize system time with an Internet time server.
Default Programs	Configures default file types for installed programs. Associates file types with a particular program. Also configures program access and computer defaults and provides access to AutoPlay options.
Device Manager	Configures hardware devices and drivers. Also displays usage of hardware resources such as IRQs, DMA channels, I/O port addresses, and memory addresses.
Ease of Access Center	Configures accessibility tools, such as Magnifier, Narrator, On-Screen Keyboard, High Contrast display, and others.
Folder Options	Sets systemwide folder view options, file associations, and indexing. The Folder Options applet is covered in detail in Chapter 26, "Tweaking the GUI."
Fonts	Adds and deletes typefaces, and displays examples of system-installed typefaces for screen display and printer output.
Game Controllers	Adds, removes, and configures game controller hardware, such as joysticks and gamepads.
Indexing Options NEW	Configures what locations are indexed and how indexing is performed. Indexing is covered in detail in Chapter 26.
Internet Options	Sets Internet Explorer options. Internet Options are covered in Chapter 15, "Using Internet Explorer 7."
iSCSI Initiator NEW	Configures connections to iSCSI storage devices.
Keyboard	Sets key repeat rate, cursor blink rate, language of your keyboard, keyboard type, and drivers, and includes keyboard troubleshooting wizards.
Mouse	Configures mouse properties such as motion speed, double-click, button orientation, cursor shapes, and other proprietary settings dependent on your mouse driver.

continues

TABLE 25.12 CONTINUED

Applet	Function
Network and Sharing Center NEW	Manages all network connections, including LAN, dial-up WAN, and VPN. Configures networking components (clients, services, and protocols) and file/folder devices. These connections are covered throughout Part V, "Networking."
Offline Files NEW	Configures settings for offline files (copies of files stored on the network). Offline Files is covered in Chapter 38, "Hitting the Road."
Parental Controls NEW	Configures user-based restrictions on computer use, gameplay, Internet access, and program access.
Pen and Input Devices NEW	Configures pen actions and motions for Tablet PCs. For more information, see Chapter 41, "Tablet PC Features."
People Near Me NEW	Enables programs such as Windows Meeting Space to find you and invite you to a meeting. Windows Meeting Space is covered in Chapter 39, "Meetings, Conferencing, and Collaboration."
Performance Information and Tools NEW	Displays Windows Experience Index and provides access to performance configuration options.
Personalization	Configures window and desktop appearance, screen savers, audio sound schemes, mouse pointers, desktop themes, and display settings. For details, see Chapter 26.
Phone and Modem Options	Adds, removes, and sets the properties of the modem(s) connected to your system. Using this applet, you can declare dialing rules (long-distance numbers, call waiting, credit card calling, and so on). You also can add and remove telephony drivers. This applet is discussed in Chapter 14, "Getting Connected."
Power Options	Configures power settings ("power plans"), power and sleep buttons, and other power management issues. See Chapter 38 for laptop-specific recommendations. Basic power options are discussed in this chapter.
Printers	Adds, modifies, removes, and manages physical printer and print drivers such as Microsoft's new XPS Document Writer. Using this applet, you can manage the print queue for each printer and enable direct faxing from applications. The Printers applet is covered in Chapter 6.
Problem Reports and Solutions NEW	Tracks computer problems and solutions. For more information on Windows troubleshooting using this and other features, see Chapter 28, "Troubleshooting and Repairing Problems."
Programs and Features	Uninstalls and changes installed programs. Enable or disable Windows features. Tracks installed Windows updates.

The Windows Vista Control Panel

Table 25.12 Continued

Applet	Function
Regional and Language Options	Sets how Windows displays times, dates, numbers, and currency through region/country settings and language preferences.
Scanners and Cameras	Adds, removes, sets properties, and troubleshoots scanners and digital cameras. For more information, see Chapter 9, "Windows Imaging Tools."
Security Center	Configures Windows Firewall, Windows Defender, automatic updates to Windows and Microsoft applications, Internet and User Account Control settings. Displays status of antivirus protection. For more information about security issues, see Part VII, "Security."
Sound	Configures audio devices or changes sound scheme.
Speech Recognition *NEW*	Configures speech recognition. For details, see Chapter 4, "Using the Windows Desktop."
Sync Center *NEW*	Configures sync partnerships such as Offline Files and others. File synchronization is covered in Chapter 38.
System	Examines and changes your identification (workgroup name, domain name, computer name) and installed devices. Displays amount of RAM available to Windows, type of processor, and processor speed. Using this applet, you can add, disable, and remove specific devices using the Device Manager; configure remote access; set up user profiles; set environment variables; configure visual effects, performance, and Data Execution Protection (DEP); configure Windows Update settings, and set emergency startup options.
Tablet PC Settings *NEW*	Configures settings for Tablet PC displays and handwriting recognition. For more information, see Chapter 41.
Taskbar and Start Menu	Sets the properties for the taskbar and Start menu. For details, see Chapter 4 and Chapter 26.
Text to Speech	Configures text-to-speech voice and speed settings. Speech features are covered in Chapter 4.
User Accounts	Adds, deletes, or configures users. Using this applet, you can assign groups, manage passwords, and set logon mode. Basic user setup is covered in Chapter 3, "The First Hour."
Welcome Center *NEW*	Provides access to various features, including Windows Easy Transfer, User Accounts, Windows Basics, Backup and Restore Center, Control Panel, and others. Provides demos of Windows Vista features and access to Microsoft add-ons for Vista. To learn more about Welcome Center, see Chapter 3.

continues

TABLE 25.12   CONTINUED

Applet	Function
Windows CardSpace [NEW]	Sets up and manages credentials for logging into secure websites, such as online stores and e-banking. To learn more about securing your web connection, see Chapter 36, "Protecting Yourself from Fraud and Spam."
Windows Defender [NEW]	Configures and manages integrated antispyware utility. To learn more about Windows Defender, see Chapter 33, "Protecting Windows from Viruses and Spyware."
Windows Firewall	Use this applet to turn on, turn off, and fine-tune the firewall that protects your computer from uninvited invasion from the Internet. To learn more about Windows Firewall, see Chapter 35, "Protecting Your Network from Hackers."
Windows Mobility Center [NEW]	One-click access to audio, power scheme, display brightness, wireless and external display configuration, Sync Center settings, and external presentation display features. To learn more about Windows Mobility Center, see Chapter 38.
Windows Sidebar Properties [NEW]	Configures Windows Sidebar and manages Sidebar gadgets. For more information, see Chapter 7, "Sidebar and Other Supplied Accessories."
Windows SideShow [NEW]	Configures Windows SideShow, which enables you to use a PDA, mobile phone, or other device to display selected Windows applications, such as email or Windows Media Player.
Windows Update	Configures how you receive updates to Windows and other Microsoft applications, such as Office. To learn more about Windows Update and Microsoft Update, see Chapter 29, "Keeping Windows and Other Software Up to Date."

In the following sections, we'll cover each of the included applets (the ones not covered in other chapters) in alphabetical order.

AutoPlay

AutoPlay isn't new to Windows Vista. Its ancestor, Autorun, has been used to automatically start programs from a CD or DVD drive since Windows 95. In Windows XP, AutoPlay was extended to USB drives and other types of removable-media drives. AutoPlay is found in the Hardware and Sound category of the Control Panel and is also available in Classic view.

What's new in Windows Vista is how AutoPlay is configured. Rather than being configured on a drive-by-drive basis through the AutoPlay tab on a drive's properties sheet, Windows Vista's AutoPlay applet (see Figure 25.12) permits you to configure AutoPlay defaults for different types of media and multimedia files on a global basis.

Figure 25.12
Using the AutoPlay applet to configure global settings for automatically recognizing media and file types.

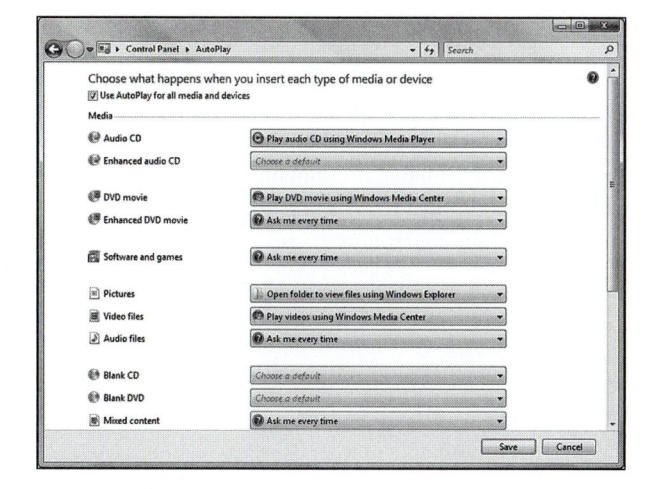

Unlike Windows XP's AutoPlay, which was primarily designed for photos, music, and video files, Windows Vista's AutoPlay also includes support for various types of CD and DVD movie discs, including HD DVD, Blu-ray Disc movies, DVD-Audio, Video CD, and Super Video CD. This is made possible in part by Windows Media Player 11's built-in support for DVD video and also enables you to use specialized players for certain types of video discs if you want.

AutoPlay also includes support for devices you connect to your system, as well as built-in devices. As in Windows XP, the exact programs available for any media or media file type vary according to the programs installed. You can also disable AutoPlay for particular media or media file types or globally.

DATE AND TIME

Date and Time is a simple applet you're sure to have used in the past to adjust the system date and time. That is, it adjusts the hardware clock in the computer, which is maintained by a battery on the motherboard. The system date and time are used for myriad purposes, including date- and time-stamping the files you create and modify, stamping email, controlling the scheduler program for automatic application running, and so on. Date and Time is found in the Clock, Language, and Region category of the Control Panel and is also available in Classic view.

> **NOTE**
>
> The Date and Time applet doesn't change the format of the date and time, only the actual date and time stored on your computer's clock. To change formats, see the description of the Regional applet later in this chapter.

When you're a member of a Microsoft network domain, you should never need to set the clock. It is kept synchronized to the domain controller (Windows 2000 Server, Windows NT

Server, or Windows Server 2003). Many network services, including authentication protocols and replication, require exact or close synchronization of all systems within the network.

If your system is part of a workgroup or just a standalone, you can sync your clocks with an Internet time server. The Date and Time applet includes a third tab for doing just that. However, this capability is not available on domain clients. The ability to sync with an Internet time server through the Date and Time applet is reserved for workgroup members, standalone systems, and domain controllers.

The Date and Time applet can also be accessed by double-clicking the clock on the taskbar or right-clicking over the clock and selecting Adjust Date/Time. To set the date and time, follow these steps:

1. Run the Date/Time applet.
2. Click Change Date and Time.
3. Alter the time and date by typing in the corrections or by clicking the arrows. The trick is to click directly on the hours, minutes, seconds, or AM/PM area first, and then use the little arrows to the right of them to set the correct value. So, to adjust the a.m. or p.m., click AM or PM, and then click the little up or down arrow. After setting the month and year, you can click the day in the displayed calendar. Click OK.
4. Click the Change Time Zone button to adjust the zone. Why? It's good practice to have your time zone set correctly for programs such as client managers, faxing programs, time synchronizing programs, or phone dialing programs. They may need to figure out where you are in relation to others and what the time differential is. Also, if you want your computer's clock to be adjusted automatically when daylight saving time changes, be sure the Automatically Adjust Clock for Daylight Saving Changes check box is selected. Click OK.

> **TIP**
>
> If your system's BIOS is also configured to automatically adjust for daylight savings time, you may find that your system's clock is set incorrectly when the time changes twice a year because the BIOS makes the adjustment and so does Windows. You should disable your system BIOS's daylight savings time adjustment and use Windows' instead. There are two reasons:
>
> First, it's easier to configure time zones and settings from within Windows than from within the BIOS setup program.
>
> Second, starting in 2007, daylight savings time will begin the second Sunday of March and end on the first Sunday of November. A Windows update or the built-in Internet time synchronization feature will enable your system to know when DST starts and ends. If you leave your computer's BIOS in charge of adjusting for DST, you will need to install a BIOS update—assuming that your PC's manufacturer is keeping up with U.S. law on this topic.

5. Click the Internet Time tab. Click Change Settings. On this tab, you can enable clock synchronization with an Internet time server. Five known time servers are provided in the pull-down list, but you can type in others. If you want to force a sync, click the Update Now button.

6. Click OK to save changes and close the applet.

When Internet synchronization is enabled, your clock is reset to match the time servers once each week. Internet synchronization should be configured only on systems with an active Internet connection. Clock synchronization does not initiate a dial-up connection. Plus, if there is a firewall or proxy server between your client and the Internet, the clock synchronization packets may be blocked.

> **TIP**
>
> You can also adjust the time and date using the TIME and DATE commands from a command prompt. For example, open a command prompt box (click Start, All Programs, Accessories, Command Prompt), type **time**, and press Enter. This command displays the current time and a prompt to enter the new time, as shown here:
>
> ```
> The current time is: 21:39:31.78
> Enter the new time:
> ```
>
> Enter the new time or press Enter to leave the time as it is. The same process applies to the date. Type **date** and press Enter. The current date is displayed with a prompt to enter the new date, as shown here:
>
> ```
> The current date is: Fri 09/29/2006
> Enter the new date: (mm-dd-yy)
> ```

DEFAULT PROGRAMS

Default Programs (see Figure 25.13), can be found in the Programs category of the Control Panel, is also available in Classic view, and can also be opened directly from the Start menu's right pane. It enables you to choose the default program you prefer for a particular file type, associate a file type with a particular program, change AutoPlay settings (see "AutoPlay" earlier in this chapter for details), and specify which programs are the defaults for web browsing, email, playing media, instant messaging, and providing Java VM support.

Figure 25.13
The Default Programs dialog box provides a variety of ways to ensure that you use the program you prefer to perform a particular task or open a particular file type.

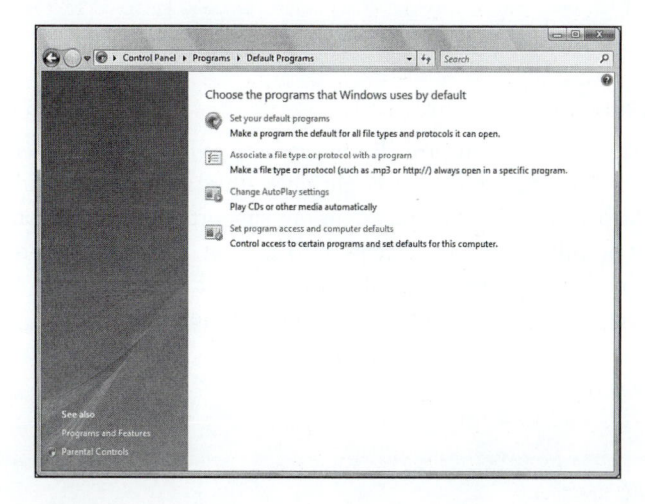

Set Your Default Programs

Select this option, and your default programs for web browsing, photo viewing, media playback, and so forth are displayed in the left pane. Select a program from the list, and select from two options listed in the right pane:

- Set This Program as Default—Choose this option to use the selected program as the default for all file types and protocols it can open.

- Choose Defaults for This Program—Choose this option to specify which file types and programs the application will open by default.

We recommend the second option. When you select it, each file and protocol type you can choose from is listed, along with the current default. To change all items listed to default to the selected program, click the Select All check box. To change only selected options, click the empty check box next to each item you want to change. Click Save to complete the process.

Figure 25.14 illustrates the process of switching some types of image files to Windows Photo Gallery as the default program association. (Note the check boxes next to .gif, .tif, and .tiff image file types.)

Figure 25.14
Selecting additional picture types to be opened by Windows Photo Gallery by default.

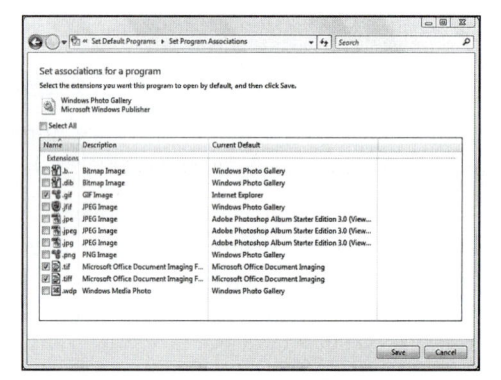

Set Associations

The Set Associations dialog box provides an easy way to change file associations from a single dialog, rather than requiring you to right-click a file, select Open With, and choose a program. Set Associations lists the file extensions supported by applications on your system and the current default. Click a file extension to select it, click Change Program, and select the program from the list of recommended programs, or click Browse to find the program you prefer. Select the program and click OK to finish the process.

Set Program Access and Computer Defaults

Select this option, and you can select from up to four different configurations for web browsing, email, and other common activities:

- Computer Manufacturer
- Microsoft Windows
- Non-Microsoft
- Custom

For maximum flexibility, choose Custom. In the Custom configuration, you can specify not only default programs but also whether to permit or deny access to non-Microsoft alternatives to the default web browser, email, media player, IM, and Java VM programs on your system, such as Firefox or Opera web browsers, Thunderbird or Eudora email clients, AOL or Trillian instant messaging clients, and so forth. Credit the existence of this feature to antitrust litigation against Microsoft for embedding Internet Explorer and other technologies into the operating system. In other words, Set Program Access and Computer Defaults enables Windows Vista to play nicely with other vendors' products.

Device Manager

Device Manager is so important in keeping your system working properly that it can be accessed from two different categories: System and Maintenance and Hardware and Sound, as well as from Classic view. When Device Manager is launched, you are presented with a category list of the devices installed in the system (see Figure 25.15). When there are no problems, the display is a bit bland (but in this case, bland is good). To see the individual devices, expand any of the listed categories. Then, to access a device's Properties dialog box, just double-click it.

Figure 25.15
The Device Manager displaying an unknown device.

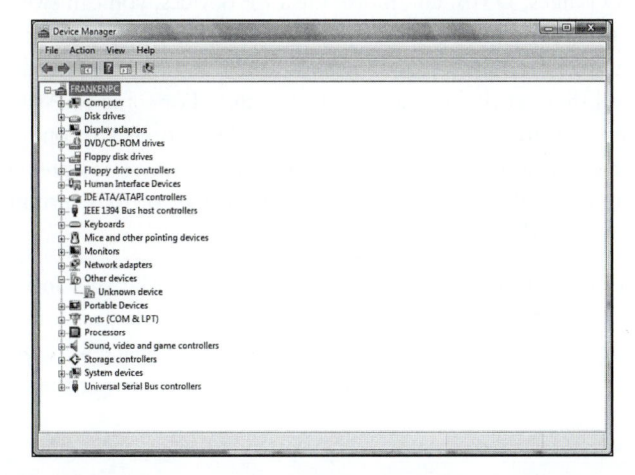

The Device Manager serves several functions, the foremost of which is to aid in the resolution of hardware problems. When any device fails to function as expected it will be highlighted with a yellow triangle or a down arrow. The yellow triangle indicates a warning or a possible problem, such as a driver that has not been loaded or an Unknown Device (see Figure 25.15). A down arrow indicates a disabled device, device conflict, or other serious error. When the Device Manager is launched and a device has an outstanding issue, its category will be expanded so that you can easily see the warning or error icon.

When a device's Properties dialog box is opened, the General tab displays basic information about the device, plus details on the device's current status. In most cases, the status report will point out exactly what is preventing the device from functioning normally. You may correct the issue on your own, or if you need help or guidance, click the Troubleshoot button on the General tab for a wizard or further guidance. This button has various labels, according to the problem you have. For example, if you have a driver problem, the button is called Reinstall Driver. If you have a resource problem, the button is called Check for Solutions. If the device is enabled, the button is called Enable Device, and so forth.

Depending on the device, there can be many other tabs in addition to the General tab. In most cases, you'll see a Driver tab, and almost as frequently you'll see a Resources tab. The Driver tab offers details about the currently installed driver for this device and enables you to update, roll back, or uninstall the driver.

Device driver rollback, just as in Windows XP, removes the current driver and restore the previous driver (assuming there was one). The ability to remove the current or newly installed driver to return to the previously used driver is often a lifesaver. I can't remember how many times I've had to remove a new driver and then had to go through the process of reinstalling the hardware just to get the old driver back. The Roll Back Driver button performs this operation with a simple click. No muss, no fuss.

The Resources tab specifies the system resources to which the device is assigned. These include IRQ, I/O ranges, DMA, and more. On PnP devices, you can switch the settings from automatic to either a predefined configuration set or a fully customized setting. On legacy cards, you may need to alter the physical device settings (such as dip switches or jumpers) first, and then set the Resources tab to match. For some PnP cards, the settings on the Resources page are read-only. In such cases, the settings are configured by the system BIOS and by the expansion slot the card is plugged into. See your system or motherboard documentation to determine how to change BIOS settings, or to determine which IRQ is assigned to a particular slot.

The Details tab, added as a standard feature to the Device Manager in Windows XP SP2, provides access to a huge list of technical details about your device. It defaults to displaying the device description (the same one you see on the main Device Manager window), but you can also view approximately 25 arcane technical details such as the Device Instance ID,

Enumerator, and so on. Some devices may list additional information. A few of the most useful ways to use this tab include

- Use the Hardware IDs and Compatible IDs selection to determine the PnP information used to install the device.
- Use the Manufacturer selection to determine the manufacturer of the device.
- Use the Power Capabilities selection to determine the device's support for various power management states.

Access the Advanced tab found on some device properties sheets to configure special settings used by that device. The Power tab on USB root and generic hubs can help you determine whether a particular hub has enough power for a particular USB device. The Power Management tab found on some devices enables you to control whether the computer can turn off a device to save power and whether the device can wake the computer from standby.

For any other tabs that may appear in a device's Properties dialog box, be sure to consult the device's user manual.

From the main Device Manager view, you can perform a few helpful actions:

- Change views between devices by type, devices by connection, resources by type (IRQ, DMA, I/O port address, and memory), and resources by connection (USB ports, legacy ports, and so forth).
- Force a scan for hardware changes.
- Update the driver for the selected device.
- Uninstall the device from the system.
- Eject or unplug a device.
- Install legacy (non-PnP) hardware.

Understanding and Resolving Hardware Conflicts

Windows, together with its Plug-and-Play technology, has grown far better at detecting and preventing hardware conflicts over the past few years. Still, system conflicts do arise, especially when you're using old ISA cards and other legacy hardware, such as integrated serial and parallel ports.

> **NOTE**
>
> By the way, if you've been longing for the day when hardware conflicts will be history, the day is closer than ever. Microsoft has announced that Windows Vista will be the last version of Windows to support the ISA bus. The ISA bus, which has been around since the beginning of the Reagan administration (in other words, it's old enough to shave, vote, have kids, and start a 529 savings plan for college), is on its last legs. When the ISA bus goes, so will such legacy hardware as PS/2 mouse and keyboard ports, parallel ports, and serial (communication) ports. Good riddance!

More often than not, configuration and installation problems are due to incorrect settings on an ISA network, I/O, sound, modem, SCSI card, or integrated ports that use ISA standards, such as the serial, parallel, and PS/2 mouse ports. The result is cards or integrated devices that conflict with one another for the same IRQ (interrupt request line), base I/O port address, DMA, or base memory address. Cards are configured by changing jumpers or DIP switches on the board, or by running a configuration program from a command prompt; a few late-model ISA cards can be configured for true Plug-and-Play operation. Onboard legacy ports are configured through the BIOS setup program.

If necessary, you can force Windows Vista to use manually selected system resources, such as IRQ, for a given piece of gear. In the Device Manager, choose the item, open its Properties dialog box, click the Resources tab, turn off Use Automatic Settings, and enter the resource or resources you want to assign. If the card uses manual configuration, you will need to set the board to the settings you select in the Device Manager.

> **CAUTION**
>
> Don't manually assign resources unless you know what you're doing. The result can be an operating system that won't boot or a bunch of other components in your system that no longer work.

Hardware uses four major resources:

- IRQ
- DMA
- I/O port addresses
- DMA channel

If you install Plug-and-Play cards (which configure themselves automatically), you seldom need to be concerned about these settings, especially if the cards use the PCI, AGP, or PCI-Express expansion slot (virtually any current card does). If your system originally ran Windows 98 or newer versions, it probably supports a feature called IRQ steering or IRQ sharing, which eliminates the major cause for hardware conflicts when you use PCI cards.

> **TIP**
>
> By default, Device Manager displays Devices by Type. To see IRQ and other hardware resources in use in Device Manager, click View, Resources by Type.

IRQs

PC architecture includes a means for a piece of hardware to quickly gain the attention of the CPU through a message called an *interrupt request*, or *IRQ*. Interrupts are sent over one of the 15 IRQ wires on the computer's bus. Such a request is a direct line to the CPU, which then services the request accordingly. A common example occurs when data comes in to your system's modem or LAN card. The modem or LAN card triggers the predetermined IRQ, and the CPU then begins to execute the program code that is appropriate for handling that interrupt. In fact, a part of the operating system called the *interrupt handler* is responsible for making it so.

Table 25.13 lists the common IRQs in an Intel-based computer. This information, in conjunction with the IRQ and the Conflicts/Sharing nodes of the Computer Management application, might help you to assign boards effectively. But remember, it's always best to let Windows make hardware assignments unless you are really stuck and something important just won't work. Also, remember that if hardware isn't on the Hardware Compatibility List (HCL), you're better off just going shopping than wasting a day tinkering with settings.

TABLE 25.13   TYPICAL IRQ ASSIGNMENTS IN 80286-BASED OR LATER x86 SYSTEMS

IRQ	Typical Assignment
0	System Timer (used by system; not available)
1	Keyboard (used by system; not available)
2	Redirected to IRQ 9; not available
3	COM2:, COM4: (can be shared only if COM 2/COM 4 are not used at the same time)
4	COM1:, COM3: (can be shared only if COM 1/COM 3 are not used at the same time)
5	LPT2: or Sound Blaster/compatible sound card
6	Floppy disk controller (used by system; never available)
7	LPT1: (printer port) can be shared only if used on a PCI card; the built-in parallel port's IRQ can't be shared
8	System clock (used by system; never available)
9	Old EGA/VGA cards or available
10	Often available
11	Often available
12	PS/2 mouse (available only on systems that don't have a PS/2-style mouse or have the port disabled)
13	Math coprocessor (not available; all modern CPUs have a built-in math coprocessor)
14	IDE hard disk controller (never available)
15	Secondary IDE hard disk controller (never available on 1995 or later systems)

On systems that feature an Advanced Programmable Interrupt Controller (APIC), PCI, AGP, and PCI-Express cards and integrated devices (such as USB ports and SATA host adapters), you can use higher IRQ settings up to 23. APIC is enabled through the system BIOS.

> **NOTE**
>
> You may see IRQs from 80 to 190 assigned to the Microsoft ACPI-Compliant System when you view IRQ assignments in Device Manager or with System Information (MSInfo32). These IRQs are new in Windows Vista.

Common add-on devices that use an IRQ include

- Modern PCI, PCI-Express, and AGP video cards
- SCSI, ATA/IDE, and SATA host adapter cards
- Fax/modem cards
- Network interface cards
- USB and FireWire (IEEE-1394) host adapter cards

Thanks to IRQ sharing and the use of APIC, there's usually enough IRQ space for all these devices in modern systems. However, on older systems that don't support APIC (such systems support only IRQs 0-15), it may be necessary to disable unused legacy ports to permit adequate IRQ resources for installed devices, even when IRQ sharing is supported.

What about ISA devices, including legacy ports? If two ISA devices (or an ISA and a PCI device) try to share an IRQ, a system lockup will usually take place, or at best, neither device will work. A common cause of this a few years ago was when a serial mouse was attached to COM 1 and a fax/modem was assigned to COM 3. As you can see from the IRQ table, both of these ports use IRQ 4. The system worked until the user tried to operate the modem; then the system locked up.

MS-DOS and old versions of Windows didn't always use the printer (LPT) ports' IRQs, enabling IRQ 7 (LPT1) and IRQ 5 (LPT2) to be used by other devices. However, Windows Vista uses the IRQs assigned to a device, so that sharing can take place only under these circumstances:

- Both devices using the IRQ are PCI devices; on most recent systems, this enables the PCI cards and any built-in PCI devices to share IRQs, as in Figure 25.16.
- When two ISA cards or an ISA and a PCI card are set to the same IRQ, Windows Vista shifts to a "polling" mode, wherein the CPU regularly checks for and services I/O requests rather than waits for IRQ lines to be activated. Obviously, this process can slow down overall system performance because it creates another software loop that the operating system has to service.

Understanding and Resolving Hardware Conflicts

Figure 25.16
IRQ sharing enables this PC to use PCI IRQ 19 for IEEE-1394 host controllers and a Linksys 10/100 Ethernet adapter and PCI IRQ 21 for both Serial ATA and USB host controllers.

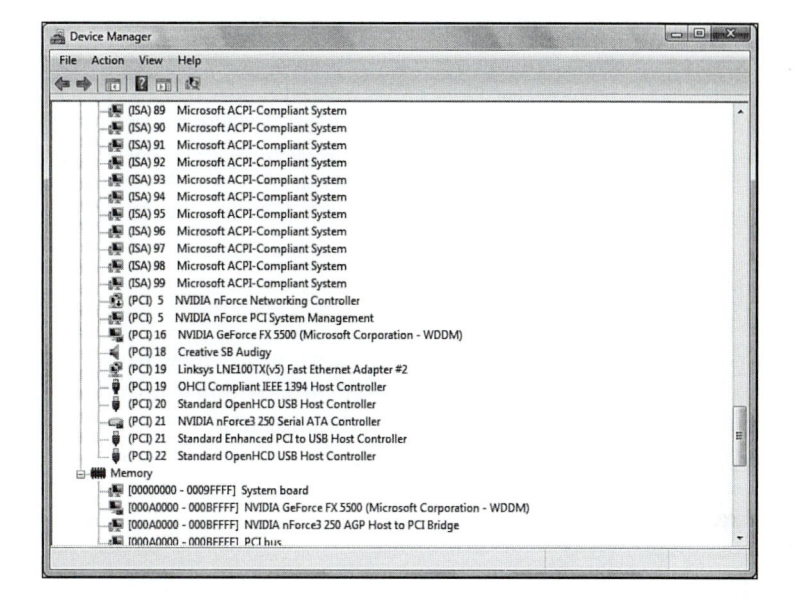

As shown in Figure 25.16, IRQ sharing is enabled automatically by Windows Vista when the system supports it. In some cases, however, some motherboards might not permit IRQs to be shared, even by PCI devices.

If you find yourself short on IRQs or if you have two devices attempting to use the same IRQ and creating a conflict, you can try these possible solutions:

- One solution with PCI cards causing conflicts is to try moving the PCI or PCI-Express card to another slot. On some machines, each PCI slot's PCI Interrupt (A through D) is mapped to an ISA-type IRQ. By simply moving a card to a neighboring slot, you may get your hardware working. Note that PCI, PCI-Express, and AGP slots all use PCI interrupts, and that some systems assign the same PCI interrupt to two slots, or to a slot and an integrated device. See your system or motherboard manual for details.

- Another workaround is to use USB, IEEE-1394, and SCSI devices in place of legacy devices (serial, parallel, PS/2). As you probably know, all these port types support multiple devices on the same wire. No IRQs are required other than for the controller, which typically takes only one, and most recent systems already have USB ports onboard and enabled. Yet USB supports up to 127 devices, IEEE-1394 up to 63 devices, and SCSI typically 7 (or 15 if your card supports Wide SCSI). If you're struggling with where to put a scanner, printer, digital camera, or additional external hard drive, consider these buses. Although you can daisy-chain devices from the parallel port, it's difficult to get more than two devices (printer and another one) working correctly. And, even the "high-speed" EPP and ECP parallel port modes are scarcely faster than USB 1.1 and are considerably slower than any form of SCSI, USB 2.0, or IEEE-1394.

TIP

> If you no longer use legacy ports, disable them in the system BIOS. By disabling legacy ports, you enable the IRQs and other hardware resources used by serial, parallel, or PS/2 mouse ports to be available for PCI, PCI-Express, and AGP devices, including integrated devices. On some systems, it may also be necessary to open the PnP/PCI dialog box in the system BIOS and assign the IRQs formerly used by legacy ports to be available for PnP/PCI devices. To determine the IRQs used by legacy ports, see Table 25.13.

DMA Channels

A typical PC has eight DMA channels, labeled 0 to 7. DMA channels are used for rapidly transferring data between memory and peripherals without the help of the CPU. Some cards even use several of these channels at once. (For example, the SoundBlaster 16 WaveEffects sound card uses two DMA channels.) Typical users of DMA channels are

- Memory access controllers
- ECP printer ports
- Floppy disk controllers
- ISA network cards
- ISA scanner cards
- ISA SCSI host adapters
- ISA sound cards

Although recent EIDE hard drives use a variation of DMA called Ultra DMA (UDMA) for fast data transfer, DMA transfers performed by PCI-based devices don't use specific DMA channels. The only time a PCI device ever needs to use a DMA channel is if it's emulating an ISA device that uses one, such as a PCI-based sound card emulating an ISA-based sound card.

Sharing DMA channels is even worse than sharing IRQs. Because DMA channels are used to transfer data, not simply to activate devices, you should *never* share DMA channels used by network cards, scanners, or SCSI host adapters because a DMA conflict could result in data loss. Fortunately, with relatively few devices requiring DMA channels today, it's normally easy to avoid sharing a DMA channel.

Table 25.14 shows the typical assignments.

TABLE 25.14 TYPICAL DMA CONTROLLER ASSIGNMENTS

Channel	Typical Assignment
0	Generally used for DMA refresh
1	Available; may be used by ISA sound cards or by PCI sound cards emulating ISA sound cards

Table 25.14	Continued
Channel	Typical Assignment
2	Floppy disk controller
3	ECP printer ports; some may use DMA 1 instead
4	DMA controller; used by system and not available
5	Available; may be used by ISA sound cards or by PCI sound cards emulating ISA sound cards
6	Available
7	Available

> **TIP**
>
> Some devices are hidden from view in the Device Manager. Hidden devices include non–Plug-and-Play devices and devices that have been physically removed from the computer but have not had their drivers uninstalled. To see hidden devices in the Device Manager list, choose View, Show Hidden Devices. A check mark should appear on the menu, indicating that hidden devices are showing. Click it again to hide them.

I/O Port Assignments

Using DMA is the fastest way to transfer data between components in the PC. However, an older technology called *memory-mapped I/O* is still in use today. (*I/O* means *input/output*.) In PC architecture, I/O ports are mapped into system memory and, therefore, are accessed by the CPU using memory addresses. As you might expect, each device that uses an I/O port must have a different port address, or data intended for one device will end up at another.

Check out the I/O folder off the Hardware Resources node in Computer Management, as shown in Figure 25.17, to see a sample list of I/O addresses and assignments. As you can see, this folder contains quite a few assignments. Note that the addresses are in standard memory-mapping parlance—hexadecimal.

> **NOTE**
>
> A common source of I/O contention occurs among video cards, SCSI devices, and network cards. However, most devices can use a choice of several I/O port address ranges to avoid conflicts.

Figure 25.17
Typical I/O assignments in a Windows Vista machine are numerous. Notice the scrollbar. Only about half the assignments are visible in this figure.

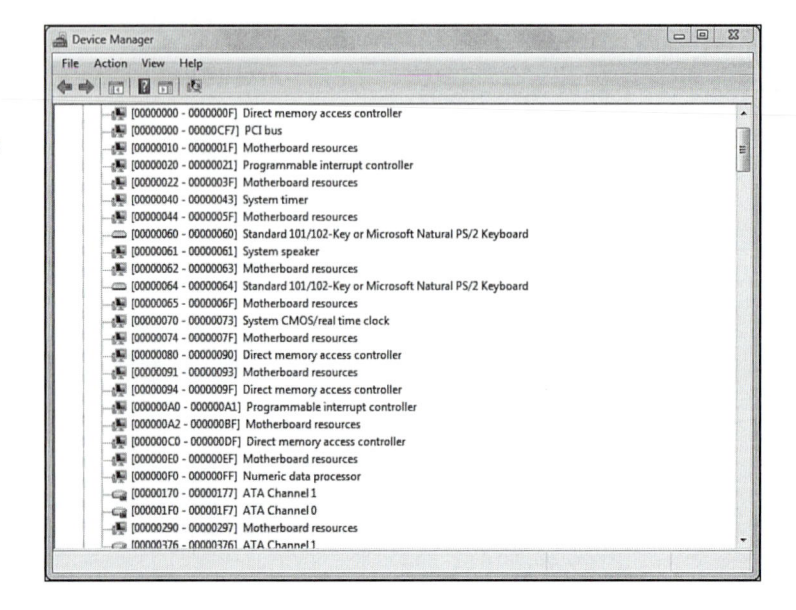

Memory Addresses

Similar to the I/O port address, the base memory address is the beginning memory address that some cards or motherboard hardware use to communicate with the CPU. Sometimes this setting is called the *RAM starting address* (or *start address*).

Some older cards (you'll notice this often with network adapters or SCSI cards, which have an onboard BIOS) must have their base memory address set by a jumper or software. Then, the device driver for that component needs its software setting to match the jumper. A typical base memory address reads like this: 0xA0000 or just A0000. Sometimes, the last digit is dropped: A000.

If you open Computer Management and go to System Information, Hardware Resources, Memory, you'll see memory addresses such as the following:

```
0xA0000-0xBFFFF    PCI bus
```

This address means the memory area between A0000 and BFFFF is assigned to the PCI bus. (The 0x indicates that it is a hexadecimal address.) So, when setting memory addressing, you need to consider not only the base addresses but also the amount of RAM space the addresses will occupy. Some cards use 16KB of space, and others use 32KB or more. Check the card's manual for options. Using more memory can, in some cases, improve the operation of the card, but it decreases your system's memory availability because that space will be occupied. The end result depends on the type of card.

When you specify a memory address for a card, the operating system reserves that memory area for it. Regular RAM in that area is not used by the CPU, to prevent conflicts that could result from trying to write data or program code into system RAM at that address. Instead, the reserved area is used only by the device driver for your piece of hardware.

Most older ISA cards use an upper memory address that falls somewhere between A000 and FFFF. However, many VL-Bus, PCI, and some ISA cards can use address space above 1MB, or even above 16MB for 32-bit cards. If your card can utilize a high address, it's better to do so because it minimizes the chances of conflicting with the operating system.

Checking a Device's Resources

To reassign a resource, click the resource in question on the Resources tab and choose Change Setting. In an attempt to prevent folks from inadvertently doing damage, the manual resource assignment dialog box keeps an eye on what you're doing. If you attempt to reassign to a resource that is already in use, you'll be warned about the conflict.

Some drivers don't have resources that can be reassigned. Others have an option button called Reinstall Driver that's useful if the system thinks that would solve a nonfunctioning-device problem. Most PCI cards don't permit their resources to be reassigned because they obtain their resource settings from Windows or from the system BIOS. Some systems allocate resources depending on which slot you use for a particular card.

> **CAUTION**
>
> Notice the Setting Based On drop-down list on the Resources tab. It lists the hardware configurations in which the currently selected device is enabled. If you choose a hardware configuration other than the default, and you change any resource settings, resource conflicts may occur when you use the default hardware configuration. Resource conflicts can disable your hardware and cause your computer to malfunction or to be inoperable.

Using Device Manager to Deal with Resource Conflicts

Although PCI, AGP, and PCI-Express cards and integrated devices are designed to share IRQs, you may see a resource conflict when you attempt to install a legacy port, such as a serial (communications) or parallel (LPT) port, or if you use a system that uses ISA cards. If the Add Hardware Wizard detects a conflict, you are alerted when you finish walking through the wizard steps. You then have the option of bailing out or continuing despite the conflict. You can also back up and choose a different model of hardware, such as one you think is compatible with what you're attempting to install. Figure 25.18 shows a typical message when a conflict is detected.

> **CAUTION**
>
> In general, be cautious about configuring resource settings manually. When you change settings manually, the settings become fixed, and Windows Vista's built-in device contention resolution is less likely to work. Also, if you install too many devices with manually configured settings, you might not be able to install new Plug-and-Play devices because none will be available. In the worst-case scenario, the system might not even boot if conflicts occur with primary hardware devices, such as hard disk controllers or video cards. If you decide to use manual configuration, make sure you know what you're doing and have the specs for the hardware in question at hand.

Figure 25.18
When a hardware conflict is detected, it's reported by the wizard at the end of the installation process.

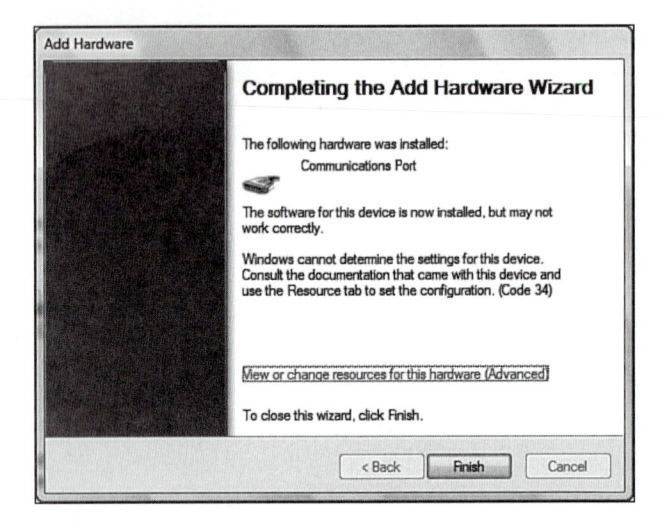

You now have the choice of setting the hardware resources for this device manually. Click View or change resources for this hardware (Advanced) to change the settings. On the next screen, click Set Configuration Manually. You'll see something similar to the dialog box shown in Figure 25.19, which is the Device Manager display of the current resources used by the device you are installing and the other device that uses the same setting.

Figure 25.19
Use caution when manually changing resources for a device. You may end up choosing an unavailable resource. In this dialog box, neither the I/O port address range nor the IRQ is available.

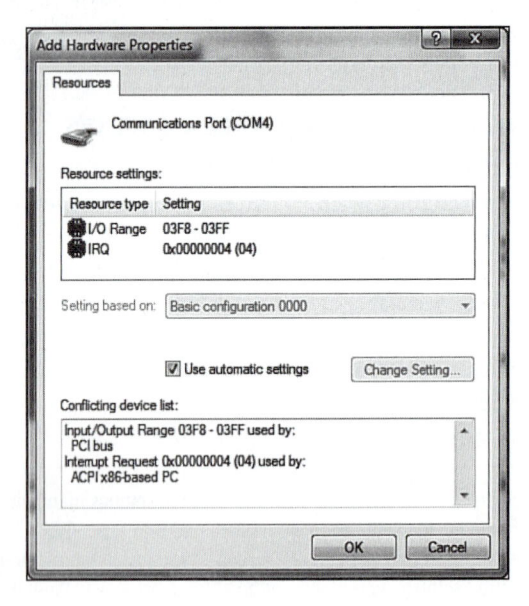

To select an alternative setting, clear the Use Automatic Settings check box; then click Change Setting to change the settings. If the system displays an error message, use the Setting Based On scroll box to try a different Basic configuration, or change the manual settings you made to alternative values. Keep trying configurations until the conflicting device listing is clear. Then, click OK and restart your computer if prompted.

If you cannot select a nonconflicting setting with the device you're installing, you have a few options:

1. Change the settings for the conflicting device with the Device Manager as discussed later in this chapter.
2. If the device you are attempting to install is an integrated legacy port, restart the system and select different settings in the BIOS setup. With a modern system, select Auto as the setting, which will enable the BIOS or Windows Vista to select a nonconflicting setting. If you must choose a particular IRQ or other hardware resource setting, make sure you don't choose a setting used by another port or card. For example, it's easy in most systems to choose the same IRQ and I/O port address range for both communication (serial) ports, causing a conflict. Be sure you choose different IRQs for each serial port.
3. In some cases, particularly with ISA cards or legacy ports, you may not be able to resolve a conflict and will need to remove one of the cards or disable the conflicting device on one of the cards with the Device Manager. PCI, PCI-Express, and AGP cards can share IRQ settings and fully support Windows Vista's Plug-and-Play feature, making them a much better choice for installation in today's crowded systems.

Ease of Access Center

The Windows Vista Ease of Access Center replaces the Windows XP Accessibility Center—in more ways than one. The Ease of Access Center, unlike its predecessor, is designed to be easy enough to enable users with visual or hearing impairments to set up their own systems, not merely use a system that has already been customized by another user for easier operation. The Ease of Access Center is in the Appearance and Personalization category of the Control Panel and is also available in Classic view.

After you open the Ease of Access Center (see Figure 25.20), Windows Vista's text-to-speech tool reads the top of the dialog box to the user and then highlights each of the tools (Magnifier, Narrator, On-Screen Keyboard, and High Contrast) in turn. To open a tool, all the user has to do is press the Spacebar when the tool is highlighted.

Figure 25.20
The Ease of Access Center talks users through selecting common accessibility tools.

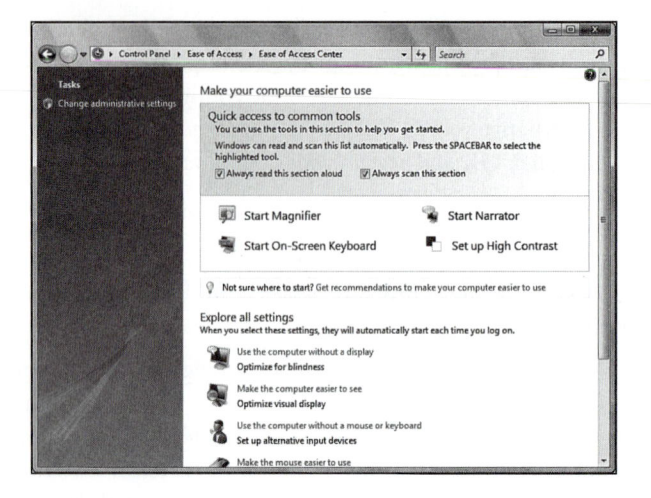

To use other Ease of Access settings, scroll down the list and select from the following:

- **Use the Computer Without a Display**—Select from options including Narrator, audio description of videos, text-to-speech setup, disabling of unnecessary animations, and adjust how long Windows dialog boxes stay open.

- **Make the Computer Easier to See**—Specifies how to turn on high-contrast displays, enable Narrator and Audio Description, adjust text and icon sizes, turn on Magnifier, increase the thickness of the focus rectangle and blinking cursor, and disable background images and unnecessary animations.

- **Use the Computer Without a Mouse or Keyboard**—Can enable the On-Screen Keyboard or open the Speech Recognition dialog box.

- **Make the Mouse Easier to Use**—Adjusts the mouse cursor size and color, enables Mouse Keys, and enables hover to switch to a window option.

- **Make the Keyboard Easier to Use**—Turns on the user's choice of Mouse Keys, Sticky Keys, Toggle Keys, or Filter Keys. See "Accessibility Keyboard Settings" later in this chapter for details.

- **Use Text or Visual Alternatives for Sounds**—Configures Sound Sentry, which can flash the active caption bar, active window, or the desktop to notify a user of a warning; configures text caption for a spoken dialog box when available.

- **Make it Easier to Focus on Tasks**—Configures accessibility keyboard settings, Narrator, and removal of background images.

You can use many combinations of accessibility features to help make computer use easier.

Accessibility Keyboard Settings

The keyboard settings deal with such problems as accidentally repeating keys or pressing combinations of keys. These options fall into three categories: *Sticky keys*, *Filter keys*, and *Toggle keys*.

Sticky keys are settings that, in effect, stay "down" when you press them once. They are good for controlling the function of the Alt, Ctrl, and Shift keys if you have trouble pressing two keys at the same time. To use them, set the Sticky keys option on; then choose the suboptions as you see fit. For some users, the shortcut of pressing the Shift key five times is a good way to activate Sticky keys. If you turn on this activation method, note that pressing the Shift key five times again turns off Sticky keys. This trick isn't explained clearly in the dialog boxes. Also, if you choose the Press Modifier Key Twice to Lock option, that means you press, for example, Shift twice to lock it. You can then press Shift twice again to unlock it.

Filter keys let you "filter" (remove) accidental repeated keystrokes if you have trouble pressing a key cleanly once and letting it up. This feature prevents you from typing multiple keystrokes. The shortcut key for turning on this feature works like the one for Sticky keys; it's a toggle. If you hold down the right shift key for eight seconds, a Filter Keys dialog box appears. Click Yes to enable Filter Keys.

> **TIP**
>
> Filter keys, when activated, can make it seem that your keyboard has ceased working unless you are very deliberate with keypresses. You have to press a key and keep it down for several seconds for the key to register. If you activate this setting and want to turn it off, the easiest solution is to use the mouse to open the Control Panel (via the taskbar), run the Ease of Access applet, turn off Filter Keys, and click Apply or OK.

The Toggle keys option, when turned on, sounds a high-pitched tone when Caps Lock, Scroll Lock, or Num Lock keys are activated and a low-pitched tone when they're turned off again.

Each of these three keyboard features can be used independently or together. Note that a slowdown in performance occurs at the keyboard if sounds are used because the sound is generated by playing a .wav file that briefly eats up your system resources. Processing of keypresses doesn't commence until after the keyboard sound finishes, which can result in jerky performance.

When Sticky keys or Filter keys are turned on, a symbol appears in the system tray. The Sticky keys feature is indicated by three small boxes with a fourth larger box above them, representative of the Ctrl, Alt, and Shift keys. The Filter keys feature is represented by the stopwatch, which is representative of the different key timing that goes into effect when the option is enabled.

ACCESSIBILITY SOUND SETTINGS

The two Accessibility sound settings—Sound Sentry and ShowSounds—are useful for those with hearing impairments, or for computer users working in a noisy environment, such as a factory floor or flight deck. Instead of playing a sound when an error message or other event that causes a sound occurs, some type of visual display appears onscreen.

With Sound Sentry, a portion of the normal Windows screen blinks. With ShowSounds turned on, a text caption or special icon will pop up over a window or dialog box when a sound is played. The information in the pop-up window will inform you of the sound played and whether the audio clue is a warning, error, and so on.

If you choose Sound Sentry, you have a choice of the visual warning to use. The options are offered in a pull-down list, which includes the Flash Active Caption Bar, Flash Active Windows, and Flash Desktop. Typically, you'll want the window of the application or at least its title bar to flash. Don't make the desktop flash because it won't indicate which program is producing the warning.

> **TIP**
>
> Some programs are finicky about the sound options, especially ShowSounds. If they're not programmed correctly, they don't display a sound. Think of it like closed captioning for TV. Not all shows have it.

ACCESSIBILITY DISPLAY SETTINGS

Special display settings in the Accessibility Options applet increase the screen contrast by altering the display scheme. Using this applet actually is just an easy way to set the display color scheme and font selection for easier reading, just as you could do from the Personalization applet, as discussed in Chapter 26. The big plus of setting the contrast here is that you can quickly call it up with a shortcut key combination when you need it. Simply press Left+Alt, Left+Shift, Prnt Scrn, and the settings go into effect. I have found this feature useful for when my eyes are tired or in imperfect lighting situations. Figure 25.21 compares the normal appearance of the Personalization menu with Aero enabled with the High Contrast White version, which as a byproduct also sets the appearance of buttons and toolbars to Windows Classic.

Figure 25.21
Windows Aero (left) compared to High Contrast White right).

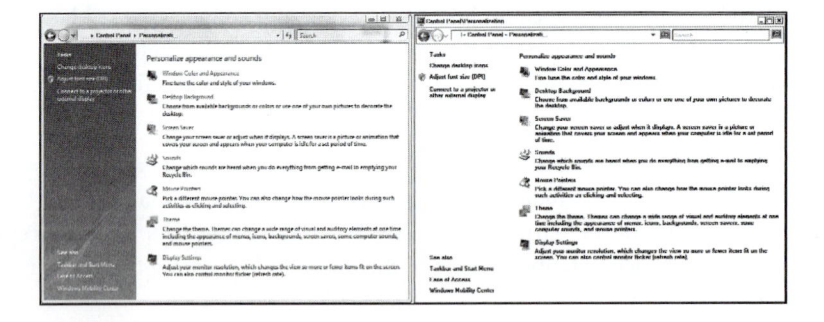

> **TIP**
>
> You get to select which predefined color scheme (both Windows provided and ones you've created through the Display applet) will be used as the high-contrast scheme. It's easier to observe the look of the schemes using the Personalization applet than in the Ease of Access Center applet. Do it there, and then decide which one you like best. Then come back to the Accessibility dialog box and make your choice.

Mouse Keys is a fourth option that enables users who have problems using a mouse to use the numeric keypad to emulate the mouse. Mouse Keys can be configured to run all the time, or only when needed by pressing the left Alt+left Shift+NumLock keys at the same time. Mouse Keys also offers options to accelerate the mouse pointer and adjust the mouse pointer speed. When Mouse Keys is active, it displays a mouse icon in the notification area (also known as the system tray).

Accessibility Mouse Settings

Using the Mouse Keys setting, you can control the mouse with the keypad if you have problems controlling your mouse's movements. This feature can bail you out if your mouse dies for some reason, too, or if you simply don't like using the mouse. As is covered in Chapter 4, you can execute many Windows and Windows application commands using the keyboard shortcut keys. But sometimes an application still responds only to mouse movements and clicks. Graphics programs are a case in point. When you use this Accessibility option, your arrow keys do double duty, acting like pointer control keys.

To use this option, simply turn on Mouse Keys from one of the dialog boxes that offers it and apply the change. Then, to activate the keys, press Left+Alt, Left+Shift, and Num Lock at the same time. The system tray should show a mouse icon. If the icon has a red line through it, Mouse keys are disabled, so press the Num Lock key to enable them.

Now you can move the pointer around the screen using the arrow keys on the numeric keypad. If you're using a laptop, you'll have to consult its manual to determine how to activate the numeric keypad, or look for an Fn key and contrasting-color keyboard markings for the numeric keypad that take effect only when Fn-NumLock is pressed first. The normal arrow keys won't cut it.

Use the Pointer Speed sliders if you need to adjust the speed settings for the arrow keys. Turn on the Ctrl and Shift options for speeding up or slowing down the mouse, assuming you can press two keys simultaneously. This setting really speeds things up.

If you adjust the configuration on the Settings dialog box, you have to click OK and then click Apply before the changes register. Then, you can go back and adjust as necessary.

Fonts

The first version of Windows to include a unified system for displaying and printing text across all Windows applications and printers was Windows 3.0. This was an attempt to catch up to the Macintosh, whose integrated support for PostScript font and graphics rendering gave it a big lead over earlier versions of Microsoft Windows. When Microsoft Windows 3.1 was introduced along with a new scalable font technology known as TrueType, Windows users had font capabilities on a par with the Macintosh. With the development of OpenType by Adobe and Microsoft, which integrates PostScript and TrueType support into a single font format, publishing and graphics users have never had it so good.

Windows Vista follows in this tradition, using the same TrueType and OpenType font outline technologies supported natively by Windows XP and Windows 2000.

FONTS 101

The Fonts folder can be accessed from the Appearance and Personalization category of the Control Panel and is also available in Classic view. Just as in, Fonts is a special system folder that features its own unique menu and right-click commands with options to let you do the following:

- Add and remove fonts
- View fonts in various ways

The word *font*, as used in Windows, refers to a typeface. Those people in typesetting circles believe the term is misused in PC jargon, and you should be calling, say, Arial a typeface. But, oh well. There goes the language (again). Fonts are specified by size as well as by name. The size of a font is measured in *points*. A point is 1/72 of an inch.

Note that all fonts except some raster fonts (see the following Tip) are scalable to any size needed. Technically, the OpenType and TrueType fonts installed on a Windows system are font outlines: Windows scales the font outline as needed for display and for printing. Although you can content yourself with picking a standard font size from a menu in Microsoft Word, CorelDraw, or Adobe Photoshop, you can enter any size you want in the Font menu or dialog box for a TrueType or OpenType font. If you need a 131.76 point font, you've got it! And, you can see it onscreen.

Windows Vista includes about 200 fonts, most of which are OpenType fonts. (A few TrueType fonts are included in that number, as are a small number of fonts.) If you have installed Microsoft or third-party office suite or graphics packages, you may have additional fonts installed.

> **TIP**
>
> OpenType fonts use an italic two-color O icon, whereas the older TrueType fonts use a two-color TT or TC icon. Fixed-size or scalable raster fonts (primarily used for command-prompt screen displays) are displayed with a red A icon.

FONT TYPES

The two primary categories of fonts are *serif* and *sans-serif* designs. Serifs are the little embellishments (often called "feet") that extend from the main *strokes* of the character. Serifs often are added to improve readability. As the name implies, sans-serif fonts lack these embellishments, making for a cleaner look. Sans-serif fonts tend to work well for headlines, whereas serif fonts are traditionally used for body text. Combining one serif and one sans-serif font in this way will look good together, but two sans-serif fonts or two serif fonts will clash. Times New Roman is a serif font, whereas Arial is a sans-serif font. The body text (the part you're reading now) of this book is a serif font; the headings in this book are sans-serif fonts.

The next major classification of fonts has to do with the spacing between characters. In *monospaced* fonts such as Courier New, every character occupies the same amount of horizontal line space. For example, *l* and *W* get the same amount of linear space.

By contrast, *proportionally spaced* fonts give differing amounts of line space, depending on the character. A *W* gets more space than an *l* or an *i*. The body text in this book uses proportionally spaced fonts, making it easier to read. The advantage of using monospaced fonts is that they allow you to easily align columns of text or numbers when you're using a simple word processor such as Notepad or sending email. You can use the Spacebar to align the items in the columns, as you would on a typewriter.

> **TIP**
>
> Aligning text in emails can be tricky. Although numbers in most proportionally spaced fonts are monospaced, each press of the Spacebar when a proportional font is in use moves the cursor only a small increment. Even if you use tabs to align text, different email clients may interpret tabs differently or might use a proportional font and replace tabs with spaces, throwing off alignment. To help align columns of text in emails, send email HTML-based (rich-text) format if the receiver can handle it, or attach a document in a common format such as MS Word that contains properly aligned text.
>
> See Chapter 16, "Windows Mail," for more details about HTML mail.

Two other categories of fonts (after headline and body text) are ornamental and nonalphabetic symbols. *Ornamental* (sometimes called *display*) fonts have limited application. They are often fun in the short term, or for a one-shot deal such as a poster or a gag. They often attract attention but are too highly stylized to be suitable for body text, and they can distract the readers' attention from your message. Windows Vista doesn't include decorative fonts, although it includes a few script fonts (which mimic handwriting). You should use ornamental fonts sparingly and only when you want to set a special mood.

Symbol or pi fonts contain special symbols such as musical notes, map symbols, or decorations instead of letters, numbers, and punctuation marks. Good examples are Symbol, Zapf Dingbats, and WingDings.

→ To learn more about symbol and other nonkeyboard characters, **see** "Character Map," this chapter, **p. 892**.

FONT AND FONT INFORMATION SOURCES

The Microsoft Typography website (www.microsoft.com/typography/default.mspx) provides a wealth of information about fonts, including tools, utilities, and links. Go to www.microsoft.com/typography/links/links.aspx?type=foundries&part=1 to find a list of all commercial, freeware, and shareware type foundries.

Some of my favorite commercial font foundries include

- **Adobe Systems** (www.adobe.com/type/index.html)—Features low-cost font libraries for educators and the Adobe Font Folio collection of more than 2,200 typefaces.
- **Bitstream** (www.bitstream.com; sales at www.myfonts.com)—This site also features WhatTheFont, a font identification service.
- **Monotype** (www.fonts.com)—Home of many Windows fonts, including Times New Roman and Arial.

Save money and find some unusual fonts with these low-cost font sources:

- **BuyFonts** (www.buyfonts.com)—Starter and professional fonts (for Windows only)
- **FontCraft** (www.fontcraft.com)—Features a huge variety of historic and specialized fonts

You can also find a lot of low-cost or free fonts online or in CD collections at retail stores.

Font Substitutions

In a perfect world, everyone working with a particular document would already have the correct fonts necessary to view and print it just as the originator intended. Unless you use only the basic fonts that every version of Windows from 3.1 to the present has included as standard (Arial, Courier New, and Times New Roman) or embed the fonts you use in a document (a feature not all applications or all fonts support), mismatches between installed fonts on the system used to create the document and on the target system are likely to happen.

To enable a document created with missing fonts to display and print in a reasonable facsimile of the original, font substitution features in applications and printer drivers are used. For example, in Microsoft Word, to determine whether font substitutions are taking place, choose Tools, Options, Compatibility, Font Substitutions. Some applications, such as CorelDraw, display a warning dialog box and provide the opportunity to select a substitute font if you open a file that contains fonts not present on your system.

Another kind of font substitution pertains only to PostScript printers. Because PostScript printers have internal fonts, printing is faster using them than forcing Windows to download a similar font file into the PostScript rasterizer and then commence printing. For example, the Windows Arial font and the PostScript Helvetica font are virtually identical. So, you can tell your PostScript printer driver to use only the Helvetica font in the printer whenever you print a document formatted with Arial. Likewise, Times can be substituted for Windows's Times New Roman.

A font substitution table is responsible for setting the relationship of the screen and printer fonts. In Windows Vista, you can find this table on the Device Settings tab of a printer's Properties dialog box.

Font Installation and Management

In Windows Vista, font management is performed by right-clicking any empty space in the Fonts folder and using the Fonts menu that appears.

You can group or sort fonts by font name, size of the font file, or font type (OpenType, TrueType, or raster). Unfortunately, Windows Vista does not offer the helpful List Fonts by Similarity feature found in Windows XP.

> **TIP**
> The only way Windows Vista provides to view the appearance of a font is to open the font file in the Fonts folder. Click the Print button to make a printed sample. This can be a tedious way to locate the right font for a project. Consider downloading a freeware or shareware font manager to use for previewing, or select your fonts from within an application that provides preview capabilities.

To install a font, select Install New Font from the right-click Fonts menu.

1. Browse to the location of the font files you want to install. Use the Network button if the files are across the LAN. It runs the Map Network Drive Wizard. After you target the source folder, all the fonts in that location are listed in the dialog box.
2. Select the fonts you want to install. Note that if you want an entire font family, you have to select all similarly named files. If you try to install a font that's already in your system, the installer won't let you, so don't worry about accidentally loading one you already have.
3. By default, a font that's not in the Fonts folder already will be copied to the folder. You can change this default, but you're better off to keep it enabled.
4. Click Install and then Continue on the User Account Control pop-up window.
5. Click Close to complete the process, or keep the Add Fonts dialog box open if you need to install more fonts from another location.

To remove fonts from your system, select them in the Fonts folder (be sure to select all variations, such as Bold, Bold Italic, and Italic), right-click the selection and choose Delete. To remove them permanently, hold down either Shift key before selecting Delete. Click Continue on the User Account Control dialog box.

> **TIP**
> If you're serious about using fonts to make your documents and websites look better, you need better font-management tools than the Fonts folder. Consider the following:
> - Printer's Apprentice—Lose Your Mind Development; www.loseyourmind.com
> - Suitcase for Windows and Font Reserve for Windows—Extensis a division of Celartern, Inc.; www.extensis.com
> - Typograf—Neuber Software; www.neuber.com/typograph/index.html
> - FontLister—Theill.com; www.theill.com/fl/default.asp

Game Controllers

If you're serious about playing games on your computer, you need a game controller, such as a joystick, flightstick, gamepad, driving wheel, and other hardware devices designed specifically for the games of your choice. If you're an extreme gamer, the type of controller you need can vary greatly with the types of games you play. Game controllers have reached the point at which serious flight simulator enthusiasts hook up a flightstick, throttle, and separate rudder foot pedals to more accurately simulate the flying experience. Sports gamers usually go for handheld digital gamepads for fast response times. And fans of racing games just aren't getting the full experience without a force feedback steering wheel with its own set of foot pedals for the gas and break (and possibly even a clutch).

This book doesn't cover gaming to any extent, but if you are a gamer, and you buy a game controller, it likely comes with an installation program. If not, Windows Vista may detect it automatically, or you may need to run the Add Hardware applet. If that doesn't seem to work, you can try adding it through the Game Controllers applet, which is found in the Hardware and Sound category of the Control Panel, or in Classic view. In most cases, USB devices have no-brainer installations. Just plug it in and you are good to go.

After you install a game controller, you can click the Advanced button if you need to alter the controller ID and the port to which it's connected. Each game controller should be assigned a different ID. You can share the same game port for a number of controllers by disconnecting one and connecting another. You might be prompted to remove a game controller from the list before a new one can be connected, however, depending on the kind of controller and the port to which it's connected.

- For a custom controller (one not listed in the Add list), click Add, and then click Custom. Fill in the settings for controller type, axes, and number of buttons; then give the controller a name.
- To choose from a list of brand-name controllers, click Add Other, and choose a manufacturer and model. (Some of the devices that show up in this list aren't game controllers, but many are.) If you have a disk for your game port or game controllers, click Have Disk, insert the diskette if necessary, or browse to the appropriate folder location.

To help provide the best gaming environment, Windows Vista introduces the latest member of the DirectX family of accelerated 3D APIs for audio and video: DirectX 10. Windows Vista SP-1 includes DirectX 10.1, an incremental improvement on DirectX 10, which was introduced by the original release of Windows Vista. DirectX 10 introduced a unified graphics architecture called Windows Graphics Foundation, which replaced separate APIs used for graphics, audio, and other features in previous DirectX versions. DirectX 10 was a complete rewrite of DirectX.

DirectX 10.1 offers additional shading and texturing capabilities (it includes the new Shader Model 4.1), improved anti-aliasing, and improved floating-point precision. DirectX 10.1 is backward-compatible with DirectX 10 and incorporates support for DirectX 9.

Keyboard

The Keyboard applet (see Figure 25.22) lets you fine-tune the way the keyboard behaves, check the keyboard driver, and perform some keyboard troubleshooting. Find it in the Hardware and Sound category of the Control Panel, or in Classic view.

Figure 25.22
Adjusting key-repeat speed and delay can be useful for avoiding unwanted characters.

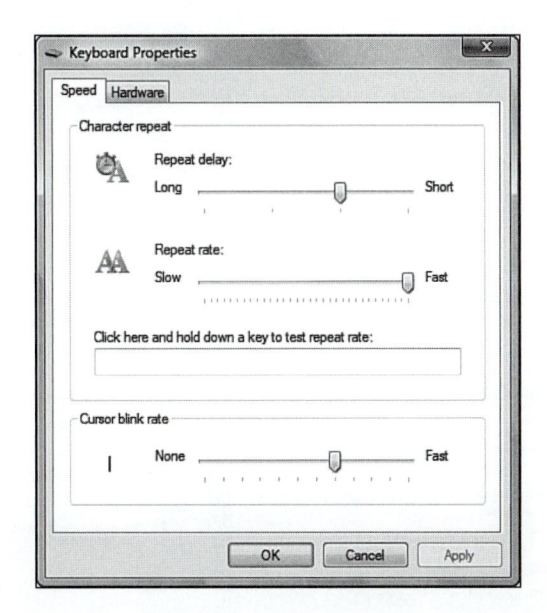

The main attractions here are the repeat rate, the repeat delay, and the cursor blink rate. By altering the key-repeat delay (the time after pressing a key before it starts to repeat) and the repeat speed, you can calm down an ill-behaved keyboard or improve usability for someone with a mobility impairment. Altering the delay before the repeat sets in might be helpful if you use applications that require extensive use of, say, the PgUp and PgDn, Enter, or the arrow keys (perhaps in a point-of-sale situation).

You also might want to change the cursor blink rate if the standard blinking cursor annoys you for some reason. You can even stop it altogether (the setting is "none"). I prefer a non-blinking one myself.

The defaults for these keyboard settings are adequate for most users and keyboards.

If you need to check keyboard properties, including the keyboard driver in use, click the Hardware tab and then click Properties. The Device Manager entry for the keyboard opens.

Mouse

It's almost impossible to use a modern computer without a mouse or equivalent pointing device. To make sure your mouse is working to your satisfaction, use the Control Panel's Mouse applet (see Figure 25.23) to fine-tune its operation. It's located in the Hardware and Sound category of the Control Panel, or in Classic view.

Figure 25.23
Setting mouse properties can help you get your work done more efficiently, though the defaults usually work fine without modification.

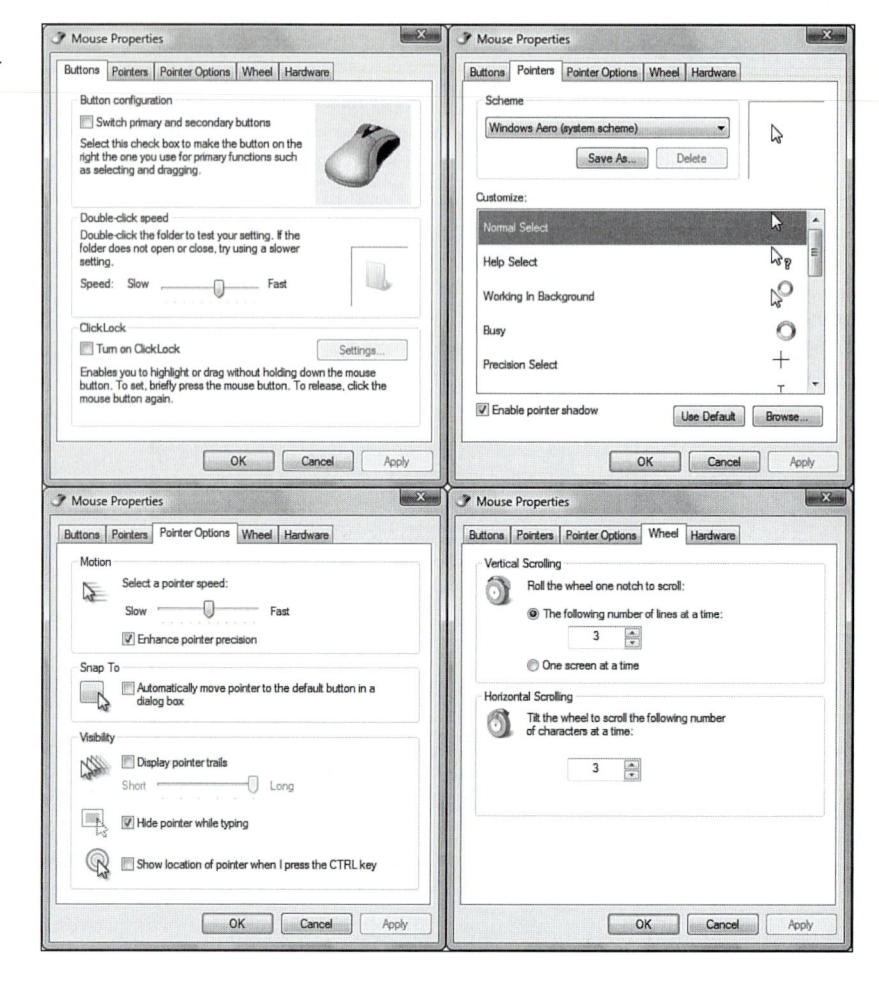

You can adjust

- Left/right button reversal
- Double-click speed
- ClickLock
- Look of the pointers
- Pointer scheme
- Pointer speed
- Enhance pointer precision
- Snap to the default button of dialog boxes
- Display pointer trails and length
- Hide pointer while typing
- Show location of pointer when Ctrl is pressed

- Set wheel scroll to number of lines or screen at a time
- Troubleshooting
- Access device properties (same controls as through Device Manager)

The options vary based on pointing device type, and sometimes you are supplied with even fancier options if your pointing device comes with a custom driver. For example, the Synaptics touchpads let you scroll a window by sliding your finger down the right side of the trackpad.

Poor lefties never get a fair shake in life, what with all the right-handed scissors and tools around. Well, they get one here (except for some types of weird, ergonomically shaped mouse devices that don't work well in the left hand). If you're left-handed, you can move the mouse to the left side of the keyboard and then reverse the function of the buttons on the Buttons tab of the Mouse applet. Right-clicks then become left-clicks. (Unfortunately, changing the setting won't make a corresponding adjustment to this book, which will continue to refer to right-clicks).

On the same tab, you can set the double-click speed. A middle-range setting is appropriate for most folks. Double-click the folder icon to try out the new double-click speed. The folder opens or closes if the double-click registered. If you're not faring well, adjust the slider, and then try again. You don't have to click Apply to test the slider settings. Just moving the slider instantly affects the mouse's double-click speed.

If all else fails and you just can't find a double-click speed to suit your needs or abilities, forget double-clicks altogether. Instead, click an icon or any selectable object in the Windows Vista environment. A single-click usually will highlight the option. Think of this as getting the object's attention. Then press Enter on the keyboard to launch, open, or execute the selected object.

As you know, the pointer cursor changes based on the task at hand. For example, when you're editing text, it becomes an I-beam. You can customize your cursors for the fun of it or to increase visibility. You can even install animated cursors to amuse yourself while you wait for some process to complete. Just as with icons and screen savers, the Web is littered with Windows cursors, if you want to collect a few thousand. Windows Vista comes with enough to keep me happy, organized into schemes. You can change individual cursors or change a set of them in one fell swoop by using the *cursor schemes*.

Like color schemes and sound schemes, cursor schemes are collections of cursor shapes. When you select a scheme, all the cursors in the scheme go into effect at once. You can choose from approximately 20 canned schemes.

NOTE

Use one of the Extra Large cursor schemes if you have trouble seeing the pointer. Also, some of the schemes change the pointer into things that don't resemble pointers and can make selecting or clicking small objects difficult because the pointer's hotspot is difficult to locate. Sometimes, the cursor is distracting and can obscure the item you want to select or click.

You can change individual cursors in a scheme, if you want. To change a cursor assignment, click a cursor in the list. Then click Browse. The default location is …\windows\cursors. Animated cursors move for you in the Browse box (a thoughtful feature). After you custom tailor a set of cursors to your liking, you can save the scheme for later recall. Click Save As and name it.

Windows Vista supports both the now-traditional scrolling wheel and the newer horizontal tilting mouse wheel with the Wheel tab. Use this tab to adjust how both types of wheels operate.

Click the Hardware tab and click Properties to open the Device Manager entry for the mouse.

PERFORMANCE INFORMATION AND TOOLS

Performance Information and Tools combines a brand-new method for rating computer performance, the Windows Experience Index, with easier access to a wide variety of performance-adjusting settings used in previous Windows versions. The principle behind Performance Information and Tools is to help you determine how well your system runs Windows Vista and to make it as easy as possible to tweak your system for better performance. It is available from the System and Maintenance category of Control Panel, or in Classic view.

THE WINDOWS EXPERIENCE INDEX

When you open Performance Information and Tools, the first item you're likely to notice on the main dialog box is the Windows Experience Index base score and component ratings (see Figure 25.24).

Figure 25.24
The Windows Experience Index includes scores from five different subsystems, but the lowest score determines your system's rating.

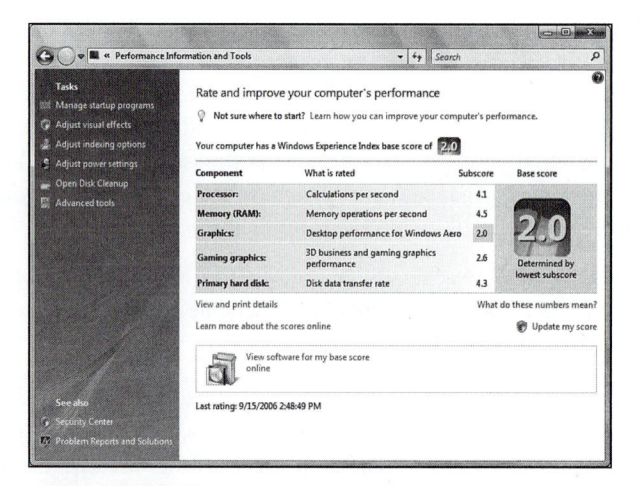

Five subsystems are evaluated to provide the basis for determining the Windows Experience Index:

- Your processor's calculations per second (CPU)
- Memory operations per second (RAM)
- Desktop performance for Windows Aero (Aero)
- 3D business and gaming graphics performance (3D)
- Your primary hard disk's data transfer rate (HD)

(The parentheticals in the preceding list identify the subsystems as listed in Table 25.15.)

Each item is scored, and the lowest score (note—*not* an average) is used to calculate the computer's Windows Experience Index. This might seem like an odd method to use, but the advantage is that it helps you determine what part of your system is the principle performance bottleneck. For example, in examining the system shown in Figure 25.24, note that the lowest scores (2.0 and 2.6) are related to the graphics card. By upgrading the graphics card to one with a more powerful GPU, the system's Windows Experience Index should increase. The other scores are 4.1 or higher, indicating satisfactory performance.

Interpreting the Windows Experience Index

How important is the Windows Experience Index (WEI) base score (the lowest of the subsystem scores) to your satisfaction with Windows Vista? According to Microsoft, computers with base scores of 2 or less will satisfactorily perform basic tasks such as office productivity or web surfing but are probably not powerful enough to run Windows Aero or advanced multimedia features. Computers with a base score of 3 can run Windows Aero but may not be powerful enough to run high-end features such as Aero across multiple displays or display HDTV. Computers with a base score of 4 or higher can use all features. The highest score, 5.9, was achieved by the fastest performing computers available when Windows Vista was released. For more information, see "What Is the Windows Experience Index?" at http://windowshelp.microsoft.com/Windows/en-US/Help/f59082f4-6385-4a61-ba7e-2de9625a780a1033.mspx.

Table 25.15 summarizes the WEI subsystem performance levels you'll want for three different types of computer usage.

Table 25.15 Desirable Windows Experience Index Subsystem Scores

Major Computer Use	CPU	RAM	Aero	3D	HD
Office productivity	4.0 or higher	4.0 or higher	2.0 or higher	2.0 or higher	2.0 or higher
Gaming and graphics-intensive programs	3.0 or higher	4.0 or higher	4.0 or higher	4.0 or higher	3.0 or higher
Media Center experience	4.0 or higher	3.0 or higher	4.0 or higher	3.0 or higher	4.0 or higher

The easiest way to improve the Windows Experience Index in a major way is to upgrade one or more of the major subsystems it rates. For example, replacing the video card can boost scores for Aero and for 3D graphics. Adding more RAM can boost memory scores. Upgrading to a faster processor can boost processor scores. Upgrading to a hard disk with a larger buffer, faster rotation rate, or both, can increase hard disk performance. Some upgrades, such as RAM and CPU, will boost performance in multiple areas.

If you decide to upgrade your system, look at the following factors:

- **Integrated video**—If you can replace integrated video with a PCI Express (PCI-E) or AGP video card that uses a GPU listed on the Windows Vista-compatible GPU list, you can significantly improve your Aero and 3D scores. Look for a unit with at least 128MB of RAM if you are primarily concerned about business graphics, or a unit with 256MB or more of RAM for 3D gaming. The latest nVidia GPUs have model numbers in the 9xxx series, whereas the latest ATI GPUs have model numbers HD 3xxx. Higher model numbers generally indicate better performance, but see the manufacturers' websites for details.

- **Processor**—Economy processors such as the AMD Sempron or Intel Celeron have slower core clock speeds, slower front side bus connections to memory, and smaller L2 cache sizes than their full-performance counterparts (AMD Phenom, 64FX, 64 X2 or Intel Core 2 Duo, Core 2 Quad). However, a processor upgrade might also require a motherboard and memory module upgrade as well. Look at other upgrades first to improve your system's base and subsystem scores.

- **Memory (RAM)**—Vista runs best with at least 1GB of RAM available to Windows. Many so-called "1GB" systems, particularly laptops, actually share as much as 128MB of RAM with the integrated graphics subsystem. Thus, for best system performance, consider upgrading systems that use shared video memory to 1.5GB or more of system memory.

    To determine the amount of memory actually available to Windows, type **DXDIAG** into the Instant Desktop Search box and press Enter. This runs DirectX Diagnostics. The System dialog indicates the amount of memory available to Windows in either Vista or Vista SP-1.

    The System properties sheet in Vista SP-1 now shows total system memory, including memory set aside for graphics memory. The difference between these amounts in Vista SP-1 is the amount of RAM used for shared video (graphics) memory.

- **Hard disk drives**—The best hard disks for desktop computers feature spin rates (RPM) of 7,200 to 10,000 and 16MB or larger buffer sizes. If your hard disk has a lower spin rate, smaller buffer size, or both, it's limiting the performance of your system. If you're considering a hard disk upgrade, keep in mind that new Serial ATA (SATA) drives are generally faster and larger than traditional PATA (ATA/IDE) drives. However, some older systems may have limited or no support for SATA drives. Laptop drives tend to feature lower spin rates, smaller buffer sizes, and smaller capacities than desktop drives.

Performance Information and Tools | 853

Click the link Learn How You Can Improve Your Computer's Performance to learn about the tools provided in the Tasks pane on the left side. Each of these tools is discussed in the following sections.

> **TIP**
> When you display your system's Windows Experience Index, you may see specific advice that a particular program, process, or setting is slowing down your system. Use this information to go directly to the best task to help improve performance. For example, if a startup program is causing system problems, you'll be advised to use the Manage Startup Programs task.

Manage Startup Programs with Windows Defender

Startup programs can slow down your system, in some cases because some startup programs might contain spyware. Consequently, when you click the Manage startup programs link from the Performance Information and Tools Tasks pane, the Windows Defender Software Explorer opens to its Startup programs listing (see Figure 25.25).

Figure 25.25
Use the Windows Defender Software Explorer to selectively disable startup programs that might slow down your system or contain spyware.

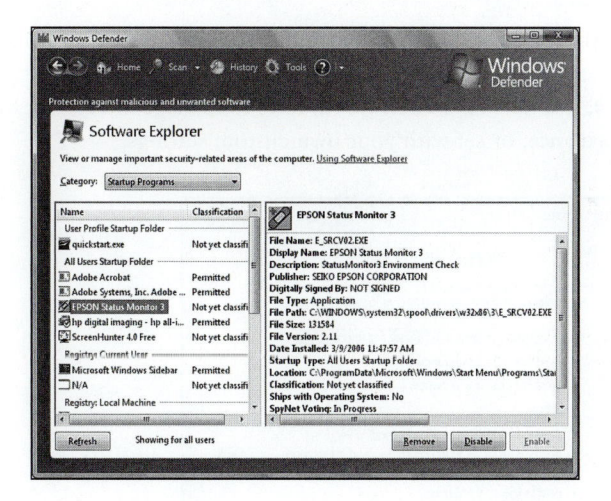

To learn more about a particular startup program, select it from the list on the left side of the dialog. The right side of the dialog box displays technical information about the program. The classification for each program (Permitted, Not yet classified, and so forth) is based on voting by SpyNet (Microsoft's antispyware community).

If you see a program listed whose status you want to adjust, click Show for All Users and provide administrator-level credentials as needed. Select the program. You can now use one of three options to adjust the program's startup capabilities:

- To prevent the program from running at startup, click Disable. This option permits you to re-enable the program to run at startup at a later point.

- To enable a disabled program, click Enable. The program will run automatically the next time you start Windows Vista.
- To remove a program from the list of startup programs, click Remove. This does not uninstall the program, but it removes it from the list of potential startup programs.

> **NOTE**
>
> If you don't select Show for All Users, very few (if any) of the programs listed can be configured.

Click the Close button when you're finished.

> **TIP**
>
> The Autoruns for Windows tool, which you can search for and download from Microsoft.com, provides an even more detailed way to view and control startup programs.

ADJUST VISUAL EFFECTS

When you select this option from the Tasks pane of Performance Information and Tools, you open the Visual Effects tab of the (Computer) Performance Options properties sheet (see Figure 25.26). Use this tab to allow Windows to manage effects, set for best appearance, set for best performance, or set with your own custom settings.

Figure 25.26
The Visual Effects tab of the Performance Options dialog box.

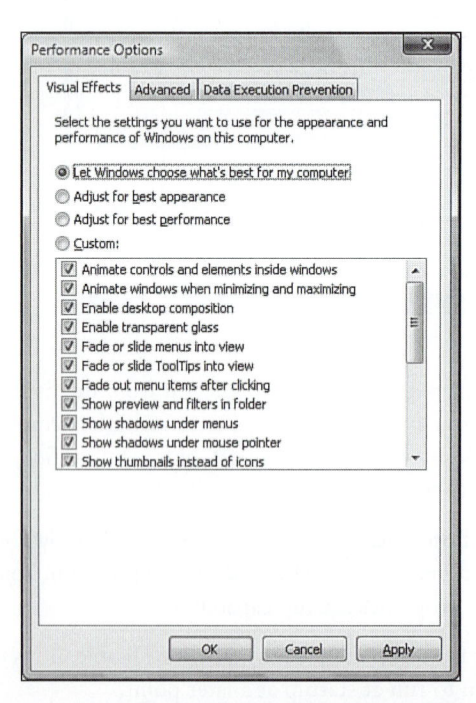

When Custom settings is selected, you can then enable or disable a long list of effects. These effects include animate resizing of windows, fade ToolTips, show shadows under menus, and use visual styles on windows and buttons.

Unless your system is low on physical RAM or uses integrated video or a PCI (not PCI Express or AGP) video card, there is little need to modify the default settings for these controls in respect to performance. However, if you think no shadows or no animation looks better, you can customize the look and feel of the user environment all you want.

> **TIP**
>
> Keep in mind that you can also boost your visual performance more significantly by switching from Aero to Vista Basic. By ditching the 3D and transparency effects in Aero, your system will display windows faster.

ADJUST INDEXING OPTIONS

One of the most important 'behind the scenes' features in Windows Vista is the integrated indexing feature. It enables you to find a file in just seconds with Instant Desktop Search and zero in on the media you want to play in Windows Media Player, to give just two examples of how indexing makes life in Windows Vistaland easier and more fun.

When you click the Adjust Indexing Options task in Performance Information and Tools, you open the Indexing Options dialog box (see Figure 25.27). The top of the dialog box lists the number of items indexed and the locations that are indexed. Click Modify to specify what to index. Click Advanced (and provide administrator-level credentials as required) to repair or rebuild indexes (Index Settings tab) or to adjust how indexing takes place for each file extension registered on the system (File Types tab). Files containing readable text (.doc, .xls, and similar) are indexed by name and contents, whereas other types of files are indexed by name only. To learn more about Indexing, see Chapter 26.

Figure 25.27
The Indexing Options dialog.

Other Performance Options

Selecting the Adjust Power Settings task opens the Power Options dialog discussed later in this chapter. Selecting the Open Disk Cleanup task opens the Disk Cleanup utility. For details, see Chapter 27.

Advanced Tools

Click the Advanced Tools task in Performance Information and Tools to open the Advanced Tools dialog (see Figure 25.28). This dialog provides see specific suggestions for improving system performance and links to seven different tools you can use to fine-tune performance.

Figure 25.28
The Advanced Tools tab for a system whose performance can be improved by changing visual settings.

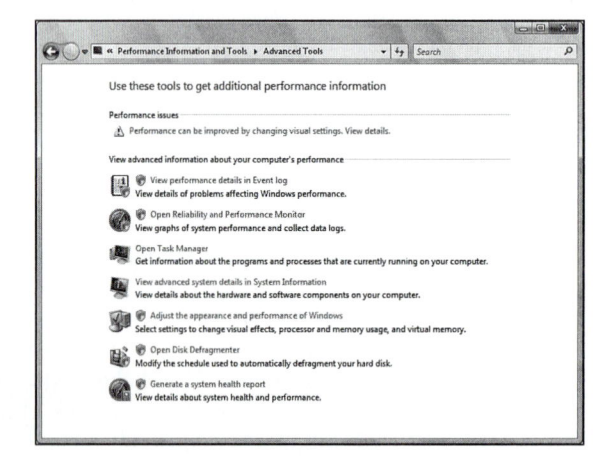

Click each item under the Performance issues category to open a pop-up window with specific recommendations for improving performance.

Table 25.16 lists the advanced information tasks and where they are discussed in this book.

TABLE 25.16   ADVANCED PERFORMANCE INFORMATION TASKS

Task	Opens	For More Information
View performance details in Event Log	Microsoft Management Console Event Viewer	"Computer Management" (this chapter, p. 876)
Open Reliability and Performance Monitor	Reliability and Performance Monitor	"Reliability and Performance Monitor" (this chapter, p. 859)
Open Task Manager	Task Manager	"Task Manager" (this chapter, p. 886)
View advanced system details in System Information	MSInfo32 (System Information) summary page	"System Information" (this chapter, p. 892)

TABLE 25.16 CONTINUED

Task	Opens	For More Information
Adjust the appearance and performance of Windows	Visual Effects and Advanced tabs of the Performance Options properties sheet	"Adjust Visual Effects and Performance Options" (this chapter, p. 890)
Open Disk Defragmenter	Disk Defragmenter	"Disk Defragmenter" (Chapter 27, p. 943)
Generate a system health report	Reliability and Performance Monitor, System Diagnostics Report	"System Diagnostics Report" (this chapter, p. 860)

RELIABILITY AND PERFORMANCE MONITOR

The Reliability and Performance Monitor provides Windows Vista users with a one-stop solution for tracking system performance along with a brand-new system reliability measurement tool.

RESOURCE OVERVIEW

Reliability and Performance Monitor opens to the Resource Overview (see Figure 25.29), which provides real-time information on CPU, disk, network, and memory subsystem performance. Although this display is somewhat reminiscent of the Performance tab in Windows XP's Task Manager, the Resource Overview provides four gauges, instead of two as in Windows XP's Performance tab, and when you click on a gauge, it displays program and process details.

Figure 25.29
Viewing the details of Memory usage with the Resource Overview.

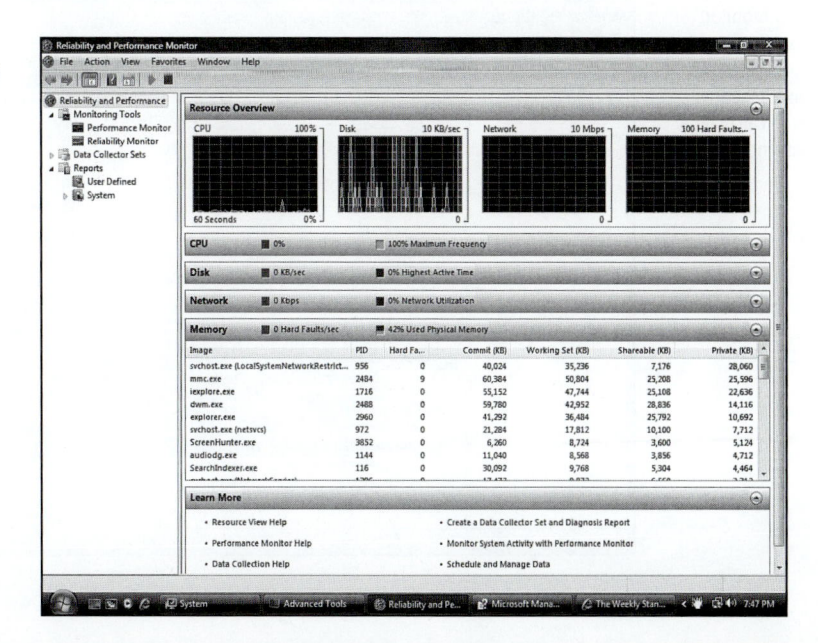

Performance Monitor

For an even more detailed and customizable look at system performance data, click the Performance Monitor node. Performance Monitor permits you to choose from dozens of performance counters ranging from .NET to iSCSI, TCP v4 and v6, WMI objects, and many others. You can monitor local or network computers with Performance Monitor, and you can view information in line, bar, or report modes. Right-click the counter area to add, edit, or remove counters; save the current image; or view properties (see Figure 25.30).

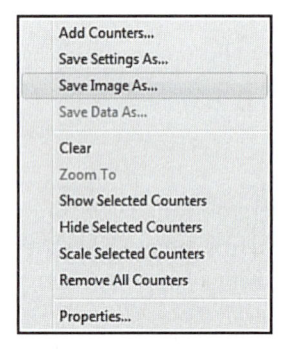

Figure 25.30
Preparing to save the current Performance Monitor counters as an image.

Reliability Monitor

How reliable is *your* system? Until now, it's been difficult to quantify the answer to that question. However, Windows Vista's brand-new Reliability Monitor (see Figure 25.31) provides solid information you can use to determine system reliability.

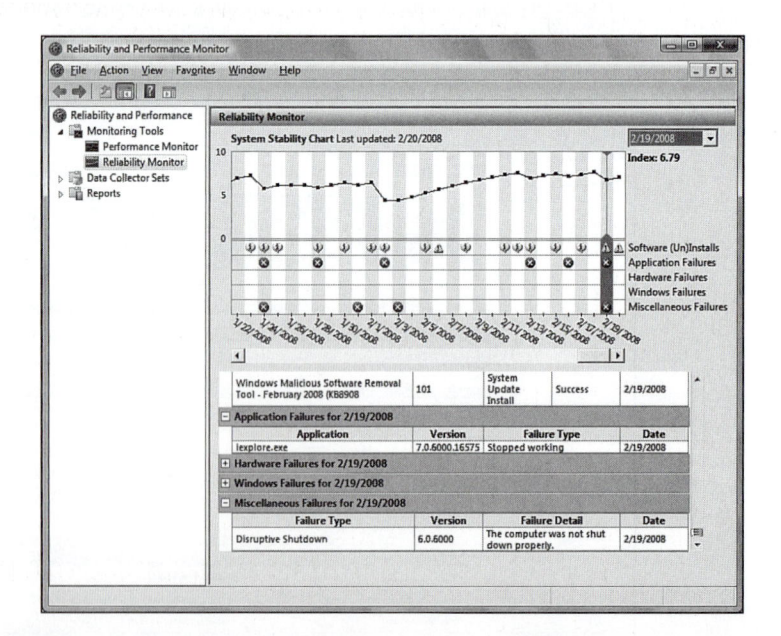

Figure 25.31
Reliability Monitor tracks application, hardware, Windows, and miscellaneous failures to calculate a reliability index.

In addition to tracking failures in four areas (applications, hardware, Windows, and miscellaneous), Reliability Monitor also tracks software installs and uninstalls (including both drivers and applications) and captures version information for drivers and applications. It also calculates a reliability index. A yellow ! symbol indicates a failed application or driver install, whereas a red X symbol indicates other types of failures.

Data Collector Sets and Reports

Reliability and Performance Monitor includes predefined four data collector sets you can use for system diagnostics: LAN Diagnostics, System Diagnostics, System Performance, and Wireless Diagnostics.

To create your own data collector set, open the Data Collector Sets node, right-click User Defined, and select New, Data Collector Set. This starts a Create New Data Collector Wizard. By selecting the option to create a data collector set from a template, you can create a Basic data collector set, which collects performance counter, configuration, and kernel trace data; a System Diagnostics collector set, which collects primarily configuration data for major hardware and system protection subsystems; or a System Performance data collector set, which collects NT Kernel and Performance counter information. You can also create customized data collector sets and create a data collector set directly from the Performance Monitor display pane.

After collecting data, you can view reports by opening the Reports node and selecting the appropriate user-defined or System report. Reports are stored in XML. Figure 25.32 shows a portion of the LAN Diagnostics wired report.

Figure 25.32
Viewing a report created with the LAN Diagnostics System data collector set.

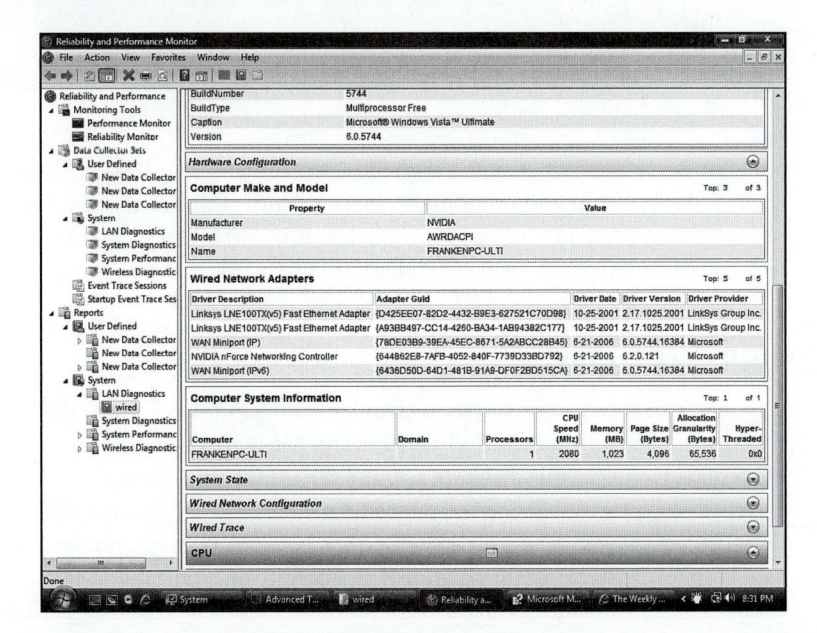

System Diagnostics Report

When you click Generate a System Health Report from the Advanced Tools menu, as shown in Figure 25.28, Windows Vista uses the Reliability and Performance Monitor to scan the system and display a System Diagnostics Report. A typical example is shown in Figure 25.33. The report includes information on system diagnostics, software configuration, hardware configuration, and CPU, network, disk, and memory subsystems, and concludes with a summary of the system and the files used to create the report.

Figure 25.33
A portion of a typical System Diagnostics Report.

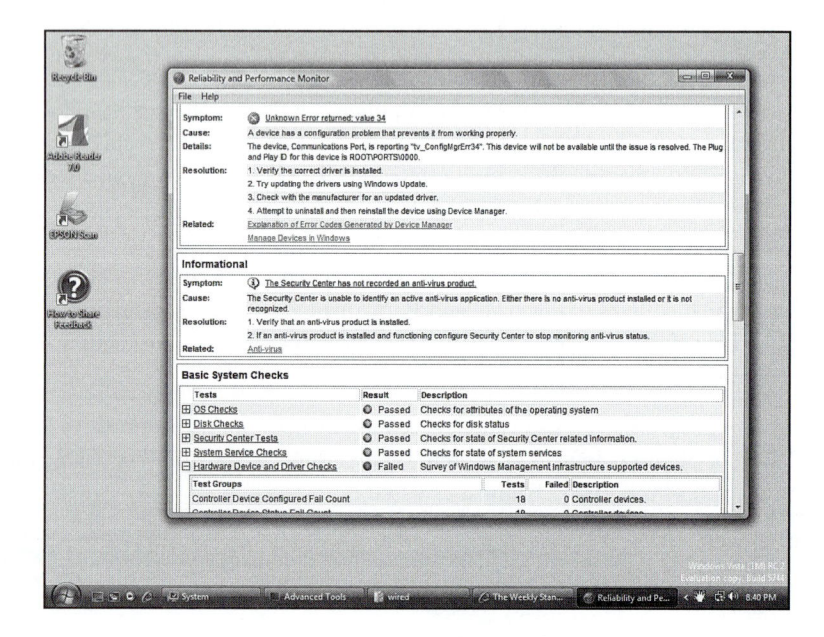

Some of the system components tracked by the System Diagnostics Report include disabled devices; device driver and other hardware problems; antivirus and firewall protection status; resource usage; system services; startup programs; SMART disk status; Windows Experience score; network interfaces; and CPU, hard disk network, and memory performance.

Power Options

Although the Power Options icon is familiar to Windows XP users, the Windows Vista version of this fundamental Control Panel utility has gone through some significant changes. On the main page of this dialog box, three different power plans (known as power schemes in earlier versions of Windows) are listed: Balanced, Power Saver, and High Performance. Balanced power plan strikes a happy medium between performance and energy savings on a desktop, or between performance and battery life on a portable system. Power Saver saves a lot of energy (provides a long battery life) but does so by reducing performance. High Performance maximizes system speed but uses a lot of energy on a desktop and provides a short battery life on a portable system. You can access Power Options through the Hardware and Sound category, or in Classic view.

→ To learn more about power settings on laptops and Tablet PCs, **see** "Getting the Most Out of Your Battery," **p. 1283**.

Programs and Features

Programs and Features performs most of the same tasks for Windows Vista that the Add or Remove Programs applet performed for Windows XP. However, there is no provision for installing programs with Programs and Features. Because this feature was hardly used in Add or Remove Programs, its absence in Programs and Features is no great loss. The major functions of Programs and Features include

- Changing or uninstalling existing programs
- Viewing installed updates
- Ordering new programs online at Windows Marketplace
- Viewing purchased software (a feature Microsoft calls the *Digital Locker*)
- Enabling or disabling Windows features

Programs and Features is available from the Programs category of Control Panel and is also available in Classic view.

Uninstall or Change a Program

You may occasionally have programs on your system that don't show up in the Uninstall or Change a Program listing you see when you open Programs and Features (see Figure 25.34). Only programs that comply with the 32-bit Windows API standard for installation have their filenames and locations recorded in the system database, allowing them to be reliably removed without adversely affecting the operation of Windows. Many older or less-sophisticated applications simply install in their own way and don't bother registering with the operating system. These programs, which are increasingly rare today, must be removed manually.

Figure 25.34
The main window of the Programs and Features applet lists programs that can be uninstalled or changed.

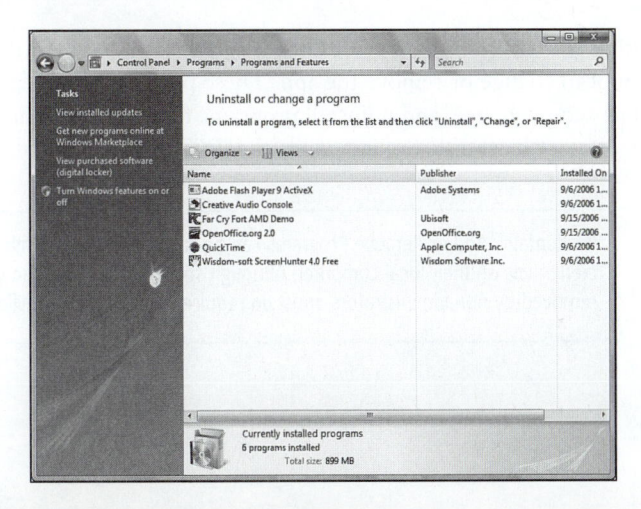

> **TIP**
>
> Never attempt to remove an application from your system by deleting its files from the \Program Files folders (or wherever). Actually, never may be too strong. Removal through manual deletion should only be done as a last resort. Always attempt to use the Programs and Features applet or the uninstall utility from the application first. Contact the vendor for help if you cannot uninstall the application. In a few cases, it might be necessary to go into the system Registry to remove pieces of an application.

What's more, the built-in uninstaller lets you make changes to applications, such as adding or removing suboptions (assuming the application supports that feature).

Use of the uninstall feature of the applet is simple:

1. Open the Programs and Features applet from the Control Panel.
2. Check the list of installed applications. A typical list appeared previously in Figure 25.34. Note that you can sort the applications by interesting criteria in the sort box, such as size or date of installation. You can use this information to find space-hogging programs you don't use.
3. Select the program you want to change or uninstall.
4. Click the Uninstall or Change buttons above the program listing. Note that program listings marked as (Remove Only) don't offer Change as an option.
5. Answer any warnings about removing an application as appropriate.
6. At the end of the process, the selected program is removed from your system and from the list of installed applications. Depending on the program you uninstalled, you may need to restart your system.

> **TIP**
>
> Obviously, removing an application can't easily be reversed by, say, restoring files from the Recycle Bin, because shortcuts on the Start menu and Registry settings are also deleted.

Some applications (for example, Microsoft Office) prompt you to insert the program CD when you attempt to change or remove the app. These prompts can be annoying, but what can you do? The setup, change, and uninstall programs for some large suites are stored on their CDs, not on your hard disk. So, just insert the disc when prompted.

> **NOTE**
>
> Incidentally, Add or Remove Programs can be run only by users with Administrator credentials on their local computer. Although some applications can be installed or removed by nonadministrators, most do require administrative privilege.

View Installed Updates

To see updates for Microsoft Windows Vista, Microsoft Office applications, and other applications that receive updates through Windows Update or Microsoft Update, click View Installed Updates in the Tasks pane of Programs and Features. All installed program (but not driver) updates are shown. Figure 25.35 shows a typical listing on a system running Microsoft Office 2003.

Figure 25.35
Viewing updates for Microsoft Office 2003 and Microsoft Windows Vista.

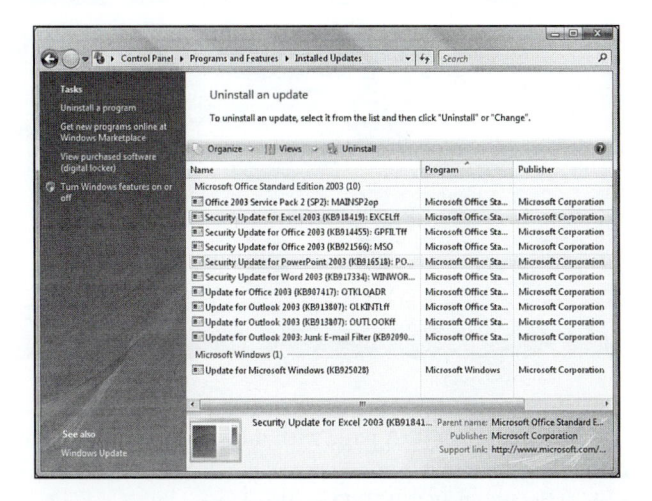

> **NOTE**
>
> To view updates for separate programs bundled with Windows Vista, such as Windows Defender and Windows Media Player, or hardware driver updates, open the Windows Update icon in the Control Panel's Classic view.

If you determine that an installed update is not working correctly, select it and click Uninstall. (Note that some updates cannot be uninstalled.)

Windows Marketplace

When you select Get New Programs Online at Windows Marketplace, your web browser opens the Windows Marketplace website. Select from Top Sellers, Windows Vista, Game Downloads, and IE Add-ons. Tens of thousands of downloads are available, so use the Narrow Your Selection categories at left to shop by category, manufacturer, vendor, price (criteria vary by category), or the new Digital Locker feature (discussed in the next section). Figure 25.36 shows a typical view of the Security Downloads category.

Figure 25.36
Viewing available software at the Windows Marketplace downloads website.

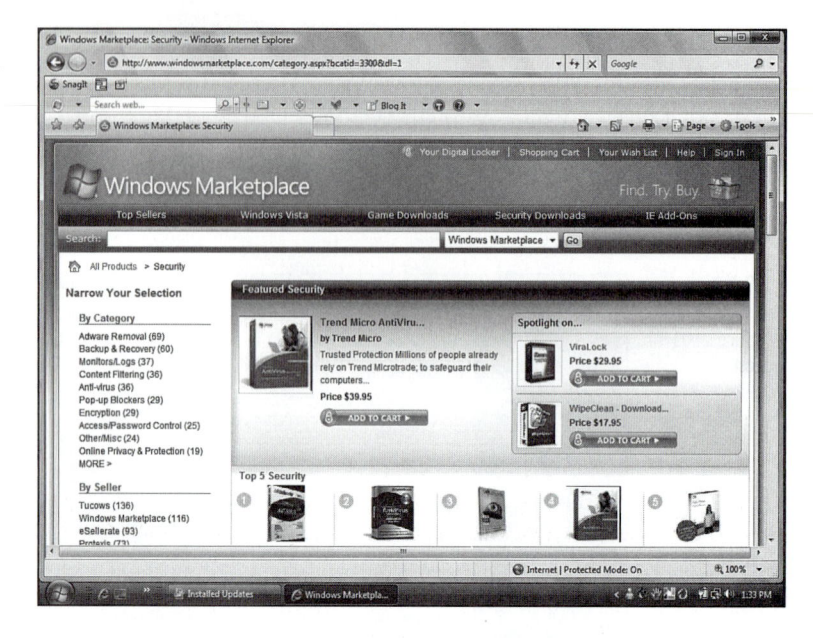

To purchase or try an item, select it. A page with more information opens. Follow the links on the page to download the item. In many cases, you'll be directed to a non-Microsoft shareware site such as Tucows or CNET Download.com.

Digital Locker

The Microsoft Digital Locker is a new concept in purchasing software online. Items that can be purchased using Digital Locker have a padlock icon in the product listing. Digital Locker has the following features:

- Uses Windows Live ID (formerly Passport) Network Credentials.
- Enables you to buy from multiple retailers with a single checkout.
- A free Digital Locker assistant program manages your downloads. This assistant is included in Windows Vista and can be downloaded for other Windows versions.
- You can access your purchased software online as needed.
- Many vendors that support Digital Locker purchase also offer free trials. When you click on a link to learn more about the program, look for the Try It First link next to the Buy and Download button.

Microsoft is trying to position Digital Locker as the greatest thing for online commerce, but, we're concerned about privacy issues surrounding Live ID.

→ To learn more about privacy concerns with Live ID, **see** "Hey, Who's Afraid of Microsoft Live ID?," **p. 465**.

Setting Up Digital Locker

To set up Digital Locker, click the Your Digital Locker button at the top of a Windows Marketplace website. Enter your username and Microsoft Passport email address and click Sign In. If you are signing in for the first time, confirm your email address and click Create Account on the next dialog box.

To add a credit (or debit) card to your account, click Profile and complete the information requested. You can add more than one card to your account; each card you add appears at the top of the dialog box.

After completing this information, you're ready to shop! If you're not planning to shop right away, be sure to click the Log Out button at the top of the dialog box.

Shopping with Digital Locker

When you go to Windows Marketplace, select Digital Locker as part of your shopping criteria to simplify your shopping experience. Otherwise, look for the green Digital Locker padlock icon next to some programs.

Click the program listing to display details. To buy and download the program with Digital Locker, click the Buy and Download button. Figure 25.37 shows a typical Digital Locker-enabled download listing.

Figure 25.37
Preparing to buy and download a program using Digital Locker.

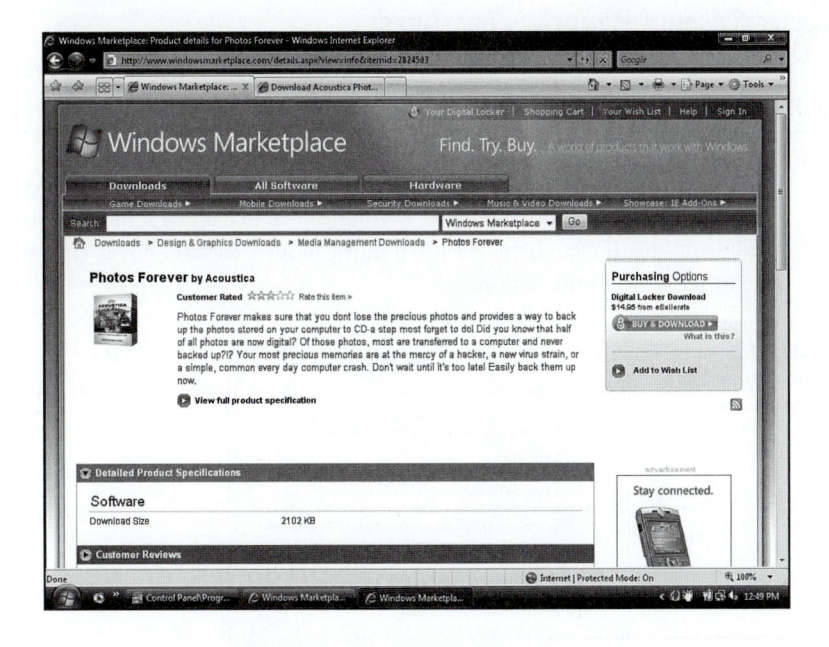

The program is added to your shopping cart. You can continue to shop until you are ready to check out. Click Checkout from the shopping cart to continue.

Sign in to Digital Locker when prompted. Select your preferred card from the Credit Card dialog box. Click Complete Purchase to complete your purchase.

From the Your Order Is Complete dialog box, click Download All to download all items purchased, or click the Download button for each item you purchased.

> **TIP**
> To make a record of your purchases, click the Printable View button when it appears and print the screen.

THE DIGITAL LOCKER ASSISTANT

You can download using your browser's file download utility, or the free Digital Locker assistant. Choose the assistant to make it easy to make a backup CD, manage your purchases, and review them whenever you want. Click Continue and then Start Digital Locker Assistant to download your purchased program. An IE Security dialog box appears, warning you that the download takes place outside the normal protected mode. Click Allow to continue.

Sign in to your Digital Locker to continue the download and installation process. To view your software purchased via Digital Locker, use the link in the Tasks menu of Programs and Features.

ENABLE/DISABLE WINDOWS FEATURES

In addition to managing add-on products and applications through the Programs and Features applet, you can also turn on or off Windows Vista features. Click the link on the Programs and Features Tasks pane to open the Windows Features dialog box shown in Figure 25.38.

Generally, you should need to add features only if you are configuring Windows Vista for specialized situations. For example, if you need to manage a remote client with Telnet, you should add the Telnet client. To learn more about a feature, hover your mouse over the feature to see a brief explanation.

Figure 25.38
Preparing to configure Windows features.

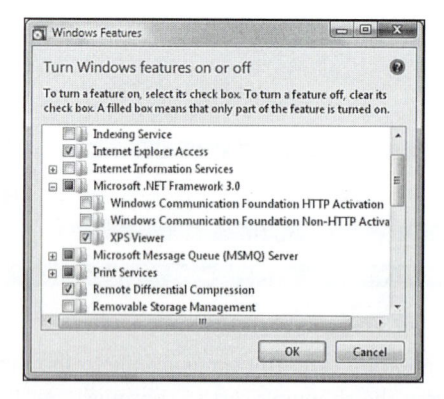

An empty check box indicates that the feature is turned off. A check mark in a box indicates that the feature is turned on. Shaded boxes indicate that only some features are turned on.

For example, note that the only active part of Microsoft .NET Framework 3.0 on this system is the XPS Viewer (which enables you to view documents created with the XPS Writer virtual printer included with Windows Vista).

To enable a feature, click an empty check box. To disable a feature, clear a check box. Click OK when you are finished.

> **NOTE** Enabling or disabling a feature doesn't change the size of your Windows Vista installation; it merely changes whether you can use the feature.

REGIONAL AND LANGUAGE OPTIONS

The Regional and Language Options settings affect the way Windows displays times, dates, numbers, and currency. When you install Windows, chances are good that the Regional settings are already set for your locale. This is certainly be true if you purchase a computer with Windows Vista preinstalled on it from a vendor in your country or area. The Regional and Language Options applet is found in the Clock, Language and Region category and is also available in Classic view.

Running this applet from the Control Panel displays the dialog box you see in Figure 25.39.

To change the settings, simply click the appropriate tab, and then click the drop-down list box for the setting in question. Examples of the current settings are shown in each section, so you don't need to change them unless they look wrong. The predefined standards are organized by language and then by country. If you can't find a standard to your liking, you can always create a customized format with the Customize This Format button.

Figure 25.39
Making changes to the Regional settings affects the display of date, time, and currency in Windows applications that use the internal Windows settings for such functions.

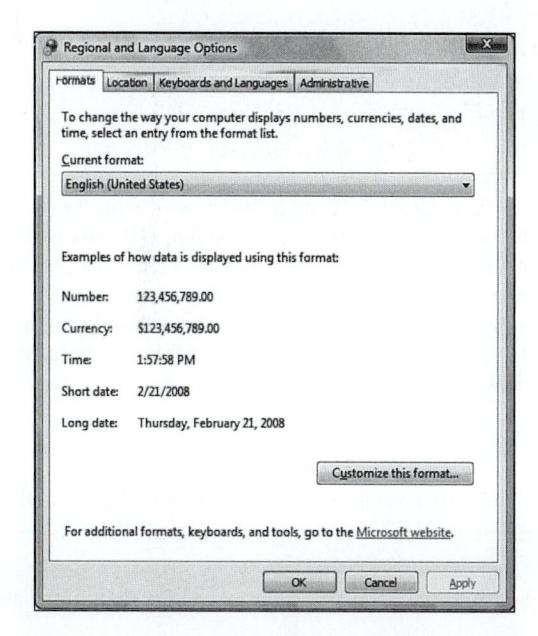

System

The System Properties sheet has long been perhaps the single most important part of the Control Panel for determining what's going on inside your system. Windows Vista has drastically remodeled the look and features of this properties sheet (see Figure 25.40) to better show you what's "under the hood." Access System from the System and Maintenance category, from Classic view, or by right-clicking Computer and selecting Properties.

Figure 25.40
The System Properties sheet in Windows Vista makes it easier than ever to view important information about your system's hardware, network settings, and performance.

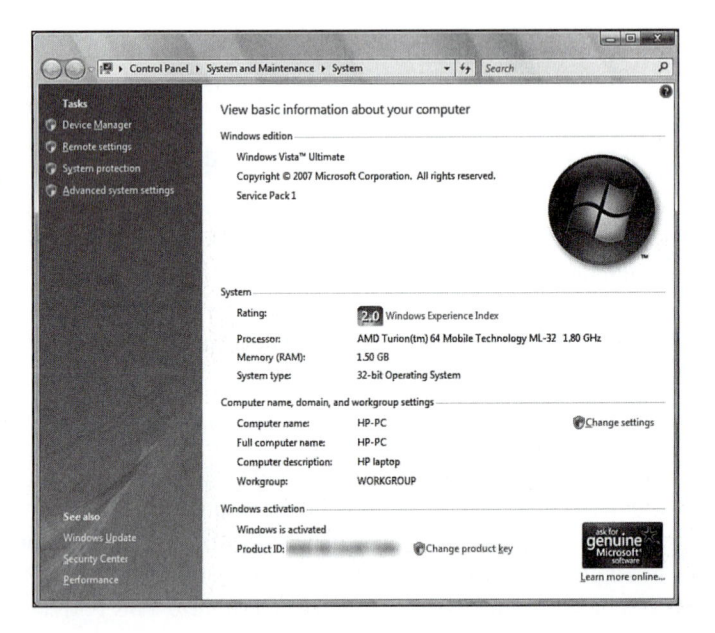

The top of the main System Properties sheet shows the Windows Vista edition in use. The System section shows the Windows Experience Index, processor and RAM information, and operating system type (32-bit or 64-bit).

> **NOTE**
>
> Virtually all "Vista-capable" systems on the market can run the 64-bit (x64) version of Vista, which enables you to use more than 4GB of RAM and create larger files. Should you? Install the x64 version only if can obtain x64 drivers for your hardware and verify that your favorite programs can run under x64 versions. Although x64 support is much more widespread today than when Vista was first released, some hardware and programs still support only the 32-bit version. Note that only signed drivers can be used by x64 versions of Vista.

Unlike in Windows XP and earlier versions, which made you dig through tabs to find the computer name, domain, and workgroup settings, they're out front in this version. If you can't connect to other computers, workgroup or domain name problems are often the culprit. Click the Change Settings button at the right to change this information.

Is your version of Windows activated? Look at the Windows Activation section of the dialog box to find out (the product key in Figure 25.40 has been altered). If you need to change the product key, click the Change Product Key button.

The Tasks pane provides access to other System functions. See "Device Manager" earlier in this chapter to learn more about this task. The other tasks are discussed in the following sections.

REMOTE SETTINGS

Click Remote Settings on System's Tasks pane to open the Remote tab of the System Properties sheet (see Figure 25.41). Use this tab to configure both Remote Assistance (top) and Remote Desktop (bottom) connections to your computer.

Figure 25.41
Use the Remote tab to configure Remote Assistance and to permit, deny, or configure Remote Desktop connections.

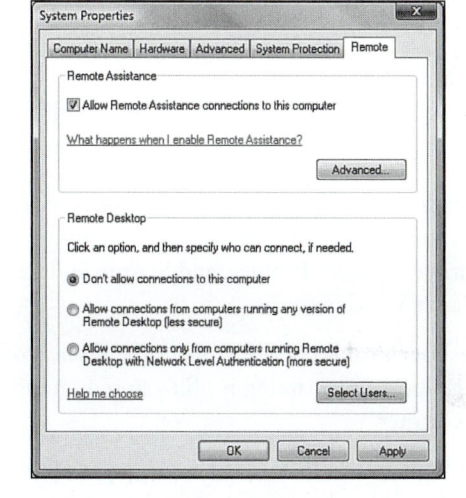

NOTE

Network Level Authentication (NLA) is the more secure type of Remote Desktop connection. Windows Vista includes NLA support. If you want to connect a Windows XP client to a Windows Vista client running Remote Desktop with NLA enabled, you must download and install the Terminal Services Client (Remote Desktop Connection v6) on the Windows XP system. The Windows XP system must be running Service Pack 2. You can also install this update on a Windows Server 2003 with Service Pack 1.

→ To learn more about Remote Assistance and Remote Desktop, **see** Chapter 40, "Remote Desktop," **p. 1329**.

SYSTEM PROTECTION

Click System Protection from the Tasks pane to open the System Protection tab (see Figure 25.42) of the System Properties sheet. This tab is used to view and create restore points that can be used by System Restore and to launch System Restore.

Figure 25.42
Use the System Protection tab to manage System Restore.

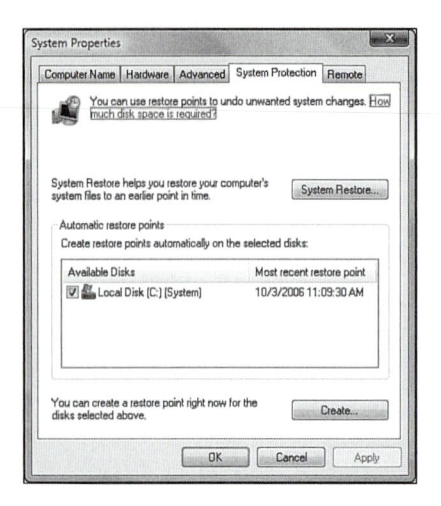

→ To learn more about System Restore, see Chapter 28, "Troubleshooting and Repairing Problems," **p. 961**.

ADVANCED SYSTEM SETTINGS

Click Advanced System Settings from the Tasks pane to open the Advanced tab of the System Properties sheet. It has four buttons. Three of these buttons are labeled Settings and are contained within the Performance, User Profiles, and Startup and Recovery sections. The fourth button is Environment Variables.

The Settings button under the User Profiles heading opens the User Profiles dialog box. This interface is used to manage local and roaming profiles stored on the local computer. User Profiles are discussed in Chapter 3.

The Settings button under the Startup and Recovery heading opens the Startup and Recovery dialog box. This interface is used to configure multibooting actions and how system failures are handled. If you have installed Windows Vista in a multiboot configuration with an earlier version of Windows, you can specify whether to run Windows Vista or the earlier version as the default. You can also specify how long to wait before starting the default operating system (30 seconds is the preset value) and whether to specify a time for displaying recovery options. By default, Windows Vista writes an event to the system log in case of system failure and restarts the system automatically. Clear check boxes to disable either or both of these features. During a system failure, Windows Vista also automatically creates a kernel memory dump called MEMORY.DMP in the root folder of the system drive (normally C:\). Other debugging operations include no memory dump, a small memory dump (64KB), or a complete memory dump. By default, a memory dump overwrites the previous one unless you disable this feature by clearing the Overwrite check box.

→ To learn more about multiboot configurations, see Chapter 2.

The Settings button under the Performance heading opens the Performance Options dialog box. The settings for both the Visual Effects and Advanced Tabs are discussed in "Adjust Visual Effects and Performance Options," earlier in this chapter.

Data Execution Prevention (DEP)

The Data Execution Prevention (DEP) tab of the Performance Options dialog box (see Figure 25.43) configures settings that prevent malicious applications from executing programs in protected areas of RAM. Protected areas of RAM, supposedly reserved for the operating system and other programs that are running, can potentially be invaded by malware, which then tries to load and execute itself in the legitimate memory space.

Figure 25.43
Use the Data Execution Prevention tab to manage DEP.

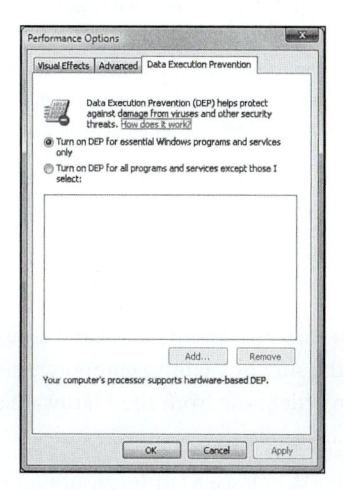

→ To learn more about DEP, **see** "Data Execution Prevention (DEP)," **p. 1142**.

Environment Variables

The Environment Variables button opens the Environment Variables dialog box. This interface is used to define user and system variables. These include TEMP and TMP, which point to storage locations where Windows can create temporary files. It also defines the PATH, which is the list of folders into which Windows looks to find programs and software components. In most cases, you should not need to edit the system variables. Chapter 32, "Command Line and Automation Tools," discusses making changes to the TEMP and PATH locations.

> **TIP**
>
> If the storage volume where your main Windows directory resides is becoming full, you can perform three operations to improve performance and keep the risk of insufficient drive space to a minimum. First, move the paging file to a different volume on a different hard drive (see "Adjust Visual Effects and Performance Options," in this chapter for details on this). Second, define the TEMP and TMP variables to point to a \Temp folder you create on a different volume on a different hard drive. Third, through Internet Options, define a location for the temporary Internet files within the alternate \Temp folder. After rebooting, the new locations will be in use. However, you may need to delete the old files from the previous temporary file location (typically \Users \<username>\AppData\Local\Microsoft\Windows\ Temporary Internet Files\). Don't forget to change permissions on the new \temp folder to permit access by the group Users. See Chapter 3 to learn how to create a group of users, and Chapter 34 to learn how to set up NTFS file permissions for a specified file or folder.
>
> Using a different hard disk for the paging file, TEMP and TMP temporary files, particularly if it's connected to a different ATA/IDE host adapter than the system hard disk or uses the SATA interface, will provide better performance than using a different drive letter on the system hard disk.

Windows SideShow

The Windows SideShow applet is used to select programs that can be displayed in a Windows SideShow auxiliary display on the side of a laptop computer, mobile phone, or other device that supports SideShow. Run SideShow from the Hardware and Sound category of the Control Panel, or find it in Classic view.

By default, Windows Media Player and the Windows Mail Inbox are on the SideShow gadgets list. (Don't confuse SideShow gadgets, by the way, with the applets that can run in the Windows Sidebar.)

To download additional gadgets, click the Get More Gadgets Online link to open the Windows Live Gallery (http://gallery.microsoft.com) and navigate to the SideShow portion.

To learn more about SideShow, go to the Windows SideShow website at www.microsoft.com/windowsvista/features/foreveryone/sideshow.mspx.

Administrative Tools

The Administrative Tools icon in the Control Panel's Classic view (it's also located in the System and Maintenance category) is not a single program, but as the name implies, it provides a convenient way to access a variety of specialized tools you can use to manage more technical aspects of your Windows Vista system:

- Computer Management*
- Data Sources (ODBC)
- Event Viewer*
- iSCSI Initiator

- Local Security Policy*
- Memory Diagnostics Tool
- Print Management*
- Reliability and Performance Monitor*
- Services*
- System Configuration
- Task Scheduler*
- Windows Firewall with Advanced Security

*Items marked with an asterisk provide direct access to the relevant portion of the Microsoft Management Console (MMC).

The following sections discuss many of these tools. Others, with the exception of ODBC Sources, are discussed elsewhere in this book. ODBC Sources is fairly complex and is used by program developers and network database integrators. In most cases, this applet is beyond what most end users or administrators will need or use.

→ To learn more about the iSCSI Initiator, **see** "Using the iSCSI Initiator," this chapter, **p. 891**.

→ For more about Windows Firewall with Advanced Security, **see** Chapter 35, **p. 1205**.

→ For a discussion of Reliability and Performance Monitor, **see** "Reliability and Performance Monitor," this chapter, **p. 857**.

→ To learn more about System Configuration, **see** "System Configuration," this chapter, **p. 881**.

→ To learn more about the Memory Diagnostic Tool, **see** "Windows Memory Diagnostic Tool," **p. 968**.

Figure 25.44 shows a typical view of the Administrative Tools folder on a Windows Vista Ultimate system. Home Premium and Home Basic versions of Vista do not include the Local Security Policy and Print Management tools.

Figure 25.44
The Administrative Tools folder.

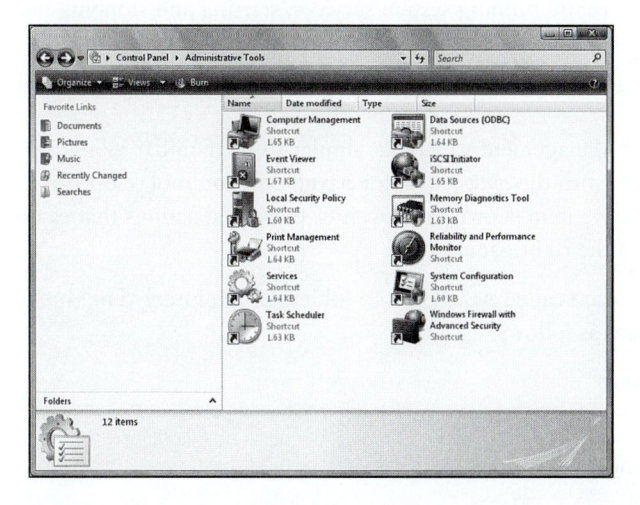

In the following sections, I discuss Computer Management and its related tools first.

Computer Management

Selecting Computer Management opens the Microsoft Management Console (MMC), a User Access Control-protected feature in Windows Vista. MMC (see Figure 25.45) provides one-stop access to the major system management features in Windows Vista, and through its use of snap-in extensions, additional management tasks as well.

Figure 25.45
The Computer Management Console (MMC) with some nodes expanded.

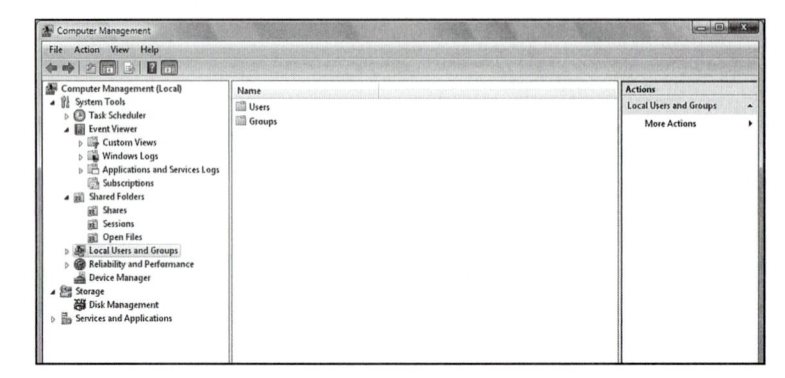

Computer Management provides easy access to the following tasks:

- Managing local users and groups
- Managing shared devices and drives
- Checking system event logs containing information such as logon times and application errors
- Seeing which remote users are logged in to the system
- Viewing currently running system services, starting and stopping them, and setting automatic startup times for them
- Managing server applications and services such as the Indexing service and web services

The Computer Management tool looks similar to the familiar Windows Explorer. It uses a three-pane view, with the *console tree* (for navigation and tool selection) in the left pane, details of the active item shown in the center pane, and actions that can be performed on the selected item in the right pane.

Items in the tree are called *nodes* (akin to folders in Explorer). The three nodes in Computer Management are as follows:

- System Tools
- Storage
- Services and Applications

The System Tools section of Computer Management contains the following tools:

- **Task Scheduler**—A utility program for automating execution of programs.
- **Event Viewer**—Used to view the event details contained in the Application, Security, and System logs. This tool is discussed later as an Administrative Tools utility in its own right.
- **Shared Folders**—Used to manage shared folders and remote users accessing shared folders.
- **Local Users and Groups**—Used to manage local user accounts and groups. This tool is discussed in Chapter 3.
- **Reliability and Performance**—New in Windows Vista, this tool was discussed earlier in this chapter.
- **Device Manager**—This tool was discussed earlier in this chapter.

The Storage area contains the Disk Management tool, which is used to define new drives as Basic or Dynamic, create/delete/manage partitions and volumes, format, assign drive letters, and so on. This tool is discussed in Chapter 27.

Services and Applications contains the Services tool, which is discussed later in this chapter, and WMI Control, which is used to configure Windows Management settings, a topic beyond the scope of this book. Additional tools may be found on some systems, depending on enabled Windows features.

As you would expect, you can conduct administrative chores by selecting a tool in the console tree and then clicking items in the center pane. When you select an item in the center pane, views and actions (right pane) change as appropriate for that item, typically displaying attributes of the item or tool you selected. For example, the Local Users and Groups branch can display the names and properties of all the users on the machine.

Explore with the interface to uncover all that is available from these three "little" nodes in the left pane. However, avoid making any changes or modifications (where possible) unless you know what effects your alterations will have. You'll be surprised. Open each node by clicking the right arrow. If you use the default Detail view, some helpful information about various items in the right pane is displayed along with the items in most cases.

By default, you manage the local computer. To manage a remote computer (assuming you have permission), right-click the topmost item in the tree—Computer Management (Local)—and choose Connect to Another Computer.

Experienced system managers may want to go to Computer Management and dig through submenus themselves, but the Administrative Tools folder, as we've already seen, provides shortcuts to the most significant features of the MMC, most of which will be discussed in the following sections.

Event Viewer

The Event Viewer is an administrative application used to view the log files that record hardware, software, and system problems and security events. You can think of an event as any occurrence of significance to the operating system. Logs are useful because, like a seismograph in earthquake country or a black box in an airplane, they provide a historical record of when events occurred. For example, you can see when services were started, stopped, paused, and resumed; or when hardware failed to start properly; when a user attempts to access protected files; or an attempt to remove a printer over which a user doesn't have control. The logs report the level of danger to the system, as you can see in Figure 25.46. The Event Viewer can be accessed directly from the Administrative Tools folder or from the Event Viewer section of the MMC. It is protected by User Account Control and contains three nodes:

- Custom views
- Windows Logs
- Applications and Services logs

You can also subscribe to logs generated by other applications.

Figure 25.46
The new Overview and Summary feature of the Event Viewer with the Critical category expanded.

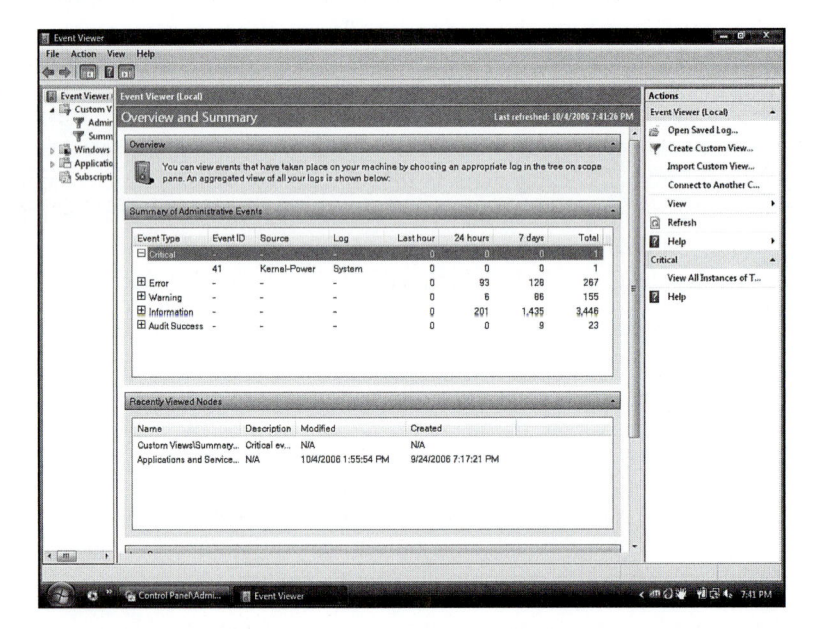

The logging features built into Windows Vista record all types of events, including many that never trigger an error message but can inform you of various problems or potential problems with your system's configuration.

Types of Log Files

Windows Vista generates three primary logs (files) in its Windows Logs category. These logs are explained in Table 25.17.

TABLE 25.17 Windows Log Files

Type of Log	Description
Application log	Contains events logged by applications or programs. For example, a database program might record a file error in the Application log. The program developer decides which events to record.
Security log	Can record security events such as valid and invalid logon attempts, as well as events related to resource use such as creating, opening, or deleting files. An administrator can specify which events are recorded in the Security log. For example, if you have enabled logon auditing, attempts to log on to the system are recorded in the Security log.
System log	Contains numerous entries pertaining to system events such as booting up, shutting down, loading drivers, and errors with hardware conflicts such as conflicts between ports, CD-ROMs, SCSI cards, or sound cards. For example, the failure of a driver or other system component to load during startup is recorded in the System log. The event types logged by system components are predetermined by Windows Vista and cannot be altered by the user or administrator.

Windows Vista also generates many additional logs in other categories. Under the Custom Views node, the Administrative Events log file displays errors and warnings derived from the Application and System logs. It's a convenient way to view problems in a single location. Under the Application and Services Logs node, Vista includes many empty log files (DFS Replication, Hardware Events, Internet Explorer, Key Management Services, and Media Center), which can be enabled by using the Windows Event Collector Utility (wecutil.exe) to subscribe to the appropriate event. Open the Microsoft and Windows nodes to view logs of many Vista features.

Now that you have a basic understanding, let's consider the Event Viewer. The Event Viewer is an application that displays each of the log files. Aside from simply displaying a log file, the Event Viewer also lets you do the following:

- Apply sorting, searching, and filtering that make it easier to look for specific events
- Control settings that affect future log entries, such as maximum log size and the time old entries should be deleted
- Clear all log entries to start a log from scratch
- Archive logs on disk for later examination and load those files when needed

NOTE

Only a user with Administrative privileges can work with the Security log. Any user can view the Application and System logs, however.

Overview and Summary

When you open the Event Viewer, it opens an Overview and Summary of administrative events, a feature new to Windows Vista. Switch the Event Viewer to full-screen mode and drag the dividers between panes as seen in Figure 25.46 to see all the details at once.

The Overview and Summary displays five categories, listed in order from most serious to least serious:

- Critical
- Error
- Warning
- Information
- Audit Success

To help you more quickly determine any trouble spots in your system, each category totals up events in the last hour, last 24 hours, last 7 days, and a grand total. On the system shown in Figure 25.46, no events have taken place in the last hour, but more than 300 events have been logged in the last 24 hours. To expand a category, click the plus (+) sign next to the category name.

Viewing Event Details

To view the details of a particular event, double-click it. Figure 25.47 displays the details for the Critical event shown in Figure 25.46.

Figure 25.47
Viewing a critical event.

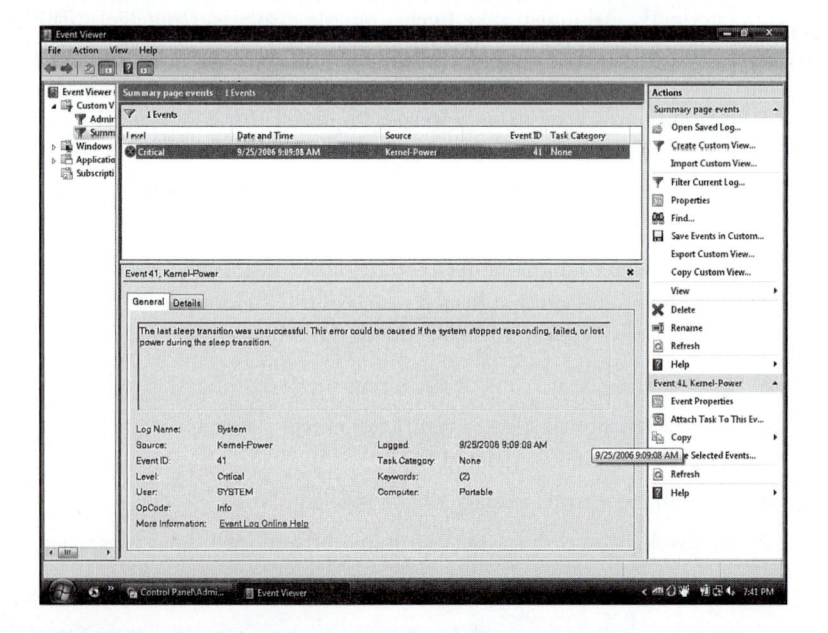

The General tab displays an overview of the log entry. To see the log entry in its native XML format, click the Details tab. XML View is selected by default. To return to the previous view, use the back (left arrow) button at the top of the Event Viewer dialog box.

Event Viewer Actions

Windows Vista's Event Viewer makes actions easy to use by displaying them in the Actions pane on the right side of the dialog box at all times. By using the Actions pane, you can create or import custom views, connect to another computer to view its events, view all instances of a particular problem or event, view event properties, save events, and filter the current log.

Shared Folders

The Shared Folders node (see Figure 25.48) includes three nodes:

- **Shares**—Allows you to manage the properties of each shared resource. For example, you can alter the access rights for a shared resource so that certain users have read-only access. You can also change share permissions for a resource in the Properties dialog box of any shared resource by right-clicking the resource and clicking Properties.
- **Sessions**—Allows you to see which users are connected to a share and optionally disconnect them.
- **Open Files**—Allows you to see which files and resources are open on a share. You also can close files that are open.

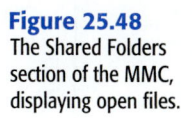

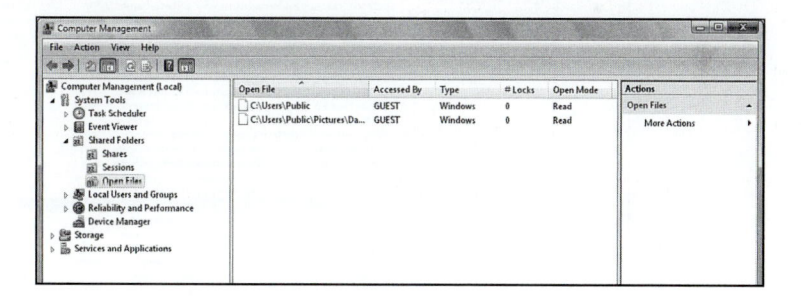

Figure 25.48
The Shared Folders section of the MMC, displaying open files.

Local Security Policy

Open the Local Security Policy shortcut in Administrative Tools to start the Microsoft Management Console's Local Security Policy snap-in. Use this snap-in to regulate network and other security policies for users of a particular system.

→ To learn more about Local Security Policy, **see** "Tightening Local Security Policy," **p. 1227**.

Print Management

If you use more than one printer, whether as a server administrator or simply a user with a laser and an inkjet printer, the Print Management shortcut in Administrative Tools opens the Microsoft Management Console Print Management snap-in. It enables you to control all the printers on your system. Custom filters show printers with jobs, printers that are not ready, printer drivers, and other information.

→ To learn more about the Print Management tool, **see** "Advanced Printer Management," **p. 225**.

SERVICES

Windows Vista is highly modular. Many of the inner housekeeping chores of the operating system are broken down into services that can be added, removed, started, and stopped at any time, without requiring a reboot. A typical Windows Vista system has 80 or more services running at any one time. You can view which services are running by using the Services shortcut in Administrative Tools. Use the Services dialog to view all installed services and their status (Automatic, Manual, or Stopped). Use this tool to start and stop services. Figure 25.49 shows a typical Services listing. To start, stop, pause, or restart a service, you can use the context menu or the VCR-like buttons on the toolbar. For deeper control of a service, such as to declare what automatic recovery steps should be taken in the case of the service crashing, which hardware profiles it should run in, and more, open its Properties dialog box.

Figure 25.49
The Services folder in the MMC.

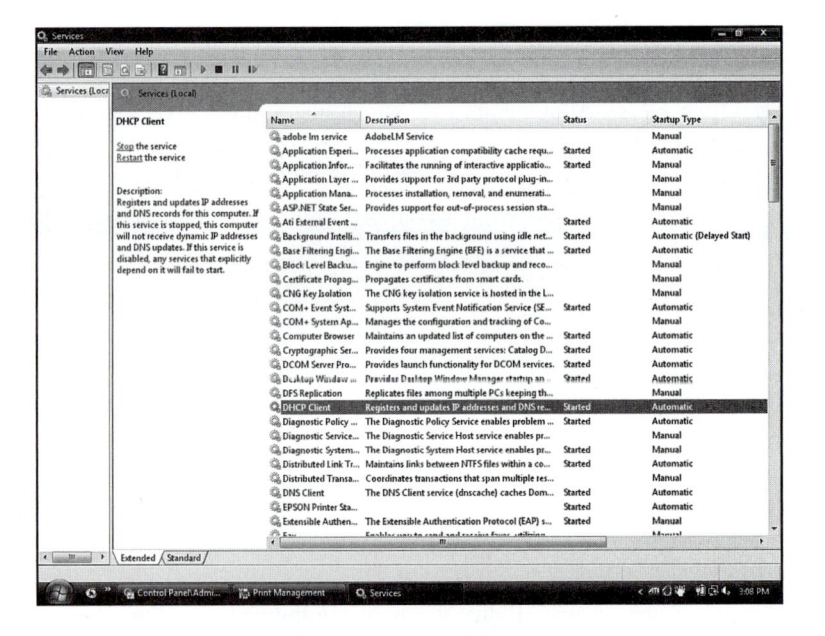

Within the Properties dialog box, you'll find controls to set a service's startup type (automatic, manual, or disabled), start/stop/pause/resume buttons, and a startup parameters field. You also can set the account under which the service is executed (Log On tab), define how a service recovers from failures—for example, restart, run a program, or reboot the system (Recovery tab), and view a list of service, program, and driver dependencies (Dependencies tab).

> **TIP**
>
> You might find websites suggesting that you can speed up your computer by disabling a bunch of Windows services. We don't recommend that you do this. Microsoft has made Vista do a *very* good job of keeping services out of your way, especially during startup and shutdown, so we suggest leaving the default set of services alone.

→ To learn more about Windows Services, **see** Appendix A, **p. 1379**.

Task Scheduler

Task Scheduler can be run from the Adminstrative Tools folder in Control Panel, the System Tools node in Computer Management, or from the Start menu (All Programs, Accessories, System Tools, and Task Scheduler). Using the Scheduled Tasks, you can set up any program or script (or even open a document) to be run automatically at predetermined times. This utility is very useful for running system maintenance programs or your own scripts and programs when you can't be around to execute them manually.

→ To learn more about Task Scheduler, **see** Chapter 32, **p. 1069**.

System Configuration

Use the System Configuration utility (msconfig.exe) to disable or enable startup programs, adjust boot options, enable or disable startup services, and run various reporting and diagnostic tools.

System Configuration can be run from the Administrative Tools menu, or by using the Run command in the Start menu. (Select Start, All Programs, Accessories, Run; type **msconfig** and click OK.)

System Configuration opens to the General tab. By default, Normal startup is selected. Normal startup runs all device drivers and services. Other options include

- **Diagnostic startup**—Runs basic devices and services only; equivalent to starting the system in Safe Mode
- **Selective startup**—Starts the system with an option to disable all system services, all startup items, or both

To adjust boot options with the built-in boot configuration data (BCD) editor, click the Boot tab (see Figure 25.50).

The options on the boot tab match the options available when you press F8 at startup and display the Advanced boot configuration menu. To boot the system to the Safe Mode GUI, click the Safe Boot check box and select Minimal. Other options include Alternative Shell (boots to the command prompt without network support); Active Directory repair (boots to the Windows GUI and runs critical system services and Active Directory); and Network (boots to Safe Mode GUI with network services enabled).

Figure 25.50
The Boot tab of System Configuration.

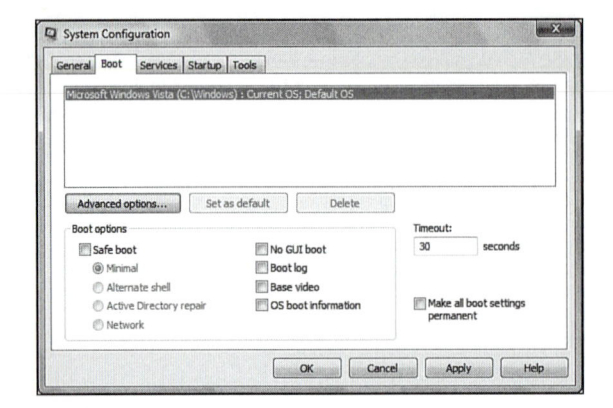

Other options you can select include No GUI boot (disables the Windows splash screen); boot log (creates a boot log of startup activities stored as ntbtlog.txt file in the default SystemRoot folder, usually C:\; base video (starts Windows GUI using standard VGA drivers); OS boot information (lists driver names as drivers are installed during boot).

Generally, these options are used for diagnostics, but if you want to make a particular combination of settings permanent (until you change them again), click the Make All Boot Settings Permanent check box.

Click the Advanced Options button if you need to specify the number of processors, lock PCI settings, detect the HAL used by the system, or configure a serial, USB, or 1394 port for remote debugging.

The Services tab is used to disable or enable Microsoft and third-party services (note that some Microsoft services cannot be disabled), whereas the Startup tab (see Figure 25.51) is used to disable or enable startup programs. Note that the Startup tab lists the date a particular startup program was disabled.

Figure 25.51
The Startup tab of System Configuration.

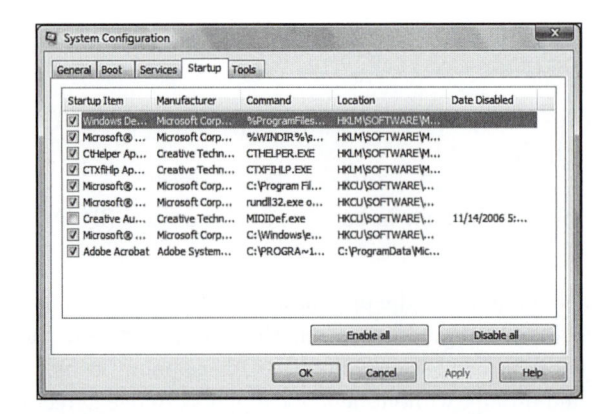

> **TIP**
>
> The Autoruns for Windows tool, which you can search for and download from Microsoft.com, provides a much better and detailed way to view and control startup programs.

The Tools tab is used to launch various reporting and diagnostic tools found in the \Windows\System32 folder, including

- About Windows
- System Information
- Remote Assistance
- System Restore
- Computer Management
- Event Viewer
- Programs
- Security Center
- System Properties
- Internet Options
- Internet Protocol Configuration
- Performance Monitor
- Task Manager
- Disable UAC (user account control)
- Enable UAC
- Command Prompt
- Registry Editor

The command line for each command is shown when you select the command, making it easy to create batch or script commands to run combinations of these tools. To start a tool, select it and click Launch.

> **TIP**
>
> To copy the command for a particular tool, select the tool, highlight the command string in the Selected Command window, and press Ctrl+C. To paste the command string into a text editor or other program in the Windows GUI, use Edit, Paste, or Ctrl+V. To paste the command string into the command-prompt environment, right-click the command-prompt window and select Paste from the right-click menu.

Task Manager

The Task Manager is one tool you're bound to use frequently, perhaps more than any other. Whenever an application crashes, you believe you're running some suspect process that you want to kill, or you want to check on the state of system resources (for example, RAM usage), you can use the Task Manager. Even as nothing more than an educational tool, the Task Manager is informative.

The fastest way to bring up the Task Manager in Windows Vista is to press Ctrl+Shift+Esc or to right-click over an empty area on the Taskbar and select Task Manager from the pop-up menu. Task Manager displays the Processes tab shown in Figure 25.52 by default.

Figure 25.52
The Task Manager shows you which applications and processes are running and lets you terminate hung programs. It also indicates some important aspects of system performance.

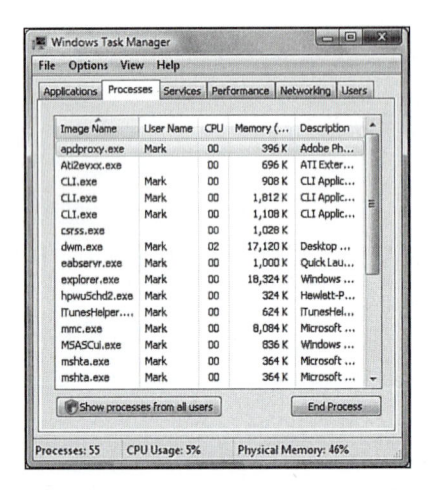

The Task Manager in Windows Vista has six tabs, up from five in Windows XP, but it does not include the Shut Down menu found in the Windows XP version.

Applications Tab

Click the Applications tab of the Task Manager to see a list of the programs currently running on the computer. Not a lot of information is displayed, only the application name and the status (running or not responding). However, this tab does provide a more complete report than you'll get by glancing at the taskbar buttons or via the dialog box you see if you press Alt+Tab.

You can sort the list by clicking the column heads. If an application has multiple documents open, the application appears only once in the list, probably with the name of the document that is foremost at the time (has the focus). Some applications don't comply with this single-document interface (SDI) approach, listing each new document as a separate application. Some examples of non-SDI applications are MS Office programs such as Word, Excel, and PowerPoint.

From this list, you can kill a hung application. If an application has hung, it is probably reported in the list as Not Responding (although this is not always true). Click the End Task button to terminate the task. If a document is open and unsaved, and if, for some unexpected reason, the program responds gracefully to Windows's attempt to shut it down (which is unlikely), you might see a dialog box asking whether you want to save. More likely, Windows Vista will just ask for confirmation to kill the application.

> *If you have killed applications and they still appear in the Applications tab listing,* **see** *"The Task Manager Is Stalled" in the "Troubleshooting" section at the end of this chapter.*

Patience, Grasshopper

Before you give an application its last rites, pause for a bit. In general, it's not a good idea to kill an application if you can avoid doing so. Terminating an application can cause instability in the operating system (even though it shouldn't in most cases because of the kernel design). Or at the least, you can lose data. Try "jiggling" the application in various ways, in hopes of being able to close it gracefully first. Switch to it and back a few times. Give it a little time. Maybe even do some work in another application for a few minutes, or take a trip to the water cooler. Try pressing Esc while the application is open.

When executing some macros in Word, for example, I noticed that one of my macros hangs for no apparent reason. It seems to crash Word. So, I killed it from the Task Manager, losing some work. I later realized the solution was to press Esc, which terminated the macro. Having slow network connections and attempting to link to nonexistent web pages, printers, or removable media can also cause apparent hangs. Try opening a drive door, removing a network cable, or performing some other trick to break a loop a program might be in before resorting to killing the program from the Task Manager. This is especially true if you've been working on a document and you might potentially lose data.

Some applications will so intensely perform calculations that the Task Manager will list them as Not Responding. If you suspect this, give the program 5 minutes or so to complete its thinking; I've learned the hard way to be patient with some applications.

Notice that you can also switch to an application in the list or run a new one. Just double-click the application you want to switch to (or click Switch To). Similarly, to run a new application, click New Task (Run), and enter the executable name or use the Browse dialog box to find it.

> *If you're frustrated because you cannot send the Task Manager to the background,* **see** *"Sending the Task Manager to the Background" in the "Troubleshooting" section at the end of this chapter.*

PROCESSES TAB

Whereas the Application tab displays only the full-fledged applications you're running, the Processes tab shown earlier in Figure 25.52 shows *all* running processes, including programs (for example, Photoshop), services (for example, Event Log), or subsystems. In addition to just listing active processes, Windows Vista displays the user or security context (that is, the user, service, or system object under which the process is executing) for each process—a great new feature not present in previous OSes. Also by default, the percentage of CPU utilization and memory utilization in bytes is listed. You can change the displayed information through the View, Select Columns command.

Almost any listed process can be terminated by selecting it and then clicking the End Process button. There are some system-level processes that even you as administrator don't have sufficient privileges to kill.

> **TIP**
>
> If for some reason the Task Manager can't seem to kill off a program that you started, try logging off and then back on. If it's still there or if you don't want to log off, try this procedure:
>
> 1. Click Start, All Programs, Accessories.
> 2. Right-click Command Prompt and select Run As Administrator. Confirm the User Account Control dialog.
> 3. Type the command `taskkill /f /im program.exe` but enter the program's actual name as it's displayed in the Processes tab in place of *program*.exe. Do not use this method to try to kill a system service. Instead, use the Services tab.

You might also discover at times that an application will fail to be killed, typically due to a programming error or a memory glitch. In those cases, you should reboot the system. You might find that sometimes a hung application also will prevent a normal shutdown. If your attempt to reboot fails, you'll have to resort to manually turning the power off and then back on. Hopefully, you saved often and didn't lose too much work.

> **TIP**
>
> At the bottom of the Processes tab is a button labeled Show Processes from All Users. If you click this, you can see not just the processes under your user account and those of the system but also those of other active users. Plus, when displayed, you can also terminate them using the End Process button. This button is protected by User Account Control.

ALTERING THE PRIORITY OF A TASK

In the beginning, all tasks are created equal. Well, most of them, at least. All the processes under your user account's security context will have Normal priority by default. Most kernel or system processes will have High priority. You might want to increase or decrease the priority of a process, though changing the priority typically isn't necessary. To do so, right-click the task and choose the new priority through the Set Priority submenu.

Avoid altering the priority of any task listed with a username of SYSTEM. This indicates the process is in use by the kernel. Altering the execution priority of such processes can render your system nonfunctional. Fortunately, process priority settings are not preserved across a reboot, so if you do change something and the system stops responding, you can reboot and return to normal. In some cases, raising the priority of an application can improve its performance. However, increase the priority in single steps instead of automatically setting it to the maximum. Throwing another top-priority application into the mix of kernel-level activities can render the system dead, too.

You can assign six priority levels to processes: Realtime, High, AboveNormal, Normal, BelowNormal, and Low. Realtime is restricted for use by administrators. You should keep away from High because it can interfere with essential OS operations (especially if you have several user processes set to High).

> **TIP**
>
> If you have a multiprocessor or multicore computer and you want to assign a task to a given processor, right-click the process and choose the Set Affinity command. Choosing this command guarantees that the process receives CPU time only from the CPU you choose.

SERVICES TAB

The Services tab is new in Windows Vista, separating services from other memory resident processes. Use it to quickly determine the services installed on your system and which ones are currently running. It lists services by name, description, status, and group. Right-click a service to stop or start it.

PERFORMANCE TAB

The Performance tab of the Task Manager indicates important conditions of your operating system. It shows a dynamic overview of your computer's performance, including CPU usage; memory usage; and totals of handles, threads, and processes (see Figure 25.53).

Figure 25.53
The Performance tab displays some interesting statistics and a chart of CPU and page file usage over time.

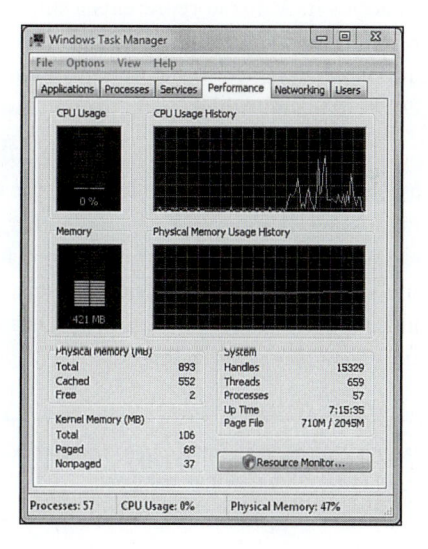

From the Performance tab, the View menu includes CPU History and Show Kernel Times. The former command is used to show different graphs for each CPU (only useful on multiple CPU systems). The latter command sets the display to show kernel activity in red and user activity in green on the CPU and Page file usage graphs. You should also notice that paging file usage is shown instead of memory usage. If your system has two or more CPUs or a dual or quad-core CPU, you will see a separate CPU gauge for each physical CPU or CPU core. (How cool is that?)

Although CPU usage is interesting, the most important of these numbers is memory usage. You can easily check in the Physical Memory area to see how much memory is installed in your system, how much is available for use by applications before disk caching begins, and how much the system is using for caching.

> **NOTE**
>
> System cache is the total current swap and RAM area allocated for system operations. When your computer has to go to a disk cache to access information, it significantly slows down overall system performance, which is why having more system RAM is almost always better.

The Kernel Memory area reports the memory in use strictly by the operating system for running the operating system internals. Nonpaged kernel memory is available only to the operating system. This memory is in physical RAM and can't be paged out to the hard disk because the operating system always needs fast access to it, and it needs to be highly protected. Paged memory can be used by other programs when necessary.

In the Totals section, you can see the number of handles, threads, and processes. Handles are tokens or pointers that let the operating system uniquely identify a resource, such as a file or Registry key, so that a program can access it. A thread represents a single subprocess. An increasing number of programs are multithreaded, running multiple subprocesses at the same time. Multithreading applications are designed to run better on multiprocessor or multicore processors such as the AMD Phenom and Athlon 64 X2, Intel Core 2 Duo and Core 2 Quad, and others.

Most of these size reports are of use only to programmers. However, the charts can offer strong, telltale signs of system overstressing. If you see, for example, that your page file usage is consistently nearing the top of its range, you are running too many programs. If the CPU is topped out most of the time, you also could be in trouble. Perhaps you have a background task running that is consuming way too much CPU time. An example could be a background program doing statistical analysis or data gathering.

> **NOTE**
>
> When the Task Manager is running, even if minimized, a green box appears in the system tray, indicating CPU usage. It's a miniature bar graph.

NETWORKING TAB

The Networking tab (see Figure 25.54) displays a bandwidth consumption history graph. As network operations occur, this graph will plot the levels of usage. If the system has two network adapters, you can determine which one is active, and separate graphs show activity on each adapter.

Figure 25.54
The Networking tab shows network traffic activity.

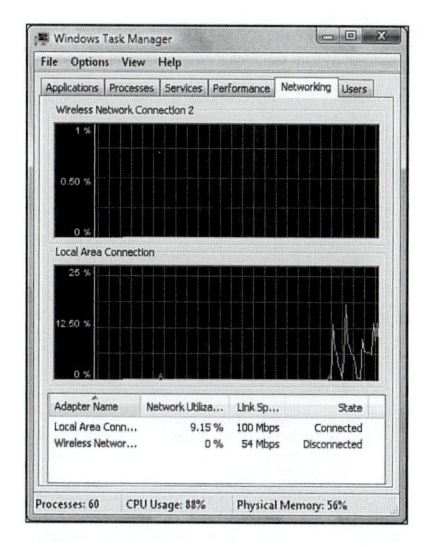

USERS TAB

The Users tab shows a list of all active users on this system or connected via the network. From here, you can disconnect a network user, log off a local user, or send a user a text message. The Users tab will be visible only if you are not participating in a Windows 2000/Windows Server 2003 Active Directory–based network or have not disabled Fast User Switching if participating in a workgroup.

SYSTEM INFORMATION

System Information is a simple but elegant tool. Opening this tool (which can also be run from the Run menu as `msinfo32`) displays detailed information about your system, its hardware resources, components, and software environment. It brings together information that's normally scattered across the main System dialog box, the Device Manager, and a myriad of other places.

Use System Information to help you determine the best configuration for a legacy device, track down software problems, or to determine the components in an unfamiliar system.

The top level, labeled System Summary, shows you basic information about your computer, operating system revision number, CPU, RAM, virtual memory, page file size, BIOS revision, and so on (see Figure 25.55).

Three nodes appear in the left pane of this figure:

- Hardware Resources displays hardware-specific settings, such as DMA, IRQs, I/O addresses, and memory addresses. The Conflicts/Sharing node identifies devices that are sharing resources or are in conflict. The Forced Hardware node indicates devices that are manually configured to share settings. This information can help you identify problems with a device.

Figure 25.55
See a summary of your system properties easily from the System Summary node.

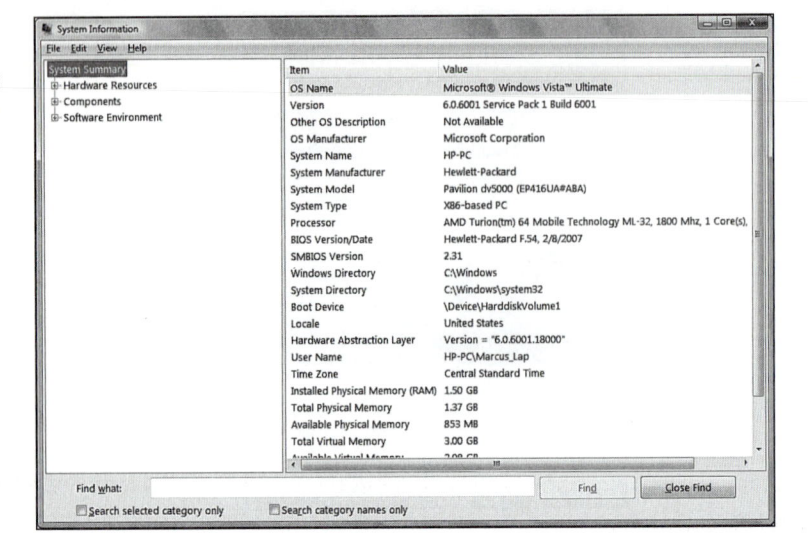

- The Components node provides a truly powerful view of all the major devices in your system. Open any subfolder and click an item. In a few seconds, information pertaining to the item is displayed, such as drive IDs, modem settings, and video display settings. In some cases, you can also see driver details. Check the folder called Problem Devices to see a list of all devices not loading or initializing properly.

- The Software Environment node is like a super Task Manager. It displays details of 12 categories of software settings. You can see the system drivers, certified drivers, environmental variables, print jobs, network connections, running tasks, loaded modules, services, program groups, startup programs, OLE registration, and Windows error reporting.

> **TIP**
>
> Ever wonder why some darned program starts up when you boot, even though it's not in your Startup group? It's probably hiding in the Software Environment, Startup Programs folder. Travel down the path from System Summary, Software Environment, Startup Programs, and take a look. I found Adobe Photo Downloader, iTunes Helper, and Picasa Media Detector there (to name just three). To disable unwanted programs from running at startup, see the documentation for the programs, or use the MSConfig System Configuration Utility's Startup tab or Windows Defender's Software Explorer to disable or enable startup items.

Adjust Visual Effects and Performance Options

If your system is having a hard time keeping up with the visual razzle-dazzle of Windows Vista, open the System applet in the Control Panel and click Advanced System Settings to open the Advanced tab of System properties.

Click the Settings button in the Performance section to open the Visual Effects dialog box. By default, Windows Vista selects the visual effects it deems appropriate for your system's performance level. To disable an item, clear its check mark. To add more pizzazz, click in an empty check box. There are more than 20 items to choose from.

To adjust how Windows uses its memory, click the Advanced tab. In the Processor Scheduling dialog box, click Programs to optimize the system to run its own applications, or click Background Services to optimize the system to provide file and other services to other systems.

If your system has less than 768MB of RAM or if you are running short of space on your system hard disk, and have another hard drive volume (preferably on a different physical hard disk), you might want to adjust the use of the paging file. Click Change to see how the paging file is configured. To make changes, clear the check box and set the paging file to a particular size, or, if you have multiple hard disk drive letters, to a particular drive. Use the fastest hard disk with plenty of available space to help speed up your system. If you change the size or location of the paging file, you must restart your system before the changes will take effect.

After making changes, click OK. To close the System properties dialog box, click Apply and then OK.

Using the iSCSI Initiator

The iSCSI Initiator is a new addition to Administrative Tools in Windows Vista. It supports iSCSI devices such as disk and tape drives, optical drives, storage libraries, and other devices that are accessed via a corporate IP network. This type of network is often referred to as a storage area network (SAN). When you run iSCSI Initiator, you must provide administrator-level credentials unless User Account Control has been disabled.

When you start the iSCSI Initiator on a system that uses the Windows Vista Firewall, you see a dialog box asking to unblock this service so that it can connect with an Internet storage name service. Click Yes. You may also be prompted to enable iSCSI Initiator to start automatically when the system starts. You should also click Yes on this dialog box if you plan to use iSCSI devices at all times. Otherwise, you must manually start iSCSI Initiator.

The iSCSI Initiator Properties sheet has six tabs. The General tab opens automatically when you start iSCSI Initiator and shows the current name of the initiator. Click Change to rename the initiator. If your iSCSI connection uses mutual CHAP authentication, click Secret to set up a CHAP secret. To set up IPsec tunneling, click Set Up.

Use the Discovery tab to set up Target portals (a target is an iSCSI device) and iSNS servers. Get the IP addresses, port numbers, and DNS names from your SAN or network administrator.

Use the Targets tab to log on to iSCSI targets and display their details. To automatically log on to a target when you restart your computer, click the Automatically Restore This Connection When the Computer Starts check box. Automatically logged in targets are listed on the Favorite Targets tab. The Volumes and Devices tab is used to autoconfigure Favorite Targets or to specify the programs or services that use a particular target. If your SAN uses RADIUS authentication services, use the RADIUS tab to specify RADIUS servers and to specify RADIUS login credentials (also known as RADIUS secrets).

System Tools Folder in Start Menu

Some of the most frequently used tools to manage your system can be accessed from the System Tools folder in the Start menu. To open the System Tools folder, click the Start orb, All Programs, Accessories, System Tools.

Table 25.18 shows the most frequently used system tools and where each is covered in this book.

TABLE 25.18 System Tools and Where Each Is Covered in This Book

System Tool	More Information
Backup Status and Configuration	"The Backup and Restore Center," Chapter 34, **p. 1150**
Character Map	"Character Map," this chapter, **p. 892**
Computer	"What's New in Windows Explorer," Chapter 5, **p. 164**
Control Panel	"The Windows Vista Control Panel," this chapter, **p. 804**
Disk Cleanup	"Disk Cleanup Utility," Chapter 27, **p. 949**
Disk Defragmenter	"Disk Defragmenter," Chapter 27, **p. 943**
Internet Explorer (no Add-ons)	Chapter 15, "Using Internet Explorer 7," **p. 423**
System Information	"System Information," this chapter, **p. 889**
System Restore	"System Restore," Chapter 28, **p. 964**
Task Scheduler	Chapter 32, "Command Line and Automation Tools," **p. 1069**
Windows Easy Transfer	"Windows Easy Transfer," Chapter 3, **p. 100**

Character Map

Character Map is a utility program that lets you examine every character in a given font and choose and easily insert into your documents special characters, such as trademark (™ and ®) and copyright symbols (©), currency symbols and accented letters (such as ¥), and nonalphabetic symbols (such as fractions, $\frac{3}{4}$), DOS line-drawing characters (+), items from specialized fonts such as Symbol and Wingdings, or the common arrow symbols (←, →, ↑, and ↓). Some fonts include characters not mapped to the keyboard. Character Map lets you choose them, too, from its graphical display. The Program Map displays Unicode, DOS, and Windows fonts' characters.

By clicking the Advanced View check box, you can also choose the character set, rearrange the items in a font (such as grouping all currency types together) to eliminate hunting, and search for a given character.

Character Map works through the Windows Clipboard. You simply choose a character you want to use and click Copy, and it moves onto the Clipboard. Switch to your destination application (typically, a word processing file), position the cursor, and choose Paste.

Using Character Map

To run Character Map, follow these steps:

1. Choose Start, All Programs, Accessories, System Tools, Character Map.
2. Choose the font you want to work with from the Font list.
3. By default, the Character Set is Unicode. This means all the characters necessary for most of the world's languages are displayed. To narrow down the selection, click the Advanced View check box and choose a language from the Character Set drop-down list.
4. To examine an individual character, click a character box, and hold down the mouse button to magnify it. You can accomplish the same thing with the keyboard by moving to the character using the arrow keys (see Figure 25.56).

Figure 25.56
Character Map with Advanced options showing. You can double-click a character to put it in the copy list.

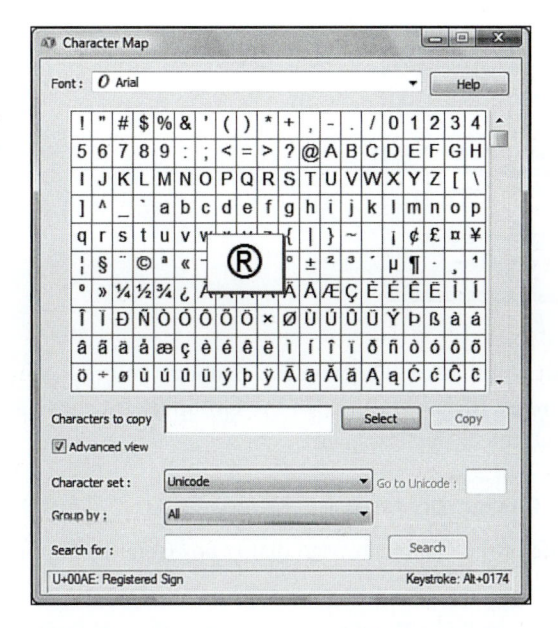

5. Double-click a character to select it, transferring it to the Characters to Copy box. Alternatively, after you've highlighted a character, you can click the Select button or press Alt+S to place it in the Characters to Copy box. You can keep adding characters to the copy box if you want to paste several into your document at once.
6. Click the Copy button to place everything from the Characters to Copy box onto the Windows Clipboard.
7. Switch to your destination application, and use the Paste command (typically on the application's Edit menu) to insert the characters into your document. In some cases, you might then have to select the inserted characters and format them in the correct font, or the characters won't appear as you expected. You can, of course, change the size and style as you want.

> **TIP**
>
> If you know the Unicode number of the item to which you want to jump, type it into the Go to Unicode field. The display scrolls as necessary, and the desired character is then highlighted, ready for copying.

Choosing from a Unicode Subrange

A useful feature of Character Map lets you choose a subrange from the Unicode. Unicode was designed intelligently with characters grouped in sets. You can choose a subset of a font's characters to help you locate a specific symbol. To check out this feature, open the Group By list and choose Unicode Subrange. When you choose this option, a box like the one shown in Figure 25.57 pops up.

Figure 25.57
Choosing a subset of a font from which to select a character.

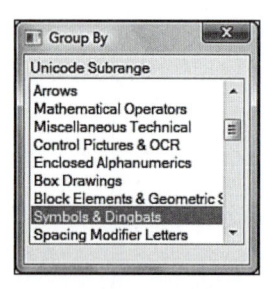

Click the subgroup that you think will contain the character you're looking for. Good examples are currency or arrows. Make sure to open the Group By list again, and choose All when you want to see all the characters again.

Entering Alternative Characters from the Keyboard

At the bottom right side of the Character Map dialog box (refer to Figure 25.56) is a line that reads Keystroke.

For nonkeyboard keys (typically, in English, anything past the ~ character), clicking a character reveals a code on this line—for example, Alt+1060. This line tells you the code you can enter from the keyboard to quickly pop this character into a document. Of course, you must be using the font in question. For example, say you want to enter the registered trademark symbol (®) into a Windows application document. Note that with a standard text font such as Arial or Times New Roman selected in Character Map, the program lists the keystrokes for this symbol as Alt+0174. Here's how to enter the character from the keyboard:

1. Press Num Lock to turn on the numeric keypad on your keyboard. (The Num Lock light should be on.)

2. Press and hold down Alt, and then press 0+1+7+4 (that is, type the **0**, **1**, **7**, and **4** keys individually, in succession) on the number pad. (You must use the number pad keys, not the standard number keys. On a laptop, you must activate the number pad using whatever special function key arrangement your laptop uses.) When you release the Alt key, the registered trademark symbol should appear in the document.

> **TIP**
>
> Not all programs accept input this way. If this approach doesn't work with a program, you'll have to resort to the standard means of putting characters into the Clipboard explained previously.

If you have pasted one or more characters from Character Map and they appear in the wrong font, **see** *"Wrong Characters Displayed When Pasting Characters from Character Map" in the "Troubleshooting" section at the end of this chapter.*

Troubleshooting

The Task Manager Is Stalled

My Task Manager seems stuck. It doesn't reflect newly opened or closed applications.

You might have this problem if you've paused the Task Manager. Choose View, Update Speed, and then choose any setting other than Paused. Another approach, if you want to keep it paused, is to choose View, Refresh Now.

Sending the Task Manager to the Background

My Task Manager doesn't drop into the background when I click another program.

Like some Help files, the Task Manager has an Always on Top option. Choose Options and turn off this setting.

Wrong Characters Displayed When Pasting Characters from Character Map

When I paste characters from the Character Map, the characters appear in the wrong font.

When you paste a character from Character Map, the application you are pasting the character into might not recognize that the character is coming from a different font. In such cases, the character is mapped to the equivalent character in the current font. For example, if you copied the Pencil (0x21) character from the Wingdings OpenType font but pasted it into a program that used the Nyala font by default, such as Windows Vista Paint, the character would change into the equivalent character in the other font (in Nyala's case, an exclamation mark). To fix this problem, select the characters you pasted from Character Map and select the correct font in the Font menu of the destination program.

Tips from the Windows Pros: Creating and Using Shortcuts to Your Favorite Control Panel Applets

Although the Control Panel's Classic view offers more than four dozen icons, you may find that you use just a few of them frequently. To make it even easier to get to your favorites, you can create shortcuts to your favorite Control Panel icon or categories on your desktop or in a customized folder in the Start menu.

To create a shortcut on your desktop, drag a Control Panel classic mode or category icon to the desktop and release it. Even if you prefer to create a customized Start menu folder, this is a good way to create shortcuts you can use for the menu.

After creating the shortcuts on the desktop, right-click each shortcut and select Rename. Delete the "- shortcut" added by Windows Vista when the shortcut was created to shorten the name. As with earlier versions of Windows, you can always tell a shortcut icon by the curved arrow.

To create the Start menu folder and add shortcuts, follow these steps:

1. Right-click the Start menu orb and select Explore (to create a folder only for you) or Explore All Users (to create a folder for all users of the computer). The Programs folder is displayed in the main pane of the Start Menu Explorer window.
2. Double-click Programs to display the folders it contains.
3. Right-click an empty area in the main pane and select New, Folder.
4. Enter a new name for the folder, such as CP Favorites.
5. Drag the shortcuts from the desktop into the new folder. (If you want to keep the shortcuts on the desktop while also making them available from the start menu, select them, right-click the group and select Copy, and then Paste them into the folder.)
6. Click the Start menu orb and then click All Programs. Click your new folder to see your new shortcuts and use them to start your favorite Control Panel applets or categories.

CHAPTER 26

TWEAKING THE GUI

In this chapter

GUI: To Tweak or Not to Tweak   898

Start Menu Pizzazz!   898

Display Properties   902

Tweak UI   919

Miscellaneous GUI Tips   920

Configuring the Recycle Bin   925

Troubleshooting   925

GUI: To Tweak or Not to Tweak

Tweaking the GUI doesn't mean anything lascivious. This chapter describes the graphical user interface and some interesting, useful, and fun stuff you can do with it—changes to help increase your computing efficiency and perhaps even make your computer more fun to use.

As you know, the GUI is the translator that interprets human input into commands the computer can interpret. It's also responsible for displaying output from computer programs and the operating system so that you can understand the results. The Windows Vista GUI is set up with factory defaults that 90 percent of users will never touch, despite its being highly programmable and easily modifiable through the Control Panel, Folder Options, properties sheets, and so on. If you're a GUI hacker, you know who you are, and if all you want to do is get your work done, well, more power to you because you're the one who's going to get the pay raise. But playing with the GUI can be fun.

Most folks won't modify their GUIs, but it's a shame they don't. Often, not even knowing there is recourse, users develop headaches from screen flicker, come down with eyestrain from tiny screen fonts, or they live with color schemes they detest. With a little effort, they can rectify these problems. Likewise, means for managing zip archives, altering the right-click Send To options, and handling numerous other functions users have to deal with every day are just a few clicks, Net downloads, Registry hacks, or properties sheet settings away. Just for fun, you can choose from hundreds of desktop themes, screen savers, wallpaper images, and so on.

Some of this chapter deals with standard display options. Other portions deal with deeper GUI tweaks and tricks. Just skim for the part that interests you.

→ This chapter doesn't cover multimonitor support because it's related more to hardware upgrades than the GUI. For coverage of multiple monitors, **see** "Installing and Using Multiple Monitors," **p. 1019**.

Start Menu Pizzazz!

The default Start menu of Windows Vista is much improved over the old classic style of Windows 2000 and even the XP style. I dread returning to Windows 2000 or earlier OSes (which I have to do from time to time) partly because of those now-old-fashioned Start menus. For those of you who do like the Classic view, you're not sunk, however. You *can* get back to it in a flash. But, for those willing to give the new look and feel a solid go, there are many nifty improvements you can take advantage of and even customize.

Tweaking the Start menu involves a right-click over the Start button (orb) to select the Properties command from the pop-up menu. This reveals the Taskbar and Start Menu Properties dialog box. The Start Menu tab is selected by default (which is strange because it's not the first tab of the dialog box). This tab offers the selections of Start menu and Classic Start menu. The default Start menu option refers, of course, to the new visual style of Vista. The Classic Start menu is that of Windows 2000 and earlier. A quick click and you can be back in the land of Windows 2000 out-of-date fashion before you can say baggy jeans. (Oops, are they back in again?)

For those of you willing to stick with Vista's classy new stylings, click the Customize button to see the almost 50 options available to you. The Customize Start Menu dialog box, shown in Figure 26.1, essentially lets you control how links, menus, and icons look and behave on the Start menu. Some of the options are

- Choose between large (default) and small icons.
- The number of recently accessed applications to be displayed.
- Which Internet (IE by default) and email (Windows Mail by default) application shortcuts to display.
- Whether to let items such as Control Panel, Computer, Documents, Music, and pictures "fly open" as menus when you click (or hover) on them, or to treat those items as links and open a separate window showing the item's contents. (See "Cascading Elements off the Start Menu" later in this chapter.)
- Whether to highlight newly installed programs (enabled by default).

Figure 26.1
The Customize Start Menu dialog box.

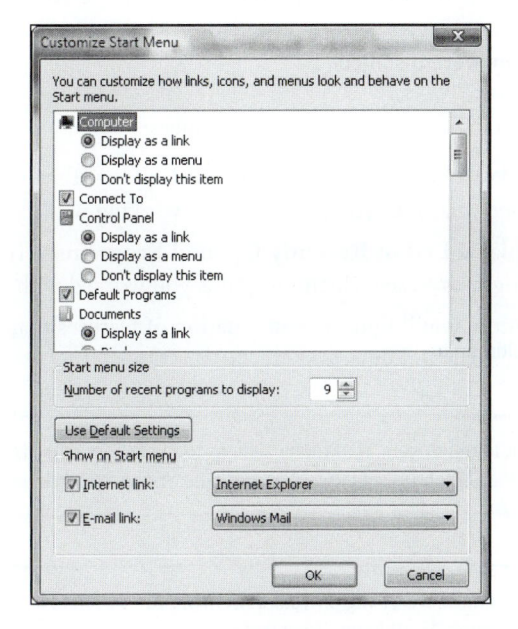

- Which items to include on the Start menu: Control Panel (enabled by default), Favorites menu, Help (enabled by default), Computer (enabled by default), Documents (enabled by default), Music (enabled by default), Pictures (enabled by default), Network (enabled by default), Printers, Search Programs (enabled by default), and Run command. Also, you can set whether the Administrative tools, such as Event Viewer and Task Scheduler will appear on the Start menu.
- Whether to list the most recently opened documents (and to clear out this list).

- There are a number of choices regarding search functions from the Start menu. These are confusing, so I will break them down:
    - ☑ **Search**—Choose whether as-you-type searches look through Internet Explorer favorites and history.
    - ☑ **Search Communications**—Choose whether as-you-type searches will comb through your emails and IM communications in addition to searching for files and folders.
    - ☑ **Search Files**—Choose whether files should be searched when conducting a search. Some people want to search only for communications, for example, and not waste time seeing listings of files they have no idea the meaning of. However, if files are included in searching, you can choose whether to search everyone's files (entire index) or only the files of the currently logged in user.
- Sort all Programs Menu by Name automatically keeps the All Programs menu organized alphabetically. In XP, you occasionally have to manually re-sort the All Programs menu as you add programs because newly installed programs just land at the end of the list, based on when they were installed.

Finally, on the Start Menu tab, you have two Privacy choices:

- ☑ **Store and Display a List of Recently Opened Files**—Turn this off if you don't want others to see what files you recently were working with.
- ☑ **Store and Display a List of Recently Opened Programs**—Turn this off if you don't want prying eyes to see which programs you worked with in the recent past.

With a bit of experimentation, you'll find the combination of features that best suits your preferred Start menu population and function.

> **TIP**
>
> If you want to return your Start menu settings to the factory defaults, there's a shortcut. Just open the Customize subtab as previously described and click Use Default Settings.

> **TIP**
>
> Technically, almost everything on your Start menu can be found in C:\ProgramData\Microsoft\Windows\Start Menu\Programs.
>
> What isn't there is in the folder under Users, for example:
>
> C:\Users\Everette\AppData\Roaming\Microsoft\Windows\Start Menu
>
> You can modify those locations if you want to add or remove shortcuts from your Start menu. Remember to only add or remove shortcuts because the Start menu is really just a collection of shortcuts to programs and documents, not the actual files themselves.

TWEAKING THE TASKBAR

The taskbar itself has configurable options; these are contained on the Taskbar tab of the Taskbar and Start Menu Properties dialog box. The taskbar can be locked so that stray mouse actions won't alter its placement or configuration; it can be auto-hidden to maximize the desktop area; and it can be set to always appear on top of other maximized windows. You'll probably recall these controls from previous Windows OSes. As in XP, there is automatic grouping of similar taskbar items but also, if you have Aero turned on, you will see live thumbnails of apps and docs when you mouse over a taskbar button.

You can turn off the Quick-Launch portion of the taskbar if you are so inclined with the Show Quick-Launch check box, although I recommend leaving it on. I put all my most-used programs on the Quick-Launch bar and run my apps from there almost exclusively.

Auto-Hide is inherited from previous Windows versions and gives you more available screen real estate by causing the taskbar to appear only if you mouse down to the bottom of the screen. A new option, Keep the Taskbar on top of other windows, is interesting in that it essentially prevents the taskbar from popping up even if you mouse down to the bottom of the screen. The only way to get it to reappear is to press the Windows key.

As you probably know, and as mentioned in Chapter 4, "Using the Windows Desktop," task buttons on the taskbar are listed from left to right in their order of launch, up to a point. When the taskbar becomes too full, buttons are grouped by similarity. For example, if you have Control Panel, My Computer, and Windows Explorer open, they can appear as a single button. This single button displays a number indicating how many applications are accessed through it (such as 4 Win…). If you click such a button, a up pop-list lets you choose the one you want to jump to.

Hide Inactive Notification Area Icons

If you're experienced with previous Windows OSes you might be familiar with how quickly the Notification Area (previously called the System Tray in XP, immediately to the left of the digital clock at the bottom of the screen) can fill up with icons. I've had systems with more than a dozen. Windows Vista manages its system tray intelligently by allowing inactive icons to be hidden. Plus, instead of displaying a long stream of active icons, only two or so are displayed with a left-facing arrow, which can be clicked to access the hidden icons. By enabling Hide Inactive Icons (which is the default), you can also customize which icons are hidden or displayed.

Reposition the Taskbar

As with previous versions of Windows, you can still drag the taskbar to any edge of your desktop: top, bottom, or sides. You can also still expand the thickness of the taskbar to allow multiple rows of task buttons. Just hover the mouse pointer near the edge of the taskbar so that it turns into a double arrow, and drag it up or down.

> **TIP**
>
> If you can't get the taskbar to resize or move, it's because it's locked. Right-click an empty part of the bar (not on a button or quick-launch shortcut) and turn off Lock the Taskbar.

DISPLAY PROPERTIES

The most obvious means for altering your GUI display settings is the Personalization dialog box. From there, you can reach a multitude of GUI settings, mostly affecting visual effects rather than GUI functionality:

- Colors and fonts for GUI elements
- Desktop background
- Screen-saver settings
- Sound effects
- Pointer and cursor shapes and sizes
- Special GUI effects such as Aero and window animations
- Device drivers
- Advanced properties such as Color depth and resolution, and hardware acceleration
- Connect to a projector or other external display

You can most easily reach the display properties by right-clicking the desktop and choosing Personalize. Figure 26.2 shows the resulting dialog box. This is a greatly redesigned box compared to the XP properties dialog box.

Figure 26.2
You can alter a multitude of display attributes from the desktop Personalization dialog box.

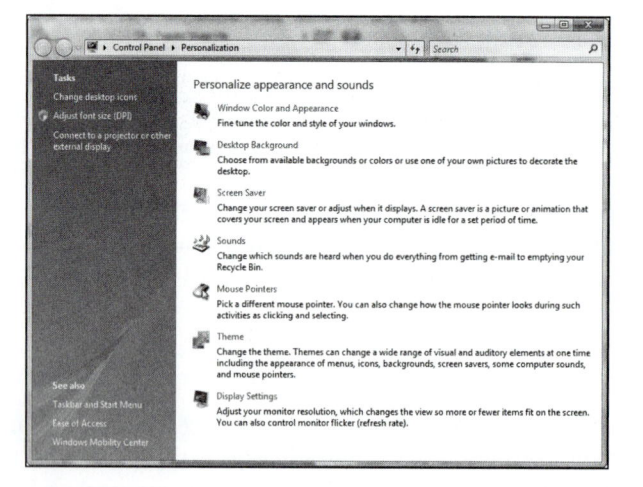

> **NOTE**
>
> You also can get to the display properties from the Control Panel. Click Start, Control Panel, Appearance and Personalization (in non-Classic view) or just plain Personalize if you're looking at the Control Panel in Classic view.

Notice that the Tasks pane includes Change Desktop Icons, Adjust Font Size, and possibly (depending on your computer, notably whether it's a laptop), Connect to a Projector or

Other External Display. In XP, you have to dive deep into some dialog boxes to find these options. It's nice that they are right up front now.

I'll briefly describe the various primary options in the following sections. You've probably used them before, so I won't belabor them; however, I will point out the basics and mention any specifics you should be aware of.

Windows Color and Appearance

From this link, what you see will vary greatly depending on whether you are running in Aero mode or the older, less flashy Windows Basic mode. Figure 26.3 shows both boxes.

Figure 26.3
The two Windows Color and Appearances boxes. You'll see the upper box if you are running Aero, the lower one if you are not.

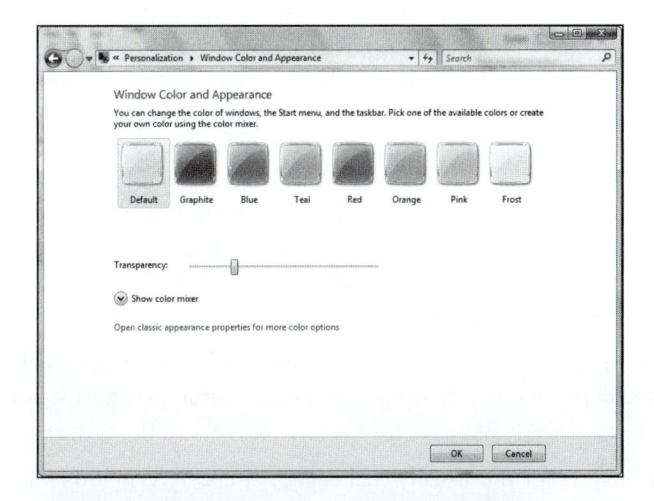

As you can see, these are like apples and oranges. I'll discuss the Aero approach first and then the non-Aero.

> **TIP**
>
> By the way, if you don't have Aero activated but you want to try it, *and* if your video hardware supports it, it will be listed in the Basic Appearances dialog box. Notice in Figure 26.3 that Aero is listed as one of the color schemes. Choose it and click OK, and it will go into effect. You can reopen that dialog from the color chooser dialog box also shown in Figure 26.3, by clicking Open Classic Appearance Properties for More Color Options.

In Aero's Window Color and Appearance box, simply click a color button, and the scheme will change. Microsoft has made it easy to choose color schemes this way, without putting you through the hassle of applying a specific color to each GUI element (title bars, document workspace, scrollbars, and so on) or choosing schemes by names that don't mean much to you, such as Wheat. (You can still assign individual colors if you want to through the Basic settings.) The effects of choosing a color button are immediately displayed across all open windows and applications when you click on it. Drag the Transparency slider to alter how translucent your window borders, title bar, and other elements will be. This effect is also instantly applied across the interface. Very slick.

Want to adjust the exact color hue, saturation, and brightness? Click the Show Color Mixer button. Three sliders show up. Adjust as you please. (Saturation means how pure the color is, by the way.)

High contrast (helpful for the visually challenged) or classic Windows looks can be achieved by opening the Basic box and scrolling through the Color Scheme options. You can do some serious mischief here, creating some egregious color schemes to attract the fashion police. Or you can design or choose schemes that improve readability on screens (or eyes) with certain limitations.

In most cases your scheme is preset to Windows Vista Basic, which is fine for most screens and users. If you prefer the look of Windows 2000 and older versions, you can go retro by selecting Windows Classic or Windows Standard from the Color Scheme list.

The old, familiar predefined color schemes such as Desert, Eggplant, and Wheat have been dropped in Vista. However, many of the schemes let you assign specific colors if you click the Advanced button (see Figure 26.4). The Advanced button opens the Advanced Appearance dialog box, which is used to alter the color settings, component size, and fonts of each individual component of a windowed display. By using the various pull-down lists or clicking in the preview area, you can fine-tune the color and font scheme.

Figure 26.4
The Advanced Appearance dialog box lets you choose high-contrast themes and control the color and font size of specific window elements.

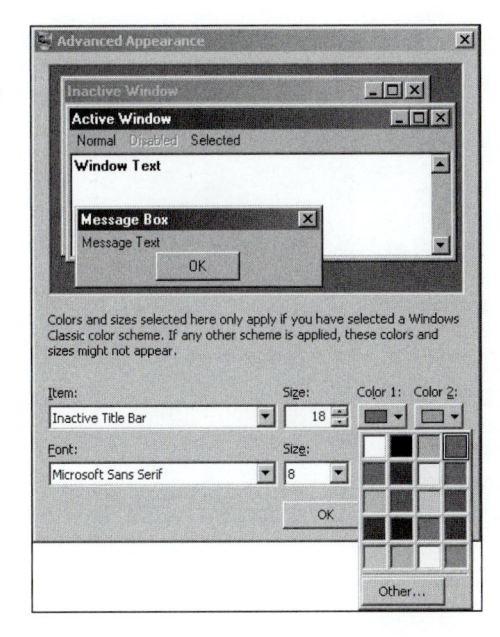

After clicking on an element in the little sample, you can click Color 1 or Color 2 and assign colors from the color picker. In some cases, two colors are assignable because some elements (for example, title bars) transition from one color to another.

> **TIP**
> If you spend considerable time creating a color, component, and font styling, be sure to save it as a theme and give it a unique name (for example, Laura's Theme). You do this by going back to the first Personalization dialog box (refer to Figure 26.2) and choosing Theme. Then click Save As. Otherwise, if you switch to another view, even for a second, you'll lose all of your previous settings.

When using the color picker, choosing a color called Other brings up the Color Refiner dialog box (see Figure 26.5). You work with two color mix controls here. One is the *luminosity bar* (which looks like a triangle arrow pointing left), and the other is the *color refiner cursor* (which looks like a set of crosshairs).

You simply drag around these cursors one at a time until the color in the box at the lower left is the shade you want. As you do so, the numbers in the boxes below the color refiner change.

- *Luminosity* is the amount of brightness in the color.
- *Hue* is the actual shade or color. All colors are composed of red, green, and blue.
- *Saturation*, as mentioned briefly earlier, is the degree of purity of the color; it is decreased by adding gray to the color and increased by subtracting gray.

You also can type in the numbers if you want, but using the cursors is easier. When you like the color, you can save a color for future use by clicking Add to Custom Colors.

Figure 26.5
The Color dialog-box lets you fine tune colors assigned to various Windows elements.

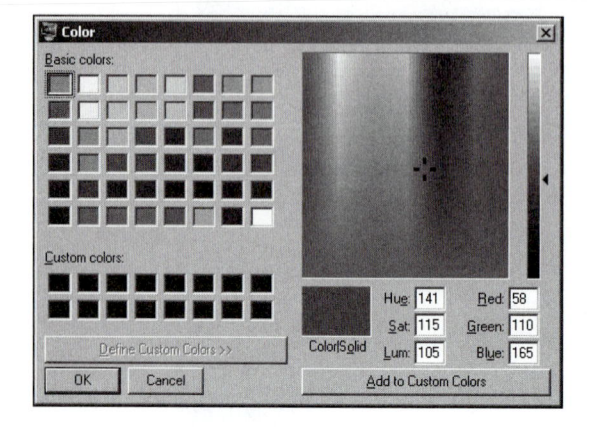

Effects Settings

The Effects button (shown previously in Figure 26.3) opens a dialog box that lets you choose from the following:

- Whether screen fonts are smoothed using the standard Windows method, or using ClearType. ClearType often improves the visibility range on older LCD displays. The ClearType method is selected by default.
- Whether to show shadows under menus (enabled by default).
- Whether to show the contents of a window while dragging (enabled by default).

> **NOTE**
> In previous versions, there was an option to hide the underlined letters for keyboard shortcuts until the Alt key is pressed. This was removed from Vista.

Desktop Background

The desktop is used to express your inner personality. It's one of the few places where you can actually customize the otherwise impersonal personal computer, isn't it? Hanging some wallpaper (such as a picture of your kids, your car, a sunset, and so forth) on your desktop gives the environment a more custom-made feeling. Microsoft includes dozens of options for you to goof around with. These include some stunning photographs, small tiles repeated across and down your screen to make a pattern, or solid colors. You can choose from a few supplied photos or supply your own, such as from your digital camera. Gone are the desktop "patterns" such as bricks and bamboo that were available in previous Windows versions, by the way.

To personalize your desktop, follow these steps:

1. Right-click on an empty spot on the desktop and choose Personalize.
2. Click Desktop Background. You see the dialog box, as shown in Figure 26.6.

Figure 26.6
Use this Desktop Background dialog box to personalize your desktop with photos, textures, and colors.

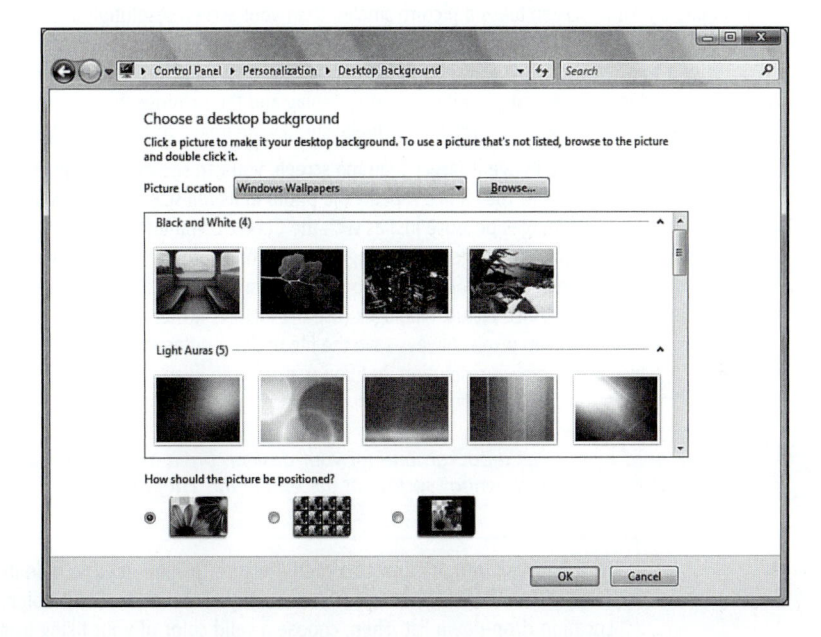

3. Click one of the images that you like or go searching for another one. From the drop-down list, choose Wallpapers, Pictures (previously My Pictures in XP), Sample Pictures, Public Pictures, or Solid Colors.

Wallpapers are high quality images designed to scale well and look good on any screen. Pictures just lets you choose from your own stockpile of photos you have stored on the hard disk somewhere, typically pulled in from your camera. Sample Pictures points to a folder supplied with Vista that includes some additional photos for you to play with. Public Pictures is a shared folder that anyone using your computer (locally or on the local area network) can see. It's a subfolder under Public. These various folder choices are just a convenience. The important point is that you're browsing for a picture to use as a desktop background, and these are the most likely places those will be stored. If you keep your photos organized elsewhere, such as I do (I use a folder called BMP Files—a throwback from before .jpg files became the popular format), just point to that folder using the Browse button and choose your image. While browsing, use the View Views control to turn on Medium Icons or larger so that you can see what you're looking at.

Acceptable photo formats are .bmp, .jpg, .jpeg, and .dib images. In addition to files already on your local system (or accessible over your local network), you can grab any image from a website by right-clicking over it and selecting Set as Background from the pop-up menu.

Making a Picture Fit Your Desktop

If an image is too small to fill up your desktop, you can always set the Position control to Stretch. You access that control by clicking How Should the Picture Be Positioned? under the list of images, as shown in Figure 26.6. From left to right, the choices are Fit to Screen, Tile, and Center (though not marked as such unless you mouse over the options). Fit to Screen takes a picture smaller than your screen resolution and enlarges it so that it fills the screen. Or conversely it takes a picture larger than the screen and shrinks it. Stretching can distort the picture or cause it to pixelate, so if you want it to look good, make sure to shoot the picture at, or convert it to, a size roughly matching the resolution setting of your display and then choose the Center option. If the image is larger than the screen's resolution, stretching actually shrinks the image to fully fit on the desktop.

If you choose Center and the image is larger than the screen, you can see only the center portion of the image that fits within your display. The Tile choice repeats the photo in its full size, numerous times on the screen. This works only with small images because just as with the Center command, large images will not even fully fit on the screen once. So shrink the image's size using an image or photo program. For example, right-click the image in question and choose Open With; then choose a program such as Paint (use the Image, Resize command in Paint) or Microsoft Office Picture Manager (use the Picture, Resize command). Experiment with resizing the picture to, say, 300×400 pixels. Always save the file under a different name first so that you don't mess up the original, which is in a higher resolution that you may want to keep.

If you've used a photo as a background for your desktop but it appears blocky, **see** *"Stretched a Bit Thin" in the "Troubleshooting" section at the end of this chapter.*

TIP

> By the way, if you don't want a pretty picture (or you need to hide the image of the sultry pin-up before your spouse returns), you can select Solid Colors in the Picture Location drop-down list. Then, choose a solid color of your liking from the resulting palette.

Setting Desktop Icons

You may want to change which basic system icons are always included on your desktop. Here's how:

1. Open the Personalize dialog box.
2. In the left pane, in the Tasks panel, click Change Desktop Icons.

Now, you can turn on or off six common shortcut icons to appear on the desktop:

- User's Files
- Computer
- Network
- Internet Explorer
- Recycle Bin
- Control Panel

You can also manage the icons used for these desktop shortcuts using the Change Icon and Restore Default buttons.

Screen Savers

We all know what screen savers are. In the Personalization dialog box, you can click Screen Saver, and you'll see the dialog box shown in Figure 26.7.

Figure 26.7
The Screen Saver Settings dialog box

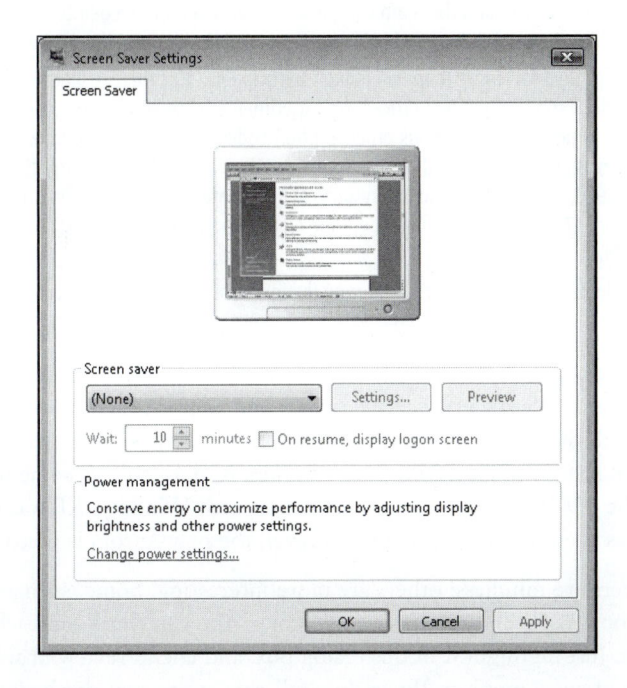

You can choose from several supplied screen savers and perhaps others that you have installed from other sources. In the old days when phosphors would "burn," screen savers actually did something useful. They prevented a ghost of the image on the screen from being burned into the screen for all time, no matter what is being displayed. Most modern CRTs don't actually need a screen saver to save anything because the phosphors are more durable. Also, LCD monitors don't need them either because they don't have any phosphors on the screen.

So, what good is a screen saver nowadays, you ask? Well, some monitor/card combinations go into low-power states when the screen is blanked, so if you choose Blank Screen, there could be some advantage. See the SETI@Home screen saver sidebar for another idea.

The SETI@home Screen Saver
Interested in space exploration? Think life might exist on other planets? If you want to become part of the largest global experiment in massive parallel processing, you can download the SETI@home screen saver to harness your computer's otherwise wasted CPU cycles to sift through signals from outer space, searching for signs of intelligent life out there. (Go to http://setiathome.ssl.berkeley.edu/ if you're interested in participating.)

SETI@home is a scientific experiment that harnesses the power of hundreds of thousands of Internet-connected computers in the Search for Extraterrestrial Intelligence (SETI). The screen saver downloads and analyzes radio telescope data captured at the world's largest radio telescope in Arecibo, Puerto Rico. There's a small but captivating possibility that your computer will detect the faint murmur of a civilization beyond Earth.

Your computer gets a "work unit" of interstellar noise, which it analyses when the screen saver comes up. A work unit requires approximately 20 hours of computing time on most computers. If an unnatural noise is detected, you and the people back at the University of California will be alerted. The scientists will attempt to confirm the finding by doing their own analysis and ruling out man-made radio sources such as radar and such. If it is finally confirmed, you and the team can pack up and head for Sweden to pick up your Nobel Prize. If nothing is found (which is somewhat more likely), your system moves on to the next work unit.

As of this writing, the project has more than five million participants. This huge, collective-computing model has set the standard by which massive parallel-processing experiments using small computers are based. Dozens of sites use this scenario to perform calculations on encryption codes, calculating PI, and even performing Internet searching and indexing. It is acknowledged by the *Guinness World Records* as the largest computation in history. With more than 900,000 computers in the system, SETI@home has the capability to compute more than 250 TFLOPS (as of April 17, 2006). For comparison, Blue Gene (one of the world's fastest supercomputers) computes 280 TFLOPS.

Now that beats the old days of screen savers featuring flying toasters, doesn't it?

Because far too many people leave their computers on all the time (it's not really true that they will last longer that way), efforts have been made by power regulators and electronics manufacturers to devise computer energy-conservation schemes. Some screen savers will turn off the video card instead of displaying cute graphics. And, of course, some screen savers are fun to watch. The 3D-Pipes screen saver that comes with Windows XP was mesmerizing actually, but it has been dropped in Vista. However, the new Aurora is pretty slick.

Some screen savers are mindless; others are more interesting. Some, such as the 3-D test, have additional options, such as font, size, and color. You can check out each one as the spirit moves you. Just highlight it in this dialog box, and click Preview or watch what happens in the little preview monitor. If you do a full-screen preview, don't move the mouse until you're ready to stop the preview, or it will stop even before it gets started. If a particular screen saver has configuration elements, click the Settings button.

You can also create a personalized screen saver by displaying selected pictures and videos as a slide show. The inclusion of videos is new to Vista. Here is how to create your own slide show as a screen saver for your Vista desktop:

1. In the Screen Saver Settings dialog box, click the drop-down list under Screen Saver and select Photos.
2. Click Settings to choose the pictures and videos you want in your slide show and other options. After you make your changes, click Save.
3. Click OK.

Note that there are two more settings in the dialog box:

- **Wait *x* minutes**—After the number of minutes you set here, the screen saver will begin. The smallest value is 1 minute. The largest is 9,999 minutes.
- **On Resume, Display Logon Screen**—A screen saver often comes on after a person leaves his desk for a while and may forget to log off or lock the computer (via Start, Lock This Computer). As a safety precaution, it is a good idea to require that the user's logon password be asked for when returning to your desk and touching a key or moving the mouse.

If you're looking to find the actual screen-saver files on your hard drive, they have an .scr extension and are stored in the windows\system32 folder. In your Vista system, they may be hidden. In a Windows Explorer window, click Organize, Folder and Search Options and then click the Search tab and turn on Include System Directories. You may have to do an Advanced Search. Most files are 200KB to 1MB in size. Double-clicking a screen saver runs it. Right-clicking and choosing Install adds it to your screen saver list. If you run it, just press a key or click the mouse to stop it.

> **NOTE**
> As of this writing, many of the 3D screen savers from XP crash in Vista due to beta graphics drivers not supporting OpenGL. Vista is not the culprit here; it's the currently provided Vista graphics drivers from video card manufacturers that do not provide openGL support. This should be fixed in time. For example, 3-D Pipes does not run on my machine but generates only an error message.

The Web is littered with screen savers. Just do a search. The following are some sources:

- **Screen Saver Heaven**—www.galttech.com/ssheaven.shtml
- **Screensaver.com**—www.screensaver.com

Between those two sources alone, you have access to more than 2,500 screen savers. Plus, many of the screen savers designed for Windows 9x/Me, Windows NT, and Windows 2000 will work on Windows Vista.

In addition to selecting the screen saver du jour, you should also define the length of time the system must be idle before the screen saver is launched, as well as whether to display the Welcome screen or return to the desktop when the system is resumed (that is, when the keyboard or mouse is activated by a user).

→ The Energy Star settings for monitors are covered under the Power applet discussion. **See** "Power Options," **p. 860**.

> **TIP**
> You can uninstall screen savers you install, but the screen savers that come with Windows can't be uninstalled.

If you are working from a portable system or are an energy conservationist, the Screen Saver Settings dialog also offers quick access to the power saving properties of Vista. Click Windows Mobility Center in the Tasks pane of the Personalization dialog box. Mobility Center is discussed in Chapter 38, "Hitting the Road."

THE SOUNDS LINK

The Sounds link on the Personalize dialog box associates Windows events with sounds. Windows Vista comes with tons of sound files, a big improvement over the measly assemblage of .wav files supplied with some earlier versions of Windows. In fact, just as with the color schemes, you can create and save sound schemes by using the Sound applet; you can set up and save personalized schemes to suit your mood. Microsoft supplies a fairly rich variety of sounds for your auditory pleasure.

Despite the diverse selection, I still use a few of the sounds I've put together using the Sound Recorder. I have one, for example, that says "New Mail" when I receive email. Sometimes, I didn't notice the generic "boop" sound when new mail arrived, so I changed it.

If you want to get fancy, you can record from a CD or tape recorder rather than from a microphone. This way, you can sample bits and pieces from your favorite artists by popping the audio CD into the computer and tapping directly into it rather than by sticking a microphone up in front of your boom box and accidentally recording the telephone when it rings. Just check out the Volume Control applet, and figure out which slider on the mixer panel controls the input volume of the CD. Then, use the Sound Recorder applet to make the recording. I have a few good ones, such as James Brown's incomparable "Ow!" for an error message sound.

> **TIP**
>
> Make sure that .wav files you intend for system sounds aren't too large. Sound files *can* be super large, especially if they are recorded in 16-bit stereo. As a rule, keep the size to a minimum for system sounds because it takes a few seconds for a larger sound to load and play.

You assign sounds to specific Windows "events" like this:

1. Right-click the desktop and choose Personalize.
2. Click Sounds. You'll see the dialog box shown in Figure 26.8.

Figure 26.8
The Sound dialog box, Sounds tab. Change system sounds from here.

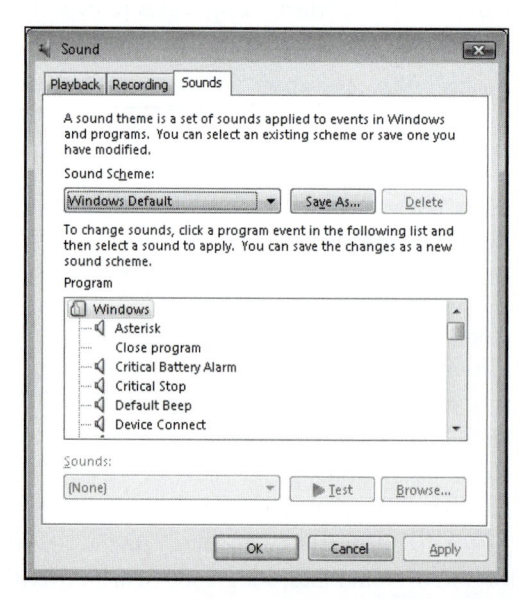

3. The Program section lists the events that can have sounds associated with them. Several classes of events are listed on a typical computer, such as New Mail Notification, the User Account Control warning, Windows Startup, Exit Windows, Low Battery Alarm, and so on. As you purchase and install new programs in the future, those programs may add their own events to your list. An event with a speaker icon next to it already has a sound associated with it. You can click it and then click the play button (the one with the triangle pointing right, just like the play button on a VCR or stereo) to hear the sound. The sound file associated with the event is listed in the Sounds box.
4. Click any event for which you want to assign a sound or change the assigned sound.
5. Open the drop-down Sounds list, and choose the .wav file you want to use for that event. Some of the event names may not make sense to you, such as Asterisk, Critical Stop, or Exclamation. These names are for the various classes of dialog boxes that Windows displays from time to time. The sounds you're most likely to hear often will be Default Beep, Menu Command, New Mail Notification, Question, Open Program, Close Program, Minimize, Maximize, and Close program. You might want to start by assigning sounds to them and then add others as you feel like it.
6. Repeat these steps for each item you want to assign or reassign a sound to. Then click OK to close the dialog box.

> **TIP**
> The default folder for sounds is \windows\media. If you have a .wav file stored in another folder and want to assign it to an event, use the Browse button to locate it. You don't have to move your sound files to the \windows\media folder for it to work. However, if you're planning on reassigning sounds regularly, you'll find that the process is easier if you move your .wav files into the media folder first.

At the top of the list of available sounds is an option called (None), which has the obvious effect: No sound will occur for that event. Assigning all events to (None) effectively silences your laptop for use in a library or other silent setting. You can also silence all sounds easily by choosing the No Sounds sound scheme as explained next.

In the same way that the Display Properties page lets you save color schemes, the Sounds applet lets you save sound schemes. You can set up goofy sounds for your humorous moods and somber ones for those gloomy days. I often tire of a sound scheme, so I have a few setups that I can easily switch to. The ones supplied with Windows Vista are pretty decent, actually, and considering the amount of work required to set up your own schemes, you'll probably make out best just trying a scheme to see if you like it. To choose an existing sound scheme, just use the Sound scheme pull-down list and select one.

You can set up your own sound schemes by assigning or reassigning individual sounds, as already explained. But unless you *save* the scheme with the Save As button, it'll be lost the next time you change to a new one. So, the moral is that after you get your favorite sounds assigned to system events, save the scheme. Then, you can call it up any time you want.

The Recording and Playback Tabs

In Figure 26.8, notice that in addition to the Sounds tab, there are also Recording and Playback tabs. Here, you can declare the default hardware you want to use for audio playback and recording, MIDI playback. Most systems offer minimal choices in these departments because typical computers have only a single sound system. You might find something strange in the sound playback and recording settings, such as the option to use your modem for these purposes (if your modem has voice messaging capability). Don't bother trying to use your modem for voice messaging unless you have multiple sound cards in the computer.

The Properties and Configure buttons for these items could be useful, however, depending on your sound system's chipset. Some offer options to adjust bass and treble; expanded stereo (sort of a wider sound based on adjustment of the "phase" of the signal going to the amplifier); sample-rate conversion options; equalization optimization based on the kind of speakers you have; amplitude gain or reduction; and hardware acceleration. (Use full acceleration if you're a gamer because it affects DirectSound used in some games.)

Clicking the Recording tab, then on a microphone icon (Mic), and then clicking Configure brings up the Speech Recognition Options dialog box. From here, you can start using speech recognition, set up your mic, take a tutorial about how to use recognition, and train your computer to better understand your voice. Speech recognition is a large topic unto itself, but for brief coverage of Vista's Speech Recognition system, see the lesson on the CD.

> **NOTE**
>
> Mouse Pointers is the next link on the Personalization dialog. However, we don't discuss it here because it's covered in Chapter 25, "Windows Management and Maintenance."

Changing Your Theme

A theme is a background plus a set of sounds, icons, and other elements to help you personalize your computer with one click. All the settings you make on the other tabs of the Personalize dialog box can be saved to a theme file on the Themes tab (see Figure 26.9). Vista includes a few themes, such as the default Windows Vista and Windows Classic theme (similar to the default theme of Windows 2000). If you make changes to desktop colors or other GUI attributes such as those described in this chapter, your theme will show up in this dialog box as Modified Theme. You can save that theme to disk so you can later reload it. Just click Save As and give it a name.

Themes are stored in files with a .themes suffix. You can browse for saved themes by opening the Theme drop-down list and choosing Browse.

Figure 26.9
You can choose an overarching desktop theme of visuals and sounds using this dialog box

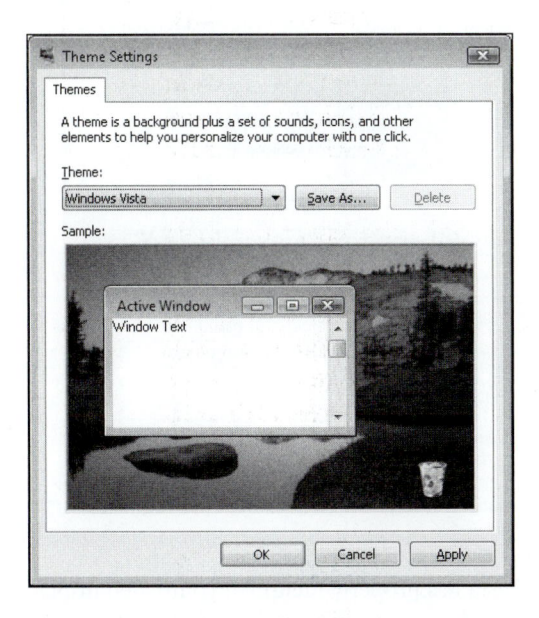

DISPLAY SETTINGS

The Display Settings link from the Personalize dialog box (refer to Figure 26.2) brings up the Display Settings dialog box, shown in Figure 26.10. From here, you can tweak the video driver's most basic settings—screen resolution (desktop size) and color quality (color depth). You can also activate multiple monitors.

> **TIP**
>
> On some slower computers that don't have fast CPUs or intelligent coprocessed video cards, you may find that running in true color at a high resolution, such as 1280×1024, can be annoying if you have Show Window Contents While Dragging turned on. When you move a window, it moves jerkily across the screen. If you play videos such as Windows Media Video, QuickTime, MPEG, or RealPlayer movies, you'll also notice that these higher color depths can slow down the movies or make them play jerkily. Try using a setting of 16-bit color depth (a.k.a. "high color") for movies and photos.

Figure 26.10
The Display Settings dialog box

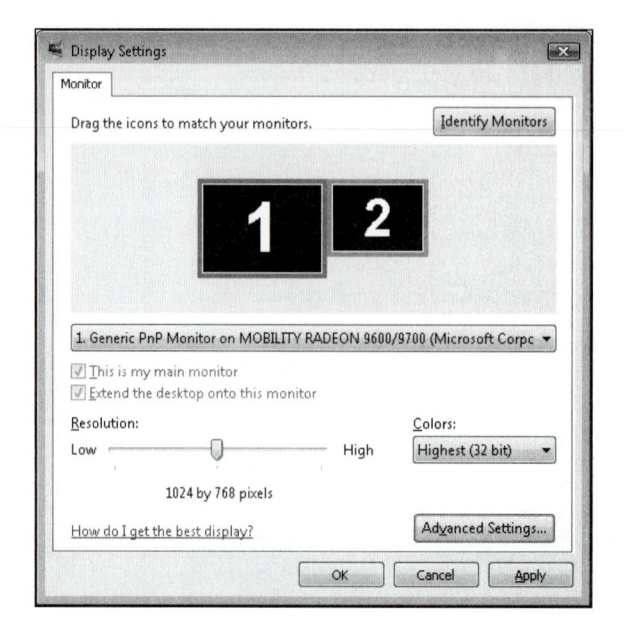

Assuming that Windows Vista has properly identified your video display card and that the correct driver is installed, the Colors drop-down list box should include all the legitimate options your card is capable of. Your color depth options are limited by the amount of video RAM on the card and the resolution you choose. The higher the resolution, the more memory is used for pixel addressing, limiting the pixel depth (number of colors that can be displayed per pixel). With many modern cards, this limitation is no biggie, and it's likely that many Windows Vista users will not have to worry about it except in cases when they have large monitors displaying 1600×1200 and want 32-bit color *and* a high refresh rate. If you find that setting the color scheme up to high color or true color causes the resolution slider to move left, this is the reason. All modern analog color monitors for PCs are capable of displaying 16 million colors, which is dubbed True Color.

> If you've changed the screen area only to find that you can no longer see some icons or open windows on the desktop, **see** "Where Did Those Icons Go?" in the "Troubleshooting" section at the end of this chapter.

You must click the Apply button before the changes are made. When you do, you are warned about the possible effects. The good thing about the no-reboot video subsystem, first introduced with Windows 98, is that the driver settings should revert within 15 seconds unless you accept them. So, if the screen goes blank or otherwise goes bananas, just wait. It should return to the previous setting.

> If, after toying with the screen resolution, you notice that your once-speedy computer seems to have lost its zip, **see** "Moving in Slow Motion" in the "Troubleshooting" section at the end of this chapter.

The Resolution setting makes resizing your desktop a breeze. Obviously, we all want to cram as much on the screen as possible without going blind. This setting lets you experiment and even change resolution on-the-fly to best display whatever you're working on. Some jobs, such as working with large spreadsheets, databases, CAD, or typesetting, are much more efficient with more data displayed on the screen. Because higher resolutions require a trade-off in clarity and make onscreen objects smaller, you can minimize eyestrain by going to a lower resolution, such as 800×600 pixels. (A *pixel* is essentially one dot on the screen.) If you find the dialog box doesn't let you choose the resolution you want, drop the color palette setting down a notch and try again.

> **TIP**
>
> All laptops, notebooks, and almost all desktop computers have LCD monitors these days. Unlike their somewhat more-versatile yet clunky and energy-hungry CRT-based progenitors, these space-saving displays are optimized for one resolution, called their *native* resolution. On LCDs, I don't suggest changing the setting from the native, (sometimes called *suggested*), resolution. Although choosing a lower resolution will result in making screen elements larger (and thus easier for some people to see), it will also produce a blockier, fuzzier display. This effect is mitigated somewhat on more intelligent displays by engineering that provides antialiasing. Trying a higher resolution than the native one typically will not work. There is a discrete number of pixels on the display, and these are of a predetermined size. Trying to jam more pixels on the screen, if it works at all, does so by creating a "virtual" screen that is larger than the actual one. This will require you to pan and scroll the screen image. Check the computer's or monitor's manual if you're in doubt about which external monitor resolutions are supported.

If you've connected an external TV monitor to your computer but cannot read the fonts on the screen, **see** "What Does That Say?" in the "Troubleshooting" section at the end of this chapter.

If you are experiencing any problems with your video system, from pop-up errors blaming the video system, to a flickering display, to even trouble resetting the resolution and color, click the Advanced Settings button and then the Troubleshoot tab. There may be some useful information there, depending on your monitor.

If the screen flicker really annoys you, **see** "Reducing Screen Flicker" in the "Troubleshooting" section at the end of the chapter.

Windows Vista allows you to display the same desktop view on two or more monitors. On a notebook where it was common to display the desktop both on the LCD panel and an external monitor, this is nothing new. But, on desktop PCs equipped with multiple video cards or a single card with dual outputs, you can now use multiple monitors. The screen resolution of each monitor is controlled from the Settings tab. Just select the monitor to set the context for the screen resolution and color quality controls.

You can also set up multiple screens such that each one is displaying different information, thus enlarging your overall desktop area (called *extended desktop*). This is covered in more detail in Chapter 30, "Installing and Replacing Hardware," but I'll briefly discuss it here.

In Figure 26.10, you can see that I have two monitors available. To activate a second monitor, plug it into the appropriate connector on your computer, and a New Display Detected dialog box opens and walks you through some settings. After you make those settings (such as whether you want a mirror arrangement or extended desktop), those settings are remembered and go into effect the next time you connect that monitor. If you unplug it, the system will revert to the previous single-monitor arrangement.

> **TIP**
>
> One drawback I've found to dual monitor setups is that I often have to disable the second display before starting up a game. Otherwise, the mouse pointer gets lost on the second screen.

If that wizard dialog box isn't coming up, open the dialog box displayed in Figure 26.10 and activate the second monitor by right-clicking it (the "2") and choosing Attached. Next, if you want your desktop icons and taskbar to be displayed on that monitor, right-click and choose Primary.

> **TIP**
>
> If using an extended desktop arrangement, you can drag the monitors around one another in the dialog box to adjust their relative position and how the mouse jumps between the monitors.

When you plug in a modern monitor, Windows usually detects it and sets the correct resolution, refresh rate, orientation, and color depth for it. Most newer monitors and projectors support Extended Display Identification Data (EDID), a standard video data format that transmits this information to the computer when you plug them in.

The Advanced Settings button on the Display Settings dialog box opens the Monitor and Adapter Properties dialog box. This dialog box has four tabs—Adapter, Monitor, Troubleshoot, and Color Management.

> **TIP**
>
> Contrary to some advertising accompanying flat-panel monitors, LCDs don't give a hoot about high refresh speed. In fact, they don't like high speeds. LCDs use a completely different technology, typically with a transistor for each pixel. The dots don't have to be refreshed as they do in a CRT. I noticed a blurry display on a desktop LCD screen once and tracked down the problem to a 72Hz refresh rate on the video card. I lowered it to 60Hz, and the image cleared up. This advice applies only to LCDs attached to analog display cards. Some outboard LCD monitors are driven by their own digital adapter cards, and refresh settings don't affect those cards.

> **CAUTION**
>
> If you specify a refresh rate that is too high for your monitor, it could damage the monitor. Also, trying to expand the desktop area to a larger size might not work. You just get a mess on the screen. If you have this problem, try using a setting with a lower refresh rate, such as 60Hz or "interlaced." The image may flicker a bit more, but at least it will be visible.

The Adapter tab displays information about the video card and offers access to configure, uninstall, update, or roll back the video driver through the Properties button. The List All Modes button is used to view the color, resolution, and refresh rate combinations supported by this video adapter.

> *If, while you're tinkering with the refresh rates for your monitor, the monitor goes blank, don't panic; instead,* **see** *"Uh-Oh, My Monitor Died" in the "Troubleshooting" section at the end of this chapter.*

The Monitor tab offers access to configure, install, upgrade, or roll back the monitor driver and to set the screen refresh rate. Use the screen refresh rate with caution because it can damage older monitors or render your desktop unviewable. Higher refresh rates reduce the flickering of the display.

> *If, after you install a new LCD monitor, you discover that the image is blurry,* **see** *"Blurry Images in LCD" in the "Troubleshooting" section at the end of this chapter.*

The Troubleshoot tab is used to set the hardware acceleration rate, anywhere between None and Full. Basically, this indicates how much video processing is offloaded to the video adapter instead of being performed by Windows Vista on the CPU. The more you can offload processing to the video card, the more smoothly your system will function. If you have problems with jitters or lockups, you may need to reduce the amount of hardware acceleration, if that option is not grayed out. (Some cards won't let you change this setting, or you won't have the privilege level necessary unless you are an administrator.)

The Color Management tab is used to set the color profile used to manage colors for your adapter and monitor. If you are performing high-end image processing you may want to investigate this feature in the Windows Vista Resource Kit.

Tweak UI

Many Windows experts have become fond of an unsupported Microsoft product called Tweak UI, which is available and freely downloadable from the Microsoft site. Tweak UI is one of the Microsoft "power toys" developed by programmers at Camp Bill in Redmond, Washington. Tweak UI worked fine on Windows XP as it did on Windows 2000 and Windows 98.

Tweak UI enabled you to make more than 100 changes to the Windows user environment, such as smooth scrolling; menu speed; covering your tracks by erasing temp files, document lists, and history files; and adding or removing drives from being displayed in My Computer. However, as of this writing, Tweak UI was not yet available for Windows Vista. You might want to Google for it and see whether it is now available. There is one commercial set of UI tweaks for Vista called Tweak VI, at www.totalidea.com/content/ tweakvi/tweakvi-index.html or www.tweakvi.com.

Miscellaneous GUI Tips

Windows Vista offers many new features and capabilities. But you don't have to settle for the out-of-the-box defaults; you can customize to your heart's content. In the following sections, we provide you with several tips to help you soup up your Windows Vista installation.

> If you've become really frustrated because single clicks are interpreted by Windows as double-clicks (and you can't seem to find any mention of the problem in this chapter), never fear; there's an easy solution. **See** "Single- or Double-Click?" in the "Troubleshooting" section at the end of this chapter.

Fonts Preview Trick

If you've ever tried to see what a font looked like before you printed it, you know how frustrating it can be. But, getting a preview of a font is now easier than ever before. Just open the Fonts applet through the Control Panel and then click any listed font. The Preview pane displays details about the font, a sample of most characters, and several sizes of characters (see Figure 26.11).

Figure 26.11
A font sampling dialog box.

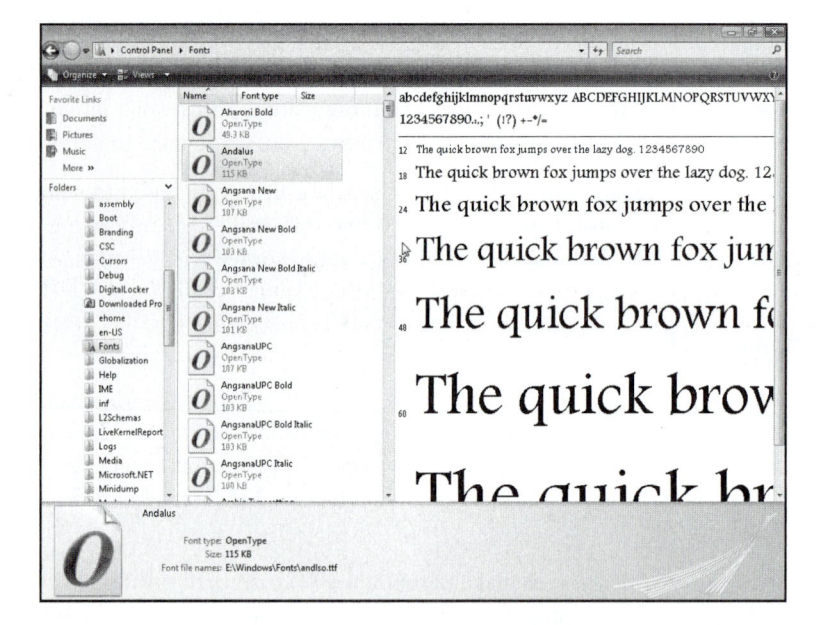

Which Windows Are You Using?

If you're dual- or multibooting between Windows Vista (using the classic interface style) and other Windows products, you may sometimes wonder which operating system you're running at any given time because the GUIs of the post-Windows 95 OSes are often virtually indistinguishable. Yes, you'll see a few giveaways, such as Computer versus My Computer, but if you're using the Classic Windows theme, the clues will be subtle.

To determine what's running, you could open the Control Panel, open the System applet, and read the dialog box. But that's a pain. Instead, you can use these techniques to remind yourself:

- Executing `winver` from the Run command or from a Command Prompt opens a dialog box that displays the OS name, version, applied Service Packs, and the amount of physical RAM installed in the system.
- Click Start and right-click Computer. From the menu that appears, click Properties. The first set of information in the System applet indicates the version of Windows you're currently using.

LIMITING FLIP 3D

If your computer does not have a high video performance rating and you have Aero turned on, using Flip 3D might be a bit slow if you have many apps and documents open at once. This can be particularly true if your windows have active video running since that consumes significant video display chip bandwidth.

One solution is to limit the number of mini-pages that Flip 3D displays when you press Windows+Tab.

WARNING Only attempt this if you know how to edit the registry. Chapter 31, "Editing the Registry," details registry editing.

1. Ensure you have Windows Aero enabled already. If you have Windows Basic running, right-click the desktop, select Personalisation, and then select Theme. From here, you can change from Windows Basic to Windows Aero. Click Apply and then OK.
2. Go to Start and then Run (or press the Windows Key + R).
3. Type in **regedit**, then press OK.
4. Navigate your way to HKEY_CURRENT_USER\Software\Microsoft\Windows\DWM.
5. In the right pane, right-click the mouse and select New; then, DWORD (32-bit) and name it Max3DWindows. Depending on your type of graphics card, your best bet is to base the value of this DWORD on the Windows System Performance Rating. If your computer has a rating of 1 to 2, set the registry value as 3. If your rating is set to 3, you can have your registry value to be 5. If your computer has a rating of 4 or 5, you can have anything over 10 as the registry value and it will still run smoothly.
6. Set the value and then press OK. Close down the Registry Editor.
7. Restart your computer for the changes to take effect.

More Visual Effects

There is another hidden location for Vista GUI settings somewhat akin to those provided by Tweak UI. For this semisecret list, follow these steps:

1. Open Control Panel.
2. Switch to Classic View.
3. Choose Performance Information and Tools.
4. Click Advanced Tools in the task pane.
5. Click Adjust the Appearance and Performance of Windows. (The UAC dialog box may appear.)

You will see the dialog box shown in Figure 26.12.

Figure 26.12
A treasure trove of UI and performance settings.

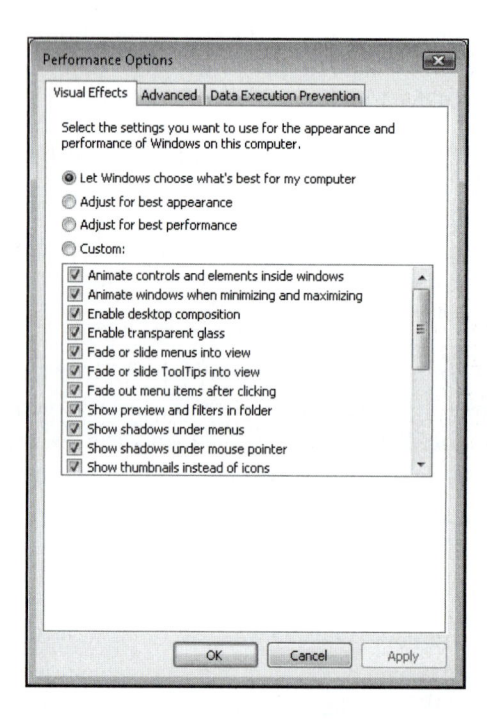

Have a ball making changes. Use care when adjusting the performance settings (processor scheduling and virtual memory). You don't want to slow down your foreground processing unless you don't mind waiting for response from your apps and input devices (keyboard and mouse). Letting Vista handle stuff like DEP and virtual memory paging size is generally the best way to go.

Administrator Tools Not Showing Up

Windows Vista is designed as an end-user operating system. Thus, most of the system-level management tools are not made readily accessible by being placed in plain sight on the Start menu. Instead, they all are contained within a subfolder of the Control Panel known as Administrative Tools. Open the Control Panel, click System and Maintenance, and choose Administrative Tools to open a folder containing these management tools.

Other than manually creating a shortcut to the Administrative Tools folder, there is no easy way to add this item to the Start menu's top level. Well, that's true if you are using the new Vista Start menu. If you revert to the Classic Start menu, you can enable the display of the Administrative Tools item within the Start menu through the Start menu's Properties, Start Menu tab, Customize button, Display Administrative Tools.

However, there is now a way to gain access to Administrative Tools without having to open the Control Panel or All Programs menu. Open the Properties for the Taskbar and Start Menu and select Customize. Scroll down to the bottom of the list and choose Administrative Tools, Display on the All Programs menu, and the Start menu.

CHANGING THE LOCATION OF THE DOCUMENTS AND OTHER SPECIAL FOLDERS

As you may know, Pictures, Documents, and so on have special qualities in that they are displayed in virtually any Windows Explorer or mini-Explorer (such as a Save To…) window. Being special system folders, it is important that Vista know where they are. But you *can* change that location for you own purposes, such as to keep all your documents on a separate drive. Some people prefer to keep their documents separated from the operating system, for example. If you are like me, you employ your own organizational scheme for saving documents and files, which does not include the Documents element. Having every Save dialog box default to Documents is a huge annoyance! It's almost enough to make you throw up your hands and surrender to saving your documents where Microsoft wants you to. In fact, that location may be pretty well hidden.

In a multiuser system, Vista creates the Documents folder under the user's name, like this:

> C:\documents and settings\bob\documents

If you're the only person using the computer, this is particularly annoying because having to "drill down" through those folders every time you want to open a document is a pain. Well, fret no more. In earlier versions of Windows, you had to hack the Registry to change the location of the Documents folder, but now changing the location is much simpler. All you have to do is the following:

1. Right-click the Documents icon on the Start menu or through Computer or Windows Explorer.
2. Choose Properties and select the Location tab.
3. Click Move and then select the new destination.

This action doesn't move the original Documents folder; it just redefines where the Documents variable actually points to. In other words, it lets you declare another preexisting folder as the default Save As and Open folder. If you already have documents stored in the original location, you'll need to copy or move them to the new location of the Documents folder.

This trick works for the properties of other special folders as well, such as Pictures. Music, and Games.

Cascading Elements off the Start Menu

Cascading is the ability to expand certain folders right off the Start menu. These expanded menus are also called *fly-open menus*. The native Windows Vista interface can be configured to add cascading menus for the Control Panel, Computer, Documents, Music, Games, Pictures, Personal Folder, Network Connections. This is the same feature we discussed earlier to gain direct Start menu access to Administrative Tools.

The process is simple:

1. Just open the Properties for the Start menu. (Right-click over the Start button and select Properties from the pop-up menu.)
2. Select the Start Menu tab and click Customize.
3. Scroll down the list of Start menu items and change the settings for the desired items to Display as a menu.

If you are running in the Classic menu mode, use steps 1 and 2 above, but click Expand Control Panel, Expand Documents, etc., as desired.

Switch Ctrl, Alt, and Caps Lock Keys

If you are frustrated by the location of the Ctrl and Caps Lock keys, there is a way to move them. Microsoft has created a document that describes the complex process of editing the Registry to alter the locations of keys on the keyboard. They provide an example of switching the left Ctrl and Caps Lock keys, but they provide instructions on how to switch around any key on the keyboard. Because Microsoft did such a great job of writing this one out, I'll leave it up to them to explain it: www.microsoft.com/whdc/device/input/w2kscan-map.mspx.

Another fix, and one that works in Vista and doesn't require that you become a programmer is a program called SharpKeys. It's available at www.randyrants.com/sharpkeys/. I love this program because I like the Ctrl key placed to the left of the A key, and Alt in the lower-left corner of the keyboard.

Auto Scrolling with a Three-Button Mouse

Do you have a three-button mouse and wish you had a wheel mouse to make it easier to scroll your web pages? Don't bother coveting your neighbor's wheel mouse because Internet Explorer, Office applications, and your three-button mouse can do the next best thing. When you're working in an Internet Explorer window, just click the center mouse button. The cursor changes to a two-headed arrow shape. Now move the mouse away or toward you, and the page scrolls. Click again or click another mouse button, and the scrolling function is terminated.

> **NOTE**
>
> If you've tried to delete a folder that looked like it was empty but an error message states the folder still contains files, you are probably dealing with hidden files. To see what's not being shown, go change the hidden files and folders Advanced setting. I've run into this issue a few times with downloaded applications that must be extracted to a temporary folder before being installed. They sometimes include files premarked as hidden.

Configuring the Recycle Bin

The Recycle Bin holds recently deleted files to provide you with a reasonable opportunity to recover them. As discussed in Chapter 4, "Using the Windows Vista Interface," the Recycle Bin holds the last deleted files that fit within its size restriction. That restriction by default is 10% of the drive space for each partition or volume on the system. However, you can and should customize the Recycle Bin for your specific needs.

The Recycle Bin's Properties dialog box (accessed by right-clicking over the icon and then selecting Properties) has a Global tab and a tab for each partition/volume on the system. The Global tab offers a control that allows you to configure your drives independently or to use one setting for all drives (the default). If you've never deleted a file by mistake and don't think you ever will, you can elect to delete files immediately without storing them in the Recycle Bin. If you'd rather just limit how much space Windows uses to store deleted files, you can set a maximum size for the Recycle Bin as a percentage of drive space. A final control on the Global tab enables a deletion confirmation dialog box—I think this should be left enabled.

Remember, if you select to configure the properties for each drive independently, you must use the provided tabs labeled for each drive on your system. Each drive will display the size of the drive and the space reserved for the Recycle Bin along with the other controls we just discussed.

When limiting the amount of space to use for deleted files, the default percentage is 10%. This is usually a good size, but as hard disk sizes increase, you may want to reduce this to 5%. Keep in mind that files moved to the Recycle Bin are not actually deleted. Instead, their path information is removed from the normal interfaces and moved into the Recycle Bin. Deleted files still remain on the drive exactly where they were before the deletion operation. This means they take up space on the drive. So, if you leave the default percentage setting at 10% on a 20GB hard drive, you can have up to 2GB of deleted files still sitting on the drive slowing down the drive's seek time.

Troubleshooting

Reducing Screen Flicker

My CRT is flickering and annoying me. How can I change it?

Increase the refresh rate of the display subsystem to at least 70Hz. Right-click the desktop, choose Properties, and then choose Settings, Advanced, Monitor. Finally, change the refresh rate. Note that this ONLY applies to older, CRT-style monitors, not thin flat panel LCD monitors. Most LCDs should be run at 60Hz for the clearest image.

WHERE DID THOSE ICONS GO?

I changed the screen resolution, and now I can't find items off the edge of the screen, and I have windows I can't close.

You might have this problem when you switch to a lower resolution from a higher one. Theoretically, Windows is good about relocating desktop icons, but some applications might not do the same. For example, the small AOL Instant Messenger dialog box can be off the edge of the screen somewhere, and when it is, you can't get to it. Closing and rerunning the program doesn't help. One trick is to switch to the application by pressing Alt+Tab. Then press Alt+spacebar and press M. This key combination invokes the Move command for the window. Then you can use the arrow keys on the keyboard to move the window (typically to the left and/or up). When you have the title bar of the window in view, press Enter. If this trick doesn't work, switch back to the previous higher resolution, reposition the application window in question closer to the upper-left corner of the screen, and then switch back to the lower resolution. It may help to remember that your screen is always decreased or increased in size starting from the lower-right corner and moving up or down diagonally.

WHAT DOES THAT SAY?

I want to use an external TV monitor, but the output text is illegible.

Some video cards and laptops can be plugged in to a TV monitor or regular TV that has video input. But displaying computer output on a TV monitor is problematic for a couple of reasons. For starters, some video display cards don't let you run the TV at anything higher than 640×480 resolution. Also, TV sets (as opposed to professional TV monitors) often *overscan*, pushing the edges of the image off the edge of the screen. The following are a few points to remember when you're using a TV or video projector, whether you're doing presentations, playing games, or giving your eyes a break by moving your focal plane back a bit:

- If your computer and TV have "S" (Super VHS) inputs, use them. They increase the clarity a bit. Don't expect miracles, though. If you're using a video projector and the computer and projector have DVI (Digital Video Interface) connectors, use those. The image should be much clearer.

- Use Display Settings to switch the output to the TV to 640×480 resolution.

- Check to see whether your Display Settings, Advanced dialog box has buttons to center the image on the TV. It's most likely off center or needs resizing when you first try it. Some drivers such as those from ATI have advanced properties for fine-tuning TV display.

- Your application may have a "zoom" control for easily increasing the size of text onscreen, without the hassle of reformatting the entire document. MS Office tools such as Excel and Word, for example, have such a feature. Try bumping up the zoom size to increase legibility.

SINGLE- OR DOUBLE-CLICK?

I seem to accidentally run programs and open documents with a slip of the finger.

You probably have Single-Click selection turned on. As a result, one click (or tap, if you're using a touchpad) runs the program or opens the document that is highlighted. Change to Double-Click selection mode by opening a folder window; choosing Organize, Folder and Search Options; and selecting Double Click to Open an Item.

UH-OH, MY MONITOR DIED

I changed my resolution or refresh rate, and now the screen is blank.

Normally, you shouldn't have this problem because Windows Vista asks you to confirm that a screen resolution works properly and switches back to the previous resolution if you don't confirm. If somehow you changed color depth and resolution, and the system is stuck with a blank screen, you can reboot, press F8 during boot, and choose Safe Mode. Right-click the desktop and choose Personalize. Choose Display Settings and reset the properties to what the computer was running at before the change. Be sure to reset both the screen resolution *and* the color depth. In the worst case scenario, start with 800×600 and 16-bit color. Then reboot normally. After you've rebooted successfully, right-click the desktop, choose Properties, click Settings, and increase the settings one step at a time. Don't change resolution *and* color depth at the same time, though. Increase one first and then the other.

> **NOTE**
>
> Some motherboards reserve F8 for a boot selection menu, which would prevent the above approach from working. If that is the case on your PC, reboot and press F6 which will bring up advanced boot options. Then choose appropriately from the resulting menu.

MOVING IN SLOW MOTION

I increased the resolution, but now the screen updates slowly when I drag windows around.

Unless you're doing high-resolution photographic-quality work, you don't need the high-resolution 24-bit or 32-bit color depth settings. These settings just serve to slow down screen redraws when you move windows about. On the Display Settings dialog box, try reducing the color depth a notch (such as to 24 or 16-bit color if you have those options) and enjoy the speed increase.

BLURRY IMAGES IN LCD

I switched to an LCD screen, and the image is blurrier than I expected.

Unlike CRTs, LCDs do not benefit from higher refresh rates. Don't try to use anything above a 60Hz refresh rate for an LCD monitor. Also, check the LCD monitor's internal settings (check its manual) for a "phase adjustment" or focus adjustment to help clear up fuzziness on small text.

Stretched a Bit Thin

I set up a picture for my desktop wallpaper, but it looks blocky.

You're stretching a small bitmap. Either use a larger image or turn off the Fit to Screen setting for the image. See the Control Panel, Personalization, Desktop Background, How Should the Picture Be Positioned option.

Screen Fonts Too Small

All my screen fonts are too small to read easily.

There are a couple of fixes. The most common one is to decrease the screen resolution. However, on LCD monitors, as explained earlier, this is not the optimum solution. Leave the screen resolution on and LCD (including laptops) at the native resolution for the screen (check the manual); then tell Vista to use a larger font. If you want *really* big and clear fonts, use the Accessibility settings from the Control Panel. Otherwise, for a modest system font size increase (up to 200%) of icons, taskbar, menus, and other common Windows elements, do the following:

1. Right-click on the desktop and choose Personalize.
2. Click Adjust Font Size (DPI).
3. Click Continue when User Account Control asks for confirmation.
4. Choose Larger Scale or click Custom DPI.

CHAPTER 27

Managing Hard Disks

In this chapter

Hard Disk Management   930

Windows Vista File and Storage Systems   930

Organizational Strategies   933

Windows Vista's Disk-Management Tools   934

Disk Management   935

Removable Storage   942

Disk Defragmenter   943

Detecting and Repairing Disk Errors   946

Convert   947

Compression: How It Works, How to Use It   948

Disk Cleanup Utility   949

Zipping or Compressing Files   953

Third-Party Management Tools   953

Hard Disk Troubleshooting   954

Tips from the Windows Pros: Quieting a Noisy System   958

Hard Disk Management

For many users and system administrators, intelligent hard disk management forms the core of efficient system management. Until a new technology evolves to replace the hard disk, we're stuck with the problems and limitations created by a crude system of motors, spinning platters, and very delicate parts, such as read/write heads floating microns above a flying surface that can be easily ruined by particles as small as those found in a puff of cigarette smoke. Perhaps someday, hard disks will be relics of the past, bookends like the 5MB drives I have on my bookshelf. (They make good doorstops, too.) Until that time, we're stuck with the peculiar vagaries of hard disks. The good news is that high-capacity drives are cheap and plentiful.

No doubt, the majority of Windows Vista users will never set up RAID arrays, multiple-booting arrangements, or dynamic disks; use encryption; or need to do any remote disk administration. Perhaps they will perform occasional disk cleanups and defragmenting, learn to share folders over the network. These tasks are enough to get by with. Yet with a bit more knowledge gleaned by reading this chapter, you can learn how extensive Windows Vista's hard disk configuration capabilities are.

> **NOTE**
>
> *RAID* is short for *Redundant Array of Independent (or Inexpensive) Disks.* In this hard disk scheme, two or more drives are connected for higher fault tolerance and performance. RAID arrangements used frequently on servers aren't generally necessary for personal or client computers.

Windows Vista File and Storage Systems

Windows Vista supports two types of storage models: basic disks and dynamic storage. Windows 2000 and Windows XP Professional also support dynamic storage. When you prepare a hard disk for use, you can choose between these storage models. The following sections explain how they differ and when to use each type.

Basic Disks

The traditional storage model of disk structure uses partition tables. Each hard drive can hold up to four *primary partitions* or up to three primary partitions and one *extended (secondary) partition*. Within this extended partition, you can create logical drives. The total number of primary partitions and logical drives cannot exceed 32 per hard drive. This disk structure is understood and can be accessed by MS-DOS, Windows, and all versions of Windows NT, as well as Windows 2000, XP, and Vista. When viewed in Disk Management, a disk drive prepared in this fashion is known as a basic disk.

The annoyances and limitations of this partition table methodology are artifacts of Microsoft operating systems—incidentally, not something imposed by hard disks themselves or their manufacturers. Some other operating systems don't suffer the same peculiarities.

> **NOTE**
>
> Storage types are separate from the file systems they contain. Both basic and dynamic disks can contain any combination of FAT16, FAT32, NTFS v4, or NTFS v5 partitions or volumes. All drives are either basic or dynamic.

The major reasons to continue using basic storage include

- Support for all versions of Windows that can read the file system used on the drives. For example, if you need to support dual-booting with Windows XP Home Edition and Vista, you must use a file system that both operating systems support. XP Home does not support dynamic disks, so you must use basic disks.
- Support for multiboot configurations. Dynamic disks don't use boot loaders, so you cannot select between operating systems; therefore, you cannot use this type of storage as your only drive in a multiboot configuration.

You can convert basic to dynamic disks without data loss, but to convert a dynamic disk back to a basic disk using Windows Vista's Disk Management, you must delete the disk structure (and, of course, the data).

> **TIP**
>
> If you need to convert a dynamic disk to a basic disk without data loss, use Avanquest Publishing USA's Partition Commander Professional 10 program (www.v-com.com/product/Partition_Commander_Home.html).

DYNAMIC STORAGE

With dynamic storage, the restraints of primary and extended partitions are gone. Under this storage model, free space on a hard drive is divided into volumes instead of partitions; these volumes can be noncontiguous and can span one or more disks. In addition, volumes on a dynamic disk can be configured as simple, spanned, mirrored, striped, or RAID-5. Basic storage partitions can be configured only as simple partitions, unless they are remnants from a previous OS retained during an upgrade.

- A *simple* volume uses free space available on a single disk. This space can be a single contiguous region or multiple concatenated regions. Under the basic storage model, each partition or logical drive is assigned a separate and distinct drive letter, and functions as a distinct region of disk space. Dynamic storage can be configured to see multiple regions of a disk as a single volume, accessed with a single assigned drive letter.
- A *spanned* volume extends the concept of a simple volume across multiple disks (up to a maximum of 32). All joined regions on these disks are seen as a single volume to programs accessing them. However, if a single unit in a spanned volume fails, the entire set is lost.

- A *mirrored* volume is a volume in which data from one disk is mirrored or duplicated on a second disk. This process provides for data redundancy, often called *fault tolerance*. If one disk fails, the data can be accessed from the second disk. A mirrored volume cannot be spanned; each volume must be contained on a single disk. Programs see only one volume, and Windows ensures that both disks are kept in sync. *Mirroring* is also known as *RAID-1*.

- A *striped* volume is a volume in which data is stored across two or more physical disks. When data is written to a striped volume space, it is allocated alternately and evenly to each of the physical disks. A striped volume cannot be mirrored or spanned via Windows Vista. (It is possible on hardware-based RAID.) *Striping*, often termed *RAID-0*, is used to increase storage system throughput. If a single unit in a striped volume fails, the entire set is lost.

- A *RAID-5* volume is a fault-tolerant version of a striped volume. When data is written to a RAID-5 volume, it is striped across an array of three or more disks, and a parity value is added. If a hard disk belonging to a RAID-5 volume fails, the remaining drives can re-create the data using this parity value. Note the difference here between a mirrored volume and a RAID-5 volume.

> **NOTE**
> A mirrored volume contains two disks; if either one fails, the operating system goes to the other for data access.
>
> A RAID-5 volume contains three or more disks, any of which can fail without the system halting. The operating system then reconstructs the missing data from the information contained on the remaining disks.

What are the advantages of dynamic storage?

- First and foremost, noncontiguous regions of multiple disks can be linked so that they appear as one large region of disk space to any program. By linking them, you can increase the size of a disk volume on-the-fly, without reformatting or having to deal with multiple drive letters.

- Second, and perhaps more important, from an administrator's point of view, disk and volume management can be performed without restarting the operating system.

However, on a multiboot system, operating systems other than Vista, Windows 2000 (Server and Professional), Windows XP Professional, and Windows Server 2003 cannot see dynamic storage drives. Unlike NTFS, which applies to only the formatted partition, dynamic storage affects the entire hard drive. Only Windows XP Pro, Windows Server 2003, and Windows 2000 can see drives configured as dynamic storage. So if you plan to use dynamic storage, plan ahead and keep other OSes on different hard drives. In addition, you must ensure that the boot drive is a basic storage drive so that the boot menu will function.

CAUTION

> Converting a hard disk to dynamic storage is a one-way process unless you use a third-party utility such as Partition Commander Professional 10. To change a dynamic disk back to a basic disk using Windows Vista's Disk Management tool, all volumes must be deleted before converting the drive back to basic storage. Also note that dynamic disks can be read by Windows Vista, Windows XP Pro, Windows Server 2003, and all versions of Windows 2000. Windows XP Home, Windows NT, Windows 98/SE/Me, and all earlier versions of Windows cannot access dynamic storage volumes. When you change the boot disk to dynamic, you can no longer multiboot into another operating system because the familiar boot loader screen disappears. Only one installation of Windows can own a set of dynamic disks, so if you are planning to use dynamic disks as your RAID solution on a multiboot computer, think about investing in a hardware-based (SCSI or SATA) RAID solution.

Organizational Strategies

Although the disk systems described in the preceding section are interesting, especially to power users and system administrators who have multiple drives available, most Windows Vista users set up their systems with standard partitions (that is, basic storage) and the NTFS file format. But what about other file systems? How should you organize multiple disks? What about preparing your disks, and what kinds of strategies should you consider?

If you're not going to stick with the straight and narrow of running only NTFS on your hard disk, consider following these alternative strategies and rules:

- Whenever possible, create a separate partition for your data files. This tip has particular relevance to users who test new software or operating systems. If you store your data on a separate partition, reinstalling an operating system is a simple matter of formatting your system partition and starting from scratch. Although you still need to reinstall your programs, using a separate data partition ensures that you didn't miss a data file somewhere along the line. It also makes backups simple and straightforward. You can do one backup of your system partition; you then need to update this backup only when you add a new device or software program. Data backups can be run on a daily or weekly basis (determined by how often your data changes) and can be set to run on your data partition. Even if you use Windows Vista's much-improved backup software, it's still easier to make backups if you separate your operating system and applications from your data.

- Use the Windows Vista Complete PC Backup utility (included in the Backup and Restore Center on Ultimate, Business, and Enterprise editions) to create an image of your system. Having such an image is worth its weight in gold if you like to "tinker" with your system and program configurations. When you have your operating system set up, your principal applications installed, and everything tweaked and configured to perfection, you can create an image of your system on a separate drive or partition. If you need to reinstall your operating system for whatever reason, the complete process—from beginning to end—should take no more than 20 minutes. When you add, delete, or reconfigure a program, or make changes to the hardware configuration of your disk subsystem, be sure to update your disk image.

The easiest way to maintain a disk image is to buy a separate hard disk (internal ATA/IDE or SATA, or USB external) just for image storage. In my office, I use external hard disks up to 250GB for image storage, but larger sizes are available.

- In many of today's systems, there's only one ATA/IDE host adapter, but four or more Serial ATA (SATA) host adapters. Even if you have only two ATA/IDE drives (a hard disk and a DVD drive), you should not put both of them on the same host adapter. DVD drives transfer data at slower rates than hard disks, slowing down operating system and application installations as well as backups to CD or DVD media. With second-generation (300MBps, native command queuing) SATA drives now selling for about the same price as IDE drives of comparable capacity, it's time to bite the bullet and switch to SATA. The disk-installation utilities provided by Seagate, Western Digital, and other drive vendors can copy your entire existing IDE drive to a new SATA drive during the installation process.

Windows Vista's Disk-Management Tools

Most of Windows Vista's disk-management tools are identical to those found in Windows XP, but Windows Vista adds the capability to shrink a volume without data loss.

The most frequently used tools are available on the Tools tab of a drive's properties sheet. To reach the properties sheet, right-click a drive in Explorer. Figure 27.1 shows the properties tabs for both a FAT drive and an NTFS drive. Notice the difference in the number of tabs—NTFS has more options because of its support for security and quota management.

Figure 27.1
Properties sheets for NTFS and FAT volumes.

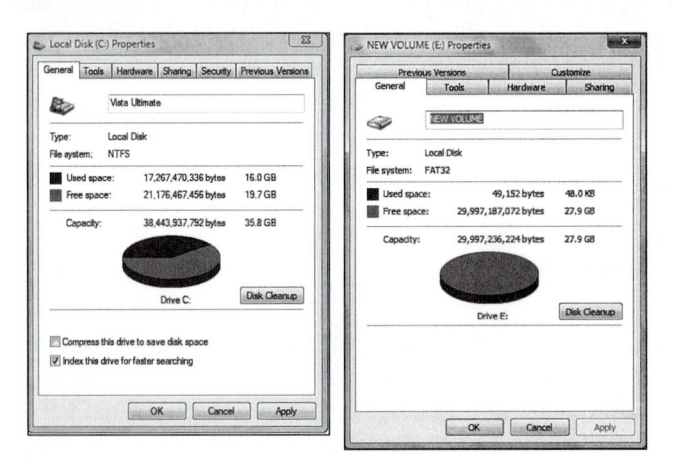

The following sections explain how to use most of the hard disk management tools included in Windows Vista.

Disk Management

The Disk Management utility (shown in Figure 27.2) is responsible for the creation, deletion, alteration, and maintenance of storage volumes in a system. This tool is located within the Computer Management interface of Administrative Tools (accessed through Start, Control Panel, Administrative Tools, Computer Management, Disk Management). It is protected by User Account Control. Another access method is right-clicking Computer and choosing Manage. Using the Disk Management utility, you also can assign the drive letters used by your DVD and hard disk drives.

Figure 27.2
The Disk Management tool as part of Computer Management.

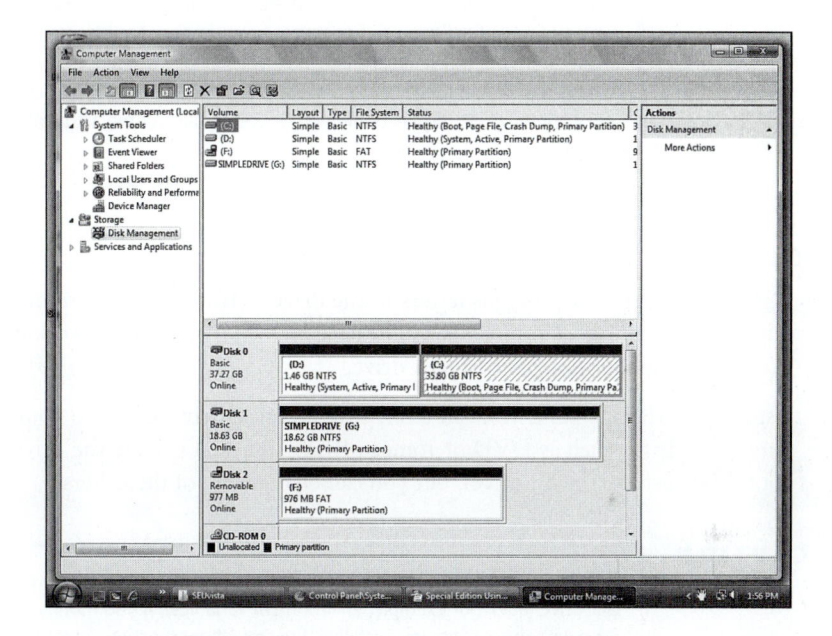

TIP

If the Administrative Tools menu selection is not displayed on the Start menu, right-click over the Start menu and select Properties, click Customize, click the Advanced tab, scroll down to the System Administrative Tools items, and then select the appropriate radio button.

If you enable the Control Panel to act as a menu, you can access Administrative Tools through it off the Start menu as well.

As discussed in Chapter 25, "Windows Management and Maintenance," this single interface lets you manage both local and remote computers using the various administration utilities shown in the left pane. Using this interface, I show you shortly how to perform different procedures on your existing and new hard disks. The process is quite simple for most of the operations because you will be presented with a wizard to complete them.

Most operations on disks can be performed by right-clicking the disk or volume you want to affect. As usual, you are presented with a context-sensitive menu from which you can perform any actions relating to the volume or disk you click. From the graphical layout in the Disk Management utility, you can also see what is going on with your disks at any given time. As always, you can select the Help option from within any menu to get an explanation of the operations available to you.

> **TIP**
>
> You can change the way specific types of volumes are displayed in Disk Management. To do this, click View, Settings. From there, you can select the color you want to use to represent any of the various disk states shown by Disk Management. By selecting the Scaling tab from the Settings dialog box, you can also change the way in which Disk Management shows the scaling of each disk. This capability is particularly useful if you want the scale display to be more representative of the actual physical sizes of your disks.

ASSIGNING DRIVE LETTERS AND JOINING VOLUMES

Windows automatically assigns letters to the drives. However, this assignment might not suit your system; for example, you might have already mapped a network drive to the same letter that Windows assigns to a new drive.

Using Disk Management, you can easily assign logical drive letters to your hard disks and removable drives such as DVD or Iomega REV. You can't change the drive letter of your boot drive (usually the C: drive), but you can change any of the others.

> **CAUTION**
>
> Note that many MS-DOS-based and Windows-based programs make references to a specific drive letter (for example, environment variables). If you modify the drive letter of a drive with these programs installed, they might not function correctly.

To change the letter, right-click the disk volume or drive in the bottom-right pane of Disk Management, and select Change Drive Letter and Paths. A dialog box appears, listing the current drive letter assignment. Click Change. Under Assign a Drive Letter, choose the desired new letter. Click OK and confirm that you really do want to make the change.

In addition to or instead of assigning a drive letter to a disk drive or partition, you can "graft" the disk volume onto another. Windows lets you specify a folder that will become the mount point for the new drive. For example, I might create a folder named C:\TEMP. Because I want lots of space for it, I can install a new hard drive and, instead of assigning it a drive letter, tell Windows to access it through C:\TEMP. My C:\TEMP files and subfolders are then stored on the alternate drive.

Disk Management | 937

> **TIP**
> By using a mount point, you can add space to the folders under the mount point folder using an available drive. This is a good way to add space in a controlled fashion for a specific purpose, such as to store scratch files or web page images.

Grafting Versus Dynamic Disks

Assigning mount points is different from what happens when you aggregate dynamic disks into one large volume. Although dynamic disks and regular (basic) disks both support the use of mount points, dynamic disks can create one large, apparently contiguous disk space. Mount points graft subsequently added drives at a folder, similar to grafting two trees by tying together a branch from each tree. Figure 27.3 illustrates the differences between the two approaches.

Figure 27.3
You can join drives two different ways: using mount points or using dynamic disk aggregation.

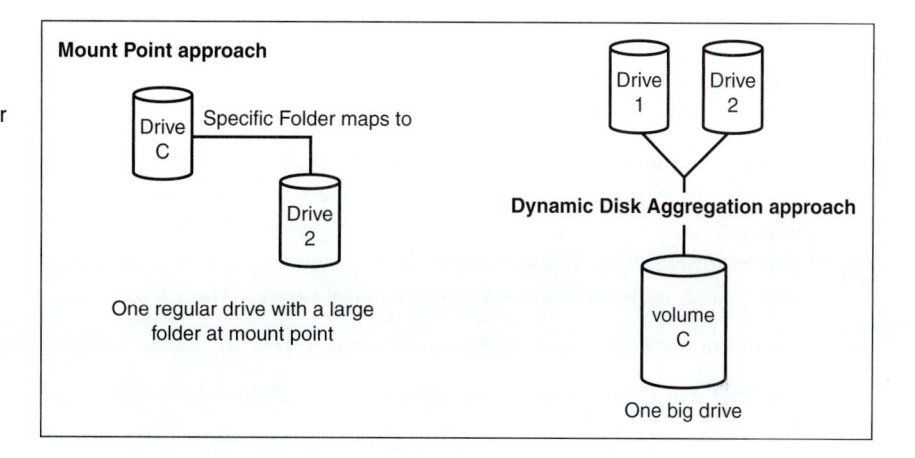

In Figure 27.4, I've grafted a hard disk containing digital photos (J:) into the mount point on drive `C:\Users\Marcus_S\Pictures\More Pix`.

> **NOTE**
> You can graft new volumes or disks onto a folder only on an NTFS-formatted drive. The new volume can have any format, however.

Figure 27.4
Assigning a partition or volume to a folder rather than a drive letter joins the volume to an existing volume. The contents of the added volume appear as subdirectories of the mount point folder.

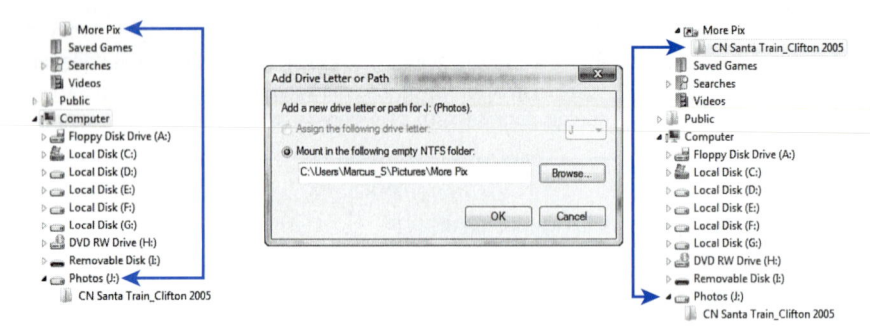

> **NOTE**
>
> If the folder you specify as the mount point already contains files, these are inaccessible as long as the drive-to-path mapping exists because that folder is now remapped into the new location. The original files reappear if you delete the drive path. Therefore, it's usually a good idea to create a new folder as a mount point or delete all the contents of an existing folder before establishing the mount point.

Even if you have several hard drives and DVD drives, you can graft them all together onto your C: drive, making it appear as one big file system. It's a great management concept: You can add space to your file system by attaching new disk volumes directly into the original folder structure. (UNIX users are probably smirking at this point because the UNIX operating system has worked this way since it was written in the 1970s.)

If you mount a drive and assign it a drive letter, you can access it through both pathways.

To graft a disk volume to an existing file system, follow these steps:

1. Create the folder that is to serve as the mount point for the new drive or volume.
2. Highlight the new drive or volume in Disk Management.
3. Right-click, select Change Drive Letter and Paths, and click Add.
4. Select Mount in the Following Empty NTFS Folder.
5. Enter the folder's pathname, or click Browse to locate it.
6. Click OK to save the path.
7. Click OK to close the dialog box.

> **TIP**
>
> When Explorer shows you free disk space on the original drive, it measures only the space on the physical drive, not space on any grafted drives. You'll actually have more space than you think because files on the grafted folders are stored on another volume. If you want, you can also assign a drive letter to the added volume so that you can view and monitor its free space directly.
>
> Alternatively, you can use the command prompt, change to the folder in the grafted volume, and use the DIR command. The DIR command lists free space on the actual current volume.

You can assign a given drive or volume to only one drive letter but an arbitrary number of paths. (It's a little strange to see the same files appear in several different places, so I recommend that you not go nuts with this feature.)

> **TIP**
> If you're running out of room on your C: drive, decide whether it makes sense in your situation to add lots of space to just one folder (for example, Documents). If it does, install and format a new hard drive, and assign it a letter. Copy the original folder to the new drive; then add a path to the new hard drive using the name of the original folder. This way, you can preserve your original data and have room for growth.

By the way, this "grafting" technique works with both basic and dynamic NTFS disks. Only Windows dynamic disks can be "grown" by changing their partition size on-the-fly. If you use a basic-formatted disk, as most users do, the grafting trick is a good one to know.

> **TIP**
> Another good time to use this feature is when you've backed up application data onto a CD or DVD disc. If you want to use the backed-up data in an emergency, you can add a path for your DVD drive to make its files appear in the original data location your application expects. That way, you can use the data off the media without restoring it to disk or reconfiguring your application. Later, you can delete the path to regain access to the "real" folder.

DYNAMIC DISK MANAGEMENT

If you are using only Windows Vista on a system, upgrading your storage devices to dynamic disks is usually the best way to go because of the many advantages of the new dynamic disk storage system. Remember, though, that you can't boot into or read your dynamic disks from any other operating system after you upgrade them. You can upgrade a disk through Disk Management, right-clicking the drive's icon in the bottom pane (click the part of the graphical display that reads "Disk 0," "Disk 1," and so on, not on the volume), and choosing Upgrade to Dynamic Disk. Then, choose the disk and click OK. Next, just follow the wizard, and you'll be set.

> **CAUTION**
> Don't upgrade to dynamic disks until you read all the material here on the topic and review the Help system's coverage of it in Disk Management. As you learned earlier in this chapter, dynamic disks cannot be changed back to basic disks using Windows Vista's Disk Management without completely destroying any partitions and reformatting the disk. If you need to do that, right-click the volume and select Delete Volume. From there, you can re-create your simple volume by right-clicking a disk and going through the applicable wizard. Also remember that other operating systems such as Windows XP Home, Windows 9x, and DOS can't use dynamic disks, so if you intend to multiboot your machine, you should not upgrade the drive. Whether a drive is basic or dynamic has no bearing on network client access to shared folders.

If you don't have the option of upgrading to dynamic disks, one of two possible reasons might be the cause. First, the disks might have already been upgraded to dynamic disks. Second, the disk is not a hard drive, but rather a CD, DVD, or removable media device.

Extending a Disk

One of the cool options available in Disk Management is the option to extend the volume on a dynamic storage drive. Extending is actually another way of "stretching" a simple volume to a specified size when unallocated space is present on the disk. Sometimes, you might want to rearrange the way you've set up your disks, so this option can come in handy.

To perform the actual extend operation on a disk, you need to have an area of the disk that is unallocated. From there, you simply right-click an existing partition and select Extend Volume to bring up the Extend Volume Wizard. The wizard enables you to specify the size that you want to extend the volume to. Finishing the operation leaves you with a disk that is now larger than before. This operation is not limited to volumes that are mounted as drive letters; you can also perform this task on volumes that are mounted into directories.

When Disk Management extends a disk, it is actually creating a new partition and mapping it to the same drive letter as the partition to be extended. It is, in effect, a spanned volume. Although this approach is a bit different from the traditional method performed by disk utilities, such as PartitionMagic, the upside of the Disk Management approach is that you can extend your disk without needing to wait for the volume to be resized and data to be shuffled around. The Disk Management approach happens very quickly, without even rebooting your system.

Shrinking a Disk

Windows Vista now supports shrinking a dynamic disk volume as well as extending it. When you shrink a volume, the space removed from the volume becomes unallocated space. You can use it for another volume or save it for a future multibooting operating system. To shrink a volume, right-click it and select Shrink Volume. The system calculates the amount of space that can be removed, and you can use all or part of this amount.

> **CAUTION**
>
> If you shrink your system's boot volume, you cannot extend it (unless you want to connect your system's hard disk to another system running Windows Vista). Before you shrink a boot volume, be sure you calculate how much room you'll need for future data, programs, and updates to Windows Vista.

Creating a Spanned Volume

A spanned volume is a volume in which the disk space spans multiple partitions and disks. Using a spanned volume is a handy way of turning a couple of small disks into one large disk, mounted under one drive letter or folder. Simple volumes can also be extended using spanned volumes, as shown in the previous section. Spanned volumes can be created only on dynamic disks. A spanned volume basically is the same as an extended volume, except that the former adds drive space from other hard drives and the latter adds drive space from the same drive.

Creating a spanned volume is just a matter of right-clicking an empty partition and selecting New Volume, which opens the New Volume Wizard. This wizard enables you to select the Spanned Volume option. Next, you are given the option to select which disks to include in your spanned volume. At this point, you also can select the amount of space to use for each disk. The total size of your spanned volume is the cumulative total of the space you select on each disk. Finally, you are prompted for the mount point and the format for your new spanned volume.

CREATING A STRIPED VOLUME

One of the procedures you can perform with Disk Management is creating a striped volume. Creating such a volume is often desirable simply because of the ease of administration and the substantial gain in speed. To create a striped volume, you must have more than one disk. For the definition of a striped volume, see "Dynamic Storage," earlier in this chapter.

When you're creating a striped volume, you are creating partitions of the same size across two or more disks. Bear this point in mind as you plan your implementation because you need to have the same amount of space available on each disk that you want to use for your set.

To create a striped volume, follow these steps:

1. Right-click one of the disks to be used in the striped volume set, and select New Volume. The New Volume Wizard opens.
2. Select Striped and then Next.
3. Select the disks you want to include as part of a striped volume. The New Volume Wizard automatically selects the first free disk as the first in the striped volume. The remaining two disks can be selected from the left column and added to the right column for the set. When you are done adding disks, click Next.

> **NOTE**
> Notice that the wizard automatically sets the size for all selected disks to the largest amount of free space that is equally available on each disk.

4. You are prompted for the mount point of your new striped set. Choose from the following three options:
    - **Assign the Following Drive Letter**—This option assigns your set one drive letter, as with any normal drive. Selecting this option is the most common method of mounting a striped set, and it suffices for most purposes.

- **Mount in the Following Empty NTFS Folder**—This option is a bit different from anything previously offered in Windows. By mounting a striped set to a folder, you are effectively creating a mount point within another disk. The mount point isn't actually on another disk, in the physical sense. The folder you use just has the amount of storage equal to the size of your striped set. This approach is more closely related to the UNIX approach, in which the actual drive letter is not used but the folder is referred to as the mount point. (Mount points were discussed earlier in this chapter.)
- **Do Not Assign a Drive Letter or Drive Path**—Selecting this option creates the striped set and leaves it for you to allocate later, using either of the two methods mentioned previously.

5. Select the Volume Format Options.
6. When you are presented with a summary of the actions to be performed by the wizard, choose the Finish button so that your new striped volume will be created and mounted under the path you chose in Step 4.

> **NOTE**
>
> In Explorer, notice that the icon for the folder mount point shows up as a hard disk. This icon appears simply so that you can differentiate between a mounted folder and a plain folder.

RAID and Dynamic Disk Information Storage

When a basic disk is made a member of a mirror, stripe, or RAID set, it's marked (or "signed") with a tiny, hidden partition at the end of the disk drive. This partition tells Windows that the disk is a member of a fault-tolerant disk set. The information about the configuration itself–for example, whether a given disk is the primary or secondary disk in a mirror set–is stored in the Registry. If you think about it, you can see that this is not a great place to store this kind of information: If a disk is damaged, Windows might not be capable of reading the Registry to find the configuration information. That's why you were always exhorted to update your Emergency Boot Disks when you made changes in the old Windows NT Disk Management; the disk configuration was stored on the emergency disks, too.

For dynamic disks, Windows creates a 4MB partition at the end of each disk drive in which it stores all the configuration information for all the dynamic drives in your computer. This redundant information helps Windows reconstruct a picture of the whole system if any drives are damaged or replaced, and it's another good reason to use dynamic disks over basic ones when you're building a Windows Vista system.

REMOVABLE STORAGE

Removable Storage is an optional tool within Computer Management. Its job is to track and catalog the data stored on removable storage devices. These devices can take the form of tape backup drives, MO drives, REV or JAZ drives, or the changers that control many removable storage devices. The Removable Storage Manager works by enabling you to create *media pools*—collections of media to which the same management properties (such as security permissions or backup routines) apply.

In Windows Vista, Removable Storage is not enabled by default. To enable it, follow this procedure:

1. Open the Control Panel.
2. Click the Programs category.
3. Click Turn Windows Features On or Off.
4. Click Continue on the User Access Control dialog box.
5. Click the empty check box in front of Removable Storage Management (see Figure 27.5).
6. Click OK. A progress bar indicates that the feature is being configured.

Figure 27.5
Enabling Removable Storage Management.

When Removable Storage is enabled, it is listed along with Disk Management as part of the Storage node. From here, you can create and manage media pools and also receive information about the physical locations for media.

As implemented, Removable Storage is limited to the small scope of hardware supported under it. But similar to many other Windows Vista features (the Indexing Service, for example), it has tremendous potential when third-party vendors develop hooks to its functions and interface. Currently, it stands as a useful tool to catalog backup media, such as tapes and optical cartridges, but little else.

Disk Defragmenter

When an operating system stores data on a hard disk, it places that information in the first available "hole" it can find that isn't already occupied by another file. However, if the disk already contains several other files, that location might not be large enough for the complete file. When this happens, the operating system places as much of the file as it can in the space available and then searches for another open hole for the balance of the file. This process continues until the entire file has been written to disk. Any files that are not written to a contiguous disk location are considered "fragmented."

The problem with fragmentation is that it slows down the rate at which your hard disk can retrieve information and supply it to the requesting program. Hard disks remain largely mechanical devices and are governed by the laws of physics. To access files stored on a disk, the drive must physically move a small arm to the correct location on a spinning platter. These movements are measured in milliseconds, but milliseconds add up, especially when a file is spread over a hundred unique locations.

Fragmentation is not always a bad thing. If an operating system had to find a contiguous section of disk space for every file it stored, your system would slow down as your drive filled up. Eventually, your system would reach a point at which the disk still had ample free space, but none of this space would be in contiguous blocks big enough to hold a file.

Disk Defragmenter addresses this fragmentation problem by reorganizing all the files on your hard disk so that they are stored as complete units on a single area of the disk. To do so, it identifies any remaining free areas, moves small files there to open up more space, and uses this newly opened space to consolidate larger files. This shuffling process repeats until all the files are moved around in this manner and the entire disk is defragmented.

In Windows Vista, unlike Windows XP, the Disk Defragmenter process is automated. You configure when it takes place, and it does the rest.

THE MFT

NTFS contains, at its core, a file called the master file table (MFT). It is similar to the file allocation table in the FAT system. At least one entry exists in the MFT for every file on an NTFS volume, including the MFT itself. The MFT also contains extended information about each file, such as its size, time, and date stamps; permissions; data content; and so forth.

As you add more files to an NTFS volume, the number of entries to the MFT grows. When files are deleted from an NTFS volume, their MFT entries are marked as free and can be reused, but the MFT does not shrink. Thus, space used by these entries is not reclaimed from the disk.

NTFS preallocates a specific amount of the volume for storage of the MFT and, in an effort to ensure high performance, tries not to fragment it. NTFS also does its best to intelligently allocate free space on the disk. If you are running low on disk space, it relinquishes reserved and unused MFT areas for your files. If the MFT is running low, it grabs space from the file area for more entries. As you would expect, if you have a large number of files, the MFT becomes larger. If you have a small number of files, the MFT is smaller.

Here's the rub: If you try to pack a zillion files onto an NTFS volume (I can't give you an exact number because it varies based on volume and file size) and you run out of disk space, you could exhaust the MFT. This can result in a major bummer when the directory table for the volume blows up—you get no warning. If you intend to store a huge number of small files on an NTFS partition and you think you might unexpectedly run out of room on the volume, you should consider a Registry hack that preallocates more room for the MFT by adjusting a value in the Registry.

CAUTION
> Allocating more room for the MFT is a Registry hack. Do I have to remind you to back up the Registry first? If you aren't a Registry whiz already, be sure to read Chapter 31, "Editing the Registry," before trying this operation.

To adjust this value, perform the following steps:

1. Click the Start orb, All Programs, Accessories, Run.
2. Type `Regedit.exe` and click OK. Click Continue if prompted by UAC.
3. Run the Registry Editor (`Regedit.exe`), and go to the following subkey:

   HKEY_LOCAL_MACHINE\System\CurrentControlSet\Control\FileSystem\NtfsMftZoneReservation
4. Double-click this value entry to open the Edit DWORD Value dialog box. Provide value data for this value entry.

   `NtfsMftZoneReservation` is a `REG_DWORD` value that can take on a value between 0 and 4, where 0 corresponds to the minimum MFT zone size (default) and 4 corresponds to the maximum. The sizes are not absolute. You might have to experiment with the sizing to determine what is best for you. Microsoft supplies no specific details about the number of file entries available under each size.
5. Close the Registry Editor and restart your computer.

Keep in mind that this is a runtime parameter, and it does not affect the format of a volume. Rather, it affects the way NTFS allocates space on all volumes on a given system. Therefore, to be completely effective, the parameter must be in effect from the time a volume is formatted throughout the life of the volume.

For more information, check the following URL:

http://support.microsoft.com/kb/q174619/

Or search the Microsoft Knowledge Base for article 174619.

Configuring Defrag

The fastest way to open Disk Defragmenter is to open your hard disk's properties sheet, click the Tools tab, and click Defragment Now. You can also access Disk Defragmenter from the Control Panel. Open the System and Maintenance category, scroll down to Administrative Tools, and click Defragment your hard drive. Click Continue if prompted by UAC.

By default, Disk Defragmenter (Figure 27.6) runs on a weekly schedule. Click Modify Schedule to specify a frequency (daily, weekly, monthly), a day of the week, and a time. To defragment your hard disk immediately, click Defragment Now.

Figure 27.6
The Disk Defragmenter dialog box in Windows Vista can schedule or run the utility immediately.

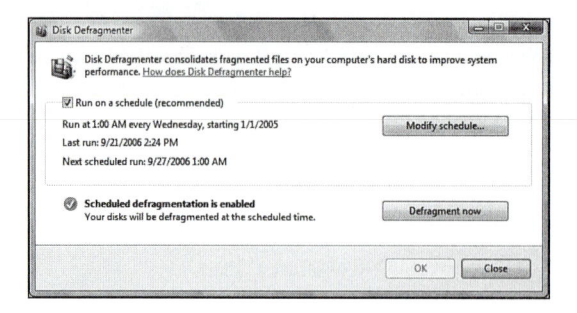

DETECTING AND REPAIRING DISK ERRORS

NTFS was introduced and billed as a "robust and self-healing" file system, as opposed to FAT, which is not. All in all, I have to agree with Microsoft on this one. I have yet to see an NTFS partition go "sour" on me in any way, shape, or form. I've had NTFS partitions that would not boot and key system files that would not run, but for the most part, these errors were self-inflicted and usually brought on by playing with fire.

The disk repair program in Windows Vista's GUI is called Error Checking. These are the command-line versions (stored in the `%SystemRoot%\System32` folder):

- `chkntfs.exe`—Works with NTFS volumes and drives
- `chkdsk.exe`—Works with FAT/FAT32 partitions and drives

For a description of how each works, just add the normal /? switch or see Windows online help. The available commands enable you to turn automatic checking on and off, and repair a "dirty" (improperly shut down) drive at bootup.

Error Checking reviews the file system for errors and the drive for bad sectors (bad spots). To run the program, do the following:

1. In Computer or the Explorer, right-click the drive you want to check.
2. On the context menu, choose Properties.
3. Click the Tools tab.
4. In the Error-Checking section, click Check Now. A dialog box appears, as shown in Figure 27.7.

You can run the error check with neither of the option boxes turned on, and you are not required to close all open files and programs. However, if you check either of the boxes, you are told that all files must be closed for this process to run. You are given the option of deferring the check until the time you restart your system.

The meaning of the options is as follows:

- **Automatically Fix File System Errors**—If file directory errors (for example, lost clusters, files without end-of-file markers, and so on) are found, this option specifies whether the program should fix them.

Figure 27.7
Checking a disk for errors in the file system.

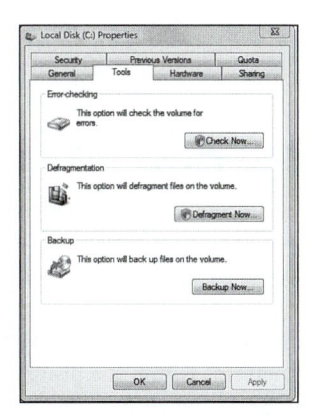

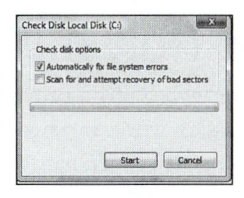

- **Scan for and Attempt Recovery of Bad Sectors**—This option specifies whether the program should attempt to locate bad sectors, mark them as bad, and recover data from them by writing it in a known, good area of the disk. If you select this option, you do not need to select Automatically Fix File System Errors; Windows fixes any errors on the disk.

> **TIP**
>
> If your volume is formatted as NTFS, Windows automatically logs all file transactions, replaces bad clusters, and stores copies of key information for all files on the NTFS volume.

CONVERT

Convert is a command-line program that converts an existing FAT16 or FAT32 partition to NTFS.

> **CAUTION**
>
> This conversion process is a one-way street. The only way to revert an NTFS partition back to a FAT partition with the native tools is to reformat the drive. To revert and not lose your data, you have to use a program such as PartitionMagic (from Symantec; www.symantec.com) or Partition Commander Professional 10 (www.v-com.com).

The command-line syntax for the Convert program is as follows:

```
CONVERT volume /FS:NTFS [/V]
```

The arguments are as follows:

    volume   Specifies the drive letter (followed by a colon), mount point, or volume name

    /FS:NTFS   Specifies that the volume should be converted to NTFS

    /V   Specifies that Convert should be run in Verbose mode

Considering the work the Convert program has to do, it's surprisingly fast, even on a well-populated disk.

COMPRESSION: HOW IT WORKS, HOW TO USE IT

Windows Vista ships with built-in provisions for file compression that is implemented via NTFS. File compression works by encoding data to take up less storage space. Digital data is compressed by finding repeatable patterns of binary 0s and 1s. The more patterns found, the more the data can be compressed. Text can generally be compressed to approximately 40% of its original size and graphics files from 20% to 90%. Some files (namely .EXE files) compress very little because of the lack of repeating data patterns within the program. The amount of compression depends entirely on the type of file and compression algorithm used.

Compressing a file or folder in Windows is a simple process:

1. Open Windows Explorer and select the file or folder you want.
2. Right-click and select Properties from the Context menu.
3. Select the Advanced button at the bottom of the Properties dialog box.
4. In the Advanced Attributes dialog box that appears, put a check mark in front of the Compress Contents to Save Disk Space option (refer to Figure 27.8).
5. When you click OK, you are prompted to choose whether you want to compress files and folders (if you're compressing a folder) recursively. Doing so is generally desirable and a safe bet.

Figure 27.8
Compressing a folder with Windows Vista.

Two caveats are in order with compression:

- A file or folder can be compressed or encrypted, but not both. These options are mutually exclusive.

- By default, compressed files are shown in blue and encrypted files are shown in green. If you choose Control Panel, Folder Options and select the View tab, you can find an option to display compressed and encrypted files or folders in an alternate color.

→ To learn more about file encryption on NTFS volumes, **see** Chapter 34, "Protecting Your Data from Loss and Theft," **p. 1149**.

CAUTION

> When using compression, keep in mind some disk space requirements. If you try to compress a volume that's running extremely low on free space, you might see this error message:
>
>   Compression Error
>   File Manager/Explorer cannot change compress attributes for:
>   "path\filename"
>
> This error message indicates that the system needs additional free space to perform compression. The system is not designed to manipulate the data in place on the disk. Additional space is needed to buffer the user data and to possibly hold additional file system metadata. The amount of additional free space required depends on the cluster size, file size, and available space.

Use compression only when expressly needed. Compression causes significant performance reduction if a sizeable number of commonly accessed files are compressed, due to the CPU processing required to decompress them for use.

Disk Cleanup Utility

In the course of daily use, Windows Vista generates thousands of temporary files to aid in system operation. These files are critical to the operation of the programs that use them. However, as most people are well aware, temporary files have a habit of being much more persistent than their name implies. And over the course of time, these files add up and consume large amounts of valuable disk space. The Disk Cleanup utility provides you with a safe and reliable way to delete these temporary files from all their various hiding spots and thus free up disk space on your hard drive.

To access this utility, do the following:

1. Disk Cleanup can be started from the System Tools folder in the Start menu, from the General tab of a drive's properties sheet, or from the Control Panel.
2. After you start Disk Cleanup, specify whether you want to clean up only your files or all users' files. If you select all users' files, User Account Control is used to confirm your selection.
3. If you are prompted to select a drive, select the drive you want to check (usually C:).
4. The program then searches this drive for files that can be safely deleted or compressed. The details of this analysis are then displayed in a dialog box similar to the one shown in Figure 27.9.

Figure 27.9
A disk cleanup analysis report.

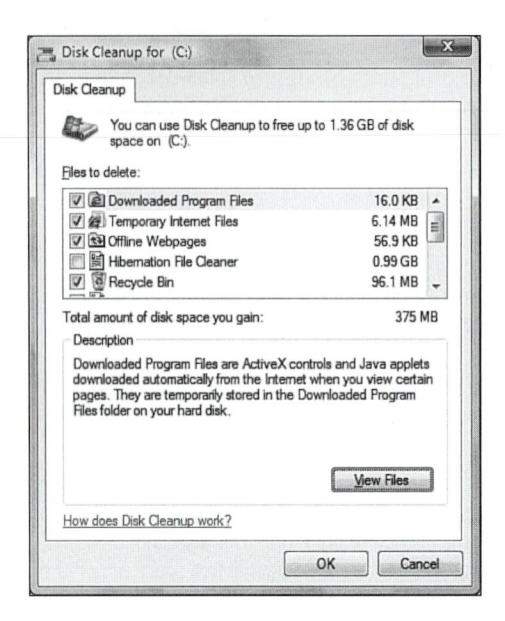

[Screenshot: Disk Cleanup for (C:) dialog box. "You can use Disk Cleanup to free up to 1.36 GB of disk space on (C:)." Files to delete: Downloaded Program Files 16.0 KB (checked); Temporary Internet Files 6.14 MB (checked); Offline Webpages 56.9 KB (checked); Hibernation File Cleaner 0.99 GB (unchecked); Recycle Bin 96.1 MB (checked). Total amount of disk space you gain: 375 MB. Description: Downloaded Program Files are ActiveX controls and Java applets downloaded automatically from the Internet when you view certain pages. They are temporarily stored in the Downloaded Program Files folder on your hard disk. Buttons: View Files, OK, Cancel.]

Near the top of the dialog box is the total amount of disk space you can free on this drive by accepting the selected recommendations listed shortly. You can exclude or include file groups from the cleanup process by placing a check mark in front of the types listed. When you select an entry, you see a description of which files that group contains and what their purpose is. By selecting a group and then the View Files button, you can see in the resulting folder window exactly which files are slated for death. Use this option if you have any doubts about a group of files, where they reside, or what they do.

The following file groupings might be listed:

- **Downloaded Program Files**—These files are ActiveX controls and Java applets used by web pages you have visited. If you delete them, they will be reloaded the next time you visit the pages.

- **Temporary Internet Files**—This one is a biggie. Every time you access a web page, your browser stores or caches the various elements of that page on the hard disk. When you revisit a page, any elements that have not changed since your last visit are reloaded from the hard disk instead of the site itself, to speed the rendering process. Deleting these temporary Internet files frees the largest amount of disk space of any of the group lists. However, if you use a modem to access the Internet, you will notice longer rendering times the next time you return to one of your favorite sites.

NOTE

Agreeing to delete temporary Internet files does not delete your *cookies* (personalized settings for websites), so don't worry about needing to re-enter user ID information or other such information for sites you frequently visit. Cookies and temporary Internet files

> are stored by default in `x:\Users\<username>\AppData\Local\Microsoft\Windows\Temporary Internet Files` (where `x:` is the volume the system is installed on).
>
> If you're concerned about web-surfing privacy, including electronic commerce and banking or confidential business matters, you should delete temporary Internet files frequently.

- **Hibernation File Cleaner**—If your computer supports hibernation but you don't use this feature, you can delete the Hibernation file by selecting this option. Deleting this file disables hibernation.

- **Recycle Bin**—Clearing this folder is the same as manually clearing your Recycle Bin. It is a good idea to have a quick look at the files stored there before choosing this option. Select this option and click the View Files button under the group description; a folder window then opens, listing the contents.

- **Setup Log Files**—These files log events during the installation of Windows Vista. They can be deleted after Windows Vista is installed and is working properly.

- **Temporary Offline Files**—Similar to cached web pages, when you connect to a network location and access a read-only file, a temporary copy is sometimes stored on your hard drive. Clearing these temporary copies does not erase the files you explicitly marked as available for offline use, so this is a safe choice.

- **Offline Files**—If you use the Synchronization features of Windows Vista (see Chapter 38, "Hitting the Road"), selected files and folders from a network connection are stored locally for access while you are disconnected. Do not delete these files unless you're sure you can work without the local copies. You'll lose any changes you made to offline files if you delete them here, so don't make this choice without synchronizing first.

- **Thumbnails**—Thumbnails are generated automatically by Windows Vista for picture, video, and document files. Deleting thumbnails forces Windows Vista to re-create thumbnails when you open a folder.

- **System archived Windows Error Reporting**—Submitted Windows Error Reports.

- **System archived Windows Error Reporting**—Windows Error Reports that have not yet been submitted.

On the Disk Cleanup dialog box, also notice the second tab marked More Options. The Programs and Features Cleanup option opens the Uninstall or change a program dialog box, so you can uninstall programs you no longer use.

The System Restore Cleanup button is used to delete all but the most recent restore points. This might free up a significant amount of drive space, but it will eliminate your capability to roll back to previous states of the system, and it also eliminates file shadow copies and older Complete PC Backup images that are part of restore points. Use this option only if you are desperate for additional space on your drive, because deleting this information could prevent you from recovering from a system problem later. (See Chapter 28, "Troubleshooting and Repairing Problems," for information on System Restore.)

> **TIP**
>
> Running Disk Cleanup weekly can do wonders to improve a system's performance, especially if you are using a hard disk that has less than 25% of its space available at any given time. The first time you run it, the program might take quite a while to run, but with regular exercise, this program speeds up because the disk stays cleaner. Once a month—after you check the contents of the individual folder groups carefully—you should empty all folders of all temporary files.

USING INTERNET EXPLORER'S CACHE CLEANUP

If you would prefer not to use the Disk Cleanup utility, you can choose a second option for clearing out those disk-hogging cached Internet files.

To access it, open the Control Panel, Network and Internet category and select the Internet Options icon. On the Internet Properties' General tab, you will find a section titled Browsing History. The Delete button opens a Delete Browsing History dialog box. You can selectively delete temporary Internet files, cookies, history, form data, or passwords, or click Delete All to delete all information in these categories.

The Settings button enables you to configure options for how often cached files are checked against their original counterparts, how much disk space these cached files are allowed to take up, and in which folder they are stored.

When the disk space setting is exceeded, files are removed on a "first in, first out" basis; that is, the oldest files are deleted to create space for newer ones.

The Move Folder option lets you specify a location where these temporary files will be stored. I think it's a great idea to change this path to a temporary folder or a drive with lots of free space. I usually redirect Internet Explorer to deposit its temporary Internet files into a \temp folder I've created on one of my drives. If you do a lot of web surfing, you'll want to map this temp location to a fast volume that is not on the same physical hard drive as your main Windows partition.

> **TIP**
>
> Changing the location for the storage of temporary Internet files is especially a good idea if the system is a client on a domain network and roaming profiles are in use. By storing the temporary files outside your profile, it will take less time to log in and log out, plus your profile will consume less space on the network server.

Zipping or Compressing Files

If you've been on the Internet for any length of time, you've run into zip files (a.k.a. `filename.zip`). Zipping files is a way to combine multiple files and even a directory structure into a single file that is compressed. Zipfiles make the transfer of data files and programs not just simpler, but faster. PKZip 2.04g was a command-line utility that was used to create zip files (its Windows descendent is known as PKZIP for Windows and supports control of user settings from within Microsoft Management Console). As zipping became popular, many third parties created utilities to perform zipping operations through GUI interfaces. These programs, such as my favorite, WinZip, continue to be popular for their ease of use. However, for basic zipfile creation, viewing, and extraction, you can use Windows Vista's integrated zipfile support.

Viewing zip files is easy. Windows Vista treats any `.zip` file as a compressed folder, no matter what utility was used to create them. Zipfiles appear as folders with a zipper. You can view and access the contents just as if they were stored in any typical folder on the file system.

You create zip files by selecting Send To, Compressed (zipped) Folder from the right-click menu in Windows Explorer, Computer, or other file-management views. After naming the folder (be sure to retain the `.zip` extension), you can drag and drop files or folder structures into it. When your files are inside the "compressed folder," you can manipulate the `.zip` file as you can any other file, including attaching to emails or uploading via FTP.

Extracting files from a `.zip` file via Windows Vista is no different than moving or copying files from normal folders; just drag and drop. Or while viewing the contents of a `.zip` file, issue the `Extract` command. This launches the Compressed (zipped) Folders Extraction Wizard, which walks you through the process of locating a destination for the contents and initiating the extraction.

Third-Party Management Tools

Table 27.1 provides a list of tools that you should not be without if you are serious about hard disk tweaking, backup, and recovery. By searching on the Web, you can easily find any of these programs because they are so popular. To determine which versions of a particular tool are compatible with Windows Vista, contact the software vendor.

Table 27.1 Third-Party Disk Management Tools

Type of Program	Vendor	Product Name
Data Recovery	Ontrack	Ontrack EasyRecovery Data Recovery
	Iolo	Search and Recover 4
	Executive Software	Undelete

continues

TABLE 27.1 CONTINUED

Type of Program	Vendor	Product Name
Disk Management	Acronis	Acronis Disk Director Suite 10
	Symantec	PartitionMagic
	Avanquest Publishing USA	System Commander, Partition Commander Professional
Compression (Zipfile)	PowerArchiver	Conexware
	WinZip International LLC[1] (**formerly Niko Mak)	WinZip
	PKWare	PKZip for Windows
	FileStream, Inc.[2]	TurboZIP
	Info-Zip	Info-Zip
	Win.rar GmbH[3]	WinRAR

[1] *Formerly Niko Mak*
[2] *Formerly Pacific Gold Coast Corporation*
[3] *Formerly Rarsoft*

Hard Disk Troubleshooting

If you work with computers long enough, you will face some form of hard disk problem. It's not a matter of *if*; it's a matter of *when*. The laws of statistics apply to everyone and everything—and that includes hard drives. In the following sections, when I speak of hard drive problems, I'm not referring to a software program that is acting petulantly or a DLL that has been overwritten by a poorly designed installation routine. I'm talking about the inability to access a critical file, a hard drive that will not boot, or one of those cryptic "Fatal Error— Cannot access hard disk" messages that cause the blood to drain from the face of even the hardiest administrator.

These sections are not meant to be comprehensive—full books have been written on solving hardware problems, and thousands of individual chapters have been written about hard drives and the multitude of problems they can exhibit. These sections will give you some tried-and-true starting points if your hard drive starts to give you grief.

Hard drive problems range from file system structures that have been twisted out of shape to catastrophic, dead-in-the-water hard drive failures. And as any seasoned administrator will tell you, the catastrophic failures are the easy ones to diagnose and fix. More often than not, the inconsistent "What the heck?" problems are the real "head-scratchers."

To keep it simple, let's begin with the most important factor in troubleshooting problems of all shapes and sizes—be it a car that will not start or a computer that will not boot. And that is....

Take the Mental Approach First

I come from a long line of tradesmen who made a living getting their hands dirty and solving mechanical problems. As a writer and computer consultant, I rarely get my hands dirty anymore, but I have discovered that the principles of problem solving that I learned when I was young are the same across all fields. You need to be methodical, and if you are going to make assumptions, they had better be good ones; otherwise, you just might steer yourself down the wrong garden path.

The very first step to take when you have a disk access problem is to stop, sit down, and think. Although this advice might seem obvious, it is seldom realized in practice. People experience what they conclude is a hard drive problem, open their case, and start ripping out components when, in fact, they have a file system problem that could have been easily resolved by running Error Checking on their drive. Similarly, others start reinstalling operating systems when the problem is not software, but a failing CMOS battery or a loose cable that is causing the motherboard to lose sight of the hard drive.

None of this exposition is meant to imply that I'm smarter or better at diagnosing problems than the next guy, and in the end, I might come to the same conclusion as the person who leapt in and started ripping his case apart. What separates us, in my humble opinion, is that the steps I use to solve a problem today will apply equally well to a completely different problem I encounter a week from now.

So when you have a hard drive problem—or what you think is a hard drive problem—before you pick up a CD-ROM or a screwdriver, get yourself a cup of coffee and take a few minutes to get a clear picture of the nature of the problem in front of you. The following are some questions you might want to ask yourself:

- When did the problem start?
- What was I doing when I first noticed the problem?
- Is the problem consistent? If so, how? If not, what is missing from the puzzle?

This last point bears some elaboration. Computers, as a whole, are extraordinarily consistent devices. Input goes in here; output comes out over there. In the case of hard drives, you lay out structures on them, and the operating system uses these structures to tell programs where their data is located. When you have inconsistencies, one of two forces is at work:

- You're not seeing or you're overlooking something.
- You could have more than one problem on your hands.

The key to this forced reflection is to have a "plan" before you react. And the cornerstone of that plan must be to do no further harm, and to figure out what the problem is without complicating matters further.

After you've pondered and had a cup of coffee, the next highly recommended tools to pick up are a notepad and a pencil. Begin by jotting down some notes on what happened, what you think the problem is, and what might be a good course of action to solve that problem. Use your notepad to reason out the problem; more often than not, eliminating a piece of flawed logic with an eraser is easier than restoring all the programs to your hard drive.

Problems and Solutions

Hard drive problems fall into two general categories:

- Hardware
- File structure

Hardware-related problems involve the hard drive itself, cabling, power, connections, or the motherboard.

File structure problems involve the tracks and partitions on the hard disk, the boot records, or the files the operating system uses to initialize itself.

If you power up your computer and the BIOS cannot find the attached hard drive, chances are, you have a hardware problem. On the other hand, if the BIOS finds and recognizes your hard drive but fails to boot, you likely have a file structure problem. Note the 'chances are' and 'likely' qualifiers in these sentences. As you read through the following scenarios, bear in mind the complications that can be brought on by compounded problems. In other words, file structure problems and hardware problems can sometimes overlap. For example, a damaged master boot record (MBR) might be the result of a failing hard drive; repairing the MBR might fix a consequence of the problem, but not the problem itself.

System Starts but Cannot Find the Hard Drive

If the computer fires up (the BIOS information appears and the floppy drive is accessed, but nothing more), you have some sleuthing to do. Follow these steps:

1. Turn off the computer, open it, and check the cables. Are the power and data cables attached to the drive? On an ATA/IDE drive, be sure pin 1 (marked as a red or speckled stripe on the edge of the cable) is lined up with pin 1 on the hard disk and motherboard. If you use only 80-wire cables, the cable is keyed, so it can't be installed wrong. However, older 40-wire cables (often used on CD and DVD drives) are not always keyed. If you use SATA drives, be sure the SATA data and power cables are firmly attached to the drive. First-generation SATA drives don't use locking mechanisms on these cables, and they can be easily removed. If you recently installed a new piece of hardware or were mucking around inside your computer case, it's very possible that you unintentionally jiggled a connection loose.

2. Check the settings on the drive to be sure they are correct. If you have a SCSI drive, check the ID number and termination, per the instruction manual for the drive. If you have an ATA/IDE drive, check the master/slave settings and channel assignment. If you have two devices on the same ATA/IDE channel, both set to master or both set to slave,

there will be a conflict. You can have only one master and one slave per ATA/IDE channel. You typically change the setting by using a little jumper block on the back of the hard drive, next to the data and power connectors (ditto for ATA/IDE-based DVD drives). Many recent systems use the CSEL or Cable Select setting for both drives. When used with an 80-wire 40-pin cable, the blue end of the cable plugs into the motherboard, the drive on the middle of the cable (gray connector) is slave, and the drive on the far end of the cable (black connector) is master. Note that many Western Digital hard disks do not use a jumper block if they are the only drive on the cable.

3. Check the BIOS settings by pressing the appropriate key during POST (Power-On Self Test) and having the computer autodetect the drive type. Be sure the drive is listed and recognized. If you have just upgraded to SATA hard disks, be sure the SATA host adapters on the motherboard are enabled in the system BIOS. On many systems, SATA functions are disabled by default. If you use an SATA host adapter card, or if the SATA ports on your motherboard use a third-party chip rather than being controlled by the motherboard chipset, you will need to install the appropriate third-party driver file before you can use SATA drives.

> **TIP**
>
> Most modern PCs and BIOSes autodetect the hard drive that's connected to the data cable after the drive gets power. You no longer need to enter all the explicit information about the drive, such as the number of heads, the sectors, the landing zone, and so on. Just set the BIOS to Autodetect.

HARD DRIVE INITIALIZES BUT WILL NOT BOOT

Windows Vista makes it easier than ever to repair a system that will not start or will not load Windows Vista. These features are useful if some of your system files become corrupt or are accidentally erased, or if you have installed software or device drivers that cause your system to not work properly. However, these features are used more to restore a system with a damaged Registry or destroyed system files rather than hard drive–specific problems. If you've already tried the actions listed in this section, to no avail, flip over to Chapter 28 for details on numerous other recovery techniques that might be of benefit to you. Be sure to check out Startup Repair, Safe Mode, and System Restore.

Editing the Boot Sequence

Windows Vista no longer uses the boot.ini file familiar from Windows NT, Windows 2000, and Windows XP installations. Instead, Windows Vista uses a new method of determining boot settings known as a boot configuration database (BCD) store. BCD is compatible with both traditional BIOS firmware and the new extensible firmware interface (EFI). EFI firmware will eventually replace BIOS firmware in new systems and also supports dual-boot installations with older Windows versions. You can make simple changes to the boot sequence (such as specifying whether Windows Vista or an older version of Windows is the default operating system) with the System Configuration tool MSConfig (see Chapter 25 for details). However, you can also use the command-line bcdedit tool to edit the boot configuration. To learn more about bcdedit, see the article "Boot Configuration Data Editor Frequently Asked Questions," available from http://technet.microsoft.com/en-us/default.aspx.

Tips from the Windows Pros: Quieting a Noisy System

Hard drives vary in the noise output they produce, but today's hard disks are much quieter than those of a few years ago—most are virtually silent when operating normally.

However, as spindle motors (the motor that turns the platters at high speed) begin to wear out, noise levels might increase. A noisy drive is particularly annoying in laptop computers if you happen to use them in a quiet place, such as a library or a home office.

In the case of serious noise (you turn on the computer and it really does sound like a garbage disposal), well, you're in trouble. This noise is a sign of your hard disk crashing. (The heads are actually rubbing on the surface of the platters.) Get out while the getting is good. Back up your data and whole drive (if you can) and replace it as soon as possible. Then, restore the data. If you don't have an up-to-date backup and your data is priceless, you can shell out big bucks for a data-recovery service to repair your drive in a clean room and try (no guarantees in situations involving mechanical failures) to retrieve your data. Backups are much cheaper.

However, before you assume that a noisy drive is a failing drive, keep in mind that you might be able to perform firmware or driver optimization to solve noise problems with some drives. For example, the Western Digital 2.5-inch Scorpio hard disk used in some laptop computers might make periodic clicking noises because of issues with power-management commands from the computer. You can download a hard-disk optimization utility from Western Digital that updates the drive's firmware to solve the problem. Some vendors, such as Samsung and Hitachi, offer downloadable utilities that adjust seek performance to reduce drive noise, although at a cost in performance. Samsung's HUTIL and Hitachi's Feature Tool are available from the vendors' websites. Maxtor once offered an acoustic management utility called SETACM.EXE, which contains the AMSET.EXE utility. It is still available from some third-party websites.

If you need to build (or upgrade to) a quiet (or, at least a quieter) PC, the hard disk choices you make can help or hurt your ability to achieve your goals.

Many of the quietest drives on the market use fluid dynamic bearings instead of mechanical bearings. If you are shopping for a quiet drive, consider drives that use fluid dynamic bearings.

A second factor in hard disk noise is the number of platters. Everything else being equal, a hard disk with fewer platters is a quieter drive. Models with similar capacities can vary in the number of platters used to achieve a given capacity. Drives that use the perpendicular recording technology need fewer platters to achieve the rated capacity and, therefore, tend to be quieter than drives that use conventional storage methods (and more platters).

Some vendors publish acoustic information, but if the drives you are considering do not offer this information, check reviews. Some hard disk review sources test acoustics along with performance information. However, even a "noisy" hard disk is far from being the loudest device in your system.

Some environments, such as recording studios, require that a computer be seen and not heard. For desktop systems, a couple of solutions exist. One is to get some long wires for the keyboard monitor, pointing device, and so on, and relegate the computer to a closet. A more practical approach is to buy an after-market kit that quiets your PC's power supply and hard disk. Check the Web for information about such kits, such as at www.quietpc.com.

The bottom line here is to check out the specs on drive noise, if you care about that. Or you can listen for a quiet computer, find out what kind of drive it has, and then order that brand and model the next time you're shopping.

In some cases, the noise you hear is not from your hard drive, but from the fans on the case, the power supply, the processor, or the North Bridge/Memory Controller Hub chip. These plastic fan blades collect dust. The dustier your environment and the higher your average humidity, the faster these fans become caked with crud. In many cases, you can use a can of compressed air to clean off the fans. But when that doesn't work, you can attempt to remove the fan's protective screen and wipe the blades clean with a slightly moist paper towel. *Don't* spray or drip any liquids into the system. Keep in mind that fans, especially those that use sleeve bearings instead of ball bearings, become very noisy as they age, especially if they get dirty and are not cleaned regularly. A noisy fan should be replaced before it causes component or system failure due to fan failure, which causes overheating.

If you find that you are cleaning your fan every month or so, you should consider getting a room filter to clean your air or attach part of an A/C filter over the air intake holes on your system. Just be sure that the airflow is not restricted, or you'll overheat the system. Keep in mind that your CPU and hard drives are air-cooled; that's why there are fans in the case. If you restrict the airflow too much, the heat will build up and cause problems. If you hear a beeping sound much like that of European police cars, that's the warning sign that the CPU is too hot. You can check fan speed for the CPU fan and some other fans on most recent systems by viewing the PC Health or Hardware Monitor section of the system BIOS. Some system and motherboard vendors also provide Windows-based utilities that display this information while you use your computer.

VIA Technologies offers a helpful web page with many links to quiet computing products and techniques. You can find it at www.via.com.tw/en/initiatives/quietcomputing/resources.jsp.

CHAPTER 28

Troubleshooting and Repairing Problems

In this chapter

Troubleshooting 101   962

Easy Repair Options at Boot Time   962

Startup Repair   963

System Restore   964

Windows Complete PC Restore   967

Windows Memory Diagnostic Tool   968

Command Prompt   970

Repairing a System That Won't Start with Regedit   970

Boot Options   972

As a Last Resort   975

Preventing Problems   976

Fixing Application Problems with the Program Compatibility Wizard   977

Using Problem Reports and Solutions   979

Finding and Using Windows Vista Troubleshooting Resources   981

Black Magic of Troubleshooting   982

Tricks of the Windows Masters: Recovering Data from the System Recovery Options Menu   983

Troubleshooting 101

Inevitably, the only time you'll ever have a problem with your computer system is the exact moment when it's not convenient—or, more specifically, the moment when any delay would be severely detrimental to the continuation of your job or life. Fortunately, the designers of Windows Vista have learned from the problems experienced by previous Windows versions, including Windows XP. Windows Vista is designed to be the most stable version yet *and* the easiest to fix.

In this chapter, I discuss many of the fault-tolerant features of Windows Vista, along with specific tools you can employ to resolve problems.

For example, if you're having a problem with a device (look for the yellow exclamation point or down-arrow over the device icon in Device Manager), open its properties sheet in Device Manager and click the solution button on the General tab. It might run a troubleshooter, update or reinstall drivers, or start the device. Type `troubleshoot` into the Windows Help and Support Center, and you'll find dozens of links. To find specific help on a problem, search on a topic and follow the links to your solution.

Easy Repair Options at Boot Time

If you cannot start your Windows Vista system, don't panic. Windows Vista makes the startup repair process easy and transparent to the user—a big change from repairing startup problems with previous versions of Windows.

If you cannot start your system from the hard disk, insert your Windows Vista installation media and use it as a boot device. After selecting the language, time, and currency formats, and the keyboard-input method on the opening screen, click Next. On the following screen, select Repair Your Computer. The system searches for recovery options. Click Repair and Restart. In some cases, this is all you need to do to fix a problem with your system.

> **NOTE**
>
> If you are using a preinstalled edition of Windows Vista, ask your hardware vendor how to access the Repair Your Computer feature. A vendor might include a special boot disc with a system or provide you with instructions on how to make a boot disc that contains the files necessary to repair your installation.
>
> Originally, Vista SP-1 was going to include a Recovery Disc maker, enabling you to boot your system in case of emergencies and run the repair tools discussed in the following sections. Although the final SP-1 release includes the executable file for the program (recdisc.exe), it does not work. Hopefully, Microsoft will make a working version of the Recovery Disc maker available in the future as an update to Vista SP-1.

Using System Recovery

However, if your system is still unable to start after running the Repair Your Computer tool discussed in the previous section, restart the system from the Windows Vista DVD and choose Repair Your Computer again. It should find your Windows installation (which it identifies by partition size and drive letter). Click Next to open a menu of System Recovery options (see Figure 28.1).

Figure 28.1
System Recovery Options provide you with a variety of repair options if your system cannot start normally.

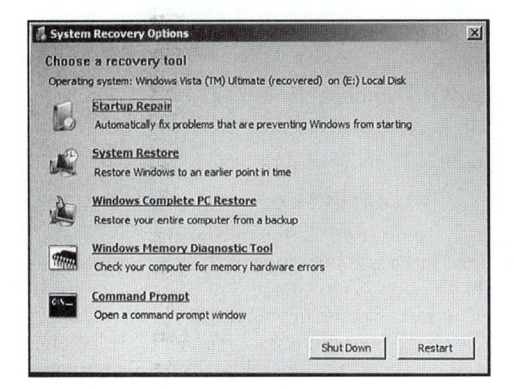

System Recovery options include these:

- Startup Repair
- System Restore
- Windows Complete PC Restore
- Windows Memory Diagnostic Tool
- Command Prompt

Each of these repair options is discussed in this chapter.

STARTUP REPAIR

Typically, the easiest repair to try when you have a system that won't boot is with the Startup Repair option, shown at the top of Figure 28.1. When you select this option, Windows performs a series of tests to determine the problem and then performs repairs. If you're not curious about what Windows did, click Finish at the end of the process to restart your system. Don't boot from the DVD; your system should start up normally.

However, to learn more, use the Click Here for Diagnostic and Repair Details link to bring up the Startup Repair dialog box. Scroll through the dialog box to satisfy yourself with the solution. In this example (see Figure 28.2), a missing or corrupt boot manager was discovered and repaired. Click Close to return to the main dialog box; then click Finish.

Figure 28.2
Startup Repair found the problem (a missing or corrupt boot manager) and repaired it, enabling the system to start normally.

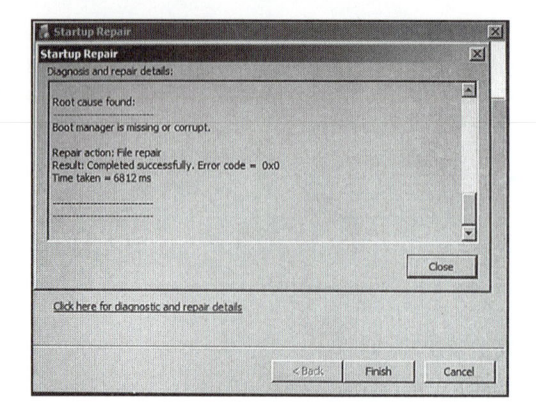

> **NOTE**
>
> Windows Vista can perform up to five startup repairs before it gives up. So, if you restart your system after performing a startup repair and you still have problems, rerun the startup repair procedure to fix additional problems. Repeat until your system starts properly, or until Windows Vista is unable to perform additional repairs. See other portions of this chapter for additional suggestions.

SYSTEM RESTORE

System Restore enables you to restore the computer to a previously saved state, so you can "roll back" your computer to the way it was working before your dog jumped on the keyboard, or before you installed that stupid program or device driver that launched your system. Here's how it works.

Performing a system restore does not affect personal files, such as documents, Internet favorites, or email. It simply reverses system-configuration changes and removes installed files to return the system to a stored state. System Restore automatically monitors your system for changes. Periodically, easily identifiable restoration points are created. Plus, you can create your own restoration points manually.

Unlike Windows XP, which requires you to start the system in Safe Mode before you can run System Restore, Windows Vista offers System Restore on its System Recovery menu.

CONFIGURING SYSTEM RESTORE

System Restore has two control interfaces. One is on the System Protection tab of the System applet. Open it by clicking the System Protection task. (It's protected by User Account Control.) The other control interface is the System Restore utility itself, accessed through Start, All Programs, Accessories, System Tools, System Restore.

System Restore is enabled or disabled for all drives in the computer via the System Restore tab (see Figure 28.3) of the System applet. It is enabled by default for the system drive.

Figure 28.3
The System Protection tab of the System applet in Windows Vista Ultimate, Enterprise, and Business. Windows Vista Home Basic, Home Premium, and Starter Editions do not support shadow copies.

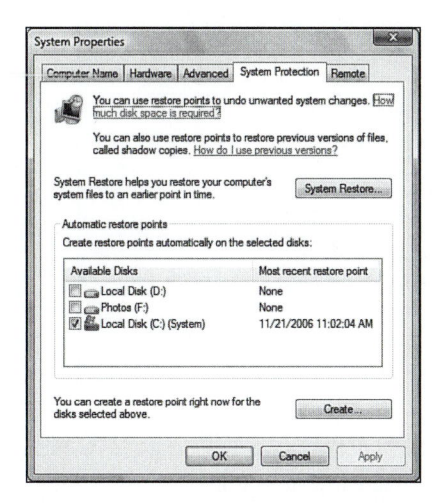

In Windows Vista, System Restore drive configuration is a simple on/off setting, unlike in Windows XP, which permitted you to adjust how much of the hard disk could be used for System Restore files. System Restores uses at least 300MB of disk space for each restore point and can use up to 15% of the space on each hard disk that has System Restore enabled.

The number of restore points retained by System Restore depends on the amount of allowed drive space use, as well as the rate and significance of changes to the system.

CREATING RESTORE POINTS

Vista creates restore points automatically whenever any one of several specific events occurs:

- On first boot after installation
- Every 24 hours of calendar time or every 24 hours of computer uptime
- When a program is installed using InstallShield or Windows Installer
- Automatic updates via Windows Update
- Any restore operation
- Installation of unsigned device drivers
- Any restore operation using Backup

As Figure 28.4 shows, these factors can result in a lot of restore points being created in a short amount of time.

Figure 28.4
Various types of restore points on a typical system.

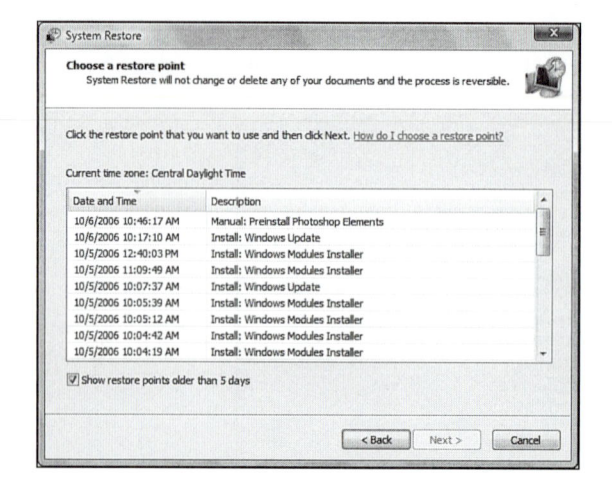

Keep in mind that not all program installations use InstallShield or Windows Installer. Thus, you should always manually create a restore point before you install applications.

To manually create a restore point, open the System Protection tab and click Create (refer to Figure 28.3). Enter a descriptive name for the restore point and click Create. The date and time are added automatically. A progress bar appears. Click OK when prompted. Your restore point is finished.

Creating a restore point at any restore operation enables you to reverse a restoration. Thus, if after a successful restoration you are not pleased with the outcome, you can reverse the restoration. The system automatically removes any failed or incomplete restoration operations.

System Restore does not replace the uninstallation process for removing an application. System Restore monitors and protects only against changes to the OS; it does not track the addition of new files to the system. Use the Add or Remove Programs utility or a vendor-provided uninstall routine to remove applications.

Restoring Your System to an Earlier Time

You can restore your system to an earlier time by running System Restore from the System Recovery menu when you boot from the Windows Vista DVD (see Figure 28.1), or by running System Restore from the System Protection tab or the System Tools menu. From the opening menu, click Next to continue.

Select a restore point from the Choose a Restore Point menu (refer to Figure 28.4).

By default, only the last 5 days' worth of restore points are listed. To select an older restore point, click the Show Restore Points Older Than 5 Days check box. (This box is checked in Figure 28.4.) After selecting a restore point, click Next to continue.

If you have more than one drive with System Restore enabled, select which drives to restore. The system drive is always selected. Click Next to continue. Click Finish. Click Yes to confirm that you want to restore your system. A progress bar appears while System Restore prepares your system, and then your system restarts.

At the end of the process, a dialog box appears, indicating that your system has been restored to the date and time of the restore point you selected.

Windows Complete PC Restore

Windows Complete PC Restore is the counterpart to Windows Complete PC Backup. Complete PC Backup makes an image backup of your system, and Complete PC Restore enables you to perform a "bare metal" restoration from the System Recovery menu.

> **CAUTION**
>
> When we say "bare metal," we mean it. All your data, files, and programs installed since the drive was imaged—everything—ends up in the big bit bucket in the sky. Be sure you want to perform a complete PC restore before you run this tool. And be ready to kiss goodbye everything you placed on your drive after it was imaged.
>
> You'll rest better if you run File and Folder backup (or a good third-party file backup program) regularly in addition to Windows Complete PC Backup. If you do, you can restore your data files after you run Complete PC Restore and get back to work.

To restore your system from a Complete PC Backup, start your system from the Windows Vista DVD and open the Repair Your Computer dialog box, as discussed earlier in this chapter. Connect the external hard disk that contains your backup. (If you backed up to DVD, have the media ready.)

When the Choose a Recovery Tool dialog box is displayed (refer to Figure 28.1), choose Windows Complete PC Restore. If you restore from an external hard disk, be sure it is connected.

By default, the most current image backup is listed. To restore from this backup, select Restore the Following Backup (see Figure 28.5). To choose an earlier backup, click Restore a Different Backup and then select it from the list. Click Next to continue.

Figure 28.5
Preparing to restore the most recent Complete PC Backup.

To simply restore the backup, click Finish. If you are installing to an unformatted hard disk or to a hard disk that is larger than your original, click the Format and Repartition Disks check box, shown in Figure 28.6, to prepare your hard disk for use; then click Finish. The restoration process starts immediately if you are restoring from a hard disk connected to the system. If you are restoring from CD, DVD, or other media, insert the media as requested.

Figure 28.6
Click the checkbox to repartition your hard disk to match the layout of the original backup.

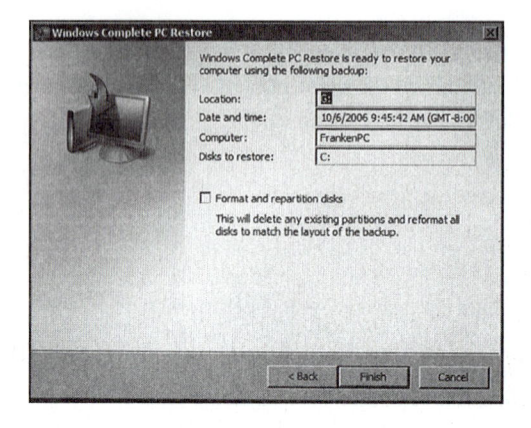

CAUTION

Do not restore to a hard disk that might still have salvageable data, even if your Windows installation no longer boots. Instead, buy a new hard disk or use one that does not contain any needed data, and use it as the restore target.

You can use programs such as Ontrack EasyRecovery DataRecovery on a working system to recover data from your crashed system hard disk, even if its file system is no longer functioning. However, the capability of any program to recover data depends upon the data areas not being overwritten. If you restore your backup over what's left of your original installation, you wipe out at least some of the data that remains.

When the restoration is finished, the system restarts normally. To get the system back to its most recent configuration, restore file backups made with Windows Vista's file-backup program or other backups.

→ For complete information about Windows Complete PC Backup and other backup/restore options, **see** Chapter 34, "Protecting Your Data from Loss and Theft," **p. 1149**.

WINDOWS MEMORY DIAGNOSTIC TOOL

If any recent version of Windows had a motto, it could very well be, "It's the RAM, stupid!" All kidding aside, if your system's memory is hosed, so is Windows. The Windows Memory Diagnostic tool is another brand-new Windows Vista feature designed to help you get help for a sick system.

The Windows Memory Diagnostics tool can be run from the Administrative Tools folder in the Control Panel (see Chapter 25, "Windows Management and Maintenance," for details), from the System Recovery menu, or from the Windows Boot Manager. If you run it from the Administrative Tools folder, it is protected by User Access Control, and you can choose to restart your system immediately for testing or to schedule testing the next time you restart your system.

Regardless of how you start it, the Windows Memory Diagnostic tool (Figure 28.7) runs before the Windows Vista GUI starts.

Figure 28.7
The Windows Memory Diagnostics tool performing a memory test.

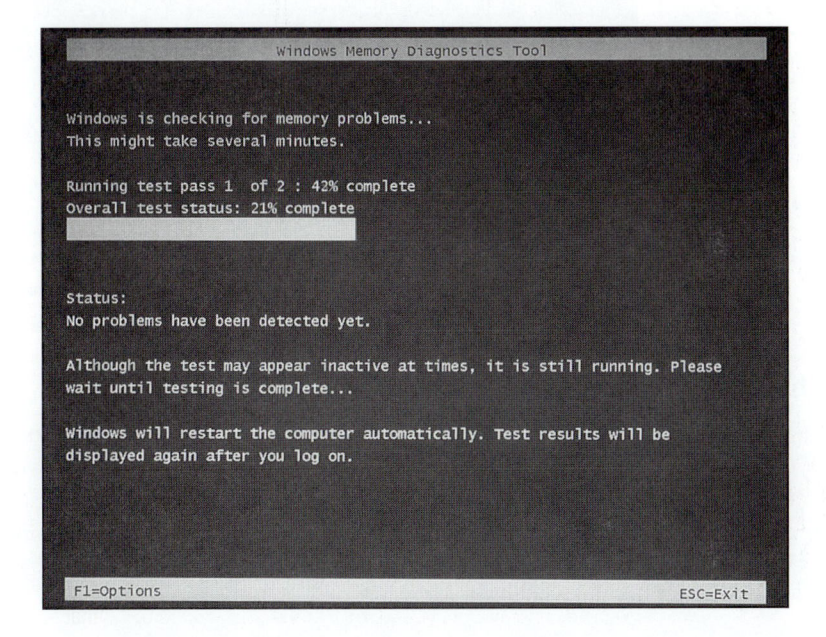

To adjust the number of test passes (the default is two), to specify how thorough a test to perform, or to configure other options, press the F1 key to display the Options dialog box, shown in Figure 28.8. You can configure three items:

- **Test type**—Basic (quick test, usually finished in about 5 minutes), Standard (adds tests to Basic), or Extended (adds tests to Standard)
- **Cache configuration**—Default (some test with cache on, some with cache off; doesn't change settings), On (turns on memory cache for all tests), Off (disables memory cache for all tests)
- **Number of test passes**—0–99 (select 0 for infinite test passes; press Esc to cancel)

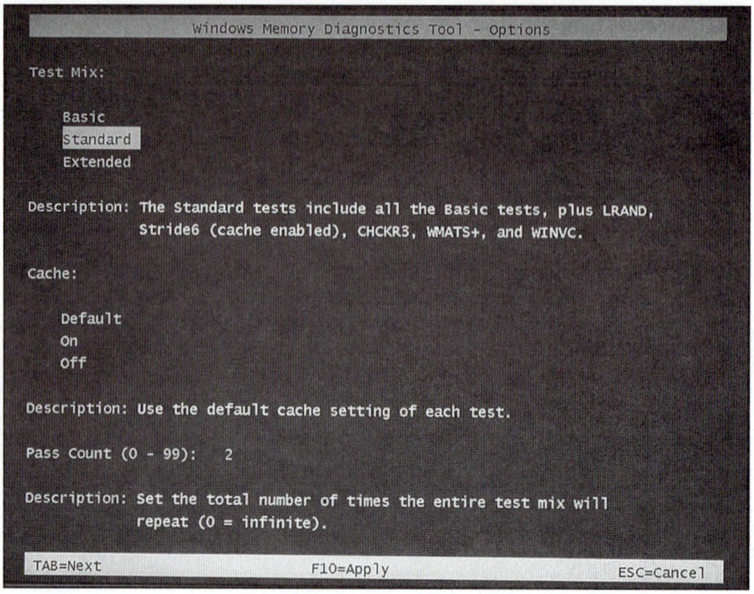

Figure 28.8
The Windows Memory Diagnostics Options dialog box.

COMMAND PROMPT

The command prompt option on the System Recovery Options dialog box opens a command-prompt interface with all the power of the command prompt environment, instead of the limited features of the Recovery Console used in Windows XP. You can run disk management, copy, delete, and other commands, just as you would from within the Windows Vista GUI. For more information about command-prompt utilities, see Chapter 32, "Command-Line and Automation Tools."

REPAIRING A SYSTEM THAT WON'T START WITH REGEDIT

One of the biggest changes in Windows Vista's startup repair features is the capability to run the Registry Editor (Regedit) from the command prompt window. If you cannot start your system because of driver or service problems or other Registry-related issues, you can use Regedit to work on your system and repair problems.

To start the Registry Editor from the System Recovery Options menu, click Command Prompt.

When the command prompt window opens, type **regedit** and press Enter. User Account Control (UAC) will pop up and ask you to confirm this action (and provide credentials if you are using a standard account) unless you have disabled UAC (which we don't recommend).

Before making any changes with Regedit, export the current registry with File, Export so that you have a backup copy, in case of problems. By default, Export saves only the current branch. To export the entire Registry, select All. Provide a name for the exported Registry

(I suggest using the computer name, if you know it) and click Save. You can use USB flash memory drives and other types of storage to save the exported Registry. However, you should not save it to the hard disk, especially if you suspect that you might need to perform data recovery operations on it later. (You don't want to overwrite any recoverable data.)

Sometimes, services running at startup crash, preventing a system from starting. Here's how to use Regedit to disable these services.

1. Select the key `HKEY_LOCAL_MACHINE`.

   NOTE If you need help running Regedit, see Chapter 31, "Editing the Registry." Don't tinker with the Registry unless you know what you're doing. And if you do tinker with it, make a backup first. Improper editing of the Registry can result in a dead computer.

2. Browse into the subkey `CurrentControlSet`, if it's displayed.
3. Browse into the `Services` key and look for the likely offending service. Under each service's key is a value named Start, with one of the following values:
   - 0 Boot driver loaded by Ntldr (Boot)
   - 1 Driver loaded at kernel initialization by Vista (System)
   - 2 Driver loaded at system startup by Session Manager or Service Controller (Auto Load)
   - 3 Driver or service loaded manually from Services, Control Panel, and so on. (Load on Demand)
   - 4 Driver or service that is not running or started (Disabled)

   Services with a Start value of 0 and 1 are used to boot Windows, and you shouldn't touch them. Services with a Start value of 2 start about the same time as the Login dialog box appears in Windows. If your Windows system boots and then promptly crashes without your help, try setting the Start value of any suspected service(s) to 3 or 4. Be sure to write down the names of the services and their original Start values before you change anything.

4. Exit Regedit.
5. Type **exit** and press Enter to close the command prompt window.
6. Remove the Windows Vista DVD and click Restart to restart your system normally.
7. If your system restarts correctly, you're finished!

You might need to repeat this process a few times, disabling a different service or two each time. In previous versions of Windows, this procedure required installing a parallel copy of Windows and some loading of the old installation's Registry into the new system's Registry editor, but thanks to the integration of Regedit into the souped-up command prompt in the System Recovery Options menu, that's not necessary in Windows Vista.

Boot Options

If you are able to start your system but it doesn't run properly, Windows Vista offers several alternate boot methods that can be used to bypass a problem or boot into a reduced environment so that you can solve the problem. For example, if you've recently installed a new device driver that caused a serious system failure (you can't complete the boot process), you can use a boot option to boot without that driver. (This is called the "Last Known Good Configuration," to be exact.)

> **TIP**
> If you can boot, but a device isn't working after you just installed a new driver, see Chapter 30, "Installing and Replacing Hardware."

The boot options of Windows Vista are accessed during the early stages of system startup. If you have more than one OS on your system, the Windows Boot Manager displays; you have until the counter reaches zero to press F8. If you have only Windows Vista on your computer, you'll see a message about pressing F8 after the computer's own Power-On Self-Test and the display of the graphical booting screen. You have only a few seconds, so keep your finger over the F8 button and press it when the message appears.

> **NOTE**
> Some systems and motherboards include a boot menu that uses the F8 key to select a boot drive. If your system includes this feature, check the documentation to determine which keys to press to display the Windows Boot Manager. For example, some Asus motherboards require that you press F6 and then F8 to display the Windows Boot Manager.

Pressing F8 at the correct moment reveals the Advanced Options menu, which contains several boot options, listed in Table 28.1.

TABLE 28.1　ADVANCED BOOT OPTIONS

Option	Description
Safe Mode	This starts Windows Vista using only basic files and drivers (mouse, except serial mouse devices; monitor; keyboard; mass storage; basic video; default system services; and no network connections).
Safe Mode with Networking	This starts Windows Vista using only basic files and drivers, plus network connections.

Option	Description
Safe Mode with Command Prompt	This starts Windows Vista using only basic files and drivers. After you log on, the command prompt is displayed instead of the Windows desktop.
Enable Boot Logging	This starts Windows Vista while logging all the drivers and services that were loaded (or not loaded) by the system to a file. This file, called `ntbtlog.txt`, is located in the `%windir%` directory. Safe Mode, Safe Mode with Networking, and Safe Mode with Command Prompt add to the boot log a list of all the drivers and services that are loaded. The boot log is useful in determining the exact cause of system startup problems.
Enable Low-Resolution Video (640×480)	This starts Windows Vista using the basic VGA driver. This mode is useful when you have installed a new driver for your video card that is causing Windows Vista to hang or start and lock up halfway into the initialization process. The basic video driver is always used when you start Windows Vista in Safe Mode (Safe Mode, Safe Mode with Networking, or Safe Mode with Command Prompt).
Last Known Good Configuration (advanced)	This starts Windows Vista using the Registry configuration information that Windows saved at the last shutdown. Use this option only if you strongly suspect that a program has written incorrect or damaging information to the Registry. The Last Known Good Configuration does not solve problems caused by corrupted or missing drivers or files. Also, any changes made since the last successful startup are lost. If this option does not help, start your system with the Vista DVD and run System Restore from the Startup Recovery Options menu. Select a recent restore point to reset your system's configuration.
Directory Services Restore Mode	This option is valid only for domain controllers.
Debugging Mode	This starts Windows Vista while sending debug information through a serial or USB cable to another computer.
Disable Automatic Restart on System Failure	Windows Vista can be configured to restart the system automatically if a `STOP` error (BSOD) occurs. This behavior can make it difficult to determine the cause. Use this option to disable automatic restart; the `STOP` error stays onscreen, so you can record the error and research a solution.

continues

TABLE 28.1 CONTINUED	
Option	Description
Disable Driver Signature Enforcement	Windows Vista can be configured to prevent the installation of unsigned device drivers. However, in some cases, an unsigned device driver might be the only way to get a system running again. Use this option to enable you to install and use unsigned device drivers if your configuration normally blocks them.
Start Windows Normally	This option boots the system without altering the normal boot operation. Use this selection to return to normal booting after you've made any other selection from the advanced menu. Selecting this option causes the normal boot to occur immediately; you are not returned to the boot menu.

After you've made a selection from the Advanced Options menu, the system boots using the startup option you selected. If you want to run Windows Memory Diagnostic before starting your system with Windows Vista, press the Esc key to display the Windows Boot Manager.

If you installed Windows Vista as a dual-boot with an older version of Windows, the Windows Boot Manager displays both options. (The older Windows version is not specifically identified.) Use the up and down arrow keys to highlight the version of Windows you want to boot, and press ENTER.

Whether you have a dual-boot installation or only Windows Vista installed, the Windows Memory Diagnostic appears in the Tools menu on the Windows Boot Manager screen. To boot Windows Vista after running the Windows Memory Diagnostic, press the Tab key to highlight Windows Memory Diagnostics, and press Enter.

Using Safe Mode, you can start your system with a minimal set of device drivers and services. For example, if newly installed device drivers or software is preventing your computer from starting, you might start your computer in Safe Mode and then remove the software or device drivers from your system. Safe Mode does not work in all circumstances, especially if your system files are corrupted or missing, or your hard disk is damaged or has failed.

> **TIP**
>
> If a symptom does not reappear when you start in Safe Mode, you can eliminate the default settings and minimum device drivers as possible causes.

In general, if you've just performed some operation that caused a system failure, the best first reboot action is to use the Last Known Good Configuration. If that fails to resolve the issue, use Safe Mode. If the problem is specific to the video drivers (or you suspect that it is), you might want to use Enable Low-Resolution Video instead of Safe Mode. If you've just recently changed video drivers or the video card itself, you might want to use the Enable Low-Resolution Video mode if things don't act normally during the reboot.

When you are able to access the system through Safe Mode, you need to resolve the issue that is causing the boot problem. In most cases, this requires you to reverse your last system alteration, application install, driver update, and so on. If your system stops booting properly and you did not make any changes, you should probably call Microsoft tech support; they might help track down the culprit and get things back on track.

If none of these boot options results in a repaired system or enables you to boot the system, you need to move on to the System Recovery Options dialog box.

AS A LAST RESORT

You can reinstall Windows Vista over a damaged Windows Vista installation. Doing so might be time-consuming, but reinstalling is useful if other repair attempts do not solve your problem. You should attempt an upgrade install first. (Start the installation by booting your system and starting the install from within Windows.) If this works, you will have repaired your OS and retained your installed applications and most system configuration settings. If upgrading fails, you must perform a fresh install, which means you have to reinstall all your applications and remake all your settings changes. Unless you format the drive, your data files remain unaffected by the upgrade or fresh install process.

> **TIP**
> If you do a fresh install, you don't have to worry that your documents and settings will get wiped out. They won't. During a reinstall, Windows Vista setup creates a folder called `Windows.old` that contains the old Windows installation. Check in this folder for the folders that belong to each user and retrieve files from those folders.

However, it is always a good idea to back up your data. See Chapter 34 to learn how to use the new backup features in Windows Vista. Keep in mind that if your system fails to boot, you can't get access to the Windows backup tool to create a backup. Although you can copy data from your system (assuming the hard disk is still readable), you won't be able to get back to work until you re-create your work environment.

> **TIP**
> If you need to recover data, there are ways to reclaim your data from the hard drive. These techniques assume that the files or folders you want to reclaim did not use NTFS encryption. First, if you have a dual-boot system, look for the `\Users\` folder on the boot drive. Drill down until you find the files you want. Keep in mind that all subfolders of users are hidden except for `Public`. Of course, this assumes that the OS you boot into can read the file system that your user files are stored under. Second, you can try to connect the drive to another computer that boots an OS that is capable of reading the volumes and folders in question. Then, go looking for the files. Find them and copy them where you'd like.

> **NOTE**
>
> If the lost data files were encrypted under NTFS, you need a *recovery key* to gain access to them. See Chapter 34 for information about EFS recovery keys.

Preventing Problems

I have never believed that having to reinstall and reconfigure an OS is a true recovery method. It's more of a start-from-scratch method. Some system failures require such far-reaching procedures, but, in many cases, you can prevent them. The most successful preventive measure is backing up. In fact, the only insurance you have from one moment to the next that your system and your data will even be accessible is a backup. Backups should be performed automatically and frequently. But just backing up is not enough; you must also verify that your backups are working properly and periodically walk through the process of restoring your system in the event of a failure.

Backups are the key to the long life of your data. Most of the repair capabilities of Windows Vista are backups. Many repair functions don't correct problems directly; instead, they restore saved functioning files over problematic ones. This includes the Last Known Good Configuration and the System Restore capability. But all these restore or repair functions focus on the OS, not on your data. Only a backup that you configure and execute will protect your data.

Read Chapter 34, "Protecting Your Data from Loss and Theft," for more details about backups.

Backups are not the only preventive measures you should take. You should also regularly check your system's performance. Chapter 25 discussed this.

It is also a good idea to use an uninterruptible power supply (UPS). A UPS conditions the power being fed to the computer and can provide several minutes of power in the event of a blackout. A UPS will prolong the life of your computer by protecting its sensitive components from electric fluctuations.

Regularly check the Event Viewer for device, driver, and service problems. Problems of this nature usually appear in the system log. They are usually indicated by a yellow triangle or a red stop sign as the event detail's icon. If you see problems related to key components of the system, you need to investigate the situation and resolve the problem. Unfortunately, the event details do not always provide enough information. You need to use the Help and Support Center, the Microsoft online Knowledge Base (support.microsoft.com), or Microsoft technical support over the phone to decipher what cryptic information is presented. In many cases, the Windows Vista troubleshooter can provide a workable solution. Otherwise, you should consult the vendor's website for updated drivers and troubleshooting instructions.

> **NOTE**
>
> Chapter 25 discusses the Event Viewer and the hardware troubleshooter.

You should also try to regularly perform drive maintenance on your system. Maintaining healthy drives reduces the number of problems related to the drive and file system. Drive maintenance involves the following:

- Manually removing old data files, via either deletion or backup
- Using Disk Cleanup to remove unnecessary files
- Using error-checking to verify that the volume is supporting its file system properly
- Using the defragmenter to consolidate files and aggregate free space

> **NOTE** Chapter 27 discusses these drive tools.

Fixing Application Problems with the Program Compatibility Wizard

Windows Vista is a big change from previous versions of Windows—even from Windows XP Service Pack 2. To enable older programs to run in Windows Vista, you can run the Program Compatibility Wizard, which is similar to the Application Compatibility Wizard featured in Windows XP.

To start the Program Compatibility Wizard, follow these steps:

1. Open Help and Support, and type **Program Compatibility** in the Search window. Press Enter. From the list of results, click Start the Program Compatibility Wizard.
2. In the next dialog box, click the link provided to run the wizard. When the wizard opens, click Next to continue.

> **CAUTION** The Program Compatibility Wizard is not designed to enable utility programs such as antivirus, backup, or other system-level programs to work. These types of programs must be made specifically for Windows Vista, or they might corrupt your system or the data they create. Use the wizard for games, educational, and office applications.

3. To work with a particular program, you can select from a list of installed programs, the program in the optical drive, or a program you search for manually. After you locate the program, select it and click Next to continue.
4. Specify the operating system the program was made for:
   - Windows 95
   - Windows NT 4.0 with Service Pack 5
   - Windows 98/Me
   - Windows 2000
   - Windows XP with Service Pack 2

5. You can also elect not to choose a compatibility mode. Click Next to continue.
6. In the next dialog box, select which display settings to use. Check boxes permit you to choose multiple options:
   - 256 Colors (a good choice for applications written for Windows 95 or NT 4.0)
   - 640×480 Screen Resolution (a good choice for applications written for Windows 95 or NT 4.0)
   - Disable Visual Themes (helpful for solving problems with title bar menus or buttons)
   - Disable Desktop Composition (helpful for solving display problems when the program runs)
   - Disable Display Scaling on High DPI Displays (helpful for solving display problems when the program runs on a high DPI display)
7. Click Next to continue.
8. Click the Run This Program as an Administrator check box if the program won't run. You must be an administrator to use this option, which is designed to help programs written for Windows 9*x* or installers and system utilities to run correctly.
9. Click Next to continue.
10. Review your settings, and click Back, if necessary, to adjust them. Click Next to run your program with the settings listed. The wizard stays open while the program runs.
11. After you run the program, return to the wizard. If the program ran correctly, click Yes. If the program did not run correctly, click No, Try Different Compatibility Settings to continue the process, or click No, I Am Finished if you want to abandon compatibility adjustments. Click Next.
12. In the next dialog box, click Yes to send compatibility information to Microsoft, or click No to skip this option. Click Next and then Finish.

ADJUSTING SETTINGS WITH THE COMPATIBILITY TAB

If you need to adjust settings without running the wizard, right-click a program, choose Properties, and select the Compatibility tab. This opens a dialog box similar to the one shown in Figure 28.9. As you can see, this tab includes the same settings as the wizard (Operating System, Display Settings, Run as Administrator). You might find that you prefer to use the Compatibility tab instead of the wizard. Note that after you use the Program Compatibility Wizard on a particular program, its settings are reflected in the program's Compatibility tab.

Figure 28.9
A program's Compatibility tab, with adjustments to mimic Windows XP Service Pack 2.

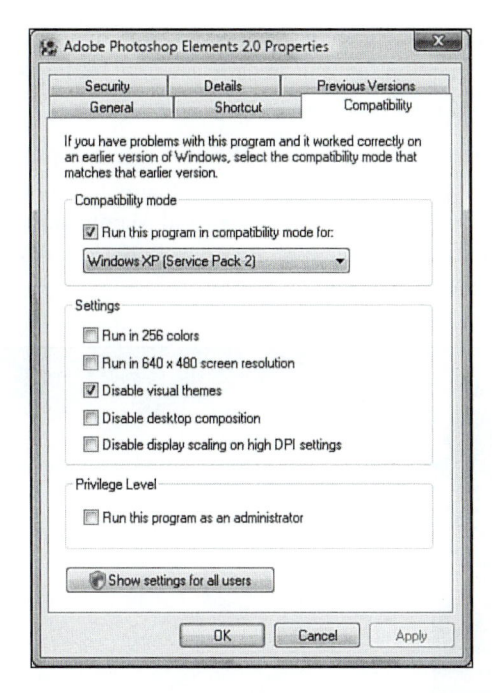

Using Problem Reports and Solutions

In Windows XP, there were troubleshooters that would walk you through solutions to common problems. There were 12 troubleshooters.

- Games and Multimedia Troubleshooter
- Display Troubleshooter
- Sound Troubleshooter
- DVD Troubleshooter
- Internet Connection Sharing Troubleshooter
- Modem Troubleshooter
- Home and Small Office Network Troubleshooter
- Hardware Troubleshooter
- Input Device Troubleshooter (keyboard, mouse, camera, scanner)
- Drives and Network Adapters Troubleshooter
- USB Troubleshooter
- Printing Troubleshooter

These troubleshooters often didn't solve your problems, though they at least walked you through a logical train of investigation for your malady, possibly leading you to a conclusion or avenue of thought you hadn't previously tried.

Vista uses a different approach to troubleshooting. When it detects a problem, you are asked if you want help with it. If your problem doesn't trigger a dialog box, open the Problem Reports and Solutions applet in Control Panel's System and Maintenance Category. (It's also available from the Classic View.) When you open Problem Reports and Solutions, you see a dialog box similar to the one shown in Figure 28.10.

Figure 28.10
The new Problem Reports and Solutions tool.

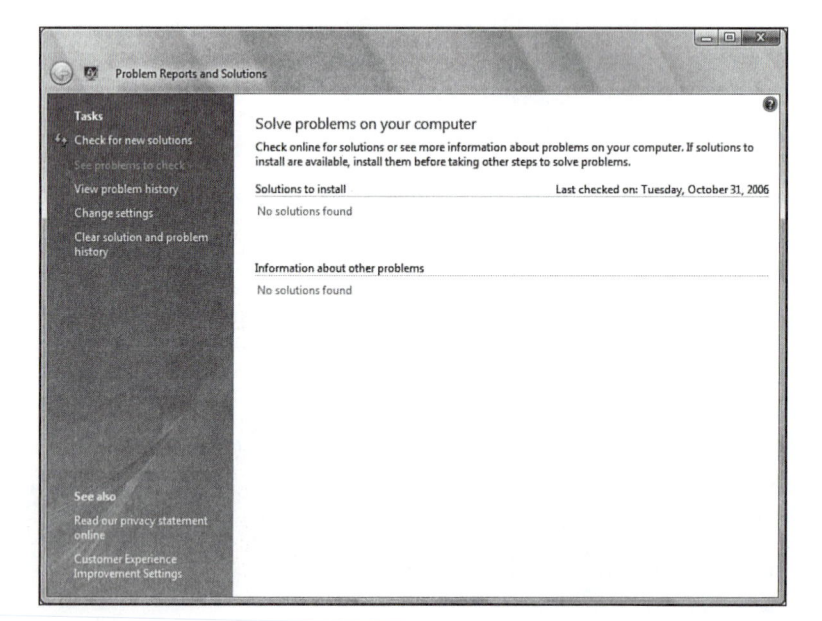

Click Check for new solutions in the left pane to check the Microsoft website for solutions to problems detected on your computer. A popup progress bar appears as messages are uploaded. You may be prompted to upload additional information to assist in finding a solution. To upload additional information, click Yes.

Click View problem history in the left pane to display a list of detected problems. Figure 28.11 shows a typical listing. Note that problems are listed by product and in newest-to-oldest chronological order.

Figure 28.11
The View Problem History dialog.

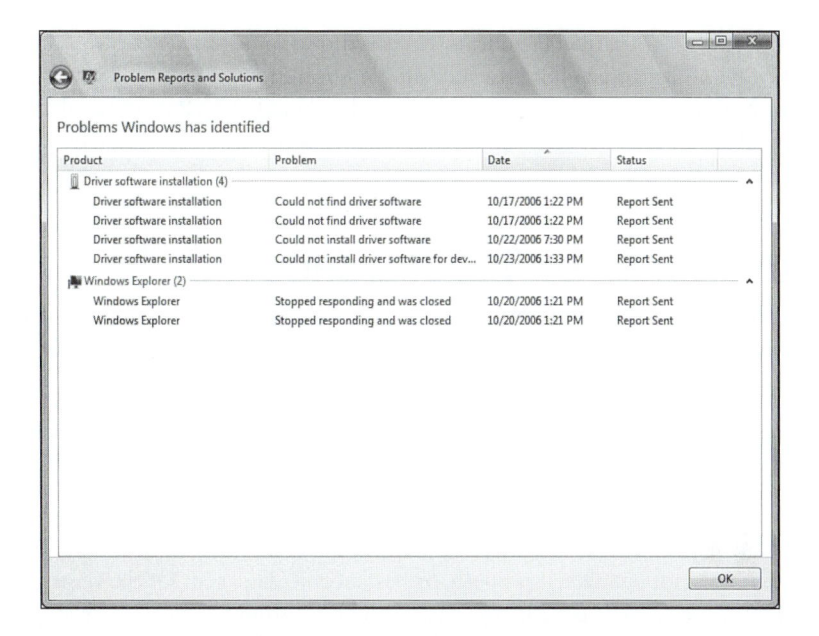

To clear the problem history list, return to the Problem Reports and Solutions main menu and click Clear Solution and Problem History. Click Clear All on the confirmation dialog box to remove this information or Cancel to return without making any changes.

> **NOTE** You should not clear the Solution and Problem History if you have unresolved problems. If you do, you may not be notified when solutions are discovered.

By default, Windows Vista automatically checks for solutions when problems are detected. To change this behavior, click Change Settings in the left pane of the Problem Reports and Solutions dialog and select Ask Me to Check If a Problem Occurs. Click OK. When you select this option, click See Problems to Check to see problems that have not yet been reported to Microsoft.

Finding and Using Windows Vista Troubleshooting Resources

If you are having problems with your system that are not handled by Windows Vista's Problem Reports and Solutions, you can get help from the Windows Vista Help and Support Center.

1. Choose Start, Help, and Support.
2. Type Troubleshooting into the search box and click the magnifying glass to start the search.
3. You will see a list of troubleshooting resources.

Windows Vista's troubleshooters, like Windows XP's, provide relevant links to operating system utilities, as well as specific help and tips. However, the 'answer a question with Yes or No to go to the next step' method used in Windows XP is not used in Windows Vista's troubleshooters. Instead, you are provided with hyperlinked resources and checklists to help you discover the problem and solutions.

Black Magic of Troubleshooting

It often seems like many professional technophiles have some sort of black magic they use when resolving problems. If you blink, you miss whatever they do to get the system back in working order. It's often as if you are working with a techno-mage.

Yes, it is true that some of our skills in resolving problems seem like hocus pocus. But in reality, it's a mixture of experience and knowledge, both of which you can gain with time and effort.

In my experience, that most computer problems are physical in nature—that is, some component is not connected properly or has become damaged. Of the remaining 5%, more than 4.99% is caused directly by the user—whether through deliberate or accidental activity. User-caused problems are typically configuration changes, installation of new drivers, or deletion of important files and folders.

When I troubleshoot a problem on my own systems, I try to mentally walk backward through whatever I've done to the system over the last few days or weeks. In many cases, I'll remember installing some downloaded application or changing some Control Panel setting that I meant to uninstall or reverse but never got around to doing. If the brainstorming fails to highlight any suspects, I check for physical issues. Is everything powered on? Are cooling fans still spinning? Are all the right cables still firmly connected?

If I don't discover anything obvious physically, I try a power-off reboot. The power-off reboot resets all hardware devices and, in many cases, resolves the problem (if it were device related). If possible, shut down the system gracefully. Then keep the power off for about 10 seconds before switching the system back on. You'll be amazed by how often this works.

My next steps always include a walk through the Event Viewer and any other types of log files I can find. Let the problem guide you in this process. For example, if the video system is failing, you probably don't need to look through the modem logs.

For me, every problem is unique and often requires a different resolution than any other problem I've tackled in the past. However, I try to follow some general rules or guidelines:

- Try only one change at a time.
- Reboot twice after each change.
- Test each change for success.
- Try the least invasive first.

- Keep a log of your changes. You might need to undo them to produce a result, or you might need the resolution process again in the future.
- Consult vendor websites for possible solutions if the problem seems to be specific to one device or software component.
- Be patient and take your time.
- After a few attempts at possible solutions, step back and re-evaluate before continuing.
- If you get frustrated, take a break. Anger and frustration are counterproductive when you need to be thinking clearly.
- Try to undo any recent changes to the system, including new hardware or software patches. You can use System Restore to undo driver or application changes, even if you can't start the system.
- Review areas of the system that caused problems in the past.
- Try to repeat the failure; knowing where, how, or why the failure occurs can lead to a solution.

Troubleshooting is both an art and a science. You need organized patience and outrageous ingenuity. Plus, knowing where to look stuff up never hurts. Keep in mind that the entire Internet is waiting at your fingertips and mouse clicks. Search groups.google.com as well as the regular Web. You'll be amazed by what you find. Be precise in your search techniques to help find the exact messages you need to read. The MS Knowledge Base is extremely helpful, too. In addition, lots of helpful information is included within the Help and Support system of Windows Vista and the Windows Vista Resource Kit. If all else fails, contact Microsoft technical support over the phone. (See support.microsoft.com for contact numbers.) In most cases, if the troubleshooting techniques in this book don't resolve the issue, it is usually beyond the end user to correct.

Not all the troubleshooting techniques applicable to Windows Vista are discussed within this one chapter. As you've no doubt noticed, we've been discussing troubleshooting within every chapter. That organizational decision was intended to group recovery information with the discussion of the related technologies, deployment, usage, and management. So before you throw your hands up in frustration that your questions are not answered or your problem is not resolved in this chapter, check out the chapter that is dedicated to the specific subject earlier in this book.

TRICKS OF THE WINDOWS MASTERS: RECOVERING DATA FROM THE SYSTEM RECOVERY OPTIONS MENU

If you decide that the only solution to a totally fouled-up Windows Vista installation is to wipe out the hard disk and start over, and if you discover that you don't have an up-to-date backup of critical data, you can use the command prompt in the System Recovery Options menu to save your data before wiping out your system.

Start by changing to the drive letter containing your Windows system. Don't assume it's the `C:` drive—for example, on a system that has been partitioned to use BitLocker; the Windows system drive might show up as the `D:` drive (even though you refer to it as the `C:` drive during normal operations).

Change to the Users folder:

```
cd\users
```

If you perform the `dir` command, you see only the Public folder. That's because all user folders are hidden. Use the command `dir /ah/p` to view the hidden user folders. For this example, let's assume that you need to retrieve files that belong to a user called Smith. Use the command `cd smith` to change to the Smith folder.

The most important user data folders include Contacts, Documents, and Favorites. Copy each folder to the target drive using `ROBOCOPY` (a souped-up version of the venerable XCOPY utility). For example, to copy Smith's Documents folder to a folder on the `F:` drive called Documents (along with any subfolders) use this command:

```
ROBOCOPY C:\Users\Smith\Documents\ F:\Documents\ /s
```

Use similar commands to copy Contacts, Favorites, Downloads, and other folders that contain irreplaceable data.

> **CAUTION**
>
> If you decide to use CD or DVD media instead of an external hard disk, USB flash drive, or network share to copy the data, be sure you know what drive letter has been assigned in the System Recovery Options Command prompt mode. It might be `D:`, `E:`, or some other letter (and not necessarily the drive letter it normally has). Here's how to tell: Insert a blank disc and type `dir x:` (substitute the drive letter you think is correct for `x:`). You see an "incorrect function" error message if you entered the correct drive letter. When you format the media, make sure it says that the old file system is RAW and the new file system is UDF before you continue the format. If you don't pay attention to these details, you could format your Windows system drive by mistake.

When you're finished, type **exit** and press Enter to close the command prompt window. Remove the media or shut down the system, and disconnect the hard disk you used for copying the data.

Go to another system, insert the media or connect the drive, and retrieve the information. If you stored it to a network share, log into the network share to retrieve the information. You might need to use the Folder Options applet in the Control Panel to enable the display of hidden files and folders to view and access the files from the other system.

CHAPTER 29

KEEPING WINDOWS AND OTHER SOFTWARE UP TO DATE

In this chapter

Windows Vista and Keeping Up to Date   986

Windows Update   986

Updating Drivers   992

Service Packs   994

"Ultimate" Extras   996

Installing and Removing Software   998

Troubleshooting   1005

Tips from the Windows Pros: Windows Update Driver Settings   1007

Windows Vista and Keeping Up to Date

Windows Vista is an ever-evolving operating system that requires new updates and maintenance constantly. These updates benefit your computer and render it more secure and stable. For Vista, Microsoft wrote a new breed of software that facilitates updating, dubbed Windows Live. Also, Windows Vista enables you to receive all the newest updates for your software and hardware via the Windows Update. As with previous versions of Windows Update, Windows Live downloads the most current updates, fixups, hotfixes, drivers, and so on for your system and then commences an installation. Updating has never been so easy and so visual.

Over a period of time, your system will accumulate many updates and newly formed software that Microsoft supplies. As you probably know, Microsoft sometimes gathers a mess of these into one package or compilation and releases it as a service pack.

As discussed throughout this book, Windows Vista comes wrapped in at least five different versions, some with and some without certain extras. The "ultimate" Vista incorporates everything that you will need in a PC. Vista Ultimate comes with many add-ons and new programs that no other operating system has ever comprised. If you are running a less-than-Ultimate version of Vista, you can upgrade (sort of easily, but not totally painlessly) to a higher level, even to Ultimate. We talk about that in this chapter. We also look at Vista's *power toys*, little goodies from Microsoft that you can download into any version of Vista.

Later in this chapter, we discuss how to install and remove applications software, including issues of running older programs. As mentioned in Chapter 1, "Introducing Windows Vista," older (16-bit) software that you have been using for years will have compatibility errors with 64-bit Vista. You learn more later in this chapter about why 64-bit Vista cannot support certain software. Also unique to Vista is how it controls side-by-side installations, and how it uses virtual registries and folders.

Understanding Windows Live

The Windows Live suite of applications available from http://get.live.com extends the online communications capabilities of Windows Vista, Windows XP, and Microsoft Office. It includes email, IM, search, social networking, photo management and publishing, blogging, event planning, online file storage, and family safety applications.

To customize the Windows Vista Sidebar, Windows Live Messenger, or Windows Live Toolbar, visit http://gallery.live.com. To use Windows Live features on a mobile device, visit http://www.gowindowslive.com/Mobile/Landing/Home/Default.aspx. To use free and low-cost web-based and email business and marketing tools, visit http://smallbusiness.officelive.com/.

Windows Update

Because this chapter is about keeping Windows and your apps updated, let's start with Windows. Windows Update is an important built-in online tool that ensures that your system gets all the latest software additions and bug fixes. Unlike the previous Windows Update in Windows XP, Windows Vista supplies users an integrated update system that does not require the user to go to the Microsoft update website. Instead of opening a web browser, the new version of Windows Update opens in the same existing window.

Windows Update has been made to be seamless to its users. Let's say a newly installed update requires a restart while you are in the process of doing important work. You can postpone that restart easily without any disruptions. Also a great new feature to Windows update is the way it handles updates for already running programs. If Windows Update has an update that needs to be installed on an already running program, Windows will save the current data for that program, close the program, install the update, and then reopen the program.

WINDOWS AUTOMATIC UPDATES

Windows users all know how important critical updates are to a system. Windows Updates can set automatic updates and guarantee that your computer acquires all the newest important updates. Windows Vista creates a scheduled time for your computer to check for system updates. Windows Update's default setting is to search for updates automatically and will only download and install critical and highest-priority updates.

> **NOTE** The Windows Update technology is rich. Among other things, systems administrators can use it to control updating many machines across a network using Windows Updates. Outside a corporate setting, though, most users will simply use their Control Panel to obtain the most current updates.

Upon installing Windows Vista, you are prompted to confirm setting for automatic update checking. In its typical hegemonic style, Microsoft does its level best to push you into allowing it to keep your system up to date automatically. You'll see a dialog strongly recommending that you leave automatic updates turned on (the default). If you do leave automatic updates on, information about your computer will be uploaded to Microsoft's Windows Update Database. Then security patches, critical updates, office updates, drivers, and operating system service packs will be automatically downloaded and installed to your computer. If you do decide to deactivate automatic updates, you are going to be bugged incessantly about it, anyway, so why fight a good thing? We believe this is good thinking on Microsoft's part.

> **NOTE** Windows does not use your name, address, email address, or any information that can be used to identify you or contact you.
>
> In Windows Vista, you have to be logged on as an administrator to install components or modify Windows automatic update settings.

Allowing Windows to download and install automatically keeps you up to date without having to remember to initiate an update check. It does not matter whether you have a broadband or dial-up connection. The Windows Update downloads just the files you need, or just the parts of the files you need, thereby keeping the downloads as small and fast moving as possible. The system is made additionally efficient by ensuring that the system downloads and installs the most crucial updates before less-important patches. So when the next virus outbreak hits, Windows users will immediately be protected. To additionally make the most of your connect time, if you disconnect from the Internet before your updates are finished, nothing is lost.

Letting Windows automatically update can sometimes cause your computer to automatically reboot by itself. A few critical updates must require a restart to successfully install. So beware when leaving update to automatic because important information and documents could be erased or damaged. For example, say that you leave your computer to automatically update at 3:00 a.m. every day, and the previous night you worked on important Word documents and left your computer on. While having those important documents on your computer, Windows downloads and installs an update that requires a restart. Windows will restart automatically, which could cause damage to your documents. This default selection may not be the best choice for you, and you may want to change these settings.

> **CAUTION**
>
> With original Windows Vista, keep in mind that with automatic updating turned on, Windows might restart your computer automatically after installing updates. Always save data and close programs if this option is activated. Otherwise, change how Windows controls automatic updates!
>
> One of the improvements in Windows Vista SP-1 is support for hotpatching. *Hotpatching* enables Vista SP-1 to install most system updates without rebooting. This is a welcome improvement, especially if you like the convenience of automatic updates but dislike having backups, remote access, or other tasks disrupted by system reboots after updates are installed.

Be aware that it is still possible that an update could damage your system. Windows Update creates a restore point for your system before installing the available updates. If a problem does occur, you can always roll back a system to its state before the update (see "Installing and Removing Software," later in this chapter), so using automatic updates is not necessarily a poor choice.

WINDOWS UPDATE APPLET AND FUNCTIONS

As you can see from Figure 29.1, the user has different options for updating her system.

On the main Windows Update applet, you can see the basic settings applied, the last time the system was updated, the time in which windows will automatically update, and what kind of updates. On the left side of the window is a list of options in which the user can select.

Figure 29.1
The Windows Update applet.

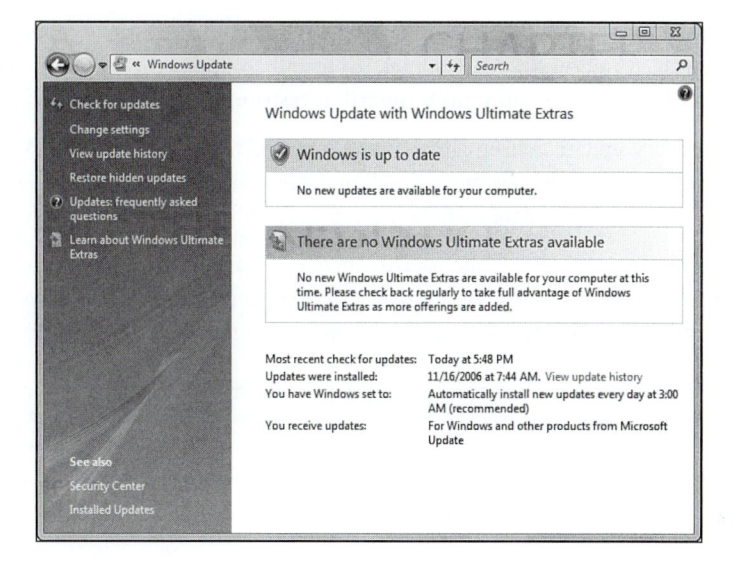

Manually Install Updates Using Windows Update

Manual Windows updating is easy and user friendly. By manually updating your system, various critical and noncritical updates can be obtained. To use Windows Update manually, follow these steps:

1. Go to the Control Panel.
2. Choose System and Maintenance.
3. Select Windows Update and then Check for Updates. Another way of getting to the Windows Update page is by clicking on the button formerly known as Start and then selecting All Programs, Windows Update.
4. Windows Update will then look for all possible updates or other available extras.
5. After a list of updates appears, you can select and install any updates that you want. Critical updates, however, will allow you no choice and will be mandatory.

Manually updating your system allows you to decide which updates you want and lets you know which updates you need.

> If Window Updates fails to install an update, **see** "Updates Do Not Install Properly," in the "Troubleshooting" section at the end of this chapter.

Other Windows Update Settings

You can also hide an update if do not want to install it. If Windows consistently asks you to install an update and you have no desire to, just hide the update. To hide an update, select the update you want to hide and click Hide Update. This is helpful because the list of installed programs can be overwhelmed by the list of installed updates. The option to filter out the updates from the list and show only installed programs makes this list easier for users to read. If you want to see hidden updates again, click Restore Hidden Update on the left side of the Windows Update applet. To install an update, it must not be hidden. If an update is hidden and you do want to install it, restore the update first and then install.

Also after every update, a user can view the installed updates by clicking View Update History, which visually shows the user all updates that were installed, when the updates were installed, whether the update installation was successful, and what priority the update was.

Windows Update also allows the user to change certain settings pertaining to updating. By clicking Change Settings, the user will see options pertaining to Windows automatic updating, recommended updates, and update service (see Figure 29.2).

Figure 29.2
Change settings in Windows Update.

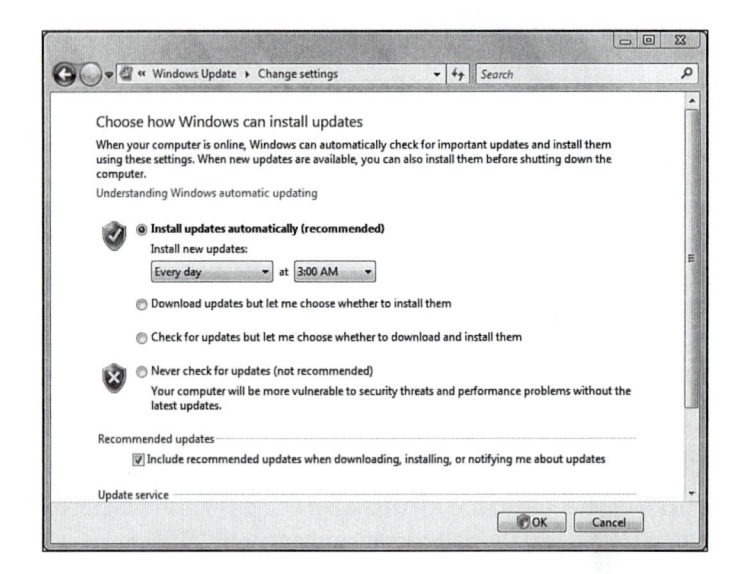

Changing settings gives four different settings to the Windows automatic updating. The default setting is to install updates automatically at a set time. You may change this setting if you want to choose which updates to install or even choose the updates before downloading. The option of selecting to install is valuable. Without choosing this option, Windows may automatically restart your system, and open or unsaved files could be damaged or even erased. We highly recommend that you change to this setting because automatic updates are important to your system, but you do not want them to ruin your important work. The last option, Never Check for Updates, is strongly discouraged by Microsoft.

When would you use the fourth option, to turn off updates altogether? In general, I'd rule that out as an intelligent option, with two exceptions:

- If you have a computer that is almost always off the Internet or a LAN, is "mission critical" (has to be up and running), and rarely if ever has new software (including email) added to it, this is a potential candidate. When I get such a dedicated system running, I haven't much interest in tempting fate with software or system upgrades.

- If you're running and maintaining PCs in a corporate setting. These PCs *are* connected to the Net and probably on a corporate network. You want to rigorously test updates before you install them across the corporation's PCs because Microsoft patches and updates can sometimes break your applications' features in subtle ways.

NOTE All updates that pertain to maintenance and support for Microsoft products are free.

Viewing and Changing Installed Updates

As stated before, some updates can cause system problems. By viewing what updates are installed on your computer you can repair critical updates and remove optional updates (see Figure 29.3).

Figure 29.3
Viewing installed updates.

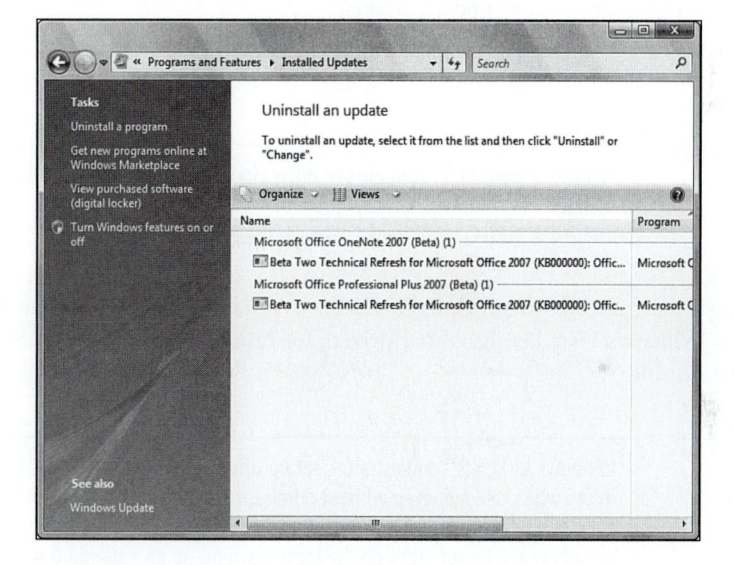

To repair or uninstall an update, follow these steps:

1. Open the Control Panel and select Programs.
2. Under Programs and Features select View Installed Updates.
3. A List of all updates should be available. Click on the update that you want to change.
4. After selecting an update, you will see various detailed information at the bottom of the window. Also on the top toolbar there will an option to repair or uninstall. Repairing will automatically repair the desired update without you really even knowing it. Uninstalling will ask for an administrative confirmation before uninstalling.

For problems with Windows uninstalling updates, **see** "Can't Uninstall Current Update," in the "Troubleshooting" section at the end of this chapter.

Updating Drivers

Keeping your system up to date also means that device drivers need to be kept up to date. Updated drivers allow your devices to work properly and will maximize compatibility. In Windows Vista, updating hardware drivers is made simple and easy.

You may have to update a driver if you encounter problems with the device—for example, if there are printing glitches or if Windows crashes with the famous "Blue Screen of Death." If you encounter this sort of problem, you may find that the support pages on the manufacturer's website direct you to download and install an updated driver. They should give you clear instructions, but here is some additional advice:

- Do you have permission to upgrade drivers? It is necessary to be logged in as Administrator or at least to have an administrator password when prompted by a User Account Control box to update drivers.
- Is it really the latest driver? Check the manufacturer's site and the Microsoft site to see what you can find.

> **TIP**
> You might want to try running Windows Update and see whether Microsoft listed updated device drivers for your system.

- Does the "new" driver work with Windows Vista? Make sure that the new driver is for Windows Vista because other drivers for other versions of Windows may not be compatible.

> **TIP**
> Windows Vista lets administrators set up drivers in a Driver Store that standard users can install when needed, even without administrative privilege. Vista also gives standard users the flexibility needed to install permitted classes of devices even if drivers aren't already in the Driver Store on the local machine. To give standard users this privilege, the administrator should open the Group Policy interface (gpedit.msc) and navigate to Computer Configuration, Administrative Templates, System, Driver Installation, Allow Non-Administrators to Install Drivers for These Devices. For more about the Driver Store and User Access Control see http://www.microsoft.com/technet/technetmag/issues/2006/11/UAC/default.aspx.

Manually Update Drivers

After you've downloaded the new driver, it is time to install using the Update Driver Software window. To access the Update Driver Software window, follow these steps:

1. Go to the Control Panel.
2. Select Hardware and Sound.

3. Either open the Device Manager or select Update Device Drivers. This will open the Device Manager either way. (If you are not logged in with administrator privileges, the Device Manager box will not open without additional input.)
4. After the Device Manager is open, you may select the device and then right-click and choose Update Driver Software.

The update driver software option opens a new window and gives you two choices, as shown in Figure 29.4.

Figure 29.4
The Update Driver Software window with the list of options.

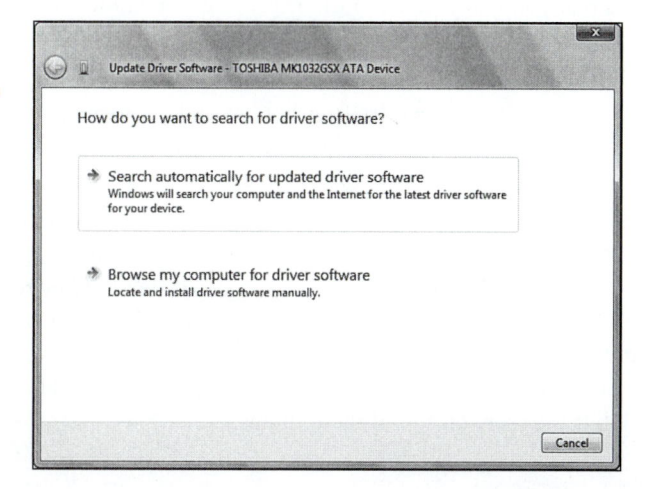

In the Update Driver Software window you can choose to let Windows search automatically for drivers, or you can manually locate drivers on your computer yourself. Selecting to search automatically will give permission to Windows to search and locate any drivers on your computer and on the Internet. After Windows searches your computer and the Internet for drivers, if a new driver is found, it will be automatically installed. If no new drivers are found then Windows will tell you that the recent driver is the latest up-to-date one. If the user already has downloaded the driver or wants to use a specific driver, he can choose to browse and locate that selected driver. When you choose to find the driver by yourself, Windows again gives you options. The first option is to manually locate the drivers. To locate the drivers you can either type in the location or click Browse. The second option is to choose drivers from a list of device drivers on the computer. When selecting to choose the driver from the list, a selection of device drivers is generated. You can decide on which driver you want and install it.

> **TIP**
> Downloadable drivers are usually stored in compressed form on the manufacturer's website. If the file is an .exe (executable) file, you will need to open it before you can use its contents; opening it might also install the driver for you. If the driver is in a .zip archive file, you will need to uncompress it. Fortunately, Windows Vista can uncompress .zip files for you. You won't need to download a separate unzipping utility.

SERVICE PACKS

Windows Vista is part of Microsoft's "New Technology" or NT family of operating systems, along with Windows XP, Windows NT, Windows 2000 Professional, the various flavors of Windows 2000 Server, and Windows Server 2003. These operating systems were designed from the ground up for stability, reliability, and security. To keep them in tip-top shape, Microsoft releases a constant stream of software updates as follows:

- *Critical updates* are just that: Fixes for bugs that are so severe or involve such serious security risks that you really *have* to install them. As you know, Vista can automatically download and install these, or at least download and offer to install them, so you don't miss out. Critical updates can be listed by using Windows Update.

- *Recommended updates* are not security fixes but are updates to accessory programs such as Messenger and Media Player, new desktop themes, and the like. Recommended Updates can be listed by using Windows Update.

- *Hotfixes* are bug fixes that affect a small enough group of users that Microsoft doesn't send them out to everyone. Instead, you have to hunt for them by searching online, or hear about them from Microsoft's Tech Support department. They're not widely advertised because if you're running into a serious-enough problem, you'll go looking for the solution, and hotfixes tend to be released in a hurry without extensive testing, so they sometimes cause new problems of their own. Hotfix users tend to be corporate IT people whose job it is to stay on top of these things.

BASIC SERVICE PACK INFORMATION

Periodically—it's supposed to be every 12 months but in practice it's less often—Microsoft gathers all the critical updates, recommended updates, and hotfixes, tests them extensively, and releases them as a service pack. Service packs, then, represent a complete, cumulative set of fixes and additions made since the initial release of an operating system. Service packs can be obtained on media disc, or can be downloaded from Microsoft's website.

You might wonder whether you really need to install service packs because you probably install the critical updates that Vista downloads and informs you of from time to time. The answer is emphatically *yes*, for two reasons. First, service packs fix those annoying but minor bugs that you may not even realize are there—that odd crash every other week, or that weird sound that Media Player makes once in a while. Vista SP-1, which was released in the spring of 2008, includes hundreds of bug fixes (many of which affected only a few users) as well as numerous performance improvements and new features. Second, application programs will eventually appear that require a certain service pack level to run correctly. Windows evolves, so you need to keep up. Those two reasons alone are enough to warrant installing any service pack.

Here are some other things that you should know about service packs:

- They're cumulative, so newer service packs include the old service packs and more. If you skipped a previous service pack, you can still install a newer one without missing anything.

- Starting about the same time that Microsoft releases a service pack to the public, new computers purchased from major vendors should come with the service pack preinstalled. (At least, it should be an option. If you're buying a new computer, ask for the latest version.) To check the current service pack level of your Windows Vista computer, open your system information.
- Shortly after Microsoft releases a service pack to the public, retail versions of the operating system will include the service pack. If you are shopping for additional copies of an operating system for upgrading existing PCs or for installation on new PCs, be sure to buy versions that include the latest service pack. A sticker or note on the package indicates whether a service pack is incorporated.
- It's likely that the procedure for installation of previous service packs will be similar for subsequent service packs as well.

> **NOTE**
> In a corporate environment, your IT department will most likely control the installation of service packs.

INSTALLATION OF SERVICE PACKS

There is a variety of ways to install a service pack, as presented in the following list:

- **Windows Automatically Updates**—If your computer was set up to automatically download critical updates, and you spend enough time connected to the Internet, a service pack will be downloaded automatically. All of the required service pack files will have already been downloaded by the time you get the notification to install them.
- **Windows Manual Update**—If the Automatic Updates feature was not enabled, you can install a service pack from the Windows Update window. Windows Update will download from Microsoft just those service pack components needed for your computer, saving some download time over the "standalone" method. However, if you have more than one or two computers to update, you'll save time by using the Standalone version.
- **Standalone**—The standalone version is the traditional service pack format. It's a compressed file that contains all of the updated files. If you have two or more computers to update, the standalone method is the one to use. Although it's bulky and contains updated components that your particular computers may not need, it's still faster to download this one large file than to have several computers download the Windows Update version independently.

Before installation of a service pack follow these guidelines:

- If you use Fast User Switching, be sure all users are logged off. Then, log on as a Computer Administrator. Close any running applications.

- We recommend that you perform a full backup of the files that you keep on your computer by using the Backup and Restore Center.

→ To learn more about the Windows Backup and Restore Center, **see** "The Backup and Restore Center," p. 1150.

- Check the websites of the manufacturers of your computer, your application software, and your antispyware and antivirus packages for updates or special instructions regarding the service pack. Some programs may need to be updated to work with the new service pack. For a list of programs that must be updated to work properly with Windows Vista SP-1, see Knowledge Base article 935796, available at http://support.microsoft.com.

- If you suspect that your computer may have viruses, spyware, adware, or other pestiential software, take steps to remove it *before* installing the service pack. These programs can cause serious networking and Internet connection problems after installation, and without a functioning Internet connection you may not be able to download the necessary clean-up tools.

- Disable any real-time virus scanners; they can slow down and possibly interfere with the installation. Disconnect from the Internet first if you do this.

- You will need free space on your hard drive for installation.

After following these suggested guidelines, you will be ready to install your service pack.

Ultimate Extras

Windows Vista Ultimate Edition is touted as the "Vista with everything" edition—and justifiably so. It includes all of the multimedia features of Windows Vista Home Premium (Windows Media Center, Windows Movie Maker 6 with HD support, DVD Maker), all of the data protection and remote access features of Windows Vista Business (Complete PC Backup and Restore, Remote Desktop Connection, Windows Fax and Scan), and the BitLocker disk encryption data security feature of Windows Vista Enterprise.

In addition to including combining all of the features of other Windows Vista editions in one package, Windows Vista Ultimate Edition also offers access to downloadable exclusive content known as Windows Ultimate Extras. When you run Windows Update on a Windows Vista Ultimate Edition system, you will be notified of any Ultimate Extras that are not yet installed on your system.

Alas, this feature of Vista Ultimate, widely touted before the introduction of Windows Vista, has been a disappointment. Instead of the flood of exclusive games and features promised by Microsoft, Windows Ultimate Extras have been few in number. As of early 2008, the following Windows Ultimate Extras can be downloaded by Windows Vista Ultimate users via Windows Update:

- Windows Hold'Em Poker Game
- Secure Online Key Backup and BitLocker Drive Preparation Tool
- DreamScene full-motion video wallpaper
- 36 language packs to support Ultimate's multi-language user interface

Figure 29.5
Windows Update on Vista Ultimate displays available Windows Ultimate Extras.

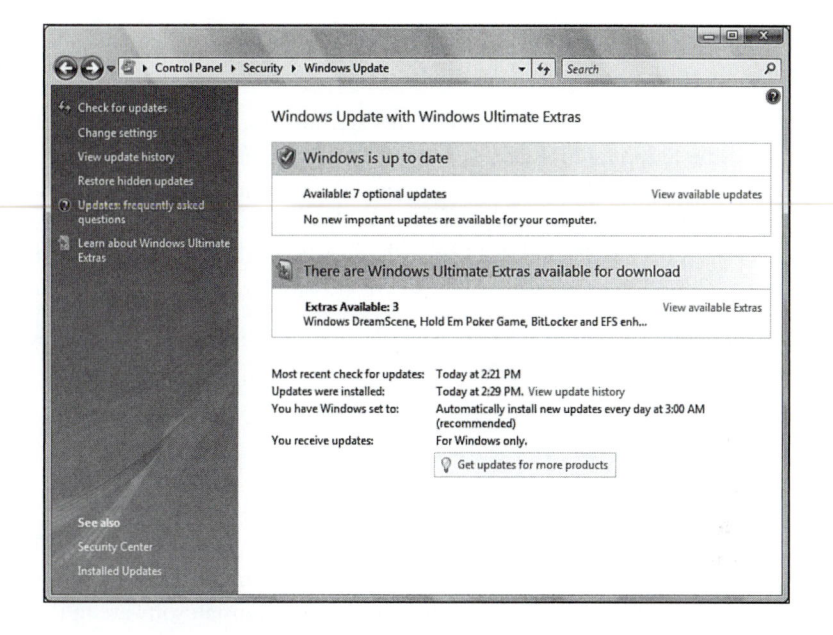

Of these, the most useful feature for most users is Secure Online Key Backup, which enables you to store EFS encryption keys online using Vista's Digital Locker secure storage technology. This update also includes the BitLocker Drive Preparation Tool, which repartitions your system drive to make it ready for BitLocker (BitLocker uses an unencrypted 1.5GB partition to store BitLocker code and boot files, and encrypts the remainder of the disk). Thanks to the BitLocker Drive Preparation Tool, users who set up their systems with a single partition can use BitLocker without needing to backup, delete, repartition, and reinstall Windows Vista.

The language packs are used to support multiple languages on a single Vista Ultimate system. They are useful for enabling different users of the same computer to run Vista using their preferred language and for students learning another language.

DreamScene full-motion video wallpaper is an enjoyable addition to Vista Ultimate, but it requires a powerful 3D graphics card. Users with integrated laptop graphics or older discrete graphics cards with limited RAM or 3D rendering capabilities are likely to discover that DreamScene reduces system responsiveness.

Windows Hold'Em enables Vista users to play the popular poker game.

Hopefully, more Ultimate Extras will be forthcoming. To stay informed about Ultimate Extras, check the official website for Ultimate Extras at windowsultimate.com.

→ To learn more about how to use Windows Update and its features, **see** "Windows Update," **p. 986**.

Power Toys

The first power toys were introduced back for Windows 95. They were extras for users that add more functionality to Windows. In fact, power toys are actually system tools designed for the user. For example, Windows XP had a power toy called Tweak UI, in which the user gained access to hidden system settings not displayed in the interface. Power toys can be very powerful, so be careful when using them.

In Vista Ultimate many of these features are built-in. Ultimate edition includes such power toys as the Snipping tool that was designed for Tablet PCs. Other PowerToys and utilities made available by Microsoft for Windows Vista Ultimate and other Vista editions include SyncToy v1.4 and above, which runs on both Windows XP and Windows Vista; Microsoft Experience Pack for Windows Vista (designed for Tablet PC users); Microsoft Ink Desktop (designed for Tablet PC users). These are available from www.microsoft.com/downloads.

Independent software developers have also developed utilities for Windows Vista that are unofficially referred to as "powertoys."

INSTALLING AND REMOVING SOFTWARE

As you know, installation of new programs is usually as simple as inserting a CD into the drive. The autorun program on most application CDs does the rest. Or, when it doesn't, you can run the Setup file on the disk, and the rest is automatic. Ditto for programs you download from the Net. The following section explains how to install software in these different ways.

> **NOTE**
> If you are using a standard user account, you will likely be prompted for an administrator password when you try to add or remove software programs. If you are logged in as an administrator, you will be prompted to Accept or OK the same procedures.

INSTALLATION VIA CD OR DVD

Installing software from a CD is user friendly and easy. Here is what you do:

1. Insert the disc into your computer.
2. Follow the onscreen instructions.

> **NOTE**
> Some software requires you to be logged in as an administrator to begin an installation or removal. You will be prompted for an administrator password or confirmation upon installing or removing this certain software.

3. Most programs will automatically try to start and begin the installation wizard. If this program automatically tries to install, you will be presented an AutoPlay dialog box that asks whether you want to run the installation wizard.
4. Some programs do not automatically run an installation wizard. In this case, check to see whether the disc comes with instructions or any information for installation. If the installation disc does not come with any instructions, open the disc to view its files. Try to find an Install.exe or Setup.exe (executable), and open that file. This should start the installation wizard and install the rest of the components.

> *For problems with Windows installing software,* **see** *"Problem Installing from Disc" in the "Troubleshooting" section at the end of this chapter.*

INSTALLATION VIA DOWNLOADED PROGRAM

Installing a program that was downloaded from the Internet is just as easy as installing a program from a disc. Before installing a program do the following:

- Make sure that you trust the publisher of the software.
- Scan the file for viruses before installing. Sometimes antivirus programs can find harmful viruses that can disrupt your system.
- Beware, some programs contain spyware and other software that can be annoying or even harmful.

After you are prepared for installation of your software, follow these steps:

1. Open your web browser and locate online where the software is.
2. After you find your software, you will be presented two choices: to open and run the program now or to run at a later time.
3. If you want to install your software immediately, click the link to the software. Select Open and follow the instructions.
4. If you want to save the software and install later, click the link and select Save. When you are ready to install this program, find the file and double-click it.

> **NOTE**
>
> Sometimes software can be downloaded as a zip or another type of compressed file. In this case, download and save the software on your computer; then right-click on the file and select Unzip to uncompress. Windows Vista has a built-in function to uncompress zip files.

UNINSTALLING OR CHANGING A PROGRAM APPLET

In Windows Vista, you can monitor and change software that is currently installed on your computer. Vista provides a helpful way to show you what software is on your computer.

As you can see in Figure 29.6, users can view information about all installed programs, including how many programs there are, who the publisher of each program is, when a program was installed, and how much space a program takes up. You can easily organize and change views however you please to better fit your likings.

By clicking on any of the installed programs on the list, you can view a program's detailed information in the lower part of the applet. This can help you see what version of the program is installed and allow you to check whether the program is up to date.

On the left side of the window, Vista gives you multiple options. You can view installed updates; these are all the Microsoft updates that your system contains.

→ To learn more about how to view and change Windows updates, **see** "Viewing and Changing Installed Updates," **p. 991**.

Figure 29.6
Uninstall or change a program applet.

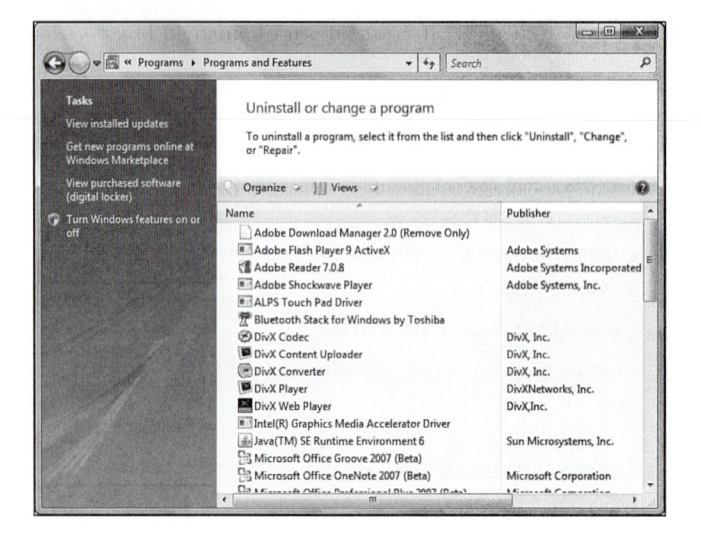

Also on the left side of the Programs and Features window is a Get New Programs Online at Windows Marketplace link and a View Purchased Software (Digital Locker) link.

Windows Marketplace is a source of new software that you can try and buy. It gives you a variety of new software and programs that can keep your computer more up to date. After purchasing and installing software from the Marketplace, it will be available in your digital locker. This digital locker holds only software that you purchase from the Windows Marketplace.

UNINSTALLING SOFTWARE

As you know, many programs come with their own installation (Setup) programs that handle all the details of installation, such as file copying, making Registry additions, making file associations, and adding items to the Start menus. An ever-growing number of applications even provide their own uninstall routine, which appears as a unique icon within their Start menu folder. But sometimes programs do not come with built-in uninstallers, or you just want Windows to handle these uninstalls.

Most modern applications are written in compliance with the Microsoft Windows standards for installation and removal. Thus, you see them in your installed applications list in the Programs and Features applet. This list is mainly the result of the PC software industry's response to kvetching from users and critics about tenacious programs that are difficult to root out after they're installed. Some ambitious programs spread themselves out all over your hard disk like oil on your garage floor with no easy way of reversing the process. Users complained about the loss of precious disk space, unexplained system slowdowns, and so forth.

INSTALLING AND REMOVING SOFTWARE | 1001

> **TIP**
>
> Never attempt to remove an application from your system by deleting its files from the \Program Files folders (or wherever). Actually, never may be too strong. Removal through manual deletion should only be a last resort. Always attempt to use the Add or Remove Programs applet or the uninstall utility from the application first.

To uninstall or change software, follow these steps:

1. Open the Programs and Features applet via the Control Panel and Programs link.
2. Select the program that you want uninstalled or changed.
3. Click on the Uninstall/Change icon.
4. Then the User Account Control will ask for administrator confirmation if this uninstall is correct.
5. Select Yes to the confirmation, and the software will automatically be uninstalled.

For problems with Windows uninstalling software, see "Uninstalling a Program" in the "Troubleshooting" section at the end of this chapter.

Also with Programs and Features you can turn on or off any Windows feature, as shown in Figure 29.7. Turning off and on a feature can customize Vista for you. For example, if you are running Vista on your desktop and only use a mouse and keyboard for input devices, you can turn off the Tablet PC optional Components. You do have the option to turn on any feature that is available as well. It is up to you the user which functions you want to use.

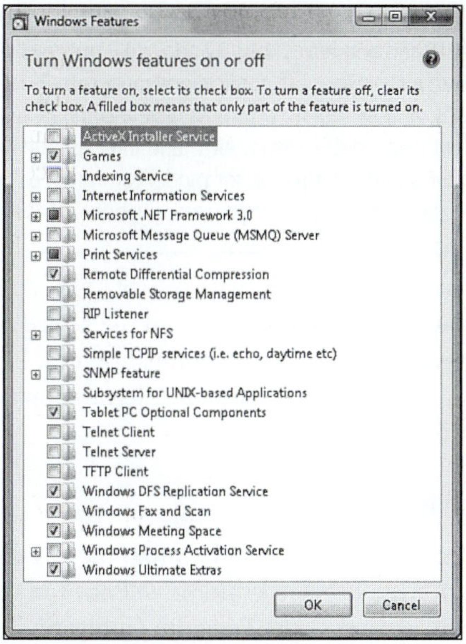

Figure 29.7
Windows features can be turned on or off.

Enabling and disabling features is easy and self-explanatory. If you want to turn on a feature, click the check box next to it to fill in the box. If you do not want a feature, just click the check box to clear it. If you do want to turn off a feature, make sure that you know what you are turning off.

> **NOTE**
>
> Turning off a feature does not uninstall it completely off your computer as in Windows XP. Instead it keeps the feature on your hard drive to give you the latter option of turning it on. This allows you to turn on and off any feature quickly but does not free up any space on your hard disk.

COMPATIBILITY ISSUES IN 64-BIT VERSION

Windows Vista 64-bit is a unique operating system that targets and utilizes 64-bit processors. It offers various benefits for users such as Virtual PC Express and a native 64-bit POSIX (portable operating system interface).

With all these great benefits comes a downside. Vista 64-bit has a number of compatibility issues and other limitations. Old 16-bit applications, legacy installer applications and 16-bit DOS, and even 32-bit drivers (you must install x64-bit drivers) are not supported in Vista 64-bit.

> **TIP**
>
> If you are planning to *upgrade* to the 64-bit version of Windows Vista, remember you can upgrade only from 64-bit Windows XP. Also you can only upgrade your 32-bit Windows XP to 32-bit Windows Vista. If you do have capability to install the 64-bit version of Windows Vista and you have 32-bit Windows XP previously installed, you must complete a new clean install. Thus, all applications must comply with the new 64-bit application standards. And of course, you must have a compatible 64-bit CPU in your machine. Most recent desktop CPUs from AMD and Intel support 64-bit versions of Vista. To determine whether a particular processor model can run in 64-bit (x64) mode, check the processor's specification sheet at the processor vendor's website.

Windows Vista incorporates a new Registry redirection and file redirection that will be responsible for all the operating system's applications compatibilities. However, 64-bit Windows Vista does not incorporate this feature, and most legacy applications will not run or install.

OTHER PROGRAM COMPATIBILITY ISSUES

While running Vista, you may decide to install an older program or game. When installing older software Vista either will not install the program or will not run the program correctly. Windows Vista sports a new version of the Program Compatibility Wizard to help work around this kind of incompatibility.

The Program Compatibility Wizard is designed to change the compatibility of a certain program and allow that program to work in Windows Vista. To open and use this wizard, follow these instructions:

1. Open the Control Panel.
2. In the Search box at the top of the screen type **Program Compatibility Wizard**.
3. The Control Panel will search for and find the wizard. When it does, click on Use an Older Program with this Version of Windows.
4. The onscreen instructions will ask you where the program is. You can choose to locate the program yourself, let Vista find the program, or use a program on a CD-ROM drive.
5. After deciding which program you want to change compatibility with, the wizard will ask you what prior version of Windows supports the program.
6. The wizard then will ask you a few options regarding the program. These options include color quality, resolution, disable visual themes, disable desktop composition, and disable scaling. Select all that apply.
7. The Program Compatibility Wizard will ask you whether administrative privileges are needed to run this software.
8. Now all the basic options that you have to choose are done. The wizard will now ask you to test the program to make sure that it works correctly. Click Next to test the program.
9. After testing is completed, you are asked whether you want to keep these settings, change the current settings, or exit the wizard.

SIDE-BY-SIDE INSTALLS

Windows 98 Second Edition provided a feature called *side-by-side DLLs*. This feature allowed a developer to use the version of DLLs required by a particular program without overwriting system DLLs (those stored in the \Windows\System folder). This feature worked *only* on Windows 98SE and only if the program developer took advantage of the feature.

Windows 2000 introduced Windows File Protection, which restored system files automatically if they were overwritten by an application when you installed it or ran it. This protected Windows from crashing but didn't do anything about a program that needed a particular system file version to run.

Side-by-side installs allow users to install multiple versions of the same product on the same computer. Many users can take advantage of side-by-side installations of programs. But sometimes using multiple programs that use a different version of the same DLL causes complications—"DLL Hell." When programs use the wrong DLL files, they crash and sometimes take the whole operating system down with them.

Windows XP Professional provided a way to handle DLL Hell. It was called *Fusion*. Fusion allowed programs to install whatever system files (DLLs and others) they needed and redirect any files that would replace system files to the program's own folder. When such a program was run, Fusion created a memory-protected virtual machine to run the program with its own DLLs. The end result was that even if two or more programs were running at the same time, using different versions of DLL or other system files that would "break" the system in past versions of Windows, both programs would run properly. No other programs could touch the area of memory granted to each program. Nor could that program or other programs gain access to the area of memory in which the basics of the operating system were running.

Windows Vista contains a different method from the Windows XP solution. Instead of a single Registry, Vista uses a virtual registry to contain multiple DLLs. These virtualized application registries eliminate any conflicts between software. So when installing two versions of Microsoft Office you can have an option to install both versions at the same time. For example, you can have Microsoft Office 97 while you have Office 2003.

Virtual Registries and Folders

Windows Vista offers a whole new level of virtual registries and virtual folders. Virtual registries, as explained earlier, can allow you the option of installing multiple versions of software at the same time. Virtual folders contain search data that can easily find and locate information.

→ To learn more about virtual folders, **see** "Searching," **p. 189**.

Virtual registries also have one other important aspect. Because Vista can create and use virtual registries for data, Microsoft applied this concept to users who do not have administrator privileges. By using virtual registers, nonadministrative guests can use a virtual registry and will not disrupt the main registry. Usually only administrators have the rights that allow one to install software that writes to the Registry. But now nonadministrators can install software and other various programs onto the system without causing any harm. Vista will continue to run and display all software installed but will not experience any permanent effect from the data on the virtual registry.

Virtual folders help users get data quickly and easily. Before creating a virtual folder, a search must first be performed (for example, using a Windows search engine). After completing the desired search a user may decide to save this search as a virtual folder. This folder can be opened up at any time and will display all the information from the search.

To create a virtual folder, follow these instructions in Vista SP-1:

1. Start a search in Vista SP-1 by typing the search text into the Start Search window above the Start button. By default, Start Search searches only Start menu items.
2. Click Search Everywhere to expand your search.
3. After the information has completely been found, click on the Save Search icon.
4. With the Save As window open, select the place where you want to save the newly created virtual folder (see Figure 29.8).

Figure 29.8
Saving a virtual folder.

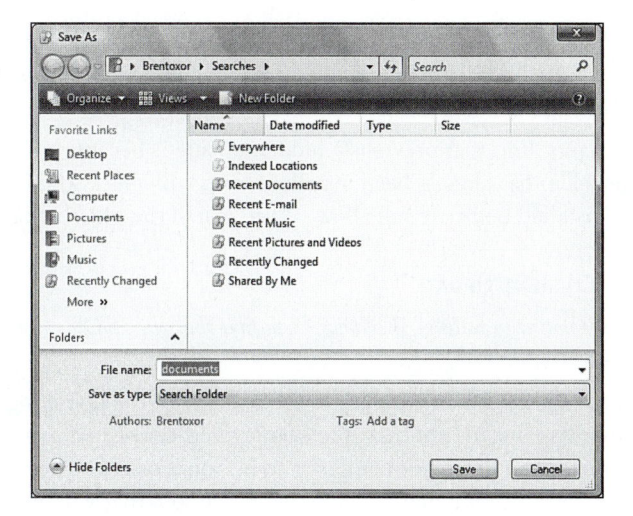

5. After you save the virtual folder you may access it whenever you want. The virtual folder will display all the information in that previous search.

Troubleshooting

Updates Do Not Install Properly

One or more of my Windows Updates did not install properly. The program failed to install and/or produces an error.

If this does occur, check the following:

- Is there enough free disk space on your computer? An update will not install if there is insufficient free space for it to install on. Free up space on your system and reinstall the update.
- Did you accidentally cancel an update while it was installing? If the update was not fully downloaded, run Windows Update again. If the update was downloaded but not installed, simply go back and reinstall the update.
- Was the Microsoft Software License Term accepted? If an error code was created about licensing, review the error code and select Try Again. When the licensing agreement opens it will ask you to review the license and agree to the terms.
- If none of the preceding solutions work, review the error code that was created and search online for more help.

Can't Find Hidden Update

After unhiding an update I decided to install it, but I cannot find the update that I unhid. Where did the update go and how can I still install it?

The reason you cannot find that previously hidden update is because a newer update that addressed that problem has already been installed. Vista will check whether a newer update has already been installed before it will allow you to install the older update.

Can't Uninstall Current Update

My current update is not uninstalling. Windows Vista says that the update cannot be uninstalled or produces an error upon uninstalling.

If an update is a critical update and applies to the security of the operating system you may not install it. Otherwise, make sure that your computer is connected to a network. Uninstalling an update requires your computer to be connected to a network due to the Group Policy. Group Policy is a network administrative tool that will manage all settings for users and other computers.

Uninstalled Update Keeps Installing

An update that I uninstalled keeps automatically installing on my computer. This update is unwanted and will not seem to be removed.

If you have Windows Update set to update automatically, you may experience this problem. To solve it, you do not have to shut off or change the setting to automatic updating. Instead of disabling features, uninstall the update and then click on Check for Updates. This will bring up a list of updates that you may install and the update that keeps automatically installing. For the update that you do not want installed, simply select Hide to hide the update.

Problems with Installed Update

Installed update seems to be causing problems, and I want to remove it. With this update certain functions of my computer are not functioning correctly and/or an error message occurs.

If this occurs make sure that you know which update is causing the problems. After you have found the offending update, you may uninstall it. If you do not know which update is the problem, search online for solutions or tips that could lead you in discovering the source of your problems.

Problem Installing from Disc

I inserted a disc into the drive, but it is not installing. Is there a problem with the disc or with my disc drive?

First make sure that you are installing the software correctly.

→ To learn more about how to install a program from a disc, **see** "Installation Via CD or DVD," **p. 1002**.

If there is still a problem with the install, check the disc to see if there are any scratches or blemishes that could create a problem. Scratches on discs can be a major problem and can make the disc reader fail to read the disc correctly. If the disc is okay, check your disc reader. If your disc drive is broken or is faulty, bring your computer to a local computer technician.

OLDER PROGRAMS NOT INSTALLING

Some of my previous programs are not installing on Vista. These programs worked correctly on an older version of Windows but will not install on Vista.

Older programs are not guaranteed to install and run correctly on Vista. Check to see whether there is a newer more recent install for this program.

→ If a program installed but is not compatible, change the compatibility by using the Windows Compatibility Wizard. **See** "Other Program Compatibility Issues," **p. 1002**.

PROGRAM DOESN'T SHOW UP

A program I installed does not show up in Programs and Features. Is the program still on my computer?

Programs and Features will only show programs that were strictly written for Windows. Any program that is not written for Windows will not show up in the Programs and Features but is still installed on your computer.

UNINSTALLING A PROGRAM

I want to uninstall a program that is not listed in Programs and Features. The program is installed on my computer but Windows does not recognize it.

If the program you want to uninstall is not listed, check for more information about the product. Programs usually come with ReadMe notes or have extra information online.

TIPS FROM THE WINDOWS PROS: WINDOWS UPDATE DRIVER SETTINGS

When installing a new device to your system, Windows usually will automatically install drivers. After installing these drivers, Vista continually looks for newer drivers online by using Windows Update. These driver checks and updates happen without you even knowing about them. But in Vista these settings can be changed. To alter these settings follow these steps:

1. Open the Control Panel and go to System and Maintenance.
2. Select System and click on the Change Settings link located on the right-hand side of the page.
3. The System Properties window should be open; click on the Hardware tab.
4. With the Hardware tab, open Windows Update Driver Settings, shown in Figure 29.9.

You can choose from three settings to instruct how Windows Update updates your drivers. The default and recommended setting is to allow Windows Update to automatically check for updated drivers. Another option is to have Windows ask you before it checks whether you want Windows Update to find new drivers. Finally, you can turn off Windows Update and disable it from checking for new device drivers.

Figure 29.9
Windows Update Driver Settings.

CHAPTER 30

INSTALLING AND REPLACING HARDWARE

In this chapter

Upgrading Your Hardware   1010

Adding Hardware   1013

Removing Hardware   1018

Installing and Using Multiple Monitors   1019

Installing a UPS   1023

How Many Upgrades Are Allowed before EULA and SPP Barf?   1028

Troubleshooting   1032

Tips from the Windows Pros: Upgrading and Optimizing Your Computer   1034

Upgrading Your Hardware

No matter how high the performance of your computer, sooner or later it will start to slow down as newer programs demanding faster hardware show up on your desktop. Chances are you'll run out of performance before you or your company is ready to pop for a replacement computer. This chapter will help you make the hardware changes—large or small—you need to get the most work and useful life out of your computer. We'll discuss how to upgrade and install hardware, add a second monitor, connect new and old hard drives, and add memory.

The single most helpful thing you can do to make your Windows Vista computer run at peak speed is give it enough system memory (or *RAM*, short for *random access memory*). Just as a reminder, your computer uses two types of memory: hard disk space and RAM. RAM holds Windows and the programs you're actually using, and Windows Vista wants *a lot* more than any previous version of Windows. As discussed in the early chapters of this book, Vista can run with as little as 512MB of RAM and an 800Mhz CPU, but it will run a bit slowly, and you'll find the experience somewhat unpleasant. Memory is inexpensive these days, and boosting your RAM up to at least 1GB will make a huge difference. I discuss adding RAM and upgrading CPUs later in this chapter.

Now, if you're already running Windows Vista on a full-bore, state-of-the-art system, and your computer has a fast video accelerator, a couple of gigs of fast memory, and fast SATA disks, there isn't much more you can do in the way of actual hardware optimizing. You might just adjust the page file sizes and certainly convert all your partitions to NTFS (which is a requirement for Vista). Some of the settings you can make are discussed in Chapter 25, "Windows Management and Maintenance;" Chapter 26, "Tweaking the GUI;" and Chapter 27, "Managing Hard Disks."

By the same token, if you're doing common, everyday tasks such as word processing, and you're already satisfied with the performance of your computer as a whole, you probably don't need to worry about performance boosters. Your system is probably running just fine, and the time you'd spend trying to fine-tune it might be better spent doing whatever it is you use your computer for (like earning a living).

If you're anywhere between these two extremes, however, you may want to look at the tune-ups and hardware upgrades we'll discuss in this chapter.

> **TIP**
>
> This chapter just scratches the surface of the ins and outs of hardware installation and updates. If you want all the details, and I mean *all* the details, get a copy of the best-selling book *Upgrading and Repairing PCs*, by Scott Mueller, published by Que.

BIOS Settings

Windows Vista depends on proper BIOS settings to enable it to detect and use hardware correctly. At a minimum, your drives should be properly configured in the system BIOS, and your CPU type and speed should be properly set (either in the BIOS or on the motherboard, depending on the system). Thanks to some clever work by Microsoft's engineers,

Windows Vista boots much faster than any other 32-bit version of Windows, but you can improve boot speed even more with these tips:

- Set up your BIOS boot order to start with drive C: so that you can skip the floppy stepper motor test.
- Disable the floppy drive seek.
- Turn off any Quick Power on Self Test. Some BIOSes have such an option that enables a quicker boot-up by skipping some of the internal diagnostics that would usually take place on startup. It makes boot-up faster but also leaves you more susceptible to errors; some problems will not be detected at startup.

If, after tinkering with your BIOS settings, you find that your computer will no longer boot up, **see** *"Altered BIOS Settings Prevent Computer from Booting" in the "Troubleshooting" section at the end of this chapter. Remember, too, that if you're looking at BIOS settings, most systems give you the option of exiting the BIOS without saving the settings. If you think you made a mistake, exit without saving and try again.*

Upgrading Your Hard Disk

One of the most effective improvements you can make to a system is to get a faster or larger hard drive, or add another drive. SCSI hard disks used to seriously one-up IDE drives, but the new breed of Ultra DMA EIDE drives (which I call Old MacDonald Disks—EIEIO!) and Serial ATA (SATA) drives are speedy and much cheaper than SCSI. An EIDE bus supports four drives (two each on the primary and secondary channels) and is almost always built in to your motherboard. Adding a CD-ROM (or CD-RW or DVD-ROM) drive claims one, leaving you with a maximum of three EIDE hard drives unless you install a separate add-on EIDE host adapter or have a motherboard with RAID support. The EIDE spec tops out at 133MB/sec. Serial ATA (SATA) supports one drive per channel, but the latest SATA II connection system can reach top transfer speeds of 300MB/sec.

TIP Many recent motherboards feature onboard IDE and even SATA RAID, which can perform either mirroring (which makes an immediate backup copy of one drive to another) or striping (which treats both drives as part of a single drive for speed). Although the RAID features on these motherboards don't support RAID 5, the safest (and most expensive!) form of RAID, they work well and are much less expensive than any SCSI form of RAID. Just remember that mirroring gives you extra reliability at the expense of speed because everything has to be written twice, and striping with only two disks gives you extra speed at the expense of reliability—if one hard disk fails, you lose everything. You can now find external Terabyte boxes with multiple drives in them that can be set up for striping or mirroring (RAID 0 or 1) at amazingly affordable prices.

The following are some essential considerations for upgrading your hard disk system:

- Don't put a hard drive and an optical drive on the same channel unless necessary. (Put the hard drive on the primary IDE1 channel and the optical drive on the secondary

IDE2 channel.) On some computers, the IDE channel negotiates down to the slowest device on a channel, slowing down the hard disk's effective transfer rate. Be sure that the hard drive containing Windows is designated as the Primary Master drive.

- Defragment the hard disk with the Defragmenter utility, which you can reach through Computer. Right-click the drive, select Properties, Tools tab, Defragment Now. Do this every week (or run Defrag and set up a schedule so it runs weekly), and the process will take just a few minutes. But, if you wait months before you try this the first time, be prepared to wait a long time for your system to finish. You can also purchase third-party defragmenting programs that do a more thorough job. For more about defragmenting, see Chapter 27.

- Get a faster disk drive (and possibly controller if necessary to support the drive): Upgrade from standard Parallel ATA (PATA) to Serial ATA (SATA) drives if possible. If you have slower (4,200 or 5,400 RPM) drives, upgrade to quicker ones such as the increasingly popular 7,200RPM or 10,000RPM drives. The faster spin rate bumps up system performance more than you might expect. Purchase drives with as large a cache buffer as you can afford. Drive technology is quickly updated, so do some web reading before purchase.

Adding RAM

Perhaps the most cost-effective upgrade you can make to any Windows-based system is to add RAM. This one is a no-brainer: If your disk is pausing and thrashing each time you switch between running applications or documents, you need more RAM. Although Microsoft says Windows Vista can run with as little as 512MB of RAM, we found that this results in only acceptable behavior. At least they were realistic about it this time around. Microsoft had claimed XP could run with 64MB, but that was a stretch. Running with 64MB caused intolerably slow performance. Vista's published minimum is 512MB, but if you run memory-intensive applications and want decent performance, you'll want to up it.

Windows automatically recognizes newly added RAM and adapts internal settings, such as when to swap to disk, to take best advantage of any RAM you throw its way. Upgrade to at least 1GB of RAM if you can afford it, especially if your system uses the economical SDRAM or DDR SDRAM DIMM modules. Memory prices fluctuate constantly, but these days 512MB memory modules are selling for under $100. This is a cost-effective upgrade indeed. But be sure to get the right memory for your motherboard. A huge variety of memory technologies are out there. At the time this was written, common technologies included SDRAM, RDRAM, DDR, DDR2, and DDR3. Memory speeds range from 100MHz (labeled PC100) to 4400MHz (labeled PC4400). And, on top of that, there are error-correcting (ECC) and nonerror-correcting varieties.

> **TIP**
>
> For more about RAM developments and technology, a good place to start is http://en.wikipedia.org/wiki/Random_access_memory.

To find out what type of memory you need, check with your computer manufacturer or the manual that came with your computer or motherboard. Get the fastest compatible memory that your CPU can use and that your motherboard supports. You can get RAM that's rated faster than you currently need, but you won't gain any speed advantage—just a greater likelihood of being able to reuse the memory if you later upgrade your motherboard. Here's a site with some good information about RAM and even possibly what kind your computer uses: www.pcbuyerbeware.co.uk/RAM.htm.

The maximum amount of RAM you can use depends on your computer's hardware and the version of Vista you are using. The following table lists the version and maximum amounts. Many last-generation computers cannot use more than 4GB of memory, even if you could plug it in, by the way, without a BIOS upgrade. Do check with the computer or motherboard manufacturer's data sheets or website to figure out whether you have to flash upgrade the system board BIOS to support more than 4GB.

Version	RAM Maximum
32-bit Home Basic	8GB
32-bit Home Premium	16GB
32-bit Business	128GB+
32-bit Enterprise	128GB+
32-but Ultimate	128GB+
64-bit Home Basic	8GB
64-bit Home Premium	16GB
64-bit all other versions	128GB+

Adding Hardware

One of the tasks that is most common for anyone responsible for configuring and maintaining PCs is adding and removing hardware. The Control Panel contains an applet designed for that purpose; it's called the Add Hardware applet (from Control Panel's Classic View). You can use it if the operating system doesn't automatically recognize that you swiped something or added something new, whether it's a peripheral such as a printer or an internal device such as a DVD-ROM, additional hard disk, or whatever.

If you're a hardware maven, you'll be visiting this applet a lot, especially if you work with non–Plug and Play hardware. Plug and Play hardware installation is often completely effortless because Windows Vista is good at detection and should install items fairly automatically, along with any necessary device drivers that tell Windows how to access the new hardware.

> **TIP**
>
> The Windows Hardware Quality Laboratories (WHQL) is the testing lab that qualifies hardware as being compatible with its software. If you want to make life easy for yourself, before you purchase hardware for your Vista system, check the compatibility lists on the Microsoft site. Or when looking on a box in a store or online, it should have the "Designed for Windows Vista" logo on it. The Windows Catalog and Hardware Compatibility List can be found at http://testedproducts.windowsmarketplace.com/.

If you've purchased a board or other hardware add-in, you should first read the supplied manual for details about installation procedures. Installation tips and an install program may be supplied with the hardware. However, if no instructions are included, you can physically install the hardware and keep reading.

> **NOTE**
>
> *Always* check the installation instructions before you install the new hardware. In some cases, the instructions tell you to install some software *before* you install the new hardware. If they do, follow this advice! They know what they are telling you. I have made the mistake of ignoring this and finding out that a driver has to be removed and reinstalled in the correct order to work correctly.

If you're installing an internal device, you'll have to shut down your computer before you open the case. I suggest that you also unplug it because most modern PCs actually keep part of the system powered up even when it appears to be off. Before inserting a card, you should discharge any potential electrostatic charge differential between you and the computer by touching the chassis of the computer with your hand. Using an antistatic wrist strap also is a good idea. Then insert the card, RAM, and so on.

> **TIP**
>
> You might be tempted to move some of the adapter cards that are plugged in to your motherboard from one slot to another, but don't do this unless you really have to. Each PCI adapter's configuration information is tied to the slot into which it's plugged. When you restart your computer, the Plug and Play system will interpret the move as your having removed an existing device and installed a new one, and this can cause headaches. In some cases, you'll even be asked to reinsert the driver disks for the device you moved, and you may have to reconfigure its software settings. (From personal experience, I can tell you that moving a modem gives Symantec PCAnywhere fits.) If you must swap slots, don't change or mess with them all at once. Change one and reboot, and then change another. Vista is better about contention and remapping resources than previous Windows versions were.

When the device is installed, power your PC back up, log on with a Computer Administrator account, and wait a minute or so. In most cases, the New Hardware Wizard automatically detects and sets up the new device.

If you're adding a USB or FireWire device, plugging in an Ethernet cable, or a digital camera card, you don't need to shut down before plugging in the new device, but you should close any programs you have running, just in case the installation process hangs the computer. The computer itself (as opposed to applications) doesn't hang often in NT-based systems such as XP and Windows Vista, so BSODs (blue screens of death) are more rare, but it can happen. Save your work and close your applications before you plug in the new device.

For non-Plug and Play hardware, or for Plug and Play stuff that isn't detected or doesn't install automatically for some reason, you can try this:

1. Run the Add Hardware applet from the Control Panel. You may have to click Continue on the UAC dialog box to give yourself permission (and possibly enter an administrator password).

2. The wizard starts by advising you to use a CD if one came with your hardware. This is good advice. If you don't have a CD, you can move ahead and use the wizard.

> **TIP**
> Another way to force a scan of legacy hardware is to open Device Manager, right-click the computer name at the top of the list, and choose Add Legacy Hardware.

3. Click Next, and the wizard asks whether you want it to search for the new hardware and figure out what it is (and try to find a driver for it), or whether you want to specify it yourself. Go for the search. If you're lucky, it will work, and you're home free. If a new device is found that doesn't require any user configuration, a help balloon appears onscreen near the system tray, supplying the details of what was located.

4. If nothing is found, the wizard asks whether you know what you're trying to install (hardware model). Assuming you do, click Next. You'll now see a list like the one in Figure 30.1.

5. Choose the correct category and click Next. Depending on the item, you'll next see a different dialog. For example, for a modem, it will offer the option of trying to detect and install it. For most other items, it will prompt you for the make and model.

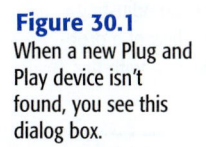

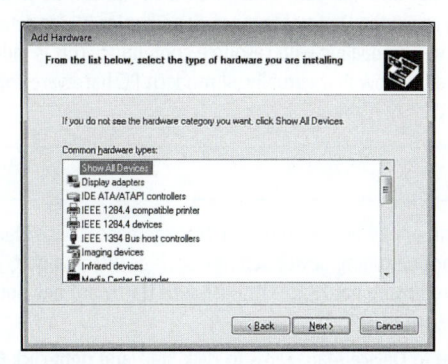

Figure 30.1
When a new Plug and Play device isn't found, you see this dialog box.

6. Choose the correct make and model. If you don't see a category that matches your hardware, click Back and then select Show All Devices. It will take a minute for the list to be populated. The box will then show every manufacturer and the devices each manufacturer sells. With some sleuthing, you may be able to find the hardware you are trying to install.

Be sure you choose the precise brand name and model number/name of the item you're installing. You might be prompted to insert your Windows Vista CD-ROM so that the appropriate driver file(s) can be loaded. If your hardware came with a driver disk, use the Have Disk button to directly install the driver from the manufacturer's driver disk or downloaded file.

Early in the wizard's steps, you have the option of specifying the hardware yourself and skipping the legacy scan. Choosing this option can save you time and, in some cases, is the surer path to installing new hardware. It also lets you physically install the hardware later should you want to. The wizard doesn't bother to authenticate the existence of the hardware; it simply installs the new driver.

> **NOTE**
>
> Vista 64-bit cannot use any legacy hardware as XP and 32-bit Vista can. All 64-bit drivers have to be digitally signed by Microsoft, or they will not be allowed to install.

If the device plugs into an external serial, parallel, or SCSI port, you might want to connect it, turn it on, and restart your system to install it. Some of these devices can't be installed via the Add Hardware Wizard if they're not present when the system is started.

> **TIP**
>
> In some cases, you are given the option of adjusting settings after the hardware is installed and possibly adjusting your hardware to match. (Some legacy cards have switches or software adjustments that can be made to them to control the I/O port, DMA address, and so forth.) You may be told which settings to use to avoid conflicts with other hardware in the system.
>
> If, for some reason, you don't want to use the settings that the wizard suggests, you can use your own settings and manually configure them. You can do so from the Add Hardware Wizard or via the Device Manager. See Chapter 25 for details on adjusting hardware resources and dealing with resource contention. This is much less of a problem than it used to be, now that virtually all modern PC hardware conforms with the Plug and Play spec.

> **TIP**
>
> You use the System applet or the Computer Management Device Manager Console, not Add Hardware, for fine-tuning device settings, such as IRQ and port, updating devices and drivers, and removing hardware. You use Add Hardware only for adding or troubleshooting hardware.
>
> A quick way to get to Device Manager is to click Start and right-click Computer. Select Properties and then click Device Manager in the Tasks pane.

Providing Drivers for Hardware Not in the List

When the hardware you're attempting to install isn't on the device list, the problem is one of the following:

- The hardware is newer than Windows Vista.
- The hardware is really old, and Microsoft decided not to include support for it.
- The hardware must be configured with a special setup program that is supplied with the hardware.

In these cases, you need to obtain the driver from the manufacturer's website. (or Microsoft's; check both) and have it at hand on floppy disk, CD-ROM, DVD, or stored on the hard disk (either locally or across an available network). If the manufacturer supplies a setup disk, forget my advice, and follow the manufacturer's instructions. However, if the manufacturer supplies a driver disk and no instructions, follow along with these steps:

1. Run the Add Hardware applet and click Next.
2. Select Install the Hardware That I Manually Select from a List and click Next.
3. Select the appropriate device category and click Next.
4. Click the Have Disk button. Enter the location of the driver. (You can enter any path, such as a directory on the hard disk or network path.) Typically, you insert a disk in your floppy or CD-ROM drive. If you downloaded the driver software from a website, locate it on your hard drive. In either case you can use the Browse button if you don't know the exact path or drive. If you do use the Browse option, look for a directory where an .INF file appears in the dialog box.
5. Assuming the wizard finds a suitable driver file, choose the correct hardware item from the resulting dialog box and follow the onscreen directions.

> **TIP**
> If you're not sure which ports and interrupts your other boards are using, you can use the Device Manager to locate available and used IRQs, ports, DMA, and so on.

If you've added some hardware and it doesn't work, **see** *"New Hardware Doesn't Work" in the "Troubleshooting" section at the end of this chapter.*

About Windows Vista Drivers
Although many Windows XP drivers will work in Vista, over time they will not be used. This is because older XP drivers were written in such a way that they ran in "kernel" mode rather than "user" mode. This means they were installed into the protected internals of the operating system where if the driver crashed, it could crash or damage the running operating system. Newer Vista drivers run in a part of system memory that keeps errant drivers away from the protected portions of the operating system and also lets you start and stop them (and restart them if necessary), the same way you can programs. If a Vista driver crashes (for example, a graphic driver), it just restarts. The screen goes black, and the driver restarts. In a few moments, you're back and running.

The user-mode driver model is called the User Mode Driver Framework, which is part of Microsoft's new driver model, Windows Driver Foundation. A user-mode driver would typically be used for devices that plug into a USB or FireWire bus, such as digital cameras, PDAs, and mass storage devices. This also allows for drivers that would typically require a system reboot (video card drivers, for example) to install or update without needing a reboot of the machine. For more about user-mode drivers, read http://en.wikipedia.org/wiki/User_Mode_Driver_Framework.

Not all Vista drivers are installed in user mode. Some drivers do need to be installed in the kernel. For extra protection, to prevent flaky or bogus drivers being installed into Vista, Microsoft is cracking down, but only for x64-based Vista (that is, the 64-bit versions). Kernel-mode drivers on x64-bit versions of Windows Vista must be digitally signed, which means they have to be tested and given the seal of approval by Microsoft. Even Administrators cannot install unsigned kernel-mode drivers. User-mode drivers can still be installed without a digital signature, however.

REMOVING HARDWARE

Before unplugging a USB, FireWire, or PCMCIA (PC Card) device, tell Windows Vista to stop using it. This prevents data loss caused by unplugging the device before Vista has finished saving all your data. You can stop these devices by clicking the PC Card icon in the system tray. Unplug the device or card only after Windows informs you that it is safe to do so.

For the most part, other hardware can be removed simply by shutting your computer off, unplugging it, and removing the unwanted hardware. When Windows restarts, it will recognize that the device is missing and will carry on without problems. As a shortcut when you don't want to power down completely, you can hibernate the computer and remove the item. Sometimes, this can prevent the computer from resuming properly though, so be cautious and save your work before you try this approach. Test it, and if it works, you can disconnect this item during hibernation in the future, knowing that Vista detects it resuming.

If you do want to completely delete the driver for an unneeded device, use the Device Manager. Double-click the device whose driver you want to remove. This opens its properties sheet. Click Uninstall Driver. Delete the drivers *before* uninstalling the hardware; otherwise, the device won't appear in the Device Manager's list.

→ For details about the Device Manager, *see* "Device Manager," **p. 825**.

> **TIP**
>
> If a USB controller doesn't install properly, especially if the controller doesn't show up in the Device Manager, the problem might be in your system BIOS. Most BIOSes have a setting that can enable or disable the USB ports. Shut down and restart. Do whatever your computer requires for you to check the BIOS settings during system startup (usually pressing the Del or Esc keys on the initial boot screen). Then, enter the BIOS setup and enable USB support.
>
> When that is done, if the USB controller still doesn't appear in the Device Manager, it's possible that the computer's BIOS might be outdated. Check with the computer's or motherboard's manufacturer for a possible update to support USB under Windows Vista.

> **TIP**
>
> If you decide to change the resources for a device using the Resource tab that appears when you view a device's properties in Device Manager, be cautious. Manually setting a device's resource assignment can result in conflicts with other installed devices, and doing so imposes restrictions on the Plug and Play system's capability to dynamically allocate resources in the future. See Chapter 28, "Troubleshooting and Repairing Problems," for more details about resource conflicts and troubleshooting.

INSTALLING AND USING MULTIPLE MONITORS

Chapter 26 discussed briefly the procedure for setting up multiple monitors. In this section, we explain a few of the more convoluted details and issues that can occur when installing additional monitors.

As you know, Windows Vista supports multiple monitors, a great feature first developed for Windows 98. You can run up to ten monitors with Windows Vista, but most commonly, you will probably run just two or three. By using multiple monitors, you can place a large amount of information on your screens at once. Use one screen for working on video editing, web design, or graphics and the other for toolbars. Leave a web or email display on at all times while you use the other monitor for current tasks. Display huge spreadsheets across both screens.

The following are some rules and tips to know about using multiple monitors:

- Some laptops support attaching an external monitor and can display different views on the internal LCD screen and on the external monitor. This feature is called DualView, and if your laptop supports it, your user's manual will show you how to enable the feature. You can ignore this section's instructions on installing a device adapter and just follow the instructions for setting the Display properties to use the second monitor.

- Because most computers don't have more than one or two PCI slots open, if you want to max out your video system, look into one of the multimonitor video cards available from Matrox, ATI, and various other vendors. In a single slot, you can drive two or four monitors with these cards. With only two slots, you can drive four to eight monitors. Multimonitor video cards are available for either AGP or PCI slots.

- The latest video interface kid on the block, dubbed PCI Express (PCIe) will be at the center of PC graphics for the foreseeable future. Even the previous video champ, AGP, is on its way out. With millions and millions of AGP systems out there, and new AGP cards being introduced all the time, it's hard to believe AGP is out of date, but it is. PCIe offers double the bandwidth of AGP 8x. PCI Express X16 slots have peak bandwidth levels of 4.0 GB/s (up to 8.0 GB/s bidirectional), compared to 2.1 GB/s of AGP 8x. PCIe cards also available in multiple-monitor versions. Look for one (be sure your system can accept it) if the highest performance (such as gaming or video work) is your aim.

- Many multimonitor arrangements consist of two cards: either two PCIs or a mix of one PCI and one AGP.

- If you mix AGP and PCI, older BIOSes sometimes have a strange habit of forcing one or the other to become the "primary" display. This is the display that Windows first boots on and the one you use for logging on. You might be annoyed if your better monitor or better card isn't the primary display because most programs are initially displayed on the primary monitor when you launch them. Therefore, you might want to flash-upgrade your BIOS if the maker of your computer or motherboard indicates that such an upgrade will improve the multiple-monitor support for your computer by letting you choose which monitor or card you want to make the primary display.

- Upon connecting a second monitor, you should be prompted with a dialog box that asks you whether you want to use a mirror arrangement, or an Extended desktop arrangement. With some luck, this wizard will be all you need to fiddle with. If not and you're unhappy with your system's choice of the primary display, you can adjust it with Display properties after both displays are running.

If you aren't having luck assigning the primary display, and your secondary card is taking over the role of primary display, see "Can't Select the Primary Display" in the "Troubleshooting" section at the end of this chapter.

- If you have updated an older system to Vista, the operating system always needs a VGA device, which becomes the primary display. The BIOS detects the VGA device based on slot order, unless the BIOS offers an option for choosing which device is to be treated as the VGA device. Check your BIOS settings to see whether any special settings might affect multimonitor display, such as whether the AGP or PCI card will default to primary display, or the PCI slot order. Slot 1 is typically the slot nearest the power supply connector.

- The design of the card itself makes it capable of operating on multiple monitors with Windows Vista and not the driver. Don't expect any vendors to add multiple monitor support simply by implementing a driver update. Either the card can support multimonitoring, or it can't. Some cards are technically capable of doing so but are not stable enough to handle the capability at this time.

- Most better laptops these days support mirror mode and extended view mode. How well they do it depends on the video card and the amount of video RAM. Note that there is a key combo on most laptops that turns off or on the output to the external monitor. Typically, it is the FN key (lower-left corner of the keyboard) combined with another key such as F4 or F5. Look closely at the little icons on your laptop's keytops. You may have to press the combination a few times to get to the desired setup (such as both the laptop screen on and the external screen on, or just one screen on).

- On some older motherboards with onboard I/O such as sound, modem, and LAN, you may have difficulties with multiple monitor configurations, especially if the devices share an IRQ with a particular PCI slot. You might want to disable any onboard devices you're not using to free up resources that can be used for additional video cards.

- Just because a set of cards supports multimonitoring under a previous version of Windows, even Windows XP, doesn't mean it can under Windows Vista. Vista has stricter hardware requirements as part of its strategy to increase reliability.

> **TIP**
>
> Microsoft doesn't provide much specific information on which video cards/chipsets work in multimonitor mode, perhaps because BIOS and motherboard issues can affect the results different users will have with the same video cards. The RealTimeSoft website contains a searchable database of thousands of working combinations and links to other multiple monitor resources, including RealTimeSoft's own UltraMon multimonitor utility. Check it out at www.realtimesoft.com.

These steps detail one likely installation scenario for a secondary display adapter for use with a multiple monitor setup. It's possible that it will be much simpler for your system. I have included details step by step mostly for those who run Vista on older systems and add a second display card. With newer systems, such as laptop with dual-monitor video display chipsets, you simply plug in the external monitor and turn it on, and Windows detects it, walks you through a wizard, and you're done.

1. Boot up your system into Windows Vista, and plug in the second monitor. Or you can right-click a blank area of your desktop. From the resulting pop-up menu, select Properties.

2. Go to the Settings tab. Confirm that your primary display adapter is listed correctly. (That is, if you have an ATI Rage Pro, ATI Rage Pro should be listed under Display.) Your display adapter *should not* be listed as plain-old "VGA," or multimonitoring will not work. If this is the case, you need to find and install correct Windows Vista drivers or consult your display manufacturer's website.

3. After you've confirmed that you have drivers loaded for your display adapter and that you are in a compatible color depth, shut down and then power off your system.

4. Disconnect the power cable leading to the back of your system and remove the case cover. Confirm that you have an available PCI slot. Before inserting your secondary display adapter, disable its VGA mode, if possible, by adjusting a jumper block or DIP switch on the card. Newer cards use the software driver or BIOS settings to enable or disable VGA mode.

If you have problems setting up your monitor, **see** *"Can't Select the Primary Display" in the "Troubleshooting" section at the end of this chapter.*

5. Insert your secondary display adapter, secure it properly with a screw, re-assemble your system, and reconnect the power. Next, connect a second monitor to the secondary display adapter.

6. Turn on both the monitors and power up the system. Allow the system to boot into Windows Vista.

7. After you log in, Windows Vista detects your new display adapter and may bring up the Add New Hardware Wizard. Confirm that it detects the correct display adapter and, when prompted, tell Windows Vista to search for a suitable driver. Then click Next.

8. Windows Vista then finds information on the display adapter. When you are prompted, insert your Windows Vista installation CD, or the driver disk that came with your adapter, and click OK.

9. Windows Vista then copies files. When the process is completed, click Finish. Windows Vista then also detects your secondary monitor (if it is a PnP monitor). When you are prompted, click Finish again.

> **NOTE**
> All of this detection may occur without intervention on your part, and a balloon may appear on the taskbar announcing that your new hardware is ready to be used.

10. After all appropriate drivers are installed, and your secondary monitor is connected and turned on, a wizard should pop up asking how you want to use the newly connected monitor: either as a mirror (repeating what is on the primary monitor) or for an extended desktop area. Answer accordingly. If you don't see the wizard, right-click a blank portion of your desktop and select Personalize. Then choose Display Settings. You will notice that two Monitor icons now appear in the center window of the display applet representing your two monitors (look ahead to Figure 30.2). Left-click the Monitor icon labeled 2, and it becomes highlighted in blue.

11. Under the displays, your secondary adapter should be displayed. In the lower-left corner below the Colors section, check the Extend My Windows Desktop into This Monitor box.

12. If Vista gives you a warning concerning compatibility, click Yes.

13. While the Monitor icon labeled 2 is highlighted, adjust the color depth and resolution for the new monitor.

14. You might want to change the way your monitors are positioned by left-clicking and dragging the Monitor icons. (Note that the displays must touch along one edge.) When you find a desirable position, just release the mouse button, and the Monitor icon is aligned adjacent to the first Monitor icon. Also note that wherever the two displays meet is the location your mouse will be able to pass from one display to the next, so a horizontal alignment is preferred for a standard desktop monitor arrangement (see Figure 30.2).

15. Click OK. Windows XP used to require a restart, but Vista does not. In a few seconds (could be almost 30 seconds), the video system resets and multimonitoring should be functional. You should have an extended desktop displayed on your second monitor. You also should be able to move your mouse into this extended desktop.

> **NOTE**
> You can set up Windows Vista with more than one secondary display adapter, up to a maximum of nine additional displays. To do so, just select another supported secondary display adapter with VGA disabled and repeat the preceding steps with another monitor attached to the additional secondary adapter.

Figure 30.2
A system running dual monitors. The relative size of monitors 1 and 2 reflects the resolution. (Monitor 1 has a higher resolution than monitor 2.)

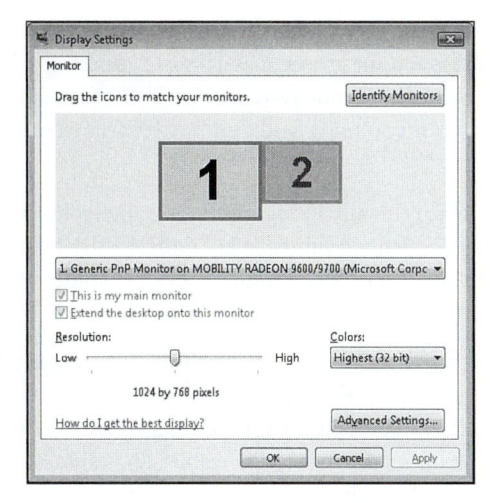

After you finish these steps, you can drag items across your screen onto alternate monitors. Better yet, you can resize a window to stretch it across more than one monitor. Things get a little weird at the gap, though. You have to get used to the idea of the mouse cursor jumping from one screen into the next, too.

> **TIP**
> If you're not sure which monitor is which, click the Identify Monitors button as shown in Figure 30.2, to display a large number across each monitor for a few seconds.

If you're having trouble getting your multimonitor setup to work, **see** *"Can't Select the Primary Display" in the "Troubleshooting" section at the end of this chapter.*

> **TIP**
> If you don't have enough open slots to install the extra adapter(s) needed for multiple monitors, look into single "multiheaded" video adapter cards that support two or four monitors.

INSTALLING A UPS

Although Windows Vista contains a backup utility that can be used to protect your data, and you may use a network drive that's backed up every night for your data, or a mirror drive, blackouts and power outages (and the data loss they cause) can happen anywhere. So in addition to regular backups, in mission-critical settings, you should also be concerned about keeping power going to your PC during its normal operation.

→ Managing backups is discussed in Chapter 20, "Creating a Windows Network," in the section "Installing and Configuring Backup Software, " **p. 656** and in Chapter 34, "Protecting Your Data from Loss and Theft," in the section "The Backup and Restore Center" **p. 1150**. "Backing Up the Registry" is covered in Chapter 31, **p. 1037**.

A battery backup unit (also called a *UPS*, which is short for *Uninterruptible Power Supply*) can provide battery power to your system for as much as 10 to 15 minutes, which is long enough for you to save your data and shut down your system. The UPS plugs into the wall (and can act as a surge suppressor), and your computer and monitor plug in to outlets on the rear of the UPS.

Electronic circuitry in the UPS continually monitors the AC line voltages, and should the voltage rise above or dip below predefined limits or fail entirely, the UPS takes over, powering the computer with its built-in battery and cutting off the computer from the AC wall outlet.

As you might imagine, preventing data loss requires the system's response time to be very fast. As soon as the AC power gets flaky, the UPS has to take over within a few milliseconds, at most. Many (but not all) UPS models feature a serial (COM) or USB cable, which attaches to the appropriate port on your system. The cable sends signals to your computer to inform it when the battery backup has taken over and to start the shutdown process; some units may also broadcast a warning message over the network to other computers. UPS units with this feature are often called *intelligent UPS* units.

> **TIP**
>
> If the UPS you purchase (or already own) doesn't come with Windows Vista-specific drivers for the shutdown and warning features, contact the vendor of the UPS for a software update.

Windows 2000 and XP had a function called the Windows 2000 UPS Services. This was a service that monitored a serial port for a warning signal from a UPS. If the UPS signaled that a power irregularity had occurred and power was about to go down, an event or series of events could be triggered. Typical events were such things as running a program or sending out an alert to all users or admins of a server about the impending doom. The message could alert users to save their work and power down the computers, for example.

Well, this service has been removed in Windows Vista. What we have now is effectively what laptop computers have—a power profile that includes battery settings. It's not different—it just works on a desktop PC. You can read about laptop power profiles in Chapter 38, "Hitting the Road," but I tell you a little about how to drill down into the power management settings here. Then later in this chapter ("Choosing a UPS" and "Installing a UPS"), you can find some tips to consider when purchasing and setting up a UPS.

If your UPS doesn't have provisions for automatic shutdown, its alarm will notify you when the power has failed. Shut down the computer yourself after saving any open files, grab a flashlight, and relax until the power comes back on.

Ideally, all your workstations assigned to serious tasks (what work isn't serious?) should have UPS protection of some sort. Although it's true that well-designed programs such as Microsoft Office have auto-backup options that help to restore files in progress if the power goes out, they are not always reliable. Crashes and weird performance of applications and operating systems are enough to worry about, without adding power loss on top. And if the power fails during a disk write, you might have a rude awakening because the hard disk's file system could be corrupted, which is far worse than having a lost file or two. Luckily, with NTFS and Previous Versions (see the section "Recovering Previous Versions of a File" in Chapter 34) and other Vista hard disk features, this is less of a specter than it used to be, but still....

My advice is that you guard against the ravages of power outages, power spikes, and line noise, at all reasonable costs. With the ever-increasing power and plummeting cost of notebook computers, one of the most economically sensible solutions is to purchase notebook computers instead of desktop computers, especially for users who change locations frequently. They take up little space, are easier to configure because the hardware complement cannot be easily altered, and have UPSes built in. When the power fails, the battery takes over.

> **TIP**
>
> When you're using laptops, be sure your batteries are still working, though. With time, they can lose their capacity to hold a charge. You should cycle them once in a while to check out how long they will run. If necessary, replace them. Also, you should set up the power options on a laptop to save to disk (hibernate) in case of impending power loss. You'll typically want to set hibernation to kick in when 5 to 10% of battery power is remaining, to ensure that the hard disk can start up (if sleeping) and write out the system state onto disk.

If you are using Windows Vista systems as servers, you'll certainly want UPS support on those, as discussed in the networking section of this book. In place of the Windows 2000 UPS Services as mentioned previously, today's USB-based UPS systems often come with proprietary programs that sit on top of the capable innards of the Vista event monitor and can work all kinds of magic, signaling users, broadcasting messages about, and so on, as the UPS battery begins to drain. Users can be warned to save their work and shut down (assuming they are running on a power source that is also functional, of course).

In addition to protecting your hardware investment from the ravages of lightning storms and line spikes, a UPS has the added advantage of alerting a remote administrator of impending server or workstation shutdowns so that appropriate measures can be taken.

Choosing a UPS

Before shelling out your hard-earned dough for UPS systems, check to see which ones are supported by Windows Vista. Consult the Hardware Compatibility List on the Microsoft site. Also, consider this checklist of questions:

- Do you want to purchase a separate UPS for every workstation or one larger UPS that can power a number of computers from a single location?
- Which kind of UPS do you need? There are three levels of UPS: Standby, line interactive, and online. *Standby* is the cheapest approach. The power to the computer comes off the AC line just as it normally does, but if the power drops or sags, the batteries

take over. There is typically a surge protector filter in the circuit to protect your computer. *Line interactive* UPS units additionally can handle temporary voltage sags without sapping the batteries, using clever electronics to stabilize the voltage. This helps keep your batteries topped up and ready in case of a major outage. *Online* UPS systems constantly convert AC to DC, filter and clean up the signal, and then convert it back to AC. The result is super clean power without spikes or sags. Batteries take over, of course, immediately in all three types, if there is a power loss.

- What UPS capacity do you need for each computer? The answer depends on the power draw of the computer box, the size of the monitor, and whether you want peripherals to work on battery, too. To fully protect your network, you should also install a UPS on network devices such as routers, hubs, bridges, modems, telephones, printers, and any other network equipment. Check the real-world specs for the UPS. The capacity is also determined by how long you want the UPS to operate after a complete power outage. If you just want enough time for you or another user to save work, a relatively small UPS will do. If you want to get through a day's work doing stock trades, you'll need a hefty unit. UPS units are rated in VA and watts. You should either measure your equipment's actual power draw or select a UPS with a wattage rating that significantly exceeds the wattage rating on your equipment. You'll also want to know how long the UPSes can run at the wattage your system will draw from it. Carefully read the vendor's battery life specifications and consider the typical length of the power outages in your area. Also compare warranties on units. You will have to replace the batteries in a couple of years. How expensive is that going to be? Are the batteries user replaceable?

- Get a unit with an alarm on it and one that is smart enough to interact with the PC and network to do something useful, such as send out alerts.

> **TIP**
> Network hardware and modems should be powered by the UPS, but printers should not be. Laser printers, in particular, have such high power requirements that your actual runtime for a given UPS unit will be just a fraction of what it would be if the laser printer were left off the UPS circuit. Because systems can store print jobs as temporary files until a printer is available to take them, there's no need to waste precious battery power to keep any type of printer running through a blackout.

- What software support do you want? Do you need to keep a log of UPS activity during the day for later analysis? What about utilities that test the UPS on a regular basis to ensure it's working?

Installing and Configuring a UPS

If you are going to use a UPS that doesn't support signaling to the computer via a data cable, you don't have to worry about the following settings because they won't make any difference. You simply plug your PC into the UPS and then plug the UPS into the wall outlet. You do your work at the computer. One day you notice that all lights in the room go off, but the computer stays on. That's your moment of grace. Save your work and shut down or hibernate the PC.

If your UPS is smarter (and it should be), you simply install it according the manufacturer's instructions. Typically, you connect the UPS to the power source, the computer to the UPS, and the USB between the UPS and the computer. After successful installation, you'll have a battery icon in your system tray near the clock, just like on a laptop.

CAUTION

If per chance your UPS is a serial-cable unit, be aware that normal serial cables do not cut the mustard for connecting a UPS to a Windows Vista machine. UPS serial cables, even between models from the same manufacturer, use different pin assignments. You're best off using the cable supplied by the maker of the UPS.

Now all you have to do is tell you system what to do during various cases of battery failure. Your system will constantly monitor the condition of the battery, just as a laptop does. So, if the AC power fails, presumably the UPS switches on, and your PC keeps running. Then, the power profile you are using comes into play. Here's how to fine-tune your profile:

1. Go to Control Panel, System and Maintenance, Power Options.
2. Under Select a Power Plan, choose the power plan you want. Under that plan, click Change Plan Settings.
3. On the next dialog box, click Change Advanced Power Settings. You'll see the dialog box shown in Figure 30.3.

Figure 30.3
Here you can set the UPS and system behavior for cases of power outage.

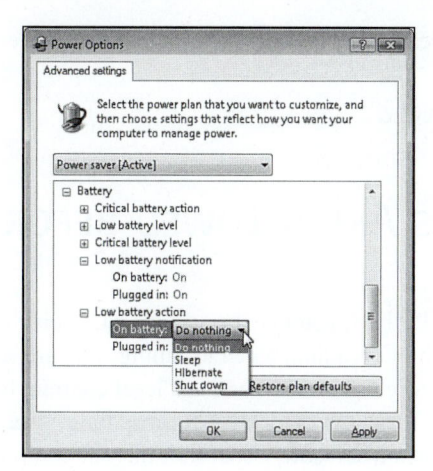

4. Click the + next to the Low Battery and Critical Battery actions and set what you want your PC to do when the power gets low. I suggest Hibernate, not Sleep, because Sleep will keep only your data in tact as long as battery power is available. Shut Down is the

next best option, but not very good, because if you are not present, unsaved work may be lost when the system shuts down.

5. Set the Low Battery notification to On for both Plugged In and On Battery. This way, if the battery level is getting low (perhaps due to a worn-out or defective battery), you'll be notified of it.

6. Set the Low Battery action for Plugged In, too, if you want to be extra cautious. You may want the computer to, for example, notify you that the power is low and then hibernate or shut down computer.

7. Set the Low Battery and Critical Battery levels after considering your computer's power needs and the capacity of your power supply. I like to play it safe and set critical to 10% and have the computer hibernate at that point. Then I can wait out the blackout, replace the UPS or battery if necessary, and start back up right where I left off. It takes a few minutes to hibernate sometimes, so you want to make sure you have enough energy in your battery to keep everything working during the wind-down.

TESTING YOUR UPS CONFIGURATION

Testing your UPS configuration from time to time is wise, to make sure you aren't let down when a real emergency occurs. Follow these steps to do so:

1. Close any open documents or programs.
2. Simulate a power failure by disconnecting the power to the UPS device. Check to see that, after disconnecting the power to the UPS device, the computer and peripherals connected to the UPS device continue operating and that a warning message appears on the screen.
3. Wait until the UPS battery reaches a low level, at which point a system shutdown should occur.
4. Restore power to the UPS device.

HOW MANY UPGRADES ARE ALLOWED BEFORE EULA AND SPP BARF?

Who is EULA, and why would SPP barf, you may be asking? EULA is the big agreement that every body clicks OK on with out reading, when installing software such as Microsoft Vista. It's short for End-User License Agreement, and is a legal contract between you and the manufacturer. When you sign (or click) the EULA for installing Vista, and when your copy of Vista is activated online with Microsoft, a snapshot of your computer system is taken (no personal data is recorded, they claim) and this is sent to Microsoft to identify your system, matching it with the serial number of the software.

Code internal to Vista that you never see unless there is trouble, called SPP (Software Protection Platform), checks your system for authenticity of Microsoft software and alerts

Microsoft if it finds inauthentic (pirated) software in your box. The purpose of SPP is to help Microsoft crack down on software privacy, and (they say) to help protect you by ensuring that you have an authentic Microsoft product. It can get upset and shut things down (barf) if it detects pirated software or other infractions of the EULA.

There was a lot of consternation among Windows Vista testers concerning whether one would have to purchase a new copy of Windows Vista each time a serious hardware upgrade was undertaken (such as when purchasing a new computer). If you see a new super fast computer and want to move Vista to it, can you legally? Will SPP prevent it? In XP, if you upgraded some magical combination of hardware parts totaling nine pieces, you could mysteriously run into a wall that would cause a warning from the WGA system (the predecessor to SPP, for Windows Genuine Advantage). Vista's SPP *was* going to work the same way, and be even stricter. For a while before Vista was released, it looked like you'd be given the option of upgrading to a completely new computer only once. After that, you had to buy a new copy of Vista. But all that was changed at the last minute before Vista was released. The original Vista EULA read

> "The first user of the software may reassign the license to another device one time. If you reassign the license, that other device becomes the 'licensed device'."

After great hue and cry, Microsoft's Vista EULA now reads:

> "You may uninstall the software and install it on another device for your use. You may not do so to share this license between devices."

And finally, here's a paragraph from product manager Nick White at Microsoft:

> "Our intention behind the original terms was genuinely geared toward combating piracy; however, it's become clear to us that those original terms were perceived as adversely affecting an important group of customers: PC and hardware enthusiasts. You who comprise the enthusiast market are vital to us for several reasons, not least of all because of the support you've provided us throughout the development of Windows Vista. We respect the time and expense you go to in customizing, building and rebuilding your hardware and we heard you that the previous terms were seen as an impediment to that — it's for that reason we've made this change. I hope that this change provides the flexibility you need, and gives you more reason to be excited about the upcoming retail release of our new operating system."

The upshot of all the hubbub is exactly this:

- If you bought a PC with Windows Vista already installed on it, you have fewer rights of reinstallation. You are not supposed to move your Windows over to another machine, and it would be difficult to do so, because you typically don't have the install DVD anyway.
- Retail copies of Windows cost much more than OEM copies do, for a reason. You can move them around between computers as you upgrade to better machines. If you bought a full retail version, you can put it on another computer and reactivate the new

one. Keep in mind, however, that this is legal, *only if* you uninstall it from the previous computer. You are supposed to format the system hard disk in the old computer. Microsoft should give you an uninstall utility so you don't have to wipe the hard disk, but they don't. Personally, I think this is because they don't really expect the average small business or home user to do this. Microsoft is simply trying to prevent a PC clone manufacturer from duplicating one copy of Windows on hundreds or thousands of PCs.

Upgrading Hardware in the Same Box and Complying with EULA

As this chapter is about hardware upgrading rather than complete computer replacement, the question raised is this: How do the EULA and SPP rules apply to upgrades? How much hardware can you upgrade without causing SPP to issue a warning, or worse, deactivate your copy of Vista? (SPP is better known to users as Windows Genuine Advantage, or WGA.)

In the original version of Windows Vista, SPP worked this way: The hardware in your system is noted when you activate Windows, as previously mentioned, and if you change too many items (notably your motherboard and hard disk drive), your system functionality is slowly reduced. Over time, portions of the operating system will be crippled and you'll be running in Reduced Functionality Mode (RFM). At first, there will only be subtle events, such as updates or Aero not working, but eventually the desktop goes black, Windows Explorer won't work, and all you can do is browse the Internet.

What can trigger the need to reactivate Windows? As intended, each hardware component is given a relative weight, and from that WGA determines whether your copy of Vista needs reactivation. The weight and the number of changes is apparently a guarded secret. If you upgrade too much at once, WGA will determine that your PC is new, and things can get messy. This triggers WGA to think you're transferring your copy of Vista to another computer and that you have to decommission the old one.

The actual algorithm that Microsoft uses is not disclosed, but we do know the weighting of components is as follows, from highest to lowest:

1. Motherboard (and CPU)
2. Hard drive
3. Network interface card (NIC)
4. Graphics card
5. RAM

If you just add a new hard disk or add new RAM, there is no issue. If you create an image of your Vista installation on another hard disk, swap that hard disk into the system and boot from it, or if you replace all your RAM and reboot, WGA will be triggered and will check to see whether you need to reactivate Vista.

In theory, the chances that you'll get stung by any of this are not great. It was widely expected that the only users who'd need to worry about reactivation would be users who'd buy a preinstalled system, image the hard disk or try to move the hard disk to a newer, faster computer, or perform a motherboard upgrade using a preinstalled copy of Vista.

Unfortunately, in practice users have been forced to reactivate after relatively modest hardware changes. In one example, a user who changed from a DirectX 9- to a DirectX 10-compatible graphics card had to reactivate his Vista installation. But wait, it gets worse: Another user had to reactivate Vista after upgrading to a newer version of the Intel Matrix Storage driver for his motherboard. Essentially, WGA mistook a driver upgrade for a significant hardware upgrade. Users who missed the three-day reactivation window (it's easy to do) found themselves in the limbo of RFM, needing to make a phone call to reactivate. Users who were hearing-impaired found that difficult to do.

Meanwhile, users of bogus Vista copies have used activation bypasses such as the Grace Timer or OEM BIOS exploits to run Vista without interference from WGA. Essentially, in the original version of Vista, Vista made it way too difficult for legitimate users to cope with systems that could not be activated normally or needed to be reactivated. Thankfully, Vista SP-1 brings those days to an end.

Windows Vista SP-1 Brings an End to Reduced Functionality Mode

Many users complained that Vista's implementation of SPP made life miserable for legitimate users while doing little to discourage piracy. Microsoft heard the complaints from users and, in Vista SP-1, has substantially changed how WGA works. To quote Alex Kochis, senior project manager for WGA, here's how WGA works in Vista SP1 (see http://blogs.msdn.com/wga/archive/2008/02/21/taking-the-next-step-with-windows-vista-sp1.aspx):

> "Reduced Functionality Mode" (RFM) has been removed from the product and replaced with a notifications-based experience. The purpose of the notifications-based experience is to differentiate between a genuine and activated copy of Windows Vista and one that is not, and do so in a way that maintains system functionality such as logon, access to the familiar desktop, etc. This new experience means that systems that are not activated during their grace periods (initial activations as well as those due to hardware changes) or that fail our validation may have this experience.
>
> After the activation grace period has been exceeded the next logon will present the user with a message that directs the customer to activate that copy of Windows. That dialog includes a fifteen-second delay before it can be dismissed. If a customer chooses to activate that copy of Windows they will be shown a number of ways to accomplish that. If they want to skip activation at that time, they can wait for the fifteen seconds and choose "Activate Later" and they will be logged into their desktop.
>
> When the desktop is loaded, the background wallpaper color will be set to black. This setting will be confirmed and reset every hour, meaning that a user can change the wallpaper to a favorite image, but each hour after being logged in, the system will reset the desktop background to black. When that happens, a system tray balloon notification will advise the customer to activate their copy of Windows.
>
> Again, if the user clicks the Activate message, they will be presented with a number of ways to activate their copy of Windows.

In other words, an unactivated copy of Windows Vista (or a copy that needs to be reactivated because of hardware changes) will continue to work more or less normally, with a few periodic nags to remind you to activate it (or to buy a legal copy). Users who cannot activate automatically will no longer be faced with an essentially useless system until they can activate by phone or otherwise.

Along with the end of the "kill switch" (as RFM was affectionately referred to by many unhappy Windows Vista users), Vista SP-1 also disables two common methods currently used to bypass activation: the so-called OEM BIOS and Grace Timer exploits. An update for both Vista and Vista SP-1 checks for these and similar exploits and provides users with help in removing them. The end result of these changes is that Vista SP-1 makes life easier for legitimate users and encourages pirates to lower their flags and get legitimate.

TROUBLESHOOTING

CAN'T SELECT THE PRIMARY DISPLAY

I can't get my multimonitor system to choose the primary display properly.

As discussed in the section "Installing and Using Multiple Monitors" (this chapter), it can be tricky to force Windows Vista to use a particular video display card as the secondary display. It usually defaults to one card and grays out Primary on the other one. If a display card isn't disabled from running in VGA mode, the computer runs the card's Power-On Self Test (POST). When that happens, Windows Vista assigns it primary display status; if the other card's VGA mode can't be disabled, you cannot use the secondary card. Most users will want to keep their first video card as the primary display, so they need to know how to prevent the POST from happening.

Generally, dual-display works best and easiest with a multihead graphics card, available in PCIe as well as the older AGP and PCI designs. However, many setups use a mix of one AGP and one PCI. This doesn't guarantee that the faster AGP video card will wind up being your primary display, though. You may need to set the system BIOS option for default video to PCI to enable an AGP+PCI dual display to work properly.

If your video card has a jumper block or switch that can be used to disable VGA mode, this option will make it easier to use the card as a secondary card because only the primary card needs VGA mode. VGA mode is used for the system's power-on self-test (POST) and to display startup options before the Windows GUI is initialized.

Many desktop systems with onboard video automatically disable the onboard video when you install a PCI or AGP video card, making it necessary to install two video cards (or a multimonitor video card) if you want multiple monitor support.

Generally, you can't tell whether a secondary card will work until after you boot Windows Vista with the secondary card in place, the system detects it and installs the drivers, and the system tries to initialize the card. If the card is initialized successfully, you should see the

Windows desktop on both screens. If the secondary monitor's screen stays black, check the Device Manager listing for the video card. If the card is listed with a yellow exclamation mark, it's not working properly. A Code 10 error on the card's properties sheet's General tab indicates the card was unable to start. Restart the system, change the default display setting in the BIOS, and retry it. If necessary, try a different slot for the card.

Something else to try is to open Desktop, Personalize, Display Properties and right click the monitor.

ALTERED BIOS SETTINGS PREVENT COMPUTER FROM BOOTING

I've altered my BIOS settings, and now the computer won't start.

Today's computer BIOSes have *so* many arcane settings that it's possible to alter one that will prevent proper booting. Before you mess with the advanced CMOS settings (not just the simple things such as time, date, boot order, power settings, ports, and so on), read the manual that came with the computer or motherboard. If you decide to change something, write down the old value before doing so. When in doubt, don't alter advanced CMOS settings that affect how the chipset works, whether and where the BIOS and video shadowing is done, and so on. The default settings are designed by the motherboard maker to work under most situations and operating systems. Because Windows is the most popular operating system, you can bet it was already tested and configured for Windows 9x, NT, 2000, or Vista (unless you have a very old motherboard).

That said, what do you do if you've changed something in the CMOS and now the computer won't boot? You can try the computer's or motherboard's manual or website for information about settings for Windows Vista. If you find nothing, you should wind back the settings to the factory defaults.

> **TIP**
> Most CMOS setups have a Set to Default or similar command you can issue. This should get you out of most any jam.

The Set to Default option might also be a good course to take if you make CMOS settings that prevent your computer from booting and you can't remember how to undo the changes. The default settings are usually conservative enough to work under most circumstances. The BIOS in some systems may also have a Fail-Safe Defaults option that sets your BIOS to its most conservative settings.

If what you've done has changed the hard disk Type, or if you manually entered the number of sectors, tracks, platters, and so on, and now it won't boot, use the Auto Detect Hard Disk BIOS setting to discover and enter those numbers automatically. (This is known as *drive autotyping.*)

New Hardware Doesn't Work

I've added some hardware, but it doesn't work.

Try these steps, in this order:

1. Try the troubleshooters included in the Help system, assuming the hardware fits into one of the neatly packaged categories. Open them through the Help and Support page as described previously.
2. Try rebooting Windows Vista.
3. Use the Computer Management Console and the Device Manager to check resources assigned to the hardware to be sure that it's not conflicting. Check the hardware's manual to determine whether you should be setting some DIP switches or jumpers on it to avoid conflicts if the device isn't a Plug and Play device.
4. Open the Device Manager, locate the device's entry, and press the Delete key to delete the entry. Then, power down, remove the device, and restart Windows.
5. Power down again, add the hardware back again (running the Add Hardware applet if the hardware isn't detected at bootup), and configure as necessary.
6. Check Google; search to see whether anyone else has written about the problem and its solution.
7. Check the manufacturer's website. If it has a "Knowledge Base" feature, search that.
8. If you purchased the hardware from a local store, contact it for assistance.
9. Contact the manufacturer via email or phone.

Tips from the Windows Pros: Upgrading and Optimizing Your Computer

Following are several tips I've learned over the years that can help save you hours of headaches.

Keep Your Eye on the Hardware Compatibility List

If you've been accustomed to thumbing your nose at Microsoft's Hardware Compatibility List (HCL) because you've been using Windows 9x, it's time to reform your behavior. In a pinch, Windows 9x could use older Windows drivers and could even load MS-DOS device drivers to make older hardware work correctly. Windows Vista, like other NT-based versions of Windows, has done away with AUTOEXEC.BAT and CONFIG.SYS, so you can't use DOS-based drivers anymore. And, although Windows Vista can use some Windows 2000 and XP drivers in an emergency, you're much better off with drivers made especially for Windows Vista. You can view the online version of the HCL by setting your browser to https://winqual.microsoft.com/hcl/ (note that you must use IE6 or higher to view this website).

The HCL also offers links to let you download drivers from either Microsoft or the manufacturer's website.

NOTE
> Some "legacy" hardware technologies no longer supported include EISA buses, game ports, Roland MPU-401 MIDI interface, AMD K6/2+ Mobile Processors, Mobile Pentium II, and Mobile Pentium III SpeedStep. ISAPnP (ISA Plug and Play) is disabled by default. Startup Hardware Profiles also have been removed.

TIP
> Hardware failures, power failures, and human error can prevent Windows Vista from starting successfully. Recovery is easier if you know the configuration of each computer and its history and if you back up critical system files when making changes to your Windows Vista configuration.
>
> A good hedge against this problem is to create a technical reference library for all your hardware and software documentation. Your reference library should include the history of software changes and upgrades for each machine, as well as hardware settings such as those described here.

Sleuthing Out Conflicts

When you're hunting down potential IRQ, memory, and I/O conflicts, try using the Device Manager to help out. Yes, Computer Management, System Information, Hardware Resources, Conflicts Sharing will show you potential conflicts, so that's a good place to look, too. But let me share a trick with the Device Manager that isn't readily apparent.

Normally, a class of devices called Hidden Devices isn't shown. To show them, open the Device Manager (either via Control Panel, System, or from Computer Management). Then, on the View menu, click Show Hidden Devices. A checkmark next to Show Hidden Devices indicates that hidden devices are showing. Click it again to clear the checkmark. Hidden devices include non–Plug and Play devices (devices with earlier Windows 2000 device drivers) and devices that have been physically removed from the computer but have not had their drivers uninstalled.

Optimizing Your Computer for Windows Vista

Finally, here's my biggest tip....

Optimizing your computer for Windows Vista is actually quite easy. I'm very impressed with this operating system's capability to keep on chugging. It doesn't cough or die easily if you mind your manners.

- If you're buying new stuff for an upgrade, consider only hardware that's on the tested products list and the Microsoft catalog and marketplace.

  http://windowsmarketplace.com/

- When you're buying a new machine, get it with Windows Vista preinstalled and from a reputable maker with decent technical support, not just a reputable dealer. The dealer might not be able to solve complex technical problems. Brand-name manufacturers such as Dell, Compaq, Gateway, Lenovo (IBM), and so on have teams of engineers devoted to testing new operating systems and ironing out kinks in their hardware, with help from engineers at Microsoft.

If you love to upgrade and experiment, more power to you. I used to build PCs from scratch, even soldering them together from parts. Then again, you can also build your own car. (I used to just about do that myself, too.) Or you can buy it preassembled from some company in Detroit or Japan. It really isn't worth spending much time fiddling with PC hardware unless you are putting together systems for a specific purpose. With the amazingly low price of computers these days, don't waste your time. And don't cut corners in configuring a new machine. For an extra 50 bucks, you can get goodies such as a modem, network card, and faster video card thrown in. Do it up front and save the hassle down the road.

- Run Windows Update frequently or set it to run itself.
- Schedule hard disk defragmentation (see Chapter 27) and make sure you have a decent amount of free space on your drives, especially your boot drive. Remember that Vista's defragmenter requires at least 15% empty space on each drive you want to defragment.
- Get an extra external hard disk of equal size or larger than your computer's internal hard disk. Use an automated backup program, such as the File and Folder Backup built into Windows Vista, to automatically back up your important stuff on a frequent basis. (Mine runs every night.) Disks are cheap these days, and your time, contacts lists, emails, and documents are valuable!

CHAPTER 31

EDITING THE REGISTRY

In this chapter

What Is the Registry?   1038

How the Registry Is Organized   1039

Registry Contents   1041

New Registry Features in Windows Vista   1043

Backing Up and Restoring the Registry   1046

Using Regedit   1050

Other Registry Tools   1061

Registry Privileges and Policies   1063

Troubleshooting   1063

Tips from the Windows Pros: Deploying Registry Settings with REG Files   1066

What Is the Registry?

The Windows *Registry* is a database in which Windows and application programs store all manner of configuration settings, startup information, hardware settings, user preferences, file locations, license and registration information, last-viewed file lists, and so on. In addition, the Registry stores the associations between file types and the applications that use them. For example, the Registry holds the information that tells Windows to use Media Player when you click on an MPG movie file. In the early days of DOS and Windows, programs stored this kind of information in a random collection of hundreds of files scattered all over your hard disk. Thankfully, those days are only a dim memory.

> **TIP**
>
> If you're already familiar with the Registry, you might want to skip this part, but be sure to read the section "New Registry Features in Windows Vista," on page 1047.

Most of the time, you can get by without giving the Registry a second thought because almost every useful Registry entry is set from a Control Panel applet, an application's Preferences dialog box, or Windows Setup. From time to time, though, you might have to roll up your sleeves to find the location of an errant device driver, you might need to remove an unwanted startup program, or you might just be curious about what kind of information Microsoft Office keeps on file about you. This chapter tells you how to go on these kinds of missions.

Registry Tweaking—Two Different Views

If you are the curious, never-satisfied-with-the-status-quo type, you may be one of those Windows users who scours the Internet for ways to eke out every little bit of extra performance you can get from your computer. And you may be tempted to edit the Registry based on advice from any of several hundred websites devoted to the intricacies of Windows. Is it a good idea? Well….

One of the advantages of having two authors for this book is that you get two viewpoints. I (Brian) must confess that I am a card-carrying tweakophobe; I think Registry tweaking is minimally useful and often leads to confusion: I really don't like it when computers don't all look and act the same way. Besides, most of the Registry hacking "tips" you'll find on the Internet are useless. Some might have been correct for earlier versions of Windows but don't work on Vista, and most of the rest are just flat-out wrong. In any case, if my computer dies, I want to be able to grab another one, plug it in, and keep going without having to make any arcane adjustments. "Stock" is the way for me.

For my co-author, Bob, the Registry is a tweaker's paradise of undocumented adjustments and fascinating Windows trivia. When he gets a new computer, he spends days changing file locations, switching the functions of the keys on his keyboard, and generally adjusting his computer to be "just so." Of course, after all these changes, nobody else can figure out how to use it but him, but he's *likes* having the Caps Lock key where the Ctrl keys belongs and *vice versa*.

To each his own, I guess. Either way, if you find Registry tweaking tips on Internet websites, do be careful to confirm that they were intended to be used on Vista. And of course, be sure that before you make any changes, either do a Registry backup or take detailed notes on how to restore the original settings. Finally, if you do make a Registry change and you don't get the results you expected, or if you see no changes at all, I would strongly urge you to undo whatever change you made.

How the Registry Is Organized

The Registry leaves the plain-text files of `AUTOEXEC.BAT` and `WIN.INI` far, far behind. It is a specialized database organized a lot like the files and folders on a hard disk.

Just as a hard disk contains partitions, the Registry contains separate sections called *top-level keys*. In each section is a list of named entries called *keys* that correspond to the folders on a hard disk. And just as a file folder can contain files and more nested folders, a Registry key can contain *values*, which hold information such as numbers or text strings, and more nested keys. Even the way that file folders and keys are described is similar: A folder might be named `\Users\brian\chapter32`, and a Registry key might be named `\HKEY_CURRENT_USER\Software\Microsoft`.

Another similarity between Registry keys and file folders is that both can have access permissions set to prevent unauthorized users from examining or modifying them. Registry security has been given quite a bit more attention in Windows Vista than in any previous version of Windows. We discuss Registry access permissions later in this chapter.

Let's look at the Registry starting with its top-level keys. The two main "top-level" keys are as follows:

- `HKEY_LOCAL_MACHINE` contains all the hardware and machine-specific setup information for your computer. For example, it lists every installed device driver and Windows service. It also holds software setup information that is common to all users.

- `HKEY_USERS` contains a key for each user account created on the computer, including the accounts used only internally by Windows services. Under each user's key, Windows stores user-specific information, such as color preferences, sounds, the location of email files, and other application configuration information.

    The keys under `HKEY_USERS` are mostly named using long numeric strings that are the user account's Security Identifier (SID) number. Usually, not all accounts' keys are visible at the same time. Each account's key is loaded into the Registry when the user logs on and is unloaded a short time after the user logs out.

The Registry editor displays three other sections that look like they are separate top-level keys but that are actually just alternate views of information inside `HKEY_LOCAL_MACHINE` or `HKEY_USERS`:

- `HKEY_CURRENT_USER` is a shortcut, of sorts—it's an alternate view of the subsection of `HKEY_USERS` that corresponds to the currently logged-on user. That is, when *you* run the Registry editor, `HKEY_CURRENT_USER` shows *your* section of `HKEY_USERS`.

- `HKEY_CURRENT_CONFIG` is a shortcut to `HKEY_LOCAL_MACHINE\System\CurrentControlSet\Hardware Profiles\Current` and contains the hardware settings specific to the hardware profile chosen when Windows was started.

- HKEY_CLASSES_ROOT is a strange beast. This Registry section stores file associations, the information that Windows uses to link file types to applications, and a huge amount of setup information for Windows software components. It's actually a combined view of the contents of two other Registry sections: HKEY_LOCAL_MACHINE\Software\Classes, which holds settings that are made for all users, and HKEY_CURRENT_USER\Software\Classes, which holds personal settings made just by the current user. If the same value is defined in both HKEY_CURRENT_USER\... and HKEY_LOCAL_MACHINE, the HKEY_CURRENT_USER value is used.

These three "virtual" top-level keys are there for convenience—it's easier to look in HKEY_CURRENT_USER than to try to find your user entry under the ugly numbered keys inside HKEY_USERS. Figure 31.1 illustrates how these virtual keys are actually alternate views of the primary ones.

An additional top-level Registry key is not visible to the Registry editor. Windows uses it internally to hold the statistics gathered by Windows' performance-monitoring system.

All this might seem a little daunting, but remember that the purpose of the Registry is to organize setup information sensibly. Instead of having this information in many mysteriously named and randomly located files, it's all here, neatly filed away in the Registry.

Figure 31.1
The Registry editor displays two true top-level keys and three "virtual" top-level keys.

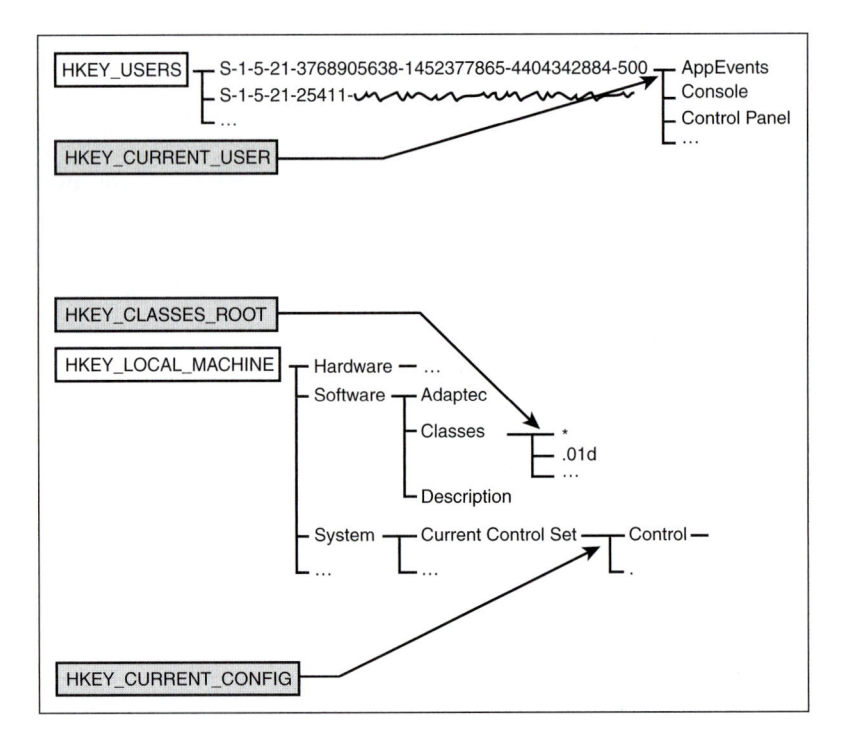

The Registry database itself is stored in several separate files, called *hives*. Most of the HKEY_LOCAL_MACHINE is stored in the folder \windows\system32\config, with its major sections stored in separate hive files: COMPONENTS, SAM, SECURITY, SOFTWARE, and SYSTEM. The exception is the `BCD00000000` section, which is stored in the file `\boot\BCD` on your computer's boot (active) partition.

Each user's subkey in `HKEY_USERS` is stored in a separate hive file. These are kept in each user's profile folder (usually under `\Users\`*username*) as a file named `NTUSER.DAT`; the exception is the `.Default User` key, which is in `\windows\system32\config\DEFAULT`. Finally, each user's list of keys that overlay `HKEY_CLASSES_ROOT` is stored in `\users\`*username*`\Local Settings\Application Data\Microsoft\Windows\UsrClass.dat`. This Registry hive also contains the user's `VirtualStore` key, which is described later in this section.

You generally can't examine, modify, or copy these hive files directly while Windows is running because Windows maintains exclusive control of them. Backup software uses special Windows program functions to get access to back them up or restore them. The exception is that the `NTUSER.DAT` files for users who are not currently logged on are not locked, so they can be copied and backed up as normal files.

Despite the fact that the information is stored in many different files, the Registry presents one collective view of the data.

Registry Contents

What's in the Registry, anyway? There's a lot to it; entire books have been written about it. Here, we give a quick overview of the Registry, to give you some idea of its organization and contents.

You just learned about the five main sections of the Registry. Let's go through them one by one now and cover some of each section's highlights.

HKEY_LOCAL_MACHINE

As you might expect, `HKEY_LOCAL_MACHINE` contains information specific to your computer—that is, all settings that aren't user specific. These include hardware settings and software information that is global for all users.

Table 31.1 describes the main keys in `HKEY_LOCAL_MACHINE`.

TABLE 31.1	Main Keys in HKEY_LOCAL_MACHINE
BCD00000000	Contains the Windows bootup configuration settings. This key is a view of the boot configuration data stored in the file `\boot\BCD`. This key is new in Windows Vista.
COMPONENTS	Contains configuration for .NET sofware components. This key is also new in Windows Vista.
HARDWARE	Contains information about the computer's hardware platform and Plug and Play devices, discovered anew each time the system is booted. No configurable settings are located here.

continues

Table 31.1	Continued
SAM and SECURITY	Contain the Windows Security Account Manager database and Group Policy settings. When viewed in the Registry editor, these keys appear to be empty because only Windows itself is allowed to read or edit the information.
SOFTWARE	Contains system-wide software settings for applications and Windows itself. This key contains many subkeys. The `Classes` subkey is special and is given its own virtual view as `HKEY_CLASSES_ROOT`. The other entries are generally named after software manufacturers. I'll describe some of the more interesting keys shortly.
SYSTEM	Contains a series of numbered `ControlSet` entries, each of which contains the settings for hardware and system services. One of them is chosen as the `CurrentControlSet` subkey. As you install or remove hardware, Windows rotates through the `ControlSet` entries, using one as the "current control set." This way, it can keep previous versions to use as a backup.

One particularly important section of `HKEY_LOCAL_MACHINE` is the key `HKEY_LOCAL_MACHINE\Software\Microsoft\Windows\CurrentVersion\Run`. This key lists programs that are started up every time any user logs on. In Windows Vista, it's much harder for viruses and other bad applications to set themselves up in this key. We talk more about this later.

If you're plagued by unwanted or buggy programs when you log in, **see** *"Tracking Down Errant Startup Programs" in the "Troubleshooting" section at the end of this chapter.*

HKEY_CURRENT_CONFIG

`HKEY_CURRENT_CONFIG` contains information that Windows uses to initialize itself during its bootup phase, and very little else. Despite its important-sounding name, you'll find virtually nothing of interest to humans in here.

HKEY_CLASSES_ROOT

`HKEY_CLASSES_ROOT` is a combined view of per-user and machine-wide settings, as discussed earlier. A large part of the `Classes` section is devoted to the associations the Explorer makes between file types (or filename extensions), such as `.doc`, and the programs that are used to open, display, or edit them. (However, just to make things confusing, this is *not* where Windows stores the Open With menu selections.)

The rest of `HKEY_CLASSES_ROOT` is the nitty-gritty linkage information that Windows uses to locate software components based on ActiveX Controls, OLE, and the COM+ interprocess communication system. These complex entries are best left completely alone.

HKEY_USERS

`HKEY_USERS` contains a subkey for each authorized user of the computer and an additional entry named `.DEFAULT`. The `.DEFAULT` section is seen as the content of `HKEY_CURRENT_USER` by services that are run under the SYSTEM account, which has no user profile loaded. (The RUNAS command with the /noprofile option can also run programs with no user profile).

The two per-user subkeys of HKEY_USERS have long numeric names. These names are the unique numeric identification numbers that Windows generates as a computer-friendly representation of the user's name. Windows uses these numbers to track users, whether local or domain-based. One of the subkeys is seen as HKEY_CURRENT_USER by all applications run under that user's logon, and the _classes subkey is merged with HKEY_LOCAL_MACHINES\Software\Classes; the combination is seen as HKEY_CLASSES_ROOT.

The subkeys are unloaded from the Registry shortly after logout and are no longer visible under HKEY_USERS. (The associated hive file is still present in the user's profile folder; it's just not attached to the Registry.) You can manually load a user's data back into the Registry for editing, if necessary, as discussed later in this chapter.

HKEY_CURRENT_USER

HKEY_CURRENT_USER contains settings, preferences, and other information specific to the currently logged-in user. This entire "section" is actually a subkey of HKEY_USERS, as discussed previously, but the HKEY_CURRENT_USER key is provided as an easy way to get to the information.

New Registry Features in Windows Vista

Windows Vista has introduced some new features to the Registry: virtualization and 64/32–bit reflection. This section gives you a brief tour. (These features are pretty gnarly and obscure, so on your first read, you might want to skip ahead to the section titled "Backing Up and Restoring the Registry.")

The main factor that distinguishes Windows Vista from its predecessors is its enhanced security achieved by limiting privileges to a bare minimum, except when absolutely necessary. In previous versions of Windows, for instance, by default, most users could modify any information in the HKEY_LOCAL_MACHINE section of the Registry—that is, the part responsible for configuring Windows itself and affecting all users. In Windows Vista, by default, the keys in HKEY_LOCAL_MACHINE can be altered only by Administrator users, and then only through a program run with elevated privileges after a User Account Control confirmation.

Although this should greatly help to control the spread of virus and spyware programs, it presents a problem for application software that in the past depended on storing shared information somewhere under HKEY_LOCAL_MACHINE. For instance, a game program might store its "highest score" information there so that the game can update this score when any user plays the game. Under Vista, unless the application's setup program knows to explicitly change its highest-score key's security settings so that any user can modify it, when the game attempts to change the highest score key, Windows will not permit it to. The game then either displays an error message or fails to update the score.

Registry Virtualization

Enter Registry virtualization, which technically is a part of User Account Control. When Registry virtualization is enabled, and Windows detects that an application has attempted to store information in HKEY_LOCAL_MACHINE and has failed because of a permissions failure, the application's data automatically and transparently is stored in a Registry key under HKEY_CURRENT_USER instead—that is, in the user's personal part of the Registry. As a result, applications that aren't aware of Vista's tighter restrictions on HKEY_LOCAL_MACHINE will run without a hitch, although their settings will be per-user instead of machinewide. For instance, the hypothetical game we discussed earlier would keep a highest-score value that's separate for each user. But at least it wouldn't crash.

As a quirk of the way Windows combines per-user and global information in HKEY_CLASSES_ROOT, the alternate, private location is HKEY_CLASSES_ROOT\VirtualStore\MACHINE. In other words, if an application attempts to write information to HKEY_LOCAL_MACHINE\Software*xxx**yyy*, it will actually be stored in HKEY_CLASSES_ROOT\VirtualStore\MACHINE\Software*xxx**yyy*. You need to know to check there when you're investigating problems with Registry settings in your system.

> *If you find that global settings or game scores don't appear the same for all users on your system,* **see** *"Configuration Changes Don't Appear for Other Users" in the "Troubleshooting" section at the end of this chapter.*

Virtualization doesn't occur under some circumstances. In those cases, the application simply is allowed to fail in its attempt to make changes to HKEY_LOCAL_MACHINE. These circumstances are listed here:

- If virtualization is disabled by your network administrator, using Group Policy on a Windows domain network.
- If the application is a 64-bit application; 64-bit applications and their installers must be designed to work correctly from the start.
- If the application program has a *manifest*, a file that describes advanced security settings. Almost all the applications that come with Windows—including Notepad; the command prompt interpreter, cmd.exe; and the Registry editor—have manifests, so almost all Windows utilities do not see virtualized settings.
- If a key is marked with a special flag that indicates that it is not to be redirected. HKEY_LOCAL_MACHINE\Software\Microsoft\Windows\CurrentVersion\Run is marked this way so that a virus that attempts to set itself up to run at logon via this key won't be capable of doing so. The command-line utility REG can modify the virtualization flag. Type **REG FLAGS /?** at the command-line prompt for more information.
- If Microsoft disables virtualization in a future service pack or version of Windows.

Virtualization is seen as a stopgap measure and will be unnecessary when most applications either store information in HKEY_CURRENT_USER or explicitly set less restrictive permissions on their keys in HKEY_LOCAL_MACHINE.

Registry Reflection

The 64-bit versions of Windows support running 32-bit Windows applications as well. This presents a problem because many Windows subcomponents are present in both 32- and 64-bit versions, and information about them (such as program filenames) is stored in the Registry under keys whose names were determined before Microsoft considered the need to distinguish between the two flavors. For a Registry value named `HKEY_CLASSES_ROOT\MyComponent\ServerFile` might be used to store the filename of a program component. The filename of the 32-bit version of the component is not the same as the filename of 64-bit version. But somehow this same Registry key has to yield the correct filename to both 64- and 32-bit applications.

To manage this, Windows stores information for 32-bit components in an alternate location and feeds the stored information to 32-bit applications when they ask for values from the original location. This is called *Registry reflection*.

These Registry sections are subject to reflection, by default:

```
HKEY_LOCAL_MACHINE\Software\Classes
HKEY_LOCAL_MACHINE\Software\COM3
HKEY_LOCAL_MACHINE\Software\Ole
HKEY_LOCAL_MACHINE\Software\EventSystem
HKEY_LOCAL_MACHINE\Software\RPC
```

Other keys can be reflected if they are designated as using Windows programming interfaces that are available to developers.

The information for 32-bit applications is actually stored under `HKEY_LOCAL_MACHINE\Software\WOW6432Node`. When a 32-bit application requests information from a reflected key using the original location, it is fed information from below `WOW6432Node`.

When working with the Registry on a 64-bit system, you need to know to look under `WOW6432Node` when looking for setup information for 32-bit components.

Alternatively, you can use the 32-bit version of `regedit`; this presents all information in the standard locations seen by 32-bit applications. When you run `regedit` from the command line, you get the 64-bit version. However, if you run `%systemroot%\syswow64\regedit.exe`, you get the 32-bit version and can edit the values seen by 32-bit applications.

> **NOTE**
>
> You must close the 64-bit version of the Registry editor before you can open the 32-bit version, and *vice versa*, unless you start the second instance of the Registry editor with the `-m` command-line argument.

For more information on reflection, see Microsoft Knowledge Base article #305097 at http://support.microsoft.com/kb/305097.

Backing Up and Restoring the Registry

Because the Registry is now the *one* place where all the Windows hardware and software settings are stored, it's also the one thing that Windows absolutely needs to run. You will hear dire warnings from Microsoft, other computer books, installation manuals, and now me: It's very important to back up the Registry before you make any significant or "experimental" changes. If you lose a critical entry or change one incorrectly (for example, one that holds the name of a driver file for your hard disk controller), Windows might not be capable of starting at all.

> If you have a Registry problem, before you attempt any drastic measures, **see** "Recovering from a Suspected Registry Problem" in the "Troubleshooting" section at the end of this chapter.

Make it a habit to back up the Registry every time you back up your hard disk. I can tell you from personal experience that without a Registry backup, something as common as a bad graphics card installation program can cost you a whole day trying to get your system to boot again. Windows has some built-in protection to help avoid this type of disaster, but you should still take your own precautions.

Backing Up the Registry

You can back up the Registry in any of four primary ways. In order of preference, these are backing up as part of a disk backup, using the Registry editor to save a key to a disk file, using a special-purpose Registry backup program, and using System Restore.

CAUTION

> The backup programs provided with Windows Vista do *not* provide a good means of backing up the Registry as insurance against accidents. Windows Backup can perform only full-volume backups, and it's helpful only if you're willing to wait for tens to hundreds of gigabytes to be copied. System Restore backs up only `HKEY_LOCAL_MACHINE`, not your own `HKEY_CURRENT_USER` data. It's okay to use only if you're modifying just `HKEY_LOCAL_MACHINE` settings.

I suggest that you use a third-party disk-backup solution to back up the Registry files every time you back up your hard disk. Before you install a piece of new hardware or a significant software package, do a full disk backup, including the Registry. Before you manually edit the Registry for other purposes, back up the Registry by any of the means I discuss in the next few sections.

Backing Up with Third-Party Disk-Backup Software

Third-party disk-backup software made for Windows Vista includes an option to back up the system portion of the Registry. Be sure to check this option whenever you are backing up your hard disk. Also, be sure to include all user profiles (everything under \User) so that personal Registry sections are saved.

Check your backup software's manual for instructions on saving Registry and system information when you back up. I suggest that you *always* include the Registry in your backups.

Backing Up with Third-Party Registry-Backup Software

Third-party programs are specifically designed to back up and restore the Registry and other critical Windows files. For example, SuperWin's WinRescue Vista program (www.superwin.com) not only can back up and restore the Registry, but also can defragment the Registry's files and work magic to revive a nonbootable Windows system. If you're a Registry hacker, it is worth buying such a Registry-backup tool.

These programs come with their own extensive instructions on backing up, restoring, repairing, and maintaining the Registry.

Backing Up with System Restore

If you will be changing only entries under HKEY_LOCAL_MACHINE, you can create a restore point to back up a copy of this part of the Registry. To create a restore point, follow these steps:

1. Click Start. Right-click Computer and select Properties.
2. Under Tasks, select System Protection. When the User Account Control dialog box appears, click Continue.
3. Be sure that the disk volume that contains Windows is checked, and click Create.

Then, edit the Registry as described later in this chapter.

Backing Up with Regedit

The Registry editor, called Regedit, has a mechanism to export a set of Registry keys and values to a text file. If you can't or won't use a more comprehensive backup system before you manually edit the Registry, at least use this editor to select and back up the key that contains all the subkeys and values you plan to modify.

That way, if it's necessary later, you can restore these exported files, recovering any changed or deleted keys and values. Remember, though, that Regedit cannot remove entries you added that were not in the Registry before the backup! So, if an entry you add causes problems, a Registry editor backup will not help you recover.

To back up a key and its subkeys and values, follow these steps:

1. To run Regedit, click Start, and type `regedit` in the Search box.
2. When Regedit appears under Programs in the search results, select it and press Enter.
3. Locate and select the key you plan to modify, or a key containing all the keys you plan to modify, in the left pane.
4. Select File, Export.

5. Choose a location and filename to use to store the Registry keys. I usually use the desktop for temporary files like this, so I'll see them and delete them later.

> **TIP**
>
> For backup purposes, I recommend *not* using the default extension .REG. This extension is associated with Registry entries in the Windows Explorer, and selecting a REG file in Explorer restores it to the Registry. This operation is far too serious to have happen with just a mouse click or two.

6. Select All Files from the Save As Type list, and enter a name (possibly with an extension other than .REG—for example, before.sav).
7. Click Save. The chosen key or keys are then saved as a text file.

> **TIP**
>
> You can use this technique to copy a set of keys and values from one section of the Registry to another. First, export the desired key and values to a file. Edit the file with Notepad, and use the Edit/Replace menu to change all of the key names to the desired new location. Then import the file back into the Registry. I have used this method to copy a group of Registry entries under HKEY_CURRENT_USER to HKEY_USERS\.Default, for example, so that all newly created user accounts will have the desired setting.

> **TIP**
>
> You can also use exported REG files to simplify the job of copying the same set of Registry entries to multiple computers. See the "Tips from the Windows Pros" section at the end of this chapter for details.

RESTORING THE REGISTRY

If you've made Registry changes that cause problems, you can try to remember each and every change you made, re-enter the original information, delete any keys you added, and thus undo the changes manually. Good luck! If you were diligent and made a backup before you started, however, you can simply restore the backup and have confidence that the recovery is complete and accurate.

> *If you think you have Registry problems,* **see** *"Signs of Registry Problems" in the "Troubleshooting" section at the end of this chapter.*

If you made a Registry backup using a third-party disk or Registry backup tool, use the instructions that came with your product to restore the Registry. If you created a restore point or used regedit, follow the steps described in the following sections.

Restoring the Registry from a Restore Point

If you created a restore point before modifying the Registry, you can back out the change by following these steps:

1. Click Start, All Programs, Accessories, System Tools, System Restore.
2. When the User Account Control dialog box appears, click Continue.
3. Select Choose a Different Restore Point.
4. Locate the restore point you created. Select it and click Next; then Finish.

Restoring the Registry from Regedit

If a Registry editing session has gone awry, and you need to restore the Registry from a Regedit backup, follow these steps:

1. In Regedit, select File, Import.
2. Select All Files from the Files of Type list.
3. Locate the file you used to back up the Registry key or keys—for example, C:\before.sav.
4. Select Open.

The saved Registry keys are then imported, replacing any changes or deletions. However, any keys or values you've added to the Registry are not removed. If they are the cause of the problem, this restore will *not* help.

If the Registry problems persist, you can try a rather drastic measure: You can use Regedit to delete the key or keys that were changed and then import the backup file again. This time, any added keys or values are removed. I suggest that you try this approach only with keys related to add-on software, *not* for any of the Microsoft software or hardware keys.

> **TIP**
> My final word on Registry repair: If you encounter problems with the Registry entries for hardware or for Windows itself, and neither the System Restore feature nor restoring the Registry helps, you are probably better off reinstalling Windows or using the System Recovery procedure than trying any further desperate measures to fix the Registry.

> **TIP**
> If you encounter what you think are Registry problems with add-on software, your best bet is to uninstall the software, if possible, and reinstall it before attempting *any* Registry restores or repairs.

Using Regedit

Most people never need to edit the Registry by hand because most Registry keys are set by the software that uses them. For example, Microsoft Office sets its own preference values, and the Control Panel applets set the appropriate Display, Sound, and Networking Registry entries. In a way, the Control Panel is mostly just a Registry editor in disguise.

However, you might need to edit the Registry by hand if you're directed by a technical support person who's helping you fix a problem, or when you're following a published procedure to make an adjustment for which there is no Control Panel setting.

In the latter case, before going any further, I need to say this one last time, to make it absolutely clear: Unless you're quite certain that you can't make a mistake, back up the Registry (or at least the section you want to change) before making any changes.

The next few sections cover the basics of the Registry editor.

Viewing the Registry

The Registry editor doesn't have a Start menu item. The easiest way to run it is to type regedit into the Search field on the Start menu. When regedit appears in the results pane under Programs, take one of the following actions, depending on your needs:

- If you are logged on as an Administrator, press Enter or click regedit. When the User Account Control dialog box appears, click Continue. The Registry editor will run with full elevated privileges.

- If you are not logged on as an Administrator but need to change settings in only the HKEY_CURRENT_USER section of the Registry, press Enter or click regedit. The Registry editor will run with reduced privileges, and you will not be able to change systemwide settings.

- If you are not logged on as an Administrator but need to change systemwide settings in HKEY_LOCAL_MACHINE, right-click regedit and select Run as Administrator. Enter an Administrator account's username and password. The Registry editor will then run with full elevated privileges.

> **NOTE**
>
> The reason for these complicated variations is that malicious programs and email attachments can easily abuse the Registry editor, so it's subject to User Account Control restrictions, for good reason. The editor must be running in elevated mode to modify Registry keys that are secured to be changeable only by the Administrator. By the way, there is no indication in the Registry editor's title bar to tell whether it's running with elevated privileges—you just have to remember.

Regedit displays a two-pane display much like Windows Explorer, as shown in Figure 31.2. The top-level keys, which are listed below Computer, can be expanded just like drives and folders in the Explorer. In the pane on the right are the values for each key. The name of the current selected key appears in the status bar.

Figure 31.2
The Regedit screen shows keys on the left and values on the right.

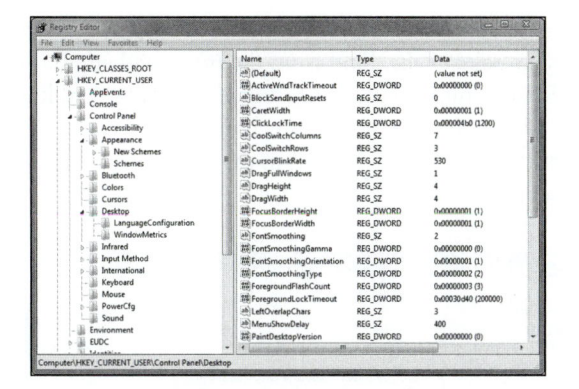

Values have names, just as the files in a folder do, and it's here that configuration information is finally stored. Each key has a (Default) value, which is the value of the key itself, and any number of named values. For example, Figure 31.2 shows the key HKEY_CURRENT_USER\Desktop. The value of HKEY_CURRENT_USER\Desktop itself is undefined (blank), and the value HKEY_CURRENT_USER\Control Panel\Desktop\DragFullWindows is 1.

Registry values have a data type, which is usually one of the types shown in Table 31.2. The Registry editor display lists values by their technical names.

TABLE 31.2   DATA TYPES SUPPORTED BY REGEDIT

Technical Name	"Friendly" Name	Description
REG_SZ	String value	Textual information, a simple string of letters.
REG_BINARY	Binary value	Binary data, displayed as an arbitrary number of hexadecimal digits.
REG_DWORD	DWORD (32-bit) value	A single number displayed in hexadecimal or decimal.
REG_QWORD	QWORD (64-bit) value	A single number displayed in hexadecimal or decimal. QWORD values are used primarily by 64-bit Windows applications.
REG_MULTI_SZ	Multistring value	A string that can contain more than one line of text.
REG_EXPAND_SZ	Expandable string value	Text that can contain environment variables (such as %TEMP%).

Other data types, such as REG_DWORD_BIG_ENDIAN and REG_RESOURCE_LIST, exist, but they are obscure and rare and can't be edited with Regedit.

SEARCHING IN THE REGISTRY

You can search for a Registry entry by key name, value name, or the contents of a value string. First, select a starting point for the search in the left pane. You can select Computer to select the entire Registry, or you can limit your search to one of the top-level keys or any subordinate key. Next, select Edit, Find from the menu and enter a search string in the Find dialog box. The Find feature is not case-sensitive, so upper- and lower-case don't matter. You can check any of the Look At boxes, shown in Figure 31.3, to designate where in the Registry you expect to find the desired text: in the name of a key, in the name of a value, or in the data, the value itself.

Figure 31.3
In the Find dialog box, you can choose whether to search key names, value names, or value data.

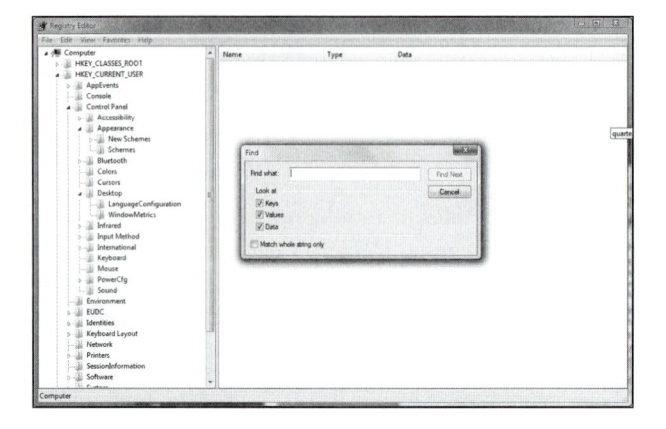

Check Match Whole String Only to search only for items whose whole name or value is the desired string.

> **NOTE**
>
> Most of the time, I check all the Look At boxes except Match Whole String Only.

Select Find Next to start the search. The Regedit display indicates the first match to your string; by pressing F3, you can repeat the search to look for other instances.

> **TIP**
>
> The search function has two limitations:
> - You can't enter a backslash (\) in the search string when looking for a key or value name; Regedit won't complain, but it won't find anything, either.
> - You can't search for the initial HKEY_xxx part of a key name. That's not actually part of the name; it's just the section of the Registry in which the key resides.
>
> For example, to find a key named HKEY_CLASSES_ROOT\MIDFile\shell\Play\Command, you can't type all that in and have Find jump right to the key. If you already know the full pathname of a key, use the left pane of Regedit to browse for the key directly.

Editing Keys and Values

Regedit has no Save or Undo menu items. Changes to the Registry happen *immediately* and *permanently*. Additions, deletions, and changes are for real. This is the reason for all the warnings to back up before you poke into the Registry.

Adding a Value

To add a value to a key, select the key in the left pane and choose Edit, New. Select the type of value to add; you can select any of the supported Registry data types, which are listed by the "friendly" names shown previously in Table 31.2. The instructions you're following indicate which type of value to add. A new value entry then appears in the right pane, as shown in Figure 31.4.

Figure 31.4
New Value adds an entry in Rename mode. Type the correct name and then press Enter.

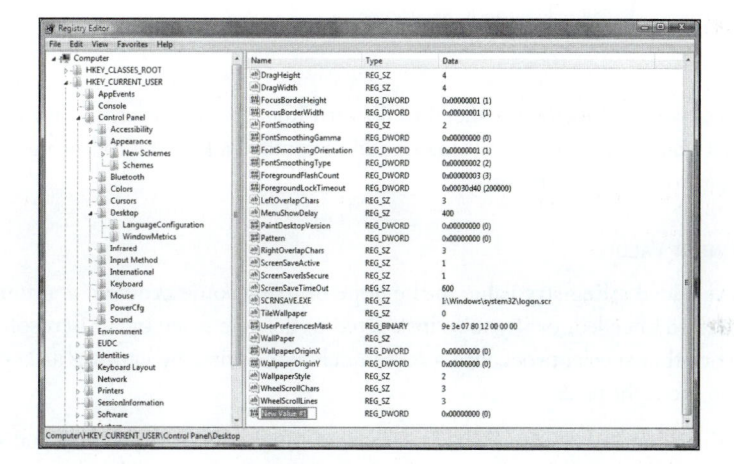

Also remember that Windows Vista might store information in some places you are not familiar with.

Enter the new value's name and press Enter to edit the value.

- For string values, enter the text of the desired string.
- For DWORD values, choose Decimal or Hexadecimal, and enter the desired value in the chosen format (see Figure 31.5).
- For binary values, enter pairs of hexadecimal characters as instructed. (You'll never be asked to do this, I promise.)

Figure 31.5
You can choose to enter a DWORD value in either decimal or hexadecimal notation.

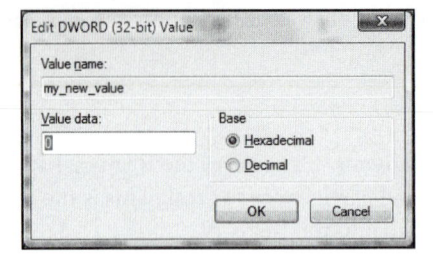

Changing a Value

If you want to change a value, double-click it in the right pane to bring up the Edit Value dialog box. Alternatively, right-click it and select. Then make the desired change and click OK.

> **NOTE**
> Many of the keys that control Windows itself have access restrictions and can be modified only by an Administrator.

That is all you will likely ever need to do with Regedit. However, in the extremely unlikely case that you want to delete a value or add or remove a key, the following sections can help see you through these processes.

Deleting a Value

If you've added a Registry value in the hope of fixing some problem and found that the change wasn't needed, or if you're instructed to delete a value by a Microsoft KnowledgeBase article or other special procedure, you can delete the entry by viewing its key and locating the value on the right pane.

Select the value and choose Edit, Delete from the menu, or right-click and select Delete from the context menu. Confirm by clicking OK.

> **CAUTION**
> There is no Undo command in the Registry editor—when you delete a value, it's gone for good. Be sure you've made a Registry backup before editing or deleting Registry keys and values.

Adding or Deleting a Key

Keys must be added as subkeys of existing keys; you can't create a new top-level key. To add a key, select an existing key in the left pane and select Edit, New, Key from the menu.

Alternatively, right-click the existing key and select New, Key from the context menu. A new key appears in the left pane, where you can edit its name, as shown in Figure 31.6. Press Enter after you enter the name.

Figure 31.6
A new key appears in Rename mode.

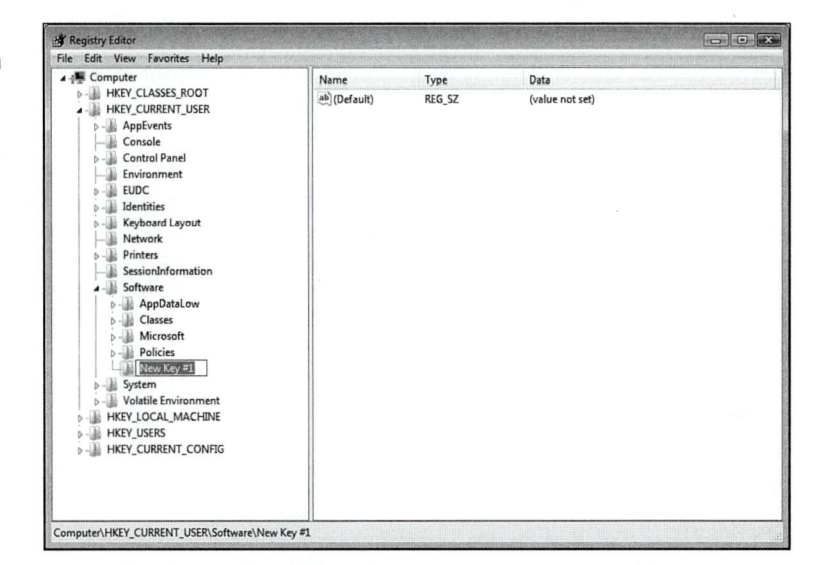

You can delete a key by selecting it in the left pane and choosing Edit, Delete from the drop-down menu, or by right-clicking it and selecting Delete from the context menu. Click OK to confirm that you intend to delete the key. Deleting a key deletes its values *and all its subkeys* as well, so without the protection of Undo (or a Registry Recycling Bin), this action is serious.

Renaming a Key

As you have probably guessed, the pattern for renaming a key follows the Explorer model exactly: Choose the key in the left pane and select Edit, Rename, or right-click the key and select Rename. Finally, enter a new name and press Enter.

> **CAUTION**
> Don't attempt to rename keys without a *very good* reason—for example, because you mistyped the name of the key you were adding. If Windows can't find specific Registry keys it needs, Windows might not boot or operate correctly.

Using Copy Key Name

As you have probably noticed by now, the names of Registry keys can be quite long, tortuous things. The Registry editor offers a bit of help to finger-fatigued Registry editors (and authors): Choosing Edit, Copy Key Name puts the name of the currently selected key into the Clipboard so you can paste it elsewhere if you need to. For example, when you've found a neat Registry trick, you might want to email your friends about it.

Advanced Registry Editing

The Registry editor has some advanced features that you'll need only if you're managing a network of Windows computers or if you run into serious problems with your Windows installation.

> **TIP**
>
> One advanced feature is the Favorites list. You can create bookmarks for Registry keys that you visit frequently. Simply locate the key of interest and click Favorites, Add to Favorites. You can change the name of the bookmark, if desired. Then press OK to create the Favorite. Later, you can select the entry from the Favorites menu to jump right to the desired Registry key.

We discuss several advanced techniques in the following sections.

Editing the Registry of a Remote Computer

The Registry editor permits Administrators to edit the Registry of other computers on a network. Of course, this operation is highly privileged; you must have Administrator privileges on the computer whose Registry you want to edit, and the Remote Management service must be running on the remote computer.

To edit a remote computer's Registry, choose File, Connect Network Registry. Next, enter the name of the remote computer, or click Advanced and then Find Now to select one graphically; then click OK.

When you're connected, the computer's Registry keys appear in the list along with your own, as shown in Figure 31.7.

> **NOTE**
>
> If you want to connect to the Registry on another computer, the Remote Registry service must be running. On Windows XP, this service is enabled by default. On Windows Vista, it is not. You must change the service's startup mode from Manual to Automatic, or you must use Windows management tools to start the service on the other machine before you can edit its Registry remotely.

Figure 31.7
Viewing and editing a remote computer's Registry.

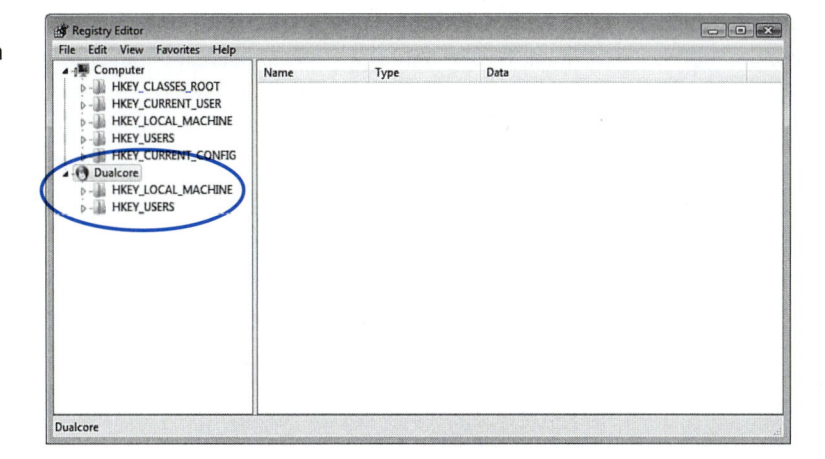

Note that only the two main "real" top-level keys appear: HKEY_LOCAL_MACHINE and HKEY_USERS—the virtual keys do not. When you have finished editing the remote computer's Registry, right-click its name in the left pane and select Disconnect.

> **CAUTION**
>
> You can't use File, Export or File, Import to save or load a remote Registry's values. These commands might appear to work, but they operate only on the local computer's Registry.

> **NOTE**
>
> The Remote Registry editing system uses TCP port 139, so before you can connect to a computer whose Registry you wish to edit, that computer must have an exception in Windows Firewall for Windows File and Printer Sharing. On Windows XP, File and Printer sharing is an item in the firewall's Exceptions list. On Windows Vista, you must enable File Sharing on its Network and Sharing Center, and you must also enable Remote Management on its firewall Exceptions tab.
>
> On both Vista and XP, you must also enable the Remote Registry service. It's set to "manual" startup by default, so you must change the service's setting to Automatic and start it on each computer that you want to manage remotely.
>
> Finally, you may not be able to edit the HKLM registry section of a computer on which User Account Control is enabled.

Editing Registry Entries for Another User

If you open a Registry editor and look under HKEY_USERS, you will find that the only available subkeys are .DEFAULT, three or more entries for system services, and your own long, numeric subkey, which is also accessible as HKEY_CURRENT_USER. As I mentioned earlier,

Windows stores various parts of the Registry in data files called hives and loads the hive containing your part of `HKEY_USER` only when you are actually logged on. When you log out, your subkey is unloaded from the Registry, and the hive file is left in your user profile folder. (If you have a roaming user profile, your profile folder is copied back to the domain server. That's how your preference settings follow you from one computer to another.)

As an administrator, you might find it necessary to edit `HKEY_USER` entries for another user. For example, a startup program in `HKEY_CURRENT_USER\Software\Windows\CurrentVersion\Run` might be causing such trouble that the user can't log on. If you can't log on as that user, you can edit his `HKEY_CURRENT_USER` Registry keys in another way:

1. Log on as an Administrator and run Regedit.
2. Select the `HKEY_USERS` window.
3. Highlight the top-level key `HKEY_USERS`.
4. Select File, Load Hive.
5. Browse to the profile folder for the desired user. For a local user account, this is in `\Users\username`. (For a Windows Server domain, look in the folder used for user profiles on the domain controller.) The folder name of this folder might have the computer name or a domain name attached. For example, on one computer, my profile folder name is `bknittel.java`.
6. Type the filename `NTUSER.DAT`. (The file will most likely not appear in the Browse dialog box because it's *super hidden*: marked with both the Hidden and System attributes.) Then click Open.
7. A dialog box appears, asking you to enter a name for the hive. `HKEY_USERS` normally loads user hives with a long numeric name, so I suggest that you type the user's logon name. Click OK. The user's Registry data is then loaded and can be edited, as shown in Figure 31.8.

Figure 31.8
An offline user's Registry hive is now loaded and can be edited.

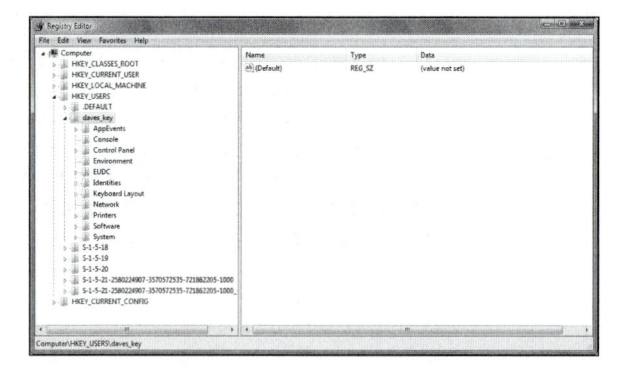

8. When you're finished editing, unload the hive. Select the key you added under `HKEY_USERS` (for example, `daves_key` in Figure 31.8), and select File, Unload Hive. Confirm by clicking Yes on the warning dialog box.

Editing Registry Entries for Another Windows Installation

If you need to retrieve Registry entries from an installation of Windows 2000, XP, or Vista on another hard disk or partition, you can load any of that installation's hive files for editing or exporting. This might happen when you do one of the following:

- Install a new hard disk and install Windows Vista on the new disk, leaving your old installation intact.
- Encounter a severe Registry error that prevents Windows from booting at all. If you can't use the usual recovery procedure to fix the problem, you can install a fresh copy of Windows onto another drive or partition. When you boot up that copy of Windows, you can load the original installation's Registry files for editing. Then, you can try to boot up the original installation.

To edit the other installation's Registry, you need to locate its hive files. They are usually found in the locations shown in Table 31.3.

Table 31.3 Usual Location of Hive Files

Key	Default Location and Hive File
HKEY_LOCAL_MACHINE\SAM	\windows\system32\config\sam
HKEY_LOCAL_MACHINE\Security	\windows\system32\config\security
HKEY_LOCAL_MACHINE\Software	\windows\system32\config\software
HKEY_LOCAL_MACHINE\System	\windows\system32\config\system
HKEY_LOCAL_MACHINE\Components	\windows\system32\config\components
HKEY_USERS\.Default	\windows\system32\config\default

To edit another Windows installation's Registry, use the technique I described under "Editing Registry Entries for Another User." But instead of locating a user's NTUSER.DAT file, locate the desired hive file on the other hard drive or partition. Unload it after you've exported or corrected the desired information.

In some cases, you will find that you cannot view or modify keys loaded from another installation. This occurs if the keys are protected with security attributes that list specific users or groups defined in the other installation. In this case, you need to first take ownership of the keys and then add yourself as a user who is authorized to read or change they keys. The next section describes this.

Editing Registry Security

Just as files and folders in an NTFS-formatted disk partition have security attributes to control access based on user and group identity, Registry keys and values also have a complete set of Access Control attributes that determine who has rights to read, write, and modify each entry. For example, the Registry keys that control system services can't be modified by non-Administrator users; otherwise, malicious programs or users could conceivably make the entries refer to programs of their choosing, which would then run at a high privilege level. Access controls on the Registry is thus an essential part of Windows security.

> **NOTE**
>
> You rarely should have to modify Registry security settings, but it does happen. The usual case is that an incorrectly designed program places information in a subkey of `HKEY_LOCAL_MACHINE\Software` that is intended to be shared and modified by all users running the program. Because Windows does not permit standard users to modify any keys in `HKEY_LOCAL_MACHINE\Software` by default, the program might malfunction. Modifying permissions so that standard users can edit the shared key is sometimes necessary to fix the problem. Microsoft also sometimes recommends modifying Registry security in one of their all-too-frequent emergency security bulletins.

If you absolutely must change permissions or auditing controls, locate the desired key or value, right-click it, and select Permissions. The Permissions dialog box looks just like the comparable dialog box for files and folders (see Figure 31.9), and lets you set read, write, and modify rights for specific groups and users. You'll find a corresponding set of audit settings.

Figure 31.9
Registry Key Permissions control which users or groups are allowed to see or modify the Registry key and its values.

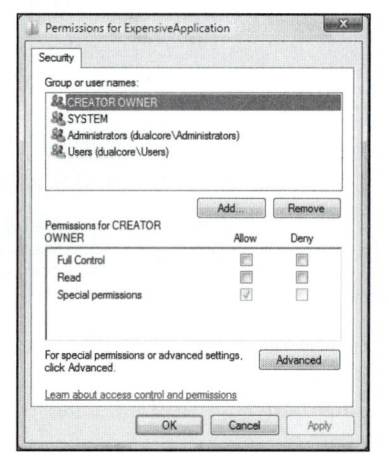

Needless to say, incorrectly changing Registry key access rights can cause profound problems with Windows, so I encourage you not to make any changes to Registry access settings unless you're explicitly instructed to do so.

In most cases, a software vendor supplies precise instructions for making changes necessary to work around an application problem. Here, I describe a general procedure to make a given key readable and writeable by all users. You might do this to make a key capable of sharing information between users, or to repair an alternate Windows installation, as mentioned in the previous section. To set more generous permissions, follow these steps:

1. Locate and select the key in the left pane.
2. Right-click it and select Permissions.

3. Select the Users entry in the top Group or User Names section. If Users is not listed, click Add, type **Users**, and press OK.
4. In the lower section, check Full Control and then Apply. If this is successful, click OK.
5. If you are unable to make the changes even though you're running the Registry editor as an Administrator, click Advanced and select the Owner tab.
6. If the Current owner is listed as unknown, select Administrators in the lower list and click OK.
7. Click OK to close the Advanced Security Settings dialog box, and return to Step 3.

Needless to say, this is a risky procedure because it could result in another user or application being unable to access its own Registry keys. Use this as a procedure of last resort.

Other Registry Tools

I've said that although Registry entries control most Windows functions, most of these settings are made using Control Panel applets, Computer Management tools, and application preferences menus. Some settings, however, can't be made using any standard Windows program.

Making these changes previously required you to directly edit the Registry. Now, however, you'll find third-party add-on tools to make these changes more safely via a nice graphical user interface. Let's go through a couple of the more popular utilities.

X-Setup Pro

X-Setup Pro by Xteq offers nearly 1,700 settings and tweaks using a slick graphical Explorer-like interface. It includes wizards for some of the more complex tasks, such as mapping file types to Explorer icons. One of its niftiest features is its capability to record a series of changes to a log file that it can then play back on other computers. The cost is US $20. You can download it from www.x-setup.net.

Registry Toolkit

Registry Toolkit is a shareware Registry editor made by Funduc software, with a nifty search-and-replace system. You can scan the Registry, changing all occurrences of one string to another, which is something that the Windows Registry editor can't do. Registry Toolkit also keeps a log of changes made so that edits can be undone. Its user interface isn't very comfortable or slick, but if you need to manage a lot of identical changes in the Registry, this is one cool tool. It's free to try, $25 to register, at www.funduc.com.

Registrar Registry Manager

Registrar Registry Manager is a powerful Registry-editing tool produced by Resplendence Software Projects (www.resplendence.com), with a drag-and-drop interface. Other features include a Registry-defragmentation tool, a Registry-compare tool, a monitoring mode to track Registry changes made by other programs, an undo capability, support for editing volatile Registry keys, and the option to edit Registry hive files on disk, allowing power users and administrators to edit Registry images of broken Windows installations. The full version costs €45, and there is a free "lite" version.

TweakVI

TweakVI, available from www.totalidea.com, combines tweaking tools with additional enhancements and optimizing tools such as a RAM disk, pop-up ad blocker, RAM reorganizer, file shredder, and so on. The cost is $39.95 for one computer, with multiple-license discounts available.

Registry-Hacker Websites

Not surprisingly, whole websites have sprung up to share Windows Registry tips and tricks. If you're interested, you might check out these two sites that I've found to be fairly useful:

www.winguides.com/registry

www.jsiinc.com/reghack.htm

To be honest, I don't find all the listed tips to be helpful or accurate, and many are not applicable to Windows Vista. Registry hacks for network tuning, in particular, will *not* work on Vista as they did on XP and earlier versions of Windows. However, these types of resources should improve considerably over time.

Google

As for so many things, when it comes to demystifying the Registry, Google is your best friend. If you're looking for the purpose and valid settings of a particular Registry key, search Google for the full key name. It's easy: Right-click the key name in the Registry editor, select Copy Key Name, and paste the name into the Google search field. If you don't get an answer, pare the name section by section, starting at the left side:

`name1\name2\name3\name4`

then

`name2\name3\name4`

then

`name3\name4`

and finally

`name4`

You can also try searching the Microsoft.com website using Microsoft's search function, but frankly, Google does a much better job of indexing Microsoft.com than Microsoft does.

Registry Privileges and Policies

In Windows NT, 2000, XP, and Vista, administrators can use the *policy* system to restrict users' ability to change their computer configuration. When you log on using a Domain user account, the policy system downloads and installs Registry settings prepared by system administrators. These Registry settings can not only help automate the setup of networking and other components, they can also restrict your ability to (mis)manage your computer.

Here's how it works: Windows looks at a boatload of Registry entries to determine what features to make available to you. For example, one value determines whether the Start menu is allowed to display the Run item; another makes the Control Panel hide the Power Management settings. These values normally don't appear in the Registry at all. However, they can be created by Group Policy settings. They're also usually entered into the Registry with security settings that prevent your changing them and may prevent your even seeing them. Thus, the policy system provides an airtight way for administrators to lock down Windows, and you can't circumvent it using the Registry editor.

→ On a computer that's a member of a Windows Domain network, the policy system is called Group Policy. On a standalone computer, it's called Local Security Policy. Local Security Policy is described in more detail under "Tightening Local Security Policy" in Chapter 35, "Protecting Your Network from Hackers and Snoops."

Troubleshooting

Signs of Registry Problems

How can I determine whether Windows problems are caused by the Registry?

Registry corruption can take two forms: Either the Registry's database files can be damaged by an errant disk operation, or information can be mangled by a buggy program or an overzealous `regedit` user. No matter what the cause, the result can be a system that won't run or one that reboots itself over and over.

These could be other signs of Registry corruption or errors:

- Drivers aren't loaded, or they give errors while Windows is booting.
- Software complains about components that aren't registered or cannot be located.
- Undesirable programs attempt to run when you log in.
- Windows does not boot, or it starts up only in Safe mode.

Recovering from a Suspected Registry Problem

How do I recover from a Registry problem?

If any of the signs of a Registry problem occur just after you install new software or hardware, after you've edited the Registry manually, or after an unexpected and unprotected power loss to the computer, you might have a Registry problem. Try these fixes, in turn, checking after each step to see whether the problem has been resolved:

1. If the problem occurred right after you installed new software, see whether the software manufacturer has released any updates for the software. If an update is available, install the updated software before proceeding. In any case, try reinstalling the software. If that doesn't fix the problem, *uninstall* it and then reinstall it.
2. If the problem occurred right after installing a new piece of hardware or updating a device driver, try updating the device driver or using the Driver Rollback feature.
3. Restart Windows, and just before the Windows startup screen appears, or when the Please Select the Operating System to Start message appears, press the F8 key. Select Last Known Good Configuration. Last Known Good Configuration uses the previous boot's version of HKEY_LOCAL_CONFIG, so good hardware settings might be preserved there.
4. If you get to this point without having gotten Windows fixed, get professional help, if it is available. (I mean professional technical help for your computer, not you personally, unless the experience has traumatized you so much that… well, let's just go on). If technical support service isn't an option, continue to Step 5.
5. Use System Restore to try to return to an earlier saved system configuration.

→ For information on the System Restore, **see** "System Restore," **p. 964**.

6. If none of these fixes solve the problem, or if you can't get Windows started, try starting Windows in Safe mode. Starting this way circumvents many display driver and service startup issues. If you suspect the problem is caused by the display driver, set Windows to use the Standard VGA driver and restart. Then, reinstall your normal graphics adapter (using the most recent updated driver).
7. If you have a backup containing the Registry (System State), restore it. This fix should return you to a state where you had a working system.
8. Use the System Recovery procedure to repair Windows (Repair mode).
9. Reinstall Windows in Repair mode.

→ For more information about reinstalling Windows, **see** "As a Last Resort," **p. 975**.

10. Reinstall Windows in Clean Install mode. This requires you to reinstall all your applications and reconfigure users, so it's an absolute last resort.

TRACKING DOWN ERRANT STARTUP PROGRAMS

How do I track down and eliminate startup programs that don't appear in the Start menu but that start anyway when I launch Windows?

When you log on, Windows examines the Startup folder in your personal Start Menu\Programs folder, as well as in the corresponding folder under \Users\All Users.

In addition, Windows examines the Startup folder in the Start Menu Programs folders of both the user logging in and the All Users folder.

Windows also looks in the Registry for values in the following keys:

    HKEY_LOCAL_MACHINE\Software\Microsoft\Windows\CurrentVersion\Run

    HKEY_LOCAL_MACHINE\Software\Microsoft\Windows\CurrentVersion\RunOnce

    HKEY_CURRENT_USER\Software\Microsoft\Windows\CurrentVersion\Run

    HKEY_CURRENT_USER\Software\Microsoft\Windows\CurrentVersion\RunOnce

The LOCAL_MACHINE entries are run for all users, and the CURRENT_USER entries are, of course, specific to each individual user.

If you're trying to determine what programs run when you start up and log on, or if you're trying to find how a particular program is getting started, your first step should be to use a tool specifically designed for this purpose: Go to microsoft.com, search for "Autoruns for Windows," download it, and run it. This will probably solve your problem faster than poking around in the Registry, even counting the download time.

But if you really want to track down a startup program by hand and it's not in your Startup folder, look in the following places:

1. In the Start menu search box, type **msconfig**. If a program of this name appears in the results pane, double-click it to run it. Select the Startup tab. This tab lists any programs in any of the locations described in the remaining steps. If you see a bad program listed, delete it.

   Otherwise, if msconfig cannot be found, search for the program manually by following the remaining steps.

2. Look for a shortcut or program in the folder \Users\Default User\Start Menu\Programs\Startup.

3. Examine the Startup folders under Programs in both your Start Menu folder and the All Users\ Start Menu folder. Right-click your Start button, and select Explore to examine these folders. Note that if your disk uses the NTFS format, you must have Administrator privileges or be a member of the Power Users group to delete an entry from the All Users folder.

4. Run Regedit and browse to the key HKEY_CURRENT_USER\Software\Microsoft\Windows\CurrentVersion. Look under any subkeys named Run, RunOnce, or RunOnceEx. Check their values for entries that are starting the undesired program. Installer programs often set the RunOnce entries to complete an installation process after rebooting and are sometimes not eliminated properly.

5. Repeat the same process with HKEY_LOCAL_MACHINE\Software\Microsoft\Windows\CurrentVersion, again looking under Run, RunOnce, and RunOnceEx.

6. Check for possible virtualized entries under HKEY_CLASSES_ROOT\VirtualStore\MACHINE\Software\Microsoft\Windows\CurrentVersion\Run, RunOnce, and RunOnceEx.

7. Finally, check for bogus items installed in a very sneaky location: `HKEY_LOCAL_MACHINE\ SYSTEM\CurrentControlSet\Control\Print\Monitors`. I have seen computer viruses install bogus software disguised as a printer driver here, which Windows runs without question. There are actually several other registry keys that list programs Windows will blithely start on the assumption that they are printer, network, or other drivers. The AutoRuns tool described previously will ferret out all of these.

> **NOTE**
>
> If you can't log in as the affected user and you suspect that the startup program is run from the `HKEY_CURRENT_USER` Registry entry, see "Editing Registry Entries for Another User," earlier in this chapter.

CONFIGURATION CHANGES DON'T APPEAR FOR OTHER USERS

When I change an application program's preference setting that should apply to all users of the program, it affects only me; the setting isn't changed when other users run the application.

Most likely, the configuration setting is stored in a Registry key under `HKEY_LOCAL_MACHINE` that isn't writeable by you. When you make the change, Windows virtualizes the Registry value, and only your account sees the change.

To fix this, first try to contact the software manufacturer for a workaround. If none exists, try this:

1. Locate the Registry key in which the setting is being saved. Either search the Registry for the setting value or use a Registry change-monitoring tool such as Registrar Registry Manager to see where the application saves your setting.
2. As an Administrator, locate the key in the left pane of the Registry editor, right-click it, and select Permissions. Select the Users entry and check Full Control.
3. Using your account, locate the virtualized copy of key under `HKEY_CLASES_ROOT\ VirtualStore` and delete it.
4. Run the application and change the setting again.

After this, everyone should share the same copy of the setting.

TIPS FROM THE WINDOWS PROS: DEPLOYING REGISTRY SETTINGS WITH REG FILES

If you find yourself having to make the same Registry settings on a whole department's or company's worth of computers, or if you frequently reinstall Windows and have to reapply the same settings every time you reload, you should know this neat way of setting a bunch of Registry entries with just a mouse click or two.

We discussed REG files earlier in this chapter as a way of backing up and restoring the Registry. You can also use REG files to automatically deploy (that is, distribute and install) a set of identical Registry settings to several computers. For example, I've used this technique to quickly copy a complicated set of file associations in the HKEY_CLASSES_ROOT Registry section to all the computers in a client's office.

The trick here is to export the relevant Registry keys and values using Regedit's Export feature, as described earlier in the chapter. Trim the resulting REG files with Notepad so that they contain *only* the exact entries that you need to copy. Then, using cut and paste, put them all into one file. The first line should contain Windows Registry Editor Version 5.00, and this should be followed by key names, with any necessary values under the keys.

REG files can also delete Registry keys or values. To delete a value, specify a single minus sign (—) after the value's equals sign. To delete a key (*and* all subkeys and values under it, so be careful!), precede the key name with a minus sign. For example, the following REG file deletes a value named GoodbyeValue and the key named HKEY_CURRENT_USER\Software\GoodbyeKey:

```
Windows Registry Editor Version 5.00

[HKEY_CURRENT_USER\Software\Some key or another]
"GoodbyeValue"=-

[-HKEY_CURRENT_USER\Software\GoodbyeKey]
```

These entries can be mixed in with other REG entries that set keys. For instance, you might want to delete a given key—thus removing any extraneous subkeys and values—before you install a clean, new version:

```
Windows Registry Editor Version 5.00

[-HKEY_CURRENT_USER\Software\MyKey]

[HKEY_CURRENT_USER\Software\MyKey]
@="Standard default Value"
value1="standard value1 setting"
value2="standard value2 setting"
```

Here's an example of how this all works. The following REG file deletes any previous associations for the file extensions .sgm and sgml, and creates an association for both to open with application sgmledit.exe:

```
Windows Registry Editor Version 5.00

[-HKEY_CLASSES_ROOT\.sgm]
[-HKEY_CLASSES_ROOT\.sgml]
[-HKEY_CLASSES_ROOT\SGML File]

[HKEY_CLASSES_ROOT\.sgm]
@="SGML File"

[HKEY_CLASSES_ROOT\.sgml]
@="SGML File"

[HKEY_CLASSES_ROOT\SGML File\shell\open\command]
@="\"c:\\program files\\SGMLEdit\\sgmledit.exe\" \"%1\""
```

To deploy the Registry settings to a given computer, double-click the REG file in an Explorer window, or type this command into a command prompt window:

```
regedit /s filename.reg
```

Replace *filename.reg* with the name of your REG file. You might need to specify the file's full path, if you're carrying it around on a USB flash disk or have it stored on a network shared folder.

In some circumstances, you might want to reset some Registry values every time a user logs on. You can do this by running the `regedit` command from a logon script. However, whereas you can prevent the Registry editor from asking to confirm reading the REG file by adding /s to the command line, you *can't* stop Windows from displaying the UAC dialog box. Thus, for logon applications, you're better off writing a script program to manipulate the Registry. The next chapter discusses scripting.

CHAPTER 32

COMMAND-LINE AND AUTOMATION TOOLS

In this chapter

Command-Line Tools   1070

The Windows Vista Command Prompt Environment   1070

Command-Line Management Tools   1081

Setting Environment Variables   1085

Setting Command Prompt Window Properties   1092

The MS-DOS Environment   1094

Batch Files   1104

Windows Script Host   1113

Task Scheduler   1123

Troubleshooting   1127

Tips from the Windows Pros: Getting More Information   1128

Command-Line Tools

Despite the ease of use of the Windows graphical user interface, the command-line interface remains a useful way to perform many maintenance, configuration, and diagnostic tasks. Many of the most important diagnostic tools such as `ping`, `tracert`, and `nslookup` are available only from the command line, unless you purchase third-party graphical add-ons to perform these functions. And although the term "batch file" might bring back uncomfortable memories of the old MS-DOS days, batch files and program scripts are still powerful tools that provide a useful way to encapsulate common management functions. For example, they can be placed in shared folders as a way of distributing management functions on a network. Together, command-line utilities, batch files, and scripts based on Windows Scripting Host provide a complete set of building blocks from which you can build high-level utilities for situations where normal Windows commands aren't sufficient for your needs.

The Windows Vista command-line utilities include many of the same programs found in DOS and earlier versions of Windows, and even UNIX. In many cases, the programs have been enhanced considerably. There are also many new utilities not found in DOS or earlier versions of Windows.

The Windows Vista Command Prompt Environment

This section gives you a quick tour to show you how command-line programs work and how to enter commands efficiently. If you're already familiar with the command-line environment, you can skip ahead to "Command-Line Management Tools" for an introduction to some of Windows Vista's more interesting command-line tools.

To open a Command Prompt window, click Start, All Programs, Accessories, Command Prompt. This will open a window in which you can type commands and review output, as shown in Figure 32.1.

Figure 32.1
The Command Prompt window is the gateway to a world of powerful Windows management tools.

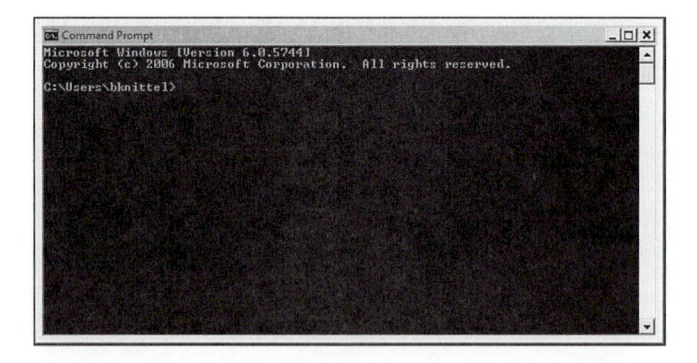

The main difference between a standard Windows application and a command-line program—which in Windows is technically called a *console program*—is that it doesn't use a graphical display or pull-down menus. Instead, you type commands into the Command Prompt window to tell Windows to do something, and the command programs type information back to you. It's a lot like an Instant Messaging program, where two people type back and forth, except here, the other person is a program.

COMMAND-LINE SYNTAX

The *prompt* part of Command Prompt window refers to the bit of text shown in Figure 32.1. The string of text that ends with > is called a prompt, and it indicates that Windows is ready for you to enter a command. When you type a command and press Enter, Windows does something, and displays another prompt only when it's ready to accept another command. As mentioned previously, it's a sort of dialog between you and the computer. The computer prints the prompt to tell you that it's your turn, and you press Enter to tell the computer it's its turn.

Each command line starts with the name of the program that you want to run, followed by additional information called *arguments*. Arguments tell the program what specifically you want to do. For example, when you use the delete file command, you have to tell it what files to delete. A delete command line might look like this:

`delete unused_document.doc`

The first word on the line tells Windows to use the `delete` program. The rest of the command line is given to the delete program to interpret. `delete` interprets the remainder as the name(s) of file(s) to delete. So, as you might expect, this command deletes the file named `unused_document.doc`.

Most commands that accept filenames on the command line allow you to type the characters * and ? as part of the filename. These are called *wildcards*, and they match any string of characters, or any one character respectively. Here are some examples:

Command	Will delete...
`delete *.doc`	All files in the current folder that end with `.doc`.
`delete b*.doc`	All files in the current folder that start with the letter b and end with `.doc`. For example, this would delete `b.doc` and `berry.doc` but not `apple.doc`.
`delete photo12?.jpg`	Files named `photo120.jpg`, `photo121.jpg`, and so on, but not photo12.doc.

Command-line programs often allow you to type additional arguments called *options*, *flags*, or *switches* that change the behavior of the program. (There's no difference between the three names; they just have different historical origins. The terms can be used interchangeably.) For example, you can add /P to a `delete` command line, as in

`delete /p *.doc`

This instructs the program to prompt you before deleting each file, so that you can double-check each one before it goes.

Each program interprets the command-line arguments its own way to meet its own needs. A big part of the learning curve of becoming a command-line guru is learning not only what commands are available but also what arguments are required or available for each one. The expected organization of the arguments and options is called the command line's *syntax*, and the documentation for each command shows the syntax using a format that looks something like this:

DEL[ETE] [/P] [/F] [/S] [/Q] [/A[[:]attributes**]]** filename **[...]**

In almost all cases, the following conventions are used:

- On Windows, items shown in uppercase *usually* can be entered in either uppercase or lowercase. The documentation for the command will usually tell you if this is not so. (This is true only for Windows programs. On the UNIX operating system, or in the Subsystem for UNIX-based Applications on Windows Vista, upper/lowercase matters, and commands must be typed exactly as shown.)
- **Boldface** indicates parts of the command line that you have to type literally, exactly as shown.
- *Italics* indicate placeholders that you must replace with appropriate information. For example, in the `delete` command, the *filename* item should be replaced with the name of a file that you want to delete. The *attributes* part of the delete command isn't self-explanatory, and you have to read the command's documentation to find out what to type.
- Square brackets [ ] indicate parts of the command line that are optional. In the `delete` command you can see that the /P switch is optional. Notice also that the command name itself can either be typed as `del` or as `delete`.
- Ellipses ... indicate that the preceding part of the command can be repeated as necessary. In the `delete` command, you can type as many filenames as necessary, with a space between each name.

You'll eventually memorize the syntax for the commands that you use the most often, and this is when knowing how to use the command line will start paying off in big time savings.

Quoting Filenames with Spaces

In the preceding example of the `delete` command, we saw that the command allows you to type several filenames on the same command line, with spaces between the names. For example, the command

`delete file1.doc file2.doc`

deletes files `file1.doc` and `file2.doc`. But what if a filename has a space in it? If I try to delete a file named `my big file.doc` with the command

`delete my big file.doc`

Windows will try to delete three files, `my`, `big`, and `file.doc`, respectively, and either it will complain that no such files exist, or worse, if I did have files with those names, it would delete them instead of the one I was after. The solution is to surround filenames that have spaces in them with quotation marks ("). What I actually need to type is

```
delete "my big file.doc"
```

THE CURRENT DRIVE AND CURRENT DIRECTORY

When you view folders in Windows Explorer, you may recall that Windows displays the contents of just one folder at a time. You can generally select a drive letter or folder in the left pane's Folder view, and see the files in the right pane. The folder whose contents are shown in the right pane is the Explorer window's *current folder*. The command-line environment also has the concept of a current folder.

Hmm, did I just say current *folder*? Folder is a relatively recent term chosen to help make computers seem more user friendly. The original term is *directory*. The terms are interchangeable. In the command-line world, though, directory is the term used most often, because it appears in the name of many commands: `mkdir` for "make directory," `cd` for "change directory," and so on. I'll use the term directory rather than folder in the remainder of this chapter. So let's try that again: The command-line environment also has the concept of a *current directory*.

When you open a Command Prompt window (as shown in Figure 32.1), Windows shows the name of the current directory just behind the > character. The prompt `c:\users\bknittel>` indicates that the current directory is `c:\users\bknittel`. If I type the command

```
del myfile.doc
```

Windows looks for `myfile.doc` in `c:\users\bknittel` only. You can work around this in several ways:

- You can manipulate files in other folders by specifying an *absolute path* for the filename. An absolute path starts with the \ character and specifies the location of the file starting at the topmost (or *root*) directory. For example, you could delete file `somefile.doc` from the Public Documents directory by typing its full path on the command line:

    ```
    del \users\public\documents\somefile.doc
    ```

- You can also specify *relative paths*—By omitting the initial \ in the path name, you can specify the location of a file relative to the current directory. When the current directory is `c:\users\bknittel`, the paths `documents\myfile.doc` and `c:\users\bknittel\documents\myfile.doc` are equivalent. The second path is a relative path because it doesn't start with \, and Windows knows to interpret `documents` as a subdirectory of `c:\users\bknittel`.

- You can change the current directory to another directory, so that you specify files and paths relative to the new location. The command

    ```
    cd \users\public
    ```

    changes the current directory to `\users\public`, so that filenames and/or relative paths use that as a starting point instead of the original location.

Windows also has the concept of a *current drive*, also called the *default drive*. In the examples we just used, the drive letter was c:, and Windows looked for the files and directories only on the c: drive. When you specify a path without typing a drive letter at the beginning, Windows looks on the current drive. You can specify an alternative drive letter in any path, or you can change the current drive by typing a command line consisting of a drive letter and a colon, like this:

d:

which makes drive D: the current drive.

This does seem a bit confusing at first, but you'll quickly get used to navigating around your drives and folders (sorry: I mean drives and directories) from the command line.

Editing Command Lines

Some commands require you to type a long series of names, options, and so on, and it's not reasonable to expect you to be able to type these long commands without making a mistake. Windows has built-in command-line editing features that help you correct mistakes, and they also save you a lot of typing when you repeat the same or similar commands several times. The usual cursor keys work as you would expect, as indicated in Table 32.1.

TABLE 32.1   CURSOR KEY EDITING IN THE COMMAND LINE

Key	Action
Backspace, Delete	Deletes the character to the left of or under the cursor, respectively.
Home, End	Moves the cursor to the beginning or end of the typed line, respectively.
Ins	Toggles between *insert mode*, where characters typed in the middle of a line shove the characters to the right of the cursor over, and *overwrite mode*, where characters typed in the middle of a line replace any existing characters.
Left, right arrow	Moves the cursor one space to the left or right.
Ctrl+left or right arrow	Moves the cursor one word to the left or right.
Up, down arrow	Scrolls through previously typed commands. Use these keys to recall a previously typed command; then modify or correct it and press Enter to reissue the command.
F3	Recalls the previously issued command from the cursor point to the end of the command. You can use this helpful key when you only need to retype the first few letters of a command. Type the first few letters of the command and then press F3 to bring back the remainder of the previous command.

When you make a mistake on a command line, it's almost always easier to recall the previous line with the up arrow key and correct it than to retype it from scratch.

FILENAME COMPLETION

Many commands involve entering filenames or directory names on the command line. The Windows Vista command shell has a feature called Command Line Completion that can make it much easier to enter these names.

Here's how it works. When you're typing a filename or directory name, you can type just the first few letters of the name and then press the Tab key to have Windows fill in the rest of the name. If more than one name matches the letter or letters you typed, Windows will pick the first matching name. If that is not the correct name, just press Tab again, and Windows will erase the first name and replace it with the next matching name. You can keep pressing Tab until the correct name appears. Windows even takes care of adding quotes to the name, if there are spaces in it.

You don't even actually have to type any letters at all—just press Tab, and Windows will type out the name of the first file in the current directory.

If you are specifying a path that involves folder names and/or filenames, you can type the \ character after Windows fills in the first name, and repeat the process with the next subfolder or filename. For example, to enter the path \Users\public\Documents, you can probably just type \, u, Tab, \, p, Tab, \, d, Tab Tab (two tabs at the end because the first fills in Desktop). If you're in front of your computer right now, give this a try, and you'll see what I mean.

> **NOTE**
>
> Normally, Filename Completion matches what you've typed to either filenames or folder names. When Windows can see that you're building a command that obviously pertains only to folders, such as cd or rmdir, it will automatically match only folder names.

If you remember to use Command Line Completion, you'll save a lot of time and make many fewer typing mistakes.

REDIRECTION AND PIPES

Most command-line commands display information in the command window itself. For example, if you open a Command Prompt window and type the command **dir** (remember to press Enter afterwards), you'll see something like this:

```
C:\Users\bknittel>dir
 Volume in drive C has no label.
 Volume Serial Number is 5C83-2321

 Directory of C:\Users\bknittel

10/13/2006  03:51 PM    <DIR>          .
10/13/2006  03:51 PM    <DIR>          ..
10/06/2006  04:51 PM    <DIR>          Contacts
10/11/2006  04:16 PM    <DIR>          Desktop
10/06/2006  04:51 PM    <DIR>          Documents
10/06/2006  04:51 PM    <DIR>          Downloads
10/06/2006  04:52 PM    <DIR>          Favorites
```

```
10/06/2006  04:51 PM    <DIR>          Links
10/06/2006  04:51 PM    <DIR>          Music
10/06/2006  04:51 PM    <DIR>          Pictures
10/06/2006  04:51 PM    <DIR>          Saved Games
10/06/2006  04:51 PM    <DIR>          Searches
10/06/2006  04:51 PM    <DIR>          Videos
               0 File(s)            0 bytes
              13 Dir(s)  6,370,185,216 bytes free
```

The display is nice to look at, but sitting there in the window you can't do much with it. Now, type the command

`dir > x.txt`

This time, nothing prints out. What has happened is that you instructed Windows to direct the output from the `dir` command into a file named `x.txt`. If you type the command `notepad x.txt` you'll see that the directory printout is in there. You can now use file `x.txt` as you want: print it, edit it, email it, or whatever.

This is called *output redirection*, and it works with all command-line programs that generate output. The > character followed by a filename instructs Windows to direct a program's output to the specified file.

If you want to run several programs and want to collect the output of each program in the same file, you might be tempted to try something like this:

```
dir *.doc > docs.txt
dir *.xls > docs.txt
dir *.pdf > docs.txt
```

However, all you'll end up with is the listing from the third command. If the file that you use after > exists when you issue the command, Windows *overwrites* the file, erasing its previous contents. Thus, the preceding example leaves us with the results of the last command only.

To properly collect the output of several programs in one file, you can use one of two techniques. The first approach is to use the *append* function. Whereas > creates a file from scratch, >> will append, or add on to, an existing file, or, if there is no existing file, it will create it. So, our three-directory listing could be done this way:

```
dir *.doc > docs.txt
dir *.xls >> docs.txt
dir *.pdf >> docs.txt
```

We start with > so that we clear out any previous version of `docs.txt`; then use >> on the next two commands to tack on successive results.

> **TIP**
>
> Windows doesn't require spaces on either side of the > or >> indicators. The commands `dir >docs.txt`, `dir>docs.txt`, and `dir > docs.txt` all work. It's good to get in the habit of using spaces, though, so that you can choose to use filename completion. If you type >>d, Tab won't work to finish the name because filename completion isn't smart enough to realize that it shouldn't be looking for a filename that starts with >>d.

A second way to redirect the output of several commands to one file is to group the commands inside parentheses. The command

```
(dir *.doc & dir *.xls & dir *.pdf) >docs.txt
```

will also have the desired effect. The & character separates the commands, and the parentheses tell Windows to redirect the output of all three together.

The < symbol redirects the *input* of a program, so that the program reads the contents of a file rather than accepting input typed into the command prompt window. For example, the command

```
ftp <get_the_file
```

runs the FTP file transfer program and tells FTP to read its commands from the file named get_the_file, rather than from your keyboard.

One other redirection operator that you should know about is called the *pipe* or *pipeline*. The | character indicates that the output of one command should be fed as the input of another. For example:

```
net view | findstr /i core
```

runs two commands. The first is net view, which lists all of the Windows computers that Windows can see on your network. The | character tells Windows to feed that listing into the second command, findstr /i core. This second command searches whatever text is fed to it and passes through only those text lines that contain the word core in either upper- or lowercase; the /i switch means to ignore case. The net result is that this command line will display the names of any computers on your network that have "core" as part of the computer name.

Although these are the most important special characters that you will use to redirect the output of command-line programs, there are a few others. Table 32.2 lists the other characters that have a special meaning when used in a command line.

TABLE 32.2   WINDOWS VISTA COMMAND-LINE SPECIAL CHARACTERS

Character	Commands
&	Separates multiple commands on the command line. For example the command `dir >x.txt & notepad x.txt` puts a directory listing into a file and then displays the file with Notepad.
&&	Separates multiple commands. The command following && runs only if the command preceding && succeeds.
|	Pipes output of one command to another. The output of the command preceding | is sent as the input to command after |. For example, `dir /b /s *.doc	sort	more` lists all .doc files in the current directory and all subdirectories; this listing is sent through sort and put into alphabetical order, and the sorted listing is fed to more, which displays it one screen at a time.

continues

TABLE 32.2 CONTINUED

Character	Commands
`││`	Separates multiple commands. The command following `││` runs only if the command preceding the `││` symbol fails. This is the opposite of the && function and has nothing to do with the pipe (`│`) function.
`( )`	Groups commands. Used primarily with the `if` and `else` commands but can also be used as follows: The command `(dir & netstat & ipconfig) │ more` prints a directory listing and runs two network information tools, and sends the collected output of the three programs through the `more` screen-at-a-time tool.
`;` or `,`	Separates arguments on a command line. This usage is a carryover from early DOS days, is generally not required, and should not be used unless required by a specific command.
`^`	This is called the escape character, and it removes the special meaning from whatever character follows it. For example, `^│` is treated as ordinary text character `│`.

CUT AND PASTE IN THE COMMAND PROMPT WINDOW

Although you will usually use output redirection to store the results of programs in files, you can also use cut and paste to move text into or out of a Command Prompt window.

To paste text into the window at the cursor location, click the window's System Menu (the upper-left corner) and select Edit, Paste, or type Alt+Space E P.

To copy text from the window to the Clipboard, click the window's System Menu, and select Edit, Mark. Alternatively, type Alt+Space E M. Use the mouse to highlight a rectangular area of the screen; then press Enter. This copies the text to the Clipboard.

By default, the mouse does not select text until you use the Mark sequence. This makes it easier to use MS-DOS programs that are mouse-aware. If you seldom use the mouse with MS-DOS applications, click the System Menu (or press Alt+Space), select Defaults, and check Quick Edit. When Quick Edit is enabled, you can use the mouse to mark text for copying to the Clipboard without having to type Alt+Space E M first.

Although I just had you change the default setting, you can change the Quick Edit setting for just a given open copy of the Command Prompt window by opening its System Menu and clicking Properties rather than Defaults.

COMMAND-LINE TIPS

The following sections offer some additional tips to help make using the command line easier.

EASY ACCESS TO THE COMMAND PROMPT WINDOW

If you're a command-line junkie like I am, locate the Command Prompt start menu item, hold down the right mouse button, and drag it to the Quick Launch bar for easy access. Select Copy Here when you release the mouse button.

Running Commands with Elevated Privileges

Some command-line programs require elevated privileges to do their job correctly. To run a command-line program with elevated privileges, you have to run it from a Command Prompt window that is itself running elevated.

To run an elevated Command Prompt window, click Start, All Programs, Accessories. Then right-click Command Prompt and select Run As Administrator.

If you find yourself doing this a lot, you might want to create a shortcut for it. Just drag the Command Prompt menu item to the desktop, or to another location in the Accessories Start menu, being sure to hold down the Ctrl key so that you make a copy. Rename the new shortcut something like "Administrator Command Prompt" or "Elevated Command Prompt." Right-click the new shortcut and select Properties. Click the Advanced button, check Run As Administrator, and then click OK.

Now, you can use this shortcut to open a privileged Command Prompt window. You will have to confirm the User Account Control (UAC) prompt every time you open it.

> **CAUTION**
>
> Be *very* careful when using an elevated Command Prompt window. Any commands you start from within this window will run with elevated privileges from the get-go, and you will receive no further UAC prompts when you start them. This includes Windows GUI programs—if you, for example, type the command `optionalfeatures`, you will get the Turn Windows Features On or Off dialog, and you will not have to confirm anything before it starts.
>
> To be safe, do not use an elevated Command Prompt window for general-purpose work. Use it only to accomplish a specific task that requires elevated privileges; then close it.

Change the Default Drive and Directory at the Same Time

You can change the default drive and directory at the same time by adding `/d` to a `cd` command. For instance, the command

`cd /d e:\setup`

changes the current drive to `e:` and the current directory to `\setup` at the same time.

Use pushd and popd to Make Backtracking Easier

As you use the `cd` command to burrow through your computer's drive and directories, you'll quickly start to miss the Explorer's Back button when you find yourself having to type long path names to get from one directory to another and back again.

The commands `pushd` and `popd` were written to help make this easier. The command `pushd` works just like `cd`, except that Windows remembers the previous current directory. `popd` returns you to the current directory before the last `pushd`. Here's how it can work, assuming that the initial directory is `c:\users\bknittel`:

Command	New Current Drive and Directory
`pushd \users\public\documents`	`c:\users\public\documents`
`popd`	`c:\users\bknittel`
`pushd \windows\system32`	`c:\windows\system32`
`pushd e:\setup`	`e:\setup`
`popd`	`c:\windows\system32`
`popd`	`c:\users\bknittel`

Note that `pushd` lets you change the current drive letter without having to type `/d`.

USE pushd TO USE NETWORK FOLDERS

If you're working with a network, `pushd` also lets you specify a path to shared folder. The command

`pushd \\myserver\public`

automatically maps a drive letter to the shared folder named `public` on computer `myserver` and makes this the current drive and directory. `pushd` starts by mapping drive `Z:` and works its way backward toward A from there. `popd` unmaps the drive.

GETTING INFORMATION ABOUT COMMAND-LINE PROGRAMS

If you haven't used the command line since Windows 98 or Me or even MS-DOS, you'll find that built-in commands have been significantly enhanced. To see a list of command-line utilities along with syntax and usage examples, open the Help and Support Center and search for Command-Line Reference. If you see an entry titled Command Line Reference A-Z, that's the one you want. If that's not present, select Command Line Reference for IT Pros, which will lead you to Microsoft's website and the A-Z reference for Windows XP and Windows Server 2003. This will hopefully be updated to include Vista.

To get information on a specific command that interests you, try the following sources, in the order listed. I'll use the `rasdial` command in the examples that follow, but you can use the same technique with any command that interests you.

- A majority of command-line commands will print help information if you add `/?` to the command line. For example, to get information for the `rasdial` command, type `rasdial /?`.

    If the command prints so much text that it scrolls out of view, use one of the following techniques to read it all:

    - Use the Command Prompt window's scrollbars to back up.
    - Press F3 to recall the command line, add ¦ **more** to the end of the line, and press Enter. This will run the help listing through the `more` command, which displays it one screen full at a time. Press Enter after reading each screen.

- Direct the help information to a file and then view the file in Notepad by typing two commands, for example:

  ```
  rasdial /? >x
  notepad x
  ```

- Type the command **help rasdial**. If too much text prints, use the techniques just listed to manage the overflow.
- Click Start, Windows Help and Support, and search for `rasdial`.
- Open Internet Explorer and type `rasdial` in the Search window.
- Browse to www.google.com, and try the following searches, in this order:

  ```
  rasdial site:microsoft.com
  windows rasdial
  rasdial.exe
  rasdial
  ```

Not every one of those information sources will work for every command, but at least one should lead you to an explanation of what the command does, what its command-line options are, and some examples of its use. The command-line options for Windows Vista, XP, and Windows Server 2003 are pretty much the same, so if you can't find any Vista-specific information, XP or Server documentation should be OK to use.

Command-Line Management Tools

In the previous section, I gave you a general overview of the command line and showed how to use it to run programs and direct output to files.

In this section, I'll outline a few of the command-line programs provided with Windows Vista that can help you perform routine maintenance and administrative tasks from the command line and from batch files.

The net use Command

I discussed the `net` command in Chapter 23, "Using a Windows Network," in the section "Managing Network Resources Using the Command Line," so I won't repeat its description here. Here I'll show you how the `net use` subcommand, which can create and delete network drive mappings, is useful in writing batch files.

→ For more information about the `net` command, **see p. 779**.

I often write small batch files to help move files around on my network, for example, to back up important files, or to publish files on a web server. I use `net use` in these batch files to make sure that the network drive mappings I need are set up correctly. You can also use `net use` in logon scripts to ensure that required network mappings are made correctly each time users log on.

For example, suppose that you wrote a batch file to perform backups and wanted to use drive R: to copy files to a specific shared folder named \\bali\officefiles. You could put the following commands in the batch file:

```
net use r: \\bali\officefiles
```

We probably don't want the batch file to continue if the drive mapping can't be made and the `net use` command fails. This might happen if the network server is down. Luckily, the net command—like most command-line programs—sets the batch file `errorlevel` to a value of 1 or higher if it can't complete its job, so we can write the command this way to stop the batch file in the event of a problem:

```
net use r: \\bali\officefiles
if errorlevel 1 (
    echo Unable to create mapping for drive R:, can't proceed
    pause
    exit /b
)
```

However, the `net use` command will also fail if drive `R:` is already in use when you start the batch file, even if it's connected to the same desired shared folder. So, before attempting to create a network mapping, the batch file should delete any preexisting connection with a command like this:

```
net use r: /delete
```

There's one last potential problem: If there was no preexisting drive mapping, this command will print an error message, even though as far as we're concerned, that's not really a problem. To avoid seeing the error message, we can redirect this command's output to the NUL file—a black hole built into Windows; information written to file NUL is simply discarded. The `delete` command should be written as

```
net use r: /delete >nul 2>nul
```

to discard messages written to the standard output and to the standard error output. Putting it all together, this is how a batch file should set up a network drive mapping:

```
@echo off
net use r: /delete >nul 2>nul
net use r: \\bali\officefiles
if errorlevel 1 (
    echo Unable to create mapping for drive R:, can't proceed
    pause
    exit /b
)
```

After this, the batch file can use drive `R:` to copy files with programs such as `copy`, `xcopy`, or `robocopy`. Then at the end of the batch file you would probably also want to delete the drive mapping, although that is optional.

Here's an actual batch file I use on my network to back up any account's Documents folder to a network server:

```
@echo off

rem *** set up drive R to point to \\server\backups
net use r: /delete >nul 2>nul
net use r: \\server\backups
if errorlevel 1 (
    echo Unable to create mapping for drive R:, can't proceed
    pause
    exit /b
)
```

```
rem *** copy the current user's Documents folder to the network
rem *** folder, inside subfolders named for this computer and user
xcopy "%USERPROFILE%\Documents" "R:\%COMPUTERNAME%\%USERNAME%" /H/K/R/E/D/I/Y
rem *** remove the drive mapping
net use r: /delete
```

THE sc COMMAND

sc is called the Service Controller program, and for good reason. sc can manage just about every aspect of installing, maintaining, and modifying system services and device drivers on local and networked Windows computers. It's another command with a huge number of options, which you can list by typing sc /?. It has so many options that after printing the /? help information, it prompts you to see whether you want to view additional information about its query and queryex subcommands. Here, I'll focus on how sc is useful in batch files.

The basic format of an sc command is as follows:

```
sc [\\computername] command [servicename [option ...]]
```

If the *computername* argument is omitted, sc operates on the local computer. There is no provision for entering an alternative username or password, so you'll need to be logged on using an account that is recognized as an Administrator if you want to do more than view the installed services on another computer.

LISTING INSTALLED SERVICES

The command sc queryex (or sc \\computername queryex) prints a long list of installed services along with their current status. A typical service listing looks like this:

```
SERVICE_NAME: Dhcp
DISPLAY_NAME: DHCP Client
        TYPE               : 20  WIN32_SHARE_PROCESS
        STATE              : 4   RUNNING
                                 (STOPPABLE,NOT_PAUSABLE,ACCEPTS_SHUTDOWN)
        WIN32_EXIT_CODE    : 0   (0x0)
        SERVICE_EXIT_CODE  : 0   (0x0)
        CHECKPOINT         : 0x0
        WAIT_HINT          : 0x0
        PID                : 844
        FLAGS              :
```

Table 32.3 details the most useful parts of this listing.

TABLE 32.3 USEFUL FIELDS IN THE sc queryex PRINTOUT

Field	Description
SERVICE_NAME	The "short" name for the service. This name can be used with the sc or net command to start and stop the service.
DISPLAY_NAME	The "long" name for the service. This name is displayed in the Services panel in Windows Management.
STATE	The service's current activity state.
PID	The service's process identifier number.

You can add type= driver or type= service (with a space after the equals sign) to the sc queryex command to limit the listing to just drivers or just services.

Starting and Stopping Services

System managers occasionally need to start and stop services for several reasons: to reset a malfunctioning service, to force a service to reinitialize itself with new startup data, or to temporarily stop a service while other services are being maintained. You can manage services using the GUI Windows Management tool, but when you have to perform this sort of task frequently, it's more convenient to use a batch file. For instance, I use a batch file to stop and restart my company's mail server after I make changes to its configuration file. Typing the batch file's name is much easier than navigating through Computer Management.

To use sc to start and stop services on a local or remote computer, you must know the service's "short" name. The easiest way to find a service's short name is to use sc queryex to get the listing of all service names, as described previously. Then you can put the command

```
sc stop servicename
```

or

```
sc \\computername stop servicename
```

into a batch file to stop a service on the local computer or on a remote computer. Likewise, you can use the command

```
sc start servicename
```

or

```
sc \\computername start servicename
```

to start the service. A stop command followed by a start command is the most useful combination because it lets you restart the service to recover from a crash or a hung condition. My mail server's downup.bat batch file contains

```
sc stop SMTPRS
sc stop SMTPDS
sc stop POP3S
sc start SMTPRS
sc start SMTPDS
sc start POP3S
```

which restarts the receiver, delivery, and post office services that are used in my mail system. This is another of those convenience batch files that I discussed earlier; it's much easier to type "downup" than to spend a minute or two poking at the Services Management tool.

> **NOTE**
>
> sc has many other commands that let you install and configure services as well as interrogate their operational status and dependency lists. The installation commands can be especially useful if you need to deploy services in an enterprise environment.

The Shutdown Command

The shutdown command can be used to log off, turn down, or restart the computer from the command line. You can see the full command line syntax by typing shutdown /? ¦ more in a Command Prompt window. The command can operate on the local computer (the computer on which the command is run), or on another computer on the network. The network option can be used to restart a computer that you are managing remotely, or perhaps to try to regain access to a computer that is failing to respond to Remote Desktop or remote management commands.

The command-line options are used primarily to determine the following things:

- Whether to perform a logoff, hibernate, shutdown, or a restart. The /l option logs off the user who runs the command. The /r option performs a restart. The /h option hibernates the computer. With the /s option, the computer is shut down. Be very careful about this if you are managing a remote computer. If you shut it down, you won't be able to use a command-line program to turn it back on again (unless the computer has a functioning wake-on-LAN feature).

- Which computer to shut down. With the /m computername on the command line, a remote computer can be shut down (or restarted, or whatever). Without /m the command affects the local computer.

- Whether to perform the action instantly, or after a delay. The default delay is 30 seconds. To perform the action instantly, add the option /t 0. To perform the action after *n* seconds, add the option /t *n*. Adding the /t option implies the /f option, which forces the shutdown to occur even if programs are running. If you don't use /t, you may want to add /f so that running applications can't stop the shutdown (of course, any work in progress will be lost, but the alternative is that the computer won't shut down as desired).

  If you use the /t feature, you can cancel an impending shutdown during the countdown by repeating the shutdown command with the /a option.

You can look at the command syntax description to see additional options. You may want to use the additional options to record a shutdown reason in the computer's Event log.

Setting Environment Variables

Environment variables are one of the ways that Windows communicates information such as the location of system files and folders—as set up on your particular computer—to programs. Environment variables indicate where temporary files are stored, what folders contain Windows program files, and other settings that affect program operation and system performance. In addition, they can be used in batch files to temporarily hold information about the job at hand.

Windows sets up a predefined set of environment variables for you, including the ones listed in Table 32.4.

NOTE

If you were familiar with the environment variables defined by Windows 2000 and XP, you'll want to take a careful look at the list for Vista because it contains many new entries that were needed to accommodate the way that Microsoft fractured the Windows Vista user profile folder structure.

If you want to write batch files that will work with user profile folders, you should not assume that you know where files are stored, but should use the most specific environment variable you can. For example, in Windows 2000 and XP the user's Application Data folder was in the user's profile folder, and you could use the path `%USERPROFILE%\Application Data`. However, on Windows Vista, it's in a different location. You should use the environment variable `APPDATA`, which will yield the correct path on all three operating systems.

→ For more information about the profile folder structure in Windows Vista, **see** "Where's My Stuff, or, the User Profile Structure," **p. 105**.

TABLE 32.4 SOME OF WINDOWS VISTA'S ENVIRONMENT VARIABLES

Variable Name	Contains
ALLUSERSPROFILE	The path to the folder that contains files visible to all users, including desktop items, Start menu items, and the Shared Documents folder.*
APPDATA	The path to the AppData\Roaming subfolder in the current user's profile. This particular folder is intended to hold user-specific information that is not machine-specific. If the user is using a roaming user profile, this folder is replicated on any computer the user logs on to.
COMPUTERNAME	The network name of this computer.*
ComSpec	The path to the command prompt shell program cmd.exe. Note the use of upper- and lowercase letters in the name; this is a change from previous versions of Windows. This will not affect batch files, but it may affect application programs.
FP_NO_HOST_CHECK	This variable appears to have something to do with Microsoft's FrontPage web page editor, but its purpose isn't even described on Microsoft's website.
HOMEDRIVE	The drive letter for the user's profile folder (the user's *home directory*).
HOMEPATH	The path of the user's profile folder, without the drive letter. The full path is thus %HOMEDRIVE%%HOMEPATH%.*
LOCALAPPDATA	The path to the AppData\Local subfolder in the current user's profile. This particular folder is intended to hold user-specific information that *is* machine-specific. The information in this folder stays on this computer.*
LOGONSERVER	The name of the computer that authenticated the current user. On a domain network, this will be the name of a domain server; otherwise, it will be the name of the local computer.*

Variable Name	Contains
OS	Always set to `Windows_NT`. You can check this value in batch files to let you know that you are running on Windows NT, 2000, XP, or Vista, as opposed to MS-DOS, Window 3.1, or Windows 9x. It does *not* let you distinguish whether a batch file is running under cmd.exe or command.com, however.*
PATH	The list of folders that Windows searches when you try to run a program by entering its name.
PATHEXT	The list of file extensions that Windows considers to indicate runnable programs: .COM, .EXE, .BAT, .CMD, and so on.
PROGRAMDATA	The path to the folder that holds application data common to all users. This folder was \Documents and Settings\All Users\Application Data on Windows XP, but it's \Program Data on Vista.
PROGRAMFILES	The path to the \Program Files folder.
PROMPT	A specification of how Windows is to display the prompt in a Command Prompt window. By default, it is `$P$G`, which displays the current drive and folder behind the >.
PUBLIC	The path to the `Public` profile folder. This was the `All Users` profile in Windows XP.
SystemDrive	The drive letter on which Windows is installed.
SystemRoot	The path to the System32 folder in the Windows installation folder.*
TEMP	The folder in which applications are to create temporary (scratch) files.
TMP	Like `TEMP`. (Some applications look at the `TMP` variable, and other applications look at `TEMP` to get the name of the temporary file folder.)
USERDOMAIN	The name of the Windows domain in which the user's account belongs. For local accounts, or for computers that are not part of a domain network, this is the computer's name.
USERNAME	The logon name of the current user.*
USERPROFILE	The path to your profile folder, the folder that contains your Documents folder, your Start menu, and so on.* The structure of the profile folder has changed significantly from Windows XP.
	→ See "User Profiles" in Chapter 5 for more information.
windir	The path to the Windows installation folder.*

These variables are informational only; changing their value doesn't change the corresponding location or name.

In DOS and Windows 9x, environment variables were usually set up in the AUTOEXEC.BAT file, using lines like this:

```
SET PROMPT=$P$G
SET TEMP=C:\TEMP
SET PATH=C:\WINDOWS;C:\DOS;C:\MOUSE;C:\BIN
```

In Windows Vista, you can still change environment variables with the SET command, but SET commands affect only the Command Prompt window in which you type them. The initial environment variables that are defined when every Command Prompt window is first opened are set up using a nifty graphical user interface, shown in Figure 32.2.

Figure 32.2
Examining the environment variables for the current user (top) and for all users of the system (bottom).

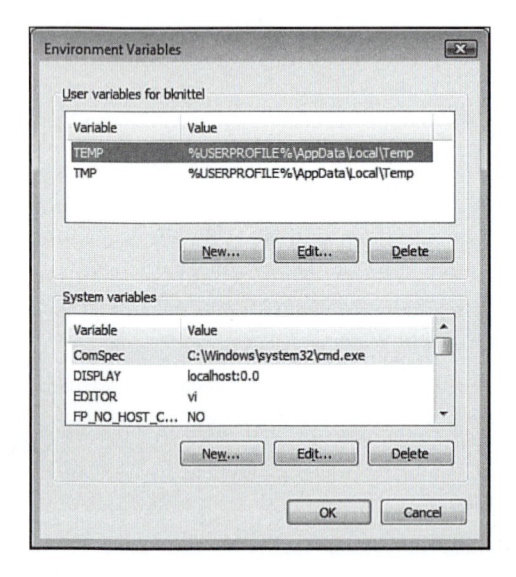

Notice that this dialog box has two sections, System Variables and User Variables. The lower System Variables part defines the environment variables set up for every user account. The upper User Variables part defines additional default environment variables just for the current user account. These can add to or override the system variables.

Getting to this dialog box is not as simple as you might hope, thanks to some quirky side effects of Vista's User Account Controls feature. Here's what you need to do:

- To edit your own account's default variables, click Start, Control Panel, User Accounts and Family Safety, User Accounts. In the task list at the left side, click Change My Environment Variables. This will bring you to the dialog, where you can edit your user account's "personal" variables in the upper list.

- To edit the systemwide default variables, click Start, right-click Computer, and select Properties. Select Advanced System Settings and confirm the User Account Control Prompt. You must be an administrator, or supply an administrator password. When the dialog box appears, you can edit the lower System Variables list.

Setting Environment Variables

CAUTION

> You might be tempted to also edit the upper User Variables list here, but take note where it says User Variables for *Accountname*. If you had to enter an administrator password to get to this dialog, you'd be editing the variables for the wrong account. If the upper part shows the wrong account name, close the dialog box and use the previous method to get to the dialog box via the Control Panel.

After you have the dialog box open, you can create new variables, delete a variable, or edit a variable using the corresponding buttons.

If you need to alter a variable, you must understand what happens if there's a conflict between environment variables defined in both the System Variables and User Variables lists. As a rule, Windows examines several locations for definitions, and the last definition seen wins. Windows sets variables in the following order:

1. System variables.
2. User variables. (At this step, the PATH variable is treated specially. See the next section for details.)
3. Variables defined by set commands in AUTOEXEC.NT. (This applies only for MS-DOS or Windows 3.x applications. See "The MS-DOS Environment" later in the chapter for more information.)
4. Subsequent definitions issued by set and setx commands typed in a Command Prompt window or encountered in a batch file. These changes apply only to that particular window and will disappear when the window is closed.

Why modify environment variables? Good question. Not many people need to. Probably the most likely reasons to modify these variables are to change the folder that applications use to create temporary work files and to add directories to the system's search path. Or, you might have particular applications that require special environment variables to be set. Finally, some command-line utilities look for environment variables to set the default value of certain options. For example, copy checks to see whether an environment variable named COPYCMD has been defined and, if it has, it interprets COPYCMD as containing default command-line switches. I'll discuss these options in the next several sections.

NOTE

> Windows Vista comes with a command-line program named setx that can also set the system or user default environment variables. It's rather complex, but you can read about it by typing setx /? in a Command Prompt window. Here's the quick and dirty version:
>
> Type setx VARIABLENAME defaultvalue to set your personal default variable, or setx VARIABLENAME defaultvalue /M to set the system default. In either case, the change won't take effect until you open a new Command Prompt window. setx must be running with elevated privileges if you specify the /M switch.

Setting the path Environment Variable

One of the most important environment variables is called `PATH`. This variable lists the folders that Windows is to search whenever you attempt to run a program by typing its name without entering a path specification. For example, if I type `regedit` into a Command Prompt window, or into the Start, Run dialog, the Registry Editor window appears. But how does Windows know that "regedit" means `C:\windows\system32\regedit.EXE`? The answer is in the `PATH` variable. On my computer, `PATH` contains this:

```
D:\Perl\bin;C:\WINDOWS\system32;C:\WINDOWS;
   ➥C:\WINDOWS\system32\WBEM;"C:\program files\scripts";
   ➥ "C:\Program Files\Symantec\pcAnywhere";c:\progra~1\winzip;
   ➥"c:\users\bknittel\scripts";c:\bin;c:\bat
```

The value of the `PATH` variable is a list of folder names separated by semicolons. (The `PATH` on your computer will almost certainly be different, depending on what software you've installed.)

When I type `regedit` as a command name, Windows searches the folders named in the `PATH` variable in order, looking for the first one that contains an executable (.exe) program whose name is `regedit`. It finds the standard Windows utility in the second folder, `c:\WINDOWS\system32`.

> **NOTE**
>
> The `PATH` variable is used for Windows GUI programs as well as command-line and MS-DOS programs; it's used any time a program is not specified with a full path.

Many applications add their own installation folders to the path during installation. Thus, you will seldom if ever need to modify the `PATH` to provide access to programs designed to run from the command line. If you write batch files or scripts, however, it's useful to put all of these into one folder and to enter this folder name into the `PATH`, so that you can run your batch files and scripts simply by typing their names.

Because it's so common for users to want to put a personal folder into the `PATH`, and because mis-editing the `PATH` variable can prevent Windows from finding applications it needs to run, Windows gives the "user variables" `PATH` definition special treatment:

- For the `PATH` variable, the User Variables definition is *appended* to the System Variable definition.

- For all other environment variables, a User Variables definition *overrides* a System Variables definition.

In other words, you can enter your own personal folder(s) into the User Variables definition of `PATH` without worrying about messing up the standard definitions.

For example, a few paragraphs back I showed my computer's `PATH` setting. It's set up this way: The System Variables `PATH` definition is

```
D:\Perl\bin;C:\WINDOWS\system32;C:\WINDOWS;C:\WINDOWS\system32\WBEM;
"C:\program files\scripts";"C:\Program Files\Symantec\pcAnywhere";
c:\progra~1\winzip;"%USERPROFILE%\scripts"
```

These folders are used for every user on my computer. My account's User Variables PATH definition contains only my personal folders:

`c:\bin;c:\bat`

When I log on, Windows automatically adds my personal folders *after* the systemwide folders.

> **TIP**
> To make it even easier to have personal PATH folders, you can automatically give each user a place to store his own personal programs by placing `%USERPROFILE%\scripts` in the System Variables PATH definition. This gives each user the option of creating a folder named `scripts` in his profile folder, into which he can put commonly used batch files, programs, and scripts.

You can also modify the PATH variable for the current Command Prompt window by directly setting the environment variable at the command prompt. It's best to do this by adding a new folder at the beginning or end of the existing path list, rather than by replacing the list entirely. Type the string `%path%` where you want the original PATH contents to appear. For example, you can add the folder `c:\myfolder` to the head of the path list by typing

`set path=c:\myfolder;%path%`

or to the end of the path by typing

`set path=%path%;c:\myfolder`

You also can use this technique to modify the path from within a batch file.

Specifying the Location of Temporary Files

Many applications create temporary files to hold information while you're working. These files are usually deleted when the application exits. Sometimes, however, they're not deleted, and they can accumulate, taking up a lot of disk space. To make management simpler, you may want to control where they are stored. By custom, most applications that do create temporary files create them in the folder named by either the TMP or TEMP environment variable.

By default, both TMP and TEMP are defined in the System Settings list as `%userprofile%\AppDdata\Local\Temp`. `%userprofile%` is an environment variable that contains the full path to your user profile folder. The net result is that, for my account, temporary files are created in `C:\users\bknittel\AppData\Local\Temp`.

Now, for maximum security, placing each user's temporary files in a different folder is a good idea. Also, with Fast User Switching active, several users could have applications running at the same time, so placing temporary files in a different folder for each user avoids the possibility of conflicts in the filenames. On my own computer, however, I am not worried about interuser security, and to make cleanup easier, I personally prefer to place temporary files for all users in a folder named `\temp` on the hard drive with the most space. On my computer this is `D:\temp`.

To specify the location of temporary files for your account alone, set the values of variables TEMP and TMP in the User Settings section. To specify the same location for *all* accounts, set the values in the System Settings section and be sure to delete any settings in the User Settings section on every account—otherwise, the User Settings will override the System Settings.

NOTE

If you designate a folder in a partition that is formatted with the NTFS file system, be sure that the user or users who are set up to use it have read and write permissions on the folder! Ensure this by editing the folder's security properties, adding the group Users, and giving Users all permissions except Full Control.

NOTE

You might be inspired to create a separate folder for each user with a setting such as `D:\temp\%username%`. This will work, but you must create the folder for each user in advance. Windows will *not* create the folders automatically, and if the folder specified by TEMP or TMP does not exist, most applications either will fail or will create temporary files in seemingly random locations.

Setting Command Prompt Window Properties

The Command Prompt window displays a text-mode window that looks a lot like a DOS computer's screen. This window is actually a true 32-bit Windows application, although it can also execute old MS-DOS applications. Settings you make in the Command Prompt window affect both the window itself and any console programs or DOS programs that run in it.

When you open a Command Prompt window or run a DOS-based program, the window defaults to a standard size, background color, and font. Configuration options on the window's Control menu allow you to alter settings for the specific session. Options in the dialog boxes also let you save the settings to establish new defaults. You can set the properties like this:

1. Click Start, All Programs, Accessories, Command Prompt. This runs the Windows Vista command prompt, a true Windows program, but the settings you'll make here are applied to console and MS-DOS programs running inside the window as well.

2. On the resulting Command Prompt window, click the upper-left corner to open the Control menu, and choose either Properties or Default:
   - Properties sets the properties for this box and optionally all other boxes with the same title (as seen in the box's title bar) in the future.
   - Default applies the settings to Command Prompt windows and DOS-based programs from here on out (even with other programs running in them).

The resulting dialog box is the same in either case; only the window title is different. You can see it in Figure 32.3.

SETTING COMMAND PROMPT WINDOW PROPERTIES 1093

Figure 32.3
Here, you can set the default properties for all Command Prompt windows.

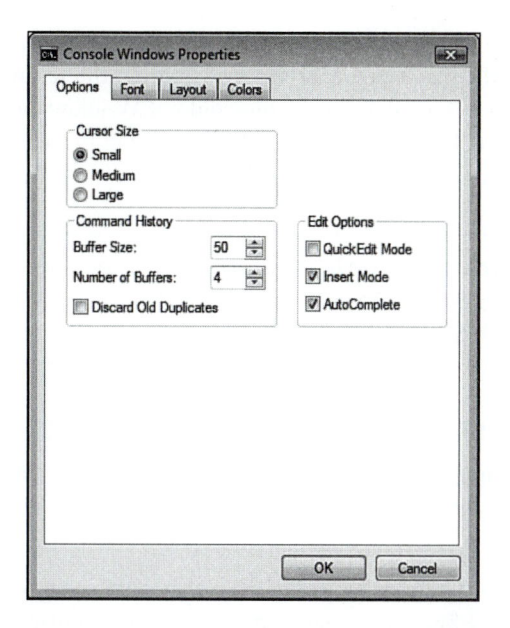

3. Click through the tabs, and notice the settings. Table 32.5 lists some of the more useful settings.
4. Make changes as necessary, and click OK.

TABLE 32.5 SOME USEFUL CONSOLE WINDOW PROPERTIES

Tab	Item	Description
Options	QuickEdit Mode	Check to enable copying to the Windows Clipboard by selecting text and pressing Enter. Uncheck if you need to use the mouse with an MS-DOS application.
	Insert Mode	Check to set insert mode as the default for command-line editing; uncheck to overwrite by default. (Press the Ins key while editing to toggle.)
	AutoComplete	Check to have the Tab key automatically complete a partial filename you've typed on the command line.
Font	Size, Font	Sets the character size in the window.
Layout	Screen Buffer Size	Sets the width and number of lines of text that are stored for the screen; if larger than the window size, you can scroll back to view previously displayed text.

If you're changing the properties for a specific window, the default is to change the properties for this window only. If you want to use these settings every time you launch this program, select Modify Shortcut That Started This Window and then click OK.

When you make this choice, Windows edits the PIF file for the DOS application in question (or the _DEFAULT.PIF in the case of a CMD window), storing the settings. PIF files are stored in the same folders as MS-DOS program files and tell Windows how the MS-DOS program is to be handled. We'll talk more about PIF files later in this chapter, in the "Editing Advanced Settings for a DOS Application" section.

> **TIP**
> Setting a large buffer size can be a real boon if you run batch files or other programs that normally cause text to scroll off the top of the screen. A large buffer enables you to scroll back the screen and check program flow and error messages.

KEEPING A COMMAND PROMPT WINDOW OPEN AFTER EXECUTION

When you run a command-line program or batch file from the Command Prompt window, the window stays open after the program completes, and you can read any messages the program has printed.

However, if you launch the program or batch file from a shortcut, or by entering its name into the Search window or the Start, Run dialog, by default the command window will close automatically as soon as the program exits. To keep the window open, follow these steps:

1. Create a shortcut to the DOS program or batch file.
2. Right-click the shortcut, and choose Properties.
3. Select the Program tab.
4. Uncheck Close on Exit. The window will now stay open after the program exits. You'll have to close it manually when you're finished reading its output.

> **TIP**
> If the command prints more text than fits on the screen and some scrolls off, you can usually simply scroll the window up to see the first part of the output. If more text is generated than the scrolling function can keep track of, you can increase the amount of stored text by editing the shortcut's properties. Select the Layout tab and increase the Screen Buffer Size Height value. Alternatively, run the program from a batch file and send its output through the more command by adding ¦ more to the end of the command line. This will display one screen at a time. Press Enter to see each successive page.

THE MS-DOS ENVIRONMENT

If you still use MS-DOS programs, you'll be glad to know that the 32-bit versions of Windows Vista still support MS-DOS programs, and the MS-DOS environment that Windows Vista uses is highly configurable.

> **NOTE**
>
> The MS-DOS and 16-bit Windows subsystems are not provided with the 64-bit versions of Windows Vista. If you use a 64-bit version and still need to run MS-DOS or Windows 3.1 applications, you can download and install the free Microsoft Virtual PC program from microsoft.com, or use VMWare from www.vmware.com. With either of these programs, you can set up a "virtual" copy of MS-DOS, Windows 3.1, or any subsequent version of Windows and run your older applications inside the simulated environment. It's not as effortless as the built-in support provided by 32-bit versions of Windows, but it works well.

→ For more information about virtual PCs, **see** "The Virtual Machine Approach," **p. 73**.

Windows Vista doesn't actually run "on top" of MS-DOS as Windows 3.1, 95, 98, and Me did. These older operating systems could run MS-DOS programs directly.

Windows Vista, XP, 2000, and NT run MS-DOS applications inside a program called `ntvdm`, which stands for *Windows NT Virtual DOS Machine*. `ntvdm` is also used by the Windows 3.x support environment. It simulates the environment that DOS programs expect and makes them work correctly under Windows. For example, DOS programs can directly access system hardware such as sound adapters, COM ports, system timers, and so on. This isn't permitted on Vista, so `ntvdm` detects a DOS program's attempts to access hardware and intercedes on the program's behalf to perform the intended action in a way that Windows permits.

`ntvdm` runs automatically when you attempt to start an MS-DOS or 16-bit Windows program. You don't have to take any special steps to activate it, but you can tune it in several ways by doing the following:

- Configure the user variables in the System dialog box, as discussed in the section "Setting Environment Variables" earlier in the chapter.
- Make selections from the DOS window's Control menu.
- Make settings in the Properties sheet for a shortcut to the DOS application.
- Set up custom AUTOEXEC.NT and CONFIG.NT configuration files so that you can address most special memory or environment variable setting requirements a DOS program might have.
- Enter environment-altering commands at the command prompt.

You can choose from many settings, including the following, all of which can be set for an individual program or as defaults to be used any time a Command Prompt window or DOS program is run. You can make the following settings:

- Set the window font (including TrueType and bitmapped font styles)
- Set the background and foreground colors for normal text

- Set the background and foreground colors for pop-up boxes
- Choose window or full-screen viewing
- Set the default window position on the screen
- Use or turn off the QuickEdit mode, which lets you copy text to the Clipboard by highlighting it on the DOS window and pressing Enter
- Use or hide the mouse pointer in the application

In addition to these settings, you can set the search path and other environment variables, specify memory requirements (for EMS and XMS), and set other nitty-gritty options using Program Information Files (PIF files) and the System option in the Control Panel. Unless specified otherwise, Windows uses the file _DEFAULT.PIF, stored in the default Windows folder (usually \windows), as the basis for MS-DOS sessions and running applications that don't have a PIF. When you alter the "properties" for DOS applications by right-clicking the application and making settings, you create a customized PIF file for that application. The result of running any DOS application, however, is that Windows creates a PIF on-the-fly and assigns the default settings to it unless other settings are specified.

NOTE In the MS-DOS subsystem all environment variable names are entirely uppercase letters. Paths in several system-defined variables are automatically converted to "8.3" format names, including the variables ALLUSERSPROFILE, APPDATA, COMMONPROGRAMFILES, PATH, PROGRAMFILES, SYSTEMDRIVE, SYSTEMROOT, and USERPROFILE. The COMSPEC variable points to COMMAND.COM rather than cmd.exe. The windir variable is not passed to the MS-DOS system.

If your MS-DOS program gives error messages when it tries to open files, **see** "MS-DOS Program Can't Open Enough Files" in the "Troubleshooting" section at the end of this chapter.

If your older MS-DOS application displays lots of strange characters on the screen, especially the combination "←[", **see** "MS-DOS Application Displays Garbage Characters" in the "Troubleshooting" section at the end of this chapter.

Customizing AUTOEXEC.NT and CONFIG.NT

You can choose to further configure the MS-DOS and Windows 3.x environment by modifying Vista's equivalent of the old CONFIG.SYS and AUTOEXEC.BAT files. In Windows Vista, as in Windows NT, XP, and 2000, these files are called CONFIG.NT and AUTOEXEC.NT. They are the files used to configure each DOS VDM when it starts up.

When you run a DOS or 16-bit Windows application, Vista creates a DOS VDM by loading the DOS environment subsystem and sort of "booting up" DOS. In the process, it reads in settings from CONFIG.NT and AUTOEXEC.NT in just the same way the original DOS read CONFIG.SYS and AUTOEXEC.BAT when it booted. The difference is the filenames and the file locations. In this case, the files are in the SYSTEM32 directory (usually \WINDOWS\SYSTEM32 or \WINNT\SYSTEM32) instead of the drive's root directory. Each time you run a DOS application in a new window (that is, each time a new VDM is created), Windows reads the CONFIG.NT and AUTOEXEC.NT files. The great thing about this capability is that you can change the settings and rerun a program, and the new settings get read and go into effect immediately. It's like rebooting DOS after fine-tuning CONFIG.SYS and AUTOEXEC.BAT—except faster.

Just remember:

- The files CONFIG.SYS and AUTOEXEC.BAT in your hard drive's root folder are completely ignored by Windows Vista. If they're there it's only to fool *really* old applications that won't run unless they see that these files exist.
- The files CONFIG.NT and AUTOEXEC.NT in \WINDOWS\SYSTEM32 *are* used but only when Windows needs to start up an MS-DOS or Windows 3.x application. The settings in these files affect *only* the one DOS or Win3.x application you're running at the time, because they're read by the VDM program before it starts up the old application.

The standard settings in CONFIG.NT as set up when Windows is installed are shown in the following listing. The REM comments have been removed for brevity. (If you upgraded your computer from an earlier version of Windows, your CONFIG.NT may be different because the installer may have retained some of your previous operating system's settings.)

```
dos=high, umb
device=%SystemRoot%\system32\himem.sys
files=40
```

> **TIP**
> On my computers, I always change the `files` setting to `files=100` and add the line `device=%SystemRoot%\system32\ansi.sys`.
> For more information about ansi.sys, see the next section.

> **TIP**
> If you need to specify different CONFIG.NT and AUTOEXEC.NT settings for various MS-DOS programs, see "Custom Startup Files" later in this chapter.

You can edit the CONFIG.NT and AUTOEXEC.NT files with a simple text editor such as Notepad. They're protected files, however, so you must use this procedure to edit them:

1. Click Start, All Programs, Accessories.
2. Right-click Notepad and select Run As Administrator.
3. Confirm the User Account Control prompt, or enter an Administrator password as requested.
4. Click File, Open, and browse to \windows\system32. Select autoexec.nt or config.nt as desired.

For some reason, Microsoft chose not to provide a comprehensive list of the settings permitted in CONFIG.NT in Vista's online Help and Support, so I've listed them in Table 32.6.

TABLE 32.6 COMMANDS AVAILABLE FOR CONFIG.NT

Command	Description
`country=`	Sets the language conventions for the session.
`device=`	Installs loadable device drivers. Be careful with drivers that attempt to address hardware directly; they likely won't work. However, you can load display drivers such as ANSI.SYS and memory managers such as EMM.SYS and HIMEM.SYS.
`dos=`	Tells Windows 2000 what to do with the Upper Memory Area (where to load DOS, as in `dos=high`).
`dosonly`	Allows only DOS programs to be loaded from a COMMAND.COM prompt. Windows and UNIX programs won't run.
`echoconfig`	Tells the VDM to print CONFIG and AUTOEXEC commands as they are executed from the files.
`EMM`	Configures the EMM (Expanded Memory Manager). Applies only when the program's properties specify that the value for EMS memory is greater than 0.
`fcbs=`	Sets the maximum number of file control blocks (FCBs). This setting is required only for truly ancient DOS programs.
`files=`	Sets the maximum number of open files. I recommend setting this to 100.
`install=`	Loads a memory-resident (TSR) program into memory before the window comes up or an application loads.
`loadhigh=`	Loads a device driver into the High Memory Area (HMA).
`lh=`	Same as `loadhigh=`.
`ntcmdprompt`	Replaces the COMMAND.COM interpreter with the Windows Vista command interpreter, CMD.EXE. After you load a TSR or when you shell out of an application to DOS, you will get CMD.EXE instead, from which you have the added benefits of the full 32-bit interpreter.
`rem`	Marks a line as a comment, causing the system to ignore it when "booting" the file.
`stacks=`	Indicates the amount of RAM set aside for stacking up hardware interrupts as they come in.

The standard settings in AUTOEXEC.NT set up when Windows is installed are shown in the following listing. The REM comments have been removed for brevity. (And again, if you upgraded your computer from an earlier version of Windows, your AUTOEXEC.NT may be different.)

```
REM Install CD ROM extensions
lh %SystemRoot%\system32\mscdexnt.EXE

REM Install network redirector (load before dosx.EXE)
lh %SystemRoot%\system32\redir
```

```
REM Install DPMI support
lh %SystemRoot%\system32\dosx
REM The following line enables Sound Blaster 2.0 support on NTVDM.
SET BLASTER=A220 I5 D1 P330 T3
```

Here's what these do:

- `mscdexnt` gives DOS programs access to CD-ROM and DVD-ROM data discs.
- `redir` gives DOS programs access to shared network resources.
- `dosx` provides expanded and extended memory services.
- `SET BLASTER` tells DOS programs, through an environment variable, how to use the simulated SoundBlaster compatible sound services provided by the VDM. If your computer has any sort of audio output hardware, MS-DOS programs can use it by acting as if SoundBlaster-compatible hardware was installed; the VDM interprets SoundBlaster commands and performs the same instructions on your computer's sound hardware.

> **TIP**
> Editing these files properly is no piece of cake. At the time this book was written, they were not even documented in Windows's Help and Support. I suggest you have at hand a good DOS reference such as Que's *Special Edition Using DOS 6.22, Third Edition*.

Issues with DOSKEY and ANSI.SYS

Two of the most common enhancements used on MS-DOS computers were DOSKEY and ANSI.SYS. DOSKEY provided enhanced command-line editing: for example, the use of the up and down arrow keys to recall previous commands. ANSI.SYS gave DOS applications a way to easily control the position and color of text output onto the screen. Both enhancements are provided with Windows Vista, although they don't work exactly as you might expect.

ANSI.SYS can be made available for MS-DOS programs simply by adding the line `device=ansi.sys` to CONFIG.NT (or an alternate CONFIG file). Unfortunately, *no* ANSI cursor support is provided for 32-bit Windows character mode (console) applications.

Conversely, DOSKEY—which has been enhanced significantly from the old DOS days—functions only in the 32-bit Windows console environment, and even if you attempt to load it in AUTOEXEC.NT, it does not function within the MS-DOS "COMMAND.COM" shell—that is, after you've run any MS-DOS program in the Command Prompt window.

You can work around this limitation by instructing Windows to use CMD.EXE as the MS-DOS shell. Just add the line `NTCMDPROMPT` to your CONFIG.NT file. However, this may not work if you need to load Terminate-and-Stay-Resident (TSR) programs before your DOS application.

> **NOTE**
>
> If you make changes to AUTOEXEC.NT or CONFIG.NT after having run an MS-DOS program from a Command Prompt window, you must close the Command Prompt window and open a new one for the MS-DOS subsystem to reload and take on the new configuration.

EDITING ADVANCED SETTINGS FOR A DOS APPLICATION

If you're experiencing difficulties while running a specific DOS program, you should read this section to learn about making deeper changes to the properties settings for them. When you manipulate the properties (via the PIF) for a program, Windows fine-tunes the VDM environment for the particular application, allowing it to run more smoothly, or in some cases simply allowing it to run at all.

MS-DOS applications were designed to run in solitude. They assume that they are the only applications running and expect to have complete control over all of the hardware in the computer.

To successfully accommodate the DOS-based applications still in use, Windows must manage computer resources such as RAM, printers, modems, mouse devices, and display I/O. Significant sleight of hand is required to pull off this task smoothly, but Microsoft has done this fairly well, partly due to the use of PIFs.

PIFs (program information files) are small files stored on disk, usually in the default Windows folder (usually \WINDOWS) or in the same folder as the application. They contain settings that Windows uses when it runs a related application. When you modify the properties of a DOS EXE (executable) file or shortcut, Windows, in turn, edits the associated PIF. With the correct settings, the program runs properly, sparing you the aggravation caused by program crashes, sluggish performance, memory shortages, and other annoying anomalies. PIFs have the same initial name as the application but use .PIF as the extension (123.PIF, for example). When you run an MS-DOS application (using any technique), Windows searches the application's directory and the system search path for a PIF with the same name as the application. If one is found, this file's settings are applied to the DOS environment by the DOS environment subsystem before running the application. If no PIF is found, Windows uses the default settings stored in a file named _DEFAULT.PIF, stored in the \WINDOWS folder. These settings work for most DOS applications but not all; games and educational programs are likely to need the most modifications.

> **TIP**
>
> In earlier versions of Windows, you may have had to edit a PIF using the PIF Editor. You no longer need to do so. For all intents and purposes, you can forget about the existence of PIFs and focus on a DOS application's properties instead by right-clicking the application and choosing Properties. However, if you have specific instructions provided with an older application for making PIF file settings, follow the advice provided for the program in configuring the application's properties.

DOS property settings can affect many aspects of an application's operation, such as (but not limited to) the following:

- The drive and folder (directory) selected as the default when an application starts
- Full-screen or windowed operation upon launch
- Conventional memory usage
- Expanded or extended memory usage
- The application's multitasking priority level
- The application's shortcut keys
- Foreground and background processing

To edit these properties for a DOS program, do the following:

1. Find the program file or a shortcut to it.
2. Right-click and choose Properties. You then see a dialog box like the one shown in Figure 32.4. (In this example, I adjusted the properties for a DOS shareware game.)

Figure 32.4
Setting the properties for a DOS application.

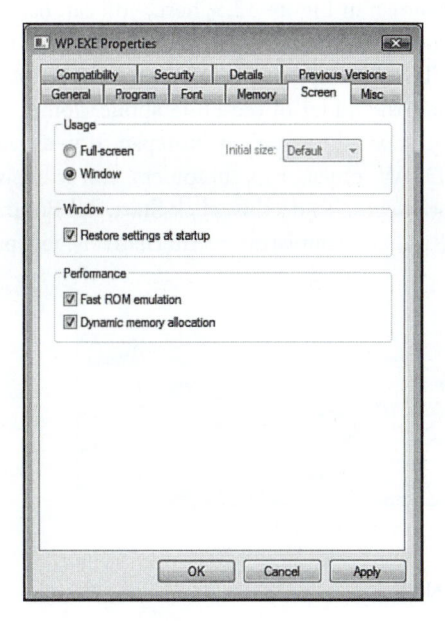

Poke through each tab, and use the ? (question mark) button for help on the settings. Educational and game programs will most often require you to adjust the Memory and Compatibility settings.

> **NOTE**
>
> On Windows Vista Business, Enterprise, and Ultimate editions, if the program is stored on an NTFS-formatted partition, the standard Security tab will also be listed in the property dialog.

TIP

> The Screen tab's Usage options determine whether the application initially comes up windowed or full-screen. You still can toggle between views by pressing Alt+Enter. Of course, in full-screen display, the mouse is surrendered to the application. When you use a mouse with a windowed application, the mouse works within the window on its menus, and with Windows when you move the mouse back to the Windows desktop. No DOS-based mouse driver is needed. Mouse support is provided automatically.
>
> If you use a shortcut to run an application that prints information to the screen, such as `tracert`, `ping`, or `dir`, see the next section to find out how to keep the window from disappearing before you can read the output.

CUSTOM STARTUP FILES

If you don't want every application's VDM to use the same AUTOEXEC.NT and CONFIG.NT settings, you can specify alternative AUTOEXEC and CONFIG files to be used instead on an application-by-application basis.

From the application's Properties page, select the Program tab and click the Advanced button. You then see the dialog box shown in Figure 32.5; here, you can name alternative files to be used. Just enter the names of the files. You should create your own modified files for this use. Start by copying CONFIG.NT and AUTOEXEC.NT from the \WINDOWS\SYSTEM32 folder to a new folder (the folder of the DOS application in question is a good spot). Then, edit them with a plain text editor such as Notepad. If you want to save the new files anywhere inside the \WINDOW folder or its subfolders, you will have to start the copy of Notepad with elevated privileges. To do this, click Start, All Programs, Accessories. Right-click Notepad and select Run As Administrator. Alternatively, just put the new files in your own profile folder.

Figure 32.5
You can specify a custom CONFIG.NT and AUTOEXEC.NT file for a given application.

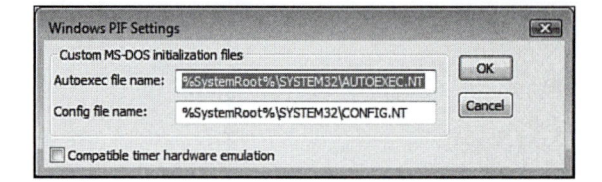

UNAVAILABLE MS-DOS COMMANDS

The MS-DOS commands in Table 32.7 are not available at the Windows Vista command prompt.

TABLE 32.7 MS-DOS COMMANDS NOT AVAILABLE IN WINDOWS VISTA

Command	New Procedure or Reason for Obsolescence
assign	Not supported in Windows Vista.
backup	Not supported.
ctty	Not supported.

Command	New Procedure or Reason for Obsolescence
dblspace	Not supported.
deltree	The `rmdir /s` command deletes directories containing files and subdirectories.
dosshell	Unnecessary with Windows Vista.
drvspace	Not currently supported.
emm386	Extended memory support is automatically provided for MS-DOS applications. It can be configured with the `EMM` command in config.nt.
fasthelp	Not available. Use `help` for help with command-line utilities.
fdisk	Use Disk Management to prepare hard disks for use with Windows Vista.
include	Multiple configurations of the MS-DOS subsystem are not supported.
interlnk	Not supported. Use the Network Connections Wizard to configure a direct connection via parallel, serial, or infrared (IR) ports.
intersrv	Not supported. Use the Network Connections Wizard to configure a direct connection via parallel, serial, or infrared (IR) ports.
join	File systems can be joined from the Disk Management console.
memmaker	Windows automatically optimizes the MS-DOS subsystem's memory use.
menucolor	Multiple configurations of the MS-DOS subsystem are not supported.
menudefault	Multiple configurations of the MS-DOS subsystem are not supported.
menuitem	Multiple configurations of the MS-DOS subsystem are not supported.
mirror	Not supported.
msav	Not supported.
msbackup	Not supported.
mscdex	CD-ROM support for MS-DOS applications is provided by `mscdexnt` run within AUTOEXEC.NT.
msd	Not supported. Use `systeminfo` instead.
numlock	Not supported.
power	Not supported.
restore	Not supported.
scandisk	Not supported.
smartdrv	Windows automatically provides disk caching for the MS-DOS subsystem.
submenu	Multiple configurations of the MS-DOS subsystem are not supported.
sys	Not supported.
undelete	Not supported.
unformat	Not supported.
vsafe	Not supported.

Batch Files

Although Windows Script Host is the most powerful tool for creating your own helpful programs, it's also useful to know how to use the batch file language. Batch files let you take advantage of the hundreds of command-line programs supplied with Windows. Although the batch file language is less powerful than VBScript, it has variables, primitive functions, and rudimentary flow-of-control commands, so it does qualify as a programming language.

A batch file, at the simplest level, is just a list of command prompt commands typed into a file whose extension is .BAT or .CMD. When you enter the name of a batch file at the command prompt, Windows looks for a file with this name in the current directory and in the folders of the PATH environment variable. Windows treats each of the lines in the batch file as a command and runs them as if you'd typed the commands by hand. At this simplest level, then, a batch file can be a big help if you find yourself typing the same commands over and over.

Batch File Basics

On every computer I own, I make a folder named c:\bat to hold my batch files and scripts, and I put this folder in the PATH. Because this folder is in the PATH, any script or batch file in it is available whenever I'm using a Command Prompt window. You may want to start by creating this folder and putting c:\bat into your PATH (in the User Variables section) too, following the instructions shown earlier under "Setting the PATH Environment Variable."

→ For more information on the PATH Environment Variable, **see** " Setting the PATH Environment Variable," **p. 1090**.

To create a new batch file, follow these steps:

1. Open a Command Prompt window.
2. Change to the folder that you'll use to contain your batch files. If you're using \bat as I do, type `cd \bat` and press Enter.
3. Type the command `notepad filename.bat`, but use the name of the batch file you want to create in place of *filename*. Press Enter, and when Notepad asks whether you want to create a new file, click Yes.
4. Type the commands that you want to put into your batch file. Then click File, Save, and File, Exit.
5. Test the batch file by typing its name on the command line.

To make changes to an existing batch file, simply repeat these steps.

Because I use the Command Prompt window a lot, I like to make batch files with one- or two-letter names, which contain commonly used commands.

For example, if I'm working for a client named "XYZ Corporation" and I have this client's files in a folder named d:\data\xyz project, I'll probably have a frequent need to have a

Command Prompt window open in this folder. So, I'll create a batch file named c:\bat\xyz.bat with this one line inside:

```
cd /d d:\data\xyz project
```

(Adding /d to the cd command sets both the current drive and the current directory.) Now, whenever I open a Command Prompt window, I can type **xyz**, and Windows will instantly switch to the right drive and directory. This may sound trivial, but this kind of batch file is a real time-saver and I personally use them every day.

Another command I use frequently is one to test whether my network's DSL connection is working correctly. Previously whenever I ran into an Internet glitch, I found myself typing the command

```
ping 65.104.11.1
```

which tests the "gateway" address for my Internet service provider. If the ping command can reach this address, it means that my Internet connection is working, and any connectivity problems must be out there on the Internet. This command goes into the file c:\bat\dsl.bat. Now I can just type **dsl** to instantly test my line without having to go look up that darned number.

Of course, batch files can contain more than just one command, but the principle remains the same: If you find yourself entering the same command or sequence of commands over and over, put them into a batch file to save wear and tear on your fingers.

Batch files become even more useful when you start using command-line arguments. Anything you type on the command line after the name of the batch file can be used to insert filenames and so on into the commands in your batch file. Anywhere that %1 appears in a batch file, the characters %1 are replaced with the first extra word on the command line. Likewise, %2 gets replaced with the second argument on the command line, and so on.

For example, if I created a batch file named bf.bat with this line inside

```
notepad c:\bat\%1.bat
```

and then typed

```
bf ibm
```

at the command prompt, Windows would see this as

```
notepad c:\bat\ibm.bat
```

and would run Windows Notepad to edit the file ibm.bat. Now I have a batch file that will let me easily edit any batch file in the folder c:\bat. It's not exactly rocket science, but you can see that with longer sequences of commands, this can really save time and trouble.

Here are a few other batch file basics:

- Normally, Windows prints out each line of a batch file as it reads through it; this is called *echoing* the commands. It can be ugly. You can suppress echoing of any line in the batch file by starting the line with an at sign (@); this is removed from the command line before it's run.

- You can permanently disable echoing in a batch file with the command `echo off`; this way you don't have to start each command with `@`. To keep this command from being echoed before it takes effect, you do need to use `@` with just this command. This is why many batch files start with the line `@echo off`.

- Any lines that start with the words `rem` or `remark` are treated as comments, not commands.

- If you have a batch file that isn't doing what you expect it to do, change the batch file's first line to `rem @echo off`. Now, without echo off, when you run the batch file, the commands will echo as they're encountered, and you can see where it's going astray. When it's fixed, remove the word `rem` to make it quiet again.

- Wherever they occur in the batch file, the sequences `%1`, `%2`, `%3`, and so on are replaced with the first, second, and third command-line arguments and so on. You can use this to specify filenames and other information at the time you run the batch file, rather than having this information hard-wired in.

- If the user types fewer command-line arguments than you expect, these command-line substitution sequences are replaced with nothing—that is, they disappear. For example, if you run a batch file with the command `mybatch one two three`, `%3` will be replaced by `three`, but `%4` will silently disappear.

- If you enter the name of an environment variable surrounded by percent signs, Windows replaces this sequence with the value of the environment variable. For example, `%USERNAME%` will be replaced with the logon name of the user running the batch file. (Environment variable names aren't case sensitive, so `%username%` does the same thing.)

- Many predefined environment variables can provide information such as the current user's logon name and the user's home and profile directories. These variables were listed earlier in the chapter in Table 32.4.

  In addition, the `cmd` command-line processor provides some "simulated" environment variables that always provide current information without ever being set. These are as follows:

  `%date%` is replaced with the current date.

  `%time%` is replaced with the current time.

  `%cd%` is replaced with the current directory.

- There is a way to extract just part of an environment variable or command-line argument. For information and examples, go to www.microsoft.com and search for the phrase "using batch files." Look at the article with that title, and view the entries "Using batch parameters" and "for." The discussion of batch parameter substitution applies to command-line parameters as well as batch parameters. The "For" command page has a section titled "Variable Substitution," and the technniques described there apply to environment variable substitution as well as to the `for` variable.

- If you need to use the percent sign itself in a command, you need to type `%%` for each one you need to indicate that you aren't calling for a replacement like the ones mentioned previously. Each `%%` is replaced with a single `%`.

If this sounds convoluted, you're catching on. Batch file programming *is* convoluted and rarely elegant. But it is also very useful.

> **TIP**
>
> In Vista, the built-in Windows Help and Support center appears not to cover the command-line environment well, but a wealth of documentation is available online. After reading this chapter, go to www.microsoft.com and search for these phrases
>
>   Command Shell Overview
>   Environment Variables
>   Using Batch Parameters
>   Using Batch Files
>   Using Command Redirection Operators
>   Cmd
>   Command-Line Reference
>
> Then, open a command prompt window and type the following commands
>
> ```
>     help cmd
>     help set
>     help for
>     help if
> ```
>
> and so on.

BATCH FILE PROGRAMMING

So far, I've described how you can place simple sequences of commands into a text file that Windows will interpret line by line. The batch file programming language has other constructs that let you perform commands repeatedly and let you test conditions and take different actions depending on the findings. They are discussed in the following sections.

THE set STATEMENT

The set statement sets environment variables. The basic form is

`set variable=value`

where `variable` is the name of the environment variable you want to set, and `value` is the text you want to assign to the variable. Many environment variables are predefined by Windows (type the command **set** with no argument to see the entire list), and you can define more in your batch files to hold information.

There are two additional ways you can use the set command. If you precede the variable name with `/a`, the set command treats the `value` part of the command as an arithmetic expression using numbers, environment variable names, and mathematical operators. The numeric result is turned into its text representation. Thus, this batch file

```
set nfiles=0
set /a nfiles=nfiles+1
set /a nfiles=nfiles+1
echo Nfiles = %nfiles%
```

prints

```
Nfiles = 2
```

The command

set /p *variable=promptstring*

lets your batch file prompt the user for the value to assign to an environment variable. For example, you can use a statement like

```
set /p filename=Please enter the filename:
```

to get the name of a file the batch file is to work with; then, later in the batch file, `%filename%` will be replaced with whatever the user typed.

> **TIP**
> I can't show blank spaces in this book, but you should put a space after the colon at the end of the prompt string; it makes the prompt look better when the script runs.

THE if STATEMENT

The `if` statement lets you execute commands if some condition is true and, if you want, other commands if the condition is false. The `if` statement can compare strings, test to see whether files exist, and can check the error status reported by the previous program run by the batch file. The basic `if` statement takes this form:

if *condition command*

where *condition* specifies something that can be determined to be true or false; the *command* is run if the condition is true. *command* can be any command-line statement.

condition can be one of the following:

exist *filename*

is true if the specified file exists. If the *filename* contains wildcards, the condition is true if any file matches the filename.

not exist *filename*

is true if the specified file does not exist; or if a wildcard is used, if no matching file exists.

string1 **==** *string2*

is true if *string1* exactly matches *string2*. If you are testing to see whether an environment variable or command-line argument matches some specific value, it's best to enclose both strings with some character like " or / so that, in the event that the environment variable or argument is blank, something will be present in the if statement at the appropriate spot. For example, you can use the statement

`if /%1/ == /debug/ then echo on`

to turn on command echoing in your script. If you don't specify a command-line argument, the command turns into `if // == /debug/ then echo on`, in which case the two strings are not equal, and the `echo on` command is not used. Without the /'s, the command would look like `if == debug then echo on`, which is not valid.

`not string1 == string2`	The reverse of `string1 == string2`; the command is run only if the strings are not equal.
`string1 compareop string2`	A more advanced string comparison. `Compareop` can be any of the following words, to perform any of the following comparisons:

EQU	exactly equal
NEQ	not equal
LSS	less than
LEQ	less than or equal to
GTR	greater than
GEQ	greater than or equal to

If both of the strings contain only digits, the comparison is made numerically. Otherwise, the comparison is made alphabetically.

`/I string1 compareop string2`

Like `string1 compareop string2`, but the string comparison is case insensitive. In most cases, you should use /I so that your script is not sensitive to the case of filenames or input.

Here are more involved versions of the if statement that let you execute more than one command or let you run alternate commands if the condition tested is not true:

if condition (command1 && command2 && ...)

if condition (
    command1
    command2
    ⋮
)

if condition (command) **else** (alternatecommand)

if condition (
    command1
    command2
    ⋮

```
) else (
    alternatecommand1
    alternatecommand2
    ⋮
)

if condition1 (
    ⋮
) else if condition2 (
    ⋮
) else if condition3 (
    ⋮
) else (
    ⋮
)
```

> **NOTE**
>
> You must be careful if you use environment variables in multiple-line `if` or `for` statements. All of the lines are read at once, and all environment variables inside % signs are replaced *immediately*, so `set` commands that modify these variables inside the block of commands statement will not take effect immediately. If you need to modify and use environment variables inside a group of statements in an `if` or `for` command, place the command `setlocal enabledelayedexpansion` at the top of your batch file, and inside the compound command, enclose environment variable names with exclamation points instead of percent signs, like this:
>
> ```
> setlocal enabledelayedexpansion
> ⋮
> if condition (
>     set var=value
>     command !var!
> )
> ```

THE goto STATEMENT

You can use the `goto` statement to tell Windows to jump to another part of the batch file and start reading commands from that point. The format of the command is

`goto label`

which directs Windows to look for a line in the batch file that starts with `:label`. `label` can be any word. The special version `goto :EOF` tells Windows to jump to the end of the batch file, which ends it. (You can also have a batch file stop in its tracks with the command `exit /b`.)

THE call STATEMENT

Batch files can contain subroutines, which let you run another batch file or jump down to a label, run a series of commands, and then return to the point that you started. It looks like this:

```
call anotherbatch xxx
call anotherbatch yyy
call anotherbatch zzz
```

This example invokes a different batch file named anotherbatch three times, with different command-line arguments. Inside the called batch file, %1 and the other command-line argument items refer to the arguments on the call command, not the command-line arguments used with the original batch file.

You can use call within the same batch file if you want. It looks like this:

```
call :mysub xxx
call :mysub yyy
call :mysub zzz...
```

other batch file commands

```
goto :EOF
```

```
:mysub...
```

subroutine's batch file commands; use %1 to pick up xxx, yyy and zzz

```
goto :EOF
```

THE for STATEMENT

The basic for statement repeats a command once for every item that appears in a list. It looks like this:

for %%v in (*list***) do** *command*

where *v* is a single letter environment variable that is to be set to the names found in the list; *list* is a list of file or folder names, or even just plain words, separated by spaces or semicolons. If an item in the list contains the characters ? or *, Windows replaces the item with any filenames matching the item using * and ? as wildcards. *command* is a command to be run once for each item in the list. In *command*, %%v will be replaced with the items. (The % sign has to be doubled up in for commands inside a batch file, but not on for commands you type directly at the command prompt.)

Here's an example. In a batch file,

```
for %%v in (a;b;c) do echo %%v
```

will print

```
a
b
c
```

You can have the for loop run several commands for each item in the list by using parentheses:

```
for %%v in (list) do (
   command 1
   command 2
   ⋮
   command n
)
```

> **NOTE**
>
> You must to be careful if you use environment variables in a multiple-line `for` statement. See the note under the `if` command, earlier in this section. Alternatively, have the `for` command call a subroutine, like this:
>
> ```
> for %%v in (list) do call :sub %%v
> ⋮
> goto :EOF
>
> :sub
> echo Working with file %1...
> set var=%1
> ⋮
> ```

On Windows Vista, the `for` command has several options that let it automatically scan for directories, read lines out of a text file, step its variable through a range of numeric values (like the `for` statement in VBScript), and more. Also, you can use special characters to indicate that Windows is to extract only part of a filename matched by a `for` statement. For more information, type **help for** at the command prompt, or view the Windows Help and Support Center entry for "Command-Line Reference A-Z" and then select For.

BATCH FILE TIPS

Table 32.8 lists several short batch files that I put on every computer that I use. These short command scripts take advantage of the batch file programming techniques discussed in this chapter, and let me edit files, change the path, view a folder with Explorer, and so on, simply by typing a couple of letters followed by a folder or filename. They don't involve fancy programming, but they can save you a significant amount of time.

TABLE 32.8 USEFUL TINY BATCH FILES

Filename	Contents and Purpose

ap.bat	`@echo off`
	`for %%p in (%path%) do if /%%p/ == /%1/ exit /b`
	`set path=%1;%path%`
	
	Adds the named folder to the PATH if it is not already listed (lasts only as long as the Command Prompt window is open).
	
	Example: `ap c:\test`

bat.bat	`cd /d c:\bat` Makes `c:\bat` the current directory, when you want to add or edit batch files and scripts. Example: `bat`

Filename	Contents and Purpose
bye.bat	`@logout`
	Logs off Windows.
	Example: `bye`
e.bat	`@if /%1/ == // (explorer /e,.) else explorer /e,%1`
	Opens Windows Explorer in Folder mode to view the named directory, or the current directory if no path is entered on the command line.
	Example: `e d:`
n.bat	`@start notepad %1`
	Edits the named file with Notepad.
	Example: `n myfile.vbs`

> **TIP**
>
> To learn how to get the most from the batch files and the command line, get Brian's book, *Windows XP Under the Hood: Hardcore Windows Scripting and Command Line Power*, published by Que. Watch for a new edition, coming out in the second half of 2008 under the title *Windows Vista Guide to Scripting, Automation, and Command Line Tools.*

Windows Script Host

In the last decade or so, Microsoft has worked diligently to provide ways for programmers to gain access to the internal functions of commercial applications such as Word and Excel and of Windows itself. The approach is based on a technology called the Component Object Model, or COM, which lets a properly designed program share its data and functional capabilities with other programs—any other programs, written in any other programming language. If you've ever written macros for Word or Excel, you've worked with scripting and COM. One product of these efforts is Windows Script Host, or WSH, which provides a fast and easy way to write your own management and utility programs. Scripts have an advantage over batch files in that they can perform complex calculations and can manipulate text information in powerful ways. They can view and change Windows settings, and take advantage of Window services through COM objects provided as a standard part of Windows. In addition, if you have COM-enabled applications such as WordPerfect, Microsoft Word, or Excel installed, scripts can even enlist these applications to present information in tidy, formatted documents and charts.

How WSH works

The Windows Script Host program itself does almost nothing. Rather, all of the real work is done by other software components that WSH recruits to do the real work, as illustrated in Figure 32.6. Windows Script Host doesn't even know how to interpret the programming language that your script is written in—it depends on a scripting engine to read and follow your instructions. And the real work of most scripts is done by *objects*, which are separate software components that represent real-world items—data, files, folders, networks, Windows user accounts, system services, and so on. I'll talk more about objects shortly.

Figure 32.6
Windows Script Host acts as an intermediary between your script program, a scripting language engine, and other program components called objects.

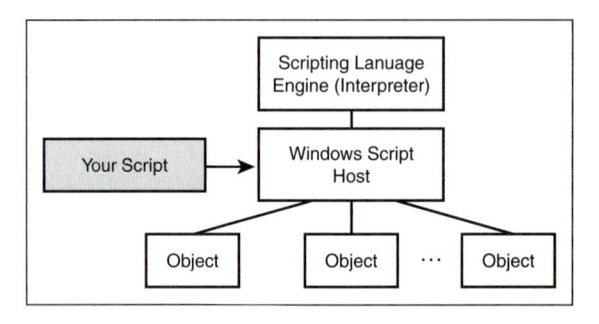

Windows XP comes with engines for two different scripting languages:

- VBScript, which is nearly identical to the Visual Basic for Applications (VBA) macro language used in Word and Excel.
- JScript, Microsoft's version of the JavaScript language, which is widely used to make web pages interactive. (JavaScript, by the way, is not the same thing as Java. Java is another programming language altogether, and it's not used by Windows Script Host.)

In addition, you can download and install other language engines. If you have a UNIX or Linux background, for example, you might want to use the Perl, Python, or TCL scripting languages. You can get free WSH-compatible versions of these languages from ActiveState Corporation at www.activestate.com.

If you are already versed in one of the scripting languages I've mentioned, by all means, use it. If you don't already know a scripting language, VBScript is probably the best one to start with because you can also use it to write macros for Microsoft's desktop applications.

CREATING SCRIPTS

Just like batch files, scripts are stored as plain text files, which you can edit with Notepad or any other text file editor. Script filenames can end in any of the extensions listed in Table 32.9.

TABLE 32.9   SCRIPT FILENAME EXTENSIONS

Extension	Description
.vbs	Script written in VBScript.
.js	Script written in JScript.
.pls	Script written in ActiveState PerlScript.
.pys	Script written in ActiveState ActivePython.

Extension	Description
.wsf	Windows Script File, a more sophisticated script file format. WSF files contain one or more script programs with special instructions written using XML markup.
.wsc	Windows Script Component file, which contains custom object programs written in a scripting language.
.vbe	Encrypted VBScript script.
.jse	Encrypted JScript script.

> **NOTE**
>
> I don't have room here to discuss WSF files, WSC files, or script encryption, but I do discuss these topics in my book *Windows Vista Guide to Scripting, Automation, and Command Line Tools*.

To create a script file, choose a descriptive name, something like "WorkSummaryReport" perhaps, and add the extension that corresponds to the language you'll be using.

As an example, I'll write a script using VBScript, which I'll call "hello.vbs." If you want to try it yourself, the steps are

1. Open a Command Prompt window by clicking Start, All Programs, Accessories, Command Prompt.
2. The Command Prompt window opens on the default directory \users*your_user_name*. If you want to create the script in another folder, you will need to type in a `cd` command to change directories. For the purposes of this example, we'll skip that and use the default directory.
3. Type the command `notepad hello.vbs`. When Notepad asks whether you want to create a new file, click Yes.
4. Type in the text

   `wscript.echo "Hello, this message comes from a script"`
5. Save the script by selecting File, Save. You can leave the Notepad window open, or close it with File, Exit.
6. Bring the Command Prompt window to the foreground.
7. Type `hello` and press Enter.

If everything works, you should see the dialog box shown in Figure 32.7. Click OK to close the message dialog.

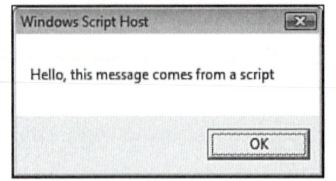

Figure 32.7
The sample script displays a simple text message.

Windows Script Host
Hello, this message comes from a script
[OK]

If VBScript (or whatever language engine you are using) finds a glaring error in the script program—for example, a missing comma or an extraneous line of text—instead of the message box, you may be treated to an error message something like that shown in Figure 32.8.

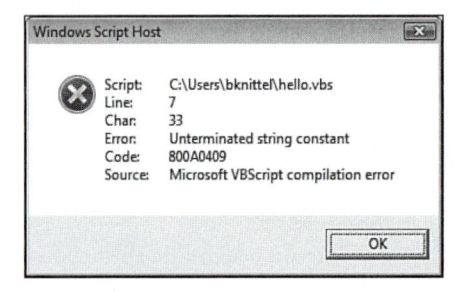

Figure 32.8
If the scripting engine finds an error, it will display a descriptive message.

Windows Script Host
Script: C:\Users\bknittel\hello.vbs
Line: 7
Char: 33
Error: Unterminated string constant
Code: 800A0409
Source: Microsoft VBScript compilation error
[OK]

In this case, VBScript is saying that the script has a problem on its seventh line.

> **TIP**
>
> To locate and correct the problematic line in the script, open the script file in Notepad. Make sure that Word Wrap is turned off. To do so, click Format, and if there is a check mark in front of Word Wrap, click Word Wrap; otherwise, press Esc to close the menu. Now, press Ctrl+G to bring up the Goto Line dialog. Enter the line number indicated in the error message and press Enter. The cursor will jump to the offending line.

To fix a problem or to change how a script works, you need to edit the script file again and alter its contents. For the sample script we created, you can type `notepad hello.vbs` again to edit the script. Or, you can locate the file in Windows Explorer, right-click it, and select Edit.

Windows Script Host can display its results in a window, as we just saw, or it can display results in the console window, as do most command-line programs. As you saw in the previous sample, the default is to display information in a window. Because you can always force WSH to display results in a window through programming, it's best to change the default so that the default mode is the text-based console output method. To do this, type this command:

`cscript //H:cscript //nologo //s`

(Notice that the slashes are doubled-up in this command.) Now, type the command `hello` again. This time the script's output should display within the Command Prompt window.

Windows Script Host 1117

> **TIP**
>
> If you're running a script in the console mode, and an error occurs, Windows Script Host will display an error message like the following:
>
> ```
> C:\Users\bknittel\hello.vbs(7, 33) Microsoft VBScript compilation
> error: Unterminated string constant
> ```
>
> Compare this to Figure 32.8, and you'll see that this is a lot more difficult to interpret than the windowed version. The thing to remember is that the first number, 7 in this example, is the line number on which the error was detected. The 33 just describes the type of the error, which is also explained in text: Unterminated string constant. In this case, it means that there is a missing quote (") mark on the indicated line.

Some Sample Scripts

We don't have room here to give you even an introductory course in VBScript programming. As I mentioned, that's a topic that can fill an entire book. What I can do is give you some examples of how Windows Script Host can be used to perform useful tasks and to manage Windows.

Disk and Network Management

Here is an example of a VBScript script that performs a reasonably useful task. The following script

```
set fso = CreateObject("Scripting.FileSystemObject")
set drivelist = fso.Drives
for each drv in drivelist
    if drv.IsReady then
        wscript.echo "Drive", drv.DriveLetter, "has", drv.FreeSpace, "bytes free"
    end if
next
```

displays the amount of free space on each of your computer's drives. Type this script into a file named freespace.vbs in your batch file directory; then type the command-line command **freespace**. On my computer this prints the following:

```
Drive C: has 15866540032 bytes free
Drive D: has 27937067008 bytes free
Drive F: has 335872000 bytes free
Drive H: has 460791808 bytes free
```

The following sample script uses WSH to display your computer's current network drive mappings:

```
set wshNetwork = CreateObject("WScript.Network") ' create the helper object

set maps = wshNetwork.EnumNetworkDrives     ' collection describes mapped drives
for i = 0 to maps.Length-2 step 2           ' step through collection by twos
    wscript.echo "Drive", maps.item(i), "is mapped to", maps.item(i+1)
next
```

Scripts can also create network drive mappings. Here is a script that ensures that drive letter
M: is mapped to the shared folder \\server\officefiles:

```
required_drive = "M:"                        ' drive letter we need
required_path  = "\\server\officefiles"      ' network path that we need

set wshNetwork = CreateObject("WScript.Network") ' create the helper object
is_mapped  = False     ' will get set True if the drive is already mapped
is_correct = False     ' will get set True if the mapping is already correct

set maps = wshNetwork.EnumNetworkDrives    ' collection describes mapped drives
for i = 0 to maps.Length-2 step 2          ' step through collection by twos
                                           ' do we see the drive we're looking for?
    if ucase(maps.item(i)) = ucase(required_drive) then
        is_mapped = True                   ' the drive we need is already mapped
                                           ' but, mapped to the correct path?
        if ucase(maps.item(i+1)) = ucase(required_path) then
            is_correct = True              ' yes: mapping is already correct
        end if

        exit for      ' no need to look at any other drives; exit this loop
    end if
next

if not is_correct then                 ' if drive mapping is not set up
    if is_mapped then                  ' if currently mapped, delete bad mapping
        wshNetwork.RemoveNetworkDrive required_drive, True, True
    end if                             ' now, map drive to desired share
    wshNetwork.MapNetworkDrive required_drive, required_path, True
end if

' At this point we can be sure that the drive is mapped to \\server\officefiles
```

Messaging and Email

Windows comes with a set of software collectively called the *Collaboration Data Objects
(CDO)*, which can be used to send text or HTML-formatted email messages from scripts,
and can even include file attachments. Here are a few reasons you might want to send email
from a script:

- Automate your workflow; you can drag files onto a desktop script shortcut to automatically mail them to a colleague.
- Report the results of scripts that are run unattended by the Task Scheduler.
- Distribute the results of scripts that generate reports, such as disk-space utilization summaries for all users on a network.

The following sample script sends an email to a specific person, containing as attachments
any file(s) named on the script's command line. You might use something like this to forward
completed documents to a co-worker. With a shortcut to this script on your desktop, all you
have to do is drag and drop a document onto the shortcut and it will automatically be mailed
out. (If you want to use this script, you'll have to change the names of the sender and the

recipient, and change the name of the SMTP mail server to the one used on your network. You must also specify the files to be sent using full pathnames.)

```
' mailfiles.vbs - mails files named on command line (or dragged onto
' shortcut) to the specified user.

if WScript.arguments.count <= 0 then     ' no files were specified
    MsgBox "Usage: mailfiles filename..., or drag files onto shortcut"
    WScript.quit 0
end if

const cdoSendUsingPort = 2               ' standard CDO constants
const cdoAnonymous     = 0

sender    = "brian@mycompanyxyz.com"     ' sender of message
recipient = "sheila@mycompanyxyz.com"    ' recipient of this message
mailserver = "mail.mycompanyxyz.com"     ' name of SMTP server

set msg  = CreateObject("CDO.Message")   ' create objects
set conf = CreateObject("CDO.Configuration")
set msg.configuration = conf

With msg                                 ' build the message
    txt = ""
    nfiles = 0                           ' count of files attached
    for each arg in WScript.arguments    ' treat each argument as a
        .AddAttachment arg               ' file to be attached
        txt    = txt & vbCRLF & arg      ' list filename in message text too
        nfiles = nfiles+1
    next
    if nfiles = 1 then plural = "" else plural = "s"
    .to       = recipient                ' address the letter
    .from     = sender
    .subject  = nfiles & " File" & plural & " for you"
    .textBody = "File" & plural & " attached to this message:" & vbCRLF & txt
End With

prefix = "http://schemas.microsoft.com/cdo/configuration/"
With conf.fields                         ' set delivery options
    .item(prefix & "sendusing")       = cdoSendUsingPort
    .item(prefix & "smtpserver")      = mailserver
    .item(prefix & "smtpauthenticate") = cdoAnonymous
    .update                              ' commit changes
End With
on error resume next        ' do not stop on errors
msg.send                    ' deliver the message
errn = err.number           ' remember error status
on error goto 0             ' restore normal error handling

if errn > 0 then            ' report results with a message box
    MsgBox "Error sending message"
else
    MsgBox "Sent " & nfiles & " file" & plural & " to " & recipient
    ' (future development: at this point it might be useful to have
    ' the script move the files to an "already sent" folder)
end if
```

Windows Management Instrumentation

Windows Management Instrumentation (WMI) is a system service that provides access to virtually every aspect of a Windows computer system, from the hardware components up to the highest level system services. For some components, WMI provides information only. Other components can be changed, and thus, as its name implies, WMI can be used to manage the system. You can use WMI to start and stop system services, monitor and stop applications, create drive mappings, share folders, and, with the appropriate updated WMI drivers installed, even manage system services such as Internet Information Services, Microsoft Exchange, and the Domain Name Service on Windows Server.

Following are three examples of WMI scripts. The first is called shownetconfig.vbs. It lists each of the network adapters in your computer and shows their IP address information. If you add a computer name or names to the command line, this script will list the information for other computers on your network. (However, this often will not work unless you are on a domain network and have administrator privileges.)

> **NOTE**
> The underscores at the ends of some lines in this script are part of the script.

```
' script to display TCP/IP info of any computer on the LAN
' Usage: shownetconfig [computername ...]

set loc = CreateObject("WBemScripting.SWbemLocator")  ' create WMI helper object

if wscript.Arguments.Length = 0 then       ' if no arguments on command line
    check "localhost"                      ' examine computer running the script
else                                       ' otherwise
    for each name in wscript.Arguments     ' check each name on command line
        check name
    next
end if

' subroutine "check" displays the network adapters and IP address info for
' the computer whose name is passed in the argument 'name'

sub check (name)
    wscript.echo
    wscript.echo "Network adapters on " & name & ":"

    on error resume next                   ' don't quit script if error occurs
                                           ' get WMI network adapter objects
    set adapters = GetObject("winmgmts:{impersonationlevel=impersonate," &_
        "authenticationlevel=pkt}!" &_
        "//" & name & "/root/CIMV2:Win32_NetworkAdapterConfiguration")

    errno = err.number                     ' get error information, if any
    msg   = err.description
    on error goto 0                        ' go back to normal stop-on-error

    if errno <> 0 then                     ' if there was an error, print info
        wscript.echo "Connect to", name, "failed"
        wscript.echo msg
        exit sub                           ' and quit working on this computer
    end if
```

```
        for each card in adapters.Instances_    ' list each network adapter
            if card.IPEnabled and not isnull(card.IPAddress) then
                wscript.echo " ", card.Caption          ' print adapter make/model
                for each addr in card.IPAddress    ' list each IP address (1 or more)
                    wscript.echo "     IP Addr ", addr
                next
                for each addr in card.DefaultIPGateway   ' list each gateway
                    wscript.echo "     Gateway ", addr
                next                                    ' list MAC address
                wscript.echo "     MAC Addr", card.MACAddress
                wscript.echo
            end if
        next
    end sub                                         ' end of subroutine
```

On my computer, the output of this script looks like this:

```
Network adapters on localhost:
  [00000004] Intel 21140-Based PCI Fast Ethernet Adapter
     IP Addr  192.168.15.106
     IP Addr  fe80::c73:fa6d:3c1:c126
     Gateway  192.168.15.1
     MAC Addr 00:03:FF:D0:CA:5F
```

> **NOTE**
>
> Due to a bug in WMI, this script can fail with an error message if your computer is sharing its Internet connection and the connection is not up.

The following sample WMI script lists the status of each system service installed on your computer. This script file can be named showservices.vbs.

```
set services = GetObject("winmgmts:{impersonationlevel=impersonate," &_
    "authenticationlevel=pkt}!" &_
    "/root/CIMV2:Win32_Service")       ' get services WMI info

for each svc in services.Instances_    ' display information for each service
    wscript.echo svc.name, "State:", svc.State, "Startup:", svc.StartMode
next
```

On my computer, the first few lines of output from this script look like this:

```
AeLookupSvc State: Running Startup: Auto
ALG State: Stopped Startup: Manual
Appinfo State: Running Startup: Manual
AppMgmt State: Running Startup: Manual
aspnet_state State: Stopped Startup: Manual
AudioEndpointBuilder State: Running Startup: Auto
```

(Remember too, that as command-line programs, you can redirect the output of these scripts into a file.) The command

```
showservices >listing.txt
```

puts the service list into file listing.txt, just as if showservices was a native Windows executable program.

As a final example, the following WMI script locates all running instances of the Windows Notepad program and terminates them:

```
set processes = GetObject("winmgmts:").ExecQuery(_
    "select * from Win32_Process where Name='notepad.exe'")

for each process in processes     ' scan objects representing Notepad instances
    process.Terminate             ' and terminate each instance
next
```

You can see that this is powerful medicine, but it can be exceptionally useful if you are developing or testing software applications.

Active Directory Scripting Interface (ADSI)

ADSI provides a way to view and administer the Windows Active Directory on a domain network. Like WMI, it's a complex yet rich programming tool that lets you manage the most complex networks using scripting tools. At the end of this chapter in the section "Tips from the Windows Pros: Getting More Information" I'll list some ADSI scripting resources.

Applications (For Example, Word)

Many Windows applications can be harnessed by scripts. As I mentioned earlier in the chapter, Microsoft Office applications such as Word and Excel use a scripting language that is similar to VBScript. And, in fact, you can start and manipulate Microsoft Office applications from Windows Script Host just as easily as you can using these applications' macro facilities.

As an example, this script lists the entire contents of your C: drive, formatting the listing into an Excel spreadsheet:

```
' script to list all of the files on the C drive into a spreadsheet

set fso       = CreateObject("Scripting.FileSystemObject") ' create helper object
set excel     = CreateObject("Excel.Application")          ' open instance of Excel
excel.visible = True                                       ' make it visible
set workbook  = excel.Workbooks.Add                        ' create an empty workbook
set worksheet = workbook.Worksheets("sheet1")              ' and select a worksheet

nfiles = 0                                                 ' we have no files yet
list fso.GetFolder("C:\")                                  ' list contents of C:

totalrow = nfiles+2                                        ' total the file sizes
worksheet.Cells(totalrow, 1).Value     = "Total"
worksheet.Cells(totalrow, 1).Font.Bold = True
worksheet.Cells(totalrow, 2).Value     = "=sum(B1:B" & ltrim(str(nfiles)) & ")"
worksheet.Cells(totalrow, 2).Font.Bold = True

set worksheet = nothing                   ' release the worksheet
set workbook  = nothing                   ' and the workbook
set excel     = nothing                   ' release Excel but leave running
' ----------------------------------------------------------------
' subroutine to list the contents of a specific folder.
' The files inside are placed into the excel spreadsheet
' and all subfolders are listed as well
' ----------------------------------------------------------------
```

```
sub list (folder)
    on error resume next                                ' if there is a permissions error,
                                                        ' just ignore the file or folder
    for each file in folder.Files                       ' scan all of the files first
        nfiles = nfiles + 1                             ' count one new file
        worksheet.Cells(nfiles, 1).Value = file.Path    ' put name in column 1
        worksheet.Cells(nfiles, 2).Value = file.size    ' put size in column 2
    next

    for each subfolder in folder.Subfolders             ' then scan each subfolder
        list subfolder
    next
end sub
```

Of course, it works only if Excel is actually installed on your computer.

> **NOTE**
>
> Microsoft has developed a new command line environment called Windows PowerShell (WPS), which is available as a free download from microsoft.com. WPS is not your father's old command prompt. For one thing, its commands pass objects between each other, not text. It's a promising tool, but it's beyond the scope of this book. For more information about WPS, check out my book *Windows Vista Guide to Scripting, Automation, and Command Line Tools* or *Windows PowerShell 2.0 Unleashed*.

Task Scheduler

The Windows Task Scheduler lets you specify programs to be run automatically at specified dates and times and on certain events like system startup, users logging on, or even the occurrence of any event that can be logged in the Event Viewer. It's especially useful with batch files and scripts, since these scheduled programs need to run without any user interaction anyway. And it's truly the ultimate automation tool because you don't even have to be there when it's working!

There are two ways to start the Task Scheduler, click Start, All Programs, Accessories, System Tools, Task Scheduler. Alternatively, you can right-click Computer, select Manage, and then select Task Scheduler. Either way you will have to confirm a User Account Control prompt or enter an Administrator password because the Task Scheduler is a privileged program.

After you define the tasks to run, the Task Scheduler service sits in the background, checking the computer's system clock and watching for various system events. When the predetermined time or a specified event occurs, the Task Scheduler runs the program as though it had been executed by the specified user. The Task Scheduler service automatically starts each time the computer boots. By itself, the Task Schedule service does not significantly affect system performance, although the tasks it runs can. However, you can instruct it not to start specified tasks when the system is busy. You might want to do this, for example, if a particular task generates a lot of disk activity.

What kinds of tasks would you run with the Task Scheduler? As I mentioned, the tasks need to run without user interaction. So, they are typically maintenance tasks such as defragmenting the hard disk, cleaning out temporary files, and so on. Windows uses the Task Scheduler for this very purpose, and you'll notice that there are several pre-installed scheduled tasks set up when Windows is installed to do this very sort of thing. The Task scheduler can also watch for the occurrence of any event that can be recorded in the Event Log, so you could use it, for instance, to run a designated program when a hardware error occurs.

You can also write your own batch files and scripts to do cleanup jobs, or perform other routine tasks. For example, I use a free spam filtering program called SpamAssassin, which is really meant for use on UNIX and Linux systems. I have a script that runs it as a Windows service, but it has some problems, and runs amok if it's left running for several consecutive days. So, I set up a scheduled task to stop and restart the service in the wee hours of every morning. I do this with a batch file that uses the net command to stop and start the mail filtering service. The batch file reads:

```
net stop pop3proxy
taskkill /f /im perl.exe
net start pop3proxy
```

These commands stop the filtering service (which is named Pop3Proxy on my computer), terminate the filtering program if it somehow is still running after its service stops, and then start it all back up again. I had developed this sequence of commands by trial and error when I was still manually dealing with the intermittent problems. Putting them into a batch file and running them every day at 2:00 a.m. made the process automatic, and it's now something I no longer have to think about.

You also can cause a specific script or program to run (1) when the system boots, (2) when a user (any user) logs on, or (3) when the system is idle. Why would you use the "when a user logs on" option, when you could just as well put a shortcut to the script or program in the Startup folder for All Users? The reason is that the Scheduled Tasks lets you specify the user account to use for the task. For example, whenever any user logs on, you can have the Scheduled Tasks run a program with Administrative privileges to record information in a protected file.

> **NOTE**
> When the Task Scheduler runs a task as a different user than the one currently logged on, the logged-on user cannot see or interact with the program. Be sure that scheduled tasks can operate without user input and exit cleanly when they've done their work. And keep in mind that once an application or service is running, even if it was launched through a scheduled task, it will affect system performance just as if you started it manually.

> **NOTE**
> Obviously, the computer has to be alive to run a task, so if you expect to do a disk cleanup at 4:00 a.m., be sure to leave the computer on. If a scheduled task is missed because the computer was turned off, Windows will perform the task the next time the computer is started, but the task will now be running while you're there, which is probably what you were trying to avoid by having it run at night.

> **TIP**
>
> If you upgraded from an older version of Windows and had automated tasks assigned there, they should have been converted or imported to the Windows Vista Task Scheduler automatically.

There are two types of tasks you can create in Task Scheduler:

- **Basic tasks** are designed to be run using the current user's account, and support a single triggering event or time.
- **Tasks** can be run using any specified user account, and can be configured to run whether the user is logged in or not. Tasks can also be run in Windows XP or Windows Server 2003 compatibility mode, and can be configured to run with higher than normal priority if necessary.

To create a Basic Task in the Task Scheduler, follow these steps:

1. Open Task Scheduler as discussed earlier in this section. Task Scheduler displays a summary list of scheduled tasks run in the last 24 hours in the top center pane and a list of active tasks below that.
2. The Add Actions pane is located on the right side. Click Create Basic Task. The Create a Basic Task wizard opens.
3. Enter the name of the task and a description. Enter whatever you want, to remind you of what the tasks does. Click Next to continue.
4. On the Task Trigger dialog, select when to run the task. You can choose daily, weekly, monthly, or one time; when the computer starts, when you log on, or when a specific event is logged.

   You can use the When a Specific Event Is Logged option to trigger the task when a specific Event Log entry is recorded. For example, you could use this to perform some sort of notification if a disk error event occurs. You'll need to enter the event's numeric ID number.

   Click Next.

   > **TIP**
   >
   > To find an event's ID number, find an occurrence of the event in the Windows Event log.

5. Specify applicable time options, such as time of day, as required. Click Next.
6. Select what you want the task to do (open a program, send an email, display a message). You will probably need to enter a command line that specifies a program, and also specifies arguments to tell the program what to do. Click Next to continue.

7. Specify the action to take place. If you select the option to open a program, use Browse to locate the program, then provide any optional switches or settings. For Windows applications, search in the \Windows or \Windows\system32 folders. For third-party applications, search in the subfolders of the Programs folder. For scripts you've written yourself, browse to the folder in which you've stored the script or batch file. If you select Send an Email, enter the information for sender, receiver, SMTP email server, message, and so forth. If you select Display a Message, enter the message title and text.
8. Review the task on the Summary dialog (see Figure 32.9). If you want to set advanced options such as idle time, what to do if the computer is running on batteries, and what to do after the task completes, mark Open Advanced Properties for This Task When I Click Finish. Click Finish to complete the task.

Figure 32.9
Completing the configuration of a basic task.

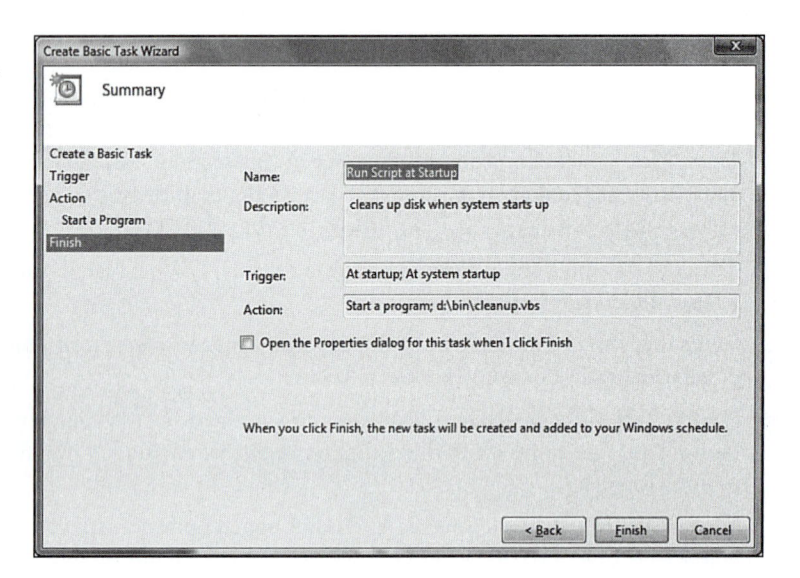

For more advanced scheduling, use the Create Task selection. The Create Task interface uses a multi-tabbed interface instead of a wizard. The General tab includes security options, while the Triggers tab permits you to specify multiple triggers for a task (the task will be performed whenever any of the triggers occurs), the Actions tab supports multiple actions in a task, the Conditions tab includes options to configure idle time, power, and network connection requirements, and the Settings tab supports conditions for running and stopping a task. Use Create Task, rather than Create Basic Task, when you need these additional settings in your task.

The Actions menu contains one additional option you can use with either type of task: AT Service Account. The Scheduled Tasks runs any commands scheduled using the `at` command-line utility, which is a carryover from Windows NT. By design, commands scheduled by `at` all run under the same login account. This option lets you specify which account is to be used. You can leave it set to the default System setting, or you can specify a user account.

Troubleshooting

MS-DOS Program Can't Open Enough Files

When I run my MS-DOS application, I get the error "Too Many Files Open" or a similar message.

By default, MS-DOS applications run by the VDM are allowed to open only 20 files. Some older programs, especially database programs, want to open more. In DOS or Windows 9x, you'd have added the line

```
FILES=100
```

to your config.sys file. In Windows Vista, you must add this line to your config.nt file. Of course, if you specified an alternate setup file for this particular application, you'll want to change that file rather than config.nt.

config.nt is normally protected against changes. To modify it, you must use the following procedure:

1. Click Start, All Programs, Accessories.
2. Locate Notepad, right-click it, and select Run As Administrator.
3. Confirm the User Account Control prompt.
4. Click File, Open, and locate \windows\system32\config.nt (or the alternate config file, if your application uses one).
5. Edit the file as necessary; then click File, Save, File, Exit.

MS-DOS Application Displays Garbage Characters

When I run an old MS-DOS application, I see lots of junk characters on the screen and many occurrences of "←[".

Some older programs that displayed text on the computer screen depended on the assistance of a display driver program called ansi.sys. Ansi.sys isn't installed by default in config.nt, so you're seeing the control messages that your program was intending for ansi.sys to interpret; these should have resulted in color changes or cursor movements.

You need to add the line

```
device=ansi.sys
```

to your config.nt file. Of course, if you specified an alternate setup file for this application, you'll want to change that file rather than config.nt.

config.nt is normally protected against changes. To modify it, you must use the procedure in the preceding Troubleshooting tip.

> **NOTE**
> If you're a software developer, you should know that ANSI.SYS works for MS-DOS applications only. There is no support for ANSI escape sequences for Win32 console applications.

Tips from the Windows Pros: Getting More Information

This chapter barely scratches the surface of what you can do with scripting, batch files, and automation. I hope that you'll check out my book *Windows Vista Guide to Scripting, Automation, and Command Line Tools*, published by Que. It contains tutorials, handy reference sections, and many more examples.

Some other books I've found helpful are

- *Windows Management Instrumentation (WMI)* by Ashley Meggitt and Matthew M. Lavy (New Riders)
- *WMI Essentials for Automating Windows Management* by Martin Policht (Sams)
- *Windows NT/2000 ADSI Scripting for System Administration* by Thomas Eck (New Riders).

In addition, numerous websites are devoted to scripting and automation. Table 32.10 lists some of the sites I've found useful.

TABLE 32.10   Free Web Resources for Scripting and Automation

Website or Newsgroup	Description
msdn.microsoft.com/scripting	The official Microsoft site.
communities.msn.com/windowsscript	Extensive FAQs, examples, links, and articles.
www.winguides.com/scripting	Nifty online reference for VBScript and WSH.
www.sapien.com	Purveyors of a nifty $169 script editing program called PrimalScript. Expensive, yes, but it beats using Notepad.

Newsgroups:
  microsoft.public.scripting.wsh
  microsoft.public.scripting.vbscript
  microsoft.public.win32.programmer.wmi
  microsoft.public.adsi.general
  microsoft.public.platformsdk.adsi
	Public newsgroups hosted by Microsoft. A great place to scout for scripting ideas and to post any questions you have. Although you won't get tech support from Microsoft employees here, the community of visitors seems to do a good job of answering questions and giving advice.

There are hundreds of others. If you find other particularly useful scripting resources, let me know by dropping me a line through the guestbook at www.helpwinxp.com.

PART VII

SECURITY

33 Protecting Windows from Viruses and Spyware   1131

34 Protecting Your Data from Loss and Theft   1149

35 Protecting Your Network from Hackers and Snoops   1205

36 Protecting Yourself from Fraud and Spam   1243

CHAPTER 33

PROTECTING WINDOWS FROM VIRUSES AND SPYWARE

In this chapter

Malicious Software: Ignorance Is Not Bliss   1132

Antimalware Strategy: Defense in Depth   1134

Tips from the Windows Pros: Avoiding Malware   1147

Malicious Software: Ignorance Is Not Bliss

Hackers and computer viruses have long been popularized in movies and the media. Although the term *hacker* was once affectionately used to describe particularly dedicated and skilled computer geeks, it is also used in negative context to describe those who would abuse that knowledge for criminal activity. As high-speed Internet connections and personal computers proliferate, these so-called "black hat" hackers continue to amass an impressive arsenal of tools. These tools are placed into a few major categories according to their primary characteristics. All of the descriptive terms, some of which you've no doubt heard in reference to computers, such as *virus*, *worm*, or *spyware*, all fall under the single category called *malware*: software designed to do bad things.

It's important to understand the differences between the major types of malware because the computer industry is still evolving to fight these threats. At this time, there is no single silver bullet that is the solution to all these problems. The computer user who understands the fundamentals of malware is in a better position to make informed decisions and avoid potentially disastrous consequences. This chapter explains the major threat categories and how, when configured properly, Windows Vista can effectively arm you better than ever against malware.

Viruses Past and Present

Not so long ago, computer viruses were a joke among computer professionals. Viruses were a scapegoat on which the uninitiated or uninformed systems administrator could blame irreproducible or incomprehensible computer problems. The word itself maintained a level of mystique, describing little-understood software that spread almost magically unseen. Respected security experts contended that viruses were mostly hype and paranoia, and certainly the least of our worries. Of course, that was during a time when the main exposure to malicious data was confined to what could be put on a magnetic diskette. As long as pervasive connectivity and complex networks remained confined to the cognoscenti, computer viruses were not a major concern.

The tipping point was reached sometime in the early 1990s, when several well-known technology companies stepped up to provide virus protection for the masses. The mainstream media heralded the disk-mangling doom of the Michelangelo virus, which was expected to strike each March 6th thereafter in a tawdry birthday celebration of its Renaissance master namesake. (It's also my, Robert Cowart's, birthday, and I am annually disappointed to not yet have a virus named after me in retaliation for all these books about Microsoft Windows.) On that fateful date, with no warning, the Michelangelo virus began destroying data on the hard disk. The system locked up, the hard disk light stayed on and, upon restart, victims discovered that disk was irrevocably erased. As it turned out, Michelangelo made a much better news story than it did a computer virus. Although forecasted to impact millions of computers, it affected relatively few.

As technology developed in complexity, so did opportunities for virus writers. Virus construction kits provided simpler power tools for evildoers, as did Microsoft Office with its macro technology. David L. Smith wrote the Melissa macro virus, which duped users into opening a malicious Microsoft Word email attachment. When opened, the macro used Microsoft Outlook to send copies of itself to 50 people in the address book. It was an effective method of propagation that in 1999 clogged email systems around the world. Melissa and subsequent variants of email macro viruses showed that one did not have to be a formidable programmer to elicit formidable mayhem. They also illustrated the defining characteristic of a computer virus that differentiates it from benign programs: the capability to self-replicate. Melissa used a combination of human and technological manipulation to accomplish its mission, but other forms of viruses spread even more effectively.

Worms: "Look, Ma! No Hands!"

Systems that hold large databases often contain key financial or business-critical information. SQL Slammer is a computer virus that infected tens of thousands of database systems in 10 minutes. It did this so quickly because it required no human interaction, aside from the initial launch, to propagate. Viruses that can move quickly between networks and carry out their mission automatically are referred to as *worms*. Each computer infected with SQL Slammer blasted network packets to thousands of random computer addresses every second. Each packet carried with it the potential to create another infected computer, which would in turn instantly spew viral packets at an equally precipitate pace. Due to the resulting network clog, bank ATMs, airline check-in systems, and Seattle's 911 emergency networks were all temporarily knocked out. Even so, SQL Slammer was a mere shadow of what it could have been. It did not directly deliver any malicious payload, steal any information, or destroy any data, but it certainly could have. Worms are the most dreaded incarnation of viruses because they spread so rapidly and have the potential to do a vast amount of damage in a short amount of time. More elaborate and sophisticated viruses continue to develop, and some experts believe we have yet to see the worst.

Spyware

More often than not, if your Internet-connected computer has become sluggish, wrought with pop-up ads, and is in a general state of malaise, it's because spyware has crept into your computer. Installed without consent, spyware can perform a range of unauthorized functions including track visited websites, force pop-up advertisements, and even capture keystrokes. Passwords, credit card numbers, and any personal information typed can all be captured on a computer that has the worst type of spyware installed. Unlike viruses, spyware does not actively reproduce itself, nor does it traverse networks the way worms do. Aside from plain and simple information theft and forced advertisements, it can apply a vast array of creative implements to inconspicuously do outright bad, or at least ethically questionable, things.

Spyware can be installed on a computer in several ways. Downloading and installing any number of ostensibly harmless components, such as weather trackers, toolbars, or games, can install spyware. The term *Trojan Horse* is often used to describe this kind of malicious software that masquerades as something else to get inside your computer. In some cases, innocently clicking the dancing monkey or visiting the wrong website can exploit a security vulnerability and install a Trojan. When installed, spyware has an uncanny knack for begetting spyware, inviting its unwelcome spyware kin, and dragging a computer to its knees. Fortunately, plenty of actions can prevent spyware from infiltrating a computer in the first place, and tools are available to remove it on the off chance it finds a way to sneak in.

Rootkits and Beyond

As if viruses, worms, and spyware are not enough, they really aren't the worst that can happen to a computer. Good hackers have known for a long time that the best way to infiltrate a system is to do it in such a way that nobody can possibly know you were there. Historically, they used a "kit" of utilities for getting the highest level of access, root, on UNIX systems.

Currently, most of the wonderful security programs that we use to keep our computers safe rely on core Windows components to ferret out unsavory software. These core components provide information about files, applications, and processes, and keep track of what's going on inside the computer. But what if these core components were wrong? What if they had been tampered with or replaced with malicious components that hid information from the antimalware programs, and even Windows itself? Rootkits attempt and often succeed at this very feat, acting as a mole in the trusted parts of the operating system. They operate below the radar of traditional security programs and are especially troublesome for antimalware writers, who must develop fresh approaches to deal with the problem. There are some ways to detect rootkits, though, and Windows Vista has the built-in security technology to help do that.

What's next? Without question, the human mind's boundless creativity and perseverance will generate additional problems and threats. Antimalware strategists must be weary after years of reactive solutions, going back and forth in a perpetual cat-and-mouse game. Although there may never be a complete end to the one-upsmanship between malware writers and their rivals, the good guys have shifted toward a more holistic strategy, developing technologies that fight not just a specific type of malware, but malware tactics in general. Windows Vista possesses several features in this vein, some of which are passive, and others that must be enabled to take maximum advantage.

Antimalware Strategy: Defense in Depth

No single solution has yet been developed that completely solves all computer security problems. At this point, the best strategy for protecting information systems is using layers of defense to stop attackers. Although security technologies can be complex, the strategy behind them is simple: Give attackers as little as possible to target, and protect what must be exposed with layers of security. The expectation is that even if one layer is defeated, another will likely stop the attack.

Think of a medieval castle on a hilltop. Tall watchtowers provide visibility in every direction. A massive outer wall surrounds the castle, as does a foul moat. Attack options are limited and grim because there are so many layers of defense to contend with. The castle's archers, catapults, and other defenses make even approaching the wall a daunting task, while the moat protects against undermining the castle walls. But even if one were to somehow penetrate the outer defenses, concentric inner walls, protected by all manner of vicious implements, stand to deliver more punishment. And then, if the inner walls are breached, the innermost keep must be stormed, which will certainly be defended most fiercely by its inhabitants. Defense in depth is not a new security strategy, but it is an effective one. Besieging a castle was a formidable task. Eventually, of course, new technology in the form of gunpowder rendered these defenses obsolete. Such is the nature of an arms race.

Windows Security Center

The easiest way to get a high-level security overview of your computer's own defense in depth strategy is to check the Control Panel's Security Center, shown in Figure 33.1. It monitors the state of the main security components on the system: Firewall, Malware Protection, Automatic Updating, and Other Security Settings, which contains User Account Control and Internet Security Settings. If there are any immediate security concerns, a yellow or red shield icon with a "!" or "X," respectively will appear on the taskbar to indicate the severity of the issue. In such a case, you can right-click on the shield to launch the Security Center and find out why. Common reasons for these states include virus definitions that are out of date, security updates that need to be applied, or a firewall that has been disabled, perhaps for troubleshooting purposes.

Figure 33.1
Security Center provides an overview of key security components.

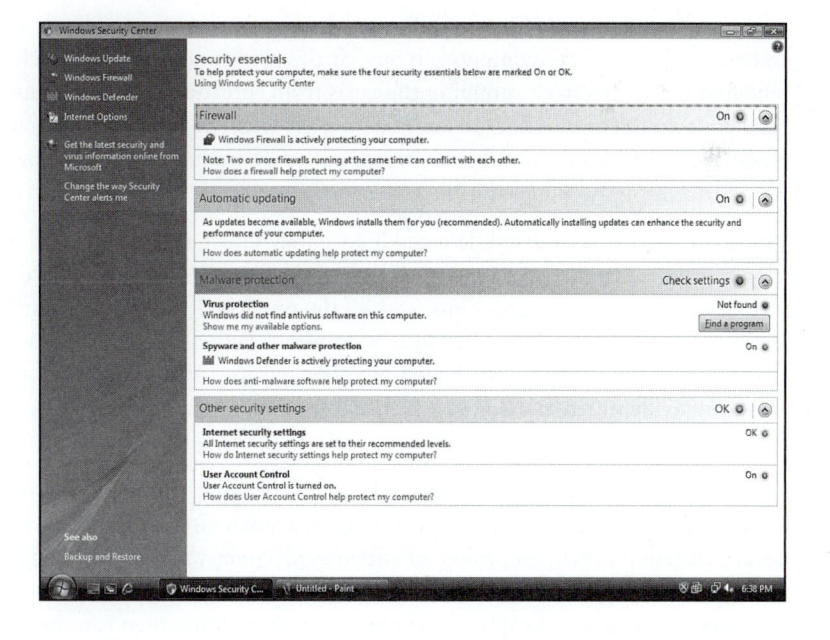

Microsoft graciously covers three out of four of the main security categories right out of the box. With no action on your part, Firewall, Automatic Updating, and even Other Security Settings light up with a pleasant green color. One section, however, may be yellow even on a brand-new computer. Although it is a universally recommended component, and you'd be remiss to get on the Internet without one, an antivirus protection program does not come with Windows Vista. Spyware protection is included in the form of Windows Defender, but an antivirus product is left for you to procure. If you buy Vista with a new PC, the manufacturer may include antivirus software, improved firewalls, or a spyware solution other than Windows Defender. You can monitor these programs in the Security Center as well.

> **TIP**
>
> Software vendors sometimes bundle security software, including antivirus and firewall products, that can install on top of the existing Windows solutions. Overlapping security programs that perform the same function, when installed at the same time, can cause conflicts and unpredictable results. You do not want two different firewall programs, for example, operating concurrently. You can select which firewall to run in the Security Center, or if you choose to use the built-in Windows Firewall, simply uninstall the secondary firewall from the Programs section in Control Panel.

CHOOSING AND INSTALLING AN ANTIVIRUS CLIENT

Antivirus software works primarily by comparing the contents of the computer with a list of known viruses (virus definitions) to see whether any part of the computer is infected. It does this in two different ways. The first is by scheduling recurring scans, daily or perhaps weekly at a time of your choosing, during which the program ploddingly reads through all endangered areas of the computer. If any viruses are found, they can be cleaned, deleted, or rendered inert, effectively stopping the virus from spreading. Several prominent companies offer antivirus scans of this type for free on their websites. This cleaning approach works magnificently in some cases. In other cases, after a computer is compromised, cleaning a virus is like trying to push a bullet back into a gun.

Viruses are best detected and defeated before they infect and damage a computer, which is why web-based scans alone are not enough. Real-time protection is the second major feature of modern antivirus programs, and it's the one worth paying for. With real-time protection, computer activity is constantly monitored. Whenever a file is read, opened, or modified, it is checked against the list of known viruses. With this level of protection, a virus can be identified and stopped before it has the opportunity to spread or cause any damage, and that is a valuable service indeed.

Most modern antivirus programs provide both scheduled scans and real-time protection, but both features are only as good as the list of known viruses they can identify. Virus writers are an active bunch, and using an antivirus program with an outdated list is not much better than running nothing at all. When a new virus is detected in the wild, antivirus vendors race to identify and capture its unique signature. Only then can the vendor's virus definition lists be updated and distributed to customers, so in addition to the quality of the software itself, the experience and knowledge of the response team is of paramount importance. Good antivirus vendors deliver timely and effective virus definition updates, so seek a vendor with a proven record of responsiveness. The heavyweights in the industry are currently McAfee, Symantec, and Trend Micro, but a number of well-respected smaller vendors do a fine job, some of whose products might be a better alternative.

If you subscribe to a high-speed Internet service, it's likely that your provider will supply you with an antivirus program free of charge. Although Internet service providers are in general an outstanding bunch, their generosity is far from altruistic. ISPs provide free antivirus programs because if they don't, unprotected systems can bog down their networks, erode trust in their service, and cause a string of headaches. Many hackers first go for easy targets, and an unprotected system on a public network is soon mincemeat, or worse, can be used as a launching pad for further attacks. If your ISP provides free antivirus protection, the ISP usually has done the homework to select a reputable vendor and can often provide some level of support with the product. You may cross the margin of diminishing utility by paying more for a different antivirus program, so unless you have a specific need, try your ISP's recommended antivirus software if you don't already have some installed.

If your computer manufacturer did not include any, and your ISP does not offer any gratis, you may need to buy antivirus software yourself. This can be challenging at first glance because there are many features to consider and the product lines are updated frequently. For contemporary advice on antivirus software, consult reputable periodicals such as *PC World* or *PC Magazine*, both of which have up-to-date information on their websites.

> **TIP**
>
> The antivirus business is a $2 billion dollar market, and the initial cost of the software product is quickly outweighed by the cost of the recurring subscription service to provide updates. When selecting a product, take into account the yearly subscription costs over the expected life of your computer. Multiyear subscriptions may provide valuable discounts, but as competition increases, subscription prices may drop.

> **TIP**
>
> We don't get kickbacks for unsolicited advertising in our books (too bad), but we're occasionally moved to give tips to readers about products we like a lot. One of these is Avast! antivirus. For individual users, the price is right—it's free. What's more, it's easy to use, doesn't drag down my system speed like some other antivirus programs have done, and it's a real-time virus scanner, protecting against malicious code cloaked inside IMs, emails, web browsing, network communications, P2P transfers, and web pages and downloads. For more information visit www.avast.com.

It's great when viruses are stopped before they have a chance to take root, but sometimes they're discovered only after the damage is done. The primary job of your antivirus software is to detect and prevent viruses. Most programs can clean and repair simple infections, but more complex and destructive viruses require a separate, specifically designed removal tool. If you're not careful, even if a virus is successfully cleaned, the infection can recur the second you lift your finger from the mouse button. Regardless of which software protects your computer, here are the steps to break the cycle and effectively get rid of a virus:

1. Manually run Windows Update to fix any new security vulnerabilities in Windows. To be thorough, also check vendors' websites for updates to any additional software you may have installed. Remember, if you remove a virus but remain vulnerable to a relapse, you might be in for a long day.

2. Update your virus definitions to detect the latest threats. Most antivirus software uses definition files that become stale quickly. Don't bring a knife to a gun fight.

3. Run a virus scan to find and eliminate any viruses. If you clean or quarantine a virus this way, run a follow-up scan to make sure it's truly dispatched. If not, at least you have identified the name of the threat and can proceed to the next step.

4. Visit your antivirus vendor's website and search for the identified threat. Most likely they have instructions and tools to help remove the virus from your computer. After a removal attempt, run another scan to confirm success. If needed, a general web search can often reveal alternative methods of treatment.

If all else fails, the fifth step to virus removal is tried and true: reinstall Windows from scratch. Make sure to delete and re-create the hard disk partitions during the install, and pat yourself on the back for having a recent backup of your critical data.

Windows Defender for Spyware Protection

Mark Twain famously said, "There are lies, damned lies, and statistics." No matter whose statistics you believe, reports and personal experiences indicate that most if not the vast majority of Internet-connected systems have some form of spyware installed. It's a big enough problem that Microsoft has included antispyware capabilities in the box with Windows Vista. Windows Defender evolved from Microsoft's 2005 free beta release of Microsoft AntiSpyware and is built with technology gained from Microsoft's acquisition of Giant Company Software, Inc. Spyware protection is its chief focus, but as the name implies, Windows Defender does not limit itself exclusively to spyware protection and takes on the remainder of malware that antivirus programs can leave behind.

After spyware gets onto a system, it can be difficult to remove. Let's assume you have a cousin named Heather who, after admittedly visiting suspicious links on MySpace, is convinced something bad has happened to her computer. Performance has degraded noticeably. Pop-ups abound. Like many, Heather is an avid fan of toolbars and neat programs that do wonderfully cute things. They have cute names such as BearShare and Bonzi Buddy, and at first seem to make the computer more fun than it ever deserved to be. If her suspicion is correct and the system is indeed infested with spyware, it could take a seasoned computer expert many, many hours to be *almost* certain that the system was rid of malware. Almost certain because, once a computer is compromised, it's difficult to know with absolute certainty that it is clean unless drastic measures are taken. Even after scouring the system with a variety of antispyware tools, intermediate-level system cleaners, and ultimately the more advanced power tools, it's difficult to be convinced that a previously compromised system is truly clean because just as layered defenses are so effective at preventing malware, layered deception can be equally effective at hiding it. A more efficient and effective route in severe cases may be to reinstall from scratch. Not a quick or easy fix.

As with viruses, by far the best way to prevent spyware is to stop it before it gets into the system, and Windows Defender monitors several system locations that are the main targets. It does its best to scan for rootkits, keystroke loggers, and other threats that do not fall into the worm or virus category. Along with real-time protection, Windows Defender provides the capability to periodically scan the computer, at a time and frequency you select, against the list of known spyware agents. A quick scan of the usual suspect areas is the default configuration, designed for optimal performance and daily use, whereas a full scan exhaustively covers every file and process on the computer. A full scan may result in slow performance while it runs, so is intended to run only occasionally, or when you think spyware may be lurking. To ensure the most up-to-date scanning capability, Windows Defender will automatically check for updated spyware definitions before each scheduled scan and download them beforehand if necessary. For both real-time protection and scheduled scans, spyware alerts are classified as severe, high, medium, low, or unknown. Finely granular control is provided for each alert level, including whether to automatically remove detected spyware. Because false positives are a risk, Windows will create a restore point before each automatic spyware removal to enable recovery if needed. The sensitivity and scope of real-time protection can be fine-tuned in even greater detail or disabled altogether. Windows Defender is found in the Security section of Control Panel alongside Vista's other security tools. Its behavior is highly configurable as detailed in the Options section of the Tools menu, shown in Figure 33.2. Thankfully, the default options will suit most users, although enough flexibility is provided to please discriminating tastes.

> **NOTE**
>
> Real-time protection is comprised of nine software agents that protect different parts of the system. It's recommended to leave all of them on, but each can be independently disabled. That way, compatibility or other issues with a single agent can be alleviated while the rest stay active. The Options section in Figure 33.2 provides an "Understanding real-time protection" link with detailed information on each agent.

Arcane tweaks aside, the method for rooting out spyware is fairly straightforward in most cases. In the Security section of Control Panel, just click Scan for Spyware and Potentially Unwanted Software. If you have a healthy level of paranoia, which does *not* mean they're not after you, a Full system scan may be selected in the Options section. When the scan completes, Windows Defender indicates any potentially unwanted software as shown in Figure 33.3. At that point, if you've had enough of this spyware nonsense and just want it gone, click Remove All. To control exactly what will be removed and what will stay, peruse the Review Items section. It includes detailed information on each item detected, and relevant links to Microsoft's online Malicious Software Encyclopedia if applicable. After you've removed the unwanted software, or quarantined it if you'd rather put it in the penalty box and investigate further, you can verify a clean bill of health with a follow-up scan.

Figure 33.2
Windows Defender real-time protection allows fine-tuning.

Figure 33.3
Removing spyware with Windows Defender.

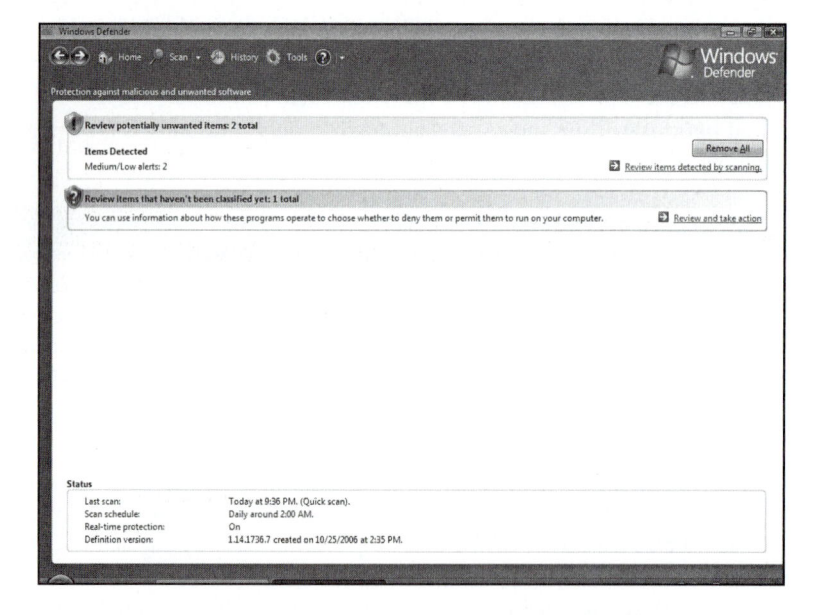

The Software Explorer feature in Windows Defender provides a detailed, consolidated view of software running on your computer. For casual users, it provides a more detailed way to check up on suspicious software. In the main view, there is a list of active software, and the Classification column makes it easy to tell at a glance whether the software is a "Permitted" or known good program. With a single click on any program title, more detailed information is available in the right pane, including the name, description, publisher, and most importantly the digital signature. If there is no digital signature, all of the aforementioned categories are suspect because anyone could have made it up. Malware is not usually digitally signed because its authors are not often interested in being identified. Which programs are set to Auto Start can also provide clues about persistent malware, which prefers to restart automatically when the computer is rebooted. Software Explorer is a layer of defense that provides an entry point to manual malware detection and removal. It's a welcome addition to Vista, and may whet the armchair malware hunter's appetite for more advanced tools.

> **TIP**
>
> For advanced malware detection and removal tools, few sources can match the Sysinternals website, a widely respected provider of free Windows power tools. Vista's Software Explorer touches the surface of manual malware detection and removal, but the reigning champion of its ilk is none other than Process Explorer, available for download at http://www.sysinternals.com. Winternals, the sole sponsor of Sysinternals, is now owned by Microsoft. Unlike antivirus programs, which can interfere with each other, it's safe (and recommended) to have multiple antispyware programs on your system. In addition to Windows Defender and Process Explorer, we also recommend Spybot Search & Destroy, available from http://www.safer-networking.org/.

The most interesting feature of Windows Defender is its use of Microsoft SpyNet. There is strength in numbers, and SpyNet seeks to use the collective wisdom of all participating users to inform our decisions about installing unknown or suspicious software. In the television quiz show *Who Wants to Be a Millionaire*, contestants are asked to answer multiple choice trivia questions for cash. Once per game, when stumped, contestants cam choose to "Ask the Audience" for assistance. The studio audience members each electronically enter her best answer, and the contestant is instantaneously presented with a graph indicating which answers are most favored by the audience. SpyNet works much like "Ask the Audience," but instead of cash, you're playing for the safety of your computer. When Windows Defender detects suspicious changes that it has yet to classify, you can see how other SpyNet members responded to the alert and make an informed choice about how to proceed. Not quite as exciting as a quiz show, perhaps, but a fresh approach to spyware defense. It's important to note that on the television show, "Ask the Audience" is a mixed bag. The audience is often correct on pop culture or general knowledge questions, but sometimes, they are wrong.

It's also important to note that participation in SpyNet is elective and turned off by default. When joining, participants must select either Basic or Advanced membership, which controls how much information will be sent to Microsoft about the potential spyware on your computer. Sending any information of this kind involves a degree of trust and is not appropriate for everyone. Essentially, Basic membership will send detailed information about files, complete URLs, and possibly search terms, in addition to what actions you took in response to the potential threat and some general computer information. Advanced membership can contain personal information from file paths and may provide memory dumps, which could provide valuable information to Microsoft engineers but could also contain the most sensitive data on your computer. For detailed information about what kind of information is sent based on membership type, and how Microsoft promises to protect your privacy, a link to the Windows Defender Privacy Statement Online is provided in the SpyNet section of Windows Defender.

Personal Firewalls: A Layer of Protection from Worms

Because worms spread across networks without user interaction, antivirus programs that seek to prevent users from launching viruses do not well apply. Defense against worms is a layered approach, with the first layer being a good network firewall.

→ For more detailed discussion about Windows Firewall, **see** "Windows Firewall," **p. 1213**.

> **TIP**
>
> As evidenced by the layout of the Security Center, there is often one program to block spyware, another to fight viruses, and yet another to provide a network firewall on a single computer. The industry trend, however, is toward convergence in this field. Many antivirus programs now use their scanning technology to identify and remove spyware, and some include a personal firewall as well. Some packages even include rootkit and phishing protection in various forms. In the coming years we may see the evolution of an Integrated Security Client rather than a smattering of specialized applications, or at least more cohesive suites of products.
>
> Comprehensive personal computer management services, which include malware defense, are another interesting development. In May 2006, Microsoft launched the Windows Live OneCare program, an attempt at a more holistic approach to PC management including malware protection, preventative maintenance, backups, and tech support.

Automatic Updates: Remove the Side Doors

In conjunction with antivirus, antispyware, and personal firewall capabilities, automatic updates are a critical part of the security strategy because they shut down avenues of attack as soon as they are discovered. Malware often relies on flaws found in software to perform its mission. These flaws are akin to open side doors to your home that, hopefully, nobody knows about. There they stand as an open invitation for malware to walk in. Automatic updates don't just shut the door; they usually remove the door entirely and put a permanent wall in its place. You can enable and configure Automatic updates in the Security section of the Control Panel. If daily updates at 3:00 a.m. do not suit you, the time and frequency can be adjusted as you like.

→ For a detailed discussion of the important automatic update technologies in Windows Vista, **see** "Windows Vista and Keeping Up to Date," **p. 986**.

Data Execution Prevention (DEP)

The infamous Internet Worm, launched in 1988 by then Cornell University student Robert Morris, was the first worm to publicly demonstrate the risk of buffer overflow attacks. It infected thousands of systems on the Internet, frustrating military and university researchers at the time. Modern malware writers continue to exploit the same type of vulnerability on a much larger scale. The Internet has grown exponentially, connecting banks, corporations, government agencies, and private homes. The recent generation of worms, such as MS Blaster and Sasser, have attracted mass media attention as they delayed British Airways flights and affected networks from public hospitals in Hong Kong to the Sydney train system—all made possible by a single category of security vulnerability.

Buffers are fixed-length memory locations used to hold data. They can be adjacent to other memory locations also used to hold data. If a program attempts to write more data into the buffer than will fit, the remaining data can overflow into the adjacent memory location and overwrite its previous contents with malicious code. It is an esoteric task that requires a high degree of skill, but if the malicious code can then be *executed*, what was once a fine upstanding member of the computer community is now, potentially, a minion of evil.

The effects of buffer overflow exploits have been dramatic and complex, yet the root cause, and effective remedies, have been known for some time. Computer programs can be written and compiled in ways that check and prevent these conditions, but for decades, many traditional tools and practices of software engineers have not addressed the problem.

New programming tools and conscientious coding can thwart buffer overflows, but because rebuilding all computer code in existence is impractical, techniques have been developed to mitigate the risk. Executable Space Protection techniques, as implemented through Microsoft's Data Execution Prevention, disallow code execution in areas of memory where it is not expected, and thereby significantly reduce the threat of buffer overflow attacks. It's technology with a proven track record of success. Several critical exploits have already been proven to fail on DEP-enabled systems—but not all DEP is created equally.

Modern processors from both AMD and Intel come with hardware-based Data Execution Prevention technology. Windows Vista can take full advantage of this important security feature, but it will not do so by itself. As installed, DEP is enabled only for core Windows components. To take full advantage of DEP for non-Windows programs, you must find the Data Execution Prevention menu, nestled deep in the user interface, and turn on DEP for all programs. Microsoft did not enable this setting because some programs will not work with DEP enabled. This should not deter you from taking full advantage of DEP because, as shown in Figure 33.4, there is an exception list, and the trouble is worth the extra security.

To enable DEP, follow these steps:

1. Select Start, Control Panel, System and Maintenance.
2. Choose System, Change Settings, (and Continue if UAC is enabled).
3. Select Advanced, Settings (under Performance), Data Execution Prevention.
4. Turn on DEP for All Programs.
5. Select OK three times.
6. Restart your computer.

Figure 33.4
Enable DEP for all programs.

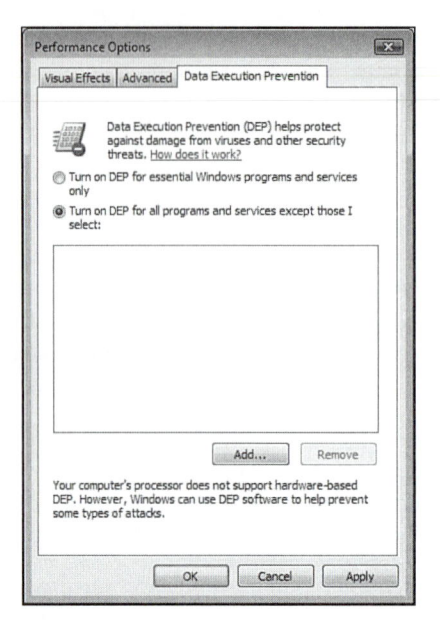

Hardware DEP will take advantage of the processor's inherent security features, but even if your computer does not have an AMD processor with NX (No Execute) or an Intel processor with XD (Execute Disabled) features, Windows Vista can still provide some level of buffer overflow protection using Software DEP. Although not a hardware DEP equivalent, Software DEP has shown to be effective against real-world exploits. It can protect the exception handling processes in Windows and provides better protection when programs are built specifically to support Software DEP.

> **NOTE**
>
> In addition to DEP, Windows Vista uses Address Space Layout Randomization to combat malicious code execution. Without ASLR, key operating system components load in predictable locations that are more easily targeted. Randomizing the location of executable images adds a new level of difficulty for would-be exploiters but not for you. This protection activates and selects new random locations automatically at startup.

USER ACCOUNT CONTROL (UAC)

Systems administrators of sensitive computer systems, on which thousands or even millions of people depend, have to be careful about what users are allowed to do—especially themselves. They have unfettered access to every aspect of the system, which allows them to quickly diagnose and correct any number of complex problems that might arise. Computers can be efficient in carrying out voluminous tasks, which is good when those tasks are performing useful work but potentially devastating in the case of human error, particularly when those errors are made by someone with complete access to destroy massive amounts of data with the stroke of a key. Experienced computer professionals know that it is bad juju to perform casual work on a system using a full-fledged administrator account because it is far too easy to blow things up. Instead, they create two different accounts for themselves: a limited access account that has enough power to get daily tasks done but is restricted enough to keep them out of serious trouble, and a second unrestricted administrative account for use only when they need to perform perilous tasks.

Once relegated to the humble personal computer, Microsoft Windows is now the world's premier operating system in an interconnected world where personal computers have become critically important. Through the release of Windows XP, unless you were conscientious enough to create a separate user account, the standard practice was to use the system with full administrator rights all the time. This is convenient for deft users who rarely make mistakes, but even more convenient for those who would install malware on the computer. If a user constantly operates as an unrestricted administrator, even the most mundane task, such as opening an email or downloading a simple program, acts as a supreme being, ready to create or destroy without limits.

User Account Control is Vista's answer to the problem. Even if you don't want to go to the extent of creating a standard user account for perilous tasks, you still have some degree of protection. There are two basic levels of users in Windows Vista: standard users and administrators. Like Windows XP before it, the default user account in Vista still has full administrator privileges to the system, but now, before you get into any serious trouble, you will be asked for permission to continue. The administrator account normally runs with the same permissions as a standard user. When called on to do something that requires administrator privileges, the account can elevate to the administrator level for that task only. That means some actions that would have been performed without question in previous versions of Windows now pop up with additional information and require consent. At first, the notifications can seem like an annoyance, but when heeded, provide a superior level of protection. They warn of potential danger and use an intuitive color-coded scheme according to the perceived level of risk. User Account Control is highly recommended for improved system security. For intrepid travelers who laugh at spyware and taunt viruses with a quick wink of the eye, User Account Control can be disabled in the User Accounts section of Control Panel. And in that case, you may also be interested in dog-earing the section of this book on Installing Windows.

→ For information on installing Windows, **see** "Performing a New Installation of Windows Vista" **p. 49**.

CHANGING UAC BEHAVIOR

If you need to provide different levels of User Account Control for different users of the computer, Vista provides two options for how to handle this. When using a standard user account, if a task is attempted that requires administrator level access, the user can either be prompted to enter an administrator username and password or be flat-out denied. The default approach in this case is to prompt the user for credentials so that an over-the-shoulder parent or systems administrator can authorize privileged actions. If you would rather that such requests simply be denied, you can use the Local Security Policy Console (click start; then type `secpol.msc` in the Search box) to change the setting highlighted in Figure 33.5. See Local Policies, Security Options for this setting.

Figure 33.5
Use the Local Security Policy Console to change UAC settings.

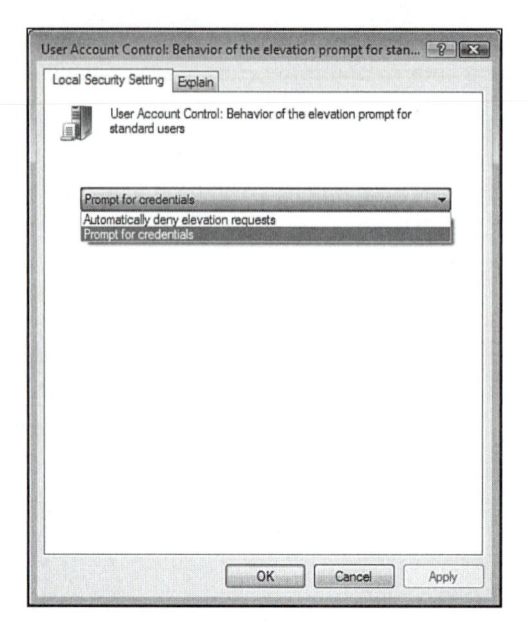

Service Hardening

In addition to the security improvements that can be configured, several improvements in Windows Vista may go unnoticed to all but software developers, including malware writers. Microsoft has more closely adhered to the well-known security principle of Least Privilege, which means that people or things should have access only to what they need, and nothing more. It's a sound idea that, had it been followed more closely in earlier version of Windows, would have prevented numerous security exploits.

Core Windows programs called services have in the past been favorite targets because many of them are always running, and they often have a wide scope of access to the system. When a service could be compromised, it provided many avenues for further exploration and exploitation. This time around, Microsoft has limited the access of services to only what they need to do. For example, a service's capability to write to the disk or Registry is based strictly on the requirements of the service. This is a real security improvement, which will continue to pay unsung dividends as long as Vista exists.

> **NOTE** Some features of Windows Vista are available only if you have a 64-bit processor and purchase the 64-bit version of Vista. The 64-bit version requires digitally signed kernel-mode drivers, the core software that controls various devices on the computer. Iffy drivers have long been a source of computer crashes and instability. Malicious drivers can be a path to kernel-mode rootkits, which are difficult to detect. The desire to ensure that drivers come only from reputable sources, then, is apparently to help improve stability and security. It may also, however, help prevent the installation of sneaky drivers that do things such as circumvent audio or video copy protection.

Internet Explorer 7 Malware Protection

Internet Explorer has several new features specifically designed to increase security. First, the default Protected Mode of operation limits the capability to write to any locations other than the one for temporary Internet files. Any attempts to access user or system areas now require user action. This will reduce furtive software installs that take place through Internet Explorer.

ActiveX—the name sends shivers down the spines of computer security professionals everywhere. A wonderful and powerful technology when used within the safety of a protected network, on the Internet frontier ActiveX has proven to be a terrible thing in the hands of the wicked. Rather than being available whether they are needed or not, most native ActiveX controls are now disabled with IE 7 unless you specifically enable them with the Information Bar. This feature is called ActiveX Opt-In and is in line with the Principle of Least Privilege. It prevents taking advantage of security holes in components that weren't even used but were there anyway, just waiting to be exploited.

Previous versions of IE contained multiple functions to process URL data, each a potential point of entry for attack. Hackers used specially crafted URLs to cause buffer overflow conditions and compromise the system. Problems parsing malformed URLs were common causes of security threats and resulted in a fair percentage of IE patches. With IE 7, the URL handling has been rewritten such that there is a single and more robust mechanism, which should result in fewer opportunities and greater difficulties for attackers.

→ For a discussion of more security enhancements in Internet Explorer, **see** the section on phishing, **p. 1244**.

Tips from the Windows Pros: Avoiding Malware

Taking a minimalist approach to installing software on your computer goes a long way toward avoiding malware. It also saves space, avoids bogging down your computer, and can make the computer simpler and easier to use. That doesn't mean to take a Spartan stance and forego all the software gadgetry that makes computers useful and fun, but it does mean to take a more deliberate attitude toward installing software. As with many areas in life, when it comes to installing software from the Internet, installing a CD purchased at the dollar store, or downloading content from a peer-to-peer program, less is more.

Whenever seemingly innocuous software is installed, be it a toolbar, cute purple gorilla, weather program, or anything at all, you are potentially transferring full ownership of your computer to somebody else. Now of course, one would expect that before such a transition of ownership, the previous owner would ceremoniously sign a title or perform some similar ritual, but just clicking OK is usually all it takes.

The best way to prevent an unintentional computer donation is to never install software from a source you don't trust. Once installed, malware can and will take substantial liberties with your computer. Malware writers go to amazingly creative and destructive lengths to achieve their goals—whether profit by directing you to advertisements, theft of personal information, or worse. If your computer is infected with malware and performing slowly, it may be busy doing a lot of work in the background on someone else's behalf. Computer criminals have been known to control an army of thousands, or even more than a million compromised computers and then extort money from online businesses by threatening to use the army of "zombies" to barrage a commercial website, shutting it down for hours or days. It's a credible threat.

You'll find many long lists of things you can to do avoid malware and keep your computer from becoming a zombie. Here are three essential things to remember to protect your Windows Vista computer:

- Install an antivirus program with real-time protection.
- Keep the Security Center green.
- Only install software from sources you trust.

CHAPTER 34

Protecting Your Data from Loss and Theft

In this chapter

The Backup and Restore Center   1150

Creating a File and Folder Backup   1153

Restoring Data from a File and Folder Backup   1157

Creating a Complete PC (Image) Backup   1160

Restoring a Complete PC Backup Image   1172

Encrypted File System (EFS)   1173

Disk Organization for Data Safety   1181

BitLocker Disk Encryption   1182

Recovering Previous Versions of a File   1190

NTFS File Permissions   1192

Security Policy Configuration Options   1199

Third-Party Disc-Backup Tools   1200

Troubleshooting   1201

Tips from the Windows Pros: Restoring NTBACKUP Files   1203

The Backup and Restore Center

After years of providing slow backup and restore programs that ignored the widespread availability of rewriteable DVD and CD drives, Microsoft has made a big turnaround in Windows Vista with the introduction of the Backup and Restore Center. Although the features of the Backup and Restore Center vary by Vista edition, all Vista editions provide a fast and easy-to-use File and Folder Backup Wizard (occasionally referred to as SafeDocs backup) that supports rewriteable CD and DVD drives, as well as external USB and FireWire hard disks and internal hard disks.

Differences in the Backup and Restore Center

Microsoft's nomenclature leads to confusion here. The Volume Shadow Copy Service (VSS) is present in all Vista and XP versions, and it's what permits reliable backup of open files, for *all* versions of XP and Vista. Vista has the capability to keep *persistent* shadow copies. This is the basis of System Restore on Vista versions, and the Complete PC Backup and "previous versions" features on Vista Business/Enterprise/Ultimate. When they refer to Volume Shadow Copies on Vista, they're usually referring to these latter applications.

Although all Windows Vista versions support file and folder backup, some Windows Vista editions support additional backup options:

- Capability to back up to and restore from network shares
- Scheduled incremental file and folder backup
- Previous versions, which permits the user to revert to the previous version of a file or folder
- Complete PC Backup, which makes an image backup of a complete system and permits a "bare-metal" restore to the same hard disk, same-size replacement, or larger replacement hard disk

> **NOTE**
>
> Previous Versions depends upon System Protection restore points (the same restore points used for System Restore). By default, System Protection is enabled for the system drive (usually, the C: drive). However, it must be enabled manually for other hard disk drives. If you configure your system to store documents, photos, and other types of files on a different drive, be sure to enable System Protection for that drive. See Chapter 28, "Troubleshooting and Repairing Problems," for details.

Table 34.1 lists the backup and restore features supported by each Windows Vista edition.

The Backup and Restore Center

Table 34.1   Backup and Restore Center Features

Vista Edition	File and Folder Backup	File and Folder Backup to Network Share	Scheduled File and Folder Backup	Previous Versions	Complete PC Backup*
Home Basic	Yes	No	No	No	No
Home Premium	Yes	Yes	Yes	No	No
Business	Yes	Yes	Yes	Yes	Yes
Enterprise	Yes	Yes	Yes	Yes	Yes
Ultimate	Yes	Yes	Yes	Yes	Yes

*Complete PC Backup does not support backing up to network shares.

Figure 34.1 shows the Backup and Restore Center as it appears in Windows Vista Home Basic and Home Premium.

Figure 34.1
The Backup and Restore Center in Windows Vista Home Basic and Home Premium offers only file backup and restore.

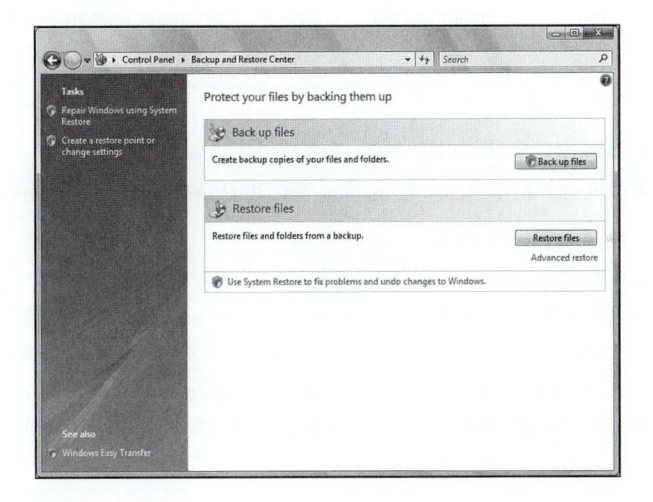

Although the Backup and Restore Center interface is the same in Home Basic and Home Premium, Home Premium has two additional backup capabilities:

- Home Premium can back up to a network share, whereas Home Basic can back up to only local devices.
- Home Premium's file backup runs on a schedule, whereas Home Basic's file backup runs manually.

The Backup and Restore Center in Windows Vista Business and Ultimate includes Complete PC Backup and previous version support, as shown in Figure 34.2.

Figure 34.2
The Backup and Restore Center in Windows Vista adds support for Complete PC Backup and previous versions.

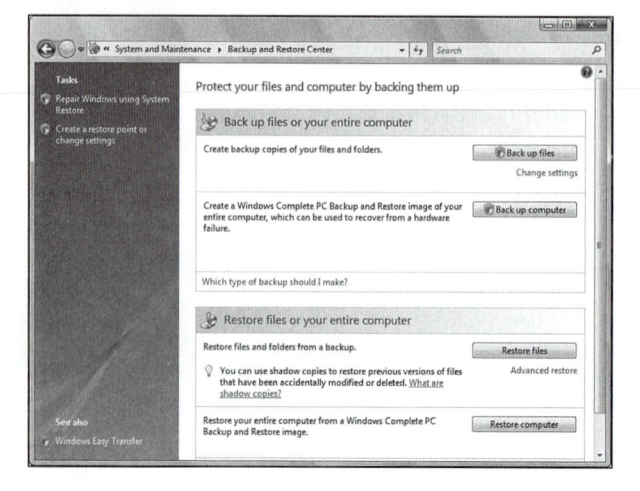

> **NOTE**
> You must be an administrator or provide administrator-level credentials to perform backups.

File and Folder Backups Versus Complete PC Backups

File and folder backups differ from Complete PC Backup and Restore image backups in several ways:

- You can restore individual files directly from a file and folder backup.
- File and folder backups are designed to protect an individual user's data files, favorites, and settings (including email messages), but not the operating system.
- Complete PC backups can be used to restore a system from a "bare metal" hard disk but are not designed to permit the restoration of individual files and folders.

> **TIP**
> If you need to restore a file from a Complete PC backup, you can mount the .VHD backup file created by Complete PC backup in Microsoft's Virtual PC or Virtual Server and retrieve individual files and folders, or you can use the command-line wbadmin tool. If you don't want to install the entire Virtual PC or Virtual Server package, you can perform a custom installation of Virtual Server 2005 and install only the VHDMount utility. VHDMount enables you to access individual files using the command line. See "Using VHDMount with Complete PC Backup Images," in this chapter, **p. 1164**.

Because of the differences in how file and folder backups and Complete PC Backup and Restore image backups work, your best backup strategy on systems that support Complete PC Backup and Restore backups is to do the following:

1. Create a Complete PC backup after configuring your system.
2. Set up automatic file and folder backups on a schedule that works for you.

By following this procedure, you can recover from a system crash by

1. Restoring a Complete PC Backup and Restore image backup.
2. Restoring file and folder backups.

→ To learn how to restore a Complete PC Backup image backup from the Windows Vista Recovery environment (Recovery Options), see Chapter 28.

CREATING A FILE AND FOLDER BACKUP

Although all Windows Vista editions support file and folder backups using the Back Up Files Wizard, there are several differences in the process, depending upon the Windows Vista edition you use.

1. Click the Back Up Files button, shown in Figures 34.1 and 34.2, to get started.
2. In the next dialog box, select the location where you want to store the backup (see Figure 34.3). Most editions offer the choice of a rewriteable CD or DVD drive or hard disk (top), or a network share (bottom), but the Home Basic edition grays out the network share; it supports only local drives.

Figure 34.3
Selecting a destination drive or network share for the file backup.

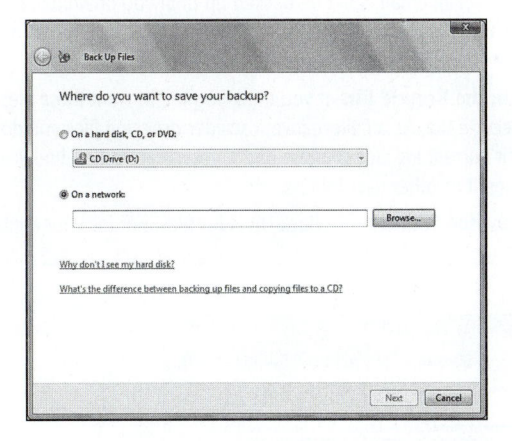

3. If you select a network share, you must log into the network share if prompted, even if you are selecting a Public folder and Public Folder Sharing is turned on.

> **TIP**
> If you want to use network shares as backup destinations, set up the user(s) and password(s) on the network destination before you start the backup process.

4. By default, the Back Up Files Wizard backs up a wide range of user-created files (see Figure 34.4).

To avoid backing up a particular category, clear the check box.

> **TIP**
>
> Use this feature to create backups of specific categories of files by clearing the checkmarks for all but a particular category.

> **CAUTION**
>
> It's important to realize that File Back Up does not back up several types of files (and one type of file system), depending upon whether you are using original Windows Vista or Vista SP-1.
>
> - **Hard disks that use the FAT file system (including FAT32)**—If you are using Windows Vista as a dual-boot with another operating system that uses FAT drives, any data on those drives must be backed up with another backup program.
>
> - **Encrypted files using the Encrypted File System (EFS)**—These files are not backed up by the Back Up Files wizard in original Windows Vista. However, in Windows Vista SP-1, EFS files are backed up by the Back Up Files wizard. This is a welcome improvement for Business, Enterprise, and Ultimate users (Home editions and Starter don't support EFS). Encrypted file and folder names are displayed in green.
>
> - **Web-based email that is not stored on your hard disk**—Your Hotmail, Yahoo! Mail, or Gmail email won't be backed up until you download it. Unfortunately, you can't use Windows Mail (Vista's successor to Outlook Express) to access these or other web-based email services.
>
> - **Files in the Recycle Bin**—If you think you might want these files, get them out of the Recycle Bin. As an alternative, consider dragging files you don't want (at least, in their current locations) into a folder you create called Junk inside of your Document or other user folders.
>
> - **User Profile Settings**—File Back Up is for files, not for your digital identity.

Figure 34.4
Clear checkmarks to skip backups of listed file types.

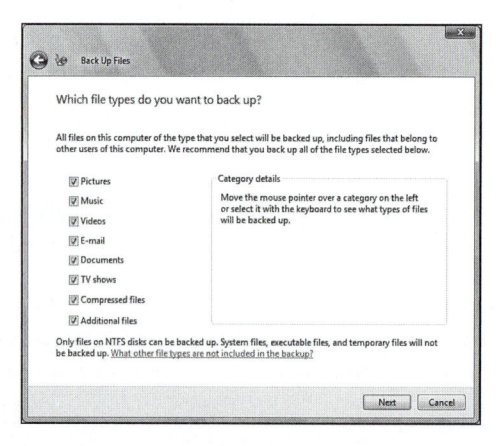

5. With Windows Vista Home Basic (and Starter) editions, click Save Settings and Start Backup to begin the backup process. With other editions, this button is part of the scheduling dialog box, shown in Figure 34.5.

Figure 34.5
The backup scheduler in Home Premium, Business, and Ultimate editions.

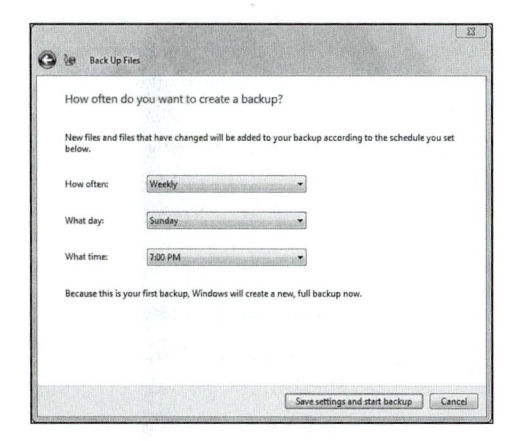

6. Select a frequency (daily, weekly, or monthly), a day of the week, and a time (any hour). Choose a time when your computer is not normally in use but will be turned on. Then click Save Settings and Start Backup.
7. A progress dialog box displays the progress of the backup. At the end of the backup, a dialog box appears indicating whether the backup was successful. Click Close.

WORKING WITH REMOVABLE MEDIA DURING BACKUPS

You can use removable-media drives such as Iomega REV or DVD-recordable drives with either Back Up Files or Complete PC Backup (Back Up Files can also use CDs). However, I don't recommend using CDs or DVDs for Back Up Files with any edition other than Home Basic (or Starter). You must format each disc (unless it's already formatted), and if you use CDs or DVDs with the scheduled backup feature in other Vista editions, the backup will fail if the medium is not in place when the backup starts.

If you use DVDs for Complete PC Backup, you'll probably be using a handful of DVDs for your backup. Instead, consider dedicating an external USB hard disk for backups. You can use the same hard disk for both Back Up Files and Complete PC Backup files.

If you use CDs or DVDs for backups, you will see dialog boxes similar to the following during the backup process when it's time to insert the medium:

- **Label and Insert a Blank Disk**—A dialog box displays the label format to use: *computername, date, time, disk #*. Click OK.
- **Are You Sure You Want to Format This Disk?**—You'll see this dialog box unless you previously formatted or used the CD or DVD. Click Format.

> **TIP**
> To save time during the process, click the empty Don't Ask Again for This Backup check box. When this box is checked, unformatted media is formatted automatically.

A format process bar appears, and the backup continues until it's time for the next disc. If you use any type of supported DVD or CD-R, the format should take less than a minute. A CD-RW might take much longer. I recommend using DVDs instead of CDs to save time and disc swaps, but external hard disks make for faster and easier backups.

How Backups Created with Back Up Files Are Stored

If you're concerned that Back Up Files has unleashed another incompatible file format upon the world, relax. Back Up Files actually uses the venerable PKZip file format. When viewed in Computer or other views, the files it creates feature the same folder with a zipper icon used by any other Zip-compression archive. Each backup file has a maximum size of 200MB, making it easy to transfer from a network share or external hard disk to CD, DVD, or other medium for long-term archiving.

Figure 34.6 shows the internal structure of a Back Up Files backup, as shown in Windows Explorer. The first-level folder is the computer name, followed by nested folders listing the backup set name and date. The actual backup file is listed next, along with a catalog folder.

Figure 34.6
The folder structure of a typical DVD created with Back Up Files.

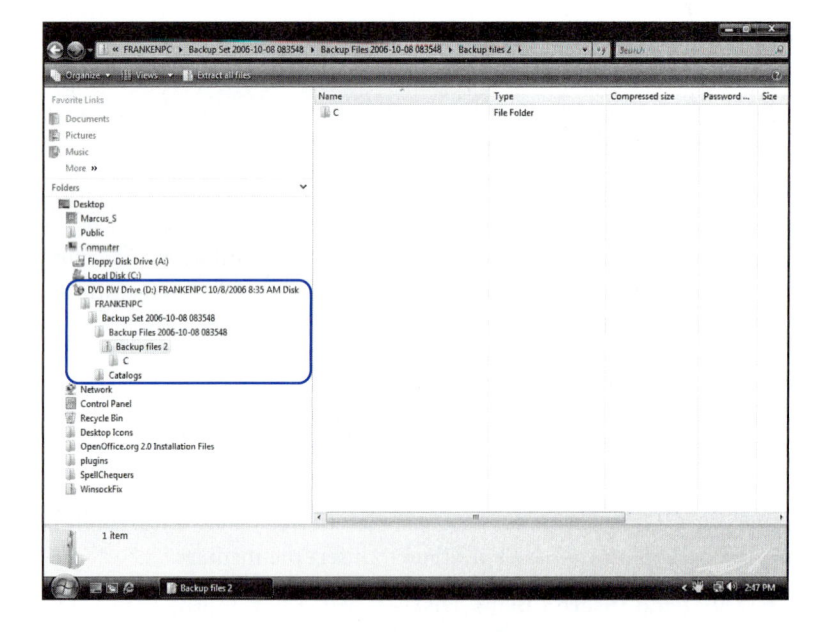

> **TIP**
>
> In an emergency, you can access a backup made with Back Up Files on a computer running Windows XP using its integrated Zip file support.

Restoring Data from a File and Folder Backup

To restore data files from your backup, click Restore Files from the Backup and Restore Center dialog boxes shown in Figures 34.1 and 34.2. The Restore Files dialog box prompts you to select whether you want to restore the most recent backup or an earlier backup. Home Basic (and Starter) editions permit you to restore backups made on the same computer by the current user only; other editions also feature options to restore all users' data or data from another computer.

Restoring the Current User's Data

Select Restore Files and choose whether to restore files from the latest backup or an earlier backup. Click Next to continue. In the next dialog box, click Add Files to specify individual files to restore, Add Folders to specify folders to restore, or Search to specify search terms to locate items to restore. The backup catalog stored with the backup (refer to Figure 34.6) enables you to navigate your backup as you would use Windows Explorer to navigate a drive. After you navigate to the appropriate location and select Add, the files or folders are listed (see Figure 34.7). Click Next to continue.

Figure 34.7
Selecting a folder to restore with Restore Files.

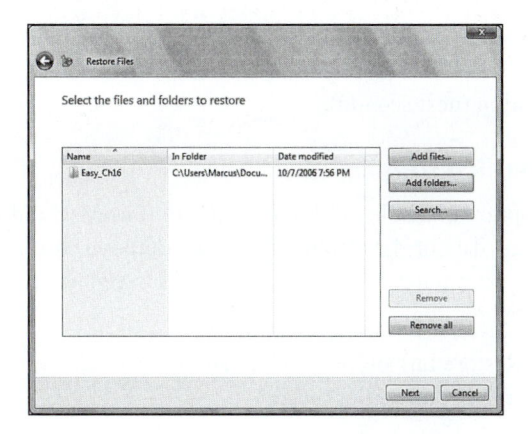

Specify where to save the restored files (see Figure 34.8). By default, the files are returned to their original location. However, you can also use the Browse button to specify a particular location (a helpful feature for testing a backup). If you select the option to choose a location, you can also specify whether to restore the files to their original subfolder and whether to create a subfolder for the drive letter. After specifying options, click Start Restore.

If the backup drive or removable medium is not already present, connect the backup drive or insert the appropriate medium when prompted. Click OK to continue the restore. At the end of the process, a dialog box appears indicating whether the restore was successful. Click Finish to close the dialog box.

Figure 34.8
Preparing to restore a folder with Restore Files.

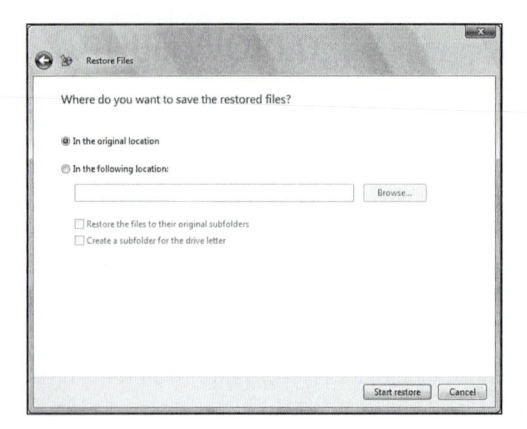

> **NOTE**
>
> If you click Stop Restore after the system has started copying files to your system, the files that already have been restored remain on the system.

The process is quick and easy because the backup catalog on the system is used to select the files or folders to restore. If the backup catalog is lost, the files can still be restored by using the Advanced Restore option (next section).

PERFORMING AN ADVANCED RESTORE

The Advanced Restore option available in Home Premium, Business, and Ultimate editions supports restoring all users' data or data from a different computer. It can also be used to restore data from the same computer if the backup catalogs were lost. To perform an Advanced Restore, follow these steps:

1. Click the Advanced Restore link on the Backup and Restore Center dialog box. This link is located below the Restore Files button.

2. The Advanced Restore link opens the Backup Status and Configuration dialog box. Select Advanced Restore to restore all users' files or files from a different computer. Click Restore Files to perform a restoration of the current user's files only, as described in the previous section.

3. From the Restore Files (Advanced) dialog box, select whether to restore files from the latest backup, a previous backup, or a backup from a different computer. Click Next to continue.

4. Specify the location of the backup (see Figure 34.9). To enable the system to detect the backup source, be sure to insert the backup medium or connect the backup hard disk. Click Next to continue.

5. A list of backups by date and time appears. Select the appropriate backup from the list and click Next to continue.

6. In the next dialog box, use Add Files, Add Folders, or Search to locate the files or folders to restore. Click Next to continue.

Figure 34.9
Selecting a backup source for an advanced restore.

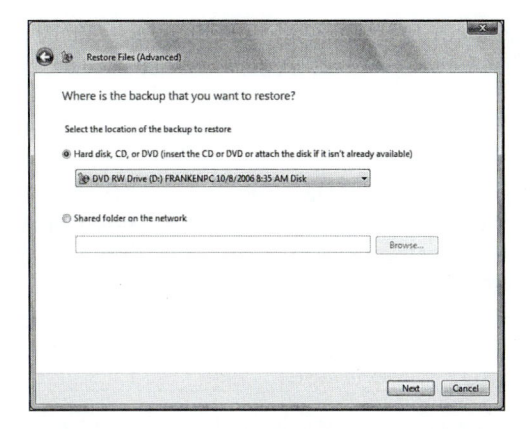

> **CAUTION**
>
> The files and folders selection dialog box includes a check box to restore everything in the backup. Don't check this box unless you want to restore favorites, game shortcuts, and other items from the backup. Restoring these items can cause problems for your system because they might not match settings in your system.

7. Just as with the standard restore, you can specify where to restore the files. Figure 34.10 shows an alternative location for restoration. If you are restoring data from another system, you must restore it to your system's Public folder if it came from a different computer.

Figure 34.10
Specifying an alternative destination for an advanced restore from a different computer.

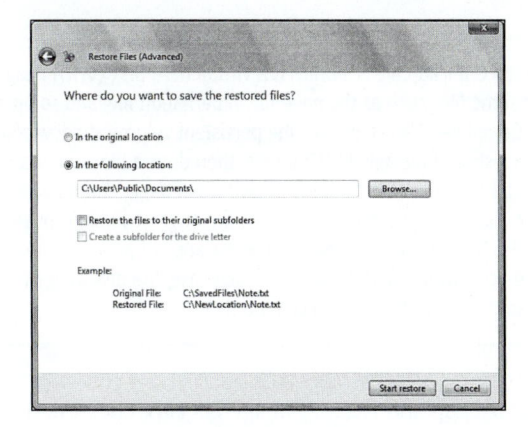

If you are restoring data from a different computer, the original user account might not match any user on your computer. In such cases, a Missing User Account dialog box appears. You have two options for restoring the data:

- Create a user with the same name on your system before continuing
- Click the check box to restore files without reassigning security permissions

Follow the option that makes the most sense in your situation, and click Continue. The restoration begins immediately. Swap media, if prompted. Click Finish at the end of the restoration process.

> **NOTE**
> If the files are being transferred to a computer that will be used by the owner of the original files, create a user with the same name so the files can have that user's permissions. However, if file ownership is not important, click the check box and assign the files to a particular owner later.

> **TIP**
> It would be a good idea to test your backup before things go wrong. Create a new folder and restore selected files or folders to it. If they restore correctly, you know your backup works. If not, you've discovered a problem before it's too late.

If you are having difficulty restoring files from a multi-disc backup set, see "Can't Locate File to Restore from a Multidisc Backup Setup" in the "Troubleshooting" section at the end of the chapter.

Creating a Complete PC (Image) Backup

If your edition of Vista supports it, you should create a Complete PC Backup as soon as you have installed Windows Vista and configured it to your liking. By doing so, you create a baseline configuration that you can return to in case of a major system crash.

> **NOTE**
> A Complete PC Backup file is stored as a virtual hard disk (VHD) image of the entire disk, excluding some files such as the page file, hibernation file, and so on. For subsequent backups, Complete PC Backup uses the persistent volume shadow copy mechanism to retain a snapshot of the initial VHD image, then does a block-by-block image update of the VHD. The VHD now has the most recent disk image, and the shadow copy presents the earlier image (that is, Windows retains the original versions of all changed blocks). Complete PC Backup can keep quite a few backups of previous versions this way, depending upon available disk space. In each case, the disk image copy is performed on a temporary VSS snapshot of the live hard disk.

To create a Complete PC Backup and Restore image backup, click the Back Up Computer button from the Backup and Restore Center dialog box (refer to Figure 34.2). Click Continue on the User Account Control dialog box.

Select the location for the backup (a hard disk or DVD). Click Next. Review the backup location, the amount of space needed on the target drive, and the drive to be backed up, and click Start Backup to begin (see Figure 34.11).

Figure 34.11
Starting a Complete PC Backup.

> **TIP**
> Before you start the Complete PC Backup process, insert the medium or connect the external drive (and make sure Windows Vista recognizes it). Complete PC Backup ignores empty removable media or optical drives, and can use removable hard disks only if they are formatted using the NTFS file system.

If you back up to an external hard disk (my recommendation for reliability and easy restoration), just sit back and watch the progress bar.

If you use DVDs, follow the prompts to label and format the medium when it is inserted. After the medium is formatted, the backup process continues. When a backup to DVD is complete, you are prompted to insert each disc to verify the backup. This feature is designed to protect you against backup failures caused by scratched or otherwise defective media.

> **TIP**
> Click the Don't Ask Again for This Backup option to avoid being asked to format your medium each time.
>
> You can also format your media in advance with Windows Explorer to avoid backup failures if one or more of your discs fails to format correctly. DVDs are formatted using the widely supported UDF disk format.

When you store a Complete PC Backup on a hard disk, the backup is not compressed. However, DVD backups are compressed. The backup is stored in a folder called WindowsImageBackup.

If you decide to create another Complete PC Backup image in the future, you can use the same target drive, and Vista will back up only the files that have changed since the original image backup.

WBADMIN Command-Line System Backup and Restore

To use a network share or for other advanced complete PC Backup and Restore options, including scripted restores, use the command-line backup tool wbadmin. Originally developed for Windows Server, wbadmin provides many options for backing up and restoring a system image. You can also use wbadmin to restore files from an image backup.

- Use the WBADMIN START BACKUP command to start a backup.

    Usage:
    ```
    WBADMIN START BACKUP
          -backupTarget:{TargetVolume | TargetNetworkShare} -
          include:VolumesToInclude
          [-noVerify]
          [-quiet]
    ```
    Runs a backup immediately using the specified options.

-backupTarget	Storage location for this backup. Requires drive letter or UNC path to shared network folder.
include	Comma-delimited list of volume drive letters, volume mount points, or GUID-based volume names to include in backup. Should be used when -backupTarget is specified.
-noVerify	If specified, backups written to removable media such as DVD will not be verified. By default, backups written to such media will be verified for errors.
-quiet	Runs the command with no user prompts.

    Example:
    ```
    WBADMIN START BACKUP -backupTarget:e: -
    include:e:,d:\mountpoint,\\?\Volume{cc566d14-44a0-11d9-9d93-806e6f6e6963}\
    ```

- Use the WBADMIN GET command to list items in a backup set.

    Usage:
    ```
    WBADMIN GET ITEMS
        -version:VersionIdentifier
        [-backupTarget:{VolumeName | NetworkSharePath}]
        [-machine:BackupMachineName]
    ```
    Lists items contained in the backup based on the options specified.

-version	Version identifier of the backup in MM/DD/YYYY-HH:MM format, as listed by WBADMIN GET VERSIONS.
-backupTarget	Specifies the storage location that contains the backups for which you want the details. Useful when the backups are stored in a different location than the normal location for backups of this computer.
-machine	Specifies the name of the computer for which you want the details. Useful when multiple computers have been backed up to the same location. Should be used when -backupTarget is specified.

Example:
```
WBADMIN GET ITEMS -version:03/31/2005-09:00
```

- Use the WBADMIN STOP command to stop a backup:

Usage:
```
WBADMIN STOP JOB [-quiet]
```

Cancels currently running backup or recovery. Canceled jobs cannot be restarted.

-quiet   Runs the command with no user prompts.

- Use the WBADMIN START RECOVERY command to restore files, volumes, or apps.

Usage:
```
WBADMIN START RECOVERY
    -version:VersionIdentifier
    -items:VolumesToRecover¦AppsToRecover¦FilesOrFoldersToRecover
    -itemtype:{Volume ¦ App ¦ File}
    [-backupTarget:{VolumeHostingBackup ¦ NetworkShareHostingBackup}]
    [-machine:BackupMachineName]
    [-recoveryTarget:TargetVolumeForRecovery ¦ TargetPathForRecovery]
    [-recursive]
    [-overwrite:{Overwrite ¦ CreateCopy ¦ Skip}]
    [-notrestoreacl]
    [-quiet]
```

Runs a recovery immediately based on the options specified.

Option	Description
-version	Version identifier MM/DD/YYYY-HH:MM format of backup to recover from, as listed by WBADMIN GET VERSIONS.
-items	Comma-delimited list of items to recover. If itemtype is Volume, can be only a single volume. If itemtype is App, can be only a single application. If itemtype is File, can be files or directories, but should be part of the same volume and should be under the same parent.
-itemtype	Type of items to recover. Must be volume, app, or file.
-backupTarget	Drive letter or shared network folder path of the backup. Useful when the backup to use for recovery is different than the location where backups of this computer are usually stored.
-machine	The computer whose backup you want to use for recovery. Useful when multiple computers were backed up to the same location. Should be used when -backupTarget is specified.
-recoveryTarget	Drive letter of volume to restore to. Useful if the volume to restore to is different than the volume that was backed up.
-recursive	Valid only when recovering files. Recursively recovers files under the specified path. By default, only files that reside directly under the specified folders will be recovered.
-overwrite	Valid only when recovering files. Specifies the action to take when a file being recovered already exists in the same location. Skip causes recovery to skip the existing file and continue with recovery of the

next file. `Createcopy` causes recovery to create a copy of the existing file; the existing file will not be modified. `Overwrite` causes recovery to overwrite the existing file with the file from the backup.

`-notrestoreacl` — Valid only when recovering files. Does not restore the security ACLs of files being recovered from backup. By default, the security ACLs would be restored. Default is `true`.

`-quiet` — Runs the command with no user prompts.

Examples:
```
WBADMIN START RECOVERY -version:03/31/2005-09:00 -itemType:Volume -items:d:
WBADMIN START RECOVERY -version:03/31/2005-09:00 -itemType:App -items:SQL
WBADMIN START RECOVERY -version:03/31/2005-09:00 -itemType:File -items:d:\folder -recursive
```

Remarks: To view a list of items available to recover from a specific version, use `WBADMIN GET ITEMS`. When the `itemtype` is `App`, you can use `ADExtended` to recover all the related data needed for Active Directory.

Using VHDMount with Complete PC Backup Images

As you learned in the previous section, WBADMIN, the command-line counterpart of Complete PC Backup, can be used to create backup images compatible with Complete PC Backup and Complete PC Restore, and can restore backup images or selected files and folders. However, because WBADMIN works from the command line and features complex syntax, it can be a challenging tool to use for restoring individual files and folders from a backup image.

As an alternative, consider using the VHDMount component included in Virtual Server 2005. As you will learn in this section, VHDMount, although it is normally used as a command-line tool, can also be used within the Windows Explorer GUI to retrieve individual files from an image backup created with Complete PC Backup or WBADMIN.

> **NOTE**
>
> WBADMIN and Complete PC Backup create backups that are stored as .vhd (virtual hard disk) files. These files are compatible with Virtual PC 2007 and Virtual Server 2005.
>
> Microsoft distributes trial versions of many operating systems and applications as VHD images for use with either Virtual PC 2007 and Virtual Server 2005. For details, see "Run IT on a Virtual Hard Disk" at http://technet.microsoft.com.

Obtaining VHDMount

VHDMount is a component of Virtual Server 2005 R2 SP-1, a free virtualization host program available from Microsoft. To download Virtual Server 2005 R2 SP1, go to www.microsoft.com/technet/virtualserver/software/default.mspx. Free registration is required for this download, which is available in 32-bit and 64-bit versions.

After you download the appropriate version of Virtual Server 2005 R2 SP-1, run the Setup.exe installer. When prompted, select Custom as the setup type. On the Custom Setup dialog, select This Feature Will Not Be Available for all modules except VHDMount. For VHDMount, be sure to select This Feature Will Be Installed on Local Hard Drive (see Figure 34.12).

Figure 34.12
Performing a custom install of Virtual Server 2005 R2 to install only VHDMount.

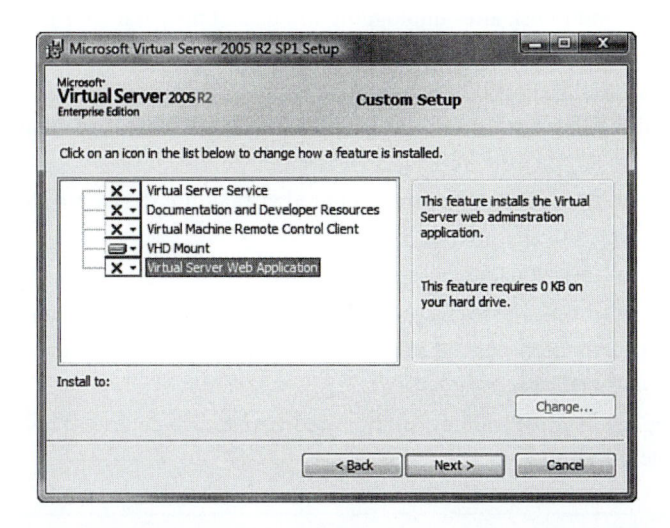

After you complete the installation, you will find the following new folder structure within your system's Program Files folder:

- Microsoft Virtual Server\VHDMount

The VHDMount program (`vhdmount.exe`) is in the VHDMount folder.

USING VHDMOUNT FROM THE COMMAND LINE

VHDMount can be used from the command line, using the following syntax:

```
VHDMOUNT /p [/f] VHDFileName
VHDMOUNT /m [/f] VHDFileName [DriveLetter]
VHDMOUNT /u [/c ¦ /d] VHDFileName ¦ All
VHDMOUNT /q VHDFileName ¦ All
```

By default, VHDMount creates an Undo Disk in current user's temporary folder. All changes to the mounted disk are written to this Undo Disk. Use /c to commit or /d to discard these changes at the time of unplugging the disk device. Use the /f option to mount a VHD without an Undo Disk.

- /p—Plugs in the specified VHD as a virtual disk device without mounting the volume.
- /m—Plugs in the specified VHD as a virtual disk device and mounts the volume.

- /f—Performs the specified operation without creating an Undo Disk. This parameter is applicable for /p and /m. All changes to the mounted disk are directly written to the specified VHD.

- /u—Unplugs the virtual disk device for the specified VHDFileName.

- /c—Updates the original VHD with all changes that were stored in the Undo Disk and deletes the Undo Disk after unplugging the disk. This parameter is only applicable if the VHD was mounted without using /f.

- /d—Discards all changes to the mounted disk and deletes the Undo Disk after unplugging the disk. This parameter is only applicable if the VHD was mounted without using /f.

- /q—Displays the disk name of the mounted virtual disk device for the specified VHDFileName.

- VHDFileName—VHD name including full path.

- DriveLetter—Optional parameter for the /m option. If the drive letter is specified, the volumes are mounted starting at the specified drive letter. If the drive letter is not specified, it is automatically assigned.

- All—Applies the operation on all mounted virtual disk devices. This parameter is applicable for /u and /q.

NOTE

VHDMount must be run from an elevated command prompt. To do so, right-click Command Prompt (All Programs, Accessories) and select Run As Administrator.

However, you **cannot** mount a VHD image with VHDMount until the appropriate drivers are installed in Device Manager. And, if you want to configure your system to use VHDMount to open .vhd files in Windows Explorer, you must create new registry entries to enable this capability and configure VHDMount to Run As Administrator. The following sections discuss how to perform these tasks.

CREATING REGISTRY ENTRIES TO ENABLE VHDMOUNT TO RUN IN WINDOWS EXPLORER

Thanks to the ingenuity of Ben Armstrong, a program manager on the core virtualization team at Microsoft, you can create a set of registry entries that will enable VHDMount to mount and dismount VHD images in Windows Explorer and view them as additional disk drive letters after the appropriate drivers are also installed.

At his Virtual PC Guy's Weblog (http://blogs.msdn.com/virtual_pc_guy/archive/2007/06/20/double-clicking-on-a-vhd-to-mount-it-take-2.aspx), Ben has posted the following registry entries. Copy this text and insert it into an empty Notepad document:

```
Windows Registry Editor Version 5.00
[HKEY_LOCAL_MACHINE\SOFTWARE\Classes\Virtual.Machine.HD]
➥@="Virtual Hard Disk"
```

Creating a Complete PC (Image) Backup 1167

```
[HKEY_LOCAL_MACHINE\SOFTWARE\Classes\Virtual.Machine.HD\shell]
↪@="Plug in"
[HKEY_LOCAL_MACHINE\SOFTWARE\Classes\Virtual.Machine.HD\shell\Plug in]
↪@="&Plug in"
[HKEY_LOCAL_MACHINE\SOFTWARE\Classes\Virtual.Machine.HD\shell\Plug in\command]
↪@="\"C:\\Program Files\\Microsoft Virtual Server\\Vhdmount\\vhdmount.exe\" /p
↪\"%1\""
[HKEY_LOCAL_MACHINE\SOFTWARE\Classes\Virtual.Machine.HD\shell\Unplug (discard
changes)]
@="Unplug (&discard changes)"
[HKEY_LOCAL_MACHINE\SOFTWARE\Classes\Virtual.Machine.HD\shell\Unplug (discard
↪changes)\command]
@="\"C:\\Program Files\\Microsoft Virtual Server\\Vhdmount\\vhdmount.exe\
↪" /u /d \"%1\""
[HKEY_LOCAL_MACHINE\SOFTWARE\Classes\Virtual.Machine.HD\shell\Unplug (commit
↪changes)]
@="Unplug (&commit changes)"
[HKEY_LOCAL_MACHINE\SOFTWARE\Classes\Virtual.Machine.HD\shell\Unplug (commit
↪changes)\command]
@="\"C:\\Program Files\\Microsoft Virtual Server\\Vhdmount\\vhdmount.exe\" /u /c
↪ \"%1\""
[HKEY_CLASSES_ROOT\.vhd]
@="Virtual.Machine.HD"
```

To save this text as a `.reg` (Registry) file in Notepad, be sure to use double-quote marks around the name and extension when you save it. For example: `"VHDMount_R.reg"`.

After saving this file to a folder (such as your Documents folder), add it to your Registry:

1. Browse to the folder containing the file.
2. Double-click the file.
3. Provide administrator-level credentials as prompted.
4. Click Yes when asked whether you want to continue.
5. Click OK.

Configuring VHDMount.exe to Run as Administrator

If you want to make VHDMount.exe easier to use from the command line or with Windows Explorer, you also need to configure it to Run as Administrator:

1. Open Computer.
2. Browse to the location of VHDMount.exe. On most systems, it will be located in C:\Program Files\Microsoft Virtual Server\VHDMount\.
3. Right-click VHDMount.exe and select Properties.
4. Click the Compatibility tab and select Run This Program as an Administrator (Figure 34.13).
5. Click Apply, then OK.

Figure 34.13
Configuring `VHDMount.exe` to Run as Administrator.

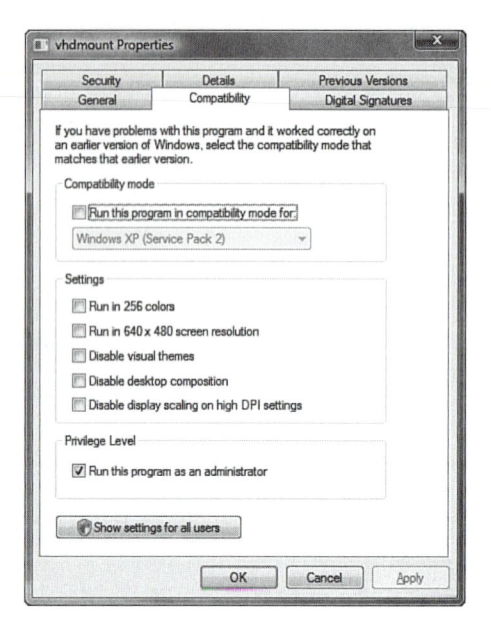

INSTALLING DRIVERS NEEDED FOR VHDMOUNT

A full installation of Virtual Server 2005 R2 SP1 will install the following drivers into Device Manager for use by VHDMount:

- MS Virtual Server SCSI Disk Driver (Disk Drives category)
- Microsoft Virtual Server Storage Device01 (Microsoft Virtual Server Storage Devices category)

However, if you install only VHDMount as described in a previous section, these drivers will not be installed automatically. Follow these procedures to install these drivers and make VHDMount ready to use. These procedures are adapted from http://www.eggheadcafe.com/software/aspnet/31023132/installing-virtual-server.aspx forum posts and from Greg Duncan's http://coolthingoftheday.blogspot.com/2008/01/tell-me-vhd-mount-story-installing-just.html illustrated discussion.

To begin driver installation:

1. Open Control Panel and switch to Classic View.
2. Open Add Hardware and provide administrator-level credentials as prompted.
3. Click Next.
4. Select Install the Hardware That I Manually Select From a List (Advanced). Click Next.
5. Highlight Show All Devices. Click Next.
6. Click Have Disk (it is not necessary to wait until the list of devices is displayed).
7. Click Browse and navigate to the location of VHDMount. On most systems, it will be C:\Program Files\Microsoft Virtual Server\VHDMount.

Creating a Complete PC (Image) Backup

8. Select vhdbus.inf and click Open.
9. Click OK.
10. Verify that Microsoft Virtual Server Storage Bus appears in the Add Hardware window (shown in Figure 34.14). Click Next.
11. Click Next on the confirmation window.
12. Click Finish.

Figure 34.14
Installing the driver for Microsoft Virtual Server Storage Bus.

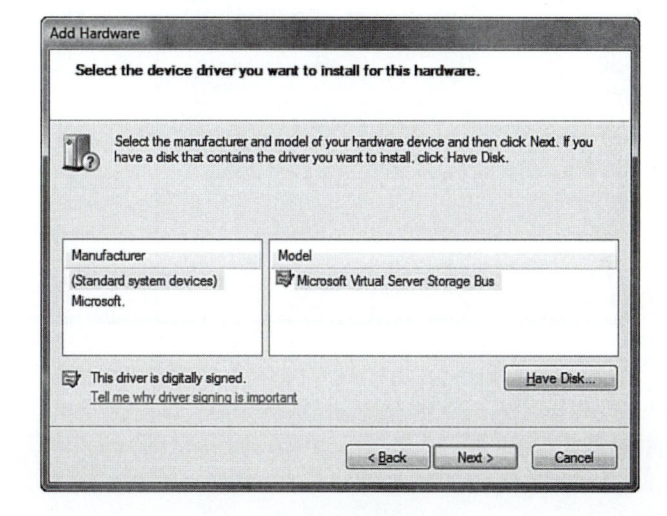

At this point, no new drivers are yet visible in Device Manager. To complete driver installation, it is necessary to attempt to use VHDMount so an error message is triggered.

1. Browse to the location containing the .vhd file you want to open. On the backup medium, it will be stored in a folder called \WindowsImageBackup*computername*\Backup *date_id* (replace *computername* with the actual name of the computer, and *date_id* with the actual date of the last image backup and an ID number).
2. Right-click the .vhd file and select Plug In (see Figure 34.15). Provide administrator-level credentials as prompted.
3. A command prompt window appears. In the Notification area, a message indicates that device driver software is being installed. This message is replaced by one indicating that the device driver could not be installed. Eventually, the command prompt window closes when the vhdmount command fails.
4. Open Control Panel in Classic View.
5. Open Device Manager and provide administrator-level credentials as prompted.
6. Navigate to the Disk Drives category. Microsoft Virtual Server Storage Device01 should be displayed with a yellow triangle, indicating a driver problem.
7. Double-click the Microsoft Virtual Server Storage Device01 entry.

Figure 34.15
The right-click menu for .vhd files contains Plug In and Unplug entries after VHDMount commands are added to the system Registry.

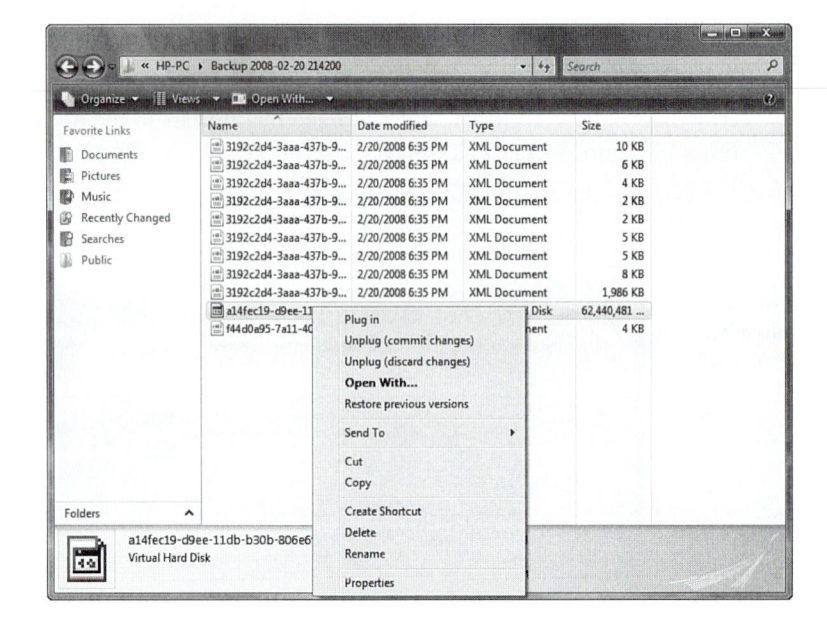

8. Open the Driver tab.
9. Click Update Driver.
10. Select Browse My Computer for Driver Software.
11. Make sure the Search window lists the location of the Vhdmount program. On most systems, it should read:

    C:\Program Files\Microsoft Virtual Server\Vhdmount.

    If this location is not listed, use the Browse button to navigate to the folder. Click Next to install drivers.

12. Click Close to close the update window, then click OK to close the properties sheet.

If you open Device Manager after Step 12, you will see a new entry in the Disk Drives category: MS Virtual Server SCSI Disk Device. You will also see a new category: Microsoft Virtual Server Storage Device. This category contains one device: Microsoft Virtual Server Storage Device01 (Figure 34.16).

WORKING WITH .vhd FILES IN WINDOWS EXPLORER

To access the .vhd file in Windows Explorer, navigate to the .vhd file, right-click it, and select Plug In. Provide administrator-level credentials as prompted. You will see a command prompt window appear briefly and "Installing Device Driver" messages appear in the Notification area. When the .vhd file is mounted, you might see an AutoPlay window appear (see Figure 34.17). Select Open Folder to View Files to view the contents of the .vhd file in Windows Explorer (where it is displayed as a new drive letter), or open Computer to access the new drive letter.

Creating a Complete PC (Image) Backup

Figure 34.16
Device Manager contains new entries for MS Virtual Server storage devices after drivers are installed and updated.

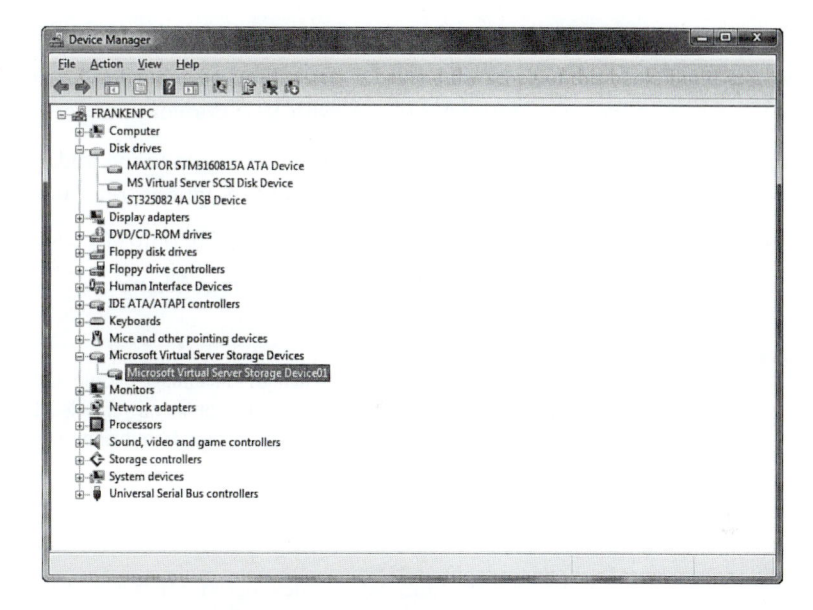

Figure 34.17
VHDMount assigns the .vhd file the next available drive letter and enables you to work with the files it contains in various ways.

As you navigate through the folders of the virtual drive the first time you use VHDMount, you might see "You Don't Currently Have Permission to Access This Folder." Click Continue and provide administrator-level credentials on the Edit Security dialog as prompted to continue. It might take a few moments to change the security settings for some folders; the green progress bar that appears behind the address window moves as the security settings are changed.

You can copy files and folders from any location on the backup to your system, and you can also add, rename, or delete files and folders in the backup. See the next section, "Closing Your .vhd File Safely," to learn how to disconnect safely from your backup.

Closing Your .vhd File Safely

Whether you leave the Windows Explorer drive letter view of your backup open or close it, the backup is still plugged into your system with VHDMount until you unplug it.

To safely disconnect the backup from your system, navigate to the folder containing the .vhd file, right-click the file, and select one of the following options (refer back to Figure 34.15):

- If you do not want to save any changes, select Unplug (Discard Changes).
- If you want to keep changes, select Unplug (Commit Changes).

CAUTION

It is usually not advisable to make changes to an image backup. Unless you have deliberately made changes to the backup image, I recommend you select Unplug (Discard Changes). This option prevents accidental changes from being saved to your backup image.

In either case, you must provide administrator-level credentials as prompted. A command prompt window appears as the image is being unplugged, and closes after the process is complete. If you choose the option to Commit Changes, it might take some time to save the changes to the backup image before completing the process.

Restoring a Complete PC Backup Image

You should restore a Complete PC Backup image only in drastic circumstances, such as a complete system failure. Basically, if Windows Vista won't start and you've already tried everything else *and* you've made a Complete PC Backup image, it's time to restore it. A Complete PC Restore sets your system to its exact condition at the time of backup. Unlike System Restore, which leaves current data files behind although it resets the Windows Vista Registry to the specified earlier time, a Complete PC Restore formats your hard disk, wiping out any remaining information and replacing it with whatever you backed up. It's not called a "bare metal" restore for nothing!

NOTE

After you restore a Complete PC Backup, restore all the file and folder backups available to bring your system as close to its prefailure condition as possible.

To restore a Complete PC Backup image from within the Backup and Restore Center, click Restore Computer. However, if you need to restore your system from outside the Vista GUI, use the Windows Recovery Environment, which is accessed by booting from the Windows Vista DVD and selecting Repair Your Computer.

→ To learn more about restoring a Complete PC Backup image, **see** Chapter 28.

Encrypted File System (EFS)

If you need to protect files on your system from being read by unauthorized users, you can use the Encrypted File System (EFS) feature of the NTFS file system. Note that Vista Home Basic, Home Premium (and Starter Edition) do not support EFS. When a file is encrypted, the data stored on the hard disk is scrambled in a very secure way. Encryption is transparent to the user who encrypted the file; you do not have to "decrypt" an encrypted file before you can use it. You can work with an encrypted file just as you would any other file; you can open and change the file as necessary. However, any other user or an intruder who tries to access your encrypted files is prevented from doing so. Only the original owner and the computer's designated recovery agent can get into encrypted files. Anyone else receives an "Access Denied" message when trying to open or copy your encrypted file.

Folders can be marked as encrypted, too. This means that any file created in or copied to an encrypted folder is automatically encrypted. The folder itself isn't encrypted, though; anyone with the proper file access permissions can see the names of the files in it.

> **NOTE**
>
> EFS encryption protects the files only while they reside on the NTFS volume. When they are accessed for use by an application, they are decrypted by the file system drivers. This means that files that are encrypted on the drive are not encrypted in memory while being used by an application. This also means that transferring files over the network is done without encryption. Any file action that performs a copy (which includes moves across partitions or volumes) inherits the settings of its new container. In other words, if the new container is not encrypted, the new file will not be encrypted, either, even if it was encrypted in its previous location. If you back up EFS-protected files, they are stored on the backup media in their normal form, not as encrypted. EFS protects files only on the hard drive, nowhere else. Use EFS only when expressly needed. EFS causes significant performance reduction if a significant number of commonly accessed files are encrypted, due to the CPU processing required to decrypt them for use.

You encrypt or decrypt a folder or file by setting the encryption property for the folder or file just as you set any other attribute (such as read-only, compressed, or hidden), through a file or folder's Advanced Attributes dialog box (see Figure 34.18).

Figure 34.18
Setting encryption for a specific folder.

After you set the option to encrypt a folder and click OK on a folder's properties dialog box, you are prompted to confirm the attribute change. From this dialog box, you can set the option to encrypt all the subfolders and files within the folder you are encrypting.

It is recommended that you encrypt at the folder level rather than mark individual files so that new files added to the folder will also be encrypted. This point is crucial because most editing programs write a new copy of the file each time you save changes and then delete the original. If the folder containing an encrypted file isn't marked for encryption, too, editing an encrypted file results in your saving an unencrypted version.

If you upgrade a Windows XP system with EFS-encrypted files or folders, the files or folders will be encrypted in Windows Vista as well.

How File Encryption Works

As a kid, you probably played around with simple codes and ciphers in which you exchanged the letters of a message: *D* for *A*, *E* for *B*, and so on. You might look at this as the process of "adding three" to each letter in your message: Each letter gets bumped to the third-next letter in the alphabet. To decode a message, you subtracted three from every letter to get the original message. In this code, you could say that the "key" is the number 3. Anyone who knew the technique and possessed the key could read and write these secret messages.

Although this example is very simplistic, it illustrates the basic idea of numeric encryption. The cryptographic system used by Windows for the Encrypted File System also uses a numeric technique, but it's extremely complex and uses a key that is 128 digits long. Such a large number means many possible choices, and that means it would take someone a very long time to guess a key and read an encrypted file.

When you mark a file for encryption, Windows randomly generates such a large number, called a unique *file encryption key (FEK)*, which is used to scramble the contents of just that one file. This unique key is itself scrambled with your own personal file encryption key, an even longer number stored in the Windows Certificate database. The encrypted unique key is then stored along with the file.

When you're logged in and try to open an encrypted file, Windows retrieves your personal key, decodes the unique key, and uses that key to decode the contents of the file as it's read off the hard disk.

The reason for the two-step process is to let Windows use a different and unique key for each file. Using different keys provides added security. Even if an attacker managed to guess the key to one file, he or she would have to start fresh to find the key to other files. Yet your personal key can unscramble the unique key to any file you've encrypted. It's a valuable thing, this key, and I'll tell you how to back it up in a certificate file for safekeeping.

As a backup in case your personal key gets lost, Windows lets each computer or domain administrator designate recovery agents, users who are allowed to decode other people's encrypted files. Windows also encrypts the unique FEK for each of the recovery agents. It, too, is stored along with the file, and anyone who possesses a recovery key can also read your encrypted files. You'll learn about the benefits and risks of this system in "Protecting and Recovering Encrypted Files," later in this chapter.

You can use EFS to keep your documents safe from intruders who might gain unauthorized physical access to your sensitive stored data (by stealing your laptop, for example).

NOTE
> Files encrypted with EFS are not backed up by the version of File and Folder Backup provided with the original version of Windows Vista. However, in Vista SP-1, File and Folder Backup does back up EFS-encrypted files.

Using CIPHER

You also can encrypt or decrypt a file or folder using the command-line program CIPHER and the following syntax. If you've previously used CIPHER on a Windows XP system, keep in mind that the syntax that CIPHER uses in Windows Vista is almost entirely new. Several existing parameters have been removed, many new parameters have been added and, by default, CIPHER runs even if an error is encountered, unless you use the new /B parameter. In Windows XP, CIPHER stopped on error.

Omitted parameters: /F, /I, /Q

New parameters: /B, /C, /W, /X, /Y, /ADDUSER, /REKEY, /REMOVEUSER

(The following is not an exhaustive list of the cipher syntax; execute **cipher /?** at a command prompt for the complete list of parameters and syntax.)

```
CIPHER [/E ¦ /D ¦ /C]
       [/S:directory] [/B] [/H] [pathname [...]]
CIPHER /K
CIPHER /R:filename [/SMARTCARD]
CIPHER /U [/N]
CIPHER /W:directory
CIPHER /X[:efsfile] [filename]
CIPHER /Y
CIPHER /ADDUSER [/CERTHASH:hash ¦ /CERTFILE:filename]
       [/S:directory] [/B] [/H] [pathname [...]]
CIPHER /REMOVEUSER /CERTHASH:hash
       [/S:directory] [/B] [/H] [pathname [...]]
CIPHER /REKEY [pathname [...]]
```

The arguments (parameters) are as follows:

/B	Abort if an error is encountered. By default, CIPHER continues executing even if errors are encountered (new option).
/C	Displays information on the encrypted file (new option).
/D	Decrypts the folder and halts any further encryption on that folder until reactivated.
/E	Encrypts the specified directories. Directories are marked so that files added afterward will be encrypted.
/H	Displays files with the hidden or system attributes. These files are omitted by default (new option).
/K	Creates a new certificate and key for use with EFS. If this option is chosen, all other options are ignored (new option).

/N	Works only with /U. Prevents keys from being updated. This is used to find all the encrypted files on the local drives (new option).
/R	Generates an EFS recovery agent key and certificate, and then writes them to a .PFX file (containing certificate and private key) and a .CER file (containing only the certificate). An administrator can add the contents of the .CER to the EFS recovery policy to create the recovery agent for users and can import the .PFX to recover individual files. If SMARTCARD is specified, it writes the recovery key and certificate to a smart card. A .CER file is generated (containing only the certificate). No .PFX file is generated.
/S	Performs the specified operation on directories in the given directory and all subdirectories.
/U	Tries to touch all the encrypted files on local drives. This updates the user's file encryption key or recovery agent's key to the current ones if they are changed. This option does not work with other options except /N.
/W	Removes data from available unused disk space on the entire volume. If this option is chosen, all other options are ignored. The directory specified can be anywhere in a local volume. If it is a mount point or points to a directory in another volume, the data on that volume will be removed (new option).
/X	Backs up the EFS certificate and keys into file *filename*. If efsfile is provided, the current user's certificate(s) used to encrypt the file will be backed up. Otherwise, the user's current EFS certificate and keys will be backed up (new option).
/Y	Displays your current EFS certificate thumbnail on the local PC (new option).
/ADDUSER	Adds a user to the specified encrypted file(s). If CERTHASH is provided, CIPHER will search for a certificate with this SHA1 hash. If CERTFILE is provided, cipher will extract the certificate from the file (new option).
/REKEY	Updates the specified encrypted file(s) to use the configured EFS current key (new option).
/REMOVEUSER	Removes a user from the specified file(s). CERTHASH must be the SHA1 hash of the certificate to remove (new option).
directory	A directory path.
filename	A filename without extensions.
pathname	Specifies a pattern, file, or directory.
efsfile	An encrypted file path.

Used without parameters, CIPHER displays the encryption state of the current directory and any files it contains. You can use multiple directory names and wildcards. You must put spaces between multiple parameters.

Rules for Using Encrypted Files

When you work with encrypted files and folders, keep in mind the following points:

- Only files and folders on NTFS volumes can be encrypted.
- You cannot encrypt files or folders that are compressed. Compression and encryption are mutually exclusive file attributes. If you want to encrypt a compressed file or folder, you must decompress it first.
- Only the user who encrypted the file and the designated recovery agent(s) can open it. (You'll learn more about recovery agents shortly.)
- If you encrypt a file in a shared directory, it is inaccessible to others.
- Windows Vista displays encrypted files and folders in green (compressed files and folders are displayed in blue).
- Encrypted files become decrypted if you copy or move the file to a volume or partition that is not formatted with NTFS.
- You should use Cut and Paste to move files into an encrypted folder. If you use the drag-and-drop method to move files, they are not automatically encrypted in the new folder.
- System files cannot be encrypted.
- Encrypting folders or files does not protect them against being deleted, moved, or renamed. Anyone with the appropriate permission level can manipulate encrypted folders or files. (These users just can't open them.)
- Temporary files, which are created by some programs when documents are edited, are also encrypted as long as all the files are on an NTFS volume and in an encrypted folder. I recommend that you encrypt the Temp folder on your hard disk for this reason. Encrypting your original files keeps them safe from prying eyes, but programs often leave behind temp files—usually in the Temp folder—and these files remain vulnerable.
- The paging file (used for virtual memory) can be encrypted in Windows Vista through Group Policy settings. You can also configure the Local Security Policy to clear the pagefile when you shut down the system. Just enable the Shutdown: Clear Virtual Memory Pagefile policy under the Local Policies, Security Option section.
- On a domain network, you can encrypt or decrypt files and folders located on a remote computer that has been enabled for remote encryption. Check with your system administrator to see whether your company's servers support this capability. Keep in mind, however, that opening an encrypted file over a network still exposes the contents of that file while it is being transmitted. A network administrator should implement a security protocol such as IPSec to safeguard data during transmission.
- You should encrypt folders instead of individual files so that if a program creates temporary files and/or saves new copies during editing, they will be encrypted as well.
- Encrypted files, like compressed folders, perform more slowly than unencrypted ones. If you want maximum performance when folders or files in the folders are being used extensively (for example, by database programs), think twice before encrypting them.

You might want to perform benchmark tests using encrypted and unencrypted folders with similar data to determine whether your system can handle the performance hit.

Suggested Folders to Encrypt

I recommend that you encrypt the following folders:

- Encrypt the Documents folder if you save most of your documents there. Encrypting this folder ensures that any personal documents saved there are automatically encrypted. However, a better alternative would be to create a subfolder under Documents for personal files and encrypt just this folder. This approach relieves you from having to track which files are encrypted and which are not.

- Encrypt your Temp folder so that any temporary files created by programs are automatically encrypted.

> **CAUTION**
>
> If someone steals your laptop computer or gains physical access to your desktop computer, it's possible that even with all of Windows Vista's file access security and file encryption, that person can gain access to your files. How? A trick allows this to happen, and you should guard against it. Here's how it works: By reinstalling the operating system from a DVD drive, a thief can set up himself or herself as the system administrator. If the default file recovery certificate is still on the computer at this point, the intruder can view encrypted files. To guard against this situation, you should export the file recovery certificate to a floppy disk or other drive and remove it from the computer. I show you how in the next section.
>
> Another method you can use is to configure your system to use BitLocker full drive encryption (available on Vista Ultimate and Enterprise editions). To learn more about BitLocker, see "BitLocker (Disk Encryption)," later in this chapter.

Protecting and Recovering Encrypted Files

Encrypted files are supposed to be very secure; only the user who creates an encrypted file can unscramble it. But this security hangs on your own personal file encryption key, which is stored in the Windows Certificate database (see the sidebar "How File Encryption Works," earlier in this chapter). Where would you be if you accidentally deleted your file encryption certificate, or if your user account was deleted from the system? Could the secret recipe for Aunt Dottie's zucchini fritters be lost forever this way? Probably not. The Encrypted File System has a "back door" that lets designated recovery agents open any encrypted file.

The availability of this back door is both good news and bad news. The good news is that encrypted files can be recovered when necessary. The bad news is that this capability opens a potential security risk, and you need to be sure you take measures to protect yourself against it.

Securing the Recovery Certificate

Your capability to recover encrypted files hinges on two factors:

- Being listed by the Windows Local or Group Security Policy as a designated recovery agent
- Possessing the file recovery certificate that holds the recovery key data

With a few dirty tricks, it's possible for someone who steals your computer to get himself or herself in as an administrator and pose as the recovery agent. If you really want to ensure the privacy of your files with the Encrypted File System, you have to save the file recovery certificate on a floppy disk or other removable medium and remove the certificate from your computer.

To back up and remove the recovery certificate, do the following:

1. Be sure that at least one file on your computer has been marked Encrypted by any user.
2. Log in as the local administrator (*XXXX*\Administrator, where *XXXX* is the name of your computer).
3. Start the Microsoft Management Console by choosing Start, All Programs, Accessories, Run. Then type **mmc** and press Enter.

> **NOTE** Unless User Account Control (UAC) has been disabled, you must be an administrator or provide administrator-level credentials to back up the recovery certificate.

4. Choose File, Add/Remove Snap-In. Next, highlight the Certificates snap-in and click Add. Select My User Account and click Finish. Finally, click OK.
5. In the left pane, expand the Certificates node, Current User, Personal, Certificates.
6. In the right pane, you should see a certificate listed with its Intended Purposes shown as Encrypting File System, as shown in Figure 34.19. If this certificate is not present and you're on a domain network, your domain administrator has done this job for you and you don't need to proceed any further.
7. Right-click the EFS certificate entry and select All Tasks, Export to launch the Certificate Export Wizard.
8. Click Next and then select Yes, Export the Private Key, and click Next. Select Personal Information Exchange, and then click Next.
9. Enter a password twice to protect this key. (You must remember this password!) Then click Next.

Figure 34.19
Certificate Manager showing the Administrator's file recovery certificate.

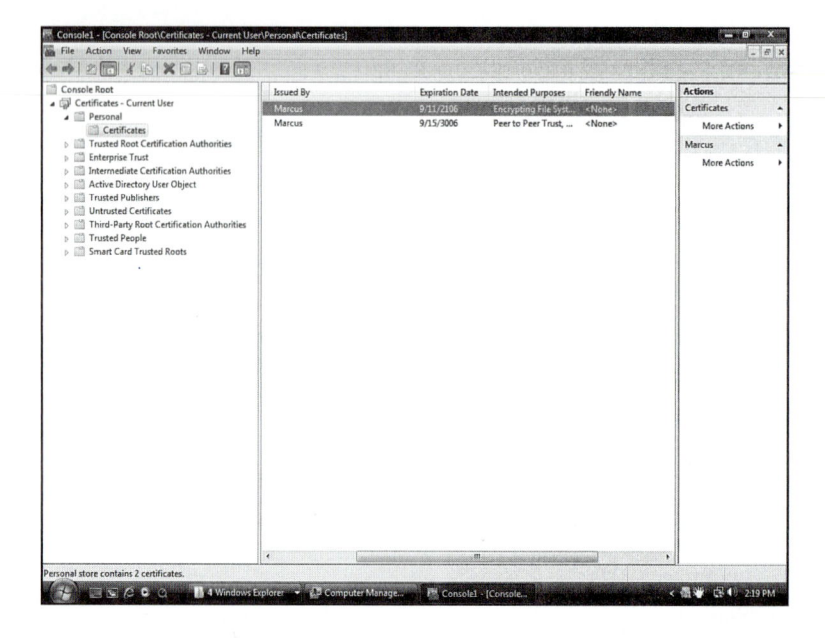

10. Specify a path and filename to be used to save the key. If your system has a floppy drive, insert a blank, formatted floppy disk and type the path and filename, such as `A:\RECOVERY.PFX` (not case sensitive). Otherwise, you can insert a writeable CD or DVD (recommended) or a USB flash memory drive (not recommended for permanent storage) and type the path and filename. If you use CD or DVD media, click Next and then Finish. A dialog box appears stating that the export was successful; click OK.

11. Right-click the certificate entry again and select Delete.

12. Label the floppy disk clearly as "EFS Recovery Key for *XXX*," where *XXX* is the name of your computer. Store this disk in a safe place away from your computer.

13. Restart your computer. After it's restarted, log on as Administrator again, and confirm that you can't view the file you encrypted as another user.

> **CAUTION**
>
> You should back up and delete the Administrator's recovery certificate (that's the procedure you just performed), but don't delete Administrator as the recovery agent from the Local Security Policy. Leave the Local Security Policy alone. If you delete the entries there, you'll disable EFS.

Protecting Your Own File Encryption Certificate

If your user account is lost or you accidentally delete your own file encryption certificate some day, you might lose access to your own files. The recovery agent could still help, but you can protect yourself by exporting your own personal EFS certificate. Basically, follow the same procedure as for the local administrator while logged in as a user. Just be sure to have at least one encrypted file before starting the process. Once complete, label the disk

"EFS for *UUU* on *XXX*," where *UUU* is your user account name and *XXX* is your computer name. Store it in a safe place.

Recovering Encrypted Files on Your Own Computer

If your user account is deleted or you end up reinstalling Windows from scratch, you'll lose access to your encrypted files because the Encryption database will be lost. You can log on as Administrator and reinstall the encrypted file recovery certificate, or you can log on as yourself and reinstall your file encryption certificate to get the files back with the following procedure:

1. Choose Console, select File, and select Add/Remove Snap-In. Next, highlight the Certificates snap-in and click Add. Select My User Account and click Finish. Finally, click Close and then click OK.
2. In the left pane, expand the Certificates node, Current User, Personal, Certificates.
3. In the right pane, right-click and select All Tasks, Import to start the Certificate Import Wizard.
4. Click Next.
5. Enter the name of the certificate file—for example, `a:\recovery.pfx`. Otherwise, you can click Browse and navigate to the drive and folder containing the certificate. To see it, select Personal Information Exchange (`*.pfx, *.p12`) as the certificate type. Select it and click Open. Click Next.
6. Enter the password for the certificate, and check Mark the Private Key As Exportable. Click Next twice, and then click Finish.
7. Click OK on the status box.

You should now be able to access the encrypted files. I suggest that you remove the Encrypted checkmark from these files. Log on again as the Normal user of these files, and re-encrypt them if you want.

> **NOTE**
> If you use a migration utility to move EFS-encrypted files and folders from a Windows XP system to a Windows Vista system, be sure to export your EFS certificate from the Windows XP system and import it to the Windows Vista system as described here. Otherwise, you will not be able to access your files.

Disk Organization for Data Safety

RAID arrays are no longer exotic. Most late-model desktop computers have provision for RAID 0 or RAID 1 arrays, and many systems have four or more SATA host adapters, making RAID 0+1 arrays possible. Which are the safest types of RAID arrays in common use?

RAID 5 provides maximum safety. With RAID 5, which requires the use of three or more hard disks in a single array, you can rebuild the contents of the array even if one drive fails.

RAID 5 sets aside space on each drive for the information needed to rebuild the array in case of drive failure. However, RAID 5 is not yet implemented in desktop computers' onboard host adapters. You must purchase a RAID 5 host adapter and compatible SATA or SCSI hard disks.

RAID 0+1 combines data striping (for performance) and mirroring (for safety). It requires four drives and is supported on many recent desktop computers. It provides a high level of data safety against failures and is inexpensive to implement with SATA or ATA/IDE (PATA) drives.

RAID 1 mirrors the contents of one drive to a second hard disk. It is supported on many desktop systems that are up to four years old, through either a motherboard RAID host adapter chip or the motherboard's integrated chipset. It is inexpensive to implement with SATA or IDE drives.

RAID 0 stripes data across two drives to improve read/write performance. If either drive fails, the array is wiped out. Thus, RAID 0 actually has no redundancy. It should be used only on drives that do not contain data.

To learn more about implementing RAID arrays in Windows, see Chapter 27, "Managing Hard Disks."

BITLOCKER DISK ENCRYPTION

With the widely reported loss or theft of laptops containing sensitive personal and financial information in the last year, hundreds of thousands of people have been forced to change credit card information and worry about identity theft. Thus, the time is ripe for a new approach to protecting hard disk contents from unauthorized use: BitLocker.

BitLocker, available on Enterprise and Ultimate editions, encrypts the entire system hard disk. Originally known as Secure Startup, BitLocker stops unauthorized access, even if the hard disk is moved to a different computer.

> **CAUTION**
>
> It's now known that a thief can get around BitLocker's protection if he steals your computer while it's suspended (sleeping), hibernating, or powered up. To truly protect your computer, you must completely shut it down when you finish using it, and don't let it out of your sight for at least 10 minutes after shutdown. This time frame is especially important because Princeton University researchers have discovered that memory chips can be frozen with "canned air," preserving their contents for retrieval, even after the system has been turned off. See http://citp.princeton.edu/memory/ for details.
>
> Following these procedures is especially important with laptops because the default action when you close the lid or click the little power button on the Start menu is "suspend." You must instead click the options arrow and select Shut Down. When you power up the computer, it should display the black BitLocker protection screen. If it goes directly to Windows, your computer was not protected!

> For greater protection, you can use the Power Options dialog in Control Panel to change the default actions for closing the lid or pushing the power button on the Start menu to shut down. You should also use file encryption to further protect any sensitive files on your hard drive.

BitLocker System Requirements

BitLocker requires that your hard disk have a second partition of at least 1.5GB that is used for the BitLocker encryption tools. You must also have a way to provide credentials to permit the system to recognize you as the authorized user, such as a Trusted Platform Module (TPM) microchip and BIOS or, for systems that lack onboard TPM 1.2 support, a USB flash memory drive. BitLocker in the original version of Windows Vista can only be used to encrypt the system (C:) partition, but in Vista SP-1, BitLocker can also encrypt additional volumes on the system drive.

Using the BitLocker Drive Preparation Tool

If you install Windows Vista Ultimate or Enterprise on an empty hard disk, you can follow the instructions in the section "Manual Preparation of the Hard Disk for Use with BitLocker," later in this chapter. However, if you want to run BitLocker on a system that is already in use, there's an easier way to prepare the hard disk—the BitLocker Drive Preparation Tool.

To determine whether you need to obtain this tool, follow this procedure:

1. Open the Security category in Control Panel and click BitLocker Drive Encryption (a UAC-protected program). Provide administrator-level credentials when prompted.
2. Unless your hard disk is already properly partitioned for BitLocker, you will see a message informing you that the drive configuration is not suitable for use with BitLocker. Go to Step 4.
3. If you do not see a message informing you that that drive configuration is unsuitable for use with BitLocker, stop. You can proceed to the section "Enabling the TPM," later in this chapter.
4. Follow the appropriate procedure to obtain the BitLocker Drive Preparation Tool:
   - If you use Windows Vista Ultimate Edition, download the BitLocker and EFS Enhancements Ultimate Extra with Windows Update.
   - If you use Windows Vista Enterprise, you can request it through Microsoft Support Customer Services. To learn more about this tool, see Knowledge Base article 930063 at http://support.microsoft.com.
5. After installing the tool, run it by clicking Start, All Programs, Accessories, System Tools, BitLocker, Bit Locker Drive Preparation Tool.

> **NOTE**
>
> To run BitLocker Drive Preparation Tool from the command line with advanced options, view the Readme file. A shortcut to this file is stored in the Start menu folder BitLocker Drive Preparation Tool – Readme.

The BitLocker Drive Preparation Tool is a UAC-protected program; provide administrator-level credentials when prompted.

Click I Accept after reviewing the EULA to run the program. The program repartitions the C: drive to create a new 1.5GB drive named S:, which is used to boot the system and run BitLocker encryption on the C: drive and, in Vista SP-1, can also encrypt other drive volumes on the system drive. Before clicking Continue to start the process, note the cautions provided by the tool:

- Back up critical files and data before continuing.
- The process might take anywhere from several minutes to several hours, depending upon how long it takes to defragment the C: drive.
- Do not use drive S: (the new active drive) to store important data and files; it is unencrypted and very small.

First, the tool reduces the C: drive in size to make room for the new S: drive. Next, it creates the new S: drive and then sets up the drive for BitLocker. When all three tasks are complete, click Finish. Then click Restart Now to restart the system, or Restart Later if you have other tasks to finish later. Note that the system drive (C:) is not yet protected by BitLocker.

If you are performing a clean install of Windows Vista Ultimate or Enterprise and do not want to use the BitLocker Drive Preparation Tool, follow the instructions in the "Manual Preparation of the Hard Disk for Use with BitLocker" section.

MANUAL PREPARATION OF THE HARD DISK FOR USE WITH BITLOCKER

If you are preparing a new hard disk for use with Windows Vista Enterprise or Ultimate editions and BitLocker and do not want to use the BitLocker Drive Preparation Tool, follow this procedure:

1. Boot the system with the Windows Vista product DVD.
2. Configure the installation language, time, currency format, and keyboard layout. Click Next to continue.
3. Click System Recovery Options.
4. Open the command prompt window.
5. Type `Diskpart` and press Enter. You can now enter a series of commands to partition the hard disk.
6. Enter the command `select disk 0`.
7. Enter the command `clean`. This erases the existing partition table (if any).

8. Enter the command **create partition primary size=1500**. This partition will be used to boot the system, so it must be configured as a primary partition.
9. Enter the command **assign letter=S**. This partition will be called S:.
10. Enter the command **active** to make this partition the active partition.
11. To use the remainder of the disk, enter the command **create partition primary**. You will install Windows Vista on this larger partition.
12. To configure this partition as the C: drive, enter the command **assign letter=C**.
13. Enter **list volume** to see a display of all the volumes on this disk. You will see a listing of each volume, volume numbers, letters, labels, file systems, types, sizes, status, and information. Make sure two volumes are listed, that they are NTFS, and that you know the labels.
14. Enter the command **exit** to close diskpart.
15. Enter the command **format c: /y /q /fs:NTFS** to format the C: drive.
16. Enter the command **format s: /y /q /fs:NTFS** to format the S: drive.
17. Enter the command **exit** to leave the command prompt and return to the System Recovery Options dialog box.
18. In the System Recovery Options window, use the Close icon in the upper right (or press Alt+F4) to close the window to return to the main installation screen. (Do not click Shut Down or Restart.)
19. Click Install Now and proceed with the Windows Vista installation process. Install Windows Vista on the larger partition, C: (the operating system volume).

At the end of the installation process, your system will use the C: drive as it normally does, but the boot files reside on S:, making BitLocker encryption possible.

ENABLING THE TPM

The easiest way to use BitLocker is to use your computer's TPM microchip (if it has one). To determine whether your system supports TPM 1.2 and to learn how to enable this feature in the system BIOS, see your system's documentation. A lot of 2006 and newer laptops have onboard TPM 1.2, but older laptops (and most desktops) don't support it.

After you enable TPM in the system BIOS, use the TPM Management Console (tpm.msc) to turn on TPM support in Windows (use the Turn On the TPM Security Hardware dialog box) and set up a TPM password (use the Create the TPM Owner Password dialog box). A TPM password is saved as *computer_name.tpm*. Thus, if your computer is named WildThing, the password is stored as WildThing.tpm.

> **TIP**
> Be sure to print your TPM password using the Print option and save it to a location you can access later, such as a CD or DVD.

If your system doesn't support TPM, you can still use BitLocker, despite the BitLocker Drive Encryption utility in Control Panel statement that you must have a TPM. However, to use BitLocker without a TPM, you must use a USB flash memory drive to store your credentials, and it must be plugged into the system to permit the system to boot. You must also enable BitLocker drive encryption with the Group Policy Object Editor:

1. Click Start, All Programs, Accessories, Run.
2. Type `gpedit.msc` and click OK to open the Group Policy Editor. Click Continue or provide administrator-level credentials (if prompted by UAC) to continue.
3. Open Computer Configuration.
4. Open Administrative Templates.
5. Open Windows Components.
6. Open BitLocker Drive Encryption.
7. Open Control Panel Setup: Enable Advanced Startup Options.
8. Select Enabled. Verify that the option Allow BitLocker Without a Compatible TPM is checked (see Figure 34.20).
9. Click Apply, then OK.
10. Close the Group Policy Object Editor.

Figure 34.20
Enabling BitLocker support on a system that does not have a compatible TPM.

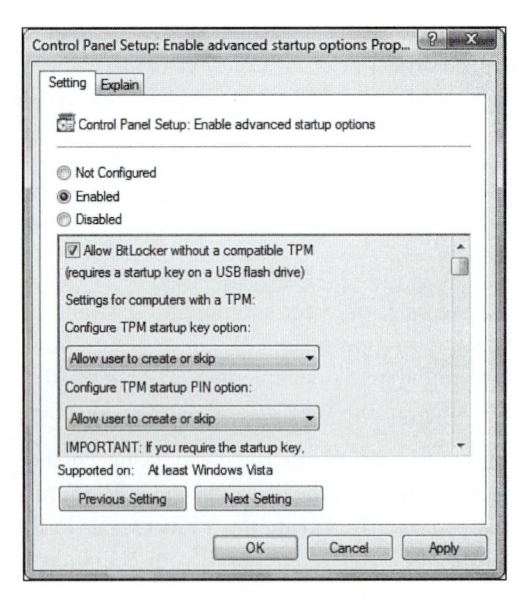

Encrypting the Drive with BitLocker

To start the encryption process, open the BitLocker Drive Encryption icon in the Control Panel and select Turn on BitLocker. If your system has a TPM, you can choose either to use the TPM chip along with your logon password to access an encrypted BitLocker volume or to assign a PIN number that is used along with the TPM. If your system does not have a

TPM, you must use a Startup USB key. Make sure you have a USB flash drive available to use for BitLocker key storage.

When you create the BitLocker volume, you must create a recovery key password, in case BitLocker enters a locked state. If you lose the password, you can be locked out of your data; be sure to save the password to an accessible location and print it for safekeeping. Note that this is not the same as the TPM management password discussed in the previous section.

If you choose to store the recovery key password on a USB drive or in a folder, it is stored in a plain-text file. The name of the file matches the administrative password ID: four hex digits, followed by three groups of two hex digits, followed by six hex digits:

aabbccdd-ee-ff-gg-001122334455.txt

The password recovery key file contains the name of the disk volume, the drive letter, and the date of encryption as well as the password itself, which is stored as eight groups of six digits each:

000000-111111-22222-333333-444444-555555-666666-777777

Recovery keys can be stored on Active Directory servers for systems that are members of a domain.

After you store and print the recovery key password, BitLocker performs a system check to ensure that the recovery and encryption keys can be read before beginning the encryption process. If you use a USB device to enable BitLocker, insert it when prompted. After the system check is performed successfully, BitLocker restarts your system and encrypts your system drive. During the encryption process, an icon in the notification area appears. Hover your mouse over the icon or double-click it to see encryption progress. You can pause encryption if necessary, but you can use your computer normally while encryption progresses. When you start your system, you must provide the appropriate credentials (entering the PIN number when prompted or inserting the USB flash drive before starting the system or when prompted). Otherwise, the system will not boot.

In Vista SP-1, after BitLocker encrypts the system volume and you restart your system, you can encrypt any other volumes on the system drive. To encrypt additional volumes, open the BitLocker Disk Encryption tool in Control Panel and turn the encryption status from Off to On for other system drives you want to encrypt.

If you are unable to use BitLocker, see "Unable to Use BitLocker" in the "Troubleshooting" section at the end of this chapter.

BitLocker Drive Encryption Recovery

If you do not provide the appropriate credentials when you attempt to boot a BitLocker-encrypted volume, you are prompted to press the Enter key to enter into the Windows BitLocker Drive Encryption Password Entry dialog. The drive label, system drive letter, BitLocker encryption date, and key filename are provided so you can locate the correct recovery key password.

Instead of using the normal 1–9 keys on the keyboard, use F1–F9 for digits 1–9, and F10 for 0. If you use the normal 1–9 keys, the password will not work. As soon as you correctly enter the recovery key password, the system starts normally.

How BitLocker Protects Your Information

During normal use, a BitLocker-encrypted volume appears as a normal drive using the NTFS file system, and you can use EFS or disk compression on individual files and folders as with any normal NTFS volume.

> **NOTE**
>
> Backups made of a BitLocker-encrypted drive with Windows Complete PC Backup or other backup utilities are not encrypted. Keep them in a safe place.
>
> Once data is transferred from a BitLocker-encrypted drive, it is no longer encrypted.

However, if you attempt to bypass BitLocker security by booting the system from a Windows DVD and using the Recovery Environment, BitLocker Drive Encryption Recovery will prompt you to provide the password from removable media or by entering it (see Figure 34.21). When you provide the password, you can access the volume for repair or data-recovery processes.

Figure 34.21
BitLocker encryption prevents access to a hard disk unless you have the recovery password.

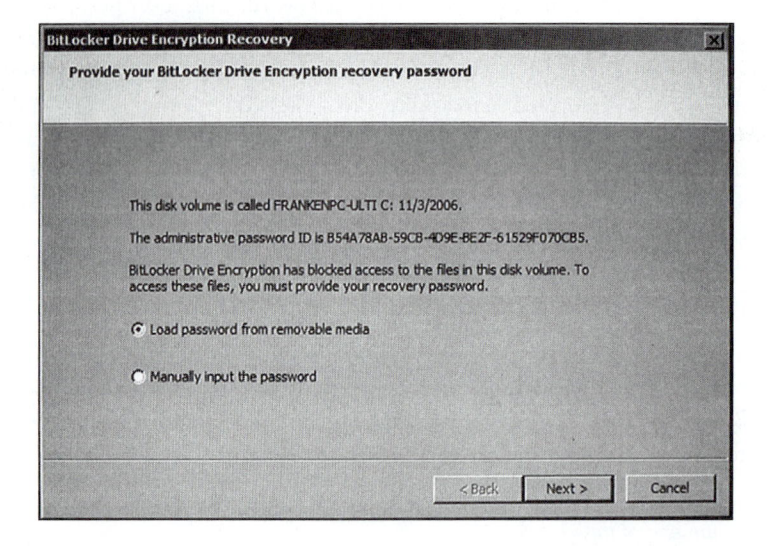

If you cancel the recovery process, the Recovery Environment will continue, but you will not be able to access the drive without providing the recovery password.

If you attempt to access the drive from the Recovery Console command prompt, you will see this message: "This volume is locked by BitLocker Drive Encryption. Return to the control panel to unlock volume."

If you connect a BitLocker-encrypted volume to another computer running Windows Vista and attempt to access its contents, the volume shows up as a drive letter in Windows Explorer with a size of 0MB, no disk label, and no file system.

If you connect a BitLocker-encrypted volume to another computer running Windows XP or other operating systems, the file system is listed as RAW (unformatted). Third-party data-recovery programs are unable to determine the file system or other information about the drive. The drive can be formatted, but its contents cannot be accessed.

BitLocker prevents access to the drive by unauthorized Windows Vista systems, and prevents other operating systems from detecting the file system. BitLocker does this by encrypting the drive with a full volume encryption key using AES encryption, and then encrypting that key with a volume master key, also using AES encryption. The volume master key is unlocked when you provide the proper credentials at boot time and it, in turn, unlocks the full volume encryption key that is used by a file system driver to unencrypt the volume. In recovery mode, the recovery password (eight groups of six digits) unlocks the volume.

> **NOTE**
>
> By default, BitLocker's AES encryption method uses a 128-bit key and uses the Diffuser algorithm, which protects against ciphertext manipulation key-cracking methods while providing excellent performance. Through the Group Policy Object Editor, you can select other options, including 128-bit without Diffuser, 256-bit with Diffuser, and 256-bit without diffuser. To select other options, open Computer Components, Administrative Templates, Windows Components, BitLocker Drive Encryption, Configure Encryption Method. Click the Enabled radio button, and select the desired encryption method. Click Apply, then OK.

DIFFERENCES BETWEEN BITLOCKER AND EFS ENCRYPTION

Although EFS encryption is familiar to many Windows Vista users because of previous experience with Windows 2000 and Windows XP, it may be useful to review the differences:

- In the initial version of Windows Vista, secures the entire system volume, but not other volumes (drive letters) on a system, while EFS encryption can be used on any volume formatted with NTFS. However, Vista SP-1's version of BitLocker can secure additional volumes on the system drive at the user's option.
- BitLocker uses a TPM chip or a USB flash memory drive to provide credentials, while EFS uses a personal certificate stored as part of the operating system to provide credentials.
- Neither EFS nor BitLocker encryption protects files once they have been copied to another drive. However, when EFS files are transferred via a file migration program, they retain their encryption attributes and the original user's EFS certificate must be exported from the source system and imported to the target system to enable encrypted files to be opened on the target system.

- EFS encryption is retained when files are backed up, but BitLocker volume encryption is not retained on a backup of a BitLocker volume.
- EFS encryption can be used by Windows Vista editions that do not support BitLocker, and on systems that are not compatible with BitLocker.
- BitLocker encryption cannot protect files on systems in sleep or hibernate mode, although EFS encryption can protect files on systems in these modes provided that the user has configured the system to request a strong password when waking up the system.

As you can see, BitLocker and EFS are complementary security features. You can use EFS to protect files on removable hard disks that are not secured with BitLocker, but you can use BitLocker to prevent anyone from using a stolen laptop or desktop computer.

> **NOTE**
>
> Use the Vista command-line utility `robocopy.exe` with the `/EFSRAW` option to migrate EFS-encrypted files from Vista to another system.

Recovering Previous Versions of a File

Windows Vista Business, Enterprise, and Ultimate editions enable you to restore a previous version of a file. This is handy if a data file has been edited and the changes are not an improvement, or if a user who intended to save a new version of a file with File, Save As accidentally clicked File, Save instead and overwrote the previous version.

There are two sources for previous versions:

- Backup copies (created with the Back Up Files wizard)
- Shadow copies (created as part of a volume restore point)

> **TIP**
>
> Although Previous Versions can be a lifesaver, it's no replacement for making backup copies of important files or saving different versions of a file in progress. The last-available previous version might be days or weeks old in some cases, so you might need to reconstruct changes you performed on the current version. In such cases, you may want to use the Open or Copy, rather than the Restore option with the most recent previous version.
>
> If you use a drive other than the system drive for data, be sure to enable restore points (System Protection) on that drive if you want shadow copies. A drive without restore points cannot provide shadow copies. In such cases, only backup copies (if they exist) will be available as previous versions. System Restore uses up to 15% of each NTFS drive of at least 1GB in size for restore points. On systems with limited disk space, Vista removes older restore points, which can also cause shadow copies to be lost. If you upgrade to Vista SP-1 on a system with limited disk space, all existing restore points will be removed and replaced with a single restore point before SP-1 is installed. See KB945681, available from http://support.microsoft.com.

If you have overwritten a file and want to retrieve a previous version, right-click the file and select Properties. Click the Previous Versions tab to see what backup or shadow copies may exist (see Figure 34.22).

Figure 34.22
Viewing the previous version of a file.

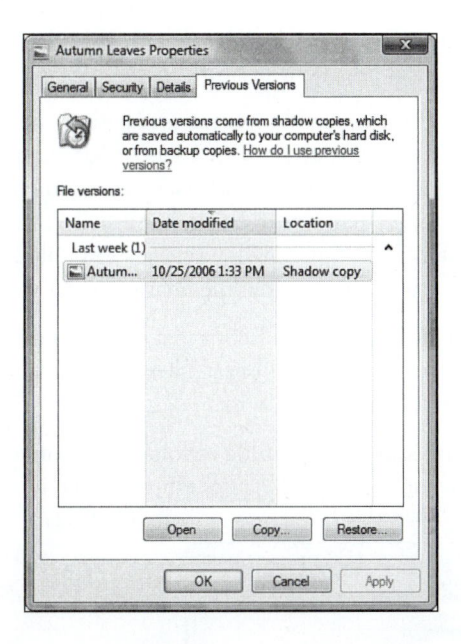

If more than one previous version exists, select the one you want to use, and choose from the following options:

- **Open**—The previous version is opened by the default application for the file type. The current version is retained.
- **Copy**—The previous version is copied to the destination you specify.
- **Restore**—The previous version replaces the current version. After selecting this option, you must click Restore to confirm the operation.

CAUTION

If you use Windows XP and Windows Vista in a dual-boot configuration and Windows XP mounts drives that contain Windows Vista system restore points, Windows Vista will delete those restore points the next time Vista is booted. When the restore points are deleted, any shadow copies contained there are also deleted.

If you use a dual-boot XP/Vista configuration, don't mount Vista drives with Window XP. To prevent Vista drives from being mounted by Windows XP, use the techniques described in KB926185, available at http://support.microsoft.com. These methods include creating a new registry subkey in Windows XP, which prevents XP from mounting the specified drive letter, or using BitLocker on the Ultimate or Enterprise editions of Vista to prevent XP from mounting encrypted drives.

NTFS File Permissions

All versions of Windows Vista use the NTFS (NT File System) directory structure, including Home Basic and Home Premium. NTFS enables you to assign control of who is permitted to access files and folders on a per-user or per-group basis. NTFS permissions can be used to control access for either local folders or network shares.

Windows XP Home Edition and Professional supported installation on disks formatted with the FAT32 file system, or the NTFS file system. Many users of XP did use NTFS formatted disks, either by choice, or because their computer manufacturers set their computer up that way. The user-based file permission system was in effect, but usually without the users even knowing it—on XP Home Edition, NTFS permission settings were hidden from the user, and on XP Professional, you had to disable Simple File Sharing to see them.

On the other hand, on Windows Vista, use of NTFS is mandatory, and the security settings are available to see and modify on *all* versions of Vista. Therefore, all Windows Vista users should understand how NTFS File Permissions work.

To display or modify NTFS permissions, select a file or folder in Computer or Windows Explorer, right-click Properties, and select the Security tab, as shown in Figure 34.23.

Figure 34.23
You can use the NTFS Permissions dialog box to designate a folder to restrict access to both network and local users.

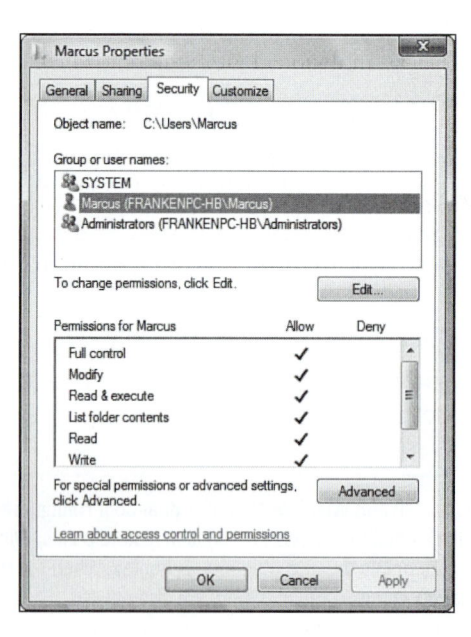

In the top part of the dialog box is the list of users or user groups with access to the file or folder. You can select any of the names in the list to view their associated permissions in the bottom half of the dialog.

The permission properties can each be granted or revoked individually. The permissions are Full Control, Modify, Read & Execute, List Folder Contents, Read, and Write. Their properties are listed in Table 34.2.

TABLE 34.2 NTFS FILE PERMISSION SETTINGS AND THEIR FUNCTIONS

Permission	Properties
Full Control	Gives all the rights listed below, plus lets the user change the file's security and ownership settings.
Modify	Lets a user modify a file's contents or delete a file.
Read & Execute	Allows a user to read a file's contents and/or run an executable file as a program.
List folder contents	Allows a user to view the contents of the folder.
Read	Lets a user read a file's contents only.
Write	Lets a user create a new file, or write data in an existing file, but not read a file's contents. For a folder, lets users add new files to the folder but not view the folder's contents.

Note that each permission has both Allow and Deny check boxes. To get access to a given resource, a user must be explicitly listed with Allow checked or must belong to a listed group that has Allow checked, and must not be listed with Deny access or belong to any group with Deny marked. Deny preempts Allow.

All these permissions are additive. In other words, Read and Write can both be checked to combine the properties of both. Full Control could be marked Allow but Write marked Deny to give all access rights except writing. (This permission would be strange but possible.)

The most productive use of NTFS file permissions is to assign most rights by group membership. One exception is with user home directories or profile directories, to which you usually grant access only to the Administrators group and the individual owner.

Editing NTFS file permissions is protected by UAC (unless you've disabled it). So, expect to see a lot of prompts to Continue (if you're an administrator) or to provide an administrator password (if you're a standard user) when you perform these operations.

TIP

If you edit Permissions, before you click OK or Apply, click the Advanced button and view the Effective Permissions tab, as discussed later in this chapter. Enter a few usernames to see that the permissions work out as you expected. If they do, only then should you click OK.

If you find that even if an Administrator can't gain the rights to delete a file or folder, **see** *"Administrator Can't Delete File or Folder" in the "Troubleshooting" section at the end of this chapter.*

Inheritance of Permissions

Normally, permissions are assigned to a folder (or drive), and all the folders and files within it *inherit* the permissions of the top-level folder. This makes it possible for you to set permissions on just one object (folder), managing possibly hundreds of other files and folders contained within. If necessary, explicit permissions can be set on a file or subfolder to add to or override the inherited permissions. Permissions displayed in the Security tab (as in Figure 34.23) will be grayed out if they have been inherited from a containing folder.

You can view or change the inheritance setting for a file or folder by clicking the Advanced button on the Security properties page. In Figure 34.24, the folder has a check in Inherit from Parent the Permission Entries That Apply to Child Objects.

Figure 34.24
The Advanced Permissions dialog box lets you control the inheritance of permissions, and set detailed permissions for user and groups.

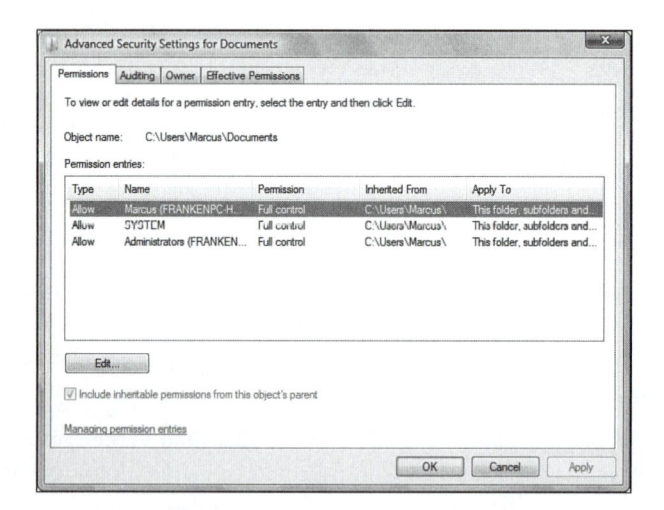

To change inheritance settings, click Edit. You can then uncheck the Inherit from Parent… box. If you uncheck the box, Windows gives you the option of starting with a blank permissions list (Remove) or keeping a copy of the settings it had before (Copy). In either case, the item now has its own independent list of access rights, which you can edit at will.

When you change permissions on a folder, you may want to cancel any manually added permissions set on the files and folders it contains. Checking the Replace All Existing Permission Entries on All Descendents… box will reset the permissions on all files in this folder and in subfolders, and will force all subfolders to inherit permissions from this folder.

CAUTION

Changing the permissions of the root folder of the drive containing Windows may make your system unusable. It's best not to mess with the permissions of your boot (usually C:) drive.

Advanced Security Settings

If you edit access permissions in the Advanced Security Settings dialog, you can exercise more "fine grained" control over permissions. It's rarely necessary, but for your reference, Table 34.3 lists the available permission settings.

TABLE 34.3   NTFS Advanced File Permission Settings and Their Functions

Permission	Properties
Traverse Folder/Execute File	For folders, this special permission allows a user the right to move through a folder to which he or she doesn't have List access, to reach a file or folder to which he or she does have access. For files, this permission allows the running of applications. (This permission is necessary only if the user wasn't granted the Group policy "Bypass Traverse Checking.")
List Folder/Read Data	For folders, allows the user to view the names of files or subfolders inside a folder. For files, allows the user to read the data in a file.
Read Attributes	Allows the user to view the attributes of the file or folder (that is, Hidden, Read-Only, or System).
Read Extended Attributes	Allows the user to view extended attributes of files or folders as defined by another program. (These attributes vary depending on the program.)
Create Files/Write Data	For folders, allows the user to create new files inside the folder. For files, allows the user to add new data or overwrite data inside existing files.
Create Folders/Append Data	For folders, allows the user to create new subfolders. For files, allows the user to append data to the end of an existing file. This permission does not pertain to deleting or overwriting existing data.
Write Attributes	Allows the user to change the attributes of the file or folder.
Write Extended Attributes	Allows the user to change the extended attributes of a file or folder.
Delete Subfolders and Files	For a folder, allows the user to delete subfolders and their contents. This permission applies even if the Delete permission has not been expressly granted on the individual subfolders or their files.
Delete	Allows or denies the user to delete the file. Even if Delete is denied, a user can still delete a file if he or she has Delete Subfolders and Files permission on the parent folder.
Read Permissions	Allows the user to view the file's or folder's permissions assigned to a file or folder.
Change Permissions	Allows the user to change the file's or folder's permissions.
Take Ownership	Allows the user to take ownership of a file or folder.

Viewing Effective Permissions

The Effective Permissions tab on the Advanced Security page lets you enter a username and see what privileges the user will have as a result of the current security settings on the file or folder, as shown in Figure 34.25.

This dialog box displays the effective permissions *as edited*, before they are applied to the file folder. This lets you verify that the permissions you have set operate as desired before committing them to the file by clicking OK or Apply.

Figure 34.25
Effective Permissions shows you how edited Permissions settings will work before they're actually applied to the file.

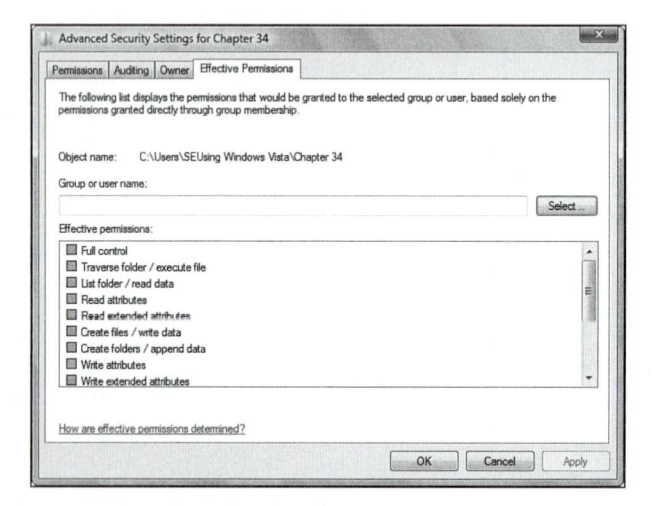

Access Auditing

The Advanced Security Settings dialog provides a way for you (if you are an administrator) to monitor access to files and folders through the Event Log. The Auditing tab (see Figure 34.26) lets you specify users and access types to monitor, and decide whether to record log entries for successful access, failure to access, or both. Auditing can be set for the use of each access attribute that you can set with Permissions: List Folder, Write Data, and so on.

Auditing is useful in several situations:

- To determine what files and folders an errant application program is attempting to use
- To monitor users for attempts to circumvent security
- To keep a record of access to important documents

To enable auditing, locate the folder or file you want to monitor, view its Security properties, click Advanced, view the Auditing page, and click Add. Select a specific user or group (or Everyone), and check the desired events to audit. You can prevent a new audit setting from propagating into subfolders by checking Apply These Auditing Entries to Objects and/or Containers Within This Container Only. You can enable the resetting of audit properties of all subfolders and files by checking Replace All Existing Auditing Entries on All Descendants....

Figure 34.26
Auditing properties record events in the Security Event log whenever the selected access privileges succeed and/or fail.

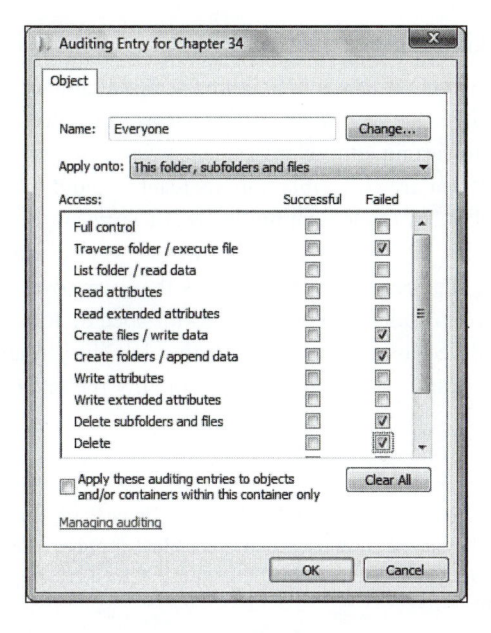

An entry is made in the Security Event log for each audited access, so be careful if you are enabling auditing on the entire hard drive!

Taking Ownership of Files

Sometimes files or folders have security attributes set so stringently that even Administrator can't read or modify them. Usually this occurs when the file has permissions set only for its owner and not the usual list: Owner, Administrator, System. This can occur when a user account is deleted. It can also happen when you have reinstalled Windows or are using a disk drive taken from another Windows computer. Whatever the cause, the symptom is that even a Computer Administrator user is not able to access the files in some folder. If you absolutely need to access such files, you can take ownership of the file or folder, and then assign permissions to read and write as appropriate. To take ownership of a file or folder

1. Log on as Administrator.
2. View the file or folder in Explorer, right-click it, and choose Properties.
3. View the Security tab and click Advanced.
4. View the Owner tab, and click Edit.
5. Select Administrator (the user) or Administrators (the group) from the list. You may want to check the Replace Owner on Subcontainers and Objects box to change subfolders as well.
6. Click OK.
7. Add privileges as necessary to grant access to the desired user(s).

Assigning Permissions to Groups

It's common in an office environment to want shared folders that are accessible by some users and not by others. For instance, you may wish to put payroll information in a shared folder and grant access only to certain administrative employees. In a school environment, you might want some folders that are accessible only by teachers, and others accessible only by members of a particular class. At home, you might want to prevent the children from getting access to the parent's folder. The best practice in this case is to create local *user groups*, which are collections of users that can be given privileges that carry over to the group's members. You can add the group and assign permissions for specific folders and files without having to list each of the qualified users separately. Another benefit is that you can add and remove users from the group later on without having to modify the settings of the various folders.

> **NOTE**
>
> You cannot create local user groups with Windows Home Basic, Home Premium (or Starter Edition) using the Local Users and Groups tool. If you're a hard-core Windows hacker, you *can* use the command-line technique that we'll explain in the tip at the end of this section.

To create local user groups, follow these steps:

1. Right click Computer, click Manage, and open Local Users and Groups; or, on a domain computer, click the Advanced button on the Advanced tab of the User Accounts control panel applet.
2. Right-click the Group entry in the left pane.
3. Select Actions, New Group.
4. Enter a name for the new group, such as Accounting.
5. Click Add and select users to add to the group.

To grant the group permissions to specific folders

1. Highlight the folder or file in Windows Explorer.
2. Right-click and select Sharing and Security.
3. Select the Security tab and click Add.
4. Select the group name (on a domain computer you may select domain groups or local groups by selecting Location and choosing a domain name or the local computer name).
5. Click OK, and then check the appropriate permissions for the group to have.
6. If Everyone or other groups are listed as having rights to this folder, you may want to select the group(s) and uncheck any undesired privileges. If the entry is grayed out, the privileges are inherited from a containing folder. In this case, select Advanced, uncheck Inherit from Parent, and choose Copy to retain copies of the current settings. You can then remove the entries you don't want.

7. **Important:** Before you click OK to commit the changes, use the Effective Permissions tab on the Advanced Properties dialog to check the effective rights of a few different users to be sure that the rights are what you intend. Be sure that Administrator has at least taken ownership privileges.

> *If you find that a user has access to something he or she shouldn't,* **see** *"A User Has Access to a Restricted Object" in the "Troubleshooting" section at the end of the chapter.*

> **TIP**
>
> On Vista Home versions, if you're willing to work with the command-line interface, you *can* create local groups. Open a Command Prompt window and type the command
>
> `net localgroup groupname /add`
>
> but in the place of *groupname* type the name of the group you'd like to create. Then, to add a user to the group, type the command
>
> `net localgroup groupname username /add`
>
> and again, in place of *groupname* type the name of the group you created, and in place of *username*, type the name of a user on your computer. Repeat this command as necessary to add other users. The same command with /delete at the end instead of /add removes a user from the group.

Securing Your Printers

If you have a printer that uses expensive paper or ink, and are concerned that guests, kids, or unauthorized persons might use your printer, you should know that printers can be secured in the same way that access is controlled for files and folders: through user and group privileges. In the case of printers, the privileges allow users to add jobs to the printer, delete other people's jobs, and so on.

On a domain network, the network manager usually takes care of this. And on a workgroup it's generally not important to restrict access to printers. If you are using Simple File Sharing, it's not even possible to set up specific printer access privileges.

If you decide to, however, you can set printer access permissions by right-clicking a printer in your Printers folder and selecting Properties. The Security properties tab resembles the properties tab of files and folders, and can be modified in the same way.

Security Policy Configuration Options

USB flash memory drives are becoming ubiquitous. I carry one around most of the time for quick and easy file transfers, and they've found their way onto many keychains and even a few ballpoint pens and Swiss Army Knife models. Although USB flash memory drives are handy for data transfer, for improving Windows performance with ReadyBoost, and as a method for providing BitLocker credentials, they are a two-edged sword: They can also be used to steal confidential data, even from systems that use BitLocker or EFS encryption.

After all, these encryption methods block unauthorized users from gaining access to data, but they can't stop the authorized user from walking off with data.

In the past, institutions have used fairly crude methods for blocking access by USB devices, even to the point of literally gluing USB ports closed. However, in an era in which parallel, serial, and PS2 devices have been relegated to the boneyard by USB devices, more intelligent management of USB device security is needed. In Windows Vista, you can use various Group Policy settings, including the following, to prevent removable-media drives, including USB flash memory drives, from being used to snatch data, while still permitting legitimate uses for printing, input devices, and so forth.

- Removable Disks Deny Write Access
- All Removable Storage Classes Deny Write Access

You can also block installation of unapproved devices, such as USB flash memory drives, or permit only installation of approved devices. For details, see "Step-By-Step Guide to Controlling Device Installation and Usage with Group Policy," at the Microsoft TechNet website.

Third-Party Disc-Backup Tools

Although Windows Vista breaks new ground for Microsoft in its support for both image and file/folder backups, you might still prefer to use third-party backup tools for the following reasons:

- **Support for existing backup file types**—If you want to be able to access existing backups with Windows Vista, you need to use a version of your existing backup software that works with Windows Vista. Consult your backup software vendor for specific recommendations.

- **Capability to extract files from an image backup without scripting**—The most recent versions of leading image-backup programs such as Acronis TrueImage and Symantec Norton Ghost also support individual file/folder restoration from an easy-to-use GUI. Windows Vista's Complete PC Backup can be used for file/folder restoration only through the use of the `wbadmin` command-line tool, or by installing the VHDMount program included as part of Virtual Server 2005. See "Using VHDMount with Complete PC Backup Images," **p.xxx**, earlier in this chapter.

- **Support for advanced backup options such as compression, splitting of a backup into smaller files, password protection, and others**—If you want these or other advanced options, you must use a third-party backup program.

- **Support for tape backups and tape libraries**—Windows Vista's backup features do not include support for tape backups and tape libraries, although many third-party backup programs support tape as well as external drives, network shares, and CD or DVD backups.

Because of the extensive changes Windows Vista makes to the structure of user file storage and how the operating system works, you will probably need to upgrade existing backup programs to versions made especially for Windows Vista. Contact your backup vendor for details.

TROUBLESHOOTING

BACKUP HARDWARE NOT WORKING

The easiest way to determine whether your backup hardware (hard disk or CD/DVD drive) is failing or has failed is to swap the unit for another unit. During the writing of this chapter, I had a number of problems working with rewriteable DVDs during backups. I swapped drives with another system, and the problems went away. The result: I now have a dead DVD rewriter on my junk shelf.

If the problem happens only after an update to Windows, try using System Restore to revert your system to its condition before the update (see Chapter 28 for details). Use the drive's properties sheet in Device Manager to roll back to a previous driver version if you suspect that an updated device driver isn't working as well as the old driver.

USB BACKUP DEVICE NOT RECOGNIZED

If a USB-based hard disk or other backup device is not recognized, try a different port. On some systems, you can control the number of active USB ports in the system BIOS/CMOS setup. Thus, it's possible that a port that's physically present might be disabled.

If you plug the drive into a front-mounted USB port and it is not recognized, try a port on the rear of the system. Front-mounted USB ports must be connected to the motherboard, and some motherboards might not have the connections needed to support front-mounted ports, the connections on the port might be disabled, or the ports might be miswired.

Finally, make sure Group Policy options are not preventing USB drives from working. If your company has standardized on a particular brand and model of USB external hard disk, a Group Policy setting can be created to permit those drives to work, while blocking unauthorized models.

USB BACKUP DEVICE RUNS VERY SLOWLY

If the drive plugs into a USB port and works, but runs very slowly, a USB 2.0 (Hi-Speed USB) port might be configured as a USB 1.1 port in the system BIOS/CMOS program, or the system might have a mixture of USB 1.1 and USB 2.0 ports. Use only USB 2.0 ports for best performance (USB 2.0 runs at 480Mbps, while USB 1.1 runs at a top speed of 12Mbps). You will normally see a warning that you have plugged a Hi-Speed USB device into a low-speed port, but if USB warnings are disabled, you won't see such a warning.

NOT ENOUGH ROOM FOR BACKUP ON TARGET

The Windows Vista Complete PC Backup and Backup Files Wizards are easy to use for basic backup and restore, but if you use advanced options such as network shares or restores from a different system, the possibilities of problems increase. Make sure users check the target location for adequate space for a backup. If a drive has only a bit more space than the backup requires, the backup might fail or might run very slowly, especially if the drive has not been defragmented lately. Defragment the target drive before using it for backup storage. On a network drive, verify that the user has read/write access to the drive. If storage quotas are in use, verify that the user has been provided with an adequate amount of storage on the network drive.

Can't Locate File to Restore from a Multidisc Backup Setup

If the user needs to restore a multidisc (CD or DVD) file backup from a different computer, insert the last backup disc first when prompted for media. This ensures that the catalog will be read properly. Because file backups are stored in separate .zip files of no more than 200MB each, each disc can be restored separately.

CIPHER Produces Unexpected Results

Although using encryption (EFS) via the right-click menu works the same way as in previous NT-based versions of Windows, changes in the CIPHER command-line encryption tool can cause problems, particularly for users who are accustomed to how CIPHER worked in Windows XP. As with wbadmin, some practice time with noncritical files is a good idea.

Unable to Encrypt Files or Folders

If you are unable to use EFS on a particular drive, make sure that it is not compressed and that the drive uses the NTFS file system. Compressed files and folders are displayed in blue; encrypted (EFS) files and folders are displayed in green in Windows Explorer. A file on an NTFS drive can be encrypted or compressed (or neither), but not both. To check the file system used by a drive, right-click the drive in Computer, select Properties, and view the General tab. A FAT or FAT32 drive must be converted to NTFS to support encryption or compression. Keep in mind that home editions (and Starter) of Vista do not support EFS, although they do use NTFS as their native file system.

Unable to Use BitLocker

If you are unable to use BitLocker, check the following:

- Is the hard disk properly partitioned? The hard disk must have a 1.5GB primary partition and a separate system partition for Windows (it can be any size above the minimum requirements for Vista). You cannot enable BitLocker on a system with a single hard disk partition.
- If the system has a TPM chip, is the feature enabled in the system BIOS? If it is, check with the system or motherboard vendor for a BIOS upgrade.
- If the system does not have a TPM chip, follow the procedure to enable BitLocker in the Group Policy Object Editor.
- If you get the error message BitLocker could not be enabled. The system firmware failed to enable clearing of system memory on reboot after restarting your system

during the BitLocker setup process, it means that BitLocker has determined your system does not clear out memory during the reboot process. Hackers could analyze the contents of memory for the BitLocker encryption key and use it to bypass BitLocker encryption.

To enable your system to run BitLocker, contact your system vendor for a BIOS upgrade that includes the clearing of system memory upon reboot option. If this option is not available, you cannot run BitLocker on the system.

A User Has Access to a Restricted Object

A user in the Users local group has access to an object that the Users local group is not assigned permissions for.

Check to see whether the user belongs to any other groups that have been assigned permissions. Remember that permissions accumulate through groups. If necessary, you can remove groups from those listed as having access to the file, or you can list specific users and/or groups and check the Deny boxes to remove access rights.

Administrator Can't Delete File or Folder

I have found some files or folders that can't be deleted even by Administrator. They don't have the Read-Only attribute set, but Windows informs me that access is denied.

Sometimes a file or more often a folder is set with access controls such that even Administrator can't access or delete it. To erase such a folder, take ownership of it as described earlier in this chapter. Give Administrator full access rights. Use the Advanced Security button to view Advanced Permissions, and check Replace Permission Entries on All Child Objects. Click OK and Apply, and then try to delete the folder again.

Tips from the Windows Pros: Restoring NTBACKUP Files

Windows Vista is not designed to work with backups made by older Windows backup programs, nor can it work with tape backup drives. If you need access to existing .BKF (NTBackup) files and don't have a system running Windows XP or 2000, use the Windows NTBackup—Restore Utility available from the Microsoft Download Center at www.microsoft.com/downloads.

You must also enable the Removable Storage Management service to use the utility. See Chapter 27 for details on starting this service.

CHAPTER 35

PROTECTING YOUR NETWORK FROM HACKERS AND SNOOPS

In this chapter

It's a Cold, Cruel World   1206

Network Security Basics   1210

Advantages of a NAT (Shared) Connection and Separate Router   1212

Passwords Versus Passwordless File Sharing   1217

Testing, Logging, and Monitoring   1219

Disaster Planning: Preparation for Recovery After an Attack   1222

Specific Configuration Steps for Windows Vista   1224

Configuring Windows Firewall   1230

Windows Firewall with Advanced Security   1235

More About Security   1240

Troubleshooting   1240

Tips from the Windows Pros: Having Professionals Audit Your Network   1242

It's a Cold, Cruel World

You might be considering connecting your LAN to the Internet, or you might have done so already. Connecting will probably be a bit more work than you expect (even with, or due to, my advice), but the achievement will be gratifying. After you make just a few keystrokes, a friend in Italy will be able to log on to your network. Millions of potential customers can reach you. You'll be one with the world.

I don't want to spoil your day, but the cruel fact is that, besides your customers, friends, mother, and curious, benign strangers, your computer and your LAN will be exposed to pranksters, hackers, spammers, information bandits, thieves, and a variety of other bottom-feeders and bad guys who, like anyone else, can probe, prod, and test your system. Will your network be up to the task? Even if you have a single computer that is only occasionally connected to the Internet by modem, you're at risk.

By this point in the book, you are aware that network design is foremost a task of planning. It's especially true in this case: *Before* you connect to the Internet, you must plan for security, whether you have a single computer or a large local area network (LAN).

Explaining everything that you can and should do would be impossible. In this chapter, I give you an idea of what network security entails. I talk about the types of risks you'll be exposed to and the means people use to minimize this exposure; then I end with some tips and to-do lists. If you want to have a network or security consultant take care of implementation for you, that's great. This chapter gives you the background to understand what the consultant is doing. If you want to go it on your own, consider this chapter to be a survey course, with your assignment to continue to research, write, and implement a security plan.

Who Would Be Interested in My Computer?

Most of us don't give security risks a second thought. After all, who is a data thief going to target: me or the Pentagon? Who'd be interested in my computer? Well, the sad truth is that thousands of people out there would be delighted to find that they could connect to your computer. They might be looking for your credit card information, passwords for computers and websites, or a way to get to other computers on your LAN. Even more, they would love to find that they could install software on your computer that they could then use to send spam and probe other people's computers. They might even use your computer to launch attacks against corporate or governmental networks. Don't doubt that this could happen to you. Much of the spam you receive is sent from home computers that have been taken over by criminals through the conduit of an unsecured Internet connection. The problem has gotten so bad in the past few years that, starting with Windows XP Service Pack 2, when you install Windows software, Microsoft enables the strictest network security settings by default instead of requiring you to take explicit steps to enable them. There were just too many Windows computers—perhaps millions—with no protection whatsoever. And with the advent of high-speed, always-on Internet connections, the risks are increasing because computers stay connected and exposed for longer periods of time.

In this chapter, I explain a bit about how network attacks and defenses work. I tell you ways to prevent and prepare for recovery from a hacker attack. And most importantly, I show you what to do to make your Windows Vista system secure.

> **NOTE**
>
> If your computer is connected to a Windows domain–type network, your network administrators probably have taken care of all this for you. In fact, you might not even be able to make any changes in your computer's network or security settings. If this is the case, you might find it frustrating, but it's in the best interest of your organization.

Even if you're not too interested in this and you don't read any other part of this chapter, you should read and carry out the steps in the section titled "Specific Configuration Steps for Windows Vista."

Think You're Safe? Think Again

I want to give you a practical example of what can happen over the Internet. Just to see how easy it might be, one night at 1:00 a.m., I scanned the Internet for computers with unprotected Windows File Sharing. I picked a block of IP addresses near mine and used common, completely legal programs to find computers that were turned on and connected. Within a few minutes, I had found 20. I went through these 20 to see whether they had shared files or folders. My efforts didn't take long; on the fourth try, I was presented with the contents of someone's entire hard drive. Of course, I immediately closed the display, but not before noticing that one of the folders on the hard drive was named Quicken and probably contained all this person's checking and savings account information.

Within 10 minutes, I had hacked into someone's computer, and I wasn't trying very hard or using one of the many sophisticated tools available. I didn't even have to attempt to break a password. But even if I'd had to, would that person have noticed his or her computer's hard disk light flickering at 1:00 a.m.? Would you?

To make matters worse, in a business environment, security risks can come from *inside* a network environment as well as from outside. Inside, you might be subject to highly sophisticated eavesdropping techniques or even simple theft. I know of a company whose entire customer list and confidential pricing database walked out the door one night with the receptionist, whose significant other worked for the competition. The theft was easy; any employee could read and print any file on the company's network. Computer security is a real and serious issue. And it only helps to think about it *before* things go wrong.

Types of Attack

Before I talk about how to defend your computer against attack, let's briefly go through the types of attacks you're facing. Hackers can work their way into your computer and network using several methods. Here are some of them:

- **Password cracking**—Given a user account name, so-called "cracking" software can tirelessly try dictionary words, proper names, and random combinations in the hope of guessing a correct password. If your passwords aren't complex (that is, composed of upper- and lowercase letters, numbers, and punctuation characters), this doesn't take long to accomplish. If you make your computer(s) accessible over the Internet via

Remote Desktop or if you run a public FTP, web, or email server, I can *promise* you that you will be the target of this sort of attack.

- **Address spoofing**—If you've seen the caller ID service used on telephones, you know that it can be used to screen calls: You answer the phone only if you recognize the caller. But what if telemarketers could make the device say "Mom's calling"? There's an analogy to this in networking. Hackers can send "spoofed" network commands into a network with a trusted IP address.

- **Impersonation**—By tricking Internet routers and the domain name registry system, hackers can have Internet or network data traffic routed to their own computers instead of the legitimate website server. With a fake website in operation, they can collect credit card numbers and other valuable data.

- **Eavesdropping**—Wiretaps on your telephone or network cable, or monitoring of the radio emissions from your computer and monitor can let the more sophisticated hackers and spies see what you're seeing and record what you're typing.

- **Exploits**—It's a given that complex software has bugs. Some bugs make programs fail in such a way that part of the program itself gets replaced by data from the user. Exploiting this sort of bug, hackers can run their own programs on your computer. It sounds farfetched and unlikely, but exploits in Microsoft's products alone are reported about once a week. The hacker community usually hears about them a few weeks before anyone else does, so even on the most up-to-date copy of Windows, there are a few available for use.

- **Back doors**—Some software developers put special features into programs intended for their use only, usually to help in debugging. These back doors sometimes circumvent security features. Hackers discover and trade information on these and are only too happy to use the Internet to see if they work on your computer.

- **Open doors**—All the attack methods I described previously involve direct and malicious actions to try to break into your system. But this isn't always necessary: Sometimes a computer can be left open in such a way that it just offers itself to the public. Just as leaving your front door wide open might invite burglary, leaving a computer unsecured by passwords and without proper controls on network access allows hackers to read and write your files by the simplest means. Simple File Sharing, which I discuss later in the chapter, mitigates this risk somewhat.

- **Viruses and Trojan horses**—The ancient Greeks came up with the idea 3,200 years ago, and the Trojan horse trick is still alive and well today. Shareware programs used to be the favored way to distribute disguised attack software, but today email attachments are the favored method. Most email providers automatically strip out obviously executable email attachments, so the current trend is for viruses to send their payloads in .ZIP file attachments. File and music sharing programs, Registry cleanup tools, and other "free" software utilities are another great source of unwanted add-ons commonly called spyware, adware, and malware.

- **Social engineering**—A more subtle approach than brute-force hacking is to simply call or email someone who has useful information and ask for it. One variation on this approach is the email that purports to come from a service provider such as AOL, saying there was some sort of account glitch and asking the user to reply with his or her password and Social Security number so the glitch can be fixed. P. T. Barnum said there's a sucker born every minute. Sadly, this works out to 1,440 suckers per day, or more than half a million per year, and it's not too hard to reach a lot of them with one bulk email.

Recently, there has been an upsurge in the form of social engineering called *phishing*, in which spammers send an email that purports to be from your bank or eBay or other such vendor, with a link to a website that looks official and a request that you sign on with your username, password, and other personal information. (We'll talk more about phishing in the next chapter.)

- **Denial of service**—Not every hacker is interested in your credit cards or business secrets. Some are just plain vandals, and it's enough for them to know that you can't get your work done. They might erase your hard drive or, more subtly, crash your server or tie up your Internet connection with a torrent of meaningless data. In any case, you're inconvenienced. For an interesting write-up on one such attack, see www.grc.com/dos/drdos.htm.

- **Identity theft**—Finally, one type of attack that has recently gained a lot of attention is identity theft. Hackers steal personal information, such as your name, date of birth, address, credit card, and Social Security number. Armed with this, they can proceed to open credit card and bank accounts, redirect your mail, obtain services, purchase goods, obtain employment, and so on, all without your knowledge. This is one of the most vicious attacks and can have a profound effect on victims. Computers can expose you to identity theft in several ways: You might provide personal information to a phishing scheme or to an unscrupulous online seller yourself. Hackers could break into your computer or that of an online seller and steal your information stored there. Or, criminals could tap into your home or business network, a wireless network in a public space, or even tap into the wiring at an Internet service provider and capture unencrypted information flowing through the network there.

If all this makes you nervous about hooking your LAN up to the Internet, I've done my job well. Before you pull the plug, though, read on.

Your Lines of Defense

Making your computer and network completely impervious to all these forms of attack is quite impossible, if for no other reason than that there is always a human element that you cannot control, and there are always bugs and exploits not yet anticipated.

You *can* do a great deal, however, if you plan ahead. Furthermore, as new software introduces new features and risks, and as existing flaws are identified and repaired, you have to keep on top of things to maintain your defenses. The most important part of the process is that you spend some time thinking about security.

The following sections delve into the four main lines of computer defense:

- Preparation
- Active defense

- Testing, logging, and monitoring
- Disaster planning

You can omit any of these measures, of course, if you weigh what you have at risk against what these efforts will cost you, and decide that the benefit isn't worth the effort.

What I'm describing sounds like a lot of work, and it can be if you take full-fledged measures in a business environment. Nevertheless, even if you're a home user, I encourage you to consider each of the following steps and to put them into effect with as much diligence as you can muster. Just think of that poor sleeping soul whose hard disk I could have erased that morning at 1:00 a.m. (If you missed this poignant example, see the sidebar titled "Think You're Safe? Think Again," earlier in the chapter.)

Network Security Basics

Preparation involves eliminating unnecessary sources of risk before they can be attacked. You should take the following steps:

- Invest time in planning and policies. If you want to be really diligent about security, for each of the strategies I describe in this chapter, outline how you plan to implement each one.

- Structure your network to restrict unauthorized access. Do you really need to allow users to use their own modems to connect to the Internet? Do you want to permit access from the Internet directly into your network, indirectly via a virtual private network (VPN), or not at all? Eliminating points of access reduces risk but also convenience. You have to decide where to strike the balance.

    If you're concerned about unauthorized in-house access to your computers, be sure that every user account is set up with a good password—one with letters and numbers and punctuation. Unauthorized network access is less of a problem with Password File Sharing because *all* network users are treated the same, but you must ensure that an effective firewall is in place between your LAN and the Internet. I show you how to use the Windows Firewall later in this chapter.

- Install only needed services. The less network software you have installed, the less you'll have to maintain through updates, and the fewer potential openings you'll offer to attackers.

    For example, don't install SMTP or Internet Information Services (IIS) unless you really need them.

    The optional Simple TCP Services network service provides no useful function, only archaic services that make great denial-of-service attack targets. Don't install it.

- Use software known to be secure and (relatively) bug-free. Use the Windows Automatic Updates feature. Update your software promptly when fixes become available. Be *very* wary of shareware and free software, unless you can be sure of its pedigree and safety.

- Properly configure your computers, file systems, software, and user accounts to maintain appropriate access control. We discuss this in detail later in the chapter.

- Hide from the outside world as much information about your systems as possible. Don't give hackers any assistance by revealing user account or computer names, if you can help it. For example, if you set up your own Internet domain, put as little information into DNS as you can get away with. Don't install SNMP unless you need it, and be sure to block it at your Internet firewall.

> **TIP**
>
> The most important program to keep up-to-date is Windows Vista itself. I suggest that you keep up-to-date on Windows Vista bugs and fixes through the Windows Automatic Updates feature *and* through independent watchdogs. Configure Windows to notify you of critical updates. Subscribe to the security bulletin mailing lists at www.microsoft.com/security, www.ntbugtraq.com, and www.sans.org.
>
> If you use Internet Information Services to host a website, pay particular attention to announcements regarding Internet Explorer and IIS. Internet Explorer and IIS together account for the lion's share of Windows security problems.

Security is partly a technical issue and partly a matter of organizational policy. No matter how you've configured your computers and network, one user with a modem and a lack of responsibility can open a door into the best-protected network.

You should decide which security-related issues you want to leave to your users' discretion and which you want to mandate as a matter of policy. On a Windows 200x domain network, the operating system enforces some of these points, but if you don't have a domain server, you might need to rely on communication and trust alone. The following are some issues to ponder:

- Do you trust users to create and protect their own shared folders, or should this be done by management only?
- Do you want to let users run a web server, an FTP server, or other network services, each of which provides benefits but also increases risk?
- Are your users allowed to create simple alphabetic passwords without numbers or punctuation?
- Are users allowed to send and receive personal email from the network?
- Are users allowed to install software they obtain themselves?
- Are users allowed to share access to their desktops with Remote Desktop, Remote Assistance, NetMeeting, Carbon Copy, PCAnywhere, or other remote-control software?

Make public your management and personnel policies regarding network security and appropriate use of computer resources.

If your own users don't respect the integrity of your network, you don't stand a chance against the outside world. A crucial part of any effective security strategy is making up the rules in advance and ensuring that everyone knows.

Advantages of a NAT (Shared) Connection and Separate Router

Active defense means actively resisting known methods of attack. Active defenses include these:

- Firewalls and gateways to block dangerous or inappropriate Internet traffic as it passes between your network and the Internet at large
- Encryption and authentication to limit access based on some sort of credentials (such as a password)
- Efforts to keep up-to-date on security and risks, especially with respect to Windows Vista

When your network is in place, your next job is to configure it to restrict access as much as possible. This task involves blocking network traffic that is known to be dangerous and configuring network protocols to use the most secure communications protocols possible.

Set Up Firewalls and NAT (Connection-Sharing) Devices

Using a firewall is an effective way to secure your network. From the viewpoint of design and maintenance, it is also the most efficient tool because you can focus your efforts on one critical place, the interface between your internal network and the Internet.

A firewall is a program or piece of hardware that intercepts all data that passes between two networks—for example, between your computer or LAN and the Internet. The firewall inspects each incoming and outgoing data packet and permits only certain packets to pass. Generally, a firewall is set up to permit traffic for safe protocols such as those used for email and web browsing. It blocks packets that carry file-sharing or computer administration commands.

Network Address Translation (NAT), the technology behind Internet Connection Sharing and connection-sharing routers, insulates your network from the Internet by funneling all of your LAN's network traffic through one IP address—the Internet analog of a telephone number. Like an office's switchboard operator, NAT lets all your computers place outgoing connections at will, but it intercepts all incoming connection attempts. If an incoming data request was anticipated, it's forwarded to one of your computers, but all other incoming network requests are rejected or ignored. Microsoft's Internet Connection Sharing and hardware Internet Connection Sharing routers all use a NAT scheme.

→ To learn more about this topic, **see** "NAT and Internet Connection Sharing," **p. 706**.

The use of either NAT or a firewall, or both, can protect your network by letting you specify exactly how much of your network's resources you expose to the Internet.

Windows Firewall

One of Windows Vista's features is the built-in Windows Firewall software.

Windows Firewall is enabled, or attached, on any network adapter or dial-up connection that directly connects to the Internet. Its purpose is to block any traffic that carries networking-related data, so it prevents computers on the Internet from accessing shared files, Remote Desktop, Remote Administration, and other "sensitive" functions.

In fact, Windows Firewall is designed so that on all but large corporate LANs, it can be used on all network interfaces without interfering with day-to-day networking use. This can help prevent the spread of viruses from one computer to another across your LAN if one becomes infected.

Windows Firewall is enabled by default when you install Windows Vista. You can also enable or disable it manually by selecting the Change Settings task on the Windows Firewall window. (I tell you how to do this later in the chapter, under "Specific Configuration Steps for Windows Vista.") You also can tell the firewall whether you want it to permit incoming requests for specific services. If you have a web server, for example, you need to tell Windows Firewall to permit incoming HTTP data.

> **NOTE**
>
> Windows Firewall has the advantage that it can permit incoming connections for programs such as Remote Assistance. On the other hand, it's part of the very operating system it's trying to protect, and if either Windows Vista *or* the firewall gets compromised, your computer's a goner.
>
> If I had the choice between using Windows Firewall and an external firewall device such as a commercial firewall server, or a connection-sharing router with filter rules, I'd use the external firewall. But Windows Firewall is definitely better than no firewall.

Packet Filtering

If you use a hardware Internet Connection Sharing router (also called a residential gateway) or a full-fledged network router for your Internet service, you can instruct it to block data that carries services you don't want exposed to the Internet. This is called *packet filtering*. You can set this up in addition to NAT, to provide extra protection.

Filtering works like this: Each Internet data packet contains identifying numbers that indicate the protocol type (such as TCP or UDP) and the IP address for the source and destination computers. Some protocols also have an additional number called a port, which identifies the program that is to receive the packet. The WWW service, for example, expects TCP protocol packets addressed to port 80. A domain name server listens for UDP packets on port 53.

A packet that arrives at the firewall from either side is examined; then it is either passed on or discarded, according to a set of rules that list the protocols and ports permitted or prohibited for each direction. A prohibited packet can be dropped silently, or the router can reject the packet with an error message indicating that the requested network service is unavailable. (If possible, I prefer to specify the silent treatment. Why tell hackers that a desired service is present even if it's unavailable to them?) Some routers can also make a log entry or send an alert indicating that an unwanted connection was attempted.

> **NOTE**
>
> For a good introduction to firewalls and Internet security in general, I recommend *Practical Firewalls* (Que, 2000; ISBN 0789724162) *Maximum Windows 2000 Security* (Sams, 2001; ISBN 0672319659), and *Firewalls and Internet Security: Repelling the Wily Hacker* (Addison-Wesley Professional, 2003; ISBN 020163466X). A good introductory-level book is *Absolute Beginner's Guide to Security, Spam, Spyware & Viruses, Second Edition* (coming from Que in Spring 2007, 0-7897-3459-1).

Configuring routers for filtering is beyond the scope of this book, but Table 35.1 lists some relevant protocols and ports. If your router lets you block incoming requests separately from outgoing requests, you should block incoming requests for all the services listed, unless you are *sure* you want to enable access to them. If you have a basic gateway router that doesn't provide separate incoming and outgoing filters, you probably want to filter only those services that I've marked with an asterisk (*).

TABLE 35.1 Services That You Might Want to Block

Protocol	Port	Associated Service
TCP	20–21	FTP—File Transfer Protocol.
TCP	22	SSH—Secure Shell protocol, an encrypted version of Telnet
TCP *	23	Telnet—Clear-text passwords are sent by this remote terminal service, which also is used to configure routers.
TCP	53	DNS—Domain name service. Block TCP mode "zone" transfers, which reveal machine names.
TCP+UDP	67	BOOTP—Bootstrap protocol (similar to DHCP). Unnecessary.
TCP+UDP	69	TFTP—Trivial File Transfer Protocol. No security.
TCP	110	POP3—Post Office Protocol.
UDP * TCP *	137–8 139	NetBIOS—Three ports are used by Microsoft File Sharing.
UDP *	161–2	SNMP—Simple Network Monitoring Protocol. Reveals too much information and can be used to reconfigure the router.
TCP *	445	SMB—Windows File Sharing can use port 445 as well as ports 137–139.
TCP	515	LPD—UNIX printer-sharing protocol supported by Windows Vista.
UDP TCP	1900 5000	Universal Plug and Play—can be used to reconfigure routers.

As I said, if you use a hardware router to connect to the Internet, I can't show you the specifics for your device. I can give you a couple of examples, though. My Linksys cable/DSL–sharing router uses a web browser for configuration, and there's a page for setting up filters, as shown in Figure 35.1. In this figure, I've blocked the ports for Microsoft file-sharing services.

Figure 35.1
Configuring packet filters in a typical Internet Connection Sharing router.

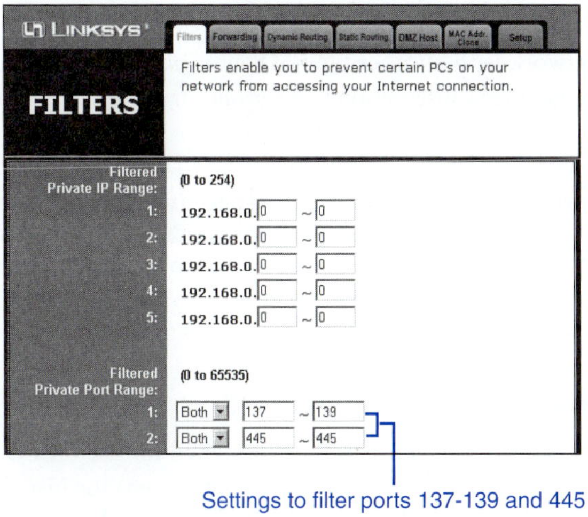

Settings to filter ports 137-139 and 445

If you use routed DSL Internet service, your ISP might have provided a router manufactured by Flowpoint, Netopia, or another manufacturer. As an example, filtering is set up in a Flowpoint router through a command-line interface, as shown here:

```
remote ipfilter append input drop -p udp -dp 137:138 internet
remote ipfilter append input drop -p tcp -dp 139 internet
remote ipfilter append input drop -p tcp -dp 445 internet
```

These are complex devices, and your ISP will help you set up yours. Insist that your ISP install filters for ports 137, 138, 139, and 445, at the very least.

USING NAT OR INTERNET CONNECTION SHARING

By either name, Network Address Translation (NAT) has two big security benefits. First, it can be used to hide an entire network behind one IP address. Then, while it transparently passes connections from you out to the Internet, it rejects all incoming connection attempts except those that you explicitly direct to waiting servers inside your LAN. Packet filtering isn't absolutely necessary with NAT, although it can't hurt to add it.

→ To learn more about NAT, **see** "NAT and Internet Connection Sharing," **p. 706**.

You learned how to configure Windows Internet Connection Sharing in Chapter 22, "Connecting Your Network to the Internet," so I don't repeat that information here.

> **CAUTION**
>
> Microsoft's Internet Connection Sharing (ICS) blocks incoming access to other computers on the LAN, but unless Windows Firewall is also enabled, it does *not* protect the computer that is sharing the Internet connection. If you use ICS, you must enable Windows Firewall on the same connection. Together, they provide adequate firewall protection for all your computers.

If you have built a network with another type of router or connection-sharing device, you must follow the manufacturer's instructions or get help from your ISP to set it up.

> **TIP**
>
> Not all ISPs will help you set up a connection-sharing router. These devices just cut into their revenues. Your ISP might even forbid their use. Better check first before you ask for help in installing one. Personally, I think that the additional security they provide justifies their use, even if the ISP doesn't like them.

ADD-ON PRODUCTS FOR WINDOWS

Commercial products called *personal firewalls are* designed for use on PCs. These types of products, Norton Internet Security 2007 (www.symantec.com) for instance, range in price from free to about $50. Now that Windows includes an integral firewall, add-on products might no longer be necessary, but you still might want to investigate them for the additional reporting and more intelligent outbound traffic monitoring they can provide.

SECURE YOUR ROUTER

If you use a router for your Internet connection and rely on it to provide network protection, you *must* make it require a secure password. If your router doesn't require a password, *anyone* can connect to it across the Internet and delete the filters you've set up. As configured by the manufacturers and ISPs, most routers *do not* require a password.

To lock down your router, you have to follow procedures for your specific router. You'll want to do the following:

- Change the router's administrative password to a combination of letters, numbers, and punctuation. Be sure to write it down somewhere.
- Change the SNMP read-only and read-write community names (which are, in effect, passwords) to a secret word or a very long random string of random characters.
- Prohibit write access via SNMP or disable SNMP entirely.
- Change all Telnet login passwords, whether administrative or informational.

If you don't want to attempt to lock down your router, your ISP should do it for you. If your ISP supplied your router and you change the password yourself, be sure to give the new password to your ISP.

Passwords Versus Passwordless File Sharing

Windows Vista supports password and passwordless file sharing. Before I explain this, I give you some background. In the original Windows NT/2000 workgroup network security model, when you attempted to use a shared network resource, Windows would see if your username and password matched an account on the remote computer. One of four things would happen:

- If the username and password exactly matched an account defined on the remote computer, you got that user's privileges on the remote machine for reading and writing files.
- If the username matched but the password didn't, you were prompted to enter the correct password.
- If the username didn't match any predefined account, or if you failed to supply the correct password, you got the privileges accorded to the Guest account, if the Guest account was enabled.
- If the Guest account was disabled—and it usually was—you were denied access.

The problem with this system is that it required you to create user accounts on each computer you wanted to reach over the network. Multiply, say, 5 users times 5 computers, and you had 25 user accounts to configure. What a pain! (People pay big bucks for a Windows Server–based domain network to eliminate this very hassle.) Because it was so much trouble, people usually enabled the Guest account.

Enter Passwordless File Sharing, which can make sharing folders and files much easier. Passwordless File Sharing makes the contents of the Public folder accessible to everyone on the network, regardless of whether they have a user account and password on your computer. This is ideal if you want to share everything in your Public folder and do not need to set sharing permissions for individuals.

> **NOTE** Actually, technically, on Windows Vista the feature is called Password Protected File Sharing, and it appears on the File Sharing on the Network and Sharing Center screen. When you uncheck Password Protected File Sharing, passwords are not used, and this is what I'm calling passwordless file sharing. Passwordless file sharing was called Simple File Sharing on Windows XP.

From a security perspective, only a few folders are accessible with passwordless file sharing, and although anybody with access to the network can access them, the damage an intruder can do is limited to stealing or modifying just the files in a few folders that are known to be public.

Passwordless file sharing has two downsides: First, and most important, it's *crucial* that you have a firewall in place. Otherwise, everyone on the Internet will have the same rights in your shared folders as you. (That's one of the reasons for Windows Firewall and why Windows Vista is so adamant about either installing the Firewall or disabling file sharing.)

The second downside is less troublesome and probably less noticeable to most people: If you attempt to use a shared folder from another computer on which you have the same username and password, you won't get the full rights that you'd have locally. You'll be a guest, like anyone else. In particular, the very handy whole-drive administrative shares such as C$ do not work when passwordless file sharing is in use.

By default, Windows Vista uses password-protected file sharing, which is much more secure. It limits access to the Public folder and all other shared folders to users with a user account and password on your computer. This method provides for finer granularity of control because you can set sharing permissions for individuals and groups. You can also give individuals different permissions, depending on the type of access they need.

If you want to make the Public folder accessible to everyone on your network, you can disable password-protected file sharing. Click Start, Control Panel, Network and Internet, Network and Sharing Center. Under Sharing and Discovery, click the drop-down arrow beside Password Protected Sharing, click Turn Off Password Protected Sharing, and click Apply.

SET UP RESTRICTIVE ACCESS CONTROLS

Possibly the most important and difficult step you can take is to limit access to shared files, folders, and printers. You can use the guidelines shown in Table 35.2 to help organize a security review of every machine on your network. I've put some crucial items in boldface.

TABLE 35.2   RESTRICTING ACCESS CONTROLS

Access Point	Controls
File Sharing	Don't share your computers' entire hard drives. Share only folders that need to be shared, and, if possible, choose only folders in your Documents folder (for simplicity). Use Password Protected File Sharing.
Passwords	Set up *all* accounts to require passwords. You can configure your computers to require long passwords if you want to enforce good internal security. I show you how to do this later in the chapter.
Partitions	If you install IIS and want to make a website or FTP site available to the Internet, set up a separate NTFS partition on your hard drive *just* for website files. I discussed this in Chapter 18, "Hosting Web Pages with Internet Information Services."
Access Control	Don't use Administrator or any other Computer Administrator account for your day-to-day work. If you accidentally run a Trojan horse or virus program using an Administrator account, the nasty program has full access to your computer. Instead, create and use Power User and Limited User accounts to the greatest extent possible.
FTP	If you install a public FTP server, do not let FTP share a FAT-formatted drive or partition. In addition, you must prevent anonymous FTP users from writing to your hard drive. I discussed this in Chapter 18.

Access Point	Controls
SMTP	Configuring an email system is beyond the scope of this book. But if you operate an email server, consider storing incoming mail in a separate partition, to avoid getting overrun with too much mail. Also, you *must* prohibit "relaying" from outside SMTP servers to outside domains, lest your server be used as a spam relay site.
HTTP (Web)	Don't enable both Script/Execute permission and Write permission on the same folder. Enabling both permissions would permit outside users to install and run arbitrary programs on your computer. You should manually install any needed scripts or CGI programs. (The FrontPage extensions can publish scripts to protected directories, but they perform strong user authentication before doing so.)
SNMP	This network-monitoring option is a useful tool for large networks, but it also poses a security risk. If installed, it could be used to modify your computer's network settings and, at the very least, will happily reveal the names of all the user accounts on your computer. Don't install SNMP unless you need it, and if you do, change the "community name" from public to something confidential and difficult to guess. Block SNMP traffic through your Internet connection with filtering.

Testing, Logging, and Monitoring

Testing, logging, and monitoring involve testing your defense strategies and detecting breaches. It's tedious, but who would you rather have be the first to find out that your system is hackable: you or "them?" Your testing steps should include these:

- Testing your defenses before you connect to the Internet
- Monitoring Internet traffic on your network and on the connection to your Internet service provider or other networks
- Detecting and recording suspicious activity on the network and in application software

You can't second-guess what 100 million potential "visitors" might do to your computer or network, but you should at least be sure that all your roadblocks stop the traffic you were expecting them to stop.

Test Your Defenses

Some companies hire expert hackers to attempt to break into their networks. You can do this, too, or you can try to be your own hacker. Before you connect to the Internet, and periodically thereafter, try to break into your own system. Find its weaknesses.

Go through each of your defenses and each of the security policy changes you made, and try each of the things you thought they should prevent.

First, connect to the Internet, visit www.grc.com, and view the Shields Up page. This website attempts to connect to Microsoft Networking and TCP/IP services on your computer to see whether any are accessible from the outside world. Click the File Sharing and Common Ports buttons to see whether this testing system exposes any vulnerabilities. This is a great tool. (Its author, Steve Gibson is a very bright guy and has lots of interesting things to say, but be forewarned that some of it is a bit hyperbolic.)

> **NOTE**
>
> If you're on a corporate network, contact your network manager before trying this. If your company uses intrusion monitoring, this probe might set off alarms and get you in hot water.

As a second test, find out what your public IP address is. If you use a dial-up connection or Internet Connection Sharing, go to the computer that actually connects to the Internet, open a command prompt window, and type `ipconfig`. Write down the IP address of your actual Internet connection (this number will change every time you dial in, by the way). If you use a sharing router, you need to get the actual IP address from your router's Status page.

Then enlist the help of a friend or go to a computer that is *not* on your site but out on the Internet. Open Windows Explorer (*not* Internet Explorer) and, in the Address box, type `\\1.2.3.4`, but in place of `1.2.3.4`, type the IP address that you recorded earlier. This attempts to connect to your computer for file sharing. You should not be able to see any shared folders, and you shouldn't even be prompted for a username and/or password. If you have more than one public IP address, test *all* of them.

> If you are able to view your computer's shared folders, **see** "Shared Folders Are Visible to the Internet" in the "Troubleshooting" section at the end of this chapter.

If you have installed a web or FTP server, attempt to view any protected pages *without* using the correct username or password. With FTP, try using the login name anonymous and the password guest. Try to copy files to the FTP site while connected as anonymous—you shouldn't be able to.

> If you are able to view your computer's shared folders, **see** "Sensitive Web Pages or FTP Folders Are Visible to the Internet" in the "Troubleshooting" section at the end of this chapter.

> If you are not able to view protected web pages or folders even after providing the correct password, **see** "Can't View Protected Web Pages" in the "Troubleshooting" section at the end of this chapter.

Use network-testing utilities to attempt to connect to any of the network services you think you have blocked, such as SNMP.

> If sensitive network services are found to be accessible, **see** "Network Services Are Not Being Blocked" in the "Troubleshooting" section at the end of this chapter.

Attempt to use Telnet to connect to your router, if you have one. If you are prompted for a login, try the factory default login name and password listed in the router's manual. If you've blocked Telnet with a packet filter setting, you should not be prompted for a password. If you are prompted, be sure the factory default password does not work, because you should have changed it.

If you can access your router, see *"Router Is Accessible via Telnet" in the "Troubleshooting" section at the end of this chapter.*

Port-scanning tools are available to perform many of these tests automatically. For an example, see the Shields Up web page at www.grc.com. I caution you to use this sort of tool in addition to, not instead of, the other tests I listed here.

NOTE
You can also use professional auditing services that will probe your network and web server for security problems. For more information, see the "Tips from the Windows Pros" section at the end of this chapter.

MONITOR SUSPICIOUS ACTIVITY

If you use Windows Firewall, you can configure it to keep a record of rejected connection attempts. Log on using a Computer Administrator–type account. Choose Start, All Programs, Administrative Tools, and Windows Firewall with Advanced Security. Click Windows Firewall Properties, click one of the available profile tabs (such as Public Profile) and click the Customize button within the Logging area to get to the window shown in Figure 35.2.

Inspect the log file periodically by viewing it with Notepad.

Figure 35.2
Enable logging to see what Windows Firewall is turning away.

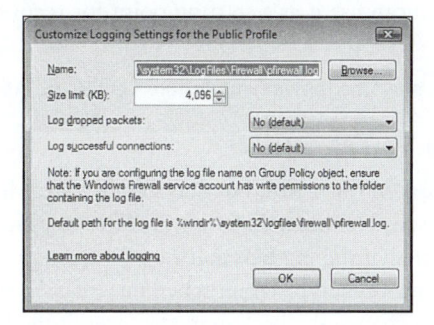

NOTE
If you use a dial-up connection, the firewall log is less useful. It will accrue lots of entries caused by packets left over from connections made by the dial-up customer who had your temporary IP address before you got it. They'll continue to arrive for a while, just as junk mail does after a tenant moves out.

Disaster Planning: Preparation for Recovery After an Attack

Disaster planning should be a key part of your security strategy. The old saying "Hope for the best and prepare for the worst" certainly applies to network security. Murphy's law predicts that if you don't have a way to recover from a network or security disaster, you'll soon need one. If you're prepared, you can recover quickly and may even be able to learn something useful from the experience. Here are some suggestions to help you prepare for the worst:

- Make permanent, archived "baseline" backups of exposed computers *before* they're connected to the Internet and anytime system software is changed.
- Make frequent backups once online.
- Prepare written, thorough, and *tested* computer restore procedures.
- Write and maintain documentation of your software and network configuration.
- Prepare an incident plan.

A little planning now will go a long way toward helping you through this situation. The key is having a good backup of all critical software. Each of the points discussed in the preceding list is covered in more detail in the following sections.

Make a Baseline Backup Before You Go Online

You should make a permanent "baseline" backup of your computer before you connect with the Internet for the first time so you know it doesn't have any virus infections. Make this backup onto a removable disk or tape that can be kept separate from your computer, and keep this backup permanently. You can use it as a starting point for recovery if your system is compromised.

→ To learn more about making backups, **see** "The Backup and Restore Center," **p. 1150**.

Make Frequent Backups When You're Online

I hate to sound like a broken record on this point, but you should have a backup plan and stick to it. Make backups at some sensible interval and always after a session of extensive or significant changes (for example, after installing new software or adding users). In a business setting, you might want to have your backup program schedule a backup every day automatically. (You *do* have to remember to change the backup media, even if the backups are automatic.) In a business setting, backup media should be rotated off-site to prevent against loss from theft or fire.

Write and Test Server Restore Procedures

I can tell you from personal experience that the only feeling more sickening than losing your system is finding out that the backups you've been diligently making are unreadable. Whatever your backup scheme is, be sure it works!

This step is difficult to take, but I urge you to try to completely rebuild a system after an imaginary break-in or disk failure. Use a sacrificial computer, of course, not your main computer, and allow yourself a whole day for this exercise. Go through all the steps: Reformat hard disks, reinstall Windows or use the Complete PC Restore feature, reinstall tape software (if necessary), and restore the most recent backups. You will find this a very enlightening experience, well worth the cost in time and effort. Finding the problem with your system *before* you need the backups is much better than finding it afterward.

Also be sure to document the whole restoration process so that you can repeat it later. After a disaster, you'll be under considerable stress, so you might forget a step or make a mistake. Having a clear, written, tested procedure goes a long way toward making the recovery process easier and more likely to succeed.

WRITE AND MAINTAIN DOCUMENTATION

It's in your own best interest to maintain a log of all software installed on your computers, along with software settings, hardware types and settings, configuration choices, network number information, and so on. (Do you vaguely remember some sort of ordeal with a DMA conflict when you installed the tape software last year? How *did* you resolve that problem, anyway?)

In businesses, this information is often part of the "oral tradition," but a written record is an important insurance policy against loss due to memory lapses or personnel changes. Record all installation and configuration details.

> **TIP**
>
> Windows has no utilities to print the configuration settings for software and network systems. I use Alt+PrntScrn to record the configurations for each program and network component, and then paste the images into WordPad or Microsoft Word.

Then *print a copy* of this documentation so you'll be able to refer to it if your computer crashes.

Make a library of CD-ROMs, repair disks, startup disks, utility disks, backup CDs, Zip disks, tapes, manuals, and notebooks that record your configurations and observations. Keep them together in one place and locked up, if possible.

PREPARE AN INCIDENT PLAN

A system crash or intrusion is a highly stressful event. A written plan of action made now will help you keep a clear head when things go wrong. The actual event probably won't go as you imagined, but at least you'll have some good first steps to follow while you get your wits about you.

If you know a break-in has been successful, you must take immediate action. First, disconnect your network from the Internet. Then find out what happened.

Unless you have an exact understanding of what happened and can fix the problem, you should clean out your system entirely. This means that you should reformat your hard drive, install Windows and all applications from CDs or pristine disks, and make a clean start. Then you can look at recent backups to see whether you have any you know aren't compromised, restore them, and then go on.

But most off all, have a plan. The following are some steps to include in your incident plan:

- Write down exactly how to properly shut down computers and servers.
- Make a list of people to notify, including company officials, your computer support staff, your ISP, an incident response team, your therapist, and anyone else who will be involved in dealing with the aftermath.
- Check www.first.org to see whether you are eligible for assistance from one of the many FIRST response teams around the world. The FIRST (the Forum of Incident Response and Security Teams) Secretariat can tell you which agencies might best be able to help you in the event of a security incident; call 301-975-3359.
- The CERT-CC (the Computer Emergency Response Team Coordination Center) might also be able to help you, or at least get information from your break-in to help protect others. Check www.cert.org. In an emergency, call 412-268-7090.

    You can find a great deal of general information on effective incident response planning at www.cert.org. CERT offers training seminars, libraries, security (bug) advisories, and technical tips as well.

Specific Configuration Steps for Windows Vista

Many of the points I've mentioned in this chapter so far are general, conceptual ideas that should be helpful in planning a security strategy, but perhaps not specific enough to directly implement. The following sections provide some specific instructions to tighten security on your Windows Vista computer or LAN. These instructions are for a single Windows Vista computer or a workgroup without a Windows 200x Server. Server offers more powerful and integrated security tools than are available with Windows Vista alone (and happily for you, it's the domain administrator's job to set it all up).

If You Have a Standalone Windows Vista Computer

If you have a standalone system without a LAN, you need to take only a few steps to be sure you're safe when browsing the Internet:

- Enable Macro Virus Protection in your Microsoft Office applications.
- Be very wary of viruses and Trojan horses in email attachments and downloaded software. Install a virus scan program, and discard unsolicited email with attachments without opening it. If you use Outlook or Windows Mail, you can disable the preview pane that automatically displays email. Several viruses have exploited this open-without-asking feature.

- Keep your system up-to-date with Windows Update, service packs, application software updates, and virus scanner updates. Check for updates every couple weeks, at the very least.

  NOTE
  > Unfortunately, the Windows Automatic Updates pop-up appears only when you are logged in using a Computer Administrator account. Unless you've configured Windows Automatic Updates to automatically install the updates, you need to log on as an administrator at least once every week or two to see if anything new has been downloaded.

- Make the Security Policy changes I suggest later in this chapter under "Tightening Local Security Policy."
- Use strong passwords on each of your accounts, including the Administrator account. For all passwords, use uppercase letters *and* lowercase letters *and* numbers *and* punctuation; don't use your name or other simple words.
- Be absolutely certain that Windows Firewall is enabled on all network and dial-up connections to the Internet. To enable Windows Firewall, use the steps shown later in this chapter under "Enabling Windows Firewall."

IF YOU HAVE A LAN

If your computer is connected to others through a LAN, follow the first five suggestions from the list in the preceding section. Make the Security Policy changes on *each* computer.

If you use a wireless network, you *must* use encryption to protect your network. Otherwise, thanks to passwordless file sharing, random people passing by could have the same access to your shared files as you do. Use WPA2 encryption if all of your computers and routers support it; otherwise, see whether you can use WPA. Use WEP only if you have devices that don't support WPA.

ENABLING WINDOWS FIREWALL

If you use the Internet, whether directly from your computer or through a network connection, you must be sure that some sort of firewall is in place to prevent Internet denizens from reaching into your computer. If you use a hardware Internet Connection Sharing device, that will protect you to some extent, and I gave specific tips for adding more protection in the previous section. But unless you're on a professionally secured corporate network or you use a third-party firewall product, you should also use Microsoft's Windows Firewall. Windows Firewall is turned on by default, and you should already be using it. You can use the following procedure to verify or manually enable the firewall:

1. Log on using a Computer Administrator-type account. Click Start, Control Panel, and then click Security.
2. Click Windows Firewall.
3. Windows Firewall should be listed as on. If it is, you're all set.
4. If it isn't, click Change Settings. Check On (Recommended), as shown in Figure 35.3.

Figure 35.3
Click On to enable Windows Firewall.

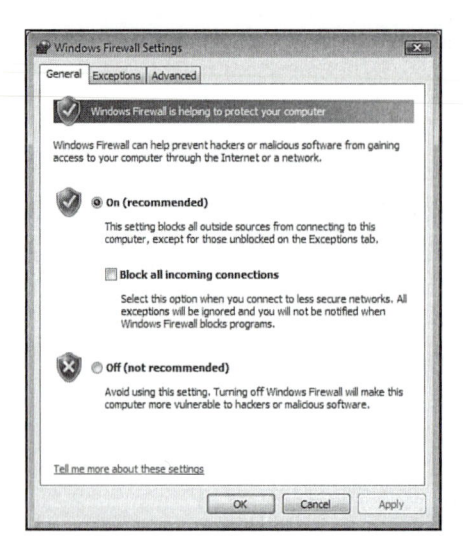

5. Click OK. Windows Firewall should now be enabled.

As you will see later in the chapter, you can enable Windows Firewall on one connection but disable it on another.

If you want to run a web server, email system, or other network services that you want to have made available to the outside world, you'll have to "open" the firewall for these services. See "Configuring Windows Firewall," later in this chapter, for details.

Keep Up-to-Date

New bugs in major operating systems and applications software are found every week, and patches and updates are issued almost as frequently. Even Microsoft's own public servers have been taken out by virus software.

Software manufacturers, including Microsoft, have recently become quite forthcoming with information about security risks, bugs, and the like. It wasn't always the case; they mostly figured that if they kept the problems a secret, fewer bad guys would find out about them, so their customers would be better off (and it saved them the embarrassment of admitting the seriousness of their bugs). Information is shared so quickly among the bad guys now that it has become essential for companies to inform users of security problems as soon as a defensive strategy can be devised.

You can subscribe to the Microsoft Email Updates security bulletin service at www.microsoft.com/security. The following are some other places to check out:

www.ntbugtraq.com
www.sans.org
www.cert.org
www.first.org

www.cs.purdue.edu/coast/

www.greatcircle.com

Usenet newsgroups: comp.security.*, comp.risks

Some of these sites point you toward security-related mailing lists. You should subscribe to Microsoft Security Advisor Bulletins at least. Forewarned is forearmed.

Tightening Local Security Policy

You should set your machine's own (local) security policy whether you have a standalone computer or are on a LAN. The Local Security Policy lets Windows enforce some common-sense security rules, such as requiring a password of a certain minimum length or requiring users to change their passwords after a certain number of days.

> **NOTE**
>
> Local Security Policy settings are not available on Windows Vista Home versions.

If your computer is part of a Windows domain–type network, your local security policy settings will likely be superseded by policies set by your domain administrator, but you should set them anyway so that you're protected if your domain administrator doesn't specify a so-called global policy.

To configure local security policy, log in as a Computer Administrator and choose Start, All Programs, Administrative Tools, and Local Security Policy. (If the Administrative Tools icon doesn't appear on the menu, the Administrative Tools Control Panel applet can get you there. You can also customize the Start menu to display the Administrative Tools.)

A familiar Explorer view then appears, with several main security policy categories in the left pane, as shown in Figure 35.4. I list several policy items you might want to change.

Figure 35.4
The Local Policy Editor lets you tighten security by restricting unsafe configuration options.

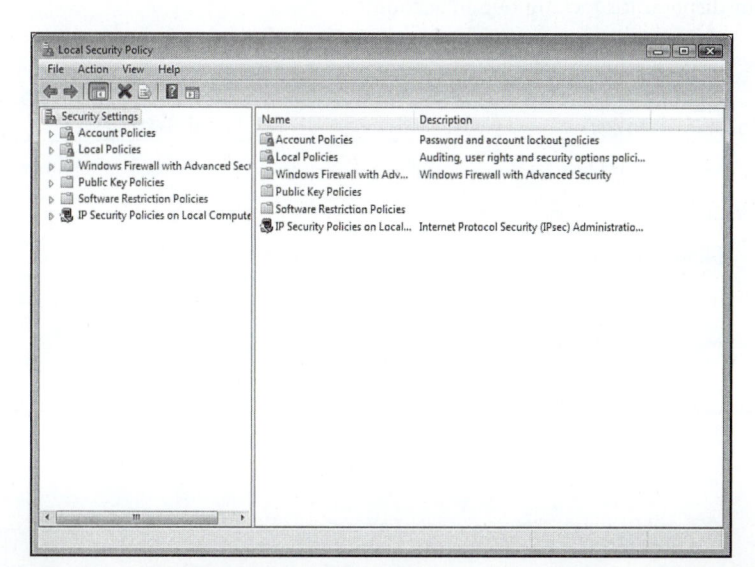

To change the settings, select the policy categories from the left pane and double-click one of the policy names listed in the right pane. Appropriate Properties dialog boxes appear for each; Figure 35.5 shows an example.

Figure 35.5
Each security policy item has a properties dialog box. You can enter the settings shown in the tables in the following sections.

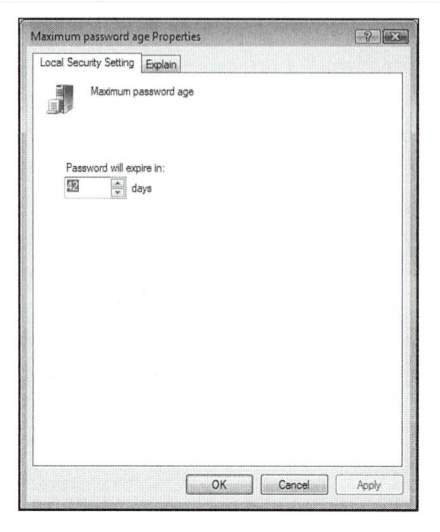

You don't need to change all the policies; I list the important ones in the following sections.

ACCOUNT POLICIES

Account policies can be used to enforce long, difficult, frequently changed passwords and make it hard for users to recycle the same passwords when forced to change. You should lock out accounts that fail several login attempts, locally or over the LAN. Table 35.3 shows the password policies and recommended altered settings, and Table 35.4 shows the options at your disposal for locking out an account.

TABLE 35.3   PASSWORD POLICY SETTINGS

Password Policy	Local Setting
Enforce password history	10 passwords remembered
Minimum password age	1 day
Maximum password age	70 days
Minimum password length	8 characters
Passwords must meet complexity requirements	Enabled
Store password using reversible encryption	Disabled

Table 35.4 Account Lockout Policy Settings

Account Lockout Policy	Local Setting
Account lockout duration	30 minutes
Account lockout threshold	5 invalid logon attempts
Reset account lockout counter after	30 minutes

LOCAL POLICIES

You should have Windows make an entry in the Event Log whenever someone oversteps his or her bounds. Table 35.5 shows the audit policies and recommended settings.

Table 35.5 Audit Policy Settings

Audit Policy	Local Setting
Audit account logon events	Failure
Audit account management	Failure
Audit directory service access	Failure
Audit logon events	Failure
Audit object access	Failure
Audit policy change	Success, Failure
Audit privilege use	No auditing *
Audit system events	Failure

* You should not audit Privilege Use because hundreds of spurious entries appear for no apparent reason.

No changes are necessary in the User Rights assignments section, but you might want to view these entries to see what sorts of permission restrictions Windows uses.

Finally, go through the security options, as listed in Table 35.6. Security options are used to restrict what users can do with system options.

> **NOTE**
>
> If you're interested in how Windows regulates the operation of your computer, take a look at the settings under User Rights Assignment and Security Options. You'll probably never need to change any of these settings, but these two sections are the heart of Windows's security controls.

Table 35.6 Security Options Settings

Security Option	Local Setting
Interactive logon: Do not require Ctrl+Alt+Del	Enabled *
Interactive logon: Message text for users attempting to log on	You can display a sort of "Posted: No Trespassing" warning with this entry.
Devices: Prevent users from installing printer drivers	Disabled. If you want to prevent users from installing potentially untested printer and hardware drivers, check out the options for these settings.
Audit: Shut down system immediately if unable to log security audits	A common hacker trick is to fill up audit logs with junk messages and then break in. If you want, you can have Windows shut down when the Security Event Log fills. The downside is that it makes your security system a denial-of-service risk. (Microsoft's public "hack me if you can" Windows 2000 Server was shut down just this way.)

When you log out and back in, the new restrictive security policies will take effect.

Configuring Windows Firewall

The purpose of Windows Firewall is to examine all incoming network data, looking for attempts to connect to your computer. The firewall maintains a list of networking services for which incoming connections should be permitted, within a given range of network addresses. For example, by default, Windows Firewall permits file-sharing connections only from computers on the same "subnet" or local area network as your computer. Attempts by users outside your immediate network to contact your computer are rebuffed. This prevents Internet users from examining your shared files. (Outgoing requests, attempts by your computer to connect to others, are not restricted.)

The Firewall also monitors application programs and system services that announce their willingness to receive connections through the network. These are compared against a list of authorized programs. If an unexpected program sets itself up to receive incoming network connections, Windows displays a pop-up message similar to the one shown in Figure 35.6, giving you the opportunity to either prevent the program from receiving any network traffic (Keep Blocking) or add the program to the authorized list (Unblock). This gives you a chance to prevent "spyware" and Trojan horses from doing their dirty work. Firewall-aware programs such as Windows Messenger automatically instruct the Firewall to unblock their data connections.

Figure 35.6
Windows Firewall displays a pop-up message if an unauthorized program asks to receive network connections.

To view Windows Firewall's setup dialog boxes, open Windows Firewall and select Change Settings.

> **NOTE**
>
> On a corporate network, your network manager might enforce or prevent its use and may restrict your capability to change Firewall settings while your computer is connected to the network.

The remainder of this section discusses the various setup options for Windows Firewall.

Enabling and Disabling the Firewall

The Firewall's General tab (refer to Figure 35.3) lets you enable or disable the firewall function. When the firewall is on, you can additionally check the Block All Incoming Connections option to prevent *all* incoming connections from other computers. This can provide an extra level of safety when you are using an unsecured public network such as a wireless hot spot in a hotel, airport, or café.

If you use Windows Live Messenger, and Messenger file transfers fail after enabling Windows Firewall, **see** *"Windows Messenger Can't Send Files" in the "Troubleshooting" section at the end of this chapter.*

Enabling Exceptions

In most cases, you *do* want other computers to be able to make connections to yours; for instance, this is how other people get to folders and printers you are sharing. Windows Firewall lets you determine what network services it will let in and, for each, which other users (as specified by their computers' network address) will be allowed to make contact. These are called *exceptions*.

Exceptions can be defined in terms of network protocols and port numbers, which correspond to particular network services, or in terms of specific application program filenames.

When a protocol and port is listed, any program that wants to receive connections for that network service is permitted to. When a program filename is listed, that program is permitted to receive connections for any protocol or port it wants to.

The range of network addresses that are allowed to contact your computer is called a *scope*. This can be specified as any of the following:

- Any computer (including those on the Internet)
- My Network (subnet) only
- Custom list (a list of network addresses or subnet specifications separated by commas)

CAUTION

> The My Network selection permits access by any computer in the same subnet (local network group) of *any* of your computer's network connection, which can include more than just your own LAN. When your computer has a direct broadband or dial-up Internet connection, in most cases, there can be up to 252 other random computers assigned to the same subnet as your computer, and they'll have access to your computer.
>
> The workaround is to not run sensitive services on a computer that is sharing its own Internet connection. This is not a problem when you are using a shared connection or a sharing router.

The Firewall's Exceptions tab, shown in Figure 35.7, has a predefined list of programs and network services for which exceptions can be created.

Figure 35.7
Predefined list of programs and network services for which exceptions can be created.

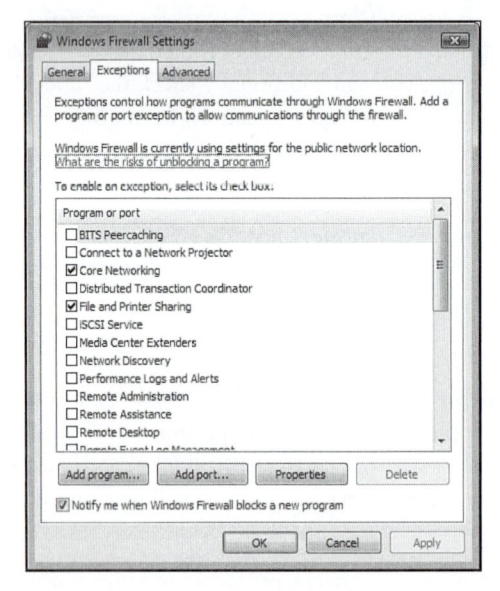

If you run a service such as a web server or an application program that will need to receive network connections, you can get an exception placed into this list by letting Windows display a pop-up warning of the type shown in Figure 35.6, or you can manually add an exception for this program.

To manually add an application exception, which lets the program receive any network connections it wants, view the Exceptions tab and click Add Program. Click Browse to locate the program's executable (.EXE) file if you do not see it in the Programs list, and click Change Scope to set the range of network addresses that should be able to access the program's services.

To manually add a port (service) exception, which lets any program receive network connections on the specified network ports, view the Exceptions tab and click Add Port. Enter a name to describe the network service, enter the port number, and select TCP or UDP. Click Change Scope to set the range of network addresses that should be able to access this service.

For example, to permit access to a web server running on your computer, you add the information shown in Figure 35.8. The Scope could be set to Any, to permit access by the entire Internet, or Subnet, to restrict access to your LAN only.

Figure 35.8
Adding an exception for a web server.

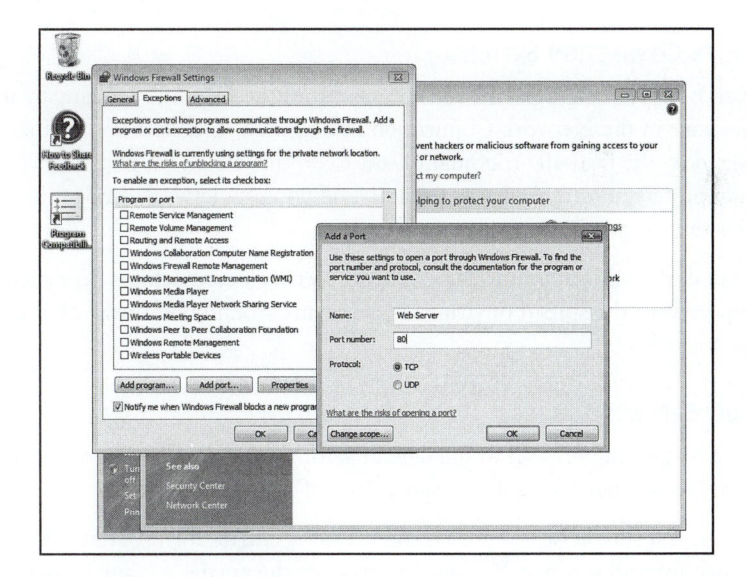

You can later highlight any entry and select Delete or Properties to remove or modify these settings. You can also uncheck an entry to temporarily block the program or service.

> **TIP**
>
> Curious to know what programs and services on your computer are listening for incoming network connections? Just follow these convoluted steps:
>
> 1. Log on as a Computer Administrator, click Start, and, in the search box, type the letters `cmd`.
> 2. In the search results, right-click `cmd.exe` and select Run As Administrator. Confirm the User Account Control prompt.
> 3. When the command prompt window opens, type the command `netstat -ab | more`. (This might take quite a long time.) A list of open ports is listed along with the names of the programs that are using them.
>
> If you don't recognize a program's name, use Google to see if it's discussed on any web pages; this might help you determine whether it's a legitimate Windows program or some sort of malware.

Advanced Firewall Settings

The Firewall's Advanced tab lets you remove the firewall from particular network connections, enable logging of rejected data, control how Internet control packets are treated, and restore the Firewall to the default, factory-fresh settings.

Network Connection Settings

You can remove some network connections from the firewall's scrutiny by unchecking these connections in the Network Connection Settings list. This leaves the other connections still protected by the firewall. You might want to do this when, for instance, your LAN is professionally protected by a hardware firewall, and you use network services on your LAN that the firewall has trouble with.

In general, though, it's best to leave all your network connections protected by the firewall, to help prevent the spread of viruses and Trojans around your network if one computer is compromised.

Default Settings

You can restore the firewall to the default settings provided by Microsoft by clicking the Restore Default button on the Advanced tab of the Windows Firewall Settings window.

However, you should be aware that this removes entries for programs that might have added their own firewall settings. You need to recheck the entries for any services that you want to make available.

Windows Firewall with Advanced Security

New to Windows Vista is Windows Firewall with Advanced Security. In a nutshell, this is a host-based firewall that can monitor and block both incoming and outgoing connections based on the configuration settings you specify.

> **CAUTION**
>
> Typical end users need to work within only the simpler Windows Firewall Control Panel tool. This is where general configuration of Windows Firewall takes place, such as enabling the firewall and adding exceptions. Windows Firewall with Advanced Security is for more advanced users or corporate network managers.

Windows Firewall with Advanced Security introduces a slew of new features and enhancements, summarized in Table 35.7, that are not available in previous versions of the firewall.

TABLE 35.7 NEW FEATURES OF WINDOWS FIREWALL WITH ADVANCED SECURITY

Feature	Description
Windows Service Hardening	Prevents attackers from exploiting Windows Services. Any abnormal activity, as defined by the Windows Service Hardening network rules, is blocked.
Outbound filtering	The firewall is capable of filtering outbound traffic as well as inbound traffic.
Granular rules	Through Windows Firewall with Advanced Security, more granular rules can be configured for inbound and outbound filtering.
Firewall profiles	Different rules can be configured for different profiles. Firewall profiles include domain, private, and public. These choices refer to the type of network your computer is connected to.
Authenticated bypass rules	The firewall can be configured to bypass blocks for specific computers that have been authenticated.
Active Directory support	The firewall can filter based on Active Directory account information.
IPv6	The firewall provides support for IPv6 environments.

> **TIP**
>
> You can use the Windows Firewall with Advanced Security console to configure firewall settings on either the local computer or a remote computer. Alternatively, these advanced settings can be deployed through Group Policy.

Configuring Windows Firewall with Advanced Security on a Local Computer

To open the firewall, click Start, All Programs, Administrative Tools, Windows Firewall with Advanced Security. The console shown in Figure 35.9 appears.

Figure 35.9
Console for configuring Windows Firewall with Advanced Security.

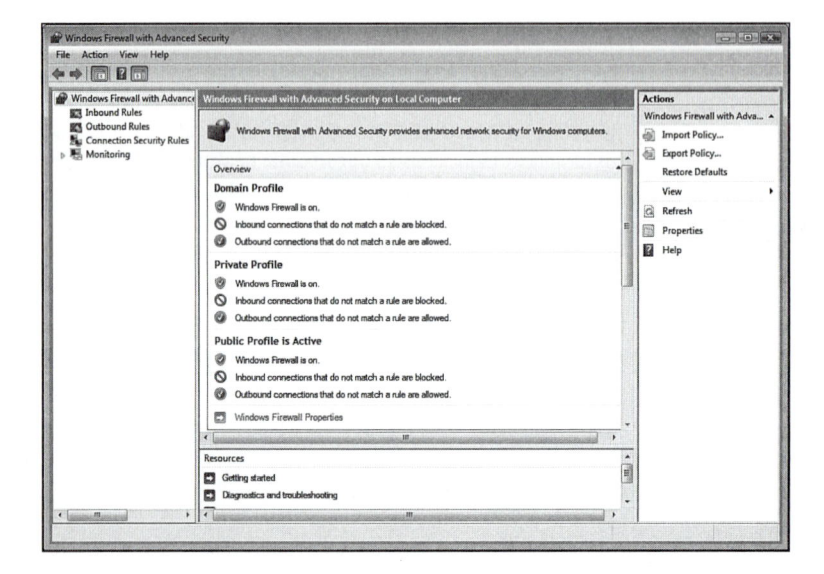

The Overview pane gives you a quick summary of how each firewall profile is currently configured. You can see from Figure 35.9 that when Windows Firewall is enabled for the Public Profile, inbound connections that do not match a rule are blocked and outbound connections that do not match a rule are allowed. This default setting makes Windows Vista behave as Windows XP did after Service Pack 2 was installed.

The Actions pane, to the right of the Overview pane, presents a list of actions that can be performed. This list changes depending on what you are viewing within the console. The tree displayed on the left side of the window provides access to rules and monitoring.

Firewall Properties

You can begin configuring firewall properties by selecting the Windows Firewall Properties link in the Overview pane. The Windows Firewall with Advanced Security on Local Computer window appears with four tabs, as shown in Figure 35.10.

Figure 35.10
Configuring Windows Firewall with Advanced Security Settings.

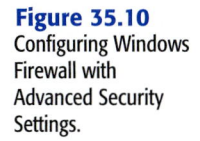

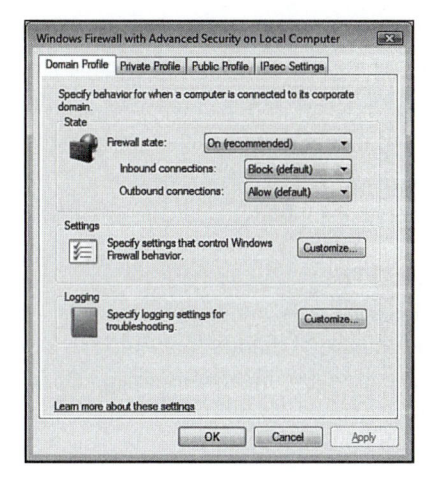

I do not go into to detail about each of the tabs because the first three tabs contain identical options. They enable you to configure firewall settings for the different profiles. Windows uses just one profile at a time, based on the Network Type setting currently in effect. For example, the settings on the Public Profile tab determine how your computer behaves when it is connected to a public network, such as the Internet.

The Firewall state, shown in Figure 35.10, is used to enable or disable the firewall for a profile. This means that you might have the firewall turned on for the Public profile but turned off when connected to your corporate domain network.

The next two options are used to configure inbound and outbound connections. Use the drop-down arrows to select one of the rules.

Inbound connections:

- **Block (default)**—Connections that do not match any active firewall rules are blocked.
- **Block All Connections**—All inbound connections are blocked, regardless of firewall rules.
- **Allow**—Connections that do not match any active firewall rules are allowed.

Outbound connections:

- **Allow (default)**—Connections that do not match any active firewall rules are allowed.
- **Block**—Connections that do not match any active firewall rules are blocked.

You can further customize the behavior of the firewall by selecting the Customize button within the Settings area. The following options can be configured:

- **Display Notifications to the User When a Program Is Blocked from Receiving Inbound Connections**—When enabled, users will receive notification when an inbound connection has been blocked by the firewall.

- **Allow Unicast Response to Multicast or Broadcast Requests**—The firewall will allow unicast response to outgoing multicast or broadcast requests.
- **Apply Local Firewall Rules**—When this option is enabled, local firewall rules configured by administrators are applied in addition to rules applied through Group Policy.
- **Allow Local Connection Security Rules**—When this option is enabled, local security rules configured by administrators are applied in addition to rules applied through Group Policy.

The Customize button within the Logging area was discussed earlier in the chapter under "Monitor Suspicious Activity." You can have Windows Firewall keep a record of connection requests that it receives and rejects, or even of connections accepted and rejected. This might be useful in determining why network connections to your computer are failing and also to identify when your computer is under attack.

IPSec

Internet Protocol Security (IPSec) is a set of protocols that protect data being sent between two hosts on an IP network. IPSec is generally used within a server environment and configured by network administrators. When you configure IPSec on a computer, you configure a set of rules that are applied network communications.

Windows Firewall with Advanced Security now integrates with Internet Protocol Security (IPSec). This is accomplished by configuring Security Rules that allow and block connections based on security certificates, Kerberos authentication, and encryption.

If by chance you have worked with IPSec in previous versions of Windows, you probably know that configuring it can a little messy. Fortunately in Windows Vista, a wizard will walk you through the process and do most of the dirty work for you. By creating a Connection Security rule, the New Connection Security Rule will walk you through the entire process.

> **CAUTION**
>
> This is an advanced topic that most home and small business users will not need to touch upon. And on a corporate network, your network administrator will most likely prevent you from viewing or changing these settings.

Firewall Rules

You create firewall rules to allow programs, services, and protocols to pass through the firewall. You can view the rules currently configured by selecting either Inbound Rules or Outbound Rules, as shown in Figure 35.9. The list of rules is displayed in the center pane. You can enable or disable a rule using the Action list mentioned earlier. For example, to enable a rule, select the appropriate rule from the list and select Enable Rule from the Action list.

Windows Firewall with Advanced Security 1239

Creating a new rule is not quite as simple and requires you to have some knowledge of the protocols and ports that are used by programs and services. The following steps provide an example of how to configure an outbound rule to block communications on a specific port.

1. Click Outbound Connections. From the list of actions, click New Rule. The New Outbound Rule Wizard appears.
2. From the Rule Type window, click Port. Click Next to continue.
3. Select the protocol that the rule will apply to: TCP or UDP. For this example, click TCP.
4. Select the Specific Local Ports option, shown in Figure 35.11, and type the port number in the port field that you want to block access to. Click Next.

Figure 35.11
Specify the protocol and port number for the outbound firewall rule.

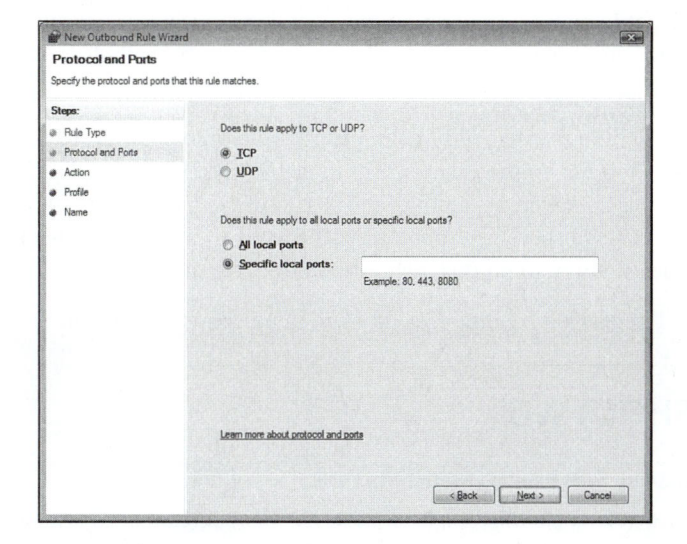

5. From the Action page, specify what the firewall should do when it receives inbound traffic on the port. In this case, I want to block traffic, so I clicked Block the Connection. Click Next.
6. The Profile page lets you tell the firewall which profiles the rule will apply to. Click Next.
7. Type in a name and description for the rule. This should be something that will help you recognize the rule in the list. Click Finish.

> **TIP**
>
> Along with TCP and UDP, the Internet makes extensive use of the *Internet Control Message Protocol (ICMP)*, which takes care of housekeeping details such as informing computers of routing problems and data-transmission errors. It's also used by the `ping` program, a very important networking diagnostic tool.
>
> By default, Windows Firewall does not permit any ICMP data to pass through the firewall. This prevents outside computers from sending you bogus ICMP data that could disrupt your use of the network. You can create inbound and outbound rules for ICMP in Windows Firewall with Advanced Security to instruct the firewall to pass these types of messages.

continues

> In most cases, ICMP Echo Request (`ping`) is the only ICMP message that you definitely want to process. Happily, you don't have to manually check this; Windows Firewall automatically passes these packets if the exception for File and Printer Sharing is enabled.

More About Security

This chapter just barely scratched the surface of what there is to know and do about network security. Lots of great books have been published on the topic, and I've mentioned several of them in this chapter.

You also can get lots of information on the Web. First, www.sans.org and www.cert.org are great places to start looking into the security community. Steve Gibson has plenty to say about security at www.grc.com—it's educational and entertaining.

Finally, you might look into additional measures you can take to protect your computer and your network. You can configure networks in many ways. For example, it's common to keep public web or email servers separate from the rest of your LAN. For additional security, you even can buy or build special-purpose firewall routers to place between your LAN and the Internet. One nifty way to do this is shown at http://pigtail.net/LRP/index.html.

In any case, I'm glad you're interested enough in security to have read this far in the chapter.

Troubleshooting

Shared Folders Are Visible to the Internet

When I use Explorer to view my computer across the Internet, I am prompted for a username and password, and/or shared folders are visible.

If you have this problem, Microsoft-file sharing services are being exposed to the Internet. If you have a shared connection to the Internet, you need to enable Windows Firewall or enable filtering on your Internet connection. At the very least, you *must* block TCP/UDP ports 137–139 and 445. Don't leave this unfixed.

If you have several computers connected to a cable modem with just a hub and no connection-sharing router, you should read Chapter 22 for alternative ways to share your cable Internet connection.

Sensitive Web Pages or FTP Folders Are Visible to the Internet

When I access my website from the Internet using a web browser or anonymous FTP, I can view folders that I thought were private and protected.

First, you must be sure that the shared folders are not on a FAT-formatted disk partition. FAT disks don't support user-level file protection. Share only folders from NTFS-formatted disks.

You must restrict access on the shared folders using NTFS permissions. View the folders in Windows Explorer on the computer running IIS. View the folders' Securities Properties tab.

Be sure neither Everyone nor IUSR_*XXXX* (where *XXXX* is your computer name) is granted access. On these protected folders, grant read and write privileges only to authorized users. In the Internet Information Services management console, you can also disable Anonymous access on the website's security page.

CAN'T VIEW PROTECTED WEB PAGES

When I try to view protected web pages or change to a protected directory in FTP, I can't view the pages or folders.

View the virtual folder's Properties page in the Internet Information Services management applet. On the Directory Security tab, click Edit under Anonymous Access and Authentication Control. Be sure that Digest Authentication and Integrated Windows Authentication are checked. If they were checked already, view the folder's Security settings in Windows Explorer, as described in the previous troubleshooting tip. Make sure that the desired users or groups are granted appropriate NTFS access permissions on the folder and its files and subfolders.

NETWORK SERVICES ARE NOT BEING BLOCKED

I can connect to my computer across the Internet with remote administration tools such as the Registry Editor, with SNMP viewers, or with other tools that use network services. How do I prevent this access?

Look up the protocol type (for example, UDP or TCP) and port numbers of the unblocked services, and configure filters in your router to block these services. Your ISP might be able to help you with this problem. You might have disabled Windows Firewall by mistake.

WINDOWS MESSENGER CAN'T SEND FILES

When you attempt to send someone a file using Windows Live Messenger, that person can't receive the file.

When you send someone a file, what actually happens is that the other person's copy of Windows Messenger contacts your computer to pick up the file. If Windows Firewall is blocking Windows Messenger data, the other person's copy of Messenger will not be able to retrieve the file. Check the Windows Firewall configuration dialog box to ensure that Block All Incoming Connections is not checked (at least temporarily) and that an exception exists for Windows Messenger.

Also, if you are using a file-sharing router, enable Universal Plug and Play (UPnP) on the router so that Messenger can tell it how to route incoming file-transfer connections.

ROUTER IS ACCESSIBLE VIA TELNET

I can connect to my Internet service router through Telnet across the Internet without providing a secret administrative password. How do I prevent this access?

Configure your router to require a sensible password for access. Choose a password with uppercase letters, lowercase letters, and numbers. Be sure you write it down and also give it to the technical support department of your ISP. The ISP might even be able to help you change the password.

Tips from the Windows Pros: Having Professionals Audit Your Network

A question I asked earlier in this chapter is "Who would you rather have be the first to find out your system is hackable: you or them?" You can spend hours upon hours locking down your computer, but unless you test your defenses, there is no way of knowing if you have been successful—until of course, a hacker discovers a way in.

Protecting your computer and network against attacks requires you to take a proactive approach by regularly testing your defenses for possible vulnerabilities. It isn't as difficult or time-consuming as it may sound, especially with the free tools available on the Internet.

Consider, for example, FreeScan by Qaulys. It is a free-trial, quick, and accurate and doesn't require you to install any additional software on your computer. It scans your computer for thousands of vulnerabilities that attackers are looking to exploit. These include many known problems with various Windows services such a file sharing, database access, and the Internet Information Services web server. In many cases, the FreeScan report can tell you the name of a specific Microsoft Knowledge Base article or hotfix download that will help you take care of the problem.

Along with this, the results of the scan are in a detailed report describing the vulnerabilities that have been identified, the severity of any threats, and the potential impact. You initiate your FreeScan at www.qualys.com/products/trials.

CHAPTER 36

PROTECTING YOURSELF FROM FRAUD AND SPAM

In this chapter

Phishing (Fishing) for Information   1244

Spam Not Fit for Consumption   1252

Tips from the Windows Pros: Take Action Against Email Abuse   1257

Phishing (Fishing) for Information

At one time, obtaining a free Internet access account was as simple as using a program to generate a fake credit card number and then filling out an AOL application with false information. By the time AOL figured out the credit card number was no good, quite a bit of free online access could be had. This reproachable practice ended when AOL fixed the problem, at which time even more reproachable practices ensued. A perpetrator would use specially designed programs to send a barrage of instant messages to subscribers, posing as an AOL representative, and lure them into providing personal account information. The use of diffuse targets, social engineering, and technology, all used together to steal information, is the essence of phishing.

This particular method of stealing information has become more prevalent in recent years and, by most accounts, is highly successful. Studies done on human susceptibility to specific, concocted phishing scams have varied greatly in results, from as few as 3% to as great as 70% susceptible. But if even one in a hundred falls prey, the number of potential victims is alarming.

> **NOTE**
>
> In 1994, AOHell was a popular program used to wreak havoc on the AOL system. It provided power tools for phishing exploits. A quick read of the user manual provides insight into the mentality of some of those who phish.

Live Phish: A Real-World Example

If gauged by the inbox, phishing is becoming more popular. The recent vein of email typically claims to come from one of many pervasive online services such as eBay, financial institutions, or any commercial service you can imagine. The typical example tends to report that some questionable account activity has taken place and require that you click a web link to attend to this matter immediately. Most certainly, this involves divulging personal information, and the criminals hope that, in your haste to rectify the problem, you share enough to be useful.

Fate is a funny thing. I received the email in Figure 36.1 just as I was beginning to write this chapter about Internet fraud.

Figure 36.1
Email from the PayPal Security Center <service5@hfsfcu.org>.

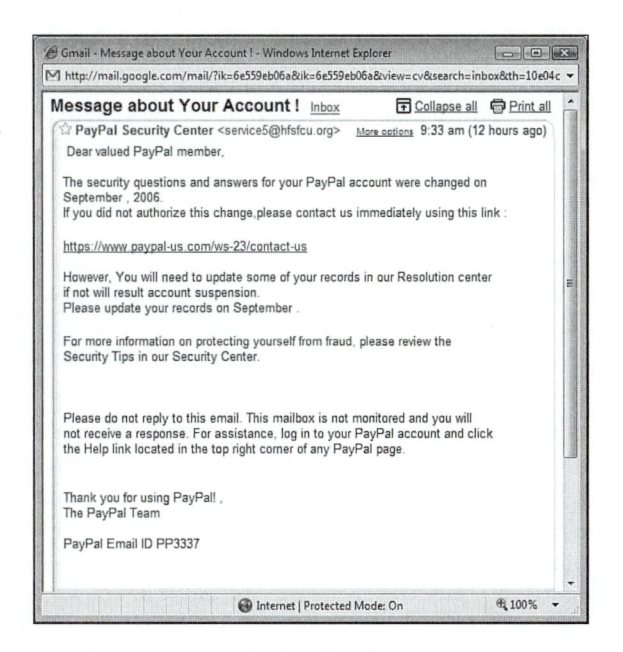

As an avid user of online auction sites and a frequent PayPal customer, I remember when I update my security question information, and I have not done so recently. On the surface, it appears that someone has changed my account without authorization, and PayPal has appropriately sent notification to my email address. They courteously referred to me as a "valued member" and provided a handy link for me to click on. It shows that it's pointing to www.paypal-us.com. The message has an official-looking PayPal Email ID code, and I absolutely do not want my account to be suspended. That would mean postponement of my habitual consumption of goods and services for a few hours, maybe days! That will not do.

Yet you might think something isn't quite right about this, and you'd be right. Our human race has not trudged through hardship and peril only to be outdone by a sloppy fake email. The first thing that might tip us off is the very first line of the email. Although it purports to be from the PayPal Security Center, the actual email address does not match. Communication from the real PayPal Security Center would come from an address with the paypal.com suffix, not hfsfcu.org. What is hfsfcu.org, anyway? Too many consonants make for a rough domain name. Second, the subject doesn't seem quite right. PayPal is a professional, reputable organization and is not known for alarmist tactics. Why is there a scary and somewhat intense exclamation point at the end of the sentence? PayPal would want me to act thoughtfully and deliberately, not out of panic and fear. I'd expect something more sedate and businesslike from them. Strange.

Take a careful look at the first paragraph. The greeting is not to anyone in particular, but rather a "valued PayPal member," yet PayPal knows its customers' usernames and would address them as such. Also, it is missing the date on what is assumed to be a computer-automated email, and there are several formatting errors. There is no space after the comma, an unnecessary space before the colon, and a forced carriage return. Okay, so the formatting issue may be nitpicking, but PayPal's business is dealing with monetary transactions. How often are banks lax with dates or haphazard in any kind of correspondence? Incorrect dates, bad formatting, and punctuation errors continue throughout the email. The PayPal Email ID seems way too short to be legitimate because it isn't. Even with all this, we have not yet arrived at the major, glaring, red-flag tip off.

The main clues that this email is not really from PayPal lie in the web link. First, www.paypal-us.com is not PayPal. The web address for PayPal is www.paypal.com. Those three extra characters are significant because www.paypal-us.com is owned by a totally different entity, probably waiting and hoping that someday PayPal will buy the domain name. Second, it doesn't really matter what any blue underlined link says because it is just an arbitrary description of the underlying URL, which is where the link directs you. The familiar blue underlined text could say "Click Here" or anything you can imagine, and it would still take you to the same underlying URL. There's an easy way to tell where you will actually be sent once you click on a link. Simply hover over the link with the mouse, and look in the status bar in the lower-left part of the browser. In this case, the www.paypal-us.com link does not go anywhere near PayPal. It is pointing to an unrelated website registered to a company in Hong Kong.

> **TIP**
>
> Another way to find the URL behind the link description is to right-click the link and select Properties. If the link is too long to fit in two lines, you might not see it entirely, but if you click and drag over the link, it will scroll to display the entire link.

And what about hfsfcu.org? This is a legitimate Federal Credit Union in Hawaii. The HFS Federal Credit Union was not manipulated into sending this email; it didn't come from them at all. Their good name just happened to be forged by the criminals perpetrating this scam. The fact is, the From address on an e-mail is one of the easiest things to manipulate and is never an authoritative indicator of who actually sent the email. A visit to the HFS Credit Union's website prominently displays a warning in bold red letters, stating that they are the target of a phishing scam.

This fraudulent email is a prime example of a phishing lure. The initial purpose of this elaborate (and it gets better) hoax is to trick the victim into clicking a web link. Unfortunately, security vulnerabilities in web browsers, including Microsoft's Internet Explorer, have proven that just clicking a malicious link can be a risky activity that, in past cases, has allowed a computer to be compromised. In this case, the link itself is harmless. The criminal's aim is not to compromise or control a computer, but to steal account credentials, which in some cases are directly linked to a bank account.

Although the astute observer finds many things about this email that make the Spidey Sense tingle, it's highly possible that a bleary-eyed, unsuspecting computer user who has not yet had morning coffee might miss some of these warning signs. This is where Microsoft's Phishing Filter comes in. Figure 36.2 shows what is presented when the link is clicked.

Figure 36.2
The Internet Explorer Phishing Filter at work.

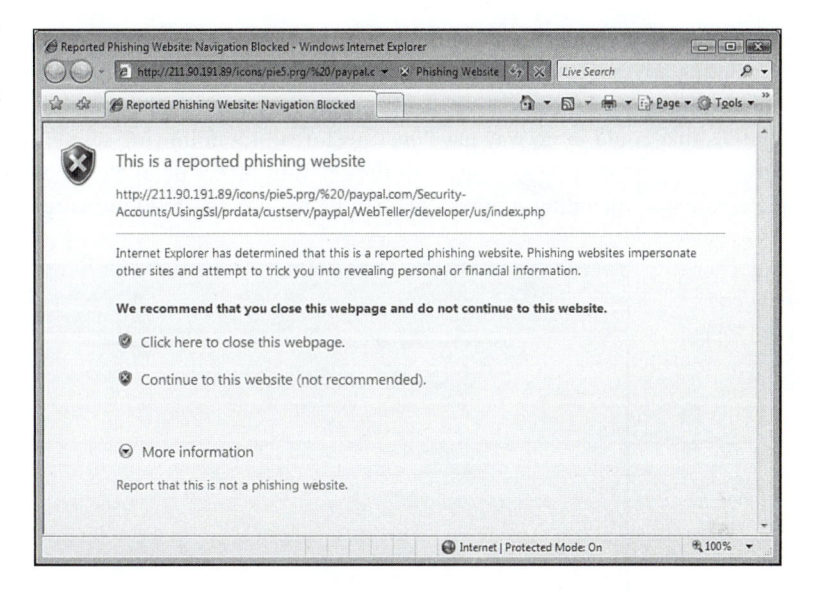

Ah-ha! Just as suspected, that link did not lead to PayPal, and Windows Vista's Internet Explorer 7 has communicated in no uncertain terms that it is a known dangerous site. It's fully correct. It provides the option to continue to the web page, if desired, but it explicitly states that clicking the link to proceed is absolutely not recommended—which is why, of course, at least for this example, the link must be clicked. If you decided to throw caution to the wind and proceed, or if you did not have the benefit of the Phishing Filter, you would see the site in Figure 36.3.

Figure 36.3
Looks like PayPal.

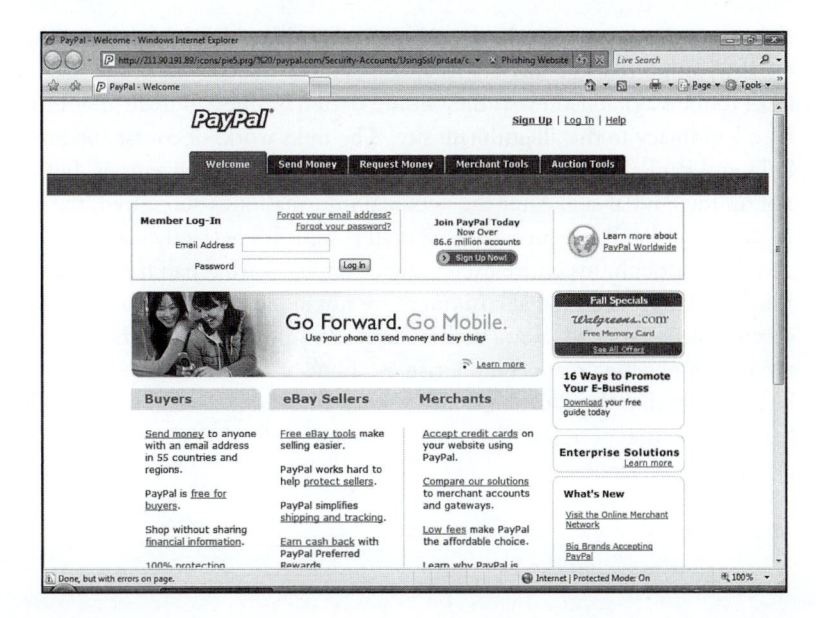

Figure 36.4 is a very convincing replica of the PayPal site, complete with the exact same circulating advertisements, links, format, and, most important for the phishing criminals, a Member Account Login section. After supplying fictitious and incredibly colorful login credentials that could in no way have ever been real, the following screen is presented, along with the opportunity to give away all the relevant pieces of an electronic identity to a complete stranger, including mother's maiden name, just for good measure.

Figure 36.4
Give it away, give it away, give it away now!

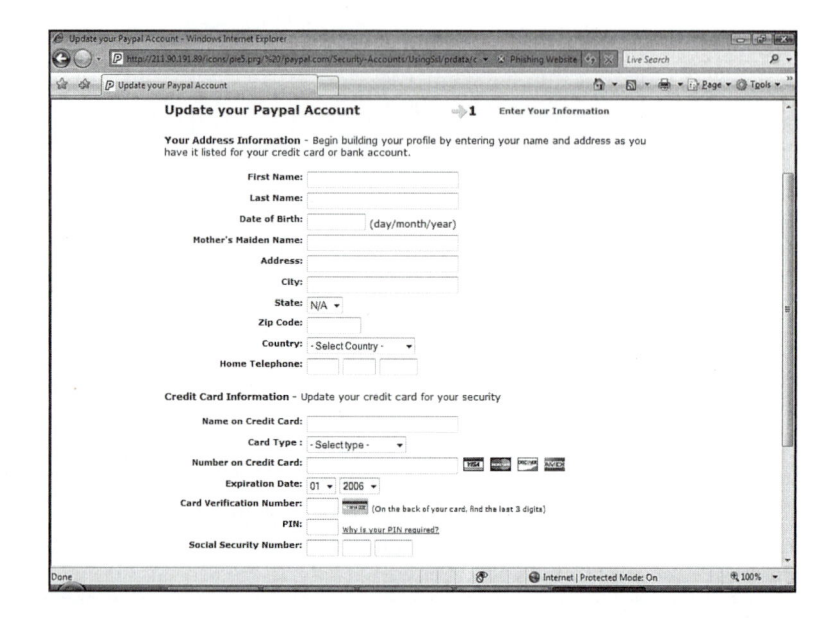

Entering yet more erroneous data showed that this phishing form actually did some decent data validation to avoid any bogus entries, and at the bottom of the form were legitimate links to the PayPal listings at the Online Better Business Bureau and TRUSTe, to add some false legitimacy to this illegitimate site. The links work, of course, because they are valid links and PayPal is really affiliated with both of those organizations, but nevertheless we are not on the PayPal site. After the personal information is submitted, the victim is directed to the actual PayPal login screen, as if all is well. It's perfectly conceivable that someone could go through this entire exercise and not know what had happened, were it not for the Phishing Filter, and PayPal customers are not alone. Citigroup and Bank of America have recently been targeted, along with a litany of respectable organizations you know well. With the rate of phishing scams on the rise, no filter based on a discreet list of bad sites will ever be complete, but the Phishing Filter service is updated several times per hour and also uses heuristics so that even if a malicious site is not explicitly listed, it can still be detected.

> **NOTE**
>
> The "ph" in *phishing* probably comes from the early days of hacking computer and phone systems, when "phone phreaks" used wit and cunning to manipulate and control the telephone system, and underground electronic magazines like *Phrack*, the original phreak/hack journal, ruled the day. It has nothing to do with Phish, the Vermont-based eclectic rock band.

MORE HELP FROM INTERNET EXPLORER

In addition to the Phishing Filter, Microsoft has improved a bit upon the venerable Gold Lock. Once stuck discreetly at the bottom of the browser, the new and improved Gold Lock is bigger, better, and more prominently placed right next to the URL it describes. The lock still signifies that the site you are currently browsing is using encryption to protect your session, but it has a few new twists. You can now view the site's certificate information with 50% fewer clicks (it is now a single click), and it will show up against a red background if there is anything odd about the site's certificate. It also highlights sites with Extended Validation (previously High Assurance SSL) certificates in green for those sites that have submitted to the more rigorous identification process and paid for the new certificate type.

In previous versions of IE, hackers used to be able to hide the true URL being visited in a number of ways, which could mask the fact that you were directed to a suspicious site. Now there will always be a URL bar in every window, so that kind of misdirection will be easier to spot.

> **CAUTION**
>
> On the other hand, IE 7 introduces something that will make bad URLs harder to spot: internationalized domain names (IDN). With previous versions, you had to worry about only your native alphabet or character set in the URL bar, but now you can get international character sets that could look similar to something in your native language yet be a different site entirely. IDN requires a keen eye to watch for accent marks and umlauts.

Finally, the new browser makes it much easier to clean up your personal information trail. If you were meticulous about cleaning up your personal information before, you had to painstakingly navigate to different areas of Windows to clean temporary Internet files, clear the history, erase autocomplete, clear the history for the Run line, and so on. Now, when you're in the browser, two clicks are all you need: Tools, Delete Browsing History. Use it whenever you are in public places or are shopping for secret presents.

> **TIP**
>
> The commonly recognized site names that end with suffixes such as `.com`, `.org`, and `.gov` should be immediately preceded by the core organization name and immediately followed by a slash. For example:
>
> Good URLs:
>
> www.mybanksite.com/
>
> http://accounts.mybanksite.com/
>
> Potential phishing URLs:
>
> www.mybanksite.com.elsewhere.com/
>
> http://mybanksite.com.phishcity.org/
>
> http://202.12.29.20/mybanksite.com/
>
> In some exceptions, good organizations use bad URLs, but you are right to be suspicious in those cases.

Two-Way Authentication

Authentication is proving that you are who you claim to be. The frequent use of bogus websites demonstrates the need not only for the users to prove their identity to a site, but also for a site to prove its identity to the users. One way to accomplish this type of two-way authentication is for the user to choose a secret symbol, such as a small picture of a tropical sunset, that is known only between the user and the site. Henceforth, whenever that user visits the site, the tropical sunset picture is displayed alongside the rest of the site information. A malicious site replica will not know which symbol to produce, so even if a user is tricked into visiting one, it will be clear that the site is not authentic. Sounds like an improvement, and it is.

The system works by placing a unique signature on the user's computer. When the customer visits the site and provides a valid account, the site verifies that the computer is the right one. If it is, the picture of the sunset is displayed along with the password prompt. The customer will recognize the picture, know it's the right site, and type in the password. Nice plan. But what if you are at a computer that you don't usually use? In that case, in addition to your username and password, you have to provide the answer to another security question before the site displays the secret symbol.

Two-Factor Authentication

The most pervasive example of single-factor authentication is having a password to prove that you are who you say you are. Two-factor authentication involves both something you know and something you have. A password or PIN is something you know. Something you have can come in many different forms but is usually either an electronic token of some sort or a biological property, such as a fingerprint or retina, that can be used to identify you. Using two factors to prove who you are is much better than using a password alone because whereas a password can be electronically stolen, obtaining both a password and a unique physical device—or a finger, for that matter—is substantially more difficult.

One challenge with two-factor authentication is that the computer must be capable of validating the "something you have." That usually means extra, specialized hardware. For example, to scan your finger for authentication, the computer must be equipped with a fingerprint reader. To use a special electronic token, you need a piece of equipment that can validate the token. When you consider that some institutions have millions of customers, the cost of extra hardware adds up.

RSA Security's solution to this problem is the SecurID token, a small device that fits on a keychain. It possesses a wristwatchlike LCD display that updates every 60 seconds with a six-digit code. The code is generated using a combination of an embedded clock and a random code generated specifically for each SecurID device. Websites that use this technology require not only a password or PIN, but also the six-digit code that is currently displaying on the corresponding token. Shortly after the number expires from the screen, it no longer works on the site. This effectively changes the password approximately every minute so that even if someone electronically stole the complete combination, they'd have all of 1 minute to make use of it. That works well against many types of phishing schemes, but not all. Although two-factor authentication adds measurably more security to authentication, it is still vulnerable to some type of attacks. A passive, bogus website that waited for victims to give away their information and then saved it for later use would be hopeless against a SecurID strategy. Imagine that instead of warehousing the stolen information, the bogus website immediately sent that information to the legitimate website, connected on the customer's behalf, and carried out a few miscellaneous transactions. It has already happened.

Identity-Management Software

Because no centralized or standard system exists for managing usernames and passwords across different websites, users are forced to improvise solutions for managing their various electronic identities. The most rudimentary solutions to this problem involve using the same or similar usernames and passwords for different sites, using usernames and passwords based on some type of mnemonic system, or even cutting and pasting the information from a Word document.

All these solutions leave much to be desired and become unwieldy as the number of identities increases. Identity is a tricky subject. Just ask any philosopher or information systems architect. The computer industry is still wrestling with this problem. Several solutions are on the table, some relatively simple and direct, and others that attempt to address the system as a whole.

A detailed discussion about the identity problem in the information systems world is way too big for this chapter, but satisfying workarounds available today run independently on Windows Vista. Password-management programs keep track of all your various usernames and passwords, and store them in a safe, encrypted format. They often have browser-integrated features that, with your permission, automatically fill in your credentials by site. These programs help circumvent keystroke loggers because there are no keystrokes. If you were ever in the habit of clicking the Remember My Password on This Computer check box at any number of websites, that bad habit can be alleviated by using a password manager. Programs such as Roboform, Login King, and Account Logon all provide one-click logons and enable you to use diverse and more complex usernames and passwords because you don't have to remember them. It's nice to know that with so many people focused on making life difficult with malware, innovative and pragmatic software developers are making life on the Web easier.

Avoiding Phishing

When visited with earlier browser versions, the bogus PayPal site in the previous example yields no additional clues to its true nature, but the numeric address in the URL bar is a tip that something might be amiss. For several technical reasons, it's uncommon for professional websites to use strictly numeric addresses (IP addresses) in their URLs. Here is a brief review of some key ways to avoid phishing attempts:

- Do not click links in email. Type in the known good URL yourself. You can also hover over a suspicious link or right-click and check Properties to see the true URL before visiting.
- Independently find the security department email address of the organization in question, usually on the main web page, and forward the suspicious email to them. They will tell you if it actually came from them and will act on the situation, if it did not.
- When visiting a website, pay attention to the URL. It usually contains a readable name that you expect, not just numbers. With internationalized domain names, now you also have to watch out for accents and umlauts that don't belong.
- Make a habit of clicking the Gold Lock to check the site certificate, and trust your gut. If you feel like something is amiss, it probably is.

> **TIP**
> The Anti-Phishing Workgroup keeps a large library of past antiphishing scams, including screen shots of the bogus websites. Hopefully, these won't look familiar to you, but they do serve as fine examples of what to look for. Check out www.antiphishing.org.

Spam Not Fit for Consumption

Email users of the world, especially in Hawaii, are no doubt nostalgic for a time when Spam was just a tasty shoulder-pork and ham product. Now it is the scourge of email systems throughout the world, as unsolicited email messages from an ever-increasing number of junk-mail senders congest mail systems and take up space on our computers. Spam is such a problem because, on the scale of subversive electronic activities, it is fairly easy to do, fairly difficult to be caught, and very inexpensive for the sender. Despite ridiculously low response rates, spammers continue to dupe shady advertisers into paying for it, and there is no need to reproduce any spam example here. With very few exceptions, every Internet email user has, or will very soon, receive some. In fact, if you have not been able to resist the temptation to click on some of the most tantalizing junk email links, you may have inadvertently volunteered your computer to be another spam sender, making it even more difficult for the actual perpetrators to be found and reducing their overhead costs.

Perhaps the most important cost involved with spam is in human time: time spent reading, deleting, and otherwise dealing with it. Thankfully, antispam technology continues to get better, and there are several practical things you can do to both make spam less of a nuisance and reduce the risk that it will lead to even more serious problems, such as email-borne viruses or information theft.

> **NOTE** According to the Merriam-Webster Online Dictionary, the origin of the word *spam* when used to refer to unsolicited email messages originates from a skit on the British television series *Monty Python's Flying Circus*. A quick search of the Web, however, reveals a rich etymology.

Antispam Tactics

To avoid spam, it helps to understand a bit about how it occurs. Spammers generally find email addresses by harvesting them from public sources, such as message boards or web pages. They also use special programs called spambots to methodically crawl the Web for email addresses wherever they might be, or programmatically generate likely (and not-so-likely) email addresses using common names and domain suffixes. Because little cost or penalty is associated with sending spam to the wrong email address, spammers trade and compile enormous email lists, with many incorrect and probably some legitimate addresses as well. If your email address ends up on one of these lists, it will probably stay there, so the best defense is to keep your email address off the list in the first place.

> **TIP** To make it more challenging for spam tools to guess an email address, use uncommon combinations instead of common naming conventions. Although it's less intuitive than john_doe@myemail.com, using initials and meaningful (to you) combinations of numbers, such as jhd0213@myemail.com, makes you a more difficult spam target.

Protect Your Email Address

The best way to avoid getting on spammers' lists is to share your email address only when necessary and only with the trusted few. One of the simplest ways that information is inadvertently shared is bad email etiquette. When a single email is sent to multiple people, it's best to use the BCC field and keep the names out of the To or CC lines. The exception to this rule is when you are on a private network, such as a corporate email system, where the email will not generally travel over the Internet unprotected.

Another way to reduce spam is to use multiple email addresses for different purposes. One email could be a primary address for trusted friends or merchants, and another could be for sites that are less familiar, or for times you need to register with a site for a one-time use. Keeping one address for important communications and another for "junk email" is not only effective at reducing spam, but it also can help protect you in other ways. In the phishing example earlier in this chapter, when an email arrived from PayPal at the junk email address, and I knew I had provided them with the trusted email address instead, it was a clear red flag. This works even better if you have yet more specific email addresses for important lines of communication. Free email address services abound. Many of them have good spam-filtering capabilities, so they make good choices for a junk email address.

Use Spam Filtering

Despite good faith and antispam tactics, an email address might eventually receive some spam. Spammers are innovative, but equally innovative people are at work preventing spam from taking valuable time away from your life. Spam filters analyze email and relegate spam to a "junk mail" folder or the like. They use various methods, including some similar to other antimalware programs, to detect and get rid of spam before it hits your inbox.

Many aftermarket spam filters also are available with a range of features, and there's even some plug-in hardware devices that protect from spam at the network level. Windows Mail, included with Vista, has a built-in junk mail filter itself and some powerful tools for dealing with spam. Take a look at the Junk E-Mail options from the Tools menu, in Figure 36.5.

Figure 36.5
Junk E-Mail filter options in Windows Mail.

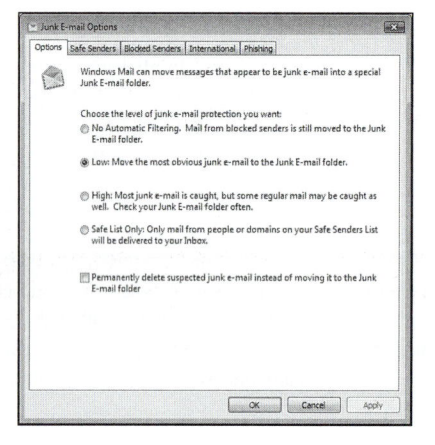

Three levels of automatic spam filtering exist. The rub is, the more aggressively spam is filtered, the more likely a well-intentioned email from a legitimate source ends up in the junk email folder. When calibrating, if Windows Mail is instructed to use the High level of filtering, it's best to leave the Permanently Delete Suspected Junk Email option unchecked.

Safe Senders List: Don't Call Us, We'll Call You

Executives of large corporations and others for whom privacy is very important sometimes use the most aggressive and effective way to make sure that email communication remains under control. Instead of filtering out the bad stuff, they filter in the good stuff. Only email that is on a designated "white list" is allowed to appear in the inbox, and all other email is discarded or relegated to junk mail. Though possible, it's not necessary to specify each and every email address allowed. Instead, if you wanted to receive mail from everyone at mycompany.com, you can simply add the domain mycompany.com to the Safe Senders list. And whether or not the Safe Senders list is used, the Blocked Senders tab can be used to filter mail by domain or by a specific "black list" of banned email addresses.

International Filtering: Isolationism for Email

Although the merits of profiling have been the topic of heated debate, when it comes to spam, top-level domain profiling is a wonderful thing. For better or worse, most of us limit our circle of communication to a limited number of countries. In some cases, maybe all our email contacts are in a single country. Windows Mail provides the capability to filter based on the last letters of the email address, or the top-level domain, that can represent the country or geographic region from which it originates. Because a person generally knows which countries or regions valid email will come from, and because spammers are usually lax about respecting international borders, the International tab provides two great options for limiting international spam from reaching your inbox. In Figure 36.6, all incoming email from the Kingdom of Lesotho, a land-locked country in the middle of South Africa, has been blocked. Instead, a resident of the kingdom could elect to receive email only from within, as could the resident of any nation, by simply selecting the corresponding check boxes.

Figure 36.6
Blocking email from the Kingdom of Lesotho.

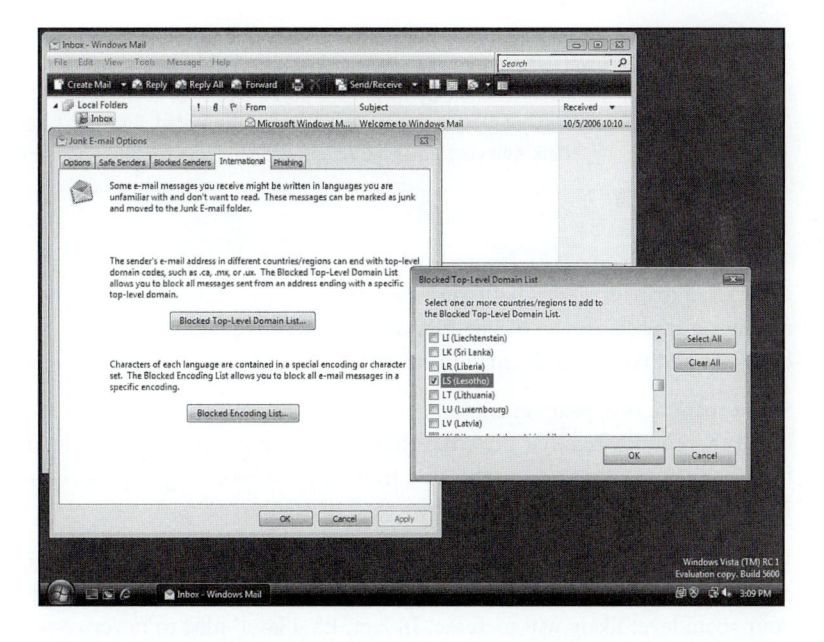

Unfortunately, as observed in the section about phishing, the From line in the email address is not always accurate. For those cases, Windows Mail has implemented one of my favorite tricks for eliminating spam. The Internet is a wide and wild place. Adventurous web surfers or those who occasionally click the wrong link through a momentary lapse of judgment can sometimes end up with a seemingly endless stream of totally incomprehensible spam in a foreign language. With some email programs, one way to deal with this is to create an email rule to search for common characters or pictograms that appear only in the foreign language, and filter spam based on their occurrence. It's a very effective method, and with Vista, an even better variation on this theme has been implemented. Windows Mail enables the user to block by Encoding List, the character set used in the email text. For example, if you have not yet had the opportunity to study Russian, yet somehow Russian spam has an affinity for your mailbox, you can remedy this international dilemma with a mouse click to exclude Cyrillic text.

INBOX PHISHING PROTECTION AND MORE

Although eliminating spam before it gets to the inbox goes a long way toward preventing phishing emails, Windows Mail has another layer of defense. The phishing filter that proved so useful in the PayPal email scam is not only used with Internet Explorer, but it also verifies email-embedded web links. Additionally, Windows Mail automatically blocks harmful attachments that are often used to install malware. Pictures that were once automatically downloaded and displayed now require that you choose to download and view them. This reduces the number of processes that malware writers can exploit and is in line with Vista's strategy to "reduce the attack surface."

> **TIP**
>
> If you need to put your email address on a public web page, instead of posting it in clear text that is readable by spammers, post a picture of it. The picture will be readable by humans, but most spambots aren't that sophisticated. And, don't create a "mailto:" hyperlink with your email address in it. Spammers eat those up like candy.

AVOIDING SPAMMERS' TRICKS

All these antispam tactics help, but spammers have hundreds or maybe thousands of tricks up their grimy sleeves to bypass filters. Still, there are plenty of simple things to do to limit exposure and reduce junk email in its various forms.

Some spammers appear repentantly courteous. That is, they have violated your inbox by being there uninvited, but now that they have your attention, please don't be offended because you can simply click this link to opt out of receiving any more spam from them. Honest.

Do not reply to spam that claims to provide an "opt out" link. Often, by clicking the link in an attempt to stop receiving spam, you are confirming that your email address is good, and your spam level likely will increase. In fact, it's a good idea to never respond to spam, especially to buy anything. Although it is possible some well-intentioned but ill-advised vendors are using spam to sell legitimate products, all purveyors of spam are suspect simply because of the insidious nature of the communication: unsolicited, unauthorized, unwelcome, and often illegal. Avoid spam like the plague it is. If you suspect an email message is spam, you're probably right. Don't opt out. Don't even open it; just delete it.

Read the terms of use and privacy policies when you register with a website, to make sure they will not sell or share your information. Often at the end of the form are preselected check boxes indicating that you'd love to receive email from them, their sponsors, their affiliates, and so on. Clicking those boxes is considered opting in and permits them to legally bombard you with spam. Many spammers disregard the law anyway, but it's never a good idea to give them carte blanche with your inbox.

The right way for an upstanding website to manage an email list is called "confirmed opt-in," and you've probably used it before. Good citizens of the Internet will not start sending email to you until they have confirmed, by receiving email from your email address, that you actually want it. Without such confirmation, anyone could type your email address into a hundred different Send Me Mail forms, some of which are perhaps distasteful, and every day you'd have an inbox full of junk. This is such an important premise that, in general, if it's not a confirmed opt-in, it might as well be spam.

Junk email can come from the most unlikely sources. Well-intentioned relatives bent on protecting their loved ones from syringes on movie seats, international kidney thieves, or cancer-causing agents in shampoo are responsible for spam that's hard to avoid because, although it might be tempting, you don't want to filter *everything* from them. If you are one of those who likes to be in close contact through email, sharing the trials and tribulations of life with your loved ones by forwarding electronic messages, there is help for you. Instead of forwarding something, consider writing an original heartfelt message to be treasured and appreciated. And if you must forward a tantalizing or tender tidbit, before others spend time reading the message, take a moment to search and make sure it's true. Whatever you do, never send chain mail; it will not bring good luck or take it away, but it will turn you into a spammer.

> **NOTE**
>
> Several Internet sites have evolved to fight electronic chain letters, spam, and especially urban legends that compel so many people to send massive amounts of ultimately groundless email. Snopes.com has emerged as an excellent source to determine whether an email is fact or fiction. Use it often. Your friends and relatives will thank you.

Tips from the Windows Pros: Take Action Against Email Abuse

So far, this chapter has taken the Aikido route to spam and fraud defense: avoidance and being "like water." Among our many techniques, we sidestep dangerous links, make email addresses slippery to spambots, and use identity management software to leave would-be keyloggers with a sieve-fisted find. These are useful defensive techniques, but sometimes a more offensive approach to vanquishing online foes is more effective and satisfying. With enough complaints on file, and if they haven't bought off an unscrupulous service provider, spammers can be identified and their "license to spam" revoked. Once discovered, phishing sites can be quickly put out of business. Many commercial Internet sites provide readily available tools to report suspicious activity. Ebay and PayPal request that you forward suspected fake emails to spoof@ebay.com or spoof@paypal.com respectively. They will quickly take appropriate action. Responsible sites display security or fraud-related links on the front page, so it's easy to find their preferred mode of communication. If you suspect a phishing scam, take a moment to find the right email address and report it. You may save someone else a lot of heartache, and will validate your own sleuthiness. If you stumble upon a suspected phishing site with Internet Explorer, you can click Report This Site in the Tools menu to aid other Phishing Filter users.

Reporting spam can be easy, too. Free email services used with a web browser often provide a "report spam" button that can automatically notify the provider to take action. If you prefer to use a separate email program, such as Windows Mail, there are a plethora of add-ons that can help report and eliminate most spam. Some of the most interesting and effective ones use collaborative networks. Like the free email services that have potentially millions of users, these add-ons are based on the premise that humans can filter spam better than any algorithm alone. When a number of users identify a particular message as spam, the other members of the network can be spared the trouble. It's a successful strategy used by companies like Cloudmark, and there are other successful strategies as the field continues to evolve to provide convenient, active ways to fight spam.

On the other hand, there are not-quite-so-convenient yet more active ways for those who desire to "get medieval" on spammers. With a little practice, it's not difficult to track down email headers using publicly available Internet resources. You can often identify the service provider whose network was used to send spam, and they can opt to shut down the spammer's Internet access if enough complaints are received. Additionally, the Federal Trade Commission encourages you to forward spam to spam@uce.gov. The FTC may not respond to individual complaints, but in true democratic fashion, they will tally the votes and go after the worst spammers.

PART VIII

Windows On the Move

37 Wireless Networking 1261

38 Hitting the Road 1279

39 Meetings, Conferencing, and Collaboration 1311

40 Remote Desktop 1329

41 Tablet PC Features 1355

CHAPTER 37

WIRELESS NETWORKING

In this chapter

Wireless Networking in Windows Vista   1262

Wireless Security Issues   1262

Joining a Wireless Network   1267

Ad Hoc Networks and Meetings   1271

Managing Wireless Network Connections   1271

Troubleshooting   1273

Tips from the Windows Pros: The Wireless Command Line   1277

Wireless Networking in Windows Vista

Wireless networks are everywhere. From home to work to just about everywhere on the road, it seems like you can fire up a wireless-capable device and get connected no matter where you are. Wireless networks are popular for several reasons, including low costs to get started and, more important, ease of configuration and use.

With the rapid growth of wireless networking has come evolving standards. The 802.11 series of standards was implemented in wireless hardware and software to ensure interoperability among vendors. However, that hasn't stopped wireless hardware vendors from extending their hardware with proprietary add-ons. One thing is certain: The standards that define wireless networking change rapidly. Although the upcoming 802.11*n* standard has not yet been ratified, it will be an important step in the evolution of wireless networking.

Microsoft recognized the popularity of wireless networks among its users. This recognition translates directly into a much improved and enhanced wireless networking experience in Windows Vista. Wireless networking is now part of the native networking stack in Windows: Drivers have been updated and improved, and tools such as the Network Diagnostics Framework help in troubleshooting when things go wrong. Microsoft has even taken steps to reduce some of the security problems inherent in wireless networking.

> **NOTE**
> This chapter shows you how to use wireless networks that have already been set up.

→ For information on creating a new wireless network for your home or office, **see** "Installing a Wireless Network" on **p. 635**. For information on using wireless networking with the Windows Meeting Space collaboration tool, see Chapter 39, "Meetings, Conferencing, and Collaboration."

Types of Wireless Networks

Most wireless networks use a wireless router, base station, or access point. These are called *infrastructure networks*; all communications on the network are between the computers and the access point. You can also tie a group of computers together without an access point, and this is called an *ad hoc network*. In this type of network the computers talk directly to each other. A common scenario where an ad hoc network is used is a group of business people connecting together at a conference table in order to share files and information.

Wireless Security Issues

Many of the same security issues surrounding radio communications in World War II affect today's wireless networking. In World War II, radio transmissions between military units and other military installations were routinely intercepted and used by the enemy. This led to advances in the areas of mathematics and cryptography, to better encrypt and protect those transmissions. However, even encrypting transmissions didn't prevent interception and eventual decryption.

Worse yet, arrogance about the security of the ciphers used to encrypt communications led to or assisted in those ciphers being broken. For example, during WWII, even when there was evidence that certain ciphers had been broken, they were still used. This is also the case for some of today's wireless networking ciphers, such as WEP, which we'll discuss shortly.

When something traverses the air, whether it is a radio transmission or data from a wireless-connected computer, it can be heard not only by the intended recipient, but also by anyone else who happens to be listening. It is helpful to keep this in mind when considering the security footprint of wireless networking. The reason that we wanted to begin this chapter on wireless networking with a sort of guided tour of its limitations and dangers is that we want you to be *very* sure to take advantage of the security features that Vista makes available to you.

The next couple of sections discuss what you might call the hairy details of wireless, so if you want you can skip ahead to the "Longer Is Better" section.

Plain Old Snooping

All the data that gets sent between your computer and the wireless access point is visible to anyone within range, just as a conversation can be heard by anyone within earshot of the parties conversing. On a wireless network that offers no encryption (frequently called an unsecured wireless network), everything that passes between your computer and the Internet or other connected computers can also be seen by someone else in range. Tools exist that can help the eavesdropper literally see what you see, including web pages and email. An eavesdropper on a wireless network can potentially see it all.

What can you do to secure a wireless network? Not too long ago, the answer was, not a lot. Today, the answer is, a little bit. The first thing—and, luckily for Windows Vista users, one of the easiest things—to do is enable encryption on the wireless network. Windows Vista encrypts wireless connections by default, and it will warn you if you connect to an unsecured wireless network.

Windows Vista offers several different encryption methods for wireless networks. Working with so many methods helps ensure compatibility between and among wireless networks and wireless hardware vendors. Of course, if you're setting up a new wireless network, as we discuss in Chapter 20, you'll want to be sure Vista uses the most powerful encryption scheme that's supported by your computers and your wireless networking hardware. However, there is no guarantee that the attacker won't attempt to decrypt the data or break the encryption key, both of which take resources in terms of time and computing power.

The bottom line is that wireless networking is not as secure as its wired counterpart. Even with encryption, it's possible to gain unauthorized access. However, using encryption is better than nothing at all.

Man in the Middle

Another security risk with wireless networks is known as man in the middle (MITM). An MITM attack occurs when an attacker spoofs an access point. The attacker discovers the identity of the real access point by listening to traffic on the network. The attacker then causes his or her equipment to act like the real access point, claiming its identity. When your computer attempts to connect to the access point, the attacker's access point claims to be the real access point, and suddenly all your traffic goes through the attacker's equipment, enabling him or her to see all your traffic.

Previous versions of Windows were susceptible to this type of attack because they broadcast the preferred network list every 60 seconds. An attacker running a rogue access point could then see the connection attempt and act like that access point, in hopes of getting the computer to connect.

Windows Vista makes MITM attacks more difficult. When broadcasting the preferred network list, Windows Vista also includes a fictitious wireless network name. The computer never really uses this name to connect to a wireless network; it is just created for the purposes of preventing MITM attacks. If an access point attempts to connect to this fictitiously named network, Windows Vista marks it as being a potential rogue access point. In this way, the chance of falling victim to an MITM attack is reduced with Windows Vista.

Wireless Security Keys

Security keys for wireless connections are created through varying processes, which depending on the type of key, can include an Initialization Vector (IV) along with shared keys. For the Wired Equivalent Privacy protocol (WEP), the encryption key along with the IV are combined and sent to a pseudo-random number generator to create a key. WEP uses the RC4 stream cipher. Due to security problems inherent in WEP, WiFi Protected Access (WPA) encryption was developed.

Like WEP, WPA uses the RC4 stream cipher. Unlike WEP, WPA uses the Temporal Key Integrity Protocol (TKIP). TKIP automatically changes the key used in order to make an active attack more difficult. It should be noted that an attacker could still capture the data and could potentially still decipher the key and thus decrypt the data. However, since TKIP changes the key, the attacker would only be able to decrypt a finite portion of data using the deciphered key. Therefore, a protocol that uses TKIP can be said to limit the amount of information that an attacker can gain from a single key.

The WPA2 wireless specification is the next generation of the WPA security specification. WPA2 is fully supported in Windows Vista and features the Advanced Encryption Standard (AES) in place of the RC4 cipher for encryption.

Longer is Better

Besides depending on the encryption method (WPA2, WPA, WEP), the strength of wireless encryption is also dependent on the length of the private key that you select when you set up the network. In general for a given encryption scheme, the more binary bits in the key, the stronger the protection. Strength of an encryption scheme reflects in the amount of work, time, and resources an attacker needs to use in order to break or decipher the encrypted data. In other words, by definition, a stronger encryption mechanism is one that takes more effort for an attacker to break than a weaker scheme.

The bottom line is this: for wireless networks, WPA2 is stronger then WPA, and WPA is stronger than WEP. And for any of these encryption methods, the longer the key, the greater the security.

An encryption key is specified as a hexadecimal number (a number composed of the digits 0 through 9 plus the letters A through F), or as a *passphrase*, which is a word or phrase using any letters or symbols. If you use the passphrase method, Windows mangles the passphrase characters to construct a somewhat longer hexadecimal key. Table 37.1 lists the key lengths that may be selected in Windows Vista, along with the lengths of the corresponding hexadecimal or passphrase.

> **NOTE**
>
> Windows Vista will let you connect to an *existing* wireless network that uses 40-bit WEP security, but the wireless network setup wizard will not let you create a *new* network with 40-bit WEP security.

For example, to specify a 108-bit key, you could enter 13 ASCII (text) characters like this: `abnormalities` or a 26-digit hexadecimal number like this: `3F985B1C89E00CDE1234434ED4`. You must use the same key on all of your computers and your wireless router or access point, if you have one.

> **NOTE**
>
> Despite its irritating length, it's usually better to use the hexadecimal format if you are inventing a wireless key for your network. The reason is that the hexadecimal format specifies the actual key, where the passphrase format has to be converted by some software scheme into a hexadecimal key, and not every wireless device and operating system uses the same scheme. For example, the passphrase `abnormalities` might turn into one key on a Linksys router, and a different key on Windows Vista. Thus, you could type the same passphrase into your router and into Windows, and the network would not work. To be safe, use a hexadecimal key.

If you are joining an existing wireless network, you have to use the network key that was set by whomever set up that network. If you are creating a new network, use the strongest encryption method and the longest key that is supported by *all* of the devices and computers on your network. This means that if you have even one computer that doesn't support WPA, you need to use WEP, and if you have even one computer that doesn't support 256-bit keys, you have to use a 128-bit key. If you have a router, access point, or network adapter that doesn't support WPA, it's worth checking to see if you can update its internal software (firmware) or drivers to support this stronger encryption method.

> **NOTE**
>
> Support for WPA2 can be added to Windows XP through the use of a hotfix. Search for KB893397 in Microsoft's Knowledge Base for more information on this patch for Windows XP.

Table 37.1 WEP/WPA Key Formats

Encryption Strength	PassPhrase/Key Format
40 bit (also called 64 bit) WEP	5 ASCII characters (any character) or 10 hexadecimal digits (0–9, A–F)
104 bit (also called 128 bit) WEP	13 ASCII characters or 26 hexadecimal digits
256-bit WPA or WPA2	8-63 ASCII characters or 64 hexadecimal digits

Take Care When You Share

Because wireless networking involves just another network connection type for Windows, file and printer sharing is also available. This is a blessing and a curse. Wireless users can work with your shared files and folders just as if you were connected to a wired network. However, you must take special care when connecting at a public location or when using an unsecured, unencrypted wireless network because everyone else can see those same files and folders. At the very least, you should have Password Protected Sharing enabled when using a wireless connection in a public location; the paranoid among us also entirely disable sharing when connecting at a public location.

Windows Vista's Network Location feature helps to keep track of the relative safety of various networks to which your computer connects and enables and disables services based on the type of network. These locations include a Domain network, a Public network, and a Private network. In more detail, the standard types are as follows:

- **Public**—A network where other computers can't be trusted and your own network traffic has not been secured with encryption. This could be the Internet at large, or any network where other computers that share the same connection should not be trusted. The Public network location should be selected for any network link that is directly connected to the Internet, a network in a café, airport, university or other public location, or a home or office that you are visiting. When you designate a network as a Public network, Windows file and printer sharing is blocked to protect your computer.

- **Private**—A network that is trusted to be secure. If the network has an Internet connection, you know it to be protected by a firewall or a connection sharing router. You trust the users and the other computers on the network to access files and printers shared by your computer (with or without a password, depending on the Password Protected Sharing setting in the Network and Sharing Center window). Examples of Private networks are home or business networks managed by you or someone you trust.

- **Domain**—A network that is managed by one or more computers running a Windows Server operating system. This is a trusted network, and the security of the network and its member computers is managed by network administrators.

Select the appropriate Network Location when you first connect to a given network. You can view the current setting through the Network and Sharing Center. On Domain networks, this location is automatically set but it can be changed for other types of networks through the Network and Sharing Center.

Several settings that affect the security of the computer are changed automatically by Windows Vista when you connect to these various types of networks. On Domain networks, Group Policy configures the settings for Network Discovery and File and Printer Sharing alike. When you connect to a Public network, Windows disables Network Discovery File and Printer Sharing. When you connect to a Private network, Network Discovery is enabled but File and Printer Sharing is still disabled by default.

After connecting, you can change these default settings, but you really should *not* enable File and Printer Sharing when you're connected to a network that might contain computers that are unknown to you or are not under your control.

CAUTION
> Be sure to select the appropriate Network Location when Windows prompts you after you've connected to a new network. If in doubt, select Public. You can always change it to a less restrictive setting later if you find that you can't use the network services you need.

JOINING A WIRELESS NETWORK

Windows Vista makes configuring wireless connections easier than ever. A new wizard-driven interface is included with Windows Vista to help with the configuration. The wizard automatically selects many secure defaults, which helps keep the connections more secure without much effort on your part.

This section shows you how to connect to wireless networks in some common—but distinctly different—scenarios.

IN THE CORPORATE ENVIRONMENT

Wireless networks in a business setting are frequently configured using automated means. For large enterprises, your computer will be preloaded with a certificate, a sort of digital fingerprint that identifies your computer as being authorized to use the corporate network, and the wireless network will be configured for you. Wireless network clients can now be configured via Group Policy (Group Policy is short for "By other people, and there's nothing you can do about it") and through the command line by using new `netsh` commands for wireless.

AT HOME OR THE SMALL OFFICE

A wireless network at home or in a small office usually doesn't have the same configuration needs as in a large enterprise setting, and home users and small offices usually don't have domain controllers and Group Policy infrastructures at their disposal. Wireless network configuration is usually done manually in these environments, first by purchasing and obtaining an access point, then by configuring that access point, and finally by configuring one or more wireless client computers to connect to the wireless network.

Chapter 37 Wireless Networking

> **TIP**
> Always be sure to change the default passwords on any access points or routers that you purchase. One of the most common attack vectors is through the use of default passwords that were left on devices. Even if it means writing the password on a piece of paper and taping it to the bottom of the device, this is still more secure than leaving the default password in place.

When you first plug a Windows-compatible wireless adapter into the computer (or if your computer has an adapter built in), you can begin the process of connecting to a wireless network. A good place to start is the Network and Sharing Center. To open the Network and Sharing Center, click on the Start button and then right-click on Network and select Properties. This opens the Network and Sharing Center, shown in Figure 37.1.

Figure 37.1
The Network and Sharing Center is used to begin configuring wireless settings.

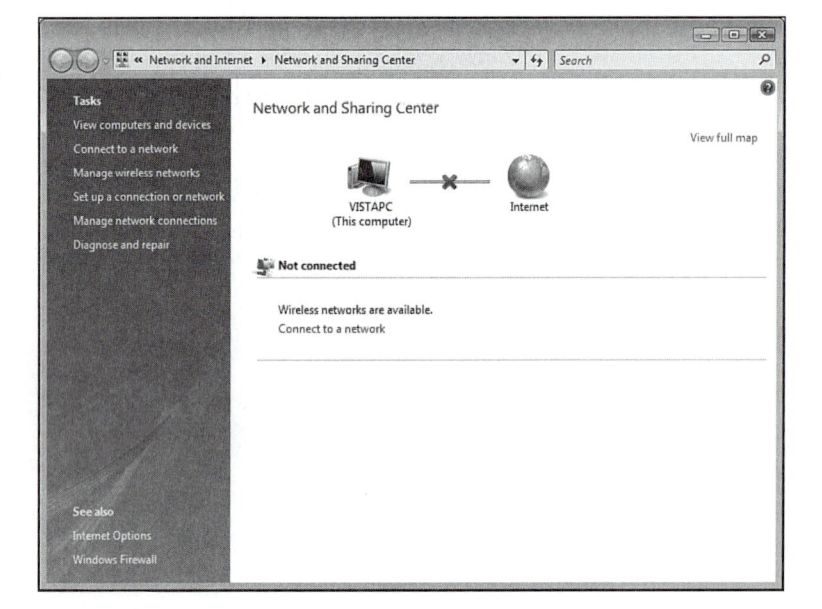

If Windows Vista was capable of finding wireless networks in range, you'll see a message indicating that wireless networks are available. To begin the process of connecting, click on Connect to a Network. This invokes the Connect to a Network dialog, shown in Figure 37.2. You will then see a list of available networks. In the case of Figure 37.2, only one network is available, HOUSE, so that's the one I selected.

Highlight the network that you want to connect to and click on Connect. This connects to the network, possibly prompting you for the network's security key. This will be a hexadecimal number or passphrase in one of the formats described earlier in Table 37.1.

> **TIP**
> If you want to view or change the settings, right-click on the wireless network and select Properties instead of clicking Connect.

Figure 37.2
Beginning the process of connecting by selecting a network.

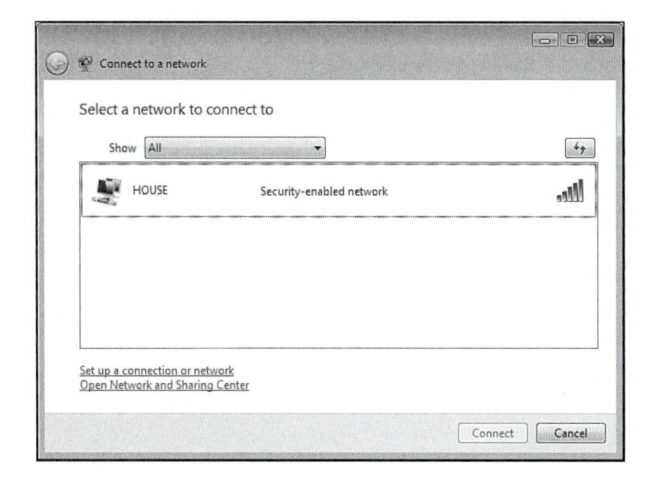

When the connection has been made, you'll see confirmation that the setup was successful, similar to Figure 37.3.

Figure 37.3
A successful connection to a wireless network.

When you're connected, you can configure file and printer sharing from the Network and Sharing Center. For more information on sharing files and folders, see Chapter 23, "Using a Windows Network."

IN SOMEONE ELSE'S OFFICE

When you're away from home or the home office, you might find yourself connecting to another person's wireless network. A common scenario is business workers going to another office and needing to access files on the network, or people on that network needing to access files on your computer.

When connecting to a different network, it's important to make sure that you're not inadvertently sharing files and folders that you don't want to share. Refer to Chapter 23 for additional information on sharing files safely. You should keep these things in mind when connecting to another wireless network:

- If the people at the new network won't need to access files that are located on your computer, disable file sharing entirely through the Network and Sharing Center. You can enable it again when you return to your network.
- If you need to share files from your computer, make sure that Password Protected Sharing is enabled. You can also accomplish this from the Network and Sharing Center.

    1. Open the Network and Sharing Center by clicking on Start, right-clicking on Network, and selecting Properties.
    2. Click on Password Protected Sharing and then click on Turn on Password Protected Sharing.

Connecting to another network involves the same process as configuring your first network in Windows Vista. Begin at the Network and Sharing Center (refer to the previous section to find out how to get to the Network and Sharing Center). Within the Tasks pane, choose Connect to a Network; you'll see a list of available wireless networks in range. Simply highlight the new network and click Connect.

> **TIP**
> You can also right-click on the Network icon in the taskbar and select Connect to a Network.

AT A PUBLIC HOT SPOT

Public wireless network hot spots are quite helpful when you're on the road and need to check email, get travel information, or just surf the Web. Public hot spots can also be places for would-be attackers to find easy victims. On open, unsecured public hot spots, it's quite common to have eavesdroppers listening to other people's wireless traffic. On networks secured with encryption, it's still possible for an eavesdropper to listen to traffic after the encryption key has been decrypted.

Another path for attack at a public hot spot is through files that client computers accidentally share. Before connecting to a public hot spot, you should either disable file sharing entirely or enable Password Protected Sharing; both can be configured in the Network and Sharing Center.

1. Open the Network and Sharing Center by clicking on Start, right-clicking on Network, and selecting Properties.
2. Click on File Sharing if you need to disable it or Password Protected Sharing if you need to enable it.

Ad Hoc Networks and Meetings

Earlier in the chapter, I discussed using a wireless network's "infrastructure" mode, which essentially ties computers with wireless adapters into a wired network that connects to other computers and to the Internet using a base station called an access point or a wireless router.

Another use of wireless networking, called ad hoc networking, involves two or more computers with wireless connections that can communicate directly with each other without an access point or router. Windows Vista's Windows Meeting Space features ad hoc networking, allowing people to use their wireless connections to collaborate and share files in the context of a meeting room. For more information on Windows Meeting Space, see Chapter 39.

Managing Wireless Network Connections

If you travel and connect to different networks, you will soon collect a list of several preferred (preconfigured) networks. To view the list of available networks, double-click the wireless connection icon in the task tray and select Connect or Disconnect. The Connect to a Network dialog is shown, an example of which can be seen in Figure 37.2.

When Windows is not currently connected to any wireless network, Windows scans through this list of preferred networks in order and automatically connects to the first one that is in range. In most cases, you will only be within range of one of the networks you want to use, and this system will work without any adjustments. Windows will automatically connect to a network that you have previously selected, and will ignore any other networks that are in range.

Switching Between Wireless Networks

If you find that your computer is in range of more than one of your preferred networks, you may have to manually instruct Windows as to which one you wish to use, because given a 50/50 chance of picking the wrong one, 9 times out of 10 it will. One way to do this is to view the list of available networks by double-clicking the Wireless Connection icon in the Notification Area (or clicking View Wireless Networks on the Wireless Networks Properties page).

If you really don't want Windows to connect to the original network, right-click on the Wireless Connection icon in the Notification Area and select Disconnect From and select the current network. Then, select the desired network and click Connect.

This has a permanent side effect; from this point on, Windows will not automatically connect to the original network when it becomes available. To use the original network in the future, you'll have to manually select it in this list and click Connect.

To switch networks without disabling the original one, don't use the Disconnect From function; just select the desired network and click Connect.

Advanced Wireless Network Settings

In this section, I'll list some of the more advanced wireless network configuration options. These can come in handy if you work with crowded or unconventional wireless network situations.

Setting Preferred Network Order

If you work in a place where multiple preferred networks are available and find that Windows is consistently connecting to the wrong network, you can change the ordering of the preferred network list. While viewing the available network list (see Figure 37.2), select the network you wish to use most often, and click Move Up to raise it above the less commonly used network(s).

You can also delete a network from the list if you don't plan on using it again in the future.

Selecting Automatic or Manual Connections

If you work in an area that has more than one wireless network that you actually do use, you can leave the less commonly used networks in the preferred network list and indicate that Windows is just not to connect to them automatically. To do this, double-click the wireless connection icon in the task tray and select the Network and Sharing Center. Click on the Manage Wireless Networks in the Tasks pane, right-click on the network you'd like to modify, and select Properties. This brings up the Wireless Networks dialog shown in Figure 37.4. Uncheck the Connect Automatically When This Network Is in Range check box.

Figure 37.4
The Wireless Connection Properties Dialog Checking the status of the wireless network.

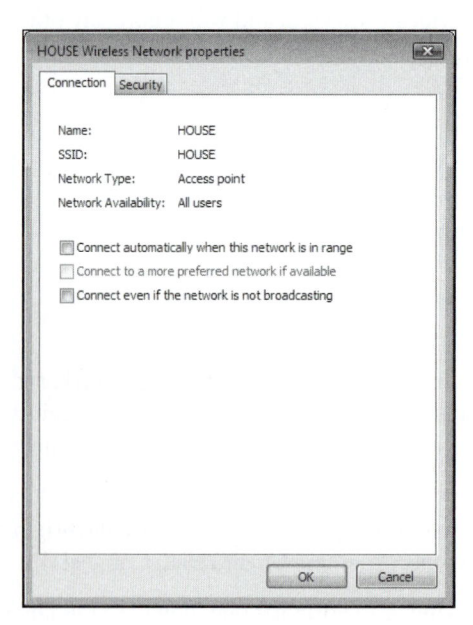

Now, Windows will not connect to this network unless you deliberately select it from the list of available networks and click Connect.

ADDING A NETWORK MANUALLY

A network that does not broadcast its network name (SSID) will not appear in the list of available networks. To connect to such a network, you must enter its connection information manually by following these steps:

1. Bring up the Wireless Connection Properties dialog by double-clicking the Wireless Connection icon in the Notification Area and clicking Connect or Disconnect.
2. Click the Setup a Connection or Network link, then select Manually Connect to a Wireless Network and click Next.
3. Enter the network name (SSID).
4. If the network is unencrypted, change the Data Encryption setting to Disabled, click OK, and you're finished.
5. If the network is encrypted, in most cases you will have to enter the encryption key. Then click OK.

The network will now appear in the list of available networks when it is in range.

CONNECTING TO MANUALLY CREATED AD HOC NETWORKS

By default, Windows will connect to either infrastructure or ad hoc networks but assumes that networks you define manually are infrastructure networks.

To connect to an ad hoc network, open the Network and Sharing Center by double-clicking on the wireless network icon in the Notification Area and selecting Network and Sharing Center. Click on Manage Wireless Networks and then click Add. Select Create an Ad Hoc Network.

TROUBLESHOOTING

One of the areas in which Windows Vista shows most improvement is troubleshooting. This is especially true for wireless networking. With the help of the Network Diagnostics Framework, Windows attempts to diagnose and correct many common issues with wireless networking. The Windows Vista mantra is to present options instead of errors.

WINDOWS IS UNABLE TO FIND ANY NETWORKS

The list of available wireless networks is empty, and the Refresh List command doesn't help.

With wireless communication, there is a chance that your computer isn't within range of a wireless access point. I've been in hotel rooms where the wireless signal is almost nonexistent in one room but excellent in a nearby room. Radio interference is just one of the causes of weak or no signal when connecting to a wireless network. Unfortunately, there is little that can be done about this problem aside from moving closer to the access point or, in the case of interference, removing the source of the interference.

When you start the Connect to a Network Wizard, and Windows can't find any networks in range, you can use a wizard to help in the troubleshooting process. From the Connect to a Network dialog box, clicking on Diagnose Why Windows Can't Find Any Networks starts the network troubleshooter, shown in Figure 37.5. This wizard attempts to diagnose the problem and then presents you with options for solving the problem.

→ We talk about the Network Diagnostics tool in more detail in Chapter 24, "Troubleshooting Your Network."

Figure 37.5
The Windows Network Diagnostics is troubleshooting a wireless connection problem.

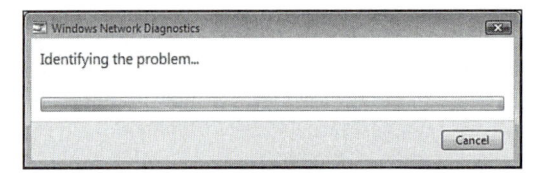

Closely related to Windows not being able to find any networks is a lossy network or one in which the signal is weak. This situation can be extremely frustrating because the connection goes up and down unexpectedly.

Windows Vista shows the signal strength of the various in-range networks by clicking on the Connect to a Network link within the Network and Sharing Center. Figure 37.6 shows a wireless network with excellent signal strength, as depicted by the five vertical green bars toward the right of the network listing.

Figure 37.6
Examining signal strength for a wireless network.

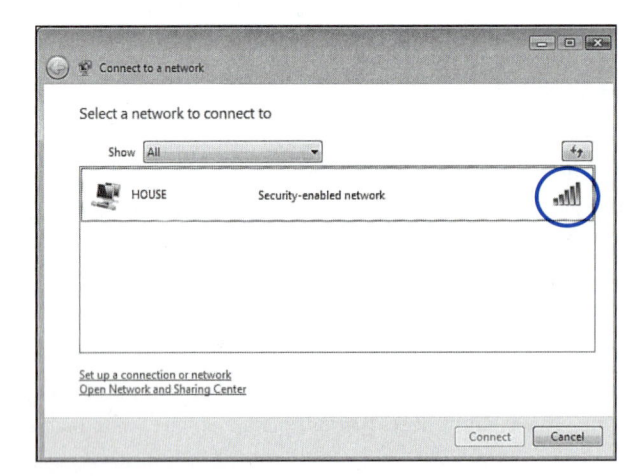

Unable to Connect to Wireless Network

When I attempt to connect to a wireless network, I am never asked to enter a key, or the connection never completes.

For several reasons, you might not be able to connect to a wireless network even though Windows says that the network is otherwise in range and available. With anything from an incorrectly typed encryption key to problems with the wireless access point or DHCP server, the range of problems that can arise when connecting to a wireless network seems limitless.

Windows Vista uses the Windows Network Diagnostics Framework to assist in correcting problems with networks—and not just those of the wireless variety. When a wireless connection can't be made, Windows keeps attempting to connect while informing you that the process seems to be taking longer than expected, as shown in Figure 37.7.

Figure 37.7
Attempting to connect to a wireless network.

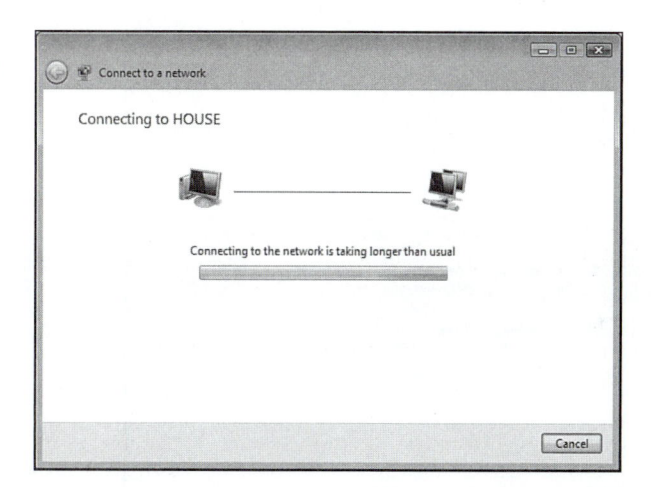

If Windows cannot connect, a dialog box appears, informing you of the status. This dialog box, shown in Figure 37.8, gives you the opportunity to diagnose the problem. If you choose to have Windows diagnose the problem, the Network Diagnostics Framework is invoked (see Figure 37.5 for an example).

In some cases, you are presented with several options to help solve the problem. Figure 37.9 shows an example of this scenario.

Figure 37.8
An unsuccessful attempt to connect to a network.

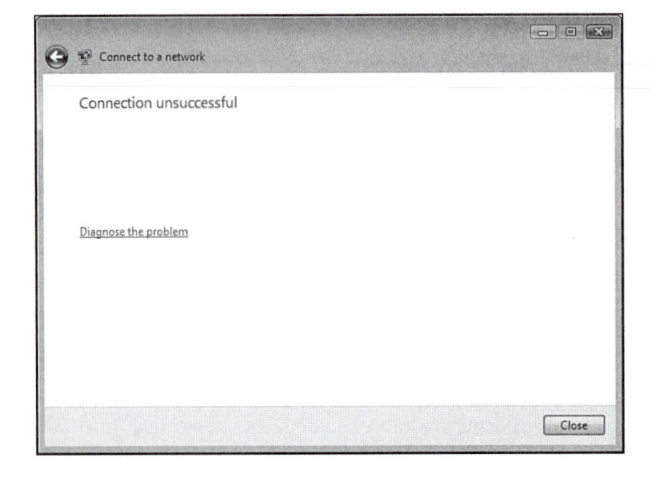

Figure 37.9
The Network Diagnostics Framework dialog box presenting options for solving the connectivity issue.

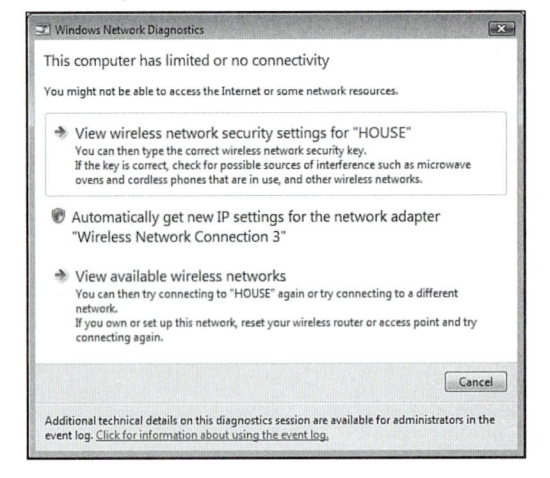

In this case, I suspect that the WEP key is incorrect. Therefore, I chose the top option to examine the security settings for the network named HOUSE. This, in turn, opens the Security tab of the Wireless Properties dialog box for this network, as shown in Figure 37.10.

I changed the encryption key for this network and clicked OK. The Diagnostics Framework continued after this point, as illustrated by Figure 37.11.

I chose the Click Here When You Are Done So That Windows Can Check If the Problem Is Resolved option because I believed I'd solved the problem. Windows successfully connected to the network.

> **NOTE**
>
> If the Network Diagnostics Framework still cannot correct the problem, you are given the option of connecting manually to the network. This step is sometimes necessary for the connection to apparently be reinitialized before it is successful.

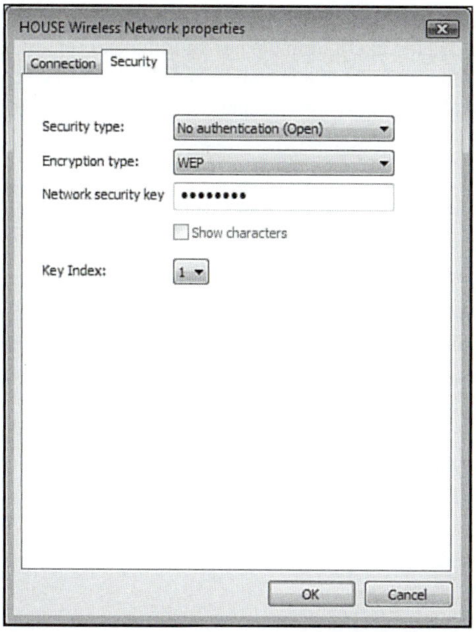

Figure 37.10
Viewing the network properties to set the encryption key.

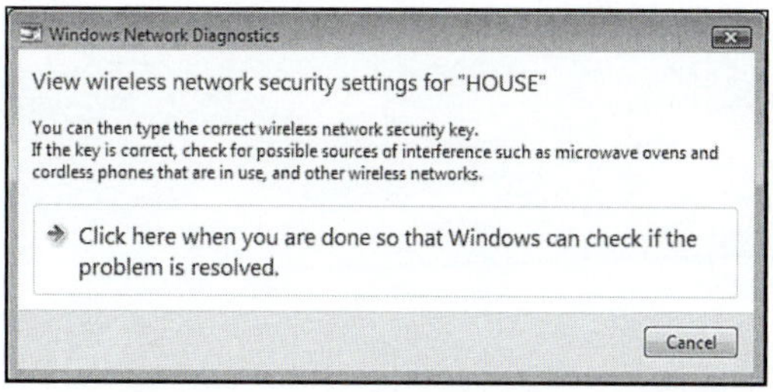

Figure 37.11
Continuing the Network Diagnostics.

Tips from the Windows Pros: The Wireless Command Line

Microsoft has learned a lot from its competitors, as evidenced by the effort to include command-line utilities with Windows Vista (and other forthcoming versions of Windows). The netsh command-line utilities are available for managing wireless connections in Windows Vista. Help desk staff can use these powerful tools to troubleshoot wireless connectivity issues. IT administrators also use the command-line tools to quickly provision wireless clients or script changes within an enterprise. However, the command-line tools aren't just limited to enterprise use; advanced home users can benefit from them, too.

The first step in using the command-line tools is to get to a command prompt within Windows Vista. Click on Start, type **cmd** in the Start Search box, and press Enter. This brings up a command prompt. You can invoke the netsh command line by simply typing netsh in a command prompt window. You're then placed in the netsh command context.

> **TIP**
>
> Type `exit` at any time to exit from the `netsh` command context or from the command line. You can also type `help` at any time from within the `netsh` command context to see help on what commands are available.

From within the `netsh` command context, type **wlan** to be placed into the `netsh wlan` context. Typing **help** from within the `netsh wlan` context shows the options that are available within this context, including add, connect, delete, disconnect, dump, export, set, and show. IT administrators can use export to save a known-good configuration, which can then be imported onto another computer. For this example, typing **show networks** shows the available networks. You can also use connect, disconnect, dump, set and several additional parameters from within the `netsh wlan` tools.

Experiment with the `netsh` tools; they can be helpful not only for wireless connections, but also for all other networking settings in Windows Vista.

CHAPTER 38

HITTING THE ROAD

In this chapter

Windows Unplugged: Mobile and Remote Computing   1280

Managing Mobile Computers   1280

VPN and Dial-Up Networking   1286

Incoming VPN and Dial-Up Access   1297

Offline Folders   1301

Multiple LAN Connections   1308

Troubleshooting   1308

Tips from the Windows Pros: Manually Adding Routing Information   1309

Windows Unplugged: Mobile and Remote Computing

Some people predict that some day, a global Internet will cover every inch of the Earth's surface, giving us an always-on, always-available stream of data they call the "Evernet." We're not quite there yet, but today the Internet is available in pretty much any city you might visit, and it has become easy to stay in touch with home while you're traveling.

Windows Vista supports you when you're away from home or the office with some pretty spiffy portability and networking features, including these features that are covered in other chapters:

- Wireless networking support lets Vista stay connected when you're on the go. This was covered in Chapter 37, "Wireless Networking."
- Vista makes it easier to use a portable or laptop computer to make business or school presentations. Presentations are covered in Chapter 39, "Meetings, Conferencing, and Collaboration."
- Vista has a nifty Remote Desktop feature that lets you use your own computer from somewhere else, over the Internet. This is covered in Chapter 40, "Remote Desktop."

This chapter covers several other Vista features, which are mostly related to mobile (portable, laptop, notebook, or tablet) computers:

- For laptops, the Windows Mobility Center puts a bunch of important settings in one window so you can manage your computer's display, power consumption, and networking features.
- Dial-up and VPN networking let you access a remote network when you're traveling, and you can even set up remote access to your own home or office network.
- Offline Folders let you automatically keep up-to-date personal copies of files that are stored on network folders, so you really can "take it with you."

Let's start with the Mobility Center.

Managing Mobile Computers

Mobile computers (which I also call laptops, notebooks, or portables) are no longer an expensive perk provided only to jet-setting executives. They're now standard equipment for most people who work at least part time out of their office, and consumers now buy more portable computers than desktops for home and personal use. Consequently, portables have become powerful and inexpensive, and support for their special needs by Windows has grown considerably.

Managing Mobile Computers 1281

Windows Mobility Center

If you have a mobile computer (that is, a notebook, pen, portable, tablet, or laptop computer), you'll find that Windows Vista provides a tool called the Windows Mobility Center and a special control panel that desktop computers don't have. To open the Mobility Center, click Start, All Programs, Accessories, Windows Mobility Center. It's shown in Figure 38.1.

Figure 38.1
The Windows Mobility Center is found in the Accessories menu.

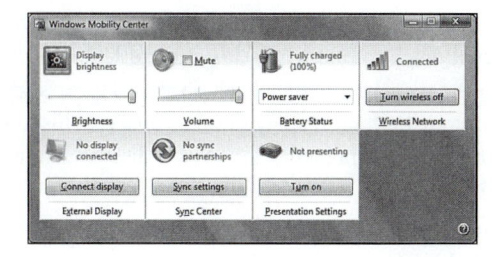

> **TIP**
>
> If you like using the Mobility Center, drag its shortcut from the Start Menu to the Quick Launch Toolbar or to the upper part of the Start Menu so that it is easily accessible. You can also bring it up by typing **mblctr** into the Search box on the Start menu..

The Mobility Center is designed to bring together in one window most of the settings that you'll want to change while using your computer remotely. The settings pertain mostly to power management, so you can make your laptop's battery last as long as possible, and display management, because many people use their laptops to make business and school presentations. Your computer's Mobility Center may display some or all of the following controls:

- **Brightness**—The slider lets you increase or decrease your screen's backlight brightness. A lower brightness setting should make your computer run longer on its battery charge. Windows remembers separate brightness settings for battery and AC-powered operation, stores them as part of a power profile, and resets the brightness when the power status changes. You can fine-tune the setting with this control.

- **Volume**—The slider controls your computer's speaker volume and the Mute check box lets you instantly shut the sound off. This may be useful, for example, if you're in a meeting and someone keeps sending you noisy instant message pop-ups.

- **Battery Status**—The icon shows you whether you are running on AC or battery-only power. (The power plug in the icon shown in Figure 38.1 indicates that the computer is on AC power.) The battery icon and the text tell you the battery's charge level. The drop-down list lets you select a power profile. Power profiles let you choose a balance between lower power consumption and greater performance. We'll discuss Power Profiles in more detail in the next section, "Getting the Most Out of Your Battery."

- **Wireless Network**—The icon shows whether you have an active wireless network connection, and the button can enable or disable your computer's wireless adapter to conserve power or gain privacy. If your laptop has a physical switch that turns the wireless adapter on and off, it's likely that both the switch and this setting have to be turned on for the wireless adapter to work.

- **Screen Rotation**—On tablet PCs, this control lets you switch the display between portrait (taller than wide) and landscape (wider than tall) orientation. Generally, in portrait orientation it's easier to read documents, and in landscape it's easier to watch movies.

- **External Display**—When an external display monitor or projector has been connected to your computer's external display connector, this control lets you choose to turn the external display off, have the display mirror what's on your laptop's screen, or treat the display as an extension of your built-in display desktop space. This lets you control what attendees see when you're making a presentation. We'll discuss External Display in more detail in Chapter 39.

- **Sync Center**—The Sync Center is used to copy files to or from an external device like a Windows Mobile handheld device, or to update copies of network server files that you've obtained using the Offline Files feature. We'll discuss Sync Center later in this chapter, under "Offline Folders."

- **Presentation Settings**—When you turn Presentation Settings on, Windows suppresses some behaviors that could disrupt your presentation. We'll discuss Presentation settings in Chapter 39.

> **NOTE**
>
> Your computer manufacturer may have added additional controls not listed here.

In addition to the Windows Mobility Center, mobile computers have an extra Control Panel section titled Mobile PC. If you click Mobile PC in the Control Panel, the page shown in Figure 38.2 appears.

Figure 38.2
The Mobile PC Control Panel page is available only on portable computers.

Many of the functions on this Control Panel are also found on the Windows Mobility Center. Some of the additional settings that you may want to remember are as follows:

- **Power Options**—Lets you specify the exact settings to use in each of the three power profile selections. We'll discuss this in the next section.

    (The Change Battery Settings and Change When the Computer Sleeps items lead to the same settings.)

- **The Change What the Power Buttons Do**, under Power Options—This lets you choose whether the computer goes into sleep mode, hibernate mode, or completely shuts down when you press your portable computer's power button or close its lid while it's running.

    (The Change What Closing the Lid Does item leads to the same settings.)

- **Change Settings Before Giving a Presentation**, under Personalization—Lets you specify types of interruptions that you want to prevent during presentations. This will be discussed in more detail in Chapter 39.

GETTING THE MOST OUT OF YOUR BATTERY

Portable computers seem like a great idea until you actually try to port one. The problem is that we've gotten used to blazing-fast processor speeds, mind-bending graphical effects, and heaps of memory in our desktop computers, and we demand the same performance from our laptops. The problem is that all that speed and glory has to be purchased with electrical power—lots and lots of it. A high-end desktop computer can consume a sustained 500 watts of power, which is a *lot* to demand of a battery small enough to fit in your pocket, light enough to carry over your shoulder and, while we're at it, capable of keeping this up long enough to watch all of *Gone With The Wind* on a transcontinental flight.

Keeping laptop power requirements at manageable levels while providing the performance we demand is no easy feat, and laptop makers and chip makers have invested an amazing amount of effort and money into making today's laptops a reality. Improved battery technology is a part of it, but the biggest part of the picture is very careful attention to power management. While running on battery power, a laptop has to carefully consider how to dole out its limited energy allotment.

The central processor unit (CPU) chip and graphical processor unit (GPU) chip can be the two biggest energy guzzlers in a computer, but in most cases, they spend little of their time actually working. For example, as I type this chapter, my brain may be "processing" pretty much constantly, but my computer's CPU takes less than a millisecond to react to each keystroke and decide how to change the display, and the GPU takes less than a millisecond to move the pixels around and display each added character. To them, and probably to you, too, if you were here watching, this book-writing business is about as exciting as watching ice melt. Thus, they may be occupied with useful work much less than 0.1% of the time. Laptop processors take advantage of the relatively long lulls by slowing their processing speed or *clock speed* way down between bursts of activity, and this significantly reduces power consumption.

Additionally, laptops can conserve energy by dimming the backlight lamp that illuminates the display, and by turning off hardware devices like the disk drive, DVD or CD drive, network adapter, and modem when they are not actively being used—even the devices' interface electronics can be shut down.

Of course, when you're watching a movie (which requires a lot of processor effort to decode the DVD's data into millions of pixels per second) or performing heavy-duty calculations, power consumption can go way up.

On Windows Vista, you can adjust how Windows manages hardware power consumption, and how fast the processor is allowed to run, by creating power profiles, which are collections of settings that can be applied in different situations. Windows Vista allows you to adjust the settings for three default profiles:

- **Power Saver**—Select this profile when you want to extend the battery life as long as possible, even if it noticeably slows the processor and eliminates some graphical effects.
- **High Performance**— Select this profile when you want maximum speed, or when your computer is running on AC power.
- **Balanced**—Select this profile to strike a fair balance between power savings and performance.

To view the power profiles, click Start, Control Panel, Mobile PC, Power Options (or Control Panel, Hardware and Sound, Power Options). This will display the Select a Power Plan screen, which lets you select the profile you want to use at any given time. (The Windows Mobility Center also lets you select a power profile.)

> **NOTE**
>
> If you have a scenario that's begging for its own profile, you can add a new one to this list. To do so, view the Power Options control panel and click Create a Power Plan in the left pane.

To select what settings are put into effect by each profile, click the phrase Change Plan Settings under a profile name. This displays the window shown in Figure 38.3. Here, you can select how long Windows should wait before darkening the screen and putting the computer to sleep (suspend mode) when idle, under AC power, and battery power.

If you rarely stop while you are actually working, but tend to leave for a while when you do stop, you might gain additional battery life by reducing the time before turning off the display or shutting down when on battery power. Dimming the display can help, too, if you're not working outdoors.

To really change the speed versus power compromise, click Change Advanced Power Settings to get the dialog shown in Figure 38.4. Here, you can change quite a number of power-related delays and rates. Each setting has two values: one to use when on AC power, and another to use on battery power.

Figure 38.3
Click Change Advanced Power Settings to select a compromise of speed versus power consumption.

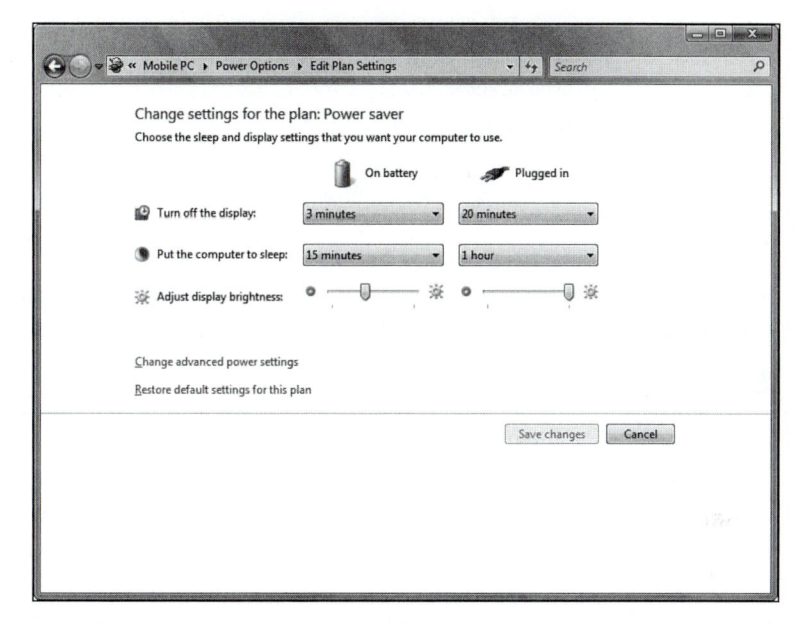

Figure 38.4
The Power Options Advanced Settings dialog box lets you control speed and power in detail.

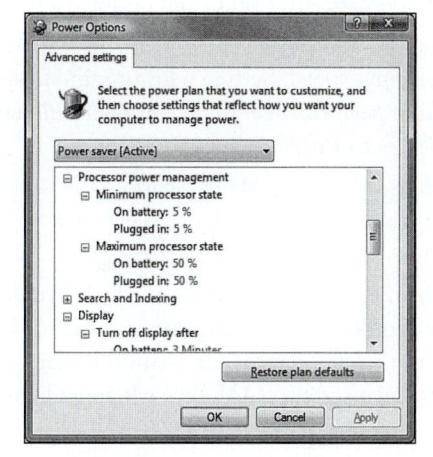

> **TIP**
>
> The default settings should be adequate. But, if you'd like to get maximum time on battery power while getting full performance on AC power, select the Power Saver plan, and make these changes:
>
> Wireless Adapter Settings, Power Saving Mode
>   Plugged in: Maximum performance
>
> PCI Express, Link State Power Management
>   Plugged in: Off
>
> Processor Power Management, Minimum Processor State
>   Plugged in: 50%

continues

continued

> Processor Power Management, Maximum Processor State
>   Plugged in: 100%
>
> Display, Adaptive Display
>   Plugged in: Off
>
> Save the changes to the profile, and select Power Saver as your active power profile.

If you really do love tweaking, you might want to look at some of the more interesting advanced settings:

- **Hard Disk**—Set the time that the disk is allowed to spin after being used. The default time on battery is 3 minutes. If your usage pattern usually spins the disk up right after it shuts down, you might increase this time.
- **Wireless Adapter Settings**—You can choose any of four settings, from Maximum Performance to Maximum Power Saving (and presumably slower and less reliable data transfer). If your wireless access point is nearby, Maximum Power Saving might help extend battery life.
- **Sleep**—Hybrid sleep is a mode where Windows will wake the computer up after a certain time in sleep mode (the Hibernate After time) and perform a full hibernate.
- **Processor Power Management**—You can set the lowest and highest processor states (speeds), in terms of % of maximum speed. Setting a low minimum speed increases battery life without costing much in performance. Reducing the maximum speed also helps battery life, but also takes a bite out of performance.
- **Multimedia Settings**—If you use Windows Media Sharing, this setting can prevent Windows from going to sleep while it's sharing media. Sleep cuts off your remote players.
- **Battery**—You can select the battery percentage levels at which Windows takes action to warn you about power loss or shutdown, and what actions to take at low and critically low power levels. You should not select Sleep as the Critical Battery Action, because Windows might not be able to keep system RAM alive when the battery level falls even further.

VPN and Dial-Up Networking

Windows can connect to a remote Windows network via a modem or via a protected connection that's routed through the Internet called a Virtual Private Network (VPN). Using these services, all file sharing, printing, and directory services are available just as if you were directly connected (albeit much slower in some cases). Just connect, open shared folders, transfer files, and email as if you were there, and then disconnect when you're finished.

The receiving end of VPN and Dial-Up Networking is usually handled by the Remote Access Services (RAS) provided by Windows 200x/NT4 Server or third-party remote connection devices manufactured by networking companies such as Cisco and Lucent. But

Windows Vista and XP Professional come with a stripped-down version of RAS so you can set up your own Windows computer to receive a single incoming modem connection. You can use this, for example, to get access to your office computer and LAN from home, provided that your company's security policies permit this.

I'll discuss how to allow incoming connections later in the chapter.

Virtual Private Networking

Most of us are familiar with using a modem to connect a computer to the Internet. Establishing a dial-up or VPN networking connection is no different; the remote network is just a bit smaller than the Internet.

Virtual Private Networking deserves a bit more explanation. In a nutshell, a Virtual Private Network (VPN) lets you connect to a remote network in a secure way. VPNs create what is effectively a *tunnel* between your computer and a remote network, a tunnel that can pass data freely and securely through potentially hostile intermediate territory like the Internet. Authorized data is encapsulated in special packets that are passed through your computer's firewall and the remote network's firewall, and is inspected by a VPN server before being released to the protected network.

Figure 38.5 illustrates the concept, showing a Virtual Private Network connection between a computer out on the Internet and a server on a protected network. The figure shows how the computer sends data (1) through a VPN connection that encapsulates it (2) and transmits it over the Internet (3). A firewall (4) passes VPN packets but blocks all others. The VPN Server verifies the authenticity of your data, extracts it (5), and transmits the original packet (6) on to the desired remote server. The encapsulation process allows for encryption of your data, and allows "private" IP addresses to be used as the endpoints of the network connection.

Figure 38.5
A Virtual Private Network encapsulates and encrypts data that is passed over the Internet.

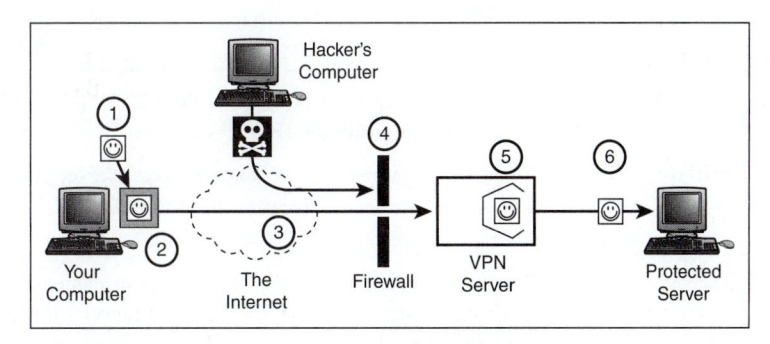

VPN connections work like dial-up connections. After you have an Internet connection established (via modem or a dedicated service), Windows establishes the link between your computer and a VPN server on the remote network. After it's connected, the VPN service transmits data between your computer. In effect, you are now a part of the distant LAN.

You can use Windows Vista's VPN service to allow incoming VPN connections to your computer as well. Windows Firewall protects your computer against hackers, yet you can still connect to your computer through the Internet to retrieve files from afar.

Now let's see how to use VPN or dial-up networking to connect to a remote Windows network.

Setting Up VPN and Dial-Up Networking

To create a VPN or dial-up connection to a remote network or computer, you need a working Internet connection or modem, respectively. You learned how to install both of these in Chapter 14, "Getting Connected," so if you haven't done so already, start there to install and configure your modem and Internet connection.

You also must get or confirm the information shown in Table 38.1 from the remote network's or computer's manager.

Table 38.1 Information Needed for a VPN or RAS Dial-Up Connection

Information	Reason
For Dial-up:	
Telephone number	You must know the receiving modem's telephone number, including area code.
Modem compatibility	You must confirm that your modem is compatible with the modems used by the remote network; check which modem protocols are supported (V.90, V.32, and so on).
For VPN:	
VPN Server	You need either the hostname or IP address of the remote VPN server computer.
For Either:	
Protocols in use	The remote network must support TCP/IP. Windows Vista does not support networking with the IPX/SPX or NetBEUI protocols.
TCP/IP configuration	You should confirm that the Remote Access Server assigns TCP/IP information automatically (dynamically) via DHCP. Usually, the answer is yes.
Mail servers	You might need to obtain the IP addresses or names of SMTP, POP, Exchange, Lotus Notes, or Microsoft Mail servers if you want to use these applications while connected to the remote network.
User ID and password	You must be ready to supply a username and password to the remote server. If you're calling into Windows Vista, XP, 200x, or NT RAS server, use the same Windows username and password you use on that remote network.

Armed with this information, you're ready to create a connection to the remote network. To do so, follow these steps:

1. Click Start, Network, Network and Sharing Center.
2. Under Tasks, select Set Up a Connection or Network.
3. Select Connect to a Workplace and click Next.
4. Select No, Create a New Connection and click Next.
5. For a VPN connection, select Use My Internet Connection (VPN). For a dial-up connection, select Dial Directly.
6. If you are setting up a VPN connection, enter the hostname of the IP address of the remote VPN server.

   If you are setting up a dial-up connection, enter the telephone number of the remote computer, including area code, in the appropriate format. For telephone numbers in the North American Numbering Plan, the format is (###) ###-####, where # represents a digit. Then click Dialing Rules to double-check that your current location and area code are set correctly. Change it if necessary, and click OK.
7. Change the Destination Name from "Dial-up Connection" to something meaningful to you, such as "Dial-up office network" or "VPN to Big Client."
8. If you want to make the connection available to other users of your computer, check Allow Other People to Use This Connection. If your network uses Smart Card authentication (your network Administrator will tell you so), check Use a Smart Card. You will usually not need to check either of these.
9. Check Don't Connect Now; Just Set It Up So I Can Use It Later. Then click Next.
10. Enter the username and password that you use when logging on to the remote computer, or use the name and password assigned by your network administrator. If this is a Windows domain logon, enter the domain name in the Domain (Optional) field. You can check Show Characters if you want to verify that you typed the password correctly.

    If you want to have Windows remember the password so that you can connect without having to type it every time, check Remember This Password. However, if earlier you checked Allow Other People to Use This Connection, this would let others connect using your network credentials, so think carefully whether you want to allow that.
11. Click Close.
12. In the Network and Sharing Center window, under Tasks, click Manage Network Connections.

There should now be an icon for the new connection in the Network Connections window. Before you use it, you should view and check its properties settings, as described in the next section.

SETTING A VPN OR DIAL-UP CONNECTION'S PROPERTIES

There are several ways you can edit the properties of a VPN or dial-up connection. For example, from the Network Connections window, you can right-click the icon and select

Properties. The easiest way, though, is to click Start, Connect To. Then right-click the desired connection name and select Properties.

The connection's properties page has five tabs and a heap o' parameters. Most of the time, the default settings will work correctly, but you might need to change some of them. I've listed the most important parameters in Table 38.2.

TABLE 38.2 IMPORTANT DIAL-UP CONNECTION PROPERTIES

Tab	Property	Description
General (VPN)	Hostname or IP address Dial Another Connection First	Contact information for the VPN server. Check this box and select a dial-up or PPPoE connection name if you need this to establish an Internet connection before attempting the VPN connection.
General (Dial-up)	Area Code Phone Number Country/Region Code	Set the appropriate dialing information here. If the remote server has more than one phone number (or more than one hunt group), you can click Alternate to specify alternate telephone numbers.
	Use Dialing Rules	Check to have Windows determine when to send prefixes and area codes. If you want to use this, enter the area code and phone number in their separate fields. This feature is useful if you will be calling the same number from several locations with different dialing properties.
Options	Prompt for Name and Password Use Windows Logon Domain Redialing Options	Check to have Windows allow you to change previously stored credentials. Check if you are connecting to a Windows Server computer. You can change these settings to change how Windows deals with busy signals and dropped connections, and what to do if you leave the connection unused for a long time.
Security		Your network administrator may instruct you to change these settings; otherwise the default settings should work. Be sure to leave Data Encryption set to Require Encryption.
	Automatically Use My Windows Logon Name and Password	Check this box if your Windows Vista account uses the same logon name and password (and domain, if you are on a domain network) that you need to enter on the remote network, *and* if you want to let connections be made without your having to reenter your password.

Tab	Property	Description
Networking		Usually, all protocols and services should be checked except File and Printer Sharing. This option should be disabled so remote network users cannot use your computer's shared folders and printers. If you really do want to let the remote network's users see your shares, check File and Printer Sharing.
	Internet Protocol Version 4 (TCP/IP)	Normally, a Remote Access Server automatically assigns your connection the proper IP and DNS addresses. In the very unlikely event that the network administrator tells you that you must set TCP/IP parameters yourself, select Internet Protocol Version 4 (TCP/IP) from the Components list, and click Properties. Enter the required IP address and DNS addresses there.

If the network to which you're connecting is a safe, protected corporate network with its own firewall, *and* you are instructed to do so by your network administrators, you can disable Windows Firewall for this particular connection. To do this, follow these steps:

1. Click Start, Control Panel. Select Security, Windows Firewall.
2. Click Change Settings and confirm the User Account Control prompt.
3. Select the Advanced Tab and uncheck the VPN or dial-up connection in the Network Connections list. Then click OK.

Again, you should not do this unless you are instructed to do so by your network administrator.

CALLBACKS

Some dial-up servers are set up so that after you dial up and sign in, the server will hang up and call you back. Your modem will pick up the incoming call and reestablish the connection. One purpose of this is to shift the cost of the telephone call to the network owner (your company, for instance). Callback can also be used as a security measure by ensuring that users can access the network from only certain, validated telephone numbers.

If your remote network uses callbacks, and you *always* call from the same location and telephone line, you can set up a default callback number so that you don't have to provide it to the remote server every time you connect. Here are the steps:

1. View the Network Connections folder. Press and release the Alt key. On the menu, select Advanced, Remote Access Preferences.
2. Select the Callback tab, and select Always Call Me Back at the Number(s) Below.

3. Select the entry for your modem and click Edit. Enter your telephone number, including area code if necessary, as it should be specified to the remote network server. Then click OK and close the windows.

If you later connect to a different telephone line, be sure to change the telephone number or select Ask Me During Dialing When the Server Offers, so that the remote server doesn't try to call you back at the old number.

GATEWAY SETTINGS

If you are connecting to a complex, multisubnet remote network, or if you want to browse the Internet through your regular Internet connection while you're also using the dial-up or VPN connection, you must deal with the network gateway issue, which I'll discuss later in this chapter under "Routing Issues." To change the gateway setting

1. Select Internet Protocol Version 4 and choose Properties. Then click the Advanced button.
2. If the remote network has only one subnet, *or* if you will set routes to multiple subnets manually, uncheck Use Default Gateway on Remote Network.

After you've finished making any changes to the connection's options, select OK. You can now double-click the icon to start the connection process.

MANAGING DIAL-UP CONNECTIONS FROM MULTIPLE LOCATIONS

As you've seen already, Windows lets you enter your current telephone area code and dialing prefix requirements so that when you're making modem calls, Windows uses the customs and prefixes appropriate for your local phone system. This capability is great if you use a portable computer. For example, at home, you might be in area code 415. At the office, you might be in area code 707 and have to dial 9 to get an outside telephone line. When you're visiting Indianapolis, you're in area code 317 and might need to use a telephone company calling card when making long-distance calls.

Windows offers great support for these variations by letting you define "locations," each with a separate local area code and dialing rules. When you use one of your Network Connections icons, as long as you've told Windows your current location, it can automatically apply the correct set of rules when making a dial-up connection.

→ For instructions on establishing locations and dialing rules, **see** "Adjusting Dial-Up Connection Properties," **p. 409**.

However, if you use an ISP with access points in various cities, or your company has different access numbers in various regions, you'll find that this Locations system does not let you associate a different dial-up number with each location. It would be great if it did, but no such luck.

If you want to use different "local" dial-up numbers for the various locations you visit with your computer, you must set up a separate Network Connections icon for each access number and use the appropriate icon when making a connection at each location.

> **TIP**
>
> Set up and test the first access number you need. Then when you need to add a new access number, view the Network Connections folder, right-click the connection icon, select Create Copy, rename it, and change its telephone number. I name my icons based on the location of the local number: Office-Berkeley, Office-Seattle, and so on.
>
> When you travel and want to make a dial-up connection, select the appropriate dial-up icon and set your location before you click Dial.

> **TIP**
>
> If you travel, you'll find that having your Internet Options set to dial a particular connection automatically is not a great idea. It would dial the chosen connection no matter where you were (and remember, if there's a 50-50 chance of things going wrong, 9 times out of 10 they will). So, if you travel with your computer, you might want to open Internet Explorer and click Tools, Internet Options. Select the Connections tab and choose Never Dial a Connection. This way, you won't be blindsided by an inadvertent call to Indiana while you're in India.

Establishing a VPN or Dial-Up Connection

Making a remote network dial-up or VPN connection is no more difficult than connecting to the Internet.

Check Your Current Location

If you're making a dial-up connection and you've changed area codes or phone systems since the last time you made a modem connection, check your location setting by following these steps before dialing into the network:

1. Open the Control Panel, select Hardware and Sound, and click Set Up Dialing Rules under Phone and Modem Options.
2. Check your current location in the list of configured dialing locations using the Dialing Rules tab.
3. Click OK to close the dialog box.

Windows should now use the correct area code and dialing prefixes.

Make the Connection

To connect to a remote network, follow these steps:

1. Click Start, Connect To.

2. Windows will open the connection dialog box, as shown in Figure 38.6. Enter your login name, password, and Windows domain name (if appropriate). You can also select Properties to adjust the connection's telephone number or dialing properties. The Dialing From choice appears only if you checked Use Dialing Rules and have defined more than one dialing location.

Figure 38.6
In the Connect dialog box, enter your username and password for the remote network.

TIP

If you're connecting to a remote Windows Server domain, you can enter *domain\username* or *username@domain* in the User Name field.

3. Click Connect or Dial. Windows shows you the progress of your connection as it dials or contacts the remote server through the Internet, verifies your username and password, and registers your computer on the remote network.

If the connection fails, unless you dialed the wrong number, you'll most likely get a reasonable explanation: The password or account name was invalid, the remote system is not accepting calls, and so on. If you entered an incorrect username or password, you are usually given two more chances to reenter the information before the other end hangs up on you.

If the connection completes successfully, a new connection icon appears in the notification area. If you hover your mouse over it, a panel pops up showing the active network connections, as shown in Figure 38.7.

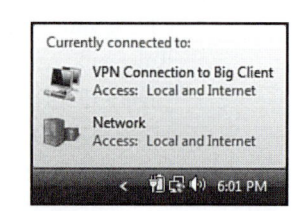

Figure 38.7

You can now use the remote network's resources, as discussed next.

Using Remote Network Resources

When you're connected, you can use network resources exactly as if you were on the network. The Network folder, shared folders, and network printers all function as if you were directly connected.

The following are some tips for effective remote networking by modem:

- Don't try to run application software that is installed on the remote network itself. Starting it could take quite a long time!
- If you get disconnected while using a remote network, it's annoying to have to stop what you're doing and reconnect. You can tell Windows to automatically reconnect if you're disconnected while you're working. Click Start, Network, Network and Sharing Center, Manage Network Connections. Press and release the Alt key. From the Advanced menu, choose Remote Access Preferences, and select the Autodial tab. Check any locations from which you would like Windows to automatically reconnect you.

> **TIP**
>
> If you get disconnected while you are editing a document that was originally stored on the remote network, I suggest that you immediately save it on your local hard disk the moment you notice that the connection has been disrupted. Then, when the connection is reestablished, save it back to its original location. This will help you avoid losing your work.

- You can also place shortcuts to network folders on your desktop or in other folders for quick access.
- If the remote LAN has Internet access, you should be able to browse the Internet while you're connected to the LAN. You don't need to disconnect and switch to your ISP. You might need to make a change in your personal email program, though, as I'll note later under "Email and Network Connections."
- If you use several remote networks, you can create a folder for each. In them, put shortcuts to the appropriate connection and to frequently used folders on those networks. Put all these folders in a folder named, for example, Remote Networks on your desktop. This way you can open one folder and be working within seconds.

Email and Network Connections

If you use your computer with remote LANs as well as an ISP, you might need to be careful with the email programs you use. Most email programs don't make it easy for you to associate different mail servers with different connections.

Although most email servers allow you to *retrieve* your mail from anywhere on the Internet, most are very picky about whom they let *send* email. Generally, to use an SMTP server to send mail out, you must be using a computer whose IP address is known by the server as belonging to its network. You can usually send mail out only through the server that serves your current connection.

See if your favorite email program can configure separate "identities," each with associated incoming and outgoing servers. If you send mail, be sure you're using the identity that's set up to use the outgoing (SMTP) server that belongs to your current VPN or dial-up connection.

Monitoring and Ending a VPN or Dial-Up Connection

While you're connected, note that the notification area connection icon flashes to indicate incoming and outgoing data activity. (If it doesn't, right-click the icon and select Turn On Activity Notification.)

To check the status of the connection, click Start, Connect To. When the list of connections appears, locate the active connection (it will say Connected). Right-click it and select Status. The connection status dialog box appears, as shown in Figure 38.8. From the status dialog box, you can get to the connection properties, or click Disconnect.

The easiest way to end the connection is to click Start, Connect To, then select the connection from the displayed list and click Disconnect.

Figure 38.8
The connection status dialog box displays current connection statistics and lets you disconnect or change connection properties. Right-clicking the connection icon in the taskbar is a quicker way to disconnect.

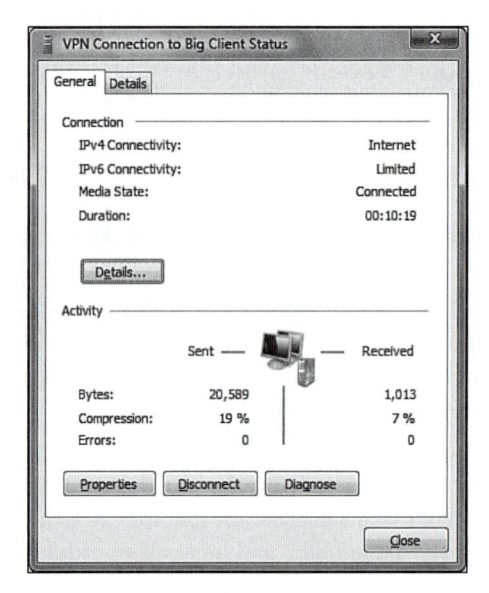

Routing Issues

If the remote network you want to use is a simple, small network with only one subnet or range of IP addresses, you can skip this section. Otherwise, we have to address an issue with TCP/IPv4 routing here, even though it's a real can of worms.

When you establish a VPN connection to another network, your computer is assigned an IP address from that other network for the duration of your connection. This address might be a private, non-Internet-routable address like 192.168.1.100. All data destined for the remote network is packaged up in PPTP, SSTP, or L2TP packets and sent to the remote host. But what happens if you want to communicate with two servers—a private server through the tunnel and a public website on the Internet—at the same time?

When you send data to an IP address that doesn't clearly belong to the private network's range, Windows has two choices: It can pass the data through the tunnel and let the network on the other end route it on, or it can pass the data without encapsulation and let it travel directly to the Internet host.

It would seem sensible that Windows should always use the second approach because any IP address other than, for instance, 192.168.1.xxx obviously doesn't belong to the private network and doesn't need protection. That's right as long as the remote network has only one such subnet. Some complex corporate networks have many, with different addresses, so Windows can't always know just from the address of the VPN connection which addresses belong to the private network and which go direct.

If you plan to use a VPN connection and your Internet connection at the same time, you must find out whether your remote network has more than one subnet. Then follow this advice:

- If the remote network has only one subnet, tell Windows not to use the remote network as the gateway address for unknown locations. This is the easy case.
- If the remote network has more than one subnet, tell Windows to use the remote network as its gateway, so you can connect to all servers on the remote network. But Internet access goes through the tunnel, too, and from there to the Internet. It slows things down.
- Alternatively, you can tell Windows not to use the remote network gateway and you can manually set routes to other subnets while you're connected. It's tricky and inconvenient. I'll show you how I do it at the end of the chapter, under "Tips from the Windows Pros."

When you know how you'll resolve the gateway issue, refer to the "Gateway Settings" heading earlier in this chapter to make the appropriate settings on the connection's Networking properties tab.

Incoming VPN and Dial-Up Access

Windows Vista has a stripped-down Remote Access Server (RAS) built in, and you can use it to connect to your computer by modem, or through the Internet, from another location using any computer running Windows 2000, XP, or Vista. After you're connected, you can access your computer's shared files and printers just as you can on your home or office network. This incoming dial-up and VPN feature is available even on the Home versions of Windows Vista. To use this feature, your computer must have a modem and/or a dedicated, always-on Internet connection. At most, one remote user can connect at a time.

Setting up a modem to receive calls is straightforward: Just connect to a phone line, and you can dial in from anywhere. Setting up an incoming Internet connection is substantially more difficult because you need an always-on Internet connection, whose external IP address you know and can reach from the Internet at large. We talked about ways to establish an Internet hostname using static addressing or dynamic DNS providers in Chapter 18, under the heading "Name Service," so I won't repeat that discussion here. Besides a discoverable IP address, you will have to configure your Internet router or Windows Internet Connection sharing service to forward VPN data through the firewall to the computer that you're going to set up to receive VPN connections. We'll discuss this in more detail shortly, under "Enabling Incoming VPN Connections with NAT."

> **NOTE**
> Windows Firewall doesn't have to be told to permit incoming VPN connections, because it knows to let them in.

> **CAUTION**
> Incoming connections are not too difficult to set up, but beware: Permitting remote access opens up security risks. Before you enable incoming access on a computer at work, be sure that your company permits it. In some companies, you could be fired for violating the security policies.

The process for enabling VPN access is the same as for enabling dial-in access. Let's walk through that process now.

Setting Up VPN and Dial-Up Access

To enable VPN or dial-up access, follow these steps:

1. Open the Network and Sharing Center, and then click Manage Network Connections.
2. If the standard menu bar (File, Edit, View, Tools, Advanced, Help) isn't displayed, press and release the Alt key. Then click File, New Incoming Connection, and confirm the User Account Control prompt.
3. Select the user accounts that will be permitted to access your computer remotely, as shown in Figure 38.9. This step is very important: Check only the names of those users whom you really want and need to give access. The fewer accounts you enable, the less likely that someone might accidentally break into your computer.

> **NOTE**
> You can use the Add Someone button to create a new account and use the Account Properties button to set the password on a selected account.

Figure 38.9
Here you can choose users who will be granted the right to remote access of your computer. Check only the names of those users really needing access.

> **CAUTION**
>
> Under no circumstances should you enable Guest, IIS_USR, IUSR_*xxx*, or IWAM_*xxx* (where *xxx* is the name of your computer) for remote access. These are accounts that require no password and would make your computer available to anyone who tried to connect.
>
> Check only the names of users who need access and who have good (long, complex) passwords.

4. After selecting users, click Next. Then select the means that you will use for remote access. Check Through the Internet to enable incoming VPN connections, and/or Through a Dial-Up Modem to enable dial-up access. If you enable dial-up access, select the modem that is to be used. Then click Next.

   > **NOTE**
   >
   > If you enable dial-up access, the selected modem will answer all incoming calls on its telephone line.

5. Windows displays a list of network protocols and services that will be made available to the dial-up connection. Select the Internet Protocol Version 4 (TCP/IP) entry, and click Properties. Uncheck Allow Callers to Access My Local Area Network, and then click OK.

   > **NOTE**
   >
   > Incoming connections could also be set up to allow remote computers to access other computers on your network, but this requires expertise in TCP/IP addressing and routing issues that are beyond the scope of this book.

6. Make sure that Internet Protocol Version 4 (TCP/IP) is checked and that Internet Protocol Version 6 (TCP/IP) is unchecked. Then click Allow Access. When the final window appears, click Close.

When the incoming connection information has been entered, a new Incoming Connection icon appears in your Network Connections window, as shown in Figure 38.10. This icon shows that incoming connections are enabled, and also indicates whether the connection is being used.

Figure 38.10
Incoming Connections can be monitored in the Network Connections Window.

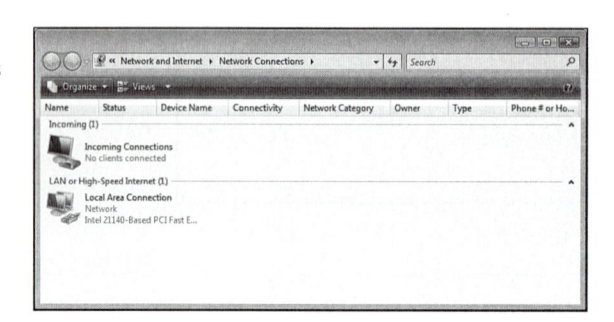

When someone connects to your computer, a second icon appears in the Network Connections folder showing their username. If necessary you can right-click this to disconnect them.

Enabling Incoming VPN Connections with NAT

Microsoft's Internet Connection Sharing and DSL/cable sharing routers use an IP-addressing trick called Network Address Translation (NAT) to serve an entire LAN with only one public IP address. Thus incoming connections, as from a VPN client to a VPN server, have to be directed to a single host computer on the internal network.

If you use a shared Internet connection, only one computer can be designated as the recipient of incoming VPN connections. If you use Microsoft's Internet Connection Sharing, that one computer should be the one sharing its connection. It will receive and properly handle VPN requests.

If you use a hardware sharing router, the VPN server can be any computer you want to designate. Your router must be set up to forward the following packet types to the designated computer:

> TCP port 1723
>
> GRE (protocol 47. This is not the same as port 47!)

Unfortunately, many inexpensive commercial DSL/cable connection sharing routers don't have a way to explicitly forward GRE packets. There are several ways around this:

- Some routers know about Microsoft's Point to Point Tunneling Protocol (PPTP) and you can specify the computer that is to receive incoming VPN connections.
- If you enable Universal Plug and Play (UPnP) on your router, Windows can tell the router to forward incoming VPN connections. UPnP is discussed in Chapter 22, "Connecting Your Network to the Internet."

- If neither of these options is available, you may designate the VPN computer as a DMZ host so that it receives *all* unrecognized incoming packets. This is relatively dangerous, however.

> **CAUTION**
>
> If you designate a computer as a DMZ host, that computer can be vulnerable to hacker attacks. You *must* enable Windows Firewall on this computer's network connection, and you must disable exceptions. You must also configure your router to block Microsoft File Sharing packets, at the very least. Set up filtering to block TCP and UDP ports 137 through 139 and 445.

→ To learn more about forwarding network requests on a shared Internet connection, **see** "Enabling Access with a Sharing Router," **p. 732**.

Offline Folders

You might recognize the "Offline" problem: If you have a portable computer that you sometimes use with your office network, and sometimes use out in the field, you probably make copies of important "online" documents—documents stored on the network server—on your laptop. But, if you make changes to one of your "offline" copies, the network's copy will be out of date. Likewise, if someone updates the original on the network, your copy will be out of date. And, trying to remember where the originals came from and who has the most recent version of a given file is a painful job. I admit that more than once I've accidentally overwritten somebody's work because I wasn't paying attention to the files' date and time stamps.

Windows Vista has a solution to this housekeeping problem: Offline Folders and the Sync Center. Here's the skinny: When you use a network folder and tell Windows to make it available for offline use, Windows stashes away a copy or *caches* the folder's files somewhere on your hard drive, but all you see is the original shared folder on your screen. When you disconnect, the shared file folder remains on your screen, with its files intact. You can still add, delete, and edit the files. Meanwhile, network users can do the same with the original copies. When you reconnect later, Windows will set everything right again thanks to a program called the Sync Center.

> **NOTE**
>
> Offline Files are available only on Windows Vista Business, Enterprise, and Ultimate editions. The Sync Center is present on Vista Home versions, though, because it can also work with handheld devices such as PDAs and cell phones. If your version of Vista doesn't support offline files (or even if it does), you should know about Microsoft's Sync Toy tool, which is a free program you can download from Microsoft.com. Sync Toy can do a pretty good job of copying new and updated files back and forth between a network location and a folder on your portable computer. It's not quite as seamless as Offline Files, but it can do just as good a job. To get this tool, visit microsoft.com and search for "Synctoy." You want version 2.0 or a later version.

You'll find that Offline Folders really work and are more powerful than they seem at first glance. The following are some of the potential applications:

- Maintaining an up-to-date copy of a set of shared files on both a server (or desktop computer) and a remote or portable computer. If you keep a project's files in an offline folder, Windows keeps the copies up to date on all your computers.

- "Pushing" application software or data from a network to a portable computer. If software or data is kept in an offline folder, your portable can update itself whenever you connect or dock to the LAN.

- Automatically backing up important files from your computer to an alternative location. Your computer can connect to a dial-up or network computer on a timer and refresh your offline folders automatically.

It's very easy make folders available offline, as you'll see in the next section.

Identifying Files and Folders for Offline Use

You can mark specific files, subfolders, or even entire shared folders from a "remote" server for offline use.

> **NOTE**
> The server I'm talking about might be in the next room, which isn't very "remote" at all, but that's what I'll call it for simplicity's sake. In this section, a "remote" server refers to some other computer that you access via networking.

> **NOTE**
> Before you mark a folder for offline use, check to make sure that you don't have any of its files open in Word, Excel, or so on. Open files can't be copied.

While you're connected to the remote network, view the desired items in Windows Explorer or, if you've mapped a drive letter to the shared folder, you can select it under Computer as well.

When you find the folder or folders you want to use while offline, select them, right-click, and select Always Available Offline. Be cautious about marking entire shared drives or folders available offline, though, unless you're sure how much data they contain, and you're sure you want it all. You could end up with gigabytes of stuff you don't need.

If Always Available Offline isn't displayed as an option, **see** *"Can't Make File Available Offline" in the "Troubleshooting" section at the end of this chapter.*

The first time you mark a folder for offline use, Windows copies it, and all its contents, to your hard drive. This may take a while if there is a lot to copy or if your network connection is slow. If any files cannot be copied, you can click the Sync Center link to see their names and the reasons for the problem.

NOTE

The most common reason a file can't be copied is that it is open and in use by an application. If this is the case for any of your files, close the application and perform another sync, as discussed later in this section. Another common problem is that `thumbs.db`, a hidden file Windows creates in folders that contain pictures, is sometimes in use by Windows Explorer and can't be copied. You can ignore problems with `thumbs.db`—right-click the file's name in the Sync Results window and select Ignore.

CAUTION

If the files that you're copying from your network contain sensitive information, you may want to ask Windows to encrypt the copies stored on your computer. To see how to do this, skip ahead to "Managing and Encrypting Offline Files" later in this chapter.

When the folder or folders have been copied, you will be able to use the network folders whether you're connected to the network or not.

Using Files While Offline

When you've marked a folder or network drive as Always Available Offline, a small green "sync center" icon appears on each folder and file icon to show that it's been marked as available, as shown in Figure 38.11.

Figure 38.11
When a folder or network drive is Always Available Offline, a "sync center" mark is displayed on each icon.

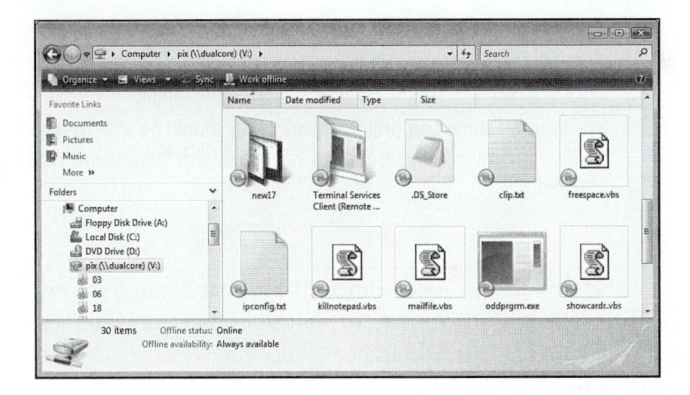

Notice that two new buttons are displayed in the Explorer window: Sync and Work Offline:

- Use the Sync button when you've been disconnected from the network and have reconnected. This will reconcile any changes you have made to your copy of the files and changes others made to the originals on the network.
- You can use the Work Offline button to disconnect this shared folder from the network (other network connections remain intact), so that you can make changes to files locally, and later sync them to the network.

Now, if you disconnect from the network or use the Work Offline button, offline files and folders will remain in the Explorer display.

> **TIP**
>
> If your network or VPN connection is unreliable, you may find that your applications may sometimes hang trying to save your work to a network folder. If this happens to you frequently, the Work Offline button is your new best friend. With it you can *force* Windows to use a local, cached copy of a document while you edit it, then sync it back up after you've saved your changes. Here's how to do it: Locate a network folder in Windows Explorer. Mark it "Make Available Offline." Open the folder, and click the button labeled "Work Offline." Edit the file(s) you need to edit, then click "Work Online." This should run the Sync Center, and copy your changes back to the network.

> **NOTE**
>
> Folders that were not marked Always Available Offline will disappear from the display when you disconnect from the network.

While offline, you can add new files, delete files, or edit files in the remote folder. If you had mapped a drive letter to the network folder, the drive letter still functions.

You can also rename files, and the network copy of the file will be renamed the next time you connect and sync up.

> **NOTE**
>
> In most cases, you cannot rename folders while offline.
>
> However, on some corporate networks, you should be able to rename "redirected" folders if your network administrator has enabled this feature and Vista Service Pack 1 is installed.

This process works so well that it's disconcerting at first because the effect is… well, because there is no effect at all. You can happily work away as if you were really still connected to the network. The only difference is that your changes won't be visible to others on the network until you reconnect.

> **CAUTION**
>
> If you delete a file from a network folder, either while you are offline or online, it will be deleted immediately and permanently. Deleted network files are *not* saved in the Recycle Bin.

When you do reconnect, you should synchronize your offline folders with the network folders so that both sets will be up to date.

Sync Center

You can synchronize files anytime you are connected to the network that contains the original shared folder, whether you connect by LAN, modem, or VPN. You can start a synchronization in any of several ways:

- Click Start, All Programs, Accessories, Sync Center. Then click Sync All.
- Right-click a specific shared file or folder and select Sync.
- Click the Sync button in Windows Explorer.
- If you have a portable computer, you can click the Sync button in the Windows Mobility Center window.

Synchronization can also occur automatically

- When you reconnect to the network and Windows is idle.
- When you click Work Online in the folder view.
- When you log on and off.
- At specified times and days of the week. For a scheduled synchronization, Windows can even automatically make a dial-up connection.

The Sync Center has the job of reconciling changes made to the online and offline copies of the files.

Reconciling Changes

The Sync Center will automatically copy new or changed files from your computer to the network, and vice versa. However, three situations exist in which it will need some help:

- If both you and another user have changed the same file, you'll have to pick which version to keep.
- If you deleted a file while you were disconnected, you'll have to decide if you want to also delete the network's copy.
- If a network user deleted a file while you were disconnected, you'll have to confirm that you want to delete your copy.

If any problems occur while syncing files, the Sync Center icon in the notification area on your taskbar will display a yellow warning triangle. Double-click the Sync Center icon to display the Sync Center, then click View Sync Conflicts in the tasks list. This displays the Conflicts page, as shown in Figure 38.12.

Double-click the first listed file. This displays an explanation of why Sync Center can't update the file, and you see a selection of choices to resolve the issue. For example, if both you and a network user modified the same file while you were disconnected, the dialog box will look like the one shown in Figure 38.13.

Figure 38.12
The Sync Conflicts page lists files that cannot be reconciled without help.

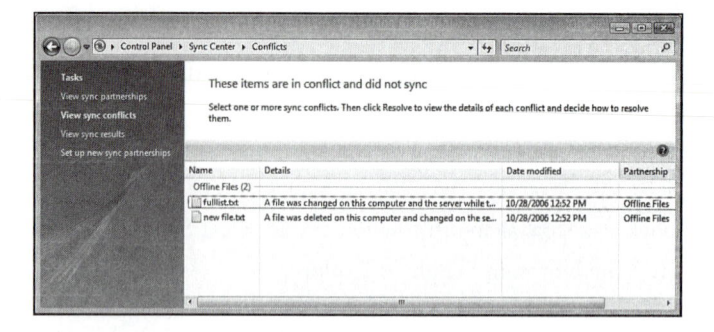

Figure 38.13
When two users have modified the same file, you can choose to keep one or both versions. The selected version(s) will be copied to your computer *and* the network.

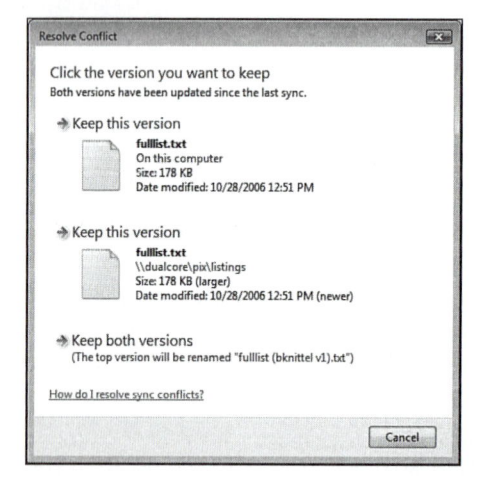

Continue through the conflict list to resolve each problem.

> **CAUTION**
>
> If the sync process fails because a file is in use, you should repeat the synchronization when no one is editing files in the shared folder; otherwise, you might lose changes to some files.

Managing and Encrypting Offline Files

To manage the Offline Files feature, click Start, Control Panel. Select Network and Internet and click Offline Files. The following are tabs on this dialog box:

- **General**—Here you can enable or disable the Offline Files feature entirely. You can also see a list of all files that have been copied to your hard disk for offline use.
- **Disk Usage**—This tab lets you monitor or limit the amount of disk space used by offline file copies.
- **Encryption**—Here you select to encrypt the network files that are stored on your hard disk. This makes them safe from theft should your computer fall into the wrong hands.

- **Network**—If Windows detects that you have a slow (dial-up, for instance) network connection, Windows can automatically elect to work with offline copies and will sync them up periodically while you continue to work.

Finally, remember that you can uncheck Make Available Offline on a file or folder anytime to remove it from the cached file list. This will delete the cached copies of the files in that folder.

MAKING YOUR SHARED FOLDERS AVAILABLE FOR OFFLINE USE BY OTHERS

When you've marked a network file for offline use, Windows makes a copy of the file on your hard disk. While you're connected to the network, it would be faster to use the local copy to access the file; this could really save time, for example, if you are running an application from a network folder. On the other hand, this would not be appropriate for files that change frequently or for database files that are used by multiple users concurrently.

Windows has to know whether or not it's appropriate to serve up the cached copy for online use, and it leaves the choice up to the person who shares the network folder. When you share folders on your computer, you should specify the way Windows will make this folder available for offline use by others.

Normally, Windows will not give users a cached file when the network copy is available. It's useful to change the default settings only when you are sharing a folder with read-only documents and application programs. In this case, you may be able to give users faster access by following these steps:

1. Use Explorer or Computer to locate the folder you're sharing. Right-click it and select Properties.
2. View the Sharing tab. Click the Advanced Sharing button and confirm the User Account Control prompt. If Share This Folder is not checked, check it.
3. Click the Caching button.
4. Select Automatic Caching of Programs and Documents.

    If you want Windows to automatically have remote users keep an offline copy of files and programs even if they haven't selected Always Available Offline, also check Optimized for Performance.
5. Click OK to close the Offline Settings dialog box, and then click OK to close the Advanced Sharing dialog box.

The amount of disk space allocated to "automatically" available offline files is limited to an amount set in the Offline Files properties page.

If you can't find a file that was marked for offline use, **see** *"Offline Files Are Missing" in the "Troubleshooting" section at the end of this chapter.*

Multiple LAN Connections

Most desktop computers sit where they are installed, gathering dust until they're obsolete, and they participate in only one LAN. But portable computer users often carry their computers from office to office, docking or plugging into several local LANs. Although Microsoft has made it easy for you to manage different dial-up and VPN connections, it's difficult to manage connections to different LANs if the network configuration settings are manually set.

Internet Protocol settings are the difficult ones. If your computer is set to use automatic TCP/IP configuration, you won't encounter any problems; your computer will absorb the local information each time you connect.

If your TCP/IP settings are set manually, things aren't so simple. Microsoft has come up with a partial solution called Alternate Configuration, which is available in Windows Vista and XP. You can configure your computer for automatic IP address assignment on most networks, and manual assignment on one. The way this works is that Windows looks for a DHCP server when it boots up, and if it doesn't find one it uses the Alternate Configuration. This can be a static IP address, or the default setting of Automatic Private IP address assignment, whereby Windows chooses a random address in the 169.254 subnet. (The Automatic Private IP technique was the only option in Windows 98, Me, 2000.)

This means that your computer can automatically adjust itself to multiple networks, at most one of which requires manual IP address settings.

To set up Alternate Configuration, open your Network Connections folder, view the Local Area Connection's properties, and double-click Internet Protocol Version 4 (TCP/IP). Be sure the General tab uses the Obtain an IP Address Automatically setting—if not, this discussion doesn't apply to your computer. View the Alternate Configuration tab and choose User Configured to enter the static LAN's information.

If you need to commute between multiple networks that require manual configuration, you'll have to change the General settings each time you connect to a different network. I suggest that you stick a 3-by-5-inch card with the settings for each network in your laptop carrying case for handy reference.

Troubleshooting

VPN Connection Fails Without Certificate

When I attempt to make a VPN connection, I receive the message `Unable to negotiate the encryption you requested without a certificate.`

You are trying to connect to a VPN server with a higher level of encryption than your computer or the other computer is configured to carry out. Contact your network administrator to get the appropriate certificate installed.

Can't Make File Available Offline

The choice Make File Available Offline doesn't appear when I right-click a file or folder.

To useOffline Folders, you must be using Windows Vista Business, Enterprise, or Ultimate edition—the Home versions don't have it. The feature might also be disabled. To check, click Start, Control Panel, Network and Internet, Offline Files. If there is a button labeled Enable Offline Files, click it. Finally, your network manager may have disabled Offline Files via group policy—in this case you're out of luck.

When I mark files or folders for offline use, I receive the error Files of this Type Cannot Be Made Available Offline.

Some file types (for example, Microsoft Access .mdb database files) should usually not be available offline, because such files are usually used by multiple LAN users simultaneously, and there's no way to reconcile changes made by offline and online users. Your network manager may have designated one or more files as being unavailable for offline for this reason. Ask your network manager to check Group Policy entry Computer Configuration\Administrative Templates\Network\Offline Files\Files not cached.

Offline Files Are Missing

I can't find files or folders I've clearly marked for offline use.

You might not have synchronized after marking the file, its folder, or a containing folder for offline use. The solution is to go back online and synchronize. Then check the Sync Conflicts page to see if Windows says that it couldn't copy your file for some reason.

Tips from the Windows Pros: Manually Adding Routing Information

As I discussed previously (the bit about a can of worms), if you use Virtual Private Networking to connect to a remote network with more than one subnet, you can let Windows set the default gateway to be the remote network. This way, you can contact all the hosts on the remote network and its subnets. Unfortunately, all your Internet traffic will travel through the tunnel, too, slowing you down. The remote network might not even permit outgoing Internet access.

The alternative is to disable the use of the default gateway and manually add routes to any subnets known to belong to the private network. To make these changes, you have to work in a Command Prompt window with elevated privileges. To open one, click Start, All Programs, Accessories. Right-click Command Prompt and select Run As Administrator. Then confirm the UAC prompt.

To add information about remote network subnets, use the route command, which looks like this:

```
route add subnet mask netmask gateway
```

The *subnet* and *netmask* arguments are the addresses for additional networks that can be reached through the gateway address *gateway*. To add a route, you must know the IP address and mask information for each remote subnet and your gateway address on the VPN.

You must get the subnet information from the network administrator on the remote end. You can find the gateway address from your own computer. Connect to the remote VPN, and type **ipconfig** in the command prompt window. One of the connections printed should be labeled PPP Adapter, SSTP Adapter or L2TP Adapter. Note the gateway IP address listed. This address can be used as the gateway address to send packets destined for other subnets on the remote network.

Suppose you're connecting to a VPN host through a connection named VPN to Client and you find these connection addresses:

```
PPP adapter VPN to Client:
    IP Address. . . . . . . 192.168.5.226
    Subnet Mask . . . . . . 255.255.255.255
    Default Gateway . . . . 192.168.5.226
```

Now suppose you know that there are two other subnets on the remote network: 192.168.10.0 mask 255.255.255.0 and 192.168.15.0 mask 255.255.255.0. You can reach these two networks by typing two route commands:

route add 192.168.10.0 mask 255.255.255.0 192.168.5.226
route add 192.168.15.0 mask 255.255.255.0 192.168.5.226

Each route command ends with the IP address of the remote gateway address (it's called the *next hop*).

Check your work by typing **route print** and looking at its output. In the IPv4 Route Table section, you should see only one destination labeled 0.0.0.0; if you see two, you forgot to disable the use of the default gateway on the remote network. Verify that the two routes you added are shown.

To avoid having to type all this every time, you can use another neat trick. You can put a rasphone command and route commands in a batch file, like this:

```
@echo off
rasphone -d "VPN to Client"
route add 192.168.10.0 mask 255.255.255.0 192.168.005.225
route add 192.168.15.0 mask 255.255.255.0 192.168.005.225
```

The rasphone command pops up the connection dialer. When the connection is made, the two routes will be added, and you're all set. With this setup, you'll need the network administrator to give you the real RAS gateway address of the remote VPN server to use as the "next hop" of the route commands. With a shortcut to this batch file, you can connect and set up the routes with just a click.

When you disconnect the VPN connection, Windows removes the added routes automatically.

CHAPTER 39

MEETINGS, CONFERENCING, AND COLLABORATION

In this chapter

Vista: Plays Well with Others   1312

Making Presentations with a Mobile Computer   1312

Windows Meeting Space   1315

Remote Assistance   1322

Tips from the Windows Pros: It's Not All About the Bullets   1328

Vista: Plays Well with Others

Today's computers are no longer seen as tools used in isolation. They've become portals through which people can communicate and work just as easily from across the globe as from across the room. Business users and students are increasingly relying on computers to make presentations and give reports (making them at least more colorful, if not more interesting).

In this chapter, we'll cover several Windows Vista features that make it easier for you to work with others:

- When you use your computer to display a business or class presentation, the Presentation Settings feature lets you tell Vista not to disrupt your presentation with messages, noises, or the screen saver.
- If you use a laptop computer, Vista's External Display tool makes it easy to control an external monitor or a projector.
- Windows Meeting Space lets you and other Windows Vista users work collaboratively, using wireless networking.
- If you need help with your computer, or if you want to demonstrate some computer task or application to others using their computer, Remote Assistance may be just what you need.

We'll start by looking at Vista's support for making presentations.

Making Presentations with a Mobile Computer

If you use a mobile (laptop or tablet) computer, Windows Vista has two features that are designed to make giving presentations smoother and easier. The features are Presentation Settings and External Display, part of the Windows Mobility Center that we discussed in Chapter 38, "Hitting the Road." External Display lets you manage an external monitor or a projector, and Presentation Settings keep Windows from interrupting your presentation.

Adjusting Presentation Settings

One of Vista's more thoughtful additions is the Presentation Settings feature in Windows Mobility Center. When you indicate that you are making a presentation, Vista takes steps to keep itself out of your way. It can make the following accommodations:

- Display a screen background chosen to minimize distraction or promote your company logo.
- Disable the screen saver, so that if you leave the computer alone for a few minutes, your audience isn't treated to an animated aquarium or a slide show that includes pictures of you getting dressed up for a Halloween party in really bad drag.
- Disable pop-up notifications and reminders from Windows services.

Making Presentations with a Mobile Computer

- Set the speaker volume so that you aren't bothered by sounds associated with events like mouse clicks, Window resizing, and the like.
- Disable automatic shutdown so that your computer won't go to sleep while you're talking. (There is unfortunately no corresponding setting for the audience.)

> **NOTE**
>
> Presentation Settings and the Windows Mobility Center are available only if you are using a mobile (laptop or tablet) computer.

To use the Presentation settings, first select the accommodations you'd like Windows to make. To do this, click Start, Control Panel, Mobile PC, and then click Adjust Settings Before Giving a Presentation, found under the Windows Mobility Center heading. The Presentation Settings dialog box appears, as shown in Figure 39.1.

Figure 39.1
Presentation Settings lets you keep Windows quiet during a presentation.

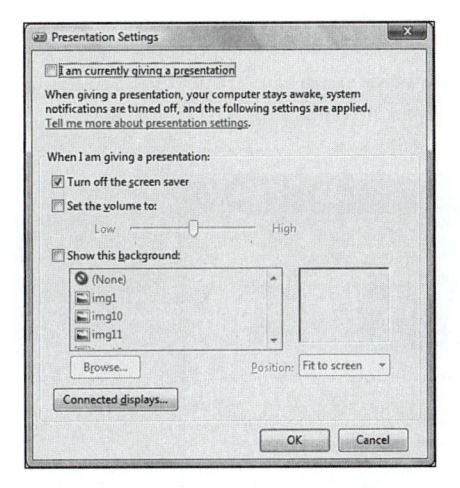

Set the check boxes next to the desired accommodations, and preselect the sound volume and desktop background if desired.

If you use a certain external monitor or projector whenever you give presentations, you can instruct Windows to invoke presentation settings automatically whenever the display is connected. To do this, attach the display(s), click Connected Displays, and check I Always Give a Presentation When I Use This Display Configuration.

Save your presentation settings preferences by clicking OK.

Now, whenever you are making a presentation, open the Windows Mobility Center by typing Windows+X, or by clicking Start, All Programs, Accessories, Windows Mobility Center. Then in the Presentation Settings tile, click Turn On.

> **TIP**
>
> If you use the Mobility Center a lot, that Windows+X hot-key shortcut will save you a lot of time and clicking! You could also put a shortcut to Windows Mobility Center on your Quick Launch Toolbar to make it easily accessible.

→ **See** "Set Up the Quick Launch Bar" on **p. 96** for more information on customizing the Quick Launch bar.

EXTERNAL DISPLAY

The External Display tile on Windows Mobility Center lets you control what appears on any connected external display or monitor attached to your computer.

To start, attach your external monitor or projector, or connect to a network-attached projector as described in the next section. Then, open Windows Mobility Center: click Start, All Programs, Accessories, Windows Mobility Center.

In the Windows Mobility Center window, click the Connect Display button in the External Display tile. The New Display Detected dialog box appears, letting you choose how to use the added screen real estate, as shown in Figure 39.2.

Figure 39.2
Select whether to extend or duplicate your desktop on the new display.

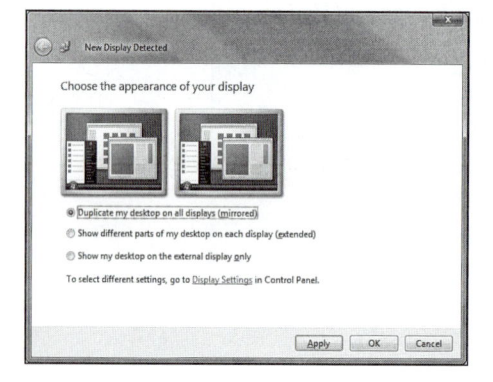

Then make one of the following choices:

- To display the same thing on the new display as you see on your laptop screen, select Duplicate My Desktop on All Displays.
- To show your audience one thing while you view something else on your laptop's screen, select Show Different Parts of My Desktop on Each Display. With this selection, you can drag application windows back and forth between your laptop's screen and the external display.
- To black out your laptop's screen and use the attached display only, select Show My Desktop on the External Display Only.

Click OK to save the setting.

> **NOTE**
>
> If you select the Duplicate option, your screen's resolution may be changed. Windows will use the highest reasonable screen resolution supported by both monitors. If both displays don't have the same shape, the external display might look pinched or stretched. If this happens, right-click the desktop, select Personalize, select Display Settings, and adjust the resolution slider to find a more acceptable setting. Click Apply after making each adjustment.
>
> Later, when you disconnect the external display, Windows probably won't reset your laptop's screen resolution to its original setting. To reset it manually, right-click the desktop, select Personalize, select Display Settings, and move the Resolution slider to the laptop display's native resolution—usually the rightmost position.

→ To learn about Vista's other accessories for mobile computers, **see** "Windows Mobility Center," **p. 1281**.

→ For more information about managing external displays, **see** "Installing and Using Multiple Monitors," **p. 1019**.

NETWORK PROJECTORS

Windows Vista includes support for connecting to video projectors that are reached over a network, rather than requiring them to be attached directly to your computer. Network attached projectors are becoming a more common feature in corporate conference rooms that are also outfitted with wireless or Ethernet network ports.

To use a network-attached projector, follow these steps:

1. Ensure that you have an active wireless or wired connection to the network that leads to the projector.
2. Click Start, All Programs, Accessories, Connect to a Network Projector.
3. If Windows asks for permission to allow the network projector to communicate through Windows Firewall, click Yes, and confirm the User Account Control prompt.
4. Click Search for a Projector. If the projector appears in the list of available devices, select its name and click Connect. If the projector can't be found, click the back button (the left arrow in the upper-left corner of the window), and click Enter the Projector Address. Type in the projector's network path, as provided by your network administrator. Enter the projector's password, if a password is required. Then click Connect.

Next, follow any additional prompts to direct your presentation output to the connected projector.

WINDOWS MEETING SPACE

Windows Meeting Space is a program that lets you and other Windows Vista users collaborate on a project by sharing files and sharing a view of a common Windows desktop. What makes Windows Meeting space different from and better than its predecessor, Microsoft

NetMeeting, is that Windows Meeting Space can use wireless networking to connect the meeting's participants without any setup—the program does all the work of creating and managing an ad hoc wireless network. An *ad hoc network* is one that connects two or more computers directly without requiring the use of a hardware access point or router—you and the other meeting participants simply have to be within wireless radio range of each other. Of course, you don't have to be sitting in the same room—Meeting Space works just as well across the Internet as over a wireless network.

Windows Meeting Space lets the participants share a set of files, and when anyone changes a file, everyone in the meeting automatically receives an updated copy. Cool, no? The one downside is that Windows Meeting Space is available only on Windows Vista, and NetMeeting isn't included, so Windows XP users and Vista users can't collaborate using either of these free tools. Also, if you use Vista Home Basic edition, you can join into a meeting set up by others, but you can't create a new meeting yourself. This means that at least one participant in the meeting has to have a higher-level version of Vista.

> **NOTE**
>
> The network connection that you use for Windows Meeting Space must support the IPv6 protocol—some older wireless network adapters can't. If yours doesn't, you might be able to upgrade the network driver to do so. Also, you cannot use Windows Meeting Space from the Guest user account.

Setting Up Windows Meeting Space

To start Windows Meeting Space, click Start, All Programs, Windows Meeting Space. When the program starts for the first time, it will ask you to begin the setup process. Click Yes, Continue Setting Up Windows Meeting Space. You'll have to confirm a User Account Control prompt to proceed.

The setup process will do three things:

- Enable People Near Me, which is a network service that lets other computers on your local area network (or wireless network) know who you are and that you are connected.
- Enable Distributed File Replication Service, which monitors a set of files and copies updates between computers.
- Create exceptions in Windows Firewall to pass Windows Meeting Space traffic.

The first screen asks you to enter your name as you'd like it to be advertised to other potential meeting participants, as shown in Figure 39.3.

Figure 39.3
Enter your name as you'd like it to be displayed to other meeting participants.

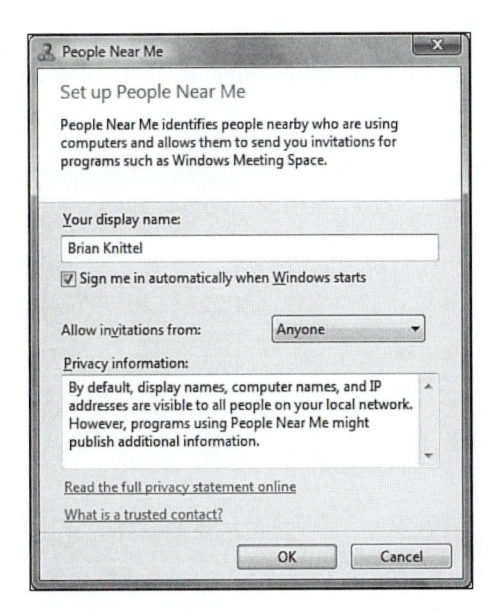

If you check Sign Me In Automatically When Windows Starts, the People Near Me service will always be available. (There's probably no need to do this—anytime the service isn't on when you start Windows Meeting space, Windows will prompt you with this screen.)

> **NOTE**
>
> People Near Me is used only by Windows Meeting Space, but future applications may use it as well. Its purpose is to make it easy to use collaboration and communication software with other users on your local network. You can manage the People Near Me application from the Control Panel Control—just click Network and Internet, People Near Me. You might want to do this if you later decide not to have it start up every time you log on.

You can also change Allow Invitations From to prevent strangers from contacting you through People Near Me. If you select Trusted Contacts only, you'll have to install contact certificates provided by others before they can invite you into a meeting. You can also select No One, which means that you must always initiate an invitation to a meeting, never the other way around. For now, leave the setting on Anyone and click OK.

The Windows Meeting Space window will then appear, as shown in Figure 39.4. One person must start the meeting by creating a meeting name. If you want to do this yourself, click Start a New Meeting. Then follow these steps:

Figure 39.4
Start by creating or selecting a meeting.

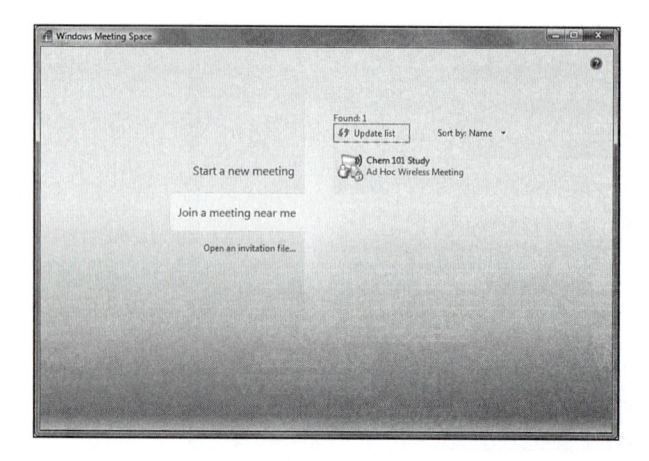

1. Enter a name for the meeting, such as Chem 101 Study. If you plan to use the ad hoc wireless network feature to connect the participants, keep the meeting name to 15 characters or fewer.
2. Unless you're afraid that some sort of spy is peering over your shoulder, check Show Characters so that you can see what you're about to type and can catch any typos.
3. Enter a password. Other users will need to use this password to connect to the meeting. It has to be eight characters long and simple enough to tell to the other participants without confusion.
4. If the other participants' computers are already connected to yours through an existing wired or wireless network, click Options, uncheck Create a Private Ad Hoc Wireless Network, and then click OK. Otherwise, if you do want to let Windows Meeting Space connect you using its wireless network feature, leave this option alone.
5. Click the right arrow (the Next button).

Windows Meeting Space prepares the ad hoc wireless network if necessary, and then displays the Windows Meeting Space window, as shown in Figure 39.5. Wait for others to join the meeting before proceeding. When your group is ready to go, skip ahead to "Working in Windows Meeting Space."

Figure 39.5
The Windows Meeting Space window shows a shared desktop or application, a list of participants, and a list of shared files.

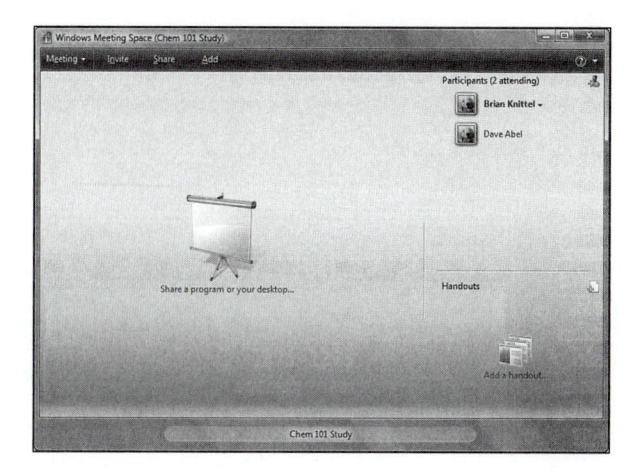

Joining an Existing Meeting

If you want to join a meeting that someone else has created, start Windows Meeting Space, and if necessary, enter your name as you'd like it to be displayed to others, as described in the previous section.

The Windows Meeting Space window should display a list of available meetings, as shown in Figure 39.4. If the meeting you want to join doesn't appear, click Update List.

Click the desired meeting name, enter the password, and press Enter. The Windows Meeting Space window will appear, and your name will be added to the list of participants.

You can start to work as soon as you join, or you can wait for others to join before proceeding.

Working in Windows Meeting Space

Meeting participants can all share a view of a common Windows desktop or a single application. To share an application on your desktop, click Share a Program or Your Desktop. A list of active applications appears, as shown in Figure 39.6. You can make one of the following choices:

Figure 39.6
Select the desktop or a single application to share with the other participants.

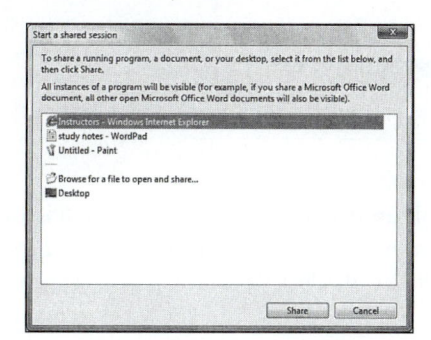

- To share the window of just one application, select the application from the upper part of the list and click Share.

- To open a document in its associated application and then share that application window, click Browse for a File to Open and Share, locate and select the file, and then click Open.
- To share your entire desktop, select Desktop, and click Share.

Now the selected application or your entire desktop will be made visible to the other meeting participants. You can use the application as you normally would.

> **TIP**
> If you have selected to share an application rather than the full desktop, the other participants will see the application window just as you do, with the rest of the screen blacked out. Maximize the application to let the others get a better view.

Click Stop Sharing in the Windows Meeting Space window to cancel sharing or let others share their desktop.

When someone else has shared an application or a desktop, you'll see a somewhat shrunken view of it in the Windows Meeting Space window, as shown in Figure 39.7. You can maximize the Windows Meeting Space window to improve the view.

Figure 39.7
A shared application appears within the Windows Meeting Space window.

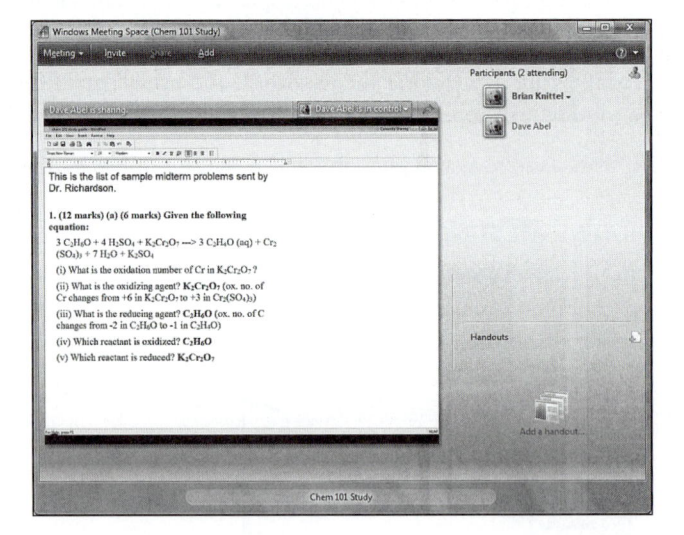

You'll see the same view of the application that its owner sees, including the mouse cursor. If you want to make changes or run the application yourself, click the *Person's Name* Is in Control box at the top of the window, and select Request Control. When the other user grants permission, you'll be able to use your mouse and keyboard to make changes.

Sharing Documents as Handouts

You can easily share documents with other meeting participants. Just drag a file from your desktop or Windows Explorer to the Handouts section of the Windows Meeting Space window. Alternatively, click the small Add (+) icon in the Handouts area and browse for a file.

The selected file will be copied to everyone in the meeting and will appear in everyone's Windows Meeting Space window, as seen in Figure 39.8.

Figure 39.8
Handouts are files that are automatically copied to each participant.

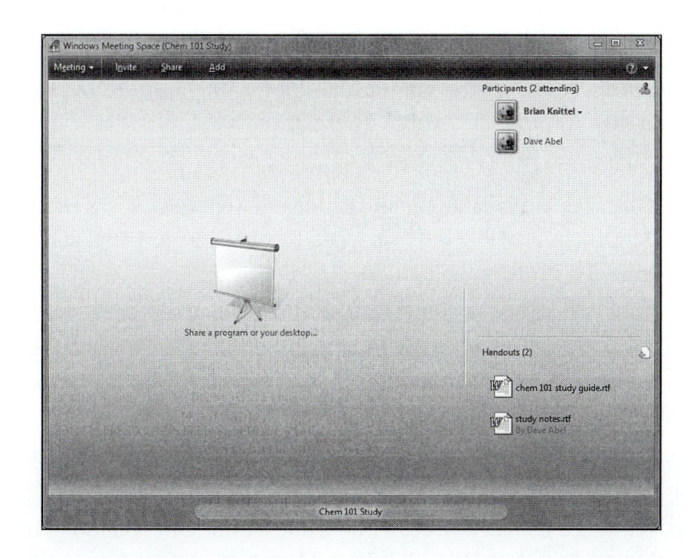

Anyone can open any handout document and view its contents. If anyone edits and saves the document, the changed version will automatically be copied to everyone else in the meeting (although, if they're viewing the document at the time, they'll need to close their old copy and reopen the file to see your changes).

If you contribute a handout, your original copy of the file that you dragged into the Handouts section will *not* be changed. Everyone in the meeting works with a copy that's stored in a temporary file on each member's hard disk. So, if you want to keep the changed version of the document you shared, you'll need to save a copy of the document when you leave the meeting.

Leaving a Meeting

At the end of the meeting, you can save a copy of the final version of the handout files by clicking Meeting, Save Handouts. You'll be prompted for a location into which to save the file(s). You also will be asked if you want to save handouts when you leave the meeting.

You can leave the meeting anytime by clicking Meeting, Leave Meeting. When the last person leaves, if you used an ad hoc wireless network, the network setup will automatically be deleted.

Remote Assistance

Remote Assistance lets two people work collaboratively on one Windows computer—one at the computer and one remotely, over the Internet. While Windows Meeting Space, which we discussed in the previous section, is designed to let a group of people work together on a project, Remote Assistance is designed to let people get technical assistance from someone else at a remote location. It's not so much a "let's all work together" tool as a "let me help you with this" tool. In fact, some computer manufacturers advertise that they'll use Remote Assistance to help you with your computer after you purchase it.

Remote Assistance is based on the same technology as the Remote Desktop feature we'll discuss in Chapter 40, "Remote Desktop." There are some similarities, and several significant differences, between the two:

- Remote Assistance is available on all versions of Windows Vista and XP, whereas Remote Desktop is available only on Vista Business, Enterprise, and Ultimate editions, and Windows XP Professional.
- With Remote Assistance, both the local and remote users see the same screen at the same time, and both can move the mouse, type on the keyboard, and so forth. With Remote Desktop, when a remote user is working, the computer's monitor displays the Welcome screen.
- Remote Assistance doesn't make the local computer's hard drives available, nor does it transmit sound, as Remote Desktop does.
- Remote Assistance connections can't be made ad lib. One Windows user must invite another through email or Windows Live Messenger. Or one user can offer assistance to another using Messenger. In any case, the procedure requires the simultaneous cooperation of users at both ends of the connection.
- Remote Assistance allows you to use a text chat window or voice chat while the desktop session is active.

A big plus with Remote Assistance on Windows Vista is that it should work even if you are using a shared Internet connection. This is a big improvement over Remote Assistance on Windows XP, which rarely worked over a shared connection. The reason is that on Vista, Remote Assistance uses Internet Protocol Version 6 and Teredo tunneling to safely pass data through Internet connection sharing routers and firewalls.

> **NOTE**
> To take advantage of the new, more reliable connection method, both you and the person who is helping you—or the person you are helping—must be using Windows Vista, *and* you must change a setting, as described in the next section. You and the other person should also have Windows Vista Service Pack 1 installed, or any later service pack.

Enabling Remote Assistance

Remote Assistance is usually enabled by default when you install Windows, but before you try to use it to get help, you should confirm that it is enabled. Furthermore, if you want to use the new, more reliable connection method to work with another Vista user, you must change a setting by following these steps:

1. Click Start, right-click Computer, and select Properties.
2. In the Tasks list on the left, click Remote Settings. A User Account Control prompt will appear. Click Continue, or enter an Administrator password, as requested.
3. Check to be sure that Allow Remote Assistance Connections to This Computer is checked. If it isn't, check it.
4. Click the Advanced button.
5. If you use an Internet connection sharing router, check Create Invitations That Can Only Be Used from Computers Running Windows Vista or Later. You will only be able to invite other Windows Vista users to help you, not XP users, but at least it will work.

    You can also change the number of hours that an invitation to help remains active.

Finally, click OK to save your changes.

REQUESTING REMOTE ASSISTANCE

To invite a friend or colleague to work with you on your computer, first contact your friend and confirm that she has Windows Vista or XP and is ready to work with you.

Before you start, you may need to change settings, depending on whether the person you are asking for help is running Windows Vista or Windows XP:

If the other user is using Windows Vista:

- Use the instructions in the previous section to check the box labeled Create Invitations That Can Only Be Used from Computers Running Windows Vista or Later.

If the other user is using Windows XP:

- Use the instructions in the previous section to *uncheck* the box labeled Create Invitations That Can Only Be Used from Computers Running Windows Vista or Later.
- We have found that sometimes the XP version of Remote Assistance crashes when it opens a request for assistance from a Vista user. We hope that Microsoft is working on fixing this.
- If you are using an Internet connection sharing router, or if you are on a business network that uses a firewall, the odds of your friend's computer being able to connect to yours are fairly slim. If you can, try to enable Universal Plug and Play (UPnP) in your router before you issue the Remote Assistance request. That may help.

After you've made those adjustments, follow these steps to request assistance:

1. Select Start, Help and Support.
2. Click Use Windows Remote Assistance to Get Help from a Friend or Offer Help.
3. Select Invite Someone You Trust to Help You.

4. Select Use Email to Send an Invitation.

5. Make up and enter a password of at least six letters or numbers. You'll have to give this password to your friend before your friend can assist you. Send it to them via email or call them by phone and tell them.

6. Your selected email program will pop up with an email ready to address and send. Enter your friend's email address and send the email. The important part is the attachment, which is a file named something along the lines of `RATicket.MsRcIncident`. Don't delete the attachment!

7. Windows will display a window that says Waiting for an Incoming Connection. Leave this window alone until your friend receives the invitation and responds.

NOTE

If you use a dial-up Internet connection or a DSL service that requires you to sign on, your Internet IP address changes every time you connect. The Remote Assistance invitation uses this address to tell the other person's computer how to contact you, so it will work only if you stay connected from the time you send the invitation to the time your friend responds. If you have a fixed (static) IP address, this won't be a problem.

If you sent your request via Windows Live Messenger, you should get a response within a few seconds. If you sent the request by email, it could be some time before the other party reads and receives it.

NOTE

At Step 4, you also can select Save This Invitation as a File. You can use this choice to transfer the invitation by means such as a network folder or removable disk.

When someone responds to your request for assistance, a dialog box will appear on your screen, asking if it's okay for him to connect. Click Yes, and after a short while—a minute or so—a window will appear with which you can control the Remote Assistance session, as shown in Figure 39.9.

Figure 39.9
When your Remote Assistant has connected, you can use this window to chat and control the connection.

At this point, your friend can see your screen and can watch what you do with it, but he can't actually do anything with your computer. The friend first has to ask to take control, and you have to consent. Then, either of you can type, move the mouse, and otherwise poke around and use your computer.

By default, Remote Assistance makes it easy for you to take back control, presumably so that you can stop someone from doing something you don't like. All you have to do is to press the Esc key, and the person is once again locked out. The problem is that if your friend presses the Esc key, the same thing happens: that person loses the ability to work with your computer. This can be *really* annoying. So, if you trust the person who's helping you, you can save everyone a lot of grief by making the following setting change right away:

1. Click Settings.
2. Uncheck Use ESC Key to Stop Sharing Control.
3. Click OK.

Now the Esc key will no longer bring him to a crashing halt.

When a friend asks to take control of your computer, a request will pop up on your screen. If he's just going to work with a normal Windows application such as Word, just click Yes to let him take control. However, if he needs to manage Windows itself, you have to decide who is going to handle the User Account Control prompts that will appear. By default, he won't be able to see or respond to them. You have two options:

- If you want to respond to any User Account Control prompts yourself, just click Yes to let him connect. If he performs an action that requires security confirmation, his screen will go black for a moment, and you'll have to respond to the User Account Control prompt.
- If you want to let him change Windows settings without your intervention, check Allow *username* to Respond to User Account Control Prompts, then click Yes. You will be asked to confirm a User Account Control prompt yourself at this point.

> **NOTE**
>
> If you don't have administrator privileges on your computer, you won't be able to give your friend permission to perform administrative actions, either. There are two ways to work around this.
>
> If the remote user knows an administrator password and will tell you what it is, check Allow *username* to Respond to User Account Control Prompts and click Yes. When the prompt appears, select the account and enter the password he gave you.
>
> The second workaround requires Vista Service Pack 1 and some advance setup *before* you need to use Remote Assistance. An Administrator has to perform these steps: Click Start, All Programs, Administrative Tools, Local Security Policy. Under Local Policies, Security Options, enable User Account Control: Allow UIAccess Applications to Prompt for Elevation Without Using the Secure Desktop. Then restart Windows (on a corporate network, this option can be enabled through Group Policy). With this option enabled, the remote user will be able to respond to User Account Control prompts even if you don't know an administrator password.

Now your friend should be able to work your keyboard and mouse, and help you.

The Windows Remote Assistance toolbar has a few other features that you will find useful:

- If you want a moment of privacy, perhaps to read email or look at a sensitive file, click Pause. This will black out the other person's view of your screen without disconnecting that person. Click Continue to restore the view.
- To communicate with your friend via text messaging, click Chat. The Remote Assistance toolbar will enlarge. Type your comments into the lower box on the window and press Enter (or click Send), and your friend will see what you type. You'll see your friend's responses in the upper part of the window. Click the Chat button again to shrink the toolbar back to its original size.
- To send your friend a file or document, click Send File. Select the file and click Open. The Sending File dialog box will remain on the screen until your friend accepts the file and it has been transferred.
- To take control away from your friend, click Stop Sharing. Your friend will still be able to see your screen, but can only watch. He has to request control again to do anything.

When you're finished, click Disconnect to end the Remote Assistance session.

Responding to an Assistance Request

When someone invites you to connect by Remote Assistance, you'll either see a pop-up box in Windows Live Messenger, or you'll receive an email. You might also receive a file, with a name something like `Invitation.MsRcIncident`.

You can directly respond to an instant message invitation as indicated in the message window. To accept an email invitation, open the message's attachment. (How you do that depends on your email program—in Windows Mail, click the paper clip icon and select the attachment whose name ends with `.MsRcIncident`. When Windows Mail asks `Do you want to open this file?` click Open.) Opening the attachment should activate the Remote Assistance connection. If you receive the invitation as a file, just double-click to open the file in Windows Explorer.

You will be asked to enter the password associated with the invitation—the person who invited you will have to tell you what it is.

Assuming you both say yes, at this point patience is called for because it can take more than a minute for the required software to load up and for the other user's desktop to appear on your screen, as shown in Figure 39.10.

> **NOTE**
>
> If Windows is unable to establish a connection to the person who invited you, ask her what operating system she's using. If it's XP and it doesn't work the first time, the chances that it's ever going to work are slim. If she's using Vista, ask her to check the box labeled Create Invitations That Can Only Be Used From Computers Running Windows Vista or Later, as described in the "Enabling Remote Assistance" section earlier in this chapter. Then have her send you a new invitation.

Figure 39.10
The Remote Assistance screen has a control panel at the top and a view of the remote user's screen underneath. Click Request Control if you want to manipulate the remote computer.

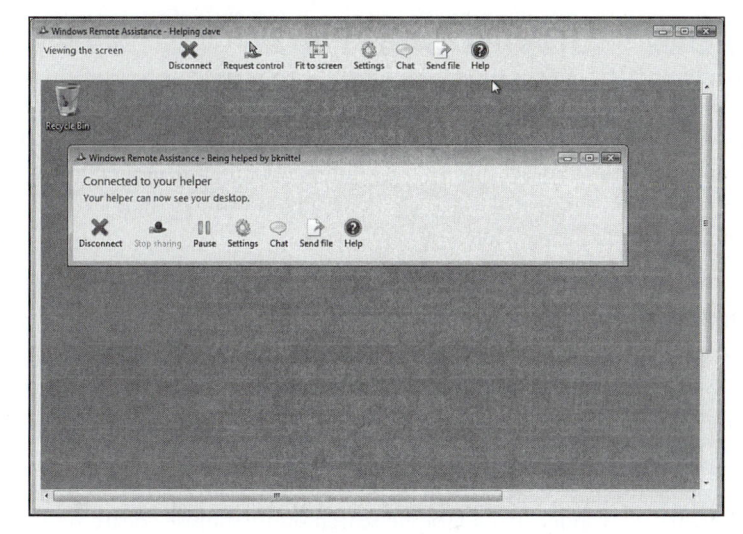

Across the top is a menu of controls. The choices are

- **Disconnect**—Click this to close Remote Assistance.
- **Request Control**—Click this to begin using the other computer's mouse and keyboard. The remote user will have to grant permission. After you have control of the other computer, both of you can use your mouse and keyboard.

    Watch out for the Esc key—it can instantly disconnect your keyboard and mouse from the other computer. To prevent this, click Settings, uncheck Use ESC Key to Stop Sharing Control, and then click OK.

- **Fit to Screen**—Click this to shrink the view of the other computer's screen so that it fits perfectly in the Remote Assistance window. You won't have to use the scrollbars to see the far corners anymore.
- **Settings**—Click to turn off the recording of the remote session that Windows makes by default.
- **Chat**—Click this to open a text chat panel in the left side of the Remote Assistance window. Type your messages into the small box at the bottom of the Chat area.
- **Send File**—Click to transfer a file to your friend. Browse and select the file you want to send, then click Open. You may have to wait a while, until the other person agrees to receive the file and the file is sent.
- **Help**—Displays online help for Remote Assistance.

If your friend clicks the Stop Sharing button, or either of you presses the Esc key while it's still set to cancel sharing, you'll lose control of the remote screen. Just click Request Control again to resume working.

Tips from the Windows Pros: It's Not All About the Bullets

If you make a lot of presentations with your computer, you're probably one of the millions of people who uses PowerPoint to help out. PowerPoint is an application that's part of Microsoft Office, and it makes it easy to design and show "slides" that are projected to and watched by the audience while you talk.

PowerPoint does make the design part easy, with a huge assortment of background patterns and predefined templates that help you organize the information you want to present. Unfortunately, there is no corresponding assistance in helping you decide what you should actually say or show. Large numbers of presentations consist of an endless series of slides that the presenter simply reads aloud while the audience watches. We've all been subjected to that, and knowing that you're going to get the same set of slides in printed form after it's all over just adds to the frustration—you could just read the handout yourself in five minutes. It's no wonder that a Google search on the phrase "death by PowerPoint" returns more than 70,000 hits.

Making an effective presentation takes more than just filling in the empty spots next to the three bullet points that PowerPoint puts on each slide. If you have to make presentations as part of your job, you probably know that effective graphical communication is a fascinating and complex skill. It's worth learning as much as you can about the ways that information should be communicated graphically, and ways to make the visual part of your presentation complement and enhance your oral presentation, rather than simply mirror it.

There are many books and courses devoted to the topic, but I suggest that you get started with Edward Tuft's essay *The Cognitive Style of PowerPoint*, which you can get at www.edwardtufte.com. It's contrarian, and a bit of a ramble, but it shows so many ways that visual presentations can go horribly wrong that you'll definitely think in a very different way the next time you start up PowerPoint.

CHAPTER 40

REMOTE DESKTOP

In this chapter

Using Your Computer Remotely   1330

Setting Up Access to Your Own Computer   1332

Connecting to Other Computers with Remote Desktop   1342

Troubleshooting   1350

Tips from the Windows Pros: Making More Than One Computer Available   1351

Using Your Computer Remotely

Windows Vista Business, Enterprise, and Ultimate editions (as well as Windows XP Professional) have a spiffy feature called Remote Desktop that lets you connect to and use your computer from another location. You can see your computer's screen, move the mouse and type on the keyboard, open files, and even print, just as if you were really sitting in front of your own computer. The neat part is that you can do this from just about any computer, as long as it's running some version of Windows or Mac OS X.

Figure 40.1 shows how this works.

Figure 40.1
You can use any computer running Windows or Macintosh OS X to connect to and control your computer.

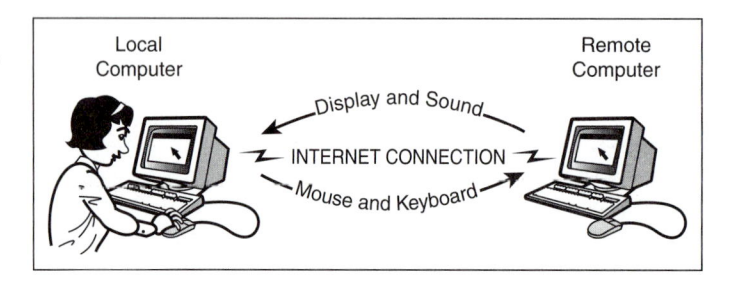

This is just what you need when you're out of town and need to read a file you left on the computer back home, or if you want to read your office email from home.

I've been using this feature since it appeared in Windows XP Professional, and I love it.

You also can use the Remote Desktop Client program to attach to computers running Windows Server 2003, Windows 2000 Server, and Windows NT Terminal Services Edition. The client program lets you log on to these computers to access applications or for administration and maintenance.

> **NOTE**
> You don't have to be miles away to take advantage of Remote Desktop, either. You can also use it to access other computers in your home or office, using your local area network. For instance, you can use it to start a lengthy computing or printing job on someone else's computer without leaving your own desk.

This chapter consists of two parts. The first part shows you how to set up your computer so that you can access it remotely. The second part shows you how to connect to another computer using the Remote Desktop Client.

NOTE

The Remote Desktop Service, which lets you connect to your own computer from another computer, is available only on Windows Vista Business, Enterprise, and Ultimate Editions, as well as Windows XP Professional. If you have one of the Home versions of Windows Vista, the part of this chapter that talks about setting up access to your own computer does not apply to your version of Windows.

On the other hand, the Remote Desktop Client, which is the application you use to connect to a remote computer and which is discussed in the second part of the chapter, is included with *all* Windows Vista and XP versions. It can also be downloaded for Windows 98, Me, and Mac OS X.

NOTE

You can also get tiny, special-purpose computers called "thin clients" that have the Remote Desktop Client software built in. I purchased a used Wyse WinTerm on eBay for $15 and added a used LCD monitor, USB mouse, and USB keyboard. It's plugged into my network at home in the kitchen. The little computer is small enough to stick to the back of the monitor with Velcro. Now I can check email and browse for recipes while cooking dinner, by connecting to my office computer. Be careful, though: If you shop for a thin client, be sure to get one that has the Remote Desktop Protocol (RDP) software preinstalled. Mine came with an alternate protocol called Citrix ICA, and it was a real pain finding and installing the Remote Desktop software module because my used WinTerm was old and no longer supported.

Third-party programs such as Carbon Copy, PC Anywhere, Timbuktu, GoToMyPC, and VNC also provide this type of remote access capability; some of these products have some more sophisticated features, but Remote Desktop is built into Windows and it's essentially free (well, it's free after you've paid for Windows).

Remote Desktop is a scaled-down version of Windows Terminal Services, a component of the Windows Server versions that lets multiple users run programs on one central server. By "stripped down," I mean that only one person is allowed to connect to Windows Vista at a time, either remotely or with the regular monitor and keyboard. So if you connect remotely, the local user is temporarily kicked out to the welcome screen. And if a local user logs on while you're connected remotely, *you'll* be disconnected. You won't lose your work—you can reconnect later—but the upshot is that only one person at a time is allowed to use a Windows Vista computer.

When Remote Desktop is set up, you can use any Windows or Macintosh computer to reach your computer, using the Remote Desktop Connection Client program. The Remote

Desktop Client software (which you use to view the remote computer) works on any 32- or 64-bit version of Windows, and a version also exists for Mac OS X.

Setting Up Access to Your Own Computer

This first half of the chapter tells you how to set up remote access to your own computer. If you want to use the Remote Desktop Connection client to access another computer, skip ahead to "Using the Remote Connection," later in the chapter.

Across a local area network (that is, between computers in your home or office), Remote Desktop Connection works right "out of the box"—you just have to enable the feature.

However, if you want to use Remote Desktop to reach your computer over the Internet, you have to set up several other things in advance. I'll give you step-by-step instructions shortly, but to give you an overview, the requirements are as follows:

- You must enable Remote Desktop; it's disabled by default. You also have to specify which user account(s) are to be given access.
- A password has to be set for any user account that you want to use when connecting remotely. You can't use Remote Desktop to connect to an account that has no password.
- Your host computer must be reachable over the Internet whenever you want to connect to it; this means that it needs an always-on Internet connection. Cable Internet service usually works this way. If you have a DSL connection that requires you to sign on every time you use it, you need to either use a connection-sharing router device and tell it to keep the connection up 24×7, or use third-party software to tell Windows to keep your connection open. I'll show you how shortly.
- Your Internet connection either needs a *static* (fixed) IP address, or you need to use a dynamic DNS service so that your computer's IP address can be determined from afar. With most cable and DSL Internet service, your connection's IP address can change from day to day. You might be able to ask your ISP for a static address for an added monthly fee. If that's not an option, I'll show you shortly how to install some free add-on software or use a connection-sharing router that supports dynamic DNS (DDNS).
- Finally, if you use a shared Internet connection, the router or sharing computer has to be set up to forward incoming requests to the computer you want to reach by Remote Desktop.

This sounds complex, but it really isn't that bad. Let's go through the process step by step. You can go about this in other ways, of course, but what I give you here is a procedure that's suitable for a home user with Windows Vista Ultimate edition or a small-office user with the Business version.

CAUTION

> If your computer is part of a corporate network, check with your network administrators before attempting to make any changes to the Remote Desktop settings. In fact, in all likelihood, these settings will be locked down and you won't be able to change them anyway. If this is the case, your network admins will have to set up Remote Desktop access for you.

ENABLING REMOTE DESKTOP ACCESS TO YOUR COMPUTER

To enable Remote Desktop connections to your computer, follow these steps:

1. Click Start, right-click Computer, and select Properties.
2. Under Tasks, click Remote Settings and then confirm the User Account Control prompt.
3. Select Allow Connections from Computers Running Any Version of Remote Desktop. (The "more secure" version works only on corporate networks using IPSec security).
4. By default, all Administrator level accounts will be allowed to connect to the computer. If you want to grant Remote Desktop access to any Limited users, click Select Users, Add, Advanced, Find Now, and then locate the desired name in the Search Results section. Double-click it. To add another name, click Advanced and Find Now again.
5. Click OK to close all the dialog boxes.

NOTE

> A password must be set on a user's account before that user can connect to the computer remotely.

CAUTION

> Be *sure* that every user account that can be reached via Remote Desktop (that is, every Administrator account and any Limited accounts that you entered in Step 4) has a strong password. This means a password with uppercase letters *and* lowercase letters *and* one or more numbers *and* punctuation, and at least 8 characters in length.

At this point, you should do two things to be sure that Remote Desktop has been set up correctly:

- Click Start, Control Panel. Under Security, select Allow a Program Through Windows Firewall and confirm the User Account Control prompt. On the Exceptions tab, find Remote Desktop in the Exceptions list and be sure it's checked. If it isn't, check it. On the General tab, be sure that Block All Incoming Connections is *not* checked.
- If your computer is connected to a local area network in your home or office, use one of your other computers to test Remote Desktop before you get involved in the Internet part. Use the instructions in the second part of the chapter to open the Remote Desktop client on another computer on your network. As the host name, type

in the name of the computer you just set up. Make sure that you can connect over your own local network before proceeding.

If you just want to use Remote Desktop within your home or office network, you're finished and can skip ahead to the part of the chapter titled "Connecting to Other Computers with Remote Desktop."

However, if you want to reach your computer through the Internet, you have more work to do.

Establishing 24×7 Access

Because you won't be there at your home or office to turn on your computer and establish an Internet connection, you have to set things up so that your computer and connection are always working. If the power goes out at your home or office and your computer doesn't start itself up again automatically, you won't be able to connect. Your computer must start up automatically.

To set this up on a desktop computer, you need to get to the BIOS setup screen. You can get there when you first power up the computer, or by restarting Windows and waiting for the screen to go black. Be prepared to press the BIOS Setup hot key. The screen tells you what key to press; it's usually the Del or F2 key.

When you've gotten to the BIOS setup screen, look for the Power Management settings. Find an entry titled AC Power Recovery, or something similar. Some computers have an option labeled Last Setting, which turns the computer on only if it was already on when the power failed. If it's available, that's the one to use. Otherwise, select the setting that turns your computer on whenever the AC power comes on. Then save the BIOS settings and restart Windows.

> **NOTE**
>
> Automatic startup is generally not an option with a laptop computer. If you want remote access to your laptop, you just have to leave it on and hope that the battery takes it through any brief power outages.

Besides a 24×7 computer, you need a 24×7 Internet connection. If you have cable Internet service or a type of DSL service that does not require you to enter a username or password, you have an always-on Internet connection already and can skip ahead to the next section.

For Internet service that requires sign-on, you need some means of automatically reestablishing the connection whenever your computer starts up or the connection goes down. Microsoft's built-in Broadband connection sign-on software does not provide a reliable way by itself to keep the Internet connection permanently open. You can work around this in three ways:

- You can see if your DSL provider can upgrade your service to provide a static IP address and always-on service. This *might* be inexpensive enough to make it worthwhile.

- You can use a hardware connection-sharing router. The router connects to your DSL modem and your computer(s) to the router. The router makes the DSL connection for you, and you can configure it to keep it going all the time.

    If you don't have a router already, it's a worthwhile investment to buy one. They cost between $0 (after rebate, when there's a sale) and $75, and can also provide wireless networking capability for your home or office.

    Chapter 22, "Connecting Your Network to the Internet," tells how to set up a router for DSL service, so I don't cover that here. Be sure to enable the router's "keepalive" feature so that your connection is kept going all the time. Otherwise, the connection might be allowed to close when there is no activity from inside your LAN, and you might not be able to connect later.

- If you use the Broadband connection feature built into Windows Vista, you can add a third-party program to force Windows to keep the connection open all the time. Although I personally prefer the first two options, the DynDNS Updater program that I'll discuss later can do this for you, so you can forgo the router if you want to.

Next, you must make sure you can locate your computer from out on the Internet.

STATIC IP ADDRESS OR DYNAMIC DNS

All Internet connections are established on the basis of a number called an *IP address*, which is to your Internet connection as your telephone number is to your phone. Your IP address uniquely identifies your computer among all the millions of connected computers worldwide. If you use a shared connection, all your network's computers share one *public* IP address, much as the phone extensions in an office share one outside telephone number.

The question is, when you're somewhere else, how do you find your computer's IP address so that Remote Desktop can establish a connection to it?

If you have purchased a static IP address from your ISP, the answer is, they'll tell you. It has four sets of numbers separated by periods and looks something like this: 64.220.177.62. This will always be your computer's number. You can simply type this in when using the Remote Desktop client to connect to your computer. However, static addresses usually carry a monthly surcharge, and some ISPs simply cannot or will not provide them. So although this is worth looking into, it might not be an option. (My home ISP is sonic.net and static addresses are *not* expensive, but this is the exception instead of the rule.)

In most cases, dial-up, DSL, and cable Internet connections use *dynamic* addressing, in which a different IP address is assigned to you every time you or your router connects to your ISP (or, in the case of cable service, whenever your cable modem is reset). Thus, your computer's IP address can change at any time, and you won't necessarily know what it is when you want to connect from somewhere else.

The solution to this problem is to use a free dynamic domain name service (DDNS). It has two parts: First, on a DDNS provider's website, you register a *host name*, a name of your own choice, attached to one of several domain names that the provider makes available. For example, you might register the host name `mycomputer` in the domain `homedns.org`. Second, you set up dynamic DNS client software that periodically contacts the DDNS provider and informs it of your current IP address. Some Internet connection-sharing routers have a DDNS client built in, or you can download and install a software version on your computer. When this is all set up, you can use the name (`mycomputer.homedns.org`, in our example) to connect to your computer from anywhere on the Internet.

> **NOTE**
>
> Many DDNS providers exist, most of which are free services. You can find them easily enough by doing a Google search for "free DDNS service." In addition, for a fee, some DDNS providers will let you use your own personal domain name instead of using one provided by the service. Here I give you step-by-step instructions for setting up service with dyndns.com because it's free and it's directly supported by many hardware connection-sharing routers.

To set up dynamic DNS service at dyndns.com, follow these steps:

1. View www.dyndns.com in Internet Explorer. Click Create Account. Make up a username and password, and enter these along with your email address in the registration form. Be sure to jot down the username and password.

2. Read and acknowledge the terms of service, check I Will Create Only One Free Account, and click Create Account. (You're allowed only one free account, but you can use it to register several computers, if you want.)

3. Await the confirmation email, and follow its instructions to activate your account and sign on.

4. When you are at the dyndns.com website and have logged on, click Services, Dynamic DNS, Add Dynamic DNS.

5. Enter a host name that you can easily remember, and select a domain name from the pull-down list. Leave the other information as is and click Add Host. If someone else has claimed the name you chose, change the name or domain and try again until you succeed. Be sure to write down the host name and domain name that you eventually select.

Now your DDNS service is set up. Next, you need to set up the DNS client, so that changes to your IP address are sent to dyndns.com.

If you are using an Internet connection-sharing router that supports DDNS, use your router's setup screens to enable DDNS using your dyndns.com login name, password, and full host name, including the domain name that you selected. For example, this might be `mycomputer.homedns.org`. Your router's setup screen will likely differ from this, but it will generally look something like the one in Figure 40.2.

Setting Up Access to Your Own Computer

> **TIP**
>
> If you don't know how to connect to your router, try this: Click Start, All Programs, Accessories, Command Prompt. Type the command `ipconfig` and press Enter. Note the gateway address for the local area connection entry, which will be something like 192.168.0.1; the third number might be different. Close this window and open Internet Explorer. In the address bar, type // followed by the gateway address you noted earlier. For example, //192.168.0.1.

Figure 40.2
Configure your router to update your host name using dynamic DNS.

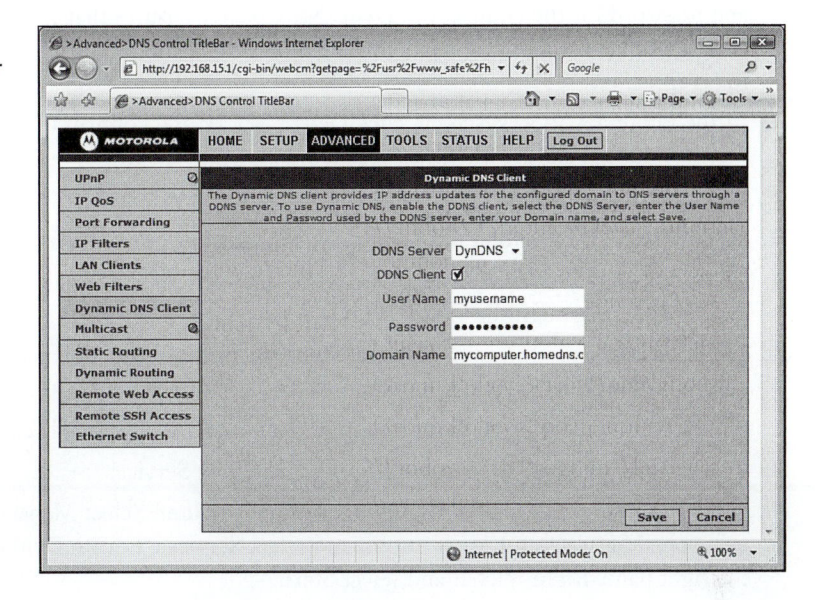

If your router doesn't have a DDNS client built in, or if you are not using a hardware router, you have to install a software DDNS client to do the job. You want one that doesn't require any manual intervention to get started and that always runs even when nobody is logged on. This means that you need one that operates as a Windows *service* rather than as a regular desktop application. The free DynDNS Updater program available from dyndns.com fits this bill nicely. Here's how to set it up.

If you use Windows Internet Connection Sharing, perform this procedure on the computer that shares its connection with the Internet, whether or not it's the computer that you're enabling for Remote Desktop access. Otherwise, do this on the computer that you're enabling for Remote Desktop access.

1. Log on as an Administrator. Open Internet Explorer and view www.dyndns.com/support/clients. Download `dyndns-setup.zip` by following the link on this page.
2. After downloading, open `dyndns-setup.zip` and drag `setup.exe` to your desktop.
3. Right-click `setup.exe` and select Run As Administrator. Confirm the User Account Control dialog box and then click Allow to run the downloaded program.
4. Step through the installation screens. At the last screen, check Launch DynDNS Updater and click Finish.

5. Follow the wizard's instructions, clicking Next after you fill in any required information on each page.

   On the first page, if you have dial-up or DSL service that requires a logon and password *and the connection is made directly from your computer*, click Dial-Up. If you have cable Internet service or you have a router that establishes the connection for you, select Local Area Network.

6. If you selected Dial-Up, select the correct connection name and provide the username and password for the connection. DynDNS Updater ensures that your dial-up or DSL connection is kept going permanently, reconnecting as necessary if the connection is interrupted.

7. At the Public IP Address screen, click Detect MY IP and confirm that the address matches the one shown when you registered at dyndns.com.

8. On the Hostname Group page, enter `my group`.

9. On the Login Information page, enter your dyndns.org username and password.

10. At the Entering Host Name page, select Yes, Do Automatic Download. (When you click Next, there might be a considerable delay.)

11. On the Host Name Information page, check the entry for the host name and domain name you selected for your computer.

12. On the Automatic Update page, leave Enable Automatic Update checked.

13. On the Program Start Options page, select Install As Service.

14. To start the service, click Start and right-click Computer. Select Manage. In the left pane, open Services and Applications, and select Services. Locate DynDNS Updater in the right pane. Right-click it and select Start.

15. Wait a few moments and then click Start, All Programs, DynDNS Updater, DynDNS Updater. View the Log tab. You should see a notification that the updater successfully updated your IP address information at dyndns.org, as shown in Figure 40.3. (The log file's time stamps are UTC, formerly known as Greenwich Mean Time, so the times shown are several hours ahead of U.S. local time.)

To be sure that it's working, click Start, All Programs, Accessories, Command Prompt, and type the command `ping` followed by the hostname and domain name you chose for your computer; for example, `ping mycomputer.homedns.org`. Press Enter and be sure that the command finds your IP address, and doesn't print "`Could not find host`."

Now your registered host name will always point to your computer, even when your IP address changes. After a change, it might take up to an hour for the update to occur, but changes should be infrequent.

Port Forwarding

The last setup step is to make sure that incoming Remote Desktop connections from the Internet make it to the right computer. If your computer connects directly to your cable or DSL modem, you can skip this step.

Figure 40.3
The DynDNS Updater log should show a successful update.

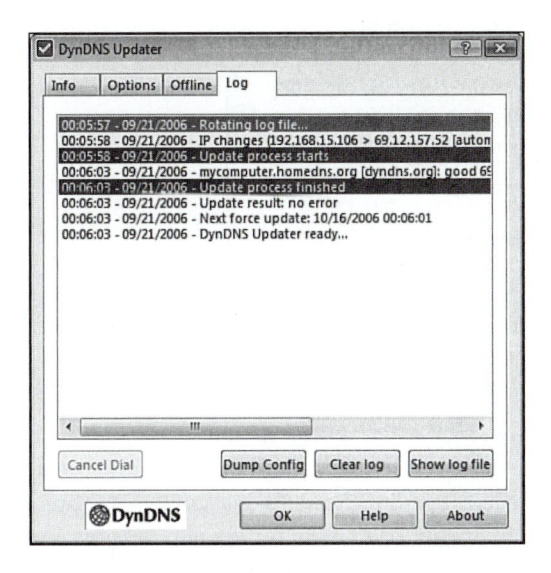

However, if you use Internet Connection Sharing or a connection-sharing router, you have to instruct your sharing computer or router to forward Remote Desktop data through to your computer. To be precise, you have to set up your sharing computer or router to forward incoming requests on TCP port 3389 to the computer you want to reach by Remote Desktop.

The procedure depends on whether you are using the Internet Connection Sharing service built into Windows or a hardware-sharing router. Use one of the procedures described in the next two sections.

Port Forwarding with Internet Connection Sharing

If you use the built-in Internet Connection Sharing service provided with Windows to share an Internet connection on one computer with the rest of your LAN, the forwarding procedure is pretty straightforward using these steps:

1. Go to the computer that is sharing its connection (whether or not it's the one that you want to reach via Remote Desktop) and log on as an Administrator.

2. View the Properties dialog box for the local area connection that corresponds to the Internet connection itself. On Windows Vista, click Start, Control Panel, Network and Internet, Network and Sharing Center. In the Tasks list, select Manage Network Connections.

3. Locate the connection that goes to your Internet service. This might be a broadband icon if you use DSL service, or a local area connection icon for cable service. It should have the word *Shared* next to it. Right-click the icon, select Properties, and view the Sharing tab.

4. Click Settings and, under Services, check Remote Desktop. The Service Settings dialog box appears, as shown in Figure 40.4. Enter the name of the computer that you want to make available via Remote Desktop and click OK.

Figure 40.4
Enter the name of the computer that you want to make available via Remote Desktop.

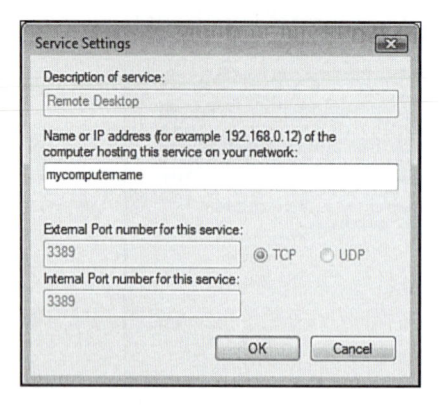

5. If you want to make additional computers available, as discussed at the end of the chapter, you can click Add to add entries for the additional computer. Enter external port numbers 3390, 3391, and so on, but enter 3389 for the internal port number in each case.

6. When you're finished, click OK to close all the dialog boxes.

Now you should be able to reach your computer from anywhere on the Internet. If the connection doesn't work, check the "Troubleshooting" section at the end of the chapter for some suggestions.

Port Forwarding with a Router

If you are using a hardware connection-sharing router, setup is a bit more difficult but is worthwhile. First, because your router doesn't know your computers by their names, you have to set up a fixed IP address on the computer that you will be using via Remote Desktop, using these steps:

1. Click Start, All Programs, Accessories, Command Prompt.

2. Type the command `ipconfig /all` and press Enter. Locate the local area connection part of the printout, which will look in part something like this:

```
Ethernet adapter Local Area Connection:

        Connection-specific DNS Suffix  . : quarterbyte.com
        Description . . . . . . . . . . . : NVIDIA nForce Networking Controller
        Physical Address. . . . . . . . . : 00-50-8D-D7-CA-5F
        Dhcp Enabled. . . . . . . . . . . : Yes
        Autoconfiguration Enabled . . . . : Yes
        IP Address. . . . . . . . . . . . : 192.168.15.102
        Subnet Mask . . . . . . . . . . . : 255.255.255.0
        Default Gateway . . . . . . . . . : 192.168.15.1
        DHCP Server . . . . . . . . . . . : 192.168.15.1
        DNS Servers . . . . . . . . . . . : 192.168.15.1
```

The important information is noted in bold. (On your computer, the numbers will be different—use your numbers, not these!)

3. Click Start, Control Panel, Network and Internet, Network and Sharing Center, Manage Network Connections.

Setting Up Access to Your Own Computer

4. Right-click your local area connection icon and select Properties. Confirm the User Account Control prompt.
5. Select the Internet Protocol Version 4 (TCP/IPv4) entry and click Properties.
6. Check Use the Following IP Address. Enter the first three parts of your original IP address exactly as you see it in your command prompt window, but replace the last part with **250**. For example, on my computer, I'd enter 192.168.15.250.
7. For the subnet mask and default gateway, enter the same numbers that were displayed in the command prompt window.
8. Check Use the Following DNS Server Addresses. Enter the one or two addresses that were displayed in the command prompt window.
9. Click OK.

(If you need to set up any other computers with a fixed IP address, use the same procedure but use addresses ending in .249, .248, .247, and so on, counting backward from .250.)

Now you have to instruct your router to forward Remote Desktop connections to this computer. You need to use the router's setup screen to enable its Port Forwarding feature, which some routers call Virtual Server or Applications and Gaming. There you need to enter the fixed IP address that you assigned to your computer and tell the router to forward connections on TCP port 3389 to this address. Every router uses a slightly different scheme, but Figure 40.5 shows a typical router. If a range of port numbers is required or external and internal numbers are entered separately, enter **3389** in all fields.

Figure 40.5
Use your router's setup system to forward TCP port 3389 to your computer.

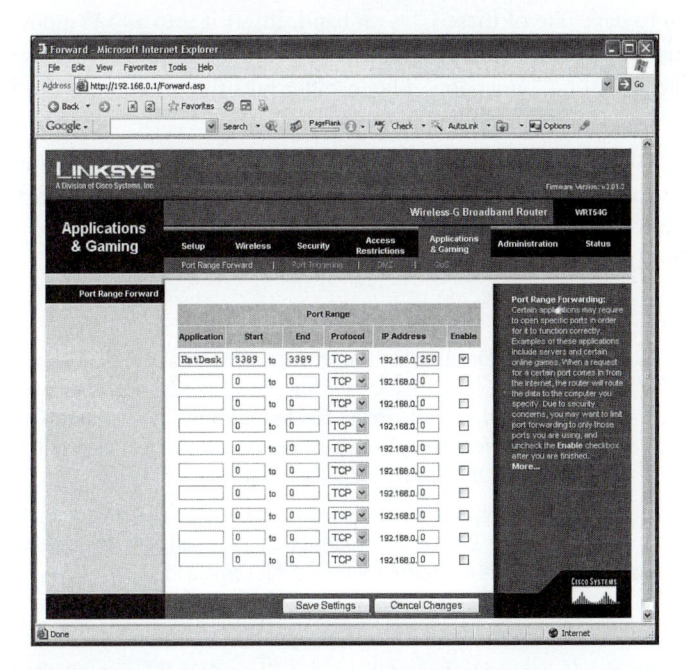

→ To learn more about forwarding network requests on a shared Internet connection, **see** "Enabling Access with a Sharing Router," **p. 732**.

Now you should be able to reach your computer from anywhere on the Internet. If the connection doesn't work, check the "Troubleshooting" section at the end of the chapter for some suggestions.

CONNECTING TO OTHER COMPUTERS WITH REMOTE DESKTOP

To establish a connection to another computer using the Remote Desktop system, you need a copy of the Remote Desktop Client, which is also sometimes called the Terminal Services Client. You can get this program in several ways:

- It's preinstalled on all Windows Vista computers, on all editions. Select Start, All Programs, Accessories, Remote Desktop Connection.

- It's preinstalled on all Windows XP computers, on all editions. Select Start, All Programs, Accessories, Communications, Remote Desktop Connection. However, the version provided with XP lacks support for multiple monitors and plug-and-play devices. You can upgrade the version on XP by downloading and installing the new version, as described in the next paragraph.

- You can download it from www.microsoft.com. Search for "Remote Desktop Client." This is handy if you're traveling and don't have your Windows CD with you. Two versions exist, one for Windows (Windows 98 and up) and one for Mac OS X.

- Every Windows XP Setup CD-ROM also has a somewhat out-of-date version, if you happen to have one of these CDs on hand. Insert it into any Windows 98, Me, or 2000 computer. From the setup program, select Perform Additional Tasks and then Set Up Remote Desktop Connection. The installer puts the program in the Start menu under Accessories, Communications.

- Finally, a Remote Desktop Client version works as an add-on to Internet Explorer. If you have your own web server, or if you've set up a website on a hosted service, you can use a web-based version of the client. I talk about that later in the chapter in the section "Setting Up the Web-Based Client."

> **TIP**
>
> If your local computer has two or more monitors that are the same height (that is, have the same vertical resolution) and are aligned side by side, you can use the spanned monitors for the remote connection by following this procedure: Click Start and, in the Windows Search box, type `mstsc /span`. Press Enter. When you connect to the remote computer, set the Display size to Full Screen.
>
> This works only on the new version of the Remote Desktop Connection client provided with Windows Vista or downloaded from microsoft.com. If it does work well for you, you can create a shortcut containing this command.

When you run the Remote Desktop Client, you'll see the Remote Desktop Connection dialog box, shown in Figure 40.6.

Figure 40.6
The Remote Desktop Connection dialog box enables you to configure the connection and select the remote computer to use.

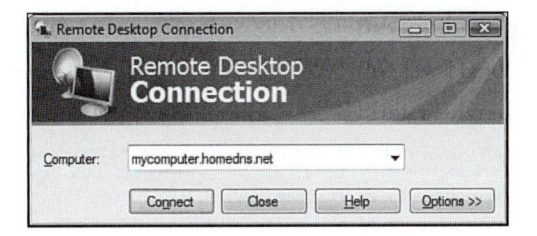

Enter the IP address or registered DNS name of the computer you want to use. If you have set up a dynamic DNS host name, as described in the first part of this chapter, the name might look something like `mycomputer.homedns.org`. (And if you've set up multiple computers, as described in the "Tips from the Windows Pros" section at the end of the chapter, add a colon and the desired port number, as in `mycomputer.homedns.org:3390`.)

At this point, you can select options that control how the remote connection is made, how large a window to use, and so on.

Connection Options

At the Remote Desktop Connections Computer selection prompt, you can set several connection options. In most cases, you can use the default settings and simply click Connect to start the connection, but several of the options can be quite useful.

To view the option categories, click the Options button. The dialog box expands to show six pages of settings, which you can select by clicking on the tab names across the top. Table 40.1 describes the properties tabs.

TABLE 40.1 REMOTE DESKTOP CONNECTION PROPERTIES

Tab	Properties
General	Connection Settings enables you to save your desired default option settings and to save setups for particular remote computers as shortcuts for quick access later.
Display	With this option, you can set the size and color depth of the window used for your remote connection's desktop. Display size can be set to a fixed window size or Full Screen.
Local Resources	This option connects devices on the local computer so that you can use them as if they were part of the remote computer. (This feature does not work when connecting to Windows NT and Windows 2000 Terminal Services.) You can use this feature to hear sound and use the disk drives, COM ports, and certain other USB and plug-and-play devices on the local computer during your remote session. The Keyboard setting determines whether special Windows key commands, such as Alt+Tab, apply to your local computer or the remote computer.
Programs	This option enables you to automatically run a program on the remote computer upon logging on.

continues

Table 40.1 Continued

Tab	Properties
Experience	With this option, you can indicate your connection speed so that Windows can appropriately limit display-intense features such as menu animation.
Advanced	This option enables you to specify whether Network Level Authentication, an advanced network security feature, is required. You can also configure use of a Terminal Services Gateway to access computers on a corporate network through a single Internet host.

You will rarely need to adjust any of these settings. However, some situations might require you to change settings before making a Remote Desktop Connection. Table 40.2 lists these situations.

Table 40.2 Some Reasons to Change Remote Desktop Settings

Situation	Setting Change
You *always* connect across the Internet and/or your remote network does not support IPSec.	On the Advanced tab, set Authentication Options to Always Connect Even If Authentication Fails.
You are using a dial-up Internet connection.	On the Experience tab, change the Connection Speed to Modem (56K). On the Local Resources tab, set Sound to Do Not Play.
You need to work with the local and remote screens simultaneously.	On the Display tab, change the resolution to a size smaller than your local screen, perhaps 800×600.
You need to see as much of the remote computer's screen as possible.	On the Display tab, change the resolution to Full Screen.
You need to be able to print from the applications on the remote computer and get the printouts where you are working.	On the Local Resources tab, check Printers.
You don't need to print while connected.	On the Local Resources tab, uncheck Printers.
You want remote applications to be able to access files on the computer where you are working.	On the Local Resources tab, click More and then click the boxes next to the drive letter(s) that you want to be made visible to the remote computer.
You need to use an application that uses a device attached to a COM port (for example, a Palm Pilot) or other local device.	On the Local Resources tab, click More, and then click the ports or other devices that you want to make visible to the remote computer.

The Full Screen setting is very useful if you have serious work to do on the remote computer because it gives you the maximum amount of desktop space on which to work. Although the resulting connection will fill your local computer's screen, you can still switch back and forth between remote and local work, as I describe in the next section.

When you have made the necessary settings, you might want to save them as the default settings for future connections. To do this, select the General tab and click Save.

> **TIP**
>
> If you routinely make connections to different computers using different settings, you can set up Remote Desktop Connection files with the computer name and all options preset. To do this, make the settings, click Save As, and select a filename. You can create shortcuts to the saved files and put them on your desktop, in your Start menu, or in your Quick Launch bar.

Finally, after you have made any necessary option settings, click Connect to begin the connection.

The program prompts you to enter the username and password for the remote computer, as shown in Figure 40.7. (This is new to Vista: Previous versions of the Remote Desktop client let the remote computer prompt you for your password.)

Figure 40.7
Windows prompts you to enter your username and password before establishing the connection.

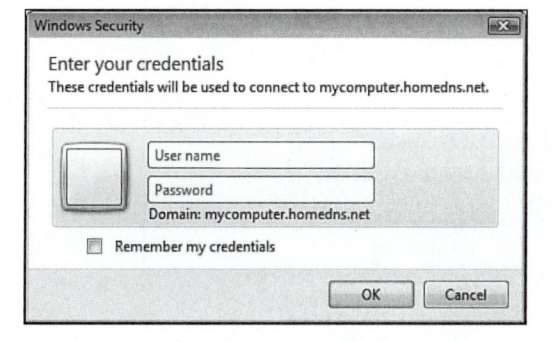

Type in the username and password you use on the *remote* computer, the one to which you're connecting. Entering the password is optional and, in most cases, it's safer not to enter it here. Let the remote system prompt you for your password.

> **NOTE**
>
> If you are connecting to a Windows Server Domain computer, by default, you use your domain logon. If you need to specify a local machine account, enter your username in the form `machinename\username`, as in `mycomputer\Administrator`.

If you want the logon name and password to be stored (relatively securely) in the local computer so that future connections can be automatic, click Remember My Credentials. *Do not* do this on any computer that is not your own or is not secure because anyone who has access to the account will be able to connect to the same remote computer using your logon.

Finally, click OK to begin the connection.

> **If the connection to the remote computer fails,** see "Can't Connect to Remote Computer" in the "Troubleshooting" section at the end of this chapter.
>
> **If the remote computer connects but will not let you sign on,** see "Logon Is Denied" in the "Troubleshooting" section at the end of this chapter.

If Network Level Authentication is being used and the connection to the remote computer does not use the IPSec network security protocol, you might see the dialog box shown in Figure 40.8 warning you that the remote computer's identity cannot be validated. (Thus, you could be supplying your password to a counterfeit computer.) In most cases, this is not a problem, so you can click Yes. You can also check Don't Prompt Me Again for Connections to This Computer, or you can use the Advanced tab in connections options, as described earlier, to prevent this warning from reoccurring.

Figure 40.8
If the remote computer cannot be authenticated, Windows might issue this warning.

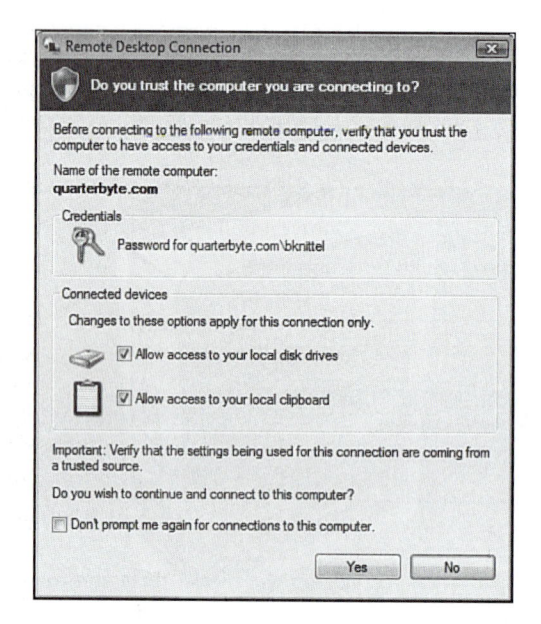

Using the Remote Connection

When you're logged on, you'll see the remote computer's desktop, and can use it as if you were actually sitting in front of it. In a full-screen connection, the title bar at the top of the screen tells you that you're viewing the remote computer's screen. The title bar might slide up out of view, but you can hover the mouse near the top of the screen to bring it back. You can also click on the Minimize button to hide the remote screen, or click on the Maximize button to switch between a windowed or full screen view.

Keyboard, mouse, display, and sound (unless you disabled it) should be fully functional. It all works quite well—it can even be difficult to remember which computer you're actually using!

Figure 40.9
The remote computer's drives can be brought to your local computer.

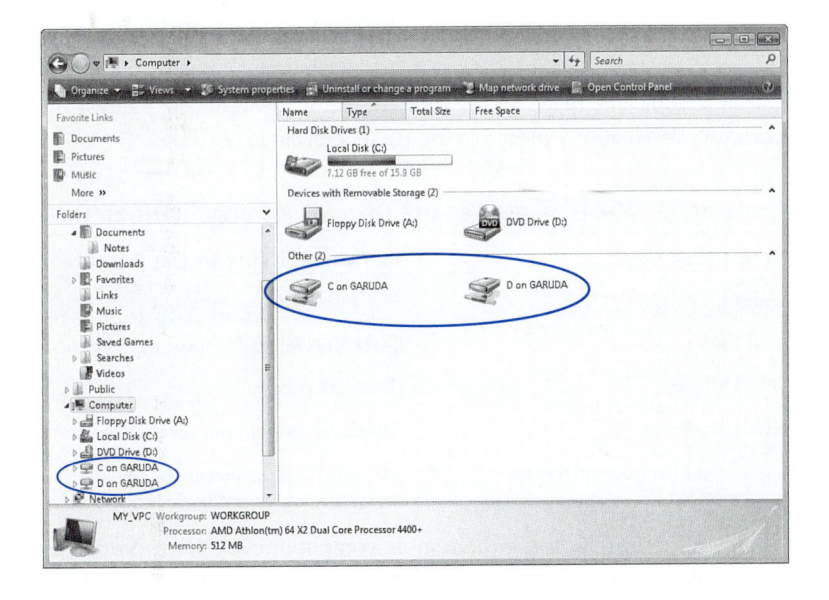

> **TIP**
>
> If the computer to which you're connecting has more than one monitor or a larger monitor than the one you're currently using, when you start an application, its window might not be visible. The problem is that when the application was last used, its window was placed on one of the alternate monitors and its position is now completely off the Remote Desktop screen. To make it visible, right-click the application's button on the taskbar and click Move (or Restore, then Move). Then press and hold the arrow keys to slide the window into view. Press Enter when it's visible, then finish positioning it with your mouse.

If you elected to connect the local computer's disk drives in the connection options dialog box, the local computer's drives appear in Windows Explorer view, as shown in Figure 40.9. Because you're theoretically viewing the remote computer's screen (computer MY_VPC in the figure), the remote computer's drives are labeled normally. The drives on the local computer (computer GARUDA in the figure) are labeled. Access to these drives is fairly slow and annoying. Still, you can take advantage of this to copy files between the local and remote computers.

In addition, any printers attached to your local computer will appear as choices if you print from applications on the remote computer, as long as a compatible printer driver is available on the *remote* computer. Printers might not work if you are connecting from a Macintosh computer or a computer that is running an older version of Windows.

Keyboard Shortcuts

While you're connected, you might want to use keyboard shortcuts such as Alt+Tab to switch between applications. This can confuse Windows, which won't know whether to switch applications on the local computer or the remote computer. You can specify where special key combinations should be interpreted on the Connection Options Local Resources tab, as I described earlier, or you can use alternate key combinations to ensure that the desired actions take place on the remote computer. Table 40.3 shows the alternate keyboard shortcuts. Personally, I prefer to use these alternate shortcuts.

TABLE 40.3   SOME OF THE REMOTE DESKTOP KEYBOARD SHORTCUTS

Use These Keys:	To Transmit This to the Remote Computer:
Alt+PgUp, Alt+PgDn	Alt+Tab (switch programs)
Alt+End	Ctrl+Alt+Del (task monitor)
Alt+Home	(Displays the Start menu)
Ctrl+Alt+Break	Alt+Enter (toggle full screen)
Ctrl+Alt+Plus on numeric pad	Alt+PrntScrn (screen to Clipboard)

When you've finished using the remote computer, click Start. Notice that the Disconnect button has replaced the usual Sleep button, as shown in Figure 40.10. You can end your session in two ways:

Figure 40.10
The Disconnect (X) button appears where Sleep normally appears.

- Click the right arrow button and click Log Off to log off the remote computer and end the connection.
- Click the X button to disconnect but not log off, leaving your applications still running on the remote computer. This is the equivalent of using Switch Users. Your account

stays active on the remote computer until you reconnect and log off, or until you log on physically at the remote computer and log off from there.

Alternately, you can disconnect by clicking the close box on the Remote Desktop window or the title bar at the top of the screen.

I use Remote Desktop to use my work computer at the office and from home, and I've found that I save a lot of time by never logging off entirely. When I finish at work, I just press Windows+L to switch out to the welcome screen. Then I can reconnect from home and pick up where I left off without waiting for all those darn startup programs to get going. Likewise, at home, when I'm finished, I simply disconnect, so I never actually log off.

> **NOTE**
>
> Windows Vista permits only one person to use each computer. If you attempt to connect to a computer with Remote Desktop while another user is logged on, you have the choice of disconnecting yourself or forcing that user off. If Fast User Switching is enabled, the other user is switched out to the welcome screen; otherwise, the user is summarily logged off. This is somewhat brutal; the other user might lose work in progress.
>
> If you log on using the same username as the local user, though, you simply take over the desktop without forcing a logoff.
>
> If someone else logs on to the remote computer while you're connected from afar, your session is disconnected. Again, if Fast User Switching is enabled, you can reconnect later and pick up where you left off. Otherwise, the same deal applies: If it is a different user, your applications shut down.

If you're using Remote Desktop to use your own computer, this probably won't matter to you because you'll probably never see what happens on the other screen. But if you use Remote Desktop to work on someone else's computer, you should let that person know what will happen before starting; otherwise, the two of you could get into a tussle, repeatedly kicking the other person off the computer, with neither of you knowing that the other person is there trying to get something done.

SETTING UP THE WEB-BASED CLIENT

If you set up Remote Desktop so that you can access your work computer from home or vice versa, you're probably using Windows Vista or XP at both locations, so you can count on having the Remote Desktop Client program available. However, older Windows 2000, 98, and Me computers likely don't have the client program preinstalled, and they're still in use in some places. If you need to be able to reach your computer while traveling, you might encounter situations where the only computer you have access to doesn't have the Remote Desktop Connection client installed—and, worse, you don't have permission to download and install the client.

Fortunately, if you have a website of your own (even a free one)—or if you have installed Internet Information Services on your own computer, as described in Chapter 18, "Hosting Web Pages with Internet Information Services," and if you've prepared for this in advance—you'll still be able to connect to home.

Here's what you need to do:

1. Download the Remote Desktop Connection Web Connection program `tswebsetup.exe` from www.microsoft.com/windowsxp/downloads/tools/rdwebconn.mspx. Microsoft rearranges its site frequently, so you might have better luck just searching microsoft.com for "remote desktop web connection download."

2. If your web server is IIS and you have direct access to the computer that's running IIS, run `tswebsetup.exe` on that computer. Save the package's files in `\inetpub\wwwroot\tsweb`.

    Otherwise, if you're using a different web server, run `tswebsetup.exe` on any Windows computer and have it put the files in some convenient folder. Then transfer the files into the appropriate folder on your web server, preferably in a folder named `tsweb` in your home directory. The web server itself won't be required to interpret any of these files, so it needn't even be running Windows—you can put these files on any web server, including one of the free hosting services such as `geocities.com`.

Now, if your site's Internet URL is www.mysite.com, the URL www.mysite.com/tsweb will run a Remote Desktop client inside an Internet Explorer window. Likewise, if you are using a free dynamic DNS hostname, your URL might be something along the lines of `mycomputername.homedns.org/tsweb`. The remote computer must be an Intel-based computer running Windows, and the web browser must support Active-X plug-ins. The first time you open the `tsweb` page, you have to confirm that you want to enable the ActiveX plug-in.

TROUBLESHOOTING

CAN'T CONNECT TO REMOTE COMPUTER

When I try to connect to my computer over the Internet, the connection fails.

The problem could be in any of several areas. Look at the following items, and make sure that.

- The computer is turned on.
- Remote Desktop is enabled.
- An exception is open for Remote Desktop in Windows Firewall.
- The host computer's Internet connection is working. (Can it view www.google.com using Internet Explorer?)
- If you use a shared Internet connection, port forwarding on TCP port 3390 is set up and points to the right computer. Open a command prompt window and type the `ipconfig` command on the host computer to verify its IP address. Check that against the port-forwarding setup screen you used.
- The IP address or host name you're using to make the connection matches the public IP address at your host computer. Open a command prompt window at the remote computer and type `ping` followed by the name or IP address you're trying. See if `ping` displays and tests the correct IP address. If echoes are returned, that's good. However, some routers don't return echoes, by default, so a failure to get replies might not indicate a problem.

Logon Is Denied

When I try to sign on via Remote Desktop, Windows tells me that my account has a user account restriction.

The account you tried to use might have a blank password or might be a Limited account that was not entered as an account authorized to connect remotely. See "Enabling Remote Desktop Access to Your Computer," earlier in the chapter, for instructions on authorizing accounts. An account must have a password set before you can use it remotely, even if it's authorized.

Tips from the Windows Pros: Making More Than One Computer Available

If you have more than one computer on your network that you want to reach with Remote Desktop over the Internet, you need to do some additional setup work. It can be well worth the effort, though. I have a Windows Server at my office, and I've found it very helpful to be able to administer the server from home, as well as be able to connect to my own desktop computer to work and check email. It has saved quite a number of emergency trips to the office on weekends!

Now, if you can connect to your office network through a virtual private network (VPN), or if you have a Windows Server with the Terminal Services Gateway service installed, you can use either of those technologies to first connect to your office and then connect to the desired computer.

However, these services aren't available on a home network. Even in a larger office environment, these services depend on that Windows Server computer to assist in making the connection. If the server is having problems, you could be out of luck. I'll show you a way to set up Remote Desktop access to any number of computers that works even on a home network and even if the corporate server is down.

You set up different network *port numbers* for the Remote Desktop service for each computer so that each can be addressed directly from over the Internet. It's sort of like giving each telephone in an office its own direct telephone number so that outside callers don't have to go through a switchboard operator to reach someone. By default, Remote Desktop uses network port number 3389. But we can use other port numbers, using different numbers to identify the computer to which we want to connect.

Suppose I have three computers. To be able to reach all three of them using Remote Desktop, I could configure my Internet-sharing router to forward incoming connections on TCP port 3389 to port 3389 on the first computer, incoming connections on port 3390 to port 3389 on the second computer, and incoming connections on port 3391 to the third computer.

This way, the router sorts out the incoming connections and forwards incoming connections to the correct computer using the port number that Windows expects.

To make this work, each of the computers must be set up with a static IP address. Chapter 22 describes how to do this. For example, if I have three computers on my network, I might assign them static IP addresses 192.168.0.248, 192.168.0.249, and 192.168.0.250. Then my Internet router would be set up with forwarding information like this:

Protocol	External Port	Internal Port	IP Address
TCP	3389	3389	192.168.0.248
TCP	3390	3389	192.168.0.249
TCP	3391	3389	192.168.0.250

With this setup, I could connect to the computers from out on the Internet by specifying the appropriate port number when I make the connection using the Remote Desktop Client, by typing connection names like this: `mycompany.com:3389`, `mycompany.com:3390`, or `mycompany.com:3391`. The colon and number after the host name tell the Remote Desktop Connection client to use an alternate port number when making the connection.

If your router's Port Forwarding setup screen doesn't allow you to specify different external and internal port numbers, you have to change the port that Remote Desktop "listens" on by editing the Registry. Find the key named `HKEY_LOCAL_MACHINE\System\CurrentControlSet\Control\Terminal Server\WinStations\RDP-Tcp` and locate the value `PortNumber`, as shown in Figure 40.11.

Figure 40.11
Change the `PortNumber` value to make Remote Desktop listen on an alternate TCP port.

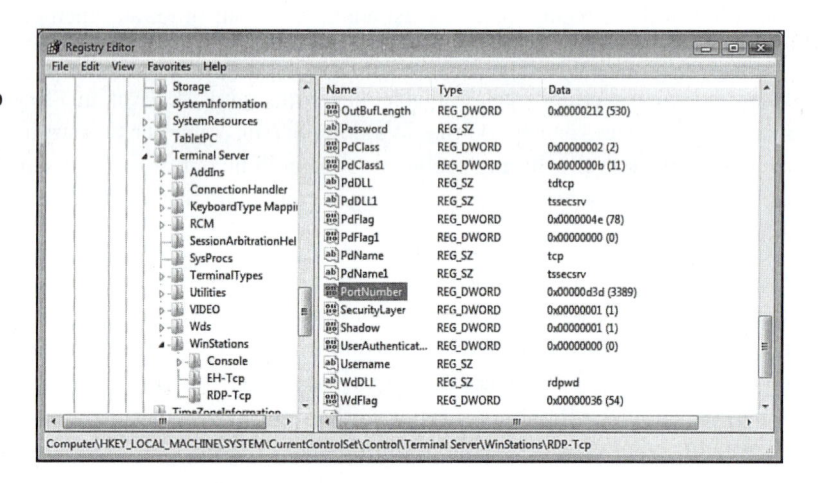

You can change this value (select Decimal mode to make it easier): Use `3390` for the second computer, `3391` for the third, and so on. The first computer should be left alone, to listen on the standard port number `3389`.

In this case, the router would be provided with the following forwarding information:

External Port	Internal IP Address
TCP 3389	192.168.0.248
TCP 3390	192.168.0.249
TCP 3391	192.168.0.250

You need to restart the computers to make the port number change take effect.

Finally, and this is very important, you have to manually create exceptions in the Windows Firewall on the computers to which you've assigned alternate port numbers. The built-in "Remote Desktop" exception works for port 3389 only.

To create the exception, click Start, Control Panel, and select Allow a Program Through Windows Firewall. Confirm the UAC prompt. On the Exceptions tab, click Add Port. For the name, enter Remote Desktop Alternate Port and, for the port number, enter the alternate number you used on this particular computer: 3390, 3391, or whatever number you chose. Click OK and close the Port dialog box; then click OK to close the Firewall dialog box.

CHAPTER 41

TABLET PC FEATURES

In this chapter

Importance of Handwriting   1356

History of Tablets   1356

Who Needs a Tablet?   1358

What Does Tablet Vista Have That Regular PCs Don't?   1359

What's New in Tablet Vista?   1360

Choosing a Tablet PC   1360

Using Your Tablet PC—Differences and Similarities of Functions   1361

Input Methods Using the Input Panel   1361

Gestures and Pen Flicks   1363

Handwriting Recognition   1364

AutoComplete   1366

Sticky Notes and the Snipping Tool   1366

Windows Journal   1369

Tablet PC Settings and Pen and Input Devices   1370

Troubleshooting   1374

Tips from the Windows Pros: A Whole New Level of Pen Flicks   1375

Importance of Handwriting

Nowadays, the old "pencil and paper" approach to creating documents has certainly gone the way of the dinosaur. If you're like me, without a keyboard you're lost. I can barely remember how to sign my name on a check. The use of electronic file editing has almost totally put an end to basic handwriting. But what about the times you have to write out in longhand? We need longhand when taking basic notes at home or at a business meeting, developing a quick graph or sketch, or even jotting down a shopping list. With these thoughts in mind, how can we connect the digital world with the analog world? One way has been through PocketPCs—those little PDAs that sport handwriting recognition and turn your scribbles into text. I use one daily, and it's pretty amazing how good the recognition is. Still, it's just a little PDA, not a full-blown computer. I can scribble into Pocket Word or Pocket Excel, which is pretty cool, but the screen is small, and I mostly use it for email, contacts, and organizing my calendar. But while the PDA was evolving in the foreground and capturing our attention as it merged with cell phones, the Tablet PC was quietly climbing out of the water onto dry land and growing legs.

History of Tablets

The idea of a fully functional Tablet PC has been a vision for many engineers and a select group of computer users since the 1980s. In the '80s, handwriting recognition was a new and developing technology, with numerous companies developing basic handwriting recognizers that could interpret basic text and numbers.

A decade later, in 1991, the pen was seen as a major competitor to the standard mouse. At this time, Microsoft developed Windows for Pen Computing, a basic pen extension for Windows 3.1. One year later, another program, PenPoint (from GO Computing), was developed to allow a user to write in longhand notation. Both PenPoint and Windows for Pen Computing created a new interest for other companies to create new hardware to utilize these programs. Pen computing created a lot of hype in the marketplace. As the first pen recognition computers were developed, there was a huge interest for them. But in the end, the pen computer flopped and did not sell. Many companies poured millions of dollars into research and development of pen computers only to go belly up. IBM's first ThinkPad was actually a pen computer based on PenPoint. Only later did ThinkPads include a keyboard and normal Windows operating system. Along the way, pen computers from EO, GRiD, Samsung, NEC, Fujitsu, NCR, TelePad, and others bit the dust. Figure 41.1 shows some examples of different kinds of tablets that were pioneers in Tablet PC history.

Figure 41.1
From left to right, Fujitsu Stylistic 3500 Tablet PC and the Newton MessagePad 2000.

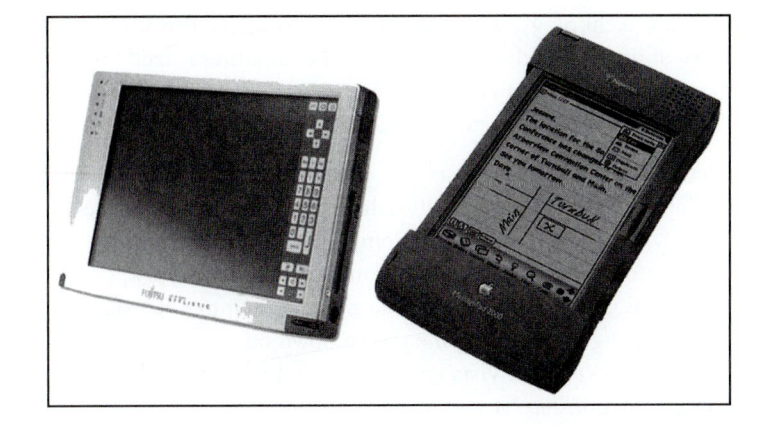

Around 1993, the Apple Newton was released, stuffed with handwriting recognition technology claimed by Apple to be truly workable. Although the Newton was clever and innovative in many ways, and filled a void between the PDA and the laptop, its handwriting recognition was flawed too, and it soon fell prey to critical reviews.

By 1995, pen computer technology was essentially dead. Multiple companies made attempts to bring it back but to no avail. For customers who did need a pen alternative, one remaining leader was PenX from Communication Intelligence Corporation who specializes in electronic signature input.

Even though everyone thought pen computing was dead, one major supporter really drove the development of the new era of pen computing. This major advocate was Bill Gates, who believed in pen computing technology ever since it was first created. In 1995, along with Windows 95, Windows Pen Services 2.0 was released with little fanfare and was a disappointment, lacking promised features and not working as well as hoped.

Things were fairly quiet in the second half of the '90s except for a little band of gadgets called *webpads* that began to spring up. The leader of this field was Zenith with its CruisePad in 1995, followed by National Semiconductor and a few others. Webpads were wireless pen-based systems connected to the Internet and could be walked around in an office building. None of these really took off.

The next short-lived chapter in pen computing was an effort called MIRA. We wrote about MIRA a bit in previous editions of this book on Windows XP. MIRA was an initiative to have "smart displays"—a screen connected to your desktop PC that you could pick up out of a docking station and then walk around with. It would stay wirelessly connected to your host PC and also have pen activation. Take it to a meeting, pass your Excel spreadsheet around the conference table, that sort of thing. MIRA was a bust too, with no follow-up.

But Tablet PC was not giving up the ghost yet. In 2000 at Comdex, keynote speaker Microsoft CEO Bill Gates excitedly presented a webpad and reintroduced the Tablet PC almost as a new technology. Those in the know could see this was hype, but Gates did spark a new flurry of interest in the technology. Pen computing is trudging along and is improving. Pen-based XP and Vista computers are now readily available and actually work. The name Tablet PC is actually starting to stick as of about 2005.

The Tablet PC comes with two varieties, the *slate* and the *convertible* as shown in Figure 41.2. The slate Tablet PC is a basic no-frills tablet that requires you to use handwriting because there is no keyboard. By contrast, the convertible Tablet PC has both a keyboard and a pen. By having a laptop with a keyboard you can, if a proficient typist, enter basic documents quickly and easily. But then by converting that laptop into a flat slate (either by removing the keyboard or rotating and flipping the screen down on top of the keyboard), you are then fully pen-enabled. Windows Vista employs the full functions of the Tablet PC. A variety of programs and functions are at your pen tip. In this chapter, you see all the benefits you can have by owning a Tablet PC.

Figure 41.2
Toshiba M400 Convertible Tablet PC with the HP Slate Tablet PC TC1100 to its right.

NOTE

Of course, because a Tablet PC is a fully functioning XP or Vista machine, it can run speech recognition software such as Dragon, ViaVoice, or the voice recognition built into Vista. So if you hate to type, check out the possibility of getting a headset and using speech recognition with a Vista tablet. We cover speech to text in "Using Speech Recognizer" in Chapter 4, "Using the Windows Desktop."

WHO NEEDS A TABLET?

Is a Tablet PC in your future? Possibly. Some would argue that a Tablet PC is for everyone, whereas others are too addicted to the keyboard. After you get used to touching the screen instead of pointing with the mouse, you may never go back because this approach is so much more direct and intuitive.

Tablet functions are easy to use and great for work, school, or personal use. Because they are so portable, almost like a sheet of paper, and because you can easily draw pictures, diagrams, and maps, as well as write longhand text that translates into typed text, a Tablet PC can replace scratch paper, Post-It notes, and other desk-cluttering trivia. Eliminate that mess and invest in a Tablet PC. With Windows Vista, a Tablet PC can be an efficient means of staying organized.

What Does Tablet Vista Have That Regular PCs Don't?

The most obvious answer to this question is that Tablet Vista provides you the ability to use handwriting on your computer. Using a pen both as a mouse and for writing increases your computer options. The handwriting recognizer can distinguish your handwriting and transform that writing into typed text.

With Vista, users who have a Tablet PC get extra fun goodies. These include special software and hardware that a normal PC does not have. A few basic extras include

- A stylus pen shown in Figure 41.3 that acts like a mouse and keyboard. Use the stylus to click and accomplish other functions just like a mouse. A stylus has many improved functions over a mouse, discussed later in this chapter.

Figure 41.3
Wacom stylus pen with multiple functionalities.

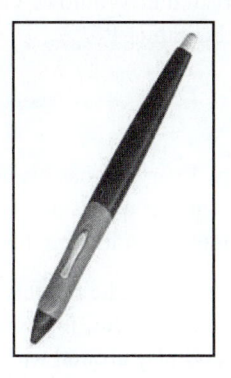

- Touch-screen monitors on a tablet are also pressure-sensitive and offer more than a normal monitor. The Tablet PC screen recognizes how hard you push and displays that as a lighter or darker line.
- Convertible Tablet PCs have the added technology of the swivel screen, seen in Figure 41.2. This swivel screen can be rotated and closed flat to cover the keyboard and provide a full-layout tablet.
- New software that can only be fully utilized by using a pen.

What's New in Tablet Vista?

The tablet functions in Vista are a superset of Windows XP Tablet Edition. All the existing items for tablets in the previous XP version are in the Vista version. In addition, a few things are new for tablets in Vista:

- **Enhanced stylus graphics**—New visual effects are added in Vista that the previous XP did not have. As you can see when using Vista, your computer will recognize the stylus and create a new pointer for your pen. Clicking has also been enhanced to present a ripple effect and a halo for right-clicks.

- **Pen flicks**—Increasing your usage yet again with great added functionality, pen flicks improve how you browse online and how you can edit documents. This new feature is discussed later in this chapter.

- **Better handwriting recognition**—Vista improved the recognizer so that it is more capable of accurately recognizing different handwriting styles. No longer will you have to comply with a standard writing style. Why change your style when you can just change how Vista understands it?

- **Improved tablet input panel**—This is a great improvement to the Tablet Input Panel and makes handwriting sentences much easier. Increased size of the writing field and some added options expedite input.

These are but a few improvements that Microsoft created in Windows Vista. Later in this chapter, you see in depth what Vista has done with the Tablet PC.

Choosing a Tablet PC

Choosing a Tablet PC can be difficult for new buyers. Everyone has his own distinct likes and dislikes of certain PC styles and layouts. Add to that, the quirks of a tablet and the choice becomes a conundrum. Here are two things to consider when looking for a Tablet PC:

- Most stores do not have Tablet PCs displayed because of the fragility of the swivel screen of the convertible type. Lately a few stores—Best Buy, for example—have let you touch one before you buy it. Go to these stores and play around with the Tablet to see whether a Tablet PC is for you.

- Tablets come in two different types, and it's your choice which one to buy. Beware that most slate Tablet PCs are not sold in local stores. If having a keyboard is a must for you, but you like the lighter weight and size of the slates (for example, Motion makes a nice small one), consider a fold-up Bluetooth or IR keyboard made for PDAs. If the tablet you want has Bluetooth or IR, you can carry a keyboard in your pocket. I use the one from Think Outside.

Using Your Tablet PC—Differences and Similarities of Functions

Using a Tablet PC can be very different from a regular PC, depending on the type. With slate design Tablet PCs, you are required to use only the pen for every function (unless you are using voice input). After you become accustomed to a slate Tablet PC, you will not miss a keyboard. If you do miss a keyboard, you can obtain an external one and plug it in via USB or wirelessly with Bluetooth.

Convertible Tablet PCs are just like a normal laptop but with the added feature of the stylus pen. Unlike slate Tablet PCs, convertibles have a built-in keyboard. One downfall to the built-in keyboard is that it will add more weight and bulk to the computer.

Either design of Tablet PC comes with a stylus and all the tablet functions. Using a pen on the screen is no different from using a mouse—you simply point and click, but in this case, a click is done with the pressure of the pen or a switch on the side of the pen. It could be argued that using a pen is actually faster and more immediately intuitive. As icing on the cake, Vista's tablet features include some shortcuts called *flicks* and *gestures* that make tablet computing even more efficient.

Input Methods Using the Input Panel

As with a Pocket PC (if you have used one), Tablet PCs, offer a variety of ways to input data and text. In Windows XP Tablet Edition, Microsoft introduced three new ways for a user to input text and phrases. In Vista, the new inclusion of the *Input Panel* simplifies input matters further.

The basic Input Panel contains a variety of functions and extras. The Input Panel lets you choose where to dock it—it can be docked anywhere on the screen. When not using the Input Panel it will quietly minimize where you docked it and be ready for you to use whenever you click it. This is a bit like the taskbar on any XP or Vista computer when set to auto-hide. You can open the Input Panel without having to go to the tab on the side of the screen. Simply hold the stylus over a text box or text area, and a little Tablet Panel icon will show next to your stylus. Clicking this icon will open a floating Input Panel for you to quickly and easily input text. Figure 41.4 illustrates the basic Input Panel. As you can see, it has a nicely sized text frame for you to write in. Windows Vista gives you a large enough text frame to input a decent size sentence.

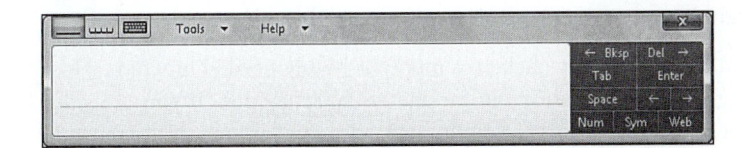

Figure 41.4
Tablet Input Panel.

Writing Methods Using the Input Panel

In Figure 41.1, you can see three different boxes on the top left of the Input Panel. These boxes are the three ways that you can input your handwriting and transform that into typed text. The boxes are as follows:

- **Writing Pad**—The first panel on the left is a free-form-based writing field. You can write full words and sentences, and Vista will do its best to transform that into text. Also, Vista will recognize words fairly well even from the start and display the word you wrote on the bottom of the Input Panel. If a certain word you wrote is not recognized correctly by Vista, you can click the word that Vista created and edit it with a version of the Character Pad.

- **Character Pad**—This text panel looks like the previous XP-Tablet-based panel except that lines separate the input areas. Instead of free-form writing with your hand, you write a letter into each block. The writing pad will transform the letter you wrote in the text block straight to a typed text letter in the same block. This approach is most useful for entering unique words, phrases, or idioms that don't exist in the Windows database.

- **On-Screen Keyboard**—Vista incorporates a full-size keyboard to fit your needs for using a stylus. This includes all the basic keys situated in the same spot as a normal keyboard. On-Screen Keyboard is a handy tool that will help you with such things as creating a certain password or ID name that may likely include a mix of letters and numbers.

> **TIP**
>
> The Tablet Input Panel can be inserted into your taskbar. Just right-click the taskbar and click Toolbars, Tablet PC Input Panel.

Stylus Pen

The stylus is the tablet owner's best friend. It will never leave your computer (and if it does, you're up the creek because it's essential to tablet use). A lot of functionality is packed into the stylus when using a Vista tablet. Briefly, here's how it works.

When using the Input Panel, you can see your pen point as a small white dot. Vista detects that you are using a pen automatically and will change the cursor from an arrow to a small dot when you are writing rather than just pointing and clicking icons, buttons, and other interface items. Also, Vista detects pen clicks and will display a neat ripple effect. One tap on the screen with the stylus will create one ripple and represents an onscreen click. So, one ripple equals one click and two ripples equal a double-click. Now if that weren't 'neat enough, Vista incorporated an even neater right-click.

As you know the right-click on a mouse is highly needed function. Most styli incorporate this right-click as a button on the side of the actual pen. If you press this button and tap on the screen, the result is a right-click. Vista will automatically recognize the pen and the right-click and will open the right-click menu. Also you will see a lighted halo at the spot you right-clicked.

The tip of the pen is a great feature, but why don't we use more of the pen? Windows utilizes not only the front of the stylus but also the back end. When writing a note you may want to delete a small mistake in your text. Instead of clicking the onscreen eraser, erasing with the stylus, and then clicking on the pen button again to continue writing, you can just flip your pen backward and erase. The end of the stylus (shown in Figure 41.2) serves as an onscreen eraser, just like on a real pencil. Vista will always recognize the back end of the pen as the eraser—very slick and intuitive.

INPUT PANEL OPTIONS

Of course, with many Windows option dialog boxes, there is no dearth of option settings. The Input Panel gives you the basic Tools drop-down and Help drop-down. The Tools drop-down allows you to select Personalize Handwriting Recognition (described later in this chapter), ways to dock the Input Panel, and Tablet PC Options (also described later in this chapter). The Help drop-down includes all the basic Windows help functions for all new beginners.

Under the Tools drop-down, you can select different docking styles. You have the option to dock the Input Panel at the top or bottom of the screen, or to have it float on the screen. Floating the Input Panel is great when you want to write small, quick text, such as a username and password. The set docking styles will take the entire width of your screen and maximize how much you may write. Most tablet users will agree that docking on the bottom of the screen is the best strategy. Docking the Input Panel on the bottom not only allows you to write but also is least invasive of other documents that are likely to be on your screen.

GESTURES AND PEN FLICKS

Gestures and pen flicks are basic stylus options that let you write and browse even faster and easier. Gestures are quick scribbles with the stylus that effectively scratch out text, or enter the keyboard keys of Backspace, Delete, Space, and Enter. Using pen flicks makes scrolling through documents and browsing the Internet easy. With pen flicks, you can scroll up and down and go back and forward in your current web browser with just a few quick motions of the pen.

SCRATCH-OUT GESTURES

The most important gesture of all the tablet stylus options is the Scratch-out gesture. With a Tablet PC, you will be doing a lot of writing with the stylus. Sometimes, when writing with the stylus, you will misspell words and make mistakes. Instead of using the back end of the pen to erase an entire word, you can use a Scratch-out. Simply draw a line through the words you want to erase. You can scratch out not only words but entire sentences also. The best Scratch-out in Vista is called the *Z-shape*, which is a "Z" shape that you make with the stylus. This Scratch-out is the one that Vista will never mistake for a word or phrase. By using the Z-shape, you are able to erase any letters or words that are unwanted without having to use the end of your pen.

One negative effect of Scratch-outs is the accidental erase. Sometimes when you write a word or phrase, Windows will recognize your input as a Scratch-out. Is this something to worry about? Depending on your handwriting style, it could be a problem. However, there is a simple solution available via the Tablet PC Settings where you can change the way Vista recognizes your Scratch-out. You can set only certain types of Scratch-outs and eliminate the one that is causing the problem.

Pen Flicks

The stylus pen enables you to view and scroll through documents and web pages easier than you can with a touchpad. With a stylus, you are free to touch anywhere on the screen with the pen and instantly click where you need to go. Windows Vista now makes browsing even faster with the introduction of pen flicks.

Pen flicks are common actions that can be done using the stylus pen. For example, suppose you are browsing the Internet and you want to go back a page. You could click the Back button once or scroll through the list of web pages you visited to get there. A faster way is to just touch the screen at any spot with the pen and flick the pen toward the left direction. With one flick of the wrist you will automatically go back to the previous web page. Conversely, flicking to the right moves forward, analogous to clicking the Forward button on the browser toolbar.

If you think going back and forward is simple, scrolling up and down in a web page is just as easy. Scrolling in a web page using the stylus used to require you to hold your pen on the scrollbar on the screen just as you would do with a mouse. With pen flicks, instead of holding the scrollbar you can flick up or down to scroll in the respective direction.

> **TIP**
> Flicking is a little tricky at first. To use pen flicks correctly, you may need to practice. Vista supplies a pen flick trainer located in the Tablet PC folder under All Programs, Tablet PC.

Handwriting Recognition

When you first start using your Tablet PC, Vista may not recognize certain words or phrases correctly. This can be a software issue, or, as with a few us, your handwriting just stinks. This can easily be solved by using the Handwriting Recognition tool that allows you to teach Vista how you write. Because everyone has a distinct handwriting style, teaching Vista how to recognize your style can help Vista better read and understand what you are writing. To teach Windows Vista about your handwriting use the Handwriting Personalization window (see Figure 41.5).

Figure 41.5
Handwriting personalization.

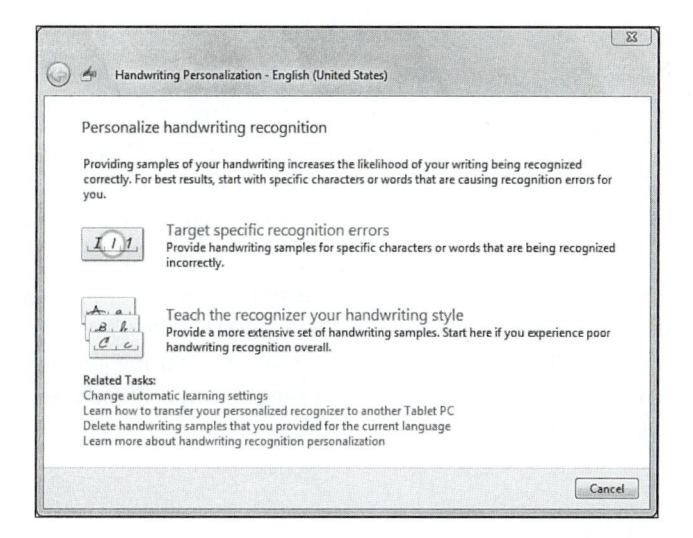

The Handwriting Personalization window will ask you to demonstrate your handwriting to allow Vista to understand your handwriting better. To open the Handwriting Personalization window, follow these steps:

1. Click the Start button and select All Programs.
2. Select Tablet PC.
3. Select Personalize Handwriting Recognition. You can also get to Personalize Handwriting Recognition from the Input Panel, Tools.

Specific Handwriting Recognition Errors

With the Handwriting Personalization window open, you are given two options. The first option is to target specific handwriting errors that constantly occur. The second option is to allow Vista to better learn how you write.

Automatic correction of common errors in Vista's handwriting recognition can save you time. Constantly fixing that one word that Vista always misrecognizes can be really annoying. You can make Vista correct those mistakes and improve how it reads your handwriting with the Handwriting Recognition tool.

Teach the Recognizer Your Style

Teaching the Recognizer how you write can improve its accuracy significantly, especially if your handwriting is sloppy. This process lets you keep your current handwriting style and changes how Vista reads it. If you have trained a speech recognition program to understand your vocal patterns, you'll be familiar with the idea. There are two basic ways that you can change the Recognizer to improve its capability to understand your writing.

- **Numbers, Symbols, and Letters Recognition**—Teach the Recognizer how to read your handwriting by individual words and numbers. The Handwriting Personalization applet will ask you to write the entire alphabet in caps and lowercase, and write all numbers from zero to nine. This way of teaching the recognizer is basic and quick.

- **Sentences Recognition**—When using this option, you will be asked to write a variety of sentences so that Recognizer can get better recognition of your style and sentence compilation. Beware, though, Vista will want you to write a total of 50 sentences for it to fully understand your handwriting. But instead of writing all 50 right away you can save and do this incrementally. Spend the time to finish this setting. It will save you a lot of time correcting words later.

AutoComplete

The AutoComplete function for tablets is the same as the AutoComplete function used on a regular PC, such as in Internet Explorer or Office. Windows will suggest what word or URL you are typing and give you the option to select it without typing the entire word or URL. With the Tablet Input Panel, you have the same power with your stylus.

Most people log in to an email account or type a URL in their browser everyday. Browsers commonly use the AutoComplete function due to the length of the URL. The stylus input works the same way as if you were typing that URL on your keyboard.

To write a URL in your browser, open the Tablet Input Panel and select the address line. Instead of a keyboard, you are left with the option of handwriting the URL in the Tablet Input Panel. While you are writing the URL into the text field, Windows creates a list of suggestions for you. Choose one of the suggestions if it is what you are writing.

> **NOTE**
>
> You may have noticed, that if you highlight a phrase such as a URL and then open the Table Input Panel, the word will appear in a separate Character Pad. If only small changes are needed, you can enter them in that Character Pad. This helps decrease the amount of writing that you have to do.

Sticky Notes and the Snipping Tool

Both Windows XP and Vista Tablet Editions include two tools specifically designed for the tablet operating system: Sticky Notes and the Snipping Tool. This section describes them and how they work.

Sticky Notes

Sticky Notes, shown in Figure 41.6, are analogous to Post-It™ notes. You might take their function for granted because they look like simple Post-It notes. However, they are quite sophisticated and can be a boon to Tablet users.

Figure 41.6
Sticky Note.

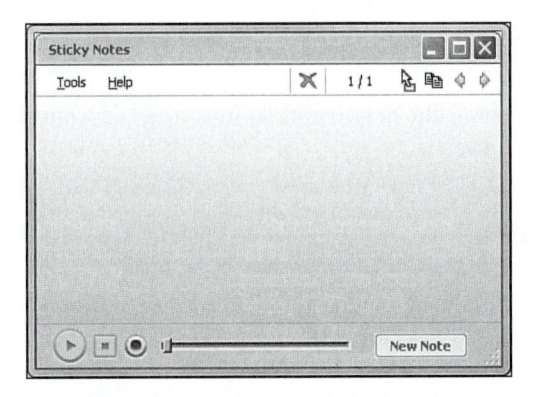

Sticky Notes can be organized as a stacked pad of notes. So, instead of having many different notes stuck on your physical desk or on the edges of your computer monitor, you have just one little pad and can easily scroll through all the notes. The note itself is written using your stylus. This enables you to write whatever you want and even draw a small picture. Take Sticky Notes into consideration the next time you need to jot down a list of important items, such as a grocery list.

Another neat feature of Sticky Notes is its capability to record a sound. This sound is stored by the Sticky Note and can be played as many times as you want or need. Little verbal reminders can be a great way to keep you updated. To leave a short verbal reminder, click on the red record dot. After clicking the red dot, Sticky Notes will start recording. Click the stop button when you are done recording or when the time of recording has run out. To play the sound, click the play button. The sound can be played as many times as you want and will be deleted only when you delete the note or record over the sound.

Snipping Tool

No Tablet PC is complete without the Snipping Tool, which lets you use your stylus to snip any object on your screen. You can crop any box anywhere on the screen and then write on and edit it as a picture. When snipping items on your screen, you are able to freely change and modify just like Paint. To open the snipping tool, go to All Programs, Accessories, and then Snipping Tool.

Using the Snipping Tool is easy and requires only a few clicks of the mouse. When you open the Snipping Tool, your entire screen will fade, a toolbox will appear(shown in Figure 41.7), and your mouse will turn into a pair of scissors. The toolbox will offer a few options regarding snipping types that will become useful. Other smaller options do exist as well in the Options drop down. These options refer to the cropping line color and other various tasks.

Figure 41.7
Snipping Tools Window.

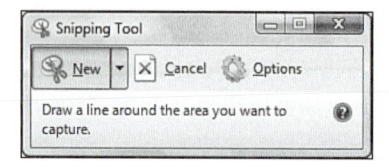

The different types of snips that you can do from the screen are as follows:

- **Rectangular Snip**—This is the most common snip. You take your stylus and make a rectangular box on the screen.
- **Full-Screen Snip**—A snip of the full screen is done fast and with a tap of the pen.
- **Window Snip**—Snip any window that you have open on your screen. Simply select the window that you want, and it will automatically be snipped.
- **Free-form Snip**—Using the pen makes this snip a lot easier to use. This snip gives you any shape—for example, a circle—that you want to make into a snip.

Each snip will be shown in a defaulted red frame unless otherwise changed in the options. This frame will let you see exactly which section you are snipping. The Snipping Tools Window will also disappear when selecting your snip. After you have decided how you want to snip the current screen, you simply left-click and hold the mouse while dragging around the snipping areas. With the entire screen faded, the selected snip on the screen will be unfaded and outlined in default red if not changed from the default, seen in Figure 41.8.

Figure 41.8
Selecting the Area using the Snipping Tool.

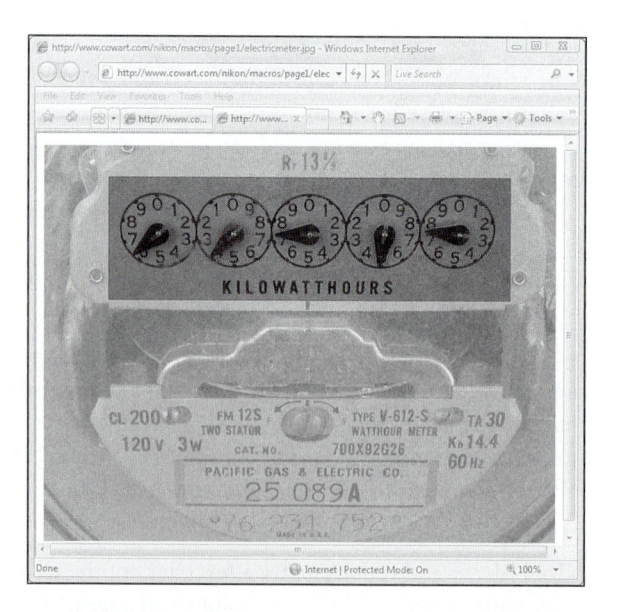

After the area is selected, the snipped area will automatically be sent to a separate window, the Snipping Tool editing window shown in Figure 41.9. This window will allow you to draw, erase, highlight, and save the snipped area.

Figure 41.9
Snipping Tools Editing Window.

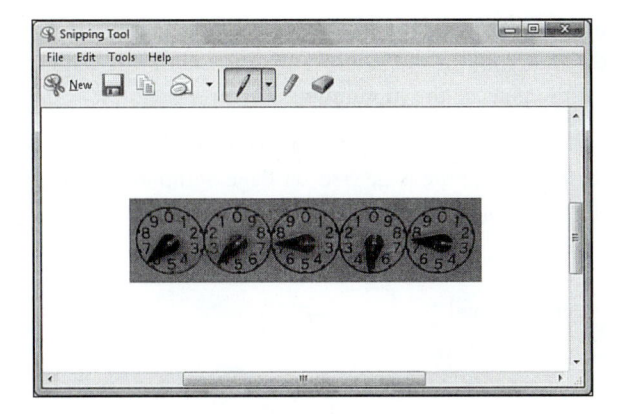

When saving the snip, you are offered a variety of file extensions. You can save the snip as an HTML file, PNG, GIF, or JPEG file extension. Once saved, you are allowed to reopen the snip with your Internet Browser for HTML files or your Paint program for picture extensions. Snips also can be directly copied from the Snipping Tool window and can be pasted anywhere as a picture type. This is a great feature if you have to copy a few words out of a document that is in a picture form or PDF. Snipping tools really benefit tablet users because a stylus pen makes snips more precise and to be used on-the-fly.

Windows Journal

If you like to keep notes or even a diary, this is the program for you. Windows Journal looks like a basic sheet of paper but on your tablet (see Figure 41.10). You can write anything you want, draw graphs and charts, or just doodle.

Figure 41.10
Windows Journal.

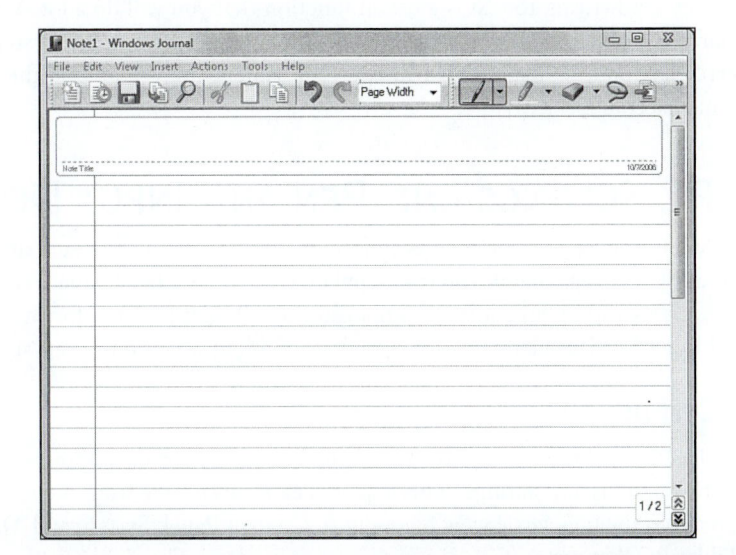

At first blush, Windows Journal might look like Microsoft Word. True, it is similar, but the primary difference is that you can use handwriting instead of just plain text. You can easily change the colors of the pens or the highlighters if you take notes.

When you first open Windows Journal, you may wonder why the page is so small. Not a problem. You can easily change the page size via Page Setup under the File tab. Remember this is a program that is supposed to be used mainly for notes, so the default size is small.

Two options in particular are worth checking out:

- Convert Selection to E-mail
- Convert Handwriting to Text

Both of these options are useful. After scribbling up a set of notes, you may want to consider converting them to text so that you can place them in a Word document. To do so, follow these steps:

1. Complete the handwritten text that you want converted.
2. Select the Lasso tool and select all the text that you want converted. The Lasso tool has a weird pivot system that is at first awkward to use. Instead of the red dots being the selector of the text, the Lasso tool uses the white dotted line that comes from the focus point. Also if the white dotted line selects about 70% more of the handwriting, it figures out what you are trying to select and will select all of that content.
3. After you select the text you want converted, select Actions in the toolbar and then select Convert Handwriting to Text.
4. A new window appears asking you whether the words that it recognized are correct. You can then change any words that are incorrect.

Converting handwriting to text is a useful function that you will do a lot. You can also convert your text to an email if you want. Follow the preceding steps, but at step 3, click Convert Selection to E-mail. This will open the same window and send the data to your profile mail account.

Tablet PC Settings and Pen and Input Devices

If you are left-handed, certain menus and items may be difficult to reach or pull up. With the Tablet PC Settings menu, you can stipulate that you are left-handed. As discussed previously, the stylus and its functions are important to a Tablet PC, and for that reason, the Vista Pen and Input Devices menu gives you multiple options about how your stylus works.

Tablet PC Settings Menu

The Tablet PC Settings menu, shown in Figure 41.11, is a primary applet that offers many handwriting and display settings. This applet is easily accessible from the classic view Control Panel, or from the nonclassic view by going to Control Panel, System and Maintenance, and then Tablet PC Settings.

Figure 41.11
Tablet PC
Settings menu.

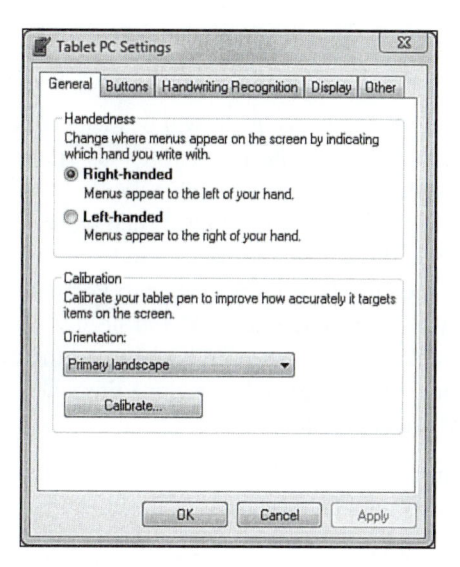

The first option the Tablet PC menu offers lets you designate your handedness. As a result of your choosing Left-Handed or Right-Handed, the Tablet Input Panel will either appear on the left or right side of the screen. One of the most important options that displays on the General tab is the Calibration option. From time to time, you will have to recalibrate your stylus with your tablet. Every few months, take the time to recalibrate your pen. Having the pointer uncalibrated can cause annoying pen misbehavior such as the inability to grab the scrollbar.

The next option in the Tablet PC Settings menu is the Buttons tab. Every tablet comes with a few sets of buttons on the side or next to the screen. These buttons perform certain shortcut actions and can save you pen strokes. Take the time to set each button to what you want. Setting a button to a function such as opening your Windows Journal can be a huge benefit. Obviously, you'll want to set your buttons to launch programs or execute functions that you use most frequently.

As previously stated in this chapter, handwriting recognition is an important tool when writing text. Vista has a great capacity to learn how to recognize your handwriting style. In the Handwriting Recognition tab, you can turn off the Recognizer and turn off the automatic learning. Vista keeps each setting on by default, and we recommend that you not change them. Keep the default settings unless you have a personal vendetta against the handwriting Recognizer. Let your computer learn to better recognize your handwriting over time. Your efficiency will increase markedly.

The last two option tabs in the Tablet PC Settings menu are basic screen settings and links to other settings. You can change the orientation of the screen however you want. If you have a "pure" Tablet PC (no keyboard), choose Portrait mode as the default if it isn't already selected. Portrait gives more of a "paper" feel, as the layout of the screen is more like a piece of paper. If you are having problems with the screen changing layout, check the

Troubleshooting section "Screen Does Not Change Layouts for Convertibles" at the end of the chapter.

In portrait layout, word documents and full page items will be easier to read and will require less scrolling. The only time I would suggest you change to Landscape is when you are watching a full-screen movie or slideshow. Most convertible Tablet PCs come with a swivel screen that changes the layout when rotating and closing. When typing on the physical keyboard with a convertible Tablet PC, the screen must be in Landscape mode if you want to read what you are writing. On some models, you can change to Portrait orientation while typing on the keyboard, but do you want to have to cock your head 90 degrees to the side the entire time? (This setting could be useful, however, if you stood the computer on its side and used an external USB or Bluetooth keyboard. I have done this when I really wanted to type and also had a vertical page orientation.)

The links on the Other tab are just basic links to the Pen and Input Device menu and the Tablet PC Panel options. Vista incorporated these links in this menu just to give you quick access to those settings.

PEN AND INPUT DEVICES MENU

Changing options to the stylus pen lets you customize your tablet. With the Pen and Input Devices menu, shown in Figure 41.12, you can change such things so that a single-click with the stylus registers as a double-click.

Figure 41.12
The Pen and Input Devices menu.

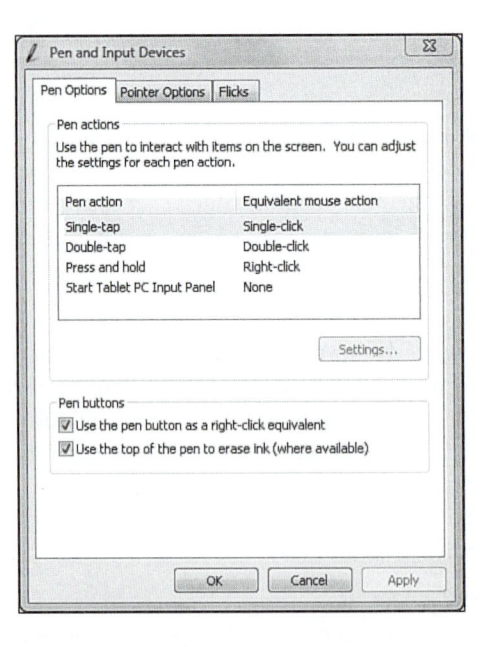

The Pen and Input Devices menu gives you three options: Pen Options, Pointer Options, and Flicks. Most of these options are perfect left in the default settings. The main reason for this panel is to give you the option to personalize the stylus a bit should you feel the need. Let's go over the options briefly:

- The general Pen Options tab gives you options for how the pen interacts with the screen. Changing how the stylus implements such functions as a right-click can better help you customize your tablet. Other options here let you turn off the right-click equivalent and the back-end eraser. Most likely, you will never want to change these settings.

- The next tab in the Pen and Input Devices menu is what we call the "visualization" tab. The Pointer Options tab allows for minor display modifications that won't change your tablet experience markedly. They only spice it up. In the Pointer Options tab, you can turn on and off the visualizations of the pointer and the various clicks. In Vista, default visualizations are small halos and when clicking on the screen with the pen, produces a ripple type effect. This Pointer tab also allows you to change the pointer type of your pen. By default, the pen cursor is a small white dot. You can turn this feature off and display a regular mouse cursor if wanted. The only time recommended to turn off these settings is when your Tablet PC has a poor graphics card or a slow processor. If your system is not up to par, you may have to turn off these visualization effects. But if your computer has no problem running these effects, why turn down a free gift?

- The last tab is the basic Flicks tab. If you are new to using pen flicks, leave these settings alone. After a bit of practice, you will be efficient in using pen flicks. You can increase pen flick usage by changing your settings by using *Customize Flicks window*. Customize Flicks window offers additional flicks that can do basic functions such as undo, delete, copy, and paste. This also is customizable to whatever keys you want.

Change your different pen flicks to your liking by simply using the customizing window shown in Figure 41.13.

Figure 41.13
Customizing pen flicks.

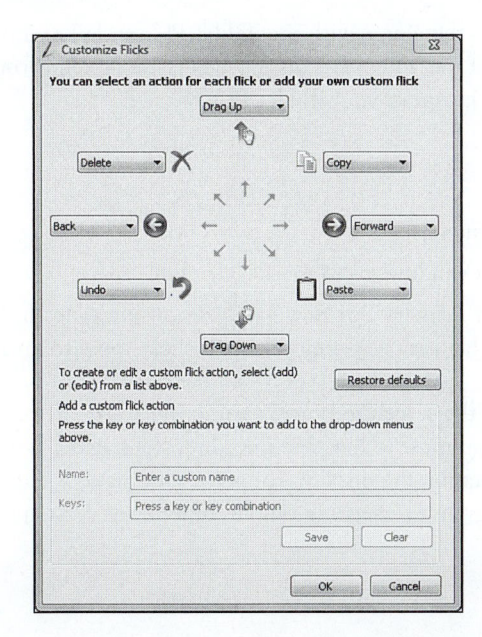

→ To learn more about how to use pen flicks and its features, **see** "Gestures and Pen Flicks," **p. 1363**. (Chapter 41)

TROUBLESHOOTING

PEN CURSOR PROBLEM

My pen cursor is off center. What do I do? With the pen cursor off center, I have a hard time clicking on various items.

The Tablet PC stylus pen will need recalibration after a period of time. To recalibrate the pen check the "Tablet PC Settings, and Pen and Input Devices" section earlier in this chapter.

PEN FLICKS NOT WORKING

I cannot get my pen flicks to work correctly. Pen Flicks will not work at all or only works very scarcely.

This is a common mistake to new Tablet PC owners. First, make sure that pen flicks are turned on. Refer to the "Pen Flicks" section earlier in this chapter.

If pen flicks are turned on, you might just be having a problem implementing a flick. Go to the pen flicks training in the Tablet PC folder in All Programs. This will guide you in how to successfully use pen flicks.

SCREEN DOES CHANGE LAYOUT FOR CONVERTIBLES

I own a convertible Tablet PC and when I rotate the screen to go into tablet mode, the screen does not change orientation. The screen should be in portrait layout but stays in landscape.

Sometimes, rotation programs that come with the Tablet PC can fail to initialize. Rotation programs control the layout of the Tablet PC display when the screen is rotated. Follow the following steps to change the layout of your Tablet PC.

1. Open the Control Panel.
2. Click on the Mobile PC.
3. Select the Tablet PC Settings.
4. In the Tablet PC Settings window, go to the Display tab.
5. Under Orientation, select Primary Portrait. The preview underneath the option will show a screen in portrait landscape. When selected, click Apply to save changes.

When changing the layout of the screen to portrait using the above method, when you want to revert back to landscape, you must follow the preceding steps again. Using the preceding method is a manual way of rotating the display. To fix the automatic rotation utility program, try reinstalling the program or checking online for a newer version of the software.

Tips from the Windows Pros: A Whole New Level of Pen Flicks

After using your Tablet PC long enough, you can become proficient at using pen flicks. If you haven't already customized your pen flicks, here is a great tip to make your friends envious.

Vista incorporates a 3-D Windows Switcher that is a great visual substitution for the Alt+Tab method. As you know from Chapter 1, "Introducing Windows Vista," it's called Flip 3-D. You can utilize this function by using only your stylus pen. Follow these basic steps to change your pen flick:

1. Open the Pen and Input Devices Menu and go to the Flicks tab.
2. Make sure that flicks are enabled and that Navigational Flicks and Editing Flicks are enabled.
3. Select Customize to open the Customize Flicks window.
4. Make your choice for which pen flicks you want to change. Assign one direction of your flicks to be interpreted as the keypress Ctrl+Windows+Tab. Be sure that you add the Ctrl key there because if you don't, the Window Switcher will not stay open.
5. After setting one flick to the actual switcher, you can switch between the actual slides of the Windows Switcher by using the same Pen Flick. To select the window that you want, simply click the slide that you want open.

PART IX

APPENDIXES

- **A** Windows Programs and Services 1379
- **B** What's New in Service Pack 1 (SP-1) 1421

APPENDIX A

WINDOWS PROGRAMS AND SERVICES

In this appendix

Windows Programs 1380
  Executable Programs 1382
  MS-DOS Applications 1401
  Control Panel Applets 1402
  Microsoft Management Console Plug-Ins 1403
  Screensavers 1404
Windows Services 1405

# Windows Programs

Table A.1 lists the standard programs, Microsoft Management Console snap-ins, and Control Panel applets that are installed as part of Windows Vista Ultimate Edition. Other versions of Vista might not include all of these programs. Many of the listed programs are installed by default with Windows. Other programs are installed only when an option is checked in the Turn Windows Feature On and Off Control Panel. Certain hardware support packages might install additional programs not listed here.

Executable Programs

Filename	Description
ACW.exe	Microsoft Guided Help
AdapterTroubleshooter.exe	Display Adapter troubleshooter
AgentSvr.exe	Microsoft Agent Server
alg.exe	Application Layer Gateway service
appcmd.exe	Application Server command-line admin tool
AppLaunch.exe	Microsoft .NET ClickOnce launch utility
ARP.EXE	TCP/IP diagnostic command
aspnetca.exe	ASP.NET setup custom actions
aspnet_compiler.exe	ASP.NET compiler
aspnet_regbrowsers.exe	Installs .NET browsers into the Global Assembly Cache
aspnet_regiis.exe	Associates ASP.NET scripts with correct .NET CLR version
aspnet_regsql.exe	Associates MS SQL databases with ASP.NET applications
aspnet_state.exe	Microsoft ASP.NET State service
aspnet_wp.exe	ASP.NET Worker process
at.exe	Scheduled task command-line interface
AtBroker.exe	Transitions accessible technologies between desktops
attrib.exe	File attribute editor
audiodg.exe	Windows Audio Device Graph Isolation
audit.exe	Part of Windows setup
auditpol.exe	Audit Policy command-line tool
autochk.exe	Boot-time disk check
autoconv.exe	Boot-time file system conversion
autofmt.exe	Boot-time disk format

Filename	Description
AxInstUI.exe	ActiveX Installer service
bcdedit.exe	Boot Configuration Data editor (command-line tool)
BdeHdCfg.exe	BitLocker Drive Preparation Tool (Windows Ultimate Extra)
bfsvc.exe	Boot File Servicing utility
BitLockerWizard.exe	BitLocker Drive Encryption Wizard
bitsadmin.exe	BITS administration utility
bootcfg.exe	Command-line tool to modify `boot.ini` (not used by Vista)
bridgeunattend.exe	Network Bridge setup component
bthudtask.exe	Bluetooth Uninstall Device Task
cacls.exe	File access settings editor (`icacls` is now preferred)
calc.exe	Calculator application
CaptureWizard.exe	Import video
CasPol.exe	Microsoft .NET Framework CAS Policy Manager
cbsra.exe	Windows Update component (added by Service Pack 1)
Cclitesetupui.exe	Win32 Cabinet Self-Extractor
CertEnrollCtrl.exe	Certificate enrollment component
certreq.exe	Certificate request command-line tool
certutil.exe	Certificate management command-line tool
change.exe	Terminal Services utility
charmap.exe	Character Map application
Chess.exe	Chess game
chglogon.exe	Terminal Services utility
chgport.exe	Terminal Services utility
chgusr.exe	Terminal Services utility
chkdsk.exe	Check Disk utility
chkntfs.exe	NTFS `checkdisk` component
choice.exe	Offers the user a choice (batch file tool)
CIDAEMON.EXE	Indexing Service filter service
cipher.exe	File encryption command-line tool
CISVC.EXE	Content Index service

Filename	Description
cleanmgr.exe	Disk Cleanup applet
cliconfg.exe	SQL Client Configuration utility
clip.exe	Redirects input/output to Clipboard (batch file tool)
clrgc.exe	.NET Framework utility
cmd.exe	Windows command-line shell
cmdkey.exe	Credential Manager command-line utility
cmdl32.exe	Microsoft Connection Manager component
cmmon32.exe	Microsoft Connection Manager Monitor component
cmstp.exe	Microsoft Connection Manager Profile installer
cofire.exe	Corrupted File Recovery Client
colorcpl.exe	Color Management Control Panel
comp.exe	File compare utility
compact.exe	File compress utility
CompMgmtLauncher.exe	Computer Management window launcher
ComputerDefaults.exe	Program Access and Computer Defaults Control Panel
comrepl.exe	COM+ Server Replication
ComSvcConfig.exe	COM+ Service Model Integration configuration utility
conime.exe	Console Input Method Editor (IME)
consent.exe	User Account Control component
control.exe	Control panel main window
convert.exe	File system conversion utility
credwiz.exe	Stored Usernames and Passwords Backup and Restore Wizard
csc.exe	Visual C# compiler
cscript.exe	Windows Script Host text-mode interpreter
csrss.exe	Client Server Runtime Process (core Windows service)
csrstub.exe	16-bit Windows component
ctfmon.exe	CTF Loader
cvtres.exe	Resource File to COFF Object converter
dcomcnfg.exe	COM+ configuration

Filename	Description
Defrag.exe	Disk Defragmenter utility
DeviceEject.exe	Eject Device control panel
DeviceProperties.exe	Device Properties component
DFDWiz.exe	Windows Disk Diagnostic User Resolver
dfrgfat.exe	Disk Defragmenter component
dfrgifc.exe	Disk Defragmenter component
DfrgNtfs.exe	Disk Defragmenter component
dfrgui.exe	Disk Defragmenter window
dfsr.exe	Distributed File System Replication
dfsvc.exe	Distributed File System service
dialer.exe	Phone Dialer
diantz.exe	Cabinet-file compression
digitalx.exe	Digital Locker component
diskpart.exe	Disk partition utility
diskperf.exe	Disk performance monitoring enabler (obsolete)
diskraid.exe	RAID disk config utility
dispdiag.exe	Display diagnostic tool
dllhost.exe	COM object host process
dllhst3g.exe	COM object host process
dnscacheugc.exe	DNSCache Unattend Generic command
doskey.exe	Command-line alias and editing extension—a 32-bit Windows console application, not the MS-DOS version
dpapimig.exe	DPAPI Key Migration Wizard
DpiScaling.exe	DPI Scaling control panel
dplaysvr.exe	DirectPlay component
dpnsvr.exe	DirectPlay component
driverquery.exe	Lists installed drivers
drvinst.exe	Driver Installation module
DRWATSON.EXE	Windows fault-detection utility
DVDMaker.exe	Windows DVD Maker
dvdplay.exe	dvdplay placeholder application; runs Windows Media Player
dvdupgrd.exe	Setup/upgrade component

Filename	Description
dw20.exe	Microsoft .NET Error Reporting component
dwm.exe	Desktop Window Manager (Windows component)
DWWIN.EXE	Windows fault-detection utility
dxdiag.exe	Microsoft DirectX Diagnostic Tool
efsui.exe	File Encryption user interface component
ehexthost.exe	Media Center component
ehmsas.exe	Media Center component
ehprivjob.exe	Media Center component
ehrec.exe	Media Center component
ehrecvr.exe	Media Center component
ehsched.exe	Media Center component
ehshell.exe	Media Center component
ehtray.exe	Media Center component
ehvid.exe	Media Center component
esentutl.exe	Extensible Storage Engine command-line tool
eudcedit.exe	Private character editor
eventcreate.exe	Creates custom event in an event log
eventvwr.exe	Event Viewer
evntcmd.exe	Event Translator Configuration Tool
evntwin.exe	Event Translator config tool
expand.exe	Zip/CAB file expansion utility
explorer.exe	Windows Explorer
extrac32.exe	CAB file-extract utility
fc.exe	File Comparing utility
find.exe	Find String (grep) utility
findstr.exe	Find String (QGREP) utility
finger.exe	TCP/IP "finger" command
FirewallControlPanel.exe	Windows Firewall Control Panel window
FirewallSettings.exe	Windows Firewall Settings dialog box
fixmapi.exe	MAPI Repair Tool
FlickLearningWizard.exe	Pen Flicks Training Wizard
fltMC.exe	Filter Manager Control Program
fontview.exe	Windows Font Viewer
forfiles.exe	Executes a command on selected files

Windows Programs

Filename	Description
format.com	Formats fixed and removable disks
FreeCell.exe	FreeCell Game
fsquirt.exe	Bluetooth File Transfer Wizard
fsutil.exe	File system maintenance command-line utility
ftp.exe	File Transfer Protocol client
fvenotify.exe	BitLocker Drive Encryption Notification utility
fveupdate.exe	BitLocker Drive Encryption Servicing utility
FXSCOVER.exe	Microsoft Fax Cover Page Editor
FXSSVC.exe	Fax service
FXSUNATD.exe	Microsoft Fax setup component
GDI.EXE	Windows Graphics Device Interface core component
getmac.exe	Displays network adapter MAC information
gpresult.exe	Query Group Policy RSOP Data
gpscript.exe	Group Policy Script Application
gpupdate.exe	Group Policy Update utility
grpconv.exe	Windows 3.1 Program Manager Group Converter
hdwwiz.exe	Add Hardware Wizard
Hearts.exe	Hearts game
help.exe	Command-line help utility
HelpPane.exe	Help and support
hh.exe	HTML help application
HoldEm.exe	Texas Hold-Em game (Windows Ultimate Extra)
HOSTNAME.EXE	Displays computer name
iashost.exe	IIS component
icacls.exe	Edits, saves, and restores access settings on files (command-line tool)
icardagt.exe	Windows CardSpace User Interface Agent
icsunattend.exe	Internet Connection Sharing setup component
ie4uinit.exe	IE per-user initialization utility
iedw.exe	IE crash detection
IEExec.exe	Microsoft IE Execute shell
ieinstal.exe	Internet Explorer Add-on Installer

Filename	Description
ieUnatt.exe	IE 7.0 setup component
ieuser.exe	Internet Explorer (protected mode version)
iexplore.exe	Internet Explorer
iexpress.exe	Wizard to build application deployment and setup packages
iisreset.exe	IIS control command-line utility
iisrstas.exe	Internet Information Services reset control
iissetup.exe	IIS Setup
ilasm.exe	Microsoft .NET Framework IL assembler
ImagingDevices.exe	Imaging Devices Control Panel
IMCCPHR.exe	Microsoft Chinese IME (Input Method Editor) PhraseUI Tools
IMEPADSV.EXE	Microsoft IME component
IMJPDADM.EXE	Microsoft IME component
IMJPDCT.EXE	Microsoft IME component
IMJPDSVR.EXE	Microsoft IME component
IMJPMGR.EXE	Microsoft IME component
imjppdmg.exe	Microsoft IME component
IMJPUEX.EXE	Microsoft IME component
imjpuexc.exe	Microsoft IME component
IMSCPROP.exe	Microsoft Pinyin IME Property Setting
IMTCPROP.exe	Microsoft IME component
inetinfo.exe	Internet Information Services service
InetMgr.exe	IIS v7 Manager
InetMgr6.exe	IIS v6 Admin Program
InfDefaultInstall.exe	Windows setup component
infocard.exe	Windows CardSpace
inkball.exe	InkBall game
InkWatson.exe	Handwriting Recognition Error Reporting Wizard
InputPersonalization.exe	Input Personalization Server
InstallUtil.exe	.NET Framework installation utility
ipconfig.exe	IP Configuration utility
IpsOptInSrv.exe	Input Personalization Opt-In dialog box
irftp.exe	Infrared File Transfer

Filename	Description
iscsicli.exe	iSCSI Discovery tool
iscsicpl.exe	Microsoft iSCSI Initiator Configuration Tool
Journal.exe	Windows Journal
jsc.exe	JScript Compiler
krnl386.exe	Windows kernel component
ktmutil.exe	Kernel Transaction Management utility
label.exe	Disk Label command-line tool
lnkstub.exe	Broken link target placeholder
loadmxf.exe	Windows Media Center MXF Loader
Locator.exe	Rpc Locator service
lodctr.exe	Load PerfMon Counters
logagent.exe	Windows Media Player component
logman.exe	Performance Log utility
logoff.exe	Session Logoff utility
LogonUI.exe	Windows Logon User Interface Host
lpksetup.exe	Language Pack Installer
lpq.exe	TCP/IP printing `lpq` command
lpr.exe	TCP/IP printing `lpr` command
lpremove.exe	MUI Language pack cleanup
lsass.exe	Local Security Authority Process service
lsm.exe	Local Session Manager service
Magnify.exe	Screen Magnifier
Mahjong.exe	Mahjong Titans game
makecab.exe	Cabinet Maker
manage-bde.wsf	Bitlocker management script (Ultimate only)
mblctr.exe	Windows Mobility Center
mcbuilder.exe	Resource cache builder tool
McrMgr.exe	Media Center Extender Manager
mcspad.exe	Media Center SPAD Configuration utility
mcupdate.exe	Windows Media Center Store Update Manager
Mcx2Prov.exe	MCX2 Provisioning library
MdRes.exe	Memory diagnostic tool
MdSched.exe	Memory diagnostic tool
memtest.exe	Memory diagnostic tool

Filename	Description
mfpmp.exe	Media Foundation Protected Pipeline EXE
MigAutoPlay.exe	Windows Easy Transfer component
mighost.exe	Migration plug-ins host program
MigRegDB.exe	COM+ setup component
MigSetup.exe	Windows Easy Transfer component
migwiz.exe	Windows Easy Transfer Wizard
MineSweeper.exe	Minesweeper game
mmc.exe	Microsoft Management Console
mobsync.exe	Sync Center
mofcomp.exe	Managed Object Format (MOF) Compiler
more.exe	Text file display tool
mount.exe	Client for NFS export/share mount utility
mountvol.exe	Mount Volume utility
MOVIEMK.exe	Windows Movie Maker
MpCmdRun.exe	Windows Defender command-line utility
mpnotify.exe	Windows NT Multiple Provider Notification application
mqbkup.exe	Message Queuing Backup/Restore utility
mqsvc.exe	Message Queuing service
mqtgsvc.exe	Message Queuing Trigger service
MRINFO.EXE	Multicast Information
mrt.exe	Malicious Software Removal tool
MSASCui.exe	Windows Defender User Interface
MSBuild.exe	Application build utility; part of .NET framework
msconfig.exe	System Configuration utility
mscorsvw.exe	.NET Runtime Optimization service
msdt.exe	Microsoft Support Diagnostic tool
msdtc.exe	MS Distributed Transaction Coordinator console program
msfeedssync.exe	Microsoft Feeds Synchronization
msg.exe	Computer-to-computer message utility
mshta.exe	Microsoft HTML Application host
msiexec.exe	Windows installer
msinfo32.exe	System Information

Filename	Description
msoobe.exe	Windows Machine OOBE (Out of the Box Experience, the initial setup and welcome screens)
mspaint.exe	Paint accessory
msra.exe	Windows Remote Assistance
mstsc.exe	Remote Desktop Connection client
mtedit.exe	Group Policy Management Migration Table Editor
mtstocom.exe	COM+ component
MuiUnattend.exe	Multilanguage User Interface setup component
NAPSTAT.EXE	Network Access Protection Client UI
Narrator.exe	Narrator accessory
nbtstat.exe	TCP/IP NetBIOS information utility
net.exe	File sharing command-line control utility
net1.exe	Net command component
netbtugc.exe	NetBT setup component
netcfg.exe	Network installer setup utility
NETFXSBS10.exe	Microsoft .NET Installation Hook
netiougc.exe	Network installer setup component
Netplwiz.exe	Advanced User Accounts Control Panel (on Windows XP, this was `control userpasswords2`)
NetProj.exe	Connect to a Network Projector
netsh.exe	Network configuration shell
NETSTAT.EXE	TCP/IP status command
newdev.exe	Device driver software installation
nfsadmin.exe	Services for NFS administration utility
nfsclnt.exe	Client for NFS service
ngen.exe	Microsoft Common Language Runtime native compiler
notepad.exe	Notepad accessory
nslookup.exe	Name server lookup tool
ntkrnlpa.exe	Windows kernel component
ntoskrnl.exe	Windows kernel component
ntprint.exe	Printer driver software installation component

Filename	Description
ntvdm.exe	MS-DOS and Win16 compatibility component
ocsetup.exe	Windows Optional Component Setup
odbcad32.exe	ODBC Administrator
odbcconf.exe	ODBC Driver command-line setup tool
oobeldr.exe	OOBE (initial setup) component
openfiles.exe	Displays list of currently open files; requires kernel flag to be set first.
OptionalFeatures.exe	Turn Windows Features On or Off control panel
osk.exe	On-Screen Keyboard
p2phost.exe	People Near Me service
pathping.exe	TCP/IP pathping command
pcaelv.exe	Program Compatibility Assistant component
pcalua.exe	Program Compatibility Assistant component
pcaui.exe	Program Compatibility Assistant User Interface
pdialog.exe	Windows Journal Note Writer Progress dialog box
PenTraining.exe	Tablet PC Pen Training
perfmon.exe	Reliability and Performance Monitor
ping.exe	TCP/IP ping command
pipanel.exe	Microsoft Tablet PC Component
PkgMgr.exe	Windows Package Manager
plasrv.exe	Performance Logs and Alerts component
PnPUnattend.exe	PnP setup component
PnPutil.exe	Microsoft PnP utility—tool to add, delete, and enumerate driver packages
poqexec.exe	Primitive Operations Queue Executor
posix.exe	Subsystem for UNIX-Based Applications Console Session Manager
powercfg.exe	Power Settings command-line tool
PresentationFontCache.exe	Windows Presentation Foundation Font Cache service
PresentationHost.exe	Windows Presentation Foundation Host
PresentationSettings.exe	Mobile PC Presentation Settings configuration dialog

Filename	Description
prevhost.exe	Preview Handler Surrogate Host
PrintBrm.exe	Printer migration command-line tool
PrintBrmEngine.exe	Printer migration service
PrintBrmUi.exe	Printer migration application
printfilterpipelinesvc.exe	Print Filter Pipeline Host
printui.exe	Printer setup tool
proquota.exe	Disk quota enforcement pop-up
psxrun.exe	SUA Subsystem Session Manager
psxss.exe	SUA Subsystem Server
PurblePlace.exe	Purble Place game
PushPrinterConnections.exe	Sets up printers based on Group Policy
qappsrv.exe	Query Terminal Server utility
qprocess.exe	Query Process utility
query.exe	MultiUser Query utility
quser.exe	Query User utility
qwinsta.exe	Query Session utility
RacAgent.exe	Reliability analysis metrics-calculation program
rasautou.exe	Remote Access dialer component
rasdial.exe	Remote Access command line dialing tool. Works for VPNs, too.
raserver.exe	Windows Remote Assistance COM Server
rasphone.exe	Remote Access Phonebook
rdpclip.exe	RDP Clip Monitor
rdrleakdiag.exe	Microsoft Windows Resource Leak Diagnostic
recdisc.exe	Recovery disc creation tool (added by Service Pack 1)
recover.exe	Recover Files utility
reg.exe	Command-line Registry editor/query tool
RegAsm.exe	Microsoft .NET Assembly Registration utility
regedit.exe	Registry Editor
regedt32.exe	Registry Editor (old name)
regini.exe	Registry Initializer
RegisterMCEApp.exe	Media Center Application registration

Filename	Description
RegSvcs.exe	Microsoft .NET Services Installation utility
regsvr32.exe	Registers COM/ActiveX components
rekeywiz.exe	Encrypted File System certificate manager/wizard
relog.exe	Performance Relogging utility
RelPost.exe	Windows Diagnosis and Recovery
replace.exe	Replace File command-line tool
reset.exe	Terminal Services Reset utility
RMActivate.exe	Windows Rights Management component
RMActivate_isv.exe	Windows Rights Management component
RMActivate_ssp.exe	Windows Rights Management component
RMActivate_ssp_isv.exe	Windows Rights Management component
RmClient.exe	Restart Manager LUA Restart Client
Robocopy.exe	Spiffy file tree copying tool
ROUTE.EXE	TCP/IP route-setup tool
rpcinfo.exe	Services for NFS ONCRPC registration admin utility
RpcPing.exe	RPC Ping diagnostic utility
rrinstaller.exe	R&R installer
rsm.exe	Removable Storage Command-Line Interface
rsmllsv.exe	Removable Storage MLL Layer
rsmsink.exe	Removable Storage Sink Layer
rsmui.exe	Removable Storage UI Layer
rstrui.exe	System Restore Wizard
runas.exe	Run-As utility
rundll32.exe	Calls DLL function from command line
RunLegacyCPLElevated.exe	Runs a legacy control panel applet with elevated permissions
runonce.exe	Run Once Wrapper
rwinsta.exe	Reset Session utility
sapisvr.exe	Speech Recognition
SBEServer.exe	Burn CD/DVD plug-in component
sbunattend.exe	Windows Sidebar setup component
sc.exe	Service control command-line tool
schtasks.exe	Manages scheduled tasks

Filename	Description
scrcons.exe	WMI (Windows Management Instrumentation) Standard Event Consumer—scripting
sdbinst.exe	Application Compatibility Database installer
sdchange.exe	Remote Assistance component
sdclt.exe	Windows Backup setup
SearchFilterHost.exe	Microsoft Windows Search Filter Host component
SearchIndexer.exe	Microsoft Windows Search Indexer component
SearchProtocolHost.exe	Microsoft Windows Search Protocol Host component
SecEdit.exe	Windows Security Configuration command-line tool
secinit.exe	Security Init component
ServiceModelReg.exe	.NET Framework component
services.exe	Services and Controller app
sethc.exe	Accessibility shortcut keys
Setup.exe	Windows Installation and Setup
setupcl.exe	SetupCL utility
setupSNK.exe	Launch Wireless Network Setup Wizard program
setupugc.exe	Setup component
setup_wm.exe	Microsoft Windows Media Configuration utility
setx.exe	Sets environment variables from command line
sfc.exe	System integrity check and repair
shadow.exe	Terminal Services session remote control utility
ShapeCollector.exe	Personalize Handwriting Recognition UI
showmount.exe	Services for NFS mount information query utility
shrpubw.exe	Share Creation Wizard
shutdown.exe	Windows Shutdown and Annotation Tool
sidebar.exe	Windows Sidebar accessory
sigverif.exe	File Signature Verification

Filename	Description
SLLUA.exe	Software Licensing Admin Access Provider
SLsvc.exe	Microsoft Software Licensing service
SLUI.exe	Windows Activation Client
SMConfigInstaller.exe	WCF Generic Command for Vista Setup
smi2smir.exe	WMI SNMP MIB Compiler
smss.exe	Session Manager service
SMSvcHost.exe	Windows Communication Foundation component
SndVol.exe	Volume Control Applet
SnippingTool.exe	Snipping Tool
snmp.exe	SNMP service
snmptrap.exe	SNMP Trap service
Solitaire.exe	Solitaire game
sort.exe	Text file sort utility
SoundRecorder.exe	Windows Sound Recorder
SpiderSolitaire.exe	Spider Solitaire game
spoolsv.exe	Print spooler component
spreview.exe	Displays "Finished" message after installing Service Pack 1
srdelayed.exe	System Restore Delayed File Renamer
StikyNot.exe	Sticky Notes accessory
suagc.exe	Services for UNIX-Based Applications component
subst.exe	Maps file path to virtual drive letter (MS-DOS ancestry, but this is a Windows application)
svchost.exe	Host Process for Windows Services—runs services whose code is contained in DLLs
sxstrace.exe	Side-by-Side tracing tool
sysedit.exe	Windows System Editor (for Win16 compatibility)
syskey.exe	Security and Accounts database-lockdown tool
sysprep.exe	System Preparation Tool (for cloning/deployment)
systeminfo.exe	Displays system information

Filename	Description
SystemPropertiesAdvanced.exe	Advanced System Settings dialog box (these System Properties*XXX* programs do the jobs of the tabs on Windows XP's System Properties dialog box)
SystemPropertiesComputerName.exe	Change Computer Settings dialog box
SystemPropertiesDataExecution-Prevention.exe	Change Data Execution Prevention Settings dialog box
SystemPropertiesHardware.exe	Hardware Settings dialog box
SystemPropertiesPerformance.exe	Change Computer Performance Settings dialog box
SystemPropertiesProtection.exe	System Protection Settings dialog box
SystemPropertiesRemote.exe	System Remote Settings dialog box
systray.exe	Systray .exe stub
tabcal.exe	Digitizer Calibration Tool
TabTip.exe	Tablet PC Input Panel accessory
takeown.exe	Takes ownership of a file
TapiUnattend.exe	Telephony setup component
taskeng.exe	Task Scheduler service
taskkill.exe	Terminates processes from command line
tasklist.exe	Lists the current running tasks
taskmgr.exe	Windows Task Manager
tcmsetup.exe	Telephony Administration Setup
tcpsvcs.exe	TCP/IP network services component
telnet.exe	Command-line Telnet client
tftp.exe	Trivial File Transfer Protocol client
timeout.exe	Batch file "sleep" command
tlntadmn.exe	Telnet service configuration tool
tlntsess.exe	Microsoft Telnet Server Helper
tlntsvr.exe	Telnet service
TouchTraining.exe	Tablet PC Touch Training
TpmInit.exe	TPM Initialization Wizard
tracerpt.exe	Event Trace Report Tool
tracert.exe	TCP/IP traceroute command
tree.exe	Displays directory structure
TrustedInstaller.exe	Windows Modules Installer

Filename	Description
tscon.exe	Terminal Services Session Connection utility
tscupgrd.exe	Setup Custom Action DLL
tsdiscon.exe	Terminal Services Session Disconnection utility
tskill.exe	Terminal Services End Process utility
tssetup.exe	Terminal Server Custom Action setup tool
TSTheme.exe	Themes service
tswpfwrp.exe	Terminals Server (remote desktop) WPF wrapper component (added by Service Pack 1)
twunk_16.exe	TWAIN (Scanner) 16-bit software support module
twunk_32.exe	TWAIN (Scanner) 32-bit software support module
typeperf.exe	Command-line performance monitor
tzupd.exe	Time zone/daylight savings time database update utility
ucsvc.exe	Boot File Servicing utility
UI0Detect.exe	Interactive services detection
umount.exe	Client for NFS export/share unmount utility
unattendedjoin.exe	Domain join setup component
unlodctr.exe	Unloads PerfMon Counters
unregmp2.exe	Microsoft Windows Media Player setup component
unsecapp.exe	Sink to receive asynchronous callbacks for WMI client application
upnpcont.exe	UPnP Device Host Container
USER.EXE	Windows User-interface core component
userinit.exe	Logon processing component
Utilman.exe	Ease of Access control panel
vbc.exe	Visual Basic command line compiler
vds.exe	Virtual Disk service
vdsldr.exe	Virtual Disk service loader
verclsid.exe	Extension CLSID Verification Host
verifier.exe	Driver Verifier Manager
VideoCameraAutoPlayManager.exe	Windows Video Camera Auto Play Manager
vsp1ceip.exe	Vista Service Pack 1 Customer Experience tracking utility

Filename	Description
vsp1cln.exe	Removes archive of files replaced by SP-1. Recovers disk space and removes uninstall option
vssadmin.exe	Command-line interface for Volume Shadow Copy service
VSSVC.exe	Volume Shadow Copy service
w32tm.exe	Windows Time service diagnostic tool
w3wp.exe	IIS Worker Process
wab.exe	Contacts (address book) editor
wabmig.exe	Contacts Import Tool
waitfor.exe	Waits for or sends a signal over a network
wbadmin.exe	Windows Backup command-line interface
wbemtest.exe	WMI Test Tool
wbengine.exe	Block Level Backup Engine service
wecutil.exe	Event Collector command-line utility
wercon.exe	Problem Reports and Solutions
WerFault.exe	Windows Problem Reporting
WerFaultSecure.exe	Windows Fault Reporting
WerManifestDownload.exe	Windows Message Reporting manifest download program
wermgr.exe	Windows Problem Reporting
wevtutil.exe	Eventing command-line utility
wextract.exe	Win32 Cabinet Self-Extractor
wfs.exe	Microsoft Windows Fax and Scan
where.exe	Locates files in the search path
whoami.exe	Displays logged-on user
wiaacmgr.exe	Windows Picture Acquisition Wizard
win.com	Does nothing; provided for compatibility with obsolete software installers
WinCal.exe	Windows Calendar
WinCollab.exe	Windows Meeting Space
windeploy.exe	Windows Deployment Loader
WindowsMailGadget.exe	Windows Mail Gadget for Windows SideShow–capable devices
WindowsPhotoGallery.exe	Windows Photo Gallery
WinFXDocObj.exe	WinFX Runtime components

APPENDIX A WINDOWS PROGRAMS AND SERVICES

Filename	Description
winhelp.exe	Windows Help engine
winhlp32.exe	Windows Help component
wininit.exe	Windows startup component
winload.exe	Windows startup component
winlogon.exe	Windows Logon component
WinMail.exe	Windows Mail
WinMgmt.exe	WMI service control utility
winresume.exe	Resume-from-hibernate boot application
winrm.vbs	Remote management tool with extensive capabilities
winrs.exe	Windows Remote Shell management tool
winrshost.exe	Windows Remote Shell service
WinSAT.exe	Windows System Assessment Tool
winspool.exe	16-bit Windows print spooler component
winver.exe	Version Reporter applet
wisptis.exe	Microsoft Tablet PC Input component
wlanext.exe	Windows Wireless LAN 802.11 Extensibility Framework
wlrmdr.exe	Pops up balloon reminder at logon
wmdSync.exe	User session Windows Mobile device handler
WMIADAP.exe	WMI Reverse Performance Adapter Maintenance utility
WmiApSrv.exe	WMI Performance Reverse Adapter
WMIC.exe	WMI command-line utility
WmiPrvSE.exe	WMI Provider host
wmlaunch.exe	Windows Media Player Launcher
wmpconfig.exe	Windows Media Player Configuration
wmpenc.exe	Windows Media Player Encoder Helper
wmplayer.exe	Windows Media Player
wmpnetwk.exe	Windows Media Player Network Sharing service
wmpnscfg.exe	Windows Media Player Network Sharing service configuration application
wmprph.exe	Windows Media Player Rich Preview handler
wmpshare.exe	Windows Media Player Folder Sharing

Filename	Description
WMPSideShowGadget.exe	Windows Media Player Gadget for Windows SideShow–capable devices
WMSvc.exe	IIS Manager service
wordpad.exe	Wordpad accessory
WOWDEB.EXE	16-bit Windows Debugging Helper
WOWEXEC.EXE	16-bit Windows Application Launcher
wpcer.exe	WPC Exemption Requester
wpcumi.exe	Windows Parental Control Notifications
WPDShextAutoplay.exe	Windows Portable Device Shell Extension Autoplay Handler
wpnpinst.exe	Support .exe for Internet Printing
write.exe	Windows Write accessory
WsatConfig.exe	Windows Communication Foundation WS-AtomicTransaction configuration utility
wscript.exe	Windows Script Host Window-based interpreter
WSManHTTPConfig.exe	WSMan HTTP Configuration File
wsqmcons.exe	Windows SQM Consolidator
wuapp.exe	Windows Update Application Launcher
wuauclt.exe	Automatic Updates client
WUDFHost.exe	Windows Driver Foundation—User-mode Driver Framework Host Process
wusa.exe	Windows Update standalone installer
WUSetupV.exe	Windows Update component
XamlViewer_v0300.exe	XAML Viewer
xcopy.exe	Extended file copy command line
XPSViewer.exe	XPS Viewer

MS-DOS Applications

MS-DOS applications are provided with 32-bit versions of Windows Vista versions for compatibility with legacy MS-DOS applications and batch files. MS-DOS applications are not provided with Windows Vista 64-bit versions.

Filename	Description
append.exe	Networking utility
chcp.com	Changes MS-DOS Code Page
command.com	MS-DOS command shell

Filename	Description
debug.exe	MS-DOS debugger
diskcomp.com	Compares floppy disks
diskcopy.com	Disk Copy Utility
dosx.exe	MS-DOS subsystem component
edit.com	MS-DOS text editor
edlin.exe	Text file editor
exe2bin.exe	Application development utility
fastopen.exe	Disk speed-up utility (placebo)
format.com	Disk Format utility
graftabl.com	Graphics code page switch
graphics.com	Loads MS-DOS graphics driver
kb16.com	Configures MS-DOS keyboard for specified language
loadfix.com	Loads MS-DOS program
mem.exe	Free memory display tool
mode.com	DOS Device MODE Utility
more.com	Page-by-page file display
mscdexnt.exe	Compatibility component (CD driver)
nlsfunc.exe	Language setting utility
print.exe	File print tool
redir.exe	Networking subsystem component
setver.exe	Program compatibility tool
share.exe	Networking subsystem component (placebo)
tree.com	Directory tree printing tool
win.com	Empty program; present to appease old MS-DOS and 16-bit Windows applications

Control Panel Applets

You can run control panel applets directly from the command line by typing **start** *filename*.**cpl**.

Filename	Control Panel Function
appwiz.cpl	Install/uninstall program
bthprops.cpl	Bluetooth
collab.cpl	People Near Me (used by Meeting Space)
desk.cpl	Desktop settings
Firewall.cpl	Windows Firewall

Filename	Control Panel Function
`hdwwiz.cpl`	Add Hardware
`inetcpl.cpl`	Internet Options
`infocardcpl.cpl`	Windows CardSpace
`intl.cpl`	International settings
`irprops.cpl`	Infrared
`joy.cpl`	Game controllers
`main.cpl`	Mouse and keyboard
`mmsys.cpl`	Sound
`ncpa.cpl`	Network Connections
`powercfg.cpl`	Power Management
`sapi.cpl`	Speech
`sysdm.cpl`	System properties
`TabletPC.cpl`	Tablet PC
`telephon.cpl`	Telephony
`timedate.cpl`	Time and date
`wmdConn.cpl`	Windows Mobile Device Center
`wscui.cpl`	Security Center

NOTE

> Windows Vista has fewer CPL control panel applets than previous versions of Windows. To accommodate the needs of User Account Control, many control panel functions are now EXE files. For example, the Add/Remove Windows Components function is now performed by `optionalfeatures.exe`.

MICROSOFT MANAGEMENT CONSOLE PLUG-INS

You can run management plug-ins directly from the command line by typing **start** *filename*`.msc`.

Filename	Management Console
`azman.msc`	Authorization Manager
`certmgr.msc`	Certificates
`CIADV.MSC`	Indexing service
`comexp.msc`	Component Services
`compmgmt.msc`	Computer Management (multiple plug-ins)
`devmgmt.msc`	Device Manager
`diskmgmt.msc`	Disk Management
`eventvwr.msc`	Event Viewer

Filename	Management Console
fsmgmt.msc	Shared Folders
gpedit.msc	Group Policy Object Editor
gpmc.msc	Group Policy Management (removed by Service Pack 1)
iis.msc	Internet Information Services (v7)
iis6.msc	Internet Information Services (v6)
lusrmgr.msc	Local Users and Groups
NAPCLCFG.MSC	Network Access Protection (NAP) Client Configuration
nfsmgmt.msc	NFS Management
ntmsmgr.msc	Removable Storage Manager
ntmsoprq.msc	Removable Storage Operator Requests
perfmon.msc	Performance
printmanagement.msc	Print Management
rsop.msc	Resultant Set of Policy
secpol.msc	Local Security Settings
services.msc	Services
taskschd.msc	Task Scheduler
tpm.msc	Trusted Platform Module Management
WF.msc	Windows Firewall with Advanced Security
WmiMgmt.msc	Windows Management Instrumentation Management

SCREENSAVERS

Filename	Description
Aurora.scr	Aurora
Bubbles.scr	Bubbles
logon.scr	Logon
Mystify.scr	Mystify
PhotoScreensaver.scr	Photos
Ribbons.scr	Ribbons
scrnsave.scr	Blank
ssBranded.scr	Windows Energy
ssText3d.scr	3D Text

Windows Services

This section lists services installed with Windows Vista. Not all versions of Vista include all of these services, and not all services will be enabled on a given Vista installation. Some services are installed only when optional Windows features are enabled. The services descriptions listed in this section are derived from the full Microsoft description displayed in each service's Properties dialog box.

The file listed for each service is the name of the file that implements the service. Some services are implemented as Dynamic Link Library (DLL) files that are run by the `svchost.exe` generic service container program. When you view Processes in the Windows Task Manager, `svchost.exe` is the program listed for these services. Some program modules implement more than one service, and thus these `.exe` and `.dll` files might be listed more than once.

ActiveX Installer (AxInstSV)

File: `AxInstSV.dll` via `svchost.exe`

Enables the installation of ActiveX controls based on enterprise policy.

Application Experience (AeLookupSvc)

File: `aelupsvc.dll` via `svchost.exe`

Processes application-compatibility cache requests for applications as they are launched.

Application Information (Appinfo)

File: `appinfo.dll` via `svchost.exe`

Facilitates the running of interactive applications with additional administrative privileges (Run As Administrator).

Application Layer Gateway Service (ALG)

File: `alg.exe`

Provides support for third-party protocol plug-ins for Internet Connection Sharing.

Application Management (AppMgmt)

File: `appmgmts.dll` via `svchost.exe`

Processes installation, removal, and enumeration requests for software deployed through Group Policy.

ASP.NET State Service (aspnet_state)

File: `aspnet_state.exe`

Provides support for out-of-process session states for ASP.NET.

Background Intelligent Transfer Service (BITS)

File: `qmgr.dll` via `svchost.exe`

Transfers files in the background using idle network bandwidth.

Base Filtering Engine (BFE)

File: `bfe.dll` via `svchost.exe`

Manages firewall and Internet Protocol security (IPSec) policies and implements user-mode filtering.

Block Level Backup Engine Service (wbengine)

File: `wbengine.exe`

Engine to perform block-level backup and recovery of data.

Certificate Propagation (CertPropSvc)

File: `certprop.dll` via `svchost.exe`

Propagates certificates from smart cards.

Client for NFS (NfsClnt)

File: `nfsclnt.exe`

Enables this computer to access files on NFS shares.

CNG Key Isolation (KeyIso)

File: `lsass.exe`

Provides key process isolation to private keys and associated cryptographic operations, as required by Common Criteria. The service stores and uses long-lived keys in a secure process complying with Common Criteria requirements.

COM+ Event System (EventSystem)

File: `es.dll` via `svchost.exe`

Supports System Event Notification Service (SENS), which provides automatic distribution of events to subscribing Component Object Model (COM) components.

COM+ System Application (COMSysApp)

File: `dllhost.exe` / Process ID: `{02D4B3F1-FD88-11D1-960D-00805FC79235}`

Manages the configuration and tracking of Component Object Model (COM)+–based components.

Computer Browser (Browser)

File: `browser.dll` via `svchost.exe`

Maintains an updated list of computers on the network and supplies this list to computers designated as browsers.

Cryptographic Services (CryptSvc)

File: `cryptsvc.dll` via `svchost.exe`

Confirms the signatures of Windows files and allows new programs to be installed, adds and removes Trusted Root Certification Authority certificates from this computer, retrieves root certificates from Windows Update and enable scenarios such as SSL, and helps enroll this computer for certificates.

DCOM Server Process Launcher (DcomLaunch)

File: `rpcss.dll` via `svchost.exe`

Provides launch functionality for DCOM services.

Desktop Window Manager Session Manager (UxSms)

File: `uxsms.dll` via `svchost.exe`

Provides Desktop Window Manager startup and maintenance services.

DFS Replication (DFSR)

File: `DFSR.exe`

Replicates files among multiple PCs, keeping them in sync. Used to roam folders between PCs.

DHCP Client (Dhcp)

File: `dhcpcsvc.dll` via `svchost.exe`

Registers and updates IP addresses and DNS records for this computer.

Diagnostic Policy Service (DPS)

File: `dps.dll` via `svchost.exe`

Along with the following two services, enables problem detection, troubleshooting, and resolution for Windows components.

Diagnostic Service Host (WdiServiceHost)

File: `wdi.dll` via `svchost.exe`

Enables problem detection, troubleshooting, and resolution for Windows components.

Diagnostic System Host (WdiSystemHost)

File: `wdi.dll` via `svchost.exe`

Enables problem detection, troubleshooting, and resolution for Windows components.

Distributed Link Tracking Client (TrkWks)

File: `trkwks.dll` via `svchost.exe`

Maintains links between NTFS files within a computer or across computers in a network.

Distributed Transaction Coordinator (MSDTC)

File: `msdtc.exe`

Coordinates transactions that span multiple resource managers, such as databases, message queues, and file systems.

DNS Client (Dnscache)

File: `dnsrslvr.dll` via `svchost.exe`

Caches Domain Name System (DNS) names and registers the full computer name for this computer.

Extensible Authentication Protocol (EapHost)

File: `eapsvc.dll` via `svchost.exe`

Provides network authentication in such scenarios as 802.1x wired and wireless, VPN, and Network Access Protection (NAP). Provides application programming interfaces (APIs) used by network access clients, including wireless and VPN clients, during the authentication process.

Fax (Fax)

File: `fxssvc.exe`

Sends and receives faxes, utilizing fax resources available on this computer or on the network.

FTP Publishing Service (MSFTPSVC)

File: `inetinfo.exe`

File Transfer Protocol (FTP) server.

Function Discovery Provider Host (fdPHost)

File: `fdPHost.dll` via `svchost.exe`

Host process for Function Discovery providers.

Function Discovery Resource Publication (FDResPub)

File: `fdrespub.dll` via `svchost.exe`

Publishes information about this computer and resources attached to this computer so they can be discovered over the network.

Group Policy Client (gpsvc)

File: `gpsvc.dll` via `svchost.exe`

Applies settings configured by administrators for the computer and users through the Group Policy component.

Health Key and Certificate Management (hkmsvc)

File: `kmsvc.dll` via `svchost.exe`

Provides X.509 certificate and key management services for the Network Access Protection Agent (NAPAgent).

Human Interface Device Access (hidserv)

File: `hidserv.dll` via `svchost.exe`

Enables generic input access to Human Interface Devices (HID), which activates and maintains the use of predefined hot buttons on keyboards, remote controls, and other multimedia devices.

IIS Admin Service (IISADMIN)

File: `inetinfo.exe`

Enables this server to administer metabase FTP services.

IKE and AuthIP IPSec Keying Modules (IKEEXT)

File: `ikeext.dll` via `svchost.exe`

Hosts the Internet Key Exchange (IKE) and Authenticated Internet Protocol (AuthIP) keying modules used for authentication and key exchange in Internet Protocol security (IPSec).

Indexing Service (CISVC)

File: `CISVC.EXE`

Indexes contents and properties of files on local and remote computers; provides rapid access to files through flexible querying language.

Interactive Services Detection (UI0Detect)

File: `UI0Detect.exe`

Enables user notification of user input for interactive services, which enables access to dialog boxes created by interactive services when they appear.

Internet Connection Sharing (ICS) (SharedAccess)

File: `ipnathlp.dll` via `svchost.exe`

Provides Network Address Translation, addressing, name resolution, and/or intrusion prevention services for a home or small office network.

IP Helper (iphlpsvc)

File: `iphlpsvc.dll` via `svchost.exe`

Provides automatic IPv6 connectivity over an IPv4 network.

IPSec Policy Agent (PolicyAgent)

File: `ipsecsvc.dll` via `svchost.exe`

Enforces IPSec policies created through the IP Security Policies snap-in or the command-line tool `netsh ipsec`.

KtmRm for Distributed Transaction Coordinator (KtmRm)

File: `msdtckrm.dll` via `svchost.exe`

Coordinates transactions between MSDTC and the Kernel Transaction Manager (KTM).

Link-Layer Topology Discovery Mapper (lltdsvc)

File: `lltdsvc.dll` via `svchost.exe`

Creates a network map, consisting of PC and device topology (connectivity) information, and metadata describing each PC and device.

Message Queuing (MSMQ)

File: `mqsvc.exe`

Provides a messaging infrastructure and development tool for creating distributed messaging applications for Windows-based networks and programs.

Message Queuing Triggers (MSMQTriggers)

File: `mqtgsvc.exe`

Provides rule-based monitoring of messages arriving in a Message Queuing queue and, when the conditions of a rule are satisfied, invokes a COM component or a standalone executable program to process the message.

Microsoft .NET Framework NGEN v2.0.50727_X86 (clr_optimization_v2)

File: `mscorsvw.exe`

Microsoft .NET Framework Native Image Generation service.

Microsoft iSCSI Initiator Service (MSiSCSI)

File: `iscsiexe.dll` via `svchost.exe`

Manages Internet SCSI (iSCSI) sessions from this computer to remote iSCSI target devices.

Microsoft Software Shadow Copy Provider (swprv)

File: `swprv.dll` via `svchost.exe`

Manages software-based volume shadow copies taken by the Volume Shadow Copy service.

Multimedia Class Scheduler (MMCSS)

File: `mmcss.dll` via `svchost.exe`

Enables relative prioritization of work based on system-wide task priorities, mainly for multimedia applications.

Net.Msmq Listener Adapter (NetMsmqActivator)

File: `SMSvcHost.exe -NetMsmqActivator`

Receives activation requests over the `net.msmq` and `msmq.formatname` protocols and passes them to the Windows Process Activation Service.

Net.Pipe Listener Adapter (NetPipeActivator)

File: `SMSvcHost.exe`

Receives activation requests over the `net.pipe` protocol and passes them to the Windows Process Activation Service.

Net.Tcp Listener Adapter (NetTcpActivator)

File: `SMSvcHost.exe`

Receives activation requests over the `net.tcp` protocol and passes them to the Windows Process Activation Service.

Net.Tcp Port Sharing Service (NetTcpPortSharing)

File: `SMSvcHost.exe`

Provides capability to share TCP ports over the `net.tcp` protocol.

Netlogon

File: `lsass.exe`

Maintains a secure channel between this computer and the domain controller for authenticating users and services.

Network Access Protection Agent (napagent)

File: `qagentRT.dll` via `svchost.exe`

Enables Network Access Protection (NAP) functionality on client computers.

Network Connections (Netman)

File: `netman.dll` via `svchost.exe`

Manages objects in the Network and Dial-Up Connections folder, in which you can view both local area network and remote connections.

Network List Service (netprofm)

File: `netprofm.dll` via `svchost.exe`

Identifies the networks to which the computer has connected, collects and stores properties for these networks, and notifies applications when these properties change.

Network Location Awareness (NlaSvc)

File: `nlasvc.dll` via `svchost.exe`

Collects and stores configuration information for the network and notifies programs when this information is modified.

Network Store Interface Service (nsi)

File: `nsisvc.dll` via `svchost.exe`

Delivers network notifications (for example, interface addition/deleting) to user-mode clients.

Offline Files (CscService)

File: `cscsvc.dll` via `svchost.exe`

Performs maintenance activities on the Offline Files cache, responds to user logon and logoff events, implements the internals of the public API, and dispatches interesting events to those interested in Offline Files activities and changes in cache state.

Parental Controls (WPCSvc)

File: `wpcsvc.dll` via `svchost.exe`

Enables Windows Parental Controls on the system.

Peer Name Resolution Protocol (PNRPsvc)

File: `p2psvc.dll` via `svchost.exe`

Enables Serverless Peer Name Resolution over the Internet.

Peer Networking Grouping (p2psvc)

File: `p2psvc.dll` via `svchost.exe`

Provides Peer Networking Grouping services.

Peer Networking Identity Manager (p2pimsvc)

File: `p2psvc.dll` via `svchost.exe`

Provides Identity service for Peer Networking.

Performance Logs & Alerts (pla)

File: `pla.dll` via `svchost.exe`

Collects performance data from local or remote computers based on preconfigured schedule parameters, and then writes the data to a log or triggers an alert.

Plug and Play

File: `umpnpmgr.dll` via `svchost.exe`

Recognizes hardware changes and configures hardware automatically.

PnP-X IP Bus Enumerator (IPBusEnum)

File: `ipbusenum.dll` via `svchost.exe`

Manages the virtual network bus, discovers network-connected devices using the SSDP/WS discovery protocols, and gives them presence in PnP.

PNRP Machine Name Publication Service (PNRPAutoReg)

File: `p2psvc.dll` via `svchost.exe`

Publishes a machine name using the Peer Name Resolution Protocol. Configuration is managed via the `netsh` context `p2p pnrp peer`.

Portable Device Enumerator Service (WPDBusEnum)

File: `wpdbusenum.dll` via `svchost.exe`

Enforces Group Policy for removable mass-storage devices. Enables applications such as Windows Media Player and the Image Import Wizard to transfer and synchronize content using removable mass-storage devices.

Print Spooler (Spooler)

File: `spoolsv.exe`

Loads files to memory for later printing.

Problem Reports and Solutions Control Panel Support (wercplsupport)

File: `wercplsupport.dll` via `svchost.exe`

Provides support for viewing, sending, and deleting system-level problem reports for the Problem Reports and Solutions control panel.

Program Compatibility Assistant Service (PcaSvc)

File: `pcasvc.dll` via `svchost.exe`

Provides support for the Program Compatibility Assistant.

Protected Storage (ProtectedStorage)

File: `lsass.exe`

Provides protected storage for sensitive data, such as passwords, to prevent access by unauthorized services, processes, or users.

Quality Windows Audio Video Experience (QWAVE)

File: `qwave.dll` via `svchost.exe`

Networking platform for Audio Video (AV) streaming applications on IP home networks. Enhances AV streaming performance and reliability by ensuring network quality-of-service (QoS) for AV applications.

ReadyBoost (EMDMgmt)

File: `emdmgmt.dll` via `svchost.exe`

Provides support for improving system performance using ReadyBoost. Caches frequently used programs on attached solid-state disks.

Remote Access Auto Connection Manager (RasAuto)

File: `rasauto.dll` via `svchost.exe`

Creates a connection to a remote network whenever a program references a remote DNS or NetBIOS name or address.

Remote Access Connection Manager (RasMan)

File: `rasmans.dll` via `svchost.exe`

Manages dial-up and virtual private network (VPN) connections from this computer to the Internet or other remote networks.

Remote Procedure Call (RPC) (RpcSs)

File: `rpcss.dll` via `svchost.exe`

Serves as the endpoint mapper and COM Service Control Manager.

Remote Procedure Call (RPC) Locator (RpcLocator)

File: `locator.exe`

Manages the RPC name service database.

Remote Registry (RemoteRegistry)

File: `regsvc.dll` via `svchost.exe`

Enables remote users to modify Registry settings on this computer.

Removable Storage (NtmsSvc)

File: `ntmssvc.dll` via `svchost.exe`

Manages and catalogs removable media, and operates automated removable media devices.

RIP Listener (iprip)

File: `iprip.dll` via `svchost.exe`

Listens for TCP/IP network route updates sent by routers that use the Routing Information Protocol Version 1 (RIPv1).

Routing and Remote Access (RemoteAccess)

File: `mprdim.dll` via `svchost.exe`

Offers VPN and advanced dial-up and routing services in local area and wide area network environments.

Secondary Logon (seclogon)

File: `seclogon.dll` via `svchost.exe`

Enables starting processes under alternate credentials.

Security Accounts Manager (SamSs)

File: `lsass.exe`

Manages the user/privilege database.

Security Center (wscsvc)

File: `wscsvc.dll` via `svchost.exe`

Monitors system security settings and configurations.

Server (LanmanServer)

File: `srvsvc.dll` via `svchost.exe`

Supports sharing of files, printer, and named pipes by this computer.

Shell Hardware Detection (ShellHWDetection)

File: `shsvcs.dll` via `svchost.exe`

Provides notifications for AutoPlay hardware events.

Simple TCP/IP Services (simptcp)

File: `tcpsvcs.exe`

Supports the following TCP/IP services: Character Generator, Daytime, Discard, Echo, and Quote of the Day.

SL UI Notification Service (SLUINotify)

File: `SLUINotify.dll` via `svchost.exe`

Provides Software Licensing activation and notification.

Smart Card (SCardSvr)

File: `SCardSvr.dll` via `svchost.exe`

Manages access to smart cards read by this computer.

Smart Card Removal Policy (SCPolicySvc)

File: `certprop.dll` via `svchost.exe`

Allows the system to be configured to lock the user desktop upon smart card removal.

SNMP Service (SNMP)

File: `snmp.exe`

Enables Simple Network Management Protocol (SNMP) requests to be processed by this computer.

SNMP Trap (SNMPTRAP)

File: `snmptrap.exe`

Receives trap messages generated by local or remote Simple Network Management Protocol (SNMP) agents and forwards the messages to SNMP management programs running on this computer.

Software Licensing (slsvc)

File: `SLsvc.exe`

Enables the download, installation, and enforcement of digital licenses for Windows and Windows applications.

SSDP Discovery (SSDPSRV)

File: `ssdpsrv.dll` via `svchost.exe`

Discovers networked devices and services that use the SSDP discovery protocol, such as UPnP devices. Announces SSDP devices and services running on the local computer.

Superfetch (SysMain)

File: `sysmain.dll` via `svchost.exe`

Maintains and improves system performance over time.

System Event Notification Service (SENS)

File: `sens.dll` via `svchost.exe`

Monitors system events and notifies subscribers to COM+ Event System of these events.

Tablet PC Input Service (TabletInputService)

File: `TabSvc.dll` via `svchost.exe`

Enables Tablet PC pen and ink functionality.

Task Scheduler (Schedule)

File: `schedsvc.dll` via `svchost.exe`

Allows users to configure and schedule automated tasks on this computer.

TCP/IP NetBIOS Helper (lmhosts)

File: `lmhsvc.dll` via `svchost.exe`

Provides support for the NetBIOS over TCP/IP (NetBT) service and NetBIOS name resolution for clients on the network.

TCP/IP Print Server (LPDSVC)

File: `tcpsvcs.exe`

Enables TCP/IP–based printing using the Line Printer Daemon protocol.

Telephony (TapiSrv)

File: `tapisrv.dll` via `svchost.exe`

Provides Telephony API (TAPI) support for programs that control telephony devices on the local computer and, through the LAN, on servers that are also running the service.

Telnet (TlntSvr)

File: `tlntsvr.exe`

Enables a remote user to log on to this computer and run programs, and supports various TCP/IP Telnet clients, including UNIX-based and Windows-based computers.

Terminal Services (TermService)

File: `termsrv.dll` via `svchost.exe`

Enables users to connect interactively to this computer using Remote Desktop or Remote Assistance.

Terminal Services Configuration (SessionEnv)

File: `sessenv.dll` via `svchost.exe`

Manages Remote Desktop–related configuration and session-maintenance activities, such as per-session temporary folders, TS themes, and TS certificates.

Terminal Services UserMode Port Redirector (UmRdpService)

File: `umrdp.dll` via `svchost.exe`

Allows the redirection of printers/drives/ports for Remote Desktop connections.

Themes (Themes)

File: `shsvcs.dll` via `svchost.exe`

Provides user experience theme management.

Thread Ordering Server (THREADORDER)

File: `mmcss.dll` via `svchost.exe`

Provides ordered execution for a group of threads within a specific period of time.

TPM Base Services (TBS)

File: `tbssvc.dll` via `svchost.exe`

Provides hardware-based cryptographic services to system components and applications (Trusted Platform Module).

UPnP Device Host (upnphost)

File: `upnphost.dll` via `svchost.exe`

Allows UPnP devices to be hosted on this computer.

User Profile Service (ProfSvc)

File: `profsvc.dll` via `svchost.exe`

Loads and unloads user profiles.

Virtual Disk (vds)

File: `vds.exe`

Provides management services for disks, volumes, file systems, and hardware disk array objects.

Volume Shadow Copy (VSS)

File: `vssvc.exe`

Manages and implements Volume Shadow Copies used for backup and other purposes.

Web Management Service (WMSvc)

File: `wmsvc.exe`

Enables remote and delegated management capabilities for administrators to manage for the web server, sites, and applications present on this machine.

WebClient (WebClient)

File: `webclnt.dll` via `svchost.exe`

Enables Windows-based programs to create, access, and modify Internet-based files.

Windows Audio (Audiosrv)

File: `Audiosrv.dll` via `svchost.exe`

Manages audio for Windows-based programs.

Windows Audio Endpoint Builder (AudioEndpointBuilder)

File: `Audiosrv.dll` via `svchost.exe`

Manages audio devices for the Windows Audio service.

Windows Backup (SDRSVC)

File: `SDRSVC.dll` via `svchost.exe`

Provides Windows Backup and Restore capabilities.

Windows CardSpace (idsvc)

File: `infocard.exe`

Securely enables the creation, management, and disclosure of digital identities.

Windows Color System (WcsPlugInService)

File: `WcsPlugInService.dll` via `svchost.exe`

JHosts third-party Windows Color System color device model and gamut map model plug-in modules.

Windows Connect Now—Config Registrar (wcncsvc)

File: `wcncsvc.dll` via `svchost.exe`

Acts as a Registrar and issues network credentials to Enrollees.

Windows Defender (WinDefend)

File: `mpsvc.dll` via `svchost.exe`

Scans computer for unwanted software, schedules scans, and keeps the latest unwanted software definition list up-to-date.

Windows Driver Foundation—User-mode Driver Frame (wudfsvc)

File: `WUDFSvc.dll` via `svchost.exe`

Manages user-mode driver host processes.

Windows Error Reporting Service (WerSvc)

File: `WerSvc.dll` via `svchost.exe`

Allows errors to be reported when programs stop working or responding, and allows existing solutions to be delivered. Also allows logs to be generated for diagnostic and repair services.

Windows Event Collector (Wecsvc)

File: `wecsvc.dll` via `svchost.exe`

Manages persistent subscriptions to events from remote sources that support the WS-Management protocol. This includes Windows Vista event logs, hardware, and IPMI-enabled event sources.

Windows Event Log (Eventlog)

File: `svchost.exe -k LocalServiceNetworkRestricted`

Manages events and event logs. Supports logging events, querying events, subscribing to events, archiving event logs, and managing event metadata.

Windows Firewall (MpsSvc)

File: `mpssvc.dll` via `svchost.exe`

Protects the local computer by preventing unauthorized users from gaining access through the Internet or a network.

Windows Image Acquisition (WIA) (stisvc)

File: `wiaservc.dll` via `svchost.exe`

Provides image-acquisition services for scanners and cameras.

Windows Installer (msiserver)

File: `msiexec /V`

Adds, modifies, and removes applications provided as a Windows Installer (`*.msi`) package.

Windows Management Instrumentation (Winmgmt)

File: `WMIsvc.dll` via `svchost.exe`

Provides a common interface and object model to access management information about the operating system, devices, applications, and services.

Windows Media Center Extender Service (Mcx2Svc)

File: `Mcx2Svc.dll` via `svchost.exe`

Allows Windows Media Center Extender devices to locate and connect to the computer.

Windows Media Center Receiver Service (ehRecvr)

File: `ehRecvr.exe`

Windows Media Center Service for TV and FM broadcast reception.

Windows Media Center Scheduler Service (ehSched)

File: `ehsched.exe`

Starts and stops recording of TV programs within Windows Media Center.

Windows Media Center Service Launcher (ehstart)

File: `ehstart.dll` via `svchost.exe`

Starts Windows Media Center Scheduler and Windows Media Center Receiver services at startup if TV is enabled within Windows Media Center.

Windows Media Player Network Sharing Service (WMPNetworkSvc)

File: `wmpnetwk.exe`

Shares Windows Media Player libraries to other networked players and media devices using Universal Plug and Play.

Windows Modules Installer (TrustedInstaller)

File: `TrustedInstaller.exe`

Enables installation, modification, and removal of Windows updates and optional components.

Windows Presentation Foundation Font Cache 3.0.0.0 (FontCache3.0.0.0)

File: `PresentationFontCache.exe`

Optimizes performance of Windows Presentation Foundation (WPF) applications by caching commonly used font data. (WPF applications start this service automatically.)

Windows Process Activation Service (WAS)

File: `iisw3adm.dll` via `svchost.exe`

Provides process-activation, resource-management, and health-management services for message-activated applications.

Windows Remote Management (WS-Management) (WinRM)

File: `WsmSvc.dll` via `svchost.exe`

Implements the WS-Management protocol for remote management. Listens on the network for WS-Management requests and processes them. Must be configured using the `winrm.cmd` command-line tool or through Group Policy for it to listen over the network.

Windows Search (WSearch)

File: `SearchIndexer.exe /Embedding`

Provides content indexing and property caching for file, email and other content (via extensibility APIs).

Windows Time (W32Time)

File: `w32time.dll` via `svchost.exe`

Maintains date and time synchronization on all clients and servers in the network.

Windows Update (wuauserv)

File: `wuaueng.dll` via `svchost.exe`

Enables the detection, download, and installation of updates for Windows and other programs.

WinHTTP Web Proxy Auto-Discovery Service (WinHttpAutoProxySvc)

File: `winhttp.dll` via `svchost.exe`

Implements the client HTTP stack and provides developers with a Win32 API and COM Automation component for sending HTTP requests and receiving responses. Provides support for autodiscovering a proxy configuration via its implementation of the Web Proxy Auto-Discovery (WPAD) protocol.

Wired AutoConfig (dot3svc)

File: `dot3svc.dll` via `svchost.exe`

Performs IEEE 802.1x authentication on Ethernet interfaces.

WLAN AutoConfig (Wlansvc)

File: `wlansvc.dll` via `svchost.exe`

Enumerates WLAN adapters and manages WLAN connections and profiles.

WMI Performance Adapter (wmiApSrv)

File: `WmiApSrv.exe`

Provides performance library information from Windows Management Instrumentation (WMI) providers to clients on the network.

Workstation (LanmanWorkstation)

File: `wkssvc.dll` via `svchost.exe`

Creates and maintains client network connections to remote servers using the SMB protocol.

World Wide Web Publishing Service (W3SVC)

File: `iisw3adm.dll` via `svchost.exe`

Provides Web connectivity and administration through the Internet Information Services Manager.

APPENDIX B

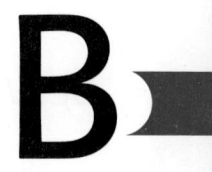

WHAT'S NEW IN SERVICE PACK 1 (SP-1)

In this appendix

Service Packs, Updates, and Hotfixes, Oh My!   1422

Windows Vista Service Pack 1   1423

Obtaining and Installing Service Pack 1   1424

Free Support from Microsoft   1427

   Standalone Method   1427

Uninstalling Service Pack 1   1428

Making Service Pack 1 Permanent   1428

Service Packs, Updates, and Hotfixes, Oh My!

No computer operating system ever made has been without bugs, and Windows is no exception. Bugs cause problems that range from merely annoying (such as the ones that make applications get stuck) to frightening (such as the ones that let criminals take over your computer through your Internet connection). Many of these bugs are found and reported by Microsoft employees, users, and security experts. Windows also has automatic reporting mechanisms that—with your permission—send information about application crashes, driver failures, and other problems to Microsoft, which sorts through the reports and addresses them based on their severity and frequency of occurrence. Finally, Microsoft occasionally adds new features to existing versions of Windows, such as support for new types of hardware, new connection technologies, and new security mechanisms. The result is that Windows improves and evolves over time.

You, like most users, probably do want to receive these updates and improvements as soon as possible, but there is a catch—making a change to an operating system as complex as Windows carries the risk that the cure might be worse than the disease, so to speak. There are thousands of different hardware devices and application programs out there, some of which weren't designed very well, in an infinite variety of combinations. Microsoft goes to great lengths to test its updates in a wide variety of situations, but testing takes time, and it's impossible to test every software fix on every hardware and software combination. And sometimes a fix exposes a bug in an application, or causes an improperly designed device driver to stop working. Whatever the reason, it's incredibly frustrating when installing a "fix" breaks a working system.

To help balance between the need to quickly distribute updates to software bugs versus the need to ensure that a fix won't cause more problems than it addresses, Microsoft uses different means to distribute different types of fixes, and it applies different levels of testing to these fixes, depending on their nature:

- Fixes that address security risks are designated *critical updates*, and these are delivered through the "Automatic Updates" method, as well as through Windows Update. These fixes receive extensive testing before they're released. Critical updates are released weekly. Some weeks there are none, and some weeks there are two or three. In a corporate environment, network managers might delay delivery of automatic updates until the fixes can be tested to be sure that they don't break any critical business applications.

- Fixes that apply to most users, but don't involve security risks and just add new or improved functionality, are designated as *optional updates*. These appear on Windows Update, but are not sent out through automatic updates. These fixes also receive extensive testing to be sure that they will work on all systems.

- Fixes that don't involve a security risk, and which apply only in a narrow range of circumstances (such as problems with a specific manufacturer's hardware, or problems that occur only after a specific sequence of events under very limited conditions) are designated as *hotfixes*. These are made available for download from Microsoft's support website, but you have to know to look for them. They are less extensively tested so that they can be released more quickly, and Microsoft assumes that a hotfix will only be installed by users who are experiencing the particular problem that the hotfix addresses. Hotfixes are usually only located and installed by corporate IT departments. Microsoft typically produces between 200–600 hotfixes per year in the first few years after a new Windows version is released.

- Occasionally, a large group of hotfixes are collected and packaged as a *rollup*, a package containing all or most of the hotfixes released since the last Service Pack, covering all of Windows or just a specific area, such as Internet Explorer.

Other features and changes are put on hold until Microsoft puts together a *Service Pack*, which is a massive cumulative update that includes all critical and optional updates, virtually all hotfixes, and other random additions made since the initial release of the operating system.

Before they're released to the public, Service Packs get extensive testing under a wide variety of conditions, so the hotfixes can be finally be made available to all Windows users. Although some users might never have run into the problems addressed by the majority of hotfixes, other users find that a Service Pack fixes many odd problems that they ran into from time to time. Service Packs are produced at intervals of a year or two, and less often after an operating system has been out for several years.

In general, Service Packs don't introduce many new features, and they're not supposed to (Windows XP Service Pack 2 was the notable exception). They might include new versions of some Windows applications such as Internet Explorer or Windows Media Player, which are made available for download separately, anyway. The job of a Service Pack is mainly to increase reliability and improve performance.

At the time this book was written, Microsoft had just released the first Service Pack for Windows Vista, which is imaginatively named Service Pack 1, or SP-1. This appendix tells you how to get SP-1 and what it will do for your computer. These instructions will also apply to subsequent service packs when they're released.

> **NOTE**
>
> If you purchased a computer or a Windows Vista disc after April 2008, SP-1 might already be installed. Click Start, Computer, System Properties, and look under Windows Edition. Below the Microsoft copyright notice, it will say "Service Pack 1" if the service pack has been installed.

Windows Vista Service Pack 1

Microsoft finalized Service Pack 1 for Windows Vista in January, 2008. SP-1 includes fixes for more than 500 bugs detected and fixed in the first year since Vista was released. It also includes a whole slew of improvements in the speed of network and Internet file transfers, adds support for some new networking protocols, and adds improvements that will be of interest only to corporate network managers. In addition, there are a very small number of minor visible changes. Here is a *very* brief summary of the included changes:

- All previously released critical and optional updates.
- Improvements to the BitLocker drive encryption mechanism, so that drives other than just the boot drive can be encrypted, and so that a USB drive and/or a PIN code can be required to unlock the computer.
- The capability for third-party antivirus programs to interact more deeply with the Windows kernel on 64-bit versions of Vista.
- Improved mechanisms for encrypting data.
- Improvements to the speed of network file transfers.
- Faster suspend, resume, and hibernate operations under some circumstances.
- Improvements to the Network Diagnostics wizard.
- The Disk Defragmenter now allows you to select which drive(s) to defragment.
- Support for the exFAT file system, which can be used on Flash memory devices such as USB drives and some camera memory cards. There is also support for faster DMA transfers to and from upcoming Secure Digital (SD) memory devices.
- Direct3D 10.1 for improved gaming graphics and performance.
- Secure Socket Tunneling Protocol (SSTP) support for Virtual Private Network access to corporate networks.
- Increased likelihood that Remote Assistance will actually work.
- Security policy changes that make it easier for network managers to assist and fix computers using Remote Assistance.

You can see the entire list of SP-1 changes by visiting technet.microsoft.com. Search for "Windows Vista Technical Library" and select the item with this name. Find the Windows Vista Service Pack 1 entry in the left-hand Table of Contents pane. Under it, check out the "Overview of…" and "Hotfixes and Security Updates Included In…" articles.

Obtaining and Installing Service Pack 1

At the time this book was written, Microsoft planned SP-1 for English, Japanese, German, Spanish, and French versions of Vista to be released on the following schedule, with the remaining languages following about a month later:

- By mid-March 2008, most users will see SP-1 listed as an optional update in Windows Update. It will be downloadable from the Download Center on www.microsoft.com. It should also start appearing preinstalled in new computers, depending on the manufacturer.
- By mid-April 2008, SP-1 will become an automatic update. If automatic updates are enabled on your computer, it will be downloaded automatically, and you should be prompted to install it the next time you log on after that.

However, not every user will see SP-1 on Windows Update or receive it through Automatic Updates, at least at first. It turns out that the installation process for SP-1 can disable some device drivers if the installation software didn't do the setup job correctly. These devices might be working now, but they'd stop working if SP-1 is installed. Microsoft says that it knows most or all of the device drivers that are subject to this problem, so if you have one of these devices, Windows Update will not list SP-1 as an optional update or deliver it as an Automatic Update until the hardware manufacturer can produce and deliver a fix for your driver—automatically, hopefully, through Windows Update. After the driver update has been installed, SP-1 will appear. If it all works as planned, you won't have to do anything; they'll work this out for you, and SP-1 will arrive—eventually.

If you don't want to wait, you can download SP-1 from www.microsoft.com. Search for the term "Vista Service Pack 1" and follow the download instructions from there. We'll tell you how to install it later in this appendix in the "Standalone Method" section.

NOTE
You must have at least 5GB of free space on your hard disk to install SP-1. It won't take up all of this space after it's been installed, but it does need at least this much to perform the installation.

NOTE
The Service Pack installation clears out all saved System Restore points. After the service pack has been installed, earlier System Restore points will not be available.

NOTE
Computer resellers and corporate IT staff who perform image-based deployment can integrate SP-1 into their disk images.

Windows Update Method

When SP-1 has been released to the public, it will initially appear as an optional update, then as an automatic update. If your computer is set up to receive updates automatically, you'll be notified when the service pack is ready to install. If you do not use automatic updates or if you want to install it manually, follow these steps:

1. Be sure that your Internet connection is working correctly.
2. Click Start, All Programs, Windows Update.
3. Select View Available Updates.
4. If Service Pack 1 is listed, be sure that it's checked, and click Install.

Now follow the prompts. The update will take a while to download.

> **NOTE**
>
> If Service Pack 1 does not appear, it could be that you have a device driver that Microsoft identified as one that will not work after SP-1 is installed. You can wait for Microsoft to deliver a fix for this driver, you can visit the manufacturer's website to see whether an update is available, or you can download and install the update manually (see the next section for instructions). After installing SP-1, reinstall the driver for the problem device as discussed earlier in this appendix.
>
> You cannot receive the final version of Vista SP-1 via Windows Update if you have installed one of the release candidates (RC/RC2) or earlier beta versions of SP-1. To uninstall a prerelease version of SP-1, see the Microsoft Knowledge Base article 936330 at http://support.microsoft.com/?kbid=936330. After you uninstall a prerelease version, you must wait at least an hour before Windows Update will provide links to the final release or to prerequisite files required to install the final release of SP-1.

The Update Process Itself

The service pack will take up to an hour to install, and Windows will restart at least once during the process. After Windows restarts, the update process will continue for a while before the Welcome screen appears.

The first time you log on after installing SP-1, Windows might ask you (again) to participate in the Customer Experience program, in which Windows sends information to Microsoft about problems you encounter with software: application hangs, programs that refused to close, driver failures, and so on. In general, it's helpful to permit this, as the information Microsoft collects helps it identify bugs that still need to be fixed.

If your system has one of the devices that has the installation problem we discussed earlier, it might stop working after you install SP-1. If this happens, just reinstall the device driver. To do this, follow these steps:

1. Click Start, right-click Computer, and select Manage. Confirm the User Account Control prompt.
2. Select Device Manager in the left-hand pane.
3. The problematic device should appear in the right-hand pane with a small yellow exclamation point next to its name.
4. Right-click the problem device and select Uninstall. Repeat this for any other devices that stopped working after you installed SP-1.
5. Right-click the top item in the Device Manager list (the name of your computer) and select Scan for Hardware Changes. Follow the New Hardware wizard's instructions from there. You might need to reinsert the driver CD or other disk that came with your hardware.

If the device still does not work, visit the manufacturer's website for support information. They might suggest downloading an updated driver or recommend using a different procedure.

Free Support from Microsoft

Microsoft has taken the unusual step of offering free technical support to any Windows Vista user who has problems with Service Pack 1, either during installation, or with application or device driver compatibility after installation. (It's unusual in that Microsoft usually offers free support only to users who purchase full-price retail versions of their operating systems, not to users whose copy of Windows came preinstalled on a new computer.) At the time this was written, Microsoft stated that free SP-1 support would be offered until March 18, 2009.

If you have problems getting Service Pack 1 installed, or if you have problems with Vista, your applications, or devices after installing it, you might try to get help from Microsoft. To start, visit the Microsoft support website at http://support.microsoft.com. On the left, under Top Solutions Centers, select Windows Vista. At the right, under Need More Help?, select Contact a Support Professional by Email, Online, or Phone. Under Select a Product, click Windows Vista Service Pack 1 (All Languages).

For most users, the support options are to either converse with Microsoft support staff via email or through an online chat system. Free telephone support is available for people with various support, subscription, or partnership agreements. (Presumably, telephone support is also available to everyone else, but for a fee.)

Standalone Method

If you want, you can download an installation file for SP-1 from www.microsoft.com and use this to update your computer. This method is helpful if you have more than one computer to update, so you don't have to wait for Windows to download the entire service pack separately for each computer.

To use the standalone method, visit www.microsoft.com and search for "Windows Vista Service Pack 1." Locate the download page and select the language and CPU version that corresponds to your version of Vista. (The 32-bit x86 version is used by most users. The 64-bit x64 version is less commonly used.) The download might be named something like `Windows6.0-KB936330-X86-wave0.exe`. Save the file to a location on your hard disk—the Desktop is fine. The download will take a while, as the x86 version weighs in at over 450MB.

If you have just one computer to update, run the downloaded file. You will have to confirm a User Account Control prompt. Now skip back to the section titled "The Update Process Itself" in this appendix for further instructions.

If you have several computers to update, you can burn the downloaded update file to a CD or DVD and take it around to your other computers. You can also move the file into a shared network folder so that you can run it over the network from other computers.

> **NOTE**
>
> Previous Microsoft Service Packs allowed you to expand the individual component files of a Service Pack into a shared network folder, so that each computer didn't have to expand the files during the update process. Vista SP-1 does not support this update option. You must run the full SP-1 installer program on each computer.

After you've downloaded all of your computers, delete the downloaded file.

Uninstalling Service Pack 1

Vista saves a copy of every system file that was changed by the service pack, so if you run into insurmountable problems after you've installed Service Pack 1, you can have Windows uninstall it. (If you just have a device that will no longer function, you might not need to take this time-consuming step—you might be able to simply install the device's driver. See the section titled "The Update Process Itself" earlier in this appendix for details.)

Although we believe that it should be unnecessary to do so, to uninstall SP-1, follow these steps:

1. Click Start, Control Panel.
2. Under Programs, select Uninstall a Program.
3. Under Tasks, select View Installed Updates. It might take a while for the list to be filled in.
4. Select Service Pack for Microsoft Windows (KB936330).
5. Click the Uninstall button.

The uninstall process will take up to an hour, and then Windows will restart. After the uninstall is complete, four small updates will still be present, and these cannot be uninstalled. They pertain to Windows Update and the Service Pack installation system itself.

> **NOTE**
>
> You might be able to remove SP-1 by using Windows Update. For instructions, see Microsoft Knowledge Base article 948537, available at http://support.microsoft.com/kb/948537/en-us.

Making Service Pack 1 Permanent

When SP-1 is installed, Windows collects and archives the original version of all the files that are being replaced so that you can later uninstall the Service Pack should you so desire. This archive of files takes up a fair amount of space. (It took up 650MB on my Vista Ultimate Edition system, for example.) After you've had SP-1 installed and working for a while and are *certain* that you want to keep it, you can delete the archive and recover the space it takes up by following these steps:

1. Click the Start button.
2. In the Search box, type **vsp1cln** and press Enter.
3. Confirm the User Account Control prompt.
4. When the program asks whether it's OK to proceed, press **Y**.

When the window closes, the option to uninstall Service Pack 1 will no longer be available, and you should find about 650MB more free space on your disk, give or take. (The cleanup program itself won't be deleted, and it won't complain if you run it again, but it won't be able to recover any additional disk space.)

INDEX

NUMBERS

2 Sides option (Printer Properties dialog), 217
8P8C connectors, 593
10BASE-T Ethernet, 618-620
10BASE5 Ethernet, 593
32-bit versions of Windows Vista, 32
64-bit processors, software compatibility, 1002
64-bit versions of Windows Vista, 32
100BASE-T Ethernet, 618-620
802.11i protocol (WPA2), 599
1000Mbps Ethernet (Gigabit), 620

A

Access Control attributes (Registry), 1059-1060
access controls, restrictive configuration, 1218
access permissions. *See* permissions
Access Points (AP), wireless networks, 623
access privileges, Active Directory, 608
accessibility settings
    display, 840-841
    keyboards, 838-839
    mouse, 841
    sound, 839-840
active application buttons (taskbar), 140
active defenses (attacks)
    access controls, restricting, 1218
    firewall configuration, 1212-1213
    NAT device configuration, 1212, 1215-1216
    packet filtering, 1213-1215
    passwords versus passwordless file sharing, 1217-1218
    routers, securing, 1216
Active Desktop items, 234-235
Active Directory
    distributed databases, 607
    domain name system (DNS) integration, 608
    function of, 607
    Group Policies, 607
    groups
        access privileges, 608
        containers, 607-608
    networks
        advanced search tool, 752
        computer searches, 750
        domain-type searches, 748
        file/folder searches, 750-752
        missing printers, 781
        policy-based restrictions, 741
        printer searches, 750, 760
        publishing shared folders, 751-752
        resource search functions, 741
Active Directory Scripting Interface (ADSI), 1122
Active Server Pages (ASP), site development, 586
ActiveX controls
    add-ons (IE7), 445
    unsigned controls, 455
ad hoc networks, 1262, 1271-1273
adapter cards, movement within motherboards, 1014
adapters (network), 625-627
Add Favorite dialog (IE7), offline browsing options, 432
Add Hardware applet (Control Panel), 1013-1016
Add or Remove Programs applet (Control Panel), 140-145, 998-1000
Add Printer Wizard, installing
    networks, 759
    printers, 210-213
add-ons (IE7)
    crash detection, 448
    download protections, 445-446
    invalid signatures, 447
    management of, 30, 447-448
    scripting functions, 445
Address bar (IE7), 428-430
Address Book (Windows Mail 7), 495
    backups, maintaining, 506-507
    distribution lists, 493-494
    entries
        adding, 492-493
        deleting, 493
        editing, 493

address spoofing, 1208
Administrative Tools, 872-873, 922-923
administrators
　accounts
　　accessing, 115-116
　　troubleshooting, 1203
　Registry entries, editing, 1057-1058
　VHDMount (Virtual Server 2005) operation, 1167
Adobe Acrobat Reader, 468-469
ads (pop-ups/unders), IE7
　blocking in, 457-458
　exceptions in, 458-459
ADSI (Active Directory Scripting Interface), 1122
ADSL (Asymmetric Digital Subscriber Line), 395-396
Advanced System Settings option (System Properties), 870
Advanced tab, Printer Property sheets, 216
Aero desktop environment, 13-14. *See also* glass
　adding items to, 131
　default appearance, 125-126
　efficient use of, 159-161
　files, saving on, 132-134
　icons, 127-130
　Recycle Bin, 125-128
　shortcuts, creating, 131-132
　Sidebar gadgets, 126
　taskbar, 125
　visual color palette, 124-125
Agent tool (newsgroups), 526
AGP video cards, 1019-1020
album art, updating, 284-285
All Users, 1087
ALLUSERSPROFILE environment variable, 1086
Alt+F4 keystroke, foreground window closure, 159
Alternate Configuration features, 1308
always-on connections (broadband), configuring, 413-416
analog camcorders, 325

analog modems
　installing, 401-406
　Internet access, 394-395
anonymous web access, 572
ANSI.SYS, MS-DOS environment optimization, 1099
antivirus software, 1136-1138
AOHell, 1244
AP (Access Points), wireless networks, 623
ap.bat, 1112
APPDATA, 1086
Appearance and Personalization applet (Control Panel), 902
Appearance and Personalization view (Category view), 812
Apple Newton, 1357
AppleTalk, 598
　AFP (AppleTalk File Protocol), 683
　printers, configuring on Windows networks, 765
Application Compatibility Wizard. *See* Program Compatibility Wizard
applications. *See also* software
　adding, 143-144
　compatibility
　　Linux, 37-38
　　virtualization, 110-111
　crashes, handling, 156-157
　DOS applications, printing from, 222-223
　flipping via Flip 3D, 159
　installing
　　new installations (Add or Remove Programs applet), 145, 998
　　via networks, 145
　launching, 145-146
　　Computer, 147-149
　　Start button, 147
　　Windows Explorer, 147-149
　MS-DOS environments
　　ANSI.SYS issues, 1099
　　AUTOEXEC.NT customization, 1096-1099
　　CONFIG.NT customization, 1096-1099

　　configuring for optimal performance, 1092-1102
　　DOSKEY issues, 1099
　partitions, separating from data partitions, 933
　removing via Add or Remove Programs applet, 140-142
　transferring between computers via Windows Easy Transfer Companion, 102-103
　troubleshooting via Program Compatibility Wizard, 977-979
　Windows applications, printing from, 220-222
Applications tab (Task Manager), 884-885
appointments (Calendar), entering, 248-249
archiving via photos, 305-306
arguments (command-line), 1071-1072
ASP (Active Server Pages), site development, 586
assigning
　drive letters, 936
　permissions
　　restricted objects, 1203
　　to user groups, 1198-1199
　sounds with events, 911-913
　tasks via Scheduled Tasks utility, 1125
AtomFilms.com website, 342
attachments
　newsgroups
　　binaries, 524
　　multi-part, 524-525
　　multimedia, 525-526
　Windows Mail 7
　　opening via, 485
　　sending via, 485
　　virus prevention, 486
attacks (networks)
　address spoofing, 1208
　back door attacks, 1208
　defense measures, 1209
　　active defenses, 1212-1218
　　preparations, 1210-1211
　DoS (Denial of Service), 1209

eavesdropping, 1208
email hoaxes, 1208
exploits, 1208
identity theft, 1209
impersonation, 1208
open doors, 1208
password cracking, 1207
phishing, 1209
social engineering, 1208
Trojan horses, 1208
viruses, 1208

audio
accessibility settings, 839-840
CDs/DVDs
bit rates, 268
file format selection, 268
playing, 265-266
ripping, 266-268
events, associating with, 911-913
Internet Explorer 7
MP3s, downloads (Windows Media Player), 441-442
streaming (Windows Media Player), 439-440
Web elements, 436-438
MP3 files
copyright controversies, 441
downloading (Windows Media Player), 441-442
MP3 Pro format, 442
MP3.com website, 441
portable players, 441
streaming audio, 439-440
playback, 914
recording, 914
Volume Control settings, 351-353, 360
Windows Movie Maker, exporting to, 332
Windows Sound Recorder, 350-351

auditing
networks for vulnerabilities, 1242
permissions, 1196-1197
policies, local settings, 1229-1230

authentication
Kerberos, 610
two-factor authentication, 1250-1251
two-way authentication, 1250
web servers, 571-572
Authenticode, software downloads, 444
auto playlists, creating, 279-280
auto-scrolling, three-button mouse, 924
AutoComplete feature
enabling/disabling (IE7), 429-430, 461
Tablet Vista, 1366
AUTOEXEC.NT, MS-DOS environment optimization, 1096-1099
automatic caching, offline folders, 1307
automatic updates, 1142
IIS, 582
SP2 (Service Pack 2), 995
Windows Update, 987-988
AutoMovie, 343-344
AutoPlay, 820-821
AVI video format, 438

B

back door attacks, 1208
backgrounds
changing, 96
GUI display properties, setting, 908
Backup and Restore Center, 23-24
Complete PC backups
creating, 1160-1161
restoring, 1172
WBADMIN command-line tool, 1162-1164
features, 1150-1152
file and folder backups
Complete PC backups versus, 1152-1153
creating, 1153-1155
format of, 1156
restoring, 1157-1160
removable media for backups, 1155-1156

backups. *See also* **restoring**
Address Book (Windows Mail 7), 506-507
Backup and Restore Center, 23-24
Complete PC backups, 1160-1164, 1172
file and folder backups, 1152-1160
features of, 1150-1152
removable media for backups, 1155-1156
baseline backups, 1222
Complete PC backups, 24
creating, 1160-1161
restoring, 1172
WBADMIN command-line tool, 1162-1164
email
web-based email, 1154
Windows Mail 7, 505, 508
FAT file system and, 1154
multi-disc backups, finding files in, 1202
network shares, 1153
NTBackup files, restoring, 1203
recovery certificates, 1179-1181
Recycle Bin, 1154
Registry
Regedit utility, 1047-1048
system restore, 1047
third-party utilities, 1046-1047
security disaster planning, 1222
software, 656-658
System Recovery Options menu, creating from, 983-984
systems, network media selections, 616
third-party backup tools, 1200-1201
troubleshooting, 1201-1202
UPS (Uninterruptible Power Supplies)
configuring, 1027-1028
installing, 1023-1026

How can we make this index more useful? Email us at indexes@quepublishing.com

BACKUPS

selecting, 1025-1026
testing configuration, 1028
user profiles, 1154
VHDMount (Virtual Server 2005)
   Administrator operation, 1167
   command-line syntax, 1165-1166
   downloading, 1164
   driver installation, 1168-1170
   installing, 1165
   Windows Explorer operation, 1166-1167, 1170
Balanced profile (power usage), 1284
basic disks, 930-931
Basic Tasks, creating in Task Scheduler, 1125-1126
batch files, 1104
   ap.bat, 1112
   basics of, 1104-1107
   creating, 1104-1105
   e.bat, 1113
   ping, 1105
   programming
      call statement, 1110-1111
      for statement, 1111-1112
      goto statement, 1110
      if statement, 1108-1110
      set statement, 1107-1108
batteries
   mobile computing, 1283-1286
   power profiles, 1284
Battery Status icon (Mobility Center), 1281
BCD (Boot Configuration Databases), editing, 957
Berkeley "r" commands, Internetworking via UNIX and Linux, 680-682
Berners-Lee, Tim, 424
bidirectional satellite dishes, 397
binary attachments (newsgroups), 524
bindings (networks), 690-691
BIOS
   altered settings, troubleshooting, 1033
   hardware, boot order, 1010

settings, correct configuration of, 1010-1011
USB controllers, port settings, 1018
bit rates (audio CDs/DVDs), selecting, 268
BitLocker, 1182
   Drive Preparation tool, 1183-1184
   EFS (Encrypted File System) versus, 1189-1190
   encryption process, 1186-1189
   manual hard disk preparation, 1184-1185
   recovery process, 1187
   system requirements, 1183
   TPM (Trusted Platform Module), 1185-1186
   troubleshooting, 1202
Blackberry devices, receiving email on, 255-256
Blackcomb (codename), 4
blocking
   network services
      packet filtering, 1214-1215
      troubleshooting, 1241
   pop-up/under ads (IE7), 457-458
Boot Configuration Databases (BCD), 957
boot manager, changes to, 67-68
boot menu, editing entries, 74-76
boot process
   troubleshooting, 957, 972-975
   wrong BIOS settings, 1033
breadcrumbs, 82
   Computer folder, 172-175
   Windows Explorer, 165, 170-171, 175-177
bridges, disparate networks, 658-659
Brightness control (Mobility Center), 1281
broadband connections
   configuring, 411-416
   ICS (Internet Connection Sharing), 718-719
   PPPoE configuration, 412
broadband DSL, 703

broadcasting television programs to TV or projector, 381-383
browsing
   network printers, 760
   Windows Media Player, 263-265
bug fixes, IIS, 582
burning
   CDs
      custom CDs, 272-274
      music CDs, 262
      photo CDs, 300-303
   DVDs
      DivX files, 390
      images to, 357-360
      Windows Media Center, 383-384
buy.com website, 613

C

cable modems
   installing, 401-406
   Internet connections, 396
   configuring, 411-416
   troubleshooting, 536-537
cable service, LAN, 705
   Internet connections, 710-713
   multiple computer LAN configurations, 724-726
   troubleshooting, 736
cabling
   covers, 628
   crimp-on connectors, 630
   general installation guidelines, 629-630
   network printers, 616, 624-625
   networks
      10/100BASE-T Ethernet, 618-620
      1000Mbps Ethernet, 620
      HomePlug, 622
      HomePNA, 620-621
      IEEE 802.11g Wireless, 622-623
      selection criteria, 617-618
      testing, 794
      updating older systems, 624

plenum, 629
Practical Network Cabling, 630
testing, 794
troubleshooting, 659
UTP (Unshielded Twisted-Pair), 594-595
wired Ethernet, 593-594
wiring channels, 659
cache cleanup, Internet Explorer, 952
Cailliau, Robert, 424
Calculator, 147, 252
Calendar, 25, 247
  appointments, entering, 248-249
  configuring, 251-252
  creating, 248
  publishing, 249-250
  subscribing to, 249
  tasks, setting up, 251
call statements, batch file programming, 1110-1111
callbacks, dial-up/VPN networks, 1291
cameras (digital)
  Windows Photo Gallery, 292-295
  zooming, 348
Caps Lock key, altering location on keyboard, 924
car stereos, playing portable media players through, 285-286
Carbon Copy (CC), 1331
cascade ports (hubs), 634-635
cascading elements, Start menu, 924
CataList website, mailing list repository, 510
Category view (Control Panel), 805-806, 810
  Appearance and Personalization category, 812
  Classic Mode applets, 814-820
  Clock, Language, and Region category, 813
  Ease of Access category, 813
  Hardware and Sound category, 809
  Mobile PC category, 811

Network and Internet category, 808
System and Maintenance category, 807
User Accounts and Family Safety category, 811
CAUCE (Coalition Against Unsolicited Commercial Email), 508-509
CD-RW drives, archiving photos via, 305
CDO (Collaboration Data Objects), 1118
CDs
  audio CDs/DVDs
    bit rates, 268
    file formats, 268
    playing, 265-266
    ripping, 266-268
  backups on, 1155-1156
  burning
    custom CDs, 272-274
    music to, 262
    photo CDs, 300-303
  installing software from, 998, 1106
  movies, HighMAT technology, 342
censorship, news servers, 511
CERN (European Laboratory for Particle Physics), Web browser development, 424
CertEnroll folder
  Windows 200x Server shared status, 748
certificates
  digital signatures, 490
  file encryption certificates, 93
  IE verification, 446
  missing VPN, 1308
  SSL encryption, 456
  VeriSign, 456
CGI (Common Gateway Interface) scripts, 558, 573
Change Advanced Power Settings, 1284
Change What the Power Buttons Do setting (Mobility Center, Power Options), 1283

Character Map, 252-253, 892-895
Character Pad (Input Panel), 1362
CIFS (Common Internet File System), 673
CIPHER command-line tool, 1175-1176, 1202
Classic Mode applets (Control Panel), 814-820
clean installations of Windows Vista, 49-62
clicks (stylus pen), 1362
clients
  Client for Microsoft Networks
    adding, 642-644
    file and printer sharing functions, 602
  client programs (email), 475
  client/server networks, 592
  Remote Desktop Client, 1342, 1346-1349
Clinton, William, 424
clips (video), Windows Movie Maker
  assembling, 333-334
  editing, 334-336
  effects, adding, 337
  narration, adding, 338-339
  organizing, 332-333
  titles, adding, 339-340
  transitions, adding, 336-337
Clock, Language, and Region view (Category view), 813
cmd command, 1277
CMOS (Complementary Metal-Oxide Semiconductors), 1033
codenames for Windows Vista, 4
Collaboration Data Objects (CDO), 1118
collection bin (Windows Movie Maker), video clips
  assembling, 333-334
  editing, 334-336
  organizing, 332-333
color
  correction, movies, 347
  depth, configuring GUI display properties, 915-919

COLOR

hue, 905-906
luminosity, 905-906
photos, adjusting in Windows Photo Gallery, 296
saturation, 905-906
schemes, configuring GUI display properties, 903-905
Color Management tab, Printer Property sheets, 216
Color Refiner dialog, GUI settings, 905-906
COM (Component Object Model), 604
COM(serial) ports, printer installations, 210-212
COM+ distributed applications, network interaction, 604
COM/DCOM Unleashed, 604
Command Line completion, 1075
command prompt
  backups, creating from, 983-984
  command-line
    editing, 1074
    syntax, 1071-1072
  commands, running with elevated privileges, 1079
  current folders, 1073-1074
  default drives and directories, changing at the same time, 1079
  filenames
    completing, 1075
    quoting with spaces, 1072-1073
  pipes, 1075-1078
  pushd, 1079-1080
  redirection, 1075-1078
  special characters, 1077
  troubleshooting from, 970
Command Prompt window
  cut and paste, 1078
  keeping open after execution, 1094
  opening, 1070, 1078
  properties, 1092-1094

command-line, 1070
Command Prompt environment
  command-line syntax, 1071-1072
  editing via, 1074
  commands, 1071, 1078, 1102-1103
  management tools
    net use command, 1081-1083
    sc command, 1083-1084
    shutdown command, 1085
  network resources, managing via, 778-779
  programs, information about, 1080-1081
  syntax, Command Prompt environment, 1071-1072
  TCP/IP diagnostics, 543
    ipconfig, 544-545
    pathping, 547-548
    ping, 545-546
    route, 548-549
    tracert, 546-547
  utilities
    list of, 1080
    network administration, 782-783
commercials, skipping, 374
Common Gateway Interface (CGI) scripts, 558, 573
Common Internet File System (CIFS), 673
compatibility
  hardware requirements, checking with Windows Vista Upgrade Advisor, 43-48
  junction points and symbolic links, 109-110
  planning for, Internetworking with Macintosh, 683-684
  software, Program Compatibility Wizard, 1002-1003
  virtualization, 110-111
  Windows applications with Linux, 37-38
compatibility mode, 130

Compatibility tab (Program Compatibility Wizard), 978-979
Complete PC backups, 24
  creating, 1160-1164
  file and folder backups versus, 1152-1153
  restoring, 1172
Complete PC Restore tool. *See* Windows Complete PC Restore tool
Component Object Model (COM), 604
compression (files), 198-202, 948-949, 953
Computer Associates Arcserve, 616
computer identification, checking, 796-797
Computer Management utility, 778
Computer Name Changes dialog, 414
COMPUTERNAME environment variable, 1086
ComSpec, 1086
CONFIG.NT, MS-DOS environment optimization, 1096-1099
configuring
  BIOS settings, 1010-1011
  calendars, 251-252
  default user profile, 116-117
  Dial-Up Networking, RAS, 1289-1292
  Disk Defragmenter, 945-946
  fax service (Windows Fax and Scan), 309
    cover pages, 310-311
    fax receiving options, 310
    fax settings, 312
    sender information, 310
  gadgets, 242-243
  Guide (Windows Media Center), 372-374
  Internet connections, 94, 406
    broadband connections, 411-416
    dial-up connections, 409-411
    high-speed setup, 411-416

ISP accounts, 407-409
   manually, 407-409
   New Connection
      Wizard, 406
Internet Explorer 7,
   448-453
multiple monitors, 917-918
networks
   checking for problems,
      790-791, 795-797
   checking network config-
      uration, 795-797
   client additions, 642-644
   protocol additions,
      642-644
   service additions,
      642-644
parental controls in
   Windows Media Center,
   385-386
peer-to-peer networks, 642
   TCP/IP, 644-646
   Windows Firewall,
      652-653
printers, 206-207
   print documents,
      225-226
   properties of, 214-219
Recycle Bin, 925
simple websites, 567-569
sound playback and recording, 914
System Restore tool,
   964-965
TCP/IP, 646-649
UPS, 1027-1028
VPN connections, 1292
Windows Firewall,
   1230-1231
Windows Firewall with
   Advanced Security,
   1236-1238
Windows Media Center
   hardware, 368-370
conflicts (hardware)
   HCL (Hardware
      Compatibility List),
      1034-1035
   hidden devices, 1035
   resolving, 827-837
   troubleshooting, 1035

connections
   Dial-Up Networking
      current location checks,
         1293
      disconnecting, 1296
      monitoring, 1296
      multiple location man-
         agement, 1292-1293
      without roaming profiles,
         1293-1294
   forwarding, 580-581
   FTP Server, disconnecting,
      579
   IIS installation require-
      ments, 560
   Internet
      analog modems, 394-395
      cable modems, 396
      changing default connec-
         tions, 418-419
      choosing, 397-400
      configuring, 406-416
      dial-up connections,
         416-418
      Dial-Up Networking,
         1289-1292
      DSL (Digital Subscriber
         Line), 395-396
      equipment, 400
      ISDN(Integrated
         Services Digital
         Network), 395
      mobile connections,
         421-422
      modem installation,
         401-406
      multiple connections,
         419-420
      ordering services, 401
      satellite service, 397
      status checks, 418
      troubleshooting, 420-421
      wireless access, 397
   Internet connections, con-
      figuring, 94
   networks, checking for
      problems, 797-798
   sharing routers, 703
   Windows Media Center and
      Xbox 360, 380-381
**connectivity (networks), test-
   ing, 797-798**

connectors
   Gigabit Ethernet
      (1000Mbps), 620
   wiring order, 630-631
console programs, 1070
**Console Window properties,
   1093**
**Consumer Reports website,
   printer reviews, 230**
**Consumer Search website,
   printer reviews, 230**
contacts, Windows Mail 7
   disabling auto-additions,
      520
   sending via, 508
**containers, Active Directory,
   607-608**
Content Advisor (IE7)
   ratings resources, 461
   site objectionable content,
      controlling, 459-461
**Content Controls, Internet
   Explorer 7, 459-461**
**Control Panel, 83-84, 139,
   804**
   Add Hardware applet,
      1013-1016
   Add or Remove Programs
      applet, 140-145, 998-1000
   Administrative Tools,
      872-873
   Appearance and
      Personalization applet, 902
   applets list, 1400-1401
   Category view, 805-820
   default display, 805
   Default Programs, 823
      Set Associations option,
         824
      Set Program Access and
         Computer Defaults
         option, 825
      setting, 824
   Fonts applet, 920
   GUI modifications, 898
   Keyboard applet, 847
   Mouse applet, 847-850
   Performance Information
      and Tools applet, 850, 856
      Adjust Indexing options,
         855
      Visual Effects, 854-855

Control Panel

Windows Defender, 853-854
Windows Experience Index, 850-853
Phone and Modem Options, property settings, 541-542
Printers applet, 205
Regional and Language Options, 867
shortcuts, creating, 895-896
System applet, updating device drivers, 992-993
System Properties, 868-872
System Tools applet, Scheduled Task utility, 1124-1125
Task Scheduler, 881
Visual Effects dialog, 890-891
Windows SideShow, 872

Convert utility, 947-948
convertible Tablet PC, 1358, 1361
converting
handwriting to text, 1370
hard disks to dynamic storage model, 933
recorded television programs to DivX files, 388-389
cookies
deleting, 950
website preferences, setting (IE7), 455
copy protection (music), 262
copying web pages to home directories (IIS), 567, 569
copyright restrictions, 262
MP3 audio files, 441
online graphics (IE7), 436
corporate environments, wireless networks, 1267
corporate networks
ban on personal websites, 555
Windows Vista features, 39-40
corrupted files (Registry), troubleshooting, 1063
cover pages (faxes), customizing, 310-311
crashes
add-ons (IE7) as cause, 447
Ctrl+Alt+Del keystroke, troubleshooting, 158

forced shutdowns, 158
Fusion prevention mechanism, 1003
handling, 156-157
crimp-on connectors (cabling), 630
critical updates, 95, 994, 1422
cropping photos in Windows Photo Gallery, 296
crossover cables, network wiring installations, 632-633
Ctrl key, altering location on keyboard, 924
Ctrl+Alt+Del keystroke, forced shutdowns, 158
Ctrl+F6 keystroke, open window cycling, 161
current drivers, 1074
current folders, Command Prompt environment, 1073-1074
custom CDs, burning, 272-274
Customize Flicks window, 1373
Customize Start Menu dialog, 899-900
customizing. *See also* **personalizing**
color, GUI display properties, 905-906
environment variables, 93
fax cover pages, 310-311
playlists, 279-280
Recycle Bin, 127
sounds associated with events, 911-913
Start menu, 98, 898-900
Taskbar, 900-901
cut and paste, Command Prompt window, 1078
Cutler, Dave, 7

D

Data Collector Sets (Reliability and Performance Monitor), 859
data encapsulation, VPN, 1287

Data Execution Prevention (DEP), 871, 1142-1144
data forks (Macintosh), 683
data partitions, separating from application partitions, 933
data security, 23-24
data transfers, Windows Easy Transfer, 100-103
Date and Time applet, 821-823
Dazzle DV-Editor SE, 345
DCOM (Distributed COM), 604
DDNS (Dynamic Domain Name Services)
DynDNS Updater, 1337
Remote Desktop, 1335-1336
DDR SDRAM modules (RAM), 1012
Debugging Mode boot option, 973
deep searching, 190
Default Datatype option (Printer Properties dialog), 217
default documents, web server home directories, 556-557, 572
default drivers, 1074
default email programs, 476
default firewall settings, restoring, 1234
default home pages (Internet Explorer 7), 426
default Internet connections, changing, 418-419
default mail preferences, setting (IE7), 453
Default Programs (Control Panel), 823
Set Associations option, 824
Set Program Access and Computer Defaults option, 825
default search engine, setting in Internet Explorer 7, 99
default Start menu, resetting, 900
default user profiles, configuring, 116-117
defragmenting hard disks, 943-946, 1012

DIAGNOSTIC TOOLS 1439

deja.com Web-based news server, 510
deleting
 cookies, 950
 email (Windows Mail 7), 483
 files
  Disk Cleanup utility, 949-952
  from printer queues, 224
  Internet Explorer, 952
  media files, 281-282
  troubleshooting, 1203
 gadgets, 245-246
 history (IE), 31
 print jobs from queues, 224
 user accounts, 90
demand-dialing, ICS (Internet Connection Sharing), 703, 714-717
Denial of Service (DoS) attacks, 1209
DEP (Data Execution Prevention), 1142-1144
Department of Justice (DOJ), Microsoft consent decree, 426
Derfler, Frank, 630
desktop, 15-16
 Active Desktop items, 234-235
 arranging, 182
 backgrounds, changing, 96
 drag-and-drop support, 181
 icons, 127-129, 908
 images
  block-like appearance, 928
  GUI display properties, 906-908
 immediate access, Windows key+M, 159
 Meeting Space, sharing views in, 1319-1320
 Recycle Bin, manually emptying, 128
 Screen Rotation control (Mobility Center), 1282
 See user interface (UI), 125
 shortcuts
  alias designation, 132
  troubleshooting, 157-158
 Sidebar, hiding, 241-242

desktop environment (Aero)
 adding items to, 131
 efficient use of, 159-161
 files, saving, 132-134
 icons, 127-130
 Recycle Bin, 125-128
 shortcuts, creating, 131-132
 Sidebar gadgets, 126
 taskbar, 125
 visual color palette, 124-125
Details pane, 167, 183
device drivers. *See* drivers
Device Manager, 793-794, 825-827
 Add Hardware applet (Control Panel) versus, 1016
 devices, removing, 1018
 network diagnostic functions, 793
 resource conflicts, resolving, 835-837
Device Settings tab, Printer Property sheets, 216
DHCP (Dynamic Host Configuration Protocol), 413-416
DHCP servers, TCP/IP automatic configuration, 647-648
diagnostic tools, 22, 804. *See also* testing; troubleshooting
 AutoPlay, 820-821
 Control Panel, 804
  Administrative Tools, 872-873
  Category view, 805-820
  default display, 805
  Default Programs, 823-825
  Keyboard applet, 847
  Mouse applet, 847-850
  Performance Information and Tools applet, 850-856
  Regional and Language Options, 867
  shortcuts, 895-896
  System Properties, 868-872
  Task Scheduler, 881

 Visual Effects dialog, 890-891
 Windows SideShow, 872
Date and Time applet, 821-823
Device Manager, 793-794, 825-827
Ease of Access Center, 837
 display settings, 840-841
 keyboard settings, 838-839
 mouse settings, 841
 sound settings, 839-840
Event Viewer, 792-793
game controllers, 846
ipconfig, 795-796
iSCSI Initiator, 891
MMC (Microsoft Management Console), 874-875
 Event Viewer, 876-879
 Services folder, 880
 Shared Folder node, 879-881
Network and Sharing Center, 789-790
Network Diagnostics, 790-791
network problems
 Device Manager, 793
 Event Viewer, 792-793
 Network window, 788
Network window, 788-789
ping, 797-798
Power Options icon, 860-861
Program and Features, 861-867
Reliability and Performance Monitor
 Data Collector Sets, 859
 Performance Monitor, 858
 Reliability Monitor, 858-859
 Resource Overview, 857
System Configuration utility, 881-883
System Diagnostics Report, 860
System Information, 889-890
System Tools folder, 892-895

How can we make this index more useful? Email us at indexes@quepublishing.com

Task Manager, 883
    Applications tab, 884-885
    Networking tab, 888-889
    Performance tab, 887-888
    Processes tab, 885-886
    Services tab, 887
    Users tab, 889
    troubleshooting, 895
    Windows Firewall, 791-792
dial-up networks, 605
    callbacks, 1291
    configuring, 1288-1289
    connections
        callbacks, 1291
        configuring, 409-411
        current locations, checking, 1293
        disconnect status, 1296
        email connections, 1295
        enabling (RAS), 1297, 1300
        ending, 1296
        establishing, 1293-1294
        hanging up, 418-419
        Internet connections, 530
        ISP dialing process, 420-421
        launching, 416-418
        managing from multiple locations, 1292-1293
        modifying accounts, 409-410
        monitoring, 1296
        multiple locations, managing, 1292-1293
        software configuration problems, 535-536
        terminating, 416-418
        troubleshooting, 420-421, 530, 535-536
        without roaming profiles, 1293-1294
    gateway settings, 1292
    incoming access, 1297-1300
    properties tables, 1290-1291
    RAS (Remote Access Services), 1286-1287
        enabling dial-up connections, 1297, 1300
        connection properties, 1289-1292

required setup information, 1288-1289
remote networks, 1295-1296
routing issues, 1296-1297
Dial-Up Properties dialog
    Advanced tab, 1292
    General tab, 1290
    Networking tab, 1291
dialing rules (Windows x and Scan), 315
digital cameras
    Windows Photo Gallery, 292-295
    zooming, 348
digital certificates, software safety (Internet Explorer 7), 446
digital IDs, 490-491
Digital Locker, 143-144
digital media receivers, 277
digital signatures, 447, 490
Digital Video Magazine website, 345
directories
    browsing, IIS, 557, 572-573
    folders versus, 129
    structure of, 105-108
        junction points and symbolic links, 109-110
        virtualization, 110-111
    virtual directories, IIS, 574
Directory Services Restore Mode boot option, 973
Disable Automatic Restart on System Failure boot option, 973
Disable Driver Signature Enforcement boot option, 974
disabling
    copy protection (music), 262
    hidden file extensions, 97-98
    logon at startup, 93-94
    updates via Windows Update, 990
    Windows features, 1001
    Windows Firewall, 1231
disaster planning, network security, 1222-1224
Disk Cleanup utility
    cleanup analysis reports, 950
    file groupings, 950-951
    frequency of execution, 952
    function of, 949

Disk Defragmenter, 943-946
disk drives
    PATA, 1012
    SATA, 1012
    shared drives, 753
    speed upgrades, 1012
disk files, printing to, 227-228
disk management
    Disk Management utility, 935
        drive letters, assigning, 936
        dynamic disk management, 939
        extending hard disks, 940
        joining hard disks, 937-939
        joining volumes together, 936-937
        shrinking hard drives, 940
        spanned volume creation, 940-941
        striped volume creation, 941-942
    WSH (Windows Script Host), 1117-1118
disk storage requirements, Windows Media Center, 374-376, 388-389
disparate networks, bridging, 658-659
display fonts, 843
display properties, modifying, 902-905
Display Settings dialog, 915-919
display settings. *See* screen settings
displaying
    effective permissions, 1196
    file extensions, 97-98
    gadgets, 245
    hidden files, 925
    images
        screen savers, 356-357
        slideshows, 355-356
        via Windows Explorer, 354-355
    installed software, 999-1000
    PDF documents from websites, 468-469
    print documents, 225-226
    protected web pages, 1241

Registry, Regedit utility, 1050-1051
television programs on HDTV or projector, 380
updates via Windows Update, 990
Windows Boot Manager, 972
workgroup networks, absent computers, 660-661
distributed applications (networks)
  COM+, 604
  Peer-to-Peer networking service, 604
  remote procedure calls (RPCs), 603
Distributed COM (DCOM), 604
distribution lists, Address Book (Windows Mail 7), 493-494
DivX files
  DVDs, burning to, 390
  television programs, converting to, 388-389
DLL (Dynamic Link Libraries), 1003-1004
DMA channels, 832-833
DNS (Domain Name Service)
  Active Directory, 608
  cost, 561
  dynamic, 561, 710
  IIS configuration guidelines, 560-562
  Inverse, 710
  ISP, free services, 709
DNSSuffix dialog, 415
documents
  disaster planning, 1223
  faxing, 228
  filename extension associations, 222
  Meeting Space, sharing in, 1321
  opening, application launches, 146
  printing
    configuring, 225-226
    offline, 222
    Print Manger, 221
    print queue properties, 225
    to disk files, 227-228
    troubleshooting, 228-230
    via Internet (IPP), 762-763
    XPS (XML Paper Specification), 226-227
Documents folder, 149-150, 165, 923-924
domain networks, 740
  joining, 653-655
  policy-based restrictions, 741
  printers, setting permissions, 773
  roaming user profiles, 741
  searching, 748
  Windows 200x Server, 748-749
  wireless networks, 1266
  workgroup networks versus, 742
domains
  Inverse DNS, 710
  registering, 561, 709
DOS applications
  editing advanced settings, 1100-1102
  printing from, 222-223
DoS attacks (Denial of Service), 1209
DOSKEY, MS-DOS environment optimization issues, 1099
dosx, 1099
double-click mode
  mouse, 135, 927
  stylus pen, 1362
downloading
  critical updates, 95
  gadgets, 239-241
  MP3 files, 441-442
  multimedia, Internet Explorer 7, 435-448
  program files, deleting (Disk Cleanup utility), 950
  Service Pack (SP2), setup files, 995
  software
    add-on crash detection (IE7), 448
    add-on management (IE7), 447-448
    digital certificates (IE7), 446
    Download.com, 442
    drive-by (IE7), 445-446
    installing, 999
    invalid signatures (IE7), 447
    mirror sites, 442
    progress bar, 443
    Tucows.com, 442
    version updates, 443
    virus scanning, 443
    ZIP compression, 443
  Tweak UI tool, 919
  websites, offline browsing (IE7), 432
drag-and-drop support, 137-138, 181
DreamScene wallpaper (Ultimate Extras), 997
Drive Preparation tool (BitLocker), 1183-1184
drive-by software downloads (Internet Explorer 7), 445-447
drivers, 204
  Command Prompt environment, 1074
  devices
    removing (Device Manager), 1018
    updating (System applet), 992-993
  inbox drivers, 204
  installing, VHDMount (Virtual Server 2005) operation, 1168-1170
  kernel-mode drivers, 1018
  missing, troubleshooting, 1017
  printers, 204
    network printer installations, 772-773
    Property sheets, 214-216
  searching (Microsoft Downloads Site), 213
  updates
    manual updates, 992-993
    Windows Update settings, 1007-1008
  user-mode drivers, 1018
  WIA drivers, opening, 321

How can we make this index more useful? Email us at indexes@quepublishing.com

1442 DRIVES

drives
  autotyping, 1033
  drive letters
    hard disk assignments (Disk Management), 936
    non-existent letters, mapping shared folders, 757
    unused letters, mapping shared folders, 754-757
  maintenance, 997
  mapping (net use command), 779-780
DSL (Digital Subscriber Line), 395-396
  connections
    high-speed connections, 411-416
    Remote Desktop, 1334
  modems, troubleshooting Internet connections, 536-537
  services, LAN, 710, 736
dual-boot systems, 38
DualView feature, 1019
dubbing television programs to VHS via Windows Media Center, 384
DV camcorders, 325, 346
DVD Maker, 357-360
DVDs
  audio CDs/DVDs
    bit rate, 268
    file formats, 268
    playing, 265-266
    ripping, 266-268
  backups on, 1155-1156
  burning
    DivX files, 390
    Windows Media Center, 383-384
  decoders, 260-261
  installing software from, 998, 1006
  keyboard shortcuts in Windows Media Center, 386
  playing
    in Windows Media Center, 378-379
    troubleshooting, 260-261
  recording to, 357-360

DVR (Digital Video Recorders), 373. *See also* television
dynamic disks
  aggregation, joining hard disks, 937-939
  upgrades, 939
dynamic DNS services, 561, 710
dynamic IP addressing, 413-415
dynamic storage models, hard disks, 931-933
dynamic web pages, 557
DynDNS Updater, 1337

E

e.bat, 1113
Ease of Access Center, 837
  display settings, 840-841
  keyboard settings, 838-839
  mouse settings, 841
  sound settings, 839-840
Ease of Access view (Category view), 813
Easy Microsoft Windows Vista, 126
eavesdropping, 1208
editing
  BCD (Boot Configuration Databases), 957
  boot menu entries, 74-76
  command-lines, Command Prompt environment, 1074
  DOS application settings, 1100-1102
  metadata, 15
  movies
    alternatives to Windows Movie Maker, 345
    nonlinear editing, 325
    Windows Movie Maker, 334-345
  recorded television programs via Windows Movie Maker, 384
  Registry keys via Regedit utility, 1053-1055

  remote computers, Registry entries (Regedit utility), 1056-1057
  user computers, Registry entries (Regedit utility), 1057-1058
Effects dialog, GUI settings, 906
EFS (Encrypted File Systems), 1173-1174
  BitLocker versus, 1189-1190
  CIPHER command-line tool, 1175-1176, 1202
  encrypted files
    restoring, 1181
    securing, 1178-1181
  folder recommendations for, 1178
  rules for usage, 1177-1178
  troubleshooting, 1202
elevated privileges, 85-86, 567
email
  accounts (Windows Mail 7)
    configuring, 478-480
    modifying, 495-496
    multiple management for single users, 498-500
  addressing (Windows Mail 7), 483-484
  backups
    account information, 508
    maintaining (Windows Mail 7), 505
    web-based email, 1154
  Blackberry devices, receiving on, 255-256
  checking while traveling (Windows Mail 7), 503-505
  client programs, 472, 475
  creating (Windows Mail 7), 483-484
  default programs, 476
  deleting (Windows Mail 7), 483
  filtering (Windows Mail 7), 501-502
  formatting, 490
    complaints from recipients (Windows Mail 7), 520
    HTML 489

messages, 523-524
plain text, 489
hoaxes, 1208
links, troubleshooting (IE7), 467
Microsoft E-Mail Updates Service, 1226
newsgroups
   availability after synchronization, 522
   marking news indicators, 522
   size options (Windows Mail 7), 526
organizing (Windows Mail 7), 500-506
out of office auto replies (Windows Mail 7), 503
PDA (Personal Data Assistants), receiving on, 255-256
phishing
   AOHell, 1244
   avoiding, 1252
   example, 1244-1248
   Gold Lock, 1249
   identity management software, 1251-1252
   overview, 1244
   Phishing Filter, 1246, 1248
   two-factor authentication, 1250-1251
   two-way authentication, 1250
photos, sharing via Windows Photo Gallery, 299
PPC (Pocket PCs), receiving on, 255-256
reading (Windows Mail 7), 481-483
receipt requests (Windows Mail 7), 488
remote networks, retrieval issues, 1295-1296
replying to (Windows Mail 7), 482
scans, emailing, 319
secure email (Windows Mail 7), 490-491
sending (Windows Mail 7), 484

signature setup (Windows Mail 7), 487
spam
   avoiding, 1256-1257
   filtering, 1254
   international filtering, 1255-1256
   overview, 1252-1253
   Phishing Filter, 1256
   protecting email addresses from, 1253-1254
   reporting, 1257-1258
   Safe Senders list, 1254-1255
transfer protocols (Windows Mail 7)
   HTTP, 481
   IMAP, 480
   POP3, 480
   SMTP, 480
VPN/dial-up network connections, 1295
web-based email, 1154
WSH (Windows Script Host), 1118-1119
EMF (Enhanced Metafile Format), 204
Empty Recycle Bin command (File menu), 128
emulation, WOW64 emulation layer, 33
Enable Advanced Printing Features option (Printer Properties dialog), 217
Enable Bidirectional Support option (Printer Properties dialog), 217
Enable Boot Logging startup option, 973
Enable Low-Resolution Video boot option, 973
encryption
   BitLocker, 1182
      Drive Preparation tool, 1183-1184
      EFS (Encrypted File Systems) versus, 1189-1190
      encryption process, 1186-1189
      manual hard disk preparation, 1184-1185

      preparation for use, 1185
      recovery process, 1187
      system requirements, 1183
      TPM (Trusted Platform Module), 1185-1186
      troubleshooting, 1202
   EFS (Encrypted File Systems), 1173-1174
      CIPHER command-line tool, 1175-1176, 1202
      folder recommendations for, 1178
      restoring encrypted files, 1181
      rules for usage, 1177-1178
      securing encrypted files, 1178-1181
      troubleshooting, 1202
   file encryption certificates, managing, 93
   Internet Explorer 7, 456
   IPP (Internet Printing Protocol), 762
   keys, 1174
   numeric encryption, 1174
   offline folders (mobile computing), 1306
   wireless networks, 636
enterprise management, LAN monitoring, 799
enterprise networks, 592
Environment Variables option (System Properties), 871-872
erasing via stylus pen, 1363
Error Checking tool, 946-947
error messages
   File Sharing Is Turned Off, 789
   Network Discovery Is Turned Off, 788
   printers, troubleshooting, 228
error reports, deleting (Disk Cleanup utility), 951
Ethernet
   10BASE-T, 618-620
   10BASE5, 593
   100BASE-T, 618-620
   1000Mbps, 620

How can we make this index more useful? Email us at indexes@quepublishing.com

bridging via phone line networks (HomePNA), 658-659
cabling installation guidelines, 628-629
IEEE 802.11 (Wireless Ethernet), 596-597
Eudora mail client, 475
EULA (End-User License Agreements), 1028-1031
Event Viewer, 792, 976
log entry sources, 793
Microsoft Management Console (MMC), 876-879
network diagnostic functions, 792-793
events, associating sounds with, 911-913
exchanging files via FTP Server, 577-579
executable Windows programs list, 1380-1399
execute attribute (CGI scripts), 558
existing documents, opening, 146
existing email accounts, modifying (Windows Mail 7), 495-496
existing network adapters, checking configurations, 626-627
existing wireless networks, joining, 641-642
exploits, 1208
Explorers, 17-18
exposure (photos), adjusting in Windows Photo Gallery, 296
extended desktops, 917
extended partitions, 930-931
extended view mode (laptop computers), 1020
extending hard disks, Disk Management utility, 940
exterior TVs, troubleshooting, 926
External Display control (Mobility Center), 1282
External Display tile (Mobility Center), 1314
external routers
purchasing advice, 709
ICS (Internet Connection Sharing) versus, 708

F

F11 key, Full Screen view (Internet Explorer), 160
F5 refresh key, 161
Family Safety Settings, 32
Fast Ethernet, 594
FAT file system
backups and, 1154
volumes, property sheets, 934
FAT16 partitions, converting to NTFS (Convert utility), 947-948
FAT32 partitions, converting to NTFS (Convert utility), 947-948
fault tolerances, 932
Favorites Center, 30
Fax Options dialog, 312
fax service (Windows Fax and Scan)
configuring, 309
cover pages, 310-311
fax receiving options, 310
fax settings, 312
sender information, 310
dialing rules, 315
faxing slides and transparencies, 322
hardware and software requirements, 308-309
monitoring outgoing faxes, 315
overview, 308-309
previewing faxes, 314
printing received faxes, 316
receiving faxes, 316
sending faxes, 313-315
troubleshooting, 230, 320-322
faxes
fax service (Windows Fax and Scan)
configuring, 309-312
dialing rules, 315
faxing slides and transparencies, 322
hardware and software requirements, 308-309
monitoring outgoing faxes, 315
overview, 308-309
previewing faxes, 314
printing received faxes, 316
receiving faxes, 316
sending faxes, 313-315
troubleshooting, 230, 320-322
sending, 228
Windows Fax and Scan, 25
WinFax Pro software, 228
feeds (news), 511
FEK (File Encryption Keys), 1174
File and Printer Sharing for Microsoft Networks, 602, 642-644
File menu commands, 128
File Sharing Is Turned Off (error message), 789
file systems
IIS
installation requirements, 560
security, 583
navigating, 177-179
meta-information views, 182-184
multiple item selection, 181-182
right-clicking, 180
files
Active Directory networks, searching in, 750-752
Administrator accounts, troubleshooting, 1203
AFP (AppleTalk File Protocol), 683
attachments (Windows Mail 7)
opening, 485
sending, 485
virus prevention, 486
backups
Complete PC backups, 1152-1153
creating, 1153-1155
file format of, 1156
multi-disc backups, 1202
restoring, 1157-1160
compression, 948-949
Computer files, 149
custom startup files, MS-DOS, 1102
data forks (Macintosh), 683

Disk Cleanup utility, 949
  cleanup analysis reports, 950
  frequency of execution, 952
  groupings, 950-951
encryption, 1173-1174
  certificate management, 93
  CIPHER command-line tool, 1175-1176, 1202
  EFS (Encrypted File System) versus BitLocker, 1189-1190
  folder recommendation, 1178
  restoring encrypted files, 1181
  rules for usage, 1177-1178
  securing encrypted files, 1178-1181
  troubleshooting, 1202
extensions, viewing, 97-98
formats
  audio CDs/DVDs, 268
  backups, 1156
  Windows Movie Maker, 326
FTPServer, exchanging via, 577-579
hidden files, 149, 925
icons, 127
In Use by Another User error message, 781
Internet Explorer, cache cleanup, 952
managing
  third-party management tools, 953-954
  Windows Explorer, 135-136
MIME mappings, 573-574, 585
multiple files, selecting, 181-182
My Computer, Tiles view, 149
naming
  completion, Command Prompt environment, 1075
  extensions, document associations, 222

Internetworking compatibility, 684
Macintosh compatibility, 684
quoting with spaces, Command Prompt environment, 1072-1073
resetting associations (media) in Windows Media Player, 438
networks, naming in, 743-744
NTBackup files, restoring, 1203
Offline Folders
  automatic caching options, 1307
  identifying for use, 1302
  inability to mark availability, 1309
  marking for sharing, 1307
  missing, 1309
  synchronizing, 1305-1306
  typical uses, 1307
  use guidelines, 1304
ownership, taking, 1197
packing, 198-200
permissions
  IIS installation, 567
  NTFS, 1192-1199
previous versions, restoring, 1190-1191
Print Manager, dragging to, 221-222
print-to-disk option, 227-228
printer queues, deleting from, 224
program files, moving, 129
resource forks (Macintosh), 683
restoring
  encrypted files, 1181
  NTBackup files, 1203
  previous versions, 1190-1191
  Recycle Bin, 127-128
saving to desktop, 132-134

searches
  changing settings, 190-193
  deep searching, 190
  grouping and stacking, 197-198
  intermediate searching, 189-190
  Search pane, 195-196
  troubleshooting, 201-202
  while typing, 192-195
security, 200-201
sharing, 742, 799
  enabling, 790
  file names, 743
  Internetworking with Windows XP and 2000, 667-669
  Network and Sharing Center, 744-746
  passwords versus passwordless file sharing, 1217-1218
  UNC (Universal Naming Convention), 743-744
  wireless networks, 1266-1267
troubleshooting, 799, 956
types of
  associations, 1038
  Windows Media Player support, 260
views, customizing, 185-187
Windows Photo Gallery, importing to, 290
zipped files, 198-202, 953
filters
  email (Windows Mail 7), 501-502
  junk mail, 19
  movies, adding to, 337-338
  Phishing Filter, 1246-1248
  photos in Windows Photo Gallery, 289
  routers, 726-727
  spam, 1254-1256
  video effects, adding to clips (Windows Movie Maker), 337
Find Printers dialog, 760

How can we make this index more useful? Email us at indexes@quepublishing.com

firewalls, 19, 1142
   configuring, 1212-1213
   enabling, 1225-1226
   function of, 1212-1213
   personal firewalls, 1216
   website availability, incoming port settings, 581
   Windows Firewall, 792
      checking for inadvertent blockages, 791
      configuring, 791, 1213, 1230-1231
      default settings, 1234
      disabling, 1231
      enabling, 1225-1226, 1231
      exceptions, 12131-1234
      function of, 1213
      improvements to, 606
      monitoring suspicious activities, 1221
      network connection settings, 1234
      opening for IIS, 566
      peer-to-peer network configurations, 652-653
   Windows Firewall with Advanced Security, 1235
      configuring, 1236-1238
      rules creation, 1238-1240
FireWire (IEEE-1394)
   crossover cable connections, 632-633
   laptop cards, 345
   Maxtor external 1394 FireWire hard drive, 345
   printer ports, 208-209
   Windows Movie Maker, 326
FIRST (Forum of Incident Response and Security Teams), 1224
fixed IP addresses
   assigning, 727
   configuring, 415-416
fixes
   Critical Updates, 1422
   hotfixes, 1422
   Optional Updates, 1422
flat cuts (transitions), 336-337
Flip-3D, 13, 921, 1375
flowcharts (Internet connection diagnostic tool), 532-534

fly-open menus, 134, 924
Folder list (Windows Mail 7), 477
Folder Options dialog (Control Panel), 187-189
Folder view, 137-138
folders
   Active Directory networks, searching in, 750-752
   Administrator accounts, deletion problems with, 1203
   compressing, 948-949
   current folders, Command Prompt environment, 1073-1074
   directories
      comparisons, 129
      junction points and symbolic links, 109-110
      virtualization, 110-111
   Documents folder, 149-150, 165
   email folders, creating (Windows Mail 7), 500-506
   encryption, 1173, 1178
   Folder view
      creating in, 138
      deleting, 138
      dragging/dropping, 137-138
   hidden files, viewing, 925
   monitored folders, changing in Windows Media Player, 271
   moving, 138
   multiple items, selecting, 181-182
   Music, 149-150
   offline folders, 767
      automatic caching options, 1307
      identifying for use, 1302
      marking for sharing, 1307
      synchronizing, 1305
      synchronizing manually, 1306
      typical uses, 1307
      use guidelines, 1304
   organization of, 767
   permissions, inheritance of, 1194

   Pictures, 149-150
   Printers folder, 205-206, 219
   searching, 189
      changing settings, 190-193
      deep searching, 190
      grouping and stacking, 197-198
      intermediate searching, 189-190
      Search pane, 195-196
      troubleshooting, 201-202
      while typing, 192-195
   security, 200-201
   sharing, 747-748, 768-771, 790
   shortcuts, creating, 767
   views, customizing, 185-189
   virtual folders, 1004-1005
   Windows Explorer, viewing in, 137-138
Folders Options Control Panel applet, 169-170
Font Substitution option (Printer Properties dialog), 217
fonts, 841
   information sources, 843-844
   installing, 845
   monospaced fonts, 843
   ornamental fonts, 843
   points, 842
   previewing, 920
   proportionally spaced fonts, 843
   size, changing, 96
   small screen fonts, troubleshooting, 928
   strokes, 842
   substitutions, 844
   types, 842
Fonts applet (Control Panel), 920
for statements, batch file programming, 1111-1112
forced shutdowns, 158
foreground windows, closing via Alt+F4, 159
forgotten passwords
   password reset disks, 91-92
   recovering, 112-115

forks, 683
form factors, Windows Media Center PCs, 365-366
Form-to-Tray Assignment option (Printer Properties dialog), 217
formatting email messages (Windows Mail 7), 489-490, 523-524
forwarding
    non-standard services to DMZ hosts (routers), 734-735
    TCP Services, routers, 733-734
    UDP Services, routers, 733-734
FPNOHOSTCHECK, 1086
fragmented hard disks, repairing, 944
frame relays, LAN Internet connections versus DSL service, 711
fraud. *See* phishing attacks
FreeBSD, 36
Freed, Les, 630
FreeNews.net website, free news servers listings, 511
FreeScan, 1242
frequent backups, security disaster planning, 1222
FTP folders, visibility of, 1240
FTP Server
    disconnecting from, 579
    file exchanges, 577-579
    IIS components, installing, 565
    secure settings, establishing, 575-576
    website content, publishing, 576-577
Fusion, 1004, system stability, 1003
FxsSrvCp$ folder, Windows 200x Server shared status, 749

G

gadgets, 16-17, 234-235
    adding, 238-239, 244
    configuring, 242-243
    downloading, 239-241
    moving, 243-244
    opacity, changing, 245
    removing, 245-246
    troubleshooting, 254
    viewing, 245
Game Explorer, 32
games
    controllers, 846
    Windows Hold'Em feature (Ultimate Extras), 997
garbage character displays (MS-DOS applications), troubleshooting, 1127
garbled text (printers), troubleshooting, 229
Gates, Bill, 1357
gateway settings, dial-up/VPN networks, 1292
General tab
    Folders Options Control Panel, 169
    Printer Property sheets, 215
gestures, 1363-1364
GIF file format, IE7 support, 436
Gigabit Ethernet (1000Mbps), 594, 620
glass, 13. *See also* Aero interface
GNU, 37
GoBack, 24
Gold Lock, 1249
Google.com, 464
    newsgroups, message size options, 526
    Registry keys, name searches, 1062
    Web-based news server, 510
Gore, Albert, 424
goto statements, batch file programming, 1110
GoToMyPC, 1331
grassroots networking, 661
Group Policies, 607

groups
    access privileges, Active Directory, 608
    containers, Active Directory, 607-608
    searches, 197-198
    user groups
        assigning permissions to, 1198-1199
        restricted objects permissions, 1203
Guest user accounts, 91
GUI (Graphical User Interfaces), 898
    Administrative Tools folder, easy access method, 922-923
    Aero desktop environment
        default appearance, 125-126
        icons, 127-130
        putting items on, 131
        Recycle Bin, 125, 127-128
        shortcuts, 131-132
        Sidebar gadgets, 126
        taskbar, 125
        visual color palette, 124-125
    Caps Lock key, altering location on keyboard, 924
    Ctrl key, altering location on keyboard, 924
    display properties
        color depth settings, 915-919
        color schemes, 903-905
        custom color creation, 905-906
        desktop icons, 908
        effects, 906
        modifying, 902-911, 914-919
        resolution settings, 915-919
        screen savers, 909-911
        themes, 914-915
        wallpaper images, 906-908
    Documents folder, changing location of, 923-924
    efficient use of, 159-161

GUI

exterior TV, troubleshooting, 926
logins, 123-124
modifying, 898
Monitor and Adapter Properties dialog, 918-919
new features, 12
   Aero interface, 13-14
   desktop, 15-16
   Explorers, 17-18
   metadata editing, 15
   searches, 14-15
   Sidebar, 16-17
   speech recognition, 18
   Start button (orb), 14
   Start menu, 15
Recycle Bin, configuring, 925
Start menu
   customizing, 898-900
   fly-open menus, 924
   resetting defaults, 900
taskbar, 138-142, 900-901
three-button mouse, auto-scrolling, 924
tips
   Flip 3D limitations, 921
   font previews, 920
   OS version determination, 920-921
   visual effects tools, 922
Tweak UI tool, 919
Windows Explorer, file management, 135-138
Windows Media Center, 370-371
Windows Media Player
   browsing and searching, 263-265
   menu tabs, 261-263
Guide (Windows Media Center)
   setting up, 372-374
   television programs
      recording, 373
      selecting, 372

H

hackers, 1207-1208, 1132
handedness, specifying, 1371
handouts, sharing in Meeting Space, 1321

handwriting
   converting to text, 1370
Handwriting Personalization window, 1364-1365
Handwriting Recognition tool, 1364-1366, 1371
   importance of, 1356
hanging up, dial-up connections, 418-419
hard disks
   boot problems, troubleshooting, 957
   defragmenting, 943-946, 1012
   drive letters, assigning (Disk Management), 936
   dynamic storage model, 931-933
   encryption via BitLocker, 1182
      EFS (Encrypted File System) versus, 1189-1190
      encryption process, 1186-1189
      preparation for, 1185
      recovery process, 1187
      system requirements, 1183
      TPM (Trusted Platform Module), 1185-1186
      troubleshooting, 1202
   error handling, 946-947
   extending (Disk Management utility), 940
   joining, 936-939
   management tools
      Disk Management utility, 935-939
      FAT volumes, 934
      NTFS volumes, 934
      Removable Storage utility, 942-943
      third-party, 953-954
   manual preparation via BitLocker, 1184-1185
   media files, playing, 266
   organizational strategies, NTFS alternatives, 933-934
   primary IDE channel, 1011
   RAID, 930, 942, 1181-1182
   SCSI, 1011

   secondary IDE channel, 1011
   Serial ATA, 1011
   shrinking (Disk Management utility), 940
   spanned volumes, creating (Disk Management utility), 940-941
   striped volumes, creating (Disk Management utility), 941-942
   traditional storage model, 930-931
   troubleshooting
      file structure problems, 956
      hardware problems, 956
      overview, 954
      strategies, 955-956
      unrecognized hard disks, 956-957
   Ultra DMA EIDE, 1011
   upgrading, 1011
hardware
   conflicts, 827-837, 1035
   Device Manager, network diagnostic functions, 793
   devices
      drivers, 1017
      resource reassignment, 1019
   drivers
      device drivers, 1017
      updating, 992-993
   hard disks
      defragmenting, 1012
      troubleshooting, 956
   HCL (Hardware Compatibility Lists), 1034-1035
   installing, 1013-1016
   Internet connections
      installing, 401-406
      selection criteria, 400
      troubleshooting, 539-543
   monitors, multiple installations, 1019-1023, 1032-1033
   noisy systems, quieting, 958-959
   non-working hardware, troubleshooting, 1034
   optimization tips, 1035

printers
  configuring, 206-207
  installing, 206-213
  missing drivers, 212-213
  troubleshooting, 210-212
removing, 1018
small network requirements, 613
upgrading, 48-49
  BIOS settings, 1010-1011
  EULA, 1028-1031
  hard disks, 1011
  page file sizes, 1010
  RAM, 1010-1013
  SPP, 1028-1030
  Windows Vista Upgrade Advisor, 43-48
UPS (Uninterruptible Power Supplies)
  configuring, 1027-1028
  installing, 1023-1026
  intelligent units, 1024
  selecting, 1025-1026
  testing configuration, 1028
Windows Media Center
  configurations, 368-370
  requirements, 364-365
Windows Movie Maker requirements, 326
wireless networks, 623
Hardware and Sound category (Category view), 809
Hardware Compatibility Lists (HCL), 619, 1034-1035
HDTV, Windows Media Center
  requirements for, 364-365
  television programs, viewing, 380
Help and Support Center (Start menu), 125, 139, 153-154, 981-982
Help System, 122, 153-154
Hibernate mode, 21, 104, 155-156
Hibernation files, deleting (Disk Cleanup utility), 951

hiding
  devices, conflicts, 1035
  files
    Computer, 149
    disabling extensions, 97-98
    viewing, 925
  icons, Notification Area, 901
  Sidebar, 241-242
  updates
    troubleshooting, 1006
    via Windows Update, 989
  Welcome Center, 81
High Performance profile (power usage), 1284
high-speed Internet connections, 411-416
hiring professionals, network installations, 615
histories
  IE, deleting, 31
  Tablet PC/pen computing, 1356-1358
  Windows, 6-8
  Windows Media Center, 363
hives (Registry), 1039-1040, 1059
HKEY_CLASSES_ROOT key (Registry), 1040-1042
HKEY_CURRENT_CONFIG key (Registry), 1039-1041
HKEY_CURRENT_USER key (Registry), 1041-1043
HKEY_LOCAL_MACHINE key (Registry), 1039-1042
HKEY_USERS key (Registry), 1039-1042
Hold Mismatched Documents option (Printer Properties dialog), 217
home directories
  IIS, copying web pages to, 567-569
  web servers, default documents, 556-557, 572
  websites
    setting file permissions, 567
    URL filename translation, 556

home networks, sharing media files, 277-278
home pages (IE7), 556-557, 572
  default pages, 98-99, 426
  multiple home pages, 30
home theater systems. See Windows Media Center
home wireless networks, 1267-1269
HOMEDRIVE, 1086
HOMEPATH, 1086
HomePlug (HomePlug Powerline Alliance), 597, 622, 628
HomePNA (Home Phoneline Networking Association), 597, 620-621, 628
host file (networking), 699-700
HotBot.com search engine, 464
hotfixes, 994, 1422
hotpatching, 988
HP-compatible printers, property settings, 216-218
HTML (Hypertext Markup Language), 425
  editors, 451-453
  Windows Mail 7
    formatting email, 489
    scripting protection, 498
HTTP (Hypertext Transfer Protocol), 429, 481
hubs, 593
  cascade ports, 634-635
  cost ranges, 613
  N-way autosensing, 624
  network wiring, multiple connections, 634-635
  switching, 624
  troubleshooting, 659-660
hue (color), 905-906

I

I/O
  cancellation, 22
  port assignments, 833
ICMP (Internet Control Message Protocol), 1240

icons
  desktop, 127-130
  files, 127
  GUI display properties, setting, 908
  hidden icons, Notification Area, 901
  shortcuts, 129-130
    settings alteration, 129
Icons view (Computer), 149
ICS (Internet Connection Sharing), 606, 625
  broadband DSL, 703
  broadband schemes, 718-719
  demand dialing, 703
  dial-up schemes, 714-717
  external routers versus, 708
  function of, 1215-1216
  outside network access, enabling, 728-732
  Remote Desktop connections, 1337-1339
  residential gateways, 706-709
IDE channels, hard disk assignment, 1011
IDE drives, switching to SATA drives, 934
identification (network computers), setting, 651-652
identity management software, 1251-1252
identity theft, 1209
IE7 (Internet Explorer 7). *See* **Internet Explorer 7 (IE7)**
IEEE 801.11g (Wireless G), 596
IEEE 802.11 Wireless Ethernet, 596-597
IEEE 802.11g Wireless networking, 622-623
IEEE-1394 (FireWire)
  crossover cable connections, 632-633
  laptop cards, 345
  Maxtor external 1394 FireWire hard drive, 345
  printer ports, 208-209
  Windows Movie Maker, 326
if statements, batch file programming, 1108-1110

IIS (Internet Information Services), 692. *See also* **web servers**
  components of, 565, 575-579
  connection limits, Windows Vista, 558-559
  default document searches, 556-557, 572
  directories
    browsing, 557, 572-573
    home directories, 556, 567-569
    virtual directories, 574
  DNS (Domain Name Service), 560-562
  domain registration, 561
  installing
    Administrator user logins, 562
    components listing, 562-564
    connection requirements, 560
    critical security fixes, 565
    decision guidelines, 559-560
    file system requirements, 560
    home directory file permissions, 567
    opening firewall, 566
    security warnings, 555
    welcome page, 566
  licensing restrictions, Windows Vista, 558-559
  localhost, 566
  log files, 580
  memory requirements, 560
  MIME mappings, 573-574
  program execution options, 557-558
  scripting, enabling, 573
  security
    automatic updates, 582
    bug fixes, 582
    file systems, 583
    tools, 555
  simple websites, configuring, 567-569
  SMTP server settings, 574-575
  supported features, 554

  troubleshooting
    bad links, 585
    server access, 584
    site connections, 584
    unresponsive servers, 584
    wrong web page versions, 585
  websites
    availability settings, 580-581
    home directories, 556
    managing (IIS Manager), 569-575
    simple configurations, 567-569
    virtual directories, 556
  Windows File Types Registry, 557
images
  backups
    Complete PC backups, 1160-1164
    VHDMount (Virtual Server 2005), 1164-1170
  burning to
    CDs, 300-303
    DVDs, 357-360
  GIF file format, 436
  Internet Explorer 7
    copyright restrictions, 436
    mouse over action, 436
    resizing, 436
    supported file formats, 435-436
  JPEG file format, 435-436
  Pictures folder, 288
  PNG file format, 436
  scanning, 317
  screen savers setting as, 356-357
  slideshows, viewing as, 355-356
  Windows Explorer
    burning images to CD, 300-301
    viewing via, 354-355
  Windows Movie Maker, 324
    importing into, 332
    movie production, 325
    video clip capturing, 327-333

INSTALLING 1451

video clip conversion, 333-334
video formats, 325-326
Windows Photo Gallery, 288
  adding to, 289, 294-295
  adjusting color in, 296
  adjusting exposure in, 296
  archiving via, 305-306
  burning images to CD, 301-303
  cropping in, 296
  filtering in, 289
  fixing in, 295-296
  importing into, 290
  organizing in, 290
  previewing in, 290
  printing from, 297-298, 303-304
  red eye fixes, 296
  sharing via, 299
IMAP (Internet Message Access Protocol), 480
impersonation, 1208
importing
  audio tracks into Windows Movie Maker, 332
  digital still images into Windows Movie Maker, 332
  photos to Windows Photo Gallery, 290
In Use by Another User error messages, 781
in-place upgrades, Windows Vista, 62-65
in-wall wiring, network installations, 631-632
Inbox (Windows Mail 7), 476-477
inbox drivers, 204
incident plans (disaster plan development), 1223-1224
incoming calls, VPN connections, 1300-1301
incoming messages (Windows Mail 7)
  deleting, 483
  reading, 481-483
  replying to, 482

incoming network connections
  by modem, 605
  Remote Assistance, 606
  Remote Desktop, 605
  Terminal Services, 605
  Windows Meeting Space, 606
indexing, 190-193
Indexing Options dialog, 855
"information superhighway," notion of, 424
infrared printer ports, 208-209
infrastructure wireless networks versus ad hoc networks, 1262
inheritance (permissions), 1194
inkjet printers, 231
Input Panel (Tablet PCs), 1361-1363
installing
  antivirus software, 1136-1138
  backup software for networks, 656-658
  fonts, 845
  hardware
    Internet connection hardware, 401-406
    methods of, 1013-1016
  IIS (Internet Information Services)
    components listing, 562-564
    connection requirements, 560
    critical security fixes, 565
    decision on use guidelines, 559-560
    file system requirements, 560
    home directory file permissions, 567
    memory requirements, 560
    opening firewall, 566
    security warnings, 555
    welcome page, 566
  internal ISDN adapters, 404
  Internet connection hardware, 401-406

LLDP responder, Windows XP, 667
modems, 401-406
multiple monitors, 1023
  secondary display adapters, 1021-1022
  troubleshooting areas, 1020-1021
  video card support, 1019
network adapters, 405-406, 625-627
networks
  hiring professionals, 615
  optional components, 691-694
  SNMP, 694-696
  wireless networks, 635-642
  wiring for, 628-635
new applications, 145, 998
printers, 206-207
  COM (serial) ports, 210-212
  extra drivers, 772-773
  local printers, 208-213
  network printers, 759-761, 766
  non-listed printers, 212-213
programs from networks, 145
service packs, 994-996, 1424-1427
software, 998
  antivirus software, 1136-1138
  backup software, 656-658
  from CD/DVD, 998
  from Internet download, 999
  side-by-side installs, 1003-1004
  troubleshooting, 1006-1007
  viewing installed software, 999-1000
SUA (Subsystem for UNIX-Based Applications), 681-682
UPS (Uninterruptible Power Supplies), 1023-1026

How can we make this index more useful? Email us at indexes@quepublishing.com

INSTALLING

VHDMount (Virtual Server 2005), 1165, 1168-1170
Windows Vista
  clean installations, 49-62
  in-place upgrades, 62-65
  multiboot installations, 66-70
  network installations, 50
  troubleshooting on notebook computers, 55
  virtual machine process, 73
wireless networks, 635, 641-642
  SSID (Service Set Identifier), 636
  Wireless Network Setup Wizard, 638-641
wiring for networks, 628-630
  crossover cables, 632-633
  in-wall, 631-632
  multiple hub connections, 634-635
  patch cables, 630
  punchdown blocks, 632
Intel Corporation website, Speed Check tool, 549
intelligent UPS units, 1024
IntelliMirror, 132, 609
interactive website scripts, 585-586
intermediate searching, 189-190
internal ISDN adapters, installing, 404
international spam filtering, 1255-1256
Internet, 609
  connections
    analog modems, 394-395
    cable modems, 396
    changing default connections, 418-419
    checking connection status, 418
    configuring, 94, 406-416
    dial-up connections, 409-410, 416-421
    DSL (Digital Subscriber Lines), 395-396, 1334
    high-speed connections, 411-416
    installing equipment, 401-406

IP addresses, 1335-1336
ISDN (Integrated Services Digital Networks), 395
internal ISDN adapter installations, 404
international travel tips, 421-422
mobile connections, 421-422
multiple connections, 419-420
Remote Desktop connections, 1337-1339
satellite service, 397
selecting equipment, 400
troubleshooting, 420-421
wireless access, 397
equipment, choosing, 400
ICS (Internet Connection Sharing), 606, 625
  broadband DSL, 703
  broadband schemes, 718-719
  demand dialing, 703
  dial-up schemes, 714-717
  external routers versus, 708
  function of, 1215-1216
  outside network access, enabling, 728-732
  Remote Desktop connections, 1337-1339
  residential gateways, 706-709
Internet 7, 452
ISP (Internet Service Providers), choosing, 397-401
LAN (Local Area Networks), 394, 702
  cable services, 705, 710-713
  configuring, 713-721, 724-727
  connection sharing routers, 703
  DSL services, 710
  frame relays, 711
  ICS (Internet Connection Sharing), 703, 714-719
  IP address management, 705-709
  ISDN service, 713

  overview, 703-705
  Remote Desktop, 709-710
  routed services, 705
  shared DSL/cable services, 736
  shared modems, 736
  speed requirements, 702-703
  VPN, 709-710
  wireless, 711-712
modems
  installing, 401-406
  shared modems, 736
  wireless modems, 406
multiple connections, managing, 419-420
network adapters, installing, 405-406
port forwarding, Remote Desktop, 1338-1341, 1351-1352
satellite dishes, 397
troubleshooting
  dial-up connections, 530, 535-536
  flowchart diagnosis, 532-534
  ipconfig command, 529, 544-545
  LAN problems, 537-539
  methodology, 531-532
  modem problems, 536-537
  network cabling diagrams, 530
  Network Connections settings, 530
  network hardware problems, 539-543
  pathping command, 547-548
  ping command, 545-546, 551-552
  route command, 548-549
  software configuration problems, 535-539
  TCP/IP utilities, 543
  TraceRoute.org reverse tracert tools, 550
  tracert command, 529, 546-547
  tSpeed Check, 549
  Whois Database, 550
Windows Calendar, 452

INTERNETWORKING | 1453

Windows Mail, 452
Windows Media Center, 452
Windows Media Player, 452
Windows Photo Gallery, 452
Internet Connection Sharing (ICS). *See* **ICS (Internet Connection Sharing)**
Internet Control Message Protocol (ICMP), 1240
Internet Explorer 7 (IE7)
  Address bar, 428
  audio
    MP3 files, 441-442
    streaming (Windows Media Player), 439-440
    Web elements, 436-438
  bad downloads, protecting against, 443-445
  cache cleanup, 952
  certificate verification, 446
  Content Controls, 459-461
  default home pages, 426
  default mail settings, configuring, 451-453
  default news settings, configuring, 451-453
  default search engine, setting, 99
  email links
    troubleshooting, 467
  F11 key (full screen view), 160, 426-427
  GIF image format, 436
  graphics, 436
  hacker targeting, 464
  home page, setting, 98-99
  HTML editor programs, 451-453
  JPEG image format, 435-436
  launching, 426
  Links bar, 427-428
  Live Search box, 425
  malware protection, 1147
  Microsoft Live ID, 465-466
  multimedia, downloading, 435-448
  new features, 30-31, 425
  Parental Controls, 459
  PNG image format, 436
  preference settings, 448
    advanced, 450, 456
    AutoComplete, 450, 461
    background image printing, 462
    certificates, 450
    connections, 450
    content advisor, 450
    default mail, 453
    fonts, 450
    general, 449
    HTML editor, 453
    multimedia, 450
    newsgroups, 453
    objectionable content controls, 459-461
    pop-ups/unders, 457-459
    privacy, 450
    programs, 450
    search options, 462
    security, 450, 453-455
    site history, 449
    temporary file cache, 449
  safer alternatives, 464
  Search Companion, 462-464
  security
    add-on downloads, 447-448
    digital certificates, 446
    drive-by software downloads, 445-446
  site navigation, 428
  tabbed pages, browsing, 430-433
  URL, 428-430
  video
    AVI format, 438
    fps (frames-per second), 437
    MPEG format, 438
    playback (Windows Media Player), 438-439
    streaming (Windows Media Player), 439-440
    Web elements, 436-438
    WMV format, 438
  web feeds, automatic searches for, 425
  web pages
    crashes caused by, 467
    graphic errors, 467
    load errors, 467
    offline browsing, 432
    page not available errors, 467
    saving for later viewing, 434-435
  websites, software
    download progress, 443
    downloading, 442
    mirror sites, 442
    version updates, 443
    virus scanning, 443
    ZIP compression, 443
  working offline, 433-434
Internet Information Services (IIS). *See* **IIS (Internet Information Services)**
Internet Options dialog
  Advanced tab, 450, 456
  Certificates tab, 450
  Connections tab, 450
  Content tab, 450
  General tab, 449-450
  Multimedia tab, 450
  Privacy tab, 450, 454-455
  Programs tab, 450, 453
  Security tab, 450, 453-455
Internet Printing Protocol. *See* **IPP (Internet Printing Protocol)**
Internet Properties dialog, 419
Internet Protocol (TCP/IP)
  adding, 642-644
  IPSEC, 599, 1238
  IPv6, 599
  Properties page, 645-646
Internet-based storage services, 754
Internetworking, 664
  Linux, 672-673
    Berkeley "r" commands, 680-682
    CIFS protocol, 673
    NFS, 678-679
    Samba, 673-676
    SMB protocol, 673
    Telnet, 676-678
  Mac OS X, 685-687
    applications, lost file associations, 698
    applications, running concurrently, 698
    compatibility planning, 683-684

How can we make this index more useful? Email us at indexes@quepublishing.com

INTERNETWORKING

file data forks, 683
file name compatibility, 684
file resource forks, 683
shared printers on Windows, 690
Windows printers on Mac, 688
Telnet sessions, Telnet Host Service (UNIX), 677-678
UNIX, 672-673
    Berkeley "r" commands, 680-682
    CIFS (Common Internet File System) protocol, 673
    mangled line feed/carriage returns, 697
    NFS, 678-679
    Samba, 673-676
    SMB (Server Message Block) protocol, 673
    SUA (Subsystem for UNIX-Based Applications), 680
    Telnet sessions, 676-678
Windows 95, 670-672
Windows 98, 667, 670-672
Windows Me, 667, 670-672
Windows XP, 665
    installing LLDP responder for Windows XP, 667
    password protection and simple file sharing, 667-669
    TCP/IP as default network protocol, 666-667
Windows 2000, 665
    installing LLDP responder for Windows XP, 667
    password protection and simple file sharing, 667-669
    TCP/IP as default network protocol, 666-667
InterNIC website, Whois Database, 550
interrupt handlers, 829
intranet tools list, 609
Inverse DNS, 710

IP addresses
    computer assignments, 644-646
    DDNS (Dynamic Domain Name Services), Remote Desktop connections, 1335-1336
    fixed IP addresses
        assigning, 727
        configuring, 415-416
    Inverse DNS, 710
    LAN (Local Area Networks), Internet connection management, 705-709
    NAT (Network Address Translation), 706-709
    static IP addresses, 709, 1335
IPC$ folder, Windows 200x Server shared status, 749
ipconfig command
    DNS settings, 544-545
    function of, 544-545
    host name, 795
    Internet connections, troubleshooting, 529
    IP address ranges, 795
    LAN (Local Area Network) connections, testing, 537-539
    network configuration checks, 795-796
    network masks, 796
ipconfig/all command, 538-539
ipMonitor, LAN monitoring tool, 800
iPods versus PlaysForSure compatible devices, 272
IPP (Internet Printing Protocol), 762-764
IPSEC (Internet Protocol Security), 599, 1238
IPSentry, 800
IPv6 (Internet Protocol version 6), 28, 599
IR blasters, 382
IRQ (Interrupt Requests), 828-829
IR receivers, 382
IR signals, broadcasting television programs to TV, 381-383

ISA buses, 827
iSCSI Initiator, 891
ISDN (Integrated Services Digital Network), 395
    internal adapter installations, 404
    LAN Internet connections, 713
ISP (Internet Service Providers)
    accounts, configuring, 407-409
    choosing, 397-400
    dial-up process, troubleshooting, 420-421
    DNS service, 561
    domains, registering, 709
    frequent traveler options, 399-400
    mobile connections, 421-422
    news servers, 511
    selection criteria, 398-399
    services, ordering, 401
    static IP addresses, 709
    troubleshooting, 420-421

J

JavaScript controls, 445
joining
    domain networks via Windows 200x Server, 653-655
    existing wireless networks, 641-642
    hard disks via
        dynamic disk aggregation, 937-939
        mount points, 937-939
    networks, 612
    volumes (Disk Management), 936-937
    wireless networks in
        home offices, 1267-1269
        corporate environments, 1267
        public hot spots, 1270
        small offices, 1267-1269
        someone else's office, 1269-1270
JPEG file format, IE7 support, 435-436

JScript, 1114
junction points, 109-110
Junk E-Mail options, 1254
junk mail filtering, 19

K

Keep Printed Documents option (Printer Properties dialog), 217
Kerberos authentication, 610
kernel-mode drivers, 1018
Keyboard applet (Control Panel), 847
keyboards
　accessibility settings, 838-839
　Caps Lock key, altering location of, 924
　Ctrl key, altering location of, 924
　shortcuts
　　DVDs in Windows Media Center, 386
　　listing, Help and Support Center, 125
　　Remote Desktop, 1347-1349
keys, 1039
　encryption, 1174
　Registry
　　Access Control attributes, 1059-1060
　　adding, 1054
　　copy name function, 1055
　　deleting, 1055
　　editing, 1053-1055
　　meanings (Google), 1062
　　renaming, 1055
Keyspan 1394 FireWire laptop card, 345
keystrokes
　Alt+F4 (foreground window closure), 159
　Ctrl+F6 (open window cycling), 161
　Windows key+M (immediate desktop), 159

L

L2TP (Layer 2 Tunneling Protocol), 599
LAN (Local Area Networks), 394
　Alternate Configuration features, 1308
　backup software, installing, 656-658
　bridging, 658-659
　computer setup, security guidelines, 1225
　ICS (Internet Connection Sharing), 606, 703
　　broadband schemes, 718-719
　　dial-up schemes, 714-717
　Internet connections, 702
　　cable services, 705, 710-713, 724-726, 736
　　configuring, 713-721, 724-727
　　connection sharing routers, 703
　　DSL services, 710, 736
　　frame relays, 711
　　IP address management, 705-709
　　ISDN service, 713
　　overview, 703, 705
　　Remote Desktop, 709-710
　　routed services, 705, 726-727
　　shared modems, 736
　　shared routers, 719-721
　　speed requirements, 702-703
　　testing, 537-539
　　VPN, 709-710
　　wireless, 711-712
　IPP-capable printers, 763-764
　multiple connections, 1308
　network monitoring, 799-800
　peer-to-peer, 612
　physical media
　　HomePlug powerline, 597
　　HomePNA phoneline, 597
　　IEEE 802.11 (Wireless Ethernet), 596-597
　　NIC (Network Interface Cards), 593
　　UTP (Unshielded Twisted-Pair) cabling, 594-595
　　wired Ethernet networks, 593-594
　testing via ipconfig command, 537-539
laptop computers
　DualView feature, 1019
　extended view mode, 1020
　mirror mode, 1020
Last Known Good Configuration boot option, 973
Layer 2 Tunneling Protocol (L2TP), 599
Layout flyout menu, 184
LCD monitors
　blurry images, 927
　native resolution settings, 917
　refresh rates, 918
legacy program installations, troubleshooting, 1007
licenses (IIS), Windows Vista licensing restrictions, 558-559
Link Level Discovery Protocol. *See* LLDP (Link Level Discovery Protocol)
links, troubleshooting (IIS), 585
Links bar (IE7), 427-428
LinkSys Powerline EtherFast 10/100 Bridge, 622
Linux, 37
　internetworking, 672-673
　　Berkeley "r" commands, 680-682
　　NFS, 678-679
　　Samba, 673-676
　　SMB/CIFS protocol, 673
　　Telnet, 676-678
　Windows application compatibility, 37-38
　Windows Vista versus, 38-39
List view (Computer), 149

listing installed services via sc command, 1083-1084
listservs. *See* mailing lists
Live File System option (Windows Photo Gallery), 302
Live ID, 465-466
Live Search box (Internet Explorer 7), 425
live thumbnails, 13
LLDP (Link Level Discovery Protocol), 603, 665, 799
LLDP responder, Windows XP installations, 667
LMHash, 671
local account policies, configuring, 1228-1229
local area connections, checking network configurations, 797
local area network (LAN). *See* LAN (Local Area Networks)
local audit policies, configuring, 1229-1230
local password policies, configuring, 1228-1229
Local Policy Editor, 1227-1230
local printers
  connections
    FireWire, 208-209
    infrared port, 208-209
    parallel port, 208-209
    serial port, 208-212
  installing, 208-213
  missing drivers, searching, 212-213
  troubleshooting, 210-212
local security policies, configuring, 1227-1228
local user groups. *See* user groups
LOCALAPPDATA, 1086
localhost (IIS), 566
LocalTalk, 598
locking down. *See* securing
log files (IIS), 580
logins, 79
  at startup, disabling, 93-94
  logoff process, 105, 139, 155
  Remote Desktop, 1349
  Security Center, balloon notifications, 123
  Welcome screen, 123-124

LOGONSERVER, 1086
Longhorn (codename), 4
LPR and LPD Print Services, 602
LPR-based printers (UNIX), configuring on Windows networks, 764-765
luminosity (color), 905-906

M

Mac OS X
  applications
    lost file associations, 698
    running concurrently, 698
  Internetworking with, 685-687
    AFP (AppleTalk File Protocol), 683
    compatibility plans, 683-684
    files, data forks, 683
    file name compatibility, 684
    files, resource forks, 683
    Mac shared printers on Windows, 690
    Windows printers, 688
  printers
    AppleTalk protocol on Windows networks, 765
    Mac shared printers on Windows, 690
    Windows printers, 688
macros, benefits of, 161
mailing lists, 510
Malicious Software Removal Tool (MSRT), 19
malware
  avoiding, 1147-1148
  defending against, 1134
    antivirus software, 1136-1138
    automatic updates, 1142
    DEP (Data Execution Prevention), 1142-1144
    firewalls, 1142
    Internet Explorer 7 malware protection, 443-445, 1147
    service hardening, 1146

    UAC (User Account Control), 1144-1145
    Windows Defender, 1138-1139, 1141
    Windows Security Center, 1135-1136
  rootkits, 1134
  spyware, 1133-1134
  viruses, 1132-1133
  worms, 1133
Man In The Middle (MITM), 1264
Management Console plug-ins list, 1401-1402
management tools
  AutoPlay, 820-821
  Control panel, 804
    Administrative Tools, 872-873
    Category view, 805-820
    default display, 805
    Default Programs, 823-825
    Keyboard applet, 847
    Mouse applet, 847-850
    Performance Information and Tools applet, 850-856
    Regional and Language Options, 867
    shortcuts, 895-896
    System Properties, 868-872
    Task Scheduler, 881
    Visual Effects dialog, 890-891
    Windows SideShow, 872
  Date and Time applet, 821-823
  Device Manager, 825-827
  Ease of Access Center, 837-841
  game controllers, 846
  iSCSI Initiator, 891
  MMC (Microsoft Management Console), 874-875, 881
    Event Viewer, 876-879
    Services folder, 880
    Shared Folder node, 879
  Power Options icon, 860-861
  Programs and Features, 861-867

Reliability and Performance Monitor
  Data Collector Sets, 859
  Performance Monitor, 858
  Reliability Monitor, 858-859
  Resource Overview, 857
System Configuration utility, 881-883
System Diagnostics Report, 860
System Information, 889-890
System Tools folder, 892-895
Task Manager, 883-884
  Applications tab, 884-885
  Networking tab, 888-889
  Performance tab, 887-888
  Processes tab, 885-886
  Services tab, 887
  Users tab, 889
troubleshooting, 895
manual updates
  driver updates, 992-993
  Windows Update, 989
mapping
  network drives, net use command, 779-780
  shared folders
    to unused drive letters, 754-757
    without drive letters, 757
Marketplace (Windows), 143-144
master file table (MFT), NTFS pre-allocation to volumes, 944-945
Mastered option (Windows Photo Gallery), 302
Maxtor external 1394 FireWire hard drive, 345
media
  pools, managing devices (Removable Storage utility), 942-943
  sharing, 790
  updating information, 282-284
Media Center (Windows). See Windows Media Center

Media Center Extender, 370
media files
  album art, updating, 284-285
  deleting, 281-282
  media information, updating, 282-284
  organizing, 281-282
  sharing via home networking, 277-278
Media Player (Windows). See Windows Media Player
Meeting Space, 1315
  configuring, 1316-1318
  leaving meetings
    joining existing, 1319
    leaving, 1321
  sharing
    desktop views, 1319-1320
    documents, 1321
Melissa virus, 1133
memory
  addresses, 834-835
  DDR SDRAM modules (RAM), 1012
  IIS installation requirements, 560
  MS-DOS program settings, editing, 1100-1102
  RAM
    adding, 1012-1013
    DDR SDRAM modules, 1012
    maximum requirements, 1013
    SDRAM modules, 1012
    upgrading, 1010
  SDRAM modules (RAM), 1012
  troubleshooting, Windows Memory Diagnostic tool, 968-970
memory-mapped I/O, 833
metadata, 167
  editing, 15
  viewing, 182-184
MGI VideoWave, 345
Michelangelo virus, 1132
Microsoft Backup Utility, 616
Microsoft Client for Microsoft Networks, 642-644

Microsoft Downloads Site, 213
Microsoft HighMAT technology, 342
Microsoft Live ID, obtaining, 465-466
Microsoft Management Console (MMC), 874-875
  Event Viewer, 876-879
  Shared Folder node, 879-881
Microsoft Message Queue, 692
Microsoft SpyNet, 1141
Microsoft Technet website
  IIS security tools, 555
  Service Pack 2 (SP2) downloads, 995
Microsoft Technical Support, OS desupport dates, 122
Microsoft Typography website, 843
Microsoft Virtual PC, 74
MIME (Multipurpose Internet Mail Extensions), 557
  mappings, 573-574, 585
  message format (Windows Mail 7), 489
  web browser interpretation, 557
MIRA, 1357
mirror mode, laptop computers, 1020
mirroring
  RAID, 1011
  volumes, dynamic storage model (hard disks), 932
  websites, downloading software from, 442
missing
  files (offline folders), troubleshooting, 1309
  hard disks, troubleshooting, 956-957
  print jobs, troubleshooting, 229
  printers (Active Directory networks), troubleshooting, 781

MIT (Massachusetts Institute of Technology), Kerberos authentication, 610
MITM (Man In The Middle), 1264
mixed networking, updating older systems, 624
MMC (Microsoft Management Console), 874-875
  Event Viewer, 876-879
  Services folder, 880
  Shared Folder node, 879-881
mobile computing, 1280. *See also* Remote Desktop
  battery optimization, 1283-1286
  Internet connections, 421-422
  LAN (Local Area Networks), multiple connections, 1308
  Mobility Center, 1281-1282
  offline folders, 1301
    encrypting, 1306
    identifying, 1302
    making shared folders available to others, 1307
    managing, 1306
    synchronizing, 1305
    troubleshooting, 1309
    using offline, 1303-1304
  presentations, 1312-1315, 1328
  RAS dial-up networking, 1286
    callbacks, 1291
    configuring, 1288-1289
    email connections, 1295
    ending connections, 1296
    establishing connections, 1293-1294
    gateway settings, 1292
    incoming access, 1297-1300
    managing connections from multiple locations, 1292-1293
    monitoring connections, 1296
    properties tables, 1290-1291
    remote network resources, 1295
    routing issues, 1296-1297
  VPN (Virtual Private Networks), 1287
    callbacks, 1291
    configuring, 1288-1289
    email connections, 1295
    ending connections, 1296
    establishing connections, 1293-1294
    gateway settings, 1292
    incoming access, 1297-1300
    manually adding router information, 1309-1310
    monitoring connections, 1296
    properties tables, 1290-1291
    remote network resources, 1295
    routing issues, 1296-1297
    troubleshooting, 1308
Mobile PC view (Category view), 811
Mobility Center, 21
  Battery Status icon, 1281
  Brightness control, 1281
  External Display control, 1282
  External Display tile, 1314
  Power Options, 1283
  Presentation Settings, 1282, 1312-1313
  Screen Rotation control, 1282
  Sync Center, 1282
  Volume control, 1281
  Wireless Network icon, 1281
modems
  analog modems, 394-395
  cable connections, troubleshooting software configuration problems, 536-537
  cable modems, 396
  connectivity problems, diagnosing, 542-543
  dial-up process, troubleshooting, 420-421
  DSL connections, troubleshooting software configuration problems, 536-537
  hardware problems, diagnosing, 540-542
  installing, 401-406
  types, changing, 404
  wireless modems, 397, 406
Monitor and Adapter Properties dialog, 918-919
monitoring
  LAN (Local Area Networks), 799-800
  networks
    remote connections, 1296
    suspicious activities, 1221
  outgoing faxes, 315
  Windows Media Player folders, 271
monitors
  blank monitors, troubleshooting, 927
  CRT versus LCD, 917
  LCD
    blurry images, 927
    CRT versus, 917
    refresh rates, 918
  Monitor and Adapter Properties dialog, 918-919
  multiple monitors
    configuring, 917-918
    installing, 1019-1023
    troubleshooting, 1032-1033
  refresh rates, potential damage from, 918
  resolution, changing, 96
  screen flicker, reducing, 925
  Screen Rotation control (Mobility Center), 1282
  screen savers list, 1402
  slow motion, troubleshooting, 927
  window edges off screen, troubleshooting, 926
monospaced fonts, 843
Mosaic Web browser, 424
motherboards
  adapter cards, movement of, 1014
  RAID features, 1011
  RAM compatibility, 1013

mount points, joining hard disks, 937-939
mouse
  accessibility settings, 841
  double-click mode, 135
  Double-Click option, 927
  right-click context menus, 132
  single-click mode, 135
  Single-Click option, 927
  three-button mouse, autoscrolling, 924
Mouse applet (Control Panel), 847-850
mouse over action, online graphics (IE7), 436
movies
  assembling video clips into, 333-334
  AutoMovie, creating via, 343-344
  color correction, 347
  converting, 333-334
  editing
    nonlinear editing, 325
    Windows Movie Maker, 334-344
  effects, adding, 337
  filters, adding to, 337-338
  improving, 346-348
  Microsoft HighMAT technology (Windows Movie Maker), 342
  narration, adding, 338-339
  producing in Windows Movie Maker, 325-326
  saving in Windows Movie Maker, 340-343
  sharing over Web, 342
  titles, adding to, 339-340
  transitions, adding between clips, 336-337
  troubleshooting, 345-346
  Windows Movie Maker
    alternatives to, 345
    assembling video clips, 333-334
    audio tracks, 332
    AutoMovie, 343-344
    clip capture process, 325-332
    compatible file formats, 325-326
    converting clips to movies, 333-334
    digital still images, 332
    DV camcorder compatibility, 346
    editing in, 325, 334-345, 384
    effects, 337
    hardware requirements, 326
    launching, 327, 331
    Microsoft HighMAT technology, 342
    narration, 338-339
    organizing video clips, 332-333
    playback controls, 334
    producing movies in, 325-326
    saving in, 340-343
    titles, 339-340
    transitions, 336-337
    troubleshooting, 345-346
  Windows Photo Gallery
    adding to, 289
    organizing, 290
moving
  gadgets on Sidebar, 243-244
  program files, 129
MP3 files, 441, 526
MP3 players. *See* **portable media devices**
MP3 Pro format, 442
MP3.com website, 441
MPEG video file format, 438
MS-DOS, 1094
  ANSI.SYS, 1099
  applications
    advanced memory settings, 1100-1102
    garbage characters displays, 1127
    list of, 1399-1400
    too many files open error message, 1127
  AUTOEXEC.NT, 1096-1099
  CONFIG.NT, 1096-1098
  custom startup files, 1102
  DOSKEY, 1099
  editing advanced settings for DOS applications, 1100-1102
  environment
    ANSI.SYS issues, 1099
    AUTOEXEC.NT customization, 1096-1099
    CONFIG.NT customization, 1096-1099
    configuring for optimal program performance, 1092-1102
    DOSKEY issues, 1099
  history of Windows, 6
  ntvdm, 1095
  troubleshooting, 1127
  unavailable commands, 1102-1103
MSMQ (Microsoft Message Queuing), 692
MSN Media, streaming audio, 440
msodexnt, 1099
MSRT (Malicious Software Removal Tool), 19
multi-disc backups, finding files in, 1202
multi-part attachments, newsgroups, 524-525
multibooting Windows Vista, 66-70, 73
multiheaded video cards, 1023
multimedia. *See* movies; music; video
multimonitor video cards, 1019-1021
multiple email accounts (Windows Mail 7), checking, 520
multiple computers, enabling access on (Remote Desktop), 1342, 1346-1353
multiple home pages, 30
multiple hubs, connecting, 634-635
multiple Internet connections, managing, 419-420
multiple items, selecting, 181-182
multiple monitors
  configuring, 917-918
  DualView feature, 1019
  installing, 1019-1023
  primary displays, inability to select, 1032-1033

How can we make this index more useful? Email us at indexes@quepublishing.com

troubleshooting, 1032-1033
video cards, 1019-1021
multiple network adapters, installing, 627
Multipurpose Internet Mail Extensions (MIME). *See* **MIME (Multipurpose Internet Mail Extensions)**
music. *See also* **audio CDs/DVDs**
   CDs, burning to, 262
   copy protection, disabling, 262
   online stores, 269-270
   Windows Media Center, playing in, 378
   photos, adding to, 377
   playlists, creating, 279-280
   Windows Media Center, playing in, 378
Music folder, 149-150
My Computer
   applications, launching, 146
   files, Icons view, 149
My Documents (Start menu), 139
My Network Places (Start menu), 139
My Pictures (Start menu), 139

N

N-way autosensing hubs, 624
name servers. *See* **DNS service**
naming
   computers, 56
   networks
      files, 743-744
      printers, 743-744, 759
NAP (Network Access Protection), 20
narration, adding to movies/video, 338-339
NAT (Network Address Translation), 1300-1301
   devices, configuring, 1212, 1215-1216
   Internet Connection Sharing (NCS), 706-709
   VPN connections, enabling incoming calls, 1300-1301

National Center for Supercomputing Applications (NCSA), 424
National Public Radio (NPR), streaming audio, 439
navigation tools (IE7), 428
Neptune (codename), 8
net command, 779
.NET initiative, 604
net use command
   command-line management tools, 1081-1083
   drives, mapping, 779-780
NETLOGON folder, Windows 200x Server shared status, 748
Netmeeting. *See* **Windows Meeting Space**
netsh command, 1278
network adapters
   10/100BASE-T costs, 613
   configuration checks, 626-627
   high-speed connections, configuring, 411-416
   installing, 405-406, 625-627
   types of, 619
   wireless networks, 623
Network Address Translation (NAT). *See* **NAT (Network Address Translation)**
Network and Internet category (Category view), 808
Network and Sharing Center, 744-746, 789-790
network cards, 613
Network Connection Properties dialog, Networking tab, 1292
Network Diagnostics Framework dialog, 28, 790-791, 1275-1276
Network Discovery, 655, 790
Network Discovery Is Turned Off error message, 788
Network Explorer, 766
Network File Sharing (NFS), 602
Network File Systems (NFS). *See* **NFS (Network File Systems)**

Network Interface Cards (NIC). *See* **NIC (Network Interface Cards)**
Network Location Awareness API, 28
Network News Transport Protocol (NNTP), 509
Network Setup Wizard
   ICS (Internet Connection Sharing)
      broadband scheme configuration, 718-719
      dial-up scheme configuration, 714-717
      peer-to-peer networks, configuring, 642, 644-646
Network Troubleshooting Wizard, 790
Network window, 789
   network diagnostic functions, 788
   troubleshooting, 660
Networking tab (Task Manager), 888-889
networks, 27-28, 665
   Active Directory, 741
      access privileges, 608
      advanced search tool, 752
      computer searches, 750
      containers, 607-608
      distributed databases, 607
      DNS (Domain Name System) integration, 608
      file searches, 750-752
      folder searches, 750-752
      Group Policies, 607
      printer searches, 750
   adapters
      10/100BASE-T costs, 613
      existing, checking, 626-627
      high-speed connections, 411-416
      installing, 405-406, 625-627
      types of, 619
      wireless networks, 623
   Alternate Configuration features, 1308
   appliances, 664

NETWORKS

backups
  shares, 1153
  software installations, 656-658
  system media selections, 616
beneficial uses of, 590
bindings, 690-691
bridging, 658-659
cables
  10/100BASE-T Ethernet, 618-620
  1000Mbps Ethernet, 620
  cabling diagrams, 530
  Home Plug, 622
  HomePNA, 620-621
  IEEE 802.11g Wireless, 622-623
  physical challenges, 659
  selection criteria, 617-618
  updating older systems, 624
  UTP (Unshielded Twisted-Pair), 594-595
  wired Ethernet networks, 593-594
command-line utilities, administration of, 782-783
common uses of, 590
computer identification, configuring, 651-652
computer usage, managing via Computer Management utility, 778
connections, troubleshooting, 530
configuring manually, 642-644
corporate networks, features of, 39-40
costs of, 591
creating, overview of, 612
defenses, testing, 1219-1221
dial-up networking
  connecting without roaming profile, 1293-1294
  connection monitoring, 1296
  current connection location options, 1293
  disconnection, 1296

  effective use of resources, 1295
  email retrieval issues, 1295-1296
  multiple connection locations, 1292-1293
  RAS (Remote Access Services), 1286-1292
distributed applications interaction
  COM+, 604
  Peer-to-Peer networking service, 604
  RPC (Remote Procedure Calls), 603
domain networks, 740
  searching, 748
  workgroups versus, 742
drives, mapping via net use command, 779-780
files
  In Use by Another User error message, 781
  names, 743-744
  sharing, 602
folders
  offline, 767
  sharing, 747-748
  shortcuts, 767
grassroots networking, 661
home networks, sharing media files, 277-278
HomePlug wiring guidelines, 628
HomePNA wiring guidelines, 628
host files, 699-700
hubs, 593
  cost ranges, 613
  N-way autosensing, 624
  non-working lights, 659-660
  switching, 624
ICS (Internet Connection Sharing), 606, 625
installing, 50, 615
IntelliMirror, 609
Internet services and tools, 609
Internet-based file storage services, 754
intranet services and tools, 609
joining, 612

LAN (Local Area Networks)
  monitoring, 799-800
  multiple connections, 1308
location of, 649-650
managing, WSH (Windows Script Host), 1117-1118
missing computers, troubleshooting, 696
monitoring tools, 800
.NET software framework, 604
Network and Sharing Center, 744
  finding network shares, 745-746
  network map, 745
  sharing and discovery area, 745
  status area, 745
Network Explorer, 766
offline folders, 1301
  automatic caching options, 1307
  file/folder identification for use, 1302
  file/folder manual synchronization, 1306
  file/folder synchronization, 1305
  file/folder use guidelines, 1304
  inability to mark for availability, 1309
  marking shared folders, 1307
  typical uses, 1307
older networks, organization of, 767
online documentation, 767
optional components, installing, 691-694
outside access, enabling, 728-735
passwords, managing, 93
peer-to-peer networks, 642-646, 652-653, 740
performance, improving, 624
physical media
  HomePlug powerline, 597
  HomePNA phoneline, 597

NETWORKS

IEEE 802.11 (Wireless Ethernet), 596-597
NIC (Network Interface Cards), 593
UTP (Unshielded Twisted-Pair) cables, 594-595
wired Ethernet networks, 593-594
planning
  adequate capacities, 616
  tasks overview, 612-613
power issues, UPS (Uninterruptible Power Supplies), 617
printers, 208
  AppleTalk protocol, 765
  cabling, 616, 624-625
  extra driver installations, 772-773
  installing, 759-761, 766
  LPR/LPD protocol (UNIX), 764-765
  management privileges, 761-762
  names, 743-744, 759
  overview, 757-758
  permissions, setting, 773
  pooling, 776
  separator pages, 776-777
  sharing, 602, 771-775
  spool directory location, 775
  user tracking, 774-775
projectors, presentations over mobile networks, 1315
protocols
  AppleTalk, 598
  configuring, 646-649
  definition of, 598
  IPSEC (Internet Protocol Security), 599
  IPv6 (Internet Protocol Version 6), 599
  L2TP (Layer 2 Tunneling Protocol), 599
  LLDP (Link Layer Discovery Protocol), 603
  LocalTalk, 598
  NFS (Network File Sharing), 602

PPP (Point-to-Point Protocol), 598
PPPoE (Point-to-Point Protocol over Ethernet), 598
PPTP (Point-to-Point tunneling Protocol), 599
SSTP (Secure Socket Tunneling Protocol), 599
TKIP (Temporal Key Integrity Protocol), 1264
WEP (Wired Equivalent Privacy), 1264
WPA (Wi-Fi Protected Access), 599
WEP (Wired Equivalency Privacy), 598
Registry entries, setting all at once, 1066-1068
remote access
  connections, 605-606
  implementation, 625
Remote Assistance
  enabling, 1322
  features of, 1322
  requesting, 1323-1325
  responding to requests, 1326-1327
Remote Desktop
  connections, 1342-1347, 1351
  enabling, 1332-1333
  function of, 1331
  multiple computer access, 1342, 1346-1353
remote networks, 741
resources, 599, 778-779
roaming user profiles, 603
security, 655
  assessing personal risk, 1206-1207
  attacks, 1207-1218
  disaster planning, 1222-1224
  firewall guidelines, 1225-1226
  FTP folders, 1240
  holes, 1206-1207
  Kerberos authentication, 610

LAN guidelines, 1225
local policy configuration, 1227-1230
Network Discovery, 655
protected Web pages, viewing, 1241
router access to Telnet, 1241
scanning for vulnerabilities, 1242
sensitive web pages, visibility of, 1240
shared folders, visibility of, 1240
standalone guidelines, 1224-1225
updates, 1226-1227
Windows Firewall with Advanced Security, 1235-1240
Windows Firewall, 1230-1234
services, 600-602
  inability to block, 1241
  packet filtering, 1214-1215
share backups, 1153
shared disk drives, enabling, 753
shared folders, mapping
  drive letters, 754-757
  without drive letters, 757
shared resources, 748-749
small networks, hardware requirements, 613
SNMP (Simple Network Management Protocol), 694-696
storage, 664
suspicious activities, monitoring, 1221
switches, 593
troubleshooting, 696, 787
  cables, 794
  carriage returns, 697
  configuration checks, 790-791, 795-797
  connectivity checks, 797-798
  Device Manager, 793-794
  diagnostic questions, 786-787
  diagnostic tools, 788, 792-793

NEWSGROUPS

Event Viewer, 792-793
file sharing problems, 799
general categories, 787
line feeds, 697
Macintosh issues, 698
missing computers, 696
Network and Sharing Center, 789-790
Network Diagnostics, 790-791
Network window, 788-789
overview, 786
printer sharing problems, 799
questions to ask, 786-787
Windows Firewall, 791-792
types of, 591-592
UNC (Universal Naming Conventions), 743-744
UPnP (Universal Plug and Play), 606
VPN (Virtual Private Networks), 591, 605, 1287
  adding manual routing information, adding, 1309-1310
  callbacks, 1291
  configuring, 1288-1289
  connection process, 1287
  connection properties, 1292
  data encapsulation, 1287
  email connections, 1295
  enabling computer access, 1297, 1300-1301
  enabling incoming calls via NAT, 1300-1301
  ending connections, 1296
  establishing connections, 1293-1294
  gateway settings, 1292
  incoming access, 1297-1300
  manually adding router information, 1309-1310
  missing certificates, 1308
  monitoring connections, 1296
  properties tables, 1290-1291

  remote network resources, 1295
  routing issues, 1296-1297
  troubleshooting, 1308
  tunnels, 1287
Windows 200x Server
  joining, 653-655
  XP Pro versus, 613-614
Windows Firewall, 606
wireless networks
  ad hoc networks, 1262, 1271-1273
  adding manually, 1273
  automatic connections, 1272
  command-line tools with, 1277-1278
  domain, 1266
  encryption keys, 636
  encryption protocols, 636
  infrastructure networks, 1262
  installing, 635-642
  joining, 1267-1270
  manual additions, 1273
  manual connections, 1272
  overview, 1262
  preferred network order, 1271-1273
  private networks, 1266
  public networks, 1266
  security, 1262-1267
  SSID (Service Set Identifier), 636
  switching between, 1271
  troubleshooting, 1273-1276
wiring
  correct order in connectors, 630-631
  installing, 628-635
workgroups
  domains versus, 742
  searching, 748
  XP Pro versus Windows 200x Server, 613-614
New Connection Wizard, 406
New Driver option (Printer Properties dialog), 217
New Fax dialog, 313

New Hardware Wizard, 1014-1016
News Rover tool (newsgroups), 526
news servers
  accessing, 509-510
  feeds, censorship of, 511
  FreeNews.net, 511
  locating, 511
  missing connections, troubleshooting, 523
  missing newsgroups, troubleshooting, 521
  monthly cost, 511
  NNTP (Network News Transport Protocol), 509
  UUCP (Unix-to-Unix Copy Protocol), 509
  Web-based servers, 510-511
Newsbin Pro tool (newsgroups), 526
newsgroups
  accessing, 509-510
  account configuration (Windows Mail 7), 512-513
  Agent tool, 526
  attachments
    binaries, 524
    multi-part, 524-525
    multimedia, 525-526
  evolution of, 509, 524
  Google.com, 526
  locating via Windows Mail 7, 513-514
  mailing lists versus, 510
  messages
    managing (Windows Mail 7), 517-518
    marking new indicators, 522
    posting (Windows Mail 7), 515-517
    reading offline (Windows Mail 7), 518-519
    unavailability after synchronization, 522
  missing from news servers, troubleshooting, 521
  News Rover tool, 526
  Newsbin Pro tool, 526
  preferences, setting (IE7), 453

How can we make this index more useful? Email us at indexes@quepublishing.com

reading in Windows Mail 7, 513-517
subscribing to (Windows Mail 7), 514-515
Usenet, 10, 509-510
viruses, safety measures, 524
Xnews tool, 526
Newsguy.com Web-based news server, 511
newsreader tools, 526
NFS (Network File Systems), 602, 678-679
NIC (Network Interface Cards), 593, 619
noisy devices, quieting, 958-959
non-booting computers, troubleshooting BIOS settings, 1033
non-linear editing (movies/video), 325
non-listed printers, installing, 212-213
non-Plug and Play device, installing, 1014-1016
NorthernLight.com search engine, 464
notebook computers, troubleshooting Windows Vista installations, 55
Notepad, 253-254
Notification Area (taskbar), 139, 901
Novell NetWare, internetworking, 665
NTBackup files, restoring, 1203
NTFS (New Technology File Systems)
   alternative organizational strategies, 933-934
   FAT16/32 partitions, converting to (Convert utility), 947-948
   file permissions, 1192-1193
      advanced settings, 1195
      assigning to groups, 1198-1199
      auditing, 1196-1197
      inheritance of, 1194
      taking ownership of files, 1197
      viewing effective permissions, 1196

IIS installation requirements, 560
MFT (Master File Tables), pre-allocations to volumes, 944-945
printer permissions, 1199
volumes, property sheets, 934
ntvdm (Windows NT Virtual DOS Machine), 1095
numeric encryption, 1174

O

O'Hara, Shelley, 126
objectionable content, controlling (IE7), 459-461
Odyssey (codename), 8
offline
   browsing, Web pages (IE7), 432
   printing, 222
   working, Internet Explorer 7, 433-434
offline files, deleting (Disk Cleanup utility), 951
Offline Files Wizard, 1302
offline folders, 767, 1301
offline folders
   automatic caching options, 1307
   availability, inability to mark, 1309
   identifying for, 1302
   missing, 1309
   mobile computing, 1301-1304
      encrypting, 1306
      managing, 1306
      shared folders, making available to others, 1307
      troubleshooting, 1309
   sharing, marking for, 1307
   synchronizing, 1305-1306
   typical uses, 1307
   use guidelines, 1304
older programs. *See* legacy programs
On-Screen Keyboard (in Input Panel), 1362
online stores, Windows Media Player and, 269-270

opacity, changing in gadgets, 245
open door attacks, 1208
open windows, cycling through via Ctrl+F6, 161
OpenGL support, screen savers and, 911
OpenType font outline technology, 841-844
optimization
   environment variables, setting, 1085-1091
   program environments, configuring, 1092-1102
   temporary files, specifying location of, 1091-1092
   tips, system hardware, 1035
Optional Updates, 1422
orb (Start button), 14
organizing
   email, folder creation (Windows Mail 7), 500-506
   media files, 281-282
   photos in Windows Photo Gallery, 290
   video clips in Movie Maker, 332-333
Orientation option (Printer Properties dialog), 217
ornamental fonts, 843
OS (Operating Systems), 1087
   Microsoft desupport dates, 122
   networking with other operating systems, 664-665
OS environment variable, 1087
OS X (Macintosh), Internetworking, 685-687
OS/2, history of Windows, 7
out of office auto replies (email), Windows Mail 7, 503
Outlook 2000, 474-475
Outlook 2003, 474-475
Outlook 97, 474-475
Outlook 98, 474-475
Outlook Express. *See* Mail
outside network access, enabling, 728-735
ownership of files, taking, 1197

P

PA Server Monitor, 800
packets
  filtering
    blocking network services, 1214-1215
    routers, 1213-1215
  size, pinging, 551-552
  testing (ping tool), 545-546
packing files, 198-200
page file sizes, upgrading, 1010
Page Order option (Printer Properties dialog), 218
Page Protect option (Printer Properties dialog), 218
Paint, 253
parallel printer ports, 208-209
parental controls, 32, 90
  Internet Explorer 7, 459
  Windows Media Center, 385-386
partitions, separating applications and data, 933
passphrases, 1265
Password Protected Sharing, 672
passwords
  Administrator accounts, 115-116
  changing, 90
  cracking, 1207
  email accounts (Windows Mail 7), troubleshooting, 519
  forgotten passwords, recovering, 112-115
  IPP (Internet Printing Protocol), 762
  network passwords, managing, 93
  passwordless file sharing versus, 1217-1218
  policies, local settings, 1228-1229
  protection
    internetworking with Windows XP and 2000, 667-669
    sharing, 790
  recovery disks, 115
  reset disks, 91-92

Remote Desktop, 1333
  sharing, 790
PATA (Parallel ATA) disk drives, 1012
patch cables, wiring guidelines, 630
PATH environment variable, 1087, 1090-1091
PATHEXT environment variable, 1087
pathping (TCP/IP utility), 547-548
pausing print jobs, 224-225
PC Anywhere, 1331
PC emulation, 74
PC form factors, Windows Media Center, 365-366
PC Magazine website, 230
PCIe (PCI Express), 1019-1020
PCT (Private Communication Technology), IE7 encryption, 456
PDA (Personal Data Assistants), receiving email on, 255-256
PDF (Portable Document Format) documents, 468-469
peer-to-peer (P2P) networks, 28, 591, 604, 612, 740
  configuring, 642
    TCP/IP, 644-646
    Windows Firewall, 652-653
  folders, sharing, 769-771
  Internet Protocol (TCP/IP) Properties page, 645-646
  searching, 748
Pen and Input Devices menu, 1372-1373
pen computing, 1356-1358, 1374. *See also* Tablet PC, Tablet Vista
pen flicks, 1363-1364, 1373-1375
pending documents, viewing network printers, 761-762
PenPoint, 1356
performance
  hard disk defragmentation, 1012
  new features, 20-21

Performance Information and Tools applet (Control Panel), 856
  Adjust Indexing options, 855
  Visual Effects, 854-855
  Windows Defender, 853-854
  Windows Experience Index, 850-853
Performance Monitor (Reliability and Performance Monitor), 23, 858
Performance tab (Task Manager), 887-888
Perl scripts, site development, 585
permissions, 1192-1193
  advanced settings, 1195
  assigning to groups, 1198-1199
  auditing, 1196-1197
  for printers, 1199
  IIS installation, 567
  inheritance of, 1194
  printers, setting, 773
  restricted objects, assigning, 1203
  taking ownership of files, 1197
  viewing effective permissions, 1196
personal firewalls, 1142, 1216
Personalization dialog, 902
  color depth settings, 915-919
  color schemes, 903-905
  custom color creation, 905-906
  desktop icons, 908
  effects, 906
  resolution settings, 915-919
  screen savers, 909-911
  sounds, 911-914
  themes, 914-915
  wallpaper images, 906-908
personalizing screen settings, 95-96. *See also* customizing
phishing attacks, 1209
  AOHell, 1244
  avoiding, 1252

example of, 1244-1248
Gold Lock, 1249
identity management software, 1251-1252
overview, 1244
Phishing Filter, 1246-1248, 1256
preventing, 456
two-factor authentication, 1250-1251
two-way authentication, 1250
Phone and Modem Options (Control Panel), property settings, 541-542
phoneline networks (HomePNA)
    bridging via Ethernet, 658-659
    disadvantages of, 621
    monthly costs of, 621
    wiring guidelines, 628
Photo Gallery, 26, 288, 452
    adding photos to, 289, 294-295
    archiving photos in, 305-306
    burning photos to CD, 301-303
    cropping photos in, 296
    digital cameras, 292-295
    filtering photos in, 289
    fixing photos in, 295-296
    importing files to, 290
    Live File System option, 302
    Mastered option, 302
    organizing photos in, 290
    previewing photos in, 290
    printing photos from, 297-298, 303-304
    scanners, 290-292, 304-305
    sharing photos via, 299
photos. *See also* **images**
    burning to
        CDs, 300-301
        DVDs, 357-360
    Pictures folder, 288
    scanning, 317
    screen savers, setting as, 356-357
    Windows Explorer, burning photos to CD, 300-301

Windows Media Center printing from, 377
    slideshows, 376-377
Windows Photo Gallery, 288
    adding to, 289, 294-295
    adjusting color in, 296
    adjusting exposure in, 296
    archiving via, 305-306
    burning photos to CD, 301-303
    cropping in, 296
    filtering in, 289
    fixing in, 295-296
    organizing in, 290
    previewing in, 290
    printing from, 297-298, 303-304
    red eye fixes, 296
    sharing via, 299
physical paths (web servers), changing, 571
PICS (Platform for Internet Content Selection), site content ratings, 461
pictures. *See* **images; photos**
Pictures folder, 149-150, 288
ping command
    batch files, 1105
    function of, 545-546
    LAN connections, testing, 537-539
    larger packets, 551-552
    network connectivity, checking, 797-798
    packet testing, 545-546
pipes, Command Prompt environment, 1075-1078
PKZip utility, 953
plain text formatting (email), 489
planning networks, 612-613, 616
playback (sound), configuring, 914
playing
    audio CDs, 265-266
    DVDs, 265-266
        troubleshooting, 260-261
        Windows Media Center, 378-379
    hard disk media files, 266

music in Windows Media Center, 378
portable media players through car stereo, 285-286
playlists, creating, 279-280
PlaysForSure compatible devices, 272-274
plenum cables, 629
Plug and Play hardware devices, installing, 1013-1016
PNG image format, IE7 support, 436
Point-to-Point Protocol (PPP), 598
Point-to-Point Protocol over Ethernet (PPPoE), 412-413, 598
Point-to-Point Tunneling Protocol (PPTP), 599
points (fonts), 842
pooled printers, configuring, 776
POP (Post Office Protocol), 480
pop-up/under ads (IE7), 457-459
popd (Command Prompt environment), 1079-1080
port forwarding, Remote Desktop connections, 1338
    Internet Connection Sharing, 1339
    routers, 1340-1341, 1351-1352
portable entertainment systems, 365
portable media players
    MP3 audio files, 441
    PlaysForSure compatible devices versus iPods, 272
    playing through car stereo, 285-286
    synchronizing with Windows Media Player, 274-276
Portrait mode (Tablet PC), 1371
Ports tab (Printer Property sheets), 215
posting newsgroup messages (Windows Mail 7), 515-517

PRINTING/PRINTERS 1467

PostScript printers
  print-to-disk option, 227-228
  property settings, 216-218
power supplies
  UPS (Uninterruptible Power Supplies), 617
    configuring, 1027-1028
    installing, 1023-1026
    selecting, 1025-1026
    testing configuration, 1028
  usage profiles, 1284
Power Options (Mobility Center), 1283
  Change Settings Before Giving a Presentation, under Personalization setting, 1283
  Change What the Power Buttons Do setting, 1283
Power Options Advanced Setting dialog, 1286
Power Options icon, 860-861
Power Saver profile (power usage), 1284
power toys, 997-998
powerline networks (HomePlug)
  bridges, 622
  typical network setup, 622
  wiring guidelines, 628
PPC (Pocket PCs), receiving email on, 255-256
PPP (Point-to-Point Protocol), 598
PPPoE (Point-to-Point Protocol over Ethernet), 412-413, 598
PPTP (Point-to-Point Tunneling Protocol), 599
Practical Firewalls, 610
Practical Network Cabling, 610, 630
Practical Network Peer Networking, 610
preferred network order (wireless networks), 1271-1273
prefetching, 20
Presentation Settings feature (Mobility Center), 1282, 1312-1313

presentations
  Change Settings Before Giving a Presentation, under Personalization setting (Mobility Center, Power Options), 1283
  mobile computers, 1312-1315, 1328
Preview pane (Windows Mail 7), 185, 477
previewing
  faxes, 314
  fonts, 920
  photos in Windows Photo Gallery, 290
primary display adapters, inability to select multiple monitors, 1032-1033
primary partitions, 930-931
Print Directly to the Printer option (Printer Properties dialog), 218
Print Manager, 204
  files, dragging to, 221-222
  Printers folder, 205-206
Print Server Properties dialog, 774-775
Print Spooled Documents First option (Printer Properties dialog), 218
print$ folder, Windows 200x Server shared status, 749
print-to-disk option, PostScript printers, 227-228
Printer Memory option (Printer Properties dialog), 218
Printer Properties dialog, 217-219
Printers and Faxes (Start menu), 139
Printers applet (Control Panel), 205
Printers folder, 206
  printers
    management features, 205
    removing from, 219
  Windows 200x Server shared status, 749

printing/printers
  Active Directory networks
    missing, 781
    searching, 760
  background image controls (IE7), 462
  by dragging files to Print Manager, 221-222
  configuring, 206-208
  consumer review sites, 230
  cost-saving procedures, 230-231
  disk files, 227-228
  documents
    configuring, 225-226
    rendering, 204
  DOS application files, 222-223
  drivers, 204
  EMF (Enhanced Metafile Format), 204
  error messages, troubleshooting, 228
  extra drivers, installing, 772-773
  faxes, 228, 316
  garbled text, troubleshooting, 229
  ink usage, conserving, 231
  installing, 206-208
    COM(serial) ports, 210-212
    non-listed printers, 212-213
  IPP-capable printers, LAN connections, 763-764
  local printers
    FireWire connection, 208-209
    infrared port connection, 208-209
    installing, 208-213
    parallel port connection, 208-209
    serial port connection, 208-212
    troubleshooting, 210-213
  management of (Printers folder), 205
  mangled line feed/carriage returns, troubleshooting (UNIX), 697
  missing jobs, troubleshooting, 229

How can we make this index more useful? Email us at indexes@quepublishing.com

multiple default settings, 216
network printers, 208
  AppleTalk protocol, 765
  browsing, 760
  cabling issues, 616
  installing, 759-761, 766
  LPR/LPD protocol (UNIX), 764-765
  management privileges, 761-762
  names, 743-744
  naming, 759
  overview, 757-758
  permissions, 773
  spool directory location, 775
  user tracking, 774-775
no output, troubleshooting, 229
offline print option, 222
permissions, 1199
photos
  from Windows Media Center, 377
  Windows Photo Gallery, 297-298, 303-304
pooling, 776
preprinting checklist, 220-221
Print Manager, 204-206
print-to-disk option, 227-228
Printers folder
  management features, 205
  removing from, 219
  Windows 200x Server shared status, 749
print jobs, 204
  launching DOS applications, 222-223
  launching Windows applications, 220
  printing via Internet (IPP), 762-763
  sending to other printers, 781
  usage patterns, recording, 774-775
properties, changing, 214-219
Properties dialog options, 216-218

Property sheets, 215-216
purchasing, advice on, 230-231
queues, 204
  canceling all print jobs, 224
  deleting files from, 224
  managing, 223-224
  modifying document properties, 225
  offline jobs, 222
  pausing, 224-225
  restarting, 224-225
  resuming, 224-225
  UNIX queues from Windows, 675
  viewing, 223-225
removing, 219
searching for, 750
selecting by
  URL (IPP), 762-763
  website (IPP), 763
separator pages
  creating, 776-777
  predefined files, 777
  substitution sequence, 777
sharing printers, 771-775
  cable requirements, 624-625
  diagnosing problems, 799
  enabling, 790
  troubleshooting file and printer sharing problems, 799
  wireless networks, 1266-1267
spooling, 204
stalled jobs, sending to other printers, 781
troubleshooting, 228-230
UNIX queues from Windows (Samba), 675
UPS (Uninterruptible Power Supplies), 1026
Windows application files, 220-222
Windows printers from UNIX, 675-676
XPS (XML Paper Specification), 226-227

Printing Defaults option (Printer Properties dialog), 218-219
privacy preferences, setting (IE7), 454-455
Private Communication Technology (PCT), IE7 encryption, 456
private wireless networks, 1266
privileges. *See also* **permissions**
  elevated privileges, 85-86
  Registry security controls, 1063
  UAC (User Account Control), 85
Problem Reports and Solutions applet, 979-981
problems. *See* **troubleshooting**
Processes tab (Task Manager), 885-886
Product Activation, 70-72
productivity, 29-30
profiles
  dial-up networks, connecting without, 1293-1294
  roaming profiles, 603, 741, 1293-1294
  scan profiles, 318-319
  user profiles, 79
    backups, 1154
    changing settings, 93
    default profile configuration, 116-117
    directory structure, 105-111
Program Compatibility Wizard, 977-979, 1002-1003
PROGRAMDATA, 1087
PROGRAMFILES, 1087
Programs and Features applet, 861-867, 1007
progress bar, downloading software, 443
projectors, television programs
  broadcasting to, 381-383
  viewing via Windows Media Center, 380
PROMPT environment variable, 1087

Properties dialog, 132
  HP-compatible printer options, 216-218
  PostScript printer options, 216-218
property sheets, 133, 214-216
  Advanced tab, 216
  changing drivers, 214-216
  Color Management tab, 216
  Device Settings tab, 216
  General tab, 215
  multiple default settings, 216
  Ports tab, 215
  Security tab, 216
  Sharing tab, 215
  Utilities tab, 216
protected Web pages, viewing, 1241
PUBLIC, 1087
Public Folder Sharing feature, 769-771
public wireless networks, 1266
Published folder, Windows 200x Server shared status, 749
publishing
  calendars, 249-250
  shared folders, Active Directory, 751-752
  software, Authenticode verification, 444
  website content via FTP Server, 576-577
punchdown blocks, network wiring installations, 632
purchasing
  printers, advice on, 230-231
  routers, 709
pushd, Command Prompt environment, 1079-1080

Q

QoS Packet Scheduler, 642-644
queues (printers), 204
  deleting files from, 224
  managing, 223-224
  pausing, 224-225
  print jobs, canceling, 224
  restarting, 224-225
  resuming, 224-225
Quick Launch Bar, 139
  enabling, 96-97
  item capacity, 160
  launching applications, 145
  Show Desktop icon, 149
  Windows Explorer shortcut, 136
QuickTime Player, 440
quieting noisy systems, 958-959
quoting filenames with spaces, Command Prompt environment, 1072-1073

R

RAID (Redundant Array of Independent Disks), 930
  arrays, 1181-1182
  dynamic disk storage, 942
  mirroring, 1011
  striping, 1011
RAID 0, 932, 1182
RAID 1, 932, 1182
RAID 5, 932, 1181
RAM (Random Access Memory)
  adding, 1012-1013
  available technologies, 1012
  compatibility with motherboard, 1013
  cost fluctuations, 1012
  DDR SDRAM modules, 1012
  requirements, 1012-1013
  minimum size, 1010
  SDRAM modules, 1012
  starting addresses, 834-835
  upgrading, 1010
RAS (Remote Access Service), dial-up networks, 605, 1286
  callbacks, 1291
  configuring, 1288-1289
  connections
    email connections, 1295
    ending, 1296
    establishing, 1293-1294
    managing from multiple locations, 1292-1293
    monitoring, 1296
  gateway settings, 1292
  incoming access, 1297-1300
  properties tables, 1290-1291
  remote network resources, 1295
  routing issues, 1296-1297
raw spooling, 204
read attribute (CGI scripts), 558
ReadyBoost, 20
ReadyDrive, 21
RealPlayer, downloading/installing, 440
receipt requests, messages (Windows Mail 7), 488
receiving faxes, 310, 316
Recent Documents (Start menu), 139
Recommended Updates, 994
recording
  narration for movie clips (Windows Movie Maker), 338-339
  sound, 914
  television programs
    converting to DivX files, 388-389
    disk storage requirements, 374-376
    editing with Windows Movie Maker, 384
    Windows Media Center, 373
recovering. *See also* **restoring**
  BitLocker encrypted drives, 1187
  forgotten passwords, 112-115
recovery certificate backups, 1179-1181
Recycle Bin, 125
  backups, 1154
  configuring, 925
  customizing, 127
  emptying, 128
  files
    deleting (Disk Cleanup utility), 951
    restoring, 127-128
  storage capacity, 127

red eye (photos), fixing in Windows Photo Gallery, 296
redir, 1099
redirection
    Command Prompt environment, 1075-1078
    web servers, 556
Redundant Array of Independent Disks (RAID). See RAID (Redundant Array of Independent Disks)
reflection (Registry), 1045
refresh key (F5), 161
refresh rates (monitors), 918
REG files (Registry), 1066-1068
Regedit utility (Registry editor)
    data types, 1051
    other user computers, editing, 1057-1058
    Registry
        adding keys, 1054
        backups creation, 1047-1048
        deleting keys, 1055
        editing keys, 1053-1055
        entries, searching, 1051-1052
        key copy name functions, 1055
        key value additions, 1053
        key value changes, 1054
        key vale deletions, 1054
        renaming keys, 1055
        viewing, 1050-1051
    Registry restoration, 1049
    remote computers, editing, 1056-1057
    startup repair with, 970-971
    supported data types, 1051
Regional and Language Options (Control Panel), 867
registering domain names, 561
Registrar Registry Manager tool, 1061

Registry
    associations, 1038
    backups
        Regedit utility, 1047-1048
        system restore, 1047
        third-party utilities, 1046-1047
    errant startup programs, removing, 1064-1066
    exporting, 970
    file corruption, signs of, 1063
    function of, 1038
    hives, 1039-1040, 1059
    HKEY_CLASSES_ROOT keys, 1040-1042
    HKEY_CURRENT_CONFIG keys, 1039-1041
    HKEY_CURRENT_USER keys, 1041-1043
    HKEY_LOCAL_MACHINE keys, 1039-1042
    HKEY_USERS keys, 1039-1042
    keys, meanings of (Google), 1062
    mass entries, setting across networks, 1066-1068
    modification, dangers of, 1038
    organization of, 1039
    privileges, security controls, 1063
    recovery process, 1063-1064
    reflection, 1045
    Registrar Registry Manager, 1061
    Registry Toolkit, 1061
    restoring, 1046-1049
    retrieving entries from other Windows installations, 1059
    security attributes, editing, 1059-1060
    troubleshooting, 1066
    TweakVI, 1062
    virtual registries, 1004-1005, 1044
    website resources, 1062
Registry Editor. See Regedit
REG_BINARY data type, 1051

REG_DWORD data type, 1051
REG_EXPAND_SZ data type, 1051
REG_MULTI_SZ data type, 1051
REG_SZ data type, 1051
reinstalling
    uninstalled updates, troubleshooting, 1006
    Windows Vista for startup repair, 975-976
Reliability and Performance Monitor, 22, 857-859
remote access, network implementation, 625
Remote Access Service (RAS). See RAS (Remote Access Service)
Remote Assistance
    enabling, 1322
    features, 1322
    remote client access, 606
    requesting, 1323-1325
    responding to requests, 1326-1327
remote computing, 1280
    battery optimization, 1283-1286
    LAN (Local Area Networks), multiple connections, 1308
    Mobility Center, 1281-1282
    offline folders, 1301
        encrypting, 1306
        identifying, 1302
        making shared folders available, 1307
        managing, 1306
        synchronizing, 1305
        troubleshooting, 1309
        using offline, 1303-1304
    RAS dial-up networking, 1286
        callbacks, 1291
        configuring, 1288-1289
        email connections, 1295
        ending connections, 1296
        establishing connections, 1293-1294
        gateway settings, 1292
        incoming access, 1297-1300

managing connections
   from multiple locations,
   1292-1293
monitoring connections,
   1296
properties tables,
   1290-1291
remote network
   resources, 1295
routing issues,
   1296-1297
Registry entries, editing,
   1056-1057
VPN (Virtual Private
   Networks), 1287
   callbacks, 1291
   configuring, 1288-1289
   email connections, 1295
   ending connections, 1296
   establishing connections,
      1293-1294
   gateway settings, 1292
   incoming access,
      1297-1300
   manually adding router
      information, 1309-1310
   monitoring connections,
      1296
   properties tables,
      1290-1291
   remote network
      resources, 1295
   routing issues,
      1296-1297
   troubleshooting, 1308
Remote Desktop. *See also*
mobile computing
   availability of, 1331
   Client, accessing, 1342,
      1346-1349
   Connection dialog, 1342,
      1346-1349
   connections
      DDNS, 1335-1336
      disconnecting, 1349
      DSL, 1334
      establishing, 1333
      Internet Connection
         Sharing, 1337-1339
      networks, 1342-1347,
         1351
      port forwarding,
         1338-1341, 1351-1352

properties table, 1343
reasons for changing,
   1344-1345
routers, 1336
static IP addresses, 1335
troubleshooting, 1350
VPN, 1351
enabling, 1332-1333
function of, 1331
keyboard shortcuts,
   1347-1349
LAN Internet connections,
   709-710
logins, 1349-1351
multiple computer access,
   1342, 1346-1349,
   1351-1353
passwords, 1333
properties, 1346
remote client access, 605
testing, 1333
web-based client configuration, 1349
remote networks, 741
   connections
      disconnect status, 1296
      modems, 605
      monitoring, 1296
   dial-in access, enabling,
      1297, 1300
   effective use of resources,
      1295
   email, retrieval of,
      1295-1296
   Remote Assistance, 606
   Remote Desktop, 605
   Terminal Services, 605
   VPN access, enabling, 1297,
      1300
   Windows Meeting Space,
      606
Remote Procedure Calls
(RPC), 603
Remote Settings option
(System Properties), 869
remote workstations, 591
removable media
   backups, 1155-1156
   USB flash drives, security,
      1199-1200
Removable Storage utility,
media pools, 942-943
residential gateways (ICS),
706-709

resizing
   desktop images, 908
   online graphics (IE7), 436
   Taskbar, 901
resolution
   desktop images, 908
   GUI display properties,
      configuring, 915-919
   monitors, changing, 96
   native settings, 917
   slow motion, troubleshoot-
      ing, 927
   window edges off screen,
      troubleshooting, 926
   Windows Fax and Scan, 318
Resolution option (Printer
Properties dialog), 218
resource forks (Macintosh),
683
Resource Overview
(Reliability and
Performance Monitor), 857
Restart Manager, 21
restarting print jobs, 224-225
restoring. *See also* **recovering**
   Complete PC backups, 1172
   default firewall settings,
      1234
   disaster planning proce-
      dures, 1222-1223
   files
      backups, 1157-1160
      encrypted files, 1181
      Recycle Bin, 127
   folder backups, 1157-1160
   System Recovery Options
      menu backups, 983-984
   from Windows Complete
      PC Restore tool, 967-968
   NTBackup files, 1203
   previous versions of files,
      1190-1191
   Registry, 1046-1048
      from restore point, 1049
      problem diagnosis,
         1063-1064
      via Regedit utility, 1049
   restore points
      creating, 965-966
      deleting (Disk Cleanup
         utility), 951
      restoring from, 966-967,
         1049

restricting
  access controls, 1218
  permission assignments, 1203
resuming print jobs, 224-225
reverse tracert tool, route testing, 550
Review Fax Status window, 316
RFM (Reduced Functionality Mode), 1031
right-clicking
  context menus, 132-135
  manipulating objects, 180
  shortcuts, 160
  stylus pen, 1362
ripping audio CDs/DVDs, 266-268
RJ-45 connectors, 593
roaming user profiles
  domain networks, 741
  remote networks, connecting without, 1293-1294
  Vista networking, 603
root folders, sharing disk drives, 753
rootkits, 1134
routed services, 705, 726-727
routers
  blockages, checking (tracert tool), 546-547
  cost, 620
  DMZ host forwarding, 734-735
  external routers versus ICS (Internet Connection Sharing), 708
  filters, 726-727
  locking down, 1216
  network protection measures, 726
  packet filtering, 1213-1215
  purchasing advice, 709
  Remote Desktop connections, 1336, 1340-1341, 1351-1352
  shared routers
    broadband configuration, 719-721
    dial-up configuration, 719-721
    UPnP (Universal Plug and Play), 722-723

TCP Services, forwarding, 733-734
Telnet access, preventing, 1241
traffic tests, checking (pathping tool), 547-548
UDP Services, forwarding, 733-734
VPN (Virtual Private Networks)
  connections, 1296-1297
  manual additions, 1309-1310
  wireless networks, 623
routing tables, management of (route tool), 548-549
Roxio.com website, 345
RPC (Remote Procedure Calls), 603
RSS feeds, 30
rules (firewalls), creating, 1238-1240
Run (Start menu), 139

S

Safe Mode boot option, 972
Safe Mode with Command Prompt boot option, 973
Safe Mode with Networking boot option, 972
Safe Senders list, 1254-1255
Samba
  client tools, 673-674
  downloading, 673
  features, 673
  Internetworking with UNIX and Linux, 673
  printing to
    UNIX queues from Windows, 675
    Windows printers from UNIX, 675-676
  server tools, 674-676
sans-serif fonts, 842
SATA drives, 934, 1012
satellite dishes, 397
satellite modems, 406
satellite service, Internet access, 397
saturation (color), 905-906

saving
  files on desktop, 132-134
  movies in Windows Movie Maker, 340-343
  Web pages, later viewing option (IE7), 434-435
  Windows Sound Recorder files, 350-351
sc command, command-line management tools, 1083-1084
sc queryex, 1083-1084
Scan dialog, 316
Scan Profiles dialog, 319
scanner service (Windows Fax and Scan), 25
  configuring, 316
  emailing scans, 319
  faxing scans, 319
  hardware and software requirements, 308-309
  manipulating scanned images, 319
  overview, 308-309
  scan profiles, 318-319
  scanning photos, 317
  scanning slides and transparencies, 322
  troubleshooting, 320-322
scanners, Windows Photo Gallery, 290-292, 304-305
scanning
  networks for vulnerabilities, 1242
  photos, 317
Scheduled Tasks utility, 749, 1124-1125
Scratch-out gesture, 1363-1364
screens (monitors)
  flicker, reducing, 925
  personalizing settings, 95-96
  rotation, 1282, 1374
  screen savers
    changing, 96
    configuring GUI display properties, 909-911
    creating from photos, 356-357
    list of, 1402
    SETI@home Project, 909-910
script attribute (CGI scripts), 558

scripts
    ASP, 586
    dangers of, 586
    filename extensions, 1114
    IIS (Internet Information Services), 573
    Perl, 585
    WSH (Windows Script Host), 1114-1117
SCSI hard disks, 1011
SDRAM modules (RAM), 1012
Search command (Start menu), 146
Search Companion (IE7), 462-464
search engines, 99, 464
Search for Extraterrestrial Intelligence (SETI), screen saver project, 909-910
Search tool (Start menu), 202
searches, 14-15
    Active Directory
        advanced options, 752
        networks, 750-752
        printers, 750, 760
    device drivers, 1017
    domain networks, 748
    IE7 (Internet Explorer 7) options, 462
    printers
        Active Directory, 750, 760
        drivers, 212-213
    Registry, Regedit utility, 1051-1052
    Search pane, 195-196
    stacking, 197-198
    Start menu, 82
    troubleshooting, 201-202
    while typing, 192-195
    Windows Media Player, 263-265
    workgroup networks, 748
secondary display adapters, multiple monitor installations, 1021-1022
secure email (Windows Mail 7), sending/reading, 490-491
Secure Online Key Backup feature (Ultimate Extras), 997

Secure Socket Tunneling Protocol (SSTP), 599
Secure Sockets Layer (SSL), IE7 encryption, 456
security, 18-20
    access controls, restricting, 1218
    bulletins, subscribing to, 1211
    cable services, LAN Internet connections, 712-713
    corporate networks, ban on personal websites, 555
    data security, 23-24
    encryption
        BitLocker, 1182-1190, 1202
        EFS (Encrypted File Systems), 1173-1181, 1202
        file encryption certificates, managing, 93
        Internet Explorer 7, 456
        IPP (Internet Printing Protocol), 762
        keys, 1174
        numeric encryption, 1174
        offline folders (mobile computing), 1306
        wireless networks, 636
    files, 200-201
    firewalls
        configuring, 1212-1213
        personal firewalls, 1216
        Windows Firewall, 791-792
    FTP Server configuration, 575-576
    hackers, 1132
    IIS (Internet Information Services)
        automatic updates, 582
        bug fixes, 582
        file systems, 583
        level of risk, 555
        tools, 555
    Internet Explorer 7
        add-on crash detection, 448
        add-on management, 447-448

digital certificates, 446
hacker targeting, 464
software download protections, 445-447
malware
    avoiding, 1147-1148
    defending against, 1134-1147
    overview, 1132
    rootkits, 1134
    spyware, 1133-1134
    viruses, 1132-1133
    worms, 1133
Microsoft E-Mail Updates Service, 1226
NAT devices, configuring, 1212, 1215-1216
networks, 655
    active defenses, 1212-1218
    assessing personal risk, 1206-1207
    attacks, 1207-1218
    disaster planning, 1222-1224
    firewall guidelines, 1225-1226
    FTP folders, 1240
    holes, 1206-1207
    Kerberos authentication, 610
    LAN guidelines, 1225
    local policy configuration, 1227-1230
    monitoring suspicious activities, 1221
    Network Discovery, 655
    protected Web pages, 1241
    routers, 1216, 1241
    scanning for vulnerabilities, 1242
    sensitive web pages, visibility of, 1240
    shared folders, 1240
    standalone guidelines, 1224-1225
    Telnet, 1241
    testing defenses, 1219-1221
    updates, 1226-1227

SECURITY

Windows Firewall with Advanced Security, 1235-1240
Windows Firewall, 1230-1234
offline folders (mobile computing), 1306
packet filtering, 1213
permissions, 1192-1193
    advanced settings, 1195
    assigning to groups, 1198-1199
    auditing, 1196-1197
    for printers, 1199
    inheritance of, 1194
    taking ownership of files, 1197
    viewing effective permissions, 1196
phishing
    AOHell, 1244
    avoiding, 1252
    example, 1244-1248
    Gold Lock, 1249
    identity management software, 1251-1252
    overview, 1244
    Phishing Filter, 1246-1248
    two-factor authentication, 1250-1251
    two-way authentication, 1250
preferences, setting (IE7), 453-455
RAID arrays, 1181-1182
RAS (Remote Access Service), 1297, 1300
routers
    locking down, 1216
    network protection measures, 726
    packet filtering, 1213-1215
scripts, dangers of, 586
Service Packs, 994
USB flash drives, 1199-1200
UAC (User Account Control), 84-87
user groups, creating, 112-113
website resources, 1226, 1240

Windows Firewall, 606, 652-653
Windows Mail 7, 496-498
wireless networks, 1262
    file and printer sharing, 1266-1267
    MITM (Man In The Middle), 1264
    security keys, 1264-1266
    snooping, 1263
Security category (Category view), 808
Security Center, balloon notifications, 123
Security tab, Printer Property sheets, 216
Select Recipients dialog, 313
selecting
    bit rates for audio CDs/DVDs, 268
    file formats for audio CDs/DVDs, 268
    multiple items, 181-182
    online music stores, 269-270
    Tablet PC, 1360
    television programs in Windows Media Center, 372
    UPS (Uninterruptible Power Supplies), 1025-1026
    Windows Vista Premium Ready PC, 48
sender information, configuring (Windows Fax and Scan), 310
sending
    attachments (Windows Mail 7), 485
    email (Windows Mail 7), 484
    faxes, 228, 313-315
Separator File option (Printer Properties dialog), 218
separator pages, 776-777
serial (COM) ports, printer installations, 210-212
Serial ATA hard disks, 1011
serial printer ports, 208-212
serif fonts, 842
Server Message Block protocol (SMB), 673

server-side scripts
    attributes of, 558
    enabling, 573
Servers Alive LAN monitoring tool, 800
service hardening, 19, 1146
service packs
    checking for latest versions, 995
    Critical Updates, 994
    cumulative nature of, 994
    Hotfixes, 994
    installing, 994-996
    Service Pack 2 (SP2), 496, 995-996
    Service Pack-1 (SP-1), 1423-1428
    types of updates in, 994
service recovery, 22
Services dialog (MMC), 880
Services tab (Task Manager), 887
Set Associations option (Control Panel), 824
Set Program Access and Computer Defaults option (Control Panel), 825
set statements, batch file programming, 1107-1108
SETBLASTER, 1099
SETI@home Project website, screen saver/parallel processing project, 909-910
setting up. *See* configuring
setup log files, deleting (Disk Cleanup utility), 951
shadow copies. *See* volume shadow copies
Shared Documents folder, 747-748
Shared Folder node (MMC), 879-881
sharing
    desktop views in Meeting Space, 1319-1320
    disk drives, enabling, 753
    documents in Meeting Space, 1321
    enabling, 790
    files, 742
        file names, 743
        media files via home networking, 277-278

SOFTWARE | **1475**

Network and Sharing Center, 744-746
troubleshooting, 799
UNC (Universal Naming Convention), 743-744
folders, 747-748, 768
　mapping drive letters, 754-757
　mapping without drive letters, 757
　offline folders (mobile computing), 1307
　organization of, 767
　passwords versus passwordless file sharing, 1217-1218
　publishing (Active Directory), 751-752
　Shared Documents folder, 747-748
　Shared Folder node (MMC), 879-881
　visibility of, 1240
　Windows 200x Server, 748-749
　workgroup networks, 769-771
modems, inability to access on LAN (Local Area Networks), 736
movies over Web, 342
over wireless networks, 1266-1267
photos via Windows Photo Gallery, 299
printers, 771-775
　cabling requirements, 624-625
　troubleshooting, 799
routers
　broadband connections, 719-721
　dial-up connections, 719-721
　outside network access, 732-735
　UPnP (Universal Plug and Play), 722-723
Sharing tab, Printer Property sheets, 215

shortcuts
　alias designation, 132
　Control Panel applets, creating, 895-896
　desktop, creating for, 131-132
　folders, creating for, 767
　icons, 129-130
　right-click, 160
　settings alteration, 129
　troubleshooting, 157-158
　Windows Explorer, creating for, 136
Show Desktop icon (Quick Launch Bar), 149
shuffling playback in Windows Media Player, 266
shutdown command, command-line management tools, 1085
shutdown process
　options for, 104-105
shutdowns, 154
　forced shutdowns, 158
　Hibernate option, 155-156
　Log Off option, 155
　process of, 104-105
　Sleep, 155-156
　Switch User, 155
side-by-side DLL (Dynamic Link Libraries), 1003
side-by-side installs, 1003-1004
Sidebar, 16-17, 234-235
　gadgets
　　adding, 238-239
　　adding multiple times, 244
　　configuring, 242-243
　　downloading, 239-241
　　moving, 243-244
　　opacity, 245
　　removing, 245-246
　　troubleshooting, 254
　　viewing, 245
　hiding, 241-242
　running, 235-238
SideShow (Control Panel), 872
signatures
　digital certificates, 490
　email (Windows Mail 7), 487

SIIG 1394 FireWire laptop card, 345
simple volumes, dynamic storage model (hard disks), 931
single-click mode (mouse), 135
Single-Click mouse option, 927
skipping commercials, 374
slate Tablet PC, 1358, 1361
Sleep button, 104
Sleep mode, 21, 155-156
slides
　faxing or scanning, 322
　slideshows, 355-356, 376-377
small networks
　hardware requirements, 613
　wireless networks, 1267-1269
small screen fonts, troubleshooting, 928
SMB (Server Message Block) protocol, 673
Smith, David L., 1133
SMTP (Simple Mail Transfer Protocol), 480
SMTP server, IIS settings, 574-575
Snipping Tool, 1367-1369
SNMP (Simple Network Management Protocol)
　installing, 694-696
　LAN monitoring, 799
　security risks, 695
social engineering, 1208
software
　antivirus software, 1136-1138
　compatibility, Program Compatibility Wizard, 1002-1003
　compatibility mode, enabling, 130
　downloading, 442
　　add-on crash detection (IE7), 448
　　add-on management (IE7), 447-448
　　digital certificates (IE7), 446
　　drive-by (IE7), 445-446

How can we make this index more useful? Email us at indexes@quepublishing.com

from mirror sites, 442
invalid signatures (IE7), 447
progress bar, 443
version updates, 443
virus scanning, 443
ZIP compression, 443
firewalls, 1142
identity management software, 1251-1252
installing
  CD installations, 998
  DVD installations, 998
  Internet downloads, 999
  side-by-side installations, 1003-1004
  troubleshooting, 1006-1007
  viewing installed software, 999-1000
Internet configuration problems
  dial-up problems, 535-536
  LAN problems, 537-539
  modem problems, 536-537
  troubleshooting, 535-539
malware
  avoiding, 1147-1148
  defending against, 1134-1147
  overview, 1132
  rootkits, 1134
  spyware, 1133-1134
  viruses, 1132-1133
  worms, 1133
uninstalling, 1000-1002, 1007
updates, 994
Windows Defender, 1138-1139, 1141
Software Protection Platform. *See* **SPP**
sound
  accessibility settings, 839-840
  CDs/DVDs
    bit rates, 268
    file format selection, 268
    playing, 265-266
    ripping, 266-268
  events, associating with, 911-913

Internet Explorer 7
  MP3s, downloads (Windows Media Player), 441-442
  streaming (Windows Media Player), 439-440
  Web elements, 436-438
MP3 files
  copyright controversies, 441
  downloading (Windows Media Player), 441-442
  MP3 Pro format, 442
  MP3.com website, 441
  portable players, 441
  streaming audio, 439-440
playback, 914
recording, 914
Volume Control settings, 351-353, 360
Windows Movie Maker, exporting to, 332
Windows Sound Recorder, 350-351
SP-1 (Service Pack-1)
  installing, 1424-1427
  testing, 1423
  uninstalling, 1428
  Vista changes to, 1423-1424
SP2 (Service Pack), 496, 995-996
spam
  avoiding, 1256-1257
  CAUCE (Coalition Against Unsolicited Commercial Email), 508-509
  filtering, 1254
  international filtering, 1255-1256
  legal measures, 508-509
  overview, 1252-1253
  Phishing Filter, 1256
  protecting email addresses from, 1253-1254
  reporting, 1257-1258
  Safe Senders list, 1254-1255
  Windows Mail 7 limitation features, 496-498
spanned volumes
  dynamic storage model (hard disks), 931
  hard disks, creating (Disk Management utility), 940-941

speakers, Volume Control settings, 351-353, 360
special characters, Command Prompt environment, 1077
special effects, adding to clips (Windows Movie Maker), 336-337
speech recognition, 18, 150-153
Speed Check tool, Internet transfer speed monitor, 549
spool directories, 775
spooling documents (printers), 204
SPP (Software Protection Platform), 1028-1030
SpyNet, 1141
spyware
  overview, 1133-1134
  protecting against with Windows Defender, 1138-1141
SQL Slammer worm, 1133
SRT (Startup Repair Tool), 22, 963-964
SSID (Service Set Identifiers), wireless network setup, 636
SSL (Secure Sockets Layer), IE7 encryption, 456
SSTP (Secure Socket Tunneling Protocol), 599
stacking searches, 197-198
Standard Ethernet, 594
Standard user accounts, 88-90
Standby mode, 21
Start button
  opening Start menu, 81
  orb, 14
  programs, running from, 147
Start menu, 15, 81-82
  columns, dual arrangement, 138
  Control Panel, 139
  customizing, 98, 898-900
  default items, 138
  errant programs, eliminating, 1064-1066
  fly-open menus, 924
  Help and Support, 139
  Help and Support Center, 153-154

icons, 127
Log Off, 139
My Documents, 139
My Network Places, 139
My Pictures, 139
opening, 81
Printers and Faxes, 139
properties, 898
Quick Launch Bar, 139
Recent Documents, 139
recently access applications, 138
resetting defaults, 900
Run, 139
searches, 82, 146, 194-196, 202
shortcuts, troubleshooting, 157-158
Switch User command, 155
Turn Off, 139

Start Windows Normally boot option, 974
startup files, MS-DOS, 1102
startup process
  logins at startup, disabling, 93-94
  performance, 20
  secure startups, 19
  troubleshooting
    boot options, 972-975
    command prompt, 970
    creating backups from System Recovery Options menu, 983-984
    Regedit, 970-971
    reinstalling Windows Vista, 975-976
    Startup Repair tool, 963-964
    System Recovery options, 962-963
    System Restore tool, 964-967
    Windows Complete PC Restore tool, 967-968
    Windows Memory Diagnostic tool, 968-970
  unwanted startup programs, eliminating, 1064-1066
Startup Repair tool, 22, 963-964

static IP addresses
  assigning, 727
  ISP assignment, 709
  Remote Desktop, 1335
static web pages, web servers, 557
Sticky Notes, 1367
storage capacity (Recycle Bin), 127
storage devices, upgrading to dynamic disks, 939
streaming
  audio, 439-440
  video
    minimum connection speeds, 439
    playback (IE7), 437
    sources, 439-440
stretching desktop images, 908
striped volumes
  dynamic storage model (hard disks), 932
  hard disks, creating (Disk Management utility), 941-942
strokes (fonts), 842
stylus pens, 1362
  gestures, 1363-1364
  Pen and Input Devices menu, 1372-1373
  pen flicks, 1363-1364
SUA (Subsystem for UNIX-Based Applications), 36, 680-682
subfolder driver letters, mapping, 756-757
subscriptions
  calendars, 249
  newsgroups, Windows Mail 7, 514-515
substitutions (fonts), 844
superfetching, 20
Switch User command (Start menu), 155
switches
  10/100BASE-T Ethernet, 619
  network switches, 593
switching
  between wireless networks, 1271
  hubs, 624
  users, 105

symbolic links, 109-110
Sync Center (Mobility Center), 29-30, 1282, 1305
Synchronization Manager, 1305
synchronizing
  newsgroups, 522
  offline folders, manual settings, 1306
  portable media players with Windows Media Player, 274-276
System and Maintenance category (Category view), 807
System applet (Control Panel), updating device drivers, 992-993
System Configuration utility, 881-883
System Diagnostics Report, 860
system file recovery, 22
System Information tool, 889-890
system management
  new features, 22-23
  Scheduled Tasks, 1124-1125
system performance
  environment variables, setting, 1085-1091
  program environments, 1092-1102
  temporary files, specifying location of, 1091-1092
System Properties (Control Panel), 868-872
System Protection option (System Properties), 869-870
System Recovery options, 962
  backups, creating from, 983-984
  command prompt, 970
  Startup Repair tool, 963-964
  System Restore tool, 964-967
  Windows Complete PC Restore tool, 967-968
  Windows Memory Diagnostic tool, 968-970
system restore, Registry backup creation, 1047

System Restore tool
 configuring, 964-965
 creating restore points, 965-966
 restoring from restore points, 966-967
system stability, 1003
System Tools applet (Control Panel), 1124-1125
System Tools folder, Character Map, 892-895
System Tray. *See* **Notification Area**
SystemDrive, 1087
SystemRoot environment variable, 1087
SYSVOL folder, Windows 200x Server shared status, 749

T

tabbed browsing, 30, 430-433
Tablet PC
 gestures, 1363-1364
 history of, 1356-1358
 Input Panel, 1361-1363
 pen flicks, 1363-1364, 1375
 regular PCs versus, 1359, 1361
 selecting, 1360
 Settings menu, 1370-1372
 stylus pens, 1362-1363
 troubleshooting
  pen cursor, 1374
  pen flicks, 1374
  screen rotation, 1374
 uses for, 1358-1359
Tablet Vista, 29
 AutoComplete, 1366
 Handwriting Personalization window, 1364-1365
 Handwriting Recognition tool, 1364-1366
 new features, 1360
 Pen and Input Devices menu, 1372-1373
 Snipping Tool, 1367-1369
 Sticky Notes, 1367

 Tablet PC Settings menu, 1370-1372
 Windows Journal, 1369-1370
Task Manager, 883-884
 Applications tab, 884-885
 applications, launching, 146
 Networking tab, 888-889
 Performance tab, 887-888
 Processes tab, 885-886
 Services tab, 887
 troubleshooting, 895
 Users tab, 889
Task Scheduler, 881, 1123-1126
taskbar, 125, 141-142
 active application buttons, 140
 customizing, 900-901
 drag-and-drop support, 181, 901
 Notification Area, 139, 901
 repositioning, 140
 resizing, 901
 Start menu, dual column arrangement, 138
Taskbar and Start Menu Properties dialog, 140, 900-901
tasks (calendars), scheduling, 251, 1125
TCP Services, forwarding (routers), 733-734
TCP/IP
 auto-configuration via DHCP servers, 647-648
 default network protocol, Internetworking with Windows XP and 2000, 666-667
 configuring, 646-649
 Internet problems, troubleshooting, 543-549
 ipconfig command, 544-545
 pathping command, 547-548
 peer-to-peer networks, configuring, 644-646
 ping command, 545-546
 route command, 548-549
 tracert command, 546-547
television. *See* **TV**

Telnet
 Internetworking with UNIX and Linux, 676-678
 router access, preventing, 1241
Telnet session (UNIX), 676-678
TEMP environment variable, 1087
Temporal Key Integrity Protocol (TKIP), 1264
temporary files
 Internet files, 950
 location of, specifying, 1091-1092
 offline files, deleting (Disk Cleanup utility), 951
Teredo IPv6 Tunneling support, 28
Terminal Services, remote client access, 605
testing. *See also* **diagnostic tools; troubleshooting**
 fax modem, 320
 networks
  cables, 794
  configurations, 795-797
  connectivity, 797-798
  defenses, 1219-1221
  Remote Desktop, 1333
  scanner, 321
  SP-1 (Service Pack-1), 1423
  UPS configurations, 1028
text, converting handwriting to, 1370
thin clients, 1331
ThinkPad, 1356
third-party utilities
 backup tools, 1046-1047, 1200-1201
 disk management tools, 953-954
 Internet problems
  reverse tracert, 550
  Speed Check, 549
  troubleshooting, 549-550
  Whois Database, 550
three-button mouse, auto-scrolling, 924
thumbnails
 deleting (Disk Cleanup utility), 951
 live thumbnails, 13
 Thumbnails view (Computer), 149

Tiles view (Computer), 149
Timbuktu, 1331
titles, adding to movies/video clips, 339-340
TiVo
    Tivo-To-Go, 274
    Windows Media Center versus, 372
TKIP (Temporal Key Integrity Protocol), 1264
too many files open error message, MS-DOS applications, 1127
top-level keys (Registry), 1039-1042
Torvalds, Linus, 37
TPM (Trusted Platform Module), 19, 1185-1187
TraceRoute.org website, 550
tracert tool (TCP/IP utility), 529-530, 546-547
transferring data between computers, Windows Easy Transfer, 100-103
transitions
    flat cuts, 336-337
    video clips, adding (Windows Movie Maker), 336-337
transparencies, faxing or scanning, 322
Travan tape storage, 616
Trojan horses, 1133, 1208
troubleshooting, 962. *See also* diagnostic tools; testing
    absent computers, workgroup networks, 660-661
    application crashes, 156-157, 977-979
    backups, 1201-1202
    BitLocker, 1202
    blank monitors, 927
    boot process, 957
    Character Map, 895
    devices, missing drivers, 1017
    dial-up networks
        ISP, 420-421
        routing issues, 1296-1297
    DVDs, playing, 260-261
    EFS (Encrypted File System), 1202

errant startup programs, Registry entries, 1064-1066
fax services, 230
files
    In Use by Another User error message, 781
    compressing, 202
    deleting, Administrators account, 1203
folders, deleting, 1203
garbage characters display, MS-DOS applications, 1127
hard disks
    file structure problems, 956
    hardware problems, 956
    overview, 954
    strategies, 955-956
    unrecognized, 956-957
hardware
    conflicts, 1035
    general guidelines, 1034
Help and Support Center, 981-982
hidden updates, 1006
hubs, 659-660
IIS (Internet Information Services), 584-585
installing
    software, 1006-1007
    Windows Vista, notebook computers, 55
Internet connections, 420-421, 528
    dial-up problems, 535-536
    dial-up settings, 530
    flowchart diagnosis, 532-534
    hardware configuration problems, 539-543
    ipconfig command, 544-545
    ipconfig tool, 529
    LAN problems, 537-539
    methodology, 531-532
    modem problems, 536-537
    Network Connections settings, 530

pathping command, 547-548
ping command, 545-546
pinging with larger packets, 551-552
route command, 548-549
router configuration, 530
software configuration problems, 535-539
Speed Check, 549
TCP/IP utilities, 543
TraceRoute.org reverse tracert tools, 550
tracert command, 529, 546-547
tracert network cabling diagram, 530
Whois Database, 550
Internet Explorer 7, 467
LAN (Local Area Networks), shared connections, 736
Macintosh networking
    inability to run concurrent applications, 698
    lost application associations, 698
mangled line feed/carriage returns
    UNIX networking, 697
missing
    computers from networks, 696
    printers, Active Directory networks, 781
monitors
    LCD monitors, 927
    multiple monitors, 1020-1021, 1032-1033
    resolution, 927
    screen flicker, 925
    screen savers, 911
    wallpaper images, 928
    window edges off screen, 926
mouse clicks, 927
movies, 345-346
MS-DOS, 1127
Network window, 660, 788-789

How can we make this index more useful? Email us at indexes@quepublishing.com

networks, 696-698
  cables, 659, 794
  configuration checks, 790-791, 795-797
  connectivity checks, 797-798
  Device Manager, 793-794
  diagnostic questions, 786-787
  diagnostic tools, 788, 792-793
  Event Viewer, 792-793
  file and printer sharing problems, 799
  file sharing problems, 799
  general categories, 787
  LAN monitoring, 799-800
  Network and Sharing Center, 789-790
  Network Diagnostics, 790-791
  overview, 786
  printer sharing problems, 799
  questions to ask, 786-787
  services, 1241
  types of network problems, 787
  Windows Firewall, 791-792
news servers, 523
newsgroups, 521-522
non-booting computers, BIOS settings, 1033
Notepad, 254
offline folders, 1309
output to exterior TVs, 926
passwords, email accounts (Windows Mail 7), 519
photos, printing, 303-304
printing, 210-213, 228-230, 781
problem prevention, 976-977
Problem Reports and Solutions applet, 979-981
Programs and Features window, 1007
re-installing uninstalled updates, 1006

Registry
  configuration changes don't appear for other users, 1066
  corrupted files, 1063
  recovery process, 1063-1064
Remote Desktop, 1350-1351
screen flicker, 925
screen savers, 911
searches, 201-202
shared connections (LAN)
  cable connections, 736
  DSL connections, 736
  modem connections, 736
shortcuts, 157-158
Sidebar gadgets, 254
small screen fonts, 928
startup process
  boot options, 972-975
  command prompt, 970
  creating backups from System Recovery Options menu, 983-984
  Regedit, 970-971
  reinstalling Windows Vista, 975-976
  Startup Repair tool, 963-964
  System Recovery options, 962-963
  System Restore tool, 964-967
  Windows Complete PC Restore tool, 967-968
  Windows Memory Diagnostic tool, 968-970
Tablet PC, 1374
Task Manager, 895
tips for, 982-983
too many files open error message, MS-DOS applications, 1127
uninstalling
  software, 1007
  updates, 1006
Volume Control, 360
VPN (Virtual Private Networks), 1296-1297, 1308
wallpaper images, 928

Windows Fax and Scan, 320-322
Windows Mail 7, 520-521
Windows Media Center, 387-388
Windows Messenger, 1241
Windows Update, 1005
wireless networks, 1273-1276
Wordpad, 255
TrueType font outline technology, 841-844
Turn Off (Start menu), 139
TV tuner, troubleshooting, 387
Tweak UI tool, 919
TweakVI tool, editing Registry, 1062
two-factor authentication, 1250-1251
two-way authentication, 1250
typefaces, 841
  information sources, 843-844
  installing, 845
  points, 842
  substitutions, 844
  types, 842
Typography (Microsoft) website, 843

U

UAC (User Account Control), 19, 84-87, 1079, 1144-1145
UDP Services, forwarding (routers), 733-734
UI (User Interfaces), 122
  Aero, 124
    default appearance, 125-126
    icons, 129-130
    putting items on, 131
    Recycle Bin, 125-128
    shortcuts, 131-132
    Sidebar gadgets, 126
    taskbar, 125
    visual color palette, 124-125
  breadcrumbs, 172-175
  efficient use of, 159-161

file system navigation, 177-184
file views, 185-187
folder views, 185-189
logon process, 123-124
panes, toggling, 184-185
taskbar, 138-142
Windows Explorer, 135
  breadcrumbs, 165, 170-171, 175-177
  Details pane, 167
  file management, 135-138
  new features, 164-167
  toolbar, 165-166
  WebView, 167-170
Ulead Video Studio, 345
Ulead.com website, 345
Ultimate Extras, 997
Ultra DME EIDE hard disks, 1011
UNC (Universal Naming Convention), 743-744
unidirectional satellite dishes, 397
uninstalling
  applications, 141-142
  programs, 140
  software, 1000-1002, 1007
  SP-1 (Service Pack-1), 1428
  updates
    troubleshooting, 1006
    with Windows Update, 991
University of Illinois, Mosaic Web browser development, 424
UNIX, 35-36
  carriage returns, troubleshooting, 697
  Internetworking, 672
    Berkeley "r" commands, 680-682
    CIFS (Common Internet File System) protocol, 673
    NFS, 678-679
    Samba, 673-676
    SMB (Server Message Block) protocol, 673
    SUA (Subsystem for UNIX-Based Applications), 680
    Telnet, 676-678

mangled line feeds, troubleshooting, 697
printers, LPR/LPD protocol, 764-765
UUCP (Unix-to-Unix Copy Protocol), news server protocol, 509
unrecognized hard disks, troubleshooting, 956-957
updates
  album art, 284-285
  automatic updates, 1142
  Critical Updates, 1422
  critical updates, downloading, 95
  driver updates
    manual updates, 992-993
    Windows Update settings, 1007-1008
  hardware, device drivers, 992-993
  hidden updates, troubleshooting, 1006
  hotfixes, 1422
  importance of, 1211, 1226-1227
  media information, 282-284
  Microsoft E-Mail Updates Service, 1226
  networks, mixed types, 624
  Optional Updates, 1422
  re-installing uninstalled updates, troubleshooting, 1006
  service packs, 994-996
  software, downloading, 443
  uninstalling, troubleshooting, 1006
  Windows Update
    automatic updates, 987-988
    changing update settings, 990
    disabling updates, 990
    hiding updates, 989
    manual updates, 989
    repairing/uninstalling updates, 991
    SP-1 installation, 1425-1426
    troubleshooting, 1005
    viewing updates, 990

upgrades
  hard disks, 1011
  hardware, 48-49
    EULA, 1028-1031
    overview, 1010
    SPP, 1028-1030
  older operating systems, Microsoft desupport dates, 122
  page file sizes, 1010
  RAM, 1010
  storage devices to dynamic disk model, 939
  Windows Media Center, 367-368
  Windows Vista, 62-65
    options for, 35
    versions of, 66
Upgrading and Repairing Networks, Fourth Edition, 610
UPnP (Universal Plug and Play), 606
UPS (Uninterruptible Power Supplies), 617, 976
  configuring, 1027-1028
  installing, 1023-1026
  intelligent units, 1024
  selecting, 1025-1026
  testing configuration, 1028
URGE online music store, 269
URL (Uniform Resource Locators), 428
  AutoComplete feature (IE7), 429
  components of, 429
  entry of, 429-430
  error messages, 429
  filename translation, website home directories, 556
  home pages, 556-557, 572
  HTTP protocol, 429
  IIS, localhost, 566
  IPP printers, selecting by, 762-763
  websites, virtual directories, 556
US-CERT (Computer Emergency Response Team), browser security advice, 464
USB backup devices, troubleshooting, 1201

USB controllers, BIOS settings, 1018
USB flash drives, security, 1199-1200
Use Printer Halftoning option (Printer Properties dialog), 218
Usenet
   lack of oversight authority, 509
   newsgroups versus, 510
User Account Control (UAC), 19, 84-87, 1079, 1144-1145
user accounts
   Administrator accounts, accessing, 115-116
   changing settings, 90-93
   creating, 89-90, 270
   deleting, 90
   logins
      disabling at startup, 93-94
      process of, 123-124
   password recovery disks, 115
   password reset disks, 91-92
   switching, 105
   types of, 88
   user groups, creating, 112-113
User Accounts and Family Safety view (Category view), 811
user groups
   creating, 112-113
   permissions, assigning to, 1198-1199, 1203
   restricted objects, permission assignments, 1203
user interface (UI). *See* UI (User Interfaces)
user profiles, 79
   backups, 1154
   changing settings, 93
   default user profile, configuring, 116-117
   directory structure, 105-108
      junction points and symbolic links, 109-110
      virtualization, 110-111
   roaming, 603, 741
User Variables, 1089
user-mode drivers, 1018

USERDOMAIN, 1087
USERNAME, 1087
usernames, changing, 90
USERPROFILE environment variable, 1087
Users tab (Task Manager), 889
Utilities tab, Printer Property sheets, 216
UTP (Unshielded Twisted-Pair) cables, 594-595, 618-620
uuencode message format, 489

V

VBScript, 1114
vCards, sending via Windows Mail 7, 508
VeriSign, certificate issuances, 456
Veritas Backup Exec, 616
VHDMount (Virtual Server 2005)
   Administrator operation, 1167
   command-line syntax, 1165-1166
   downloading, 1164
   driver installation, 1168-1170
   installing, 1165
   Windows Explorer operation, 1166-1167, 1170
VHS, dubbing television programs to (Windows Media Center), 384
video
   analog camcorders, 325
   acquisition sources, 325
   clips (Windows Movie Maker)
      assembling in, 333-334
      capture process, 327-332
      converting to movies, 333-334
      editing in, 334-336
      effects, adding, 337-338
      file formats, 325-326
      filters, 337-338
      hardware requirements, 326

      launching, 327, 331
      media associations, 438
      narration, 338-339
      organizing, 332-333
      saving projects, 340-343
      titles, 339-340
      transitions, 336-337
      troubleshooting, 387-388
   DV camcorders, 325
   DVDs, burning to, 357-360
   editing tools, 345
   Internet Explorer 7
      AVI format, 438
      fps (frames per second), 437
      MPEG format, 438
      playing (Windows Media Player), 438-439
      streaming, 437-440
      Web elements, 436-438
      WMV format, 438
   non-linear editing, 325
   online stores, 269-270
   Web cameras, 325
   Windows Media Center, playing, 378-379
video cards, 1019-1021
VideoMaker magazine website, 345
View tab (Folders Options Control Panel), 170
virtual directories
   IIS, 574
   redirection, 556
   websites, 556
virtual domains, 559
virtual folders, 1004-1005
virtual machines, 73, 130
Virtual PC, 74
Virtual Private Networks (VPN). *See* VPN (Virtual Private Networks)
virtual registries, 1004-1005
Virtual Server 2005, VHDMount
   Administrator operation, 1167
   command-line syntax, 1165-1166
   downloading, 1164
   driver installation, 1168-1170
   installing, 1165
   Windows Explorer operation, 1166-1167, 1170

WEB SERVERS 1483

virtualization, 110-111, 1044
viruses, 1208
  attachments, 486
  history of, 1132-1133
  Melissa, 1133
  Michelangelo, 1132
  newsgroups, safety measures, 524
  software downloads, scanning, 443
Vista SP-1, RFM, 1031
Vista Ultimate, 996-998
Vista (Windows). *See* Windows Vista
visual color palette, desktop environment, 124-125
Visual Effects dialog (Control Panel), 890-891
Visual Effects tab (Computer Performance Options property sheets), 854-855
visual effects tools, 922
visualizations, Windows Media Player, 262
VMWare, 74
voice commands. *See* speech recognition
Volume Control, 351-353, 360, 1281
volumes
  MFT (Master File Tables), pre-allocations, 944-945
  shadow copies, 24, 1150, 1190
VPN (Virtual Private Networks), 605
  callbacks, 1291
  computer access, enabling, 1297, 1300-1301
  configuring, 1288-1289
  connections
    failures, missing certificates, 1308
    LAN Internet connections, 709-710
    process of, 1287
    properties, 1292
    routing issues, 1296-1297
  data encapsulation, 1287
  email connections, 1295
  enabling (RAS), 1297, 1300
  ending connections, 1296
  establishing connections, 1293-1294
  gateway settings, 1292
  incoming access, 1297-1301
  monitoring connections, 1296
  properties tables, 1290-1291
  Remote Desktop connections, 1351
  remote network resources, 1295
  router information, manually adding, 1309-1310
  routing
    information, manual additions, 1309-1310
    issues with, 1296-1297
  troubleshooting, 1308
  tunnels, 1287

W

wallpaper (desktops)
  block-like appearance, 928
  DreamScene (Ultimate Extras), 997
  GUI display properties, setting, 906-908
WBADMIN command-line tool, 1162-1164
Web browsers. *See also* Internet Explorer 7
  alternatives to Internet Explorer 7, 464
  Berners-Lee, Tim, 424
  Cailliau, Robert, 424
  function of, 555
  MIME types, interpretation of, 557
  Mosaic, 424
  virtual directories, redirection, 556
web cameras, 325
web feeds, automatic searches for Internet Explorer 7, 425
web pages
  Address bar, length reduction (IE7), 428
  audio
    elements, 436-438
    streaming (Windows Media Player), 439-440
  enlarging view (Internet Explorer 7), 426-427
  GIF image file format, 436
  graphics
    copyright restrictions, 436
    mouse over action, 436
    resizing, 436
    troubleshooting (IE7), 467
  home directories (IIS), copying to, 567-569
  JPEG image file format, 435-436
  Links bar, 427-428
  loading errors, troubleshooting, 467
  MP3 audio
    copyright controversies, 441
    downloading (Windows Media Player), 442
    playing (Windows Media Player), 441
  navigation tools (IE7), 428
  offline browsing (IE7), 432
  page not available errors, troubleshooting (IE7), 467
  PNG image file format, 436
  saving for later viewing, 434-435
  troubleshooting, 467
  video
    AVI format, 438
    elements, 436-438
    fps (frames per second), 437
    MPEG format, 438
    playing (Windows Media Player), 438-439
    streaming (Windows Media Player), 439-440
    WMV format, 438
web servers. *See also* IIS (Internet Information Services)
  access, troubleshooting, 584
  authentication, 571-572
  function of, 555
  home directories, default documents, 556-557, 572
  MIME types, file labeling, 557

How can we make this index more useful? Email us at indexes@quepublishing.com

physical paths, changing, 571
programs
    dynamic pages execution, 557
    execution options, 558
    server-side scripts, 558, 573
    static pages execution, 557
unresponsive servers, troubleshooting (IIS), 584
virtual directories, redirection, 556
Windows File Types Registry, MIME types, 557
web-based clients, Remote Desktop configuration, 1349
web-based email, backups, 1154
web-based news servers, 510-511
webpads, 1357
websites
    Apple.com, 440
    AtomFilms.com, 342
    availability settings (IIS), connection forwarding, 580-581
    background images, print controls, 462
    buy.com, 613
    CataList, 510
    connections
        forwarding, 580-581
        troubleshooting, 531-532, 584
    Consumer Reports, 230
    Consumer Search, 230
    content rating systems, 461
    cookies, enabling/disabling (IE7), 455
    Digital Video Magazine, 345
    Download.com, 442
    FreeNews.net, 511
    home directories
        setting file permissions, 567
        URL filename translation, 556

IIS (Internet Information Services)
    managing, 569-575
    security tools, 555
Intel Corporation, Speed Check tool, 549
InterNIC, Whois Database tool, 550
IPP printers, selecting by, 763
Microsoft Downloads, 213
Microsoft Technet, IIS security tools, 555
mirror sites, software downloads, 442
MSN Media, 440
National Public Radio (NPR), 439
objectionable content, controlling, 459-461
offline browsing (IE7), 432
PC Magazine, 230
PDF documents, viewing, 468-469
personal websites, banned on corporate networks, 555
pop-ups/unders ads
    blocking, 457-458
    exceptions, 458-459
publishing via FTPServer, 576-577
Real Broadcast Network, 440
Registry tips and tricks, 1062
Roxio.com, digital editing tools, 345
scripts
    ASP, 586
    dangers of, 586
    Perl, 585
search options
    Search Companion (IE7), 462-464
    setting (IE7), 462
security 454-456, 459-461, 1240
server connections, encrypted sessions, 456
SETI@home Project, 909-910

software downloads
    add-on crash detection (IE7), 448
    add-on management (IE7), 447-448
    certificates (IE7), 446
    drive-by (IE7), 445-446
    invalid signatures (IE7), 447
    mirror sites, 442
    progress bar, 443
    version updates, 443
    virus scanning, 443
    ZIP compression, 443
TraceRoute.org, reverse tracert tool, 550
Tucows.com, 442
Ulead.com, digital editing tools, 345
URL (Uniform Resource Locators)
    AutoComplete, 429, 461
    components of, 429
    entry of, 429-430
    error messages, 429
    filename translation, 556
    HTTP protocol, 429
VideoMaker magazine, 345
virtual directories, 556
Windows Marketplace, 619
wrong page versions, troubleshooting (IIS), 585
WebView, 167-170
Welcome Center, 80-81
welcome page (IIS), 566
Welcome screen, 78-79
WEP (Wired Equivalency Privacy), 598, 1264
Whistler (codename), 8
White, Nick, 1029
Whois Database tool, domain registration information, 550
WHQL (Windows Hardware Quality Laboratories), 1014
Wi-Fi Alliance, IEEE 802.11 Wireless Ethernet, 596
WIA drivers, 321
wildcards, command-line tools, 1071
windir environment variable, 1087

Windows 2000
- history of Windows, 8
- Internetworking with, 665
  - password protection and simple file sharing, 667-669
  - TCP/IP as default network protocol, 666-667

Windows 2003 Server, 592

Windows 200x Server
- domain networks, joining, 653-655
- shared administrative folders, 748-749
- XP Pro versus, 613-614

Windows 3.x, history of Windows, 6

Windows 95
- history of Windows, 6
- Internetworking, 670-672

Windows 98
- history of Windows, 6
- Internetworking, 667, 670-672

Windows 98 Second Edition, history of Windows, 6

Windows Anytime Upgrade, 66

Windows Backup and Restore Center. *See* **Backup and Restore Center**

Windows Boot Manager, 972

Windows Calendar. *See* **Calendar**

Windows Communication Foundation HTTP Activation, 692

Windows Complete PC Restore tool, 967-968

Windows Defender, 19, 853-854, 1138-1141

Windows Disk Diagnostics, 22

Windows Driver Foundation, 1018

Windows DVD Maker, 357-360

Windows Easy Transfer, 100-102

Windows Easy Transfer Companion, 102-103

Windows Experience Index, 850-853

Windows Explorer, 82, 97, 135
- applications, launching, 146
- breadcrumbs, 165, 170-177
- CDs, burning photos to, 300-301
- Details pane, 167
- Documents folder, 149-150, 165
- elevated privileges, running with, 567
- files
  - customizing views, 185-187
  - managing, 135-136
  - security, 200-201
  - system navigation, 177-184
  - viewing extensions, 97-98
  - zipping and packing, 198-202
- folders
  - customizing views, 185-189
  - deleting, 138
  - viewing, 137-138
- images, viewing with, 354-355
- indexing, changing settings, 190-193
- Music folder, 149-150
- new features, 164-167
- panes, toggling, 184-185
- Pictures folder, 149-150
- programs, running from, 147-149
- screen appearance, 136
- searches
  - changing settings, 190-193
  - deep searching, 190
  - grouping and stacking, 197-198
  - intermediate searching, 189-190
  - Search pane, 195-196
  - troubleshooting, 201-202
  - while typing, 192-194
- shortcuts, creating, 136
- toolbar, 165-166

VHDMount (Virtual Server 2005) operation, 1166-1167, 1170

WebView, 167-170

Windows Fax and Scan, 25
- dialing rules, 315
- emailing scans, 319
- fax service configuration, 309
  - cover pages, 310-311
  - fax receiving options, 310
  - fax settings, 312
  - sender information, 310
- faxing
  - scans, 319
  - slides and transparencies, 322
- hardware and software requirements, 308-309
- manipulating scanned images, 319
- monitoring outgoing faxes, 315
- overview, 308-309
- previewing faxes, 314
- printing received faxes, 316
- receiving faxes, 316
- scanning
  - photos, 317
  - profiles, 318-319
  - settings, 316
  - slides and transparencies, 322
- sending faxes, 313-315
- troubleshooting, 320-322

Windows File Protection, 1003

Windows File Types Registry, MIME types, 557

Windows Firewall, 791-792
- configuring, 791, 1213, 1230-1231
- default settings, 1234
- disabling, 1231
- enabling, 1225-1226, 1231
- exceptions, enabling, 1231-1234
- IIS (Internet Information Services), opening for, 566
- network connection settings, 1234
- peer-to-peer networks, configuring for, 652-653

security, 606
suspicious activities, monitoring, 1221
Windows Firewall with Advanced Security, 1235
   configuring, 1236-1238
   creating rules, 1238-1240
Windows for Pen Computing, 1356
Windows for Workgroups, history of Windows, 6
Windows Hardware Quality Laboratories (WHQL), 1014
Windows Hold'Em feature (Ultimate Extras), 997
Windows Journal, 1369-1370
Windows key+M keystroke, immediate desktop access, 159
Windows Live, 986
Windows Mail 7, 452
   accounts
      checking multiple accounts, 520
      configuring, 478-480
      information backups, 508
      modifying existing accounts, 495-496
      multiple user accounts, 498-500
      newsgroup accounts, 512-514
   Address Book
      backups, 506-507
      distribution lists, 493-494
      entries, adding, 492-493
      entries, deleting, 493
      entries, editing, 493
      looking up people who aren't in, 495
   attachments
      opening, 485
      sending, 485
      virus prevention, 486
   contacts
      disabling auto-additions, 520
      sending, 508
   data backups, 505
   earlier Outlook versions versus, 474-475
   email
      addressing, 483-484
      checking while traveling, 503-505
      creating, 483-484
      filtering, 501-502
      formatting complaints from recipients, 520
      formatting messages, 523-524
      formatting options, 489-490
      organizing, 500-506
      out of office auto reply, 503
      receipt requests, 488
      secure, 490-491
      sending, 484
      signature setup, 487
      transfer protocols, 480-481
   HTML scripts, security protections, 498
   identity on outgoing mail, 520
   Inbox
      appearance of, 476-477
      Folders list, 477
      Microsoft welcome letter, 476
      Preview pane, 477
   incoming messages
      deleting, 483
      reading, 481-483
      replying to, 482
   initial startup, 476
   launching, 476
   missing folders, troubleshooting, 521
   missing mail servers, troubleshooting, 521
   newsgroups
      accessing, 509-510
      locating accounts, 513-514
      managing, 517-518
      message size options, 526
      messages, marked as new, 522
      posting, 515-517
      reading, 513-517
      reading offline, 518-519
      setting up accounts, 512-513
      subscribing to, 514-515
   overview, 472-474
   passwords, 519
   SP2 (Service Pack 2), security features, 496
   spam
      legal measures, 508-509
      limitation features, 496-498
   vCards, sending, 508
Windows Management Instrumentation (WMI), WSH (Windows Script Host), 1120-1122
Windows Marketplace, 143-144, 619, 1000
Windows Me
   history of Windows, 6, 8
   Internetworking, 667, 670-672
Windows Media Center, 362, 452
   DVDs
      burning television programs to, 383-384
      keyboard shortcuts, 386
      playing, 378-379
   hardware
      configuration, 368-370
      requirements, 364-365
   history of, 363
   interface, 370-371
   Media Center Extender, 370
   music, playing, 378
   parental controls, setting, 385-386
   PC form factors, 365-366
   photo slideshows, 376-377
   television
      broadcasting to TV or projector, 381-383
      burning DivX files to DVDs, 390
      burning to DVDs, 383-384
      converting to DivX files, 388-389
      disk storage requirements, 374-376
      dubbing to VHS, 384
      Guide setup, 372-374

Windows Photo Gallery

program selection, 372
recording programs, 373
viewing on HDTV or projector, 380
troubleshooting, 387-388
upgrading to, 367-368
Windows Vista version based on, 366
Xbox 360 connections, 380-381

Windows Media Player, 452
audio
  streaming audio, 439-440
CDs
  bit rate, 268
  burning, 272-274
  file formats, 268
  playing, 265-266
  ripping, 266-268
copy protection, disabling, 262
DVDs
  bit rate, 268
  file formats, 268
  playing, 265-266
  ripping, 266-268
file types supported, 260
hard disk media files, playing, 266
home networking and, 277-278
interface
  browsing and searching, 263-265
  menu tabs, 261-263
media associations, setting, 438
media files
  deleting, 281-282
  organizing, 281-282
  updating album art, 284-285
  updating media information, 282-284
monitored folders, changing, 271
MP3 audio
  downloading, 442
  playing, 441
online stores, 269-270
playlists, creating, 279-280

PlaysForSure compatible devices versus iPods, 272
portable media players
  playing through car stereo, 285-286
  synchronizing with, 274-276
shuffling playback, 266
streaming audio/video, 439-440
video
  playback support, 438
  playing, 438-439
  streaming, 439-440

Windows Meeting Space, 25, 606, 1315

Windows Memory Diagnostic tool, 22, 968-970

Windows Messenger, 1241

Windows Mobility Center Mobility Center, 21
Battery Status icon, 1281
Brightness control, 1281
External Display control, 1282
External Display tile, 1314
Power Options, 1283
Presentation Settings, 1282, 1312-1313
Screen Rotation control, 1282
Sync Center, 1282
Volume control, 1281
Wireless Network icon, 1281

Windows Movie Maker, 347-348
alternatives to, 345
assembling video clips, 333-334
audio tracks, importing, 332
AutoMovie, 343-344
clip capture process, 325-332
converting clips to movies, 333-334
digital still images, importing, 332
DV camcorders, control compatibility, 346

editing, 334-344
  alternative editing tools, 345
  non-linear editing, 325
  recorded television programs, 384
effects, adding, 337
file formats, 325
  compatible formats, 326
  Microsoft HighMAT technology, 342
filters, adding, 337-338
hardware requirements, FireWire port, 326
launching, 327, 331
narration, 338-339
organizing clips, 332-333
playback controls, 334
producing movies, 325-326
saving projects, 340-343
titles, 339-340
transitions, 336-337
troubleshooting, 345-346

Windows NT, history of Windows, 7

Windows NT Virtual DOS Machine (ntvdm), 1095

Windows OS, version determination, 920-921

Windows Pen Services, 1357

Windows Photo Gallery, 26, 288, 452
adding photos to, 289, 294-295
archiving photos in, 305-306
burning photos to CD, 301-303
cropping photos in, 296
digital cameras, 292-295
filtering photos in, 289
fixing photos in, 295-296
importing files to, 290
Live File System option, 302
Mastered option, 302
organizing photos in, 290
previewing photos in, 290
printing photos from, 297-298, 303-304
scanners, 290-292, 304-305
sharing photos via, 299

How can we make this index more useful? Email us at indexes@quepublishing.com

Windows Script Host (WSH). *See* WSH (Windows Script Host)
Windows Search Engine (WSE), 15
Windows Security Center, 1135-1136
Windows Server 2003, 592
Windows services, list of, 1403-1420
Windows SideShow (Control Panel), 872
Windows Sound Recorder, 350-351
Windows Task Scheduler, 881, 1123-1126
Windows Update, 986
  automatic updates, 987-988
  changing update settings, 990
  disabling updates, 990
  driver update settings, 1007-1008
  hiding updates, 989
  manual updates, 989
  repairing/uninstalling updates, 991
  SP-1 (Service Pack-1) installation, 1425-1426
  SP2 (Service Pack 2) installation, 995
  troubleshooting, 1005
  viewing updates, 990
  website, 994
Windows Vista
  activating, 70-72
  boot menu, editing entries, 74-76
  corporate network features, 39-40
  development codenames, 4
  exiting, 154-156
  hardware requirements, 42-48
  improvements over Windows XP, 5
  installing
    clean installations, 49-62
    in-place upgrades, 62-65
    network installations, 50
    reinstalling, 975-976
    troubleshooting on notebook computers, 55
  Linux versus, 38-39

logging process, 123-124
multibooting, 66-70, 73
new features, 8-11
  accessories, 24-27
  for data security, 23-24
  for entertainment, 31-32
  for networking, 27-28
  for performance, 20-21
  for productivity, 29-30
  for stability, 22-23
  for system security, 18-20
  in interface, 12-18
  in Internet Explorer, 30-31
reinstalling for startup repair, 975-976
updates, downloading, 95
upgrading
  options for, 35
  versions of, 66
versions of, 4-5
  compared, 32-35
  with Windows Media Center, 366
Windows Vista Premium Ready PC, 48
Windows Vista Ultimate Edition
  power toys, 997-998
  Ultimate Extras, 996
    downloading, 996
    DreamScene wallpaper, 997
    Secure Online Key Backup feature, 997
    Windows Hold'Em feature, 997
Windows Vista Upgrade Advisor, 43-48
Windows XP
  compatibility, junction points and symbolic links, 109-110
  history of Windows, 7-8
  internetworking with, 665
    installing LLDP responder, 667
    password protection and simple file sharing, 667-669
    setting TCP/IP as default network protocol, 666-667
  Windows Vista improvements over, 5

Windows XP Professional, 613-614
WINE, 37
WinFax Pro software, 228
WinRescue utility, Registry backups, 1046-1047
Wired Equivalency Privacy (WEP), 598, 636, 1264
wired Ethernet networks, 593-594
Wireless Connection Properties dialog, 1273
Wireless Ethernet (IEEE 802.11)
  current standards, 596
  security vulnerabilities, 597
  Wi-Fi Alliance, 596
wireless Internet access, 397
wireless modems, 397, 406
Wireless Network icon (Mobility Center), 1281
Wireless Network Setup Wizard, 638-642
wireless networks (IEEE 802.11g), 622
  ad hoc networks, 1262, 1271-1273
  adding manually, 1273
  automatic/manual connections, selecting, 1272
  command-line tools with, 1277-1278
  domain, 1266
  encryption keys, 636
  encryption protocols, 636
  existing networks, joining, 641-642
  features overview, 623
  hardware requirements, 623
  infrastructure networks, 1262
  installing, 635-636, 638-642
  Internet connections on LAN (Local Area Networks), 711-712
  joining, 1267
    at home or small offices, 1267-1269
    existing networks, 641-642
    in corporate environments, 1267
    in public hot spots, 1270
    in someone else's office, 1269-1270

manual additions, 1273
overview, 1262
preferred networks, 1271-1273
private networks, 1266
public networks, 1266
security
  file and printer sharing, 1266-1267
  MITM (Man In The Middle), 1264
  overview, 1262-1263
  security keys, 1264-1266
  snooping, 1263
  SSID (Service Set Identifier), 636
switching between, 1271
troubleshooting, 1273-1276
wiring networks
  correct order in connectors, 630-631
  installing, 628-635
wiring channels, 659
wiring guides, Windows Media Center, 368-370, 380-381
WMI (Windows Management instrumentation), WSH (Windows Script Host), 1120-1122
WMV video format, 438
Wordpad, 254-255
workgroup networks, 740
  computers, absence of, 660-661
  domain networks versus, 742
  file sharing, troubleshooting, 799
  folders, sharing, 769-771
  printer sharing, troubleshooting, 799
  searching, 748
World Wide Web (WWW)
  growth of, 424
  HTML (Hypertext Markup Language), 425
  origins and development, 424
  site registrars, 424
worms, 1133
WOW64 emulation layer, 33

WPA2 (Wi-Fi Protected Access 2), 599
Writing Pad (in Input Panel), 1362
WSE (Windows Search Engine), 15
WSH (Windows Script Host), 1113
  ADSI, 1122
  applications (Windows), 1122-1123
  disk and network management, 1117-1118
  messaging and email, 1118-1119
  scripts, creating, 1114-1117
  WMI, 1120-1122
WSH (Windows Script Host), 1113

X - Y - Z

Xbox 360, Windows Media Center connections, 380-381
Xnews tool (newsgroups), 526
XPS (XML Paper Specification), print output, 226-227

zipped files, 198-200, 443
  creating, 953
  troubleshooting, 202
zones (security), 454
zooming (cameras), 348

How can we make this index more useful? Email us at indexes@quepublishing.com

IN DEPTH

Essential advice and techniques to get the job done.

In Depth provides tested and proven solutions to the problems you run into everyday – things other books ignore or oversimplify. An *In Depth* book is the only book you will need to master everything there is to know on all the essential topics

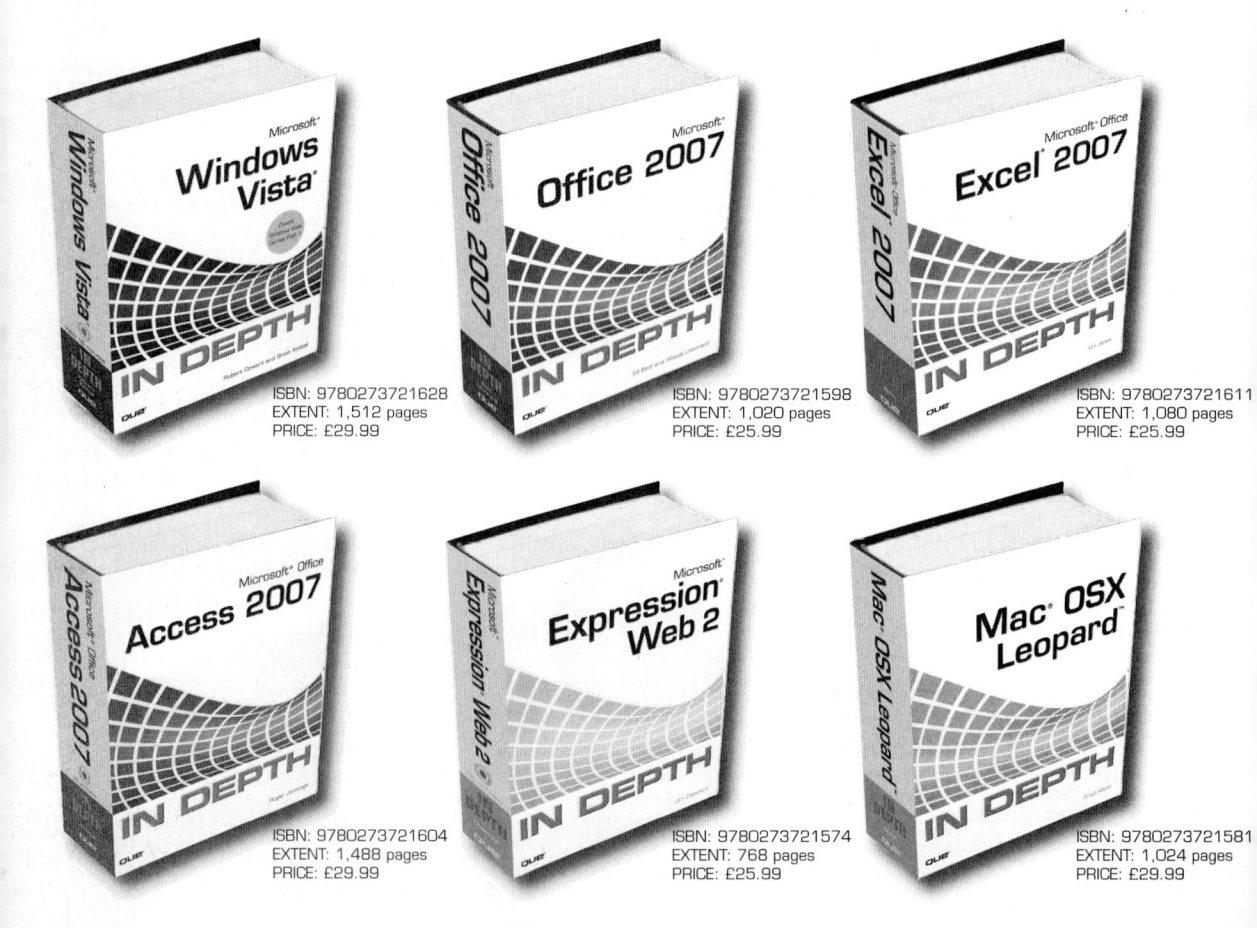

Microsoft Windows Vista
ISBN: 9780273721628
EXTENT: 1,512 pages
PRICE: £29.99

Microsoft Office 2007
ISBN: 9780273721598
EXTENT: 1,020 pages
PRICE: £25.99

Microsoft Office Excel 2007
ISBN: 9780273721611
EXTENT: 1,080 pages
PRICE: £25.99

Microsoft Office Access 2007
ISBN: 9780273721604
EXTENT: 1,488 pages
PRICE: £29.99

Microsoft Expression Web 2
ISBN: 9780273721574
EXTENT: 768 pages
PRICE: £25.99

Mac OSX Leopard
ISBN: 9780273721581
EXTENT: 1,024 pages
PRICE: £29.99

All you need to know – In Depth

que